D0289583

Russia
& Belarus

Simon Richmond

Mark Elliott, Patrick Horton, Steve Kokker, John Noble,
Robert Reid, Regis St Louis, Mara Vorhees

BELARUS (p654)
Marvel at the monumental Brest Fortress war memorial, the idyllic countryside and the sparkling clean streets of Minsk in this Soviet throwback of a country

ST PETERSBURG (p224)
Visit tsarist palaces and enjoy many wonderful museums, including the Hermitage, in Russia's most elegant and European city

MOSCOW (p120)
Savour the power and pleasures of the nation's awe-inspiring capital in Red Square, and its plethora of museums, shops, restaurants and clubs

VELIKY USTYUG (p401)
Deliver your wishes directly to Russia's own Santa Claus in this delightfully quaint town

NOVGOROD (p327)
Relish Russia's history in the country's first capital, home of the Byzantine Cathedral of St Sophia and a restored kremlin

TOMSK (p515)
Discover Siberia's most attractive city, an old university town packed with charming wooden architecture and a youthful outlook

YEKATERINBURG (p436)
Explore the gently rolling Ural Mountains from this historic city where the Romanovs met their violent end

CAUCASUS MOUNTAINS (p481)
You don't have to climb Mt Elbrus, Europe's premier peak, to enjoy the beauty of this southern Russian range

ALTAI REPUBLIC (p521) & REPUBLIC OF TUVA (p546)
Raft, ski and hike in these remote, picturesque and culturally distinct Siberian regions

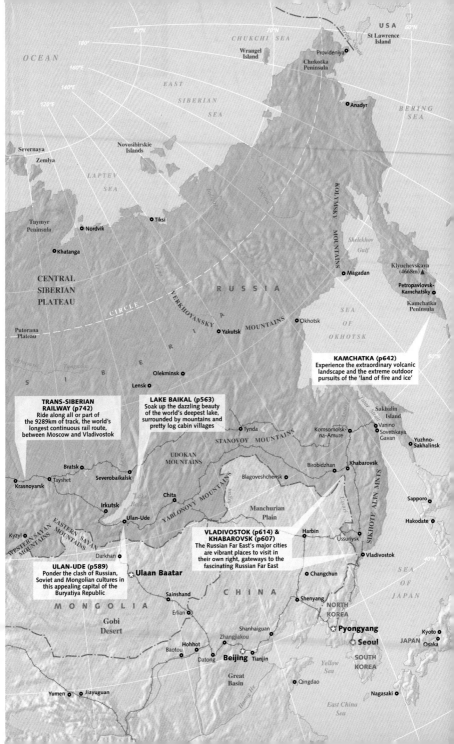

TRANS-SIBERIAN RAILWAY (p742)
Ride along all or part of the 9289km of track, the world's longest continuous rail route, between Moscow and Vladivostok

LAKE BAIKAL (p563)
Soak up the dazzling beauty of the world's deepest lake, surrounded by mountains and pretty log cabin villages

KAMCHATKA (p642)
Experience the extraordinary volcanic landscape and the extreme outdoor pursuits of the 'land of fire and ice'

VLADIVOSTOK (p614) & KHABAROVSK (p607)
The Russian Far East's major cities are vibrant places to visit in their own right, gateways to the fascinating Russian Far East

ULAN-UDE (p589)
Ponder the clash of Russian, Soviet and Mongolian cultures in this appealing capital of the Buryatiya Republic

Destination Russia & Belarus

Famously described by Winston Churchill as 'a riddle wrapped in a mystery inside an enigma', Russia is the globe's most rewarding and misunderstood destination. From St Petersburg's glittering palaces to Kamchatka's bubbling volcanoes nine time zones away, the world's largest country offers unparalleled geographic and cultural marvels, plus incredible hospitality and a refreshing break from the norm. The last few years have seen noticeable changes, many for the better – the Russia you'll find today is a vastly different place from that of the Soviet years.

Whether you attend a ballet at the Bolshoi, go white-water rafting in the Altai Mountains, or trundle across country on a trans-Siberian train, Russia's range of holiday possibilities is practically limitless. Moscow and St Petersburg are fabulous cities, up there with the best of Europe in terms of sights, sleeping and dining options. Vast areas of the country, previously off limits or undeveloped for tourism, are now open and easily accessible through Russia's comprehensive rail system, making Russia an adventure traveller's dream.

Neighbouring Belarus is the nation with arguably the closest geographical and cultural ties to Russia. This authoritarian dinosaur of a country is an unlikely place for a holiday, but its cosmopolitan capital, Minsk, and the historic towns of Hrodna, Vitsebsk and Brest all have their charms. The countryside also retains a haunting, old-fashioned beauty.

It's not all good news. Dealing with bureaucracy, corrupt police and tolerating some discomfort remains an integral part of the whole Russian travel experience. Don't be put off: this guide will help you break through Russia's sometime gruff exterior, allowing you to discover the renowned warmth of its people and its epic-scale natural beauty. So ditch those preconceptions – come shed your own shaft of light on the world's largest mystery.

JONATHAN SMITH

Historic Russia

Come face-to-face with Russian history at awe-inspiring Red Square (p147), Moscow

Cruise past elegant the buildings lining St Petersburg's (p224) Moyka Canal

OTHER HIGHLIGHTS

- Want to get off the beaten track? There is no beaten track on Kamchatka (p642), Russia's land of fire and ice
- Delve into the extremes of Russia's history at the Solovetsky Islands (p391), site of so much heroism, endurance, suffering and cruelty
- Take a break from icons and onion domes with a visit to the revitalised Buddhist *datsans* at Tsugol and Aginskoe (p601)

Walk in the footsteps of Russia's most powerful at the mighty Moscow Kremlin (p138)

Historic Russia

Contemplate Russia's countless fallen in Yekaterinburg (p436), home to this powerful war memorial

SIMON RICHMOND

MARTIN MOOS

Don't forget to bring your sunglasses when viewing Moscow's lurid landmark St Basil's Cathedral (p149)

Water tumbles from the elaborate Grand Cascade out to the Gulf of Finland at Peter the Great's stunning estate, Petrodvorets (p295)

GEORGI S SHABLOVSKY

Indulge in world-class opera or ballet at St Petersburg's historic Mariinsky Theatre (p262)

Admire ancient Novgorod's (p327) beautiful old churches and magnificent kremlin

Take the time to explore intriguing Vladivostok (p614), launch pad for a million adventures

Scenic Russia

SIMON RICHMOND

Sunrise breaks over spectacular Lake Baikal (p563)

Climbers unload their gear on Mt Elbrus
(p487), Europe's highest peak

WADE EAKLE

CHRISTINA DAMEYER

Explore rustic old Siberia at the Taltsy Museum of
Wooden Architecture (p575), near Lake Baikal

Tackle Mt Cheget's (p488) challenging
piste, or just revel in the stunning views

Massive snow-capped mountains loom over the
deep Alibek Valley, Dombay (p481)

Be dwarfed by the towering Lena Pillars (p631), sandstone formations that line the Lena River

Cultural Russia & Belarus

Climb the Jordan Staircase and explore the artistic bounty of the Hermitage (p244)

Traditional Russian peasant costume on display at Kizhi Island (p361)

Relive the Soviet glory days at the All-Russian Exhibition Centre (p164)

The amazing Transfiguration Church (p361) of Kizhi Island was constructed without a single nail

JEFF GREENBERG

The Grand Palace dominates the Petrodvorets estate (p295)

JONATHAN SMITH

Brest Fortress (p684) is an overwhelming, not-to-be-missed tribute to its heroic defenders

JONATHAN SMITH

Active Russia

Take advantage of the famous Russian winters; go skiing at Mt Elbrus (p487)

PATRICK HORTON

JONATHAN SMITH

Discover the latest in St Petersburg's thriving live music scene (p286) at venues like Money Honey

All aboard; make your own odyssey across Russia on the legendary Trans-Siberian Railway (p742)

CHRISTINA DAMEYER

Contents

14 CONTENTS

Regional Map Contents

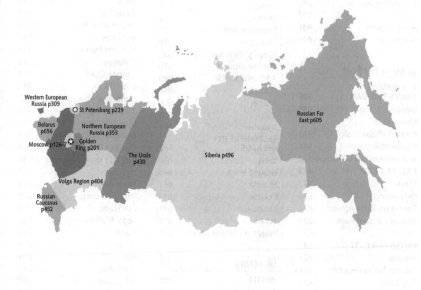

Western European Russia p309
St Petersburg p229
Belarus p656
Moscow p126–7
Northern European Russia p353
Golden Ring p201
The Urals p430
Siberia p496
Russian Far East p605
Volga Region p404
Russian Caucasus p452

The Authors

SIMON RICHMOND
Coordinating Author, St Petersburg

The globetrotting descendant of Eastern European immigrants to the UK, Simon knows there must be some Russian blood flowing in his veins, such has been the constant pull of Russia. After studying Russian history and politics at university, his first visit to the country was in 1994 when he wandered goggle-eyed around gorgeous St Petersburg and sank beers at the Australian embassy in Moscow (hard to believe there were few decent pubs in the capital back then!). Having coauthored both the 1st edition of Lonely Planet's *Trans-Siberian Railway* in 2001 and the previous edition of *Russia & Belarus* in 2002, Simon was back in the driving seat for the current edition.

My Favourite Trip

Group tours are not my thing, but when it comes to Kamchatka, unless you have bucketloads of cash or time to spare there's no other option. Temperamental weather kept our group grounded for a few days in the regional capital Petropavlovsk-Kamchatsky (p644), where I learnt more than I cared to know about the peninsula's even more unpredictable 68 active volcanoes, several within easy lava-flow distance. But, oh how magnificent those volcanoes are! I'll never forget choppering into the lush, steaming Valley of the Geysers (p650), or reaching the sulphur-stained summit of Mt Mutnovskaya (p649). Best of all though was spending a night at the camp of Even reindeer herders, another thrilling helicopter flight from the pretty alpine village of Esso (p650).

MARK ELLIOTT
Siberia

Mark updated and expanded the Siberia chapter. He first fell in love with Eastern Europe 30 years ago when dragged most willingly to Romania by parental caravan. Since joining Prague's 1989 Velvet Revolution he has been venturing ever further east. Beneath their deadpan exteriors, it's the great humanity and warmth of Russians' souls that keep drawing Mark back to Siberia. Where else can one drink birch sap with Vissarion devotees, vodka with Rasputin's alter ego, or *samagon* firewater with off-duty mercenaries while bathing outdoors at –25°C? He now lives in Belgium with the lovely Danielle, who he met while jamming blues harmonica in a Turkmenistan club.

LONELY PLANET AUTHORS

Why is our travel information the best in the world? It's simple: our authors are independent, dedicated travellers. They don't research using just the Internet or phone, and they don't take freebies in exchange for positive coverage. They travel widely, to all the popular spots and off the beaten track. They personally visit thousands of hotels, restaurants, cafés, bars, galleries, palaces, museums and more – and they take pride in getting all the details right, and telling it how it is. For more, see the authors section on www.lonelyplanet.com.

PATRICK HORTON
Russian Caucasus

Patrick has been intrigued by Russia ever since he saw a jet engine mounted on a truck blasting away the snow outside a Moscow hotel. Inside the service was equally icy and unmelting in the face of his charm. Oh those Soviet days! He's even more intrigued now that western Russia is becoming more European and every visit reveals more change. Patrick has travelled across Russia from St Petersburg to the Mongolian border by train but is still drawn to the emotional majesty of the Caucasus. He is however intrigued that women seem to run the Russian railways; is that why they're generally efficient and run on time?

STEVE KOKKER
Belarus

Steve is a die-hard Eastern Europe lover, having spent most of his time since 1996 living away from his native Montreal. He bases himself in his father's homeland of Tallinn, Estonia, despite a dislike of Scandinavian techno, sour cream and pickles. A film critic, filmmaker, freelance writer and photographer, he's lived in Russia and has had a ball in places most travellers avoid, like Belarus, Kaliningrad, Moldova, northern Russia and Chornobyl. He's been writing and photographing for Lonely Planet since 1998.

JOHN NOBLE
Northern European Russia

John, with colleague John King, pioneered Lonely Planet's coverage of Russia back in the *perestroika* days by writing *USSR*, a magnum opus about a country that abolished itself while the book was at the printer. So John turned to writing Lonely Planet guides to the Soviet successor states: *Baltic States & Kaliningrad* 1, *Central Asia* 1 and *Russia, Ukraine & Belarus* 1. He then took a 10-year breather in other countries before returning to Russia for this edition. He found the country as beautiful and challenging as ever, its people far happier and its restaurants in a whole new league!

ROBERT REID
Russian Far East

Prompted by rebellion and the library's air-con on hot Oklahoma days, Robert picked up old copies of *Soviet Life* as a kid, then Dostoevsky paperbacks as a college kid. He studied Russian and spent the 'first summer of Russia' (1992) in St Petersburg and Moscow, where he also volunteered at Echo Moscow radio. He's travelled around Eastern Europe loads, updating Bulgaria for Lonely Planet's *Eastern Europe* guide. While updating coverage of Russia's Far East he counted 151 moustaches along Russian pavements, railways and boats. He lives barefaced in Brooklyn, New York.

REGIS ST LOUIS   Western European Russia

Raised with an unhealthy dread of nuclear annihilation, Regis became deeply interested in Russia after watching evil-empire films like *Threads, Red Dawn* and *Rocky III*. In high school, a teacher introduced him to Dostoevsky, and from that point on he was hooked. At Indiana University he immersed himself in the world of Rus, spending an academic year at Moscow State University and majoring in Slavic languages and literature. Since then, his interest in Russia has led him to Cuba (the unsightly legacy of Soviet engineers lives on), Mexico (Trotsky's home when he was assassinated) and Japan (site of the historic, but ineffectual, Shimoda peace treaty). He lives in New York City.

MARA VORHEES   Moscow, Golden Ring, Volga Region, Urals Region

Mara has been travelling to Russia since the days of the Cold War and communism. After the Soviet collapse, she lived for two years in Yekaterinburg, where she worked on a foreign aid project. In her adventures as a travel writer, she has spent two months riding the Trans-Siberian Railway, four weeks cruising the Volga River, two weeks circling the Golden Ring and seven seconds swimming in Lake Baikal. She is the author of Lonely Planet's guide to *Moscow* and coauthor of the *Trans-Siberian Railway*.

CONTRIBUTING AUTHOR

Leonid Ragozin devoted himself to beach dynamics when he studied geology at the Moscow State University. But for want of really nice beaches in Russia, he helped Australian gold prospectors in Siberia, then sold InterRail tickets and Lonely Planet books to Russian backpackers. He's been on Auntie's service for seven years now, lately focusing on its burgeoning Russian-language website. Leonid is based in Moscow, though when it gets cold he is likely to be spotted in London or South America. Leonid wrote the Chechnya, Dagestan and Ingushetia sections of this guide.

Getting Started

WHEN TO GO

Early summer and autumn are many people's favourite periods for visiting Russia and Belarus. By May all of the winter's snow has usually disappeared and temperatures are pleasant, while the golden autumnal colours of September and early October are stunning.

July and August are the warmest months and the main holiday season for both foreigners and Russians (which means securing train tickets at short notice can be a problem). They're also the dampest months in most parts of Belarus and European Russia, with as many as one rainy day in three. In rural parts of Siberia and the Russian Far East, May and June are peak danger periods for encephalitis-carrying ticks, though June and July are worse for biting insects. By September the air has cleared of mosquitoes.

See Climate Charts (p700 & p716) for more information.

Winter brings the Russia of the imagination to life. If you're prepared for it, travel in this season is recommended: the snow makes everything picturesque, and the insides of buildings are kept warm. Avoid, though, the first snows (usually in late October) and the spring thaw (April), which turn everything to slush and mud.

COSTS & MONEY

It's not unusual for a foreigner to be charged 10 times what Russians are charged to enter museums, not entirely unfairly given the vast disparity between average Western and Russian incomes. Remember your extra money is desperately needed to protect the very works of art and artefacts you've come to see.

While it's possible to travel on next to nothing (p731), on the whole, Russia and Belarus are not cheap destinations. Avoid the major cities and use the *platskartny* ('hard' class, or 3rd class) carriages of overnight trains as an alternative to hotels and it's possible to live on US$30 per day (US$20 in Belarus). However, if you visit the main cities, eat Western-style meals in restaurants and travel on *kupeyny* (2nd class) trains, US$80 per day is a more realistic figure. Prices drop away from the metropolises, but not significantly, but in remote areas, such as the Russian Far East, everything can cost considerably more.

In both countries dual pricing is also an issue. As a foreigner you'll find yourself pretty much always paying more than a local as far as entrance to museums and tourist sites is concerned and sometimes at hotels, too (although not in Moscow or St Petersburg where hotel prices are the same for everyone). It's often fair game for taxi drivers and sometimes market sellers to try to charge foreigners more – check with locals for prices, but don't expect that knowledge to be much use unless you can bargain in Russian. You'll rarely be short-changed by staff in restaurants, cafés and bars, though.

DON'T LEAVE HOME WITHOUT...

- Getting a visa – we'll guide you through the paperwork (p713)
- Checking the security situation – travel to areas such as Chechnya and Dagestan is dangerous and not recommended
- Very warm clothes and a long, windproof coat, if you're visiting during winter
- Thick-soled, waterproof, comfortable walking shoes
- Strong insect repellent for summer
- A sense of humour
- A stash of painkillers or other decent hangover cure

TOP TENS

Must-See Movies

Hollywood did Russia proud in David Lean's romantic epic *Doctor Zhivago* and spy thrillers such as *Gorky Park* and *The Russia House,* but otherwise its interest in the country as a location has been limited. No matter, as Russia has its own illustrious movie-making record. Check out the following classic movies, listed in chronological order, and for more on Russian cinema see p88.

- *Battleship Potemkin* (1925) Sergei Eisenstein
- *Ivan the Terrible* (1945) Sergei Eisenstein
- *The Cranes Are Flying* (1957) Mikhail Kalatozov
- *Irony of Fate* (1975) Eldar Ryazanov
- *Stalker* (1980) Andrei Tarkovsky
- *My Friend Ivan Lapshin* (1982) Alexey German
- *Burnt by the Sun* (1994) Nikita Mikhalkov
- *Brother* (1997) Alexey Balabanov
- *Russian Ark* (2002) Alexander Sokurov
- *The Return* (2003) Andrei Zvyagintsev

Great Reads

Russian literature flourished in the 19th century when leviathans such as Pushkin, Gogol, Chekhov and Dostoevsky were wielding their pens. However, 20th- and 21st-century Russia has also bred several notable wordsmiths whose works afford a glimpse of the country's troubled soul. For more on Russian literature go to p89.

- *War and Peace* Leo Tolstoy
- *Dr Zhivago* Boris Pasternak
- *The Master and Margarita* Mikhail Bulgakov
- *Quiet Flows the Don* Mikhail Sholokhov
- *Crime and Punishment* Fyodor Dostoevsky
- *Eugene Onegin* Alexander Pushkin
- *The Overcoat* Nikolai Gogol
- *Fathers and Sons* Ivan Turgenev
- *Kolyma Tales* Varlam Shalamov
- *A Hero's Daughter* Andrei Makine

Quintessential Experiences

- Bunk down on a train – even if you don't have time for the full trans-Siberian trip (p742), taking an overnight train is a rite of passage in Russian travel.

- Scrub yourself in a *banya* – wallow in a steamy communal sauna and allow yourself to be thrashed with birch leaves (p71).

- Whisper your wishes to Father Frost – Russia's Santa Claus holds court in the picturesque village of Veliky Ustyug (p401).

- Drink vodka – any time, any place. And if you want to learn something of the history of this great national drink head to the vodka museums in St Petersburg (p262) and Smolensk (p325).

- Sail down the Volga – the greatest of Russia's rivers is best experienced from the deck of one of the many boats that cruise its length each summer (p406).

- Weekend at a dacha – accept any invitation you get to a Russian's rural retreat (p72).

- Take the cure at a sanatorium – sign up for relaxation, health regimes and medicinal baths in Soviet-era spas, some of which are grand enough for a tsar, such as those at Sochi (p467).

- Attend a Victory Day parade – be reminded of Russia's indomitable fighting spirit and tumultuous past during the colourful street marches in early May (p706).

- Swim in Lake Baikal – locals claim a full body dip in the frigid waters of this supreme Siberian lake (p563) will grant you several decades of good health.

- Attend the ballet or opera – Moscow's Bolshoi (p182) and St Petersburg's Mariinsky (p287) theatres are the obvious choices, but many other Russian cities have grand performance halls, including Siberia's Novosibirsk (p513).

TRAVEL LITERATURE

Andrew Meier's *Black Earth: A Journey Through Russia after the Fall* is acutely observed and elegiac. In dispatches from Chechnya, Norilsk, Sakhalin and St Petersburg, as well as Moscow, he sums up Russia's current situation superbly. Also worth dipping into is Vanora Bennett's lyrical *The Taste of Dreams*, in which she heads south to the Caspian Sea in search of news and the luxurious grey eggs.

Black Earth City, an eloquent account of Charlotte Hobson's year studying in Voronezh in the turbulent period following the dissolution of the Soviet Union, captures eternal truths about the Russian way of life. The 1960s USSR encountered by Laurens van der Post in *Journey into Russia* seems awfully familiar, too, as does the Russia that Colin Thubron details in *Among the Russians* (published in some countries as *Where Nights Are Longest*). More up to date is Thubron's *In Siberia*, a fascinating but often sombre account of the author's journey from the Urals to Magadan.

Mark Taplin's *Open Lands: Travels through Russia's Once Forbidden Places* is an engrossing read, covering some of Russia's once off-limits cities, including Vladivostok and Nizhny Novgorod.

The Trans-Siberian Railway has been a rich source of inspiration for many writers. Paul Theroux covers the journey, caustically as usual, in both *The Great Railway Bazaar* and, a decade later, *Riding the Iron Rooster*. Eric Newby's classic *The Big Red Train Ride* is a hilarious account of hopping on and off the *Rossiya* between Moscow and Nakhodka. The legendary Dervla Murphy hobbles through Siberia on a crook leg in *Through Siberia by Accident*, characteristically taking the less glamorous BAM route to Tynda.

In *The Bronski House*, Philip Marsden travels with his friend back to her childhood village of Mantuski, now in Belarus; it's a poignant and evocative read.

INTERNET RESOURCES

Russia
CIA World Factbook (www.cia.gov/cia/publications/factbook/geos/rs.html) Read what the US spooks have on the Russkies.
Lonely Planet (www.lonelyplanet.com) Russian travel tips and blogs plus the Thorn Tree bulletin board.
Moscow Times (www.moscowtimes.ru) All the latest breaking national news plus links to sister paper the *St Petersburg Times* and a good travel section.
Tourism Department of Russian Federation (www.russiatourism.ru/eng) The official tourist website has a few useful bits of information.
Trans-Siberian Railway Web Encyclopaedia (www.transsib.ru/Eng) The best trans-Siberian site, regularly updated with tons of useful information and a huge photo library. (There's also a German-language version at www.trans-sib.de.)
Way to Russia (www.waytorussia.net) This incredibly useful Russian travel site is written and maintained by Russian backpackers. Lots of cool information, including details on arranging visas.
Your Train (www.poezda.net/en/) Invaluable site for planning train journeys to, from and inside Russia.

Belarus
A Belarus Miscellany (www.belarus-misc.org) Not the most user-friendly interface, but this site has tons about current news and historical facts from a patriotic view.
Karta Minska (www.kartaminska.by.ru/belorussian-tours.htm) Much of this made-in-Russia site is in Russian, but it's the funkiest one around about Minsk and Belarus, chock-full of cheeky and amusing photos.
Virtual Guide to Belarus (www.belarusguide.com) Well-organised site containing more than you could ever want to know about Belarus.

HOW MUCH?

In Russia/ Belarus
3-star double room R3500-4000/ BR110,000-170,000
1hr online R50/BR2000
Meal & drink in a decent restaurant R600-1000/ BR20,000-35,000
Short taxi ride R100/ BR6000
1L of petrol R15-20/ BR2400-2600

LONELY PLANET INDEX

In Russia/ Belarus
1L of bottled water R12/BR1200
Bottle of local beer R70/BR900
Souvenir *matryoshka* doll R150-300/ BR15,000-20,000
Blin R30/BR1500
Metro ticket R10/BR360

Itineraries
CLASSIC ROUTES

RUSSIAN CAPITALS
Two Weeks

If you've never been to Russia before, start with the awe-inspiring capital **Moscow** (p120) and the spellbinding imperial capital **St Petersburg** (p224); Russia's tumultuous history and fast-evolving future are writ large across both. Moscow highlights include the historic **Kremlin** (p138), glorious **Red Square** (p147) and classic **Tretyakov Gallery** (p160), while in St Petersburg do not miss the incomparable **Hermitage** (p244) and the **Russian Museum** (p252), or cruising the city's **rivers and canals** (p272). Enjoy nights dining and drinking at some of the best restaurants and bars in Russia, witnessing first-rate performances at the **Bolshoi** (p182) or **Mariinsky Theatres** (p287), or relaxing in a *banya* such as Moscow's luxury **Sanduny Baths** (p167). St Petersburg is ringed by glittering palaces set in beautifully landscaped grounds such as **Petrodvorets** (p295), **Tsarskoe Selo** and **Pavlovsk** (p299). From Moscow you have easy access to the historic Golden Ring towns of **Sergiev Posad** (p221), **Suzdal** (p206) and **Vladimir** (p203), where you will be rewarded with a slice of rural Russian life far from the frenetic city pace. Also leave time for ancient **Novgorod** (p327), home to an impressive kremlin, the Byzantine Cathedral of St Sophia and the riverside Yurev Monastery.

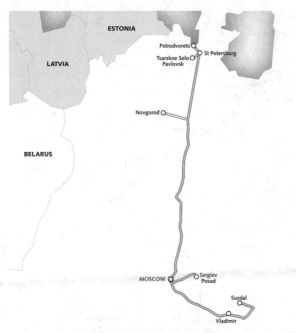

Moscow and St Petersburg are linked by a 650km-long railway. A week is the absolute minimum needed if you want to experience the cream of both cities. Add on another week if you plan on visiting the Golden Ring towns, the palaces around St Petersburg, and Novgorod, where it's best to stay at least one night.

FROM THE BALTIC TO THE CASPIAN   Three Weeks

There's plenty to see and do in European Russia as this itinerary from the Baltic coast to the Caspian Sea shows. Kick off in the geographically separate region of Kaliningrad, Russia's most westerly outpost, sandwiched between Poland and Lithuania. Check out the evolving maritime city of **Kaliningrad** (p342) and the World Heritage area **Kurshkaya Kosa** (p350), the Russian half of the sandy Curonian Spit, then head south through Poland to enter Belarus at the historic border town **Brest** (p682). Pause to marvel at the Brest Fortress, a colossal WWII memorial, and enjoy Belarus' most laid-back city before spotting mammoth bisons in the centuries-old oak and pine forests of the **Belavezhskaja Pushcha National Park** (p686). Head to the squeaky-clean capital **Minsk** (p666), where the heart of the Soviet Union still beats loud, then take a side trip to the artistic town of **Vitsebsk** (p691), birthplace of Marc Chagall. Reentering Russia, linger in the charming walled city of **Smolensk** (p322), which has a connection to the composer Mikhail Glinka, before indulging in the bright lights and big nights of **Moscow** (p120). If it's summer, consider booking a berth on one of the cruise ships that frequently sail down Mother Russia's No 1 waterway, the **Volga River** (p406). Possible stops along the route include Russia's 'third capital' **Nizhny Novgorod** (p406), with its mighty kremlin and the Sakharov Museum; the Tatar capital **Kazan** (p411), also with a World Heritage–listed kremlin; and **Volgograd** (p422), sacred site of Russia's bloodiest battle of WWII. Follow the river to its delta on the Caspian Sea and you'll arrive at **Astrakhan** (p425), which has a lively market and a well-preserved kremlin, but is most famous for its black gold: caviar.

Combining the possibilities of travelling by road, rail and river this 2500km route takes you from the Baltic coast to the Caspian Sea and the very edge of Central Asia. Remember to sort out a multiple-entry visa to Russia and a visa to Belarus and you'll be ready for a full exploration of western European Russia.

THE BIG TRANS-SIBERIAN TRIP   Two to Four Weeks

The classic Russian adventure is travelling the **Trans-Siberian Railway** (p742), one of the 20th-century's engineering wonders and a route that holds together the world's largest country. Although it can be done in either direction we suggest going against the general flow by boarding the train in the port of **Vladivostok** (p614), at the far eastern end of Russia, so you can finish up with a grand party in either **Moscow** (p120) or, better yet, **St Petersburg** (p224). Vladivostok, situated on a stunningly attractive natural harbour, merits a couple of days of your time, and it's also worth considering a stop off at **Khabarovsk** (p607), a lively city of some charm on the banks of the Amur River – it's just an overnight hop to the west. Save a couple of days for **Ulan-Ude** (p589), a fascinating city where Russian, Soviet and Mongolian cultures coexist, and from where you can venture into the steppes to visit Russia's principal Buddhist monastery, **Ivolginsk Datsan** (p594). Just west of Ulan-Ude the railway hugs the southern shores of magnificent **Lake Baikal** (p563). Allow at least three days (preferably longer) to see this beautiful lake, basing yourself on beguiling **Olkhon Island** (p578); also check out historic **Irkutsk** (p563) on the way there or back. **Krasnoyarsk** (p553), on the Yenisey River, affords the opportunity for scenic cruises along one of Siberia's most pleasant waterways. Crossing the Urals into European Russia, the first stop of note is **Yekaterinburg** (p436), a historic, bustling city well stocked with interesting museums and sites connected to the murder of the last tsar and his family. Your last stop before Moscow could be either of the Golden Ring towns of **Yaroslavl** (p213) or **Vladimir** (p203), both packed with ancient onion-domed churches.

The 9289km journey between Moscow and Vladivostok can be done, nonstop, in a week, but unless you're into extreme relaxation we recommend hopping on and off the train, making more of an adventure of it. Spend time seeing the sights in Moscow and St Petersburg and you could easily stretch this trip to a month.

ROADS LESS TRAVELLED

Travel junkies will relish this off-beat trip involving overnight train journeys, hopping around on planes and helicopters, and possibly a bumpy ride by bus through forbidding stretches of taiga and tundra. In summer there's also the chance to relax on a languid river cruise between Khabarovsk and Komsomolsk-na-Amure.

RUSSIAN FAR EAST CIRCUIT   One Month

Travel in the Russian Far East isn't so much a holiday as an expedition. From the 'wild east' port of **Vladivostok** (p614) head north to **Khabarovsk** (p607), with a possible detour to the World Heritage–listed **Sikhote-Alin Nature Reserve** (p623). An overnight train from Khabarovsk heads to the lively border town **Blagoveshchensk** (p606) – China is on the opposite bank of the Amur River. Another overnight train from here will transport you to **Tynda** (p623), headquarters of the Baikal-Amur Mainline (BAM) construction company and a great place to refresh at the local *banya*. From here there's a choice. Train and hard-travel fanatics should head to **Neryungri** (p624) from where there's a very bumpy and erratic bus to **Yakutsk** (p627), the extraordinary permafrost-bound capital of Sakha Republic. Alternatively, stick with the BAM route through to the proudly Soviet city of **Komsomolsk-na-Amure** (p624) and back to Khabarovsk, from where there are flights to Yakutsk. Once in Yakutsk, make time to cruise to the scenic **Lena Pillars** (p631), and to visit the city's fascinating **Permafrost Institute** (p627). A flight from either Khabarovsk or Vladivostok will take you over the Sea of Okhotsk to the highlight of this far-eastern odyssey: **Kamchatka** (p642). Cap off your adventures by climbing one of the snowcapped volcanoes rising behind the rugged peninsula's capital, **Petropavlovsk-Kamchatsky** (p644), which hugs breathtakingly serene Avacha Bay, and by visiting **Esso** (p650), as charming an alpine village as you could wish for at the end of a long bumpy road.

TYUMEN TO TUVA:
SIBERIA OFF THE BEATEN TRACK
One to Two Months

Far from the forbidding land of the popular imagination, Siberia is a vast, glorious, adventure-travel playground where you could spend months happily exploring areas away from the well-travelled trans-Siberian route. For a journey covering some of Siberia's lesser-known locations begin in the oil-rich city of **Tyumen** (p497), which for all its contemporary bustle includes several picturesque areas of traditional architecture. Journey northeast in the footsteps of the Siberian conqueror Yermak Timofeevich, the exiled writer Fyodor Dostoevsky and the last tsar to **Tobolsk** (p501), whose splendid kremlin lords it over the Tobol and Irtysh Rivers. Upriver and back on the main trans-Sib route is **Omsk** (p504), a pleasant, thriving city, from where you can head directly to the backwater of **Tomsk** (p515), a convivial university town dotted with pretty wooden gingerbread-style houses. Journey south next to **Barnaul** (p522), gateway to the mountainous **Altai Republic** (p520). Here you can arrange a white-water rafting expedition or plan treks out to **Lake Teletskoe** and the arty village of **Artybash** (p528), or along the panoramic **Chuysky Trakt** (p531), a helter-skelter mountain road leading to yurt-dotted grasslands, first stopping in **Gorno-Altaisk** (p526) where you'll have to register your visa. A train journey via **Novokuznetsk** (p536) will get you to **Abakan** (p538), where you can arrange onward travel to the wild republic of **Tuva** (p546). This remote and little-visited region, hard up against Mongolia (with which it shares several cultural similarities), is famed for its throat-singing nomads and mystic shamans. Use the uninspiring capital **Kyzyl** (p548) as a base for expeditions to pretty villages and the vast Central Asian steppes.

Direct overnight trains link the major cities on this Siberia-wide itinerary, save Kyzyl, which is best reached either by flight from Barnaul or by a shared taxi from Abakan along the spectacular mountain route, the Usinsky Trakt. In summer a two-day boat trip between Tobolsk and Omsk is also possible.

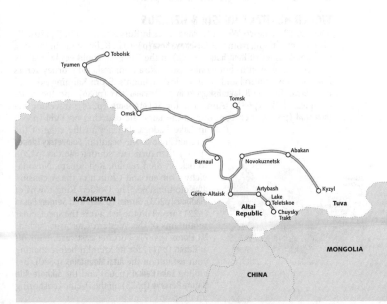

TAILORED TRIPS

LITERARY RUSSIA

A tour of the locations associated with Russia's literary giants gives you an insight into what inspired their work, and makes for an offbeat trip across Russia, from the Baltic to the Pacific and back to the Black Sea. **St Petersburg** (p224) is arguably Russia's city of letters, with museums in the former homes of Fyodor Dostoevsky, Alexander Pushkin and the poet Anna Akhmatova. You can also pay your respects at Dostoevsky's summer hideaway in **Staraya Russa** (p333) and the Siberian prisons in which he languished in **Tobolsk** (p501) and **Omsk** (p504). In contrast Anton Chekhov, whose country estate is at **Melikhovo** (p198), made a voluntary trip across Siberia ending up on Sakhalin; a small museum in the island's capital, **Yuzhno-Sakhalinsk** (p635), commemorates the writer's epic journey. Boris Pasternak's dacha in the writers' colony of **Peredelkino** (p198) is open for inspection, as is **Yasnaya Polyana** (p199), Leo Tolstoy's estate, which is surrounded by apple orchards, and **Spasskoe-Lutovinovo** (p319), the family manor of Ivan Turgenev. Recite your favourite Pushkin verses at his home in **Mikhailovskoe** (p339) before heading south, as the poet did in exile, to the romantic, troubled Caucasus and the resort of **Pyatigorsk** (p472), where fellow poet Mikhail Lermontov is commemorated all over town at a grotto, gallery, museum and gardens.

WORLD HERITAGE RUSSIA & BELARUS

There are 21 Unesco World Heritage sites in Russia and two in Belarus. To visit many of them, from the **Kurshkaya Kosa** (p350) in Kaliningrad in the west to the volcanoes of **Kamchatka** (p642) in the Far East, could easily swallow up a couple of months but would also make an unparalleled journey across both nations' cultural and geographical highlights. From Kaliningrad head to Belarus for the **Belavezhskaja Pushcha National Park** (p686) and the castle complex at **Mir** (p681). Aim next for **St Petersburg** (p224), travelling via **Novgorod** (p327), then continue to the fairy-tale churches on **Kizhi** (p361) in Lake Ladoga. Journey to the edge of the Arctic Circle to the beautiful **Solovetsky Islands** (p391), then turn back south to **Moscow** (p120), to tick off the Kremlin, Red Square, Novodevichy Convent and Church of the Ascension at Kolomenskoe. The Golden Ring towns of **Vladimir** (p203), **Suzdal** (p206) and **Sergiev Posad** (p221) are all on the list, as are the spectacular mountains of the Western Caucasus such as **Mt Elbrus** (p487). Turning eastward, stop off at **Kazan** (p411) for its kremlin before making your assault on the **Altai Mountains** (p520). Beguiling **Lake Baikal** (p563) and the **Sikhote-Alin Nature Reserve** (p623) on the Pacific coast bring up the rear.

Snapshot

Normalno. That's the word Russians most commonly use to describe their lives – not good, not bad, just *normalno.* So, is Russia, after the authoritarianism of the Soviet era and the economic chaos of the Yeltsin years, becoming a more 'normal' (ie Western) country under Vladimir Putin? In some ways yes, but in others no.

In economic terms it's clear that Russia, coasting along on a wave of petrodollar profits, is in far better shape than at any time in recent memory. Growth is running at over 7% per annum. Inflation – rampant in the 1990s – is under control, with a consequent stabilisation of the rouble. Three-quarters of state enterprise has been either fully or partially privatised (albeit with much corruption along the way). In all the major cities you'll notice a burgeoning middle class, and the commercial trappings that go with it.

Despite these improvements, Russia's economy still has a way to go before it can be said to have fully capitalised on its astonishing natural resources. The boom and bust period of the late 1990s as well as the abandonment of the social safety net provided by communism has left many people worse off. According to World Bank figures published in 2004, 20% of Russians live below the poverty line, defined as a monthly income of R1000 (less than €30 or US$38). At least 5.5 million people are unemployed, although many others considered 'employed' have jobs with little work and less pay.

Democracy is another sticky subject. In the December 2003 elections the propresidential party United Russia won two-thirds of the Duma's seats, while in the subsequent presidential election Putin comfortably romped home for a second (and probably final) term of office, but few people would say that either of these victories reflected the true political opinions of Russians. More telling was the nose dive in Putin's popularity, from a high of 70% to around 40%, in the wake of a series of spontaneous public protests across the nation in early 2005 as the government passed controversial laws replacing important transport, housing and utility subsidies for pensioners, invalids and army veterans with extra pension payments. Nonetheless, Putin still remains the most popular of Russia's often dubious bunch of politicians.

A substantial part of the public's growing cynicism with the Kremlin boils down to the failure of Russia to become what is seen in the West as a fully democratic country. In 2005 increased control of the media, politicisation of the law enforcement system and the imposition of central government control on local government caused the US-based organisation Freedom House to classify Russia as 'not free', for the first time since the demise of the Soviet Union in 1991. The KGB might be history, but ordinary Russians now look over their shoulder for Putin's shadowy *siloviki* (power people), an unholy alliance of power-hungry law enforcers and bureaucrats who many believe really run the country.

Putin has been accused of exploiting the recent wave of terrorist attacks, such as the 2004 hostage crisis in Beslan (p69) and the bombing of Moscow's metro, to further curb civil liberties (not a topic the former KGB agent has ever shown much true concern over anyway). The Kremlin insists that life in the breakaway republic of Chechnya is getting back to normal, but human rights groups beg to differ, accusing government forces of regularly abducting innocent civilians for interrogation. The

FAST FACTS: RUSSIA

Population: 143.4 million

Surface area: 17 million sq km

Time zones: 11

National symbol: double-headed eagle

Extent of the Russian rail network: 87,000 km

State pension: about R2000 per month

Net worth of the 27 richest Russians: US$90.6 billion

Per capita consumption of alcohol: 15.1L per year

Number of languages spoken (other than Russian): over 100

Number of Nobel Prize winners: 20

assassination by Russian special forces in March 2005 of separatist leader Aslan Maskhadov, one of the few figures in the Chechen resistance to offer peace talks with Moscow, did nothing to bring the conflict any nearer to resolution.

The international fight against terrorism has brought Russia well and truly out of the diplomatic cold. However, a neat illustration of the delicate position that Russia finds itself in with regard to foreign policy came with the celebration of the 60th anniversary of WWII. President Bush standing side by side with Putin in Red Square watching a very Soviet-style parade of Russian military might spoke volumes about how far relations between the former Cold War enemies have progressed. But the fact that Bush had visited Latvia beforehand, supporting the Baltic States' calls for apologies from Russia for the post-WWII annexation of their countries into the Soviet Union, also showed how far Russia still has to go before it's fully trusted in the region again.

Having seen popular revolutions recently sweep away the old guard in Ukraine and Kyrgyzstan, there is understandably a certain nervousness in the Kremlin that similar events could happen in Russia in the run-up to the 2008 presidential election. Meanwhile in neighbouring Belarus, Alexander Lukashenka, its autocratic leader, has proclaimed that no revolutions, coloured or otherwise, would be happening there. 'Batka' (Daddy, or Little Father, as he's ironically dubbed by many locals) gives the impression that his hands guide every shimmer and sway of society. While most city folk don't regard him favourably, be cautious about your anti-Batka proclamations – being against the system is a touchy subject here!

Privately the debate in Belarus is all about whether to open up to or close off from the rest of the world. While the government erects barriers against the evil West, ordinary folk are caught between the desire to maintain stability, and wanting to make a decent living in a free and open society. In Minsk especially you are bound to be drawn into conversations about the latest ludicrous law or street name change; it's also where you'll most feel the surreal mix of Belarus as both a living Soviet museum and modern European city.

Russia

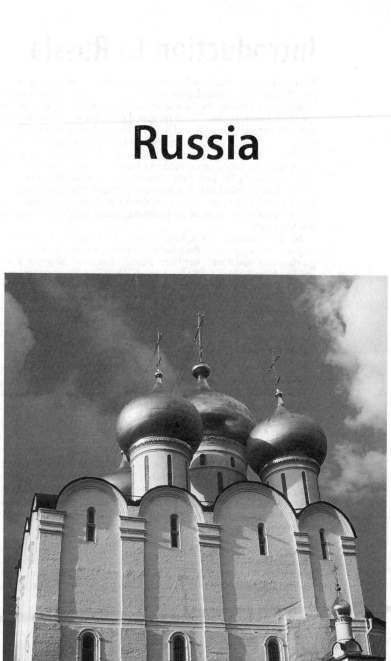

JONATHAN SMITH

Introduction to Russia

Your experience of Russia will depend very much on where you choose to go. While our Itineraries chapter can help you sort through the multiple options, the following should also provide a clearer idea of how best to spend your time. In short, those interested primarily in Russia's cultural and architectural highlights, and those whose need for creature comforts is high, should stick to European Russia, which is all of the country west of the Ural Mountains. If you don't mind occasionally roughing it and are in search of Russia's great outdoors, train your eye on the vast spaces of Siberia and the Far East. Even if you restrict your travels to European Russia, bear in mind that this area is still bigger than any European country, with terrain stretching from the frozen tundra that borders the Arctic Ocean to the peaks of the Caucasus, Europe's highest mountains, 3000km south.

Between these extremes lie Russia's two greatest cities and biggest tourist draws: Moscow and St Petersburg. Here tsars reigned and the world's greatest communist state was born, Russia's unique architecture developed and the Russian Orthodox Church flourished. Here too, modern Russia is most evident – as any traveller can experience in flashy, contemporary hotels, shops and restaurants or while sampling the pumping nightlife. Still, within a few hundred kilometres of either of these cities are dozens of appealing towns and villages where you can witness the timeless beauty of Russia's gentle landscape and agrarian culture: check out the highlights of both the Golden Ring and Western European Russia chapters for some ideas of where to go.

You don't need to head all the way to Siberia to find wilderness. North of St Petersburg in northern European Russia lie huge tracts of largely unexplored forest, lakes, marshes and tundra, ideal for outdoor pursuits. Among the more touristed sites are Kizhi Island, with its extraordinary assemblage of old wooden architecture; the venerable churches and monasteries of Vologda; and, especially popular with Russians, Father Frost's charming home town of Veliky Ustyug.

East from Moscow, then south, flows the Volga River. One of Russia's historic highways, the Volga links many cities of both ancient and modern importance – among them Yaroslavl (a key city in the famous Golden Ring), Nizhny Novgorod, Kazan, Volgograd and Astrakhan – along its course to the Caspian Sea. Numerous ethnic minorities, whose religious beliefs range from Islam to Buddhism to animism, live in or near to the Volga Basin. They are reminders of European Russia's proximity to Asia and its long history of invasion, migration and cultural exchange.

Forming a low barrier between European Russia and Siberia, the Ural Mountains stretch from Kazakhstan in the south to the Arctic Kara Sea in the north. Apart from opportunities to hike and undertake some gentle river rafting, here you'll find major cities, such as historic Yekaterinburg, and Russia's main downhill ski centre at Magnitogorsk.

The other great European Russian waterway, the Don River, flows south from near Moscow to the Sea of Azov, an offshoot of the Black Sea, near Rostov-on-Don, which is known as the gateway to the Northern Caucasus. South of here, along the Black Sea and centred around Sochi, is a coastal riviera to which Russians flock for summer holidays, while heading east is the Kuban Steppe, part of the great rolling grasslands (now largely given over to agriculture) that continue through to Mongolia. The

Caucasus Mountains, a range of spectacular beauty and home to an incredible jigsaw of ethnic groups, rise on Russia's southern fringe. Many of these people were not conquered by Russia until the 19th century; today, some are tragically mired in bloody conflicts with each other or with Russia, putting parts of this region firmly off limits to tourism.

The images traditionally associated with Siberia and the Russian Far East – prison camps, snowbound exile, frozen wastelands – are also less than welcoming. So it's a great surprise to many Westerners to discover that Siberian summers can be a blistering 35°C, that there are beachside rave parties in Novosibirsk, great new restaurants in most of the cities, and that icy cold March is actually the best time to visit as frozen lakes and rivers turn into motorable roads.

Certainly the region has a tragic history. Used by the tsars and then by the Soviet regime to dispose of 'undesirable elements', it took in first criminals, then political dissenters, the suspiciously wealthy, the religious, the stubborn citizens of troublesome nationalities and eventually virtually anyone for no reason at all. The writer Maxim Gorky gave voice to the national dread of Siberia when he described the region as 'a land of chains and ice'.

At the same time though, Russians have also long viewed this vast slab of land as a place of adventure, discovery and immense riches. This was where brave explorers and rapacious plunderers pushed forward the boundaries of the Russian Empire. Of the early exiles, many chose to stay on after their sentences had ended, seduced by the wide open spaces and, strangely enough, the sense of freedom.

The population of this great land is only three times that of metropolitan Moscow, with most of it huddled along the railways in the south, so with a handful of exceptions don't come here in search of manmade wonders. Instead be prepared to discover the serenity of Lake Baikal, the pristine geometry of the Altai Mountains, the fiery volcanic landscapes of Kamchatka, and the lush semitropical forests of the Sikhote-Alin Nature Reserve on the Pacific coast.

Travellers today still write, not of trips in Siberia, but of odysseys, hypnotised by unending views of taiga (Siberian forest) from the cocoon of a Trans-Siberian Railway carriage. By magnifying the difficulties for literary effect, such semifactual travelogues have helped to scare tourists into taking the 'rush through' approach. And travel agents are all too happy to oblige by perpetuating the 'tour only' myth. However, it's reasonably straightforward to hop across the region, taking one overnight train at a time, using the railway as a hotel, and spending the long summer days exploring.

History

Epic is the only word for Russia's history, which within the last century alone has packed in an indecent amount of world-shaking events and spawned larger-than-life characters from Rasputin to Boris Yeltsin. Even now, over a decade since the end of the Soviet Union, the official record is still in flux as long-secret documents come to light and then, just as mysteriously, become classified again. What is clear is that from its very beginnings Russia has been a multiethnic country, its inhabitants a colourful and exhausting list of native peoples and invaders, the descendants of whom are still around today.

Until 30 January 1918 the Russian calendar was 12 days behind that used in the West in the 19th century, and 13 days behind in the 20th century.

EARLY HISTORY

Human activity in Russia stretches back a million years, with evidence of Stone Age hunting communities in the region from Moscow to the Altai and Lake Baikal. By 2000 BC a basic agriculture, relying on hardy cereals, had penetrated from the Danube region as far east as the Moscow area and the southern Ural Mountains. At about the same time, peoples in Ukraine and southern areas of European Russia domesticated the horse and developed a nomadic, pastoral lifestyle.

Ex-diplomat Sir Fitzroy Maclean has written several entertaining, intelligent books on the country. *Holy Russia* is a good, short Russian history, while *All the Russias: The End of an Empire* covers the whole of the former USSR.

While central and northern European Russia remained a complete backwater for almost 3000 years, the south was subject to a succession of invasions by nomads from the east. The first written records, by the 5th-century-BC Greek historian Herodotus, concern a people called the Scythians, who probably originated in the Altai region of Siberia and Mongolia and were feared for their riding and battle skills. They spread as far west as southern Russia and Ukraine by the 7th century BC. The Scythian empire, which stretched south as far as Egypt, ended with the arrival of another people from the east, the Sarmatians, in the 3rd century BC.

In the 4th century AD, came the Huns of the Altai region, followed by their relations the Avars, then by the Khazars, a grouping of Turkic and Iranian tribes from the Caucasus, who occupied the lower Volga and Don Basins and the steppes to the east and west between the 7th and 10th centuries. The crafty and talented Khazars brought stability and religious tolerance to areas under their control. Their capital was Itil, near the mouth of the Volga. In the 9th century they converted to Judaism, and by the 10th century they had mostly settled down to farming and trade.

A History of Russia, by Nicholas Riasanovsky, is one of the best single-volume versions of the whole Russian story through to the end of the Soviet Union.

SLAVS

The migrants who were to give Russia its predominant character were the Slavs. There is some disagreement about where the Slavs originated, but in the first few centuries AD they expanded rapidly to the east, west and south from the vicinity of present-day northern Ukraine and southern Belarus. The Eastern Slavs were the ancestors of the Russians; they were still spreading eastward across the central Russian woodland belt in the 9th century. From the Western Slavs came the Poles, Czechs, Slovaks and others. The Southern Slavs became the Serbs, Croats, Slovenes and Bulgarians.

TIMELINE **c 20,000 BC**

Humans settle in Don River basin

AD 862

Rurik of Jutland founds Novgorod

The Slavs' conversion to Christianity in the 9th and 10th centuries was accompanied by the introduction of an alphabet devised by Cyril, a Greek missionary (later St Cyril), which was simplified a few decades later by a fellow missionary, Methodius. The forerunner of Cyrillic, it was based on the Greek alphabet, with a dozen or so additional characters. The Bible was translated into the Southern Slav dialect, which became known as Church Slavonic and is the language of the Russian Orthodox Church's liturgy to this day.

VIKINGS & KYIVAN RUS
The first Russian state developed out of the trade on river routes across Eastern Slavic areas – between the Baltic and Black Seas and, to a lesser extent, between the Baltic Sea and the Volga River. Vikings from Scandinavia, called Varyagi by the Slavs, had been nosing east from the Baltic since the 6th century AD, trading and raiding for furs, slaves and amber, and coming into conflict with the Khazars and with Byzantium, the eastern centre of Christianity. To secure their hold on the trade routes, the Vikings made themselves masters of settlements in key areas – places such as Novgorod, Smolensk, Staraya Ladoga and Kyiv (Kiev) in Ukraine. Though by no means united themselves, they created a loose confederation of city-states in the Eastern Slavic areas.

Predslava's Russian History Trivia page (members.aol.com /Predslava/RussianHistory TriviaPage.html) abounds with intriguing details, such as the fact that surnames didn't exist in Russia for most of the Middle Ages.

The founding of Novgorod in 862 by Rurik of Jutland is traditionally taken as the birth of the Russian state. Rurik's successor, Oleg, became Kyiv's ruler two decades later, and the Rurikid dynasty, though soon Slavicised, maintained its hold, and produced the dominant rulers in Eastern Slavic areas until the end of the 16th century.

The name Rus may have been that of the dominant Kyivan Viking clan, but it wasn't until the 18th century that the term Russian or Great Russian came to be used exclusively for Eastern Slavs in the north, while those to the south or west were identified as Ukrainians or Belarusians.

Prince Svyatoslav made Kyiv the dominant regional power by campaigning against quarrelling Varangian princes and dealing the Khazars a series of fatal blows. After his death, his son Vladimir made further conquests, and persuaded the Patriarch of Constantinople to establish an episcopal see – a Church 'branch' – in Kyiv in 988, marking the birth of the Russian Orthodox Church. He also introduced the beginnings of a feudal structure to replace clan allegiances, though some principalities – including Novgorod, Pskov and Vyatka (north of Kazan) – were ruled democratically by popular *vechi* (assemblies).

Geoffrey Hosking's *Russia and the Russians* is a definitive one-volume trot through 1000 years of Russian history by a top scholar.

Kyiv's supremacy was broken by new invaders from the east – first the Pechenegs, then in 1093 the Polovtsy sacked the city – and by the effects of European crusades from the late 11th century onwards, which broke the Arab hold on southern Europe and the Mediterranean, reviving west–east trade routes and making Rus a commercial backwater.

NOVGOROD & ROSTOV-SUZDAL
The northern Rus principalities began breaking from Kyiv after about 1050. The merchants of Novgorod joined the emerging Hanseatic League, a federation of city-states that controlled Baltic and North Sea trade. Novgorod became the league's gateway to the lands east and southeast.

988	1108
Russian Orthodox Church established in Kyiv	Vladimir Monomakh of Kyiv founds Vladimir

NAMING RUSSIAN RULERS

In line with common usage, names of pre-1700 rulers are directly transliterated, anglicised from Peter the Great until 1917, and again transliterated after that – thus Andrei Bogolyubov not Andrew, Vasily III not Basil; but Peter the Great not Pyotr, Catherine the Great not Yekaterina etc.

Ivan the Great was the first ruler to have himself formally called tsar. Peter the Great began using emperor, though tsar remained in use. In this book we use empress for a female ruler; a tsar's wife who does not become ruler is a *tsaritsa* (in English, tsarina). A tsar's son is a *tsarevitch* and his daughter a *tsarevna*.

As Kyiv declined, the Russian population shifted northwards and the fertile Rostov-Suzdal region northeast of Moscow began to be developed. Vladimir Monomakh of Kyiv founded the town of Vladimir there in 1108 and gave the Rostov-Suzdal principality to his son Yury Dolgoruky, who is credited with founding the little settlement of Moscow in 1147.

Rostov-Suzdal grew so rich and strong that Yury's son Andrei Bogolyubov sacked Kyiv in 1169 and moved the court to Vladimir. The Church's headquarters remained in Kyiv until 1300. Rostov-Suzdal began to gear up for a challenge against the Bulgars' hold on the Volga-Ural Mountains region. The Bulgars were a people who had originated further east several centuries before and had since converted to Islam. Their capital, Bolgar, was near modern Kazan, on the Volga.

The Secret History of the Mongols, Mongolia's most famous book about the life and deeds of Chinggis Khaan, has no known author. You can find several English translations including a 1990 one by Urgunge Onon.

TATARS & THE GOLDEN HORDE

Meanwhile, over in the east, a confederation of armies headed by the Mongolian warlord Chinggis (Genghis) Khaan (1167–1227) was busy subduing most of Asia, except far northern Siberia, eventually crossing Russia into Europe to create history's largest land empire. Russians often refer to these mainly Mongol invaders as Tatars, when in fact the Tatars were simply one particularly powerful tribe that joined the Mongol bandwagon. The Tatars of Tatarstan actually descended from the Bulgars and are related to the Bulgarians of the Balkans.

In 1223 Chinggis' forces met the armies of the Russian princes and thrashed them at the Battle of Kalka River. This push into European Russia was cut short by the death of the warlord, but his grandson Batu Khaan returned in 1236 to finish the job, laying waste to Bolgar and Rostov-Suzdal, and annihilating most of the other Russian principalities, including Kyiv, within four years. Novgorod was saved only by spring floods that prevented the invaders from crossing the marshes around the city.

Batu and his successors ruled the Golden Horde (one of the khanates into which Chinggis' empire had broken) from Saray on the Volga, near modern Volgograd. The Horde's control over its subjects was indirect: although it raided them in traditional fashion if they grew uppity, it mainly used local princes to keep order, provide soldiers and collect taxes.

ALEXANDER NEVSKY & THE RISE OF MOSCOW

One such 'collaborator' was the Prince of Novgorod, Alexander Nevsky, a Russian hero (and later a saint of the Russian Church) for his resistance to German crusaders and Swedish invaders. His victory in 1240 over the

| Vladimir's son Yury Dolgoruky builds Moscow's Kremlin | Mongol hordes overrun Russian principalities |

THE COSSACKS

The word 'Cossack' (from the Turkic *kazak*, meaning free man, adventurer or horseman) was originally applied to residual Tatar groups and later to serfs, paupers and dropouts who fled south from Russia, Poland and Lithuania in the 15th century. They organised themselves into self-governing communities in the Don Basin, on the Dnipro (Dnepr in Russian) River in Ukraine, and in western Kazakhstan. Those in a given region, eg the Don Cossacks, were not just a tribe; its men constituted a *voysko* (army), within which each *stanitsa* (village-regiment) elected an ataman, or leader.

Mindful of their skill as fighters, the Russian government treated the Cossacks carefully, offering autonomy in return for military service. Cossacks were the wedge that opened Siberia in the 17th century. By the 19th century there were a dozen Cossack armies from Ukraine to the Russian Far East.

But they still raised hell when things didn't suit them. Three peasant uprisings in the Volga-Don region – 1670, 1707 and 1773 – were Cossack-led. After 1917 the Bolsheviks abolished Cossack institutions, though some cavalry units were revived in WWII. Since 1991 there has been a major Cossack revival. Cossack regiments have been officially recognised, there is a presidential advisor on Cossacks, and some Cossacks demand that the state recognise them as an ethnic group.

Swedes on the Neva River, near present-day St Petersburg, earned him his nickname, 'Nevsky'. Later, in 1252, Batu Khaan put him on the throne as Grand Prince of Vladimir.

Nevsky and his successors acted as intermediaries between the Tatars and other Russian princes. With shrewd diplomacy, the princes of Moscow obtained and hung on to the title of grand prince from the early 14th century while other princes resumed their feuding. The Church provided backing to Moscow by moving there from Vladimir in the 1320s, and was in turn favoured with exemption from Tatar taxation.

But Moscow proved to be the Tatars' nemesis. With a new-found Russian confidence, Grand Prince Dmitry put Moscow at the head of a coalition of princes and took on the Tatars, defeating them in the Kulikovo Pole battle on the Don River in 1380. For this he became Dmitry Donskoy (of the Don) and was canonised after his death.

The Tatars crushed this uprising in a three-year campaign but their days were numbered. Weakened by internal dissension, they fell at the end of the 14th century to the Turkic empire of Timur (Tamerlane), which was based in Samarkand (in present day Uzbekistan). Yet the Russians, themselves divided as usual, remained Tatar vassals until 1480.

MOSCOW VS LITHUANIA

Moscow (or Muscovy, as its expanding lands came to be known) was champion of the Russian cause after Kulikovo, though it had rivals, especially Novgorod and Tver. More ominous was the rise of the Grand Duchy of Lithuania, which had started to expand into old Kyivan Rus lands in the 14th century. The threat became real in 1386 when the Lithuanian ruler Jogaila married the Polish queen Jadwiga and became king of Poland, thus joining two of Europe's most powerful states.

With Jogaila's coronation as Wladyslaw II of Poland, the previously pagan Lithuanian ruling class embraced Catholicism. The Russian Church

1325	1326
Ivan I (Ivan the Moneybags) starts a major building programme in the Kremlin	Seat of the Orthodox Church shifts from Vladimir to Moscow

portrayed the struggle against Lithuania as one against the pope in Rome. After Constantinople (centre of the Greek Orthodox Church) was taken by the Turks in 1453, the metropolitan or head of the Russian Church declared Moscow the 'third Rome', the true heir of Christianity.

Meanwhile, with the death of Dmitry Donskoy's son in 1425, Muscovy suffered a dynastic war. The old Rurikids got the upper hand – ironically with Lithuanian and Tatar help – but it was only with Ivan III's forceful reign from 1462 to 1505 that the other principalities ceased to oppose Muscovy.

Ivan III, also called Ivan the Great, brought most of the Great Russian principalities to heel. Novgorod was first, in 1478, as it was no longer able to rely on the Tatars as a diversion. Two years later a Russian army faced the Tatars at the Ugra River southwest of Moscow. Though they parted without a fight, after that Ivan simply stopped paying tribute to the Golden Horde.

Tver fell to Moscow in 1485, and far-flung Vyatka in 1489. Pskov and Ryazan, the only states still independent at the end of Ivan's reign, were mopped up by his successor, Vasily III. Lithuania and Poland, however, remained thorns in Russia's side.

Ivan III was the first Russian emperor to adopt the use of the double-headed eagle as the symbol of state.

SERVANTS & SERFS

When Ivan III took Novgorod he installed a governor, exiled the city's influential families and ejected the Hanseatic merchants, turning Russia's back on Western Europe for two centuries. The exiles were replaced with Ivan's administrators, who got temporary title to confiscated lands for good performance. This new approach to land tenure, called *pomestie* (estate), characterised Ivan's rule. Previously, the boyars (feudal landholders) had held land under a *votchina* (system of patrimony) giving them unlimited control and inheritance rights over their lands and the people on them. The freedom to shift allegiance to other princes had given them political clout, too. Now, with few alternative princes left, the influence of the boyars declined in favour of the new landholding civil servants.

Sergei Eisenstein takes on yet another key figure in Russian history in his 1938 movie *Alexander Nevsky*, focusing on the saviour of Russia's epic battle with the Teutonic knights.

This increased central control spread to the lower levels of society with the growth of serfdom. Before the 1500s, peasants could work for themselves after meeting their master's needs, and could even change jobs during the two weeks around St George's Day in November. These rights were less frequently bestowed by the new masters, who lacked the old sense of obligation, and peasants became a permanent fixture on the land.

IVAN IV (THE TERRIBLE)

Vasily III's son, Ivan IV, took the throne in 1533 at age three, with his mother as regent. After 13 years of court intrigue he had himself crowned 'Tsar of all the Russias'. The word 'tsar', from the Latin *caesar*, had previously been used only for a great khan or for the emperor of Constantinople.

Ivan IV's marriage to Anastasia, from the Romanov boyar family, was a happy one – unlike the five that followed her death in 1560, a turning point in his life. Believing her to have been poisoned, Ivan instituted a reign of terror that earned him the sobriquet *grozny* (literally 'awesome'

1382	Late 1400s
Mongols invade again, slaughtering half of Moscow's population	Ivan III (Ivan the Great) rebuilds the Kremlin and defeats Mongols

but commonly translated as 'terrible') and nearly destroyed all his earlier good works. In a fit of rage he even killed his eldest son and heir, Ivan.

His subsequent career was indeed terrible, though he was admired for upholding Russian interests and tradition. During his active reign (1547–84), Russia defeated the surviving Tatar khanates of Kazan (in 1552) and Astrakhan (in 1556), thus acquiring the whole Volga region and a chunk of the Caspian Sea coast, and opening the way to Siberia. His campaign against the Crimean Tatars, however, nearly ended with the loss of Moscow.

Ivan's interest in the West and obsession with reaching the Baltic Sea foreshadowed Peter the Great, but he failed to break through, only antagonising the Lithuanians, Poles and Swedes, and setting the stage for the Time of Troubles. His growing paranoia led to a savage attack on Novgorod that finally snuffed out that city's golden age.

A potted history of Ivan the Terrible can be found on the BBC's history website at www.bbc.co.uk/history/programmes/ivan/ivanmain.shtml.

BORIS GODUNOV & THE TIME OF TROUBLES

When Ivan IV died of poisoning in 1584, rule passed to his second son, the hopeless Fyodor I, who had the sense to leave government to his brother-in-law, Boris Godunov, a skilled 'prime minister' who repaired much of Ivan's damage. Fyodor died childless in 1598, ending the 700-year Rurikid dynasty, and Boris ruled as tsar for seven more years.

Then a Polish-backed Catholic pretender arrived on the scene claiming to be Dmitry, another son of Ivan the Terrible, who had died in obscure circumstances – murdered on Boris Godunov's orders, some said. This 'False Dmitry' gathered a huge ragtag army as he advanced on Moscow. Boris Godunov conveniently died, his son was lynched and the boyars acclaimed the pretender tsar.

Thus began the Time of Troubles, or Smuta (1606–13); a spell of anarchy, dynastic chaos and foreign invasions. At its heart was a struggle between the boyars and central government (the tsar). The False Dmitry was murdered in a popular revolt and succeeded by Vasily Shuysky (1606–10), another boyar puppet. Then a second False Dmitry challenged Shuysky. Swedish and Polish invaders fought each other over claims to the Russian throne, Shuysky was dethroned by the boyars, and from 1610 to 1612 the Poles occupied Moscow.

Eventually a popular army rallied by merchant Kuzma Minin and noble Dmitry Pozharsky, both from Nizhny Novgorod, with support from the Church, removed the Poles. In 1613 a Zemsky Sobor, or Assembly of the Land, with representatives of the political classes of the day, elected 16-year-old Mikhail Romanov tsar, the first of a new dynasty that was to rule until 1917.

You can view the first two episodes of Sergei Eisenstein's powerful trilogy of movies on Ivan the Terrible, but only 20 minutes of the third episode were shot before the director's death in 1948.

The story of Boris Godunov inspired both a play by Alexander Pushkin in 1831 and an opera by Modest Mussorgsky in 1869.

17TH-CENTURY RUSSIA

Though the first three Romanov rulers – Mikhail (1613–45), Alexey (1645–76) and Fyodor III (1676–82) – provided continuity and stability, there were also big changes that foretold the downfall of 'old' Russia.

Acquisitions

The 17th century saw a huge growth in the Russian lands. In 1650 Tsar Alexey commissioned the Cossack trader Yerofey Khabarov (after whom Khabarovsk is named) to open up the far-eastern region. By 1689 the

1547	1584
Ivan IV (Ivan the Terrible) crowns himself Tsar of all the Russias	Boris Godunov effective ruler behind official Tsar Fyodor I

Russians were in occupation of the northern bank of the Amur. The Treaty of Nerchinsk sealed a peace with neighbouring China that lasted for more than 150 years.

Additionally, when Cossacks in Ukraine appealed for help against the Poles, Alexey came to their aid, and in 1667 Kyiv, Smolensk and lands east of the Dnepr came under Russian control.

Serfdom

http://artsci.shu
.edu/reesp/documents
/index.html is Seton
Hall University's online
source book of primary
documents on Russia,
including proclamations
by the tsars and speeches
by Lenin and Stalin.

Authority in the countryside collapsed during the Time of Troubles, with thousands of peasants fleeing to Cossack areas or to Siberia, where serfdom was unknown. Landlords, in despair, found support from the government. The peasants' right to move freely was abolished in 1646. In 1675 they lost all land rights and, in a uniquely Russian version of serfdom, could be sold separately from the estates they worked – slavery, in effect.

In 1670–71 Cossacks, runaway serfs and adventurers joined in a huge uprising in the Volga-Don region, led by the Cossack Stepan (Stenka) Razin. Razin's army of 200,000 seized the entire lower Volga basin before he was captured and killed. He remains a folk hero today.

The Church

Internal conflicts transformed the Church into a friend of authority, distrusted as much as the government was. In the mid-17th century, Patriarch Nikon tried to bring rituals and texts into line with the 'pure' Greek Orthodox Church, horrifying those attached to traditional Russian forms.

The result was a bitter schism between Nikon's New Believers and Old Believers who, under government persecution, formed a widespread, occasionally fanatical religious underground. In the end Nikon himself was sacked by Tsar Alexey over the issue of Church authority in the newly acquired Ukrainian territories, while Old Believers survive to this day (see p77).

PETER THE GREAT

Benson Bobrick's East
of the Sun is a rollicking
history of the conquest
and settlement of Siberia
and the Russian Far East,
packed with gory details.

Peter I, known as 'the Great' for his commanding 2.24m frame and his equally commanding victory over the Swedes, dragged Russia kicking and screaming into Europe, and made it a major world power.

Born to Tsar Alexey's second wife in 1672, Peter spent much of his youth in royal residences in the countryside, organising his playmates into military regiments. Energetic, inquisitive and comfortable in any circle, he often visited Moscow's European district to learn about the West. Dutch and British ship captains in Arkhangelsk gave him navigation lessons on the White Sea.

When Fyodor III died in 1682, Peter became tsar, along with his feeble-minded half-brother Ivan V, under the regency of Ivan's ambitious sister, Sofia. She had the support of a leading statesman of the day, Prince Vasily Golitsyn. The boyars, annoyed by Golitsyn's institution of a stringent ranking system, schemed successfully to have Sofia sent to a monastery in 1689 and replaced as regent by Peter's unambitious mother.

Few doubted Peter as the true monarch, and when he became sole ruler, after his mother's death in 1694 and Ivan's in 1696, he embarked on a modernisation campaign, symbolised by his fact-finding mission

1606	1613
Start of the Time of Troubles and the claims of the false Dmitrys	Romanov dynasty begins when 16-year-old Mikhail Romanov is elected new tsar of Russia

to Europe in 1697–98; he was the first Muscovite ruler ever to go there. Historical literature abounds with tales of his spirited visits to hospitals, workshops and trading houses, his stint as a ship's carpenter in Amsterdam and his hiring of some 1000 experts for service in Russia.

He was also busy negotiating alliances. In 1695 he had sent Russia's first navy down the Don River and captured the Black Sea port of Azov from the Crimean Tatars, vassals of the Ottoman Turks. His European allies weren't interested in the Turks but shared his concern about the Swedes, who held most of the Baltic coast and had penetrated deep into Europe.

Peter's alliance with Poland and Denmark led to the Great Northern War against Sweden (1700–21), the focal point of his career. The rout of Charles XII's forces at the Battle of Poltava (1709) heralded Russia's power and the collapse of the Swedish empire. The Treaty of Nystadt (1721) gave Peter control of the Gulf of Finland and the eastern shores of the Baltic Sea, and in the midst of this (1707), he put down another peasant rebellion, led by Don Cossack Kondraty Bulavin.

On land taken from the Swedes, Peter founded a new city, which he named St Petersburg after his patron saint. In 1712 he made it the capital, symbol of a new, Europe-facing Russia.

Peter the Great – His Life & World by Robert K Massie is a good read about one of Russia's most influential rulers and contains much detail on how he created St Petersburg.

PETER'S LEGACY

Peter's lasting legacy was mobilising Russian resources to compete on equal terms with the West. His territorial gains were small, but the strategic Baltic territories added ethnic variety, including a new upper class of German traders and administrators who formed the backbone of Russia's commercial and military expansion.

Peter was also to have the last word on the authority of the Church. When it resisted his reforms he simply blocked the appointment of a new patriarch, put bishops under a government department and in effect became head of the Church himself.

Vast sums of money were needed to build St Petersburg, pay a growing civil service, modernise the army and launch naval and commercial fleets. But money was scarce in an economy based on serf labour, so Peter slapped taxes on everything from coffins to beards, including an infamous 'Soul Tax' on all lower-class adult males. The lot of serfs worsened, as they bore the main tax burden.

Even the upper classes had to chip in: aristocrats could serve in either the army or the civil service, or lose their titles and land. Birth counted for little, with state servants subject to Peter's Table of Ranks, a performance-based ladder of promotion, with the upper grades conferring hereditary nobility. Some aristocrats lost all they had, while capable state employees of humble origin, and even foreigners, became Russian nobles.

In his efforts to modernise Russia Peter the Great ordered all his administrators and soldiers to shave off their beards.

In 1648 the Cossack Semyon Dezhnev sailed round the northeastern corner of Asia, from the Pacific Ocean into the Arctic, 80 years before Vitus Bering.

AFTER PETER

Peter died in 1725 without naming a successor. For the next 37 years Russia suffered ineffectual rulers. Day-to-day administration was handled by a governing body called the Supreme Privy Council, staffed by many of Peter's leading administrators. Dominated by the Dolgoruky and Golitsyn boyar families, the council elected Peter's niece Anna of Courland (a small principality in present-day Latvia) to the throne, with a contract

1639	1660
Having traded their way across Siberia, Russians reach Pacific coast at Okhotsk	Patriarch Nikon is deposed after creating a schism in Russian Orthodox Church

RUSSIANS IN AMERICA

Peter the Great commissioned Vitus Bering, a Danish officer in the Russian navy, to head the Great Northern Expedition, which was ostensibly a scientific survey of Kamchatka (claimed for the tsar in 1697 by the explorer Vladimir Atlasov) and the eastern seaboard. In reality the survey's aim was to expand Russia's Pacific sphere of influence as far south as Japan and across to North America.

Bering succeeded in discovering Alaska, landing in 1741. Unfortunately, on the return voyage his ship was wrecked off an island just 250km east of the Kamchatka coast. Bering died on the island, and it, too, now carries his name. (Archaeologists digging on the island in 1991 discovered his grave and the bones were flown to Moscow for scientific examination. They've since been returned to the island and reburied with full naval ceremony.)

Survivors of Bering's crew brought back reports of an abundance of foxes, fur seals and otters inhabiting the islands off the mainland, triggering a fresh wave of fur-inspired expansion. An Irkutsk trader, Grigory Shelekhov, landed on Kodiak Island (in present-day Alaska) in 1784 and, 15 years later, his successor founded Sitka (originally called New Archangel), the capital of Alaska until 1900.

In 1804 the Russians reached Honolulu, and in 1806 Russian ships sailed into San Francisco Bay. Soon afterwards, a fortified outpost was established at what is now called Fort Ross, California. Here the imperial flag flew and a marker was buried on which was inscribed 'Land of the Russian Empire'.

stating that the council had the final say in policy decisions. Anna ended this experiment in constitutional monarchy by disbanding the council.

Anna ruled from 1730 to 1740, appointing a Baltic German baron, Ernst Johann von Bühren, to handle affairs of state. His name was Russified to Biron, but his heavy-handed, corrupt style came to symbolise the German influence on the royal family that had begun with Peter the Great.

During the reign of Peter's daughter, Elizabeth (1741–61), German influence waned and restrictions on the nobility were loosened. Some aristocrats began to dabble in manufacture and trade.

Catherine the Great: Life and Legend, by John T Alexander, is a highly readable account of the famous empress, making a case for the veracity of some of the more salacious tales of her life.

CATHERINE II (THE GREAT)

Daughter of a German prince, Catherine came to Russia at the age of 15 to marry Empress Elizabeth's heir apparent, her nephew Peter III. Intelligent and ambitious, Catherine learned Russian, embraced the Orthodox Church and devoured the writings of European political philosophers. This was the time of the Enlightenment, when talk of human rights, social contracts and the separation of powers abounded.

Catherine later said of Peter III, 'I believe the Crown of Russia attracted me more than his person'. Six months after he ascended the throne she had him overthrown in a palace coup led by her current lover (it has been said that she had more lovers than the average serf had hot dinners); he was murdered shortly afterwards.

Catherine embarked on a programme of reforms, though she made it clear that she had no intention of limiting her own authority. She drafted a new legal code, limited the use of torture and supported religious tolerance. But any ideas she might have had of improving the lot of serfs went overboard with the violent peasant rebellion of 1773–74, led by the Don

1689	1703
Russia settles Siberian land squabbles with China in Treaty of Nerchinsk	Peter I (Peter the Great) begins building St Petersburg

Cossack Yemelyan Pugachev, which spread from the Ural Mountains to the Caspian Sea and along the Volga. Hundreds of thousands of serfs responded to Pugachev's promises to end serfdom and taxation, but were beaten by famine and government armies. Pugachev was executed and Catherine put an end to Cossack autonomy.

In the cultural sphere, Catherine increased the number of schools and colleges and expanded publishing. Her vast collection of paintings forms the core of the present-day Hermitage collection. A critical elite gradually developed, alienated from most uneducated Russians but also increasingly at odds with central authority – a 'split personality' common among future Russian radicals.

TERRITORIAL GAINS

Catherine's reign saw major expansion at the expense of the weakened Ottoman Turks and Poles, engineered by her 'prime minister' and foremost lover, Grigory Potemkin (Potyomkin). War with the Turks began in 1768, peaked with the naval victory at Çesme (Chesma) and ended with a 1774 treaty giving Russia control of the north coast of the Black Sea, freedom of shipping through the Dardanelles to the Mediterranean, and 'protectorship' of Christian interests in the Ottoman Empire – a pretext for later incursions into the Balkans. Crimea was annexed in 1783.

Poland had spent the previous century collapsing into a set of semi-independent units with a figurehead king in Warsaw. Catherine manipulated events with divide-and-rule tactics and even had another former lover, Stanislas Poniatowski, installed as king. Austria and Prussia proposed sharing Poland among the three powers, and in 1772, 1793 and 1795 the country was carved up, ceasing to exist as an independent state until 1918. Eastern Poland and the Grand Duchy of Lithuania – roughly, present-day Lithuania, Belarus and western Ukraine – came under Russian rule.

After wrapping up the periodic table, Mendeleyev devoted much of his remaining 38 years of life to searching for the universal ethers and rarefied gases that allegedly rule interactions between all bodies.

RUSSIA'S SCIENTIFIC LEGACY

The Russian Academy of Sciences was established in 1726 and has since produced great results. Students the world over learn about the conditional reflex experiments on Ivan Pavlov's puppies, and about Dmitry Mendeleyev's 1869 discovery of the periodic table of elements. Yet you may be surprised to hear from locals about Russia's invention of the electric light and radio (didn't you know?).

In the USSR science, hampered by secrecy, bureaucracy and a lack of technology, was dependent on the ruling party. Funding was sporadic, often coming in great bursts for projects that served propaganda or militaristic purposes. Thus the space race received lots of money, and even though little of real scientific consequence was achieved during the first missions, the PR was priceless. In other fields, however, the USSR lagged behind the West; genetics, cybernetics and the theory of relativity were all at one point deemed anathema to communism.

Physics – especially theoretical and nuclear – was supported and Russia has produced some of the world's brightest scientists in the field. Andrei Sakharov (1921–89), 'father of the H-bomb', was exiled to Gorky (now Nizhny Novgorod, p407) in 1980, five years after receiving the Nobel Peace Prize for his vocal denunciations of the Soviet nuclear programme and the Afghan War. He was one of the most influential dissidents of his time.

1762	1812
Catherine II (Catherine the Great) overthrows her husband Peter III and becomes empress	Napoleon's armies invade then retreat from Moscow

The roots of the current Chechen war began when Catherine sought to expand her empire into the Caucasus; see the boxed text, p124.

ALEXANDER I

When Catherine died in 1796 the throne passed on to her son, Paul I. A mysterious figure in Russian history (often called the Russian Hamlet by Western scholars), he antagonised the gentry with attempts to reimpose compulsory state service, and was killed in a coup in 1801.

Paul's son and successor was Catherine's favourite grandson, Alexander I, who had been trained by the best European tutors. Alexander kicked off his reign with several reforms, including an expansion of the school system that brought education within reach of the lower middle classes. But he was soon preoccupied with the wars against Napoleon, which were to dominate his career.

After Napoleon defeated him at Austerlitz, north of Vienna, in 1805 and then at Friedland, near modern Kaliningrad, Alexander came to the negotiating table. The Treaty of Tilsit (1807) left Napoleon in charge as Emperor of the West and Alexander as Emperor of the East, united (in theory) against England.

1812 & AFTERMATH

The alliance lasted only until 1810, when Russia resumed trade with England. With his Grand Army of 700,000 – the largest force the world had ever seen for a single military operation – a furious Napoleon decided to crush the tsar.

The vastly outnumbered Russian forces retreated across their own countryside through the summer of 1812, scorching the earth in an attempt to deny the French sustenance and fighting some successful rearguard actions. Napoleon set his sights on Moscow, the symbolic heart of Russia. In September, with the lack of provisions beginning to bite on the French, the Russian general Mikhail Kutuzov finally decided to turn and fight at Borodino, 130km from Moscow (p197). The battle was extremely bloody, but inconclusive, with the Russians withdrawing in good order.

Before the month was out, Napoleon entered a deserted Moscow; the same day, the city began to burn down around him (by whose hand has never been established). Alexander ignored his overtures to negotiate. With winter coming and his supply lines overstretched, Napoleon was forced to retreat. His starving troops were picked off by Russian partisans. Only one in 20 made it back to the relative safety of Poland, and the Russians pursued them all the way to Paris.

At the Congress of Vienna, where the victors met in 1814–15 to establish a new order after Napoleon's final defeat, Alexander championed the cause of the old monarchies. His legacies were a hazy Christian fellowship of European kings, called the Holy Alliance, and a system of pacts to guard against future Napoleons – or any revolutionary change.

Meanwhile Russia was expanding its territory on other fronts. The kingdom of Georgia united with Russia in 1801. After a war with Sweden in 1807–09, Alexander became Grand Duke of Finland. Russia argued with Turkey over the Danube principalities of Bessarabia (essentially, modern Moldova) and Wallachia (now in Romania), taking Bessarabia

Vincent Cronin's *Catherine, Empress of all the Russias* paints a more sympathetic portrait than usual of a woman traditionally seen as a scheming, power-crazed sexpot.

Learn about the fascinating life of Grigory Potemkin, lover of Catherine the Great and mover and shaker in 18th-century Russia in Simon Sebag Montefiore's *Prince of Princes: The Life of Potemkin*.

Adam Zamoyski's *1812: Napoleon's Fatal March on Moscow* is packed with graphic detail and individual stories that bring the famous defeat to life.

1825	1851
Decembrists attempt to overthrow Nicholas I	Moscow to St Petersburg railway opens

in 1812. Persia ceded northern Azerbaijan a year later and Yerevan (in Armenia) in 1828.

DECEMBRISTS & OTHER POLITICAL EXILES

Alexander died in 1825 without leaving a clear heir, sparking the usual crisis. His reform-minded brother Constantine, married to a Pole and living happily in Warsaw, had no interest in the throne.

Officers who had brought back liberal ideas from Paris in 1815 preferred Constantine to Alexander's youngest brother, the militaristic Nicholas, who was due to be crowned on 26 December 1825. Their show of force in St Petersburg was squashed by troops loyal to Nicholas; five of these 'Decembrists' (Dekabristy) were executed and more than 100 – mostly aristocrats and officers – were sent to Siberia along with their families for terms of hard labour, mostly in rural parts of the Chita region. Pardoned by Tsar Alexander II in 1856, many of these exiles chose to stay on in Siberia, their presence having a marked effect on the educational and cultural life in their adopted towns.

Following a failed uprising in Poland in 1864 huge numbers of Polish rebels, many well educated, were also shipped to Siberia. In the late 19th century other famous intellectual exiles followed in their footsteps including novelist Fyodor Dostoevsky and, in the early 20th century, Leon Trotsky, Josef Stalin and Vladimir Lenin, who spent nearly three years at Shushenskoe near Abakan.

NICHOLAS I

Nicholas I's reign (1825–55) was a time of stagnation and repression under a tsar who put his faith in his army. The social revolutions that were shaking Europe passed Russia by.

There were positive developments, however. The economy grew, and grain exports increased. Nicholas detested serfdom, if only because he detested the serf-owning class. As a result, peasants on state lands, nearly half the total, were given title to the land and, in effect, freed.

In foreign policy, Nicholas' meddling in the Balkans was eventually to destroy Russian credibility in Europe. Bad diplomacy led to the Crimean War of 1854–56 against the Ottoman Empire, Britain and France, who declared war after Russian troops marched into the Ottoman provinces of Moldavia and Wallachia – ostensibly to protect Christian communities there. At Sevastopol an Anglo-French-Turkish force besieged the Russian naval headquarters. Inept command on both sides led to a bloody, stalemated war.

ALEXANDER II & ALEXANDER III
The 'Great Reforms'

Nicholas died in 1855. His son, Alexander II, saw the Crimean War stir up discontent within Russia and accepted peace on unfavourable terms. The war had revealed the backwardness behind the post-1812 imperial glory, and the time for reform had come.

All serfs were freed in 1861. Of the land they had worked, roughly a third was kept by established landholders. The rest went to village communes, which assigned it to the individual ex-serfs in return for

'Nicholas I detested serfdom, if only because he detested the serf-owning class'

'redemption payments' to compensate former landholders – a system that pleased nobody.

Abolition of serfdom opened the way for a market economy, capitalism and an industrial revolution. Railways and factories were built, and cities expanded as peasants left the land. Foreign investment in Russia grew during the 1880s and 1890s, but nothing was done to modernise farming, and very little to help peasants. By 1914, 85% of the Russian population was still rural, but their lot had barely improved in 50 years.

Revolutionary Movements

The reforms raised hopes that were not satisfied. The tsar refused to set up a representative assembly for all of Russia. Peasants were angry at having to pay for land they considered theirs by right. Radical students, known as *narodniki* (populists), took to the countryside in the 1870s to rouse the peasants, but the students and the peasants were worlds apart and the campaign failed.

Other populists saw more value in cultivating revolution among the growing urban working class, or proletariat, while yet others turned to terrorism: one secret society, the People's Will, blew up Alexander II in 1881.

Not all opponents to tsarism were radical revolutionaries. Some moderates, well off and with much to lose from a revolution, called themselves liberals and advocated constitutional reform along Western European lines, with universal suffrage and a *duma* (national parliament).

The terrorist groups were genuinely surprised that there was no uprising after Alexander II's assassination. Most were rounded up and executed or exiled, and the reign of his son Alexander III was marked by repression of revolutionaries and liberals alike.

Discontent was sometimes directed at Jews and took the form of violent mass attacks, or pogroms. At their height in the 1880s, these were often fanned by the authorities to divert social tension onto a convenient scapegoat. Tending towards intellectual and commercial professions, Jews were hated as shopkeepers and moneylenders by the lower classes and as political radicals by the authorities.

'The abolition of serfdom opened the way for a market economy, capitalism and an industrial revolution'

Territorial Expansion

During the reigns of Alexander II (1855–81) and Alexander III (1881–94), Central Asia (modern Kazakhstan, Uzbekistan, Turkmenistan, Kyrgyzstan and Tajikistan) came fully under Russian control.

In the east, Russia acquired a long strip of Pacific coast from China and built the port of Vladivostok. At the same time it was forced to sell the Alaskan territories (see the boxed text, p42) to the USA in 1867 – its only supporter during the Crimean War – for the then enormous amount of US$7.2 million, in the wake of the economic crisis following the conflict.

Marxism

Many revolutionaries fled abroad. Georgy Plekhanov and Pavel Axelrod went to Switzerland; they converted to Marxism, founding the Russian Social-Democratic Workers' Party in 1883. As Marxists they believed that

1867	1877
Alaska sold to the USA; Karl Marx writes *Das Kapital*	War breaks out with Turkey

Russia was passing through a capitalist phase on its way to socialism, and that the urban proletariat was the only class with revolutionary potential.

One of their converts was young, upper-middle-class Vladimir Ulyanov, better known by his later pseudonym, Lenin. In 1895 he took charge of Russia's first Marxist cell in St Petersburg, which earned him three years of Siberian exile. On his release in 1899 he went to Europe, where he remained (except for a few secret visits) until 1917, rising to joint leadership of the Social Democratic Workers' Party with Plekhanov.

Social democrats in Europe were being elected to parliaments and developing Marxism into 'parliamentary socialism', improving the lot of workers through legislation. But in Russia there was no parliament, and an active secret police, to boot. At a meeting of the Socialist International movement in London in 1903, Lenin stood for violent overthrow of the government by a small, committed, well-organised party, while Plekhanov stood for mass membership and cooperation with other political forces. Lenin won the vote through clever manoeuvring, and his faction came to be known as the Bolsheviks, or majority people; Plekhanov's faction became the Mensheviks, or minority people. The Mensheviks actually outnumbered the Bolsheviks in the party, but Lenin clung to the name, for obvious reasons. The two factions coexisted until 1912, when the Bolsheviks set up their own party.

RUSSO-JAPANESE WAR

Nicholas II, who succeeded his father, Alexander III, in 1894, was a weak man who commanded less respect than his father, but was equally in opposition to representative government.

The most serious blow to his position was a humiliating defeat by Japan when the two countries clashed over their respective 'spheres of influence' in the far east – Russia's in Manchuria, Japan's in Korea. As in Crimea 50 years before, poor diplomacy led to war. In 1904 Japan attacked the Russian naval base at Port Arthur (near Dalian in present-day China).

Defeat followed defeat for Russia on land and sea. The ultimate disaster came in May 1905, when the entire Baltic fleet, which had sailed halfway around the world to relieve Port Arthur, was sunk in the Tsushima Straits off Japan. In September 1905 a badly beaten Russia signed the Treaty of Portsmouth (New Hampshire), under the terms of which it gave up Port Arthur, Dalny and southern Sakhalin as well as any claims to Korea – but at least retained its preeminent position in Manchuria.

It wasn't all bad news in the Siberia and the far east. In 1886 Alexander III authorised the building of 7500km of railroad between Chelyabinsk (then Russia's eastern railhead) and Vladivostok, shifting up development in Siberia several gears. In less than 25 years up to 1911, the immigrant population leapt above eight million. Most were peasants, who put Siberian agriculture at the head of the class in grain, stock and dairy farming (before the October Revolution, Europeans had Siberian butter on their tables).

1905 REVOLUTION

Unrest across Russia became widespread after the fall of Port Arthur. On 9 January 1905 a priest named Georgy Gapon led a crowd of some 200,000 workers – men, women and children – to the Winter Palace in St Petersburg to petition the tsar for better working conditions. Singing

Edmund Wilson's *To the Finland Station* (1940) is the most authoritative account of the development of socialism and communism in Russia.

1881	1875
Alexander II assassinated by People's Will group	Pyotr Tchaikovsky commissioned to write *Swan Lake*

'God Save the Tsar', they were met by imperial guards, who opened fire and killed several hundred. This was 'Bloody Sunday'.

The country was breaking into anarchy, with wild strikes, pogroms, mutinies, and killings of landowners and industrialists. Social democrat activists formed soviets (workers' councils) in St Petersburg and Moscow. These councils, with representatives chosen by acclaim, proved remarkably successful: the St Petersburg Soviet, led by Mensheviks under Leon Trotsky, declared a general strike, which brought the whole country to a standstill in October.

The tsar gave in and promised a *duma*. General elections in April 1906 gave it a leftist majority and it demanded further reforms. The tsar disbanded it. New elections in 1907 pushed the *duma* further to the left. It was again disbanded and a new electoral law, limiting the vote to the upper classes and Orthodox Christians, ensured that the third and fourth *duma* were more cooperative with the tsar, who continued to choose the prime minister and cabinet.

The capable prime minister, Pyotr Stolypin, abolished the hated redemption payments in the countryside. Enterprising peasants were now able to buy decent parcels of land, which could be worked efficiently; this led to the creation of a new class of kulaks (big farmers), and to a series of good harvests. It also made it easier for peasants to leave their villages, providing a mobile labour force for industry. Russia enjoyed unprecedented economic growth and radical activists lost their following.

Still, Stolypin was assassinated in 1911, and the tsarist regime again lost touch with the people. Nicholas became a puppet of his strong-willed, eccentric wife, Alexandra, who herself fell under the spell of the sinister Siberian mystic Rasputin (see the boxed text, opposite).

WWI & FEBRUARY REVOLUTION

Russia's involvement with the Balkans made it a main player in the world war that began there in 1914. The Russian campaign went badly from the start. Between 1915 and 1918 the theatre of the war was mostly around Russia's western border and often on enemy territory. Much, if not most, of fighting was with Austro-Hungarians in Galitsia, rather than with Germans who didn't make major advances into Russian territory until 1918, by which time an estimated two million Russian troops had been killed and Germany controlled Poland and much of the Baltic coast, Belarus and Ukraine.

The tsar responded to antiwar protests by disbanding the *duma* and assuming personal command in the field, where he couldn't make much headway. At home, the disorganised government failed to introduce rationing, and in February 1917 in Petrograd (the new, less 'German' name for St Petersburg), discontent in the food queues turned to riots, kicking off the February Revolution. Soldiers and police mutinied, refusing to fire on demonstrators. A new Petrograd Soviet of Workers' & Soldiers' Deputies was formed on the 1905 model, and more sprang up elsewhere. The reconvened *duma* ignored an order to disband itself and set up a committee to assume government.

Now there were two alternative power bases in the capital. The soviet was a rallying and debating point for factory workers and soldiers; the *duma* committee attracted the educated and commercial elite. In Febru-

---

Edvard Radzinsky's *Rasputin: The Last Word* is certainly *not* going to be the last word on this notorious subject, but it's a good read nonetheless, drawing on recently discovered government files.

By turns anecdotal and specific, *A People's Tragedy: The Russian Revolution 1891–1924* by erudite scholar Orlando Figes paints a vivid picture of this tumultuous period in Russian history.

| Alexander III OKs construction of Trans-Siberian Railway | Russia occupies Manchuria |

ary the two reached agreement on a provisional government that would demand the tsar's abdication. The tsar tried to return to Petrograd but was blocked by his own troops. On 1 March he abdicated.

OCTOBER REVOLUTION

The provisional government announced general elections for November, and continued the war despite a collapse of discipline in the army and popular demands for peace. On 3 April Lenin and other exiled Bolsheviks returned to Petrograd via Scandinavia in a sealed railway carriage provided by the German army. Though well and truly in the minority in the soviets, the Bolsheviks were organised and committed. They won over many with a demand for immediate 'peace, land and bread', and believed the soviets should seize power at once. But a series of violent mass demonstrations in July (the 'July Days'), inspired by the Bolsheviks, was in the end not fully backed by the soviets and was quelled. Lenin fled to Finland, and Alexander Kerensky, a moderate Social Revolutionary, became prime minister.

In September the Russian military chief of staff, General Kornilov, sent cavalry to Petrograd to crush the soviets. Kerensky turned to the left for support against this insubordination, even courting the Bolsheviks, and the counterrevolution was defeated. After this, public opinion massively favoured the Bolsheviks, who quickly took control of the Petrograd Soviet

THE PRIEST OF SEX

Cult figure of the early 1900s, Grigory Rasputin was born in the Siberian village of Pokrovskoe in 1869. Though not a monk as is sometimes supposed, Rasputin did pray a lot. In his mid-20s, he experienced a vision of the Virgin while working in the fields and left Pokrovskoe to seek enlightenment. On his wanderings he came to believe, as did the contemporary Khlyst (Whip) sect, that sinning (especially through sex), then repenting, could bring people close to God.

On reaching St Petersburg, Rasputin's racy brand of redemption, along with his soothing talk, compassion and generosity, made him very popular with some aristocratic women. His magnetic personality was apparently heightened by what the French ambassador called 'a strong animal smell, like that of a goat'.

Eventually Rasputin was summoned by Tsaritsa Alexandra and seemed able, thanks to some kind of hypnotic power, to cure the uncontrollable bleeding of her haemophiliac son, Tsarevitch Alexey, the heir to the throne. As he continued his drunken, lecherous life, replete with famous orgies, Rasputin's influence on the royal family grew to the point where he could make or break the careers of ministers and generals. He became increasingly unpopular and many blamed him for the disasters of WWI.

His end finally came late in 1916 when Prince Felix Yusupov and others decided to assassinate him. According to Yusupov's own account of the affair this proved to be easier said than done: Rasputin survived poisoning, several shots and a beating, all in the one evening at St Petersburg's Yusupov Palace (p261). Apparently he died only when drowned in a nearby river.

However, new evidence has recently come to light that Rasputin actually died from his bullet wounds, one of which might have been delivered by a British secret agent working in conjunction with the Russian plotters. For the fascinating background to this version of events see www.bbc.co.uk/history/war/wwone/rasputin_murder_01.shtml or read Andrew Cook's *To Kill Rasputin*. Even more incredible are efforts by a small but vocal group within the Orthodox Russian Church to have Rasputin canonised, an idea that the Orthodox Patriarch Alexey II has called 'madness'.

1903	1904
Russian Social-Democratic Workers' Party splits into Bolsheviks and Mensheviks	Japan successfully attacks Russian naval base Port Arthur and wins Russo-Japanese War

(chaired by Trotsky, who had joined them) and, by extension, all the soviets in the land. Lenin decided it was time to seize power, and returned from Finland in October.

During the night of 24–25 October 1917, Bolshevik workers and soldiers in Petrograd seized government buildings and communication centres, and arrested the provisional government, which was meeting in the Winter Palace. (Kerensky managed to escape, eventually dying in the USA in 1970.) Within hours, an All-Russian Congress of Soviets, meeting in Petrograd, made the soviets the ruling councils in Russia, headed by a 'parliament' called the Soviet Central Executive Committee. A Council of People's Commissars became the government, headed by Lenin, with Trotsky as commissar for foreign affairs and the Georgian Josef Stalin as commissar for nationalities.

Local soviets elsewhere in Russia seized power relatively easily, but the coup in Moscow took six days of fighting. The general elections scheduled for November could not be stopped, however. More than half of Russia's male population voted. Even though 55% chose Kerensky's rural socialist party, and only 25% voted for the Bolsheviks, when the Founding Assembly met in January, the Bolsheviks disbanded it after its first day in session, thus setting the antidemocratic tone for the coming decades.

> Seventeen Moments in Soviet History (www .soviethistory.org) is a well-designed site that covers all the major events during the life of the USSR.

CIVIL WAR

The Soviet government wasted no time introducing sweeping measures. It redistributed land to those who worked it, signed an armistice with the Germans in December 1917 and set up its own secret police force, the Cheka; Trotsky, now military commissar, founded the Red Army in January 1918. In March the Bolshevik Party renamed itself the Communist Party and moved the capital to Moscow.

> *Ten Days That Shook the World*, by US journalist John Reed, the only American buried in Moscow's Kremlin wall, is a melodramatic, enthusiastic and contemporary account of the Bolsheviks' 1917 power grab.

Straight after the revolution Lenin proclaimed the independence of Finland and Poland, and the Founding Assembly gave independence to Ukraine and the Baltic states. Further concessions were made in the Treaty of Brest-Litovsk in March 1918 so the Soviet regime could concentrate on internal enemies. These were becoming numerous in the countryside due to food requisitions by armed trade-union detachments.

In July 1918 the former tsar and his family, who had been interned for months, were killed by their Communist guards in Yekaterinburg (see the boxed text, p437). Two months later, the Cheka began a systematic programme of arrest, torture and execution of anyone opposed to Soviet rule.

Those hostile to the Bolsheviks, collectively termed 'Whites', had developed strongholds in the south and east of the country. But they lacked unity, including as they did tsarist stalwarts, landlord-killing social revolutionaries (who were opposed to the Treaty of Brest-Litovsk), Czech POWs, Finnish partisans and Japanese troops. The Bolsheviks had the advantage of controlling the heart of Russia, including its war industry and communications. Full-scale civil war broke out in early 1918 and lasted almost three years. The main centres of opposition to the Bolsheviks were:

1905	1911
Hundreds killed as troops fire on crowds in St Petersburg, sparking first Russian revolution	Reforming prime minister Pyotr Stolypin assassinated

- In the south, home to tsarist and liberal sympathisers under generals Kornilov and Denikin, plus Cossacks clamouring for autonomy.
- Ukraine, which was under German control until November 1918, and then was occupied variously by nationalists, the army of newly independent Poland, and Denikin's troops.
- Admiral Kolchak's government of 'all Russia' in Omsk, which was supported by 45,000 Czech prisoners of war, the most formidable fighting force the Red Army had to deal with (see the boxed text, p52).
- The Baltic provinces and Finland, which waged successful wars of independence.
- British, French, US and Japanese troops who made mischief round the periphery. The Japanese were the biggest threat as they established themselves in large tracts of the Russian Far East, but they eventually pulled out in 1922.
- Uprisings by peasants as a result of famine in 1920–21, and by sailors at the Kronshtadt naval base near Petrograd in 1921 (see the boxed text, p303).

By 1921 the Communist Party had firmly established one-party rule, thanks to the Red Army and the Cheka, which continued to eliminate opponents. Some opponents escaped, joining an estimated 1.5 million citizens in exile.

WAR COMMUNISM

During the civil war, a system called War Communism subjected every aspect of society to the aim of victory. This meant sweeping nationalisations in all economic sectors and strict administrative control by the Soviet government, which in turn was controlled by the Communist Party.

The Party itself was restructured to reflect Lenin's creed of 'democratic centralism', which held that Party decisions should be obeyed all the way down the line. A new political bureau, the Politburo, was created for Party decision-making, and a new secretariat supervised Party appointments, ensuring that only loyal members were given responsibility (Stalin became Party general secretary in 1922).

War Communism was also a form of social engineering to create a classless society. Many 'class enemies' were eliminated by execution or exile, with disastrous economic consequences. Forced food requisitions and hostility towards larger, more efficient farmers, combined with drought and a breakdown of infrastructure, led to the enormous famine of 1920–21, when between four and five million people died.

THE NEW ECONOMIC POLICY

Lenin suggested a strategic compromise with capitalism. The New Economic Policy (NEP), was adopted by the 10th Party congress in 1921 and remained in force until 1927. The state continued to own the 'commanding heights' of the economy – large-scale industry, banks, transport – but allowed private enterprise to reemerge. Farm output improved as the kulaks consolidated their holdings and employed landless peasants as wage earners. Farm surplus was sold to the cities in return for industrial

Robert Service is the writer of both a biography of Lenin and the *History of Twentieth-Century Russia*, both excellent introductions to the dawn and progress of the Soviet era.

1914	1917
World War I begins	Vladimir Lenin takes charge after October Revolution

KOLCHAK'S LAST STAND

A general counterrevolution swept across Siberia in May 1918, sparked by a force of 45,000 Czechoslovakian POWs. The Czechoslovaks, who had been fighting alongside the Russians against the Germans, were heading home via Vladivostok when caught out by the revolution and Russia's decision to pull out of WWI. Convinced that the new Soviet government was going to hand them over to the Germans, the fully armed Czechoslovaks seized virtually the entire Trans-Siberian Railway. The regional Bolshevik government in the Russian Far East was thrown into retreat and by mid-September all Siberia was 'White'.

Meanwhile, the tsarist Admiral Alexander Kolchak, stranded in the USA by the revolution, landed at Vladivostok and headed west at the head of a White army. His cause was boosted when the entire area from the Pacific to Lake Baikal was occupied by foreign troops – 72,000 Japanese, 7000 Americans, 6400 British, 4400 Canadians and others – all there, ostensibly, to help the Czechoslovaks.

In November 1918, Kolchak pushed into European Russia. Joining with armies from the Don Basin and northwest Russia, he very nearly overthrew the Bolsheviks before being pushed back to Omsk, where his forces were decisively routed. Kolchak hastily retreated to Irkutsk. There he was captured and shot in 1920, which all but ended the Civil War – except in the Russian Far East, where it raged on until the Red victory at Volochaevka, west of Khabarovsk, in February 1922.

products, giving rise to a new class of traders and small-scale industrialists called 'Nepmen'.

In the state sectors, wages were allowed to reflect effort as professional managers replaced Party administrators. By the late 1920s, agricultural and industrial production had reached prewar levels.

But the political tide was set the other way. At the 1921 Party congress, Lenin outlawed debate within the Party as 'factionalism', launching the first systematic purge among Party members. The Cheka was reorganised as the GPU (State Political Administration) in 1922, gaining much greater powers to operate outside the law; for the time being it limited itself to targeting political opponents.

The Union of Soviet Socialist Republics (USSR), a federation of theoretically independent Soviet Socialist Republics (SSRs), was established in 1922. The initial members were the Russian, Ukrainian, Belarusian and Transcaucasian SSRs. By 1940 the number had reached 15, with the splitting of the Transcaucasian SSR into Georgian, Armenian and Azerbaijani SSRs and the addition of five Central Asian republics.

STALIN VS TROTSKY

In May 1922 Lenin suffered the first of a series of paralysing strokes that removed him from effective control of Party and government. He died aged 54 in January 1924. His embalmed remains were put on display in Moscow, Petrograd was (again) renamed Leningrad in his honour and a personality cult was built around him – all orchestrated by Stalin.

But Lenin had failed to name a successor, and had expressed a low opinion of 'too rude' Stalin. The charismatic Trotsky, hero of the civil war and second only to Lenin as an architect of the revolution, wanted collectivisation of agriculture – an extension of War Communism – and

1918	1920
Nicholas II and family are murdered in Yekaterinburg	End of Russian Civil War

worldwide revolution. He attacked Party 'bureaucrats' who wished to concentrate on socialism in the Soviet Union.

But even before Lenin's death, the powers that mattered in the Party and soviets had backed a three-man leadership of Zinoviev, Kamenev and Stalin, in which Stalin already pulled the strings. As Party general secretary, he controlled all appointments and had installed his supporters wherever it mattered. His influence grew with a recruiting drive that doubled Party membership to over a million.

Trotsky and his diminishing group of supporters were expelled from the Party in 1927. Two years later Trotsky went into exile, ending up in Mexico, where an agent of Stalin wielding an ice pick finished him off in 1940.

FIVE-YEAR PLANS & FARM COLLECTIVISATION

With Trotsky out of the way, Stalin took up Trotsky's farm collectivisation idea as part of a grand plan to turn the USSR into an industrial power. The first Five-Year Plan, launched in 1929, called for a quadrupling of output by heavy industry, such as power stations, mines, steelworks and railways. Agriculture was to be collectivised to get the peasants to fulfil production quotas, which would feed the growing cities and provide food exports to pay for imported heavy machinery.

The forced collectivisation of agriculture destroyed the country's peasantry (who were still 80% of the population) as a class and as a way of life. Farmers were required to pool their land and resources into kolkhozes (collective farms), usually consisting of about 75 households and dozens of square kilometres in area, which became their collective property, in return for compulsory quotas of produce. These kolkhozes covered two-thirds of all farmland, supported by a network of Machine Tractor Stations that dispensed machinery and advice (political or otherwise).

Stalin once remarked that the death of one person was tragic, the death of a million 'a statistic'.

Farmers who resisted – and most kulaks did, especially in Ukraine and the Volga and Don regions, which had the biggest grain surpluses – were killed or deported to labour camps in their millions. Farmers slaughtered their animals rather than hand them over, leading to the loss of half the national livestock. A drought and continued grain requisitions led to famine in the same three regions in 1932–33, in which a further six million or more people died. Some say Stalin deliberately orchestrated this to wipe out opposition. An estimated 20 million country people had left for the cities by 1939, by which time virtually all those left were 'collectivised'.

In heavy industry, if not in consumer goods, the first two Five-Year Plans produced faster growth than any Western country ever showed. By 1939 only the USA and Germany had higher industrial output.

THE GULAG & PURGES

Many of the new mines and factories were built in Central Asia or the resource-rich, but thinly populated, region of Siberia. A key labour force was provided by the network of concentration camps – begun under Lenin and now referred to as the Gulag, from the initial letters of *Glavnoe Upravlenie Lagerey* (Main Administration for Camps) – which stretched from the north of European Russia through Siberia and Central Asia to the far east (see the boxed text, p54).

1922	1923
Josef Stalin becomes general secretary of the Communist Party	Formation of Union of Soviet Socialist Republics (USSR)

Stalin: The Court of the Red Czar by Simon Sebag Montefiore is a highly readable account of the Soviet Union's most notorious leader that sheds light on a man traditionally viewed as a monster.

Many of the early camp inmates were farmers caught up in the collectivisation, but in the 1930s the terror shifted to Party members and other influential people not enthusiastic enough about Stalin. In 1934 the popular Leningrad Party secretary and Stalin's second-in-command, Sergei Kirov, who favoured alleviating the lot of the peasants and producing more consumer goods for urban workers, was murdered by an agent of the secret police (now called the NKVD, the People's Commissariat of Internal Affairs). This launched the biggest series of purges yet. That year 100,000 Party members, intellectuals and 'enemies of the people' disappeared or were executed in Leningrad alone. In 1936 the former Party leaders Zinoviev and Kamenev made absurd public confessions, admitting to murdering Kirov and plotting to kill Stalin, and were executed.

This was the first of the Moscow show trials, whose charges ranged from murder plots and capitalist sympathies to Trotskyist conspiracies. The biggest was in 1938 against 17 leading Bolsheviks, including Party theoretician Bukharin. Throughout 1937 and 1938, NKVD agents took victims from their homes at night; most were never heard of again. In the non-Russian republics of the USSR, virtually the whole Party apparatus was eliminated on charges of 'bourgeois nationalism'. The ghastly business clawed its way into all sectors and levels of society – even 400 of the Red Army's 700 generals were shot. Its victims are thought to have totalled 8.5 million.

THE GERMAN-SOVIET PACT

In 1939 the UK and France tried to persuade Stalin to join them in declaring war on Germany if it should invade Poland. They were coolly received. If the Germans were to walk into Poland they would be on the

---

THE GULAG

The Siberian exile system was abolished at the turn of the 20th century, but Stalin brought it back with a vengeance, expanding it into a full-blown, homegrown slave trade. It was during his rule that Siberia became synonymous with death. He established a vast bureaucracy of re-settlement programmes, labour colonies, concentration camps and special psychiatric hospitals, commonly known as the Gulag.

The Gulag's inmates – some of whose only 'offence' was to joke about Stalin or steal two spikelets of wheat from a kolkhoz field – cut trees, dug canals, laid railway tracks and worked in factories in remote areas, especially Siberia and the Russian Far East. A huge slice of the northeast was set aside exclusively for labour camps, and whole cities such as Komsomolsk-na-Amure and Magadan were developed as Gulag centres.

The Gulag population grew from 30,000 in 1928 to eight million in 1938. Prisoners were underfed, mistreated and literally worked to death; the average inmate died after just two years in the camps, and 90% of inmates died. The Gulag continued well after WWII; Boris Yeltsin announced the release of Russia's 'last 10' political prisoners from a camp near Perm in 1992.

Anne Applebaum, author of the Pulitzer Prize–winning, definitive history *Gulag: A History*, reckons at least 18 million people passed through the camp system. Many more suffered, though. Nadezhda Mandelstam, whose husband Osip Mandelstam, a highly regarded poet, was exiled to Siberia in 1934, wrote that a wife considered herself a widow from the moment of her husband's arrest. She was almost right – Osip lasted four years before dying at the Vtoraya Rechka transit camp in Vladivostok.

1924	1929
Lenin dies; Stalin begins power struggle with Leon Trotsky	Trotsky exiled; first of Stalin's Five Year Plans

Soviet border, and ready, if the USSR was hostile, to roll on to Moscow. Stalin needed time to prepare his country for war, and saw a deal with the Germans as a route to making territorial gains in Poland.

On 23 August 1939 the Soviet and German foreign ministers, Molotov and Ribbentrop, signed a nonaggression pact. A secret protocol stated that any future rearrangement would divide Poland between them; Germany would have a free hand in Lithuania, and the Soviet Union in Estonia, Latvia, Finland and Bessarabia, which had been lost to Romania in 1918.

Germany invaded Poland on 1 September; the UK and France declared war on Germany on 3 September. Stalin traded the Polish provinces of Warsaw and Lublin with Hitler for most of Lithuania, and the Red Army marched into these territories less than three weeks later. The Soviet gains in Poland, many of which were areas inhabited by non-Polish speakers and had been under Russian control before WWI, were quickly incorporated into the Belarusian and Ukrainian republics of the USSR.

The Baltic states were made republics of the USSR in 1940 (along with Moldavia, they brought the total of SSRs up to its final number of 15). But the Finns offered fierce resistance, fighting the Red Army to a standstill.

THE GREAT PATRIOTIC WAR

'Operation Barbarossa', Hitler's secret plan for an invasion of the Soviet Union, began on 22 June 1941. Even though Russia was prepared for war by this time, Stalin, in one of the great military blunders of all time, refused to believe that the Germans were preparing to attack, even as reports came to Moscow of massive German preparations along the border. The disorganised Red Army was no match for the German war machine, which advanced on three fronts. Within four months the Germans had overrun Minsk and Smolensk and were just outside Moscow; they had marched through the Baltic states, most of Ukraine, and laid siege to Leningrad. Only an early, severe winter halted the advance.

The Soviet commander, General Zhukov, used the winter to push the Germans back from Moscow. Leningrad held out – and continued to do so for 2¼ years, during which over half a million of its civilians died, mainly from hunger (see the boxed text, p225). In 1942 Hitler ordered a new southern offensive towards the Caucasian oilfields, which became bogged down in the battle for Stalingrad (now Volgograd). Well aware of the symbolism of a city named after the Great Leader, both Hitler and Stalin ordered that there be no retreat (see the boxed text, p424).

The Germans, with insecure supply lines along a front that stretched more than 1600km from north to south, also faced scorched earth and guerrilla warfare. Their atrocities against the local population stiffened resistance. Stalin appealed to old-fashioned patriotism and eased restrictions on the Church, ensuring that the whole country rallied to the cause with incredible endurance. Military goods supplied by the Allies through the northern ports of Murmansk and Arkhangelsk were invaluable in the early days of the war. All Soviet military industry was packed up, moved east of the Ural Mountains, and worked by women and Gulag labour.

The Soviet forces slowly gained the upper hand at Stalingrad, and on 2 February 1943 Field Marshal von Paulus surrendered what was left of the encircled German Sixth Army. It was the turning point of the war.

Melancholy lingers over the beautifully filmed *Burnt by the Sun*, Nikita Mikhalkov's 1994 Oscar-winning movie dramatising the awful effects of Stalin's purges.

Eugenia Ginzburg's *Journey Into the Whirlwind* is her memoir of 18 years in Stalin's prisons and labour camps.

1933	1938
More than six million die in famines following forced collectivisation of farms	Moscow show trials reach their peak under Stalin's purges

The Red Army had driven the Germans out of most of the Soviet Union by the end of the year; it reached Berlin in April 1945.

Siberia was never a battlefield in WWII but in virtually the closing days of the war, with Japan on its knees, the Soviet Union occupied the Japanese territories of southern Sakhalin Island and the Kuril Islands. Japan accepted the loss of Sakhalin but continues to this day to maintain a claim to the southern islands in the Kuril chain, which at their closest point are approximately 14km from Hokkaido.

The 900 Days: The Siege of Leningrad, by Harrison Salisbury, is the most thorough and harrowing account of that city's sufferings in WWII.

The USSR had borne the brunt of the war. Its total losses, civilian and military, may never be known, but they probably reached at least 26 million. The Battle for Stalingrad alone is estimated to have cost the live of some one million Soviet troops, over two times more than the combined US casualties in all theatres of the war.

The successes of the Red Army meant that the US and British leaders, Roosevelt and Churchill, were obliged to observe Stalin's wishes in the postwar settlement. At Tehran (November 1943) and Yalta (February 1945), the three agreed each to govern the areas they liberated until free elections could be held.

Soviet troops liberating Eastern Europe propped up local communist movements, which formed 'action committees' that either manipulated the elections or simply seized power when the election results were unfavourable.

Jean-Jacques Annaud's Enemy at the Gates is a harrowing 2001 WWII movie about the bloody siege of Stalingrad, seen through the pretty-boy eyes of Jude Law and Joseph Fiennes.

POSTWAR STALINISM

Control over Eastern Europe, and a postwar modernisation of industry with the aid of German factories and engineers seized as war booty, made the Soviet Union one of the two major world powers. The development of a Soviet atomic bomb as early as September 1949 demonstrated its industry's new power. But the first postwar Five-Year Plan was military and strategic (more heavy industry); consumer goods and agriculture remained low priorities.

A cold war was shaping up between the communist and capitalist worlds, and in the USSR the new demon became 'cosmopolitanism' – warm feelings towards the West. The first victims were the estimated two million Soviet citizens repatriated by the Allies in 1945 and 1946. Some were former prisoners of war or forced labourers taken by the Germans; others were refugees or people who had taken the chance of war to escape the USSR. They were sent straight to the Gulag in case their stay abroad had contaminated them.

Stalingrad by Antony Beevor, a superb work based on new access to long-secret archives, concentrates on the human cost of WWII.

Party and government purges continued as Stalin's reign came to resemble that of Ivan the Terrible, with unpredictable, often shattering decisions.

In 1947 US president Harry Truman initiated a policy of 'containment' of Soviet influence within its 1947 limits. The US, British and French forces occupying western zones of Germany unified their areas. The Soviet troops in eastern Germany retaliated by blockading western Berlin, controlled by the Western powers, in 1948; it had to be supplied from the air for a year. The long-term division of Germany followed.

In 1949 the North Atlantic Treaty Organization (NATO) was set up to protect Western Europe against invasion. The Soviet Union replied with a series of military alliances that led to the Warsaw Pact in 1955.

1939	1941
Russia signs nonaggression pact with Germany	Hitler invades Russia

THE KHRUSHCHEV THAW

After Stalin died in 1953, allegedly of a stroke, power passed to a combined leadership of five Politburo members. One, Lavrenty Beria, the NKVD boss responsible under Stalin for millions of deaths, was secretly tried and shot (and the NKVD was reorganised as the KGB, the Committee for State Security, which was to remain firmly under Party control). In 1954 another of the Politburo members, Nikita Khrushchev, a pragmatic Ukrainian who had helped carry out 1930s purges, launched the Virgin Lands campaign, bringing vast tracts of Kazakhstan and Central Asia under cultivation. A series of good harvests did his reputation no harm.

During the 20th Party congress in 1956, Khrushchev made a famous 'secret speech' about crimes committed under Stalin. It was the beginning of de-Stalinisation (also known as the Thaw), marked by the release of millions of Gulag prisoners and a thaw in the political and intellectual climate. The congress also approved peaceful coexistence between communist and noncommunist regimes. The Soviet Union, Khrushchev argued, would soon triumph over the 'imperialists' by economic means. Despite the setback of the 1956 Hungarian rebellion, which was put down by Soviet troops, in 1957 he emerged the unchallenged leader of the USSR.

In October 1957 the world listened to radio 'blips' from the first space satellite, Sputnik 1, and in 1961 Yury Gagarin became the first person in space. The Soviet Union seemed to be going places. But foreign crises undermined Khrushchev. In 1961 Berlin was divided by the Wall to stop an exodus from East Germany. In 1962, on the pretext of supplying the USSR's Caribbean ally Cuba with defensive weapons, Khrushchev stationed medium-range missiles with nuclear capability on the US doorstep. After some tense calling of bluff that brought the world to the brink of nuclear war, he withdrew the missiles.

A rift opened between the Soviet Union and China, itself now on the road to superpower status. The two competed for the allegiance of newly independent Third World nations and came into conflict over areas in Central Asia and the Russian Far East that had been conquered by the tsars.

At home, Khrushchev started the mass construction of cheap and ugly apartment blocks – by the end of his reign most people who had lived in communal flats now had their own, but the cityscapes changed forever. The agricultural sector also performed poorly and Khrushchev upset Party colleagues by decentralising economic decision-making. After a disastrous harvest in 1963 forced the Soviet Union to buy wheat from Canada, the Central Committee relieved Khrushchev of his posts in 1964, because of 'advanced age and poor health'.

THE BREZHNEV STAGNATION

The new 'collective' leadership of Leonid Brezhnev (general secretary) and Alexey Kosygin (premier) soon devolved into a one-man show under conservative Brezhnev. Khrushchev's administrative reforms were rolled back. Economic stagnation was the predictable result, despite the exploitation of huge Siberian oil and gas reserves. But despite increased repression, the 'dissident' movement grew, along with samizdat (underground publications). Prison terms and forced labour did not seem to have the desired effect,

Officially Russia and Japan are still fighting WWII, having never signed a peace treaty because of a dispute over the sovereignty of the Kuril Islands (known as the Northern Territories in Japan).

See both the BBC's www.bbc.co.uk/history/war/coldwar/index.shtml and CNN's http://edition.cnn.com/SPECIALS/cold.war/ for background features on the Cold War and the collapse of the USSR.

1943	1949
Russia wins Battle of Stalingrad at a cost of one million–plus troops	Development of Soviet atomic bomb heats up Cold War

STALIN'S COMEBACK

It's hard to believe that the reputation of an acknowledged tyrant who, at a conservative estimate, was responsible for the deaths of 20 million Russians is currently under rehabilitation in Russia. But such is the case with Josef Stalin.

Four decades after Stalin was purged from Soviet society, his image is making a comeback. Volgograd is possibly to be the home of yet another controversial statue by the artist Zurab Tsereteli (see the boxed text, p158), this time of Stalin, Roosevelt and Churchill in their famous pose at the 1945 Yalta conference. Similar statues are planned in other cities as local politicians call for the federal government to rehabilitate the wartime leader. Prime time TV shows have also begun to show Stalin in a positive light, reflecting a view held by many ordinary Russians, who look back on his murderous rule with rose-tinted glasses and see a time when the country was a superpower.

The revisionism hasn't all been one way. Access to old KGB files has allowed historians to compile a more accurate picture of just what went on, and who was in control, during the paranoid days of Stalin's rule. Many books previously banned about the era are now freely available and a more accurate history is taught in schools. In January 2003 a law was also passed granting Stalin's victims and their children a small measure of compensation: R92 a month, one free train ride a year, half-price medicine and free false teeth! Polls conducted in April and May 2005 also showed that a healthy majority of Russians are against rehabilitating Stalin.

and in 1972 the KGB chief, Yury Andropov, introduced new measures that included forced emigration and imprisonment in 'psychiatric institutions'.

The growing government and Party elite, known as nomenklatura (literally, 'list of nominees'), enjoyed lavish lifestyles, with access to goods that were unavailable to the average citizen. So did military leaders and some approved engineers and artists. But the ponderous, overcentralised economy, with its suffocating bureaucracy, was providing fewer and fewer improvements in general living standards. Incentive and initiative were dead; corruption began to spread in the Party and a cynical malaise seeped through society.

Repression extended to countries under the Soviet wing. The 1968 Prague Spring, when new Czechoslovak Party leader Alexander Dubcek promised 'socialism with a human face', was crushed by Soviet troops. The invasion was later defended by the 'Brezhnev Doctrine' – that the Soviet Union had the right to defend its interests among countries that fell within its sphere of influence. In 1979 Afghanistan would be one such country. Relations with China fell to an all-time low with border clashes in 1969, and the military build-up between the two countries was toned down only in the late 1980s.

Despite all this, the Brezhnev era also included the easing of superpower tensions, a process known as détente. US president Richard Nixon visited Moscow in 1972 and the two superpowers signed the first Strategic Arms Limitation Talks (SALT) treaty, restricting the number of nuclear ballistic weapons.

ANDROPOV & CHERNENKO

Brezhnev was rarely seen in public after his health declined in 1979. Before he died in 1982, he came to symbolise the country's moribund state of affairs. His successor, the former KGB chief Andropov, replaced

1953

Stalin suffers fatal stroke; Nikita Khrushchev becomes first secretary

1955

Signing of Warsaw Pact

some officials with young technocrats and proposed campaigns against alcoholism (which was costing the economy dearly) and corruption, later carried out under Gorbachev. He also clamped down on dissidents and increased defence spending.

As the economy continued to decline, Andropov died in February 1984, only 14 months after coming to power. Frail, 72-year-old Konstantin Chernenko, his successor, didn't even last that long, dying after a year in the top job.

GORBACHEV
Glasnost

Mikhail Gorbachev, a sprightly 54-year-old Andropov protégé, was waiting to step up as general secretary. Articulate and energetic, he understood that the Soviet economy badly needed sparking back into life, and soon departed radically from past policies. He launched an immediate turnover in the Politburo, bureaucracy and military, replacing many of the Brezhnevite 'old guard' with his own, younger supporters, and he clamped down vigorously on alcohol abuse.

'Acceleration' in the economy and *glasnost* (openness), first manifested in press criticism of poor economic management and past Party failings, were his initial slogans. The aim was to spur the dangerously stagnant economy by encouraging some management initiative, rewarding efficiency and letting bad practices be criticised.

However, the bloody clampdowns on nationalist rallies in Alma-Ata (now known as Almaty) in 1986, Tbilisi in 1989, and Vilnius and Riga in early 1991 made an alliance between Gorbachev, the interregional group in the parliament and the Democratic Russia movement impossible.

Foreign Affairs

In foreign policy, Gorbachev discontinued the isolationist, confrontational and economically costly policies of his predecessors. At his first meeting with US president Ronald Reagan in Geneva in 1985, Gorbachev suggested a 50% cut in long-range nuclear weaponry. By 1987 the two superpowers had agreed to remove all medium-range missiles from Europe, with other significant cuts in arms and troop numbers following. During 1988–89 the 'new thinking' also put an end to the Afghan War which had become the Soviet Union's Vietnam. Relations with China improved, too.

Perestroika

At home, Gorbachev quickly found that he could not expect a programme of limited reform to proceed smoothly and that there were hard choices to be made. The Chornobyl (Chernobyl in Russian) nuclear disaster in April 1986 led to one step along this road. Gorbachev announced there would be greater openness in reporting embarrassing things such as disasters; it had taken the authorities 18 days to admit the extent of the disaster at the power station in Ukraine, and even when they did, it was in a heavily expurgated form.

The antialcohol campaign was very unpopular and won little support. The end result was a huge growth in illegal distilling, and before long the campaign was abandoned.

Memorial (www.memo .ru/eng/index.htm) is a human rights movement that preserves the memory of those who suffered under the political repressions of the Soviet Union.

In *Koba the Dread* author Martin Amis lambasts the left for soft-pedalling on Stalin's murderous reign and the failure of communism.

1956	1957
Soviet troops crush Hungarian uprising	Space race kicks off with launch of Sputnik I

But above all it was becoming clear that no leader who relied on the Party could survive as a reformer. Many Party officials, with their privileged positions and opportunities for corruption, were a hindrance to, not a force for, change. In the economy, *perestroika* (restructuring) became the new slogan. This meant limited private enterprise and private property, not unlike Lenin's NEP, plus further efforts to push decision-making and responsibility out towards the grass roots. New laws were enacted in both these fields in 1988, but their application met resistance from the centralised bureaucracy.

Glasnost was supposed to tie in with *perestroika* as a way to encourage new ideas and counter the Brezhnev legacy of cynicism. The release at the end of 1986 of a famous dissident, Nobel Peace Prize–winner Andrei Sakharov (p407), from internal exile in Nizhny Novgorod was the start of a general freeing of political prisoners. Religions were allowed to operate more and more freely.

'The Brezhnev Doctrine gave way to the 'Sinatra Doctrine' letting Eastern Europe do it their way'

Political Reform

In 1988 Gorbachev appealed over the Party's head to the people by announcing a new 'parliament', the Congress of People's Deputies, with two-thirds of its members to be elected directly by the people, thus reducing the power of the bureaucracy and Party. The elections were held and the congress convened, to outspoken debate and national fascination, in 1989. Though dominated by Party apparatchiks (members), the parliament also contained outspoken critics of the government such as Sakharov.

End of the Empire

Gorbachev sprang repeated surprises, including sudden purges of difficult opponents (such as the populist reformer Boris Yeltsin), but the forces unleashed by his opening up of society grew impossible to control. From 1988 onwards, the reduced threat of repression and the experience of electing even semirepresentative assemblies spurred a growing clamour for independence in the Soviet satellite states. One by one, the Eastern European countries threw off their Soviet puppet regimes in the autumn of 1989; the Berlin Wall fell on 9 November. The Brezhnev Doctrine, Gorbachev's spokesperson said, had given way to the 'Sinatra Doctrine': letting them do it *their* way. The formal reunification of Germany on 3 October 1990 marked the effective end of the Cold War.

In 1990 the three Baltic states of the USSR also declared (or, as they would have it, reaffirmed) their independence – an independence that for the time being remained more theoretical than real. Before long, most other Soviet republics either followed suit or declared 'sovereignty' – the precedence of their own laws over the Soviet Union's. Gorbachev's proposal for an ill-defined new federal system, to hold the Soviet Union together, won few friends.

Rise of Yeltsin

Also in 1990, Yeltsin won the chairmanship of the parliament of the giant Russian Republic, which had three-quarters of the USSR's area and more than half its population. Soon after coming to power, Gorbachev had promoted Yeltsin to head the Communist Party in Moscow, but had then

1961	1962
Yury Gagarin first man in space	Cuban missile crisis with the USA

dumped him in 1987–88 in the face of opposition to his reforms there from the Party's old guard. By that time, Yeltsin had already declared *perestroika* a failure, and these events produced a lasting personal enmity between the two men. Gorbachev increasingly struggled to hold together the radical reformers and the conservative old guard in the Party.

Once chosen as chairman of the Russian parliament, Yeltsin proceeded to taunt and jockey for power with Gorbachev. He seemed already to have concluded that real change was impossible not only under the Communist Party but also within a centrally controlled Soviet Union, the members of which were in any case showing severe centrifugal tendencies. Yeltsin resigned from the Communist Party and his parliament proclaimed the sovereignty of the Russian Republic.

At street level, organised crime and black-marketeering boomed, profiting from a slackening of the law-and-order system, and preying on many of the fledgling private businesses by running protection rackets.

In early 1990 Gorbachev persuaded the Communist Party to vote away its own constitutional monopoly on power, and parliament chose him for the newly created post of executive president, which further distanced the organs of government from the Party. But these events made little difference to the crisis into which the USSR was sliding.

Economic Collapse & Old-Guard Reaction

Gorbachev's economic reforms proved too little to yield a healthy private sector or a sound, decentralised state sector. Prices went up, supplies of goods fell, people got angry. Some wanted all-out capitalism immediately; others wanted to go back to the suddenly rosy days of communism. In trying to steer a middle course, to prevent a showdown between the radical reformers and the conservatives in the Party, Gorbachev achieved nothing and pleased no-one.

Much of the record 1990 harvest was left to rot in fields and warehouses because the Party could no longer mobilise the machinery and hands to bring it in, while private enterprise was not yet advanced enough to do so. When Gorbachev, still trying to keep a balance, backed down in September 1990 from implementing the radical '500 Day Plan' – to shift to a fully fledged market economy within 500 days – many saw it as submission to the growing displeasure of the old guard, and a lost last chance to save his reforms.

His Nobel Peace Prize, awarded in the bleak winter of 1990–91, when fuel and food were disappearing from many shops, left the average Soviet citizen literally cold. The army, the security forces and the Party hardliners called with growing confidence for the restoration of law and order to save the country. Foreign minister Eduard Shevardnadze, long one of Gorbachev's staunchest partners but now under constant old-guard sniping for 'losing Eastern Europe', resigned, warning of impending hardline dictatorship.

FALL OF THE SOVIET UNION

Even before June 1991, when he was voted president of the Russian Republic in the country's first-ever direct presidential elections, Yeltsin was more powerful than the beleaguered Gorbachev. Yeltsin demanded devolution

> 'Gorbachev's Nobel Peace Prize, awarded in the bleak winter of 1990–91, when fuel and food were disappearing from many shops, left the average Soviet citizen literally cold'

1964	1968
Leonid Brezhnev takes over as Khrushchev is relieved of duties	Soviet troops stamp on Prague Spring

of power from the Soviet Union to the republics, and banned Communist Party cells from government offices and workplaces in Russia. Gorbachev won some respite by fashioning a new union treaty, transferring greater power to the republics, which was to be signed on 20 August.

The Coup

Matters were taken out of Gorbachev's hands, however, on 18 August, when a delegation from the 'Committee for the State of Emergency in the USSR' arrived at the Crimean dacha where he was taking a holiday and demanded that he declare a state of emergency and transfer power to the vice president, Gennady Yanayev. According to his sometimes disputed version, Gorbachev refused and was put under house arrest. The old-guard coup had begun.

The eight-person Committee for the State of Emergency, which included Gorbachev's defence minister, prime minister and KGB chief, planned to restore the Communist Party and the Soviet Union to their former status. On 19 August the coup leaders sought to arrest Yeltsin, tanks appeared on Moscow's streets, and it was announced that Yanayev had assumed the president's powers.

Dominic Lieven's *Empire* is an astute, scholarly book written with great love and understanding of Russia.

But Yeltsin escaped arrest and went to the Moscow White House, seat of the Russian parliament, to rally opposition. Crowds gathered at the White House, persuaded some of the tank crews to switch sides, and started to build barricades. Yeltsin climbed on a tank to declare the coup illegal and call for a general strike. Troops that had been ordered to storm the White House refused to do so.

The following day huge crowds opposed to the coup gathered in Moscow and Leningrad. The leaders of Ukraine and Kazakhstan rejected the coup, and Estonia declared full independence from the Soviet Union. Coup leaders started to quit or fall ill. On 21 August the tanks withdrew; the coup leaders fled and were arrested.

Demolition

Gorbachev flew back to Moscow on 22 August 1991, but his time was up. The old-style Soviet Union and the Communist Party were already suffering the consequences of their humiliation in the failed coup. Yeltsin had announced that all state property in the Russian Republic was under the control of Russia, not the Soviet Union. On 23 August he banned the Communist Party in Russia. Gorbachev resigned as the USSR Party's leader the following day, ordering that its property be transferred to the Soviet parliament.

Latvia followed Estonia by declaring independence on 21 August – Lithuania had already done so in 1990 – and most of the other republics of the USSR followed suit. International, and finally Soviet, recognition of the Baltic states' independence came by early September.

Gorbachev embarked on a last-ditch bid to save the Soviet Union with proposals for a looser union of independent states. In September the Soviet parliament abolished the centralised Soviet state, vesting power in three temporary governing bodies until a new union treaty could be signed. But Yeltsin was steadily transferring control over everything that mattered in Russia from Soviet hands into Russian ones.

1973

Publication of Alexander Solzhenitsyn's *The Gulag Archipelago*

1979

Russia invades Afghanistan

On 8 December Yeltsin and the leaders of Ukraine and Belarus, meeting near Brest in Belarus, announced that the USSR no longer existed. They proclaimed a new Commonwealth of Independent States (CIS), a vague alliance of fully independent states with no central authority. Russia kicked the Soviet government out of the Kremlin on 19 December. Two days later eight more republics joined the CIS, and the USSR was pronounced finally dead.

Gorbachev, now a president without a country, formally resigned on 25 December, the day the white, blue and red Russian flag replaced the Soviet red flag over the Kremlin.

RUSSIA UNDER YELTSIN
Economic Reform & Regional Tensions

Even before Gorbachev's resignation Yeltsin had announced plans to move to a free-market economy, appointing in November 1991 a reforming government to carry this out. State subsidies were to be phased out, prices freed, government spending cut, and state businesses, housing, land and agriculture privatised. Yeltsin became prime minister and defence minister, as well as president, as an emergency measure.

With the economy already in chaos, some local regions of Russia started hoarding scarce foodstuffs or declaring autonomy and control over their own economic resources. All of the 20 nominally autonomous ethnic regions scattered across Russia, some of them rich in resources vital to the Russian economy, declared themselves autonomous republics, leading to fears that Russia might disintegrate as the USSR had just done. These worries were eventually defused, however, by a 1992 treaty between the central government and the republics; by a new constitution in 1993, which handed the other regions increased rights; and by changes in the tax system.

Some benefits of economic reform took hold during 1994 in a few big cities, notably Moscow and St Petersburg (the name to which Leningrad had reverted in 1991), where a market economy was taking root and an enterprise culture was developing among the younger generations. At the same time crime and corruption seemed to be spiralling out of control. One of Yeltsin's advisers reported in 1994: 'Every, repeat every, owner of a shop or kiosk pays a racketeer.'

Night of Stone: Death and Memory in Twentieth-Century Russia by Catherine Merridale is an enthralling read, viewing the country's bleak recent history through the prisms of psychology and philosophy.

Conflict with the Old Guard

The parliament, although it had supported Yeltsin against the coup in 1991, could not tolerate the fast pace of his economic reforms, the weakening of Russian power that stemmed from his demolition of the Soviet Union, his arms-reduction agreements with the USA and his need for Western economic aid. Elected in 1990 under Gorbachev-era voting rules, the parliament was dominated by communists and Russian nationalists, both opposed to the course events were taking.

As early as April 1991 Yeltsin's ministers were complaining that their reforms were being stymied by contradictory legislation from the parliament. As the austerity caused by economic reform continued to bite – though there was more in the shops, ordinary people could buy less because they had no money – Yeltsin's popularity began to fall and his opponents in parliament launched a series of increasingly serious

1980	1982
Summer Olympic Games held in Moscow	Brezhnev dies from heart attack and is succeeded by Yury Andropov

challenges to his position. Organised crime was steadily rising and corruption at all levels seemed more prevalent than before.

Yeltsin sacrificed key ministers and compromised on the pace of reform, but the parliament continued to issue resolutions contradicting his presidential decrees, leaving overall policy heading nowhere. In April 1993 a national referendum gave Yeltsin a big vote of confidence, both in his presidency and in his economic reform policies. Yeltsin began framing a new constitution that would kill off the existing parliament and define more clearly the roles of president and legislature.

Finally, matters came down to a trial of strength. In September 1993 Yeltsin 'dissolved' the parliament, which in turn 'stripped' the president of all his powers. Yeltsin sent troops to blockade the White House, ordering the members to leave it by 4 October. Many did, but on 2 and 3 October the National Salvation Front, an aggressive communist-nationalist group, attempted an insurrection, overwhelming the troops around the White House and attacking Moscow's Ostankino TV centre, where 62 people died. The next morning troops stormed the White House, leaving at least 70 dead. Yeltsin's use of force won him few friends.

David Remnick's
Lenin's Tomb and
*Resurrection: The Struggle
for a New Russia* are both
notable volumes by the
Washington Post's
award-winning
ex-Moscow
correspondent.

1993 Elections & Constitutional Reform

Elections to a new two-house form of parliament were held in December 1993. The name of the more influential lower house, the State Duma (Gosudarstvennaya Duma), consciously echoed that of tsarist Russia's parliaments. At the same time as the elections, a national referendum endorsed the new Yeltsin-drafted constitution, which gave the president a clear upper hand over parliament.

This system, however, does have potential flaws in that the president and the parliament can (and do) both make laws and can effectively block each other's actions. In practice, the president can usually get his way through issuing presidential decrees. During Yeltsin's time this happened often, while his successor Vladimir Putin has worked harmoniously with the Duma.

The president is the head of state and has broad powers. They appoint all government ministers, including the prime minister, who is effectively number two and who would assume the presidency should the president die or become incapacitated. The Duma has to approve the president's appointees, which has led to showdowns. Presidential elections are held every four years.

The Duma's upper house, the Federation Council (Sovet Federatsii), had 178 seats at the time of research, occupied by two representatives from each of Russia's administrative districts (see the boxed text, p66). Representatives are the top officials from these areas and as such are not elected to this body. Its primary purpose is to approve or reject laws proposed by the lower house.

The lower house, the State Duma, oversees all legislation. Its 450 members are equally divided between representatives elected from single-member districts and those elected from party lists. Obviously this gives extra clout to the major parties, and efforts to replace its system of representation with a purely proportional system have been shunned. Elections are held every four years in the December preceding the presidential elections.

1984	1985
Andropov dies; 72-year-old Konstantin Chernenko dodders up to the post	Mikhail Gorbachev takes Kremlin top job

The 1993 constitution also enshrines the rights to free trade and competition, private ownership of land and property, freedom of conscience, and free movement in and out of Russia, and bans censorship, torture and the establishment of any official ideology.

War in Chechnya

Yeltsin's foreign policy reflected the growing mood of conservative nationalism at home. The perceived need for a buffer zone between Russia and the outside world and the millions of ethnic Russians living in the former Soviet republics (many already moving to Russia as political tides turned against them) were chief concerns. Russian troops intervened in fighting in Tajikistan, Georgia and Moldova with the aim of strengthening Russia's hand in those regions, and by early 1995 Russian forces were stationed in all the other former republics except Estonia and Lithuania.

In Chechnya, however, this policy proved particularly disastrous. Russia wanted to bring to heel this Muslim republic of around one million people in the Caucasus, which had declared independence from Russia in 1991. Chechnya, prone to internal conflicts and noted as the homeland of many of the most powerful and violent gangsters in Russia, also sits across the routes of the pipelines that bring oil from the Caspian Sea to Russia.

Attempts to negotiate a settlement or have Chechnya's truculent leader Dzhokhar Dudayev deposed had got nowhere by the end of 1994. Yeltsin ordered the army and air force into Chechnya for what was meant to be a quick operation to restore Russian control. But the Chechens fought bitterly, their resistance fuelled by anti-Russian resentments stemming from 1943–45, when the Chechens were deported en masse from the Caucasus to Central Asia for alleged collaboration with the invading Germans (the surviving Chechens were allowed back in the 1950s).

By mid-1995 at least 25,000 people, mostly civilians, were dead, and the Russians had only just gained full control of the Chechen capital, Grozny, which had been reduced to rubble. Some 300,000 or more people fled their homes, Dudayev was still holding out in southern Chechnya, and the guerrilla warfare continued unabated. Criticism of Yeltsin surged and in national elections in December 1995, communists and nationalists won control of 45% of the Duma.

In December 2004 the BBC brought together a panel of ordinary Chechens to answer online questions about life in Chechnya; read the results at http://news.bbc.co.uk/2/hi/talking_point/4078049.stm.

1996 Elections

By early 1996 Yeltsin seemed a shadow of the vigorous man who had leapt atop a tank in August 1991. Frequent bouts of various ill-defined sicknesses kept him from public view. Worse for his hold on power, when he was seen in public he often seemed confused and unstable.

But even as the communists under Gennady Zyuganov seemed set to rise from the dead on a wave of discontent, those who had grown rich under Russia's five-year flirtation with capitalism – the oligarchs (see p68) – came to Yeltsin's aid. These media moguls and financiers made certain that the only message the Russian voters received was Yeltsin's. The communists were kept off TV. Meanwhile one of Yeltsin's young protégés – Anatoly Chubais – ran a brilliant campaign that among other things had a temporarily revived Yeltsin appear on stage dancing at a rock concert to show his supposed strength.

1986	1989
Perestroika and *glasnost* enter Soviet political language	Soviet troops leave Afghanistan

---

THE RUSSIAN FEDERATION

Following the consolidation of the Perm Oblast and the Komi-Permyak Autonomous Area into the Perm Kray in late 2005, the Russian Federation is now made up of 88 constituent parts, including 19 semiautonomous *respubliki* (republics), 49 *oblasti* (regions), seven *kraya* (territories), 10 autonomous areas, one autonomous region, and the two federal cities of Moscow and St Petersburg. Republics have their own constitution and legislation. Territories, regions, federal cities, autonomous regions and autonomous areas have their own charter and legislation.

The consolidation of administrative areas is set to continue with both the sparsely populated Taymyr and Evenkia autonomous areas voting in referendums in April 2005 to merge with Krasnoyarsk territory. There's likely to be more of these mergers in the future as the presidential administration would prefer to deal with fewer separate regions across Russia.

The current structure is partly a hangover from the old Soviet system of nominally autonomous republics for many minority ethnic groups. After the collapse of the Soviet Union, all these republics declared varying degrees of autonomy from Russia, the most extreme being Chechnya, in the Caucasus, which unilaterally declared full independence.

Yeltsin struck deals with the republics, which largely pacified them, and the 1993 constitution awarded regions and territories much the same status as republics and declared that federal laws always took precedence over local ones. Putin has endeavoured to bring control back to the Kremlin by creating seven large federal districts – Central, South, North West, Volga, Ural, Siberia and Far East – each with an appointed envoy. According to opinion polls only around 20% of Russians have any idea who these envoys are and what they do.

In the June 1996 elections, Zyuganov and a tough-talking ex-general, Alexander Lebed, split the opposition vote, and Yeltsin easily defeated Zyuganov in a run-off in early July (although the strain of dancing at concerts and other stunts had taken their toll because Yeltsin again disappeared from view for several weeks). The communists and other opposition parties returned to their grousing in the Duma, while Lebed unwisely accepted an offer from Yeltsin to try to negotiate an end to the fighting in Chechnya. Given little leeway, Lebed proved to be the fall guy for the entire botched affair and his political star was greatly dimmed by the time a peace settlement was reached and Russian troops began withdrawing in late 1996.

Meanwhile Yeltsin's health deteriorated to the point where even the Kremlin had to admit he might be suffering from something worse than 'a cold'. In November he underwent quintuple heart bypass surgery. While Yeltsin slowly recuperated, much of 1997 saw a series of financial shenanigans and deals that became known variously as the 'War of the Oligarchs' or the 'War of the Bankers'. These were nothing more than power grabs by the various Russian billionaires. On occasion Yeltsin would make a grand show of exerting his authority, as he did in 1998 when he sacked the government for its bad economic management.

Economic Collapse & Recovery

In the spring of 1998 signs that the Russian economy was in deep trouble were everywhere. Coal miners went on strike over months of unpaid wages that were part of more than US$300 billion owed to workers across the country. This, added to well over US$100 billion in foreign debt, meant that Russia was effectively bankrupt.

During the summer of 1998 the foreign investors who had propped up the Russian economy fled. On 17 August the Yeltsin government took the inevitable but fateful step of devaluing the rouble. In a repeat of scenes that had shaken the West during the Depression of 1929, many Russian banks closed, leaving their depositors with nothing.

The economy would eventually benefit from the rouble devaluation. Following the initial shock, the middle class, mostly paid in untaxed cash dollars, suddenly realised that their salaries had increased threefold overnight (if counted in roubles) while prices largely remained the same. This led to a huge boom in consumer goods and services. Things such as restaurants and fitness clubs that were previously only for the rich suddenly became available to many more people. The situation also gave a great chance to Russian consumer-goods producers; 1999 saw imported products being rapidly substituted by high-quality local ones.

The Oligarchs: Wealth and Power in the New Russia by David Hoffman gives a blow-by-blow account of the rise and sometimes fall of the 'robber barons' of modern Russia.

Rise of the Nationalists

Given the circumstances it was no surprise that various nationalist groups like the communists would enjoy growing support. Their cause received a major boost on 24 March 1999 when NATO forces, led by the USA, began bombing Yugoslavia over the Kosovo crisis. This attack on the Serbs, who are regarded by Russians as ethnic kin, inflamed long-dormant passions among Russians, who turned out in Moscow to stone the US embassy.

Prior to the NATO attacks, a poll had shown that 57% of Russians had favourable feelings about the Western democracies. After 24 March that figure fell to 14%.

Moscow bureau chief of the *Financial Times*, Andrew Jack, sums up the thorny political, economic and social issues facing the country in the recent *Inside Putin's Russia: Can There Be Reform Without Democracy?*

In September 1999 a series of explosions in Moscow that virtually demolished three apartment blocks left more than 200 people dead. This unprecedented terrorism in the nation's capital fuelled unease and xenophobia. The Moscow government introduced oppressive measures against ethnic minorities, especially those from the southern republics such as Chechnya. There was a widespread, although unproven, belief that Chechen terrorists were responsible for the bombings. The authorities have blamed non-Chechen Islamists from the North Caucasus for these blasts. Some of these terrorists have been sentenced, others killed in Chechnya. Although a theory about FSB (Federal Security Service, successor to the KGB) involvement in the apartment bombings is still doing the rounds, now, after proven terrorists attacks in Dubrovka and Beslan, people tend to believe the government's official line.

In 2005, Revolution Day, commemorating the Bolshevik uprising of October 1917, was replaced by People's Unity Day (November 4), celebrating the day Polish troops marched out of Moscow in 1612.

Seizing upon public opinion, the Russian government launched a brutal new military campaign centred on Grozny, the Chechen capital. Tens of thousands of civilians fled to the countryside to escape the bombardment and there was a huge number of casualties. Human rights abuses on both sides have been rampant and the ongoing conflict threatens to eclipse the Afghan War as Russia's Vietnam; see p492 for more details.

VLADIMIR PUTIN

On New Year's Eve 1999, in a move that caught everyone on the hop, Yeltsin announced his immediate resignation, entrusting the caretaker duties of president to the prime minister Vladimir Putin, a former director of the FSB.

1992	1994
Boris Yeltsin heads the government of the Russian Federation	War in Chechnya begins

Putin's sweeping victory in the March 2000 presidential elections did not surprise anyone. He wasted no time in establishing his strongman credentials by boosting military spending, clawing back power to the Kremlin from the regions and cracking down hard on the critical media. Despite the international protests that accompanied actions such as the takeover of independent TV station NTV (see p76) and the increasingly bloody conflict in Chechnya, Putin's home support remained solid, particularly as the economy began to recover on the back of rising oil and gas prices.

As if the Chechen war wasn't bad enough, Russia's military suffered a humiliating tragedy in 2001 when the submarine *Kursk* exploded in the Barents Sea, taking its crew of 118 to a watery grave. Much soul-searching

THE OLIGARCHS' SCORE CARD

Vladimir Putin has set his sights on Russia's so-called oligarchs, a group of billionaire businessmen who made their fortunes in the economic free-for-all following the demise of the Soviet Union. The aim of this has been to reconsolidate control of Russia and its economic resources within the Kremlin rather than through the machinations of the super-rich. At first none too gentle warnings were issued that the oligarchs stick to the law and keep out of politics. Later, as Mikhail Khodorkovsky has learnt to his cost, the courts were brought in to mete out a uniquely Russian version of justice. Here we rate the prospects of various key players.

Mikhail Khodorkovsky 0/10 – Once reckoned to be Russia's richest man, Khodorkovsky has been sentenced to nine years in jail for fraud and tax evasion, following a trial widely held to be unfair and during which he watched the government dismantle his company Yukos Oil, at one time the world's fourth-largest oil company.

Boris Berezovsky 3/10 – Granted political asylum in the UK in 2003, the one-time media baron and wannabe politician was a major power broker during the Yeltsin years. He now lives under the name of Platon Yelenin, and although stripped of his Russian media interests remains a wealthy and committed opponent of Putin.

Vladimir Gusinsky 5/10 – The former theatre director and media baron is a somewhat more bohemian character than his fellow oligarchs. He was hounded out of Russia and arrested on fraud charges which were subsequently dropped. He now shuttles between Israel and the US, busying himself with religious and humanitarian causes.

Anatoly Chubais 5/10 – In March 2005 the so-called Father of the Oligarchs (he was Yeltsin's deputy prime minister in charge of privatisation) survived an assassination attempt. In May, following a meltdown of Moscow's electricity supply, Chubais, now head of Russia's power monopoly Unified Energy Systems, was called to account in a criminal investigation by the prosecutor general's office.

Mikhail Fridman 9/10 – Chairman of the Alfa group controlling a major bank and the TNK-BP oil company, Fridman is reckoned to be worth at least US$4 billion. One of the big seven oligarchs who bankrolled Yeltsin's 1996 reelection, he keeps a low profile these days and has his wife and family living safely in Paris.

Vladimir Potanin 9/10 – His company owns Norilsk Nickel, the world's largest nickel, platinum and palladium producer. Although worth around US$1 billion, pocket money compared to the wealth of other oligarchs, Potanin's international reputation is strong, especially since he took a seat on the board of the trustees of the Guggenheim Museum, to which he donates US$1 million annually.

Yelena Baturina 10/10 – The only woman on the 2005 list of the country's richest businesspeople compiled by *Forbes* magazine, this property developer is also Russia's only female billionaire, worth an estimated US$1.46 billion. She has good connections, being the wife of Yury Luzhkov, the powerful mayor of Moscow.

Roman Abramovich 10/10 – The governor of the Russian Far East province of Chukotka, Abramovich is also, currently, Russia's richest tycoon. He recently sold his share of the oil firm Sibneft to Gazprom for US$13.09 billion making him even richer than he was previously, which was pretty damn rich anyway. The youngest of the oligarchs (he was born in 1966) he keeps a generally low profile despite being the owner of Chelsea Football Club.

1998	2000
Economy on skids as rouble is devalued	Yeltsin resigns and names Vladimir Putin as his successor; he is elected to the role later in year

ensued over the decrepit state of the nation's infrastructure, a situation underscored by the devastating blaze at Moscow's Ostankino TV tower.

In wake of the events of 11 September in New York, Putin's immediately cooperative stance and support for the US-led assault on Afghanistan won him increased respect in the West. Subsequent meetings with George W Bush were notably friendly and relaxed, although the two former foes had to agree to differ over the Iraq War of 2003. By the time of Putin's reelection in 2004 (p29) the two presidents were back to praising each other.

Terrorism remains a major thorn in Putin's side, and one he seems to be making little headway with. The tragic events at Moscow's Palace of Culture Theatre in October 2002, when Chechen guerrillas took more than 700 hostages, underlined his uncompromising stance. Security forces stormed the building, leaving more than 100 of the hostages dead from the nerve gas used to subdue the terrorists. Other terrorist attacks in Moscow have followed; see the boxed text, p124. Worse was the aftermath of the September 2004 siege of a school in Beslan, again involving Chechen terrorists: out of 1200 hostages, 344 people died, half of them children.

> Want to know what Vladimir Putin is currently up to? Check out his personal portal at http://president.kremlin.ru/eng/.

WHO IS VLADIMIR PUTIN?

Saviour of Mother Russia or, as one of his most outspoken critics has called him, a 'KGB snoop' in democrat's clothing? Well into his second term of office as president of the Russian Federation, the verdict on Vladimir Putin remains out.

As a man schooled in the arts of espionage and state control, it's little wonder that Putin comes across as a shady figure. In an effort to strip away some of the mystery, a group of journalists interviewed Putin, family members, friends and acquaintances in 2000. The resulting book, published in English under the title *First Person: An Astonishingly Frank Self-Portrait by Russia's President Vladimir Putin* sheds some light, but ultimately poses more questions than it answers.

Born in St Petersburg in 1952 to a toolmaker (father) and janitor (mother), Putin had a poor childhood in a communal apartment where he poked at rats in the stairwell for fun. Initially disinterested in school, Putin settled down once he discovered martial arts (he's a judo black belt) and a burning desire to join the KGB. After completing a law degree at Leningrad State University he did indeed join the KGB. There, as he later told a friend, he became 'a specialist in human relations'.

In 1983 he married Lyudmila, a flight attendant. Masha, the first of his two daughters (the other is Katya) was born in 1985, the year he was transferred to Dresden in the former East Germany. This is where he stayed, gathering information, until the fall of the Berlin Wall in 1990. Claiming disillusion with the crumbling Soviet Union and rejection of all it had stood for, Putin resigned from the KGB in 1991 (although in the KGB they say, 'we have no retirees, just temporarily inactive members'), eventually joining the fiercely prodemocratic government of St Petersburg under one of the main leaders of the Russian democratic movement, Anatoly Sobchak.

His quiet achievements in St Petersburg saw him called to Moscow in 1996, where he progressed steadily through a series of important posts to become FSB director in 1998. In August the following year he was appointed prime minister and by the year's end Yeltsin was announcing Putin as acting president.

Putin remains very popular although he is vilified by the intelligentsia for his clampdown on critical media. Resolving the war in the north Caucasus, he claims, is his 'historical mission' (seemingly at almost any cost). He also talks about the need to make Russia a civil society, integrated with Europe, where the rule of law holds sway: some might say that this is an even tougher proposition than sorting out Chechnya.

2001	2004
Submarine *Kursk* sinks	Putin reelected

The Culture

THE NATIONAL PSYCHE

Within the Russian Federation, one's 'nationality' refers to one's ethnicity rather than one's passport. And Russia has dozens of nationalities. Nonetheless, despite the enormous cultural variation, there are certain elements of a common psyche. The classic image of miserable Soviet receptionists snapping *'nyet'* with a 'get-lost' shrug is still to be found in certain 'service' industries (though things are rapidly improving), but the overwhelming Russian character trait is one of genuine humanity and hospitality that goes much deeper than in most Western countries.

Russians are often coy in their initial approach to strangers. But once you've earned a small crumb of friendship, hospitality typically unfolds with extraordinary generosity. Visitors can rapidly find themselves regaled with stories, drowned in vodka and stuffed full of food. An invitation to a Russian home will typically result in all this repeating several times, even when the family can ill afford the expense. This can be especially true outside the big cities, where you'll meet locals determined to share everything they have with you, however meagre their resources.

There's a similar bipolarity in the Russian sense of humour. Unsmiling gloom and fatalistic melancholy remain archetypically Russian, but, as in Britain, this is often used as a foil to a deadpan, sarcastic humour.

You'll soon learn how deeply most Russians love their country. They will sing the praises of Mother Russia's great contributions to the arts and sciences, its long history and abundant physical attributes, then just as loudly point out its many failures. The dark side of this patriotism is an unpleasant streak of racism (see p75). Don't let it put you off and take heart in the knowledge that as much as foreigners may be perplexed about the true nature of the Russian soul, the locals themselves still haven't got it figured out either! As the poet Fyodor Tyutchev said, 'You can't understand Russia with reason...you can only believe in her'.

Russia's suicide rate hovers at around 40 people per 1000 – nearly three times the world average – and alcoholism is rampant.

Although a little out of date, *Teach Yourself World Cultures: Russia,* by Stephen and Tatyana Webber is a decent, layman's stab at decoding all aspects of Russian culture.

THE RULES OF RUSSIAN HOSPITALITY

- If you're invited to a Russian home, always bring a gift, such as wine or a cake.
- Shaking hands across the threshold is considered unlucky; wait until you're fully inside.
- If you give anyone flowers, make sure there's an odd number of flowers, as even numbers are for funerals.
- Remove your shoes and coat on entering a house.
- Once the festivities begin, refusing offered food or drink can cause grave offence.
- Vodka is for toasting, not for casual sipping; wait for the cue.
- When you are in any setting with other people, even strangers such as those sharing your train compartment, it's polite to share anything you have to eat, drink or smoke.
- Traditional gentlemanly behaviour is not just appreciated but expected, as you will notice when you see women standing in front of closed doors waiting for something to happen.

LIFESTYLE

In the world's biggest country, the way of life of a Nenets reindeer herder in Siberia is radically different from that of a marketing executive in Moscow or an Islamic factory worker in Kazan. Not only this, but as Russia grows more prosperous, the gap between rich and poor – and the lives they lead – becomes larger.

This said, there are common features to life across Russia, such as education, and weekly visits to the *banya* (hot bath, a bit like a sauna) and dacha (country home), that are worth noting.

The Banya

For centuries, travellers to Russia have commented on the particular (and in many people's eyes, peculiar) traditions of the *banya*; the closest English equivalents, 'bathhouse' and 'sauna', don't quite sum it up. To this day, Russians make it an important part of their week and you can't say you've really been to Russia unless you've visited one.

The main element of the *banya* is the *parilka* (steam room), which can get so hot that it makes Finnish saunas seem wussy in comparison. Here, rocks are heated by a furnace, with water poured onto them using a long-handled ladle. Often, a few drops of eucalyptus or pine oil (sometimes even beer) is added to the water, creating a scent in the burst of scalding steam released into the room. After this some people stand up, grab hold of a *venik* (a tied bundle of birch branches) and beat themselves or each other with it.

It does appear sadomasochistic, and there are theories tying the practice to other masochistic elements of Russian culture. At the very least it's painful, although the effect is pleasant and cleansing: apparently, the birch leaves (or sometimes oak or, agonisingly, juniper branches) and their secretions help rid the skin of toxins.

The *banya* tradition is deeply ingrained in the Russian culture that emerged from the ancient Viking settlement of Novgorod, with the Kyivan Slavs making fun of their northern brothers for all that steamy whipping. In folk traditions, it has been customary for bride and groom to take separate *bani* with their friends the night before the wedding, with the *banya* itself the bridge to marriage; a modern version of this custom is depicted humorously in every Russian's favourite film *Ironiya Sudby ili s Legkim Parom* (Irony of Fate). Husband and wife would also customarily bathe together after the ceremony, and midwives used to administer a steam bath to women during delivery. (It was not uncommon to give

> To see the funny side of the worst of Russian culture, check out the Russian Misery Tourism site www.unclepasha.com/misery_russian.htm – for the 'sophisticated misanthrope'.

A GUIDE TO BANYA ETIQUETTE   *Steve Kokker*

At the same time every week, people head out to their favourite *banya* (hot bath, a bit like a sauna) to meet up with a regular crowd of people (the Western equivalent would be your gym buddies). Many bring along a Thermos filled with tea that's mixed with jam, spices and heaps of sugar. (A few bottles of beer and some dried fish also do nicely.)

After stripping down in the sex-segregated changing room, wishing *'Lyogkogo* (pronounced *lyokh*-ka-va) *para!'* to their mates (meaning something like 'May your steam be easy!'), bathers head off into the *parilka* (steam room). After the birch-branch thrashing (best experienced lying down on a bench, with someone else administering the 'beating'), bathers run outside and, depending on their nerve, plunge into the *basseyn* (ice-cold pool).

With eyelids draped back over their skull, they stagger back into the changing room to their mates' wishes of *'S lyogkim parom!'* (Hope your steam was easy!). Finally, they drape themselves in sheets and discuss world issues before repeating the process – most *banya* experts go through the motions about five to 10 times over a two-hour period.

a hot birch minimassage to the newborn.) The *banya*, in short, is a place for physical and moral purification.

This said, many city *bani* are run down and unappealing (with a few classy exceptions, including Moscow's splendid Sanduny Baths, p167); grab any chance you get to try a traditional one in a countryside log cabin.

The Dacha

For the vast majority of urban Russians, home is within a drab, ugly housing complex of Soviet vintage. Although quite cosy and prettily decorated on the inside, these apartments are typically cramped and come with no attached garden. Instead, a large percentage of Russian families have a dacha, or small country house. Often little more than a bare-bones hut (but sometimes quite luxurious), these retreats offer Russians refuge from city life and as such figure prominently in the national psyche. On half-warm weekends, places such as Moscow begin to empty out early on Friday as people head to the country (see the boxed text, p193).

One of the most important aspects of dacha life is gardening. Families grow all manner of vegetables and fruits to eat over the winter. Flowers also play an important part in creating the proper dacha ambience, and even among people who have no need to grow food the contact with the soil provides an important balm for the Russian soul.

Country Studies (www
.country-studies.com
/russia/) includes a
comprehensive series of
essays on many aspects
of Russian life.

Education

From its beginning as an agrarian society in which literacy was limited to the few in the upper classes, the USSR achieved a literacy rate of 98% – among the best in the world. Russia continues to benefit from this legacy. Russian schools today emphasise basics such as reading and mathematics, and the high literacy rate has been maintained.

Students wishing to attend a further two years of secondary education must pass rigorous tests. The hurdles are even tougher for those wishing to attend a university, but many are prepared to go through with them – particularly men who can delay or avoid compulsory national service by going on to higher education.

Technical subjects such as science and mathematics are valued and bright students are encouraged to specialise in a particular area from a young age. While Russian teachers and professors are held in high regard by their international peers, at home they are among the worst victims of Russia's new economy, their government-paid salaries being among the lowest in the land.

POPULATION

The last century has wrought enormous changes on Russia's population. The country of peasants has become an urban one with close on three quarters of Russia's 143.4 million people living in cities and towns. There are 13 cities with populations in excess of one million (in order: Moscow, St Petersburg, Novosibirsk, Nizhny Novgorod, Yekaterinburg, Samara, Omsk, Kazan, Rostov-on-Don, Chelyabinsk, Ufa, Volgograd and Perm). Rural communities are withering – according to the 2002 census, of Russia's 155,000 villages, 13,000 had been deserted and 35,000 had populations of less than 10 people.

Russia is also facing an alarming natural decline in its population – around 0.45% per year. In the last decade alone the population has plummeted by some 6 million people. The average life expectancy for a Russian man is 59 years, for a woman 73: at current rates the population will

decline to 123 million by 2030. Much of this is due to the population's
staggering health problems, problems inherent in a diet high in alcohol
and fat. Accidental deaths due to drunkenness are also frequent.

About 81.5% of Russia's people are ethnic Russians. The next largest
ethnic groups are Tatars with 3.8%, followed by Ukrainians (3%), Chuvash (1.2%), Bashkirs (0.9%), Belarusians (0.8%) and Moldavians (0.7%).
The remaining 8.1% belong to dozens of smaller ethnic groups, all with
their own languages and cultural traditions (in varying degrees of usage),
and varied religions.

Tatars

Russia's biggest minority is the Tatars, who are descended from the
Mongol-Tatar armies of Chinggis (Genghis) Khaan (p36) and his successors, and from earlier Hunnic, Turkic and Finno-Ugric settlers on the
middle Volga. Tatars lived in Siberia before Russians (see p501). There's
a famous painting in Moscow's Tretyakov Gallery that shows the Tatar
stronghold of Sibir being conquered by Cossacks in 1582.

Today the Tatars are mostly Muslim, and some 1.8 million of them form
nearly half the population of the Tatarstan Republic, the capital of which is
Kazan, on the Volga River. A couple more million or so Tatars live in other
parts of Russia and the Commonwealth of Independent States (CIS). For
more details, see **Tatarstan on the Internet** (www.kcn.ru/tat_en/index.htm).

Russiatrek (www
.russiatrek.com) is a
useful website with
concise background
information on the
various Russian republics,
including details of native
peoples, cultures and
links to other relevant
sites.

Chuvash & Bashkirs

Two other important groups in the middle Volga region are the Chuvash
and the Bashkirs. The Chuvash, descendants of the pre-Mongol Tatar

---

WEDDINGS RUSSIAN STYLE

Cohabitation remains less common in Russia than in the West, so when young couples get
together they often as not get married. During any trip to Russia you will not fail to notice the
number of people getting hitched, particularly on Friday and Saturday when the registry offices
(called ZAGS) are open for business. Wedding parties are particularly conspicuous, as they tear
around town in convoys of cars making lots of noise and having their photos taken at the official beauty and historical spots.

Church weddings are now fairly common; the Russian Orthodox variety go on for ages, especially for the best friends who have to hold crowns above the heads of the bride and the
groom during the whole ceremony. But for a marriage to be officially registered all couples
need to get a stamp in their passports at a ZAGS. Most ZAGS offices are drab Soviet buildings
with a ceremonial hall designed like a modern Protestant church less the crucifix, but there are
also *dvortsy brakosochetaniy* (purpose-built wedding palaces), and a few in actual old palaces of
extraordinary elegance.

The ZAGS ceremony has been mocked numerous times in Russian films. The registrar, typically
an ageing woman with a funny hairstyle, reads an extremely solemn speech about the virtues of
marriage with an intonation leaving no doubt that a happy marriage is something well beyond
her experience. The speech is accompanied by usually recorded classical music of the couple's
choice, though in wedding palaces there are often live musicians.

After the couple and two witnesses from both sides sign some papers, the bride and the
groom then exchange rings (which in the Orthodox tradition you wear on your right hand) and
the registrar pronounces them husband and wife. The witnesses each wear a red sash around
their shoulders with the word 'witness' written on it in golden letters. The groom's best man
takes care of all tips and other payments since it's traditional for the groom not to spend a single
kopeck during the wedding. Another tradition is that the bride's mother does not attend the
wedding ceremony, although she does go to the party.

settlers in the region, are Orthodox Christian and form a majority in the Chuvashia Republic, immediately west of the Tatarstan Republic. The capital is Cheboksary (also known as Shupashkar).

The nominally Muslim Bashkirs have Turkic roots. About half of them live in the Bashkortostan Republic (capital: Ufa), where they are outnumbered both by Russians and by Tatars.

Finno-Ugric peoples

In central and northern European Russia, several major groups of Finno-Ugric peoples are found, distant relatives of the Estonians, Hungarians and Finns. These groups include the Orthodox or Muslim Mordvins, a quarter of whom live in Mordovia (capital: Saransk); the Udmurts or Votyaks, predominantly Orthodox, two-thirds of whom live in Udmurtia (capital: Izhevsk); the Mari, with an animist/shamanist religion, nearly half of whom live in Mary-El (capital: Yoshkar-Ola); the Komi, who are Orthodox, most of whom live in the Komi Republic (capital: Syktyvkar); and the Karelians, found in the Karelia Republic north of St Petersburg.

Finno-Ugric people are also found in Asian Russia. The Khanty, also known as the Ostyak, were the first indigenous people encountered by 11th-century Novgorodian explorers as they came across the Urals. Along with the related Mansi or Voguls, many live in the swampy Khanty-Mansisk Autonomous District on the middle Ob River, north of Tobolsk.

Both www.unpo.org, the website of the Unrepresented Nations and Peoples Organization (UNPO), and *The Red Book of the Peoples of the Russian Empire* (www .eki.ee/books/redbook/) contain profiles of over 80 different ethnic groups found in the lands currently or once ruled by Russia.

Peoples of the Caucasus

The Russian northern Caucasus is a real ethnic jigsaw of at least 19 local nationalities including the Abaza (also known as the Circassians), Abkhazians, Adygeya, Kabardians, Lezgians and Ossetians. Several of these peoples have been involved in ethnic conflicts in recent years, some of which stem from Stalinist gerrymandering of their territories.

The most notorious of Caucasian peoples are the Chechens, a Muslim people almost one million strong, renowned for their fierce nationalism and for the separatist war they have been fighting against Russia for over a decade.

The National Museum of Natural History of Washington, DC, has a website (www.mnh .si.edu/arctic/features /croads) that provides a virtual exhibition on the native peoples of Siberia and Alaska.

Turkic peoples in the region include the Kumyk and Nogay in Dagestan, and the Karachay and Balkar in the western and central Caucasus.

Peoples of Siberia & the Russian Far East

Over 30 indigenous Siberian and Russian Far East peoples now make up less than 5% of the region's total population. The most numerous groups are the ethnic Mongol Buryats, the Yakuts of Sakha, Tuvans, Khakass and Altai. Each of these has a distinct Turkic-rooted language and their 'own' republic within the Russian Federation, but only Tuvans form a local majority.

Among the smaller groups are the Evenki, also called the Tungusi, spread widely but very thinly throughout Siberia. Related tribes include the Evens, scattered around the northeast but found mainly in Kamchatka (p650), and the Nanai in the lower Amur River basin; you can visit some Nanai villages near Khabarovsk (p614).

The Arctic hunter-herder Nenets (numbering around 35,000) are the most numerous of the 25 'Peoples of the North'. Together with three smaller groups they are called the Samoyed, though the name's not too popular because in Russian it means 'self-eater' – a person who wears himself out physically and psychologically. All these tribes face increasing destruction of their reindeer herds' habitat by the oil and gas industries.

The Chukchi and Koryaks are the most numerous of six palaeo-Siberian peoples of the far northeast, with languages that don't belong in any larger category. Their Stone-Age forebears, who crossed the Bering Strait ice to America and Greenland, may also be remote ancestors of the Native American. Also in the far northeast are found Eskimos, Aleuts and the Oroks of Sakhalin Island, who were counted at just 190 in the 1989 census.

MULTICULTURALISM

Scratch a Russian, a local saying goes, and you'll find a Tatar (ie under the European veneer beats an Asian heart). With a history shaped by imperial expansion, forced movements and migration over many thousands of years, it's not surprising that Russian society has multicultural traits. On paper, the USSR's divide-and-rule politics promoted awareness of ethnic 'national' identities. But the quest to mould model Soviet citizens steadily undermined real cultural differences and virtually killed off many of Russia's native non-Slavic cultures (as well as much of true Russian culture). With Sovietisation came a heavy dose of Slavic influence. Most native peoples have thus adopted Russian dress and diets, particularly those who live in the bigger towns and cities.

With the fading of the Soviet dream, ethnic tensions have risen, as have nationalism, xenophobia and racism. A clause in the Russian constitution gives courts the power to ban groups inciting hatred or intolerant behaviour. Nonetheless, neo-Nazi and skinhead groups, often violent, are reckoned to have over 50,000 members and are believed to be behind the assassination of leading antiracism campaigner Nikolai Girenko in St Petersburg in 2004. Attacks on Africans and Asians on city streets are not uncommon. Visitors of African, Middle-Eastern and Asian descent should be aware that they may not always receive the warmest of welcomes, though Russian racism seems particularly focused against Caucasian peoples (ie people from the Caucasus, not white-skinned Europeans).

Anna Reid's *The Shaman's Coat* is both a fascinating history of the major native peoples of Siberia and the Russian Far East and a lively travelogue of her journeys through the region.

What is most surprising is that racist attitudes or statements can come from otherwise highly educated Russians. Jews, targets of state-sponsored anti-Semitism during the communist reign, are more distrusted than hated, although the hatred certainly exists, especially when stirred up by right-wing political parties.

On the other hand, attitudes are broadening among younger and more-affluent Russians, notably through visa-free travel to Turkey and North Africa. The result has been a current fad for the exotic – whether it's Turkish pop music or *qalyans* (water pipes) in ever more restaurants. The country's declining population is also bringing more migrants from nearby countries such as Ukraine or the Central Asian republics to Russia to live and work. Still, the chances of Russia developing a truly multicultural society are slim and it's telling that when Russians discuss the subject they refer to their nation as a 'mosaic' of cultures, each one distinct.

MEDIA

Russia is a TV country, with radio and newspapers sidelined to a greater extent than elsewhere in Europe.

Newspapers & Magazines

Genuine freedom of speech has migrated from TV (see p76) to the newspapers, the best of which offer editorial opinions largely independent of their owners' or the government's views.

THE STYLE REVOLUTION

A sign of the changing Russian times came in March 2005 with publication of the first Russian-language edition of the global style bible *wallpaper**. Costing R150 (equivalent to the average Russian pensioner's weekly food bill) the magazine is unashamedly elitist; readers should be grateful that there are advertisers out there willing to stump up US$9100 per page. Editor Yulia Korsounskaya comes from good nomenklatura stock: her grandma was deputy minister of communications in the 1950s and '60s.

The leading paper, and one of the most respected, is *Kommersant,* owned by the anti–Vladimir Putin Boris Berezovsky (see the boxed text, p68), closely followed by *Izvestia* (bought in 2005 by Gazprom, the state-owned gas monopoly). *Gazeta* is a good liberal newspaper, and *Vedomosti,* a joint venture by the *Financial Times* and *Wall Street Journal,* is a highly professional business daily that shows little sympathy for Putin.

Novaya Gazeta is a staunchly anti-Putin tabloid, with other tabloid-type (but not necessarily format) papers being *Komsomolskaya Pravda,* the Putin-friendly *Argumenty i Fakty,* and the varying-with-the-political-wind *Moskovsky Komsomolets.* There are also a couple of good weeklies like *Kommersant-Vlast, Profil* and the Russian version of *Newsweek* headed by former NTV star, Leonid Parfenov.

Among monthlies, there are also all the international glossy magazines, and another newcomer – the Russian *Forbes,* whose American editor-in-chief Paul Klebnikov was killed last year. The authorities charged several Chechens with this murder.

Listen to the Voice of Russia state radio station on www.vor.ru/index _eng.phtml and also use its Russian Culture Navigator to learn more about aspects of Russian culture.

TV

He who controls the TV in Russia, rules the country – and no-one else understands this better than President Putin. In 2000 his administration conducted a heavy-handed legal attack on the owners of NTV, a channel that came closer than the others to matching the professional, relatively unbiased news standards adopted in the West.

The NTV staff split: some journalists stayed behind to work under the new owner, Gazprom. Others seized the life buoy thrown by oligarch Boris Berezovsky and moved to his TVS channel. But a year later Berezovsky was forced into political exile in London, while TVS met the fate of NTV and was transformed into a sports channel.

Now, in terms of independent journalism, there's little to distinguish Gazprom-owned NTV from the state-run channels. Not that Russian TV is managed by some Soviet-style spooks. In fact, the heads of the main state channels – Channel 1 and Rossiya – were among those young journalists who gave Russian audiences a taste of editorial freedom in the 1990s. Many faces on the screen are still the same, but news and analysis are increasingly uncontroversial, while entertainment is dominated by crime series in which shaven-headed veterans of the war in Chechnya pin down conspiring oligarchs and politicians.

That said, Russian TV provides a wide choice of programmes, some modelled on Western formats, some unique. Documentaries have been especially good in the last years, and the national channel Kultura, dedicated entirely to arts and culture, is always worth a look. For news, RenTV, a channel owned by the state power grid, has coverage with a bit more bite. A national military channel was launched in 2005, but most Russians have been spared from watching it so far.

The government has also stumped up US$30 million to launch a 24-hour English-language satellite news channel, along the lines of CNN, by the end of 2005. Whether this proves to be another Kremlin-managed propaganda tool remains to be seen.

RELIGION

One of the most noticeable phenomena since the end of the atheist Soviet Union has been the resurrection of religion in Russia, and in particular the Russian Orthodox Church. Since 1997 the Russian Orthodox Church has been legally recognised as the leading faith, but the Russian constitution enshrines religious freedom, ensuring the Church respects Islam, Judaism, Buddhism and the nation's myriad animist religions.

Russian Orthodox Church

After decades of persecution under the Soviet regime, the Russian Orthodox Church (Russkaya Pravoslavnaya Tserkov) is enjoying a huge revival. The religion is so central to Russian life that understanding something about its history and working will enhance any of the visits that you will inevitably make to a Russian Orthodox church.

The English-language website of the Russian Orthodox Church, containing details of its history and current practices, can be found at www.mospat.ru/e_start page/index.html.

HISTORY

Prince Vladimir of Kyiv (Kiev) effectively founded the Russian Orthodox Church in AD 988 by adopting Christianity from Constantinople (Istanbul today), the eastern centre of Christianity in the Middle Ages. The Church's headquarters stayed at Kyiv until 1300, when it moved north to Vladimir. In the 1320s it moved again, from Vladimir to Moscow.

The church flourished until 1653 when it was split in two by the reforms of Patriarch Nikon, who thought it had departed from its roots. He insisted, among other things, that the translation of the Bible be altered to conform with the Greek original, and that the sign of the cross be made with three fingers, not two. Those who couldn't accept these changes became known as Starovery (Old Believers) and were persecuted. Some fled to Siberia or remote parts of Central Asia, where in the 1980s one group was found who had never heard of Vladimir Lenin, electricity or the revolution. Only from 1771 to 1827, 1905 to 1918 and again recently have Old Believers had real freedom of worship. They probably now number over one million, but in 1917 there were as many as 20 million.

Another blow to church power came with the reforms of Peter the Great, who replaced the self-governing patriarchate with a holy synod subordinate to the tsar, who effectively became head of the church. When

---

RUSSIA'S TOP 10 RELIGIOUS BUILDINGS

Russia has returned to its religious roots in a big way. Discover some of its most impressive religious buildings by visiting these places:

- Assumption Cathedral, Smolensk (p323)
- Cathedral of St Sophia, Novgorod (p329)
- Church of the Intercession on the Nerl, Bogolyubovo (p206)
- Church of the Saviour on Spilled Blood, St Petersburg (p252)
- Grand Choral Synagogue, St Petersburg (p262)
- Kul Sharif Mosque, Kazan (p412)
- Mirozhsky Monastery, Pskov (p336)
- St Basil's Cathedral, Moscow (p149)
- Transfiguration Cathedral, Kizhi (p361)
- Trinity Monastery of St Sergius, Sergiev Posad (p222)
- Tsugol Datsan, Tsugol (p601)

the Bolsheviks came to power Russia had over 50,000 churches. Lenin adopted Karl Marx's view of religion as 'the opium of the people'. Atheism was vigorously promoted and Josef Stalin seemed to be trying to wipe out religion altogether until 1941, when he decided the war effort needed the patriotism that the church could stir up. Nikita Khrushchev renewed the attack in the 1950s, closing about 15,000 churches.

Following the end of the Soviet Union, many churches and monasteries that had been turned into museums, archive stores and even prisons, have been returned to Church hands and are being restored. There are now some 25,000 active churches in the whole country, as against fewer than 7000 in 1988, and there are 680 working monasteries, up from 21 in 1988.

HIERARCHY

Patriarch Alexey II of Moscow and All Russia is head of the Church. The patriarch's residence is the Danilovsky Monastery in Moscow, though some important Church business is still conducted at the Trinity Monastery of St Sergius at Sergiev Posad, the patriarch's residence until the late 1980s. The Cathedral of Christ the Saviour is currently the senior church in Moscow. The Church's senior bishops bear the title metropolitan.

In the past the church hierarchy was plagued by corruption to such an extent that for a few years Putin avoided appearing together with the patriarch. Most notoriously, under Boris Yeltsin, the Church – along with the National Sports Foundation – was exempted from customs duties on imported alcohol and cigarettes. Billions of dollars were generated for the Church this way. Yet, according to polls, the Church remains the most trusted institution in Russia.

Rozhdestvo (Christmas) falls on 7 January because the Church still uses the Julian calendar, a calendar the Soviet state abandoned in 1918.

BELIEFS & PRACTICE

Russian Orthodoxy is highly traditional, and the atmosphere inside a church is formal and solemn. Churches have no seats, no music (only melodic chanting) and many icons (p96), before which people will often be seen praying, lighting candles, and even kissing the ground.

The Virgin Mary (Bogomater, Mother of God) is greatly honoured; the language of the liturgy is 'Church Slavonic', the old Bulgarian dialect into which the Bible was first translated for Slavs. Paskha (Easter) is the focus of the Church year, with festive midnight services launching Easter Day.

In most churches, Divine Liturgy (Bozhestvennaya Liturgia), lasting about two hours, is held at 8am, 9am or 10am Monday to Saturday, and usually at 7am and 10am on Sunday and festival days. Most churches also hold services at 5pm or 6pm daily. Some include an *akafist,* a series of chants to the Virgin or saints.

Part of the Christian revival is the renewed celebration of name days. Just as in Catholic countries, children are traditionally named after saints. Each saint has his or her 'saint's day' set in the Orthodox calendar. The day of one's namesake saint is celebrated like a second birthday.

CHURCH DESIGN

Churches are decorated with frescoes, mosaics and icons, with the aim of conveying Christian teachings and assisting veneration. Different subjects are assigned traditional places in the church (the Last Judgement, for instance, appears on the western wall). The central focus is always an iconostasis (icon stand), often elaborately decorated. The iconostasis divides the main body of the church from the sanctuary, or altar area, at the eastern end, which is off limits to all but the priest.

CHURCH-GOING DOS & DON'TS

As a rule, working churches are open to one and all, but as a visitor you should take care not to disturb any devotions or offend sensibilities. On entering a church, men bare their heads and women usually cover theirs. Female visitors can often get away without covering their heads, but miniskirts are unwelcome and even trousers on women sometimes attract disapproval. Hands in pockets or legs or arms crossed may attract frowns. Photography at services is generally not welcome; if in doubt, you should ask permission first.

The iconostasis is composed of up to six tiers of icons. The biggest tier will be the *deisusny ryad* (deesis row), whose central group of icons, known as the deesis, consists of Christ enthroned as the judge of the world, with the Virgin and John the Baptist interceding for humanity on either side. Archangels, apostles and Eastern Church fathers may also appear on this row. Below the deesis row are one or two rows of smaller icons: the bottom one is the *mestny ryad* (local row) showing saints with local links. Above the deesis row are the *prazdnichny ryad* (festival row) showing the annual festivals of the Church, then the *prorocheskiy ryad* (prophet row) showing Old Testament prophets, and sometimes a further *praotechesky ryad* (patriarch row) showing the Old Testament patriarchs.

During a service the priest comes and goes through the Holy or Royal Door, an opening in the middle of the iconostasis.

Other Christian Churches

Russia has small numbers of Roman Catholics, and Lutheran and Baptist Protestants, mostly among the German, Polish and other non-Russian ethnic groups. Other groups such as the Mormons, Seventh-Day Adventists and the Salvation Army are sending hordes of missionaries – not all such groups are being welcomed. Courts have tried to use the 1997 religion law (asserting the Orthodox Church's leading role) to ban the Pentecostalist Church, Jehovah's Witnesses and other Christian faiths that are seen as threats by the Russian Orthodox Church.

Communities of Old Believers (p77) still survive in Siberia. Their villages tend to be neat with many wooden cottages, but apart from a preponderance of long beards, are not immediately different from other old rural Russian settlements. Also out in Siberia, Vissarion (p542) is considered by his followers to be a living, modern-day Jesus.

Islam

After Christianity, the most popular religion in Russia is Islam, with estimates of anything from 14 to 20 million followers, mainly among the Tatar and Bashkir peoples east of Moscow and a few dozen of the Caucasian ethnic groups. Nearly all are Sunni Muslims, except for some Shiah in Dagestan. Muslim Kazakhs, a small minority in southeast Altai, are the only long-term Islamic group east of Bashkortostan.

Muslim history in Russia goes back a long way, to the days of the Golden Horde (p36). In the dying days of tsarist Russia, Muslims even had their own faction in the *duma* (parliament). Soviet 'militant atheism' led to the closure and destruction of nearly all the mosques and madrasahs (Muslim religious schools) in Russia, although some remained in the Central Asian states. Under Stalin there were mass deportations and liquidation of the Muslim elite. Policies eased marginally after WWII.

Islam has, like Christianity, enjoyed growth since the mid-1980s. The Islamic Cultural Centre of Russia, which includes a madrasah, opened in

'Under Stalin there were mass deportations and liquidation of the Muslim elite'

Moscow in 1991. In 1995 the Union of Muslims of Russia was established and a political party, the Nur All-Russia Muslim Public Movement, was also formed to act in close coordination with Muslim clergy to defend the political, economic and cultural rights of Muslims.

Some Muslim peoples – notably the Chechens and Tatars – have been the most resistant of Russia's minorities to being brought within the Russian national fold since the fall of the Soviet Union in 1991, but nationalism has played at least as big a part as religion in this. In an apparent effort to ease the tensions felt between the state and Muslim communities following the war in Chechnya, Russia became a member of the influential Organisation of Islamic Conferences in 2003. However, in 2002 the courts upheld a ban on Muslim women appearing in passport photos with their heads covered.

Islam in Russia is fairly secularised – in predominantly Muslim areas you'll find women are not veiled, for example, although many will wear headscarfs; also, the Friday holy day is not a commercial holiday. Few local Muslims take Islam's antialcohol rule seriously. ('The Koran bans wine, not vodka,' laughed one Tatar Muslim.) Still, Islamic moderation means that Muslim villages in Altai tend to be safer than others where the population can too often be drunk.

Working mosques are generally closed to non-Muslims. If you are asked in, the correct form is to take off your shoes (and your socks, if they are dirty!).

Islam.ru (eng.islam.ru/) is a website full of information on Russia's Islamic communities, coming to you with the blessing of the Mufti of Dagestan Sayyidmuhammad Abubakarov.

Judaism

Jews, who number under 500,000, are considered a nation within Russia, as well as a religion. Most have been assimilated into Russian culture and do not seriously practise Judaism.

The largest communities are found in Moscow (around 200,000) and St Petersburg (around 100,000), both of which have several historic, working synagogues. There's also a small, conservative community of several thousand 'Mountain Jews' (Gorskie Yevrie) living mostly in the

---

CHURCH NAMES

Sobor	Cathedral	Собор
Tserkov	Church	Церковь
Khram	Church/Temple	Храм
Chasovnaya	Chapel	Часовня
Monastyr	Convent or Monastery	Монастырь
Blagoveshchenskaya	Annunciation	Благовещенская
Borisoglebskaya	SS Boris & Gleb	Борисоглебская
Nikolskaya	St Nicholas	Никольская
Petropavlovskaya	SS Peter & Paul	Петропавловская
Pokrovskaya	Intercession of the Virgin	Покровская
Preobrazhenskaya	Transfiguration	Преображенская
Rizopolozhenskaya	Deposition of the Holy Robe	Ризоположенская
Rozhdestvenskaya	Nativity	Рождественская
Troitskaya	Trinity	Троицкая
Uspenskaya	Assumption or Dormition	Успенская
Vladimirskaya	St Vladimir	Владимирская
Voskresenskaya	Resurrection	Воскресенская
Voznesenskaya	Ascension	Вознесенская
Znamenskaya	Holy Sign	Знаменская

Caucasian cities of Nalchik, Pyatigorsk and Derbent. Siberia was once home to large numbers of Jews but now you'll find a noticeable community only in the Jewish Autonomous Region – created during Stalin's era – centred on Birobidzhan.

After Kyiv's destruction of the Judaic Khazar empire in 965, Russia had few Jews (they were banned from Muscovy during Ivan the Terrible's reign) until the 1772–95 partitions of Poland brought in half a million. These were confined by law to the occupied lands – roughly, present-day Ukraine, Belarus, Lithuania and eastern Poland, the so-called Pale of Settlement. The notion of a 'Jewish problem' grew in the 19th century, exploding in the 1880s into pogroms and massive emigration to Western Europe and the USA.

The pogroms also led to many Jews embracing revolutionary ideas and becoming key leaders of the revolution. In Lenin's first government everybody except himself, Felix Dzerzhinsky, Stalin and Pavel Dybenko were Jewish. Hence there was a major revival of Jewish culture in the 1920s, and many talented Jews went on to enjoy government and artistic careers they could not have dreamed of under the tsar. Stalin's anti-Semitism originated in his struggle for power with Leon Trotsky, Lev Kamenev and Grigory Zinoviev (p52).

After WWII Stalin devoted himself to the destruction of Jewish cultural life, shutting schools, theatres and publishing houses. The early 1980s gave rise to the issue of 'refuseniks', as Jewish applications for emigration were denied. *Glasnost* (the free-expression aspect of the Gorbachev reforms) brought an upsurge in grass-roots anti-Semitism, and emigration grew to a flood: between 1987 and 1991 more than half a million Jews left Russia, 350,000 going to Israel and 150,000 to the US. However, since 2000 an estimated 50,000 Jews have returned to Russia after emigrating to Israel and elsewhere, despite a disturbing rise in anti-Semitism. For more on the history of Judaism in Russia see the boxed text, p165.

There are two umbrella organisations of Russian Jewry: the **Federation of Jewish Organizations and Communities of Russia** (www.fjc.ru) and the **Russian-Jewish Congress** (www.rjc.ru/en/). There are two competing chief rabbis, Russian-born Adolf Shayevich and Italian-born Berl Lazar, who is backed by Putin and is becoming increasingly influential.

Beyond the Pale: the History of Jews in Russia (www.friends -partners.org/partners /beyond-the-pale /index.html) is an online version of an exhibition on Jewish history that has toured Russia since 1995.

In the 1880s Kansk, near Krasnoyarsk, was so predominantly Jewish that it was known as the Jerusalem of Siberia.

Buddhism

There are around half a million Buddhists in Russia, a figure that has been growing steadily in the years since *glasnost*, when Buddhist organisations became free to reopen temples and monasteries.

The Kalmyks – the largest ethnic group in the Kalmyk Republic, northwest of the Caspian Sea – are traditionally members of the Gelugpa or 'Yellow-Hat' sect of Tibetan Buddhism, whose spiritual leader is the Dalai Lama. They fled to their present region in the 17th century from wars in western Mongolia, where Buddhism had reached them not long before.

The Gelugpa sect reached eastern Buryatiya and Tuva via Mongolia in the 18th century, but only really took root in the 19th century. As with other religions, Stalin did his best to wipe out Buddhism in the 1930s, destroying hundreds of *datsans* (temples) and monasteries and executing or exiling thousands of peaceable lamas (Buddhist priests). At the end of WWII, two *datsans* were opened – a new one at Ivolginsk (p594) near Ulan-Ude, which houses the largest collection of Buddhist texts in Russia, and an older one at Aginskoe, southeast of Chita (p601). The glorious 1820 Tsugol Datsan (p601) is the only other old Siberian temple to survive virtually intact. You'll also find a Yellow-Hat sect temple in St Petersburg (p267), dating from the early 20th century.

Since 1950 Buddhism has been organised under a Buddhist Religious Board based at Ivolginsk. The Dalai Lama has visited both Buryatiya and Tuva, though his planned 2002 trip was thwarted when Russia caved in to Chinese pressure not to grant him a visa. In 2004 Russian authorities reversed their decision, allowing the Dalai Lama to visit Khurul, a monastery near the Kalmyk Republic's capital of Elista.

Animism & Shamanism

Many cultures, from the Finno-Ugric Mari and Udmurts to the nominally Buddhist Mongol Buryats, retain varying degrees of animism. This is often submerged beneath, or accepted in parallel with, other religions. Animism is a primal belief in the presence of spirits or spiritual qualities in objects of the natural world. Peaks and springs are especially revered and their spirits are thanked with token offerings. Especially in Tuva and Altai, this explains the coins, stone cairns, vodka bottles and abundant prayer ribbons that you'll commonly find around holy trees and mountain passes.

Buryat shaman Sarangerel's book *Riding Windhorses* is a great general introduction to shamanism.

Spiritual guidance is through a medium or 'shaman', a high priest, prophet and doctor in one. Animal skins, trance dances and a special type of drum are typical shamanic tools, though different shamans have different spiritual and medical gifts. Siberian museums exhibit many shamanic outfits. Krasnoyarsk's regional museum (p554) shows examples from many different tribal groups. Tuva is the easiest place to encounter living, practising shamans. There are three shamanic school-clinics in Kyzyl (p550) but, like visiting a doctor, you'll be expected to have a specific need and there'll be fees for the consultation. Popular among a few New-Age groups, a less superstitious religious shamanism emphasises the core philosophical beliefs of ecological balance and respect for nature.

SPORT

To find out about the old Russian sport of *lapta*, which is a bit like softball, go to www.internationalbaseball.org/russia.htm.

Russia's international reputation in sport is well founded. Its athletes regularly reap awards at sporting meets such as the Olympics. Recently, there has been much success in the field of tennis, with Maria Sharapova, Marat Safin, Anastasia Myskina and Anna Kournikova all emerging as stars.

The most popular spectator sport is soccer, which is enjoying a boom pumped up by sponsorship deals with Russian big business. For example, LUKoil has thrown its considerable financial weight behind the all-time champion Spartak, a Moscow team that has won the Russian premier soccer league (Vysshaya Liga) every year since 1996. Some to watch out for among the other 15 teams in the league include: Lokomotiv, CSKA (2005 UEFA Cup winners and sponsored by Abramovich), Torpedo and Dynamo (all from Moscow); Alaniya (Vladikavkaz); Rostselmash (Rostov-on-Don); Zenit (St Petersburg); and Lokomotiv (Nizhny Novgorod). Grozny's Terek also played really well in the last UEFA cup. Its temporary home field is in Lermontov in Kavkazskiye Mineralnye Vody.

Despite (or maybe because of) its popularity, running a soccer club in Russia has become a risky business – in the post-Soviet era, seven soccer officials have been the victims of assassination attempts. Corruption is believed to be rife in the clubs, with match fixing a particular problem.

Canadian-style ice hockey is the second most popular spectator sport. The strongest teams are current champions Dynamo (Moscow), as well as Lada (Tolyatti), Ak Bars (Kazan), Abramovich-owned Avangard (Omsk) and Metallurg (Magnitogorsk). Russian-style ice hockey is endemic to

Nordic countries and not especially popular. Its main centres are Arkhangelsk, where you'll find the team Vodnik, and Krasnoyarsk, whose team is Yenisey.

Basketball is Russia's third favourite sport and the league is one of the strongest in Europe.

WOMEN IN RUSSIA

In her difficult procession to the bright future the woman proletarian learns to throw off all the virtues imposed on her by slavery; step by step she becomes an autonomous worker, an independent personality, a free lover.

Alexandra Kollontai, feminist and communist heroine

Madame Kollontai's hopes for her Soviet sisters were left largely unfulfilled by communist Russia. Although Soviet women were portrayed in propaganda as superwomen, equally at home with the household chores as they were heaving bricks on a construction site or operating a lathe in an industrial combine, the truth was far more familiar. Women worked out of economic necessity and were relegated to nontechnical factory work, meagre-wage service positions and low-status professions. Traditional gender roles remained firmly fixed in the Soviet home, too.

Post the Soviet break-up, it remains to be seen whether the lot of Russian women has truly improved. There is a general agreement between sociologists that women have better adapted to the changes and succeeded more than men in the last decade. There are career opportunities available to women like never before. Russia's new economy has particularly benefited young, university-educated women, who are gaining valued skills, professional experience and access to information, yielding greater economic independence and self-confidence.

But as Russian women succeed in the workplace, they have found, like their Western sisters, that this has not made their load at home any lighter. Marrying, and divorcing, young is still common, and it's almost always the woman who is left to bring up the children solo (with grandmothers often stepping in to pick up some of the strain). Some young women are rejecting traditional ideas about marriage altogether.

Career shifts have not come easily for middle-aged or unskilled women; women represent two-thirds of the unemployed. Some women have survived by finding work in Russia's seamy sex trade, while others have sought to leave the country: marriage agencies, which hook up Russian women with foreign men, do a bustling business.

> Russia has one of the highest abortion rates in Europe with nearly 13 terminations for every 10 live births.

> The Way to Russia website (www.waytorussia.net/WhatIsRussia/Women.html) has a great section on women in Russia, including travel tips for visitors.

> Alexandra Kollontai (1872–1952), a senior Communist Party figure and feminist, wrote the novel *A Great Love*, based on Lenin's affair with Inessa Armand.

ARTS

From music and dance through literature, cinema and the visual arts, Russia's contribution to the world's sum of artistic goodness is truly astounding. The following section does but skim the brim of an o'er full barrel.

Ballet

First brought to Russia under Tsar Alexey Mikhailovich in the 17th century, ballet in Russia evolved as an offshoot of French dance combined with Russian folk and peasant dance techniques. It stunned Western Europeans when it was first taken on tour during the late 19th century.

The 'official' beginnings of Russian ballet date to 1738 and the establishment by French dance master Jean Baptiste Lande of a school of dance in St Petersburg's Winter Palace, the precursor to the famed Vaganova School of Choreography (p256). Moscow's Bolshoi Theatre (p182) dates from 1776. However, the true father of Russian ballet is considered to be Marius Petipa (1819–1910), the French dancer and choreographer who acted first as principal dancer, then premier ballet master, of the Imperial Theatre in St Petersburg. All told, he produced more than 60 full ballets (including Tchaikovsky's *Sleeping Beauty* and *Swan Lake*).

Natasha's Dance: a Cultural History of Russia by Orlando Figes is a fascinating book offering plenty of colourful anecdotes about great Russian writers, artists, composers and architects.

At the turn of the 20th century – Russian ballet's heyday – St Petersburg's Imperial School of Ballet rose to world prominence, producing a wealth of superstars including Vaslav Nijinsky, Anna Pavlova, Mathilda Kshesinskaya, George Balanchine, Michel Fokine and Olga Spessivtzeva. Sergei Diaghilev's Ballets Russes took Europe by storm. The stage décor was unlike anything seen before. Painted by artists (such as Alexander Benois) and not stagehands, it shattered the audience's sense of illusion.

Under the Soviets ballet enjoyed a highly privileged status, which allowed schools like the Vaganova and companies like the Kirov and Moscow's Bolshoi to maintain a level of lavish production and no-expense-spared star searches. At the Bolshoi, Yury Grigorovich emerged as a bright, new choreographer, with *Spartacus, Ivan the Terrible* and other successes. Even so, many of Soviet ballet's brightest stars emigrated or defected, including Rudolf Nureyev, Mikhail Baryshnikov and Natalia Makarova.

For Ballet Lovers Only (www.for-ballet-lovers-only.com) has biographies of leading Bolshoi and Mariinsky dancers both past and present, as well as a good links section if you want to learn more about Russian ballet.

As the Soviet Union collapsed, artistic feuds at the Bolshoi between Grigorovich and his dancers, combined with a loss of state subsidies and the continued financial lure of the West to principal dancers, led to a crisis in the Russian ballet world. Grigorovich resigned in 1995, prompting dancers loyal to him to stage the Bolshoi's first-ever strike.

Grigorovich's successor, Vladimir Vasiliev, helped revive the Bolshoi's fortunes, and in 2004 was succeeded by rising star Alexey Ratmansky. Of Ratmansky's more than 20 ballets, *Dreams of Japan* was awarded a prestigious Golden Mask award in 1998. Grigorovich continues to play an active role on Moscow's ballet stage, and the Bolshoi Ballet often performs his classic compositions. The Bolshoi's brightest star is currently Maria Alexandrova.

Meanwhile, in St Petersburg, director Valery Gergiev at the Kirov – now known as the Mariinsky (p262) – has earned international kudos and, crucially, foreign sponsorship for his grand productions.

Note that ballet and opera are generally performed at the same venues, which are often architectural masterpieces in themselves. The

NATIVE FOLK DANCING & MUSIC

Traditional Russian folk dancing and music is still practised across the country, although as a visitor your main chance of catching it is in cheesy shows in restaurants or at tourist-orientated extravaganzas. Good companies to watch out for include Ballet Moiseyev (www.moiseyev.ru /eng/), the Osipov Russian Folk Orchestra and the Pyatnitsky Russian Folk Chorus, all offering repertoires with roots as old as Kyivan Rus, including heroic ballads and the familiar Slavic *trepak* (stamping folk dances).

In Siberia and the Russian Far East it's also possible to occasionally catch dance and music performances by native peoples. In the Altai minstrels sing epic ballads, while in Tuva *khöömei* (throat singing) ranges from the ultradeep troll-warbling of *kagara* to the superhuman self-harmonising of *sygyt*; see the boxed text, p547 for more details.

Buryat peoples retain their unique steps and patterns, which they put on show every summer at the Buryatiya festival in Ulan-Ude. The village of Esso in northern Kamchatka is home base for the folk dance group Nulgur, made up of Koryaks, Even and Itelmens. They use dance to tell stories, not just traditional myths and legends but also contemporary tales and anecdotes, done as a fluid, ensemble mime.

ballerinas in Novosibirsk may not be as fleet-footed, and the operas in Ulan-Ude may be in Buryat, but tickets can be remarkably good value.

Music

The roots of Russian music lie in folk song and dance and Orthodox Church chants. *Byliny* (epic folk songs of Russia's peasantry) preserved folk culture and lore through celebration of particular events such as great battles or harvests. More-formal music slowly reached acceptance in Russian society, first as a religious aid, then for military and other ceremonial use, and eventually for entertainment.

BUYING TICKETS FOR PERFORMANCES & EVENTS

Teatralnye kassy (theatre ticket offices or kiosks) are found across all sizable cities, although it's not difficult to buy face-value tickets from the *kassa* (ticket office) at the venue itself, typically open for advance or same-day sales from early afternoon until the start of the evening show. In provincial Russia, tickets range from R30 to R300 and only the most popular shows tend to sell out completely, so there's usually hope for same-day seats. However, in Moscow and St Petersburg competition is much greater – some venues have foreigner pricing and it can be worth falling back on a hotel service bureau or concierge to get the best tickets, even though that can mean a huge premium over face value.

Tickets for both Moscow's Bolshoi (p182) and St Petersburg's Mariinsky (p287) theatres can be booked online – this is the best way to ensure that you get the seat you want. For Moscow events also consider booking using a web-based service such as www.parter.ru or www.biletik .ru; both sites are in Russian only.

If all else fails, there are usually touts, not only professionals but also people with spares. It's standard practice to sell tickets outside the main entrance before starting time. Remember that prices are a free-for-all and you run the risk of obstructed views. Before handing any money over make sure that the ticket actually has the date, performance and section you want.

Useful Theatre Words & Phrases

theatre	*teatr*	театр
opera and ballet theatre	*teatr opery i baleta*	театр оперы и балета
drama theatre	*dramaticheskiy teatr*	драматический театр
concert hall	*kontsertnyy zal*	концертный зал
circus	*tsirk*	цирк
cinema	*kinoteatr, kino*	кинотеатр, кино
Have you got tickets for…?	*yest li u vas bilety na…?*	Есть ли у вас билеты на…?
extra tickets	*lishnie bilety*	лишние билеты
cheap tickets	*deshovye bilety*	дешёвые билеты
best tickets	*luchshchie bilety*	лучшие билеты
stalls	*parter*	партер
dress circle (one tier up from stalls)	*belye-tazh*	бель-этаж
circle	*amfiteatr*	амфитеатр
box	*lozha*	ложа
balcony	*balkon*	балкон
1st/2nd/3rd tier (eg of balcony)	*pervy/vtoroy/tretiy yarus*	первый/второй/третий ярус
row	*ryad*	ряд
inconvenient place (eg obstructed view)	*neudobnoe mesto*	неудобное место
matinee	*utrenniy spektakl*	утренний спектакль
cloakroom	*garderob*	гардероб
guest stars	*gastroli*	гастроли

PYOTR TCHAIKOVSKY

Arguably the most beloved of all Russian classical composers is Pyotr Tchaikovsky (1840–93). The former lawyer first studied music at St Petersburg's conservatory, but he later moved to Moscow to teach at the conservatory there. This was where all of his major works were composed including, in 1880, the magnificent *1812 Overture*.

Among his other famous pieces are the ballets *Swan Lake* (Lebedinoe Ozero), *Sleeping Beauty* (Spyachshchaya krasavitsa), and *The Nutcracker* (Shchelkunchik), the operas *Yevgeny Onegin* and *Queen of Spades* (both inspired by works of poet Alexander Pushkin), and his final work the *Pathetique* Symphony no 6. The romantic beauty of these pieces belies the more tragic side of the composer, who led a tortured life as a closeted homosexual. The rumour mill has it that rather than dying of cholera, he committed suicide by poisoning himself following a 'trial' by his peers about his sexual behaviour.

CLASSICAL

The defining period of Russian classical music was from the 1860s to 1900. Mikhail Glinka (see opposite) is considered the father of Russian classical music: he was born in Smolensk, where an annual festival (p325) is held in his celebration.

As Russian composers (and painters and writers) struggled to find a national identity, several influential schools formed, from which some of Russia's most famous composers and finest music emerged. The Group of Five – Modest Mussorgsky, Nikolai Rimsky-Korsakov, Alexander Borodin, Cesar Kui and Mily Balakirev – believed that a radical departure was necessary, and they looked to *byliny* and folk music for themes. Their main opponent was Anton Rubinstein's conservatively rooted Russian Musical Society, which became the St Petersburg Conservatory in 1861, the first in Russia. Triumphing in the middle ground was Pyotr Tchaikovsky (see boxed text, above), who embraced Russian folklore and music as well as the disciplines of the Western European composers.

'The rumour mill has it that rather than dying of cholera, Tchaikovsky committed suicide'

Following in Tchaikovsky's romantic footsteps were Sergei Rachmaninov (1873–1943) and Igor Stravinsky (1882–1971). Both fled Russia after the revolution. Stravinsky's *The Rite of Spring* – which created a furore at its first performance in Paris – and *The Firebird* were influenced by Russian folk music. Sergei Prokofiev (1891–1953), who also left Soviet Russia but returned in 1934, wrote the scores for Eisenstein's films *Alexander Nevsky* and *Ivan the Terrible*, the ballet *Romeo and Juliet*, and *Peter and the Wolf*, beloved of those who teach music to young children. His work was condemned for 'formalism' towards the end of his life.

Similarly, the ideological beliefs of Dmitry Shostakovich (1906–75), who wrote brooding, bizarrely dissonant works, as well as accessible traditional classical music, led to him being alternately praised and condemned by the Soviet government. Despite initial official condemnation by Stalin, Shostakovich's Symphony no 7 – the *Leningrad* – brought him honour and international standing when it was performed by the Leningrad Philharmonic during the Siege of Leningrad (see boxed text, p225). The authorities changed their minds again and banned his anti-Soviet music in 1948, then 'rehabilitated' him after Stalin's death.

Major performers to emerge in the Soviet era – though some left for the West – included violinist David Oystrakh (1908–74), pianist Svyatoslav Richter (1914–), cellist-conductor Mstislav Rostropovich (1927–) and pianist-conductor Vladimir Ashkenazy (1937–).

Progressive new music surfaced only slowly in the post-Stalin era, with outside contact limited. Alfred Schnittke's Symphony no 1, probably the most important work of this major experimental modern Russian composer, had to be premiered by its champion, conductor Gennady Rozhdestvensky, in the provincial city of Gorky (now Nizhny Novgorod) in 1974 and was not played in Moscow until 1986.

OPERA

St Petersburg became the birthplace of Russian opera when Mikhail Glinka's *A Life for the Tsar,* which merged traditional and Western influences, was performed on 9 December 1836. It told the story of peasant Ivan Susanin, who sacrifices himself to save Tsar Mikhail Romanov. He followed this up with another folk-based opera, *Ruslan and Lyudmilla* (1842), thus inaugurating the 'New Russian School' of composition.

Another pivotal moment was the 5 December 1890 premiere of Tchaikovsky's *Queen of Spades* at the Mariinsky. Adapted from a tale by Alexander Pushkin, Tchaikovsky's version surprised and invigorated the artistic community by successfully merging opera with topical social comment.

Classical opera was performed regularly in the Soviet period, and continues to be popular. Recent triumphs at the Mariinsky have included an ambitious production of Dmitry Shostakovich's *The Nose* (based on Gogol's surreal story set in St Petersburg) in 2004. In March 2005 the Bolshoi premiered its first new opera in 26 years, *Rosenthal's Children* – with music by Leonid Desyatnikov and words by Vladimir Sorokin – to a hail of protests over its allegedly pornographic plot (see boxed text, p98).

ROCK & POP

Russian music is not all about classical composers. Ever since the 'bourgeois' Beatles filtered through in the 1960s, Russians both young and old have been keen to sign up for the pop revolution. Starved of decent equipment and the chance to record or perform to big audiences, Russian rock groups initially developed underground. By the 1970s – the Soviet hippy era – the music had developed a huge following among a disaffected, distrustful youth. Although bands initially imitated their Western counterparts, by the 1980s a home-grown sound was emerging and in Leningrad (St Petersburg), in particular, many influential bands sprung up.

Mitki was a band of artists, poets and musicians, self-styled Russian hippies donning sailor gear, drinking fantastic amounts of alcohol and putting a Russian accent on the term 'bohemian'. Boris Grebenshchikov and his band Akvarium (Aquarium) from Yekaterinburg caused a sensation wherever they performed; his folk rock and introspective lyrics became the emotional cry of a generation. At first, all of their music was circulated by illegal tapes known as *magizdat,* passed from listener to listener; concerts were held, if at all, in remote halls in city suburbs, and even to attend them could be risky. Other top bands included Leningrad's DDT, Nautilus Pompilius and ChayF from Yekaterinburg and the Moscow-based Mashina Vremeni, Bravo and Brigada S.

The god of Russian rock, though, was Viktor Tsoy, originally from Kazakhstan. His group Kino was the stuff of legends. A few appearances in kung fu–type flicks helped make Tsoy the King of Cool, and his early death in a 1990 car crash ensured the legend a long life. To this day, fans gather on the anniversary of his death (15 August) and play his music. His grave, at the Bogoslovskogo Cemetery in St Petersburg, has been turned into a shrine, much like Jim Morrison's in Paris. There is also the 'Tsoy Wall' on ul Arbat in Moscow, covered with Tsoy-related graffiti.

The pseudo-lesbian performance of girl duo tATu at 2003's Eurovision Song Contest helped alert international listeners that Russian pop today

'Appearances in kung fu–type flicks helped make Viktor Tsoy the King of Cool, and his early death in a 1990 car crash ensured the legend a long life' is as good (or bad, depending on your point of view) as the rest of the world's. Switch on Russian MTV and you'll see local versions of boy bands and disco divas all doing their sometimes desultory, sometimes foot-tapping stuff. If you want to listen to something outside the mainstream, there are interesting bands such as Leningrad whose music mixes up punk rock, Latino, polka and Tom Waits with a strong brass section. Another favourite St Petersburg band is the Afro-beat-infused Markscheider Kunst (see www.wadada.net for details). Children of Picasso is a Moscow-based Armenian folk-rock band whose beautiful lead singer has an exceptional voice. Also worth searching out are Zemphira, a jazz-rock musician hailing from Ufa, and the London-based Mumiy Troll, led by the literate, androgynous Ilya Lagushenko.

Cinema
SOVIET-ERA CINEMA

Sergei Eisenstein's *Battleship Potemkin* (1925) remains one of the landmarks of world cinema. It's famous for its Odesa Steps sequence, which has been recreated in many other films, most notably Brian de Palma's *The Untouchables*. Eisenstein's *Alexander Nevsky* (1938) contains one of cinema's great battle scenes, and his *Ivan the Terrible* (1945), a discreet commentary on Stalinism, was banned for many years.

The comedy *Irony of Fate* (*Ironiya Sudby ili s Legkim Parom;* 1975) directed by Eldar Ryazanov, is a national favourite screened on TV every New Year's Eve.

Mikhail Kalatozov's *The Cranes are Flying* (1957) – a love story set during WWII – was judged best film at Cannes in 1958. Of later Soviet directors, the dominant figure was Andrei Tarkovsky, whose films include *Andrei Rublyov* (1966), *Solaris* (1972) – the Russian answer to *2001: A Space Odyssey* – and *Stalker* (1980), which summed up the Leonid Brezhnev era pretty well, with its characters wandering puzzled through a landscape of clanking trains, rusting metal and overgrown concrete. Tarkovsky died in exile in 1987.

Alexey German's *My Friend Ivan Lapshin* (1982) is widely reckoned to be one of the best Soviet films: set in 1935, it shows with a light touch the amorous and professional ups and downs of a provincial police investigator, yet catches the real horror of life under Stalin with its underlying sense of impending terror.

Glasnost brought new excitement as film makers were allowed to reassess Soviet life with unprecedented freedom, and audiences flocked to see previously banned films or the latest exposure of youth culture or Stalinism. Vasily Pichul's *Little Vera* (1989) caused a sensation with its frank portrayal of a family in chaos (exhausted wife, drunken husband, rebellious daughter) and its sexual frankness – mild by Western standards but startling to the Soviet audience.

POST-SOVIET CINEMA

By the time Nikita Mikhalkov's *Burnt by the Sun* won the best foreign movie Oscar in 1994, Russian film production was suffering. Funding had disappeared during the economic chaos of the early 1990s, and audiences stayed away from cinemas. But by the end of the decade, the local industry was back on track with hits such as Alexey Balabanov's gangster drama *Brat* (Brother; 1997) and Alexander Sokurov's *Molokh* (1999). Sokurov's ambitious *Russian Ark* was an international success in 2002, as was Andrei Zvyaginstev's moody thriller *The Return* in the following year.

Neither film approached the US$16 million box office take (in Russia alone) in 2004 of *Nochnoi Dozor* (Night Watch). Directed by Timur Bekmambetov, this glossy sci-fi fantasy thriller is a Russian mix of *The Matrix* and *Dracula*, and, in true Hollywood style, there will be a sequel in 2006. *Turetsky Gambit* (Turkish Gambit), based on the novel by Boris Akunin, was an even bigger hit in 2005, beating *Nochnoi Dozor*'s box office take in just eight weeks! Both movies were produced and financed by Channel One TV. Another 2005 blockbuster was the Akunin-penned tsarist thriller, *Statsky Sovetnik* (The State Counsellor), directed by Nikita Mikhalkov, that old warhorse of Russian cinema. Mikhalkov co-stars in it along with Oleg Menshikov, heart-throb of a million Russian housewives.

Amid all the mega-budget blockbusters there is still room for some quirky independent movies – look out for 2004's *Ya Lyublu Tebya* (You I Love) directed by Olga Stolpovskaya and Dmitry Troitsky, on the international festival circuit. It's an offbeat and sometimes charming tale of modern love in Moscow, with not a hammer and sickle in sight!

Russia is also renowned for its animation. The most famous director is Yury Norshtein whose *Hedgehog in the Mist*, very philosophical and full of references to art and literature, is considered a masterpiece.

Although many old Soviet-era cinemas remain, in the bigger cities the boom in movie-going has been accompanied by the building of state-of-the-art multiplexes such as those regularly found outside Russia.

> Directed by Andrei Zvyagintsev, *The Return* (Vozvrashcheniye; 2003) has won many awards and is a deeply involving psychological thriller set in the northern Russian town of Vyborg.

Circus

While Western circuses grow smaller and more scarce, the Russian versions are like those from childhood stories – prancing horses with acrobats on their backs, snarling lions and tigers, heart-stopping high-wire artists and hilarious clowns. With around half the population attending a performance once a year, no wonder the circus remains highly popular.

The Russian circus tradition has roots in medieval travelling minstrels called *skomirovki*, although the first modern-style circus (a performance within a ring) dates to the reign of Catherine the Great. The country's first permanent circus was established in St Petersburg in 1877, and in 1927 Moscow's School for Circus Arts became the world's first such training institution. Many cities still have their own troupes and most at least have an arena for visiting companies. Best known is Moscow's Nikulin Circus (p183). There's also a museum in Voronezh (p314) devoted to the Durovs, among the most famous of Russian circus performers.

A word of warning: Russian attitudes towards animals are often less 'humane' than in the West, and some sensitive visitors find the acts and off-stage confinement of circus animals depressing.

> If you don't have time for a visit to the Hermitage, practically the next best thing is watching Alexander Sokurov's *Russian Ark* (Russky Kovcheg; 2002), filmed inside the museum in a stunning single 96-minute tracking shot.

Literature

Although they really only got going in the 19th century, Russian writers have wasted little time in establishing themselves a prime place in the canon of world literature, producing renowned classics in the fields of poetry, plays and epic novels.

19TH-CENTURY LITERATURE

The poet Alexander Pushkin (1799–1837) is to Russia what Shakespeare is to England. Read all about him in the boxed text, p340. Together with fellow poet Mikhail Lermontov (1814–41), Pushkin launched a long tradition of conflict between writers and the state. Both died in duels widely perceived as being set up by the authorities.

The satirical *The Government Inspector* by Nikolai Gogol (1809–52), who also wrote the novel *Dead Souls,* was the first major Russian play. Gogol created some of Russian literature's most memorable characters, including Akaki Akakievich, the tragicomic hero of *The Overcoat,* and the brilliant Major Kovalyev, who chases his errant nose around St Petersburg when it makes a break for it in the absurdist short story *The Nose.*

The second half of the 19th century produced a trio of great Russian novelists. In *Fathers and Sons* by Ivan Turgenev (1818–83), the hero Bazarov became a symbol for the antitsarist nihilist movement of the time. To discover more about this writer visit his beautiful estate at Spasskoe-Lutovinovo (p319).

Fyodor Dostoevsky (1821–81) produced a string of classic works, including *The Possessed,* a satire of provincial society and an analysis of political violence, and *The Brothers Karamazov,* which deals with questions of morality, faith and salvation. Head to St Petersburg to walk the streets that inspired his masterpiece *Crime and Punishment,* and to visit his museum (p260).

As Dostoevsky is forever associated with St Petersburg, so is Leo Tolstoy (1828–1910) with Moscow. If you don't have time for his epic *War and Peace,* try the slightly smaller-scale *Anna Karenina,* the tragedy of a woman who violates the rigid sexual code of her time. There's a museum devoted to Tolstoy in Moscow (p158) and you can also visit the Tolstoy family estate at Yasnaya Polyana (p199), where the great writer is buried.

Anton Chekhov (1860–1904) is principally known for his tragicomic plays including *The Seagull, The Three Sisters, The Cherry Orchard* and *Uncle Vanya,* all of which take the angst of the provincial middle class as their theme. They owed much of their early success to 'realist' productions at the Moscow Art Theatre by Konstantin Stanislavsky, which aimed to show life as it really was. Visit Chekhov's estate at Melikhovo, south of Moscow (p198).

THE SILVER AGE

Spanning the end of the 19th century up until the early 1930s, the Silver Age of Russian literature produced more towering talents. First came the rise of the symbolist movement in the Russian arts world. The outstanding figures of this time were the philosopher Vladimir Solovyov (1853–1900), the novelist Andrei Bely (1880–1934) and the poet Alexander Blok (1880–1921).

Blok's sympathies with the revolutions of 1905 and 1917 were praised by the Bolsheviks – as was the work of Vladimir Mayakovsky (1893–1930) – as an example of an established writer who had seen the light; Blok's tragic 'The Twelve', published in 1918 shortly before his death, likens the Bolsheviks to the Twelve Apostles who herald the new world. However, he soon grew deeply disenchanted with the revolution, and in one of his last letters, wrote, 'She did devour me, lousy, snuffling dear Mother Russia, like a sow devouring her piglet'. Similarly, Mayakovsky, practically the revolution's official bard, was driven to suicide.

Pushkin's Button by Serena Vitale is a fascinating account of the duel that killed Russia's most famous poet.

A Hero of Our Time by Mikhail Lermontov makes a great travelling companion in the Caucasus, where the novel is set. Its cynical antihero, Pechorin, is an indirect comment on the climate of the times.

Leo Tolstoy's *War and Peace* offers an epic panorama of Russia during the Napoleonic Wars told through the fortunes of a vivid cast of characters.

> ## SOCIALIST REALISM
>
> In 1932 the Communist Party officially demanded Socialist Realism from art and literature. This meant 'concrete representation of reality in its revolutionary development...in accordance with... ideological training of the workers in the spirit of Socialism'. Henceforth artists and writers had the all but impossible task of conveying the Party's messages as well as not falling foul of the notoriously fickle tastes of Stalin.

Also born during the Silver Age, although her major works are firmly part of the Soviet period, was the long-suffering poet Anna Akhmatova (1888–1966). Akhmatova's life was filled with sorrow and loss – her family was imprisoned and killed, her friends exiled, tortured and arrested, her colleagues constantly hounded – but she refused to leave her beloved St Petersburg. Her work depicts the city with realism and monumentalism, particularly her epic 'Poem Without a Hero', where she writes: 'The capital on the Neva/Having forgotten its greatness/Like a drunken whore/Did not know who was taking her'.

Another key poet of this age, who suffered for his art just like Akhmatova, was Osip Mandelstam (1892–1938), who died in a Stalinist transit camp near Vladivostok. Akhmatova's and Mandelstam's lives are painfully recorded by Nadezhda Mandelstam in her autobiographical *Hope Against Hope*.

SOVIET LITERATURE

One writer who managed to keep in favour with the communist authorities was Mikhail Sholokhov (1905–84), with his sagas of revolution and war among the Don Cossacks – *And Quiet Flows the Don* and *The Don Flows Home to the Sea*. He won the Nobel Prize for Literature in 1965. Others such as the great satirist Mikhail Bulgakov (1891–1940) found their works banned for years.

The Khrushchev thaw saw the emergence of poets like Yevgeny Yevtushenko, who gained international fame in 1961 with *Babi Yar* (which denounced both Nazi and Russian anti-Semitism), as well as another Nobel Prize winner, Alexander Solzhenitsyn (see boxed text, p92), who wrote mainly about life in the Gulag system. If you're interested in this subject, read *Kolyma Tales* by Varlam Shalamov, whose camp experience was even more harrowing than Solzhenitsyn's – and Shalamov is a great literary talent.

Yet another Nobel Prize winner was the fiercely talented poet Joseph Brodsky (1940–96). In 1964 he was tried for 'social parasitism' and exiled to the north of Russia. However, after concerted international protests led by Jean-Paul Sartre, he returned to Leningrad in 1965, only to continue being a thorn in the side of the authorities. Like Solzhenitsyn, Brodsky was deported in 1972, ending up in the US.

Preceding *glasnost* was native Siberian writer Valentin Rasputin, who is best known for his stories decrying the destruction of the land, spirit and traditions of the Russian people. His 1979 novel *Farewell to Matyora* is about a Siberian village flooded when a hydroelectric dam is built.

CONTEMPORARY LITERATURE

Among the contemporary Russian writers who have made their mark are Viktor Yerofeev, whose erotic novel *Russian Beauty* has been translated into 27 languages, and Tatyana Tolstaya, whose *On the Golden Porch*, a collection of stories about big souls in little Moscow flats, made her an

Famous in the West as a movie by David Lean, *Dr Zhivago* is a richly philosophical epic novel offering personal insights into the revolution and Russian civil war. Its author, poet Boris Pasternak (1890–1960), had to smuggle it into Britain in 1958 to get it published.

Mikhail Bulgakov's *The Master and Margarita* is a wacky comic novel with a serious twist, in which the devil turns up in Moscow to cause all manner of anarchy and make idiots of the system and its lackeys.

RUSSIA'S CONSCIENCE

Still alive and kicking, and complaining, in his mid-80s, Alexander Solzhenitsyn continues to do what he's done all his life – speak out against Russia's ruling elite and speak up for Christian values and nationalism. No wonder he's known as 'the Conscience of Russia'.

Despite being decorated twice with medals for bravery during WWII, the young Solzhenitsyn fell foul of the Soviet state in 1945 when he was arrested for anti-Stalin remarks found in letters to a friend. He subsequently served eight years in various camps and three more in enforced exile in Kazakhstan.

Following Stalin's death in 1956, Solzhenitsyn was rehabilitated. The climate under Khrushchev was sufficiently tolerant for the publication in 1962 of his first novel *One Day in the Life of Ivan Denisovich*, a short tale of Gulag life. The book made the writer's name famous and in 1970 he was awarded the Nobel Prize, although he did not go to Sweden to receive it for fear that he would not be allowed to reenter the USSR. Even so, he was exiled in 1974, when he went to the USA. He finally returned to Russia in 1994.

He's best known for *The Gulag Archipelago* (recently abridged into a single volume), which describes conditions at the camps on the Solovetsky Islands, although he was never imprisoned there himself.

international name when published in the West in 1989. Viktor Pelevin's novels such as *The Yellow Arrow* have also been widely translated and he has been compared to the great Mikhail Bulgakov.

Recent years have seen a boom in Russian publishing with the traditional Russian love of books as strong as ever. Just note the number of people reading novels to while away the time on the metro or trains. One of the most popular novelists is Boris Akunin, whose series of historical detective novels featuring the foppish Russian Sherlock Holmes, Erast Fandorin, including *The Winter Queen* and *Turkish Gambit*, have also been a hit in their English translations and are now being made into movies (p89).

If you're looking to read something more highbrow, try the exquisitely written 2003 Russian Booker Prize–winning *White on Black* by Ruben Gallego, a disabled man of Spanish origins. Gallego's novel is a partly autobiographical account of enduring and surviving the bleak, cruel Soviet orphanage system. *Kys* (The Slynx) by Tatyana Tolstaya is a great novel about life after a nuclear war, which seems strangely similar to post-Soviet life in the 1990s. The award-winning novels of Andrei Makine, born in the Russian Far East but long based in France where he's won the country's top two literary awards, are also worth discovering. Definitely read his *A Hero's Daughter*, which charts the impact of the Soviet Union on a family from WWII to the 1990s.

The classic and comprehensive *A History of Russian Architecture* by William Craft Brumfield was republished in an expanded version in 2004.

Architecture

Until Soviet times most Russians lived in homes made of wood. The *izba* – single-storey log cottage – is still fairly common in the countryside, while some Siberian cities, notably Tomsk, retain fine timber town houses intricately decorated with 'wooden lace'. Stone and brick were usually the preserves of the Church, royalty and nobility; to view some key buildings, see the following recommendations and the boxed text, p77.

EARLY RUSSIAN CHURCH ARCHITECTURE

Early Russian architecture is best viewed in the country's most historic churches, such as Novgorod's Cathedral of St Sophia (p329), dating from 1050. At their simplest, churches consisted of three aisles, each with an eastern apse (semicircular end), a dome or 'cupola' over the central aisle next to the apse, and high vaulted roofs forming a crucifix shape centred on the dome.

Church architects in Novgorod, Pskov and Vladimir-Suzdal developed the pattern with varying emphases in the 11th and 12th centuries. Roofs grew steeper to prevent heavy northern snows collecting and crushing them, and windows grew narrower to keep the cold out. Pskov builders invented the little *kokoshnik* gable, which was semicircular or spade-shaped and was usually found in rows supporting a dome or drum.

Where stone replaced brick, as in Vladimir's Assumption Cathedral (p204), it was often carved into a glorious kaleidoscope of decorative images. Another Vladimir-Suzdal hallmark was the 'blind arcade' – a wall decoration resembling a row of arches. Early church-citadel complexes required protection, and thus developed sturdy, fortress-style walls replete with fairy-tale towers – Russia's archetypal kremlins.

MOSCOW

Though the architects of two of the Moscow Kremlin's three great cathedrals (see p140 and p145) built between 1475 and 1510 were Italian, they took Vladimir's churches as their models; the third cathedral (p146) was by builders from Pskov.

Later in the 16th century the translation of northern Russia's wooden church features, such as the tent roof and the onion dome on a tall drum, into brick added up to a new, uniquely Russian architecture. St Basil's Cathedral (p149), the Ivan the Great Bell Tower (p140) in the Moscow Kremlin and the Ascension Church at Kolomenskoe (p166) are three high points of this era.

In the 17th century builders in Moscow added tiers of *kokoshniki*, colourful tiles and brick patterning, to create jolly, merchant-financed churches. Midcentury, Patriarch Nikon outlawed such frippery, but elaboration returned later in the century with Western-influenced Moscow baroque, which featured ornate white detailing on red-brick walls.

> An excellent website devoted to Russian architecture is archi.ru /english/index.htm, which has an index of the country's key buildings.

BAROQUE

Mainstream baroque reached Russia with Peter the Great's opening up of the country to Western influences. The focus was on his new capital, St Petersburg, as he banned new stone buildings elsewhere. The great baroque architect in Russia was an Italian, Bartolomeo Rastrelli. He created an inspired series of buildings, the style of which merged into rococo, for Empress Elizabeth. Three of the most brilliant were the Winter Palace (p244) and Smolny Cathedral (p259), both in St Petersburg, and Catherine Place at nearby Tsarskoe Selo (p299).

CLASSICISM

In the later 18th century Catherine the Great turned away from rococo 'excess' towards Europe's new wave of classicism – an attempt to re-create the ambience of an idealised ancient Rome and Greece with their mathematical proportions, rows of columns, pediments and domes. Catherine and her successors built waves of grand classical edifices in a bid to make St Petersburg the continent's most imposing capital.

From the simpler classicism of Catherine's reign, exemplified by the Pavlovsk Palace (p301) near St Petersburg, the more grandiose Russian Empire style developed under Alexander, with such buildings as the Admiralty (p257) and Kazan Cathedral (p255) in St Petersburg. The heavy St Isaac's Cathedral (p252), built for Nicholas I, was the last big project of this wave of classicism in St Petersburg. Moscow abounds with Empire-style buildings, as much of the city had to be rebuilt after the fire of 1812 (p122).

REVIVALS & STYLE MODERNE

A series of architectural revivals, notably of early Russian styles, began in the late 19th century. The first, pseudo-Russian phase produced the state department store GUM (p149), the State History Museum (p149) and the Leningradsky vokzal (train station) in Moscow, and the Moskovsky vokzal (p261) and the Church of the Saviour on Spilled Blood (p252) in St Petersburg.

The early 20th century neo-Russian movement brought a sturdy, classical elegance to architecture across the nation culminating in the extraordinary Kazansky vokzal (p153) in Moscow, which imitates no fewer than seven earlier styles. About the same time, Style Moderne, Russia's take on Art Nouveau, added wonderful curvaceous flourishes to many buildings right across Russia. Splendid examples include Moscow's Yaroslavsky vokzal (p153) and St Petersburg's Vitebsky vokzal (p261), and the Singer Building (p255).

SOVIET CONSTRUCTIVISM

The revolution gave rein to young constructivist architects, who rejected superficial decoration in favour of buildings whose appearance was a direct function of their uses and materials – a new architecture for a new society. They used lots of glass and concrete in uncompromising geometric forms.

Konstantin Melnikov was probably the most famous constructivist and his own house off ul Arbat in Moscow (p156) is one of the most interesting examples of the style; Moscow's *Pravda* and *Izvestia* offices are others. In the 1930s the constructivists were denounced, and a 400m-high design by perpetrators of yet another revival – monumental classicism – was chosen for Stalin's pet project, a Palace of Soviets in Moscow, which mercifully never got off the ground.

Like the US and German governments of the 1930s, Stalin favoured neoclassical architecture, which echoed ancient Athens – 'the only culture of the past to approach the ideal', according to Anatoly Lunacharsky, the first soviet commissar of education. Stalin liked architecture to

ARCHITECTURE IN SIBERIA

Although you'll find traditional Russian wooden architecture across European Russia, Siberia has the best examples. Many relatively accessible villages around Lake Baikal and in the Barguzin Valley retain whole streets of *izby* (log houses), whose main decorative features are carved, brightly painted window frames. This construction style was taken further in Siberian city town houses, where the carvings of eaves and window frames became so intricate that it's now known as 'wooden lace'. The classic place to see this is Tomsk, though some great individual examples have survived in Barnaul, Krasnoyarsk, Irkutsk, Tobolsk and Tyumen.

Before the Russians colonised Siberia, native Siberians were mostly nomadic. Their traditional dwellings fall into three main types: tepee-style cones of poles covered with skins or strips of bark (the Evenki *chum*); hexagonal or cylindrical frameworks of poles covered with brush and earth (the Altai *ail* or similar western Buryatiyan equivalents); and round felt-covered tent-houses (the yurts of nomadic Tuvan and Kazakh herders). Yurts and *aily* are still used in rural Tuva and Altai, and examples of all these dwellings can be found in open-air museums, including those near Bratsk (p561), Listvyanka (p575) and Ulan-Ude (p592).

be on a gigantic scale, underlining the might of the Soviet state. Convict labour was used, with a high death toll, to create enormous structures around the country. They reached their apogee in the 'Seven Sisters', seven Gothic-style skyscrapers that appeared around Moscow soon after WWII.

Then in 1955 came a decree ordering architects to avoid 'excesses', after which a bland international modern style – constructivism without the spark, you might say – was used for prestigious buildings, while no style at all was evident in the drab blocks of cramped flats that sprouted countrywide to house the people.

CONTEMPORARY ARCHITECTURE

Since the end of the Soviet Union, architectural energies and civic funds have principally gone into the restoration of decayed churches and monasteries, as well as the rebuilding of structures such as Moscow's Cathedral of Christ the Saviour (p157). St Petersburg in particular is spending millions of roubles on renovating its stock of historic architecture (although critics say that much of the work is little more than a temporary facelift).

However, as far as contemporary domestic, commercial and cultural buildings are concerned, post-Soviet architects have not been kind to Russia. Featuring bright metals and mirrored glass, buildings tend to be plopped down in the midst of otherwise unassuming vintage buildings, particularly in Moscow, where a campaign to preserve the city's historic architecture is under way; for details go to www.gif.ru/eng/places/maps/city_578/fah_3259/. Possibly the most interesting (and certainly the most controversial) contemporary structure in Russia will be the new Mariinsky Theatre in St Petersburg (p262).

FOLK & NATIVE ART

Isolated by vast distances and long winters, Russians evolved an amazing spectrum of richly decorated folk art. Perhaps most familiar are the intricately painted, enamelled wood boxes called *palekh*, after the village east of Moscow that's famous for them; and *finift*, luminous enamelled metal miniatures from Rostov-Veliky. From Gzhel, also east of Moscow, came glazed earthenware in the 18th century and its trademark blue-and-white porcelain in the 19th. Gus-Khrustalny, south of Vladimir, maintains a glass-making tradition as old as Rus. Every region also has its own style of embroidery and some specialise in knitted and other fine fabrics.

The most common craft is woodcarving, represented by toys, distaffs (tool for hand-spinning flax) and gingerbread moulds in the museums, and in its most clichéd form by the nested *matryoshka* dolls – surely the most familiar symbol of Russia, although they actually only date from 1890 (see russian-crafts.com/nest/history.html for the history of the *matryoshka* and other crafts). Overflowing from souvenir shops you'll also find the red, black and gold lacquered-pine bowls called *khokhloma*. Most uniquely Slavic are the 'gingerbread' houses of western and northern Russia and Siberia with their carved window frames, lintels and trim. The art of carpentry flourished in 17th- and 18th-century houses and churches.

Late in the Soviet period, all manner of handicrafts could increasingly be found only in homes or in museum collections. But the coming of the free market and a revived interest in national traditions has brought much more good craftwork into the open, and the process has been boosted by the restoration of churches and mosques and their artwork. There has also been a minor resurgence of wood- and bone-carving. An even more popular craft is *beresta*, using birch bark to make containers and decorative objects, with colours varying according to the age and season of peeling. In Tuva, soapstone carving and traditional leather forming are also being rediscovered.

Visual Arts

ICONS

Up until the 17th century religious icons were Russia's key art form, though they were conceived as religious artefacts – it was only in the 20th century that they really came to be seen as 'works of art'. See p78 for the typical layout of a church's iconostasis.

Traditional rules decreed that only Christ, the Virgin, angels, saints and scriptural events could be painted on icons – all of which were supposed to be copies of a limited number of approved prototype images. Christ images include the Pantokrator (All-Ruler) and the Mandilion, the latter called 'not made by hand' because it was supposedly developed from the imprint of Christ's face on St Veronica's handkerchief. Icons were traditionally painted in tempera – inorganic pigment mixed with a binder such as egg yolk – on wood. When they faded they were often touched up, obscuring the original work.

The beginning of a distinct Russian icon tradition came when artists in Novgorod started to be influenced by local folk art in their representation of people, producing sharply outlined figures with softer faces and introducing lighter colours including pale yellows and greens. The earliest outstanding painter was Theophanes the Greek (Feofan Grek in Russian) who lived between 1340 and 1405, working in Byzantium, Novgorod and Moscow, and who brought a new delicacy and grace to the form. His finest works are in the Annunciation Cathedral of the Moscow Kremlin (p146).

Andrei Rublyov, a monk at Sergiev Posad's Trinity Monastery of St Sergius (p222) and Moscow's Andronikov Monastery (p163), was 20 years Theophanes' junior and the greatest Russian icon painter. His most famous work is the dreamy *Old Testament Trinity*, in Moscow's Tretyakov Gallery (p160).

The layman Dionysius, the leading late-15th-century icon painter, elongated his figures and refined the use of colour. Sixteenth-century icons grew smaller and more crowded, their figures more realistic and Russian looking. In 17th-century Moscow, Simon Ushakov moved towards Western religious painting with the use of perspective and architectural backgrounds.

> Originally painted by monks as a spiritual exercise, icons are images intended to aid the veneration of the holy subjects they depict, and sometimes are believed able to grant luck and wishes or even cause miracles.

PEREDVIZHNIKI

In the 18th century, when Peter the Great encouraged Western trends in art, Dmitry Levitsky's portraits were the outstanding achievement. His work foreshadowed the move to a more Western style of painting.

The major artistic force of the 19th century was the Peredvizhniki (Wanderers) movement, which saw art as a force for national awareness and social change. The movement gained its name from the touring exhibitions with which it widened its audience. Patronised by the industrialists Savva Mamontov – whose Abramtsevo estate near Moscow became an artists' colony (p192) – and brothers Pavel and Sergei Tretyakov (after whom the Tretyakov Gallery is named), they included Vasily Surikov, who painted vivid Russian historical scenes, Nicholas Ghe (biblical and historical scenes), and Ilya Repin, perhaps the best loved of all Russian artists. Repin's work ranged from social criticism (*Barge Haulers on the Volga*) through history (*Zaporizhsky Cossacks Writing a Letter to the Turkish Sultan*) to portraits of the famous; see these works and many others in St Petersburg's Russian Museum (p252), a treasure house of Russian art.

Isaac Levitan, who revealed the beauty of the Russian landscape, was one of many others associated with the Peredvizhniki. The end-

---

TOP FIVE GREAT PATRIOTIC WAR MEMORIALS

Socialist Realism rarely served a better purpose than guiding the artistic efforts of the creators of the many Great Patriotic War (WWII) memorials around Russia. Here are five of our favourites, although almost any town of note has one (and don't forget the magnificent Brest Fortress in Belarus; see p684).

- Tyl Frontu memorial, Magnitogorsk (p447)
- Victory Park, Moscow (p165)
- Malaya Zemlya, Novorossiysk (p461)
- Monument to the Heroic Defenders of Leningrad, St Petersburg (p268)
- Mamaev Kurgan, Volgograd (p423)

---

of-century genius Mikhail Vrubel, inspired by sparkling Byzantine and Venetian mosaics, also showed traces of Western influence.

MODERNISM
Around the turn of the century the Mir Iskusstva (World of Art) movement in St Petersburg, led by Alexander Benois and Sergei Diaghilev under the motto 'art pure and unfettered', opened Russia up to Western innovations such as impressionism, Art Nouveau and symbolism. From about 1905 Russian art became a maelstrom of groups, styles and 'isms' as it absorbed decades of European change in a few years before giving birth to its own avant-garde futurist movements, which in turn helped Western art go head over heels.

Natalia Goncharova and Mikhail Larionov were at the centre of the Cézanne-influenced Jack of Diamonds group (with which Vasily Kandinsky was also associated) before developing neoprimitivism, based on popular arts and primitive icons.

In 1915 Kasimir Malevich announced the arrival of Suprematism, declaring that his utterly abstract geometrical shapes – with the black square representing the ultimate 'zero form' – finally freed art from having to depict the material world and made it a doorway to higher realities. See one of his four *Black Square* paintings at St Petersburg's Hermitage (p244).

SOVIET-ERA ART
Futurists turned to the needs of the revolution – education, posters, banners – with enthusiasm, relishing the chance to act on their theories of how art shapes society. But at the end of the 1920s, formalist (abstract) art fell out of favour; the Communist Party wanted Socialist Realism (see boxed text, p91). Images of striving workers, heroic soldiers and inspiring leaders took over; two million sculptures of Lenin and Stalin dotted the country; Malevich ended up painting portraits (penetrating ones) and doing designs for Red Square parades; and Mayakovsky committed suicide.

After Stalin, an avant-garde 'conceptualist' underground was allowed to form. Ilya Kabakov painted or sometimes just arranged the debris of everyday life to show the gap between the promises and realities of Soviet existence. Erik Bulatov's 'Sotsart' pointed to the devaluation of language by ironically reproducing Soviet slogans or depicting words disappearing over the horizon. In 1962 the authorities set up a show of such 'unofficial' art at the Moscow Manezh; Khrushchev called it 'dog shit' and sent it back underground. In the mid-1970s it resurfaced in the Moscow suburbs – only to be literally bulldozed back down.

ART UNDER ATTACK

Because TV journalists have largely failed (see p76), contemporary Russian artists are now taking on President Vladimir Putin and the sacred cows of Russia's establishment. At the Russia II exhibition, part of the 2005 Moscow Biennale of Contemporary Art, protest art included works that tackled themes of terrorism, the war in Chechnya and the Russian Orthodox Church. Predictably, a group of Orthodox Christians filed a criminal complaint against the exhibition.

It's not the first time this has happened. In 2003 an art exhibit mocking the Russian Orthodox Church at Moscow's Andrei Sakharov Museum was closed following protests (p152). Agitprop artist Avdey Ter Oganyan lives in exile in Berlin because of death threats made against him. Ter Oganyan hit the headlines when he chopped up Christian icons on the street with an axe in the name of art. He was charged with incitement under the federal antihatred law.

In March 2005 the Putin-supporting youth group Moving Together picketed the Bolshoi's staging of *Rosenthal's Children*, a new opera with a libretto by Vladimir Sorokin. His novel *Goluboye Salo* (Blue/Gay Lard), depicting sex between former Soviet leaders Josef Stalin and Nikita Khrushchev, had already got him into trouble with the authorities in 2002. In a typically Soviet-style knee-jerk reaction, right-wing politicians were quick to denounce the opera as pornographic and vulgarly unfitting of the Bolshoi, despite not having seen the work.

CONTEMPORARY ART

Although many contemporary painters of note have left Russia for the riches of the West, the country is still churning out promising young artists; for a review of some of the most interesting go to www.waytorussia.net/WhatIsRussia/Art.html. A few specialist art galleries are listed in the shopping sections of the Moscow and St Petersburg chapters. At these you can find the latest works by Russians within and without the motherland.

One of the most popular painters in Russia today is the religious artist Ilya Glazunov, a staunch defender of the Russian Orthodox cultural tradition. Hundreds of thousands of people visit exhibitions of his work. More notorious than popular is the artist and architect Zurab Tsereteli, whose monumental buildings and statues (many are also monumentally ugly) grace Moscow – see the boxed text, p158 for more on Tsereteli.

Artists are now freer than they ever were in the past to depict all aspects of Russian life, but there has, of late, been several public attacks on modern art; see the boxed texts, above and p152. Somewhat balancing this disturbing trend is the **Moscow Biennale of Contemporary Art** (moscowbiennale.ru/en/), a month-long festival organised and partly funded by Russia's Ministry of Culture, with the aim of establishing the capital as an international centre for contemporary art.

Environment

THE LAND

Russia is the world's largest country, covering 13% of the globe. As you'd expect there's a vast variety of terrain, though a remarkably large proportion is relatively flat. Mountains are comparatively rare, but do reach impressive heights in the Caucasus (where 5642m Mt Elbrus is Europe's highest peak), in the magnificent volcanoes of Kamchatka and in the Altai, Sayan and Ergaki ranges of southern Siberia. Cities and towns are concentrated chiefly across central European Russia, and along the ribbon of track that constitutes the Trans-Siberian Railway, thinning out in the frozen north and the southern steppe.

Northwest Russia has a short border with Norway and a longer one with Finland. Frozen northern Russia is washed by the Barents, Kara, Laptev and East Siberian Seas. Novaya Zemlya, Europe's fourth-biggest island, is also Russian, as are the islands that make up Franz Josef Land (Zemlya Frantsa-Iosifa). Both stretch to the edge of the permanent Arctic icecap. South of Finland, Russia opens on the Gulf of Finland, an inlet of the Baltic Sea; St Petersburg stands at the eastern end of this gulf.

In the west and southwest, Russia borders Estonia, Latvia, Belarus and Ukraine. The small Kaliningrad region of Russia lies disconnected from the rest of the country, between Lithuania, Poland and the Baltic Sea. East of Ukraine, the Russian Caucasus region commands stretches of the Black Sea and rugged, mountainous borders with Georgia and Azerbaijan. East of the Caucasus, Russia has an oil-rich stretch of Caspian Sea coast, north of which the Kazakhstan border runs up to the Ural Mountains.

Beyond the Urals, Asian Russia covers nearly 14 million sq km bordering Kazakhstan, Mongolia, China and a tiny corner of North Korea. Asia's easternmost point is Russia's Big Diomede Island (ostrov Ratmanov) in the Bering Strait, just 45km from the Alaskan mainland. Contrary to popular conception, only the western section of Asian Russia is actually called Siberia (Sibir). From the Amur regions in the south and the Sakha Republic (Yakutia) in the north, it becomes officially known as the Russian Far East (Dalny Vostok). The eastern seaboard is 15,500km long, giving Russia more 'Pacific Rim' than any other country.

The Wild Russia website (www.wild-russia.org) belongs to the US-based Center for Russian Nature Conservation, which assists and promotes nature conservation across Russia.

Rivers & Lakes

Though none has the fame of the Nile or the Amazon, six of the world's 20 longest rivers are in Russia. Forming the China–Russia border, the east-flowing Amur (4416km) is nominally longest, along with the Lena (4400km), Yenisey (4090km), Irtysh (4245km) and Ob (3680km), all of which flow north across Siberia ending up in the Arctic Ocean. In fact, if one was to take the longest stretch including tributaries (as is frequently done with the Mississippi-Missouri in North America), the Ob-Irtysh would clock up 5410km, and the Angara-Yenisey a phenomenal 5550km. The latter may in fact be the world's longest river if you were to include Lake Baikal and the Selenga River (992km), which directly feed into it. Beautiful Lake Baikal itself is the world's deepest, holding nearly one-fifth of all the world's unfrozen freshwater. Europe's longest river, the Volga (3690km), rises northwest of Moscow and flows via Kazan and Astrakhan into the Caspian Sea, the world's largest lake (371,800 sq km). Lake Onega (9600 sq km) and Lake Ladoga (18,390 sq km), both northeast of St Petersburg, are the biggest lakes in Europe.

RESPONSIBLE TRAVEL

As closely as some Russians live with nature, they don't always respect it: littering and poaching are everyday pastimes. Responsible travellers will be appalled by the mess left in parts of the countryside and at how easily rubbish is thrown out of train windows. Accept that you're not going to change how Russians live, but that you might be able to make a small impression by your own thoughtful behaviour. To help preserve Russia's natural environment consider the following tips while travelling:

- Don't litter, and minimise waste by avoiding excess packaging.
- Consider using purification tablets or iodine in tap water rather than relying on bottled water.
- Avoid buying items made from endangered species, such as exotic furs and caviar that isn't from legal sources (see the boxed text, p107).
- Support local enterprises, environmental groups and charities that are trying to improve Russia's environmental scorecard. A good example is the Great Baikal Trail project, which is helping construct a hiking trail around Lake Baikal. For details visit www.earthisland.org and click through to the project directory.

Until the 20th century, boats on Russia's rivers offered the most important form of transport. Today, rivers are still economically important, but mostly as sources of hydroelectric power with dozens of major dams creating vast reservoirs. The Sayano-Shushenskaya dam near Sayanogorsk is the world's fourth biggest in power-generation terms.

WILDLIFE

Heavy on photographs is *Baikal, Sacred Sea of Siberia*, a pictorial tribute to the great lake with text by travel writer and novelist Peter Matthiessen.

Despite Russia being home to an enormous range of wildlife it's pretty rare that you actually get to see much of it! To grasp the full extent of the diversity you first have to understand the three major types of vegetation. In the northernmost extremes, fringed by the Arctic Ocean, is the icy tundra. These bleak, seemingly barren flatlands extend from 60km to 420km south from the coast. They gradually become more amicable to life and build up to taiga, the vast, dense forest that characterises and covers the greater part of Siberia. Finally is the steppe (from *stepi*, meaning plain), the flat or gently rolling band of low grassland – mostly treeless except along river banks – which runs intermittently all the way from Mongolia to Hungary.

The Moscow-based Biodiversity Conservation Center (BCC; www.biodiversity.ru/eng/) is a nonprofit, nongovernmental organisation working for the restoration and protection of pristine nature all over northern Eurasia.

There are three other distinct vegetative zones: the mountainous Caucasus in southern Russia; the active volcanic region of Kamchatka, in the far northeast of Russia; and Ussuriland, in the extreme Russian southeast, which experiences tropical air and rains. The forests covering this region – and their indigenous animals and vegetation – more closely resemble those of Southeast Asia than anything typically associated with Siberia.

Tundra

Falling almost completely within the Arctic Circle, the tundra is the most inhospitable of Russia's terrains. The ground is permanently frozen (in places recorded to a depth of 1450m) with whole strata of solid ice and just a thin, fragile carpet of delicate lichens, mosses, grasses and flowers lying on top. The few trees and bushes that manage to cling tenaciously to existence are stunted dwarfs, the permafrost refusing to yield to their roots. For nine months of the year the beleaguered greenery is also buried beneath thick snow. When the brief, warming summer comes, the permafrost prevents drainage and the tundra becomes a spongy wetland, pocked with lakes, pools and puddles.

Not surprisingly, wildlife has it hard on the tundra and there are few species that can survive its climate and desolation. Reindeer, however, have few problems and there are thought to be around four million in Russia's tundra regions. They can endure temperatures as low as −50°C and, like the camel, can store food reserves. Reindeer sustain themselves on lichen and grasses, in winter sniffing them out and pawing away the snow cover.

A similar diet sustains the lemming, a small, round, fat rodent fixed in the popular consciousness for its proclivity for launching itself en masse from cliff tops. More amazing is its rate of reproduction. Lemmings can produce five or six litters annually, each comprising five or six young. The young in turn begin reproducing after only two months. With a three-week gestation period, one pair could spawn close to 10,000 lemmings in a 12-month period. In reality, predators and insufficient food keep numbers down.

Other tundra mammals include the Arctic fox, a smaller, furrier cousin of the European fox and a big lemming fan, and the wolf, which, although it prefers the taiga, will range far and wide, drawn by the lure of reindeer meat. Make it as far as the Arctic coast and you could encounter seals, walruses (notably around Chukotka), polar bears and whales.

Taiga

Russia's taiga is the world's largest forest, covering about 5 million sq km (an area big enough to blanket the whole of India) and accounting for about 25% of the world's wood reserves. Officially the taiga is the dense, moist subarctic coniferous forest that begins where the tundra ends, and which is dominated by spruces and firs. Travelling on the Baikal-Amur Mainline (BAM) through the depths of Siberia, two or three days can go by with nothing but the impenetrable and foreboding dark wall of the forest visible outside the train: 'Where it ends,' wrote Chekhov, 'only the migrating birds know.'

Though the conditions are less severe than in the Arctic region, it's still harsh and bitterly cold in winter. The trees commonly found here are pine, larch, spruce and fir. In the coldest (eastern) regions the deciduous larch predominates; by shedding its leaves it cuts down on water loss, and its shallow roots give it the best chance of survival in permafrost conditions.

Due to the permanent shade, the forest-floor vegetation isn't particularly dense (though it is wiry and spring-loaded, making it difficult for humans to move through), but there is a great variety of grasses, moss, lichens, berries and mushrooms. These provide ample nourishment for the animals at the lower end of the food chain that, in turn, become food for others.

Wildlife flourishes here; the indigenous cast includes squirrels, chipmunks (which dine well on pine cone seeds), voles and lemmings, as well as small carnivores such as polecats, foxes, wolverines and, less commonly, the sable, a weasel-like creature whose luxuriant pelt played such a great role in the early exploration of Siberia.

The most common species of large mammal in the taiga is the elk, a large deer that can measure over 2m at the shoulder and weighs almost as much as a bear. The brown bear itself is also a Siberian inhabitant that you may come across, despite the Russian penchant for hunting it. Other taiga-abiding animals include deer, wolves, lynx and foxes.

Steppe

From the latitudes of Voronezh and Saratov down into the Kuban area north of the Caucasus, and all the way across southwestern Siberia, stretch vast areas of flat or gently undulating grasslands know as steppe. Since much of this is on humus-rich chernozem (black earth), a large

Roger Took's *Running with Reindeer* is a vivid account of his travels in Russia's Kola Peninsula and the wildlife found there.

The Russian taiga is a major carbon sink, removing an estimated 500 million tonnes of carbon from the atmosphere each year.

proportion is used to cultivate grain. Where soil is poorer, as in Tuva, the grasslands offer vast open expanses of sheep-mown wilderness, encouraging wildflowers and hikers.

The delta through which the Volga River enters the Caspian is, in contrast to the surrounding area, very rich in flora and fauna. Huge carpets of the pink or white Caspian lotus flower spread across the waters in summer, attracting over 200 species of birds in their millions. Wild boar and 30 other mammal species also roam the land.

The small saygak (a type of antelope), an ancient animal that once grazed all the way from Britain to Alaska, still roams the more arid steppe regions around the northern Caspian Sea. However, the species is under threat of extinction from hunting and the eradication of its traditional habitat.

To learn more about Kamchatka's fascinating environment go to www.kamchatkapeninsula.com, the site of vulcanologist Andrew Logan.

Caucasus

The steppe gives way to alpine regions in the Caucasus, a botanist's wonderland with 6000 highly varied plant species and glorious wildflowers in summer. Among the animals of the Caucasus are the tur (a mountain goat), the bezoar (wild goat), endangered mouflon (mountain sheep), chamois (an antelope), brown bear and reintroduced European bison. The lammergeier (bearded vulture), endangered griffon vulture, imperial eagle, peregrine falcon, goshawk and snowcock are among the Caucasus' most spectacular birds. Both types of vulture will occasionally attack a live tur.

Among several research projects in the Russian Far East, the Wild Salmon Center (www.wildsalmoncenter.org) has teamed up with Moscow State University to save the last wild steelhead salmon in Kamchatka.

Kamchatka

The fantastic array of vegetation and wildlife in Kamchatka is a result of the geothermal bubbling, brewing and rumbling that goes on below the peninsula's surface and that manifests itself periodically in the eruption of one of around 30 active volcanoes. The minerals deposited by these eruptions have produced some incredibly fertile earth, which is capable of nurturing giant plants with accelerated growth rates. This effect is at its most fantastic in the calderas (craters) of collapsed volcanoes. Here, hot springs and thermal vents maintain a high temperature year-round, creating almost greenhouselike conditions for plants. Waterfowl and all manner of animals make their way here to shelter from the worst of winter.

The volcanic ash also enriches the peninsula's rivers, leading to far greater spawnings of salmon than experienced anywhere else. And in thermally warmed pools the salmon also gain weight at a much increased rate. All of which is good news for the region's predatory mammals and large sea birds (and for local fishermen). The bears, in particular, benefit and the numerous Kamchatkan brown bears are the biggest of their species in Russia: a fully grown male stands at over 3m and weighs close to a tonne. Other well-fed fish-eaters are the peninsula's sea otters (a protected species), seals and the great sea eagle, one of the world's largest birds of prey, with a 2.5m wingspan. The coastline is particularly favoured by birds, with over 200 recognised species including auks, tufted puffins and swans.

John Massey Stewart, in his book *The Nature of Russia*, gives the example of the dropwort, normally just a small, unremarkable plant, which in Kamchatka can grow as much as 10cm in 24 hours and reach a height of up to 4m.

Ussuriland

Completely unique, Ussuriland is largely covered by a monsoon forest filled with an exotic array of plant life and animals – from tree frogs to tigers – found nowhere else in Russia. The mix of plants and animals draws from the taiga to the north, and also from neighbouring China, Korea and the Himalayas. The topography is dominated by the Sikhote-Alin Range, which runs for more than 1000km in a spine parallel to the coast. Unlike the sparsely vegetated woodland floor of the taiga, the forests of Ussuriland have a lush undergrowth, with lianas and vines twined around trunks and draped from branches. However, it's the animal life that arouses the most interest – not so much the wolves, sables or Asian black bears (tree-climbing, herbivorous cousins to the more common brown bears, also found here), as Russia's own tiger, the Siberian or Amur tiger.

The Siberian tiger is the largest subspecies of tiger and the largest member of the cat family. It has been measured at up to 3.5m in length. Little wonder that the native Nanai (Nanaytsy in Russian) used to worship this incredible beast. There are estimated to be around 300 of the tigers in Ussuriland (out of a total world population of 350 to 450), which is something of a success considering that they had been hunted down to between 20 and 30 by the 1940s. The tiger was designated a protected species in 1948, and since then six reserves have been set up in the region, partly to help monitor and safeguard the cats. The tigers' favoured prey is boar, though they've been observed to hunt and kill bears, livestock and even humans.

Ussuriland is also home to the Amur leopard, a big cat significantly rarer than the tiger, though less impressive and consequently less often mentioned. Around 30 of these leopards roam the lands bordering China and North Korea. Sadly, both the leopard and tiger are under threat from constant poaching by both Chinese and Russian hunters.

STATE NATURE RESERVES

Russia has 100 official *zapovedniki* (nature reserves) and 35 national parks, ranging from the relatively tiny Bryansk Forest (122 sq km) on the border with Ukraine to the enormous 41,692 sq km Great Arctic Nature Reserve in the Taymyr Peninsula, the nation's largest such reserve. (This remote and difficult to reach peninsula is not covered in this book, but there are some details of Arctic Russia in Lonely Planet's *Greenland &*

TOP PARKS & RESERVES

Park	Features	Best Time to Visit	Page
Kronotsky State Biosphere Reserve	Volcanoes (11 active cones), geysers, bear, caribou, seal, otter	Jul & Aug	p650
Kurshkaya Kosa National Park	World's first ornithological station	Year-round	p350
Nizhnesvirsky Nature Reserve	Lake Ladoga ringed seal, migratory birds	Apr-Oct	p307
Prielbruse National Park	Mt Elbrus, glaciers, waterfalls, bears, chamois, wild goats and an enormous range of plant life	Skiing year-round, climbing & hiking Jun-Sep	p487
Prioksko-Terrasny Biosphere Reserve	European bison	Year-round	p199
Samarskaya Luka	Zhiguli Hills, hiking along rocky ledges, and grand Volga vistas	Jun-Aug	p420
Sikhote-Alin Nature Reserve	Manchurian red deer, wild boar, subtropical forests, tigers	Jul & Aug	p623
Stolby Nature Reserve	Volcanic rock pillars	Aug-Apr	p556
Taganay National Park	Some of the southern Urals' notable ridges (Small, Middle and Big Taganay, Itsyl)	Jul-Sep	p447
Teberdinsky Nature Reserve	European bison, lynx, bears, chamois, boar and deer in a near pristine temperate ecosystem	Skiing Dec-Apr, climbing & hiking May-Sep	p481
Yuzhno-Kamchatsky State Reserve	Salmon, Steller's sea eagle, brown bears	Aug-mid-Sep	p649

WORLD HERITAGE SITES

Russia's environmental treasures inscribed on Unesco's World Heritage list:

- Virgin Komi Forests of the Urals
- Lake Baikal
- Volcanoes of Kamchatka
- Altai Mountains
- Western Caucasus
- Curonian Spit
- Central Sikhote-Alin
- Uvs Nuur Basin on the border with Mongolia
- Wrangel Island Reserve in the Chukchi Sea in the Russian Far East

the Arctic.) These are areas set aside to protect fauna and flora, often habitats of endangered or unique species, where controls are very strict. There's also 69 *zakazniki* (national parks), areas where protection is limited to specific species or seasons, and many other nature parks.

These reserves were once the pride of the Soviet government, and were – by Russian standards – lavished with resources. Scientists had ample funding to study the biological diversity of the reserves and conservation laws were strictly enforced. Now, though, the entire network is in danger of collapse due to a shortage of funds. The remaining conservation officers and scientists often grow their own food so they can eat. Some reserves are open to visitors (see the table, p103); and unlike in the old days, when your ramblings were strictly controlled, today you can sometimes hire the staff to show you around.

ENVIRONMENTAL ISSUES

Russia may have ratified the Kyoto Protocol in 2004, but the fact is that care for the environment has long been a low priority with the nation's rulers. The Soviet Union's enthusiasm for rapid industrialisation was matched only by its wilful ignorance of the often devastating environmental side effects – think of the draining of the Aral Sea. Mistakes were seldom admitted and, as the 1986 Chornobyl disaster in Ukraine most famously showed, people were not told when their lives were in danger.

Environmental awareness in Russia is rising but the booming economy is having its own detrimental effect. Higher standards of living have put more cars on the roads and substantially increased solid waste generation. The government is trying to improve its act and has passed sound environmental protection laws; enforcing these laws is another thing entirely.

See www.eia.doe .gov/emeu/cabs/russenv .html for a good overview of current environmental issues in Russia.

Air Pollution

The end of the Soviet Union was an unexpected boon to air quality in Russia, as many of the centrally planned – and massively air-polluting – industries collapsed. Still, the air quality in over 200 cities often exceeds Russian pollution limits, with levels that are likely to worsen. In industrial towns such as Norilsk the air is so defiled that there'll never be any need for tinted windscreens.

Even so, the Kyoto Protocol is a good deal for Russia. Its greenhouse gas emission targets were set in 1990 during the bad old Soviet days, and since then the actual emissions have fallen by around a third. Should the quotas market ever start functioning, Russia is currently in the position of being able to earn itself billions of dollars by selling carbon credits.

Oil & Natural Gas Issues

Russia has proven oil reserves of 60 billion barrels, and most of the reserves are located in Siberia. Approximately 14 billion barrels exist on and around Sakhalin Island. It is even more blessed with natural gas – an estimated 47.54 trillion cubic metres, more than twice the reserves in the next-largest country, Iran.

While it has undoubtedly been a great source of wealth for Russia, the oil and gas industry, through greed, inattention and a failing infrastructure, has been perhaps the country's greatest environmental desecrator. There are severe problems in Chechnya, where Grozny was a key oil-pipeline junction and an estimated 30 million barrels of oil have leaked into the ground (exacerbated by the region's black market in oil). In the Western Siberian Plain, environmental degradation from oil exploration and production has reached such levels that the huge Ob River flowing across it is almost dead.

Equally harmful has been the destabilisation of the delicate tundra ecosystem by the construction of buildings, roads and railways and the extraction of underground resources. Parts of the low-lying Yamal Peninsula at the mouth of the Ob, containing some of the world's biggest gas reserves, have been melting into the sea as the permafrost melts near gas installations. The traditional hunting and reindeer-herding way of life of Siberian native peoples, such as the Nenets, Khanty, Mansi and Nivkhi, has been further impeded by new pipelines blocking migration routes. The tundra is also suffering the effects of acid rain, most of it the result of metal smelting around Norilsk.

Marine life is also under threat. Off the coast of Sakhalin the Sakhalin-2 oil and gas project is considered a threat to the endangered western Pacific grey whale and has already caused much disruption to the island's fishing industry. Oil exploration has harmed both the island's delicate environment and the lives of its native people.

There have been some successes in environmental campaigns. The native inhabitants of the Yamal Peninsula managed to halt construction of a new railway and gas pipeline that would have interfered with reindeer migration routes. On Sakhalin, ecologists are joining with locals to block further oil exploration. A positive sign is Sakhalin Energy recently agreeing to move its facilities away from the whale breeding area.

Russia has the world's largest natural gas reserves, the second-largest coal reserves, and the eighth-largest oil reserves – just as well, as it's the world's third-largest energy consumer.

Radioactivity & Nuclear Waste

Maintenance, and security against terrorist attacks, have improved in recent years at Russia's nine nuclear power plants. Still, many of the reactors at these plants are similar to the fundamentally flawed ones that operated in Chornobyl in Ukraine and accidents and incidents continue to happen.

Over two million people still live in areas of Russia affected by the Chornobyl disaster (mostly in the west around Bryansk); there are increased rates of cancer and heart problems among these people. The same is true for residents around Chelyabinsk, where the Mayak nuclear complex suffered a meltdown of similar scale to Chornobyl in 1957. Full details of this only started to emerge in the 1990s. Today Lake Karachay, adjacent to the Mayak complex, is considered to be one of the world's most polluted spots as it is estimated to contain 120 million curies of radioactive waste.

Following 120 underground and atmospheric nuclear tests on the Arctic Novaya Zemlya Island, abnormally high cancer rates have been recorded among the local Nenets people and their reindeer herds.

Chukotka in the far northeast is another past nuclear testing site, where locals have actually been subjected to as much radiation as if they'd been at Chornobyl in 1986. Today, there is close to a 100% incidence of tuberculosis and a child mortality rate of 10%.

BAIKAL'S ENVIRONMENTAL ISSUES

Home to an estimated 60,000 Nerpa seals, Lake Baikal is beautiful, pristine and drinkably pure in most areas. As it holds an astonishing 80% of Russia's freshwater, environmentalists are keen to keep things that way. In the 1960s, despite the pressures of the Soviet system, it was the building of Baikal's first (and only) lakeside industrial plant that galvanised Russia's first major green movement. That plant, the Baikalsk paper-pulp factory, is still monitored today while the owners argue over a costly, World Bank–assisted clean-up plan.

These days some two-thirds of Baikal's shoreline falls within parks or reserves, so similar factories would not be allowed. But the ecosystem extends beyond the lake itself. Another challenge includes polluted inflows from the Selenga River, which carries much of Mongolia's untreated waste into the lake. The most contentious of recent worries is the US$16 billion Eastern Siberia oil pipeline from Taishet to the Pacific coast. The route deliberately loops north avoiding the lakeshore itself. Nonetheless, when finished some 80 million tons of oil a year will flow across the lake's northern water catchment area, an area highly prone to seismic activity. Environmentalists fear that a quake-cracked pipeline could spill vast amounts of oil into the Baikal feedwaters. Ironically, the government decree allowing the project to proceed was signed in December 2004, just days after a huge earthquake caused the disastrous Southeast Asian tsunami.

For more information see the websites of regional ecogroups **Baikal Wave** (www.baikalwave .eu.org/eng.html) and **Baikal Watch** (www.earthisland.org/baikal/) and the wonderful Baikal Web World (www.bww.irk.ru), which has lots about the wildlife, history and legends of the lake.

Post-*glasnost* (the free-expression aspect of the Gorbachev reforms) disclosures have revealed that the Russian navy secretly dumped nuclear waste, including used reactors from submarines, in the Sea of Japan, off Vladivostok, and the Arctic Ocean.

Logging & Desertification

The website of environmental foundation Bellona (www.bellona.no/en/) contains much up-to-date information on nuclear pollution issues in Russia.

Multinational logging concerns from the USA, South Korea and Japan, in partnership with Russia, are queuing up to clear-fell the Siberian forests, which are currently being devoured at an estimated 4 million hectares a year. Huge fires have swept uncontrollably through Russia's forests in recent years too, causing much damage.

There's been desertification of the Kalmyk steppe areas around the northern Caspian Sea because of overgrazing by sheep, and other areas of the steppe suffer similarly from excessive cultivation.

Water Pollution

Read the quarterly English bulletins of the World Wide Fund for Nature in Russia at www.wwf.ru/eng/.

Just over a quarter of Russia's population has tap water that is dangerously contaminated with chemicals or bacteria (or both). While by no means wonderful, this is an improvement on the past and in 2004, there was a 50% decrease in the number of people officially known to have suffered from acute water poisoning.

All of European Russia's main rivers, including the Volga, Don, Kama, Kuban and Oka, have 10 to 100 times the permitted viral and bacterial levels. The Volga, in particular, is severely polluted by industrial waste, sewage, pesticides and fertilisers. A chain of hydroelectric dams along the river blocks fish spawning routes and slows the current, which encourages fish parasites. (It now takes water 18 months to flow from Rybinsk to Volgograd, instead of the one month it used to take.)

The most documented instance of water pollution has centred on Lake Baikal. For an update on the situation, see the boxed text, above.

Food & Drink

Russia has a glorious culinary heritage enriched by influences from the Baltic to the Far East. The country's rich black soil provides an abundance of grains and vegetables used in the wonderful range of breads, salads and appetisers, and as the base of the distinctive soups that are the highlight of any Russian meal. The rivers, lakes and seas yield up a unique range of fish and, as with any cold climate country, there's a great love of fat-loaded dishes – Russia is no place to go on a diet!

STAPLES & SPECIALITIES
Breakfast

Typical *zavtrak* (breakfast) dishes include bliny (pancakes) with savoury or sweet fillings, various types of *kasha* (porridge) made from buckwheat or other grains, and *syrniki* (cottage-cheese fritters), delicious with jam, sugar and the universal Russian condiment, *smetana* (sour cream). *Khleb* (bread) is freshly baked and comes in a multitude of delicious varieties.

A Taste of Russia by Darra Goldstein offers over 200 recipes as well as some interesting short essays on local food culture.

Appetisers & Salads

Whether as the preamble to a meal or something to nibble on between shots of vodka, *zakuski* (appetisers) are a big feature of Russian cuisine. They range from olives to bliny with mushrooms, *tvorog* (cheese curd) or caviar, to delicious salads, which are universally popular and nearly always smothered in creamy mayonnaise. There are many salad recipes but popular versions found in most restaurants include *salat olivye* (chopped meat – sometimes chicken, sometimes sausage – cheese and vegetables mixed with mayonnaise) and *selyodka pod shuboi* (literally 'herrings in fur coats'), a classic fish salad from the Soviet era of cooking with all but the kitchen sink thrown in. Discovering what's actually under the salad's creamy sauce is often part of the fun, unless you happen to be vegetarian: salads often include shredded meat, fish or seafood.

RusCuisine.com (www.ruscuisine.com) is a cheery website packed with Slavic recipes and background information on Russian dining and drinking.

Soups

No Russian meal is complete without soup. *Shchi* (made from cabbage) and *solyanka* (a sometimes flavoursome concoction of pickled vegetables, meat and potato that used to be the staple winter food for the peasantry) are both popular soups that you'll find on menus across the country.

CAVIAR – IF BUYING, BUY CAREFULLY

While nothing is as evocative of Russian imperial luxury as black caviar, be aware that the sturgeon of the Caspian Sea could face extinction due to the unsustainable and illegal plunder of their roe (p428). If you do buy some, buy carefully. Purchase caviar only from shops (not on the street or at markets), in sealed jars (not loose) and, most importantly, make sure the jar or tin is sealed with a CITES (Convention on International Trade in Endangered Species) label, an international trade-control measure set up to reduce sturgeon poaching. Additionally, under international law, tourists are only permitted to bring home 250g of caviar per person. For more information go to www.cites.org, or read *The Philosopher Fish* by ecojournalist Richard Adams Carey. It's a lively investigation into the endangered life of the sturgeon and the prized caviar it provides.

Borsch, made from a base of beetroot, originates from Ukraine but is now synonymous with Russia throughout the world. It can be served hot or cold and usually with *smetana* poured on top of it. Some borsch is vegetarian (ask for *postny* borsch), although most is made with beef stock. Other commonly served soups are listed in the food glossary (p117).

A great dining bargain in most Russian cities is the set-menu *biznes lunch*, generally served from noon to 4pm, Monday to Friday. These simple but filling three-course lunch deals can cost as little as R100 to R150 (up to R250 in Moscow and St Petersburg).

Main Courses

It's worth noting the difference between traditional Russian cuisine and what passed for it during Soviet times, now referred to in some restaurants as Soviet-Russian cuisine. Traditional Russian cuisine is very meaty and quite heavy. Staples include *zharkoye* (hot pot) – a meat stew served piping hot in a little jug, *kotleta po kievsky* (better known in the West as chicken Kiev), and shashlyk (meat kebab). In Siberia the common Russian dish *myaso po monastirsky* (beef topped with cheese) is often relabelled *myaso po Sibirski* (Siberian meat).

Soviet-Russian cuisine includes Central Asian–style dishes, notably *plov* (fried rice with lamb and carrot) and *lagman* (noodles and meat in a soupy broth which gets spicier the further south you go). Ubiquitous are *pelmeni*: Russian-style ravioli (generally stuffed with pork or beef) and served either heaped on a plate with sour cream, vinegar and butter, or in a stock soup. Variations such as salmon or mushroom *pelmeni* are found on the menus of more chic restaurants.

Please to the Table by Anya von Bremzen and John Welchman is nothing if not comprehensive, with over 400 recipes from the Baltics, Central Asia and all points between, plus a wealth of background detail on Russian cuisine.

Fish is extremely popular. The range is enormous, but common staples include *osyetrina* (sturgeon), *shchuka* (pike), *losos* or *syomga* (salmon) and *treska* (chub). Beware that even relatively upmarket restaurants seem averse to filleting and the unwary can find their fish dishes viciously barbed with throat-ripping bones. Stuffed *kalmar* (squid) is usually tasty and bone-safe, though as it's generally stored frozen, avoid it if you doubt the regularity of the restaurant's electrical supply.

Most restaurant menus give the weight of portions as well as the price (easily confused when your Russian is poor). In most cases you'll be expected to choose an accompanying 'garnish' (priced separately) of *ris* (rice), various potato dishes or *grechka* (split buckwheat). The latter has long been considered low class, but a recent revival means it is no longer relegated to just the most basic *stolovye* (canteen). In Chinese

---

TRAVEL YOUR TASTEBUDS

Russia has an abundant supply of regional food specialities. Our favourites include **kalmary** (calamari), **kraby** (crab) and **grebeshki** (scallops) – all standard items on Vladivostok menus. **Manti** are steamed, palm-sized dumplings, known as *pozi* or *buuzy* in Buryatiya and *pyan-se* (a peppery version) in the Russian Far East. Two or three make a good, greasy meal. Eaten most often as a snack food with beer, **oblyoma** is a dried, salty fish found in the Volga. **Omul** is a cousin of salmon and trout, endemic to Lake Baikal and considered a great delicacy.

We dare you to...

- Tuck into horse meat fillets in the Sakha Republic.
- Chew on reindeer cartilage – a snack indulged in by the Even of Kamchatka.
- Drink *khoitpak* (fermented sour milk) in Tuva or its distilled version *araka*.
- Pig out on *salo* (pig fat).

restaurants check carefully whether there's a compulsory minimum rice order: this can occasionally double the cost of a meal when eating alone.

Russian cuisine borrows enormously from neighbouring countries, most obviously from those around the Caucasus, where shashlyk originated. Across Russia, Georgian restaurants (below) are almost as common as Indian ones in the UK, though not all offer a fully Georgian menu.

TABLE SCRAPS FROM HEAVEN   *Mara Vorhees*

Described by writer Darra Goldstein as 'Heaven's table scraps', you must try the rich, spicy cuisine of the former Soviet republic of Georgia while in Russia. Fertile Georgia – wedged between East and West – has long been the beneficiary (and victim) of merchants and raiders passing through. These influences are evident in Georgian cooking, which shows glimpses of Mediterranean and Middle Eastern flavours. The truly Georgian elements – the differences – are what make this cuisine so delectable. Most notably, many meat and vegetable dishes use ground walnuts or walnut oil as an integral ingredient, yielding a distinctive rich, nutty flavour. Also characteristic is the spice mixture *khmeli-suneli*, which combines coriander, garlic, chillies, pepper and savory with a saffron substitute made from dried marigold petals.

Georgian chefs love to cook over an open flame, and certainly grilled meats are among the most beloved items on any Georgian menu. Herbs such as coriander, dill and parsley and things like scallions are often served fresh, with no preparation or sauce, as a palette-cleansing counterpoint to the other rich dishes. Grapes and pomegranates show up not only as desserts, but also as tart complements to roasted meats. For vegetarians, Georgian eggplant dishes (notably garlic-laced *badrizhani nivrit*), *lobiyo* (spicy beans) and *khachapuri* (cheese bread) are a great blessing.

Here are a few more tried and true Georgian favourites to get you started when faced with an incomprehensible menu:

basturma – marinated, grilled meat, usually beef or lamb

bkhali or **pkhali** – a vegetable purée with herbs and walnuts, most often made with beetroot or spinach

buglama – beef or veal stew with tomatoes, dill and garlic

chakhokhbili – chicken slow cooked with herbs and vegetables

chikhirtmi – lemony chicken soup

dolmas – vegetables – often tomatoes, eggplant or grape leaves – stuffed with beef

khachapuri – the archetypal Georgian cheese bread comes in three main forms: snack versions sold at markets are flaky pastry squares. In restaurants *khachapuri po-imeretinsk* are circles of fresh dough cooked with sour, salty *suluguni* cheese, while *khachapuri po-adzharski* is topped with a raw egg in the crater (mix it rapidly into the melted cheese).

kharcho – thick, spicy rice and beef or lamb soup

khinkali – dumplings stuffed with lamb or a mixture of beef and pork

lavash – flat bread used to wrap cheese, tomatoes, herbs or meat

pakhlava – a walnut pastry similar to baklava, but made with sourcream dough

satsivi – walnut, garlic and pomegranate paste, usually used as a chicken stuffing in cold starters

shilaplavi – rice *pilaf*, often with potatoes

Wine is a crucial part of any Georgian meal. At all but the most informal occasions, Georgians call on a *tamada* (toastmaster) to ensure that glasses are raised and drinks topped up throughout the meal.

Georgian vintners utilise a process that is different from their European and New World counterparts. The grapes are fermented together with skins and stems, then stored in clay jugs, resulting in a flavour specific to the Caucasus. Noteworthy Georgian wines include:

Kindzmarauli – a sickeningly sweet, blood red wine which – appropriately enough – was the favourite of Stalin

Mukuzani – a rather tannic red, which is the best known and oldest Georgian wine

Saperavi – a dark, full-bodied red produced from grapes of the same name

Tsinandali – pale and fruity, the most popular Georgian white

Desserts

The Russian sweet tooth is seriously sweet. *Morozhenoe* (ice cream) is very good here, and Russians love it with a passion: it's not unusual to see people gobbling dishfuls at outdoor tables, even in freezing weather. Also popular are gooey *torty* (cream cakes), often decorated in lurid colours. *Pecheniye* (pastries) are eaten at tea-time in the traditional English style and are available at any *bulochnaya* (bakery).

DRINKS

'Drinking is the joy of the Rus. We cannot live without it' – with these words Vladimir of Kyiv, the father of the Russian state, is said to have rejected abstinent Islam on his people's behalf in the 10th century. And who wouldn't want to bend their minds now and then during those long, cold, dark winters? Russians sometimes drink vodka in moderation, but more often it's tipped down in swift shots, with the aim of getting legless.

The nearest thing to a pub is a *traktir* (tavern), becoming more common as the Russian taste for beer exceeds the love of vodka.

Alcohol

Both good local and foreign brands are common. That doesn't stop some locals gleefully dishing out *samogon* (home-made moonshine), which can be very bad for you.

VODKA

The classic Russian drink is distilled from wheat, rye or occasionally potatoes. The word comes from *voda* (pronounced va-*da*, water). Its flavour comes from what's added after distillation, so as well as 'plain' vodka you'll find *klyukovka* (cranberry vodka, one of the most popular kinds), *pertsovka* (pepper vodka), *starka* (apple and pear leaves), *limonnaya* (lemon), and *okhotnichya* (meaning 'hunter's', with about a dozen ingredients, including peppers, juniper berries, ginger and cloves).

> The classic recipe for vodka (a 40% alcohol to water mixture) was patented in 1894 by Dmitry Mendeleyev, the inventor of the periodic table.

Two common 'plain' vodkas are Stolichnaya (perhaps the most famous Russia vodka), which is in fact slightly sweetened with sugar, and Moskovskaya, with a touch of sodium bicarbonate. Don't get excited when you see how cheap Stoli is here – the stuff made for export is way better than the domestic version. Better Russian brands include Flagman, Gzhelka and Russky Standart (Russian Standard).

BEER

These days beer is as popular, if not more so, as vodka among Russians, not least because it's cheap and very palatable. There are now scores of breweries across the country pumping out dozens of tasty local brands, as well as famous Western brands. The local market leader is Baltika, a joint venture between Scottish & Newcastle and Carlsberg under international management based in St Petersburg. You're bound to find something to like among its 12 different kinds of beer: No 3, a light beer, is the most popular; No 8 is an unfiltered beer; No 10 has natural almond and basil aromas; Medovoye is supposedly made with a taste of honey; No 0 is alcohol-free; and No 9 is a lethal 16.5% proof.

Other brands to look out for include Stepan Razin, Nevskoye and Bochkaryov (all produced in St Petersburg), Stary Melnik (a product of the Turkish-owned Efes brewery), Klinskoye and Sibirskaya Korona. Most cities have their own brews – Krasnoyarsk's Legenda is particularly good.

DRINKING ETIQUETTE IN RUSSIA

If you find yourself sharing a table at a bar or restaurant with locals, it's odds-on they'll press you to drink with them. Even people from distant tables, spotting foreigners, may be seized with hospitable urges. If it's vodka being drunk, they'll want a man to down the shot in one, neat of course; women are usually excused. This can be fun as you toast international friendship and so on, but vodka has a knack of creeping up on you from behind and the consequences can be appalling. It's traditional (and good sense) to eat a little something after each shot.

Refusing a drink can be very difficult, and Russians may continue to insist until they win you over. If you can't quite stand firm, take it in small gulps with copious thanks, while saying how you'd love to indulge but you have to be up early in the morning (or something similar). If you're really not in the mood, one sure-fire method of warding off all offers (as well as making people feel quite awful) is to say *Ya alkogolik* (*Ya alkogolichka* for women): 'I'm an alcoholic'.

WINES & BRANDY

Many locals prefer their wine *polusladkoe* (semisweet) or *sladkoe* (sweet). The latter is little short of diluted alcoholic sugar. *Bryut* (very dry and only for sparkling wine), *sukhoe* (dry) and *polusukhoe* (semidry) reds can be found, though getting a good dry white can be pretty tough. In some restaurants wine is served by the glass but look carefully at the small print as prices are often per 100g or even 50g (about one third of a full glass).

Some Georgian dry red wines are superb, though Georgian whites are very much an acquired taste (see p109). Imported wines from Bulgaria and Moldova tend to be cheaper, as are certain French table wines which are generally of the lowest quality and worth avoiding.

Locally produced sparkling wine Shampanskoye is remarkably cheap (around R300 a bottle) and popular, and rarely anything like champagne.

Russian brandy is called *konyak* – the finest come from the Caucasus. Winston Churchill reputedly preferred Armenian *konyak* over French Cognac, and although standards vary enormously, local five-star brandies are generally a very pleasant surprise.

Nonalcoholic Drinks
WATER & MINERAL WATER

Tap water is suspect in some cities and should definitely be avoided in St Petersburg. Many stick to cheap bottled water. Local brands cost around R10 for 1.5 litres. If you buy mineral (rather than purified) water, be aware that it can be a full-on gastric work-out, as you'll discover most notably with Georgia's celebrated Borzhomi – a great hangover cure.

TEA & COFFEE

The traditional Russian tea-making method is to brew an extremely strong pot, pour small shots of it into glasses, and fill the glasses with hot water. Traditionally this was done from the samovar, a metal water urn with an inner tube filled with hot charcoal; modern samovars have electric elements, like a kettle, which is actually what most Russians use to boil water for tea these days. Putting jam instead of sugar in tea is quite common.

Tuvans and Buryats often drink tea weak and milky, while tea in the Altai traditionally has butter and *talkan* (a sort of ground muesli) added to taste.

Coffee comes in small cups; unless you buy it at kiosks or stand-up eateries, it's usually good. There's been an explosion of Starbucks-style cafés all across Russia's bigger cities – cappuccino, espresso, latte and mocha are now as much part of the average Russian lexicon as elsewhere. (In smaller towns you might want to check that the cappuccino you order isn't the instant powdered kind.)

OTHER DRINKS

Tasting not unlike ginger beer, *kvas*, fermented rye bread water, is a common Russian drink. It's often dispensed on the street, for a few roubles a dose, from big, wheeled tanks and is cool and refreshing in summer.

Sok can mean anything from fruit juice (usually in cartons rather than fresh) to heavily diluted fruit squash. *Mors*, made from all types of red berries, is a popular and refreshing *sok*. *Napitok* means 'drink' – it's often a cheaper and weaker version of *sok,* maybe with some real fruit thrown in.

Jugs of *kefir* (yogurtlike sour milk) are served as a breakfast drink, and are also recommended as a hangover cure. Milk, common and cheap in *moloko* (dairy shops), is often unpasteurised.

The Bashkirs, the Kazakhs of southernmost Altai and the Sakhans of the Sakha Republic drink kumiss (fermented mare's milk).

CELEBRATIONS

In the 16th century visitors to Russia gave drooling accounts of elaborate feasts at the tsars' courts where everything, from the traditional bread and salt to young swans, was served. Little has changed since. OK, swan isn't common, but food and drink still play a central role in many Russian celebrations from birthdays to religious holidays. It's traditional, for example, for wedding feasts to stretch on for hours (if not days in some villages) with all the participants generally getting legless.

In *A Year of Russian Feasts* Catherine Cheremeteff Jones recounts how Russia's finest dishes have been preserved and passed down through the feast days of the Russian Orthodox Church.

The most important holiday for the Russian Orthodox Church is Paskha (Easter). Coming after the six-week fast of Lent, when meat and dairy products are foresworn, Easter dishes are rich, exemplified by the traditional cheesecake (also known as *paskha*) and the saffron-flavoured buttery loaf *kulich*. Together with brightly decorated boiled eggs, these are taken in baskets to church to be blessed during the Easter service.

Bliny are the food of choice during week-long Maslenitsa (Butter Festival), which precedes Lent and is the equivalent of Mardi Gras elsewhere.

Christmas (which is celebrated on 7 January in the Russian Orthodox calendar) is not as big a festival as New Year's Eve, which is celebrated with a huge feast of *zakuski* and the like. However, it is traditional to eat a sweet rice pudding called *kutya* at Christmas. The same dish is also left as an offering on graves during funerals.

WHERE TO EAT & DRINK

In all major cities you'll find a decent range of restaurants, with Moscow and St Petersburg particularly well served; there, you can feast on anything from sushi to Brazilian barbecue, often round the clock. It's worth looking out for the combination *kafe-klub* places in both cities, one-stop entertainment places where you can eat, drink, dance, listen to live music and even buy books! It's certainly not necessary to endure poor hotel food and service. The Western-run luxury hotels will usually have a decent restaurant or two, and sometimes offer good-value lunch deals or buffets.

In general a *kafe* is likely to be cheaper yet often more atmospherically cosy than a *restoran,* many of which are aimed at weddings and banquets

---

RUSSIA'S TOP 10 RESTAURANTS

Long gone are the days when Russian restaurants were something to be endured rather than enjoyed. Check out the following places for a grand culinary tour of the country:

- Tiflis, Moscow (p177)
- Actor, Yaroslavl (p216)
- Mechta Molokhovets, St Petersburg (p279)
- Restoran Detinets, Novgorod (p332)
- Restoran Bobroff, Arkhangelsk (p390)

- Grand Cafe, Volgograd (p427)
- Le Café Valida, Perm (p434)
- Yolki Palki, Rostov-on-Don (p456)
- Restoran Zhurnalist, Omsk (p508)
- Exotic Picnic with a Farmer, Paratunka (p648)

---

more than individual diners. A *kofeynya* is generally an upmarket café with real coffee and cakes, though they often serve great meals too, as will a *pab* (upmarket pub with pricey imported beers) or *traktir* (better local pub often with 'traditional' Russian décor). A *zakusochnaya* can be anything from a pleasant café to a disreputable dive bar, but usually sells cheap beer and has a limited food menu. Increasingly common as you head east, a *poznaya* is an unpretentious eatery serving Central Asian food and, most notably, *pozi*. These are meat dumplings that you need to eat very carefully in order to avoid spraying yourself with boiling juices, as an embarrassed Mikhail Gorbachev famously did when visiting Ulan-Ude.

If you fancy a snack in an old Soviet-style hotel its *bufet* is usually the best bet and will be far cheaper than its restaurant. *Bufety* are also found in stations and serve a range of simple snacks: *buterbrod* (open sandwiches), boiled eggs, salads, pastries and drinks.

The *stolovaya*, the Russian version of the canteen, is the common person's eatery: sometimes decent (particularly the newer versions such as Pelmeshka, p180, in Moscow), often dreary, always cheap. Slide your tray along the counter and point to the food, and the staff will ladle it out. *Stolovye* will often be found in market or station areas.

Outside of major cities and towns the best restaurants and cafés rarely advertise their presence, with many hidden away with hard-to-find entrances at the back of apartment blocks. Others are in cellar rooms beneath street level, their small signs often making them initially indistinguishable from similarly positioned disreputable brawl bars.

In smaller towns the choice will be far narrower, perhaps limited to standard Russian meals such as *pelmeni* (Russian-style ravioli dumplings) and *kotlety* (cutlets); in villages there may be no hot food available at all (though there's almost always do-it-yourself pot noodles available from kiosks). The choice is particularly abysmal in Tuva (beyond Kyzyl); locals often take their own food when visiting the provinces!

It's always worth asking if a restaurant has an English-language menu. If not, even armed with a dictionary and this book's food glossary, it can be difficult deciphering Russian menus (the different styles of printed Cyrillic are a challenge), although they typically follow a standard form: first come *zakuski*, (appetisers often grouped into cold and hot dishes) followed by soups, sometimes listed under *pervye blyuda* (first courses). *Vtorye blyuda* (second courses, or mains) are also known as *goryachiye blyuda* (hot courses). They can be divided into *firmenniye* (house specials, often listed at the front of the menu), *myasniye* (meat), *ribniye* (fish), *ptitsa* (poultry) and *ovoshchniye* (vegetable).

If the menu leaves you flummoxed, look at what the other diners are eating and point out what takes your fancy to the staff. If a waiter – or

---

DINING DOS & DON'TS

- Do put your wrists on the edge of the table (not in your lap) while eating, and keep your fork in your left hand and knife in your right.
- Do eat snacks between shots of vodka.
- Don't mix or dilute your vodka with another drink – an anathema to your average Russian.
- Don't place an empty bottle of vodka on the table – it must be placed on the floor.
- Don't sit at the corner of a table if you are single, unless you don't want to get married for seven years!

---

the food – takes an eternity to appear, ponder on a Russian word given to dining's universal vocabulary. After the victory over Napoleon, impatient Russian soldiers in Paris cafés would bang their tables and shout *'Bystro, bystro!'*, meaning 'Quickly, quickly!' – from this came the word 'bistro'.

Service charges are uncommon, except in the ritziest restaurants, but cover charges are frequent after 7pm, especially when there's live music (one would often gladly pay to stop the music). Check by asking, *'Vkhod platny?'*. Tipping is becoming more of the norm in Moscow and St Petersburg (leave around 10% if the service has been good), but otherwise it's not a common practice across Russia. There is no charge for using the *garderob* (cloakroom) so do check in your coat before entering. Not doing so is considered extremely bad form in all but the shabbiest places.

For more words to help you order, check out Eat Your Words opposite.

'Every sizable town has a rynok (market), where locals sell spare potatoes and carrots from their dacha plots'

Quick Eats

There's plenty of fast food available from both local and international operations, supplemented by street kiosks, vans and cafés with tables. *Pitstsa* (pizza, often microwaved) and shashlyk are common fare, as are bliny and *pelmeni*.

All large cities now have Western-style supermarkets and food stores, with a large range of Russian and imported goods. You'll generally have to leave all bags in a locker. The old food stores (with their infuriating system of queuing three times for each purchase: once to find out the price, once to pay, once to collect) are fast converting to one-stop service (if not to full supermarket-style shopping). Many places are now open 24 hours.

As well as the supermarkets, there are smaller food stores, called *kulinariya*, which sell ready-made food and are common all over the country. There are also the ubiquitous food-and-drink kiosks, generally located around parks and markets, on streets and near train and bus stations – their products are usually poor, but the kiosks are handy and reasonably cheap.

Every sizable town has a *rynok* (market), where locals sell spare potatoes and carrots from their dacha plots (check the market fringes), while bigger traders off-load trucks full of fruit, vegetables, meat, dried and dairy goods. Take your own shopping bag and go early in the morning for the liveliest scene and best selection; a certain amount of bargaining is acceptable, and it's a good idea to check prices with a trustworthy local first.

Homes, roadside vendors and the well-stocked markets are your best bet for tasting the great range of wild mushrooms, *paporotniki* (fern tips), *shishki* (cedar nuts) and various soft fruits (red currants, raspberries) laboriously gathered by locals from the forest.

VEGETARIANS & VEGANS

Russia is tough on vegetarians, though some restaurants have caught on, particularly in Moscow, St Petersburg and other large cities. Main dishes are heavy on meat and poultry, vegetables are often boiled to death, and even the good vegetable and fish soups are usually made from meat stock. If you're vegetarian say so, early and often. You'll see a lot of cucumber and tomato salads, and – if so inclined – will develop an eagle eye for *baklazhan* (eggplant) plus the rare good fish and dairy dishes. *Zakuski* include quite a lot of meatless ingredients such as eggs and mushrooms. Genuine Georgian restaurants (p109) have some great veggie fare. During Lent, many restaurants have special nonmeat menus. Potatoes *(kartoshka, kartofel, pure)* are usually filed under 'garnish' not 'vegetable'.

EATING WITH KIDS

Children are loved in Russia and in all but the fanciest of restaurants they will be greeted with the warmest of welcomes. Kids' menus are uncommon, but you shouldn't have much problem getting the littl' uns to guzzle bliny or *bifshteks* – Russian-style hamburger served without bread, and often topped with a fried egg. Also check whether the milk is pasteurised – outside of major cities it often isn't. For more information on travelling with children see p700.

HABITS & CUSTOMS

Russians often like a fairly heavy early-afternoon meal *(obed)* and a lighter evening meal *(uzhin)*. While restaurants and cafés are common across Russia, dining out for the average Russian is not: only a small percentage of Russians eat more than one meal at a restaurant each year. So don't be surprised if outside of the main cities the choice of places to dine is limited. Entering some restaurants you might feel like you're crashing a big party. Here, the purpose of eating out is less to taste exquisite food than to enjoy a whole evening of socialising and entertainment, with multiple courses, drinking and dancing. Dress is informal in all but top-end places.

If you really want to experience Russia's famous hospitality – not to mention the best cuisine – never pass up the opportunity to eat at a Russian home. Be prepared to find tables groaning with food and hosts who will never be satisfied that you're full however much you eat or drink.

EAT YOUR WORDS

This glossary will help you navigate your way around Russian food and eateries. The italics in the pronunciations indicate where the stress in the word falls. To reflect the spoken language more accurately, in the following list of words and phrases the Russian letter 'o' is written as 'a' when it occurs in unstressed syllables; see p752 for further tips on pronunciation.

Useful Words & Phrases

MEALS

breakfast	*zav*·trak	завтрак
lunch	ab·*yed*	обед
dinner	u·*zhin*	ужин

> 'The purpose of eating out is less to taste exquisite food than to enjoy a whole evening of socialising and entertainment, with multiple courses, drinking and dancing'

PLACES TO EAT & BUY FOOD

bakery	*bu*·lach·na·ya	булочная
café/small restaurant	ka·*fe*	кафе
upmarket café/coffee house	ka·*fey*·nya	кофейня
canteen	sta·*lo*·va·ya	столовая
market	*ri*·nak	рынок
pub/tavern	trak·*tir*	трактир
upmarket pub	pab	паб
pozi diner	*poz*·na·ya	позная
restaurant	res·ta·*ran*	ресторан
snack bar	bu·*fet*	буфет
supermarket	u·ni·ver·*sam*	универсам
take-away	s sa·*boy*	с собой
cheap bar or café	za·*ku*·sach·na·ya	закусочная

ORDERING AT A RESTAURANT OR CAFÉ

Do you have a table ...?
yest' sva·*bod*·ni *sto*·lik ...
Есть свободный столик ...?

for two	na dva·*ikh*	на двоих
for three	na tra·*ikh*	на троих

Do you have an English menu?
an·*gli*·ska·e me·*nyu mozh*·na
Английское меню можно?

I'm a vegetarian.
ya ve·ge·ta·ri·*a*·nets/ya ve·ge·ta·ri·*an*·ka (m/f)
Я вегетарианец/Я вегетарианка.

I don't eat meat.
ya nye yem myas·*no*·va
Я не ем мясного.

I can't eat dairy products.
ya nye yem ma·*loch*·na·va
Я не ем молочного.

Do you have any vegetarian dishes?
u vas yest' ve·ge·ta·ri·*an*·ski·e *blyu*·da
У вас есть вегетарианские блюда?

Does this dish have meat?
e·ta *blyu*·da myas·no·e
Это блюдо мясное?

Does it contain eggs?
v e·tam *blyu*·de yest' *yay*·tsa
В этом блюде есть яйца?

I'm allergic to nuts.
u me·*nya* a·ler·*gi*·ya na a·*re*·khi
У меня аллергия на орехи.

Please bring (a/an/the) ...
pri·ne·*si*·te pa·*zhal*·sta ...
Принесите, пожалуйста ...

bill	schyot	счёт
fork	*vil*·ku	вилку
knife	nozh	нож
plate	ta·*rel*·ku	тарелку
glass of water	sta·*kan* va·*di*	стакан воды
with/without ice	so l'·*dom*/byez l'·*da*	со льдом/без льда

Food Glossary
BREAKFAST

am·*lyet*	омлет	omelette
blin·chi·ki	блинчики	bliny rolled around meat or cheese and browned
bli·*ni*	блины	leavened buckwheat pancakes; also eaten as an appetiser or dessert
ka·sha	каша	Russian-style buckwheat porridge
ke·*fir*	кефир	buttermilk, served as a drink

| ya·*ich*·ni·tsa | яичница | fried egg |
| yay·*tso* | яйцо | egg |

LUNCH & DINNER

de·*syer*·ti	десерты	sweet courses or desserts
gar·*ya*·chi·e *blyu*·da	горячие блюда	hot courses or 'main' dishes
pyer·vi·e *blyu*·da	первые блюда	first courses (usually soups)
vta·*ri*·e *blyu*·da	вторые блюда	second courses or 'main' dishes
za·*kus*·ki	закуски	appetisers

COOKING STYLES

at·var·*noy*	отварной	poached or boiled
fri	фри	fried
pe·*chyo*·ni	печёный	baked
va·*ryo*·ni	варёный	boiled
zhar·ni	жарный	roasted or fried

APPETISERS

gri·*bi* v sme·*ta*·ne	грибы в сметане	mushrooms baked in sour cream
ik·*ra*	икра	black (sturgeon) caviar
ik·*ra kras*·na·ya	икра красная	red (salmon) caviar
sa·*lat*	салат	salad
sa·*lat* iz pa·mi·*dor*	салат из помидор	tomato salad
sa·*lat* sta·*lich*·ni	салат столичный	salad of vegetable, beef, potato and egg in sour cream and mayonnaise
zhul'·*yen* iz gri·*bov*	жульен из грибов	also mushrooms baked in sour cream

SOUP

ak·*rosh*·ka	окрошка	cold or hot soup made from cucumbers, sour cream, potatoes, eggs, meat and *kvas*
borshch	борщ	beetroot soup with vegetables and sometimes meat
khar·*cho*	харчо	traditional Georgian soup of lamb, rice and spices
lap·*sha*	лапша	noodle soup
sal·*yan*·ka	солянка	thick meat or fish soup
shchi	щи	cabbage or sauerkraut soup
u·*kha*	уха	fish soup with potatoes and vegetables

FISH

a·set·*ri*·na	осетрина	sturgeon
fa·*rel'*	форель	trout
ri·ba	рыба	fish
su·*dak*	судак	pike perch
syom·ga	сёмга	salmon

POULTRY & MEAT DISHES

an·tre·*kot*	антрекот	entrecôte – boned sirloin steak
ba·*ra*·ni·na	баранина	lamb or mutton
bif·*shteks*	бифштекс	'steak', usually a glorified ham burger
bif·stra·ga·*nov*	бифстроганов	beef stroganov – beef slices in a rich cream sauce
ga·lub·*tsi*	голубцы	cabbage rolls stuffed with meat
gav·*ya*·di·na	говядина	beef
kal·ba·*sa*	колбаса	a type of sausage

kat·*lye*·ta	котлета	usually a croquette of ground meat
kat·*lye*·ta pa *ki*·ev·ski	котлета по-киевски	chicken Kiev; chicken breast stuffed with garlic butter
mya·sa	мясо	meat
mya·sa pa ma·nas·*tir*·ski	мясо по монастирски	meat topped with cheese and sour cream
pa·*zhar*·ska·ya kat·*lye*·ta	пожарская котлета	croquette of minced chicken
pel'·*mye*·ni	пельмени	small meat dumplings
plov	плов	*pilaf*, rice with lamb and carrots
po·zi	пози	large meat dumplings
pti·tsa	птица	chicken or poultry
shash·*lik*	шашлык	skewered and grilled mutton or other meat
svi·*ni*·na	свинина	pork
zhar·*ko*·e pa da·*mash*·ne·mu	жаркое по-домашнему	meat stewed in a clay pot 'home-style', with mushrooms, potatoes and vegetables

VEGETABLES

a·gur·*yets*	огурец	cucumber
bak·la·*zhan*	баклажан	eggplant/aubergine
gar·*ni*·ri	гарниры	any vegetable garnish
ga·*rokh*	горох	peas
gri·*bi*	грибы	mushrooms
ka·*pus*·ta	капуста	cabbage
kar·*tosh*·ka/kar·*to*·fel'	картошка/картофель	potato
mar·*kov'*	морковь	carrots
o·va·shchi	овощи	vegetables
pa·mi·*dor*	помидор	tomato
zye·len'	зелень	greens

FRUIT

ab·ri·*kos*	абрикос	apricot
a·pel'·*sin*	апельсин	orange
ba·*nan*	банан	banana
fruk·ti	фрукты	fruit
gru·sha	груша	pear
vi·na·*grad*	виноград	grapes
vish·nya	вишня	cherry
ya·bla·ka	яблоко	apple

OTHER FOODS

khlyeb	хлеб	bread
mas·la	масло	butter
pye·rets	перец	pepper
ris	рис	rice
sa·khar	сахар	sugar
sol'	соль	salt
sir	сыр	cheese

DESSERTS

| kam·*pot* | компот | fruit in syrup |
| ki·*syel'* | кисель | fruit jelly/jello |

| ma·*ro*·zhe·na·e | мороженое | ice cream |
| pi·*rozh*·na·e | пирожное | pastries |

DRINKS
Nonalcoholic

bez·al·ka·*gol'*·ni na·*pi*·tak	безалкогольный напиток	soft drink
chay	чай	tea
ko·fe	кофе	coffee
ma·la·*ko*	молоко	milk
mi·ne·*ral'*·na·ya va·*da*	минеральная вода	mineral water
va·*da*	вода	water
sok	сок	juice

Alcoholic

bye·la·e vi·*no*	белое вино	white wine
ig·*ris*·ta·e vi·*no*/sham·*pan*·ska·e	игристое вино/шампанское	sparkling wine/ champagne
kan·*yak*	коньяк	brandy
kras·na·e vi·*no*	красное вино	red wine
kvas	квас	fermented bread drink
pi·*vo*	пиво	beer
vod·ka	водка	vodka

MOSCOW

Moscow Москва

Sunlight glinting off gold-domed churches. Scantily clad women emerging from sleek cars. Uniformed soldiers marching across vast Red Square. This is Moscow – the political, economic and cultural capital that so defines this massive nation. Russia's medieval roots are here: the Kremlin still shows off the splendour of Muscovy's grand princes; St Basil's Cathedral still recounts the defeat of the Tatars. The city also recalls Russia's more recent history, fresh in our memories. On Red Square, the founder of the Soviet state lies embalmed. Just kilometres away, his heir rallied before the White House – leading to the demise of the same state.

Moscow has always been known for the diversity of its population and the richness of its culture. Today, more than ever, visitors and residents can enjoy events ranging from the classic to the progressive. Whether a Tchaikovsky opera or a Chekhov drama, classical performing arts in Moscow are among the best – and cheapest – in the world. The Tretyakov Gallery and Pushkin Fine Arts Museum house internationally famous collections of Russian and impressionist art. Of course, New Russia comes with new forms of art and entertainment. This bohemian side of Moscow – be it an underground club, or an avant-garde exhibit at the Museum of Modern Art – provides a glimpse of Russia's future. Sometimes intellectual and inspiring, sometimes debauched and depraved, it is *always* eye-opening.

Standout seasons to visit Russia are late spring (May or June) and early autumn (September or October), when the city's parks are filled with flowering trees or colourful leaves. The city is spruced for the May holidays and City Day, both festive times in the capital.

HIGHLIGHTS

- Being awestruck by the endless array of jewels and weapons in the **Kremlin Armoury** (p146)

- Marvelling at the artistry of the massive **Moscow metro** (p191)

- Sipping a cappuccino on the rooftop terrace at **Café Pushkin** (p176)

- Bargaining for trash and treasure at the **Izmaylovo Market** (p185)

- Paying your respects to Russia's cultural greats at **Novodevichy Cemetery** (p160)

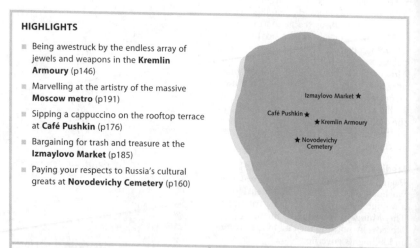

★ Izmaylovo Market

Café Pushkin ★
★ Kremlin Armoury

★ Novodevichy Cemetery

- POPULATION: 10.13 MILLION
- AREA CODE: ☎ 495

HISTORY

Today the red brick towers and sturdy stone walls of the Kremlin occupy the founding site of Moscow. Perched atop Borovitsky Hill, the location overlooks a strategic bend in the Moscow River, at the intersection of a network of waterways feeding the Upper Volga and Oka Rivers.

Early Settlement

Around the 10th century, eastern Slav tribes began to migrate to the region. For a brief time, these outlying Slavic communities enjoyed an autonomous existence far from the political and religious overlords of medieval Kyivan Rus. Present-day Moscow emerged as a trading post near the confluence of the Moscow and Yauza Rivers.

Political power gradually shifted eastward. Under Vladimir Monomakh, the Vladimir-Suzdal principality became a formidable rival within the medieval Russian realm. When Vladimir ascended to the throne of the grand prince, he appointed his youngest son, Yury Dolgoruky, to look after the region.

Legend has it that Prince Yury stopped at Moscow on his way back to Vladimir from Kyiv (Kiev). Believing that Moscow's prince had not paid him sufficient homage, Yury put the impudent boyar (high-ranking noble) to death and placed Moscow under his direct rule. Moscow is first mentioned in the historic chronicles in 1147, when Yury invited his allies to a banquet: 'Come to me, brother, please come to Moscow.'

Moscow's strategic importance prompted Yury to construct a moat-ringed wooden palisade on the hill top, the first Kremlin. Moscow blossomed into an economic centre, attracting traders and artisans to the merchant rows just outside the Kremlin's walls. In the early 13th century, Moscow became the capital of a small independent principality, though it remained a contested prize by successive generations of boyar princes.

Medieval Moscow

Beginning in 1236, Eastern Europe was overwhelmed by the ferocious Golden Horde, a Mongol-led army of nomadic tribesmen. The Mongols introduced themselves to Moscow by burning the city to the ground and killing its governor.

The Golden Horde was mainly interested in tribute, and Moscow was conveniently situated to monitor the river trade and road traffic. Moscow's Prince Ivan Danilovich readily accepted the assignment as Mongol tax collector, earning himself the moniker of Moneybags (Kalita). As Moscow prospered, its political fortunes rose too. It soon surpassed Vladimir and Suzdal as the regional capital.

Moscow eventually became a nemesis of the Mongols. In the 1380 Battle of Kulikovo, Moscow's Grand Prince Dmitry won a rare victory over the Golden Horde on the banks of the Don River. He was thereafter immortalised as Dmitry Donskoy. This feat did not break the Mongols, however, who retaliated by setting Moscow ablaze. From this time, Moscow acted as champion of the Russian cause.

Towards the end of the 15th century, Moscow's ambitions were realised as the once diminutive duchy emerged as an expanding autocratic state. Under the long reign of Grand Prince Ivan III (the Great), the eastern Slav independent principalities were forcibly consolidated into a single territorial entity. In 1480 Ivan's army faced down the Mongols at the Ugra River without a fight. The 200-year Mongol yoke was lifted.

To celebrate his successes, Ivan III imported a team of Italian artisans and masons for a complete renovation of his Moscow fortress. The Kremlin's famous thick brick walls and imposing watchtowers were constructed at this time. Next to the Kremlin, traders and artisans set up shop in Kitay-Gorod (p151), and a stone wall was erected around these commercial quarters. The city developed in concentric rings outwards from this centre.

As it emerged as a political capital, Moscow also took on the role of religious centre. In the mid-15th century, a separate Russian Orthodox Church was organised, independent of the Greek Church. In the 1450s, when Constantinople fell to the heathen Turks, Moscow claimed the title of 'Third Rome', the rightful heir of Christendom. Under Ivan IV (the Terrible), the city earned the nickname of 'Gold-Domed Moscow' because of the multitude of monastery fortresses and magnificent churches constructed within.

The once-small village grew into an urban centre. By the early 15th century, the population surpassed 50,000 people.

Contemporary visitors said Moscow was 'awesome', 'brilliant' and 'filthy'. The city was resilient against fire, famine and fighting. In the early 17th century, its population topped 200,000, making it the largest city in the world.

Imperial Moscow

Peter the Great was determined to modernise Russia. He built Moscow's tallest structure, the 90m-high Sukharev Tower, and next to it founded a College of Mathematics and Navigation. Yet Peter always despised Moscow for its scheming boyars and archaic traditions. In 1712 he startled the country by announcing the relocation of the capital to a swampland in the northwest (St Petersburg). The spurned ex-capital fell into decline.

In the 1770s Moscow was devastated by an outbreak of bubonic plague, which claimed more than 50,000 lives. The situation was so desperate that residents went on a riotous looting spree that was put down by the army. Empress Catherine II (the Great) responded to the crisis by ordering a new sanitary code to clean up the foul urban environment.

By the turn of the 19th century, Moscow had recovered from its gloom. The population climbed back over 200,000, and the city retained the ceremonial title of 'first-throned capital', where coronations were held. By this time, the city also hosted Russia's first university, museum and newspaper. Moscow's intellectual and literary scene gave rise to a nationalist-inspired Slavophile movement, which celebrated the cultural features of Russia that were distinctive from the West.

In the early 1800s Tsar Alexander I decided to resume trade with England, in violation of a treaty Russia had made with France. A furious Napoleon Bonaparte set out for Moscow with the largest military force the world had ever seen. The Russian army engaged the advancing French at the Battle of Borodino (p197), 130km from Moscow. More than 100,000 soldiers lay dead at the end of this inconclusive one-day fight. When Napoleon entered the deserted capital, defiant Muscovites had burned down two-thirds of the city rather than see it occupied. French soldiers tried to topple the formidable Kremlin, but its sturdy walls withstood their pummelling.

Moscow was feverishly rebuilt after the war. Monuments were erected to commem-orate Russia's hard-fought victory, including a Triumphal Arch and the grandiose Cathedral of Christ the Redeemer. In the centre, engineers diverted the Neglinnaya River to an underground canal and created two new urban spaces: the Alexandrovsky Garden (p147) and Teatralnaya ploshchad (p150). Meanwhile, the city's two outer defensive rings were replaced with the tree-lined Boulevard Ring and Garden Ring roads.

By midcentury, industry overtook commerce as the city's economic driving force. With a steady supply of cotton from Central Asia, Moscow became a leader in the textile industry, known as 'Calico Moscow'. By 1900, Moscow claimed over one million inhabitants. The Garden Ring became an informal social boundary line: on the inside were the abodes and amenities of businessmen, intellectuals, civil servants and foreigners; on the outside were the factories and flophouses of the toiling, the loitering and the destitute.

Red Moscow

The tsarist autocracy staggered into the new century. Exhausted by three years engaged in fighting a losing war, the old regime meekly succumbed to a mob of St Petersburg workers in February 1917. A few months later, in October, Lenin's Bolshevik party stepped into the political void and radical socialism came to power. In Moscow the Bolshevik coup provoked a week of street fighting, leaving more than 1000 dead. Fearing a German assault on St Petersburg, Lenin ordered that the capital return to Moscow.

In the early 1930s Josef Stalin launched an industrial revolution. The regime's brutal tactics created a wave of peasant immigration to Moscow. Around the city, makeshift work camps went up to shelter the huddling hordes. Moscow became a centre of military industry, whose engineers and technicians enjoyed a larger slice of the proletarian pie.

Under Stalin a comprehensive urban plan was devised for Moscow. On paper, it appeared as a neatly organised garden city; unfortunately, it was implemented with a sledgehammer. Historic cathedrals and monuments were demolished, including landmarks such as such as the Cathedral of Christ the Saviour (p157) and Kazan Cathedral (see p149). In their place appeared the marble-bedecked metro and neo-Gothic skyscrapers.

When Hitler launched 'Operation Barbarossa' into Soviet territory in June 1941 Stalin was caught by surprise. By December the Nazis were just outside Moscow, within 30km of the Kremlin – an early winter halted the advance. A monument now marks the spot of their nearest advance, near the entrance road to Sheremetyevo airport. In the Battle of Moscow, war hero General Zhukov staged a brilliant counter-offensive and saved the city from capture.

After Stalin's death in 1953, Nikita Khrushchev – a former mayor of Moscow – tried a different approach to ruling. He introduced wide-ranging reforms and promised to improve living conditions. Huge housing estates grew up round the outskirts of Moscow; many of the hastily constructed low-rise projects were nicknamed *khrushchoby*, after *trushchoby* (slums). Khrushchev's populism and unpredictability made the ruling elite a bit too nervous and he was ousted in 1964.

Next came the long reign of Leonid Brezhnev. From atop Lenin's mausoleum, he presided over the rise of a military superpower during the Cold War. The aerospace, radio-electronics and nuclear weapons ministries operated factories and research laboratories in and around the capital. By 1980 as much as one-third of the city's industrial production and one-quarter of its labour force were connected to the defence industry. As a matter of national security, the KGB secretly constructed a second subway system.

Brezhnev showed a penchant for lavish cement-pouring displays of modern architecture, such as the recently demolished Hotel Rossiya and the Kremlin Palace of Congresses (p139). Residential life continued to move further away from the city centre. Shoddy high-rise apartments went up on the periphery and metro lines were extended outward. By 1980 the city's population surpassed eight million.

Transitional Moscow

Mikhail Gorbachev came to power in March 1985 with a mandate to revitalise the ailing socialist system. He promoted Boris Yeltsin as the new head of Moscow. Yeltsin's populist touch made him an instant success with Muscovites. He embraced the more open political atmosphere, allowing 'informal' groups to organise and express themselves in public. Moscow streets such as ul Arbat (p155) hosted demonstrations by democrats, nationalists, reds and greens.

On 18 August 1991 the city awoke to find a column of tanks in the street and a self-proclaimed 'Committee for the State of Emergency in the USSR' in charge. They had already detained Gorbachev and issued orders to arrest Yeltsin. Crowds gathered at the White House (p155) and started to build barricades. Yeltsin climbed on a tank to declare the coup illegal. He dared KGB snipers to shoot him, and when they didn't, the coup was over, as was Soviet communism. By the end of the year, Boris Yeltsin had moved into the Kremlin.

The first years of transition were fraught with political conflict. In September 1993 Yeltsin issued a decree to shut down the Russian parliament. Events turned violent, and a National Salvation Front called for popular insurrection. The army intervened on the president's side and blasted the parliament into submission. In all, 145 people were killed and another 700 wounded – the worst such incident of bloodshed in the city since the Bolshevik takeover in 1917.

While the rest of Russia struggled to survive the collapse of communism, Moscow quickly emerged as an enclave of affluence and dynamism. By the mid-1990s Moscow was replete with all the things Russians had expected capitalism to bring, but which had yet to trickle down to the bulk of the population: banks, shops, restaurants, casinos, BMWs, bright lights and nightlife.

The new economy spawned a small group of 'New Russians', who are routinely derided for their garish displays of wealth. Outside this elite, Russia's transition to the market economy has come at enormous social cost. For many dedicated and talented professionals, it is now close to impossible to eke out a living. More sadly, the older generation, whose hard-earned pensions are now worth a pittance, paid the price of transition.

Within the Moscow city government, the election of Yury Luzhkov as mayor in 1992 set the stage for the creation of a big-city boss in the grandest of traditions. Through a web of financial arrangements, ownership deals and real-estate holdings, Luzhkov is as much a CEO as he is mayor. His interests range from the media to manufacturing and from five-star hotels to shopping malls.

Following decades of prudish Soviet socialism, Muscovites revelled in their new-found freedom. Liberation, libation, defiance and indulgence were all on open display. Those reared in a simpler time were no doubt shocked by the immodesty of the transition generation. After a decade, the rhythms of the city seemed to have steadied. Decadence is still for sale, but it has become more corporate. Nonetheless, Moscow remains the most freewheeling city in Russia.

ORIENTATION

Picture Moscow as being encircled by five ring roads that spread out from the centre:
Inner Ring Road About 500m north of the Kremlin; formed by the streets Mokhovaya ul, Okhotny ryad, Teatralny proezd, Novaya pl and Staraya pl. Three important squares – Manezhnaya pl, Teatralnaya pl and Lubyanskaya pl – punctuate this ring.
Boulevard Ring (Bulvarnoe Koltso) About 1km from the Kremlin. It's mostly dual carriageway, with a park strip down the middle. Each section has a different name, always ending in 'bulvar'. The Boulevard Ring ends as

---

THE CAPITAL MEETS THE CAUCASUS

The 1990s marked the revival of a war that is more than 200 years old. In the late 18th century Catherine the Great expanded the Russian empire southward into the Caucasus. The Chechens, a fiercely independent, Muslim mountain tribe, refused to recognise Russian rule.

In the 19th century Russia sought to consolidate its claim on the Caucasus, in order to maintain access to southern sea routes and to thwart British expansion into the region. The tsar ordered General Yermelov, a veteran of the Napoleonic Wars, to pacify the mountain peoples. An intense 30-year conflict ensued between Russians and Chechens, with displays of wanton savagery by both sides. The leader of the Chechen resistance, Imam Shamil, became a larger-than-life folk hero and the inspiration for today's separatist fighters.

Chechnya was tenuously incorporated into the empire through deals that Russia struck with more-cooperative Chechen clans, but separatist sentiments remained strong. Under Soviet rule, a Chechen independence revolt broke out during the Nazi invasion, even while thousands of Chechens fought the Germans. Nonetheless, towards the end of WWII Josef Stalin wreaked his revenge, terrorising villages and deporting nearly half a million Chechens to remote areas of Central Asia and Siberia. In 1969 the statue of General Yermelov in Grozny was dynamited.

National separatists declared Chechnya independent in the early 1990s. President Boris Yeltsin tried unsuccessfully to cajole, buy off and threaten Chechnya into submission. In 1994 he unleashed a military assault on the renegade republic. By 1996 fighting had subsided as Russian troops were contained to a few pockets of influence, while rebel gangs ruled the mountainous countryside in a condition of de facto independence.

In September 1999 a series of mysterious explosions in Moscow left more than 200 people dead. It was widely believed, although unproven, that Chechen terrorists were responsible for the bombings. Further provoked by the incursion of Chechen rebels into neighbouring Dagestan, the Russian military recommenced hostilities with a vengeance. For more on the continuing war in the Caucasus, see p492.

Though the Caucasus seemed far off, the repercussions of war continued to reach Moscow. In 2002 Chechen rebels wired with explosives seized a popular Moscow theatre, demanding independence. Nearly 800 theatre employees and patrons were held hostage for three days. Russian troops responded by flooding the theatre with immobilising toxic gas, resulting in 120 deaths and hundreds of illnesses.

The incident refuelled Russia's relentless and ruthless campaign to force capitulation. Chechen terrorists have responded in kind, with smaller-scale insurgencies taking place regularly.

Muscovites are all too aware of this ongoing conflict. The strike closest to home occurred in February 2004, when a bomb exploded in a metro carriage travelling between Avtozavodskaya and Paveletskaya, killing 39 and injuring more than 100. Other incidents have served as unnerving reminders, including a series of attacks that coincided with the horrific school siege in Beslan (see p491). In late August 2004 two planes that took off from Moscow exploded almost simultaneously in midair, killing all 90 passengers. A few days later, a suicide bomber failed to enter Rizhskaya metro, but still managed to kill 10 and injure 50 people on the street. Meanwhile, Chechen residents of the capital city have endured increased harassment, both officially and unofficially. And prospects for a negotiated peace appear all but nonexistent.

it approaches the Moscow River in the southwest and southeast.

Garden Ring (Sadovoe Koltso) About 2km out. Most of this ring's northern sections are called Sadovaya-something (Garden-something) ulitsa; several of its southern sections are called ulitsa-something-val, recalling its origins as a *val* (rampart). And the difference between the Garden and Boulevard Rings? The Garden Ring is the one *without* any gardens.

Third Ring (Tretoe Koltso) A new, eight-lane, high-speed motorway, recently built to absorb some of the traffic from Moscow streets. Located about 4.5km from the Kremlin, it provides motorists with a speedy route across (or rather, around) town.

Outer Ring Road (Moskovskaya Koltsovaya Avtomobilnaya Doroga; MKAD) Some 15km to 20km from the Kremlin. It forms the city limits.

Radial roads spoke out across the rings, and the Moscow River meanders across everything from northwest to southeast. The Kremlin, a north-pointing triangle with 750m sides, is at Moscow's heart in every way. Red Square lies along its eastern side while the Moscow River flows to the south.

The only elevation worth the name in the whole flat expanse is the Sparrow Hills, 6km southwest of the Kremlin, topped by the Moscow University skyscraper. This is one of seven Stalinist skyscrapers known as the 'Seven Sisters' – Moscow's most prominent buildings.

Maps

An excellent, up-to-date map in English is the *Moscow Today City Map*, published in 2004 by **Atlas Print Co** (☎ 177 8221; www.atlas-print.ru).

INFORMATION
Bookshops

Atlas (Map pp128-9; ☎ 928 6109; Kuznetsky most 9; 9am-8pm Mon-Fri, 10am-6pm Sat, 11am-5pm Sun; Kuznetsky Most) A map shop with city and regional maps covering the whole country.

Biblio-Globus (Map pp128-9; ☎ 928 3567; Myasnitskaya ul 6; 9am-9pm Mon-Fri, 10am-9pm Sat, 10am-8pm Sun; Lubyanka) A huge shop with lots of reference and souvenir books on language, art and history, and a good selection of maps and travel guides.

Bookberry (Map pp128-9; ☎ 291 8303; Nikitsky bul 17; 10am-11pm; Arbatskaya) A slick new chain that offers the city's best selection of guidebooks and maps.

House of Foreign Books (Map pp128-9; ☎ 928 2021; Kuznetsky most 18/7; 10am-8pm Mon-Sat, 11am-

7pm Sun; Kuznetsky Most) A small bookshop that specialises in foreign titles, including a decent selection of guidebooks.

Emergency

Ambulance ☎ 03, in Russian
English language emergency assistance ☎ 766 0601, 245 4387
Fire ☎ 01
Police ☎ 02

Internet Access

Besides the plethora of Internet cafés, wireless access is also becoming more common around Moscow. Take advantage of free wireless access at several upscale hotels, as well as NetLand or Time Online (see p136). A more-complete listing of clubs and cafés with wireless access is available in Russian at http://wifi.yandex.ru.

Internet Club (Map pp128-9; ☎ 292 5670; Kuznetsky most 12; per hr R60; 9am-8pm Mon-Fri, 10am-midnight Sat & Sun; Kuznetsky Most) Small, simple and very central.

NetCity Paveletskaya pl (Map p134; ☎ 969 2125; Paveletskaya pl 2/1; per hr R60; 9.30am-midnight; Paveletskaya); Kamergersky per (Map pp128-9; ☎ 292 0111; Kamergersky per 6; per hr R60; 10am-11pm; Teatralnaya) Work stations offer form more than function, but they are sufficient for surfing the Net.

(Continued on page 136)

0 — 5 km
0 — 3 miles

SLEEPING 🛏	(pp172–6)
Altai Hotel	26 C1
G&R Hostel Asia	27 F5
Golden Grain Hotel	28 D2
Hostel Sherston	29 C1
Hotel Cosmos	30 D2
Hotel Danilovsky	(see 8)
Hotel Izmaylovo (Gamma – Delta)	31 E3
Hotel Zarya	32 C1
Oksana Hotel	33 D2
Sovietsky Hotel	34 C3
Sputnik Hotel	35 B6
Travellers Guest House	36 D3

EATING 🍴	(pp176–81)
Danilovsky Market	37 C5
Rizhsky Market	38 D3

ENTERTAINMENT 🎭	(pp182–4)
Dinamo Stadium	39 B3
Great Moscow Circus	40 B6
Lokomotiv Stadium	41 E3
Luzhniki Stadium	42 B5
TsSKA Stadium	43 B3

SHOPPING 🛍	(pp184–6)
Izmaylovo Market	44 E3

TRANSPORT	(pp186–91)
Capital Shipping Company	(see 48)
Frunzenskaya Landing	45 C5
Hertz	46 A1
Kolomenskoe Landing	47 D6
Northern River Station	48 A1
Shchyolkovsky Bus Station	49 F2
Vorobyovy Gory Landing	50 B5

0   400 m
0   0.2 miles

E   **F**   **G**   **H**

ul Palikha

ul Sovetskoy Armii

☐ 25

Frunze Central
Army Park

Samarskaya pr

Kspefsky per

1

Novoslobodskaya ul

Tikhvinskaya ul

Novosushchevskaya ul

Chernyshevsky

ul Dovatorskogo

Suvorovskaya pl

Olimpiysky pr

Prospekt
Mira ⓂMira pr

2-ya vusskaya ul

Veskovsky per

Seleznevsky per

Novoslobodskaya Ⓜ

Krasnoproletarskaya ul

1-y Shchemilovsky per

Nikolayevskaya ul

ul Durova

Samarsky per

Selezvov per

usskaya pl

Dolgorukovskaya ul

Vorotnikovsky per

1-y Samotechny per

2-y Samotechny per

Olimpiysky pr

2-y Lavrsky per

3-y Lavrsky per

ul Gilyarovskogo

Shchepkina

Meshchanskaya ul

Vypolzov per

2

ul Fadeeva

Tverskaya-Yamskaya per

Seminarsky L

2-y Volkonsky per

2-y Samotechny

2-y Trotsky per

2-y Trotsky per

Troitskaya ul

Sukharevskaya Ⓜ

ul Gilyarovskogo

ul Gorlinka

50 ☐

☐ 51

Delegatskaya ul

Samotechnaya pl

Sadovaya-Samotechnaya ul

Sadovaya-Sukharevskaya ul

Sukharevskaya pl

Pankrat per

Sretensky L

2-
y per

Oruzheyny per

☐ 121

Bol Karetny per

Mal Sukharevsky per

Bol Sukharevsky per

Posledny per

Bol Golovin per

98 ☐ **3**

Mal Golovin per

Sadovaya-Triumfalnaya ul

Vorotnikovsky per

Mal Dmitrovka ul

Likhov per

Karetny per

Sredny Karetny per

Tsvetnoy Bulvar Ⓜ

Tsvetnoy bul

Bol Sukharevsky per

Pushkarev per

Bol Sergievsky per

Proxivyn per

Lukov per

Sretenka

mfalnaya pl

Mayakovskaya Ⓜ

$ 6

Staropimenovsky per

Degtyarny per

Uspensky per

Hermitage
Gardens

2-y Kolobovsky per

1-y Kolobovsky per

131 ☐

PETROVSKY

Per Kolokolnikov

per Pechatnikov

Rozhdestvensky bul

Sretensky bul

☐ 199

27

2

Blagoveshchensky per

Mamonovsky per

Nastasinsky per

Bol Putinkovsky per

101 ☐

Petrovskie 107
Vorota

Pl

Petrovsky per

Trubnaya
pl

Petrovsky bul

Rozhdestvensky bul

Bobrov per

126 ☐

☐ 36

73 ☐

48 ☐

☐ 69

Rozhdestvenka

☐ 178

35

Mal Palashevsky per

95

Tverskaya Ⓜ

☐ 58

Strastnoy bul

Petrovka

Chekhovskaya Ⓜ

Mal Kiselny per

Bol Kiselny per

Pushkinskaya Ⓜ

Pushkinskaya pl

☐ 57

☐ 104

123

Kozitsky per

130 108

☐ 134

Rakhmaninovsky per

Petrovskie linii

141 per

☐ 74

64 ☐

Nizhny Kiselny per

Zvonarsky per

TVERSKOY

Bogoslovsky per

79 ☐

118

Sandunovsky per

Varsonofevsky per

Malyuskiny per

4

☐ 42

89

Tverskoy bul

Glinishchevsky per

☐ 68

30 ☐

137 ☐

7

87

Neglinnaya

Kuznetsky most

85 ☐

103 ☐

Bol Lubyanka

Myasnitskaya ul

47

Tverskaya Ⓜ

84 ☐

4 $

105

Kuznetsky Most Ⓜ

14

116

3

110 Kuznetsky
Most Ⓜ

Pushechnaya ul

136 ☐

41 ☐

8 ●

90

Maly Gnezdnikovsky per

32 ☐

128 ☐

92 ☐

ul Petrovka

Rozhdestvenka

125

19

@

Lubyanka Ⓜ

44 ☐

132 ☐

17

114

12

122 ☐

138 ☐ Tretyakovsky
proezd

127 ☐

100 ☐

66 ☐

Mal Cherkassky per

56 ☐

60

☐ 31

Pl Nikitskie
Vorota

43 ☐

40 ☐

67 ●

76 ☐

46 ☐

Kitay-
Gorod Ⓜ

Maroseyka ul

9 ●

15 ☐

129 ☐

111 ☐

18 ☐

Teatralnaya Ⓜ

Teatralny proezd

Okhotny Ryad Ⓜ

Pl Revolyutsii

Pl Revolyutsii Ⓜ

Staryy per

53 ●

Kitay-
Gorod Ⓜ

124 ☐

Slavyanskaya pl

34 ☐

24 ☐

81 ☐

83

Pl
Arbatskie
Vorota

39 ☐

Manezhnaya
pl

ul Ilinka

Nikolsky per

139 ☐

38 ☐

5

106 ☐

5 $

Arbatskaya Ⓜ

Arbatsky per

Arbatskaya Ⓜ

Vozdvizhenka ul

Red Sq
(Krasnaya pl)

ul Varvarka

59 ☐

94 ☐

61 ☐

62 ☐

RBAT

ul Novy Arbat

ul Arbat

Mal Afanasyevsky per

Biblioteka
imeni Lenina Ⓜ

21 ☐

Alexandrovsky
Garden

Alexandrovsky
Sad Ⓜ

Borovitskaya Ⓜ

Kremlin

See The Kremlin Map p135

52 63 45 28

Hotel Rossiya

6

54 ☐

ul Znamenka

Moskvoretskaya nab

Moskvoretskaya nab

Moscow River

Kremlevskaya nab

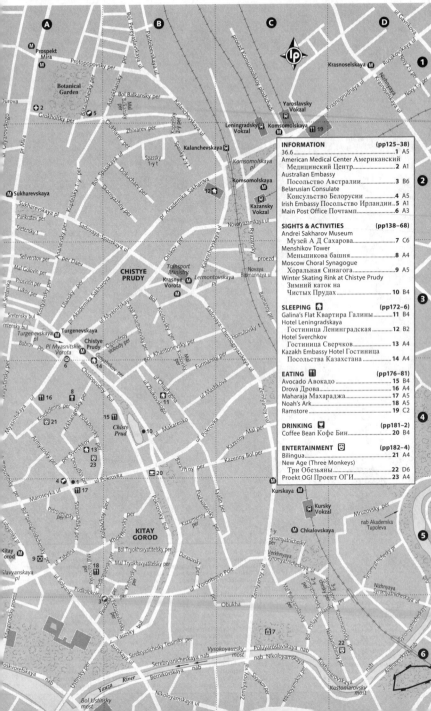

0 — 400 m
0 — 0.2 miles

INFORMATION	(pp125–38)
36.6	1 A5
American Medical Center Американский Медицинский Центр	2 A1
Australian Embassy Посольство Австралии	3 B6
Belarusian Consulate Консульство Белоруссии	4 A5
Irish Embassy Посольство Ирландии	5 A1
Main Post Office Почтамп	6 A3

SIGHTS & ACTIVITIES	(pp138–68)
Andrei Sakharov Museum Музей А Д Сахарова	7 C6
Menshikov Tower Меньшикова башня	8 A4
Moscow Choral Synagogue Хоральная Синагога	9 A5
Winter Skating Rink at Chistye Prudy Зимний каток на Чистых Прудах	10 B4

SLEEPING	(pp172–6)
Galina's Flat Квартира Галины	11 B4
Hotel Leningradskaya Гостиница Ленинградская	12 B2
Hotel Sverchkov Гостиница Сверчков	13 A4
Kazakh Embassy Hotel Гостиница Посольства Казахстана	14 A4

EATING	(pp176–81)
Avocado Авокадо	15 B4
Drova Дрова	16 A4
Maharaja Махараджа	17 A5
Noah's Ark	18 A5
Ramstore	19 C2

DRINKING	(pp181–2)
Coffee Bean Кофе Бин	20 B4

ENTERTAINMENT	(pp182–4)
Bilingua	21 A4
New Age (Three Monkeys) Три Обезьяны	22 D6
Proekt OGI Проект ОГИ	23 A4

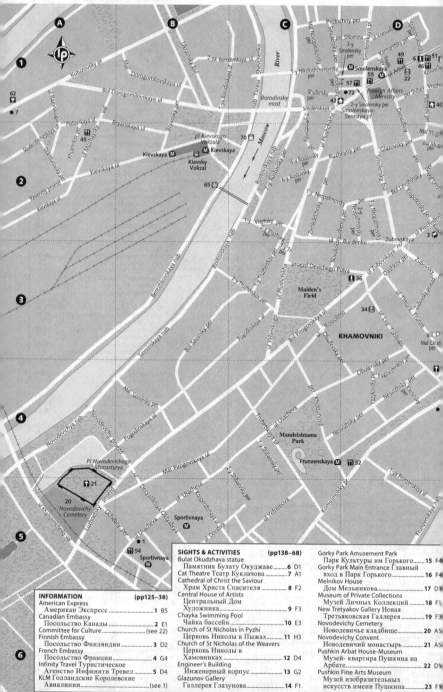

INFORMATION (pp125–38)
American Express
  Американ Экспресс 1 B5
Canadian Embassy
  Посольство Канады 2 E1
Committee for Culture .... (see 22)
Finnish Embassy
  Посольство Финляндии 3 D2
French Embassy
  Посольство Франции 4 G4
Infinity Travel Туристическое
  Агенство Инфинити Тревел 5 D4
KLM Голландские Королевские
  Авиалинии .... (see 1)

SIGHTS & ACTIVITIES (pp138–68)
Bulat Okudzhava statue
  Памятник Булату Окуджаве 6 D1
Cat Theatre Театр Куклачова 7 A1
Cathedral of Christ the Saviour
  Храм Христа Спасителя 8 F2
Central House of Artists
  Центральный Дом
  Художника 9 F3
Chayka Swimming Pool
  Чайка бассейн 10 E3
Church of St Nicholas in Pyzhi
  Церковь Николы в Пыжах.............. 11 H3
Church of St Nicholas of the Weavers
  Церковь Николы в
  Хамовниках 12 D4
Engineer's Building
  Инженерный корпус 13 G2
Glazunov Gallery
  Галлерея Глазунова........................ 14 F1

Gorky Park Amusement Park
  Парк Культуры им Горького........ 15 F4
Gorky Park Main Entrance Главный
  вход в Парк Горького.................... 16 F4
Melnikov House
  Дом Мельникова............................ 17 D1
Museum of Private Collections
  Музей Личных Коллекций 18 F1
New Tretyakov Gallery Новая
  Третьяковская Галлерея 19 F3
Novodevichy Cemetery
  Новодевичье кладбище.................. 20 A5
Novodevichy Convent
  Новодевичий монастырь 21 A5
Pushkin Arbat House-Museum
  Музей- квартира Пушкина на
  Арбате.. 22 D1
Pushkin Fine Arts Museum
  Музей изобразительных
  искусств имени Пушкина 23 F1

400 m
0.2 miles

133

eft-side labels on map:

Borovitskaya
Moskvoretskaya nab
Raushskaya nab
Moscow River
Kremlevskaya nab
Chugunny Canal
Kropotkinskaya
KROPOTKIN-SKAYA
Ovchinnikovskaya nab
Novokuznetskaya
Tretyakovskaya
Klimentovsky per
Bolotnaya pl
Vodootvodny
Mal Kamenny most
Pyzhevsky per
Park Kultury
Polyanka
ZAMOSKVORECHIE
Park Kultury
Krymsky most
Iskusstv Park
Kazansky t
Gorky Park
Kaluzhskaya pl
Oktyabrskaya
Dobryninskaya
Serpukhovskaya

Index listing

Pushkin Literary Museum
Литературный музей АС
Пушкина.....................................**24** E2
Resurrection Church in Kadashi
Церковь Воскресения в Кадашах...**25** G2
Russian Academy of Art
Российская Академия Художеств...**26** E2
St Clement's Church Церковь
Климента Папы Римского................**27** H2
St John the Baptist Church
Церковь Иоанна Предтечи.............**28** H2
Sculpture Park Парк скульптур.......**29** F3
SS Martha and Mary Convent
Марфо-Мариинская Обитель.........**30** H3
SS Mikhail and Fyodor Church
Церковь Михаила и Федора............**31** H2
State Tretyakov Gallery
Государственная
Третьяковская Галлерея................**32** H2
Statue of Peter the Great
Памятник Петру Великому.............**33** F3
Tolstoy Estate-Museum
Музей-усадьба Толстого.................**34** D3
Tolstoy Museum
Музей ЛН Толстого........................**35** E2
Tolstoy statue..................................**36** D3
Tsereteli Gallery
Галлерея Церетели.........................**37** E2
Virgin of Consolation of All Sorrows Church
Церковь Иконы всех Скорбящих
Радость..**38** H2

SLEEPING 🛏 **(pp172–6)**
Alrosa on Kazachy
Алроса на Казачих.........................**39** G3
Hotel Arbat Гостиница Арбат............**40** D1
Hotel Baltschug Kempinski
Гостиница Балчуг Кемпински.........**41** H1
Hotel Belgrad Гостиница Белград....**42** C1
Hotel Tiflis Гостиница Тифлис..........**43** E2

EATING 🍴 **(pp176–81)**
Artist's Gallery
Галлерея Художника....................**(see 37)**
Correa's..**44** H3
Dorogomilovsky Market
Дорогомиловский рынок...............**45** A2
Eastern Quarter
Восточный Квартал.......................**46** D1
Garden Art Café Арт Кафе Сад.......**47** G2
Gastronom Seventh Continent
Гастроном седьмой Континент......**48** G2
Hard Rock Café................................**49** D1
Il Patio Ил Патио............................**50** H2
Moo Moo Му-Му.............................**51** D1
Moo Moo Му-Му.............................**52** D4
Pancho Villa Панчо Вилла..............**53** F4
Ramstore...**54** B5
Smolensky Gastronom
Смоленский гастроном...................**55** D1
Starlite Diner Старлайт дайнер.......**56** G4
Stockmans Стокманс......................**57** D1
Taras Bulba Тарас Бульба................**58** H2

Tiflis Тифлис....................................**59** E2
Yolki-Palki Ёлки-Палки....................**60** H2

DRINKING 🍷 **(pp181–2)**
Coffee Bean Кофе бин.....................**61** H2
Red Bar Красный бар.......................**62** A1
Shokoladnitsa Шоколадница............**63** E1
Shokoladnitsa Шоколадница............**64** F4

ENTERTAINMENT 🎭 **(pp182–4)**
American Cinema
Американский Дом Кино................**65** B2

TRANSPORT **(pp186–91)**
Air France Эр Франс........................**66** G4
Bolshoy Kamenny most Boat Landing
Пристань Большой
Каменный мост............................**67** F1
Delta Авиалиния Дельта.................**68** E1
Gorky Park Boat Landing
Пристань Парк Горького...............**69** E4
Kievsky Vokzal Boat Landing
Пристань Киевский вокзал.............**70** C2
Krymsky most Boat Landing
Пристань Крымский мост...............**71** E3
Transaero Трансаэро.......................**72** D1

0 ————————— 400 m
0 ————————— 0.2 miles

INFORMATION	**(pp125–38)**
British Council Resource Centre	(see 1)
Foreign Literature Library Библиотека	
иностранной литературы	**1** B1
NetCity НэтСити	**2** A4

SIGHTS & ACTIVITIES	**(pp138–68)**
Andrey Rublyov Museum	
of Early Russian Culture & Art	
Музей Андрея Рублёва	(see 3)
Andronikov Monastery	
Спасо-Андроников Монастырь	**3** D1
Cathedral of St Martin the Confessor	
Храм Святого Мартина	
Исповедника	**4** C2

Church of St Nikita Beyond the Yauza	
Церковь Никиты за Яузой	**5** B1
Krutitskoe Podvorye	
Крутицкое Подворье	**6** C4
Novospassky Monastery	
Новоспасский монастырь	**7** C4
Potters' Church of the Assumption	
Церковь Успения Богородицы в	
Гончарной Слободе	**8** B2
Taganka Gates Church of St Nicholas	
Церковь Николы у Таганских	
Ворот	**9** B2

EATING	**(pp176–81)**
Il Patio Ил Патио	**10** C2

DRINKING	**(pp181–2)**
Montana Coffee Монтана Кофе	**11** A3

ENTERTAINMENT	**(pp182–4)**
Le Club Ле Клуб	(see 13)
Moscow International House of	
Music (MMDM) Московский	
Международный Дом Музыки	
(ММДМ)	**12** B3
Taganka Theatre Театр на Таганке	**13** B2

TRANSPORT	**(pp186–91)**
Novospassky most Boat Landing	
Пристань Новоспасский Мост	**14** B4
Transaero Трансаэро	**15** A4
Ustinsky most Boat Landing	
Пристань Устинский Мост	**16** A1

THE KREMLIN

0   200 m
0   0.1 miles

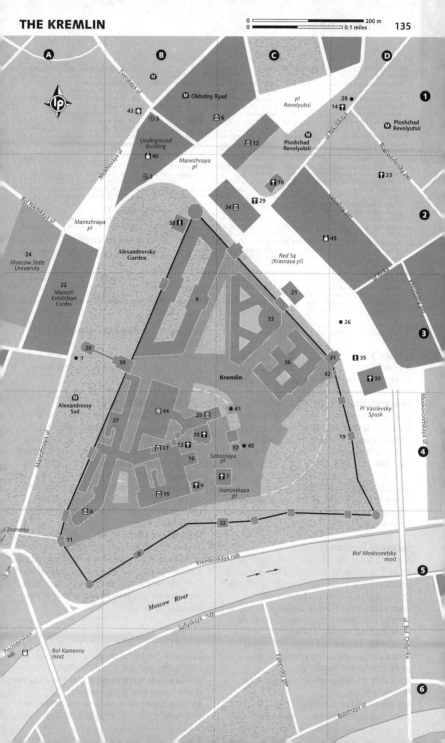

(Continued from page 125)

NetLand (Map pp128–9; ☎ 781 0923; Teatralny proezd 5; per hr R40-60; ☼ 24hr; Ⓜ Kuznetsky Most, Lubyanka) A loud, dark club that fills up with kids playing games. Enter from ul Rozhdestvenka.

Phlegmatic Dog (Map p135; ☎ 995 9545; Okhotny Ryad, 1st fl; access free; ☼ 10am-1am; Ⓜ Okhotny Ryad) Recently voted 'most stylish' Internet café in the world by Yahoo! Mail. Free Internet access with the purchase of food or drink.

Time Online Okhotny Ryad (Map p135; ☎ 363 0060; per hr R65-75; ☼ 24hr; Ⓜ Okhotny Ryad); Belorusskaya (Map pp128–9; ☎ 363 0060; Bolshoy Kondretyevsky per 7; per hr R65-75; ☼ 24hr; Ⓜ Belorusskaya) Offers copy and photo services, as well as over 200 zippy computers or free wi-fi access.

Internet Resources
See p22 for a list of mostly Moscow-based sites. The *Moscow Times* and the *Exile* (opposite) have electronic versions of their print papers. Other useful resources:

www.expat.ru Run by and for English-speaking expats living in Russia. Provides useful information about real estate, children in Moscow, social groups and more.

www.maps-moscow.com An energetic group of international journalists raising awareness of architectural preservation issues in Moscow.

www.mirkart.ru/moscow An interactive map of Moscow, in Russian.

www.moscow-taxi.com Viktor the virtual taxi driver provides extensive descriptions of sites inside and outside of Moscow, as well as hotel bookings and other tourist services.

www.moscowout.ru A full calendar of events in the capital, with links to restaurant and movie reviews, nightlife and activities for kids.

Libraries & Cultural Centres
British Council Resource Centre (Map p134; ☎ 782 0200; www.britishcouncil.org/ru; Nikoloyamskaya ul 1; ☼ noon-7pm Mon-Fri, 10am-6pm Sat; Ⓜ Taganskaya) Located at the Foreign Literature Library; take your passport.

Foreign Literature Library (Map p134; ☎ 915 3669; Nikoloyamskaya ul 1; ☼ 10am-8pm Mon-Fri, to 6pm Sat; Ⓜ Taganskaya) Home to several international libraries and cultural centres, including the American Cultural Center Library, the French Cultural Centre and the British Council Resource Centre.

Russian State Library (Map p135; ul Vozdvizhenka 3; ☼ 9am-9pm; Ⓜ Biblioteka imeni Lenina) On the corner of Mokhovaya ul, this is one of the world's largest libraries, with over 20 million volumes. If you want to peruse any of these, take along your passport and one passport photo, and fill in some forms at the information office to get a free *chitatelsky bilet* (reader's card).

Media
All of the following English-language publications can be found at hotels, restaurants and cafés around town. Numerous other publications seem to appear at random, last a few issues and then vanish.

element (www.elementmoscow.ru) This oversized newsprint magazine comes out weekly with restaurant reviews, concert listings and art exhibits. Also publishes a seasonal supplement highlighting Moscow's hottest restaurants.

The Exile (www.exile.ru) An irreverent, free weekly, with extensive entertainment listings. It is hard not to be offended by this rag, which may be why it is not as widely distributed as it used to be.

Go (www.go-magazine.ru) The *Moscow Times'* monthly entertainment guide.

Moscow Business Telephone Guide (www.mbtg.ru) A free, invaluable, bilingual phone book.

Moscow News (www.moscownews.ru) This long-standing Russian news weekly recently reappeared as an English-language publication, focusing on domestic and international politics and business.

Moscow Times (www.themoscowtimes.com) This first-rate daily is the undisputed king of the hill in locally published English-language news, covering Russian and international issues, as well as sport and entertainment. The Friday edition is a great source for what's happening at the weekend.

Medical Services

36.6 Kitay-Gorod (Map p131; ul Pokrovka 1; Ⓜ Kitay-Gorod); Kuznetsky Most (Map pp128-9; Kuznetsky most 18; Ⓜ Kuznetsky Most); Novy Arbat (Map pp128-9; ul Novy Arbat 15; Ⓜ Smolenskaya); Tverskaya (Map pp128-9; Tverskaya ul 25; Ⓜ Tverskaya, Mayakovskaya) A chain of 24-hour pharmacies.

American Medical Center (Map p131; ☎ 933 7700; www.amcenters.com; Grokholsky per 1; Ⓜ Prospekt Mira) Offers 24-hour emergency service, consultations and a full range of medical specialists, including paediatricians and dentists. Also has an on-site pharmacy with English-speaking staff.

Botkin Hospital (Map pp128-9; ☎ 237 8338, 945 7533; 2-y Botkinsky proezd 5; Ⓜ Begovaya) The best Russian facility.

European Medical Center (Map pp128-9; ☎ 933 6655; www.emcmos.ru; Spirodonevsky per 5; Ⓜ Mayakovskaya) Includes medical and dental facilities, which are open around the clock for emergencies. The staff speaks 10 different languages.

Money

Banks, exchange counters and ATMs are ubiquitous in Moscow. Rates do vary, so it may be worthwhile shopping around if you are changing a large sum. Currencies other than US dollars and euros are difficult to exchange and yield bad rates. Travellers cheques can also be problematic.

Credit cards, especially Visa and Master-Card, are widely accepted in upscale hotels, restaurants and shops. You can also use your credit card to get a cash advance at most major banks in Moscow.

Alfa Bank (☼ 8.30am-8pm Mon-Sat) Arbat (Map pp128-9; ul Arbat 4/1; Ⓜ Arbatskaya); Kuznetsky Most (Map pp128-9; Kuznetsky most 7; Ⓜ Kuznetsky Most); Marriott Grand Hotel (Map pp128-9; Tverskaya ul 26; Ⓜ Mayakovskaya) Usually changes travellers cheques. ATMs at the branches listed dispense both roubles and US dollars.

American Express (Map pp132-3; ☎ 933 6636; fax 933 6635; ul Usachova 33; ☼ 9am-5pm; Ⓜ Sportivnaya) The most reliable place to cash American Express travellers cheques. It also offers an ATM, mail holding and travel services for AmEx cardholders.

Western Union (☎ 797 2197) Contact for wire transfers of money.

Post

Service has improved dramatically in recent years, but the usual warnings about delays and disappearances of incoming mail apply. Note that mail to Europe and the USA can take two to six weeks to arrive.

Central telegraph (Map pp128-9; Tverskaya ul 7; ☼ post 8am-10pm, telephone 24hr; Ⓜ Okhotny Ryad) This convenient office offers telephone, fax and Internet services.

DHL Worldwide Express (☎ 956 1000) Air courier services. Call for information on drop-off locations and to arrange pick-ups.

FedEx (☎ 234 3400) Air courier services. Call for information on drop-off locations and to arrange pick-ups.

Main post office (Map p131; Myasnitskaya ul 26; ☼ 8am-8pm Mon-Fri, 9am-7pm Sat & Sun; Ⓜ Chistye Prudy) Moscow's main post office is on the corner of Chistoprudny bul.

TNT (☎ 797 2777) Air courier services.

UPS (☎ 961 2211) Air courier services.

Telephone

Moscow pay phones operate with cards that are widely available in shops, kiosks and metro stations. The cards are available in a range of units. The phones are fairly user friendly, and most of them have an option for directions in English. Make sure you press the button with the speaker symbol when your party answers the phone.

For international calls, it is often easier to place your call from the central telegraph office, where you prepay (R23 per minute) for the duration of your call.

Tourist Information

Moscow has no tourist information centre, but plenty of information is available at hostels and upscale hotels, as well as through travel agents.

Travel Agencies

G&R International (Map pp126-7; ☎ 378 0001; fax 378 2866; www.hostels.ru; Zelenodolskaya ul 3/2, 5th fl; Ⓜ Ryazansky Prospekt) Operates the G&R Hostel Asia, as well as organising itineraries, providing visa support and selling transport tickets.

Infinity Travel (Map pp132-3; ☎ 234 6555; www .infinity.ru; Komsomolsky pr 13; Ⓜ Park Kultury) Affiliated with the Travellers Guest House, this on-the-ball travel company offers rail and air tickets, visa support, and trans-Siberian and Central Asian packages. It's a great source for airline tickets.

DANGERS & ANNOYANCES

Unfortunately, street crime targeting tourists has increased in recent years, although Moscow is not as dangerous as paranoid locals may have you think. As in any big city, be on your guard against pickpockets and muggers. Be particularly careful at or around metro stations at Kursk Station and Partizanskaya, where readers have reported specific incidents. Watch out especially for gangs of children who are after anything they can get their hands on.

Some policemen can be bothersome, especially to dark-skinned or otherwise foreign-looking people. Practical advice from a Moscow synagogue: 'cover your kippa'.

Other members of the police force target tourists. Reports of tourists being hassled about their documents and registration have declined. However, it's still wise to carry a photocopy of your passport, visa and registration stamp. If stopped by a member of the police force, do not give him your passport! It is perfectly acceptable to show a photocopy instead.

The most common hazard is violent and xenophobic drunks. Or even worse, overly friendly drunks.

Scams

Beware of well-dressed people dropping wads of money on the streets of Moscow.

A common scam in Moscow involves a respectable-looking person who 'accidentally' drops some money on the pavement as he passes by an unsuspecting foreigner – that's you. Being an honest person, you pick up the money to return it to the careless person, who is hurrying away. A second guy sees what is happening and tries to stop you from returning it, proposing that you split the money and, well, split.

CHANGING TELEPHONE NUMBERS

Russian authorities have an annoying habit of frequently changing telephone numbers, particularly in cities. We've tried our best to list the correct telephone number at the time of research but it's likely that some will change during the lifetime of this book. As of December 2005 Moscow's telephone code has been ☎ 495, though in some areas, mainly suburbs, it is ☎ 499, and Moscow Region is ☎ 496.

This is a no-win situation. These guys are in cahoots. While you are negotiating about how to split the money – or arguing about returning it – the first guy suddenly realises he is missing his cash. He returns to the scene of the crime. But lo and behold, the cash you return to him is not enough: some money is missing and you are culpable. This leads to a shakedown or any number of unpleasantries.

The moral of the story is that the streets of Moscow are not paved with money – resist the temptation to pick up money lying on the pavement.

SIGHTS
Kremlin

The apex of political power, the **Kremlin** (Map p135; ☎ 202 3776; www.kremlin.museum.ru; adult/ student R300/150, photography permit R50; ♥ 9.30am-4pm Fri-Wed; Ⓜ Aleksandrovsky Sad, Borovitskaya, Biblioteka imeni Lenina) is the kernel not only of Moscow but of all of Russia. From here Ivan the Terrible orchestrated his terror; Napoleon watched Moscow burn; Lenin fashioned the proletariat dictatorship; Stalin purged his ranks; Khrushchev fought the Cold War; Gorbachev unleashed *perestroika* (his efforts to revive the Soviet economy); and Yeltsin concocted the New Russia.

The Kremlin occupies a triangular plot of land covering little Borovitsky Hill on the north bank of the Moscow River, probably first settled in the 11th century. Today it's enclosed by high walls 2.25km long, with Red Square outside the east wall. The best views of the Kremlin are from Sofiyskaya nab, across the river.

A 'kremlin' is a town's fortified stronghold, and the first low, wooden wall around Moscow was built in the 1150s. The Kremlin grew with the importance of Moscow's princes, becoming in the 1320s the head-quarters of the Russian Church, which had shifted from Vladimir. The 'White Stone Kremlin' – which had limestone walls – was built in the 1360s, with almost the same boundaries as it has today.

At the end of the 15th century, Ivan the Great brought master builders from Pskov and Italy to supervise new walls and towers (most of which still stand), as well as the Kremlin's three great cathedrals and more. Although Peter the Great shifted the capital to St Petersburg, the tsars continued to show up here for coronations and other celebrations.

Over the years, the biggest threat to the Kremlin was Napoleon, who blew up parts of it before his retreat in 1812. Fortunately, the timely arrival of Russian troops prevented total destruction. The citadel wouldn't be breached again until the Bolsheviks stormed the place in October 1917.

The Kremlin remained closed to the public until 1955. It was Stalin who, in 1935, had the imperial double-headed eagles removed from the wall's five tallest towers, replacing them with the distinctive red glass stars still in place today.

ADMISSION
Before entering the Kremlin, deposit bags at the **left luggage office** (Map p135; per bag R60; ☻9am-6.30pm Fri-Wed), beneath the Kutafya Tower near the main ticket office. The main ticket office is in the Alexandrovsky Garden, just off Manezhnaya pl. The ticket covers entry to all buildings except the Armoury and Diamond Fund Exhibition; it also does not include the special exhibits that are sometimes held inside Patriarch's Palace or the Ivan the Great Bell Tower.

In any case, you can and should buy tickets for the Armoury here, to avoid queuing up once inside. Arrive early before tickets sell out.

There's also an entrance at the southern Borovitskaya Tower, mainly used by those heading straight to the Armoury or Diamond Fund Exhibition.

Inside the Kremlin, police will keep you from straying into the out-of-bounds areas. Visitors wearing shorts will be refused entry.

Visiting the Kremlin buildings and the Armoury is at least a half-day affair. If you intend to visit the Diamond Fund or other special exhibits, plan on spending most of the day here.

TOURS
Numerous freelance guides tout their services near the Kutafya Tower, with prices ranging from R300 to R600 per hour, and the quality varying widely. Capital Tours (p171) offers standard daily tours of the Kremlin and Armoury, while Dom Patriarshy Tours (p171) offers more in-depth tours of the Kremlin cathedrals, sometimes including a visit to the otherwise off-limits palaces.

NORTHERN & WESTERN BUILDINGS
The main entrance is through **Kutafya Tower** (Map p135), which stands away from the Kremlin's west wall, at the end of a ramp over the Alexandrovsky Garden. The ramp was once a bridge over the Neglinnaya River, which used to be part of the Kremlin's defences; it has flowed underground, beneath the Alexandrovsky Garden, since the early 19th century. The Kutafya Tower is the last survivor of a number of outer bridge towers that once stood this side of the Kremlin.

From the Kutafya Tower, walk up the ramp and through the Kremlin walls beneath the **Trinity Gate Tower** (Map p135). The lane to the right (south), immediately inside the Trinity Gate Tower, passes the 17th-century **Poteshny Palace** (Map p135) where Stalin lived. East of here the bombastic marble, glass and concrete **State Kremlin Palace** (Map p135), formerly the Kremlin Palace of Congresses, was built from 1960 to 1961 for Communist Party congresses. It is now a concert and ballet auditorium (p182). North is the 18th-century **Arsenal** (Map p135), ringed with 800 captured Napoleonic cannons.

To the east of the Arsenal the offices of the Russian president are in the yellow former **senate** (Map p135) building, a fine, triangular 18th-century classical edifice. Next to the Senate is the 1930s former **Supreme Soviet** (Map p135) building.

PATRIARCH'S PALACE
Built for Patriarch Nikon (whose reforms sparked the break with the Old Believers) mostly in the mid-17th century, the highlight of the **Patriarch's Palace** (Map p135) is perhaps

the ceremonial **Cross Hall**, where the tsar's and ambassadorial feasts were held. The palace also contains an exhibit of 17th-century household items, including jewellery, hunting equipment and furniture. From here you can access the five-domed **Church of the Twelve Apostles**, which has a gilded, wooden iconotasis and a collection of icons by the leading 17th-century icon painters.

The Patriarch's Palace often holds **special exhibits** (adult/student R300/150), which require an additional ticket and reservation time.

ASSUMPTION CATHEDRAL

The heart of the Kremlin is Sobornaya pl (Cathedral Sq), surrounded by magnificent buildings. **Assumption Cathedral** (Map p135) stands on the northern side, with five golden helmet domes and four semicircular gables facing the square. As the focal church of prerevolutionary Russia, it is the burial place of most of the Russian Orthodox Church heads from the 1320s to 1700. The tombs are against the north, west and south walls.

The cathedral was built between 1475 and 1479 after the Bolognese architect Aristotle Fioravanti had toured Novgorod, Suzdal and Vladimir to acquaint himself with Russian architecture. His design is based on the Assumption Cathedral at Vladimir, with some Western features. It replaced a smaller 1326 cathedral on the same site.

In 1812 French troops used the cathedral as a stable, looting 295kg of gold and over five tonnes of silver, although much of it was recovered.

The church closed in 1918. However, according to some accounts, when the Nazis were on the outskirts of Moscow in 1941, Stalin secretly ordered a service in the Assumption Cathedral to protect the city from the enemy. The cathedral was officially returned to the Church in 1989, but still operates as a museum.

A striking 1660s fresco of the Virgin Mary faces Sobornaya pl, above the door once used for royal processions. The visitors' entrance is at the western end, and the interior is unusually bright and spacious, full of warm golds, reds and blues.

The tent-roofed wooden throne near the south wall was made in 1551 for Ivan the Terrible; it's commonly called the **Throne of Monomakh** because of its carved scenes from

the career of 12th-century grand prince, Vladimir Monomakh of Kyiv.

The **iconostasis** dates from 1652, although its lowest level contains some older icons, among them (second from the right) *Saviour with the Angry Eye* (Spas Yaroe Oko) from the 1340s. On the left of the central door, the *Virgin of Vladimir* (Vladimirskaya Bogomater) is an early-15th-century Rublyovschool copy of Russia's most revered image; the 12th-century original, *Vladimir Icon of the Mother of God* (now in the Tretyakov Gallery), stood in the Assumption Cathedral from the 1480s to 1930. One of the oldest Russian icons, the 12th-century red-clothed *St George* (Svyatoy Georgy) from Novgorod, is positioned by the north wall.

Most of the existing murals on the cathedral walls were painted on a gilt base in the 1640s, but three grouped together on the south wall – *The Apocalypse* (Apokalipsis), *The Life of Metropolitan Pyotr* (Zhitie Mitropolita Petra) and *All Creatures Rejoice in Thee* (O tebe Raduetsya) – are attributed to Dionysius and his followers, the cathedral's original 15th-century mural painters.

CHURCH OF THE DEPOSITION OF THE ROBE

This delicate little single-domed **church** (Map p135) beside the west door of the Assumption Cathedral was built between 1484 and 1486 by masons from Pskov. As the private chapel of the patriarch, it was built in exclusively Russian style, and the frescoes on the pillars depict the church metropolitans and Moscow princes over the centuries. The church now houses an exhibition of 15th- to 17th-century woodcarvings.

IVAN THE GREAT BELL TOWER

With its two golden domes rising above the eastern side of Sobornaya pl, the **Ivan the Great Bell Tower** (Map p135) is the Kremlin's tallest structure, a Moscow landmark visible from 30km away. (Before the 20th century it was forbidden in Moscow to build any higher than the tower.)

When designed by Italian Marco Bono in 1508 the southern tower had just two octagonal tiers beneath a drum and dome. Boris Godunov raised the tower to 81m, a public works project designed to employ the

(Continued on page 145)

Izba (traditional wooden building), Rostov-Veliky (p217)

SIMON RICHMOND

CHRISTINA DAMEYER

The Transfiguration Gate-Church,
Novodevichy Convent (p158), Moscow

The Monastery of St Jacob (p219) on the shores of Lake Nero

SIMON RICHMOND

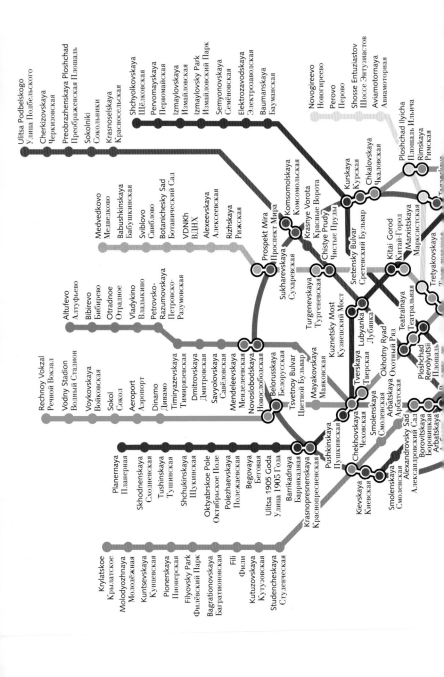

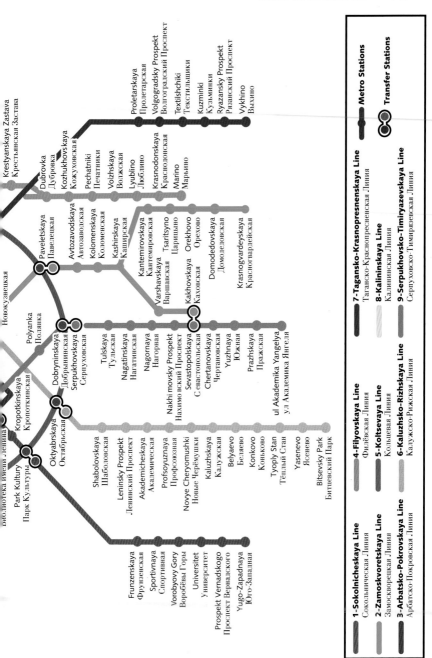

Krestyanskaya Zastava
Крестьянская Застава

Proletarskaya
Пролетарская
Volgogradsky Prospekt
Волгоградский Проспект
Textlishchiki
Текстильщики
Kuzminki
Кузьминки
Ryazansky Prospekt
Рязанский Проспект
Vykhino
Выхино

Dubrovka
Дубровка
Kozhukhovskaya
Кожуховская
Pechatniki
Печатники
Volzhskaya
Волжская
Lyublino
Люблино
Krasnodonskaya
Краснодонская
Marino
Марьино

Novokuznetskaya
Новокузнецкая

Paveletskaya
Павелецкая
Avtozavodskaya
Автозаводская
Kolomenskaya
Коломенская
Kashirskaya
Каширская
Kantemirovskaya
Кантемировская
Tsaritsyno
Царицыно
Orekhovo
Орехово
Domodedovskaya
Домодедовская
Krasnogvardeyskaya
Красногвардейская

Biblioteka imeni Lenina
Библиотека имени Ленина
Polyanka
Полянка
Varshavskaya
Варшавская
Kakhovskaya
Каховская

Park Kultury
Парк Культуры
Kropotkinskaya
Кропоткинская
Dobryninskaya
Добрынинская
Serpukhovskaya
Серпуховская
Tulskaya
Тульская
Nagatinskaya
Нагатинская
Nagornaya
Нагорная
Nakhimovsky Prospekt
Нахимовский Проспект
Sevastopolskaya
Севастопольская
Chertanovskaya
Чертановская
Yuzhnaya
Южная
Prazhskaya
Пражская
ul Akademika Yangelya
ул Академика Янгеля

Oktyabrskaya
Октябрьская

Shabolovskaya
Шаболовская
Leninsky Prospekt
Ленинский Проспект
Akademicheskaya
Академическая
Profsoyuznaya
Профсоюзная
Novye Cheryomushki
Новые Черёмушки
Kaluzhskaya
Калужская
Belyaevo
Беляево
Konkovo
Коньково
Tyoply Stan
Тёплый Стан
Yasenevo
Ясенево
Bitsevsky Park
Битцевский Парк

Frunzenskaya
Фрунзенская
Sportivnaya
Спортивная
Vorobyovy Gory
Воробьёвы Горы
Universitet
Университет
Prospekt Vernadskogo
Проспект Вернадского
Yugo-Zapadnaya
Юго-Западная

1-Sokolnicheskaya Line
Сокольническая Линия

2-Zamoskvoretskaya Line
Замоскворецкая Линия

3-Arbatsko-Pokrovskaya Line
Арбатско-Покровская Линия

4-Filyovskaya Line
Филёвская Линия

5-Koltsevaya Line
Кольцевая Линия

6-Kaluzhsko-Rizhskaya Line
Калужско-Рижская Линия

7-Tagansko-Krasnopresnenskaya Line
Таганско-Краснопресненская Линия

8-Kalininskaya Line
Калининская Линия

9-Serpukhovsko-Timiryazevskaya Line
Серпуховско-Тимирязевская Линия

● Metro Stations

◉ Transfer Stations

Church of the Saviour-over-the-Galleries,
Rostov-Veliky kremlin (p217)

Grave of Nadezhda Alliluyeva, Josef Stalin's second
wife, at Novodevichy Cemetery (p160), Moscow

Tsar Cannon (p145), Moscow Kremlin

(Continued from page 140)

thousands of people who came to Moscow during a famine. The building's central section, with a gilded single dome and a 65-tonne bell, dates from the 1530s, while the tent-roofed annexe next to the belfry was commissioned by Patriarch Filaret in 1642 and bears his name. Exhibitions from the Kremlin collections are shown on the ground level of the **bell tower** (adult/student R100/50).

TSAR BELL & CANNON

Beside the bell tower, not inside it, stands the **Tsar Bell** (Map p135), the world's biggest bell. Sadly, this 202-tonne monster never rang. In a 1701 fire an earlier 130-tonne version fell from its belfry and shattered; with these remains, the current Tsar Bell was cast in the 1730s for Empress Anna Ioanovna. The bell was cooling off in the foundry casting pit in 1737 when it came into contact with water, causing an 11-tonne chunk to chip off.

North of the bell tower is the **Tsar Cannon** (Map p135), cast in 1586 for Fyodor I, whose portrait is on the barrel. Shot has never sullied its 89cm bore – and certainly not the cannonballs beside it, which are too big even for this elephantine firearm.

ARCHANGEL CATHEDRAL

The cathedral at the square's southeastern corner was – for centuries – the coronation, wedding and burial church of tsars. The tombs of all Muscovy's rulers from the 1320s to the 1690s are here, bar one – Boris Godunov is buried at Sergiev Posad.

The **Archangel Cathedral** (Map p135), built between 1505 and 1508 by the Italian Alevisio Novi, is dedicated to Archangel Michael, guardian of Moscow's princes. Like the Assumption Cathedral, its style is essentially Byzantine-Russian, though the exterior has many Venetian Renaissance features, notably the distinctive scallop-shell gables.

Tsarevich Dmitry – Ivan the Terrible's son, who died mysteriously in 1591 – lies beneath a painted **stone canopy**. Ivan's own tomb is out of sight behind the iconostasis, along with those of his other sons: Ivan (whom he killed) and Fyodor (who succeeded him). From Peter the Great onwards, emperors and empresses were

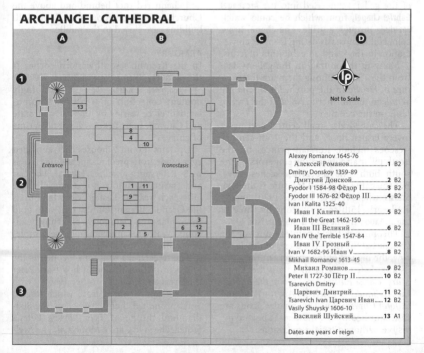

ARCHANGEL CATHEDRAL

Not to Scale

Alexey Romanov 1645-76	
Алексей Романов	1 B2
Dmitry Donskoy 1359-89	
Дмитрий Донской	2 B2
Fyodor I 1584-98 Фёдор I	3 B2
Fyodor III 1676-82 Фёдор III	4 B2
Ivan I Kalita 1325-40	
Иван I Калита	5 B2
Ivan III the Great 1462-150	
Иван III Великий	6 B2
Ivan IV the Terrible 1547-84	
Иван IV Грозный	7 B2
Ivan V 1682-96 Иван V	8 B2
Mikhail Romanov 1613-45	
Михаил Романов	9 B2
Peter II 1727-30 Пётр II	10 B2
Tsarevich Dmitry	
Царевич Дмитрий	11 B2
Tsarevich Ivan Царевич Иван	12 B2
Vasily Shuysky 1606-10	
Василий Шуйский	13 A1
Dates are years of reign	

146 MOSCOW ·· Sights   www.lonelyplanet.com

buried in St Petersburg; the exception was Peter II, who died in Moscow in 1730 and is buried here.

During restorations in the 1950s, 17th-century **murals** were uncovered. The south wall depicts many of those buried here, and on the pillars are some of their predecessors, including Andrei Bogolyubsky, Prince Daniil and his father, Alexander Nevsky.

ANNUNCIATION CATHEDRAL

Dating from 1489, the **Annunciation Cathedral** (Map p135) at the southwest corner of Sobornaya pl contains the celebrated icons of master painter Theophanes the Greek. Their timeless beauty appeals even to those usually left cold by icons.

The cathedral, built by Pskov masters, was the royal family's private chapel. Originally, it had just three domes and an open gallery around three sides. Ivan the Terrible, whose taste was more elaborate, added six more domes and chapels at each corner, and enclosed the gallery and gilded the roof.

Ivan's fourth marriage disqualified him under Orthodox law from entering the church proper, so he had the southern arm of the gallery converted into the **Archangel Gabriel Chapel**, from which he could watch services through a grille. The chapel has a colourful iconostasis dating from its consecration in 1564, and an exhibition of icons.

Many of the murals in the gallery date from the 1560s. Among them are the *Capture of Jericho* in the porch, *Jonah and the Whale* in the northern arm, and the *Tree of Jesus* on the ceiling.

The cathedral's small central part has a lovely jasper floor, and the 16th-century frescoes include Russian princes on the north pillar and Byzantine emperors on the south, both with Apocalypse scenes above. But the cathedral's real treasure is the **iconostasis**, where restorers in the 1920s uncovered early-15th-century icons by three of the greatest medieval Russian artists.

Theophanes likely painted most of the six icons at the right-hand end of the deesis row, the biggest of the six tiers of the iconostasis. Left to right, these are the *Virgin Mary*, *Christ Enthroned*, *St John the Baptist*, the *Archangel Gabriel*, the *Apostle Paul*, and *St John Chrysostom*. Theophanes' icons are distinguished by his mastery at portraying visible pathos in facial expressions.

Archangel Michael is ascribed to Andrei Rublyov, who may also have painted the adjacent *St Peter*. Rublyov is also reckoned to be the artist of the first, second, sixth and seventh (and probably the third and fifth) icons from the left of the festival row, above the deesis row. The seven at the right-hand end are attributed to Prokhor of Gorodets.

The basement – which remains from the previous 14th-century cathedral on this site – contains a fascinating exhibit on the **Archaeology of the Kremlin**. The artefacts date from the 12th to 14th centuries, showing the growth of Moscow during this period.

HALL OF FACETS & TEREM PALACE

On the western side of the square, named after its facing Italian Renaissance stone, is the square **Hall of Facets** (Map p135); its upper floor housed the tsar's throne room, the scene of banquets and ceremonies, and was reached by external staircases from the square below.

The 16th- and 17th-century **Terem Palace** (Map p135) is the most splendid of all the Kremlin palaces. Catch a glimpse of its sumptuous cluster of golden domes and chequered roof behind and above the Church of the Deposition of the Robe. Both buildings are closed to the public.

ARMOURY

In the Kremlin's southwestern corner is the **Armoury** (Map p135; adult/student R300/175; 10am, noon, 2.30pm, 4.30pm), a numbingly opulent collection of treasures accumulated over centuries by the Russian state and Church. Your ticket will specify a time of entry.

Upstairs, Room 2 houses the renowned eggs made from precious metals and jewels by St Petersburg jewellers, **Fabergé**. The tsar and tsarina traditionally exchanged these gifts each year at Easter. Most famous is the Grand Siberian Railway egg, with gold train, platinum locomotive and ruby headlamp, created to commemorate the completion of the Moscow–Vladivostok line.

The **royal regalia** in Room 7 contains the joint coronation throne of boy tsars Peter the Great and his half-brother, Ivan V (with a secret compartment from which Regent Sofia prompted them), as well as the 800-diamond throne of Tsar Alexey, Peter's father. The gold Cap of Monomakh – jewel-studded and sable-trimmed – was worn for two centuries of coronations until 1682.

Among the **coaches** in Room 9 is the sleigh that Elizabeth rode from St Petersburg to Moscow for her coronation, pulled by 23 horses at a time.

Between the Armoury and the Annunciation Cathedral stretches the 700-room **Great Kremlin Palace** (Map p135), built as an imperial residence between 1838 and 1849. Now it is an official residence of the Russian president and is used for state visits and receptions. It's not open to the public.

DIAMOND FUND EXHIBITION

If the Armoury doesn't sate your diamond lust, there's more in the separate **Diamond Fund Exhibition** (Map p135; ☎ 229 2036; adult/student R350/175; ⏰ 10am-noon, 2-5pm Fri-Wed); it's in the same building as the Armoury. The lavish collection shows off the precious stones and jewellery garnered by tsars and empresses over the centuries, including the largest sapphire in the world. The highlight is the 190-carat diamond given to Catherine the Great by her lover Grigory Orlov.

TOWERS

The Kremlin's walls have 19 distinctive towers, mostly built between 1485 and 1500, with tent roofs added in the 17th century. Some towers had to be rebuilt after Napoleonic vandalism.

The **Saviour Gate Tower** (Map p135) is the Kremlin's 'official' exit onto Red Square. The current clock dates from the 1850s. Hauling 3m hands and weighing 25 tonnes, the clock takes up three of the tower's 10 levels. Its melodic chime sounds every 15 minutes across Red Square and across the country (on the radio).

Nearby, the **Tsar Tower** (Map p135) sits atop the Kremlin wall. Legend has it that Ivan the Terrible watched executions from an old wooden tower that previously stood on this spot.

The first tower built (1485) was the **Secrets Tower** (Map p135), named for a secret passageway down to the river. During the 17th century, the **Konstantin and Yelena Tower** (Map p135) was used as a prison, earning it the nickname 'torture tower'. The **Annunciation Tower** (Map p135) is named for the miracle-working icon on the façade.

ALEXANDROVSKY GARDEN

The first public park in Moscow, **Alexandrovsky Garden** (Map p135) sits along the Kremlin's western wall. Colourful flowerbeds and impressive Kremlin views make it a favourite strolling spot for Muscovites and tourists alike.

At the north end is the **Tomb of the Unknown Soldier** (Map p135), where newlyweds bring flowers and have their pictures taken. The tomb contains the remains of one soldier who died in December 1941 at km41 of Leningradskoe sh (the nearest the Nazis came to Moscow). The inscription reads, 'Your name is unknown, your deeds immortal', along with an eternal flame and other inscriptions listing the Soviet hero cities of WWII, honouring 'those who fell for the motherland' between 1941 and 1945. The changing of the guard happens every hour.

Red Square

Immediately outside the Kremlin's northeastern wall is the infamous **Red Square** (Krasnaya ploshchad; Map p135). Commanding the square from the southern end is the building that, more than any other, says 'Russia' – St Basil's Cathedral.

Red Square used to be a market square adjoining the merchants' area in Kitay-Gorod. It has always been a place where occupants of the Kremlin chose to congregate, celebrate and castigate for all the people to see. Here, Ivan the Terrible publicly confessed his misdeeds in 1547, built St Basil's to commemorate his victories in the 1550s, and later had numerous perceived enemies executed. Red Square also saw the dismembering of the Cossack rebel Stepan Razin in 1671, as well as the en masse execution in 1698 of 2000 members of the Streltsy, Peter the Great's mutinous palace guard.

Soviet rulers chose Red Square for their military parades, perhaps most poignantly on 7 November 1941, when tanks rolled straight off to the front line outside Moscow; and during the Cold War, when lines of ICBMs rumbled across the square to remind the West of Soviet military might.

Incidentally, the name 'Krasnaya ploshchad' has nothing to do with communism or the blood that flowed here: *krasny* in old Russian meant 'beautiful' and only in the 20th century did it come to mean 'red', too.

Red Square is closed to traffic, except for the limousines that whiz in and out of the Kremlin's Saviour Gate from time to time. Most people here are sightseers, but that doesn't reduce the thrill of walking on its 400m by 150m area of cobbles, so central to Russian history. It's particularly atmospheric when floodlit at night.

The best way to enter Red Square is through the **Resurrection Gate** (Map p135). Rebuilt in 1995, it's an exact copy of the original completed on this site in 1680, with its twin red towers topped by green tent spires. The first gateway was destroyed in 1931 because Stalin considered it an impediment to the parades and demonstrations held in Red Square.

Within the gateway is the bright **Chapel of the Iverian Virgin** (Map p135), originally built in the late 18th century to house the icon of the same name.

LENIN'S MAUSOLEUM

The granite **tomb** (Map p135; ☎ 923 5527; admission free; ☼ 10am-1pm Tue-Thu, Sat & Sun; Ⓜ Ploshchad Revolyutsii) standing at the foot of the Kremlin wall is another Red Square must-see, especially since the former leader may eventually end up beside his mum in St Petersburg. For now, the embalmed leader remains as he has been since 1924 (apart from a retreat to Siberia during WWII).

From 1953 to 1961 Lenin shared the tomb with Stalin. In 1961, at the 22nd Party Congress, the esteemed (and by then ancient) Bolshevik Madame Spiridonova announced that Vladimir Ilych had appeared to her in a dream, insisting that he did not like spending eternity with his successor. With that, Stalin was removed, and given a place of honour immediately behind the mausoleum.

Before joining the queue at the northwestern corner of Red Square, drop your camera and knapsack at the left-luggage office in the State History Museum, as you will not be allowed to take it with you. Humourless guards ensure that visitors remain respectful.

After trouping past the embalmed, oddly waxy figure, emerge from the mausoleum and inspect the burial places along the Kremlin wall of Stalin, Brezhnev and other communist heavy hitters.

LENIN UNDER GLASS

Red Square is home to the world's most famous mummy, that of Vladimir Lenin. When he died of a massive stroke (on 22 January 1924, aged 53), a long line of mourners patiently gathered in winter's harshness for weeks to glimpse the body as it lay in state. Inspired by the spectacle, Stalin proposed that the father of Soviet communism should continue to serve the cause as a holy relic. So the decision was made to preserve Lenin's corpse for perpetuity, against the vehement protests of his widow, as well as his own expressed desire to be buried next to his mother in St Petersburg.

Boris Zbarsky, a biochemist, and Vladimir Vorobyov, an anatomist, were issued a political order to put a stop to the natural decomposition of the body. The pair worked frantically in a secret laboratory in search of a long-term chemical solution. In the meantime, the body's dark spots were bleached, and the lips and eyes sewn tight. The brain was removed and taken to another secret laboratory, to be sliced and diced by scientists for the next 40 years in the hope of uncovering its hidden genius.

In July 1924 the scientists hit upon a formula to successfully arrest the decaying process, a closely guarded state secret. This necrotic craft was passed on to Zbarsky's son, who ran the Kremlin's covert embalming lab for decades. After the fall of communism, Zbarsky came clean: the body is wiped down every few days, and then, every 18 months, thoroughly examined and submerged in a tub of chemicals, including paraffin wax. The institute has now gone commercial, offering its services and secrets to wannabe immortals for a mere million dollars.

In the early 1990s Boris Yeltsin expressed his intention to heed Lenin's request and bury him in St Petersburg, setting off a furore from the political left as well as more muted objections from Moscow tour operators. It seems that the mausoleum, the most sacred shrine of Soviet communism, and the mummy, the literal embodiment of the Russian Revolution, will remain in place for at least several more years.

ST BASIL'S CATHEDRAL

No picture can prepare you for the crazy confusion of colours and shapes that is **Pokrovsky Cathedral** (Map p135; ☎ 298 3304; adult/student R100/50; ☯ 11am-5pm Wed-Mon; Ⓜ Ploshchad Revolyutsii), commonly known as St Basil's. This ultimate symbol of Russia was created between 1555 and 1561 (replacing an existing church on the site) to celebrate Ivan the Terrible's capture of the Tatar stronghold, Kazan. Its design is the culmination of a wholly Russian style that had been developed building wooden churches; legend has it that Ivan had the cathedral's architect blinded so that he could never build anything comparable.

The cathedral's apparent anarchy of shapes hides a comprehensible plan of nine main chapels: the tall, tent-roofed one in the centre; four big, octagonal-towered ones, topped with the four biggest domes; and four smaller ones in between.

The misnomer St Basil's actually refers only to the northeastern chapel, which was added later. It was built over the grave of the barefoot holy fool Vasily (Basil) the Blessed, who predicted Ivan's damnation and added correctly, as the army left for Kazan, that Ivan would murder a son. Vasily, who died while Kazan was under siege, was buried beside the church that St Basil's soon replaced. He was later canonised.

The interior is open to visitors: besides a small exhibition on the cathedral itself, it contains lovely frescoed walls and loads of nooks and crannies to explore. A joint ticket (adult/student R230/115) with the State History Museum is also available.

Out the front of St Basil's is a **statue of Kuzma Minin and Dmitry Pozharsky** (Map p135), the butcher and the prince who together raised and led the army that ejected occupying Poles from the Kremlin in 1612. Up the slope is the round, walled **Place of Skulls** (Map p135), where Ivan the Terrible made his public confession and Peter the Great executed the Streltsy.

GUM

The elaborate 19th-century façade on the northeastern side of Red Square is the Gosudarstvenny Universalny Magazin (State Department Store). **GUM** (Map p135) once symbolised all that was bad about Soviet shopping: long queues and shelves empty, bar a few drab goods. A remarkable transformation has taken place since *perestroika* and today GUM is a bustling place with more than 1000 fancy shops; see p185 for more.

KAZAN CATHEDRAL

Opposite the northern end of GUM, the tiny **Kazan Cathedral** (Map p135; ul Nikolskaya 3; admission free; ☯ 8am-7pm; Ⓜ Ploshchad Revolyutsii) is a 1993 replica. The original was founded in 1636 in thanks for the 1612 expulsion of Polish invaders; for two centuries it housed the *Virgin of Kazan* icon, which supposedly helped to rout the Poles.

Three hundred years later the cathedral was completely demolished, allegedly because it impeded the flow of celebrating workers in May Day and Revolution Day parades. Evening services are now held at 8pm on Monday.

STATE HISTORY MUSEUM

At the northern end of the square, the **State History Museum** (Map p135; ☎ 292 4019; www.shm.ru; adult/student R150/75; ☯ 11am-7pm Wed-Mon; Ⓜ Ploshchad Revolyutsii) has an enormous collection covering the whole Russian empire from the Stone Age on. The building, dating from the late 19th century, is itself an attraction – each room is in the style of a different period or region, some with highly decorated walls echoing old Russian churches. Reopened in 1997, each year sees the addition of a few more galleries. A joint ticket (adult/student R230/115) allowing access to the State History Museum and St Basil's Cathedral is available at either spot.

Across the street, the former **Central Lenin Museum** (Map p135; pl Revolyutsii 2; Ⓜ Ploshchad Revolyutsii) was once the big daddy of all the Lenin museums, but was closed in 1993 after the White House shoot-out. It is sometimes used for special exhibits, but more often communist rabble-rousers congregate here.

City Centre

The heart of the city lies in the area immediately surrounding the Kremlin and Red Square. The centre is bound by an arc: Mokhovaya ul, Okhotny ryad, Teatralny proezd and Lubyansky proezd. The Moscow River encloses the arc on the south side.

AROUND MANEZHNAYA PLOSHCHAD

At the northern end of Red Square, Manezhnaya pl has been transformed with the vast underground **Okhotny Ryad Shopping Mall** (Map p135). From the square, it appears as a series of half-domes and balustrades, and a network of fountains and sculptures. See p185 for details on the shops inside.

The long, low building on the southwestern side of the square is the **Manezh Exhibition Centre** (Map p135; ☎ 292 4459; ☼ 11am-8pm Tue-Sun; Ⓜ Aleksandrovsky Sad, Borovitskaya, Biblioteka imeni Lenina), housing local art exhibitions. It is newly renovated, reopening after a fire in 2004. On the northwestern side of the square are the fine old edifices of the **Moscow State University** (Map p135; built in 1793) and **Le Royal Meridien National** (p175).

The infamous 1930s-era **Hotel Moskva** on Manezhnaya pl was finally demolished in 2004. The story goes that Stalin was shown two possible designs for the hotel and – not realising they were alternatives – approved both. The builders did not dare to point out his error, and so built half the hotel in constructivist style and half in Stalinist style. The incongruous result became such a familiar feature of the Moscow landscape that the new, high-class hotel being constructed on the site is expected to re-create its predecessor's architectural quirks.

At the base of the once and future Hotel Moskva is the entrance to the **Archaeological Museum** (Map p135; ☎ 292 4171; Manezhnaya pl 1; admission R100; ☼ 10am-5.30pm Tue-Sun; Ⓜ Ploshchad Revolyutsii, Okhotny Ryad). An excavation of the Voskresensky Bridge – which used to cross the Neglinnaya River and become the road to Tver – uncovered coins, clothing and other artefacts from old Moscow. The museum displaying these treasures is situated in an underground pavilion 7m deep, a pavilion that remains from the excavation itself.

Northeast of Manezhnaya pl, Okhotny ryad passes between the Hotel Moskva site and the glowering **State Duma** (Map pp128–9), where Russia's parliament sits. Next door, the green-columned **House of Unions** (Map pp128–9) dates from the 1780s.

TEATRALNAYA PLOSHCHAD

Teatralnaya pl opens out on both sides of Okhotny ryad, 200m from Manezhnaya pl. The northern half of the square is dominated by the **Bolshoi Theatre** (Map pp128–9), where Tchaikovsky's *Swan Lake* premiered (unsuccessfully) in 1877. Initially overshadowed by St Petersburg's Mariinsky Theatre, the

Bolshoi didn't really hit the high notes until the 1950s, when foreign tours won great acclaim for its ballet and opera companies. For ticket information, see p182. The busy streets behind the Bolshoi constitute Moscow's main shopping centre (see p185).

Across ul Petrovka from the 'big' Bolshoi is the 'small' **Maly Theatre** (see p183), a drama establishment. On Teatralnaya pl's southern half is the tiled, sculptured façade of luxurious **Hotel Metropol** (p175).

AROUND LUBYANSKAYA PLOSHCHAD

For several decades the broad square at the top of Teatralny proezd was a chilling symbol of the Komitet Gosudarstvennoy Bezopasnosti (Committee for State Security), more commonly known as the KGB.

In the 1930s, the **Lubyanka Prison** (Map pp128–9) was the feared destination of thousands of innocent victims of Stalin's purges, but today the grey building is the headquarters of the KGB's successor, the FSB (Federal Security Service). The building is not open to the public.

Behind Lubyanka is the four-room **KGB Museum** (Map pp128–9; ul Bolshaya Lubyanka 12/1; Ⓜ Lubyanka), devoted to the history, propaganda and paraphernalia of the Soviet intelligence services. The museum is not open to casual callers, but Dom Patriarshy Tours (p171) occasionally takes groups there.

From 1926 to 1990 Lubyanskaya pl was called pl Dzerzhinskogo, after Felix Dzerzhinsky, founder of the Cheka (the KGB's ancestor). A tall statue of Dzerzhinsky that dominated the square was memorably removed by angry crowds (with the assistance of a couple of cranes) when the 1991 coup collapsed. Now you can see the statue in all its (somewhat reduced) glory in the Sculpture Park (p161), where it stands among others fallen from grace.

The much humbler **Memorial to the Victims of Totalitarianism** (Map pp128–9) stands in the little garden on the square's southeastern side. This single stone slab comes from the territory of an infamous 1930s labour camp on the Solovetsky Islands in the White Sea.

The little **Moscow City History Museum** (Map pp128–9; ☎ 924 8490, 924 8058; Novaya pl 12; admission R50; ☼ 11am-5.30pm Tue-Sun; Ⓜ Lubyanka) shows how the city has spread from its starting point at the Kremlin. Across the street, the huge **Polytechnical Museum** (Map pp128–9; ☎ 923

0756; Novaya pl 3/4; adult/child R175/75; 10am-5pm Mon-Tue & Fri-Sun, 1-9pm Thu; M Lubyanka) covers the history of Russian science, technology and industry.

Kitay-Gorod

The narrow old streets east of Red Square are known as Kitay-Gorod – it translates as 'Chinatown', but this area has nothing to do with China. The name actually derives from *kita*, meaning 'wattle', and refers to the palisades that reinforced the earthen ramp erected around this early Kremlin suburb. Kitay-Gorod is one of the oldest parts of Moscow, settled in the 13th century as a trade and financial centre.

Along Teatralnaya proezd, archaeologists uncovered the 16th-century fortified wall that used to surround Kitay-Gorod, as well as foundations of the 1493 Trinity Church. Coins, jewellery and tombstones were also excavated at the site, called **Starie Polya** (Map pp128-9; M Teatralnaya). Beside the remains of the wall and the church, you can now see the memorial statue of Ivan Fyodorov, the 16th-century printer responsible for Russia's first printed book. The gated walkway of Tretyakovsky proezd leads into Kitay-Gorod.

AROUND NIKOLSKAYA ULITSA

Kitay-Gorod's busiest street was once the main road to Vladimir and used to be the centre of a busy trade in icons. The dilapidated **Church of the Zaikonospassky Monastery** (Map p135; M Ploshchad Revolyutsii), built between 1661 and 1720, stands in the courtyard of No 9. The ornate green-and-white building at No 15 is the old **Printing House** (Map p135; M Ploshchad Revolyutsii). It was here in 1563 that Ivan Fyodorov reputedly produced Russia's first printed book, *The Apostle*. (The first Russian newspaper, *Vedomosti*, was also printed here in 1703.)

The **Monastery of Epiphany** (Map p135; Bogoyavlensky per; M Ploshchad Revolyutsii) is just up the road and around the corner. Its Epiphany Cathedral was constructed in the 1690s, while the monastery itself dates from the 13th century and is the second oldest in Moscow.

AROUND ULITSA VARVARKA

From the 16th century Kitay-Gorod was exclusively the home of merchants and craftsmen, as evidenced by the present-day names of its lanes: Khrustalny (Crystal),

Rybny (Fish) and Vetoshny (Rugs). Along ul Ilinka, a block south, the **old stock exchange** (Map pp128-9; ul Ilinka 2; M Ploshchad Revolyutsii) designates Moscow's financial heart.

Ul Varvarka has Kitay-Gorod's greatest concentration of interesting buildings. They have been long dwarfed by the gargantuan Hotel Rossiya, which is next on the list for demolition. The pink-and-white **St Barbara's Church** (Map pp128-9; M Kitay-Gorod) dates from the years 1795 to 1804 and is now given over to government offices. The reconstructed 16th-century **Old English House** (Map pp128-9; ☎ 298 3952; admission R20; 11am-6pm Tue-Sun), white with peaked wooden roofs, was the residence of England's first emissaries to Russia (sent by Elizabeth I to Ivan the Terrible). It also served as the base for English merchants, who were allowed to trade duty-free in exchange for providing military supplies to Ivan. Ironically, this museum has no signs or descriptions in English.

Built in 1698, **St Maxim the Blessed's Church** (Map pp128-9; ul Varvarka 4) is now a folk-art exhibition hall. Next along is the pointed bell tower of the 17th-century **Monastery of the Sign** (Map pp128-9; ul Varvarka 8), with accompanying **monks' quarters** and a **golden domed cathedral**.

The small, though interesting, **Romanov Chambers in Zaryadiye** (Map pp128-9; ☎ 924 4529; ul Varvarka 10; admission R150; 10am-5pm Thu-Mon, 11am-6pm Wed) is devoted to the lives of the Romanov family, who were mere boyars (nobles) before they became tsars. The house was built by Nikita Romanov, whose grandson Mikhail later became the first tsar of the 300-year Romanov dynasty. Enter from the back.

The colourful **St George's Church** (Map pp128-9; ul Varvarka 12), another crafts gallery, dates from 1658. Opposite St George's Church, Ipatevsky per leads to the 1630s **Church of the Trinity in Nikitniki** (Map pp128–9), one of Moscow's finest (but still undergoing renovation). The church's onion domes and lovely tiers of red-and-white spade gables rise from a square tower, while the interior is covered with 1650s gospel frescoes by Simon Ushakov and others. A carved doorway leads into St Nikita the Martyr's chapel, above the vault of the Nikitnikov merchant family, one of whom built the church.

At the southern end of Staraya pl is **All Saints Cathedral on the Kulishka** (Map pp128–9), built in 1687. In 1380 Dmitry Donskoy built the original wooden church on this site, commemorating those who died in the Battle of Kulikovo.

Hidden among the narrow alleyways of Kitay-Gorod are more tiny churches, and ongoing renovations should produce delightful results over the next few years.

OUTER KITAY-GOROD

Moscow's oldest synagogue, the **Moscow Choral Synagogue** (Map p131; Bolshoy Spasoglinishchevsky per 10; M Kitay-Gorod), was built in 1891 by the businessman Polyakov, who made his fortune in the sugar industry. The interior is exquisite. It was the only synagogue that continued to operate throughout the Soviet period, in spite of Bolshevik demands to convert it into a workers' club.

South of Kursky vokzal (station) is a two-storey house in a small park, which contains the **Andrei Sakharov Museum** (Map p131; ☎ 923 4115; www.wdn.com/asf; Zemlyanoy val 57; admission free; ⊗ 11am-7pm Tue-Sun; M Chkalovskaya). Its displays cover the life of Sakharov, the nuclear-physicist-turned-human-rights-advocate, detailing the years of repression in Russia and providing a history of the dissident movement. Temporary expositions cover current human-rights issues (see the boxed text, below). There are signs in English and audio tours are planned. Watch for a piece of genuine Berlin Wall in front of the building.

Chistye Prudy

This area encompasses the streets off Chistoprudny bul, between uls Myasnitskaya and Pokrovka to the northeast of the Kremlin. Myasnitskaya means 'butchers' and in the late 17th century the area was known

---

CAUTION: CENSORSHIP

In January 2003 Yury Samodurov, director of the Andrei Sakharov Museum in Moscow, premiered a contemporary art exhibit entitled 'Caution: Religion'. The exhibit cast a critical eye on the clash between the nascent Orthodox revival and emerging mass consumer culture in Russia. It depicted, among others, the image of Jesus on a Coke can and the seven deadly sins as committed by an average Russian family in daily life. The theme: despite the sharp rise in citizens who identify themselves as Orthodox Christian, it is the values and identities of mass consumer culture that dominate postcommunist society.

The message elicited a shrill reaction from the Russian Orthodox Church, nationalist politicians and some patriotic hooligans, who were so offended that they vandalised the museum. The uproar attracted the attention of the state prosecutor.

The episode reveals how Russia's long tradition of dissent has evolved in postcommunist times. Throughout the Soviet period, dissent most often took political forms, correcting the lies of the regime and exposing its brutalities. As a prime example, the museum's inspiration and namesake, Andrei Sakharov, spent six years under house arrest in Nizhny Novgorod (see p407) for criticising Soviet policy. When communism collapsed, some wondered if Russia's long tradition of dissent would fade away with the commissars. As evidenced by 'Caution: Religion', dissent in post-Soviet Russia has not disappeared, but it is taking on new, cultural forms.

The case against the heretical artists also shows another side of postcommunist Russia. Under the administration of thin-skinned president Vladimir Putin, free expression has been curtailed, independent media have been intimidated and human-rights advocates silenced. The regime that began the transition espousing liberal political values has come to reflect an embattled Russian nationalism. The charges brought against the museum included inciting ethnic hatred and offending true believers. The prosecutor demanded – in the name of religious sensibility – that the exhibit should be destroyed and museum officials should be punished.

In March 2005 a Moscow court handed down the verdict. Museum director Samodurov and his deputy were found guilty and ordered to pay a fine of R100,000 each. Outside the courthouse, angry Christians were not appeased. 'These kind of people should be beaten in the face', one true believer railed.

Samodurov said that he would appeal the court's finding, taking the case, if necessary, all the way to the European Court of Human Rights in Strasbourg. The communist dictatorship may have fallen, but the ghost of Andrei Sakharov still haunts the Kremlin.

for this profession; logically, its ponds were filthy. Peter the Great gave the area to his pal Alexander Menshikov, who launched a bit of a PR campaign, renaming it Chistye Prudy (Clean Ponds). Apparently, he did actually have them cleaned first. The area boasts the first Moscow post office, founded in 1783 in one of the houses of the former Menshikov estate.

Chistoprudny bul is a pleasant stroll in itself. The pond has paddle boats in summer and an **ice-skating rink** in winter, or you can simply pick a café and (depending on the season) sip a beer or coffee while watching the boats or skaters go by.

Hidden behind the post office is the famous **Menshikov Tower** (Map p131; Krivokolenny per), built from 1704 to 1706 by the order of Menshikov at his newly founded estate. The tower was originally 3m taller than the Ivan the Great Bell Tower in the Kremlin and was one of Moscow's first baroque buildings. In 1723 it was hit by lightning during a thunderstorm and seriously damaged by fire. Today it houses the working **Church of Archangel Gabriel**.

KOMSOMOLSKAYA PLOSHCHAD

From Chistye Prudy, pr Akademika Sakharova leads northeast to Komsomolskaya pl, Moscow's transportation hub. In one square the three main railway stations capture Moscow's architectural diversity, along with diverse and dubious crowds; it's among the city's busiest and hairiest centres.

Leningradsky vokzal (Leningrad Station; Map p131), with its tall clock tower, is on the northern side of the square and is Moscow's oldest railway station (built in 1851).

Yaroslavsky vokzal (Yaroslavl Station; Map p131) – the start of the Trans-Siberian Railway – is a 1902–04 Art Nouveau fantasy by Fyodor Shekhtel.

Kazansky vokzal (Kazan Station; Map p131), on the southern side of the square, was built between 1912 and 1926. It's a retrospective of seven building styles, going back to a 16th-century Tatar tower in Kazan. (The style of its architect, Alexey Shchusev, transformed over the years – his later work includes Lenin's mausoleum.)

The 26-storey 'wedding cake' west of Komsomolskaya pl is **Hotel Leningradskaya** (p174), one of Stalin's 'Seven Sisters'.

Petrovsky District

Now restored to its prerevolutionary fashionable status, ul Petrovka constitutes Moscow's glossiest central shopping area (see p185 for more).

The **Upper St Peter Monastery** (Map pp128-9; cnr ul Petrovka & Petrovsky bul; admission free; 🕑 8am-8pm; Ⓜ Chekhovskaya) was founded in the 1380s as part of an early defensive ring around Moscow. The grounds are pleasant in a peaceful, near-deserted way. The main onion-domed **Virgin of Bogolyubovo Church** dates from the late 17th century. The loveliest structure is the brick **Cathedral of Metropolitan Pyotr** in the middle of the grounds, restored with a shingle roof. (When Peter the Great ousted the Regent Sofia in 1690, his mother was so pleased she built him this church.)

A pet project of the ubiquitous Zurab Tsereteli, the **Museum of Modern Art** (Map pp128-9; ☎ 231 4408; ul Petrovka 25; adult/student R150/75; 🕑 noon-8pm Wed-Fri, to 7pm Sat-Mon; Ⓜ Chekhovskaya) is housed in a classical 18th-century merchant's home. It contains all kinds of 20th-century paintings, sculptures and graphics, including some works by Marc Chagall, Natalia Goncharova, Vasily Kandinsky and Kasimir Malevich. Don't bypass the whimsical sculpture garden in the courtyard.

Just beyond the Garden Ring, the **Museum of Decorative & Folk Art** (Map pp128-9; ☎ 923 7725; Delegatskaya ul 3 & 5; admission R50; 🕑 10am-5pm Sat-Thu; Ⓜ Tsvetnoy Bulvar) has a good two-room *palekh* (painted lacquerwork from the town of the same name) collection, as well as lots of regional folk art.

Tverskoy District

In spite of soulless reconstruction in the 1930s, it's hard to imagine Moscow without Tverskaya ul, the beginning of the road to Tver, and therefore to St Petersburg. The bottom end of the street, near Manezhnaya pl, is the city's hub: numerous places to eat and some of Moscow's classier shops dot the slope up to Pushkinskaya pl. Trolleybuses 12 and 20 go up and down Tverskaya ul as far as Belorussky vokzal (Belarus Station).

The streets around Tverskaya ul comprise the vibrant Tverskoy District, characterised by old architecture and new commerce. Small lanes such as Kamergersky per are among Moscow's trendiest places to sip a coffee or a beer and watch the big-city bustle.

INNER TVERSKAYA ULITSA

Through the arch across the start of Bryusov per is the unexpected little gold-domed **Church of the Resurrection** (Map pp128-9; M Okhotny Ryad). The main building, built in 1629, is full of fine icons saved from churches torn down during the Soviet era; the refectory and bell tower date from 1820.

Tverskaya pl is recognisable by its **statue of Yury Dolgoruky** (Map pp128-9), the man traditionally considered Moscow's founder. The buffed-up five-storey building that faces it is the **Moscow Mayor's Office** (Map pp128-9). Behind the statue to the right is the 17th-century **Church of SS Cosma and Damian** (Map pp128-9).

On the eastern side of Tverskaya ul, shortly before Pushkinskaya pl, is the ornate **Yeliseev Grocery Store** (p180) named after its founding owner, Pyotr Yeliseev, whose bust can be seen in the central hall. Originally a mansion, the shop has been restored to its former splendour with chandeliers, stained glass, and marble columns.

AROUND PUSHKINSKAYA PLOSHCHAD

From the square that bears his name, a **Pushkin statue** (Map pp128-9) surveys his domain. It seems Pushkin has been chosen to take the place of Lenin in the New Russian ideology. Behind the statue, the recently renamed **Pushkinsky Cinema** (Map pp128-9) – formerly the Rossiya – is the main venue of Russian film makers and celebrities; Pushkinskaya metro station is underneath.

Just off Pushkinskaya pl stand the multiple tent roofs of the **Church of the Nativity of the Virgin in Putinki** (Map pp128-9; Malaya Dmitrovka ul 4; M Pushkinskaya), which curiously contributed to a ban on tent roofs on churches by Patriarch Nikon in 1652 (the year this church was completed). Nikon thought them too Russian and secular – too far from the Church's Byzantine roots.

OUTER TVERSKAYA ULITSA

North of Pushkinskaya pl is the **Contemporary History Museum** (Map pp128-9; ☎ 299 6724; www.sovr .ru; Tverskaya ul 21; admission R50; ☼ 10am-6pm Tue-Sun; M Mayakovskaya), which provides an account of Soviet history from the 1905 and 1917 revolutions up to the 1980s. The highlight is the extensive collection of propaganda posters, in addition to all the Bolshevik paraphernalia. Look for the picture of the giant Palace of Soviets (Dvorets Sovietov) that Stalin was going to build on the site of the blown-up – and now rebuilt – Cathedral of Christ the Saviour. English-language tours are available with advance notice.

PATRIARCH'S POND

This peaceful fish pond was immortalised by writer Mikhail Bulgakov, who had the devil appear here in *The Master and Margarita*, one of the most loved 20th-century Russian novels. **Bulgakov's flat** (Map pp128-9; Bolshaya Sadovaya ul 10; M Mayakovskaya), where he wrote the novel and lived up until his death, is around the corner on the Garden Ring. Although the empty flat used to be a hang-out for dissidents and hooligans, it now has tight security appropriate to this high-rent district.

ARMED FORCES MUSEUM

Covering the history of the Soviet and Russian military since 1917, the **Armed Forces Museum** (Map pp128-9; ☎ 681 6303; ul Sovetskoy Armii 2; admission R30, English-language guided tour R650; ☼ 10am-4.30pm Wed-Sun; M Novoslobodskaya) occupies 24 exhibit halls, plus open-air exhibits. It houses more than 800,000 military items, including uniforms, medals and weapons. Among the highlights are remainders of the American U2 spy plane (brought down in the Urals in 1960) and the victory flag raised over Reichstag in 1945. Take trolleybus 69 (or walk) 1.25km west from the Novoslobodskaya metro.

Barrikadnaya

The neighbourhood surrounding the intersection of Bolshaya Nikitskaya ul with the Garden Ring at Kudrinskaya pl is known as Barrikadnaya (Barricade), so-called because it saw heavy street fighting during the 1905 and 1917 uprisings.

The skyscraper at this intersection is one of the Stalinist 'Seven Sisters' neo-Gothic monstrosities.

AROUND KUDRINSKAYA PLOSHCHAD

'The colour of the house is liberal, ie red', Anton Chekhov wrote of the house on the Garden Ring, where he lived from 1886 to 1890. Appropriately, the house now contains the **Chekhov House-Museum** (Map pp128-9; ☎ 291 6154; ul Sadovaya-Kudrinskaya 6; admission R30; ☼ 11am-5pm Tue-Sun; M Barrikadnaya), with bedrooms, drawing room and study intact. One room is dedicated to Chekhov's time in Melikhovo (p198), showing photographs and manuscripts from his country estate.

Behind Kudrinskaya pl is the main entrance to the big **Moscow Zoo** (Map pp128-9; ☎ 255 6367; www.zoo.ru/moscow; cnr Barrikadnaya & Bolshaya Gruzinskaya uls; admission R80; ☒ 10am-8pm Tue-Sun May-Sep, 10am-5pm Tue-Sun Oct-Apr; Ⓜ Barrikadnaya). Popular with families, the highlight is the big cats exhibit, although the domestic animals and the kids are fun to watch too.

BOLSHAYA NIKITSKAYA ULITSA
Bolshaya Nikitskaya ul runs from the Moscow State University building, on Mokhovaya ul, to the Garden Ring. In the back streets many old mansions have survived – some renovated, some dilapidated. Most of those inside the Boulevard Ring were built by the 18th-century aristocracy; those outside by rising 19th-century industrialists. With little traffic, Bolshaya Nikitskaya ul is excellent for a quiet ramble.

On an even quieter side street, the **Matryoshka Museum** (Map pp128-9; ☎ 291 9645; Leontevsky per 7; admission free; ☒ 10am-6pm Mon-Thu, to 5pm Fri; Ⓜ Pushkinskaya) is a two-room museum showcasing designer *matryoshka* (nesting dolls) and different painting techniques. The exhibit demonstrates the history of this favourite Russian souvenir.

Pl Nikitskie Vorota, where Bolshaya Nikitskaya ul crosses the Boulevard Ring, is named after the Nikitsky Gates in the city walls, which the ring has replaced. In 1831 the poet Alexander Pushkin married Natalya Goncharova in the **Church of the Grand Ascension** (Map pp128-9; Ⓜ Arbatskaya) on the western side of pl Nikitskie Vorota. Six years later, he died in St Petersburg defending her honour in a duel; the **Rotunda Fountain** (Map pp128–9), erected in 1999 to commemorate the 200th anniversary of the poet's birthday, features the couple.

Immediately north of the church is the fascinating 1906 Art Nouveau **Gorky House-Museum** (Map pp128-9; ☎ 290 5130; Malaya Nikitskaya ul 6/2; admission free, photography permit R100; ☒ 11am-6pm Wed-Sun; Ⓜ Pushkinskaya), designed by Fyodor Shekhtel. Gifted to Gorky in 1931, the house is a visual fantasy with sculpted doorways, ceiling murals, stained glass, a carved stone staircase, and exterior tile work. Besides the fantastic décor, it contains many of Gorky's personal items, including his extensive library.

Converted to a theatre in the 1930s, the **Lyubavicheskaya Synagogue** (Map pp128-9; Bolshaya Bronnaya ul 6; Ⓜ Pushkinskaya) was still used for gatherings by the Jewish community throughout the Soviet period. The rug on the altar hides a trapdoor leading to a small cell where Jews used to hide from the communists.

WHITE HOUSE
The Russian **White House** (Map pp128-9; Krasnopresnenskaya nab 2; Ⓜ Barrikadnaya), scene of two crucial episodes in recent Russian history, stands just north of Novoarbatskaya most (still commonly known by its former name, Kalininsky most), a short walk west of the US embassy. It was here that Boris Yeltsin rallied the opposition to confound the 1991 hardline coup, then two years later sent in tanks and troops to blast out conservative rivals – some of them the same people who backed him in 1991. The images of Yeltsin climbing onto a tank in front of the White House in 1991 and of the same building ablaze after the 1993 assault are among the most unforgettable from those tumultuous years.

The White House – officially called the House of Government of the Russian Federation – fronts one of the Moscow River's stateliest bends, with the Stalinist Hotel Ukraina rising on the far bank. This corner of Moscow is particularly appealing at night when these buildings and Kalininsky most are lit up at night.

Arbat District
Bound by the Moscow River on both sides, this district includes the area south of ul Novy Arbat and north of the Garden Ring.

ULITSA ARBAT
Ul Arbat is a 1.25km pedestrian mall stretching from Arbatskaya pl on the Boulevard Ring to Smolenskaya pl on the Garden Ring. Moscow's most famous street, it's something of an art market, complete with instant portrait painters, soapbox poets, jugglers and buskers (as well as some pickpockets). The Arbat is an interesting walk, dotted with old pastel-coloured merchant houses and tourist-oriented shops and cafés.

Until the 1960s ul Arbat was Moscow's main westward artery. Then a swath was bulldozed through streets to its north to create the present ul Novy Arbat, taking out the old Arbatskaya pl, a monastery and half-a-dozen churches. Ul Arbat itself lay like a severed limb, until restored as a pedestrian precinct in the 1980s.

The evocative names of nearby lanes – Khlebny (Bread), Skatertny (Tablecloth), Serebryany (Silver), Plotnikov (Carpenters) – and that of the peaceful quarter south of the Arbat, called Staraya Konyushennaya (Old Stables), identify the area as an old settlement of court attendants (who were eventually displaced by artists and aristocrats).

Near ul Arbat's east end, the **Wall of Peace** (Map pp128-9; M Arbatskaya) is composed of hundreds of individually painted tiles on a theme of international friendship. Spasopeskovsky per, a side lanes, is home to the 17th-century **Church of the Saviour in Peski** (Map pp128-9) and the elegant **Spaso House** (Map pp128-9), residence of the US ambassador.

In a side street stands the refreshingly bizarre **Melnikov House** (Map pp132-3; Krivoarbatsky per 10; M Smolenskaya). This concoction of brick, plaster and diamond-shaped windows was built in 1927 by Konstantin Melnikov, the great constructivist architect who was denounced in the 1930s. Melnikov continued to live in the house, one of the few privately owned homes in the USSR, until his death in 1974.

The statue at the corner of Plotnikov per is of **Bulat Okudzhava** (Map pp132-3), a 1960s cult poet, singer and songwriter, much of whose work was dedicated to the Arbat (he lived at No 43; see the boxed text, below).

At the western end of the street is the **Pushkin Arbat House-Museum** (Map pp132-3; ☎ 241 4212; ul Arbat 53; admission R40; ✆ 10am-5pm Wed-Sun), a house where the Pushkins lived after they married. The museum provides some insight into the couple's home life.

NOVY ARBAT

The start of the road west to Smolensk is formed by ul Vozdvizhenka (running west from the Kremlin) and ul Novy Arbat (the continuation to the Moscow River).

The 'Moorish Castle', studded with seashells, was built in 1899 for Arseny Morozov, an eccentric merchant who was inspired by the real thing in Spain; the inside is sumptuous and equally over the top. Morozov's home is now the **House of Friendship with Peoples of Foreign Countries** (Map pp128-9; ul Vozdvizhenka 16; M Arbatskaya), which is not normally open to the public, although exhibitions are sometimes held here. The 'castle' apparently inspired Morozov's mother to

---

ARBAT, MY ARBAT

Arbat, my Arbat, You are my calling
You are my happiness and my misfortune.

Bulat Okudzhava

For Moscow's beloved bard Bulat Okudzhava, the Arbat was not only his home, it was his inspiration. Although he spent his university years in Georgia dabbling in harmless verse, it was only upon his return to Moscow – and to his cherished Arbat – that his poetry adopted the freethinking character for which it is known.

He gradually made the transition from poet to songwriter, stating that, 'Once I had the desire to accompany one of my satirical verses with music. I only knew three chords; now, 27 years later, I know seven chords, then I knew three.' While Bulat and his friends enjoyed his songs, other composers, singers and guitarists did not. The ill-feeling subsided when a well-known poet announced that '...these are not songs. This is just another way of presenting poetry.'

And so a new form of art was born. The 1960s were heady times – in Moscow as elsewhere – and Okudzhava inspired a whole movement of liberal-thinking poets to take their ideas to the streets. Vladimir Vysotsky and others – some political, some not – followed in Okudzhava's footsteps, their iconoclastic lyrics and simple melodies drawing enthusiastic crowds all around Moscow.

The Arbat today – crowded with tacky souvenir stands and overpriced cafés – bears little resemblance to the hallowed haunt of Okudzhava's youth. But its memory lives on in the bards and buskers, painters and poets who still perform for strolling crowds on summer evenings.

declare: 'Until now, only I knew you were mad; now everyone will'.

Kropotkinskaya

The Kropotkinskaya district borders the Arbat district in the north, roughly at per Sivtsev Vrazhek. It is bounded more definitively in the west by the Garden Ring and in the south by the Moscow River.

PUSHKIN FINE ARTS MUSEUM

Moscow's premier foreign-art museum is the **Pushkin Fine Arts Museum** (Map pp132-3; ☎ 203 7998; www.museum.ru/gmii; ul Volkhonka 12; adult/student R300/150, audio tour R250; ☻ 10am-6pm Tue-Sun; Ⓜ Kropotkinskaya). It is famous for its impressionist and postimpressionist paintings, but also has a broad selection of European works from the Renaissance onwards, mostly appropriated from private collections after the revolution. There is also an amazing (read: mind-numbing) array of statues through the ages.

Keep an eye open for any special exhibitions at the Pushkin. In recent years – as with the Hermitage in St Petersburg – it has revealed some fabulous art hoards that have been kept secret since their seizure from Germany by the Red Army at the end of WWII. The museum is also making an effort to mount some ambitious temporary exhibitions from its vast legitimate holdings.

The highlight of the Pushkin's permanent display is the four incredible rooms of impressionist and postimpressionist paintings and sculpture. But don't neglect the 17th-century Dutch and Flemish paintings, including several Rembrandt portraits. The excellent ancient Egyptian collection includes weapons, jewellery, ritual items and tombstones, as well as two haunting mummies that were excavated from burial sites.

Next door to the Pushkin, the **Museum of Private Collections** (Map pp132-3; ☎ 203 1546; ul Volkhonka 14; admission R40; ☻ noon-7pm Wed-Sun; Ⓜ Kropotkinskaya) shows off art collections donated by private individuals, many of whom amassed the works during the Soviet era. The collectors/donors are featured along with the art.

The elaborate empire-style mansion opposite the Pushkin Fine Arts Museum houses the **Glazunov Gallery** (Map pp132-3; ☎ 291 6949; ul Volkhonka 13; adult/student R150/100; ☻ 11am-6pm Tue-Sun; Ⓜ Kropotkinskaya), a new gallery dedicated to the work of Soviet and post-Soviet artist Ilya Glazunov. The interior is impressive: three floors filled with fanciful illustrations of historic events and biblical scenes. Glazunov is famous for huge, colourful paintings that depict hundreds of people and places and events from Russian history in one monumental scene. His most famous work is *Eternal Russia* (Bechnaya Rossiya).

CATHEDRAL OF CHRIST THE SAVIOUR

Now dominating the skyline along the Moscow River, the gargantuan **Cathedral of Christ the Saviour** (Map pp132-3; ☎ 201 2847; www.xxc.ru; admission free; ☻ 10am-5pm; Ⓜ Kropotkinskaya) sits on the site of an earlier and similar church of the same name. The original church was built from 1839 to 1883 to commemorate Russia's victory over Napoleon, but it was destroyed during Stalin's orgy of explosive secularism. Stalin planned to replace the church with a 315m-high 'Palace of Soviets' (including a 100m statue of Lenin) but the project never got off the ground – literally. Instead, for 50 years the site served an important purpose: as the world's largest swimming pool.

This time around, the church was completed in a mere two years, in time for Moscow's 850th birthday in 1997, and at an estimated cost of US$350 million. Much of the work was done by Luzhkov's favourite architect Zurab Tsereteli, and it has aroused a range of reactions from Muscovites, from pious devotion to abject horror. Muscovites should at least be grateful they can admire the shiny domes of a church instead of the shiny dome of Lenin's head.

ULITSA PRECHISTENKA

Heading southwest from Kropotkinskaya metro, ul Prechistenka is virtually a classical mansion museum; most date from empire-style rebuilding after the great fire of 1812.

The **Pushkin Literary Museum** (Map pp132-3; ☎ 202 8531; ul Prechistenka 12; admission R40; ☻ 10am-5.30pm Tue-Sun; Ⓜ Kropotkinskaya) is one of the most beautiful examples of the Moscow empire architectural style; the exhibit inside is devoted to Pushkin's life and work. In another mansion across the street, the **Tolstoy Museum** (Map pp132-3; ☎ 202 2190; www.tolstoymuseum.ru; ul Prechistenka 11; adult/student R100/50; ☻ 11am-6pm Tue-Sun; Ⓜ Kropotkinskaya) contains Leo Tolstoy's manuscripts, letters

---

LEAVING A MARK ON MOSCOW

Zurab Tsereteli is nothing if not controversial. As the chief architect of the Okhotny Ryad shopping mall and the massive Cathedral of Christ the Saviour, he has been criticised for being too ostentatious, too gaudy, too overbearing and just plain too much.

The most despised of Tsereteli's masterpieces is the gargantuan statue of Peter the Great, which now stands in front of the Krasny Oktyabr chocolate factory. At 94.5m (that's twice the size of the *Statue of Liberty* without her pedestal), Peter towers over the city. Questions of taste aside, Muscovites were sceptical about the whole idea: why pay tribute to Peter the Great, who loathed Moscow, and even moved the capital to St Petersburg? Some radicals attempted – unsuccessfully, however – to blow the thing up. Today a 24-hour guard stands watch.

Mixed reactions are nothing new to Zurab Tsereteli. An earlier sculpture of Christopher Columbus has been rejected by five North American cities for reasons of cost, size and aesthetics. Some believe that the Peter the Great statue is actually a reincarnation of homeless Chris. Despite his critics, who launched a 'Stop Tsereteli' website, this favourite artist of Moscow Mayor Yury Luzhkov does not stop. He launched the Moscow Museum of Modern Art and took over the Russian Academy of Art. He recently opened the aptly named Tsereteli Gallery, which houses room after room of the artist's primitive paintings and elaborate sculptures.

Rumour has it that Tsereteli's next project is a theme park in a northwest Moscow suburb. Apparently, a 350-hectare plot has already been designated for the so-called 'Park of Wonders', which will be based on Russian fairy tales. As one Moscow journalist observed, 'For the sake of the children, let's hope Tsereteli's fairy tale heroes are not as scary as his Peter the Great'.

---

and sketches. These museums focus on literary influences and output, as opposed to the authors' personal lives, which are on display at the house-museums (see p156 and below, respectively).

The latest endeavour of the tireless Zurab Tsereteli is the aptly named **Tsereteli Gallery** (Map pp132-3; ☎ 201 4150; ul Prechistenka 19; admission R150; ☾ noon-6pm Tue-Sun; Ⓜ Kropotkinskaya), housed in the 18th-century Dolgoruky mansion. The **Russian Academy of Art** (Map pp132-3; ☎ 201 4150; ul Prechistenka 21; admission R40; ☾ noon-6pm Tue-Sun; Ⓜ Kropotkinskaya) holds rotating exhibits next door.

Khamovniki

The Moscow River surrounds this district on three sides, as it dips down south and loops back up to the north. The northern boundary is the Garden Ring. At its intersection with ul Prechistenka, a brooding Tolstoy statue sits in the park called Maiden's Field (Skver Devichego Polya).

TOLSTOY ESTATE-MUSEUM

Leo Tolstoy's winter home during the 1880s and 1890s now houses the interesting **Tolstoy Estate-Museum** (Map pp132-3; ☎ 246 9444; www.tolstoymuseum.ru; ul Lva Tolstogo 21; adult/student R100/30; ☾ 10am-5pm Wed-Sun; Ⓜ Park Kultury). While it's not particularly big or opulent,

it is fitting for junior nobility – which Tolstoy was. Exhibits demonstrate how Tolstoy lived, as opposed to his literary influences, which are explored at the Tolstoy Museum (p157). See the salon where Sergei Rachmaninov and Nikolai Rimsky-Korsakov played piano, and the study where Tolstoy himself wove his epic tales.

At the south end of ul Lva Tolstogo, the beautiful **Church of St Nicholas of the Weavers** (Map pp132–3) vies with St Basil's Cathedral as the most colourful in Moscow. It was commissioned by the Moscow weavers' guild in 1676, which explains the name.

NOVODEVICHY CONVENT & CEMETERY

A cluster of sparkling domes behind turreted walls on the Moscow River, **Novodevichy Convent** (Map pp132-3; ☎ 246 8526; adult/student R150/75, photography permit R60; ☾ grounds 8am-8pm daily, museums 10am-5pm Wed-Mon; Ⓜ Sportivnaya) is rich with history and treasures.

The convent was founded in 1524 to celebrate the taking of Smolensk from Lithuania, an important step in Moscow's conquest of the old Kyivan Rus lands. Novodevichy was later rebuilt by Peter the Great's half-sister Sofia, who used it as a second residence when she ruled Russia as regent in the 1680s.

When Peter was 17, he deposed Sofia and confined her to Novodevichy; in 1698 she was imprisoned here for life after being implicated in the Streltsy rebellion. (Legend has it that Peter had some of her supporters hanged outside her window to remind her not to meddle.) Sofia was joined in her retirement by Yevdokia Lopukhina, Peter's first wife, whom he considered a nag.

Enter the convent through the red-and-white Moscow-baroque **Transfiguration Gate-Church**, built in the north wall between 1687 and 1689. The first building on the left contains a room for temporary exhibitions. Yevdokia Lopukhina lived in the **Lopukhin Building** against the north wall, while Sofia probably lived in the chambers adjoining the **Pond Tower**.

The oldest and most dominant building in the grounds is the white **Smolensk Cathedral**, modelled from 1524 to 1525 on the Assumption Cathedral in the Kremlin. It was unfortunately closed at the time of research, but the sumptuous interior is covered in 16th-century frescoes. The huge iconostasis – donated by Sofia – has icons from the time of Boris Godunov. The **tombs** of Sofia, a couple of her sisters and Yevdokia Lopukhina are in the south nave.

The **bell tower**, against the convent's east wall, was completed in 1690 and is generally regarded as the finest in Moscow. Other churches on the grounds include the red-and-white **Assumption Church** (1685 to 1687), and the 16th-century **St Ambrose's Church**.

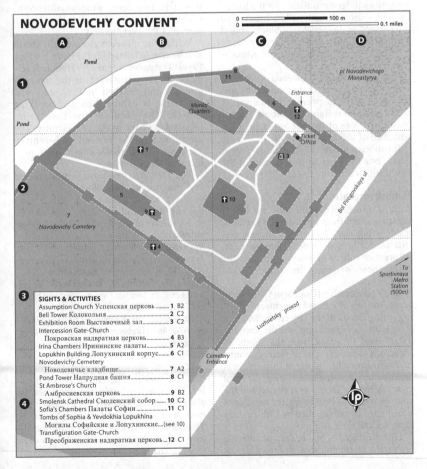

NOVODEVICHY CONVENT

0 —————— 100 m
0 —————————— 0.1 miles

MOSCOW

Boris Godunov's sister Irina lived in the building adjoining the latter church. Today, **Irina's Chambers** hold a permanent exhibit of 16th- and 17th-century religious artwork such as icons and embroidery.

Adjacent to the convent, **Novodevichy Cemetery** (Map pp132–3; admission R30; Ⓨ 9am-6pm; Ⓜ Sportivnaya) is among Moscow's most prestigious resting places – a veritable 'who's who' of Russian politics and culture. You will find the tombs of Chekhov, Nikolai Gogol, Vladimir Mayakovsky, Konstantin Stanislavsky, Sergei Prokofiev, Sergei Eisenstein, Andrei Gromyko, and many other Russian and Soviet notables.

In Soviet times Novodevichy Cemetery was used for eminent people, whom the authorities judged unsuitable for the Kremlin wall – most notably, Khrushchev. The intertwined white-and-black blocks round Khrushchev's bust were intended by sculptor Ernst Neizvestny to represent Khrushchev's good and bad sides.

The tombstone of Nadezhda Alliluyeva, Stalin's second wife, is surrounded by unbreakable glass to prevent vandalism. A recent addition is Raisa Gorbachev, the sophisticated wife of the last Soviet premier, who died of leukaemia in 1999.

If you want to investigate the cemetery in depth, buy the Russian map on sale at the kiosk, which pinpoints nearly 200 graves.

Zamoskvorechie

Zamoskvorechie (Beyond Moscow River) stretches south from opposite the Kremlin, inside a big river loop. This ancient district boasts Moscow's most famous park, its premier gallery of Russian art, and the current headquarters of the Russian Orthodox Church.

The Vodootvodny (Drainage) Canal slices across the top of Zamoskvorechie, preventing spring floods in the city centre and creating a sliver of island opposite the Kremlin. Tatars used to attack from the south, so Moscow's defensive forces were stationed in Zamoskvorechie, along with merchants and quarters devoted to servicing the royal court. After the Tatar threat abated and the court moved to St Petersburg, the merchants were joined by nobles, then by 19th-century factories and their workers.

Little damaged by Stalin, Zamoskvorechie is a varied, intriguing area, and from almost any place here you can see the giant **statue of Peter the Great** (Map pp132–3).

TRETYAKOV GALLERY

Nothing short of spectacular, the **State Tretyakov Gallery** (Map pp132-3; ☎ 951 1362, 953 5223; www .tretyakov.ru; Lavrushinsky per 10; adult/student R225/130, audio tour R120; Ⓨ 10am-6pm Tue-Sun; Ⓜ Tretyakovskaya) holds the world's best collection of Russian icons, as well as an outstanding collection of other prerevolutionary Russian art, particularly from the 18th-century Peredvizhniki (p96).

The original part of the Tretyakov building is a likeness of an old boyar castle, and was created by Viktor Vasnetsov between 1900 and 1905. The collection is based on that of the 19th-century industrialist brothers Pavel and Sergei Tretyakov (Pavel was a patron of the Peredvizhniki).

Within the museum grounds, the **Church of St Nicholas in Tolmachi** is the church where Pavel Tretyakov regularly attended services. It was transferred to the museum grounds and restored in 1997, and now functions as exhibit hall and working church. The exquisite five-tiered icon ostasis dates back to the 17th century. The centrepiece is the revered 12th-century *Vladimir Icon of the Mother of God*, protector of all of Russia.

The Tretyakov's 62 rooms are numbered and progress in chronological order from rooms 1 to 54, followed by eight rooms holding icons and jewellery. In rooms 20 to 30, the art of the most prominent **Peredvizhniki** occupies its own rooms. Look for **Ilya Repin**'s realist work, including the tragic *Ivan the Terrible and his son Ivan*, in rooms 29 to 30. A selection of **Isaac Levitan**'s landscapes are in room 37. **Mikhail Vrubel**'s masterpieces, including *Demon Seated* (1890), are in rooms 32 and 33.

Icons reside on the ground floor in rooms 56 to 62. **Andrei Rublyov**'s *Holy Trinity* (1420s) from Sergiev Posad, widely regarded as Russia's greatest icon, is in room 60.

It's worth showing up early in order to beat the queues. The entrance to the gallery is through a lovely courtyard; the **Engineer's Building** (Map pp132-3; Lavrushinsky per 12) next door is reserved for special exhibits. Thanks to a lavish renovation during the early 1990s, the entire gallery is accessible to wheelchairs.

GORKY PARK

Part ornamental park, part funfair, Gorky Park is one of Moscow's most festive places to escape the hubbub of the city. Officially the **Park of Culture** (Map pp132-3; ☎ 237 1266; ul Krymsky val; adult/child R50/15; ☼ 10am-10pm; Ⓜ Park Kultury), it's named after Maxim Gorky, and stretches almost 3km along the river upstream of Krymsky most. You can't miss the showy entrance, marked by colourful flags waving in the wind and the happy sounds of an old-fashioned carousel.

Gorky Park has a small Western-style amusement park with two roller coasters and almost a dozen other terror-inducing attractions (aside from the Peter the Great statue). Space buffs can shed a tear for the *Buran*, a Soviet space shuttle that never carried anyone into space. Most of the rides cost R30 to R60.

In winter the ponds are flooded for ice skating on and tracks are made for cross-country skiing. Skis and skates are available for rental for R50 and R80 per hour, respectively.

NEW TRETYAKOV

The premier venue for 20th-century Russian art is the State Tretyakov Gallery on ul Krymsky val, better known as the **New Tretyakov** (Map pp132-3; ☎ 238 1378; adult/student R225/130; ☼ 10am-6.30pm Tue-Sun; Ⓜ Park Kultury). This place has much more than the typical socialist realist images of muscle-bound men wielding scythes and of busty women milking cows (although there's that too). The exhibits showcase avant-garde artists like Malevich, Kandinsky, Chagall, Goncharova and Lyubov Popova.

In the same building as the New Tretyakov, the **Central House of Artists** (☎ 238 9634; adult/student R50/20; ☼ 11am-7pm Tue-Sun; Ⓜ Park Kultury) is a huge exhibit space used for contemporary art shows.

Behind the complex is a wonderful, moody **Sculpture Park** (Map pp132-3; ☎ 290 0667; ul Krymsky val 10; admission R50; ☼ 9am-9pm; Ⓜ Park Kultury). Formerly called the Park of the Fallen Heroes, it started as a collection of Soviet statues (Stalin, Dzerzhinsky, a selection of Lenins and Brezhnevs) put out to pasture when they were ripped from their pedestals in the post-1991 wave of anti-Soviet feeling. These discredited icons have now been joined by contemporary work, including an eerie bust of Stalin surrounded by heads representing millions of purge victims.

ULITSA BOLSHAYA ORDYNKA & PYATNITSKAYA ULITSA

The atmosphere of 19th-century Moscow lives on in the low buildings, crumbling courtyards and clusters of onion domes along narrow ul Bolshaya Ordynka, which runs 2km down the middle of Zamoskvorechie to Serpukhovskaya pl. Pyatnitskaya ul is roughly parallel, 200m to the east. The many churches here make up a scrapbook of Muscovite architectural styles. The name 'Ordynka' comes from *orda* (horde); until the 16th century, this was the start of the road to the Golden Horde's capital on the Volga, where Tatar ambassadors lived.

If you head south from Maly Moskvoretsky most, the first lane on the right contains the tall **Resurrection Church in Kadashi** (Map pp132-3; Ⓜ Tretyakovskaya), a restoration centre for other churches. Its rich, late-17th-century decoration is a fine example of 'Moscow baroque'. The tall and elegant belfry earned the nickname 'the candle'.

The small, white **SS Mikhail & Fyodor Church** (Map pp132-3; Chernigovsky per; Ⓜ Tretyakovskaya), dating from the late 17th century, has two rows of spade gables and five domes on a thin tower. The larger **St John the Baptist Church** (Map pp132-3), from the same period, has a landmark bell tower that was added in 1753.

The empire-style **Virgin of Consolation of All Sorrows Church** (Map pp132-3; ul Bolshaya Ordynka 20; Ⓜ Tretyakovskaya) dates from the 1830s. Klimentovsky per leads to **St Clement's Church** (Map pp132-3; Pyatnitskaya ul 26; Ⓜ Tretyakovskaya), built between 1742 and 1774, and a rare Moscow example of the true baroque style favoured by Empress Elizabeth.

The blue-and-white **Church of St Nicholas in Pyzhi** (Map pp132-3; ul Bolshaya Ordynka 27A; Ⓜ Tretyakovskaya), a working church, is a typical five-domed, mid-17th-century church, with spade gables and thin onion domes. **SS Martha & Mary Convent** (Map pp132-3; ul Bolshaya Ordynka 34A; Ⓜ Tretyakovskaya), with its pretty, single-domed Intercession Church, now houses church restoration offices. The church and gates were built between 1908 and 1912 in neo-Russian style. The church is open only for services, but the interior frescoes are worth a visit.

DANILOVSKY MONASTERY

The headquarters of the Russian Orthodox Church stand behind white fortress walls. The **Danilovsky Monastery** (Map pp126-7; ☎ 955 6757; Danilovsky val; admission free; ⏰ 7am-7pm; Ⓜ Tulskaya) was built in the late 13th century by Daniil, the first Prince of Moscow, as an outer city defence. It was repeatedly altered over the next several hundred years, and served as a factory and a detention centre during the Soviet period.

However, it was restored in time to replace Sergiev Posad as the Church's spiritual and administrative centre and to become the official residence of the patriarch during the millennial celebrations of Russian Orthodoxy in 1988. Today it radiates an air of purpose befitting the Church's role in modern Russia.

On holy days in particular, the place fills with worshippers murmuring prayers, lighting candles and ladling holy water into jugs at the tiny chapel inside the gates. Enter beneath the pink **St Simeon Stylites Gate-Church** on the north wall. Its bells are the first in Moscow to ring on holy days.

The monastery's oldest and busiest church is the **Church of the Holy Fathers of the Seven Ecumenical Councils**, where worship is held continuously from 10am to 5pm daily. Founded in the 17th century and rebuilt repeatedly, the church contains several chapels on two floors: the main one upstairs is flanked by side chapels to St Daniil (on the northern side) and SS Boris and Gleb (south). On ground level the small main chapel is dedicated to the Protecting Veil, the northern one to the prophet Daniil.

The yellow, neoclassical **Trinity Cathedral**, built in the 1830s, is an austere counterpart to the other buildings.

DONSKOY MONASTERY

Founded in 1591, the **Donskoy Monastery** (Map pp126-7; ☎ 952 1646; Donskaya ul; Ⓜ Shabolovskaya) is the youngest of Moscow's fortified monasteries. It was built to house the *Virgin of the Don* icon (now in the Tretyakov Gallery), which was credited with bringing victory in the 1380 Battle of Kulikovo (see p121). It's also said that in 1591 the Tatar Khan Giri retreated without a fight after the icon showered him with burning arrows in a dream.

Most of the monastery, surrounded by a brick wall with 12 towers, was built between 1684 and 1733 under Regent Sofia and Peter the Great. From 1918 to 1927 it was the Russian Orthodox Church headquarters; later, it was closed as a monastery, falling into neglect despite being used as an architecture museum. Restored in 1990 and 1991, it's now back in Church hands.

The **Virgin of Tikhvin Church** over the north gate, built in 1713 and 1714, is one of the last examples of Moscow baroque. In the centre of the grounds is the large, brick **New Cathedral**, built between 1684 and 1693; just to its south is the smaller **Old Cathedral**, dating from 1591 to 1593.

When burials in central Moscow were banned after a 1771 plague, the Donskoy Monastery became a graveyard for the nobility, and it is littered with elaborate tombs and chapels.

Zayauzie

Taganskaya pl on the Garden Ring is a monster intersection – loud, dusty and crowded. It's the hub of Zayauzie, the area south of the little Yauza River, and the territory of the 17th-century blacksmiths' guild; later it became an Old Believers' quarter. The square's character disappeared with reconstruction in the 1970s and 1980s, but traces remain in the streets radiating from it. This whole neighbourhood has a look of abandoned grace.

TAGANSKAYA PLOSHCHAD

The great block that dominates Taganskaya pl is the **Taganka Theatre** (Map p134; cnr Taganskaya pl & Verkhnyaya Radishchevskaya ul; Ⓜ Taganskaya), famous in the Soviet era for director Yury Lyubimov's vaguely subversive repertoire; see p183 for ticket information.

Behind metro Taganskaya is the sombre **Taganka Gates Church of St Nicholas** (Map p134), from 1712. More fetching is the **Potters' Church of the Assumption** (Map p134; ul Goncharnaya 29; Ⓜ Taganskaya), built in 1654, with its star-spangled domes and impressive tile work.

Ul Goncharnaya leads north to the **Church of St Nikita Beyond the Yauza** (Map p134), which has 15th-century foundations, 16th-century walls, 17th-century chapels and an 18th-century bell tower. The church is dwarfed by the Kotelnicheskaya apartment block, one of the Stalinist Gothic 'Seven Sisters' skyscrapers built around 1950.

Northeast of Taganskaya, you can't miss the grand **Cathedral of St Martin the Confessor**

(Map p134; Bolshaya Kommunisticheskaya ul 15; Ⓜ Tagan-skaya), built in 1792.

ANDRONIKOV MONASTERY

On the grounds of the former Andronikov Monastery, the **Andrei Rublyov Museum of Early Russian Culture & Art** (Map p134; ☎ 278 1467; Andronevskaya pl 10; adult/student R85/40; ✆ 11am-6pm Thu-Tue; Ⓜ Ploshchad Ilicha) exhibits icons from the days of yore and from the present. Unfortunately, the museum does not include any work by its namesake artist.

It is still worthwhile, not the least for its romantic location. Andrei Rublyov, the master of icon painting, was a monk here in the 15th century; he's buried in the grounds, but no-one knows quite where.

In the centre of the grounds is the compact **Saviour's Cathedral**, built in 1427, the oldest stone building in Moscow. The posy of *kokoshniki* (colourful tiles and brick patterns) is typical of Russian architecture from the era. To the left is the combined rectory

and 17th-century Moscow-baroque **Church of the Archangel Michael**. To the right, the old monks' quarters house the museum.

NOVOSPASSKY MONASTERY

Another 15th-century fort-monastery is 1km south of Taganskaya pl – the **New Monastery of the Saviour** (Map p134; ☎ 276 9570; Verkhny Novospassky proezd; admission free; ✆ 7am-7pm Mon-Sat, 8am-7pm Sun; Ⓜ Proletarskaya).

The centrepiece, the **Transfiguration Cathedral**, was built by the imperial Romanov family in the 1640s in imitation of the Kremlin's Assumption Cathedral. Frescoes depict the history of Christianity in Russia; the Romanov family tree, which goes as far back as the Viking Prince Rurik, climbs one wall. The other church is the 1675 **Intercession Church**. Under the river bank, beneath one of the monastery towers, is the site of a mass grave for thousands of Stalin's victims.

Across the road, south of Novospassky, is the sumptuous **Krutitskoe Podvorye** (Ecclesi-

---

SPACE TOURISM RUSSIAN STYLE

Ever fancied flying into space, or at twice the speed of sound? In Russia, it can be arranged – at a price. In April 2001 American billionaire Dennis Tito made history as the first paying customer of the Russian Space Agency, forking out a cool US$20 million to pay a week-long visit to the International Space Station. In April 2002 another millionaire, South African Mark Shuttleworth, followed in Titos' space boots.

Not everyone has US$20 million to spare, so the Russian aerospace company Sub-Orbital Corporation is working together with the US-based Space Adventures (which arranged the Tito and Shuttleworth jaunts) on its C-21 shuttle, designed to take one pilot and two passengers on hour-long return trips into space. For around US$100,000 passengers will zoom 100km from earth, leaving the atmosphere for about five minutes and experiencing weightlessness and the blackness of space. The companies hope to have flights scheduled by 2008.

If you can't wait that long for a space flight, Space Adventures can arrange (for US$18,995) for you to copilot a MiG-25 'Foxbat', a fighter jet that can fly at over 3000km/h (more than twice the speed of sound) to an altitude of 24,000m (the outer limit of the atmosphere, from where you can see the earth's curve). The flights take off from the formerly top-secret Zhukovsky Air Base, an hour's drive southeast of Moscow. Zhukovsky, the testing ground for Russia's newest aircraft, is home to the Gromov Flight Research Institute, one of Russia's largest centres for aviation science research and testing.

For your money you get four nights at a top Moscow hotel (including breakfast), transfers between airport, hotel and Zhukovsky Air Base, an English-speaking guide, a flight suit, a DVD with photo and ground video coverage of the flight, preflight instructions, training and a medical check. If you can't quite afford the MiG-25 experience, Space Adventures offers a range of flight programmes (including one to experience zero gravity) in other military aircraft. The cheapest is US$6995 to experience weightlessness. This package also includes three nights in Moscow, transfers, an English-speaking guide, a flight suit, tour of historic Star City where Yury Gagarin trained, a DVD with photo and video coverage of the flight, and lunch with a Russian cosmonaut. For full details contact **Space Adventures** (☎ 888-85-SPACE in USA, ☎ 703-524-7172 outside USA; www.spaceadventures.com; 4350 Fairfax Dr, Arlington, Virginia 22203).

astic Residence; Map p134; 10am-6pm Wed-Mon). It was the residence of the Moscow metropolitans from the 16th century, when they lost their place in the Kremlin as a result of the founding of the Russian patriarchate. At the northern end of the grounds are the brick **Assumption Cathedral** and an extraordinary Moscow-baroque **gate tower**.

OLD BELIEVERS' COMMUNITY

One of Russia's most atmospheric religious centres is the **Old Believers' Community** (Staroobryadcheskaya Obshchina; admission free; 9am-6pm Tue-Sun), located at Rogozhskoe cemetery, 3km east of Taganskaya pl. Old Believers split from the main Russian Orthodox Church in 1653 when they refused to accept certain reforms. They have maintained old forms of worship and customs ever since (see p77).

In the late 18th century, during a brief period free of persecution, rich Old Believer merchants founded this community, among the most important in the country. To get here, take trolleybus 16 or 26, or bus 51, east from Taganskaya pl; get off after crossing a railway. Rogozhskoe's tall, green-domed 20th-century **bell tower** is clearly visible to the north.

The yellow, classical-style **Intercession Church** contains one of Moscow's finest collections of icons, all dating from before 1653, with the oldest being the 14th-century *Saviour with the Angry Eye* (Spas Yaroe Oko), protected under glass near the south door. The icons in the deesis row (the biggest row) of the iconostasis are supposed to represent the Rublyov school, while the seventh, *The Saviour*, is attributed to Rublyov himself.

North of the church is the **Rogozhskoe Cemetery**.

Visitors are welcome at the church, but women should take care to wear long skirts (no trousers) and headscarves.

Moscow Outskirts

ALL-RUSSIA EXHIBITION CENTRE (VDNKH)

No other place sums up the rise and fall of the Soviet dream quite as well as the **All-Russia Exhibition Centre** (Vserossiysky Vystavochny Tsentr, VVTs; Map p126-7; 544 3400; www.vvcentre.ru; pavilions 10am-6pm, grounds 9am-7pm; VDNKh). The old initials by which it's still commonly known, VDNKh, tell half the story – they stand for Vystavka Dostizheny Narod-

nogo Khozyaystva SSSR (USSR Economic Achievements Exhibition).

Originally created in the 1930s, VDNKh was expanded in the '50s and '60s to impress upon one and all the success of the Soviet economic system. Two kilometres long and 1km wide, it is composed of wide pedestrian avenues and grandiose pavilions, glorifying every aspect of socialist construction from education and health to agriculture, technology and science. The pavilions represent a huge variety of architectural styles, symbolic of the contributions from diverse ethnic and artistic movements to the common goal. Here you will find the kitschiest socialist realism, the most inspiring of socialist optimism and, now, the tackiest of capitalist consumerism.

VDNKh was an early casualty when those in power finally admitted that the Soviet economy had become a disaster – funds were cut off by 1990. Today it's a commercial centre, its pavilions given over to sales of the very imported goods that were supposed to be inferior; much of the merchandise on sale is low-priced clothing and the like from China. The domed Kosmos (Space) pavilion towards the far end became a wholesaler for TV sets and VCRs, while Lenin's slogan 'Socialism is Soviet power plus electrification' still adorns the electrification pavilion to its right. Although you may not want to do your shopping here, VDNKh does host international trade exhibitions.

For tourists, it's a fascinating visit to see the remnants of socialism's achievements. Muscovites are not so easily amused, however. Fortunately the new centre also offers other distractions, including an amusement park, paint ball, a stocked fish pond and an open-air circus.

The soaring 100m titanium obelisk is a monument to Soviet space flight. In its base is the **Memorial Museum of Cosmonauts** (Map pp126-7; 283 8197; adult/child R40/20, audio tour R100; 10am-7pm Tue-Sun; VDNKh), a high-concept series of displays from the glory days of the Soviet space programme.

OSTANKINO

The pink-and-white **Ostankino Palace** (Ostankinsky dvorets; Map pp126-7), a wooden mansion with a stucco exterior made to resemble stone, was built in the 1790s as the summer pad of Count Nikolai Sheremetyev,

JUDAISM IN MOSCOW

The Jewish population in Moscow became statistically notable only in the late 18th century, when imperial Russia annexed the eastern part of the Polish Kingdom – known as the Jewish Pale. Jewish trades and traditions were regarded as a threat to the social order of the empire, however. Official policy fluctuated from forced assimilation to social isolation.

A brief respite occurred under Alexander II, the Tsar Reformer, who lifted residential restrictions on Jews with 'useful' talents, such as merchants, doctors and artisans. Jews were allowed to enter new professions, such as banking and industry, and Moscow's small Jewish community flourished during these years.

Lenin once said 'scratch a Bolshevik and you'll find a Russian chauvinist'. While the revolution provided a period of opportunity for individual Jews, the socialist regime was not tolerant towards Jewish language and customs. In 1930 Lazar Kaganovich, an ethnic Jew and Stalin crony, was made mayor of Moscow. He pleaded against the destruction of the Christ the Saviour Cathedral out of fear that he would be personally blamed and that it would provoke popular anti-Semitism (both of which happened).

Anti-Semitism became official policy again in the late Stalinist period. The Jewish quarter in the Dorogomilova neighbourhood was levelled for new building projects. Two huge apartment houses were constructed for the communist elite, at 24 and 26 Kutuzovsky pr, on top of the city's old Jewish cemetery. Systematic discrimination finally prompted the rise of a dissident movement, which battled Soviet officialdom for the right to leave the country.

In 1986 Mikhail Gorbachev announced that refusnik Anatoly Shcharansky was permitted to emigrate, signalling a more relaxed official stance. Between 1987 and 1991 half a million Soviet Jews emigrated to Israel, and another 150,000 to the USA. Moscow's Jewish community declined as a result.

Today Judaism in Moscow is enjoying a modest revival, as believers reconnect with their ancestry and traditions. As in earlier times, the new opportunities for Jews that have arisen in postcommunist Russia have also stirred anti-Semitic incidents and rhetoric.

probably Russia's richest aristocrat of the time and son of Count Pyotr Sheremetyev. Its lavish interior, with hand-painted wallpaper and intricate parquet floors, houses the count's art treasures. The centrepiece is the oval theatre-ballroom built for the Sheremetyev troupe of 250 serf actors (see p166). In 1801 Count Nikolai married one of the troupe, Praskovia Zhemchugova, and the two retired to Ostankino to avoid court gossip.

Only the **Italian Pavilion** (☎ 286 6288; admission R40; ☼ 10am-6pm Wed-Sun mid-May–Sep) is open for visits. The hours are limited and it's closed on days when it rains or when humidity is over 80%.

After a fire in the late 1990s, the 540m **Ostankino TV Tower** (Map pp126–7) is no longer open to the public, although it still provides a distinctive landmark for the area.

To reach the Ostankino Palace, walk west from VDNKh metro, across the car parks, to pick up tram 7 or 11, or trolleybus 13, 36, 69 or 73 west along ul Akademika Korolyova.

VICTORY PARK & AROUND

Following a vicious but inconclusive battle at Borodino (p197) in August 1812, Moscow's defenders retreated along what are now Kutuzovsky pr and ul Arbat, pursued by Napoleon's Grand Army. Today, about 3km west of Novoarbatsky most (formerly Kalininsky most) is the **Borodino Panorama** (Map pp126-7; ☎ 148 1967; Kutuzovsky pr 38; adult/student R5/30; ☼ 10am-5pm Sat-Thu; Ⓜ Park Pobedy, Kutuzovskaya), a pavilion with a giant 360-degree painting of the Borodino battle. Standing inside this tableau of bloodshed – complete with sound effects – is a powerful way to visualise the event.

The **Triumphal Arch** (Map pp126–7), further out, celebrates Napoleon's eventual defeat. Demolished at its original site outside Belarus Station in the 1930s, it was reconstructed here in a fit of post-WWII public spirit.

A short distance west is **Victory Park**, a huge memorial complex celebrating the Great Patriotic War. The park includes endless fountains and monuments and the memorial **Church of St George** (Map pp126–7).

The dominant monument is a 142m obelisk (each 10cm represents a day of the war).

The **Memorial Synagogue at Poklonnaya Hill** (Map pp126–7) houses the **Museum of Jewish Legacy History and Holocaust** (☎ 148 1907; Minskaya ul; admission free; ☑ 10am-6pm Tue-Thu, noon-7pm Sun; Ⓜ Park Pobedy). Admission is with a guide only, so you must make arrangements in advance, especially if you want a tour in English. Otherwise, you may be able to join an existing group.

The **Museum of the Great Patriotic War** (Map pp126–7; ☎ 142 4185; ul Bratiev Fonchenko 10; admission R30; ☑ 10am-5pm Tue-Sun; Ⓜ Park Pobedy), located within the park, has a diorama of every major WWII battle involving Soviet troops. Exhibits highlight the many heroes of the Soviet Union, as well as show weapons, photographs, documentary films, letters and many other authentic wartime memorabilia.

SPARROW HILLS
The best view over Moscow is from Universitetskaya pl on the Sparrow Hills – most of the city spreads out before you. It is also an excellent vantage point for seeing Luzhniki, the huge stadiums built across the river for the 1980 Olympics.

Behind Universitetskaya pl is the 36-storey Stalinist main spire of **Moscow State University** (Map pp126–7; Moskovsky Gosudarstvenny Universitet; Ⓜ Vorobyovy Gory), one of the 'Seven Sisters' that is visible from most places in the city thanks to its elevated site. It was built by convicts between 1949 and 1953.

KOLOMENSKOE MUSEUM-RESERVE
Set amid 4 sq km of parkland, on a bluff above a Moscow River bend, **Kolomenskoe Museum-Reserve** (Map pp126–7; ☎ 115 2768; grounds admission free, museum adult/child R300/100; ☑ grounds 10am-9pm, museum to 5pm; Ⓜ Kolomenskaya) is an ancient royal country seat and Unesco World Heritage Site. As many festivals are held here during the year, check if anything is happening during your visit.

From Bolshaya ul, enter through the 17th-century **Saviour Gate** (Map pp126–7) to the white-washed **Kazan Church**, both built in the time of Tsar Alexey. The church faces the site of his great wooden palace, which was demolished in 1768 by Catherine the Great. Ahead, the white, tent-roofed 17th-century **front gate and clock tower** mark the edge of the old inner palace precinct. The golden

double-headed eagle that tops the gate is the symbol of the Romanov dynasty.

The adjacent buildings house an interesting **museum** with a bit of everything: a model of Alexey's wooden palace, material on rebellions associated with Kolomenskoe, and Russian crafts from clocks and tiles to woodcarving and metalwork.

Outside the front gate, overlooking the river, rises Kolomenskoe's loveliest structure, the quintessentially Russian **Ascension Church** (Map pp126–7). Built between 1530 and 1532 for Grand Prince Vasily III, it probably celebrated the birth of his heir Ivan the Terrible. It is actually an important development in Russian architecture, reproducing the shapes of wooden churches in brick for the first time, and paving the way for St Basil's 25 years later. Immediately south of it are the round 16th-century **St George's Bell Tower** and another 17th-century tower.

Some 300m further south across a gully, the white **St John the Baptist Church** was built for Ivan the Terrible in the 1540s or 1550s. It has four corner chapels, which make it a stylistic 'quarter-way house' between the Ascension Church and St Basil's.

Among the old wooden buildings on the grounds is the **cabin of Peter the Great** (adult/child R200/100), in which he lived while supervising ship- and fort-building at Arkhangelsk in the 1700s.

KUSKOVO PARK
When Count Pyotr Sheremetyev married Varvara Cherkassakava in 1743, their joint property amounted to 1200 villages and 200,000 serfs. They turned their country estate at Kuskovo, 12km east of the Kremlin, into a mini-Versailles, with elegant buildings scattered around formal gardens, as well as an informal park. It's a pleasant trip out from central Moscow.

The main wooden mansion, **Kuskovo Mansion** (Map pp126–7; ☎ 370 0160; ul Yunosti 2; admission per exhibit R30-100; ☑ 10am-4pm Wed-Sun Nov-Mar, 10am-6pm Wed-Sun Apr-Oct), overlooks a lake where the count staged mock sea battles to entertain Moscow society. Across the lake to the south is the informal park. North of the mansion in the formal grounds are: an **orangery**, now housing an exhibition of 18th- to 20th-century Russian ceramics; an open-air **theatre**, where the Sheremetyev troupe of serf actors performed twice weekly; a pond-side grotto with exotic 'sea caverns'; a **Dutch house**, glazed inside with Delft tiles; an **Italian villa**; a **hermitage** for private parties; and a **church** with a wooden bell tower.

Buildings are closed when humidity exceeds 80% or when it's very cold, counting out much of the winter. To get to the park, head to Ryazansky Prospekt metro station, then take bus 133 or 208.

IZMAYLOVO

Izmaylovo is best known for its extensive arts and crafts market (p185), held every weekend. After shopping, however, Izmaylovsky Park and the crumbling royal estate are nice for a picnic or more-serious outdoor activity.

A former royal hunting preserve 10km east of the Kremlin, **Izmaylovsky Park** (Map pp126–7) is the nearest large tract of undeveloped land to central Moscow. Its 15 sq km contain a recreation park at the western end, and a much larger expanse of **woodland** (Izmaylovsky Lesopark) east of Glavnaya alleya, the road that cuts north to south across the park. Trails wind around this park, making it a good place to escape the city for hiking or biking. To get here, head south (away from the giant Hotel Izmaylovo complex) from Partizanskaya metro.

The **royal estate** (Map pp126–7) is on a small, moated island. Tsar Alexey had an experimental farm here in the 17th century, where Western farming methods and cottage industries were sampled. It was on the farm ponds that his son Peter learnt to sail in a little boat, a boat that came to be called the Grandfather of the Russian Navy.

Past an extensive 18th-century barracks (now partly occupied by the police) is the beautiful, five-domed 1679 **Intercession Cathedral** (Map pp126–7), an early example of Moscow baroque. The nearby triple-arched, tent-roofed **Ceremonial Gates** (1682) and the squat brick **bridge tower** (1671) are the only other original buildings remaining. The latter contains an **exhibition hall** (☎ 166 5881; 🕙 11.30am-5pm Wed-Sun; Ⓜ Partizanskaya).

ACTIVITIES
Banya

What better way to cope with Moscow than to have it steamed, washed and beaten out of you? There are traditional *bani* (Russian hot baths) all over town. If you aren't shy, general admission to shared facilities (though thankfully separated by gender!) is cheaper than renting a private bath. Either way, the *banya* is a sensuous, exhilarating and uniquely Russian experience. See p71 for a fuller description of the *banya* experience.

Banya on Presnya (Map pp128-9; ☎ men 255 5306, women 253 8690; Stolyarny per 7; admission R500-600; 🕙 8am-10pm Mon-Sat, 2-10pm Sun; Ⓜ Ulitsa 1905 Goda) Although lacking the old-fashioned decadent atmosphere of Sanduny, this new, clean, efficient place provides a first-rate *banya* experience.

Sanduny Baths (Map pp128-9; ☎ private 925 4631, general 925 4633; www.sanduny.ru; Neglinnaya ul 14; private room per hr from R1200, general admission per hr R500-700; 🕙 8am-10pm; Ⓜ Chekhovskaya) The oldest and most luxurious *banya* in the city. A work of art in itself, the Gothic Room has rich wood carving, and the main shower room has an almost aristocratic Roman feel to it.

Wellness (Map pp126-7; ☎ 709 5491; www.wellness -hall.ru in Russian; Volgogradsky pr 54; private room R2300-2900; Ⓜ Kuzminki) A distinctly New Russian place. Private baths for groups of up to four people include a Japanese sauna, a Greek bath and an ultrafancy 'modern hall', in addition to the Russian *banya*.

River Trips

For new perspectives on Moscow neighbourhoods, fine views of the Kremlin, or just good old-fashioned transportation, a boat ride on the Moscow River is one of the city's highlights. The main route runs between the boat landings at **Kievsky vokzal** (Map pp132–3), and **Novospassky most** (Map p134) 1km west of Proletarskaya metro (near the Novospassky Monastery). There are six intermediate stops: **Vorobyovy Gory landing** (Map pp126–7), at the foot of Sparrow Hills; **Frunzenskaya** (Map pp126–7), towards the southern end of Frunzenskaya nab; **Gorky Park** (Map pp132–3); **Krymsky most** (Map pp132–3); **Bolshoy Kamenny most** opposite the Kremlin (Map pp132–3); and **Ustinsky most** (Map p134) near Red Square.

The boats seat around 200 (most Muscovite passengers are actually going somewhere, not just enjoying the ride) and are operated by the **Capital Shipping Company** (☎ 458 9624). They run from May to September (adult/child R200/100, 1½ hours, every 20 minutes). Check at the landings for the limited weekday schedules; on weekends they run as often as every 20 minutes in either direction.

Swimming

Public pools are difficult places to take the plunge if you are a foreigner because they all insist on a Russian doctor's certificate of your good health before they'll let you in. Fortunately, the pools generally have somebody on hand who can issue the certificate on the spot (for a small fee).

Chayka Swimming Pool (Map pp132-3; ☎ 246 1344; Turchaninov per 1/3; per hr R150; ☒ 7am-10pm Mon-Sat, 8am-7pm Sun; Ⓜ Park Kultury)

Luzhniki pool (Map pp126-7; ☎ 201 0795; Luzhnenskya nab 24; ☒ 8.30am-8pm; Ⓜ Vorobyovy Gory) Part of the vast complex built for the 1980 Olympic games.

On hot summer days you can join much of the city and head to the beaches at **Serebryany Bor**, a series of lakes and channels on the Moscow River, 20km north of the city (a key detail since nothing from Moscow has yet been *flushed* into the water). There are areas that are unofficially dedicated to families, gays, nudists and even disco dancers. Take the metro to Sokol and then ride trolleybus 65 to the end of the line.

Winter Sports

There's no shortage of winter in Moscow, so take advantage of it. You can rent ice skates and see where all those great Russian figure skaters come from at **Gorky Park** (p161) or **Chistye Prudy** (p153). Bring your passport.

Izmaylovsky Park (p167) has both ski and skate rental. To get there, take bus 7 or 131 from Partizanskaya metro and get off at the third stop.

WALKING TOUR

A walk around Moscow is a chance to see some original settings from Russian literature, as well as the environs where various authors and poets lived and worked.

Start from Pushkinskaya pl on the west side of Tverskaya ul. Prepare yourself for the journey ahead with a little something at **Café Pushkin** (1; p176). Walk southwest along the promenade that runs between the two lanes of traffic of Tverskay bul. Since the 18th century this has been the most popular of Moscow's streets for walking; even the Shcherbitskiye sisters in Leo Tolstoy's *Anna Karenina* promenaded here.

The huge brown block at No 22 is the new building of the **Gorky Art Theatre (2)**, named after Maxim Gorky. Previously on this site stood the house of Praskovya Yuryevna Gagarina, a socialite who was very fond of hosting extravagant balls and opera performances. One of these infamous events is supposedly where Alexander Pushkin first met his future wife Natalya Goncharova.

In the middle of the boulevard is a **statue of Sergei Yesenin (3)**, an early-20th-century poet who was in and out of favour throughout the Soviet era. Writing about love and landscapes earned him the nickname 'the peasant poet'. His short, stormy life was torn apart by no less than five marriages and violent bouts with alcoholism. He finally ended his own life in 1925 at the age of 30.

At the foot of the street is one of the most beautiful squares in Moscow. **Nikitskie Vorota (4**; Nikitskie Gates) takes its name from the gates of a wall that stood here from the 15th to the 18th centuries. At the corner of the square, the **Rotunda Fountain (5)**, by the tireless Zurab Tsereteli, hides a statue of Pushkin and Goncharova, erected in 1999 to celebrate the poet's birthday.

Continue south on the Boulevard Ring, now called Nikitsky bul.

The classical building at No 12A now houses the **Museum of Oriental Art** (6; ☎ 202 4555; admission R60; ☒ noon-8pm Tue-Sun), but was built for the musical Lunin family. The moulded lyre on the front of the elegant house is a symbol of the many musical evenings that took place here.

The quiet courtyard at No 7 contains a statue of an emaciated, gloomy Nikolai Gogol, surrounded by some of his better-known characters in bas-relief around the base. The building on the right houses the **Gogol Memorial Rooms** (7; ☎ 291 1550; Nikitsky bul 7; admission free; ☒ noon-7pm Mon-Fri, to 5pm Sat & Sun), where the writer spent his final, tortured months. The rooms are arranged as they were when Gogol lived here; you can even see the fireplace in which he infamously threw his manuscript of *Dead Souls*.

Across the street at No 8A is an 18th-century **mansion (8)** that was home to Colonel Kiselyov, a literature fanatic and friend of Pushkin. Apparently, Pushkin and Goncharova attended a ball at the colonel's home on the day after their wedding in 1831. During the Soviet period, this building became the House of the Press, and writers such as

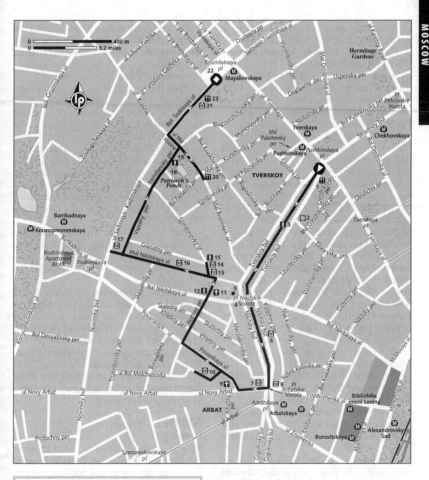

WALK FACTS

Start Pushkinskaya pl
Finish Triumfalnaya pl
Distance 3km
Duration 2–3 hours

Yesenin, Alexander Blok and Mayakovsky all presented their work here. In 1925, just two months after Yesenin recited his poem 'Flowers' here, his fans returned to pay him their last respects.

Proceed down to ul Novy Arbat and turn right; then head west for one block. Turn right in front of the 17th-century **Church of St Simeon the Stylite (9)**, Gogol's regular parish church. Head north on Povarskaya ul and take the first left on Malaya Molchanovka ul.

The pink house at No 2 was home to Mikhail Lermontov, author of *A Hero of Our Time*. It now houses the **Lermontov House-Museum (10;** ☎ 291 5298; Malaya Molchanovka ul 2; adult/child/student R30/20/25; ⏲ 2–5pm Wed & Fri, 11am–3pm Thu, Sat & Sun).

Return to Povarskaya ul and turn left, heading northwest. Povarskaya ul (meaning Cooks' St) was once inhabited by the royal court's cooks. The names of the lanes in this area still evoke the tsar's kitchen: Stolovy (Dining Room), Skatertny (Table Cloth), Khlebny (Bread) and Nozhovy (Cutlery).

Turn right on Nozhovy per and head north. Cross Bolshaya Nikitskaya ul.

The graceful **Church of the Grand Ascension** (**11**; p155) was built between 1798 and 1816 by Vasily Bazhenov and Matvei Kazakov. Pushkin married Goncharova here in 1831.

A lesser-known Tolstoy (and distant relative of Leo), **Alexey Tolstoy (12)** stands in the small park across the lane. Also a writer, Alexey Tolstoy is known primarily for his 20th-century novels about the Civil War and the revolution, the most famous being the trilogy *The Ordeal*.

Continue north on Nozhovy per until it ends at Malaya Nikitskaya ul.

Opposite the church on Malaya Nikitskaya ul is an Art Nouveau masterpiece at No 6/2 that once was the house of a wealthy merchant, Stepan Ryabushinksy. Designed by Fyodor Shekhtel, with mosaics by Mikhail Vrubel, the house was later gifted to writer Maxim Gorky, who often complained about the décor's extravagance. The building still houses the **Gorky House-Museum** (**13**; p155). Behind Gorky's house is **Alexey Tolstoy's flat (14)**.

From Malaya Nikitskaya ul, take an immediate right and then head north on ul Spiridonovka.

The statue of another early-20th-century poet, **Alexander Blok (15)**, stands a bit further up ul Spiridonovka. The revolutionary Blok believed that individualism had caused a decline in society's ethics, a situation that would only be rectified by a communist revolution.

Head back to Malaya Nikitskaya ul and turn right. The 18th-century **classical estate (16)** at No 12 once belonged to the Bobrinsky family. It was also depicted by Pushkin as the Larins' house in *Yevgeny Onegin*. At the end of ul Malaya Nikitskaya, turn right on to the Garden Ring.

The 19th-century writer Anton Chekhov lived and worked at No 6 ul Sadovaya-Kudrinskaya. Now open as the **Chekhov House-Museum** (**17**; p154), this is where he composed such masterpieces as *Three Sisters* and *The Seagull*.

Head back on Malaya Nikitskaya ul. Take the first left and walk north on Vspolny per. At the intersection with ul Spiridonovka, the name changes to Yermolayevsky. Proceed another 200m to reach the **Patriarch's Ponds (18)**.

The small park to the west of the pond has a huge statue of 19th-century Russian writer **Ivan Krylov (19)**, known to every Russian child for his didactic tales. Scenes from his stories surround the statue of the writer.

Once this area contained several ponds that kept fish for the patriarch's court (thus the name). But it is more famous as the setting for the opening scene in the novel by Mikhail Bulgakov, *The Master and Margarita*. The initial paragraph describes the area north of the pond, where the devil enters the scene and predicts the rapid death of Berlioz. If you are a real literary buff – or if you just need to refuel – grab a bite to eat at the nearby **Cafe Margarita** (**20**; p177).

Turn left on Malaya Krasina ul and head out to the Garden Ring. Turn right and walk one block north. The otherwise nondescript building at No 10 is **Bulgakov's flat** (**21**; p154).

Up ahead is Triumfalnaya pl, previously named for the poet and playwright **Vladimir Mayakovsky (22)**, whose statue stands in its centre. A favourite of the Bolshevik regime, Mayakovsky sought to demystify poetry, adopting crude language and ignoring traditional poetic techniques.

From here you can break for lunch at the **Starlite Diner** (**23**; p178) or hop on the metro at Mayakovskaya station.

COURSES
Cooking
Russian cooking classes are hard to come by, but Dom Patriarshy Tours (opposite) does offer an occasional half-day course. Learn to whip up some bliny, then eat them for lunch.

Language
Check the *Moscow Times* for advertisements for Russian tutors and short-term courses.

Center for Russian Language & Culture (☎ 939 1463; www.ruslanguage.ru; MGU; 20hr course €110) Caters mostly to students, offering semester-long courses and dormitory lodging.

Liden & Denz Language Centre (☎ 254 4991; www.lidenz.ru; 16hr course R4480) These more-expensive courses service the business and diplomatic community with less-intensive evening courses.

Russian Village (☎ 721 7294; www.rusvillage.com; weekend-/week-/month-long course from €320/770/2380)

An upscale 'country resort' language school located in the village of Pestovo, north of Moscow. Prices include lodging and meals.

Ziegler & Partner (☎ /fax 939 0980; www.study russian.com; Moscow State University, MGU) A Swiss group offering individually designed courses from standard conversation to specialised lessons in business, law, literature etc.

MOSCOW FOR CHILDREN

Got kids with you in Moscow? They may not appreciate an age-old icon or a Soviet hero but Moscow still has plenty offer the little ones.

For starters, the city is filled with parks. Patriarch's Pond (p154) and Alexandrovsky Garden (p147) both have playgrounds and plenty of room to run around. Or take them to Gorky Park (p161) – thrilling rides in summer and ice skating in winter make it the ultimate Russian experience for children. For a more post-Soviet experience, VDNKh (p164) also has amusement-park rides and video games.

Russia excels at the circus, and crazy clowns and daring acrobatics are all the rage at two locales: the huge Great Moscow Circus (p183), and the more atmospheric Nikulin Circus (p183).

Another Russian favourite is the puppet theatre. **Obraztsov Puppet Theatre & Museum** (Map pp128-9; ☎ 299 3310, 299 5563; Sadovaya Samot-yochnaya ul 3; Ⓜ Kutuzovskaya) runs performances of colourful Russian folk tales and adapted classical plays; kids can get up close and personal with the incredible puppets at the museum.

What better entertainment for kiddies than performing kitties? At the **Cat Theatre** (Map pp132-3; ☎ 249 2907; Kutuzovsky pr 25; Ⓜ Kievskaya), Yuri Kuklachev's acrobatic cats do all kinds of stunts to the audience's delight. Kuklachev says, 'We do not use the word *train* here because it implies forcing an animal to do something; and you cannot force cats to do anything they don't want to. We *play* with the cats.'

Bigger cats are the highlight of the Moscow Zoo (p155), an obvious destination for children. For a trip out of the city, take the young ones to the bison nursery at the Prioksko-Terrasny Biosphere Reserve (p199), where highly informative educational programmes are designed especially for kids.

TOURS

Capital Tours (Map pp128-9; ☎ 232 2442; www .capitaltours.ru; Gostiny Dvor, ul Ilinka 4; Ⓜ Kitay-Gorod) This spin-off of Dom Patriarshy offers a twice-daily Kremlin/Armoury tour (US$37/20, 10.30am and 3pm Friday to Wednesday) and Moscow city tour (adult/child US$20/10, 11am and 2.30pm daily). Tours depart from Gostiny Dvor.

Dom Patriarshy Tours (Map pp128-9; ☎ /fax 795 0927; http://russiatravel-pdtours.netfirms.com; Vspolny per 6, Moscow school No 1239; Ⓜ Barrikadnaya) Provides unique English-language tours on just about any specialised subject; some provide access to otherwise closed museums. Day tours range from US$16 to US$40 per person. Look for the monthly schedule at Western hotels and restaurants or online.

FESTIVALS & EVENTS

While Mayor Luzhkov is a keen proponent of bread and circuses for the masses, the festivals are an ever-changing lot from year to year; consult the Moscow newspapers for what's on. See p705 for a list of Russia-wide spectaculars.

December & January
December Nights Festival Held at the main performance halls, theatres and museums from mid-December to early January. Classical music at its best, performed in classy surroundings by the best Russian and foreign talent.

Winter Festival An outdoor fun-fest during early January, for those with antifreeze in their veins (though plenty of people use vodka for this purpose). Teams compete to build elaborate ice sculptures in front of the Pushkin Museum and on Red Square.

March & April
Golden Mask Festival (www.goldenmask.ru) Two weeks of performances by Russia's premier drama, opera, dance and musical performers, culminating in a prestigious awards ceremony. Brightens up otherwise dreary March and April.

Moscow Forum (www.ccmm.ru) A contemporary music festival held every year in April at the Moscow Conservatory.

June
Interfest (www.miff.ru) Short for the Moscow International Film Festival.

September
City Day (Den Goroda) Celebrates the city's birthday every year on the first weekend in September. The day kicks off with a festive parade, followed by live music on Red Square and plenty of food, fireworks and fun.

GAY & LESBIAN MOSCOW

Moscow is the most cosmopolitan of Russian cities, and the active gay and lesbian scene reflects this attitude. Newspapers such as the *Moscow Times* feature articles about gay and lesbian issues, as well as listings of gay and lesbian clubs. The newest publication of note is the glossy magazine *Queer* (Квир), which offers up articles and artwork aimed at, well, queers.

Some other useful resources:

www.gay.ru/english The English version of this site includes updated club listings, plus information on gay history and culture in Russia.

www.gaytours.ru While Dmitry is no longer working as a tour guide, his site is still a wealth of information about gay life in Moscow.

www.lesbi.ru An active site for lesbian issues; Russian only.

For specific venue information, see p184.

SLEEPING

Moscow is not a cheap place to stay – the small, simple hotels found elsewhere in Europe just don't exist yet, while those in the midpriced and budget ranges are mainly older Soviet-era properties that have weathered the transition to a market economy with varying degrees of grace. Many are huge labyrinths lacking any charm; however, with a bit of spirit, a stay in these places can be part of the Russian adventure.

The optimal area of the city to stay in is the centre. With the destruction of the landmark Rossiya Hotel, however, the remaining options are mostly top-end. Fortunately, a few midrange choices exist within the Garden Ring, which guarantees easy access to major sights and plenty of dining and entertainment options. The Tverskoy and Arbat Districts are particularly lively.

If you do find yourself far from the centre (which may be the case if you are on a tighter budget), look for easy access to the metro. An underground ride will whisk you from almost any stop into the centre in 20 minutes or less.

Beware that some hotels may charge a reservation fee – as much as 50% of the cost of the first night – if you reserve in advance. Prices listed include the 20% VAT (value-

added tax), but not the 5% sales tax that's charged mainly at luxury hotels.

Budget

Galina's Flat (Map p131; ☎ 921 6038; galinas.flat@mtu-net.ru; ul Chaplygina 8, No 35; dm/s/d R300/540/750; ☐; ⓜ Chistye Prudy) It's just that – a private, Soviet-era flat with a few extra rooms that Galina rents out. Staying at Galina's feels like staying in your friend's crowded apartment – cosy, comfortable and convivial. She has a total of six beds, as well as kitchen and laundry facilities, but she does not provide visa support.

Travellers Guest House (Map pp126-7; ☎ 631 4059; www.tgh.ru; Bolshaya Pereslavskaya ul 50, 10th fl; dm R690, s/d without bathroom R1350/1650, d with bathroom R1800; ☐; ⓜ Prospekt Mira) Calls itself Moscow's 'first and only' budget accommodation. Perhaps the first but no longer the only, this place is still one of the better options for budget travellers. Despite its location on the 10th floor of a drab hotel, it manages to maintain a vibrant, hostel-like atmosphere, thanks to the travellers hanging out in common lounge and to all the services available through the affiliated Infinity Travel Agency.

Hotel Izmaylovo (Gamma – Delta) (Map pp126-7; ☎ 737 7187, 737 7104; www.izmailovo.ru; Izmaylovskoe sh 71; s/d from R1440/1540; ☐; ⓜ Partizanskaya) Built for the 1980 Olympics, this hotel has 8000 beds, apparently making it Europe's biggest hotel. Four of the five buildings are budget accommodations, but Gamma – Delta is the snazziest and most service-oriented. If you need to escape the frenetic atmosphere that surrounds Izmaylovo market, it's just a few steps to lovely Izmaylovsky Park.

Hostel Sherstone (Map pp126-7; ☎ 711 2613; www.sherstone.ru; Gostinichny proezd 8/1, 3rd fl; dm/s/d R600/1200/1550; ⓜ Vladykino) The tree-lined streets west of the Botanical Gardens comprise somewhat of a hotel district (thus the name of the street, which means 'Hotel Way'). This friendly hostel occupies one floor of a hotel by the same name. Its main advantage is the English-speaking staff, but rooms and services are also satisfactory.

Hotel Zarya (Map pp126-7; ☎ /fax 788 7277; Gostinichnaya ul 4/9; s/d from R1350/1500; ⓜ Vladykino) A complex of short brick buildings, also located near the Botanical Gardens. Renovation of the rooms is ongoing, so the cheapest ones are pretty plain. But the reception is welcoming and the atmosphere is cosy. Upgraded rooms with new furniture and bathrooms are R2100 for a single, R2700 for a double.

Golden Grain Hotel (Map p126-7; ☎ 217 6356; www.zkolos.ru; Yaroslavskaya ul 15; s/d from R1090/1345; ☒; Ⓜ VDNKh) Outshone by its posher and pricier neighbour, the Dinaoda, this old-style hotel still has something to offer: pleasant service and affordable rooms. The location near the All-Russia Exhibition Centre means that it is often booked out to travelling business types.

G&R Hostel Asia (Map p126-7; ☎ 378 0001; www .hostels.ru; Zelenodolskaya ul 3/2; s/d without bathroom from R875/1400; ☐; Ⓜ Ryazansky Prospekt) It calls itself a hostel, but this is really a travel agency hiding out in a big old Soviet hotel. Unlike at the other 'hostels', your rooms may be anywhere in this monolith.

Midrange
TVERSKOY DISTRICT

East-West Hotel (Map pp128-9; ☎ 290 0404; www .eastwesthotel.ru; Tverskoy bul 14/4; s/d with breakfast R4800/6500; ☒ ☐; Ⓜ Pushkinskaya) Located on the loveliest stretch of the Boulevard Ring, this small hotel evokes the atmosphere of the 19th-century mansion it once was. It is a kitschy but charming place with 26 individually decorated rooms and a lovely fountain-filled courtyard.

Hotel Budapest (Map pp128-9; ☎ 923 1060; www .hotel-budapest.ru; Petrovskie linii 2/18; s/d with break-fast R3850/5450; ☒ ☐; Ⓜ Kuznetsky Most) This 19th-century neoclassical edifice is a perfect retreat after strolling in the surrounding swanky shopping district. Have a drink in the plush bar or dine under the crystal chandelier in the restaurant, Grand Opera. The grandeur does not extend to the rooms unless you dish out some extra cash for a suite (from R5775), but all of the accommodation is excellent value.

Hotel Peking (Map pp128-9; ☎ 209 2215; www.hotel pekin.ringnet.ru; Bolshaya Sadovaya ul 5/1; d from R2500; Ⓜ Mayakovskaya) With ongoing renovations, this Stalinist building boasts a prime location towering over Triumfalnaya pl. It's hard to see past the flashing lights and raucousness of the casino, but this place is blessed with high ceilings, parquet floors and a marble staircase. The upgraded rooms (single R3500, double R4200) – elegantly decorated in jewel tones – are worth the investment.

ARBAT DISTRICT

Hotel Arbat (Map pp132-3; ☎ 244 7628; fax 244 0093; Plotnikov per 12; s/d from with breakfast R4320/5130; Ⓜ Smolenskaya) One of the few hotels that manages to preserve some appealing Soviet camp – from the greenery-filled lobby to the mirrors behind the bar. For better or for worse, the guest rooms are decorated tastefully and comfortably. But the whole place has an anachronistic charm. Its location is

---

FIND A FLAT

Hotels in Moscow could easily break your bank. In response to the shortage of affordable accommodation, some entrepreneurial Muscovites have begun renting out flats on a short-term basis. Flats are equipped with kitchens, and sometimes with other useful amenities like Internet access. Often, a good-sized flat is available for the price of a hotel room, or less. It is an ideal solution for travellers in a group, who can split the cost.

Several websites provide information about apartments for rent. The apartments vary widely, of course, but many have photos available online. Apartments are around US$80 to US$100 per night, with prices decreasing for longer stays. Expect to pay more for fully renovated, Western-style apartments.

www.apartmentres.com Bills itself as gay-friendly lodging. Most flats include free airport transfers and international phone calls.

www.enjoymoscow.com Rick's apartments are off the Garden Ring between Sukharevskaya and Tsvetnoy Bulvar metro stations.

www.flatmates.ru/eng A site for travellers looking for somebody to share short- or long-term accommodation in Russia.

www.hofa.ru Apartments from €40 per night and homestays from €20 per night.

www.rentline.ru Offers online reservations for a variety of centrally located flats, starting from US$80 per night.

www.unclepasha.com Uncle Pasha is an unbelievable grouch, but his flat – at US$75 per night – is a great deal. He also maintains an extensive list of other budget accommodation options and will help you locate one.

MOSCOW

also very charming – on a quiet residential street, just steps from the Arbat.

Hotel Belgrad (Map pp132-3; ☎ 248 1643; www.hotel -belgrad.ru; Smolenskaya ul 8; s/d R2560/2880; Ⓜ Smolenskaya) The big block on Smolenskaya-Sennaya pl has no sign and a stark lobby, giving it a ghost-town aura. Rooms are similar – poky but functional – unless you upgrade to 'tourist' or 'business-class' accommodation, costing R4160 to R5280. The advantage is the location, which can be noisy but is convenient to the western end of ul Arbat.

ZAMOSKVORECHIE

Hotel Danilovsky (Map pp126-7; ☎ 954 0503; hotdanil@ cityline.ru; s/d incl breakfast from R3300/3660; 🖥 🖳 ✕; Ⓜ Tulskaya) Moscow's holiest hotel is on the grounds of the 12th-century monastery of the same name – where the exquisite setting comes complete with 18th-century churches and well-maintained gardens. The modern five-story hotel was built so that nearly all the rooms have a view of the grounds. The rooms themselves are simple but clean, and breakfast is modest: no greed, gluttony or sloth to be found here.

CHISTYE PRUDY

Hotel Sverchkov (Map p131; ☎ 925 4978; per Sverchkov 8; s/d with breakfast from R2600/3000; Ⓜ Chistye Prudy) On a quiet residential lane, this is a tiny 11-room hotel in a graceful 18th-century building. The hallways are lined with greenleafed plants, and paintings by local artists adorn the walls. Though rooms are nothing special, this place is a rarity for its intimacy and hominess.

Kazakh Embassy Hotel (Map p131; ☎ 208 0994; Chistoprudny bul 3; s/d with breakfast R2700/3000; Ⓜ Chistye Prudy) Caters – as you might guess – tó guests and workers of the nearby Kazakh embassy. But anyone can stay in this grand, modern building that fronts the prestigious Boulevard Ring. The rooms are a step up from the other options at this price.

Hotel Leningradskaya (Map p131; ☎ 975 1815; fax 975 1802; Kalanchevskaya ul 21/40; s/d from R2800/3600; Ⓜ Komsomolskaya) This showpiece Soviet hotel – which happens to be the shortest of Stalin's 'Seven Sisters' - is expected to reopen in early 2007 after an extensive renovation. Up until the recent closure, the hotel retained some of its grand 1950s style in the lobbies and staircases; the rooms also retained their 1950s style, though there was not

much grandeur there. This is a convenient place to stay if you are arriving or departing by train, due to the proximity to three stations. Unfortunately, the seedy atmosphere that surrounds the train stations had seeped into the hotel. Let's hope the renovation results in improved atmosphere and amenities without greatly affecting affordability.

OUTER MOSCOW

Sovietsky Hotel (Map pp126-7; ☎ 960 2000; www .sovietsky.ru; Leningradsky pr 32/2; r from R4960; 🖥 🖳 ✕ ✕; Ⓜ Dinamo) Built in 1952, this historic hotel shows Stalin's tastes in all of its architectural details, starting from the gilded hammer and sickle and the enormous Corinthian columns flanking the front door. The sumptuous lobby is graced with grand sweeping staircases, crystal chandeliers and plush carpets, and even the simplest rooms have ceiling medallions and other ornamentation. The legendary restaurant Yar – complete with old-fashioned dancing girls – is truly over the top. The location is not super convenient, but this throwback is still fun for a Soviet-style splurge.

Dinaoda Hotel (Map pp126-7; ☎ 980 6100; www .dinaoda.ru; Yaroslavskaya ul 15/2; s/d from R3630/4300; ✕ 🖳; Ⓜ VDNKh) In a classical, six-storey building, Dinaoda is a new hotel catering to business travellers. The rooms benefit from natural sunlight and spacious interiors; some are wheelchair accessible. The well-manicured miniature golf course is perhaps out of place in this elegant setting, but your kids will appreciate it.

Altai Hotel (Map pp126-7; ☎ 482 5703; Botanicheskaya ul 41; altayhotel@comail.ru; s/d with breakfast R2200/2890; 🖥 ✕; Ⓜ Vladykino) The classiest place to stay in the hotel district near the Botanical Gardens. This hotel has been completely revamped, from the elegant lobby – with chandeliers and fireplace – to the tastefully decorated guest rooms. Only a few old-school rooms remain (R800 or R1250) but they are often booked.

Sputnik Hotel (Map pp126-7; ☎ 930 3097; www .hotelsputnik.ru; Leninsky pr 38; s/d from R1960/2660; Ⓜ Leninsky Prospekt) This hulk of a hotel is rather Soviet, but its setting south of the centre has some appeal. It's just a short walk to Sparrow Hills and the leafy campus of Moscow State University. Among the many services available, the on-site Indian restaurant, Darbar, is one of the best of its type in Moscow.

Hotel Cosmos (Map pp126-7; ☎ 234 1206; www
.hotelcosmos.ru; pr Mira 150; s/d from R2240/2800;
🖳 🕿 🕱 ; Ⓜ VDNKh) This gargantuan hotel
opposite the All-Russia Exhibition Centre
is a universe to itself (appropriately enough,
for a place called Cosmos). The avant-garde
glass and steel structure houses over 1700
rooms, countless restaurants and bars and a
state-of-the-art fitness centre. Not surprisingly, a wide range of rooms are available,
some with fantastic views.

Recommended for transit travellers who
need to crash between flights:

Aerotel Domodedovo (☎ 795 3868; fax 795 3569;
Domodedovo airport; s/d with breakfast from R3500;
🕱 🕿 🕱) A new hotel within walking distance from its
namesake airport; excellent value.

Sheremetyevo-2 (☎ 578 5753/4; fax 739 4464;
Sheremetyevo-2 airport; r with breakfast from R3450) An
option that is more affordable than the nearby Novotel.
You can walk here from the airport, or use the Novotel's
free shuttle.

Top End

Hotel Metropol (Map pp128-9; ☎ 927 6000; fax 927
6010; www.metropol-moscow.ru; Teatralny proezd 1/4; s/d
from R9000/10,500; 🖳 🕿 🕱 🕱 ; Ⓜ Teatralnaya)
Nothing short of an Art Nouveau masterpiece, the historic Metropol brings an
artistic touch to every nook and cranny,
from the spectacular exterior (see the boxed
text, below) to the grand lobby to the individually decorated rooms. The overall effect
is breathtaking, but the charm lies in the
details, like stained-glass windows, Oriental rugs and early-20th-century furnishings.
Situated opposite the Bolshoi, it's worth

stopping in just to check out the exquisite
stained-glass ceiling in the restaurant.

Le Royal Meridien National (Map p135; ☎ 258
7000; fax 258 7100; www.national.ru; Okhotny ryad
14/1; old-wing r from R8960/10,360; 🖳 🕿 🕱 🕱 ;
Ⓜ Okhotny Ryad) For over a century, the National has occupied this choice location at
the foot of Tverskaya ul, opposite the Kremlin. The handsome building is somewhat
of a museum from the early 20th century,
displaying frescoed ceilings and antique
furniture. The rooms are decorated and laid
out uniquely – some have spectacular views
into the Kremlin. While the place reeks of
history, the service and amenities are up to
modern-day five-star standards.

Hotel Baltschug Kempinski (Map pp132-3;
☎ 230 6500; www.kempinskimoscow.com; ul Balchug 1;
r with breakfast weekends/weekdays from RR9450/13,125;
🖳 🕿 🕱 🕱 ; Ⓜ Kitay-Gorod) If you want to
wake up to views of the sun glinting off
the Kremlin's golden domes, this luxurious
place on the Moscow River is for you. It is
another historic hotel, built in 1898, with
230 high-ceilinged rooms that are sophisticated and sumptuous in design. The on-site
restaurant is famous for its Sunday brunch,
or 'linner', if you prefer, as it's served from
12.30pm to 6pm. Russian champagne and
live jazz accompany an extravagant buffet.

Hotel Tiflis (Map pp132-3; ☎ 733 9070; www.hotel
tiflis.com; ul Ostozhenka 32; s/d with breakfast from
R7100/9200; 🖳 🕿 🕱 🕱 ; Ⓜ Park Kultury, Kropotkinskaya) Georgians know hospitality. The proof
is in the fine restaurants – like the landmark
Tiflis (p177) – and now the proof is in this
refined, four-star hotel by the same name,

MAMONTOV'S METROPOL

The Hotel Metropol, one of Moscow's finest examples of Art Nouveau architecture, is another
contribution by famed philanthropist and patron of the arts, Savva Mamontov. The decorative
panel on the hotel's central façade, facing Teatralny proezd, is based on a sketch by the artist
Mikhail Vrubel. It depicts the legend of the *Princess of Dreams*, in which a troubadour falls in love
with a kind and beautiful princess and travels across the seas to find her. He falls ill during the
voyage and is near death when he finds his love. The princess embraces him, but he dies in her
arms. Naturally, the princess renounces her worldly life. The ceramic panels were made at the
pottery workshop at Mamontov's Abramtsevo estate (p192).

The ceramic work on the side of the hotel facing Teatralnaya pl is by the artist Alexander
Golovin. The script is a quote from Friedrich Nietzsche: 'Again the same story: when you build
a house you notice that you have learned something.'

During the Soviet era, these wise words were replaced with something more appropriate for
the time: 'Only the dictatorship of the proletariat can liberate mankind from the oppression of
capitalism.' Lenin, of course.

AUTHOR'S CHOICE

Golden Apple (Map pp128-9; ☎ 980 7000; www.goldenapple.ru; Malaya Dmitrovka ul 11; r from R9000; 🖳 🔀 ✖ ; Ⓜ Pushkinskaya, Chekhovskaya) Calling itself Moscow's first boutique hotel, this small-ish, slick hotel is indeed a novelty. The location is prime – in the heart of Moscow's shopping district and steps from the serenity of Hermitage Gardens. A classical edifice fronts the street, but the interior is sleek and sophisticated. The rooms are decorated in a modern, minimalist style – subdued whites and greys punctuated by contrasting coloured drapes and funky light fixtures. But comfort is also paramount, with no skimping on luxuries like heated bathroom floors and down-filled duvets.

Even if you can't afford to spend the night, it's worth dropping in to have a drink in the lounge – walls splashed with colour – or to dine at the relatively subdued but highly acclaimed restaurant. This is the best of New Russia: contemporary, creative and classy.

too. With only 30 rooms, the hotel offers an intimate atmosphere and personalised service. Ask for a room with a balcony overlooking the fountain-filled patio.

Alrosa on Kazachy (Map pp132-3; ☎ 745 2190; www.alrosahotels.ru; 1-y Kazachy per 4; s/d from R7000/8050; 🖳 🚲 🔀 ✖ ; Ⓜ Polyanka) Set in the heart of Zamoskvorechie, one of the oldest and most evocative parts of Moscow, the Alrosa recreates the atmosphere of an 18th-century estate. The light-filled atrium, bedecked with crystal chandelier, and 15 classically decorated rooms provide a perfect setting for old-fashioned Russian hospitality.

Hotel Marco Polo Presnja (Map pp128-9; ☎ 244 3631; www.visit-m.ru; Spiridonevsky per 9; s/d from with breakfast R6750/7425; 🖳 🔀 ✖ ; Ⓜ Pushkinskaya) Once a prestigious hotel for high-ranking Communist Party officials, this small hotel is now an excellent, straightforward business hotel operated by the Moscow city government. It is situated in Moscow's most prestigious residential neighbourhood, home to expats and diplomats. The restaurant scene is lively, and Patriarch's Pond is right around the corner.

EATING

In Soviet days eating out meant either a cheap meal at the local cafeteria, or for special occasions, nearly identical food at a cheesy hotel restaurant. Perhaps the current situation in Moscow is a reaction to this dreary sameness. These days, theme restaurants are all the rage. From the Uzbek restaurant with the live camel out the front to the French restaurant with the Gothic cathedral interior, restaurateurs are going all out to ensure that their patrons' dining experience is at least interesting.

Today many restaurants in Moscow allow the diner to experience Russian food as it is meant to be – exquisite *haute-russe* masterpieces once served at fancy feasts and extravagant balls, as well as the tasty and filling meals that have for centuries been prepared in peasant kitchens with garden ingredients.

When you tire of borscht and beef stroganoff, you will be able to find excellent European, American and Asian cuisine. Many of these restaurants have foreign chefs, foreign management, foreign standards, and foreign price levels to match. Cuisine from former Soviet republics – including Georgia (p109), Armenia, Uzbekistan and Ukraine – is popular and delicious.

Many restaurants, especially top-end eateries, accept credit cards. Discounted 'business lunch' specials are often available weekdays before 4pm. This is a great way to sample some of the pricier restaurants around town. Most upscale places require booking a table in advance, especially on weekends.

Restaurants
RUSSIAN

Café Pushkin (Map pp128-9; ☎ 229 5590; Tverskoy bul 26a; business lunch R525, meals R1500-2000; 🕒 24hr; Ⓜ Pushkinskaya) The queen mother of *haute-russe* dining, with an exquisite blend of Russian and French cuisines; service and food are done to perfection. The lovely 19th-century building has a different atmosphere on each floor, including a richly decorated library and a pleasant rooftop café.

GlavPivTorg (Map pp128-9; ☎ 928 2591; ul Bolshaya Lubyanka 5; business lunch R125-195, meals R600-1000; Ⓜ Lubyanka) At the 'central beer restaurant No 5', every effort is made to re-create an upscale apparatchik dining experience. The

Soviet fare is authentic, but not too authentic. So you may get a side of peas, but they will be fresh and sweet. Add three varieties of tasty beer brewed on site, and you've got a restaurant to suit any ideology.

Yolki-Palki (meals R200-400; ⊙ 11am-midnight) Tverskoy District (Map pp128-9; ☎ 928 5525; Neglinnaya ul 8/10; ⓜ Kuznetsky Most); Arbat District (Map pp128-9; ☎ 291 6888; ul Novy Arbat 11; ⓜ Arbatskaya); Zamoskvorechie (Map pp132-3; ☎ 953 9130; Klimentovsky per 14; ⓜ Tretyakovskaya) This excellent Russian chain is beloved for its country cottage décor and its well-stocked salad bar. Outlets all over the city specialise in traditional dishes and cheap beer.

Cafe Margarita (Map pp128-9; ☎ 299 6534; Malaya Bronnaya ul 28; meals R400-600; ⊙ noon-2am; ⓜ Mayakovskaya) With walls lined with bookshelves and a location opposite Patriarch's Pond, this offbeat café is popular with a well-read young crowd. These bookworms are pretty quiet during the day, but the place livens up in the evening, when it often hosts live music.

Meeting Place (Map pp128-9; ☎ 229 2373; Maly Gnezdnikovsky per 9/8/7; business lunch R300, meals R600-800; ⊙ noon-5am; ⓜ Pushkinskaya) The name aptly describes this club-restaurant, which attracts a constant stream of regulars. The food gets mixed reviews, but it's filling and affordable; the many varieties of *pelmeni* (Russian-style ravioli) are particularly popular. Most come for the cosy atmosphere, summertime garden café and free wi-fi access.

TsDL (Map pp128-9; ☎ 291 1515; Povarskaya ul 50; meals R1500-2000; ⊙ noon-11pm; ⓜ Barrikadnaya) The acronym stands for Tsentralny Dom Literatov (Central House of Writers), which is the historic building that houses this fancy restaurant. A glittery chandelier above, plush carpets under foot and rich oak panelling all around create a sumptuous setting for an old-fashioned Russian feast.

UKRAINIAN

Taras Bulba (meals R400-600) Tverskoy District (Map pp128-9; ☎ 200 6082; ul Petrovka 30/7; ⓜ Pushkinskaya); Zamoskvorechie (Map pp132-3; ☎ 951 3760; Pyatnitskaya ul 14; ⓜ Tretyakovskaya) With several branches around the city, this is the Ukrainian version of Yolki-Palki. There's no salad bar, but specialities like pork stuffed with vegetables and spicy smoked beef are tasty. Ukrainian tapestries and wood floors provide a homy atmosphere.

AUTHOR'S CHOICE

Tiflis (Map pp132-3; ☎ 290 2897; ul Ostozhenka 32; meals R1000-1500; ⓜ Kropotinskaya) Moscow is the best place outside the Caucasus to sample the rich, spicy cuisine of the former Soviet republic of Georgia. And Tiflis is the best place in Moscow. The name comes from the Russian word for the Georgian capital, Tbilisi, and when you enter this restaurant, you may think you're there. Its airy balconies and interior courtyards recall a 19th-century Georgian mansion – a romantic and atmospheric setting. Tiflis takes Caucasian cuisine upscale. The *kharcho* (beef soup) is thick and rich, while the *basturma* (grilled lamb) is spicy and cooked to perfection. All the menu items are particularly delectable when accompanied by the Tiflis wine, produced by the restaurateur's winery in Georgia. According to Moscow foodies, Tiflis counts among its regular customers the Russian Minister of Foreign Affairs, Igor Ivanov, who happens to be of Georgian descent.

Shinook (Map pp128-9; ☎ 255 0204; ul 1905 goda 2; meals R1000-1200; ⓜ Ulitsa 1905 Goda) In case you didn't think that Moscow's theme dining was really over the top, Shinook has re-created a Ukrainian peasant farm near the city centre. The staff wear colourfully embroidered shirts, speak with Ukrainian accents (probably lost on most tourists), and serve up the house speciality, *vareniki* (the Ukrainian version of *pelmeni*). As you dine, you can look out the window at a cheerful babushka tending the farmyard animals (who are very well taken care of, we are assured).

CAUCASIAN

Karetny Dvor (Map pp128-9; ☎ 291 6376; Povarskaya ul 52; meals R600-800; ⊙ 24hr; ⓜ Barrikadnaya) Moscow's most popular Caucasian place has a simple, relaxed interior and a green, leafy courtyard – both pleasant. Go for classic Azerbaijani fare like dolmas and lamb kebabs, accompanied by a bottle of Mukuzani (red wine).

Dioskuriya (Map pp128-9; ☎ 290 6908; Marzlyakovsky per 2; meals R400-600; ⊙ 11am-midnight; ⓜ Arbatskaya) This little house just off ul Novy Arbat is famous for its delicious *khachapuri* (Georgian cheese bread), but all of the food is highly regarded, especially for the price. The music, a trio of a capella vocalists, outclasses standard Georgian restaurant bands.

Noah's Ark (Map p131; ☎ 917 0717; Maly Ivanovsky per 9; meals R800-1000; Ⓜ Kitay-Gorod) This Armenian joint features many varieties of shashlyk (meat kebab), many more varieties of cognac and an Armenian orchestra every night. The dining hall is aromatic and atmospheric, thanks to the meat roasting over charcoal in the central brazier.

EUROPEAN

Correa's (brunch R400-600, sandwiches R200-300, meals R600-1000; Ⓨ 8am-midnight) Belorusskaya (Map pp128-9; ☎ 933 4684; Bolshaya Gruzinskaya ul 32; Ⓜ Belorusskaya); Zamoskvorechie (Map pp132-3; ☎ 725 6035; ul Bolshaya Ordinka 40/2; Ⓜ Tretyakovskaya) It's hard to characterise a place that's so simple. It is a tiny space – only seven tables. Large windows and an open kitchen guarantee that it does not feel cramped, just cosy. The menu – sandwiches, pizzas and grills – features nothing too fancy, but everything is prepared with the freshest ingredients and the utmost care. The new outlet in Zamoskvorechie is roomier, but reservations are still recommended for Sunday brunch.

Artist's Gallery (Map pp132-3; ☎ 201 2866; ul Prechistenka 19; business lunch R240, meals R600-1000; Ⓜ Kropotkinskaya) This fantastical restaurant in the Tsereteli Gallery is everything you would expect from this over-the-top artist. The five rooms follow different themes, all equally elaborate; it culminates in a huge, light-filled atrium wallpapered with stained glass and primitive paintings. The place certainly lives up to its name. The menu is a fusion of European and Asian influences, and while secondary to the art, the food is well prepared and artistically presented.

Scandinavia (Map pp128-9; ☎ 200 4986; Maly Palashevsky per 7; business lunch R490, buffet R600, meals R1500-1800; Ⓜ Pushkinskaya) There is no better place to indulge in *Shvedsky stol* (smorgasbord, or 'Swedish table' in Russian) than at a place called Scandinavia. The cold-cut buffet, however, is just the tip of the iceberg at this expat fave. A delightful summer café features sandwiches, salads and treats from the grill. Inside, the dining room offers a sophisticated menu of modern European delights.

Il Patio (business lunch R190-280, meals R400-500) Arbat District (Map pp132-3; ☎ 201 5626; ul Volkhonka 13a; Ⓜ Kropotkinskaya); Barrikadnaya (Map pp128-9; ☎ 785

6553; Novinsky bul 31; Ⓜ Barrikadnaya, Krasnopresnenskaya); Taganskaya (Map p134; ☎ 230 6662; Taganskaya ul 1/2; Ⓨ 8am-11pm; Ⓜ Taganskaya) Long-time Moscow favourite Patio Pizza has gone upscale, with a new, more Italian name, and a new, more stylish look. Fortunately, it still has a slew of outlets, each representing a different Italian city. Wood-oven pizzas and fresh salad bars are the highlights of the menu.

NORTH AMERICAN

Simple Pleasures (Map pp128-9; ☎ 207 4043; ul Sretenka 22; meals R800-1000; Ⓨ noon-midnight Mon-Fri, 2pm-midnight Sat & Sun; Ⓜ Sukharevskaya) The chef is American, but the menu is wide-ranging, including his favourite dishes from Italy, Spain and the American South. The common denominator is fresh ingredients and simple cooking techniques, an ideal match for this comfortable, uncluttered space.

Starlite Diner (meals R500-700; Ⓨ 24hr) Mayakovskaya (Map pp128-9; ☎ 290 9638; Bolshaya Sadovaya ul 16; Ⓜ Mayakovskaya); Oktyabrskaya (Map pp132-3; ☎ 959 8919; ul Korovy val 9, stroyeniye A; Ⓜ Oktyabrskaya) Outdoor seating and classic diner décor make this a long-time favourite of Moscow expats. The extensive brunch menu includes all kinds of omelettes, French toast and freshly squeezed juice. Otherwise, you can't go wrong with burgers and milkshakes, any time of day or night. A second, less pleasant outlet is near Oktyabrskaya pl.

Goodman Steakhouse (Map pp128-9; ☎ 981 4941; Novinsky bul 31; business lunch R360, meals R900-1500; Ⓜ Krasnopresnenskaya, Barrikadnaya) Inside the Novinsky shopping centre, this classic American steakhouse is done up in leather and wood, with B&W photos on the walls and old movies running on the big screen. It receives rave reviews for filet mignon and rack of lamb, and it also claims Moscow's best burger for the bargain price of R360.

Hard Rock Café (Map pp132-3; ☎ 244 8970; ul Arbat 44; sandwiches R250-300, meals R600-800; Ⓨ 24hr; Ⓜ Smolenskaya) At long last, those souvenir T-shirts reading 'Hard Rock Café Moscow' actually mean something. This is the real deal, complete with framed guitars, chicken wings and gift shop. The rock and roll memorabilia does not include enough representation from Russian rock stars, but there are a few notable exceptions. Live music on weekends.

Pancho Villa (Map pp132-3; ☎ 238 7913; ul Bolshaya Yakimanka 52; business lunch R120, meals R300-600; Ⓨ 24hr; Ⓜ Oktyabrskaya) In a new location near

Oktyabrskaya pl, this is still Moscow's top choice for 'Meksikansky' food. If the fajitas and margaritas aren't enough of a draw, come for breakfast burritos, happy hour specials (before 7pm, Monday to Thursday) or live Latin music nightly (from 9pm).

ASIAN

Eastern Quarter (Map pp132-3; ☎ 241 3803; ul Arbat 45/24; meals R400-600; M Smolenskaya) Uzbeks cooking in the open kitchen and more Uzbeks filling up the dining room are signs that this Central Asian eatery is serving some of Moscow's best international cuisine. The speciality: tasty, filling *plov* (pilaf rice with diced mutton and vegetables).

Sushi Vesla (Map pp128-9; ☎ 937 0521; ul Nikolskaya 25; sushi per piece R100-200; ⌚ noon-1am Sun-Thu, to 3am Fri & Sat; M Lubyanka) Sushi is all the rage in Moscow these days. To get in on it, head to this hip Japanese café in the basement of the Nautilus building (enter from Teatralnaya proezd). Dishes are colour-coded to indicate price; at the end of the meal the server clears the empty plates and uses them to calculate the bill.

Silk (Map pp128-9; ☎ 251 4134; 1-ya Tverskaya-Yamskaya ul 29/1; meals R600-800; ⌚ 11am-5am; M Belorusskaya) Not too expensive, but still stylish, Silk is popular for authentic Chinese fare. Connoisseurs credit fresh ingredients and bold spices. 'Bamboo Fire' comes highly recommended for those with a tough tongue.

Maharaja (Map p131; ☎ 921 7758; ul Pokrovka 2/1; meals R600-1000; ⌚ 12.30-11pm; M Kitay-Gorod) Moscow's oldest Indian restaurant features lots of spicy tandoori specialities, including several variations of kebabs and rotis hot from the tandoori oven. Vegetarians have no shortage of options here.

VEGETARIAN

During Lent (the 40-day period before Orthodox Easter), vegetarians will have a plethora of eating options, as many restaurants offer special lenten menus that feature no meat or dairy products. Only a few restaurants are exclusively veggie all year round.

Jagannath (Map pp128-9; ☎ 928 3580; Kuznetsky most 11; meals R300-500; ⌚ 10am-11pm; M Kuznetsky Most) If you are in need of vitamins, this is a funky vegetarian café, restaurant and shop. Its Indian-theme décor is more New Agey than ethnic. Service is slow but sublime, and the food is worth the wait.

Avocado (Map p131; ☎ 921 7719; Chistoprudny bul 12/2; breakfast R35-65, business lunch R140, meals R200-400; ⌚ 10am-11pm; M Chistye Prudy) Less atmospheric than Jagannath, Avocado has a more diverse menu, drawing on dishes from the world's cuisines. No-meat versions of soups and salads, pasta and *pelmeni* are all featured. Grab a seat near the window to watch the passers-by on the boulevard, because the place is otherwise rather austere.

Cafés

Loft Cafe (Map pp128-9; ☎ 933 7713; ul Nikolskaya 25; meals R800-1000; ⌚ 9am-midnight; M Lubyanka) On the top floor of the Nautilus shopping centre, next door to the luxury spa, you'll find this tiny, trendy café. An even tinier terrace gives a fantastic view of Lubyanka pl. Innovative, modern dishes fuse the best of Russian cuisine with Western and Asian influences – for example, grilled salmon with spinach, pine nuts and caviar sauce.

Pavilion (Map pp128-9; ☎ 203 5110; Bolshoy Patriarshy per; meals R600-1000; ⌚ 24hr; M Mayakovskaya) With a prime location overlooking Patriarch's Pond, this new place promises to be prominent on Moscow's thriving café scene. While the pavilion dates from the 19th century, the interior is chic and contemporary.

Garden Art Café (Map pp132-3; ☎ 239 9115; Bolshoy Tolmachevsky per; breakfast R60-100, meals R500-800; ⌚ 24hr; M Tretyakovskaya) This appropriately named café is set in the midst of flowering trees in the courtyard opposite the Tretyakov, drawing a sophisticated, artsy crowd. Wide-plank wood floors and antique furniture contrast with the modern, jazzy music and contemporary cuisine.

Donna Klara (Map pp128-9; ☎ 290 6974; Malaya Bronnaya ul 21/13; meals R300-500; ⌚ 10am-midnight; M Mayakovskaya) Specialising in flaky pastries and dark coffee, this little café is a regular stop for the French community that lives in this area.

Quick Eats

Moo-Moo (meals R100-200; ⌚ 9am-11pm) Lubyanka (Map pp128-9; ☎ 923 4503; Myasnitskaya ul 14; M Lubyanka); Arbat District (Map pp132-3; ☎ 241 1364; ul Arbat 45/23; M Smolenskaya); Khamovniki (Map pp132-3; ☎ 245 7820; Komsomolsky pr 26; M Frunzenskaya) You will recognise this place by its black-and-white Holstein-print décor. The cafeteria-style service offers an easy approach to all the Russian favourites.

Drova (meals R200-400, all-you-can-eat buffet R350; 24hr) Chistye Prudy (Map p131; ☎ 925 2725; Myasnitskaya ul 24; **M** Chistye Prudy); Arbat District (Map pp128-9; ☎ 202 7570; Nikitsky bul 8a; **M** Arbatskaya); Tverskoy District (Map pp128-9; ☎ 229 3227; Bolshaya Dmitrovka ul 7; **M** Teatralnaya) The self-serve buffet features offerings ranging from *solyanka* (a salty vegetable and meat soup) to sushi to sweet-and-sour pork. It's not the best place to sample any of these items, but the price is right. Hungry student types really take advantage of the all-you-can-eat option: it's not always pretty.

Pelmeshka (Map pp128-9; ☎ 292 8392; Kuznetsky most 4/3; breakfast R60, lunch R125, meals R150-200; 11am-midnight; **M** Teatralnaya) Serves many different kinds of *pelmeni*, the most filling of Russian favourites. This place is packed at lunchtime, a sign that it is tasty as well as cheap.

Fighting for prime retail space with McDonald's is the equally omnipresent local chain Russkoe Bistro, endorsed (and co-owned) by Mayor Luzhkov. It serves cheap, traditional goodies such as pirozhki (pastries) and bliny.

There's a handy food court in the basement of the Okhotny Ryad shopping mall.

Self-Catering
If you want to eat like an old-time Muscovite, you'll buy your food, take it home and cook it there. Russian food markets can be entertaining, and if nothing else you can buy the ingredients for a good picnic.

SUPERMARKETS
Stockmans (Map pp132-3; Smolensky Passage, Smolenskaya pl 3/5; 10am-10pm; **M** Smolenskaya) The foreign-goods supermarket in the basement of Stockmans is pricey but convenient.

Yeliseev Grocery Store (Map pp128-9; Tverskaya ul 14; 8am-9pm Mon-Sat, 10am-6pm Sun; **M** Pushkinskaya) Peek in here for a glimpse of prerevolutionary grandeur, as the store is set in the former mansion of the successful merchant Yeliseev. It now houses an upscale market selling caviar and other delicacies.

COFFEE MANIA

Moscow temperatures occasionally call for a warming drink, so it's nice to know you're never far from a fresh brewed cup o' joe. With bohemian coffee houses opening on every corner, Moscow might be called the Russian Seattle; and what, you ask, might be the Russian Starbucks?

Coffee Bean Tverskoy District (Map pp128-9; ☎ 788 6357; Tverskaya ul 10; 8am-11pm; **M** Pushkinskaya); Zamoskvorechie (Map pp132-3; ☎ 953 6726; Pyatnitskaya ul 5; 8am-10pm; **M** Tretyakovskaya); Chistye Prudy (Map p131; ☎ 923 9793; ul Pokrovka 18; 8am-10pm; Chistye Prudy) One could claim that Coffee Bean started the coffee thing in Moscow, as the original outlet on Tverskaya ul has been around for years. It's still the coolest café in the city, with high ceilings, fantastic architectural details and large windows looking out onto the main drag. Coffee drinks cost around R100; it's a rare Russian place that does not allow smoking.

Coffee Mania Kuznetsky Most (Map pp128-9; ☎ 924 0075; Pushechnaya ul; 8am-11pm; **M** Kuznetsky Most); Barrikadnaya (Map pp128-9; ☎ 290 0141; Kudrinskaya pl 46/54; 8am-midnight; **M** Barrikadnaya); Bolshaya Nikitskaya (Map pp128-9; ☎ 775 4310; Bolshaya Nikitskaya ul 13, Moscow Conservatory; 8am-1am; **M** Alexandrovsky Sad) Not quite as bohemian as Coffee Bean (and who can be surprised at this, with a name like Coffee Mania?), but it's still a cool spot, and the menu includes tasty soups, salads and sandwiches as well as coffee drinks. The Bolshaya Nikitskaya branch has a delightful outdoor seating area in front of the conservatory.

Shokolodnitsa Kuznetsky Most (Map pp128-9; ☎ 937 4639; Pushechnaya ul 7/5; 24hr; **M** Kuznetsky Most); ul Arbat (Map pp132-3; ☎ 241 0620; ul Arbat 29; 8am-11pm; **M** Arbatskaya) Oktyabrskaya pl (Map pp132-3; ☎ 238 2734; ul Bolshaya Yakimanka 58/2; 24hr; **M** Oktyabrskaya) Those with a sweet tooth will not be able to resist this place for coffee and desserts. Popular with night owls.

Montana Coffee Belorusskaya (Map pp128-9; ☎ 234 1784; Lesnaya ul 1/2; 8am-midnight Sun-Tue, 24hr Wed-Sat; **M** Belorusskaya); Teatralnaya (Map pp128-9; ☎ 292 5114; Kamergersky per 6; 9am-11pm; **M** Teatralnaya); Paveletskaya (Map p134; ☎ 235 5282; Paveletskaya pl 1; 8am-11pm Mon-Fri, 9am-10pm Sat & Sun; **M** Paveletskaya) Formerly Zen Coffee, this place offers breakfast and business lunches, as well as double espresso decaf cappuccinos. It is impossible to do a serious stroll of the trendy pedestrian strip on Kamergersky per without stopping to sip a drink at this outlet.

The well-stocked **Seventh Continent** (☎ 777 7779; 24hr) supermarkets are the most convenient and reasonable places to stock up on foodstuffs. Grab a cart and peruse the aisles, just like at home. Products available are Russian and imported – it's still expensive, but more affordable than the other places we've mentioned. Branches around the city:

Gastronom Seventh Continent (Map pp132-3; ul Serafimovicha 2; M Kropotkinskaya)

Smolensky Gastronom (Map pp132-3; ul Arbat 54/2; M Smolenskaya)

Tsentralny Gastronom (Map pp128-9; ul Bolshaya Lubyanka 12/1; M Lubyanka)

The more affordable, Turkish-owned **Ramstore** (www.ramstore.ru; 24hr; Sportivnaya Map pp132-3; ul Usachyeva 35; M Sportivnaya; Komsomolskaya Map p131; ☎ 207 3165; Komsomolskaya pl 6, Moskovsky Univermag; M Komsomolskaya; Ulitsa 1905 Goda Map pp128-9; ☎ 255 5412; Krasnaya Presnya 23; M Ulitsa 1905 Goda) includes three shopping malls, as well as a number of self-standing supermarkets in and around Moscow; of the many outlets around the city, those listed here are the most convenient. 'Club card' holders (R25) are eligible for discounts of 20% to 30% on some products. The selection is impressive, but these places can be overwhelming due to their size and the number of shoppers they attract.

MARKETS

Moscow's *rynky* (markets) are busy, bustling places, full of activity and colour. Even if you are not buying, it's fun to see what's for sale: tables piled high with fresh produce; golden honey in jars as big as basketballs; vibrantly coloured spices pouring out of plastic bags; silvery fish posing on beds of ice.

Prices are negotiable at the markets, but don't expect them to come down too much. Bring your own bag if you have one, and keep your eye on the quality of items that are popped in there. Some central markets:

Danilovsky Market (Map pp126-7; Mytnaya ul 74; M Tulskaya)

Dorogomilovsky Market (Map pp132-3; Mozhaysky val 10; 10am-8pm; M Kievskaya)

Rizhsky Market (Map pp126-7; pr Mira 94-96; M Rizhskaya)

DRINKING

There is not one area of Moscow where all the bars and pubs are clustered; indeed, the whole city is now littered with such establishments, with more opening every day. Traditionally, ul Arbat is a prime spot for the café scene, especially as it is closed to automobile traffic. Likewise, the newer and trendier Kamergersky per is a pedestrian-only street, which makes it a hot spot for strollers and drinkers.

AUTHOR'S CHOICE

Red Bar (Map pp132-3; ☎ 730 0808; Kutuzovsky pr 22-24; beers R175, meals R1400-1750; noon-3am; M Kievskaya) On the 27th floor of a skyscraper overlooking the Moscow River, Red Bar features funky décor and a fabulous view. The name refers to its colour, not its politics: the whole place is draped in swanky red, except the glistening white piano.

The menu is mostly small plates; overpriced, but tasty. The real draw is the floor-to-ceiling windows and their vantage point of the city skyline. Come for a sundown drink before heading out to paint the rest of the town red.

Bar 30/7 (Map pp128-9; ☎ 209 5951; ul Petrovka 30/7; 24hr; M Chekhovskaya) This slick new bar, located on the Boulevard Ring, is the latest place to see and be seen in Moscow. If you can snag a seat in the attached 'sun room' seating area, you will enjoy a lovely view of the boulevard promenade. Good luck, as the place gets packed on weekends.

Real McCoy (Map pp128-9; ☎ 255 4144; Kudrinskaya pl 1; business lunch R180, meals R500-1000; 24hr; M Barrikadnaya) The main features of this 'bootlegger's bar' are walls plastered in old newspapers and a dining room crowded with expats. The menu is not too memorable, except it includes BBQ ribs, seafood curry and everything in between. Nonetheless, this is a popular spot for drinking, especially the two-for-one happy hour specials (5pm to 8pm daily).

Mon Café (Map pp128-9; ☎ 250 8800; 1-ya Tverskaya-Yamskaya ul 4; meals R800-1200; 24hr; M Mayakovskaya) The hot-to-trot clientele is the décor at this otherwise minimalist French café. The vaguely European fare is tasty, if somewhat overpriced. Don your short skirts and black shirts and take a seat on the upper level for the best view of the activity below.

Tinkoff (Map pp128-9; ☎ 777 3300; Protochny per 11; ½-litre beer R120, meals R600-800; ☯ noon-2am; Ⓜ Smolenskaya) Moscow's branch of this now nationwide microbrewery features sport on the big screen, lagers and pilsners on draught, and a metre-long sausage on the menu (yikes). This hip and happening venue often hosts DJs who travel from Europe to spin for its upscale clientele.

ENTERTAINMENT

Moscow can keep anyone entertained for months. The key to finding out what's on is the weekly magazine *element* and the comprehensive weekly entertainment section in Friday's *Moscow Times*. For a laugh, try the *Exile*.

The classical performing arts remain an incredible bargain. Highly acclaimed professionals stage productions in a number of elegant theatres around the city. While the Bolshoi is Moscow's most famous theatre, other venues host productions of comparable quality, with tickets at a fraction of the Bolshoi's price.

Theatre and concert programmes are displayed at venues and ticket kiosks. Aside from the Bolshoi, you can usually purchase tickets directly from box offices on the day of the performance. Most theatres are closed between late June and early September.

Classical Music

Moscow International House of Music (Map p134; ☎ 730 1011; www.mmdm.ru; Kosmodamianskaya nab 52/8; tickets R60-600; Ⓜ Paveletskaya) A graceful, modern, glass building, this new venue opened in 2003. It has three halls, including Svetlanov Hall, which holds the largest organ in Russia. Needless to say, organ concerts held here are impressive.

Tchaikovsky Concert Hall (Map pp128-9; ☎ 299 3957; www.philharmonia.ru; Triumfalnaya pl 4/31; Ⓜ Mayakovskaya) Home to the famous State Symphony Orchestra.

Moscow Conservatory (Map pp128-9; ☎ 229 8183; Bolshaya Nikitskaya ul 13; Ⓜ Okhotny Ryad, Arbatskaya) Russia's largest music school has two venues: the Great Hall (Bolshoy Zal) and the Small Hall (Maly Zal). Every four years, the conservatory hosts hundreds of musicians at the prestigious International Tchaikovsky Competition, which will be held next in summer 2006.

Opera & Ballet

Bolshoi Theatre (Map pp128-9; ☎ 292 0050; www .bolshoi.ru; Teatralnaya pl 1; tickets R200-2000; Ⓜ Teatralnaya) An evening at the Bolshoi is still one of Moscow's most romantic options, with an electric atmosphere in the glittering six-tier auditorium. Both the ballet and opera companies perform a range of Russian and foreign works.

Since the Soviet collapse (and even before), the Bolshoi has been marred by politics, scandal and frequent turnover. Yet the show must go on – and it will. At the time of research, however, the Bolshoi was preparing to close its main stage for long-needed renovations. It is expected to reopen for the 2008 season.

In the meantime, the smaller New Stage (Novaya Stsena) – open since 2003 – will be hosting performances. In spring 2005 the New Stage showed the controversial *Children of Rosenthal*, the first world premiere performed at the Bolshoi in years (see the boxed text, p98).

In theory, tickets can be reserved by phone or Internet, or purchased directly from the box office. It's usually necessary to buy them well in advance, especially during peak tourist periods. Otherwise, the easiest way to get tickets to the Bolshoi is to go there on the day of the performance and buy them from a tout. Expect to pay upwards of R1000. Exercise caution so that you don't buy tickets for a show that was, say, last year.

State Kremlin Palace (Map p135; ☎ 928 5232; www.kremlin-gkd.ru; ul Vozdvizhenka 1; Ⓜ Alexandrovsky Sad) The Bolshoi does not have a monopoly on ballet and opera in Moscow. Leading dancers also appear with the Kremlin Ballet and the Moscow Classical Ballet Theatre, both of which perform here.

Stanislavsky & Nemirovich-Danchenko Musical Theatre (Map pp128-9; ☎ 229 8388; www.stanislavsky music.ru; Bolshaya Dmitrovka ul 17; Ⓜ Chekhovskaya) Another opera and ballet company with a similar classical repertoire and high-quality performances. This historic theatre company was founded when two legends of the Moscow theatre scene – Konstantin Stanislavsky and Vladimir Nemirovich-Danchenko – combined forces in 1941.

Theatre

Moscow has around 40 professional theatres and numerous amateur theatres, with a wide range of plays – contemporary and classic, Russian and foreign – staged each year. Most performances are in Russian. Some of the best drama venues:

MkhT (Map pp128-9; ☎ 632 4105; http://art.theatre .ru; Kamergersky per 3; Ⓜ Teatralnaya, Okhotny Ryad) Also known as the Chekhov Moscow Art Theatre, this is where method acting was founded more than 100 years ago. Watch for English-language versions of Russian classics performed by the American Studio (☎ 292 0941).

Lenkom Theatre (Map pp128-9; ☎ 299 0708; www .lenkom.ru in Russian; Malaya Dmitrovka ul 6; Ⓜ Pushkinskaya) Flashy productions and a lot of musicals keep non-Russian-speakers happy.

Maly Theatre (Map pp128-9; ☎ 923 2621; Teatralnaya pl 1/6; Ⓜ Teatralnaya) A lovely theatre founded in 1824, performing mainly 19th-century works.

Taganka Theatre (Map p134; ☎ 915 1015; Zemlyanoy val 76/12; Ⓜ Taganskaya) A legendary theatre famous for its rebellious director, Yury Lyubimov, and the unruly actor Vladimir Vysotsky. Stages top-notch contemporary productions.

Circus

Moscow has two separate circuses, putting on glittering shows for Muscovites of all ages. The show usually mixes dance, cabaret and rock music with animals and acrobats. Performance schedules are subject to change.

Great Moscow Circus (Map pp126-7; ☎ 930 2815; www.bolshoicircus.ru; pr Vernadskogo 7; tickets R100-450; Ⓨ shows 7pm Wed, Fri & Sun, 3pm Sat & Sun; Ⓜ Universitet) With 3400 seats, this circus is near Moscow University and has the best reputation, especially for its animal acts and clowns.

Nikulin Circus (Old Circus at Tsvetnoy Bul; Map pp128-9; ☎ 200 0668; www.circusnikulin.ru; Tsvetnoy bul 13; tickets R50-500; Ⓨ shows 7pm Thu & Fri, 2.30pm & 6pm Sat & Sun; Ⓜ Tsvetnoy Bulvar) More central than the Great Moscow Circus, this is in a modernised 19th-century building and produces shows around a central theme.

Nightclubs

Karma Bar (Map pp128-9; ☎ 924 5633; Pushechnaya ul 3; cover R100-200; Ⓨ 7pm-6am Thu-Sat, 11pm-6am Sun; Ⓜ Kuznetsky Most) A worldly mix of Asian food, Latin music and Russian fun. Thursday nights usually feature live music, while the other nights are for DJs and dancing (free lessons from 9pm to 11pm, Friday and Saturday). Add to the mix happy hours and hookah pipes and you've got one of Moscow's top expat clubs.

Propaganda (Map pp128-9; ☎ 924 5732; Bolshoy Zlatoustinsky per 7; meals R300-400; Ⓨ noon-7am; Ⓜ Lubyanka) This long-time favourite looks to be straight from the warehouse district, with exposed brick walls and pipe ceilings. It's a café by day, but at night they clear the dance floor and let the DJ do his stuff. This is a gay-friendly place, especially on Sunday nights.

Night Flight (Map pp128-9; ☎ 299 4165; Tverskaya ul 17; meals R1000-2000, cover incl drink R650; Ⓨ restaurant 6pm-4am, club 9pm-5am; Ⓜ Pushkinskaya) This continues to be one of Moscow's most popular spots for business travellers on expense accounts, despite – or because of – its dubious reputation. Indeed, it's hard to miss the crowds of working women hanging around this club. Nonetheless, the restaurant continues to receive rave reviews, thanks to Swedish ingredients and chefs. And the dance floor is always hopping. No cover for restaurant guests.

A Priori (Map pp128-9; ☎ 291 7783; Bolshaya Molchanovka ul 12; cover from R400; Ⓨ midnight-10am Fri & Sat; Ⓜ Arbatskaya) To really strut your stuff on the dance floor, head to this progressive house club. It has a huge bilevel dance hall, as well as an exclusive 'sofa zone'. Resident and visiting DJs host dance parties on weekends. It's a new experience every time, as the interior is redesigned every few weeks. There's strict face control, so dress the part.

Live Music

Sixteen Tons (Map pp128-9; ☎ 253 5300; www.16tons .ru; ul Presnensky val 6; cover R250-600; Ⓨ concerts 10pm or 11pm; Ⓜ Ulitsa 1905 Goda) Has a brassy English pub–restaurant downstairs, with an excellent house-brewed bitter. Upstairs, the club gets some of the best local and foreign bands that play in Moscow.

Le Club (Map p134; ☎ 915 1042; www.le-club.ru; Verkhnyaya Radishchevskaya ul 21; concerts R300-3000; Ⓨ concerts 8:30pm; Ⓜ Taganskaya) Moscow's top venue for jazz is in the building of the Taganka theatre. Top performers from all over the world come to play in this 1930s Chicago–style club.

bilingua (Map p131; ☎ 923 6683; Krivokolenny per 10/5; meals R200-500; Ⓨ 24hr; Ⓜ Chistye Prudy) Crowded with grungy, artsy student types, this café also sells books and funky clothing. If you can stand the smoke, it's a cool place to grab a bite to eat and listen to some music (nightly) or peruse the literary offerings. Despite the name, there's not much in the way of foreign-language literature.

Proekt OGI (Map p131; ☎ 927 5366; www.proekt ogi.ru in Russian; Potapovsky per 8/12; cover R50-80; ☺ 8am-11pm; Ⓜ Kitay-Gorod, Chistye Prudy) This vaguely hippy (but definitely hip) place is for student types; enter through the un-marked door in the corner of the courtyard and descend into the underground – literally and figuratively. Live music plays most nights.

Chinese Pilot Dzhao-Da (Map pp128-9; ☎ 923 2896; www.jao-da.ru in Russian; Lubyansky proezd 25; cover R150-250; ☺ concerts 11pm; Ⓜ Kitay-Gorod) A relaxed and relatively inexpensive place to hear live music. The divey basement place hosts lots of different kinds of bands – from around Europe and Russia – so check out the website in advance.

BB King (Map pp128-9; ☎ 299 8206; Sadovaya-Samotyochnaya ul 4/2; cover R200; ☺ 8pm Wed-Sun; Ⓜ Tsvetnoy Bulvar) This old-style blues club hosts an open jam session on Wednesday night, acoustic blues on Sunday (7pm) and live performances on weekends. The res-taurant is open for lunch and dinner, when you can listen to jazz and blues on the old-fashioned jukebox.

Both **Bunker** (Map pp128-9; ☎ 200 1506; Tverskaya ul 12; ☺ 10pm-7am; Ⓜ Mayakovskaya) and its succes-sor **B-2** (Map pp128-9; ☎ 209 9918; Bolshaya Sadovaya ul 8; Ⓜ Pushkinskaya) have cheap food and drinks, and live music almost every night.

Gay & Lesbian Venues

New Age (Three Monkeys) (Map p131; www.gay central.ru in Russian; Nastavnichesky per 11/1; ☺ 10pm-7am Thu-Sun; Ⓜ Chkalovskaya) The newest and best club on the gay scene. Besides the dance floor, which is hopping, the club has drag queens and go-go boys, an Internet café and a cinema. The clientele comes dressed to kill. There's no cover charge be-fore midnight.

12 Volts (Map pp128-9; ☎ 200 1506; Tverskaya ul 12; meals R400-600; ☺ 10pm-7am; Ⓜ Mayakovskaya) The founders of Moscow's gay and lesbian move-ment opened this welcoming café-cum-social club, tucked in behind the club Bunker (enter from the courtyard). Besides good food and cheap drinks, the place offers a consultation service for individuals facing homosexual is-sues. This is one of the few hang-outs that attracts lesbians as well as gay men.

911 (Map pp128-9; ☎ 292 2911; Glinishchevsky per 3; ☺ noon-2am; Ⓜ Pushkinskaya) This used to be a straight bar with a gay night, but it has grown into a gay bar with some straight guests – 'gay expansion' as described by one local in-the-know. Although the place has a small dance floor and a drag show on Saturday night, it is more of a café scene. Look for the entrance down from Studio Casino.

Cinema

American Cinema (Map pp132-3; ☎ 941 8747; Ber-ezhkovskaya nab 2; Ⓜ Kievskaya) Located inside the Radisson Slavyanskaya Hotel, this cinema shows major Hollywood movies in English. Call for information, or check the listings in the *Moscow Times* or *element*.

Sport

Vysshaya Liga, the premier football league, has six Moscow teams: Spartak, Lokomotiv, TsSKA, Torpedo, Dinamo and FC Moskva each with a loyal following. You can often buy tickets immediately before games, played at the following venues.

Dinamo Stadium (Map pp126-7; ☎ 212 3132; Leningradsky pr 36; Ⓜ Dinamo) Seats 51,000 and hosts Dinamo and TsSKA.

Lokomotiv Stadium (Map pp126-7; ☎ 161 4283; Bolshaya Cherkizovskaya ul 125; Ⓜ Cherkizovskaya) Reconstructed in 2002 and seats 30,000.

Luzhniki Stadium (Map pp126-7; ☎ 785 9717; www .luzhniki.ru in Russian; Luzhnetskaya nab 24; Ⓜ Sportiv-naya) Seats 80,000 and hosts Torpedo and Spartak.

Moscow's main entrant in the Super Liga, the top ice-hockey league, is Dinamo, which plays at the stadium of the same name.

Men's basketball has dropped in popu-larity since its days of Olympic glory in the 1980s. Moscow's top basketball team, **TsSKA** (Map pp126-7; ☎ 213 2288; Leningradsky pr 39A; Ⓜ Aeroport), does well in European league play, but all too often serves as a retirement home for the NBA, which also poaches the best players. The TsSKA women's team plays from September to May.

SHOPPING

Foreign goods cost the same or more than they would in their home countries; if an item seems like a steal, it's probably a bargain-basement counterfeit. Local items you may want to purchase are crystal, linen,

MOSCOW

traditional crafts and woollen shawls. Soviet paraphernalia is a fun novelty souvenir. If you are interested in taking home vodka or caviar, see p180.

If you'd like to take home antiques or anything else that's more than 25 years old, see p702 for details on export restrictions.

Shopping Streets

Now restored to its prerevolutionary fashionable status, ul Petrovka is Moscow's main shopping strip. It begins beside the Bolshoi Theatre and heads north, lined with upmarket boutiques, as well as a large department store (right) and a fancy shopping centre (right). It culminates in Stolesnikov per, a pedestrian strip given over to the most exclusive shops.

Ul Arbat has always been a tourist attraction; therefore, it is littered with souvenir shops and stalls.

Markets

Izmaylovo Market (Map pp126-7; admission R15; 9am-6pm Sat & Sun; M Partizanskaya) This sprawling area is packed with art, handmade crafts, antiques, Soviet paraphernalia and just about anything you may want for a souvenir. You'll find Moscow's biggest original range of *matryoshky* (nesting dolls), *palekh* and *khokhloma* (lacquer bowls) ware, as well as less traditional woodworking crafts. There are also rugs from the Caucasus and Central Asia, pottery, linen, jewellery, fur hats, chess sets, toys, Soviet posters and much more.

Feel free to negotiate, but don't expect too much flexibility in prices. Vendors normally come down in price by about 10% with little or no argument; with some hard work you can get them down further. This place is technically open every day, but many vendors come out only on weekends, when your selection will be greater.

Mayor Luzhkov has long threatened to raze this chaotic market and move the vendors indoors.

Artists set up their stalls on ul Krymsky val, opposite the entrance to Gorky Park (p161), and in the *perekhod* (underground walkway). There are also many galleries within the Central House of Artists (p161). Unlike the Izmaylovo market, this is more arts than crafts.

Malls

GUM (Map p135; ☎ 921 5763; Krasnaya pl 3; 10am-10pm; M Ploshchad Revolyutsii) On the eastern side of Red Square, this place has made the transition to a market economy in fine form: the 19th-century building is a sight in itself. It's often called a 'department store', but that's a misnomer as it is really a huge collection of individual shops spread over several floors.

Okhotny Ryad (Map p135; ☎ 737 8449; Manezhnaya pl; 11am-10pm; M Okhotny Ryad) This zillion-dollar mall was built in the 1990s. Although it was originally filled with expensive boutiques and no people, times have changed. Now the stores cater to all income levels and they are usually packed. There is a big, crowded food court on the ground floor.

Petrovsky Passazh (Map pp128-9; ☎ 928 5012; ul Petrovka 10; 10am-9pm; M Kuznetsky Most) One of Moscow's sleekest shopping arcades.

Department Stores & Speciality Shops

TsUM (Map pp128-9; ☎ 292 1157; ul Petrovka 2; 9am-8pm Mon-Sat, to 6pm Sun; M Teatralnaya) TsUM stands for Tsentralny Universalny Magazin (Central Department Store), which was built in 1909 as the Scottish-owned Muir & Merrilees. It was the first department store aimed at middle-class shoppers. It no longer is, as it is now filled with designer labels and luxury items.

Detsky Mir (Map pp128-9; ☎ 238 0096; Lubyanskaya pl; 9am-8pm Mon-Sat; M Lubyanka) This huge store – 'Children's World' in English – was the premier toy store during Soviet times. Now Detsky Mir has a mix of imported and Russian-produced toys, along with well-stocked sporting goods and homewares departments (and other toys for adults too).

Many smaller, more specialised stores offer plenty of opportunities for souvenirs:

Gus-Khrustalny Factory Store (Map pp128-9; ☎ 232 5658; www.ghz.ru; Gostiny Dvor; 10am-8pm Mon-Fri, to 6pm Sat & Sun; M Ploshchad Revolyutsii) Beautiful and reasonably priced glassware and crystal from the nearby town of Gus-Khrustalny.

La Casa de Cuba (Map p135; ☎ 737 8409; 11am-10pm; M Okhotny Ryad) Deep in the Okhotny Ryad shopping mall, Le Casa de Cuba sells a wide range of Cuban cigars.

Vologda Linen (Map pp128-9; ☎ 232 9463; www.linens.ru; Gostiny Dvor; 10am-8pm; M Ploshchad Revolyutsii) Fine clothes and linen made according to traditional Russian methods. The stuff is beautiful and good value.

World of New Russians (Map pp128-9; ☎ 241 0081; www.newrussian.net; ul Arbat 36; ⊙ 10am-9pm; Ⓜ Arbatskaya) Stocks a wide range of overpriced but amusing gifts, mostly traditional Russian items with a New Russian theme (the Gzhel mobile phone, for example).

GETTING THERE & AWAY
Air
International flights from Moscow's airports incur a departure tax, which is sometimes split between arrival and departure. In any case the taxes are included in the price of the airline ticket.

AIRPORTS
Moscow has five main airports servicing international and domestic flights. Note that the destinations served by different airports can vary, so confirm your airport when you buy your ticket. Arrive at least 90 minutes before your flight in order to navigate check-in formalities and security.

Moscow's main international airport is **Sheremetyevo-2** (☎ 956 4666; www.sheremetyevo-airport.ru), 30km northwest of the city centre. It services most flights to/from places outside the former USSR. Nearby **Sheremetyevo-1** (☎ 232 6565; www.sheremetyevo-airport.ru) services flights to/from St Petersburg, the Baltic states, Belarus and northern European Russia. The airport is across the runways from Sheremetyevo-2: bus 517 and an airport shuttle bus run between them.

Domodedovo (☎ 933 6666; www.domodedovo.ru), 48km south of the city centre, has undergone extensive upgrades in recent years in order to service more international flights.

Most notably, all British Airway flights now fly in and out of Domodedovo. It also services many flights to/from the Far East and Central Asia.

Vnukovo (☎ 436 2813; www.vnukovo-airport.ru) serves most flights to/from the Caucasus, Moldova and Kaliningrad. About 30km southwest of the city centre, this airport is also undergoing substantial renovation and is expected to expand its services significantly in future years.

The little-used **Bykovo** (☎ 558 4933) airport is about 35km southeast of the city limit on the Novoryazanskoe Hwy.

TICKETS
You can buy domestic airline tickets from most travel agents (p138) and at Aeroflot offices all over town. Convenient ticket offices:

Aeroflot (Map pp128-9; ☎ 753 5555; www.aeroflot.ru; ul Petrovka 20/1; ⊙ 9am-8pm Mon-Sat, to 4pm Sun; Ⓜ Chekhovskaya)
Transaero (☎ 788 8080; ⊙ 9am-6pm Mon-Sat) Smolenskaya pl (Map pp132-3; 2-y Smolensky per 3; Ⓜ Smolenskaya); Paveletskaya pl (Map p134; Paveletskaya pl 2/3; Ⓜ Paveletskaya)

Boat
In summer, passenger boats from Moscow ply the rivers and canals of Russia all the way north to St Petersburg, and south to Astrakhan or Rostov-on-Don.

The St Petersburg route follows the Moscow Canal and then the Volga River to the Rybinsk Reservoir; then the Volga-Baltic Canal to Lake Onega; the Svir River

DOMESTIC FLIGHTS FROM MOSCOW

Destination	Flights per day	Duration	One-way fare
Arkhangelsk	4	1hr 40min	R4200–4600
Astrakhan	4	2½hr	R4850
Irkutsk	2	5hr	R8500–9000
Kaliningrad	7	2hr	R2800–3000
Krasnodar	6	2hr	R3200–3900
Murmansk	4	2hr	R4400–5090
Novosibirsk	6	3hr	R3600–6800
Sochi	5-6	2hr	R2900–4000
St Petersburg	20	50min	R2800–3500
Yekaterinburg	11	2½hr	R5300–5400
Vladivostok	3-4	7hr	R12,500–13,800
Volgograd	4	2hr	R3400–3600

MOSCOW

to Lake Ladoga; and the Neva River to St Petersburg.

The main southbound route takes the Moscow Canal north to the Volga. It then follows the Volga east before heading south all the way downstream to Astrakhan (which is nine days from Moscow), via Uglich, Yaroslavl, Kostroma, Nizhny Novgorod, Kazan, Ulyanovsk, Samara, Saratov and Volgograd.

The Moscow terminus for these sailings is the **Northern River Station** (Severny Rechnoy Vokzal; Map pp126-7; ☎ 457 4050; Leningradskoe sh 51; Ⓜ Rechnoy Vokzal). To get here, take the metro to Rechnoy vokzal, then walk 15 minutes due west, passing under Leningradskoe sh and through a nice park.

The navigation season is generally May to September, although it depends on the route. Transit ships are operated by the **Capital Shipping Company** (Map pp126-7; ☎ 458 9624; www.cck-ship.ru in Russian; Rechnoy Vokzal, Leningradsky sh 51; Ⓜ Rechnoy Vokzal), located at the Northern River Station. Other companies offer tourist cruises that visit the cities in the Golden Ring and along the Volga. See p406 for more information.

Bus

Buses run to a number of towns and cities within 700km of Moscow. Bus fares are similar to *kupeyny* (2nd-class) train fares. Buses tend to be crowded, although they are usually faster than the *prigorodnye poezdy* (suburban trains).

To book a seat go to the long-distance bus terminal, the **Shchyolkovsky Bus Station** (Map pp126-7; Ⓜ Shchyolkovskaya), 8km east of the city centre. Queues can be bad, so it's advisable to book ahead, especially for travel on Friday, Saturday or Sunday.

Buses are best for those destinations with poor train services, including some of the Golden Ring towns.

BUSES FROM MOSCOW

Destination	Buses per day	Duration	One-way fare
Nizhny Novgorod	5	9hr	R300
Pereslavl-Zalessky	2	6hr	R236
Suzdal	1	4½hr	R145
Vladimir	4	3½hr	R120

Car & Motorcycle

See p734 for general advice about driving in Moscow.

Ten major highways, numbered M1 to M10 (but not in any logical order), fan out from Moscow to all points of the compass. Most are in fairly good condition near the city, but some get pretty bad further out:

M1 The main road from Western Europe, including Poland via Brest, Minsk and Smolensk.

M2 The first 110km of the M2 to Oryol and Ukraine are excellent dual carriageway – something you'll remember like a dream as you hit some of the bumpy, narrow roads further south.

M7 Heads east to Vladimir.

M8 Heads northeast to Yaroslavl.

M10 The road to St Petersburg; dual carriageway as far as Tver.

Moscow has no shortage of petrol stations selling all grades of fuel. Most are open 24 hours, are affiliated with Western oil companies, and can be found on the major roads in and out of town. There are service, repair and parts' specialists for many Western makes of car in Moscow – see the *Moscow Business Telephone Guide* for listings.

CAR RENTAL

While there's little reason for the average traveller to rent a car for getting around Moscow (as public transport is quite adequate), you may want to consider it for trips out of the city.

Be aware that many firms won't let you take their cars out of the city, and others will only rent a car with a driver. This latter option is not necessarily a bad one, as cars with drivers aren't always more expensive. Plus you can avoid the trouble of coping with Russian roads.

The major international rental firms have outlets in Moscow. Generally it is best to reserve your car before you arrive in Moscow – advance reservations and special offers can reduce the price by 50% or more. Prices for on-the-spot rental start at €80 per day.

The major car rental agencies will usually pick up or drop off the car at your hotel:

Avis (☎ 578 7179; www.avis-moscow.ru; Sheremetyevo-2)

Europcar (☎ 363 6418; www.europcar.ru; Domodedovo)

Hertz (Map pp126-7; ☎ 937 3274; www.hertz.ru; Smolnaya ul 24; Ⓜ Rechnoy Vokzal)

Train

Moscow has rail links to most parts of Russia, most former Soviet states, many Eastern and Western European countries, plus China and Mongolia. For representative schedules and fares, see the boxed text, below. See p737 for general information on train travel, fares and deciphering timetables.

STATIONS

Moscow has nine main stations. Multiple stations may service the same destination,

so be sure to confirm the arrival/departure station.

Belorussky vokzal (Belarus Station; Map pp128-9; ☎ 251 6093; Tverskaya Zastava pl; Ⓜ Belorusskaya) Serves trains to/from Smolensk, Kaliningrad, Belarus, Lithuania, Poland, Germany; some trains to/from the Czech Republic; and suburban trains to/from the west including Mozhaysk, Borodino and Zvenigorod.

Kazansky vokzal (Kazan Station; Map p131; ☎ 264 6556; Komsomolskaya pl; Ⓜ Komsomolskaya) Serves trains to/from Kazan, Izhevsk, Ufa, Ryazan, Ulyanovsk, Samara, Novorossiysk, Central Asia; some trains to/from Vladimir, Nizhny

---

TRAINS DEPARTING FROM MOSCOW

Trains from Moscow to St Petersburg

Train no & name	Departure time	Duration	Fare
2 Krasnaya Strela	11.55pm	8hr	R1700
4 Ekspress	11.59pm	8hr	R1700
6 Nikolaevsky Ekspress	11.30pm	8hr	R1700
24 Yunost	12.30pm	8hr	R1300 (seat)
54 Grand Express	11.24pm	9hr	R3000-13,000
160 Avrora	4.30pm	5½hr	R1300 (seat)
164 ER200	6.28pm	4½hr	R1700 (seat)

International Trains from Moscow

Destination & train no	Departure time & station	Duration	Fare
Almaty 008	10.25pm (odd days), Kazansky	78hr	R4100
Kyiv 001	11.23pm (odd days), Kievsky	14hr	R1033
Minsk 001	10.25pm, Belorussky	10hr	R1200
Rīga 001	7.11pm, Rizhsky	16hr	R2030
Tallinn 034	6.15pm, Leningradsky	15hr	R1560
Vilnius 005	7.01pm, Belorussky	15hr	R1588

Domestic Trains from Moscow

Destination & train no	Departure time & station	Duration	Fare
Irkutsk 002	9.22pm, Yaroslavsky	77hr	R6200
Kazan 028	7.28pm, Kazansky	11hr	R1150
Murmansk 382	7.28pm, Leningradsky	34hr	R1860
Nizhny Novgorod 062*	4.55pm, Kursky	4½hr	R300 (seat)
Pskov 010	7.55pm Leningradsky	12hr	R1120
Samara 010	6.50pm, Kazansky	15hr	R1888
Tver	10 daily, Leningradsky	2hr	R400
Vladimir 816*	6.04pm, Kursky	2½hr	R208
Yaroslavl	14 daily, Yaroslavsky	4hr	R340
Yekaterinburg 122	4.50pm, Yaroslavsky	28hr	R2300

*Express train; other slower trains also available.

Novgorod, the Ural Mountains, Siberia, Saratov, Rostov-on-Don; and suburban trains to/from the southeast, including Bykovo airport, Kolomna, Gzhel and Ryazan.

Kievsky vokzal (Kyiv Station; Map pp132-3; ☎ 240 1115; pl Kievskogo vokzala; Ⓜ Kievskaya) Serves Bryansk, Kyiv, western Ukraine, Moldova, Slovakia, Hungary, Austria, Prague, Romania, Bulgaria, Croatia, Serbia, Greece, Venice; suburban trains to/from the southwest, including Peredelkino and Kaluga.

Kursky vokzal (Kursk Station; Map p131; ☎ 916 2003; pl Kurskogo vokzala; Ⓜ Kurskaya) Serves Oryol, Kursk, Krasnodar, Adler, the Caucasus, eastern Ukraine, Crimea, Georgia, Azerbaijan. It also has some trains to/from Rostov-on-Don, Vladimir, Nizhny Novgorod, Perm; and suburban trains to/from the east and south, including Petushki, Vladimir, Podolsk, Chekhov, Serpukhov and Tula.

Leningradsky vokzal (Leningrad Station; Map p131; ☎ 262 9143; Komsomolskaya pl; Ⓜ Komsomolskaya) Serves Tver, Novgorod, Pskov, St Petersburg, Vyborg, Murmansk, Estonia, Helsinki; and suburban trains to/from the northwest including Klin and Tver. Note that sometimes this station is referred to on timetables and tickets by its former name, Oktyabrsky.

Paveletsky vokzal (Pavelets Station; Map p134; ☎ 235 0522; Paveletskaya pl; Ⓜ Paveletskaya) Serves Yelets, Lipetsk, Voronezh, Tambov, Volgograd, Astrakhan; some trains to/from Saratov; and suburban trains to/from the southeast, including Leninskaya.

Rizhsky vokzal (Riga Station; Map pp126-7; ☎ 631 1588; Rizhskaya pl; Ⓜ Rizhskaya) Serves Latvia, with suburban trains to/from the northwest, including Istra and Novoierusalimskaya.

Savyolovsky vokzal (Savyolov Station; Map pp126-7; ☎ 285 9005; pl Savyolovskogo vokzala; Ⓜ Savyolovskaya) Serves Cherepovets; some trains to/from Kostroma, Vologda; and suburban trains to/from the north.

Yaroslavsky vokzal (Yaroslavl Station; Map p131; ☎ 921 5914; Komsomolskaya pl; Ⓜ Komsomolskaya) Serves Yaroslavl, Arkhangelsk, Vorkuta, the Russian Far East, Mongolia, China, North Korea; some trains to/from Vladimir, Nizhny Novgorod, Kostroma, Vologda, Perm, Urals, Siberia; and suburban trains to/from the northeast, including Abramtsevo, Khotkovo, Sergiev Posad and Aleksandrov.

SUBURBAN TRAINS
When taking trains from Moscow, note the difference between long-distance and 'suburban' trains. Long-distance trains run to places at least three or four hours out of Moscow, with limited stops and a range of accommodation classes. Suburban trains, known as *prigorodnye poezdy* or *elektrichki*, run to within just 100km or 200km of Moscow, stop almost every-

where, and have a single class of hard bench seats. You simply buy your ticket before the train leaves, and there's no capacity limit – so you may have to stand part of the way.

Most Moscow stations have a separate ticket hall for suburban trains, usually called the Prigorodny Zal and often tucked away at the side or back of the station building. Suburban trains are usually listed on separate timetables, and may depart from a separate group of platforms.

TICKETS
For long-distance trains it's best to buy your tickets in advance. Tickets for some trains may be available on the day of departure, but this is less likely in summer. Always take your passport along when buying a ticket.

Tickets are sold at the train stations themselves, but it is much easier to buy tickets from a travel agent (p138) or *kassa zheleznoy dorogi* (railway ticket office). These are often conveniently located in hotel lobbies. One agency selling airplane and train tickets with many outlets around town is **GlavAgentstvo** (Lubyanka Map pp128-9; ☎ 924 8728; Teatralny proezd 5/1; Ⓜ Lubyanka; Tverskoy Map pp128-9; ☎ 290 2771; Tverskoy bul 14/5; Ⓜ Pushkinskaya). Additional outlets are in Sheremetyevo-1 airport, as well as Belorussky and Leningradsky vokzals.

GETTING AROUND
The central area around the Kremlin, Kitay-Gorod and the Bolshoi Theatre is best seen on foot. Otherwise, the fastest, cheapest and easiest way to get around is almost always on the metro, though buses, trolleybuses and trams are useful sometimes.

To/From the Airports
The easiest and surest way to get from any airport into the city is to book your transfer in advance through your hotel or travel agent (p138). This means you will be driven straight to your destination in the city and you may not have to pay any more than a normal taxi fare.

All five airports are accessible by public transportation, which usually involves taking a minivan shuttle from a metro stop. This is obviously a much cheaper, slower way to go.

BYKOVO

Prigorodnye poezdy run from Kazan station to Bykovo train station, 400m from the airport (R30, one hour, every 20 minutes). You can also pick this train up at Vykhino, near Vykhino metro. A taxi to/from the city centre is about R800 and can take 1½ hours.

DOMODEDOVO

A super convenient express train leaves Pavelets station every half-hour for Domodedovo airport (R100, 45 minutes). This route is particularly convenient, as you can check into your flight at the train station.

A taxi fare to/from the city centre is R700 to R800, with the trip taking one to 1½ hours, depending on traffic.

SHEREMETYEVO

Marshrutky (minibuses) travel between Rechnoy vokzal and Sheremetyevo-1, with Sheremetyevo-2 the middle stop in either direction. They make the journey as soon as they are full, which is about every 30 minutes or less.

At Sheremetyevo-2, *marshrutky* leave from a stop 200m in front of the terminal (just right of the car park). Make certain your shuttle is going in the right direction.

When heading to the airport, take the metro to Rechnoy vokzal, and once at Rechnoy vokzal leave the metro platform by the exit at the front end of the train. *Marshrutky* wait at the road, 100m from the metro station. The combined metro and *marshrutka* trip to/from Sheremetyevo-2 takes about one hour; to/from Sheremetyevo-1 is 70 minutes. City bus 551 also follows this route, but takes much longer.

A taxi arranged on the spot between Sheremetyevo-2 airport and the city centre takes about 45 minutes and should not cost more than R800. A better bet is to arrange one in advance through one of the companies listed (see opposite).

VNUKOVO

A new high-speed train runs between Kievsky vokzal and Vnukovo airport (R76, 35 minutes). It runs every hour between 7am and noon and between 5pm and 8pm. Outside these hours, you can take a *marshrutka* from Yugo-Zapadnaya metro (R30, 30 minutes). A taxi to/from the city

centre can take over an hour and costs about R800.

Bus, Trolleybus & Tram

Buses, trolleybuses and trams are useful along a few radial or cross-town routes that the metro misses, and are necessary for reaching sights away from the city centre. Tickets (R10) are usually sold on the vehicle by a conductor.

Metro

The metro is the easiest, quickest and cheapest way of getting around Moscow. Many of the elegant stations are marble-faced, frescoed, gilded works of art (see the boxed text, opposite). The trains are generally reliable: you will rarely wait on the platform for more than two minutes. Nonetheless, they get packed during rush hour. Up to nine million people a day ride the metro, more than the London and New York City systems combined. Sometimes it feels like all nine million are trying to get on one train.

The first station opened in 1935. The stations were meant to double as air-raid shelters, which is why the escalators seem to plunge halfway to the centre of the earth.

The 150-plus stations are marked outside by large 'M' signs. Magnetic tickets are sold at ticket booths (R13). It's useful to buy a multiple-ride ticket (10 rides for R120, 20 for R195), which saves you the hassle of queuing up every time.

Stations have maps of the system and signs on each platform showing the destinations. Interchange stations are linked by underground passages, indicated by *perekhod* signs, usually blue with a stick figure running up the stairs. The carriages now have maps inside that show the stops for that line in both Roman and Cyrillic letters. The system is fairly straightforward. The biggest confusion you may find is that when two or more lines meet, each line's interchange station often has a different name.

These days, the Moscow metro has implemented a sort of public-relations campaign. You will notice posters decorated by pretty, smiling, young ladies in uniform promising 'Good weather, any time of year.' These *devushki* (young women) bear little resemblance to the babushkas sitting at the bottom of the escalators, but let's not mull over a technicality.

Taxi

Almost any car in Moscow could be a taxi if the price is right, so get on the street and stick your arm out. Many private cars cruise around as unofficial taxis, known as 'gypsy cabs', and other drivers will often take you if they're going in roughly the same direction. Expect to pay R100 to R150 for a ride around the city centre.

Official taxis – which can be recognised by the chequerboard logo on the side and /or a small green light in the windscreen – charge about the same. No driver uses a meter (even if the cab has one), and few will admit to having any change.

Don't hesitate to wave on a car if you don't like the look of its occupants. As a general rule, it's best to avoid riding in cars that already have two or more people in-

side. Problems are more likely to crop up if you take a street cab waiting outside a nightclub, or perhaps a tourist hotel or restaurant at night.

Some reliable taxi companies (all with websites in Russian only):

Central Taxi Reservation Office (Tsentralnoe Byuro Zakazov Taxi; ☎ 927 0000; www.cbz-taxi.ru)
Eleks Polyus (☎ 707 2707; www.taxi-14.ru)
MV Motors (☎ 775 6775; www.7756775.ru)
New Yellow Taxi (☎ 940 8888; www.nyt.ru)
Taxi Bistro (☎ 327 5144; www.taxopark.ru)
Taxi Blues (☎ 105 5115; www.taxi-blues.ru)

Normally, the dispatcher will ring back within a few minutes to provide a description and licence number of the car. It's best to provide at least an hour's notice before you need the taxi.

UNDERGROUND ART

The Moscow metro is justly famous for the art and design of many of its stations. Many feature marble, bas-reliefs, stucco, mosaics and chandeliers. Diversity of theme is not their strongest point – rather, it's history, war, the happy life of the Soviet people, or a mix of all.

Ring Line Stops

Taganskaya Features a war theme, with the heads of unknown war heroes set in luscious, floral stucco frames made of white-and-blue porcelain with gold linings.
Prospekt Mira Also decorated in elegant gold-trimmed white porcelain. The bas-reliefs depict happy farmers picking fruit, children reading books, and so on.
Novoslobodskaya Features brightly illuminated stained-glass panels with happy workers, farmers, artistic types and lots of flowers.
Belorusskaya Mosaics on the ceiling depict yet more happy workers, along with farmers milking cows, dancing and taking oaths. All wear Belarusian national shirts for the occasion.
Komsomolskaya A huge stuccoed hall, its ceiling covered with mosaics depicting past Russian military heroes: Peter the Great, Dmitry Donskoy, Alexander Suvorov and more.
Barrikadnaya Done in dramatic red-and-white marble, it features bas-reliefs depicting the fateful events of 1905 and 1917.
Kievskaya The hall is decorated with labelled mosaics depicting events in Ukrainian history and goodwill between Ukrainians and Russians.

Radial Line Stops

Mayakovskaya Grand Prize winner at the 1938 World's Fair in New York. It has a central hall that's all stainless steel and marble.
Novokuznetskaya Features military bas-reliefs done in sober khaki, and colourful ceiling mosaics depicting pictures of the happy life. The elegant marble benches came from the first Church of Christ the Saviour.
Ploshchad Revolyutsii Life-sized bronze statues in the main hall and beside the escalators illustrate the idealised roles of common men and women. Heading up the escalators the themes, in order, are revolution, industry, agriculture, hunting, education, sport and child-rearing.
Partizanskaya Features floral bas-reliefs decorated with AK-47 machine guns. Unfortunately it has been covered in scaffolding for years.

AROUND MOSCOW
ПОДМОСКОВЬЕ

As soon as you leave Moscow, the fast-paced modern capital fades from view, while the slowed-down, old-fashioned countryside unfolds around you. The subtly changing landscape is crossed by winding rivers and dotted with peasant villages – the classic provincial Russia immortalised through the works of artists and writers over the centuries.

Moscow's elite have long escaped the heat and hustle of city life by retreating to the surrounding regions. The quintessential aristocratic getaway is Prince Yusupov's palatial estate at Arkhangelskoe. On a more modest scale, Tolstoy, Tchaikovsky, Chekhov and Boris Pasternak all sought inspiration in the countryside around Moscow, not to mention the countless painters and sculptors who retreated to the artists' colony at Abramtsevo. Even Lenin maintained a country estate on the outskirts of Moscow. All of these properties are now museums to inspire the rest of us.

These days, most Muscovites do not have country estates, but they still need an occasional break from the urban madness. The lovely lakes district, northwest of the capital, provides plenty of opportunities for swimming, sunning and soaking up the tranquillity of rural Russia. For some other short trip possibilities from Moscow see the Golden Ring chapter.

ABRAMTSEVO АБРАМЦЕВО

☎ 254 from Moscow, ☎ 49654 from elsewhere

Artists colony and country estate, Abramtsevo was a font of artistic inspiration for the renaissance of traditional Russian painting, sculpture and architecture.

In 1870 Savva Mamontov – railway tycoon and patron of the arts – bought this lovely estate 45km north of Moscow. Here, he hosted a whole slew of painters, who sought inspiration in the gardens and forests: Ilya Repin; landscape artist Isaak Levitan; portraitist Valentin Serov; and the quite un-Slavic painter and ceramicist Mikhail Vrubel. Other artists came to dabble at the woodworking and ceramics' workshop, and musicians (including Fyodor Chaliapin,

AROUND MOSCOW

who made his debut here) performed in the private opera.

Today the **Abramtsevo Estate Museum-Preserve** (☎ 32 470; admission R100; ✆ 10am-5pm Wed-Sun) is a delightful retreat from Moscow or addition to a trip to Sergiev Posad. Apart from the highlights mentioned here, arts and crafts exhibits occupy the other buildings on the grounds, which cost extra.

Several rooms of the **main house** have been preserved intact, complete with artwork by various resident artists. The main attraction is Mamontov's dining room, featuring Repin's portraits of the patron and his wife, and Serov's luminous *Girl with Peaches*. A striking majolica bench by Vrubel is in the garden.

The prettiest building in the grounds is **Saviour Church 'Not Made by Hand'** (Tserkov Spasa Nerukotvorny). The structure epitomises Mamontov's intentions: it's a carefully researched homage by half a dozen artists to 14th-century Novgorod architecture. The iconostasis is by Repin and Vasily Polenov. The tiled stove in the corner, still working, is exquisite.

The Slavophile painter Viktor Vasnetsov conjured up the fairy tale of Baba Yaga the witch, with his rendition of her **Hut on Chicken Legs**.

Getting There & Away

Suburban trains run every half-hour from Yaroslavsky vokzal (R50, 1½ hours). Most – but not all – trains to Sergiev Posad or Aleksandrov stop at Abramtsevo. There are also regular buses between Abramtsevo and Sergiev Posad (R20, 20 minutes).

By car, turn west off the M8 Moscow–Yaroslavl highway just north of the 61km post (signs to Khotkovo and Abramtsevo mark the turn-off) and continue over the railroad tracks.

KLIN КЛИН

☎ 224 / pop 90,000

From 1885, Tchaikovsky spent his summers in Klin, 90km northwest of Moscow. Of his country estate, he wrote, 'I can't imagine myself living anywhere else. I find no words to express how much I feel the charm of the Russian countryside, the Russian landscape and the quiet that I need more than anything else.'

In a charming house on the edge of town, he wrote the *Nutcracker* and *Sleeping Beauty*, as well as his famous *Pathetique* Symphony no 6. After he died in 1893, the estate was converted into the **Tchaikovsky House-Museum** (Dom-Muzey Chaykovskogo; ☎ 58 196; ul Chaykovskogo 48; adult/child/student R110/70/70; ✷ 10am-6pm Fri-Tue). The house and grounds are kept just as when Tchaikovsky lived here. You can peruse the photographs and personal effects, but only special guests are allowed to play his grand piano. Occasional concerts are held in the concert hall.

Klin is on the road and railway from Moscow to Tver, Novgorod and St Petersburg. Suburban trains from Moscow's Leningradsky vokzal run to Klin (R60, 1½ hours) throughout the day. Most of these continue to Tver (R42, two hours). From the station, take *marshrutka* 5 to Tchaikovsky's estate.

ZAVIDOVO ЗАВИДОВО

☎ 495

At a beautiful spot at the confluence of the Volga and Shosha Rivers, the village of Zavidovo is midway between Klin and Tver on the road to St Petersburg. On the outskirts, the **Zavidovo Holiday Complex** (☎ 937 9944; www.zavidovo.ru; Shosha village, Novo-Zavidovo; d incl breakfast from R5000/5500; ▯ ▧ ▣) offers all kinds of recreation activities, such as horseback riding, water-skiing, tennis, boating

---

GETTING BACK TO NATURE

At least 30% of Russians own a small country home, or dacha (see p72). The dacha's most remarkable feature is its garden, which is usually bursting with flowering fruit trees and veggie plants. Families today still grow all manner of vegetables and fruits, which get sold at the market or canned for the winter. Throughout winter, city dwellers can enjoy strawberry *kompot* (canned, syrupy fruit) or pickled mushrooms, and fondly recall their time in the countryside.

After playing in the dirt, the next stop is undoubtedly the *banya* (p71). While bathhouses exist in the city, the countryside *banya* experience cannot be replicated. Crowding into the tiny, wooden hothouse; receiving a beating with fragrant *veniki* (birch branches) straight from the forest; cooling down with a dip in the pond or – more extreme – a roll in the snow…now *that's* getting back to nature.

Nothing piques hunger like a *banya*, and what better way to enjoy the fruits of one's labour than with a hearty meal. Dacha cuisine evokes the peasant's kitchen: tasty soups that are the highlight of Russian cuisine; typically Russian *kasha* (porridge), which sates any appetite; and coarse, black Russian bread. These dishes often use ingredients straight from the garden, coop or pasture. Simple to prepare, rich in flavour and nourishing to body and soul, dacha fare is a perfect example of how Russians return to their rural roots for replenishment.

For an authentic dacha experience, visit **Uncle Pasha's Dacha** (☎ 910-932 5546, 916-117 1527; www.russian-horse-rides.com; d with meals R750) in the tiny village of Dubrovki (near Tver) – the setting on the Volga is magnificent. Accommodation is rustic, as it should be (read: outside toilet). Meals are included but leave something to be desired; guests are welcome to use the kitchen facilities to make their own. This place is hard to reach, so be sure to contact Uncle Pasha in advance.

and fishing. Afterwards, soothe your weary body in the tiled Turkish bath or the lakeside Russian *banya*.

In addition to the hotel complex, comfortable **cottages** (weekdays/weekends R8100/9800) sleeping four to eight people replicate various architectural styles, including Finnish cabins, Alpine chalets and Russian dachas. Suburban trains from Moscow's Leningradsky vokzal to Tver stop in Zavidovo (R75, two hours, hourly).

TVER ТВЕРЬ
☎ 4822 / pop 450,000

Tver, on the Volga 150km northwest of Moscow, was capital of an unruly ministate that was Moscow's chief rival in the 14th and 15th centuries. Little evidence of Tver's medieval heyday remains, as it subsequently went through a series of upheavals. It was punished for rising against the Golden Horde, conquered by Ivan III, savaged by Ivan the Terrible, seized by the Poles and completely destroyed by fire in 1763.

Tver experienced a renaissance when Catherine the Great made it one of her rest stops between St Petersburg and Moscow. Today classical town houses from the late 1700s and early 1800s line the main street and riverbank of this mini-Petersburg on the Volga.

In 1990 Tver dumped its Soviet name, Kalinin (after Mikhail Kalinin, Stalin's puppet president during WWII, who was

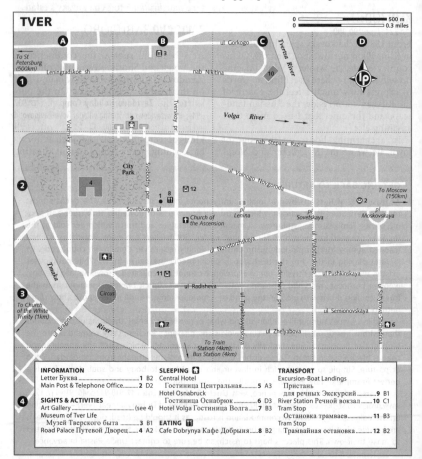

TVER

0 — 500 m
0 — 0.3 miles

INFORMATION	SLEEPING	TRANSPORT
Letter Буква **1** B2	Central Hotel	Excursion-Boat Landings
Main Post & Telephone Office........**2** D2	Гостиница Центральная...........**5** A3	Пристань
	Hotel Osnabruck	для речных Экскурсий **9** B1
SIGHTS & ACTIVITIES	Гостиница Оснабрюк **6** D3	River Station Речной вокзал **10** C1
Art Gallery ....(see 4)	Hotel Volga Гостиница Волга......**7** B3	Tram Stop
Museum of Tver Life		Остановка трамваев.............**11** B3
Музей Тверского быта **3** B1	**EATING**	Tram Stop
Road Palace Путевой Дворец......**4** A2	Cafe Dobrynya Кафе Добрыня.....**8** B2	Трамвайная остановка...........**12** B2

born here). Though Tver is not in the same league as some of the towns of the Golden Ring, it has just enough attractions to make it worth the trip from Moscow. You may also want to stop here for the same reason as Catherine the Great – to rest during your journey between Moscow and St Pete.

Orientation & Information

The Volga runs roughly from west to east through Tver, with the town centre on the southern side. Sovetskaya ul is the main east–west street. It intersects the north–south Tverskoy pr, which becomes pr Chaykovskogo further south. The train station is 4km south of the centre, at the point where pr Chaykovskogo turns 90 degrees east and becomes ul Kominterna. The bus station is 300m east of the train station.

The **main post & telephone office** (Sovetskaya ul 31; 8am-8pm Mon-Sat) is open for international phone calls 24 hours a day. You'll find a decent selection of maps at the **Letter** (Sovetskaya ul 7; 10am-8pm Mon-Fri, to 7pm Sat & Sun) bookshop.

Sights

At the west end of Sovetskaya ul, fronted by a statue of Mikhail Kalinin, stands the town's most imposing building – Catherine the Great's 1775 **Road Palace**, bedecked with ornate mouldings, marble columns and crystal chandeliers. Besides the fancy 18th-century interiors, it houses Tver's **Art Gallery** (336 243; Sovetskaya ul 3; admission R40; 11am-5pm Wed-Sun), exhibiting antique furniture and Russian paintings. The collection is not extensive, but it does feature some pieces by Levitan, Repin, Surikov and other Russian favourites.

The **City Park** on the riverbank behind the palace often hosts live concerts on summer weekends. In summer, excursion boats sail every hour from the piers.

The quaintest part of town is the streets of old wooden houses with carved eaves and window frames, west of the market on ul Bragina. In this area is Tver's oldest building, the stately **Church of the White Trinity** (Trudolyubia per), dating from 1564.

A promenade stretches along the north bank of the Volga, providing lovely views of the old houses on the southern bank. The **Museum of Tver Life** (318 404; ul Gorkogo

19/14; admission R40; 11am-5pm Wed-Sun) is housed in an 18th-century merchant's manor house. It exhibits arts, crafts, furniture and other domestic artefacts from several centuries.

Sleeping & Eating

Hotel Osnabruck (358 433; www.hotel.tver.ru; ul Saltykova-Shchedrina 20; s/d with breakfast R1800/2200;) This Western-style hotel is named for Tver's sister city in Germany, the source of investment for its construction in the late 1990s. Its 34 spacious rooms are decorated with wood furniture and rose-toned tapestries. The hotel's restaurant, fitness centre and business centre are all on par.

Hotel Volga (348 100; fax 379 557; ul Zhelyabova 1; s/d from 600/800) Overlooking the Tmaka River, the Hotel Volga is undergoing a long-term renovation process, so rooms vary widely in quality. You will pay around R1650 for an upgraded room, but don't expect a big difference in style or comfort. Nonetheless, this place is a conveniently located, reliable stand-by.

Central Hotel (489 093; fax 489 152; Novotorzhskaya ul 1; s without bathroom from R620, d with bathroom R840-1100) The darkest and dreariest option is located on the city's central square, opposite the circus.

Besides the hotel restaurants, you can dine at **Cafe Dobrynya** (321 500; Sovetskaya ul 7; meals R200-300), a convivial place with a rustic chalet interior and standard Russian food.

Getting There & Around

Tver (often still listed as Kalinin on timetables) is accessible by suburban train (R102, three hours, hourly) from Moscow's Leningradsky vokzal. Faster, long-distance trains between Moscow and St Petersburg also stop at Tver. There are also buses (R100, three hours) to/from Moscow's Yaroslavsky vokzal.

Trams 2, 5, 6 and 11 run from the bus and train stations up Chaykovskogo and Tverskoy pr to the town centre.

ISTRA ИСТРА

231

A steady stream of pilgrims makes the journey to this village, 50km west of Moscow. Their motives are diverse, as they come to worship at the grandiose New Jerusalem

Monastery, or to worship the gods of sun and fun at the nearby holiday resorts.

Sights

In the 17th century, Nikon, the patriarch whose reforms drove the Old Believers from the Orthodox Church, decided to show one and all that Russia deserved to be the centre of the Christian world. He did this by building a little Holy City right at home, complete with its own Church of the Holy Sepulchre. Thus, the grandiose **New Jerusalem Monastery** (Novo-Iyerusalimsky monastyr; ☎ 49 787; admission per exhibit adult/child R40/20, guided tour R500; 🕑 10am-4pm Tue-Sun) was founded in 1656 near the picturesque Istra River.

Unlike other Moscow monasteries, this one had no military use. In WWII the retreating Germans blew it to pieces but it's gradually being reconstructed. After years as a museum, the monastery is now in Orthodox hands and attracts a steady stream of worshippers.

In the centre of the grounds is the **Cathedral of the Resurrection** (Voskresensky sobor), intended to look like Jerusalem's Church of the Holy Sepulchre. Like its prototype, it's really several churches under one roof. The main building is still under restoration, but it is possible to enter the detached **Assumption Church** (Uspensky tserkov) in the northern part of the cathedral. Here, pilgrims come to kiss the relics of the holy martyr Tatyana, the monastery's patron saint.

Reconstruction is complete on the unusual underground **Church of SS Konstantin & Yelena** (Konstantino-Yeleninskaya tserkov), with only its belfry peeping up above the ground. Patriarch Nikon was buried in the cathedral, beneath the **Church of John the Baptist** (Tserkov Ioanna Predtechi).

The **refectory** exhibits weapons, icons and artwork from the 17th century, including personal items belonging to Patriarch Nikon. In the monastery walls, there is additional **exhibit space** displaying 20th-century drawings and handicrafts from around the Moscow region. On weekends you can sample fresh-brewed tea and homemade pastries in the **tearoom**.

Just outside the monastery's north wall, the Moscow region's **Museum of Wooden Architecture** (☎ 49 787; 🕑 May-Sep) is a collection of picturesque peasant cottages and windmills set along the river.

Sleeping & Eating

Istra Holiday Country Hotel (☎ 495-739 6198 in Moscow; www.istraholiday.ru in Russian; Trusovo; d weekdays/weekends from R4000/7100;) The quaint wooden cottages that make up this hotel sit on the shores of the lovely Istra water reserve. The place offers all the sports and outdoor activities you could hope for, from skiing to swimming to lounging on the beach. The resort is all-inclusive, with two restaurants and several cafés and bars, as well as sports facilities and spa.

Getting There & Away

Suburban trains run from Moscow's Rizhsky vokzal to Istra (R42, 1½ hour, hourly), from where buses run to the Muzey stop by the monastery. If the weather is fine, a 20-minute walk from the Istra train station is a pleasant alternative.

ARKHANGELSKOE
АРХАНГЕЛЬСКОЕ

☎ 495

In the 1780s the wealthy Prince Nikolai Yusupov purchased this grand palace on the outskirts of Moscow and turned it into a spectacular **estate** (☎ 363 1375; www.arkhangelskoe.ru; admission R150; 🕑 grounds 10am-6pm daily, exhibits 10am-4pm Wed-Sun).

During several ambassadorships and as director of the imperial museums, Yusupov accumulated a private art collection that outclassed many European museums. The **palace** consists of a series of elegant halls that display his paintings, furniture, sculptures, glass, tapestries and porcelain.

The multilevel Italianate **gardens** are full of 18th-century copies of classical statues. The majestic **colonnade** (admission R80) on the eastern side was meant to be a Yusupov mausoleum, but the family fled Russia forever after the revolution. In summer months this is the exquisite setting for live classical music **concerts** (☎ 501-453 8229; tickets R300; 🕑 5pm Sat & Sun May-Sep).

Yusupov also organised a troupe of serf actors that eventually became one of the best known of its kind, and built them a **theatre** just west of the gardens. Predating everything else is the little white **Church of the Archangel Michael** (Arkhangelskaya tserkov; 1667).

The estate is 22km west of central Moscow. Take *marshrutka* 151, 285 or 549 from

Moscow's Tushinskaya metro station to Arkhangelskoe (R20, 30 minutes).

BORODINO БОРОДИНО

☎ 238

In 1812 Napoleon invaded Russia, lured by the prospect of taking Moscow. For three months the Russians retreated, until on 26 August the two armies met in a bloody battle of attrition at the village of Borodino, 130km west of Moscow. In 15 hours more than one-third of each army was killed – over 100,000 soldiers in all. Europe would not know fighting this devastating again until WWI.

The French seemed to be the winners, as the Russians withdrew and abandoned Moscow. But Borodino was, in fact, the beginning of the end for Napoleon, who was soon in full, disastrous retreat.

The entire battlefield – more than 100 sq km – is now the **Borodino Field Museum-Preserve**, basically vast fields dotted with dozens of memorials to specific divisions and generals (most erected at the centenary of the battle in 1912). Start your tour at the **Borodino Museum** (☎ 51 546; www.borodino.ru; ☾ 10am-6pm Tue-Sun), where you can study a diorama of the battle before setting out to see the site in person.

The front line was roughly along the 4km road from Borodino village to the train station: most of the monuments are close to the road. The hill-top monument about 400m in front of the museum is **Bagration's tomb**, the grave of Prince Bagration, a heroic Georgian infantry general who was mortally wounded in battle.

Further south, a concentration of monuments around Semyonovskoe marks the battle's most frenzied fighting; here, Bagration's heroic Second Army, opposing far larger French forces, was virtually obliterated. Apparently Russian commander Mikhail Kutuzov deliberately sacrificed Bagration's army to save his larger First Army, opposing lighter French forces in the northern part of the battlefield. Kutuzov's headquarters are marked by an obelisk in the village of Gorky. Another obelisk near Shevardino to the southwest, paid for in 1912 with French donations, marks Napoleon's camp.

Ironically, this battle scene was re-created during WWII, when the Red Army confronted the Nazis on this very site. Memorials to this battle also dot the fields, and WWII trenches surround the monument to Bagration. Near the train station are two WWII mass graves.

The **Saviour Borodino Monastery** (☎ 51 057; admission R15; ☾ 10am-5pm Tue-Sun) was built by the widows of the Afghan War. Among its exhibits is a display devoted to Leo Tolstoy and the events of *War and Peace* that took place at Borodino.

The rolling hills around Borodino and Semyonovskoe are largely undeveloped, due to their historic status. Facilities are extremely limited; be sure to bring a picnic lunch.

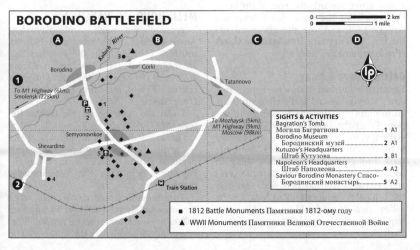

BORODINO BATTLEFIELD

0 —— 2 km
0 —— 1 mile

SIGHTS & ACTIVITIES
Bagration's Tomb Могила Багратиона	1 A1
Borodino Museum Бородинский музей	2 A1
Kutuzov's Headquarters Штаб Кутузова	3 B1
Napoleon's Headquarters Штаб Наполеона	4 A2
Saviour Borodino Monastery Спасо-Бородинский монастырь	5 A2

To M1 Highway (6km); Smolensk (228km)

Borodino
Gorki
Tatarinovo
Semyonovskoe
Shevardino
Train Station

To Mozhaysk (5km); M1 Highway (9km); Moscow (98km)

■ 1812 Battle Monuments Памятники 1812-ому году
▲ WWII Monuments Памятники Великой Отечественной Войне

Getting There & Away

Suburban trains leave in the morning from Moscow's Belorussky vokzal to Borodino (R45, two hours). A few trains return to Moscow in the evening, but be prepared to spend some time waiting. If you miss the train, you may be able to catch a bus to nearby Mozhaysk, from where there are frequent trains and buses.

Since the area is rural, visiting by car is more convenient and probably more rewarding. If driving from Moscow, stay on the M1 highway (Minskoe sh) until the Mozhaysk turn-off, 95km beyond the Moscow outer ring road. It's 5km north to Mozhaysk, then 13km west to Borodino village.

PEREDELKINO ПЕРЕДЕЛКИНО
☎ 495

Boris Pasternak – poet, author of *Doctor Zhivago* and winner of the 1958 Nobel Prize for literature – lived for a long time in a dacha in this writers' colony on Moscow's southwestern outskirts, just 5km beyond the city's outer ring road. The dacha is now the **Pasternak House-Museum** (☎ 934 5175; ul Pavlenko 3; admission R50; ☼ 10am-4pm Thu-Sun). The museum features the room where he finished *Doctor Zhivago* and the room where he died. It is open to visitors only with a guided tour (in Russian).

When Pasternak died in 1960 he was buried in the nearby cemetery, which has attracted a stream of visitors ever since. In a pine grove towards the rear of the cemetery, look for the stone slab bearing the writer's profile. Above the graveyard sits the tiny 15th-century **Transfiguration Church** (Preobrazhenskaya tserkov).

Getting There & Away

Frequent suburban trains go from Moscow's Kievsky vokzal to Peredelkino (R20, 20 minutes) on the line to Kaluga-II station. From the stop opposite Peredelkino station, you can catch a taxi or *marshrutka* to the museum. Otherwise, it is a 30-minute walk through the village. Follow the path west along the train tracks past the cemetery (where Pasternak is buried) and over the bridge. After about 400m look for the yellow two-storey building on the right-hand side, which sits on the corner of ul Pavlenko.

GORKI LENINSKIE
ГОРКИ ЛЕНИНСКИЕ
☎ 495

In Lenin's later years, he and his family spent time at the lovely 1830s manor house on this wooded estate, 32km southeast of the Kremlin. Now it is an interesting and well-maintained **museum** (☎ 548 9309; admission per exhibit R50, guided tour R350; ☼ 10am-4pm Wed-Mon).

The house was redesigned in neoclassical style by the Art Nouveau architect Fyodor Shekhtel. It is largely furnished with the incredible collection of custom-designed furniture that was commissioned by the wealthy Morozov family, who owned the estate prior to the revolution. It is set amid lovely landscaped grounds – reason enough to visit this spot on a summer afternoon.

Many of the rooms are maintained as they were when Lenin's family lived here. A special exhibit re-creates his office in the Kremlin, with many of his personal items on display. The highlight, however, is his vintage Rolls Royce – one of only 15 such automobiles in the world. Other buildings on the grounds house exhibits about 20th-century political history and peasant life in the region.

Bus 439 (R18, 30 minutes) leaves every 90 minutes for the estate from the Domodedovskaya metro station in Moscow. By car, follow the M4 highway (Kashirskoe sh) to 11km beyond the Moscow outer ring road, then turn left to Gorki Leninskie.

MELIKHOVO МЕЛИХОВО

'My estate's not much,' wrote playwright Anton Chekhov of his home at Melikhovo, south of Moscow, 'but the surroundings are magnificent'. Here, Chekhov lived from 1892 until 1899 and wrote some of his most celebrated plays, including *The Seagull* and *Uncle Vanya*.

Today the estate houses the **Chekhov Museum** (☎ 272-23 610; admission R10, tour R50; ☼ 10am-4pm Tue-Sun), dedicated to the playwright and his work. Visitors today can examine his personal effects, wander around the village and peek into the 18th-century **wooden church**.

Theatre buffs should visit in May, when the museum hosts **Melikhovo Spring** (tickets R100-150), a week-long theatre festival. Theatre groups from all over the world descend on the village to perform their interpretations of the great playwright's work.

Getting There & Away
Suburban trains (R50, 1½ hours) run frequently from Moscow's Kursky vokzal to the town of Chekhov, 12km west of Melikhovo. Bus 25 makes the 20-minute journey between Chekhov and Melikhovo, with departures just about every hour.

By car, Melikhovo is about 7km east of the dual carriageway that parallels the old M2 Moscow–Oryol road, signposted 50km south of Moscow's outer ring road.

PRIOKSKO-TERRASNY RESERVE
ПРИОКСКО-ТЕРРАСНЫЙ
ЗАПОВЕДНИК
Covering 50 sq km bordering the northern flood plain of the Oka River, a tributary of the Volga, the **Prioksko-Terrasny Reserve** (☎ 27-707 145; http://online.stack.net~ptz in Russian; admission R50, guided tour R150-350; 9am-4pm) is a meeting point of northern fir groves and marshes with typical southern meadow steppe. The reserve's varied fauna includes a herd of European bison, brought back from near extinction since WWII.

You cannot wander freely around the reserve by yourself, so it's useful to make advance arrangements for a tour. Otherwise, you could tag onto a prescheduled group tour. There is also a small **museum** near the office, with stuffed specimens of the reserve's fauna (typical of European Russia), including beavers, elk, deer and boar.

The reserve's pride, and the focus of most visits, is its **European bison nursery** (*pitomnik zubrov*). Two pairs of bison, one of Europe's largest mammals (some weigh over a tonne), were brought from Poland in 1948. Now there are about 60 and more than 200 have been sent out to other parts of the country.

Getting There & Away
Public transport is difficult. If you leave by 8am, you can take a suburban train from Moscow's Kursky vokzal to Serpukhov (two hours), then a rare bus (25, 31 or 41) to the reserve. You may also be able to negotiate a ride from the station.

Drivers from Moscow should follow Simferopolskoe sh (the extension of Varshavskoe sh). At 98km, look for the sign to the reserve or to the village of Danki.

YASNAYA POLYANA
ЯСНАЯ ПОЛЯНА
☎ 487
Located 14km south of central Tula and around 240km from Moscow, Yasnaya Polyana is the **estate** (☎ 238 6710, 517 6081; www .yasnayapolyana.ru; admission R100; 10am-5pm Tue-Sun May-Oct, 9.30am-3.30pm Tue-Sun Nov-Apr) where the great Russian writer Count Leo Tolstoy was born and buried.

Tolstoy spent much of his life in this house, which is a simple place filled with many of his possessions. Of Yasnaya Polyana, he wrote: 'All [my grandfather] had built here was not only solid and comfortable, but also very elegant. The same is true about the park he laid out near the house.' Tolstoy's nearby grave is unmarked except for bouquets of flowers left by newlyweds.

The highly recommended **Cafe Preshpekt** (meals R200-250) features hearty home-cooked Russian fare. House specialities are prepared according to recipes by Sofia Andreevna, Leo's devoted wife. There is also a simple hotel on site.

Getting There & Away
The easiest way to get to Yasnaya Polyana is on the express train from Moscow's Kursky vokzal (R180, three hours, departs 9am, returns 4.36pm). While waiting for the shuttle bus to the museum, you can amuse yourself by perusing the exhibit that shows the railway as it was during Leo Tolstoy's time.

Otherwise, you can take the *elektrichka* to Tula (R130, three hours), then take bus 261 to Yasnaya Polyana (R10, 20 minutes).

If you're driving from Moscow, it's easiest to follow Tula's western bypass all the way to its southern end and then turn back north towards Tula.

Golden Ring
Золотое Кольцо

Ancient Rus grew up in the clutch of towns northeast of Moscow that is now known as the Golden Ring. The whitewashed walls of these once-fortified cities still stand, in many cases. The golden spires and onion domes of their monasteries still mark the horizon, evoking medieval Rus. Bells ring out from towering belfries; robed holy men scurry through church doors; historic tales recall mysterious, magical times.

The Golden Ring – so called for its wealth of architectural and artistic riches – is among Russia's most enchanting destinations. Some of these spots are accessible from Moscow by day trip. But if you have a few days to spare, it is worth leaving behind the big-city bustle to immerse yourself in the age-old allure of the Golden Ring.

HIGHLIGHTS

- Sampling the varieties of *medovukha* (honey ale) at Suzdal's **Mead-Tasting Hall** (p210)
- Seeing the domes and spires of Rostov-Veliky's many monasteries from **Lake Nero** (p219)
- Lighting a candle to St Sergius in the **Trinity Cathedral** (p222), Sergiev Posad
- Strolling from church to church along the Yaroslavl **river embankments** (p214)
- Admiring the simple perfection of the **Church of Intercession on the Nerl** (p206), Bogolyubovo

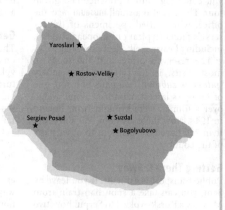

HISTORY

The 'Golden Ring' is a recently coined term that evokes a heroic distant past. Located northeast of Moscow, the Golden Ring is composed of some of Russia's oldest cities, wherein occurred the events that shaped early Russian history.

Towards the end of the 9th century, Slav tribes began to migrate into the hilly forest land of the Volga headwaters. They established small farming communities, eventually absorbing the Finno-Ugric tribes that already occupied the region. These Slav settlements made up the easternmost reaches of the Kyivan Rus principality and bordered the formidable Turkic Bulgar state of the Middle Volga.

Wary of his eastern rival, the Kyivan Grand Prince, Vladimir I, defeated the Bulgars in combat and secured his claim of sovereignty over these Slav tribes. Vladimir then made his son, Yaroslav, the regional potentate, responsible for collecting tribute and converting pagans among the locals. Upon his death, in 1015, Vladimir's realm was divided among his sons, ushering a prolonged period of violent sibling rivalry and fragmented power.

The victors who eventually emerged from this fratricidal competition were the descendants of Yaroslav's son Vsevolod, who had inherited the Rostov-Suzdal principality. As a result, the locus of power in medieval Russia gradually shifted eastward.

GOLDEN RING

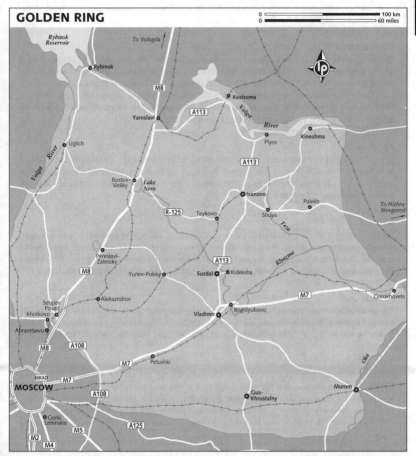

GOLDEN RING

0 — 100 km
0 — 60 miles

In this period, the Golden Ring towns prospered and expanded under a string of shrewd and able princes.

In the early 12th century, Suzdal's Vladimir Monomakh founded the fortress city of Vladimir, high above the Klyazma River. He entrusted the eastern lands to his young son, Yury Dolgoruky. In 1125, Yury took the title of Grand Prince and declared Suzdal as the northern capital of Rus. In 1157, Yury's son, Andrei Bogolyubsky, moved the Grand Prince's throne to Vladimir, which grew into the dominant city-state in the region. Andrei and his brother Vsevolod III (r 1176–1212) brought builders and artists from as far away as Western Europe to give Vladimir a Kyiv-like splendour. When the Mongols paid a

HIDDEN TREASURES

One of the charms of the Golden Ring is the proliferation of tiny villages – each populated with a handful of simple wooden houses, but always dominated by a jaw-dropping, majestic church. Recent history has not been kind to many of these idyllic spots, and the churches are in various states of disrepair. But they stand as witness to the strength of spirit, the persistence of beauty and – perhaps – the wisdom of history.

If you have your own transport, it is worth making a detour to discover some of these lesser-explored gems of the Golden Ring.

Aleksandrov

First documented in 1328, this village 120km north of Moscow (60km northeast of Sergiev Posad) gained prominence when Grand Prince Vasily III chose it as the site for his splendid royal palace. Under Ivan the Terrible, this 'Russian Versailles' served as the capital of Russia. The palace site now houses the Assumption Monastery, but little remains from the original structure. Only the 1513 Trinity Cathedral harks back to the village's glorious history: its gates were looted from Novgorod and Tver when Ivan sacked those cities in 1570.

Khotkovo

This village between Abramtsevo and Sergiev Posad is the home of the Convent of the Intercession, founded in 1308 (though the present buildings are from the 18th century or later). The parents of Sergius of Radonezh (the patron saint of Russia) are buried in the convent's recently restored Intercession Cathedral.

Murom

Locals boast that Murom, 137km southeast of Vladimir, is among the prettiest towns in Russia. Indeed, writer Maxim Gorky apparently agreed when he wrote 'Whoever has not seen Murom from the Oka River, has not seen Russian beauty.' The town is littered with 16th- to 18th-century churches and monasteries, including the elegant 1552 Saviour-Transfiguration Cathedral.

Palekh

The small village 65km east of Ivanovo on the Nizhny Novgorod road is famous for its artistry. Its namesake lacquer boxes are on display in the local museum. The Raising of the Cross Church also shows off the local craft, with a fine display of restored icons from the 14th to 19th centuries.

Yuriev-Polsky

Founded by Yury Dolgoruky in 1152, his namesake village sits on the Kaluksha River about halfway between Vladimir and Pereslavl-Zalessky. It is still surrounded by 12th-century ramparts, which provide excellent views of villagers' painted wooden houses and overflowing gardens. Within the ramparts, St George's Church – built in 1230 by Yury Dolgoruky's grandson Svyatoslav Vsyevolodovich (who is also buried here) – has a façade completely covered in elaborate stone carvings.

GOLDEN RING

TELEPHONE CODE CHANGES

In late 2005, the Russian Communications Ministry announced plans to change the area codes for 19 regions across Russia, including many towns in the Golden Ring. All codes that used to start with '0' should now start with a '4' instead, although be aware that there may be teething problems with this change. The new numbers are reflected here.

---

visit in the 13th century, Alexander Nevsky, Russia's first war hero, rebuilt Vladimir and restored the city's political status.

The heirs of Vladimir Monomakh sought to create a realm that rivalled Kyiv, the cradle of eastern Slavic civilisation. Under the reign of Andrei Bogolyubsky, in particular, the region experienced a building frenzy. Imposing towers, golden gates, fortified monasteries and elegant churches were constructed to match the cultural ambitions of its political rulers. Rostov-Veliky, Suzdal, Vladimir and Sergiev Posad each played an important part in making the Golden Ring the spiritual centre of Russian Orthodoxy.

The heyday of the Golden Ring towns was short-lived. Marauding Mongol invaders overran the towns' realm and forced their princes to pay them homage. With this change in regional politics, the erstwhile lesser principality of Muscovy rose in prominence through its role as the Golden Horde's chosen tribute collector. Gradually, the once proud principalities of the Golden Ring were absorbed into the expanding Muscovite state and reduced in status to another set of provincial capital towns.

Getting There & Around

The larger towns in the Golden Ring are accessible by train from Moscow, but it is necessary to travel by bus to visit some of the region's highlights.

The most efficient (albeit expensive) way to visit the Golden Ring is by car. Renting a car in Moscow will allow you to take a tour around the Golden Ring in a few days, stopping in some small, off-the-beaten-track destinations (see the boxed text, opposite). Alternatively, you can often hire cars with drivers at the local bus stations. Rates are about R10 per kilometre from Moscow,

but less around the smaller towns, which may be cost-effective if you're travelling in a group or are on a tight schedule.

Local Moscow-based tour agencies such as Dom Patriarshy Tours (p171) also organise excursions to most of these destinations.

VLADIMIR ВЛАДИМИР
☎ 4922 / pop 360,000 / ⏲ Moscow

High up on Vladimir's slope above the Klyazma River sits the solemnly majestic Assumption Cathedral, built to announce Vladimir's claim as capital of Rus. These days, Vladimir – 178km east of Moscow – feels more like a modern, provincial town than an ancient capital. Nonetheless, the grandeur of medieval Vladimir shines through the commotion of this busy, industrial town. Exquisite examples of Russia's most formative architecture, along with some entertaining museums, make Vladimir one of the jewels in the Golden Ring.

History

After being founded by Prince Vladimir Monomakh in the early 12th century, the city grew to become a splendid political, cultural and religious centre. See opposite for details of Vladimir's early history.

The city recovered from devastating attacks by nomadic Mongol raiders in 1238 and 1293. But its realm disintegrated into smaller principalities, with Moscow increasingly dominant. The head of the Russian Church resided here from 1300 to 1326, but then moved to Moscow. Worldly power finally shifted to Moscow around this time, too. Even so, the rulers remained nominally Grand Princes of Vladimir until the 15th century.

In the 20th century, Vladimir prospered anew on the back of textile, mechanical engineering and chemical industries.

Orientation

Vladimir's main street is Bolshaya Moskovskaya ul, although it sometimes goes by its former name, ul III Internatsionala. To make matters more confusing, other segments of the street go by different names, including simply ul Moskovskaya, which is just west of the Golden Gate. Bolshaya Moskovskaya ul is where you'll find the main attractions such as the Golden Gate and the Cathedrals of the Assumption and St Dmitry. The train and bus stations are 500m east on Vokzalnaya ul at the bottom of the slope.

Information

Internet@Salon (cnr uls Gagarina & Bolshaya Moskovskaya; per hr R30; ☺ 9am-9pm)
Post & telephone office (ul Podbelskogo; ☺ 8am-8pm Mon-Fri)
Sberbank (Bolshaya Moskovskaya ul 27; ☺ 9am-7pm Mon-Fri, 9am-5pm Sat) Exchange facilities and ATM.

Sights

ASSUMPTION CATHEDRAL

A white-stone version of Kyiv's brick Byzantine churches, the **Assumption Cathedral** (☎ 325 201; admission R100; ☺ 1.30-4.30pm Tue-Sun) was begun in 1158 – its simple but majestic form adorned with fine carving, innovative for the time. The cathedral was extended on all sides after a fire in the 1180s, when it gained the four outer domes.

The cathedral used to house the *Vladimir Icon of the Mother of God,* brought from Kyiv by Andrei Bogolyubsky. A national protector bestowing supreme status to its city of residence, the icon was moved to Moscow in 1390 and is now kept in the Tretyakov Gallery.

Inside the working church, a few restored 12th-century murals of peacocks and prophets can be deciphered about halfway up the inner wall of the outer north aisle; this was originally an outside wall. The real treasures are the Last Judgment frescoes by Andrei Rublyov and Daniil Chyorny, painted in 1408 in the central nave and inner south aisle, under the choir gallery towards the west end.

The church also contains the original coffin of Alexander Nevsky of Novgorod, the 13th-century military leader who was also Prince of Vladimir. He was buried in the former **Nativity Monastery** east of here, but his remains were moved to St Petersburg in 1724 when Peter the Great allotted him Russian hero status.

Adjoining the cathedral on the northern side are an 1810 **bell tower** and the 1862 **St George's Chapel**.

CATHEDRAL OF ST DMITRY

A quick stroll to the east of the Assumption Cathedral is the smaller **Cathedral of St Dmitry** (1193–97), where the art of Vladimir-Suzdal stone carving reached its pinnacle.

The church is permanently closed, but the attraction here is its exterior walls, covered in an amazing profusion of images.

The top centre of the north, south and west walls all show King David bewitching the birds and beasts with music. The Kyivan prince Vsevolod III, who had this church built as part of his palace, appears at the top left of the north wall, with a baby son on his knee and other sons kneeling on each side. Above the right-hand window of the south wall, Alexander the Great ascends into heaven, a symbol of princely might; on the west wall appear the labours of Hercules.

CHAMBERS

The grand building between the cathedrals is known as the **Chambers** (☎ 323 320; Bolshaya Moskovskaya ul 58; admission R150; ☺ 10am-5pm Tue-Sun) and contains a children's museum, art gallery and historical exhibit. The former is a welcome diversion for little ones, who may well be suffering from old-church syndrome on this trip. The art gallery features art since the 18th century, with wonderful depictions of the Golden Ring towns.

Across the small street, the **History Museum** (☎ 322 284; Bolshaya Moskovskaya ul 64; admission R50; ☺ 10am-4pm Tue-Sun) displays many remains and reproductions of the ornamentation from the Cathedrals of the Assumption and St Dmitry.

GOLDEN GATE

Vladimir's Golden Gate – part defensive tower, part triumphal arch – was modelled on the very similar structure in Kyiv. Originally built by Andrei Bogolyubsky to guard the main, western entrance to his city, it was later restored under Catherine the Great. Now you can climb the narrow stone staircase to check out the **Military Museum** (☎ 322 559; admission R50; ☺ 10am-4pm Fri-Wed) inside. It is a small exhibit, the centrepiece of which is a diorama of old Vladimir being ravaged by nomadic raiders. Across the street to the south you can see a remnant of the old wall that protected the city.

The red-brick building opposite was built in 1913 to house the Old Believers' Trinity Church. Now it is a **Crystal, Lacquer Miniatures & Embroidery Exhibition** (☎ 324 872; Bolshaya Moskovskaya ul 2; admission R50; ☺ 10am-4pm Wed-Mon), which features the crafts of Gus-Khrustalny and other nearby towns.

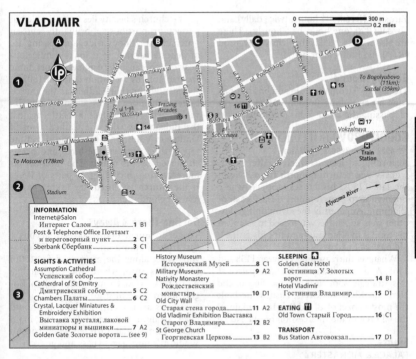

VLADIMIR

OLD VLADIMIR EXHIBIT

The red-brick water tower atop the old ramparts houses the **Old Vladimir Exhibition** (☎ 325 451; ul Kozlov val; admission R40; ☾ 10am-4pm Tue-Sun), a nostalgic collection of old photos, advertisements and maps, including a photo of a very distinguished couple taking a ride in Vladimir's first automobile in 1896. The highlight is the view from the top.

The nearby **St George Church** (Georgievskaya ul 2a) houses the Vladimir Theatre of Choral Music, where performances are often held on summer weekends.

Sleeping & Eating

Golden Gate Hotel (☎ 323 116; www.golden-gate.ru in Russian; Bolshaya Moskovskaya ul 17; s/d incl breakfast R1800/2300) The 14 rooms at this shiny new hotel are spacious and comfortable, with large windows overlooking the activity on the main street – or a central courtyard if you prefer. The attached restaurant is among the town's best, and is popular with tour groups.

Hotel Vladimir (☎ 323 042; tour@gtk.elcom.ru; Bolshaya Moskovskaya ul 74; s/d with bathroom incl breakfast

from R950/1300; P) This conveniently located option has acceptable rooms for all price ranges, including upgraded singles/doubles for R1150/1600. Rooms with shared bathroom are also available for R350 to R500 per person. It is a friendly place with lots of services, including a restaurant and bar.

Old Town (☎ 325 101; Bolshaya Moskovskaya ul 41; meals R300-400; ☾ 11am-2am) One of two side-by-side restaurants on the main drag. Choose from the cosy bar, the elegant dining room or – if the weather is fine – the lovely terrace with views of the Cathedral of St Dmitry.

Getting There & Away

The daily express train between Moscow's Kursky vokzal (Kursk train station; R208, 2½ hours) and Nizhny Novgorod (R290, 2½ hours) stops in Vladimir, as do many slower trains. Privately run buses (R100, three hours) also leave regularly from Kursky and Kazansky vokzals to Vladimir. They do not run on a timetable, but leave as they fill up.

There are also scheduled buses to/from Moscow's Shchyolkovsky bus station, as well as Kostroma (R150, five hours, three daily),

Yaroslavl (R160, 5½ hours, twice daily) and Suzdal (R20, one hour, half-hourly). There are also six buses a day to Nizhny Novgorod (R180, 4½ hours, four daily).

Getting Around
Trolleybus 5 from the train and bus stations runs up and along Bolshaya Moskovskaya ul, passing the main sights and hotels.

BOGOLYUBOVO БОГОЛЮБОВО
☎ 4922 / pop 3900 / ☯ Moscow
According to legend, when Andrei Bogo-lyubsky was returning north from Kyiv in the late 1150s, his horses stopped where Bogolyubovo now stands, 11km east of Vladimir. Apparently they wouldn't go another step, so Andrei was forced to establish his capital in Vladimir, and not his father's old base of Suzdal.

Whatever the reasoning, between 1158 and 1165, Andrei built a stone-fortified palace at this strategic spot near the meeting of the Nerl and Klyazma Rivers. Nearby, he built the most perfect of all old Russian buildings, the Church of the Intercession on the Nerl.

Sights
PALACE & MONASTERY
A tower and arch from Andrei Bogolyub-sky's palace survive amid a dilapidated but reopened 18th-century monastery (they are by the Vladimir–Nizhny Novgorod road in the middle of Bogolyubovo).

The dominant buildings today are the monastery's 1841 **bell tower** beside the road, and its 1866 **Assumption Cathedral**. Just east of the cathedral there is an arch and tower, on whose stairs – according to a chronicle – Andrei was assassinated by hostile boyars (nobles). The arch abuts the 18th-century **Church of the Virgin's Nativity**.

CHURCH OF THE INTERCESSION ON THE NERL ЦЕРКОВЬ ПОКРОВА НА НЕРЛИ
To reach this famous little church, go 200m towards Vladimir from the monastery-palace complex and turn onto ul Frunze, which winds downhill and under a railway bridge. Take the path to the left that runs along the side of a small wood. The church appears across the meadows, about 1.25km from the bridge. This walk can be precarious in spring, when the area is often flooded by the rising river.

The church's beauty lies in its simple but perfect proportions, a brilliantly chosen waterside site (floods aside) and sparing use of delicate carving. If it looks a mite top-heavy, it's because the original helmet dome was replaced by a cushion dome in 1803.

Legend has it that Andrei had the church built in memory of his favourite son, Iz-yaslav, who was killed in battle against the Bulgars. As with the Cathedral of St Dmitry in Vladimir, King David sits at the top of three façades, the birds and beasts entranced by his music. The interior has more carving, including 20 pairs of lions. If the church is closed, try asking at the house behind.

Getting There & Away
To get to Bogolyubovo, take trolleybus 1 east from Vladimir and get off at Khimza-vod. Walk along the main road for 100m to the bus stop, where you can catch a *marshrutka* (fixed-route minibus) to Bo-golyubovo (second stop).

Drivers from central Vladimir should head straight out east along the main road. From Suzdal, turn left when you hit Vladimir's northern bypass and go 5km.

SUZDAL СУЗДАЛЬ
☎ 49231 / pop 12,000 / ☯ Moscow
The gently winding Kamenka River, flower-drenched meadows and dome-spotted sky-line make this medieval capital the perfect fairytale setting. Suzdal, 35km north of Vladimir, has earned a federally protected status, which has limited development in the area. As a result, its main features are its abundance of ancient architectural gems and its decidedly rural atmosphere. Judging by the spires and cupolas, Suzdal may have as many churches as people.

History
Although the town's history dates back to 1024, Yury Dolgoruky made Suzdal the capital of the Rostov-Suzdal principality in the first half of the 12th century. Andrei Bogo-lyubsky moved the capital to Vladimir in 1157, from which time the principality was known as Vladimir-Suzdal. Set in a fertile wheat-growing area, Suzdal remained a trade centre even after Mongol-led invasions. Eventually, it united with Nizhny Novgorod until both were annexed by Moscow in 1392.

Under Muscovite rule, Suzdal became a wealthy monastic centre, with incredible development projects funded by Vasily III and Ivan the Terrible in the 16th century. In the late 17th and 18th centuries, wealthy merchants paid for 30 charming churches, which still adorn the town.

Orientation

The main street, ul Lenina, runs from north to south through Suzdal. The bus station is 2km east along Vasilyevskaya ul.

Information

Post & telephone office (Krasnaya pl; ☼ 8am-8pm) Open 24 hours for phone calls.
Sberbank (ul Lenina; ☼ 8am-4.30pm Mon-Fri) Exchange office.
Vneshtorgbank (Kremlyovskaya ul; ☼ 10am-5pm Tue-Fri, 10am-3.30pm Sat & Sun) Centrally located bank with ATM.

Sights

KREMLIN

The 1.4km-long earth rampart of Suzdal's kremlin, founded in the 11th century, today encloses a few streets of houses and a handful of churches, as well as the main cathedral group on Kremlyovskaya ul.

The **Nativity of the Virgin Cathedral**, its blue domes spangled with gold, was founded in the 1220s, but only its richly carved lower section is original white stone, the rest being 16th-century brick. The inside is sumptuous with 13th- and 17th-century frescoes and 13th-century damascene (gold on copper) west and south doors. Unfortunately, the cathedral was under restoration and closed indefinitely at the time of research.

The **Archbishop's Chambers** houses the **Suzdal History Exhibition** (☎ 21624; admission R30; ☼ 10am-5pm Wed-Mon). The exhibition includes the original 13th-century door from the cathedral, photos of its interior and a visit to the 18th-century **Cross Hall** (Krestovaya palata), which was used for receptions. The tent-roofed 1635 **kremlin bell tower** on the east side of the yard contains additional exhibits.

Just west of this group stands the 1766 wooden **St Nicholas Church**, brought from Glatovo village near Yuriev-Polsky. There's another **St Nicholas** (ul Lebedeva), one of Suzdal's own fine small 18th-century churches, just east of the cathedral group.

TORGOVAYA PLOSHCHAD

Suzdal's Torgovaya pl (Trade Sq) is dominated by the pillared **Trading Arcades** (1806–11) along its western side. Although the four churches in the immediate vicinity are closed, the five-domed 1707 **Emperor Constantine Church** in the square's northeastern corner is a working church with an ornate interior. Next to it is the smaller 1787 **Virgin of All Sorrows Church**.

SAVIOUR MONASTERY OF ST EUTHYMIUS

Founded in the 14th century to protect the town's northern entrance, Suzdal's biggest **monastery** (☎ 20746; admission to exhibits R40-50 each or all-inclusive R280; ☼ 10am-6pm Tue-Sun) grew mighty in the 16th and 17th centuries after Vasily III, Ivan the Terrible and the noble Pozharsky family funded impressive new stone buildings and big land and property acquisitions. It was girded with its great brick walls and towers in the 17th century.

Inside, the **Annunciation Gate-Church** houses an interesting exhibit on Dmitry Pozharsky (1578–1642), leader of the Russian army that drove the Polish invaders from Moscow in 1612.

A tall 16th- to 17th-century **cathedral bell tower** stands before the seven-domed **Cathedral of the Transfiguration of the Saviour**. Every 90 minutes from 10.30am to 4.30pm, a short concert of chimes is given on the bell tower's bells. The cathedral was built in the 1590s in 12th- to 13th-century Vladimir-Suzdal style. Inside, restoration has uncovered some bright 1689 frescoes by the school of Gury Nikitin from Kostroma. On summer weekends, a short but heavenly a cappella concert takes place once an hour. The **tomb** of Prince Dmitry Pozharsky is by the cathedral's east wall.

The 1525 **Assumption Church** facing the bell tower adjoins the old **Father Superior's chambers**, which houses a display of Russian icons. The **monks' quarters** across the compound contain a museum of artistic history.

At the north end of the complex is the old monastery **prison**, set up in 1764 for religious dissidents. It now houses a fascinating exhibit on the monastery's military history and prison life, including displays of some of the better-known prisoners who stayed here. The combined **hospital** and **St Nicholas' Church** (1669) features a rich museum of 12th- to 20th-century Russian applied art, much of it from Suzdal itself.

Across ul Lenina from the southeastern corner of the monastery is **Our Lady of Smolensk Church** (Smolenskaya tserkov; 1696–1707), along with Suzdal's only surviving early-18th-century **town house**.

INTERCESSION CONVENT

This **convent** (☎ 20889; ul Pokrovka; admission free; 🕙 9.30am-4.30pm Thu-Mon) is once again home to a small community of nuns, after being closed during the Soviet period. The **Intercession Cathedral** (1510–18), with its three domes, holds regular services in the centre.

Founded in 1364, the convent was originally a place of exile for the unwanted wives

of tsars. Among them was Solomonia Saburova, first wife of Vasily III, who was sent here in the 1520s because of her supposed infertility. The story goes that she finally became pregnant too late to avoid being divorced. A baby boy was born in Suzdal. Fearing he would be seen as a dangerous rival to any sons produced by Vasily's new wife, Solomonia secretly had him adopted, pretended he had died and staged a mock burial. This was probably just as well for the boy since Vasily's second wife did indeed produce a son – Ivan the Terrible.

The legend received dramatic corroboration in 1934 when researchers opened a small 16th-century tomb beside Solomonia's, in the crypt underneath the Interces-

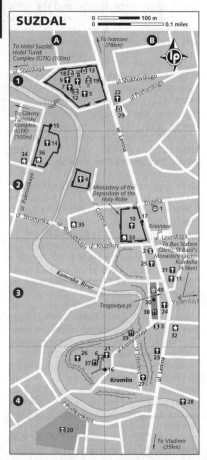

sion Cathedral. They found a silk-and-pearl shirt stuffed with rags – and no bones. The crypt is closed to visitors.

MONASTERY OF THE DEPOSITION

The Monastery of the Deposition of the Holy Robe was founded in 1207 but the existing buildings date from the 16th to 19th centuries. The monastery is now pretty dilapidated. Still, its two pyramidal entrance turrets (1688) on the south gate are exquisite. Suzdal's tallest structure, a 72m **monastery bell tower** (1813–19), rises from the east wall. The central 16th-century **Deposition Cathedral** (Rizopolozhensky sobor) is reminiscent of the Moscow Kremlin's Archangel Cathedral with its three helmet domes.

ALEXANDROVSKY CONVENT

This little white convent at the top of the river embankment stands out for its simple, quiet beauty. Reputedly founded in 1240 by Alexander Nevsky for noble women whose menfolk had been killed by nomadic raiders, its present **Ascension Church** (Voznesenskaya tserkov) and bell tower date from 1695.

MUSEUM OF WOODEN ARCHITECTURE & PEASANT LIFE

This **open-air museum** (ul Pushkarskaya; admission R50; ☯ 9.30am-3.30pm Wed-Mon May-Oct), illustrating old peasant life in this region of Russia, is a short walk across the river south of the Kremlin. Besides log houses, windmills, a barn and lots of tools and handicrafts, its highlights are the 1756 **Transfiguration Church** (Preobrazhenskaya tserkov) and the simpler 1776 **Resurrection Church** (Voskresenskaya tserkov).

OTHER SUZDAL BUILDINGS

Almost every corner in Suzdal has its own little church with its own charm. Some

other gems include the simple **Resurrection Church** (Torgovaya pl), dating from 1719; the shabby but graceful **Predtechenskaya Church** (ul Lenina), built in 1720, and the slender, multicoloured tower of **St Lazarus' Church** (Staraya ul), from 1667. The **SS Kosma & Damian Church** (1725) is picturesquely placed on a bend in the river east of ul Lenina. Suzdal's fifth monastery is the 17th-century **St Basil's** (Vasilevsky monastyr) on the Kideksha road. No doubt you'll find your own favourite.

KIDEKSHA

The 1152 **Church of SS Boris & Gleb** (Borisoglebskaya tserkov), on the Nerl River in this quiet village 4km east of Suzdal, is the oldest in the district. It was built for Yury Dolgoruky, who had a small wooden palace here.

The palace has disappeared; the church has been rebuilt many times. But a few fragments of 12th-century frescoes remain, including two figures on horseback. They probably represent Vladimir's sons, Boris and Gleb, who were the first Russian saints.

Activities

The rolling hills and attractive countryside around Suzdal are ideal for outdoor adventures, including horse riding and mountain biking. The **Hotel Tourist Complex** (GTK; ☎ 23390; ul Korovniki 45; ☯ 10am-6pm) rents bicycles, snowmobiles and skis, as well as offering horse-riding tours.

Sleeping

Pokrovskaya Hotel (☎ 20908; www.suzdaltour.ru; s/d incl breakfast R1820/2400) The cosy wooden cabins on the grounds of the Intercession Convent are rented out by Gostinichny Turistsky Komplek (GTK; Hotel Tourist Complex). Old-fashioned wooden furniture, rag rugs and fluffy quilts provide a welcoming atmosphere. A restaurant is also expected to open in the convent refectory.

Hotel Falcon (☎ 20088, 20987; www.hotel-sokol.ru in Russian; Torgovaya pl 2a; s/d incl breakfast from R1300/2200) This attractive new hotel is ideally located opposite the trading arcades. Its 40 rooms are all simply decorated and fully equipped with new wooden furniture and modern bathrooms. The elegant, bilevel restaurant is also recommended. Prices decrease significantly between October and April.

Kuchkov's Tavern (☎ 20252; fax 21507; ul Pokrovskaya 35; s/d incl breakfast R1650/2000) On a

---

AUTHOR'S CHOICE

Suzdal's most appealing place to stay, **Likhoninsky Dom** (☎ 21901; aksenova-museum @rnt.vladimir.ru; ul Slobodskaya 34; s/d incl breakfast R1500/1800), is on a quiet street near the town centre. This 17th-century merchant's house has five charming rooms and a pretty garden. It feels like home, thanks to the kindly ladies who run it.

quiet street opposite the Intercession Convent, this guesthouse has a 'New Russian' ambience that does not fit in old-fashioned Suzdal, but it is not a bad option. Its 17 rooms are comfortable but overdecorated. It also has a nice *banya* (hot bath, a bit like a sauna) and an excellent restaurant.

Hotel Rizopolozhenskaya Hotel (☎ 24314; ul Lenina; s/d incl breakfast R620/1000) Housed in the decrepit Monastery of the Deposition, this hotel is Suzdal's cheapest place to stay. Some rooms have been renovated and their quality varies widely, so it's wise to ask for a preview before you commit.

Hotel Suzdal (☎ 21530; www.suzdaltour.ru; s/d incl breakfast from R1580/1800; ✻ 🖳 🖳) One of three hotels within the GTK. This place is low on charm but high on facilities: the complex includes a fitness centre, a bowling alley, several restaurants, and a cheaper 'motel' (R1120/1340).

Eating & Drinking

Kremlin Refectory (☎ 21763; meals R300-500; ✻ 11am-11pm) The attraction here is the atmospheric location inside the Archbishop's Chambers. This place has been serving tasty, filling Russian favourites for 300 years.

Slavyansky Bar (☎ 20062; ul Kremlyovskaya 6; meals R100-200; ✻ 10am-8pm) For a quick refresher, this is a pleasant, convenient stop. The menu is mostly drinks and snacks, but hungrier patrons will also find something to satisfy them.

Mead-Tasting Hall (☎ 20803; tasting menu R120-150; ✻ 10am-5pm Mon-Fri, 10am-8pm Sat & Sun) Hidden at the rear of the trading arcades, this hall is done up like a church interior – floor-to-ceiling frescoes, arched ceilings and stained-glass windows. The menu features different varieties of *medovukha*, a mildly alcoholic honey ale that was drunk by the princes of old.

Other recommendations in the trading arcades:

Gostiny Dvor (☎ 21778; meals R200-300; ✻ 11am-midnight) A popular locals' spot for drinking and socialising.

Emelya (☎ 21011; ul Lenina 84; meals R200-300; ✻ 11am-midnight) Enjoy the lovely vista from the outside tables, especially at sunset.

Entertainment

Club Robinzon (☎ 24319; ul Lenina 63; ✻ noon-4am) Suzdal's only nightlife option offers dancing, karaoke and billiards.

Getting There & Away

The bus station is 2km east of the centre on Vasilyevskaya ul. Some long-distance buses continue on past the bus station into the centre; otherwise, a *marshrutka* will take you there.

Buses run every half-hour to/from Vladimir (R20, one hour). Otherwise, most of the buses originate elsewhere. Buses from Vladimir go to Yaroslavl (R164, five hours, twice daily) and Kostroma (R142, 4½ hours, daily), but it is often easier to go to Ivanovo (R80, two hours, four daily) and change there. One daily bus goes directly to/from Moscow's Shchyolkovsky bus station (R145, 4½ hours).

PLYOS ПЛЁС

☎ 49339 / pop 40,000 / ✻ Moscow

Plyos is a tranquil town of wooden houses and hilly streets winding down to the Volga waterfront, halfway between Ivanovo and Kostroma. Though fortified from the 15th century, Plyos' renown stems from its role as a late-19th-century artists' retreat. Isaak Levitan, Russia's most celebrated landscape artist, found inspiration here in the summers of 1888 to 1890. The playwright Anton Chekhov commented that Plyos 'put a smile in Levitan's paintings'. During the three summers in which he lived here, Levitan completed around 200 works, including 23 paintings.

The oldest part of town is along the river, as evidenced by the ramparts of the old fort, which date from 1410. The hill is topped by the simple 1699 **Assumption Cathedral** (Uspensky sobor), one of Levitan's favourite painting subjects.

The **Levitan House Museum** (Dom-Muzey Levitana; ☎ 43782; ul Lunacharskogo 4; admission R50; ✻ 9am-5pm Tue-Sun), in the eastern part of the town, across the small Shokhonka River, displays works of Levitan and other artists against the background of the Volga.

Plyos is easy to reach in summer, when hydrofoils ply the Volga from Kostroma and Yaroslavl. Otherwise, buses run regularly from Ivanovo and occasionally from Kostroma (weekends only).

KOSTROMA КОСТРОМА

☎ 4942 / pop 280,000 / ✻ Moscow

This historic town sits 300km northeast of Moscow (95km north of Ivanovo), where its namesake river – the Kostroma – converges with the Volga. The delightful historic centre dates back to the 18th century, when the old wooden structures were demolished by fire. But the pride of Kostroma is the 14th-century Monastery of St Ipaty, which poses majestically on the right bank of the Kostroma River.

History
Founded by Yury Dolgoruky in 1152, Kostroma suffered at the hands of nomadic raiders in 1238. The northern outpost was rebuilt, and served as a refuge for various grand princes throughout the 14th century.

During the Time of Troubles (1605–13), Kostroma was a centre of Russian resistance against the Poles and Cossacks. Young boyar Mikhail Romanov was in exile at the local Monastery of St Ipaty when he was elected tsar.

Orientation
The town centre lies along the northern bank of the Volga, with the bus and train stations some 4km east. The Monastery of St Ipaty is west of the centre across the Kostroma River, a Volga tributary. The central square is Susaninskaya pl.

Information
Post & telephone office (cnr uls Sovetskaya & Podlipaeva; 9am-9pm)
Sberbank (ul Sovetskaya 9; 9am-4pm Mon-Fri) Conveniently located bank with ATM.
Telecom Centre (☎ 621 162; cnr uls Sovetskaya & Podlipaeva; per hr R50; 9am-9pm) Internet access in the same complex as the post office.

Sights
MONASTERY OF ST IPATY
Legend has it that a Tatar prince named Chet (who later founded the house of Godunovs) was returning to Moscow in 1330 and fell ill. At this time he had a vision of the Virgin Mary and the martyr Ipaty of the Ganges, which aided his recovery. When he returned to Moscow he was baptised and founded the **Monastery of St Ipaty** (☎ 312 589; admission R50; 9am-5pm) to mark the occasion.

In 1590, the Godunovs built the monastery's **Trinity Cathedral** (Troitsky sobor), which contains over 80 old frescoes by a school of 17th-century Kostroma painters, headed by Gury Nikitin (plus some 20th-century additions). The fresco in the southern part of the sanctuary depicts Chet Godunov's baptism by St Ipaty. The **bell tower**, modelled after the Ivan the Great Bell Tower in Moscow, chimes concerts every hour.

The monastery's more recent history is closely tied to the Godunov and Romanov families, fierce rivals in high-level power games before the Romanovs established their dynasty. In 1600 Boris Godunov exiled the head of the Romanov family, Fyodor, and his son Mikhail to this monastery. Mikhail Romanov was here in 1613, when the all-Russia Council came to insist that he accept his position as tsar, thus ending the Time of Troubles. In honour of the event, all successive Romanov rulers came here to visit the monastery's red **Romanov Chambers** (Palaty Romanova), opposite the cathedral.

The monastery is 2.5km west of the town centre. Take bus 14 from the central Susaninskaya pl and get off once you cross the river.

MUSEUM OF WOODEN ARCHITECTURE

Behind the monastery is an attractive outdoor **museum** (☎ 577 872; admission R20, photography permit R30; 9am-5pm May-Oct) of northern-style wooden buildings, including peasant houses, windmills and churches (one built without nails). Most of the buildings are not open, but the grounds are pleasant for strolling, listening to the chirping of frogs and admiring the handiwork of the artists.

The museum is nearly indistinguishable from the surrounding neighbourhood, which also consists of storybook-like houses, blossoming gardens and pretty churches, including a **domed wooden church** directly north of the monastery.

TOWN CENTRE

Picturesque Susaninskaya pl was built after a fire in 1773, as an ensemble under Catherine the Great's patronage. Clockwise around the northern side are: a 19th-century **fire tower** (still in use and under Unesco protection); a former military **guardhouse**, housing a small **literature museum** (☎ 516 027; ul Lenina 1; admission R20; 9.30am-5pm); an 18th-century **hotel** for members of

the royal family; the **palace** of an 1812 war hero, now a courthouse; and the **town hall**.

In the streets between are many merchants' town houses. The **Art Museum** (☎ 513 829; pr Mira 5 & 7; admission to each bldg R40; 10am-6pm) comprises two elaborate neo-Russian buildings. No 5 contains 16th- to 19th-century Russian art, as well as appropriately decorated 19th-century rooms such as the White Hall (Beliy Zal). No 7, built in 1913 to celebrate 300 years of Romanov rule, houses a portrait gallery and a collection of ancient artwork.

The **monument** in the park between the arcades is to local hero Ivan Susanin, who guided a Polish detachment hunting for Mikhail Romanov into a swamp, and to their deaths. In 1967, the Soviet regime tore down the original Susanin monument and replaced it with this revolutionary figure.

CHURCHES

The **Monastery of the Epiphany** (ul Simanovskogo 26) is now the Archbishop of Kostroma's residence. The large **cathedral** in this 14th-to 19th-century complex is the city's main working church. The 13th-century icon of *Our Lady of St Theodore*, on the right-hand side of the iconostasis, is supposedly the source of many miracles.

The 17th-century **Church of the Resurrection** (ul Nizhnyaya Debrya 37), near Hotel Volga, has a bright, patterned exterior and was partly financed with a load of gold coins mistakenly shipped from London.

Sleeping

Ipatyevskaya Village (☎ 577 179; fax 319 444; ul Beregovaya 3a; d R1500-2300) Kostroma's most atmospheric lodging choice is this old-fashioned wooden house, opposite the monastery entrance. The quaint rooms feature modern amenities but old-fashioned style. Highlights include the authentic Russian *banya* and the small beach fronting the Kostroma river.

Hotel Mush (☎ 312 400; www.mush.com.ru in Russian; ul Sovetskaya 29; r incl breakfast R1300-2100) This tiny guesthouse has a central location and hospitable atmosphere. Its four rooms are spacious and elegantly furnished. Enter through the courtyard.

Rus Tourist Complex (☎ 546 163; russ@kmtn.ru; ul Yunosheskaya 1; s/d incl breakfast from R1000/1500) Kostroma's Soviet-standard hotel overlooks the Volga about 2km southeast of the centre, near the bridge. The facilities, including the restaurant, are adequate. The highlight of this place is the vista: the Volga is exquisite in the morning light with the Church of the Resurrection in the foreground.

Kostroma Intourist (☎ 390 505; hotel-intourist@ mail.ru; Magistralnaya ul 40; s/d from R1500/2100) A modern, Western-style motel with two good restaurants. Its location, about 2km south of the Volga bridge on the road to Yaroslavl and Ivanovo, is inconvenient unless you are driving. From ul Podlipaeva in front of Hotel Volga, take bus 10.

The buses that approach Kostroma from Yaroslavl or Ivanovo pass the Intourist and Volga Hotels; ask your driver to drop you off to save yourself the trek back into town from the bus station.

Eating

Horn & Hoof Café (☎ 315 240; ul Sovetskaya 2; meals R150-200; ⊙ 9am-midnight) Step off the 18th-century streets into this coffee shop that also harks back to eras past. Wrought-iron furniture and B&W photos set the atmosphere. The menu has a good selection of soups, salads and main dishes, besides pastries and coffee drinks.

White Sun (☎ 579 057; ul Lesnaya 2; meals R400-600) The décor evokes the desert at this spicy, Central Asian restaurant. When the season is right, the prime location next to the river station offers outdoor seating with views of the river. Live music nightly.

Getting There & Away
BOAT
The best way to get between Kostroma and Yaroslavl in summer is by hydrofoil, which runs twice a day in either direction. The hydrofoils depart from the main *prichal* (pier) No 4 to Yaroslavl (1½ hours) and downstream to Plyos (one hour).

Long-distance river boats between Moscow and points down the Volga as far as Astrakhan also call at Kostroma.

BUS
The bus station is 4.5km east of Susaninskaya pl on Kineshemskoe sh, the continuation of ul Sovetskaya. There are buses to/from Moscow (R308, 8½ hours, six daily), Yaroslavl (R75, two hours, six daily), and Ivanovo (R104, three hours, 10 daily). Daily trains also go to Vologda (R254, seven hours), Nizhny Novgorod (R325, 9½

hours) and Vladimir (R166, 5½ hours) via Suzdal (R150, 4½ hours).

TRAIN
The train station is 4km east of Susaninskaya pl. There are three or four daily suburban trains to/from Yaroslavl (R310, three hours).

Getting Around
Buses 1, 2, 9, 9 Expres, 14K, 19 and others run between the bus station and Susaninskaya pl, along the full length of ul Sovetskaya. Trolleybus 2 runs between the train station and Susaninskaya pl.

YAROSLAVL ЯРОСЛАВЛЬ
☎ 4852 / pop 680,000 / ⊙ Moscow
Yaroslavl, 250km northeast of Moscow, is the urban counterpart to Suzdal. This is the biggest place between Moscow and Arkhangelsk, and it has a more urban feel than anywhere else in the Golden Ring. Its big-city skyline, however, is dotted with onion domes and towering spires, not smoke stacks and skyscrapers. As a result of a trade boom in the 17th century, churches are hidden around every corner. The poet Apollon Grigoryev wrote: 'Yaroslavl is a town of unsurpassed beauty; everywhere is the Volga and everywhere is history.' And everywhere, everywhere, are churches.

History
In 1010, the Kyivan prince Yaroslav the Wise took an interest in a trading post called Medvezhy Ugol (Bear Corner). According to legend, Yaroslav subjugated and converted the locals by killing their sacred bear with his axe. So the town was founded, and its coat of arms bears both the beast and the weapon (no pun intended).

Yaroslavl was the centre of an independent principality by the time the Tatars came. Developed in the 16th and 17th centuries as the Volga's first port, it grew fat on trade with the Middle East and Europe and became Russia's second-biggest city of the time. Rich merchants competed to build churches bigger than those of Moscow, with elaborate decoration and bright frescoes on contemporary themes. Though the city's centrepiece is the Monastery of the Transfiguration of the Saviour, the merchant churches make the city unique.

Orientation

The city centre lies at the crux of the Volga and Kotorosl Rivers, inside the ring road, Pervomayskaya ul. The centre of the ring is Sovetskaya pl, from which streets radiate out to three squares: Bogoyavlenskaya pl with the landmark Transfiguration monastery; pl Volkova with the classical façade of the Volkov Theatre; and Krasnaya pl near the river station.

Information

Alfa-Bank (☎ 739 177; ul Svobody 3; ☿ 9am-6pm Mon-Thu, 9am-4.30pm Fri) Exchange office and ATM facilities.

Dom Knigi (☎ 304 751; ul Kirova 18; ☿ 10am-7pm Mon-Fri, 10am-6pm Sat) Has a good selection of maps and books.

Internet Club (☎ 726 850; pr Lenina 24; per hr R32; ☿ 9am-11pm) A dark club in the Dom Kultury that has more facilities than the post office.

Post & telephone office (Komsomolskaya ul 22; per hr R33; ☿ 8am-8pm Mon-Sat, to 6pm Sun) Also offers Internet services.

Sberbank (☎ 729 518; ul Kirova 6; ☿ 8.30am-4pm Mon-Sat) Changes money and gives credit card advances.

Sights & Activities

MONASTERY & AROUND

Founded in the 12th century, the **Monastery of the Transfiguration of the Saviour** (☎ 303 869; www.yarmp.yar.ru; Bogoyavlenskaya pl 25; grounds R10, exhibits R20-30 each, all-inclusive R50 Mon-Wed, R130 Thu-Sun; ☿ exhibits 10am-5pm Tue-Sun year-round, grounds 8am-8pm daily Oct-May) was one of Russia's richest and best-fortified monasteries by the 16th century. The oldest surviving structures, dating from 1516, are the **Holy Gate** near the main entrance by the river, and the austere **Cathedral of the Transfiguration** (admission R35; ☿ Fri-Tue).

To get a new perspective, climb the **bell tower** (admission R40; ☿ 8am-7pm daily May-Sep). The summit provides a panorama of the city and a close-up view of the spiky gold bulbs that top some of the monastery buildings.

Opposite the kremlin, the vaulted, red-brick **Church of the Epiphany** (Bogoyavlenskaya pl; admission R20) was built by a wealthy 17th-century merchant. Its rich decoration includes bright exterior ceramic tiles (a Yaroslavl speciality), vibrant frescoes and a carved iconostasis. A **statue of Yaroslav the Wise** stands in the centre of the square.

CHURCH OF ELIJAH THE PROPHET

The exquisite **church** (Sovetskaya pl; admission R60; ☿ 10am-1pm & 2-6pm Thu-Tue May-Sep) that dominates Sovetskaya pl was built by prominent 17th-century fur dealers. It has some of the Golden Ring's brightest frescoes by the ubiquitous Yury Nikitin of Kostroma and his school, and detailed exterior tiles. The church is closed during wet spells.

RIVER EMBANKMENTS

The Volga and Kotorosl embankments make for an enjoyable 1.5km walk. A pedestrian promenade runs along the bank of the Volga below the level of the street, Volzhskaya nab.

From the Church of Elijah the Prophet, head towards the river on Narodny per. Here, the **Church of St Nicholas the Miracle-Worker** (Narodny per; admission R20; ☿ 10am-5pm) was the first of Yaroslavl's stone merchant churches, built in 1622. It has a sparkling baroque iconostasis and frescoes showing the life and works of the popular St Nicholas.

The unique, private collection **Music & Time** (☎ 328 637; Volzhskaya nab 33a; admission R50; ☿ 10am-7pm) is in the little house just north of the church. Here, John Mostoslavsky enthusiastically guides visitors through his fascinating collection of clocks, musical instruments and various other antiques.

South along the embankment is the old Governor's Mansion, which now houses the **Yaroslavl Art Museum** (☎ 303 504; Volzhskaya nab 23; admission R25, special exhibits R10-30; ☿ 10am-5pm Tue-Sun), with 18th- to 20th-century Russian art. On the next block, the **History of Yaroslavl Museum** (☎ 304 175; Volzhskaya nab 17; admission R15; ☿ 10am-6pm Wed-Mon) is in a lovely 19th-century merchant's house. A **monument** to victims of war and repression in the 20th century is in the peaceful garden. Other surviving merchants' houses are nearby, such as **Dom Mateev** (cnr Volzhskaya nab & Sovetsky per).

A little further along the embankment are the **Volga Bastion**, built as a watchtower in the 1660s, and a fine early-19th-century church. The 17th-century former Metropolitan's Chambers houses the old Yaroslavl art collection of the **Art Museum** (☎ 729 287; Volzhskaya nab 1; admission R30; ☿ 10am-5pm Sat-Thu), with icons and other work from the 13th to 19th centuries.

In the leafy park behind the museum is a stone-slab **monument** marking the spot where Yaroslav founded the city in 1010. The park

YAROSLAVL

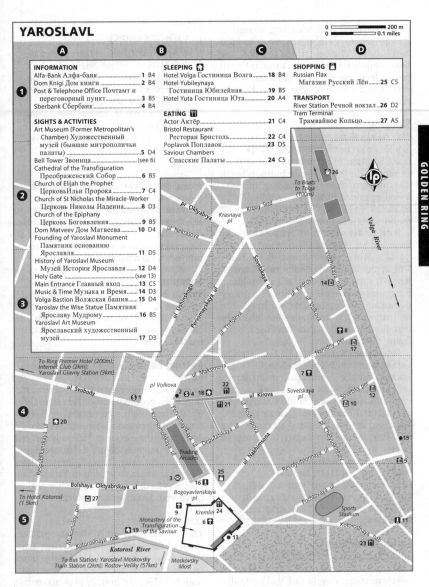

0   200 m
0   0.1 miles

INFORMATION
Alfa-Bank Алфа-банк 1 B4
Dom Knigi Дом книги 2 B4
Post & Telephone Office Почтамт и
    переговорный пункт 3 B5
Sberbank Сбербанк 4 B4

SIGHTS & ACTIVITIES
Art Museum (Former Metropolitan's
    Chamber) Художественный
    музей (бывшие митрополичьи
    палаты) 5 D4
Bell Tower Звоница ....(see 6)
Cathedral of the Transfiguration
    Преображенский Собор 6 B5
Church of Elijah the Prophet
    ЦерковьИльи Пророка 7 C4
Church of St Nicholas the Miracle-Worker
    Церковь Николы Надеина 8 D3
Church of the Epiphany
    Церковь Богоявления 9 B5
Dom Matveev Дом Матвеева 10 D4
Founding of Yaroslavl Monument
    Памятник основанию
    Ярославля 11 D5
History of Yaroslavl Museum
    Музей Истории Ярославля 12 D4
Holy Gate ....(see 13)
Main Entrance Главный вход 13 C5
Music & Time Музыка и Время......14 D3
Volga Bastion Волжская башня 15 D4
Yaroslav the Wise Statue Памятник
    Ярославу Мудрому...........................16 B5
Yaroslavl Art Museum
    Ярославский художественный
    музей 17 D3

SLEEPING
Hotel Volga Гостиница Волга........18 B4
Hotel Yubileynaya
    Гостиница Юбилейная 19 B5
Hotel Yuta Гостиница Юта...............20 A4

EATING
Actor Актёр..21 C4
Bristol Restaurant
    Ресторан Бристоль.........................22 C4
Poplavok Поплавок...............................23 D5
Saviour Chambers
    Спасские Палаты 24 C5

SHOPPING
Russian Flax
    Магазин Русский Лён....25 C5

TRANSPORT
River Station Речной вокзал ..26 D2
Tram Terminal
    Трамвайное Кольцо............27 A5

GOLDEN RING

To Boats
to Tolga
(100m)

Volga River

Pr Oktyabrya
Krasnaya pl
Krasny Sezd
ul Nekrasova
Sovetskaya ul
Yolmskaya nab
ul Kedrova
ul Volkova
ul Ushinskogo
ul Trefolova
ul Pervomayskaya
Narodny per
To Ring Premier Hotel (200m);
Internet Club (2km);
Yaroslavl Glavny Station (3km)
ul Maksimova
ul Svobody
pl Volkova
ul Kirova
Sovetskaya pl
Sovetsky per
ul Andropva
Respublikanskaya ul
Komsomolskaya ul
ul Nakhimsona
ul Depulatskaya
Revolyutsionnaya ul
Trading Arcades
Bolshaya Oktyabrskaya ul
To Hotel Kotorosl
(1.5km)
Bogoyavlenskaya pl
Mukanolov per
Monastery of the
Transfiguration
of the Saviour
Kremlin
Kotoroslnaya nab
Kotorosl River
ul Oktyabrskoy
Pochtovaya ul
Sports Stadium
Kotoroslnaya nab
To Bus Station; Yaroslavl Moskovsky
Train Station (2km); Rostov-Veliky (57km)
Moskovsky Most

stretches right onto the tip of land between the Volga and the Kotorosl Rivers. Above the Kotorosl, the raised embankments indicate the site of Yaroslavl's old kremlin.

The more time you spend, the more churches you will discover, most dating from the 17th century. There are three more along the embankment, and several south of the Kotorosl River in the settlements of Korovniki and Tolchkovo. Pick up the brochure *Yaroslavl* (available in several languages) at one of the museum gift shops.

RIVER TRIPS

There are summer services from the river station on the Volga at the northern end of Pervomayskaya ul, including a range of slow *prigorodnyy* (suburban) boats to local destinations. The best trip is to **Tolga**, one hour from Yaroslavl on the Konstantinovo route. Here, near the river, you'll find a convent with lovely buildings from the 17th century.

Sleeping

Ring Premier Hotel (☎ 581 058; fax 581 158; ul Svobody 55; s/d incl breakfast R4500/5000; ❇ ▣) The latest addition to accommodation options in Yaroslavl is this slick new business hotel. The modern six-storey building includes a well-equipped fitness centre, wheelchair-accessible rooms and an Irish pub (a must for any four-star hotel).

Hotel Yubileynaya (☎ 309 259; www.yubil.yar.ru; Kotoroslnaya nab 26; s/d incl breakfast from R1800/2600; ❇ ▣) More conventional than Hotel Volga, this hotel overlooks the Kotorosl River. It's the usual concrete slab building, but rooms are completely renovated, simply decorated and comfortably furnished. The only drawback is the fluorescent blue light that illuminates the façade (and the rooms) facing the river.

Hotel Volga (☎ 731 111; fax 728 276; ul Kirova 10; s without bathroom R600, s/d with bathroom R1500/1800) Located on the central pedestrian street, this historic hotel is a throwback to pre-revolutionary Russia. High ceilings and architectural details give it an air of faded elegance, despite the dark entrance. Size and furnishings vary between rooms, so ask for a preview.

Other recommendations:

Hotel Kotorosl (☎ 212 415; fax 216 468; kotorosl@yaroslavl.ru; Bolshaya Oktyabrskaya ul 87; s/d R1000/1500) Within walking distance of the train station.

Hotel Yuta (☎ 218 793; fax 397 86; utah@yaroslavl.ru; Respublikanskaya ul 79; s/d incl breakfast R1200/1800)

Eating & Drinking

Bristol Restaurant (☎ 729 408; ul Kirova 10; meals R200-500; ❂ noon-2am Fri & Sat, noon-midnight Sun-Thu) Downstairs, a sunlit café that's popular for lunch or drinks. Upstairs, a formal dining room with heavy drapes, high ceilings and dark wood floors.

Poplavok (☎ 314 343; meals R500-800; ❂ noon-1am) Housed on a boat on the Kotorosl River, Poplavok is Kostroma's only truly waterside dining. Seafood specials are skilfully prepared and artfully presented. Add-

itional perks include live music and alfresco dining when the weather is fine.

Saviour Chambers (☎ 304 807; Bogoyavlenskaya pl 25; meals R300-500; ❂ 11am-11pm) This place is popular with tourist groups for its atmospheric location (inside the gates of the monastery) and its tasty Russian fare.

Shopping

Russian Flax (☎ 305 670; ul Pervomayskaya 51; ❂ 9.30am-5pm Mon-Sat) Sells fine linen tablecloths, napkins and bedclothes at remarkably low prices; you can also have items made to order.

Getting There & Away

BOAT

In summer, boats depart from the river station at the northern end of Pervomayskaya ul. The hydrofoils to downstream destinations will take you to Kostroma (1½ hours) and Plyos (three hours). Tickets go on sale about 30 minutes before departure. From early June to early October, long-distance Volga passenger ships stop in Yaroslavl on their way from Moscow to cities like Nizhny Novgorod, Kazan and Astrakhan.

BUS

The bus station is on Moskovsky pr, 2km south of the Kotorosl River and near Yaroslavl's Moskovsky vokzal. One or two buses go daily to/from Moscow's Shchyolkovsky station (R236, six hours), plus about five buses stopping in transit. Most of these stop at Pereslavl-Zalessky and Sergiev Posad. Other departures include: Ivanovo (R180, three hours, two daily); Kostroma (R80, two hours, 10 daily); Uglich (R96, three hours, six daily); Pereslavl-Zalessky (R115, three hours, four daily); Rostov-Veliky (R52, 1½ hours, seven daily); Vladimir (R222, six hours, two

daily) via Suzdal (R190, five hours); and Vologda (R165, five hours, two daily).

TRAIN
The main station is Yaroslavl Glavny, on ul
Svobody 3km west of the centre. The lesser
Yaroslavl Moskovsky vokzal is near the bus
station, 2km south of town. Around 20
trains a day run to/from Moscow's Yaro-
slavsky vokzal (R350, five hours). There's
also a daily service to/from St Petersburg
(R1120, 12½ hours), as well as Nizhny
Novgorod (R900, 9½ hours) en route to
Ufa. For closer destinations such as Rostov-
Veliky (R180, two hours) or Kostroma
(R310, three hours), it's easiest to take sub-
urban trains.

Getting Around
From Yaroslavl Glavny vokzal, head 200m
to the right for the tram stop on ul Ukhtom-
skogo. Tram 3 goes along Bolshaya Oktyabrskaya ul to the tram terminal west of
Bogoyavlenskaya pl; trolleybus 1 runs along
ul Svobody to pl Volkova and Krasnaya pl.
From the bus station and Yaroslavl
Moskovsky train station, trolleybus 5 or 9
goes to Bogoyavlenskaya pl.

UGLICH УГЛИЧ
☎ 48532 / pop 39,000 / ⊕ Moscow
Uglich is a quaint but shabby town on the
Volga, 90km northwest of Rostov-Veliky.
Here the son of Ivan the Terrible, Dmitry
(later to be impersonated by the string of
False Dmitrys in the Time of Troubles), was
murdered in 1591, probably on the orders
of Boris Godunov.

Within the waterside **kremlin** (☎ 53678; each
site R34; ⊕ 9am-1pm & 2-5pm), the 15th-century
Prince's Chambers (Knyazhyi palaty) house
a historical exhibit that tells this sordid
tale. The star-spangled **Church of St Dmitry on
the Blood** (Tserkov Dmitria-na-krovi) was
built in the 1690s on the spot where the
body was found. Its interior is decorated
with bright frescoes and the bell that was
used to mourn Dmitry's death. (In 1581
the bell was used to call an insurrection on
the murder of the tsarevitch. In response,
Godunov ordered the 300kg bell to be publicly flogged and its tongue to be ripped
out before it was banished for many years
to the Siberian town of Tobolsk.) The impressive five-domed **Transfiguration Cathedral**

(Preobrazhensky sobor) and an **Art Museum**
are also in the kremlin.

Other recommendations:
Museum of City Life (☎ 24414; www.uglich.ru;
admission R60; ⊕ timed to ferry schedule) An interactive
museum with costumes and musical instruments.
Reservations recommended.
Vodka Museum (☎ 23558; ul Berggolts 9; admission
R60; ⊕ 10am-5pm) Price of admission includes samples!

If you get stuck in Uglich, you can stay at the
Assumption Hotel (Uspenskaya Gostinitsa; ☎ 51870; pl
Uspenskaya; s/d R500/700), opposite the kremlin.
It's a cheery place with comfortable rooms
and a small café. Uglich is a regular stop for
tour boats plying the Volga. Landlubbers
can come by bus from Yaroslavl (R96, three
hours, six daily). Buses to Rostov-Veliky run
sporadically, so you may have to travel via
Borisoglebsk. Otherwise, taxis wait outside
the tiny bus station.

ROSTOV-VELIKY
РОСТОВ-ВЕЛИКИЙ
☎ 48536 / pop 40,000 / ⊕ Moscow
For a place called Rostov-Veliky, or 'Rostov
the Great', this place gives the impression of
a sleepy village. Perhaps for this reason, the
magnificent Rostov kremlin catches visitors
off guard when its silver domes and whitewashed stone walls appear amid the dusty
streets. Rostov is among the prettiest of
the Golden Ring towns, idyllically sited on
shimmering Lake Nero. It is also one of the
oldest, first chronicled in 862.

Rostov is about 220km northeast of Moscow. The train and bus stations are together
in the drab modern part of Rostov, 1.5km
north of the kremlin.

Sights & Activities
KREMLIN
Rostov's main attraction is its unashamedly
photogenic **kremlin** (☎ 61717; admission grounds
R5, exhibits R15-25 each; ⊕ 10am-5pm). Though
founded in the 12th century, nearly all the
buildings here date to the 1670s and 1680s.

With its five magnificent domes, the
Assumption Cathedral dominates the kremlin, although it is just outside the latter's
north wall. Outside service hours, you can
get inside the cathedral through the door
in the church shop on ul Karla Marksa.
The cathedral was here a century before
the kremlin, while the belfry was added in

the 1680s. Each of 15 bells in the belfry has its own name; the largest, weighing 32 tonnes, is called Sysoy. The monks play magnificent bell concerts (which can be arranged through the excursions office, in the west gate) for R250.

The west gate (the main entrance) and north gate are straddled by the **Gate-Church of St John the Divine** and the **Gate-Church of the Resurrection**, both of which are richly decorated with 17th-century frescoes. Enter these churches from the monastery walls, which you can access from the stairs next to the north gate. Like several other buildings within the complex, these are open only from May to September. Between the gate-churches, the **Church of Hodigitria** houses an

exhibition of Orthodox Church vestments and paraphernalia.

The Metropolitan's private chapel, the **Church of the Saviour-over-the-Galleries**, has the most beautiful interior of all, covered in colourful frescoes. These rooms are filled with exhibits: the **White Chamber** displays religious antiquities, while the **Red Chamber** shows off *finift* (luminous enamelled miniatures), a Rostov artistic speciality.

Although the ticket office is in the west gate, you can also enter the kremlin through the north gate. Don't leave without stopping at the **gift shop** (☎ 61717; ⏰ 10am-5pm) behind the Metropolitan's House to shop for *finift* souvenirs and to sample the home-brewed *medovukha*.

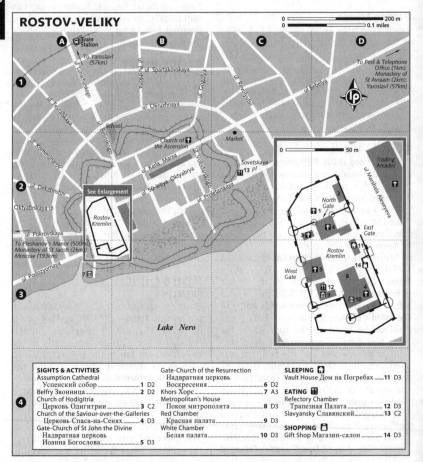

MONASTERIES & OTHER BUILDINGS

The restored **Monastery of St Jacob** is the fairy-tale apparition you'll see as you approach Rostov by road or rail. To get here you can take buses 1 or 2 1.5km to the west of the kremlin, although it's a very pleasant walk alongside Lake Nero to get here. Heading east of the kremlin, bus 1 will also bring you to the dilapidated **Monastery of St Avraam**, with a cathedral dating from 1553.

Named after a pagan sun god, **Khors** (☎ 62483; www.khors.org; ul Podozerka 30; admission free; ☙ 3-8pm Mon-Fri, 10am-9pm Sat & Sun) is a private gallery on the lakeshore behind the kremlin. The eclectic collection includes some antique household items, models of wooden churches and some exquisite enamelwork by local artist Mikhail Selishchev. The two small rooms are available for rent to 'artists passing through'. The artist who runs the place also hosts workshops on enamel and Rostov artistry.

BOAT RIDES

For a different perspective on this panorama, board the ferry **Zarya** (☎ 61717; tickets R250; ☙ 10am, 11.30am, 1pm, 2.30pm & 4pm Tue-Sun May-Sep) for a float around Lake Nero. The hour-long trip leaves from the pier near the western gate of the kremlin, and cruises past both monasteries.

Sleeping & Eating

Pleshanov's Manor (Usadba Pleshanova; ☎ 76440; www.hotel.v-rostove.ru; ul Pokrovskaya 34; r incl breakfast R1200-1500; ▧) This 19th-century manor house, once the residence of a merchant and philanthropist family, is now a welcoming inn with a nice restaurant, cosy library and wood sauna. The charm of the common areas does not extend to the rooms, which are modern and fresh, but bland. Prices decrease between October and April.

Vault House (☎ 31244; s/d without bathroom R350/600, d with bathroom R1400-1600) Right inside the kremlin, and near the east gate, this place has clean, wood-panelled rooms that vary somewhat in size and view.

Refectory Chamber (☎ 62871; meals R200-400; ☙ 9am-5pm, later in summer) The draw to the refectory is also the atmospheric location inside the kremlin, near the Metropolitan's House. The grand dining room is often crowded with tour groups supping on traditional Russian fare.

Slavyansky (☎ 62228; Sovetskaya pl 8) About 100m east of the kremlin, this semiswanky place gets recommendations from locals.

Getting There & Away

BUS

The most convenient option to get to Yaroslavsky vokzal (R52, 1½ hours, seven daily) is by bus, either transit or direct. Transit buses also pass through on the way to Moscow (four to five hours, hourly), Pereslavl-Zalessky (two hours, six daily) and Sergiev Posad (four to five hours, three daily). One lone bus goes to Uglich (three hours).

TRAIN

The fastest train from Moscow is the express service from Yaroslavsky vokzal (R180, three hours). Otherwise, some long-distance trains stop at Rostov-Veliky en route to Yaroslavl. You can also catch a suburban train, but you need to change at Aleksandrov.

Getting Around

Bus 6 runs between the train station and the town centre.

PERESLAVL-ZALESSKY
ПЕРЕСЛАВЛЬ-ЗАЛЕССКИЙ

☎ 48535 / pop 45,000 / ☙ Moscow

On the shore of Lake Pleshcheevo, almost halfway between Moscow and Yaroslavl, Pereslavl-Zalessky is a popular dacha destination for Muscovites who enjoy the peaceful village atmosphere. The southern half of the town is characterised by narrow dirt lanes lined with carved *izby* (log houses) and blossoming gardens.

Pereslavl-Zalessky (Pereslavl Beyond the Woods) was founded in 1152 by Yury Dolgoruky. The town's main claim to fame is as the birthplace of Alexander Nevsky. Its earth walls and the little Cathedral of the Transfiguration are as old as the town itself.

Orientation

Pereslavl-Zalessky is pretty much a one-street town, with the bus station at the southwestern end, 2km from the centre. Apart from the few churches in the kremlin area, most of the historic sights are out of the centre.

Information

Sberbank (Rostovskaya ul 27; ☙ 9am-7pm Mon-Sat) Exchange facility in the lobby of Hotel Pereslavl.

Yartelekom Service Centre (☎ 31595; Rostovskaya ul 20; per hr R50) Has Internet and telephone facilities.

Sights

CENTRE

The walls of Yury Dolgoruky's **kremlin** are now a grassy ring around the central town. Inside is the 1152 **Cathedral of the Transfiguration of the Saviour**, one of the oldest buildings in Russia. A bust of Alexander Nevsky stands out in front, while three additional churches across the grassy square make for a picturesque corner. These include the tent-roofed **Church of Peter the Metropolitan**, built in 1585 and renovated in 1957, and the 18th-century twin churches fronting the road.

The **Trubezh River**, winding 2km from the kremlin to the lake, is fringed by trees and narrow lanes. You can follow the northern riverbank most of the way to the lake by a combination of paths and streets. The **Forty Saints' Church** sits picturesquely on the south side of the river mouth.

Southwest of the kremlin, the **Nikolsky Women's Monastery** has undergone a massive renovation. Since its founding in 1350, this monastery has been on the brink of destruction – whether from Tatars, Poles or Communists – more than seems possible to survive. In 1994 four nuns from the Yaroslavl Tolga Convent came to restore the place, and today it looks marvellous. Rumour has it that the rebuilding is being bankrolled by a wealthy Muscovite businessperson who has benefited from the nuns' blessings.

SOUTH PERESLAVL-ZALESSKY

The **Goritsky Monastery** (☎ 38100; http://museum .pereslavl.ru in Russian; admission R50; ⏰ 10am-6pm May-Oct, 9am-5pm Nov-Apr) was founded in the 14th century, though today the oldest buildings are the 17th-century gates, gate-church and belfry. The centrepiece is the baroque **Assumption Cathedral** (Uspensky sobor; admission R40) with its beautiful carved iconostasis. The other buildings hold art and history exhibits.

The 1785 **Purification Church of Alexander Nevsky** is a working church across the main road from Goritsky. To the east, on a hillock overlooking fields and dachas, is the **Danilovsky Monastery**, whose tent-roofed **Trinity Cathedral** (Troitsky sobor) dates back to the

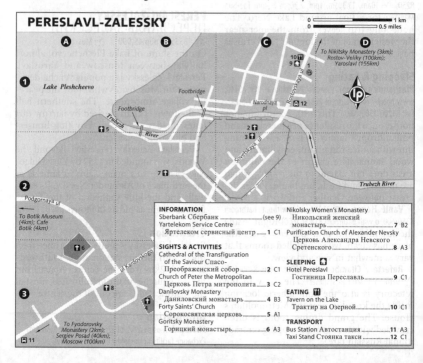

PERESLAVL-ZALESSKY

0 ————— 1 km
0 ————— 0.5 miles

To Nikitsky Monastery (3km);
Rostov-Veliky (100km);
Yaroslavl (155km)

Lake Pleshcheevo

Footbridge
Footbridge

Narodnaya pl

Trubezh River

Podgornaya ul

To Botik Museum
(4km); Cafe
Botik (4km)

Trubezh River

To Fyodorovsky
Monastery (2km);
Sergiev Posad (40km);
Moscow (100km)

1530s. There's another 16th-century walled monastery, the **Fyodorovsky Monastery**, about 2km south on the Moscow road.

BOTIK MUSEUM

Besides the birthplace of Alexander Nevsky, Pereslavl also claims to be the birthplace of the Russian Navy: Lake Pleshcheevo is one of the places where Peter the Great developed his obsession with the sea. As a young man, he studied navigation here and built a flotilla of more than 100 little ships by age 20. You can explore some of this history at the small **Botik Museum** (☎ 22788; admission R40; 🕙 10am-5pm Tue-Sun), situated 4km along the road past the Goritsky Monastery at the southern end of the lake. Its highlight is the sailboat *Fortuna*, one of only two of Peter the Great's boats to survive fire and neglect; the other is in the St Petersburg Naval Museum.

NIKITSKY MONASTERY

Founded in 1010, the Nikitsky received its current name in the 12th century, after the death of the martyr St Nikita. To punish himself for his sins, Nikita had clasped his limbs in chains and spent the end of his days in an underground cell on the monastery grounds. The handcuffs, which now hang in the main **cathedral**, are said to help cure addictions and other worldly vices. Behind the cathedral, a small chapel is being built around the dank cell where Nikita died.

Nikitsky Monastery is about 3km north of the centre on the west side of the main road. Buses 1, 3 and 4 go most of the distance, or you can catch a taxi from Narodnaya pl.

Sleeping & Eating

Hotel Pereslavl (☎ 31788; fax 32687; Rostovskaya ul 27; s/d from R650/1000) Although this hotel is only 20 years old, it is badly in need of the renovation that is ongoing. The cheapest rooms are very drab, but you can upgrade if you are willing to pay the price (R1300/1600).

    Cafe Botik (☎ 98085; Podgornaya ul; meals R200-300; 🕙 11am-11pm) This waterfront café (shaped like a boat) is in a prime location opposite the Botik museum. Stop here for lake views and lunch before or after your excursion.

    Tavern on the Lake (☎ 94264; Rostovskaya ul 27; meals R150-300; 🕙 9am-midnight) Gnaw on shashlyk to your heart's desire at this Georgian eatery. Pork, chicken, beef and sturgeon – all are grilled up and served hot and spicy.

Getting There & Away

Pereslavl is not on the train line, but buses travel frequently to Moscow (2½ hours). Not all of these stop at Sergiev Posad (one hour, three daily). Others travel to Kostroma (four hours, two daily) and Yaroslavl (three hours, two daily) via Rostov-Veliky (1½ hours).

Getting Around

Bus 1 runs up and down the main street from just south of the bus station; heading out from the centre, you can catch it just north of the river. Taxis wait at Narodnaya pl.

SERGIEV POSAD СЕРГИЕВ ПОСАД

☎ 254 (from Moscow), ☎ 49654 (from elsewhere) / pop 100,000 / 🕙 Moscow

According to old Russian wisdom, 'there is no settlement without a just man; there is no town without a saint'. And so the town of Sergiev Posad tributes St Sergius of Radonezh, founder of the local Trinity Monastery and patron saint of all of Russia. The monastery – today among the most important and active in Russia – exudes Orthodoxy. Bearded priests bustle about; babushkas fill bottles of holy water; crowds of believers light candles to St Sergius, Keeper of Russia. This mystical place is a window into the age-old belief system that has provided Russia with centuries of spiritual sustenance.

Often called by its Soviet name of Zagorsk, Sergiev Posad is 60km from the edge of Moscow on the Yaroslavl road. It is an easy day trip from Moscow – a rewarding option for travellers who don't have time to venture further around the Golden Ring.

History

St Sergius of Radonezh began his calling as a hermit monk in the forest wilderness. In 1340 he founded a monastery at Sergiev Posad, which soon became the spiritual centre of Russian Orthodoxy. Prince Dmitry Donskoy's improbable victory in battle against the Mongols in 1380 was credited to the blessing of Sergius. Soon after his death at the age of 78, Sergius was named Russia's patron saint. Since the 14th century, pilgrims have been journeying to this place to pay homage to St Sergius.

Although the Bolsheviks closed the monastery, it was reopened after WWII as a museum, residence of the patriarch and a working monastery. The patriarch and the church's administrative centre moved to the Danilovsky Monastery in Moscow in 1988, but the Trinity Monastery of St Sergius remains one of the most important spiritual sites in Russia. For its concentrated artistry and its unique role in the interrelated histories of the Russian Church and State, it is well worth a day trip from Moscow.

Orientation

Pr Krasnoy Armii is the main street, running north to south through the town centre. The train and bus stations are on opposite corners of a wide square to the east of pr Krasnoy Armii. The monastery is about 400m north of there.

Information

Post & telephone office (pr Krasnoy Armii 127A) Outside the southeastern wall of the monastery.
Sberbank (pr Krasnoy Armii; 9am-4pm Mon-Fri) Exchange facilities available, but no ATM.

Sights

TRINITY MONASTERY OF ST SERGIUS

The **monastery** (Troitse-Sergieva Lavra; ☎ 45356, 45350; admission free; 10am-6pm) is an active religious centre with a visible population of monks in residence; visitors should refrain from photographing the monks. Female visitors should wear headscarves, and men are required to remove hats before entering the churches. Guided tours cost R600 and photos R150.

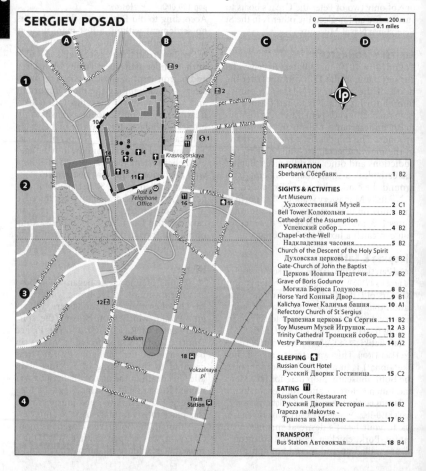

SERGIEV POSAD

Built in the 1420s, the squat, dark **Trinity Cathedral** is the heart of the Trinity Monastery. The tomb of St Sergius stands in the southeastern corner, where a memorial service for St Sergius goes on all day, every day. The icon-festooned interior, lit by oil lamps, is largely the work of the great medieval painter Andrei Rublyov and his students.

The star-spangled **Cathedral of the Assumption** was modelled on the cathedral of the same name in the Moscow Kremlin. It was finished in 1585 with money left by Ivan the Terrible in a fit of remorse for killing his son. It is closed to the general public but included as a part of guided tours. Outside the west door is the **grave** of Boris Godunov, the only tsar not buried in the Moscow Kremlin or St Petersburg's SS Peter & Paul Cathedral.

Nearby, the resplendent **Chapel-at-the-Well** was built over a spring that is said to have appeared during the Polish siege. The five-tier baroque **bell tower** took 30 years to build in the 18th century, and once had 42 bells, the largest of which weighed 65 tonnes.

The **Vestry** (admission R160; 🕑 10am-5.30pm Wed-Sun), behind the Trinity Cathedral, displays the monastery's extraordinarily rich treasury, bulging with 600 years of donations by the rich and powerful – tapestries, jewel-encrusted vestments, solid-gold chalices and more.

The huge block with the 'wallpaper' paint job is the **Refectory Church of St Sergius**, so called because it was once a dining hall for pilgrims. Now it's the Assumption Cathedral's winter counterpart, with morning services in cold weather. It is closed outside of services, except for guided tours. The green building next door is the metropolitan's residence.

The miniature imitation of the Trinity Church is the 15th-century **Church of the Descent of the Holy Spirit**. It's used only on special occasions. It contains, among other things, the grave of the first Bishop of Alaska.

OTHER MUSEUMS

A number of other museums around town showcase the monastery's rich artistic traditions.

Art Museum (☎ 45356; pr Krasnoy Armii 144; 🕑 10am-5pm Tue-Sun) Two exhibition halls featuring local artists' works.

Horse Yard (☎ 45356; ul Udarnoy Armii; 🕑 10am-5pm Wed-Sun) Exhibits on the ethnological and archaeological history of Sergiev Posad.

Toy Museum (☎ 44101; ul Krasnoy Armii 123; 🕑 11am-5pm Tue-Sat) Toys from throughout history and around the world.

Sleeping & Eating

Russian Court hotel (☎ 75392; www.zolotoe-koltso .ru/hoteldvorik in Russian; ul Mitkina 14/2; s/d incl breakfast weekdays from R1500/1900, weekends from R1700/2100) Some of the rooms at this delightful hotel boast views of the onion domes peeking out above whitewashed walls. The place is quite modern, despite the rustic style. The fanciest room even has a Jacuzzi.

Russian Court Restaurant (☎ 45114; pr Krasnoy Armii 134; meals R500-800; 🕑 10am-9pm) Not to be confused with the hotel by the same name, this restaurant is decorated like a Russian dacha. Appropriately enough, it features wait staff in peasant dress and serves hearty country cuisine. The place is popular with tour groups in summer.

Trapeza na Makovtse (☎ 41101; pr Krasnoy Armii 131; meals R500-800; 🕑 10am-9pm) Location, location, location. The highlight of this 'refectory' is alfresco dining in the shadow of the spires and cupolas. Dining is also pleasant inside, where live music plays nightly.

Getting There & Away

BUS

Services to Sergiev Posad from Moscow's VDNKh metro station depart every half-hour from 8.30am to 7.30pm (R50, 70 minutes). Three daily buses start at Sergiev Posad and run to Pereslavl-Zalessky (1½ hours). Nine daily buses stop here in transit to Yaroslavl, Kostroma or Rybinsk; all these will take you to Pereslavl-Zalessky, Rostov-Veliky or Yaroslavl if you can get a ticket.

TRAIN

The fastest transport option is the express train from Moscow's Yaroslavsky vokzal (R195, one hour). Suburban trains also run every half-hour (R55, 1½ hours); take any train bound for Sergiev Posad or Aleksandrov. To go north to Rostov-Veliky (3½ hours) or Yaroslavl (five hours), you may have to change at Aleksandrov.

GOLDEN RING

St Petersburg
Санкт Петербург

Locals call it, simply, 'Piter'. In its time – some 300 action-packed years – it has been known by several other names, all more resonant of its pivotal place in Russian history. But whatever it's called there's no denying that St Petersburg is one of the most glorious cities in Russia, if not the world. This grand dream of Peter the Great is like one gigantic museum: look up from the banks of the Neva River and the canals that meander through the heart of city and you'll gaze upon a showcase of 18th- and 19th-century palaces and mansions. Inside these you'll discover a mind-boggling collection of museums, culminating in the truly breathtaking Hermitage.

It's small wonder that such an environment has nurtured some of Russia's greatest artists and cultural movements. St Petersburg is the birthplace of Russian ballet, home to literary giants, including Pushkin and Dostoevsky, and musical maestros such as Shostakovich and Rachmaninoff. Creativity continues to throb through the city's veins manifesting itself in a hedonistic and experimental club and performing arts scenes, as well as, lately, a delicious crop of restaurants. Also make time to journey out of St Petersburg to at least one of the splendid old tsarist palace estates, such as Petrodvorets and Tsarskoe Selo. Many other rewarding day trips await those who choose to make the city their base for longer.

Not everything is perfect: St Petersburg's splendour goes hand in hand with corruption, crime, decay, squalor and pollution. If anything, though, this gritty reality makes the city's dazzling façades and lightness of spirit seem even more magical. St Petersburg's beauty is one with a human face and all the more appealing for that.

HIGHLIGHTS

- Losing yourself amid the artistic treasures and imperial interiors of the **Hermitage** (p244)
- Cruising the **canals** (p272) for a boatman's perspective on the city's architecture and pretty bridges
- Enjoying a world-class opera or ballet performance at the beautiful **Mariinsky Theatre** (p262)
- Admiring the Grand Cascade's symphony of fountains at **Petrodvorets** (p295)
- Feeling your jaw hit the parquet floor as you take in the gilded splendour of **Catherine Palace** (p299)

★ Hermitage
Mariinsky ★★ Canals
Theatre
ST PETERSBURG
★ Petrodvorets
Catherine Palace ★

■ POPULATION: 4.6 MILLION   ■ AREA CODE: ☎ 812

HISTORY

The area around the mouth of the Neva River may have been a swamp but it's been long fought over. Alexander of Novgorod defeated the Swedes here in 1240 – earning the title Nevsky (of the Neva). Sweden retook control of the region in the 17th century and it was Peter the Great's desire to crush this rival and make Russia a European power that led to the founding of St Petersburg. At the start of the Great Northern War (1700–21) he captured the Swedish outposts on the Neva, and in 1703 he began his city with the Peter & Paul Fortress.

After Peter trounced the Swedes at Poltava in 1709, the city he named, in Dutch style, Sankt Pieter Burkh (after his patron saint) really began to grow. Canals were dug to drain the marshy south bank and in 1712 Peter made the place his capital, forcing grumbling administrators, nobles and merchants to move here and build new homes. Peasants were drafted as forced labour, many dying of disease and exhaustion; it's still known as the city built upon bones. Architects and artisans came from all over Europe. By Peter's death in 1725 his city had a population of 40,000 and 90% of Russia's foreign trade passed through it.

Peter's immediate successors moved the capital back to Moscow but Empress Anna Ioanovna (1730–40) returned it to St Petersburg. Between 1741 and 1825, during the reigns of Empress Elizabeth, Catherine the Great and Alexander I, it became a cosmopolitan city with a royal court of famed splendour. These monarchs commissioned great series of palaces, government

---

THE LENINGRAD BLOCKADE

The Leningrad Blockade was the city's defining event of the 20th century. Around one million people died from shelling, starvation and disease in what's called the '900 Days' (actually 872). By comparison, the USA and UK suffered about 700,000 dead between them in all of WWII.

After the war began on 22 June 1941, with the Germans fast approaching, many residents fled. Art treasures and precious documents from the Hermitage and other museums were moved out by the train-load; factories were evacuated and relocated to Siberia; historical sculptures were buried or covered with sandbags. Yet no-one could have predicted the suffering to come.

The Nazi plan, as indicated in a secret directive, was to 'wipe the city of Petersburg from the face of the earth'. A fragile 'Road of Life' across frozen Lake Ladoga was the only (albeit heavily bombed) lifeline the city had for provisions and evacuations.

Food was practically nonexistent, and at one point rations were limited to 175g of sawdust-laden bread a day. People ate their pets, even rats and birds disappeared from the city. The paste behind wallpaper was scraped off and eaten, leather belts were cooked until chewable. Cannibalism started in the shelters for refugees from the neighbouring towns; without ration cards, they were among the first to die. The exhausted and starved literally fell over dead on the streets. There were periods when over 30,000 people per day died of hunger.

More than 150,000 shells and bombs were dropped on the city during the blockade, the effects of which are still visible on some buildings (notably on the west wall of St Isaac's Cathedral and the northwest corner of the Anichkov most). Still, life went on. Concerts and plays were performed in candlelit halls, lectures given, poetry written, orphanages opened, brigades formed to clean up the city. Most famous was the 9 August 1942 concert of Shostakovich's 7th Symphony by the Leningrad Philharmonic, broadcast nationally by radio from the besieged city.

According to survivors, random acts of kindness outnumbered incidents of robbery and vandalism, and lessons learned about the human spirit would be remembered for a lifetime. From a poem by Olga Berggolts, written after the blockade was lifted: 'In mud, in darkness, hunger, and sorrow, where death, like a shadow, trod on our heels, we were so happy at times, breathed such turbulent freedom, that our grandchildren would envy us.'

For a detailed, harrowing description of the blockade, read Harrison Salisbury's *900 Days: the Siege of Leningrad*. Otherwise, a visit to one or all of these Blockade-related sites – St Petersburg History Museum (p263), Blockade Museum (p259), Monument to the Heroic Defenders of Leningrad (p268) and Piskaryovskoe Cemetery (p268) – would greatly enrich your understanding of its history.

buildings and churches, turning it into one of Europe's grandest capitals.

The emancipation of the serfs in 1861 and industrialisation, which peaked in the 1890s, brought a flood of poor workers into the city, leading to squalor, disease and festering discontent. St Petersburg became a hotbed of strikes and political violence and was the hub of the 1905 revolution, sparked by 'Bloody Sunday' on 9 January 1905, when a strikers' march to petition the tsar in the Winter Palace was fired on by troops. In 1914, in a wave of patriotism at the start of WWI, the city's name was changed to the Russian-style Petrograd. The population at the time was 2.1 million.

In 1917 the workers' protests turned into a general strike and troops mutinied, forcing the end of the monarchy in March. Seven months later Lenin's Bolshevik Party had prevailed and the Soviet government came into being (p49). The new government moved the capital back to Moscow in March 1918, fearing a German attack on Petrograd. The privations of the Civil War caused Petrograd's population to drop to about 700,000, and in 1921 strikes in the city and a bloodily suppressed revolt by the sailors of nearby Kronshtadt (p303) helped to bring about Lenin's more liberal New Economic Policy.

Petrograd was renamed Leningrad after Lenin's death in 1924. A hub of Stalin's 1930s industrialisation program, by 1939 it had 3.1 million people and 11% of Soviet industrial output. Yet Stalin feared it as a rival power base and the 1934 assassination of the local communist chief Sergei Kirov at Smolny was the start of his 1930s Communist Party purge.

When Germany attacked the USSR in June 1941 it took them only two and a half months to reach Leningrad. As the birthplace of Bolshevism, Hitler swore to wipe it from the face of the earth. His troops besieged the city from 8 September 1941 until 27 January 1944 (p225) but Leningrad survived and, after the war, was proclaimed a 'hero city'. It took until 1960 for the city's population to exceed pre-WWII levels.

During the 1960s and '70s Leningrad developed a reputation as a dissidents' city with an artistic underground spearheaded by the poet Joseph Brodsky and, later, rock groups such as Akvarium (p87). In 1989

Anatoly Sobchak, a reform-minded candidate, was elected mayor. Two years later as the USSR crumbled the city's citizens voted to bring back the name of St Petersburg (though the region around the city remains known as Leningradskaya oblast).

During the 1990s St Petersburg became notorious for its levels of corruption and high rates of criminality. At times it seemed the local 'Mafia' were more in charge than the elected officials. In 1996 Sobchak was succeeded by his deputy Vladimir Yakovlev, and later ended up in comfortable self-exile in Paris after charges of corruption and fiscal mismanagement. Yakovlev's first act after his victory was to change the title from mayor to governor.

Romanov ghosts returned to the city on 17 July 1998, when the remains of Tsar Nicholas II, his wife, three of his five children, their doctor and three servants were buried in the family crypt at the SS Peter & Paul Cathedral within the fortress of the same name (p437). Five years later the legacy of the tsars came further under the spotlight during St Petersburg's tricentenary celebrations. With millions of dollars having been spent on restoration and refurbishment the city looks better now probably than at any other time in its history – a source of great pride to President Vladimir Putin who wastes no opportunity to return to his birthplace and show it off to visiting heads of state and other dignitaries.

In 2003 Putin lured Yakovlev into federal government (sidelining him as the envoy to the federal district of the South, including the hot potato of Chechnya), leaving the way clear for the president's ally Valentina Matvienko to assume office. She has continued to capitalise on the injection of foreign interest in Russia and business in the city is booming. Overused as the term may be St Petersburg has, in fact, reestablished itself as Russia's window on the West.

ORIENTATION

St Petersburg sprawls across and around the delta of the Neva River, at the end of the easternmost arm of the Baltic Sea, the Gulf of Finland. Entering St Petersburg at its southeastern corner, the Neva first flows north and then west across the middle of the city, dividing into several branches and forming the islands that make up the delta.

The two biggest branches, which diverge where the Winter Palace stands on the south bank, are the Bolshaya (Big) Neva and Malaya (Small) Neva; they flow into the sea either side of Vasilyevsky Island.

The heart of St Petersburg is the area spreading back from the Winter Palace and the Admiralty on the south bank, its skyline dominated by the golden dome of St Isaac's Cathedral. Nevsky pr, heading east-southeast from here, is the main drag, along and around which you'll find many of the city's sights, shops and restaurants.

The northern side of the city comprises three main areas. Vasilyevsky Island is the westernmost, with many of the city's fine early buildings still standing at the eastern end – the Strelka. The middle area is Petrograd Side, a cluster of delta islands whose southern end is marked by the tall gold spire of the SS Peter & Paul Cathedral. The third, eastern, area is Vyborg Side, stretching along the north bank of the Neva.

Maps

There's a large number of maps covering the city, all available both abroad at any good travel bookshop and in the city itself. Dom Knigi (right) has the best selection, including maps of transport routes (including *marshrutky*, fixed-rate minibuses) and several street directories.

STREET NAMES

In the early to mid-1990s, the city changed the Soviet-era names of dozens of its parks, streets and bridges back to their prerevolutionary names. Ten years on, only their 'new' names are used, though 'Griboedova Canal' will probably never revert to its tsarist-era moniker, Yekaterinsky (Alexander Griboedov was a 19th-century playwright who lived in a house on this canal).

St Petersburg has two streets called Bolshoy pr: one on Petrograd Side, one on Vasilyevsky Island. The two sides of some streets on Vasilyevsky Island are known as lines (linii), and opposite sides of these streets have different names – thus 4-ya linia (4th line) and 5-ya linia (5th line) are the east and west sides of the same street – which collectively is called 4-ya i 5-ya linii (4th and 5th lines).

INFORMATION

Bookshops

Books are for sale everywhere, but books in English are scarce. There are also many antiquarian bookshops worth rooting through for collectables and old maps; we list a couple of good options below.

Anglia (Map pp234–5; ☎ 279 8284; nab reki Fontanki 40; ☼ 10am–7pm; Ⓜ Gostiny Dvor) City's only English-language bookshop. Get your Lonely Planet guidebooks here. Entry inside the Turgenev Building.

Dom Knigi (Map pp230–1; ☎ 325 6696; Nevsky pr 62; ☼ 8am–11pm Mon-Sat, 9am–10pm Sun; Ⓜ Gostiny Dvor) You'll find a good selection of guidebooks and maps to the city on the 1st floor of St Petersburg's largest bookshop.

Na Liteynom (Map pp234–5; ☎ 275 3873; Liteyny pr 61; ☼ 9.30am–7.30pm Mon-Sat, 11am–6pm Sun; Ⓜ Mayakovskaya) Antiquarian book seller tucked away in a courtyard. Also an interesting place to browse for antiques and unusual souvenirs.

Staraya Kniga (Map pp238–9; ☎ 232 1765; Bolshoy pr 19, Petrograd Side; ☼ 10am–7pm Tue-Sat; Ⓜ Chkalovskaya) Excellent selection of old books and maps.

Cultural Centres

British Council (Map pp234–5; ☎ 718 5060; www.britishcouncil.ru; nab reki Fontanki 46; ☼ 12.30-7pm Tue-Fri, noon-5pm Sat; Ⓜ Gostiny Dvor) St Petersburg's best-organised foreign cultural centre holds classical concerts, theatre and film performances. For use of its excellent library the annual membership fee is R150 for teachers, R300 for everyone else.

Goethe Institute (Map pp230–1; ☎ 325 9835; www.goethe.de/ins/ru/pet/; nab reki Moyki 58; ☼ 9.15am–7pm Mon-Fri; Ⓜ Gostiny Dvor) Has a well-stocked German-language library.

Institut Francais (Map pp230–1; ☎ 311 0995; www.fr.spb.ru; nab reki Moyki 20; ☼ 10am–7pm Mon-Fri; Ⓜ Nevsky Prospekt) This busy centre has a library with over 12,000 French-language books, magazines, videos and CDs. It also organises numerous cultural events.

Emergency

All of the following numbers have Russian-speaking operators. If you need to make a police report and don't speak Russian, first contact the Tourist Information Centre (p243). For serious matters contact your embassy or consulate, too (p704).

Ambulance ☎ 03
Fire ☎ 01
Gas Leak ☎ 04
Police ☎ 02

ST PETERSBURG IN...

Two Days

Start in style with a tour of the **Hermitage** (p244). Enjoy an afternoon stroll in the nearby **Summer Garden** (p256) and a peek inside the beautifully restored **Sheremetyev Palace** (p258) along the Fontanka River. From here you're well placed to hop on a boat for an early evening **cruise** (p272). If you're quick, you could also squeeze in a visit to **St Isaac's Cathedral** (p252) climbing its colonnade for a bird's-eye view of the city.

Kick off day two by exploring the splendid **Russian Museum** (p252). Move on to the polychromatic **Church of the Saviour on Spilled Blood** (p252). After lunch head across the Neva River to explore the **Peter & Paul Fortress** (p264). If you have time, continue around to the **Strelka** (p263) to see the museums here, or at least take in the view.

Five Days

Following on from the previous two-day itinerary, spend a day each exploring the imperial parks and palaces at **Petrodvorets** (p295) and **Tsarskoe Selo** (p299). Consider using the fifth day to explore the city's more off-the-beaten-track sights including the **Hermitage's Storage Facility** (p267), the nearby **Buddhist Temple** (p267) and the peaceful, traffic-free park on **Yelagin Island** (p266). Cap it all off with a performance at the **Mariinsky Theatre** (p262).

Internet Access

Internet cafés are common in St Petersburg. Wi-fi is also becoming popular with hot spots popping up across the city: City Bar (p285), Ili (p282), Mirage Cinema (p286) and Zoom Café (p282) all use the **Quantum** (www .quantum.ru in Russian) network.

Café Max (Map pp234-5; ☎ 273 6655; Nevsky pr 90/92; per hr R40; ☼ 24hr; Ⓜ Mayakovskaya) Wi-fi available here. Also has a branch in the Hermitage.

FM Club (Map pp234-5; ☎ 764 3674; ul Dostoevskogo 6A; per hr R60; ☼ 10am-8am; Ⓜ Vladimirskaya)

Quo Vadis? (Map pp230-1; ☎ 571 8011; Nevsky pr 24; per hr R80; ☼ 24hr; Ⓜ Gostiny Dvor) Has 65 terminals and a café/library in which you can browse foreign newspapers and magazines.

Internet Resources

There is no shortage of information about St Petersburg on the Internet. Try the following as well as seeing individual sections in the chapter for more suggestions, and p22 for other handy sites.

http://enlight.ru/camera/index_e.htm Peter Sobolev's excellent Wandering Camera website includes some 300 albums of photos of the city.

http://petersburgcity.com/for-tourists Representing the official English-language portal for St Petersburg.

http://spb.yell.ru/eng/default.asp?site=spb Yellow Pages for St Petersburg.

www.saint-petersburg.com One of the best places to start. There's information on sights, current events and listings, a virtual city tour, online hotel booking, and a great, up-to-date traveller's message board.

www.spb.ru/eng Another starting point for St Petersburg information, with several good links.

www.eng.gov.spb.ru Official site of the St Petersburg government.

Laundry

Most hotels offer a laundry service.

Prachechnaya (Map pp240-1; ☎ 305 0886; 11-ya linia 34; ☼ 9am-9pm; Ⓜ Vasileostrovskaya) A 3kg wash costs R170, ironing an extra R105.

Stirka (Map pp230-1; ☎ 314 5371; Kazanskaya ul 26; ☼ 9am-11pm Mon-Fri, 10am-1am Sat & Sun; Ⓜ Nevsky Prospekt) Café-bar and laundrette – what a good idea! A 5kg wash costs R100 with espresso included. The dryer is R30 per 20 minutes.

Left Luggage

All the major train stations have luggage lockers and/or left-luggage services.

Media

NEWSPAPERS & MAGAZINES

Apart from the following English-language media (all of which are available free at many hotels, hostels, restaurants and bars across the city) there are a couple of useful Russian-language listing magazines. Both **Afisha** (http://spb.afisha.ru/index-spb in Russian; R20) and **Time Out** (www.timeout.ru/index.shtml in Russian; R24) are published every two weeks, with Afisha generally reckoned to have the edge in terms of features and coverage.

(Continued on page 242)

GREATER ST PETERSBURG

	0	4 km
	0	2 miles

229

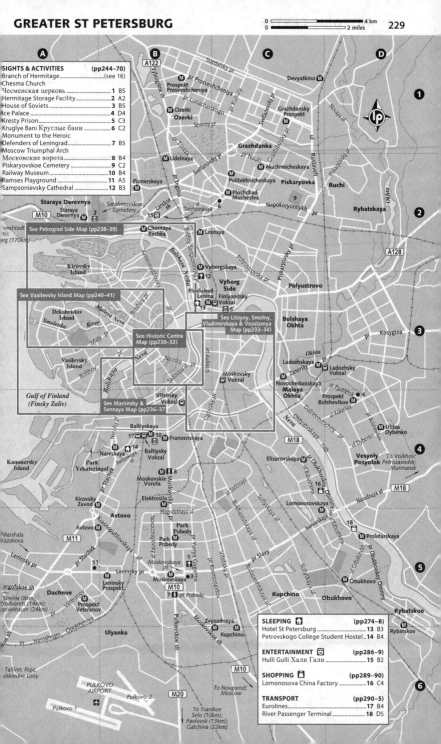

SIGHTS & ACTIVITIES (pp244–70)
Branch of Hermitage...............................(see 16)
Chesma Church
Чесменская церковь.................................**1** B5
Hermitage Storage Facility.........................**2** A2
House of Soviets.......................................**3** B5
Ice Palace...**4** D4
Kresty Prison...**5** C3
Kruglye Bani Круглые бани.......................**6** C2
Monument to the Heroic
Defenders of Leningrad.............................**7** B5
Moscow Triumphal Arch
Московские ворота..................................**8** B4
Piskaryovskoye Cemetery..........................**9** C2
Railway Museum......................................**10** B4
Ramses Playground...................................**11** A5
Sampsonievsky Cathedral...........................**12** B3

SLEEPING 🛏 (pp274–8)
Hotel St Petersburg...................................**13** B3
Petrovskogo College Student Hostel..**14** B4

ENTERTAINMENT 🎭 (pp286–9)
Hulli Gulli Хали Гали................................**15** B2

SHOPPING 🛍 (pp289–90)
Lomonosova China Factory.......................**16** C4

TRANSPORT (pp290–5)
Eurolines..**17** B4
River Passenger Terminal.........................**18** D5

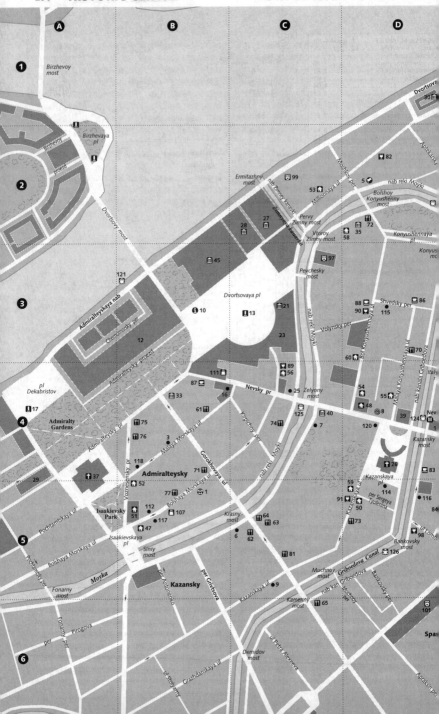

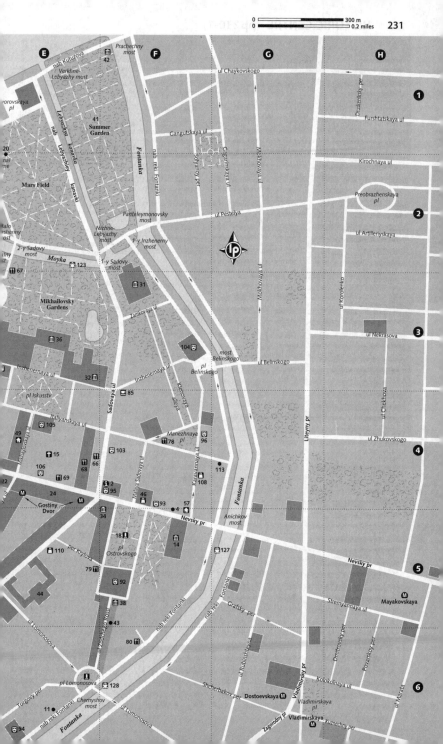

0 — 300 m
0 — 0.2 miles

E

nab Kutuzova
Verkhne
Lebyazhy most
Prachechny
most

F

ul Chaykovskogo

G

H

orovskaya
pl

Furshtatskaya ul

Druskenitsky per

20
nal
ne

Lebyazhy kanavki
nab
Lebyazhy kanavki

41
Summer
Garden

Gangutskaya ul

Solyanoy per

Chaykovskogo per

Kirochnaya ul

Preobrazhenskaya
pl

Mochovaya ul

Mars Field

nab reki Fontanki

Fontanka

Gagarinskaya ul

ul Pestelya

ul Artilleriyskaya

halo
resheny
ost
lhy
st

Panteleymonovsky
most

Nizhne-
Lebyazhy
most

Moyka

2-y Sadovy
most

1-y Inzhenerny
most

Mochovaya ul

ul Korolenko

ul Nekrasova

123

67

1-y Sadovy
most

31

Mikhailovsky
Gardens

Zamkovaya ul

104

most
Belinskogo

Litevny pr

ul Chekhova

36

pl
Belinskogo

ul Belinskogo

Inzhenernaya ul

Inzhenernaya ul

ul Zhukovskogo

32

85

Klenovaya alleya

pl Iskusstv

105

Italiyanskaya ul

Sadovaya ul

Manezhnaya
pl

78

96

49

15

103

Mikhailovskaya ul

106

66

68

108

113

Fontanka

69

2
95

Malaya Sadovaya ul

Karavannaya ul

22

24

M
Gostiny
Dvor

M

34

46

93

4

57

Nevsky pr

Anichkov
most

110

per Krylova

18

pl
Ostrovskogo

14

Nevsky pr

79

92

127

Stremyannaya ul

M
Mayakovskaya

44

38

nab reki Fontanki

Grafsky per

Dmitrovsky per

Povarskoy per

43

80

nab reki Fontanki

ul Rubinshteyna

Vladimirsky pr

Kolokolnaya ul

ul Marata

ul Lomonosova

Zodchego Rossi most

pl Lomonosova

128

Shcherbakov per

Dostoevskaya M

Vladimirskaya
pl

11

Chernyshov
most

ul Lomonosova

Zagorodny pr

Vladimirskaya M

Kuznechny per

94

Fontanka

Torgovy per

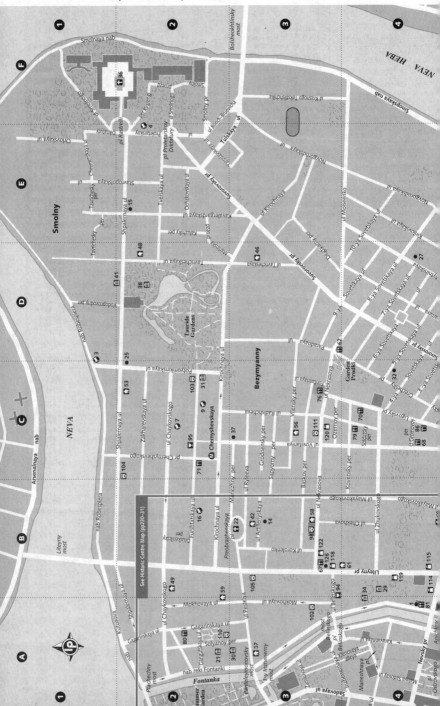

0 — 500 m
0 — 0.3 miles

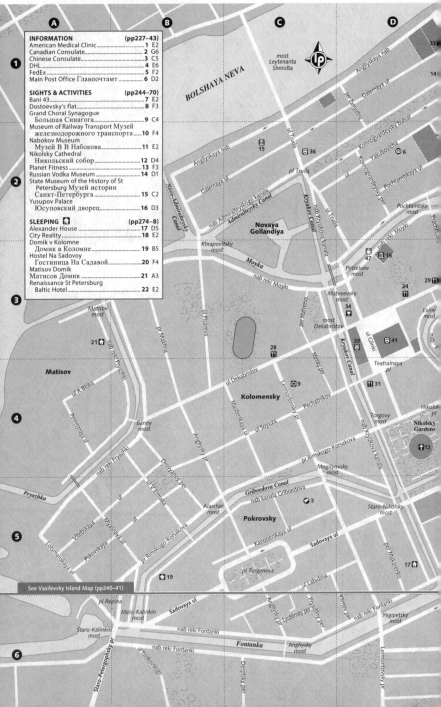

INFORMATION	(pp227–43)
American Medical Clinic	**1** E2
Canadian Consulate	**2** G6
Chinese Consulate	**3** C5
DHL	**4** E6
FedEx	**5** F2
Main Post Office Главпочтамт	**6** D2

SIGHTS & ACTIVITIES	(pp244–70)
Bani 43	**7** E2
Dostoevsky's flat	**8** F3
Grand Choral Synagogue Большая Синагога	**9** C4
Museum of Railway Transport Музей железнодорожного транспорта	**10** F4
Nabokov Museum Музей В В Набокова	**11** E2
Nikolsky Cathedral Никольский собор	**12** D4
Planet Fitness	**13** F3
Russian Vodka Museum	**14** D1
State Museum of the History of St Petersburg Музей истории Санкт-Петербурга	**15** C2
Yusupov Palace Юсуповский дворец	**16** D3

SLEEPING	(pp274–8)
Alexander House	**17** D5
City Reality	**18** E2
Domik v Kolomne Домик в Коломне	**19** B5
Hostel Na Sadovoy Гостиница На Садовой	**20** F4
Matisov Domik Матисов Домик	**21** A3
Renaissance St Petersburg Baltic Hotel	**22** E2

See Vasilevsky Island Map (pp240–41)

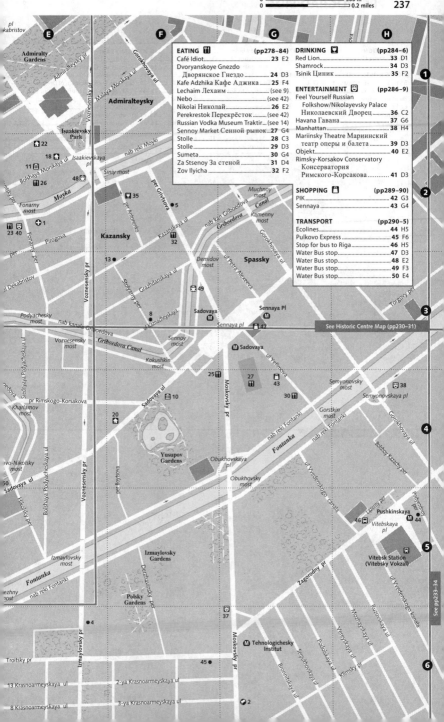

0 ——— 300 m
0 ——— 0.2 miles

EATING 🍴 (pp278–84)
Café Idiot.................................. 23 E2
Dvoryanskoye Gnezdo
  Дворянское Гнездо 24 D3
Kafe Adzhika Кафе Аджика 25 F4
Lechaim Лехаим .... (see 9)
Nebo .... (see 42)
Nikolai Николай 26 E2
Perekrestok Перекрёсток .... (see 42)
Russian Vodka Museum Traktir... (see 14)
Sennoy Market Сенной рынок ... 27 G4
Stolle 28 C3
Stolle 29 D3
Sumeta 30 G4
Za Stsenoy За стеной 31 D4
Zov Ilyicha 32 F2

DRINKING 🍷 (pp284–6)
Red Lion 33 D1
Shamrock 34 D3
Tsinik Циник 35 F2

ENTERTAINMENT 🎭 (pp286–9)
Feel Yourself Russian
  Folkshow/Nikolayevsky Palace
  Николаевский Дворец 36 C2
Havana Гавана 37 G6
Manhattan 38 H4
Mariinsky Theatre Мариинский
  театр оперы и балета 39 D3
Objekt 40 E2
Rimsky-Korsakov Conservatory
  Консерватория
  Римского-Корсакова 41 D3

SHOPPING 🛍 (pp289–90)
PIK 42 G3
Sennaya 43 G4

TRANSPORT (pp290–5)
Ecolines 44 H5
Pulkovo Express 45 F6
Stop for bus to Riga 46 H5
Water Bus stop 47 D3
Water Bus stop 48 E2
Water Bus stop 49 F3
Water Bus stop 50 E4

See Historic Centre Map (pp230–31)

See pp233–34

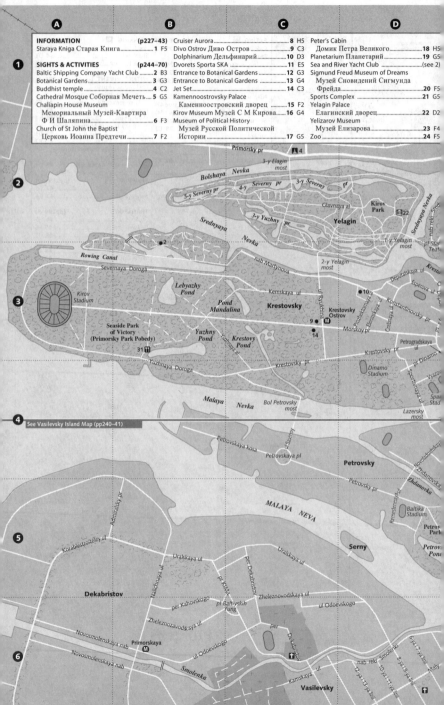

See Vasilevsky Island Map (pp240–41)

0 _____ 500 m
0 _____ 0.3 miles

Ⓐ **Ⓑ** **Ⓒ** **Ⓓ**

INFORMATION	(pp227–43)
Prachechnaya Прачечная	1 F3
Sindbad Travel	2 H4

SIGHTS & ACTIVITIES	(pp244–70)
Academy of Arts Museum Академия художеств	3 G4
Central Naval Museum (Old Stock Exchange) Центральный военно-морской музей	4 H3
Church of Mother of God the Merciful Церковь Милующей Божей Матери	5 D5
Menshikov Palace Дворец Меньшикова	6 H3
Museum of Anthropology & Ethnography (Kunstkamera) Музей антропологии и этнографии	7 H3
Museum of Zoology Музей зоологии	8 H3
Rostral Columns Ростральные колонны	9 H3

Temple of the Assumption Успенское подворье Оптиной Пустыни	10 F4
VMF ВМФ	11 D4

SLEEPING 🏠	(pp274–8)
Nevsky Prostor	12 B4
Prestige Hotel	13 F3
SPB Vergaz	14 F3

EATING 🍴	(pp278–84)
Byblos	15 F2
Restoran	16 H3
Russky Kitsch	17 G4
Staraya Tamozhnya Старая таможня	18 H3
Stolle	19 G3
Swagat	20 D5

DRINKING 🍷	(pp284–6)
Tsely Mir Целый мир	21 F3

TRANSPORT	(pp290–5)
Morskoy Vokzal Морской вокзал	22 C5
Water Bus Stop	23 H3

MALAYA NEV

Uralskaya ul

Dekabristo

Zheleznovods

pl Baltiyskih Yung

Smolensk Cemeter per

most Korablestroiteley

Novosmolenskaya nab

Smolenka

Ⓜ Primorskaya

Novosmolenskaya nab

Nalichny most

ul Odoyevskogo

Kam

Michmanskaya ul

See Petrograd Side Map (pp238–39)

ul Nakhimova

Nalichnaya ul

Smolenskoe Cemetery

Morskaya nab

pl Baltiyskogo Flota

Pribaltiyskaya pl

🏠 *Pribaltiyskaya Hotel*

Shkipersky protok

Gavan

Gavany pr

Paromnaya ul

🏠12

Grzhany Port

ul Korablestroiteley

Gavanskaya ul

ul

Sherchenko

Maly pr

11🏛

Kovsh Galernogo Forvatera

Shkipersky   protok

ul Opochina

Nalichnaya ul

Gavanskaya ul

ul Sherchenko

Veselnaya ul

Sredny pr

Kartavchnaya ul

Bolshoy pr

Detskaya ul

28-ya ?-ya liniya

Srednegavansky pr

20 🍴

🏠 5

Opachinsky Gardens

Vasilevsky

22 🚉
pl Morskoy Slavy

GULF OF FINLAND
(FINSKY ZALIV)

Kozhevennaya liniya

(Continued from page 228)

In Your Pocket (www.inyourpocket.com/russia/st_petersburg/en/) Monthly listings booklet with useful up-to-date information and short features.

Neva News Generally dull monthly broadsheet that sometimes prints useful historical features about the city.

Pulse (www.pulse.ru) Slick colour monthly with fun features and reviews.

St Petersburg Times (http://sptimesrussia.com) Published every Tuesday and Friday (when it has an indispensable listings and arts review section), this newspaper is the best source of information.

RADIO & TV

Among the more interesting FM stations to listen to are the all-jazz **Radio Hermitage** (90.1 FM), **Maximum** (102.8 FM) for pop music, and **Klassika Petersburg** (88.9 FM) for classical music.

As well as the main state TV channels, St Petersburg has several local channels, including Peterburg and Kanal 6. Satellite TV is available at all major hotels.

Medical Services

All the clinics listed below are open 24 hours and have English-speaking staff.

American Medical Clinic (Map pp236-7; ☎ 740 2090; www.amclinic.ru; nab reki Moyki 78; Ⓜ Sadovaya)

British-American Family Practice (Map pp234-5; ☎ 327 6030, 999 0949; Grafsky per 7; Ⓜ Dostoevskaya)

International Clinic (Map pp234-5; ☎ 320 3870; www.icspb.com; ul Dostoevskogo 19/21; Ⓜ Ligovsky Prospekt)

PHARMACIES

Look for the sign *apteka*, or the usual green cross to find a pharmacy. The following are two central pharmacies that are open 24 hours.

Apteka (Map pp234-5; ☎ 277 5962; Nevsky pr 83; Ⓜ Ploshchad Vosstaniya)

Apteka Petrofarm (Map pp230-1; ☎ 314 5401; Nevsky pr 22; Ⓜ Nevsky Prospekt)

Money

There are currency exchange offices all the way along and around Nevsky pr – shop around since some places offer better rates than others. ATMs are located inside every metro station, in hotels and department stores, main post offices and along major streets.

Post

Post office branches are scattered throughout St Petersburg and they vary in services, usually in proportion to size. American Express (opposite) will hold mail (letters only) for cardholders and holders of travellers cheques for up to 30 days; the mailing address is American Express, PO Box 87, SF-53501 Lappeenranta, Finland. All the major air courier services have offices in St Petersburg.

Central post office (Map pp236-7; ☎ 312 8302; www.spbpost.ru; Konnogvardeysky Bul 4; ☾ 9am-8pm Mon-Sat, 10am-6pm Sun; Ⓜ Sadovaya) While the original Style Moderne post office at Pochtamtskaya ul 9 is under renovation, the city's central post office is running out of this address around the corner. The express mail service EMS Garantpost is available here.

DHL (Map pp236-7; ☎ 326 6400; www.dhl.ru; Izmaylovsky pr 4; ☾ 8am-8pm Mon-Fri, 10am-4pm Sat; Ⓜ Tekhnologichesky Institut)

FedEx (Map pp236-7; ☎ 325 8825; www.fedex.com/ru/; per Grivtsova 6; ☾ 8am-8pm Mon-Fri, 10am-4pm Sat; Ⓜ Sadovaya)

UPS (Map pp234-5; ☎ 327 8540; www.ups.com; Shpalernaya ul 51; ☾ 8am-8pm Mon-Fri, 10am-4pm Sat; Ⓜ Chernyshevskaya)

Westpost (Map pp234-5; ☎ 327 3211; www.westpost.ru; Nevsky pr 86; ☾ 9.30am-8pm Mon-Fri, noon-8pm Sat; Ⓜ Mayakovskaya) Privately run, international mail service. Mail is transported daily from St Petersburg to Lappeenranta in Finland, and mailed from there. To the USA, a 20g letter costs US$2.20, and a 2kg parcel costs US$64. It has a full range of delivery and courier services. For mail delivery in St Petersburg they offer post boxes in Lappeenranta, with daily pick-up or delivery to the Westpost office or, for corporate clients, to an address in St Petersburg.

Telephone

Calling from a private phone is the simplest, though not necessarily the cheapest, option – except for local calls, which are free.

MOBILE PHONES

These days practically every St Petersburger has a mobile phone. See p712 for information on the main mobile providers. You can buy a local SIM card at any mobile phone shop from as little as R300, after which you only pay to make (and to a lesser extent, to receive) calls, although prices are very low. A handy place to arrange this is at the phone shop inside the Quo Vadis Internet café (p228).

PHONECARDS & CALL CENTRES

Local phonecards *(taksfon karta)* are available from shops, kiosks and metro stations and can be used to make local, national and international calls from any phone. Cards are sold in units of R25, R50 or R100.

Using a call centre (p712) is better value for international calls. There are large numbers of call centres around the city – look for the sign Mezhdunarodny Telefon. The most central is the **Central telephone office** (Map pp230-1; Bolshaya Morskaya ul 28; 24hr; Nevsky Prospekt).

Toilets

Portakabin-type toilets (R10) outside metros and the major sights are common. Shopping centres and chain cafés, such as Idealnaya Chashka and Chaynaya Lozhka, are the best places to look for a clean, odour-free loo.

Tourist Information

City Tourist Information Centre (Map pp230-1; 310 8262; www.ctic.spb.ru, in Russian; Sadovaya ul 14/52; 10am-7pm Mon-Sat; Gostiny Dvor) It speaks volumes that the city tourist office's website is a paltry affair in Russian only. The English-speaking staff are vague about most things but will do their best to help, particularly if you are a crime victim (as we can personally attest). There's also a **branch** (Map pp230-1; Dvortsovaya pl 12; 10am-7pm Mon-Sat, to 4pm Sun; Nevsky Prospekt) in a glass booth outside the Hermitage.

Travel Agencies

All the following agencies have English-speaking staff who can issue visa invitations and assist in getting a visa registered once you have arrived.

American Express (Map pp230-1; 326 4500; Malaya Morskaya ul 23; 9am-5pm Mon-Fri; Nevsky Prospekt) Only offers travel, not financial, services.

Infinity (Map pp230-1; 313 5085; www.infinity.ru; Hotel D'Angleterre, Bolshaya Morskaya ul 39; 10am-6pm; Nevsky Prospekt) Efficient travel agency. They can book you train and air tickets (and deliver them to your door if you are in a rush).

Ost-West Kontaktservice (Map pp234-5; 327 3416; www.ostwest.com; Nevsky pr 105; 10am-6pm Mon-Fri; Ploshchad Vosstaniya) The multilingual staff here can find you an apartment to rent, organise tours and tickets – heck, they'll even sell you a Lomo (they're the city's official distributor of the nifty little Russian camera).

Palladium (Map pp234-5; 279 6584; www.pallad ium.spb.ru; Hotel Rus, office 160; ul Artilleriyskaya 1; 10am-6pm; Chernyshevskaya) Small agency deep in the belly of the Hotel Rus can register both tourist visas (€30) and business visas (€50). It also offers short-term apartment rentals around the city as well as all the other normal services.

Sindbad Travel (Map pp234-5; 332 2020; www .sindbad.ru; 2-ya Sovetskaya ul 12; 9am-10pm Mon-Fri, 10am-6pm Sat & Sun; Ploshchad Vosstaniya) This is the main office of the agency owned by the HI St Petersburg International Hostel (p275); they also have a branch inside the hostel itself and one on **Vasilyevsky Island** (Map pp240-1; 324 0880; St Petersburg Philological Faculty building, Universitetskaya nab 11; 10am-6pm Mon-Fri; Vasileostrovskaya). All are genuine Western-style discount air-ticket offices, staffed by friendly, knowledgeable people. They also sell train tickets and ISIC/ITIC/IYTC cards and can book youth hostel accommodation through the IBN system.

DANGERS & ANNOYANCES
Crime & Violence

Watch out for pickpockets particularly along Nevsky pr around Griboedova Canal and in crowded places such as theatres and cinemas. It's also wise to avoid crossing directly in front of Moskovsky vokzal, unless you have to, since the police there have a nasty habit of trying to shake down foreigners for supposed infringements of visa registration rules. The same goes if you are a foreigner staggering around Nevsky pr late at night.

Non-Caucasians should be aware that St Petersburg is notorious for its incidence of race-related violent attacks. Precautions to take include not wandering around alone late at night or venturing out to the suburbs solo at any time of the day.

Environmental Hazards

It's not just the ice on the streets that you have to look out for in winter. Every year in early spring and during winter thaws, several people die when hit by child-sized, sword-shaped icicles falling from rooftops and balconies. Keep your eyes peeled to make sure one of these monsters is not dangling above your head.

From May to September mosquitoes are a nightmare. Bring along industrial-strength repellent that's at least 95% DEET (although if travelling with children its best to use low or no DEET repellent). Alternatively make sure you keep covered up. The plug-in gizmos which slowly heat repellent-saturated cardboard pads are available everywhere in the city and are pretty effective.

DON'T DRINK THE WATER

Never drink unboiled tap water in St Petersburg as it could contain harmful bacteria,
such as *Giardia lamblia*, a nasty parasite
that causes unpleasant stomach cramps,
nausea, bloated stomach, diarrhoea and
frequent gas. Metronidazole (brand name
Flagyl) or Imidazole (known as Feign) are
the recommended treatments. Antibiotics
are of no use. Symptoms may not appear
for up to several weeks after infection, and
may recur for years.

To be absolutely safe, only drink water that
has been boiled for 10 minutes or filtered
through an antimicrobial water filter (buy
one at home) and treat ice with suspicion.
While accepting tea or coffee at someone's
house should be safe, it's best to always
stick to bottled water. Brushing your teeth,
bathing, showering and shaving with tap
water should cause no problems.

If you're staying in a ground-level apartment in the city centre in early autumn,
just before the central heating is turned
on and after it starts getting cool, you may
have problems with fleas, which come up
through floorboards looking for warmth.

SIGHTS
The Hermitage
Mainly set in the magnificent Winter Palace – a stunning mint green, white and gold
profusion of columns, windows and recesses
with its roof topped by rows of classical
statues – the **State Hermitage** (Map pp230-1;
☎ 571 3465; www.hermitagemuseum.org; Dvortsovaya
nab 34; adult R350, ISIC cardholders & under 17 free, use of
camera/camcorder R100/350; ☺ 10.30am-6pm Tue-Sat, to
5pm Sun) fully lives up to its sterling reputation. You can be absorbed by its treasures for
days and still come out wishing for more.

The enormous collection (over three million items) almost amounts to a history of
Western European art, and as much as you
see in the museum, there's about 20 times
more in its vaults, part of which you can
now visit (p267). The vastness of the buildings – of which the Winter Palace alone has
1057 rooms and 117 staircases – demands
a little planning. Consider making a recon-
naissance tour first, then returning another
day to enjoy your favourite bits.

The State Hermitage consists of five
linked buildings along riverside Dvortsovaya nab. From west to east they are the
Winter Palace, the Little Hermitage, the Old
and New Hermitages (sometimes grouped
together and called the Large Hermitage)
and the Hermitage Theatre (only open for
special events, mainly concerts). The art
collection is on all three floors of the Winter
Palace and the main two floors of the Little
and Large Hermitages.

There are also separate sections of the
museum in the east wing of the General
Staff Building (p251), the Menshikov Palace on Vasilyevsky Island (p263), the Winter Palace of Peter I further east along the
embankment from the main Winter Palace, and at the Lomonosova China Factory
(p289). All have separate admission unless
you purchase a ticket for R700 which gives
you access to all the facilities over a two-day
period. See opposite for more on tickets.

HISTORY
The Winter Palace was commissioned from
Bartolomeo Rastrelli in 1754 by Empress
Elizabeth. Catherine the Great and her successors had most of the interior remodelled
in a classical style by 1837. It remained an
imperial home until 1917, though the last
two tsars spent more time in other palaces.

The classical Little Hermitage was built
for Catherine the Great as a retreat that
would also house the art collection started
by Peter the Great, which she significantly
expanded. At the river end of the Large
Hermitage is the Old Hermitage, which also
dates from her time. At its south end, facing Millionnaya ul, is the New Hermitage,
which was built for Nicholas II to hold the
still-growing art collection. The Hermitage
Theatre was built in the 1780s by the classicist Giacomo Quarenghi, who thought it
one of his finest works.

The Hermitage's collection really began
with Catherine the Great, one of the greatest art collectors of all time. She pulled off
some stunning deals, including famously
exchanging one large framed portrait of
herself for 15 Van Dykes from the collection of Sir Robert Walpole, Britain's first
prime minister. Nicholas I also greatly enriched the Hermitage's collection, which he
opened to the public for the first time in
1852. It was the postrevolutionary period

that saw the collection increase threefold in size, as many valuable private collections were seized by the state.

Throughout the 1990s, the museum has, partially thanks to partnerships with foreign museums and donors, been able to renovate its heating and temperature control system, install a new fire detection system, fit its windows with UV-filtering plastic, and to begin the first thorough, digitised inventory of its mammoth collection.

ADMISSION & TOURS
The main entrance for individuals is through the courtyard of the Winter Palace from Palace Sq. Just inside are the ticket counters, flanking a very useful information booth where you can get free colour maps of the entire museum in most major European languages. Groups enter from the river side of the Winter Palace.

Queues for tickets, particularly from May to September, can be horrendous. Apart from getting in line an hour or so before the museum opens or going late in the day when the lines are likely to be shorter, there are a few strategies you can use. The first is to book your ticket online through the Hermitage's website: US$16 gets you an entrance plus use of camera or camcorder to the main Hermitage buildings, US$24 is for the two-day ticket to all the Hermitage's collections in the city (except the storage facility). You'll be issued with a voucher which allows you to jump the queue and go straight to the ticket booth.

Joining a tour is another way to avoid queuing. These whiz round the main sections in about 1½ hours but at least provide an introduction to the place in English. It's easy to 'lose' the group and stay on until closing time. To book a tour call the museum's **excursions office** (☎ 571 8446; 🕙 11am-1pm & 2-4pm); they will tell you when they are running tours in English, German or French and when to turn up. Tours cost R1500 for up to 25 people.

Also contact the excursions office if you plan to visit the **Golden Rooms Special Collection** in Rooms 41 to 45. This costs another R350 (plus R1500 if you wish to have an English guide) and places are limited, so book early if you're interested. The focus is a hoard of fabulously worked Scythian and Greek gold and silver from the Caucasus, Crimea

and Ukraine, dating from the 7th to 2nd centuries BC.

There is a special entrance for the physically disabled from Dvortsovaya pl (the museum also has a few wheelchairs) – call in advance if you need this.

THE COLLECTION
Some of the rooms listed here will occasionally be closed without warning for maintenance or other mysterious reasons. The works on view change occasionally, too. Only a few sections have English labelling.

From the main ticket hall, the Rastrelli Gallery leads to the white marble Jordan Staircase, with windows and mirrors on all sides, which takes you up to the 2nd floor of the Winter Palace. The staircase is one of the few parts of the interior to maintain its original Rastrelli appearance.

Winter Palace, 1st floor
Rooms 1 to 33 showcase **Russian prehistoric artefacts**. Included in this are exhibits from

---

HERMITAGE HIGHLIGHTS
If your time at the Hermitage is limited, the following rooms include the highlights of the collection:
Room 100 Ancient Egypt
The Jordan Staircase Directly ahead when you pass through the main entrance inside the Winter Palace
Rooms 178–98 Imperial stateroom and apartments including the Malachite Hall, Nicholas Hall, Armorial Hall and Hall of St George
Room 204 The Pavilion Hall
Rooms 207–15 Florentine art, 13th to 16th centuries
Rooms 217–22 & 237 Venetian art, 16th century
Room 229 Raphael and his disciples
Rooms 239–40 Spanish art, 16th to 18th centuries
Rooms 244–47 Flemish art, 17th century
Rooms 249–52 & 254 Dutch art, 17th century
Rooms 228–38 Italian Art 16th to 18th centuries
Room 271 The Imperial family's cathedral

Concentrate the rest of your time here on the fabulous 3rd floor, particularly rooms 333–50 for late-19th-century and early-20th-century European art.

FRIENDS OF THE HERMITAGE

Since 1997, the **Friends of the Hermitage Society** (☎ 710 9005; www.hermitagemuseum .org) has been encouraging donations and membership to help with restoration and conservation programmes. Membership allows you access to special events hosted by the Hermitage, either at a reduced cost or for free. A US$50 annual donation will get you a free entry to the Hermitage and Menshikov Palace for a year, plus a 20% discount at their shops; for US$100 you can bring a friend along for free as well and get invitations to opening parties; US$300 allows you to bring two friends along for free and even more privileges.

the Palaeolithic (500,000–12,000 BC) and Mesolithic (12,000–3000 BC) periods in room 11. Room 12 displays Neolithic (4000–2400 BC) and Bronze Age (2000–500 BC) artefacts, including **petroglyphs** from 2500 to 2000 BC taken from the northeastern shores of Lake Onega. Bronze Age items from the western steppes dating from the 4th to the 2nd millenniums BC can be found in room 13, and Bronze Age items from southern Siberia and Kazakhstan (2000–900 BC), including fine bronze animals, are in room 14. **Scythian culture**, covering the 7th to 3rd centuries BC, is showcased in rooms 15 to 18, but the best Scythian material is in the Golden Rooms Special Collection. Exhibits from the Forest steppes (700–400 BC) are located in rooms 19 and 20, and material from Altai Mountains burial mounds, including human and horse corpses preserved for over 2000 years (complete with hair and teeth) are displayed in rooms 21 to 23, and room 26. Iron Age items from Eastern Europe, including Finno-Ugrian and Baltic items, ranging from the 8th century BC to the 12th century AD, are in room 24. The Southern steppes tribes (3rd century BC to 10th century AD) are represented in room 33 along with some **fine Sarmatian gold**.

The **Russian East** collection is spread over a few rooms, with rooms 34 to 39 and 46 to 69 covering Central Asia from the 4th century BC to the 13th century AD. Rooms 55 to 66 have items from the Caucasus and Transcaucasia from the 10th century BC to the 16th century AD. This includes **Urartu**

items from the 9th to 7th centuries BC in room 56, pieces from Dagestan (6th to 11th centuries AD) in room 59, exhibits from 14th-century Italian colonies in Crimea in room 66 and a **Golden Horde** (13th and 14th centuries) display in rooms 67 to 69.

A very fine collection from **Ancient Egypt**, much of it uncovered by Russian archaeologists, is located in room 100 but sadly has no English labelling.

Little Hermitage, 1st floor

Most of this floor is off limits but rooms 101 and 102 have displays of **Roman marble**.

Large Hermitage, 1st floor

Ancient classical culture is covered in rooms 106 to 131. **Roman sculpture**, from the 1st century BC to the 4th century AD, can be found in rooms 106 to 109 and room 127. **Ancient Greece**, from the 8th to 2nd centuries BC, is represented mostly by ceramics and sculpture in rooms 111 to 114. Material from Greek colonies around the northern Black Sea area from the 7th century BC to the 3rd century AD is located in rooms 115 to 117, and room 121. Room 128 features the huge 19th-century jasper **Kolyvanskaya Vase** from Siberia. Ancient Italy, from the 7th to 2nd centuries BC, is represented in rooms 130 and 131 by Etruscan vases and bronze mirrors.

Winter Palace, 2nd floor

This is most of what used to be called the *Hidden Treasures Revealed* exhibit and features mostly **French Art** from the 19th and 20th centuries. Rooms 143 to 146 boast oil paintings captured by the Red Army from private collections in Germany, including works by Monet, Degas, Renoir, Cézanne, Picasso and Matisse, almost all never before publicly displayed.

Russian culture and art covers rooms 147 to 189. Rooms 147 to 150 display works from the 10th to 15th centuries and room 151 covers the period of the 15th to 17th centuries. Icons, ceramics, jewellery and more from the 'Moscow baroque' period (1700–50) are shown in room 152, while room 153 features items relating to Peter the Great.

Rooms 155 to 166 showcase late 17th- and early 18th-century Russian works, including a Moorish dining room (room 155), a Rotunda with a bust of Peter the Great, and a brass Triumphal Pillar, topped by a

HERMITAGE – 1ST FLOOR

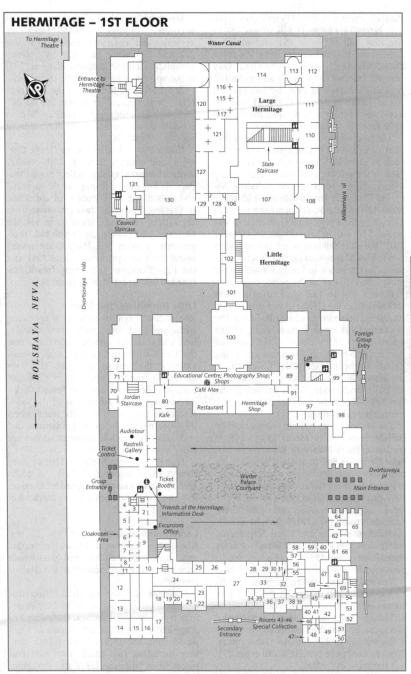

Rastrelli-created statue of Peter (room 156). The **Petrovskaya Gallereya** fills rooms 157 to the first half of room 161 and includes lathing machinery used by Peter. An ivory chandelier, partly built by the Great Guy himself, features in room 161 and room 162 contains a mosaic of Peter by Lomonosov. Room numbers 167 to 173 hold mid- to late-18th–century works (spot the bizarre 1772 tapestry image of Australia).

The next series of rooms is best viewed by starting at room 187 and working your way back to room 175. These rooms were occupied by the last imperial family, and display 19th-century interior design including Nicholas II's lovely **English Gothic-style library** in room 178 and the **Small Dining Room** in room 188 where the Provisional Government was arrested by the Bolsheviks on 26 October 1917. **Malachite Hall** is in room 189 and, with two tonnes of gorgeous green malachite columns, boxes, bowls and urns, is possibly the most impressive of all the palace rooms.

Rooms 190 to 192 are known as **Neva Enfilade** and make up one of two sets of state rooms for ceremonies and balls. Room 190 is a **Concert Hall** for small balls, and contains a now empty 18th-century silver tomb for Alexander Nevsky (his remains are in the Trinity Cathedral; see p259. Room 191 is the **Great or Nicholas Hall**, scene of great winter balls, and room 192 is known as the **Fore Hall**. All of these halls are now used for temporary exhibitions.

The second series of state rooms, or **Great Enfilade**, is located in rooms 193 to 198. It consists of the **Field Marshals' Hall** in room 193; **Peter the Great's Hall** in room 194 (with his none-too-comfy-looking throne) and the bright and gilt-encrusted **Armorial Hall** (room 195), displaying 16th- to 19th-century Western European silver. Also part of the Great Enfilade is room 197's **1812 Gallery**, hung with portraits of Russian and allied Napoleonic war leaders, and the **Hall of St George**, or **Great Throne Room** (room 198) – once a state room, now used for temporary exhibitions.

Western European tapestry, from the 16th to 19th centuries, fill rooms 200 to 202, while **German art** from the 15th to 18th centuries, including Dürer and Lucas Cranach the Elder, can be found in rooms 263 to 268.

Rooms 269 to 271 contain 18th-century Western European porcelain and room 271 was the tsars' cathedral.

French art from the 15th to 18th centuries is covered in rooms 272 to 289. Tapestries, ceramics and metalwork feature in rooms 272 and 273, while paintings by Poussin (room 279), Lorrai (280) and Watteau (284) make up part of the rest of the collection.

British art from the 16th to the 19th centuries is showcased in rooms 298 to 302 including Gainsborough's *Lady in Blue* in room 298, and works from Reynolds in rooms 299 and 300.

Room 303 is known as the 'Dark Corridor' and contains 16th- to 18th-century **Western European tapestry**, mainly from Flanders. Follow the confusing trail through 167 and 308 to get to a wonderful collection of Western European **stone engravings** from the 13th to 19th centuries in room 304, the Crimson Hall containing **English and French porcelain** in room 305, **Maria Alexandrovna's bedroom** (fit for a princess – room 306), and the Blue Bedroom containing **French, Austrian and German porcelain** in room 307.

Little Hermitage, 2nd floor

Room 204 (Pavilion Hall) is a sparkling white-and-gold room with lovely chandeliers and columns, looking onto Catherine the Great's hanging garden (under renovation at the time of research). The floor mosaic in front is copied from a Roman bath. Also here is the amazing **Peacock Clock** – a revolving dial in which one of the toadstools tells the time, and on the hour (when it's working) the peacock, toadstools, owl and cock come to life. Demonstrations are every Wednesday at 5pm.

This floor is also home to 17th-century **Flemish art** in Room 258, 11th- to 15th-century **Western European applied art** in room 259 and 15th- and 16th-century **Dutch art** in rooms 261 and 262.

Large Hermitage, 2nd floor

Room 206 features a model triumphal arch in marble, malachite and glass which announces the beginning of the Italian section.

Florentine art from the 13th to 16th centuries takes care of rooms 207 to 215. Paintings from the 15th-century, including Fra Angelico, are in room 209. Room 213 has works from the 15th and early 16th century including two small Botticellis and pieces from Filippino Lippi and Perugino.

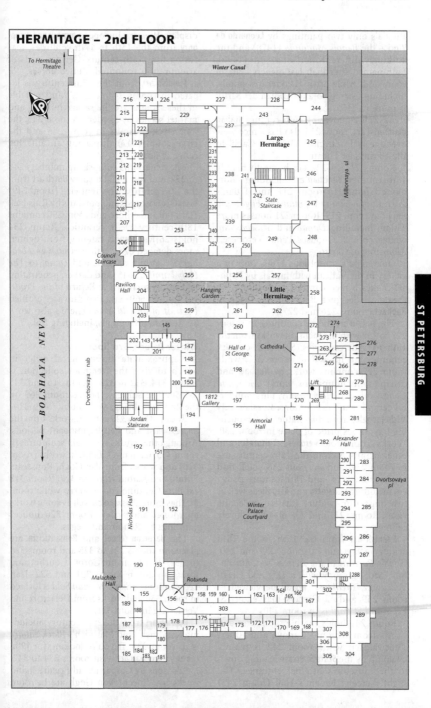

HERMITAGE – 2nd FLOOR

To Hermitage Theatre

Winter Canal

Large Hermitage

State Staircase

Millionnaya ul

Council Staircase

Pavilion Hall

Hanging Garden

Little Hermitage

BOLSHAYA NEVA

Dvortsovaya nab

Hall of St George

Cathedral

Lift

1812 Gallery

Jordan Staircase

Armorial Hall

Alexander Hall

Dvortsovaya pl

Nicholas Hall

Winter Palace Courtyard

Malachite Hall

Rotunda

Russia's only two paintings by **Leonardo da Vinci** – the *Benois Madonna* (1478) and the strikingly different *Madonna Litta* (1490), both named after their last owners – are in room 214, while art by Leonardo's pupils, including Correggio and Andrea del Sarto, is in room 215.

As well as covering 16th-century **Italian mannerist art**, room 216 also has a nice view over the little Zimnaya (Winter) Canal to the Hermitage Theatre.

Rooms 217 to 222 are home to mainly 16th century **Venetian art** including Giorgione's *Judith* in room 217 and Titian's *Portrait of a Young Woman* and *Flight into Egypt* in room 219. Room 221 houses more Titian, including *Danae* and *St Sebastian*, while room 222 houses Paolo Veronese's *Mourning of Christ*.

Quarenghi's sumptuous 1780s copy of a gallery in the Vatican with murals by Raphael makes a nice contrast to costumes by theatrical designer Bakst in the **Loggia of Raphael** (rooms 226 and 227).

The **Italian art** theme continues in rooms 228 to 238 with the focus on works from the 16th to 18th centuries. Sixteenth-century ceramics are housed in room 228, while room 229 contains works by **Raphael** and disciples, including his works *Madonna Conestabile* and *Holy Family*, plus wonderful ceramics and decorations. Russia's only **Michelangelo**, a marble statue of a crouching boy, holds pride of place in room 230. Works from Paolo **Veronese**, **Tintoretto** and other paintings from the 16th-century are in room 237, and in room 238 you'll find works from 17th- and 18th-century painters including **Canaletto** and **Tiepolo** as well as two huge 19th-century Russian malachite vases. Rooms 237 and 238 also have lovely ceilings.

Spanish art from the 16th to the 18th century gets a run in rooms 239 and 240. Goya's *Portrait of the Actress Antonia Zarate*, Murillo's *Boy with a Dog* and Diego Velazquez' *Breakfast* can all be viewed in room 239 and El Greco's marvellous *St Peter and St Paul* is in room 240.

Room 241 holds marble sculptures and works from Antonio Canova and Albert Thorwaldsen while room 242 is mainly taken up by the **State Staircase** leading down to the museum's original entrance. The slightly creepy Knight's Hall (room 243)

displays Western European **armour and weaponry** from the 15th to 17th centuries, featuring four 16th-century German suits of armour atop armoured, stuffed horses.

Flemish art from the 17th century is located in rooms 244 to 247. Most notable in these rooms are the savage hunting and market scenes by Snyders in room 245, the Van Dyck portraits in room 246 and the large room (247) displaying an amazing range of **Rubens**.

The five rooms comprising numbers 248 to 252, and room 254 display **Dutch art** from the 17th century. The Tent Hall (room 249) boasts landscapes and portraits by Ruisdael, Hals, Bol and others, and room 250 contains 18th-century Delft ceramics. Room 254 holds 26 **Rembrandts** ranging from lighter, more detailed early canvases such as *Abraham's Sacrifice of Isaac* and *Dana*, to *The Holy Family* (1645) and darker, penetrating late works such as *The Return of the Prodigal Son* (c 1669) and two canvases entitled *Portrait of an Old Man*. There's also work by Rembrandt's pupils, including Bol.

Winter Palace, 3rd floor

An approximate chronological order in which to view the **French art** collection is rooms 314, 332 to 328, 325 to 315 and 343 to 350. The staircase beside room 269 on the 2nd floor brings you out by room 314.

Rooms 316 to 320 contain works from the **Impressionist** and **Post-Impressionist** periods. Among other works are Rodin sculptures in room 315, Gauguin's Tahitian works (room 316) and works from Van Gogh, Rousseau, Forain and Latour in room 317. Room 318 exhibits Cézanne and Pissarro while room 319 has more Pissarro as well as some works by Monet and Sisley. Room 320 houses paintings by Renoir and Degas.

The **Barbizon school** and **Romanticism** are placed in rooms 321 to 325 and rooms 328 to 331. Works from Corot, Courbet and Rousseau are in rooms 321 and 322, Jean Léon Gerome's *Slave Woman Sold* is located in room 330 and works from Delacroix and Vernet are in room 331.

Russian art from the 20th century, including Kandinsky and Malevich's *Black Square* is in room 333. If you're looking for **19th-century European art**, visit rooms 334 to 342. Landscapes by Caspar David Friedrich and works by Vincent Van Gogh are in room

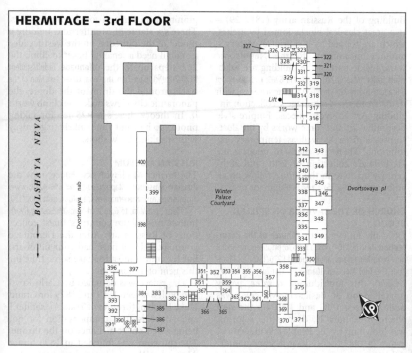

HERMITAGE – 3rd FLOOR

334. The Matisse collection covers rooms 343 to 345 and has 35 canvases, including *The Dance* and *Arab Coffeehouse*.

Rooms 346, 347 and 350 deal with 19th- to 20th-century **French art** including Bonnard, Vlaminck, Marquet, Leger and others. **Picasso** claims two rooms of his own; room 348 represents mainly his blue and cubist periods, including *The Absinthe Drinker*; while room 349 explores his cubist and later periods.

The collections swing back to the Orient and Middle East in rooms 351 to 371 and 381 to 397. The excellent collection **Art of China and Tibet** spans rooms 351 to 357 and rooms 359 to 364; **Indonesian** art is represented in room 358; while **Mongolian** (rooms 365 to 367), **Indian** (rooms 368 to 371) and **Byzantium, Near and Middle Eastern works** (rooms 381 to 387) are also shown here.

To top things off, rooms 398 and 400 have a collection of **coins**.

Historic Centre

Covered in this section are the major sights, in order of interest, found between the Neva River, the Admiralty Gardens to the west and the Fontanka River to the east and south. Bisecting the area is St Petersburg's pivotal thoroughfare Nevsky pr. The most convenient metro station is Nevsky Prospekt/Gostiny Dvor.

DVORTSOVAYA PLOSHCHAD (PALACE SQUARE)

To get to the Hermitage you'll pass through the monumental **Dvortsovaya ploshchad** (Palace Square; Mapp230-1), one of the most impressive and historic spaces in the city. Stand well back to admire the palace and the central 47.5m **Alexander Column** named after Alexander I and commemorating the 1812 victory over Napoleon. It has stood here, held in place by gravity alone, since 1834. It was in this square that tsarist troops fired on peaceful protestors in 1905 (on a day now known as Bloody Sunday), sparking the revolution of that year.

General Staff Building

Curving around the south of the square is the Carlo Rossi–designed General Staff

Building of the Russian army (1819–29) – two great classical blocks joined by arches, which are topped by a chariot of victory – another monument to the Napoleonic wars. Inside part of the building are **exhibition halls** (Map pp230-1; ☎ 314 8260; Dvortsovaya pl 6-8; adult/student R200/free; 10am-6pm Tue-Sun) with items from the Hermitage's collection including Art Nouveau pieces, Empire-style decorative art and some works by the Post-Impressionists, as well as temporary exhibitions. There are plans to relocate the Hermitage's collection of 19th- and 20th-century art here in the future following an ambitious US$155m redevelopment plan.

CHURCH OF THE SAVIOUR ON SPILLED BLOOD
Officially known as the **Church of the Resurrection** (Map pp230-1; ☎ 315 1636; http://eng.cathedral.ru; Konyushennaya pl; adult/student R270/150; 11am-7pm Thu-Tue; May-Sep 10am-8pm Thu-Tue; Nevsky Prospekt), this multidomed dazzler, partly modelled on St Basil's in Moscow, was built between 1883 and 1907 on the spot where Alexander II, despite his reforms, was blown up by the People's Will terrorist group in 1881 (hence its gruesome name).

It's now most commonly known as the church that took 24 years to build and 27 to restore. In August 1997, with much fanfare, it finally opened its doors after painstaking work by over 30 artists on the interior's incredible 7000 sq metres of mosaics – which fully justify the entrance fee. On the very spot of the assassination is the marble bust *Shatrovy Cen*, a monument to Alexander.

ST ISAAC'S CATHEDRAL
The golden dome of **St Isaac's Cathedral** (Map pp230-1; ☎ 315 9732; http://eng.cathedral.ru; Isaakievskaya pl; adult/student R270/150; 10am-8pm Thu-Mon, closed last Mon of the month) looming just south of pl Dekabristov, dominates the St Petersburg skyline. Its obscenely lavish interior is open as a museum, although services are held in the cathedral on major religious holidays.

The French architect Ricard de Montferrand won a competition organised by Alexander I to design the cathedral in 1818. It took so long to build – until 1858 – that Alexander's successor Nicholas I was able to insist on a more grandiose structure than Montferrand had planned. Special ships and a railway had to be built to carry the granite from Finland for the huge pillars. There's a statue of Montferrand holding a model of the cathedral on the west façade.

You'll need a separate ticket to climb the 262 steps up to the **colonnade** (adult/student R120/70; 10am-7pm Thu-Mon, closed last Mon of the month) around the drum of the dome; the panoramic city views make the climb worth it. In theory there's a R25 fee for taking photos up here but you're likely to get away with sneaking a few shots.

RUSSIAN MUSEUM
The former Mikhaylovsky Palace, now the **Russian Museum** (Map pp230-1; ☎ 595 4248; www.rusmuseum.ru; Inzhenernaya ul 4; adult/student R300/150; 10am-5pm Mon, to 6pm Wed-Sun; Gostiny Dvor), houses one of the country's finest collections of Russian art. After the Hermitage you may feel you have had your fill of art, but try your utmost to make some time for this gem of a museum.

The palace was designed by Carlo Rossi and built between 1819 and 1829 for Grand Duke Mikhail (brother of Tsars Alexander I and Nicholas I) as compensation for not being able to have a chance on the throne. The museum was founded in 1895 under Alexander III and opened three years later.

The Benois building, now connected to the original palace, was constructed between 1914 and 1919. Note that the façade of the palace is illuminated at night, making it a good time to take a photograph. The building is also impressively viewed from the back on a stroll through the lovely **Mikhaylovsky Gardens**.

The museum owns another three city palaces where permanent and temporary exhibitions are also held: the Marble Palace (p257), the Mikhaylovsky Castle (also known as the Engineers' Castle, p256) and the Stroganov Palace (p255). A ticket for R600, available at each palace, covers entrance to them all within a 24-hour period.

The museum's main entrance is through a tiny door on the far right side of the main building, off Inzhenernaya ul. You can also enter via the Benois wing off nab kanala Griboedova. English guided tours can be booked on ☎ 314 3448.

NEVSKY PROSPEKT
Nevsky pr is and always will be Russia's most famous street, running 4km from

the Admiralty to the Alexander Nevsky Monastery, from which it takes its name. The inner 2.5km to Moskovsky vokzal is St Petersburg's seething main avenue, the city's shopping centre and focus of its entertainment and street life.

Nevsky pr was laid out in the early years of St Petersburg as the start of the main road to Novgorod and soon became dotted with fine buildings, squares and bridges. At the beginning of the 1900s, it was one of Europe's grandest boulevards, with cobblestone sidewalks and a track down the middle for horse-drawn trams. On either side of the tracks were wooden paving blocks to muffle the sound of

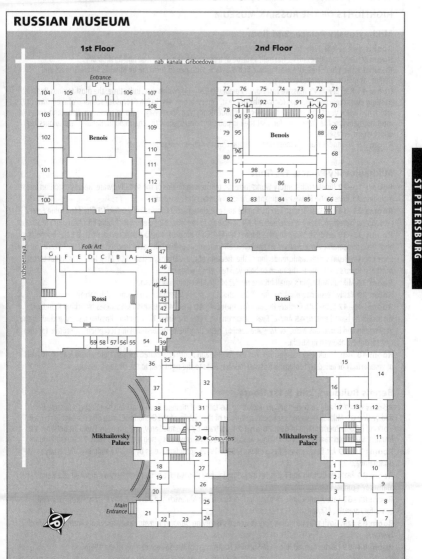

RUSSIAN MUSEUM

ST PETERSBURG

horse-drawn carriages – an innovation that was apparently the first in the world and for which the prospekt was dubbed the quietest main street in Europe.

Today, things are quite a bit noisier. The traffic and crowds can become oppressive and after a while you'll find yourself going out of your way to avoid the street. However, walking Nevsky is an essential St Petersburg experience, and if you're here on a holiday evening (such as 27 May – City Day), the sight of thousands pouring like a stream down its middle is one you'll not soon forget.

HIGHLIGHTS OF THE RUSSIAN MUSEUM

Mikhaylovsky Palace, 2nd floor

Rooms 1–4 Serene 12th- to 15th-century icons.

Room 7 Grand tapestries offset Rastrelli's statue of a pompous *Anna Ioanovna and an Arab Boy*.

Room 11 The White Hall, the most ornate in the palace, with period furniture by Rossi, is where Strauss and Berlioz, as guests, performed concerts.

Room 14 Karl Bryullov's massive *Last Day of Pompeii* (1827–33), which was, in its time, the most famous Russian painting ever; there were queues for months to see it. Petersburgers saw in it a doomsday scenario of their own city, which had a few years earlier been damaged in a huge flood. Ivan Aivazovsky's Crimea seascapes also stand out, most frighteningly *The Wave*. But don't let the big paintings overshadow the charming miniature watercolours kept under wraps in cases.

Room 15 Alexander Ivanov's most famous work, *Christ's Appearance to the People*.

Mikhaylovsky Palace, 1st floor

Rooms 18–22 Nineteenth-century works focusing on the beginnings of the socially aware 'Realist' tradition and including **21** Konstantin Flavitsky's gigantic *Christian Martyrs in Colosseum*.

Rooms 23–38 The Wanderers (Peredvizhniki) and associated artists, including **26** Nikolai Ghe's fearsome *Peter I Prosecuting Tsarevitch Alexey in Peterhof;* **31** KA Savitsky's *To the War;* **32** Polenov, including his *Christ and the Sinner*.

Rooms 33–35 and 54 Works by Ilya Repin (1844–1930), probably Russia's best-loved artist; **33** has portraits and the incomparable *Barge Haulers on the Volga*, an indictment of Russian 'social justice'; **54** contains *Meeting of the State Council,* Repin's panoramic rendering of the meeting at the Mariinsky Palace on 7 May 1901 (it's full of tsarist hotshots; there's a scheme in the room to help you tell who's who).

Room 36 Mikhail Mikeshin's small bronze model of the Millennium of Russia.

Room 39 Vasily Vershchagin's *After the Success* and *After the Defeat* plus his paintings of Japan and Israel.

Rooms 40–47 Late-19th Century Russian Art, including **40 and 41** Stunning landscapes by Arkhip Kuindzhi; **44** works by Isaak Levitan; **45** Andrei Ryabushkin on pre-Peter the Great 17th-century Russian history, including the very telling and humorous *Yedut,* or *They Are Coming,* depicting the perturbed-looking reception committee for the first foreigners allowed in Russia.

Room 48 Marc Antokolsky's sculptures *Ivan the Terrible* and *Death of Socrates*. Exits straight ahead lead to 10 halls of wonderfully detailed and colourful Russian folk art; exits to the right lead to the Benois building.

Benois Building, 2nd & 1st floors

Rooms 66–77 Early 20th-century art, including **66** father of modern Russian art Mikhail Vrubel's *Russian Hero* and *Venice;* **67** Mikhail Nesterov's religious paintings of the history of the Orthodox Church and the highly stylised works of Nikolai Roerich (also in **69**); **70 and 71** portraits by Valentin Serov, sculptures by Paolo Trubetskoy; **72** Impressionists Konstantin Korovin and Igor Grabar; **73** Boris Kustodiev's smug *Merchant's Wife.* **77** Natan Altman

Rooms 78–79 Art Between the Revolutions (1905–1917), including works by Vasily Kandinksy and Natalya Goncharova.

Room 80 Features Cubism and Futurism including Lyubov Popova, Alexander Rodchenko's *Black on Black* and Pavel Mansurov's comic *American Inhabitant*.

Room 81–82 Late Avant-Garde Painting including Kazimir Malevich and Pavel Filonov's scary *Kings Feast* and beautiful *Formula of Spring*.

Room 83 Early Soviet Art including Yury Pimenov's terrifying *Disabled Veterans* and Malevich's *Portrait of a Shock Worker*.

Room 84–85 Fascinating exhibition of Socialist Realism art of the Soviet years up to the 1950s.

The following description lists the main points of interest from the Admiralty to the Anichkov most across the Fontanka River.

Admiralty End to Kazan Cathedral

Kafe Literaturnoe (Map pp230-1), at No 18 just before the Moyka River, is where the poet Alexander Pushkin ate his last meal before his deadly duel (p340).

Across the Moyka, Rastrelli's baroque **Stroganov Palace** (Map pp230-1) is looking grand after restoration for the 2003 tricentenary. Upstairs inside the salmon-pink painted building is a branch of the **Russian Museum** (☎ 219 1608; www.rusmuseum.ru; Nevsky pr 17; adult/student R300/150; 🕑 10am-5pm Tue-Sun) displaying some beautiful examples of Imperial-era porcelain from the Gardner and Lomonosova factories in a series of splendidly restored rooms. Downstairs temporary exhibitions are held, while in the courtyard you'll find a café and the luxury restaurant Russian Empire (p280).

A block beyond the Moyka, on the southern side of Nevsky pr, the great colonnaded arms of the **Kazan Cathedral** (Map pp230-1; ☎ 318 4528; www.kazansky.ru, in Russian; Kazanskaya pl 2; admission free; 🕑 10am-7pm, services 10am & 6pm; Ⓜ Gostiny Dvor) reach out towards the avenue. Built between 1801 and 1811, its design, by Andrei Voronikhin, a former serf, was influenced by St Peter's in Rome. His original plan was to build a second, mirror version of the cathedral opposite it on the northern side of Nevsky pr. The square in front of it has been a site for political demonstrations since before the revolution. The church is well worth entering but be aware it is a working cathedral so please show some respect for the local customs (p79).

Opposite the cathedral is the **Singer Building** (Map pp230-1; Ⓜ Gostiny Dvor) a Style Moderne beauty recently restored to the splendour of when it was the headquarters of the sewing machine company. A short walk south of the cathedral, along Griboedova Canal, sits one of St Petersburg's loveliest bridges, the **Bankovsky most** (1826). The cables of this 25.2m-long bridge are supported by four cast-iron gryphons with golden wings.

Griboedova Canal to the Fontanka River

Check out the lavish **Grand Hotel Europe** (p278) built between 1873 and 1875, re- done in Style Moderne in the 1910s and completely renovated in the early 1990s. Immediately north of the hotel is the quiet **ploshchad Iskusstv** (Arts Square) named after its surrounding museums and concert halls. A statue of Pushkin, erected in 1957, stands in the middle of the tree-lined square. Both the square and Mikhaylovskaya ul, which joins the square to Nevsky pr, were designed as a unit by Rossi in the 1820s and 1830s.

Diagonally across Nevsky pr, the fashionable arcades of **Gostiny Dvor** (Map pp230-1; Ⓜ Gostiny Dvor) department store stand facing the clock tower of the **former Town Duma** (Map pp230-1; Ⓜ Gostiny Dvor), seat of the pre-revolutionary city government. One of the world's first indoor shopping malls, Gostiny Dvor (Merchant Yard) dates from 1757-85, stretches 230m along Nevsky pr (its completely restored perimeter is over 1km long) and is another Rastrelli creation. The shops inside are generally open 10am to 8pm.

On the other side of Nevsky pr, at No 42, the **Armenian Church** (Map pp230-1; Ⓜ Gostiny Dvor) built from 1771 to 1780 and one of two in St Petersburg, has been completely renovated and is open to visitors. The arcade at No 48, the **Passazh** (Map pp230-1; Ⓜ Gostiny Dvor) department store, is also beautiful to look at (notice the glass ceilings).

On Sadovaya ul, opposite the southeastern side of Gostiny Dvor, the **Vorontsov Palace** (Map pp230-1; 1749-57; Ⓜ Gostiny Dvor) is another noble town house by Rastrelli. It's now a military school for young cadets.

Ploshchad Ostrovskogo to Anichkov most

The airy square, **Pl Ostrovskogo**, commonly referred to as the Catherine Gardens after the enormous **Catherine the Great statue** (Map pp230-1; Ⓜ Gostiny Dvor), which stands amid chess, backgammon and sometimes even mah jong players that crowd the benches here, was created by Carlo Rossi in the 1820s and 1830s. At the Empress' heels are some of her renowned statesmen, including her lovers Orlov, Potemkin and Suvorov.

The square's western side is taken up by the lavish **National Library of Russia** (Map pp230-1; Ⓜ Gostiny Dvor), St Petersburg's biggest with some 31 million items, nearly one-sixth of which are in foreign languages. Rossi's **Aleksandrinsky Theatre** (Pushkin Theatre; p288) at the southern end of the square is one of

ST PETERSBURG

Russia's most important theatres. In 1896 the opening night of Chekhov's *The Seagull* was so badly received here that the playwright fled to wander anonymously among the crowds on Nevsky pr.

Behind the theatre, appropriately enough you'll find the **St Petersburg State Museum of Theatre and Music** (Map pp230-1; ☎ 311 2195; www .theatremuseum.ru/eng/; Ostrovskogo pl 6; adult/child R50/20; ⏰ 1-7pm Wed-Mon), a treasure-trove of items relating to the Russian Theatre including model sets, posters and costumes. In a newly opened section aimed at children there are great models of the Mariinksy stage and antique contraptions used to create effects like the sound of wind, rain and trains. The museum also has branches in the Sheremetyev Palace (p258), and the former homes of composer Nikolai Rimsky-Korsakov (p260) and the opera singer Fyodor Chaliapin (p266).

A continuation of Rossi's ensemble running towards pl Lomonosova, **ulitsa Zodchego Rossi** is proportion deified: it's 22m wide, lined by buildings 22m high, and 220m long. **Vaganova School of Choreography** (Map pp230-1; Ⓜ Gostiny Dvor) is situated here and is the Mariinsky Ballet's training school where, Pavlova, Nijinsky, Nureyev and others learned their art; it is not open to the public.

Returning to Nevsky, on the corner of Malaya Sadovaya ul is **Yeliseyevsky** (Map pp230-1; Nevsky pr 56; ⏰ 9am-9pm Mon-Fri, 11am-9pm Sat & Sun), the most sumptuous 'grocery store' you may have ever seen. Built in Style Moderne between 1901 and 1903, it is decorated with sculptures and statues on the outside, and a gorgeous mirrored ceiling and stained-glass windows on the inside. Pedestrianised **Malaya Sadovaya ulitsa** is also worth a look. A number of statues and sculptures have been placed here (look up near the junction with Nevsky pr to see the tiny black-and-white cats poised on ledges on either side of the street), including a marble ball with a fountain underneath which makes it spin forever. At the end of the street turn right to enter a lovely triangular square, Manezhnaya pl.

Between pl Ostrovskogo and Fontanka River is the cream-coloured **Anichkov Palace** (Map pp230-1; 1741-50; Ⓜ Gostiny Dvor). Once the city's second most important palace, worked on by a slew of architects, including Rastrelli and Rossi, it was home to several imperial favourites, including Catherine the Great's lover Grigory Potemkin. It became

the city's largest Pioneer Club headquarters after 1935 and to this day houses over 100 after-school clubs for over 10,000 children.

Nevsky pr crosses the Fontanka on the **Anichkov most**, with its famous 1840s statues (sculpted by the German Pyotr Klodt) of rearing horses at its four corners. Take note of the southwestern horse's genitals: unlike those of his anatomically correct companions, the genitals of this one are apparently created in the image of the sculptor's unfaithful wife's lover (another version has it that it's Napoleon's profile).

SUMMER GARDEN

Perhaps St Petersburg's loveliest park, the **Summer Garden** (Map pp230-1; ⏰ 10am-10pm May-Sep, 10am-8pm Oct–mid-Apr, closed mid-late–Apr; Ⓜ Gostiny Dvor) is between the Mars Field and the Fontanka River. You can enter at either the north or south end.

Laid out for Peter the Great with fountains, pavilions and a geometrical plan to resemble the park at Versailles in France, the garden became a strolling place for St Petersburg's 19th-century leisured classes. Though changed since that era, it maintains a formal elegance, with thousands of lime trees shading its straight paths and lines of statues.

St Petersburg's first palace is the modest, two-storey **Summer Palace** (Map pp234-5; ☎ 314 0456; adult/student R300/150; ⏰ 10am-5pm Wed-Mon early May–early Nov; Ⓜ Gostiny Dvor) in the garden's northeast corner. Built for Peter from 1710 to 1714, it is pretty well intact with little reliefs around the walls depicting Russian naval victories. Inside it is stocked with early-18th-century furnishings of limited appeal.

MIKHAYLOVSKY CASTLE

A much greater Summer Palace used to stand across the canal from the southern end of the Summer Garden. But Rastrelli's fairy-tale wooden creation for Empress Elizabeth was knocked down in the 1790s to make way for the bulky **Mikhaylovsky Castle** (Engineer's Castle; Map pp230-1; ☎ 313 4173; www .rusmuseum.ru; Sadovaya ul 2; adult/student R300/150; ⏰ 10am-5pm Mon, to 6pm Wed-Sun; Ⓜ Gostiny Dvor). The pale-orange painted building was briefly home of Paul I, who was suffocated in his bed only a month after moving into the castle. Later it became a military engineering school (hence its more common name Engineers' Castle). Inside are some finely restored state rooms including the lavish burgundy throne room of the tsar's wife Maria Fyodorovna and some of the original statues from the Summer Garden.

MARBLE PALACE

Between Mars Field and the Neva is another branch of the Russian Museum, the **Marble Palace** (Map pp230–1; ☎ 312 9196; www.rusmuseum.ru; Millionnaya ul 5; adult/student R300/150; ⏱ 10am-5pm Wed-Mon; Ⓜ Nevsky Prospekt), built for Catherine the Great's lover Grigory Orlov from 1768 to 1785. Designed by Antonio Rinaldi, the palace is so named because it uses 36 different kinds of marble in its construction both inside and out. Check out the grey and blue marble staircase and the fantastic Marble Hall. The art on display here is eclectic, ranging from 17th-, 18th- and 19th-century works done by foreign artists in Russia to the splendid Ludwig Museum, part of the modern art collection of chocolate billionaire Peter Ludwig. This is one of the few chances to see such a large collection of contemporary art works in the city. The monstrous equestrian statue outside the museum is of Alexander III by the sculptor Paolo Trubetskoy who famously quipped that he 'simply depicted one animal on another'.

BRONZE HORSEMAN & PLOSHCHAD DEKABRISTOV

Between the Neva River and St Isaac's Cathedral is **ploshchad Dekabristov** (Decembrists' Square; Ⓜ Nevsky Prospekt), named after the first attempt at a Russian revolution, the Decembrists' Uprising of 14 December 1825 (p45) which kicked off and quickly fizzled here.

The most famous statue of Peter the Great (practically a trademark image of the city) stands at the river end of the square. The **Bronze Horseman** (Map pp230–1) has Peter's mount rearing above the snake of treason and was sculpted over 12 years for Catherine the Great by Frenchman Etienne Falconet. The inscription reads 'To Peter I from Catherine II – 1782'.

Most of the square's western side is occupied by the Central State Historical Archives in the former Senate and Synod buildings, built in 1829–34. The **Manege Central Exhibition Hall** (Map pp230–1; ☎ 314 8253; Isaakievskaya pl 1; admission R100; ⏱ 11am-6pm Fri-Wed; Ⓜ Nevsky Pr) across the street used to be the Horse Guards' Riding School (constructed

in 1804–07 from a design by Quarenghi). It now hosts rotating art exhibitions.

ADMIRALTY

The gilded spire of the old **Admiralty** (Map pp230–1; Admiralteysky pr 1; closed to the public; Ⓜ Nevsky Prospekt), at the western edge of Dvortsovaya pl, is an unmistakable city landmark. Here was the headquarters of the Russian navy from 1711 to 1917, and today the building houses the city's largest naval college. Constructed from 1806 to 1823 to the designs of Andreyan Zakharov, it's a foremost example of the Russian Empire style of classical architecture, with its rows of white columns and plentiful reliefs and statuary. Check out the nymphs holding giant globes flanking the main gate. The gardens and fountain here are particularly lovely in summer.

MUSEUM OF ETHNOGRAPHY

To learn about Russia's fragile ethnic mosaic drop by the interesting **Museum of Ethnography** (Map pp230–1; ☎ 313 4320; Inzhenernaya ul 4/1; adult/student R250/150; gold & jewellery exhibition R100/50; ⏱ 10am-5pm Tue-Sun; Ⓜ Gostiny Dvor). There's a bit of leftover Soviet propaganda going on here, but it's a marvellous collection highlighting the traditional crafts, customs and beliefs of the more than 150 peoples covered by the USSR: the sections on Transcaucasia and Central Asia are fascinating, with rugs and two full-size yurts (nomad's portable tent-houses).

PUSHKIN FLAT-MUSEUM

Beside one of the prettiest curves of the Moyka River is the little house where the poet Pushkin died after his duel in 1837 (p340). Now the **Pushkin Flat-Museum** (Map pp230–1; ☎ 571 3531; nab reki Moyki 12; adult/student R80/40; ⏱ 10.30am-5.30pm Wed-Mon; Ⓜ Nevsky Prospekt), it has been reconstructed to look as it did in the poet's time and includes (for morbid fans) Pushkin's death mask, a lock of his hair and the waistcoat worn on the day he died. Entry includes a Russian-language tour (English tours can be arranged in advance). There's a pleasantly quiet courtyard and café in front of the museum if you just want a rest.

MARS FIELD

Once the scene of 19th-century military parades, the grassy **Mars Field** lies immediately

ST PETERSBURG

east of the Summer Garden. An **eternal flame** (Map pp230-1) burns at its centre for the victims of the 1917 revolution and the ensuing civil war. Don't take a short cut across the grass – you may be walking on graves of the communist luminaries also buried here.

Liteyny, Smolny, Vladimirskaya & Vostanniya

This section covers sights on the east side of the Fontanka Canal along and around Nevsky pr towards Alexandra Nevskogo most. It includes the governmental Smolny region, one of less-touristed areas of the city, running east from Liteyny pr towards Smolny Cathedral.

MUSEUM OF DECORATIVE & APPLIED ARTS

Also known as the **Stieglitz Museum** (☎ 273 3258; Solyarnoy per 13; adult/student R400/75; ⊙ 11am-5pm Tue-Sat; Ⓜ Chernyshevskaya), this must-see establishment is in the block opposite the eastern side of the Summer Garden; the entrance is through the Sol-Art gallery (p289). The objects displayed are gorgeous, from medieval handcrafted furniture to a rare collection of 18th-century Russian tiled stoves to the contemporary works of the students of the arts school. Their surroundings merely match their magnificence.

In 1878, the millionaire Baron Stieglitz founded the School of Technical Design and wanted to surround his students with world-class art to inspire them. He began a collection, continued by his son, that was to include a unique array of European and Oriental glassware, porcelains, tapestries, furniture and paintings. Between 1885 and 1895, a building designed by architect Max Messmacher was constructed to house the collection, and this building also became a masterpiece. Each hall is decorated in its own, unique style, including Italian, Renaissance, Flemish and baroque. The Terem Room, in the style of the medieval Terem Palace of Moscow's Kremlin, is an opulent knockout.

After the revolution, the school was closed, the museum's collection redistributed to the Hermitage and Russian Museum, and most of the lavish interiors brutally painted or plastered over, even destroyed (one room was used as a sports hall). The painstaking renovation contin-

ues to this day, despite receiving no funding from the Ministry of Education under whose direction it falls (being connected to the Applied Arts School next door).

SHEREMETYEV PALACE

Splendid wrought-iron gates, facing the Fontanka River, guard the entrance to the **Sheremetyev Palace** (1750–55), which houses two lovely little museums. In the palace itself is the **Museum of Music** (Map pp234-5; ☎ 272 4441; www.theatremuseum.ru/eng; nab reki Fontanki 34; adult/student R150/75; ⊙ noon-6pm Wed-Sun; Ⓜ Gostiny Dvor), which has a collection of musical instruments from the 19th and 20th centuries, some beautifully decorated. The Sheremetyev family was famous for the concerts and theatre it hosted at the palace. Upstairs the rooms have been wonderfully restored and you get a great sense of how cultured life must have been here. Check the local press for notices of concerts which are occasionally still held here.

In a separate wing of the palace, reached from Liteyny pr, is the charming **Museum of Anna Akhmatova in the Fountain House** (Map pp234-5; ☎ 272 2211; www.akhmatova.spb.ru/en; Liteyny pr 53; adult/student R120/80; ⊙ 10am-5.30pm Tue-Sun, closed last Wed of month; Ⓜ Mayakovskaya). Even if you know little of this celebrated early 20th-century poet you will find yourself moved by the lovingly curated exhibits here. The evocative apartment on the 2nd floor is filled with mementos of the poet and her family, all persecuted during Soviet times. Outside, in a corner of the quiet garden, is a video room where you can watch Russian-language documentaries on her life.

ALEXANDER NEVSKY MONASTERY

The working **monastery** (Map pp234-5; ☎ 274 1702; www.larva.spb.ru; Nevsky pr 179/2; entrance to main complex adult/student R70/35; ⊙ 11am-5pm Fri-Wed; Ⓜ Ploshchad Aleksandra Nevskogo), with the graves of some of Russia's most famous artistic figures, is entered from pl Alexandra Nevskogo opposite Hotel Moskva. It was founded in 1713 by Peter the Great, who wrongly thought this was the location where Alexander of Novgorod had beaten the Swedes in 1240. In 1797 it became a *lavra* (superior monastery). Today it is open to the public (but don't come wearing shorts). Sadly, the courtyard is filled with homeless beggars hoping for the charity of visitors.

For most visitors the main reason for coming here is to view the **graveyards** (adult/student R70/55; 🕘 9.30am-5.30pm Fri-Wed) either side of the main entrance; tickets are sold outside the main gate (to your right as you enter). The **Tikhvin Cemetery**, on the right, contains the most famous graves. Tchaikovsky, Rimsky-Korsakov (check out his wild tomb!), Borodin, Mussorgsky and Glinka all rest here. Turn right after entering and you'll reach the tomb of Dostoevsky. The **Lazarus Cemetery**, on the left, contains several late, great St Petersburg architects – among them Starov, Voronikhin, Quarenghi, Zakharov and Rossi.

Across the canal just outside the main *lavra* complex, the first main building on the left is the 1717–22 baroque **Annunciation Church**, now the **City Sculpture Museum** (Map pp234-5; 🕿 274 2517; adult/student R50/25; 🕘 11am-5pm Wed-Sun), featuring a large collection of the original models and designs for the city.

About 100m further on is the monastery's classical **Trinity Cathedral** (Map pp234-5; 🕘 for worship from 6am Sat, Sun & holidays) built between 1776 and 1790. Hundreds crowd in on 12 September to celebrate the feast of St Alexander Nevsky. His remains are in the silver reliquary in the main iconostasis.

Opposite the cathedral is the St Petersburg **Metropolitan's House** (Map pp234-5) built from 1775 to 1778. On the far right of the grounds facing the canal you'll see St Petersburg's **Orthodox Academy**, one of only a handful in Russia (the main one is at Sergiev Posad).

SMOLNY CATHEDRAL
The sky-blue **Smolny Cathedral** (Map pp234-5; 🕿 271 7632; eng.cathedral.ru/smolny; pl Rastrelli 3/1; Ⓜ Chernyshevskaya), one of the most fabulous of Rastrelli's buildings, is the centrepiece of a convent built mostly to the Italian architect's designs from 1748 to 1757. His inspiration was to combine baroque details with the forest of towers and onion domes typical of an old Russian monastery. There's special genius in the proportions of the cathedral (it gives the impression of soaring upward), to which the convent buildings are a perfect foil.

At time of research the cathedral was closed for renovation, but when it reopens the climb up one of the 63m **belfries** is well worth it for the stupendous views. If you don't want to make the long walk from the metro station, trolleybuses 5 and 7 from Nevsky pr end up here.

BLOCKADE MUSEUM
Next door to the Museum of Decorative and Applied Arts is the grim but engrossing **Blockade Museum** (Map pp234-5; 🕿 275 7208; Solyarnoy per 9; admission R70; 🕘 10am-4pm Tue, to 5pm Thu-Mon; Ⓜ Chernyshevskaya), opened just three months after the blockade was lifted. At that time it had 37,000 exhibits, including real tanks and aeroplanes, but three years later, during Stalin's repression of the city, the museum was shut, its director shot, and most of the exhibits destroyed or redistributed. It reopened in 1989 and the displays now contain donations from survivors, including propaganda posters from the time, and an example of the sawdust-filled tiny piece of bread Leningraders had to survive on. Book in advance for English excursions.

CATHEDRAL OF THE TRANSFIGURATION OF OUR SAVIOUR
The interior of this beautifully restored yellow **cathedral** (Map pp234-5; 🕿 272 3662; Preobrazhenskaya pl; 🕘 services 10am & 6pm; Ⓜ Chernyshevskaya) is one of the most gilded in St Petersburg. The grand gates bear the imperial double-headed eagle in vast golden busts – reflecting the fact that Empress Elizabeth ordered its construction in 1743. This is where the Preobrazhensky Guards (the monarch's personal protection unit) had their headquarters. Rebuilt in 1829 to a neoclassical design by Vasily Stasov, the cathedral is dedicated to the victory over the Turks in 1828–29; note the captured guns in the gate surrounding the church!

BELOSELSKY-BELOZERSKY PALACE
The photogenic salmon-pink backdrop to the Anichkov most is provided by the 1840s rococo **Beloselsky-Belozersky Palace** (Map pp234-5; 🕿 315 5236; a_excurse@mail.ru; Nevsky pr 41; tours R100; Ⓜ Mayakovskaya). Call or email about tours of the opulent interior here (in Russian only, but English information sheets are available), or check the posters outside for details of the concerts which are occasionally held in the palace's grandly oak-panelled and stuccoed concert hall.

ST PETERSBURG

VLADIMIRSKAYA CHURCH

The 18th-century **Vladimirskaya Church** (Map pp234-5; ☎ 312 1938; Vladimirsky pr 20; ☑ 8am-6pm; Ⓜ Vladimirskaya), designed by Quarenghi, was used as an underwear factory during Soviet times, but in 1990 it was reconsecrated and is now one of the busiest churches in town. For a brilliant view of its amazing onion domes have a drink in the 7th floor bar of the Hotel Dostoevsky across the road, part of the Vladimirsky Passazh shopping mall. If you can get past the hordes of babushkas and beggars outside, the church's interiors are also stunning (go upstairs to see the main body of the church).

DOSTOEVSKY MUSEUM

Dostoevsky lived in flats all over the city (mainly in the Sennaya area) but his final residence, where he penned most of *The Brothers Karamazov*, is preserved at the engrossing **Dostoevsky Museum** (Map pp234-5; ☎ 571 4031; www.md.spb.ru; Kuznechny per 5/2; adult/student R90/45; ☑ 11am-6pm Tue-Sun, closed last Wed of month; Ⓜ Vladimirskaya). It all looks just as it did before the writer died in 1881. There's also a rather gloomy statue of Dostoevsky outside the Vladimirskaya metro.

RIMSKY-KORSAKOV FLAT-MUSEUM

The charming **Rimsky-Korsakov Flat-Museum** (Map pp234-5; ☎ 713 3208; www.theatremuseum.ru/eng; Zagorodny pr 28; adult/student R50/30; ☑ 11am-6pm Wed-Sun; Ⓜ Vladimirskaya) remains as it was when the composer lived here in the early 20th century. Rimsky-Korsakov's tradition of holding concerts here on Wednesday evenings continues.

ARCTIC & ANTARCTIC MUSEUM

In the former Old Believers' Church of St Nicholas is the **Arctic & Antarctic Museum** (Map pp234-5; ☎ 571 2549; www.polarmuseum.sp.ru; ul Marata 24A; adult/student R100/50; ☑ 10am-6pm Wed-Sun; Ⓜ Vladimirskaya), which focuses on Soviet polar explorations. Apart from stuffed polar bears and the like, the most impressive exhibit is a wooden boat plane hanging from the ceiling. Check out the informative website though for details of Vicaar, an Arctic expedition and tourism agency linked to the museum.

WORLD OF WATER MUSEUM

The handsomely restored brick complex of 19th-century buildings between the Tau-ride Gardens and the Neva River house St Petersburg's water treatment company Vodakanal and its **World of Water Museum** (Map pp234-5; ☎ 271 9479; Shpalernaya ul. 56; adult/student R40/15; ☑ 10am-5pm Wed-Sun; Ⓜ Chernyshevskaya). Hopefully the water tower will be open to climb (it wasn't when we visited) but otherwise the museum has slick, modern displays and is informative, if you can read the Russian-only captions.

TAURIDE GARDENS, TAURIDE PALACE & FLORAL EXHIBITION HALL

The former **Tauride Gardens** (Tavricheskii Sad; entrance on Potyomkinskaya ul; Ⓜ Chernyshevskaya), now the City Children's Park, is a great place for a stroll, and there are some rusty rides for the kiddies. The view across the lake towards the **Tauride Palace**, built between 1783 and 1789 for Catherine the Great's lover Potemkin, is a fine sight. The palace (closed to the public) takes its name from the Ukrainian region of Crimea (once called Tavriya), which Potemkin was responsible for conquering. Between 1906 and 1917 the State Duma, the Provisional Government and the Petrograd Soviet all met here.

During the winter you may want to warm up at the **Floral Exhibition Hall** (Map pp234-5; ☎ 272 5448; Potyomkinskaya ul 2; admission R20; ☑ 11am-7pm Tue-Sun; Ⓜ Chernyshevskaya), a lush indoor tropical paradise, next to the gardens on the corner of Shpalernaya ul.

MUSEUM OF EROTICA

The chief attraction of this quirky **museum** (Map pp234-5; ☎ 320 7600; Furshtatskaya ul 47; admission free; ☑ 8am-10pm; Ⓜ Chernyshevskaya) housed in a venereal disease clinic, is doctor Igor Knyazkin's collection of sexually themed trinkets, the highlight being a 30cm-long grey, embalmed penis that allegedly belonged to Rasputin.

PLOSHCHAD VOSSTANIYA

Marking the division of Nevsky pr and Stary (old) Nevsky pr is **ploschad Vosstaniya** (Uprising Square; Ⓜ Ploshchad Vosstaniya), whose landmarks are the giant granite pillar with the communist star, and **Moskovsky vokzal** (opposite). The Cyrillic on top of Hotel Oktyabrskaya across from the station, translates as 'Hero City Leningrad'; several cities were designated 'hero cities' for heroism, stoicism and losses during WWII.

Mariinsky & Sennaya

This area, south and west of St Isaac's Cathedral, contains some interesting sights but is also fine just for casual wandering, particularly around the meandering Griboedova Canal which flows close to Sennaya pl (Dostoevskyland) and the theatre district of Mariinsky. Along it look for the **Lviny most**, another of St Petersburg's beautiful, beast-supported bridges, with cables emerging from the mouths of golden lions.

YUSUPOV PALACE

Best known as the place where Rasputin met his unpleasant, untimely end (p49), the interior of the **Yusupov Palace** (Map pp236-7; ☎ 314 9883; nab reki Moyki 94; adult/student R350/250; ⏰ 11am-5pm; Ⓜ Sadovaya/Sennaya Ploshchad) is also one of the city's most beautiful. A series of sumptuously decorated rooms culminate in a gilded jewel box of a theatre, where performances are still held. Admission includes an audio tour in English as well as several other languages. You have to pay extra for the *Murder of Rasputin* tour (adult/student R150/120); be warned that places are limited to 20 daily on each of the two English-language ones, so book ahead if you're interested.

SENNAYA PLOSHCHAD & AROUND

Once known as Haymarket, frenetic **Sennaya ploshchad** (Ⓜ Sennaya Ploshchad) crowded with giant kiosks and surrounded by glitzy shopping malls, is the gateway to 'Dostoevskyland'. In this area *Crime and Punishment* is set and although the cathedral that once dominated the square in Dostoevsky's time has long been demolished,

the writer would still recognise something of the area's former raffishness, if not the squalor.

Just west of the square, across the Griboedova Canal, is the **flat** (Map pp236-7; ul Kaznacheyskaya 7) where the peripatetic writer (he occupied around 20 residences in his 28-year stay in the city) wrote *Crime and Punishment*; the route taken by the novel's antihero Raskolnikov to murder the old woman moneylender passed directly under the author's window. The old woman lived at **flat 74, naberezhnaya kanala Griboedova 104**; you can visit the hallway outside the flat (residents are quite used to it). Entering from the canal side, walk straight back to entrance No 5 (apartments 22–81); the flat's on the 3rd floor.

THE MUSEUM OF RAILWAY TRANSPORT

Every trainspotter's dream is realised at the **Museum of Railway Transport** (Map pp236-7; ☎ 315 1476; www.railroad.ru/cmrt in Russian; Sadovaya ul 50; adult/student R100/50; ⏰ 11am-5pm Wed-Sun, closed last Thu of month; Ⓜ Sennaya Ploshchad/Sadovaya), a fascinating collection of scale locomotives and model railway bridges, often made by the same engineers that built the real ones. The oldest such collection in the world (the museum was established in 1809, 28 years before Russia had its first working train!), it includes models of Krasnoyarsk's *Yenisey Bridge*, the ship that once carried passengers and trains on the trans-Siberian route across Lake Baikal, and a sumptuous 1903 Trans-Siberian wagon complete with piano salon and bathtub. To see full-sized vintage trains visit the Museum of Railway Technology (p268).

ST PETERSBURG

HISTORIC RAILWAY STATIONS

As the birthplace of Russia's railway system, it's not surprising that St Petersburg has some grand stations. The oldest and most elegant is **Vitebsky vokzal** (Vitebsky Station; Map pp236-7; Ⓜ Pushkinskaya), originally built in 1837 for the line to Tsarskoe Selo. The current building dates from 1904 and is partly graced with gorgeous Style Moderne (Russian Art Nouveau) interior decoration.

While at **Moskovsky vokzal** (Moscow Station; Map pp234-5; Ⓜ Ploshchad Vostanniya) look up at the expansive ceiling mural in the main entrance hall. There's a striking giant bust of Peter the Great in the hall leading to the platforms.

Finlyandsky vokzal (Finland Station; Map p229; Ⓜ Ploshchad Lenina), rebuilt after WWII, is famous as the place where, in April 1917, Lenin arrived from exile and gave his legendary speech atop an armoured car. When the progress of the revolution began to look iffy, it was from here that Lenin hightailed if off to Finland, only to return again in October to seize power. Lenin's statue, pointing across the Neva towards the old KGB headquarters, stands outside the station.

GRAND CHORAL SYNAGOGUE
Recently restored to its full Byzantine-styled glory the **Grand Choral Synagogue** (Map pp236-7; ☎ 713 8186; Lermontovsky pr 2; ◷ 11am-3pm Mon-Wed, 11am-2pm Thu & Fri, services 10am Sat; Ⓜ Sadovaya/Sennaya Ploshchad) was designed by Vasily Stasov and opened in 1893. Its lavishness (particularly notable in the highly unusual and decorative wedding chapel to the left as you enter) indicates the pivotal role Jews played in imperial St Petersburg. All men and married women should cover their head on entering the building. The restaurant, Lechaim (p281) in the basement, is excellent.

MARIINKSY THEATRE
The pretty green-and-white **Mariinsky Theatre** (p287) has played a pivotal role in Russian ballet ever since it was built in 1859. Outside performance times you can usually wander into the foyer, and maybe peep into its lovely auditorium. To organise a full tour fax a request to **Dr Yury Schwartzkopf** (☎ 326 4141; fax 314 1744) and call back for an answer.

NIKOLSKY CATHEDRAL
Its picture-perfect canalside setting, baroque spires and golden domes make the ice-blue **Nikolsky Cathedral** (Map pp236-7; Nikolskaya pl 1/3; ◷ 9am-7pm; Ⓜ Sadovaya), just south of the Mariinsky Theatre, one of the city's best-loved churches. Nicknamed the Sailor's Church (Nicholas is the patron saint of sailors), it contains many 18th-century icons and a

finely carved wooden iconostasis. A graceful bell tower overlooks the canal, which is crossed by the Staro-Nikolsky most (from this bridge, you can see at least seven bridges, more than from any other spot in the city).

NABOKOV MUSEUM
From his birth in 1899 until 1917, when his family fled Russia, Vladimir Nabokov, author of *Lolita* and arguably the most versatile and least classifiable of modern Russian writers, lived at this lovely 19th-century townhouse now turned into a small **museum** (Map pp236-7; ☎ 571 4502; www.nabokovmuseum.org; Bolshaya Morskaya ul 47; adult/student R100/20, admission free 11am-3pm Thu; ◷ 11am-6pm Tue-Fri, noon-5pm Sat & Sun; Ⓜ Sadovaya/Sennaya Ploshchad). In Nabokov's autobiography *Speak, Memory*, he refers to it as a 'paradise lost' and it's easy to imagine why after seeing the charming carved oak interiors. There are various displays of Nabokov-related artefacts, but the museum is more of a cultural centre hosting festivals and special events.

RUSSIAN VODKA MUSEUM
Who could resist the **Russian Vodka Museum** (Map pp236-7; ☎ 312 3416; www.vodkamuseum.ru; Konnogvardeysky bul 5; admission R50, with tour R100; ◷ 11am-10pm; Ⓜ Sadovaya/Sennaya Ploshchad). The two exhibition rooms are surprisingly interesting if you opt for the English-language guided tour. There's a shot of vodka at the end for everyone, but if you really want to

---

DRAMA AT THE MARIINSKY

St Petersburg's most famous theatre was built in 1859 as the home of the Imperial Russian Opera and Ballet companies. The gilded Italianate house saw the premieres of Tchaikovsky's *Sleeping Beauty* and *The Nutcracker*. In 1935 the Soviets renamed it the Kirov Opera and Ballet Theatre, and while the theatre has reverted to its prerevolutionary name, the company is still called the Kirov. The Kirov Ballet nurtured stars including Nijinsky, Pavlova, Nureyev, Makarova and Baryshnikov.

After hard times in the 1980s, the new Mariinsky has undergone an artistic renaissance under dynamic, workaholic artistic director Valery Gergiev. New productions are paid for by Western benefactors, or staged in conjunction with overseas companies, and these days not everything is sung in Russian (even so, there will be English subtitles).

Despite the Mariinsky's revival, the fact remains that the 19th-century theatre is clapped out, with ancient equipment unable to cope with modern productions, and is in desperate need of renovation. After much heated debate in 2004, ambitious plans were finally signed off to build a second stage for the theatre behind the current building (on the site of the Palace of Culture). Dubbed the 'Golden Envelope' the design – a series of black marble structures covered by giant golden angular shell – is by French architect Dominique Perrault, responsible for the minimalist national library in Paris. The plan is for it to be ready by 2008, when it will be the most striking architectural addition to the city in decades.

do things in style, call ahead and book a spot on the special excursion (R360), which includes a proper tasting of three types of vodka plus choice of appetisers in the museum's *traktir* (tavern; p283). The food here, incidentally, is pretty good.

STATE MUSEUM OF THE HISTORY OF ST PETERSBURG

History buffs will want to check out the superb **State Museum of the History of St Petersburg** (Map pp236-7; ☎ 717 7544; Angliyskaya nab 44; adult/student R60/30; 🕑 11am-6pm Thu-Tue; M Sadovaya/Sennaya Ploshchad). Housed in the majestic Rumyantsev Mansion (1826), its main focus is the Blockade; it has the city's largest repository of documents from that time. Ask for an English guide at the ticket office.

Vasilyevsky Island

The most convenient metro station is Vasileostrovskaya but for sights around the Strelka you'd do just as well to walk over the Neva from the Hermitage or catch one of the numerous buses that run there from Nevsky prospekt.

STRELKA

Some of the best views of St Petersburg can be had from Vasilyevsky Island's eastern 'nose' known as the **Strelka** (Tongue of Land). Peter the Great's plan was to have his new city's administrative and intellectual centre here. In fact, it became the focus of St Petersburg's maritime trade, symbolised by the white colonnaded Stock Exchange (now the Central Naval Museum, p264). The two **Rostral Columns** on the point, studded with ships' prows, were oil-fired navigation beacons in

the 1800s; on some holidays such as Victory Day, gas torches are still lit on them.

MENSHIKOV PALACE

Well worth visiting is the riverside **Menshikov Palace** (Map pp240-1; ☎ 332 1112; www.hermitagemuseum.com/html_En/03/hm3_9.html; Universitetskaya nab 15; adult/student R200/100; 🕑 10.30am-4.30pm Tue-Sun; M Vasileostrovskaya), built in 1707 for Alexander Menshikov, a close friend (many now say lover) of Peter the Great. Menshikov effectively ran Russia from here for three years between Peter's death and his own exile. Now a branch of the Hermitage (p244), the palace's impressively restored interiors are filled with period art and furniture. Organ concerts are held at noon on Sunday here.

MUSEUM OF ANTHROPOLOGY & ETHNOGRAPHY (KUNSTKAMERA)

The city's first **museum** (Map pp240-1; ☎ 328 1412; www.kunstkamera.ru; entrance on Tamozhenny per; adult/student R100/50; 🕑 10.30am-6pm Tue-Sat, to 5pm Sun; M Vasileostrovskaya) was founded in 1714 by Peter himself. It's famous for its ghoulish collection of monstrosities, notably preserved freaks, two-headed mutant foetuses and odd body parts, all collected by Peter with the aim of educating the common people against superstitions. Sadly, most people rush to see these sad specimens, largely ignoring the other interesting (though not best displayed) exhibits on native peoples from around the world. Here you'll also find an exhibition devoted to the scientist and renaissance man Mikhail Lomonosov (whose statue stands beside the nearby Twelve Colleges building of the city university) with a recreation of his study-laboratory.

ACADEMY OF ARTS MUSEUM

The **Academy of Arts Museum** (Map pp240-1; ☎ 323 6469; excursions ☎ 213 3578; Universitetskaya nab 17; adult/student R200/100; English excursions R1500; 🕑 11am-6pm Wed-Sun; M Vasileostrovskaya) doesn't get many visitors but is certainly worth a look, especially if you are interested in Russian art. It's guarded by two imported Egyptian sphinxes said to be about 3500 years old. Boys would live in this building from the age of five until they graduated at age 15 – it was an experiment to create a new species of human: the artist. It mostly worked since graduates included Ilya Repin, Karl Bryullov and Anton Losenko.

ST PETERSBURG

Inside are works done by academy students and the faculty since its founding in 1775, including many studies plus temporary exhibitions. On the 3rd floor, see models of the original versions of Smolny, St Isaac's, and the Alexander Nevsky monastery. Also take a peek into the fabulous old library.

TEMPLE OF THE ASSUMPTION

The attractive 1895 neo-Byzantine **Temple of the Assumption** (Map pp240-1; ☎ 321 7473; nab Leytenanta Shmidta 27; ☒ 8am-8pm; Ⓜ Vasileostrovskaya) is again a working church, although restoration of the interior's beautiful murals continues. Closed during the Soviet period from 1957 it was turned into the city's first – and very popular – year-round skating rink. You'll find a good church shop here selling choral music and freshly baked cakes.

CENTRAL NAVAL MUSEUM

Housed in what was once the Stock Exchange, the **Central Naval Museum** (Map pp240-1; ☎ 328 2502; www.museum.navy.ru/index_e.htm; Birzhevoy proezd 4; adult/student R100/15; ☒ 11am-6pm Wed-Sun, closed last Thu of the month; Ⓜ Vasileostrovskaya), is packed with maps, excellent model ships, flags and photos relating to the Russian navy up to the present – it's a must for naval enthusiasts.

MUSEUM OF ZOOLOGY

One of the biggest and best of its kind in the world, the city's **Museum of Zoology** (Map pp240-1; ☎ 328 0112; www.zin.ru/mus_e.htm; Universitetskaya nab 1; adult/child R60/30, free Thu; ☒ 11am-6pm Sat-Thu; Ⓜ Vasileostrovskaya) was founded in 1832 and has some amazing exhibits. Amid the dio-

---

> ### DIVING IN THE CHURCH
>
> Intriguingly off limits, at the western end of Vasilyevsky Island's Bolshoy pr and on the grounds of what has long been a military training school, is the **Church of Mother of God the Merciful** (Map pp240-1), designed by V Kosyakov, who also did the Naval Cathedral in Kronshtadt (p303). The Soviets converted it into a surreal training base for submariners and for life-saving exercises. The Russian Byzantine exterior is more or less intact, but the interior has been completely gutted, and there is a 26m-high tube filled with 333 tonnes of water, in which diving exercises take place.

---

ramas and the tens of thousands of mounted beasties from around the globe is a complete woolly mammoth, thawed out of the Siberian ice in 1902, and a live insect zoo! Pay your entrance fee at the microscopic cash window just west of the main entrance.

Petrograd Side

Petrograd Side (Petrogradskaya storona) is a cluster of delta islands between the Malaya Neva and Bolshaya Nevka channels, including little Zayachy Island, where Peter the Great first broke ground for the city.

PETER & PAUL FORTRESS

Set aside a chunk of time to explore the **Peter & Paul Fortress** (Map p265; ☎ 238 4550; free entry to grounds, admission to all buildings adult/student R120/60; ☒ 11am-6pm Thu-Mon, 11am-5pm Tue; May-Sep Cathedral & Bastion 11am-6pm daily; Ⓜ Gorkovskaya) as there's plenty to do and see here. Dating from 1703, the hexahedral fortress is the oldest building in St Petersburg, planned by Peter the Great as a defence against the Swedes. It never actually saw action and its main use up to 1917 was as a political prison; famous residents included Dostoevsky, Gorky, Trotsky and Lenin's older brother, Alexander.

To get a sense of the scale of the place, and for wonderful river views, first walk the **Nevskaya Panorama** (adult/student R50/30; ☒ 10am-8pm) along part of the battlements, then head inside the **SS Peter & Paul Cathedral**, whose 122m-tall, needle-thin gilded spire is one of the defining landmarks of St Petersburg. Its magnificent baroque interior is the last resting place of all of Russia's prerevolutionary rulers from Peter the Great onward, except Peter II and Ivan VI. Mondays and Fridays at 7pm the St Petersburg male choir gives concerts here.

Worthy of a view is the fascinating history of St Petersburg exhibition inside the **Commandant's House**. Covering up to the 1917 revolution, there are some very good displays here including a vivid painting of the great flood of 1824 that all but swept the city away, and a model showing how the Alexander Column in Palace Sq was erected.

Also included in the entry ticket are: the **Engineers' House**, rotating exhibitions and a permanent display of items from the decorative arts collection of the now defunct Old St Petersburg Museum; the reconstructed prison cells of the **Trubetskoy Bastion** (closed

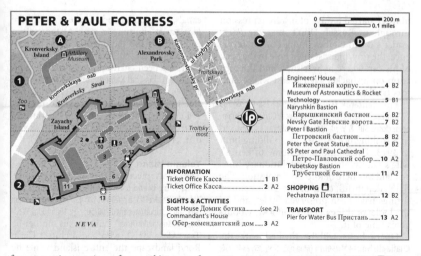

PETER & PAUL FORTRESS

INFORMATION
Ticket Office Касса 1 B1
Ticket Office Касса 2 A2

SIGHTS & ACTIVITIES
Boat House Домик ботика ....(see 2)
Commandant's House
  Обер-комендантский дом 3 A2

Engineers' House
  Инженерный корпус 4 B2
Museum of Astronautics & Rocket
  Technology 5 B1
Naryshkin Bastion
  Нарышкинский бастион 6 B2
Nevsky Gate Невские ворота 7 B2
Peter I Bastion
  Петровский бастион 8 B2
Peter the Great Statue 9 B2
SS Peter and Paul Cathedral
  Петро-Павловский собор 10 A2
Trubetskoy Bastion
  Трубецкой бастион 11 A2

SHOPPING
Pechatnaya Печатная 12 B2

TRANSPORT
Pier for Water Bus Пристань 13 A2

for renovations at time of research) – one of its first inmates was Peter's own son Alexey, whose torture Peter is said to have overseen personally; and the **Museum of Astronautics and Rocket Technology** – this was where Russia's first liquid-fuelled rocket was developed in the 1930s.

At noon every day a cannon is fired from **Naryshkin Bastion**. In the south wall is **Nevsky Gate**, where prisoners were loaded onto boats for execution. Note the plaques showing water levels of famous floods. Along the walls on any sunny day – including the rare ones in winter and spring – you'll see standing sunbathers (standing's said to give you a *proper* tan). In winter even hardier souls come here to swim in holes cut through the ice! Back inside the fortress grounds, also look out for Mikhail Shemyakin's controversial **statue of Peter the Great** with its out-of-proportion head and hands.

CATHEDRAL MOSQUE
This working **mosque** (Map pp238-9; ☎ 233 9819; Kronverksky pr 7; Ⓜ Gorkovskaya) built between 1910 and 1914 is modelled on Samarkand's Gur Emir Mausoleum. Although a serious place of worship, and decidedly not a tourist attraction, its fluted azure dome and minarets have emerged from a painstaking renovation and are stunning to view from outside.

MUSEUM OF POLITICAL HISTORY
Way more interesting than it sounds is the **Museum of Political History** (Map pp238-9; ☎ 233

7052; ul Kuybysheva 4; adult/student R150/70; Ⓥ 10am-5pm Fri-Wed; Ⓜ Gorkovskaya). This elegant Style Moderne palace once belonged to Matilda Kshesinskaya, famous ballet dancer and one-time lover of Tsar Nicholas II. The Bolsheviks made it their headquarters and Lenin often gave speeches from the balcony. Although the main exhibit details Russian politics (with English captions) to the present day, you'll also find here some of the best Soviet kitsch in town and incredibly rare satirical caricatures of Lenin published in magazines between the 1917 revolutions (the same drawings a few months later would have got the artist imprisoned, or worse). For those who really want to dig deep into Russian politics there's an **annexe** (Map pp230-1; ☎ 312 2742; Admiralteysky pr 6/2; adult/student R100/40; Ⓥ 10am-6pm Mon-Fri) opposite the Admiralty.

HOUSE MUSEUMS
The Petrograd Side includes a trio of 'house' museums that together make for an offbeat tour of St Petersburg. All are lovingly tended by small armies of babushkas who take as much care (if not more) of them as they would their own homes. Walking between each of the following will allow you also to enjoy some of the lovely Style Moderne architecture of the area.

The **Kirov Museum** (Map pp238-9; ☎ 346 0289; Kamennoostrovsky pr 26/28; admission R50; Ⓥ 11am-6pm Thu-Tue; Ⓜ Petrogradskaya) is in the 4th- and 5th-floor apartment where Sergei Kirov, one of Stalin's henchmen, spent his last days. His murder started a wave of deadly repression throughout Russia. Don't miss the Party leader's death clothes, hung out for reverence: the tiny, bloodstained hole in the back of his cap where he was shot, and the torn seam on his jacket's left breast where doctors tried to revive his heart.

The **Yelizarov Museum** (Map pp238-9; ☎ 235 3778; ul Lenina 52, flat 24; adult/student R200/50; ☽ 10am-6pm, closed Sun & Wed; Ⓜ Chkalovskaya) is housed in a striking ocean-liner-like building built in 1913. The comfortable home of Lenin's wife's family, the great revolutionary himself laid low here before the revolution. The flat's delightful turn-of-the-20th-century fittings have been preserved intact, and by the looks of things Lenin had a very bourgeois time of it.

Opera buffs will be thrilled with the **Chaliapin House Museum** (Map pp238-9; ☎ 234 1056; www.theatremuseum.ru; ul Graftio 2B; adult/student R30; ☽ noon-6pm Wed-Sun; Ⓜ Petrogradskaya), where the great singer Fyodor Chaliapin last lived before fleeing postrevolutionary Russia in 1922. The kindly babushkas in charge will happily play the singer's recordings as you wander around.

SIGMUND FREUD MUSEUM OF DREAMS
A decidedly odd conceptual exhibition based on abstractions and ideas, the **Sigmund Freud Museum of Dreams** (Map pp238-9; ☎ 235 2929; www .freud.ru; Bolshoy pr 18A; adult/student R20/10; ☽ noon-5pm Tue & Sun; Ⓜ Sportivnaya) is an outgrowth of the Psychoanalytic Institute that houses it. The two-room exhibition aims to stimulate your subconscious as you struggle to read the display symbolising what Freud himself would have dreamt of in a dimly lit, incense-scented hall.

KIROVSKY ISLANDS
This is the collective name for the outer delta islands of Petrograd Side – Kamenny, Yelagin and Krestovsky. Once marshy jungles, the islands were granted to 18th- and 19th-century court favourites and developed into bucolic playgrounds. Still mostly parkland, they remain huge leafy venues for picnics, river sports and white-nights cavorting.

Kamenny Island
This island's charm, seclusion and century-old dachas (now inhabited by the wealthy), combined with winding lanes and a series of canals, lakes and ponds, make a stroll here pleasant at any time of year. At the eastern end of the island the **Church of St John the Baptist** (Map pp238-9), built between 1776 and 1781, has been charmingly restored. Behind it the big, classical **Kamennoostrovsky Palace** (Map pp238-9), built by Catherine the Great for her son, is now a weedy military sanatorium.

Kamenny Island is a short walk south of metro Chyornaya Rechka (turn right as you exit, cross the bridge and you're there).

Yelagin Island
The centrepiece of this pedestrian-only, 2km-long **island** (admission R10 on Sat & Sun) is the **Yelagin Palace** (Map pp238-9; ☎ 430 1131; www.elagin park.spb.ru; adult/student R100/50; ☽ 10am-6pm Wed-Sun; Ⓜ Krestovsky Ostrov), built for his mother by Tsar Alexander I, who had architect Carlo Rossi landscape the entire island while he was at it. The palace, with beautifully restored interiors, is to your right as you cross the footbridge from Kamenny Island.

The rest of the island is a lovely park, with a plaza at the western end looking out to the Gulf of Finland. You can rent rowing boats in the northern part of the island.

Krestovsky Island
The biggest of the three islands, Krestovsky (Ⓜ Krestovsky Ostrov) consists mostly of the vast **Seaside Park of Victory** (Primorsky Park Pobedy), dotted with sports fields and, close to the metro, **Divo Ostrov** (Map pp238-9; ☎ 323 9705; www.divo-ostrov.ru/en; all day pass adult/child R500/250; ☽ noon-9pm Mon, noon-10pm, Tue-Fri, 11am-10pm Sat & Sun), a low-rent Disneyland-style amusement park with thrill rides that kids will adore. You can also rent bikes and in-line skates here (p269). At the island's far western end the 80,000-seat **Kirov Stadium** is set for demolition and reconstruction.

BOTANICAL GARDENS
Once the second-biggest botanical gardens in the world, behind only London's Kew Gardens, the **botanical gardens** (Map pp238-9; ☎ 234 1764; ul Professora Popova 2; grounds R20; all greenhouses R90; ☽ 11am-4pm Sat-Thu; Ⓜ Petrogradskaya) contains giant dilapidated greenhouses on a 22-hectare site and, although very much faded from its glory days, it's still a pleasant place to stroll. A highlight is the 'tsaritsa nochi' (Selenicereus pteranthus), a flowering cactus which blossoms only one

night a year, usually in mid-June, when the gardens stay open until morning for visitors to gawk at the marvel.

PETER'S CABIN

A minor historical sight is St Petersburg's first residence – a **log cabin** (Map pp238-9; ☎ 232 4576; Petrovskaya nab 6; adult/child R20/10; ☼ 10am-5pm Wed-Mon; Ⓜ Gorkovskaya) where Peter lived in 1703 while supervising the construction of the city. It's preserved inside a brick building in a patch of trees a short walk east of the fortress.

CRUISER AURORA

East along the river from the cabin is the **Aurora** (Map pp238-9; ☎ 230 8440; Petrovskaya nab; admission free; ☼ 10.30am-4pm Tue-Thu, Sat & Sun; Ⓜ Gorkovskaya), a mothballed cruiser from the Russo-Japanese War, built in 1900 and now a museum that will appeal to naval enthusiasts and kids. It was from this ship that the shot marking the start of the October Revolution was fired. So hallowed was the cruiser that during WWII, the Russians sank it to protect it from German bombs.

ALEKSANDROVSKY PARK & AROUND

Don't come to **Aleksandrovsky Park** (Ⓜ Gorkovskaya) looking for peace and quiet: this bustling hang-out is too close to traffic and perpetually thronged with people. If you have kids to entertain there are a couple of options here worth knowing about, though.

The **Planetarium** (Map pp238-9; ☎ 233 5653; Aleksandrovsky park 4; shows R50; ☼ 10.30am-6pm Tue-Sun) offers 50-minute star shows throughout the day and day-glow displays in Russian. Further west of here is the **Zoo** (Map pp238-9; ☎ 232 4828; www.spbzoo.ru/; Aleksandrovsky park 1; adult/child R100/15; ☼ 10am-8pm May-Sep, to 4pm Tue-Sun Oct-Apr). The lack of funds is pitifully evident, but all things considered, it's pretty well kept and has had remarkable success in breeding polar bears in captivity.

Vyborg Side

Peter the Great had little interest in developing the far side of the Neva. Attractions here are few and far between but many of the ones that do exist are worth seeing.

HERMITAGE STORAGE FACILITY

A superb reason for dragging out to northern St Petersburg is the **Hermitage Storage**

Facility (Map p229; ☎ 344 9226; www.hermitagemuseum .com; 37A Zausadebnaya ul; adult R200; ☼ tours at 11am, 1pm, 1.30pm & 3.30pm Wed-Sun; Ⓜ Staraya Derevnya). Inside the state-of-the art complex you'll be led through a handful of rooms housing but a fraction of the museum's collection. This is not a formal exhibition as such but the guides are knowledgeable and the examples chosen for display – paintings, furniture, carriages – are wonderful. The highlight is undoubtedly the gorgeous wool and silk embroidered Turkish Ceremonial Tent presented to Catherine the Great by Sultan Selim III in 1793 (and not opened for over 200 years!). Beside it stands an equally impressive modern diplomatic gift – a massive wood carving of the mythical Garuda bird, given by Indonesia to the city for its 300th anniversary.

The Hermitage has big plans for this site; a copy of the hanging garden at the main Hermitage is being recreated outside the building and several more buildings are due to be completed here on the large plot next to the Serafimovskoye Cemetery. The storage facility is directly behind the big shopping centre opposite the metro station.

BUDDHIST TEMPLE

A short walk south from the storage facility, overlooking Yelagin Island, is the colourfully decorated **Buddhist temple** (Map pp238-9; ☎ 239 0341; Primorsky pr 91; ☼ 10am-7pm; Ⓜ Staraya Derevnya), built between 1909 and 1915 at the instigation of Pyotr Badmaev, a Buddhist physician to Tsar Nicholas II. Like many other religious buildings it was closed during the Communist period; however, the damage was not particularly profound and the *datsan* was returned to the city's small Gelugpa, or Yellow Hat, Buddhist community in 1990. Visitors are welcome, although it's best to avoid service times (10am). There's a small Buryat café downstairs.

SAMPSONIEVSKY CATHEDRAL

Brightening up the drab industrial area of Vyborg Side, is this delightful pea-green baroque **cathedral** (Map p229; ☎ 315 4361; http://eng .cathedral.ru/sampsonievsky; 41 Bolshaya Sampsonievsky pr; adult/concession R200/100; ☼ 11am-6pm Thu-Tue; Ⓜ Vyborgskaya) dating from 1740. Catherine the Great is believed to have married her one-eyed lover Grigory Potemkin here in 1774 in a secret ceremony attended by just a couple of other people.

ST PETERSBURG

The church's most interesting feature is the calendar of saints, two enormous panels on either side of the nave, each representing six months of the year with every day decorated by a mini-icon of its saint(s). The enormous silver chandelier above the altar is also something to behold, as is the stunning baroque, green and golden iconostasis.

KRESTY PRISON

A sobering antidote to St Petersburg's high culture is a visit to its dark underbelly: **Kresty Prison** (Map p229; ☎ 542 6861; www.kresty.ru in Russian; Arsenalnaya nab 7; admission R250; ☒ tours 10.30am, noon, 1.30pm & 3pm Sat & Sun; Ⓜ Ploshchad Lenina). This deathly grim place is the city's main holding prison. Opened in 1892 with 1150 individual cells (later reconstructed and designed to hold 2065 inmates), these days close to 10,000 poor buggers are incarcerated here. Six-bed cells hold 10 to 15 people, sleeping in rotation. Tuberculosis is rife, fleas abound, and there are masked guards with ferocious dogs policing the halls.

Certainly not to everyone's taste, tours are possible of the prison and its intriguing little museum. Here the guide will tell you about past residents – such as Trotsky and the entire Provisional Government from 1917 – and you can view objects made by prisoners with lots of time on their hands. Most impressive is a chess set with a 'cops and robbers' motif made entirely from glazed bits of hardened, chewed bread. To gain entry you'll need your passport; photography is strictly forbidden.

PISKARYOVSKOE CEMETERY

Some half-million WWII victims are buried in mass graves in the **Piskaryovskoe Cemetery** (Map p229; ☎ 247 5716; Nepokoryonnikh pr; admission free; ☒ 10am-6pm; Ⓜ Ploshchad Muzhestva). Nearly 200 raised mounds are marked only by simple plaques engraved with a year and either a red star or hammer and sickle (indicating a military or civilian grave mound). At the entrance is an exhibit of photographs from the blockade that need no captions. The cemetery is about 35 minutes from the city centre on public transport. From the metro turn left, cross Nepokoryonnykh pr and take bus 123. It's the sixth stop.

Southern St Petersburg

Stalin wanted to relocate the city centre to the south and you can see some of the grand Soviet master plan along Moskovsky pr. Elsewhere, dotted around southern St Petersburg, are a few other worthwhile attractions.

MONUMENT TO THE HEROIC DEFENDERS OF LENINGRAD

On the way to or from the airport you won't miss the awe-inspiring **Monument to the Heroic Defenders of Leningrad** (Map p229; ☎ 293 6036; pl Pobedy; admission free; ☒ 10am-6pm Thu-Tue; Ⓜ Moskovskaya). Centred around a 48m-high obelisk, the monument is a sculptural ensemble of bronze statues symbolising the heavy plight of defence, and eventual victory.

On a lower level, a bronze ring 40m in diameter symbolises the city's encirclement. Haunting symphonic music creates a sombre atmosphere to guide you downstairs to the underground exhibition in a huge, mausoleum-like interior, where 900 bronze lamps create an eeriness matched by the sound of a metronome – the only sound heard by Leningraders on their radios throughout the war save for emergency announcements. Twelve thematically assembled showcases feature items from the war and Blockade. Ask to see the two seven-minute documentary films, played on large screens at the touch of a button.

RAILWAY MUSEUM

Trainspotters should hasten to view the impressive collection of full-sized locomotives at the **Railway Museum** (Map p229; ☎ 768 2063; nab Obvodnogo Kanala; adult/student R100/50; ☒ 10am-6pm; Ⓜ Baltiyskaya) behind the old Warsaw Station. Some 75 nicely painted and buffed engines and carriages are on display, including one dating from 1897.

CHESMA CHURCH

East off Moskovsky pr is the striking red-and-white 18th-century Gothic **Chesma Church** (Map p229; ☎ 443 6114; ul Lensoveta 12; admission free; ☒ 10am-7pm; Ⓜ Moskovskaya) built from 1774 to 1780 in honour of Russia's victory over the Turks at the Battle of Çesme (1770). Its relatively remote location is due to the fact that Catherine the Great was on this spot when news arrived of the victory, so that's where she ordered the church to be built.

MOSKOVSKY PROSPEKT

This long avenue, heading due south from Sennaya ploshchad to the airport, is the start of the main road to Moscow. Along it you'll find the iron **Moscow Triumphal Arch** (Map p229; **M** Moskovskiye Vorota), built in 1838 to mark victories over Turks, Persians and Poles, demolished in 1936 then rebuilt from 1959 to 1960.

Further south is **Moskovskaya ploshchad**, with its statue of Lenin and imposing **House of Soviets** (Map p229; **M** Moskovskaya), which was intended under a 1930s plan to become the new centre of St Petersburg, replacing the old tsarist centre. In a testament to the stubbornness of St Petersburgers during Stalin's terror, this plan was universally ignored.

ACTIVITIES
Banya

Tired? Frustrated by Russian bureaucracy? A good beating may be all you need – or all you need to give! Here are a few of the better *bani* (bathhouses; see p71 for correct *banya* etiquette):

Bani 43 (Map pp236-7; ☎ 571 7041; nab reki Moyki 82; **M** Sadovaya/Sennaya Ploshchad) Book this whole place out for R500 per hour at any time. The friendly guys who run it can arrange massages (R150) and will get you beer. A Russian and expat crowd often meets here on Sunday around 9.30pm.

Kruglye Bani (Map p229; ☎ 247 6409; Karbysheva ul 29A; lyux-class R140; ☑ 8am-9pm Tue-Sun; **M** Ploshchad Muzhestva) One of the city's best baths with a heated circular open-air pool. Expats meet here at 9pm Wednesday and enjoy a unisex *lyux banya*. The *banya* is opposite the metro; look for the round building across the grassy traffic island.

Mitninskaya Banya (Map pp234-5; ☎ 274 5455; ul Mytninskaya 17-19; admission R35-70; ☑ 8am-10pm Fri-Tue, last entry 8.30pm; **M** Ploshchad Vosstaniya) The last *banya* in the city to be heated with a wood furnace, just like in the countryside. You'll see lots of tattooed bodies here.

Boating, Yachting & Kayaking

Rowboats can be rented (around R150 per hour) on Yelagin Island near the bridge to the Vyborg Side. For more serious sailing contact:

Baltic Shipping Company Yacht Club (Map pp238-9; ☎ 235 3935; nab Martynova 92, Krestovsky Island; ☑ 9am-6pm Mon-Fri; **M** Krestovsky Ostrov) Arranges tours to Lakes Onega and Ladoga.

Sea and River Yacht Club (Map pp238-9; ☎ 235 0111; nab Martynova 92, Krestovsky Island; ☑ 9am-6pm Mon-Fri; **M** Krestovsky Ostrov) Come here to rent boats from private captains.

Solnechny Parus (Map pp234-5; ☎ 327 3526; www.solpar.ru; ul Vosstaniya 55; ☑ 10am-8pm Mon-Fri, to 6pm Sat; **M** Chernyshevskaya) Agency that organises yacht cruises in the Gulf of Finland.

Kayaking on Lake Ladoga can also be arranged through the friendly guys at **Wild Russia** (Map pp230-1; ☎ 313 8030; www.wildrussia.spb.ru; nab reki Fontanki 59; **M** Gostiny Dvor). They can also arrange **rock climbing** trips outside of the city.

Cycling & In-line Skating

Pancake-flat St Petersburg is a great city for cycling around (as long as you avoid the major traffic-choked roads). A good website with information on cycling events in the city is www.velopiter.spb.ru (in Russian). In-line skating is also popular; you'll often find yourself dodging young things skating down Nevsky pr and across Dvortsovaya pl. Below are listed places to rent both bikes and skates: remember to take along your passport and a sizeable chunk of roubles (around R600) for a deposit.

Jet Set (Map pp238-9; ☎ 973 2145; Pirmorsky Park Pobedy, Morskoy pr, Krestovsky Ostrov; bike rental per hr R150, per day R700, in-line skate rental per hr R100; ☑ 11am-11pm Mon-Fri, 10am-11pm Sat & Sun; **M** Krestovsky Ostrov) Also rents helmets, pads and skateboards.

Skatprokat (Map pp234-5; ☎ 8-90130 24112; www .skatprokat.ru; Goncharnaya ul 7; rental per day R300; ☑ 24hr; **M** Ploshchad Vosstaniya) They also have scooters for rent at R200 per hour.

Diving

Red Shark Dive Club (Map pp234-5; ☎ 710 2795; www.redshark.spb.ru; 5-ya Sovetskaya ul 3/13; **M** Ploshchad Vosstaniya) Offers PADI diving courses in English and can arrange wreck dives for more experienced divers in the Gulf of Finland and Lake Ladoga.

Gyms & Swimming Pools

Planet Fitness (Map pp236-7; ☎ 315 6220; Kazanskaya ul 37; entry R510, 2-week pass R2400; ☑ 7am-11pm Mon-Fri, 9am-9pm Sat & Sun; **M** Sadovaya/Sennaya Ploshchad) The cheapest and most central branch of St Petersburg's first big gym chain with eight locations citywide.

Sports Complex (Map pp238-9; ☎ 238 1632; Kronverksky pr 9A; per 90 min R100; ☑ 7am-11pm;

ST PETERSBURG

Ⓜ Gorkovskaya). Its 25m pool, under a glass roof, is heavenly and staff will let you in without the required medical certificate if you look clean. There's also a weights room.

VMF (Map pp240-1; ☎ 322 4505; Sredny pr 87, Vasilyevsky Island; admission R200; ☒ 7am-9pm; Ⓜ Vasileostrovskaya) The city's largest pool.

Ice Skating

Dvorets Sporta SKA (Map pp238-9; ☎ 237 0073; Zhdanovskaya nab 2; entry R150, skate rental per hr R60; ☒ noon-5am Fri-Sun; Ⓜ Sportivnaya) Has both indoor and outdoor rinks.

Ice Palace (Map p229; ☎ 718 6620; www.newarena .spb.ru in Russian; pr Pyatiletok1; per hr incl skates R200; Ⓜ Prospekt Bolshevikov) Fancy arena built for the 2000 World Ice Hockey Championships. Although mainly used for concerts now, it does have a public skating rink. Hours are irregular, so call for more details.

WALKING TOUR

WALK FACTS

Start St Isaac's Cathedral
Finish Krasny most
Distance 3km
Duration around two hours

The best way of experiencing St Petersburg's architectural beauty is by walking tour. This one follows a route from St Isaac's Cathedral to Palace Sq, along the loop of the Moyka River, and down the Griboedova Canal and along Gorokhovaya ul to Krasny most.

Stand in **Isaakievskaya ploshchad (1)** and admire the golden-domed **cathedral** (2; p252) and the surrounding buildings, including the **Hotel Astoria** (3; p278) and the **Mariinsky Palace (4**; not open to the public), home of the City Legislative Council. The **bronze statue (5)** is of Nicholas I on horseback, its plinth decorated with bas reliefs and figures representing Faith, Wisdom, Justice and Might.

From the square's northeast corner walk down Malaya Morskaya ul; this area was one of the wealthiest during Imperial times, hosting many financial institutions (several banks have now returned and, at No 24 Bolshaya Morksaya, the famed jewellers **Fabergé (6)**, is now the jewellers **Yakhont** (☎ 314 6415; Bolshaya Morskaya ul 24; ☒ 10am-8pm). The writers Ivan Turgenev and Nikolai Gogol

both lived at No 17 Malaya Morskaya, and Tchaikovsky died at No 13 in 1893.

On the corner of Malaya Morskaya and Nevsky pr note **Wawelburg House (7)**, a highly decorative greystone building designed after both the Doge's Palace in Venice and Florence's Palazzo Medici-Riccardi. The building is now occupied by the Central Airline Ticket Office. Cross Nevsky pr here, walk 50m east and turn left (north) at Bolshaya Morskaya ul. On the way keep an eye out for the wall of the school at **No 14 (8)** bearing a blue-and-white stencilled sign in Cyrillic maintained since WWII. It translates as 'Citizens! At times of artillery bombardment this side of the street is most dangerous!'

The most perfect way of seeing **Dvortsovaya ploshchad (9**; p251) for the first time is to approach it via Bolshaya Morskaya ul. As you turn the corner, behold the **Alexander Column (10**; p251), with the **Hermitage (11**; p244) in the background, perfectly framed under the triumphal double arch of the **General Staff Building (12**; p251). Continue walking towards the square, keeping your eyes fixed on the columns and enjoy the visual magic tricks as the perspective changes the closer you get to the arches' opening.

Head northeast across the square to Millionnaya ul, and into the **porch (13)** covering the south entrance of the New Hermitage and supported by semiclad musclemen. This was the museum's first public entrance when it opened in 1852. A favourite tourist shot is from here looking west towards St Isaac's Cathedral past the Winter Palace – you can usually fit in a few of the Atlantes, or at least a calf or two.

Walking northeast again, take the first right turn and walk along the **Zimny Canal (14)** the short block to the Moyka River (glance behind you towards the Neva for another great view). This stretch of the Moyka is lovely: cross to the east bank by the Pevchesky most and admire the views as you walk past **Pushkin's last home** (15; p257), where the poet died in 1837.

Cross the river again and head east beside the water; on the opposite bank you'll see what used to be the **Court Stables (16**; not open to the public), dating from Peter the Great's time but rebuilt in the early 19th century. One of imperial St Petersburg's flashiest streets, Bolshaya Konyushennaya ul (Big Stables St) extends south from here.

Continue along the river until you come to a very picturesque ensemble of bridges where the Moyka intersects at right angles with the start of the Griboedova Canal. While crossing over the **Malo-Konyushenny most (17)** and the pretty **Teatralny most (18)**, you'll see the **Church of the Saviour on Spilled Blood (19**; p252) across the top of the touristy souvenir kiosk canopies. Head towards the church.

Having run the gauntlet of the souvenir sellers, circle the church; on your left will be the striking Style Moderne wrought-iron fence of the **Mikhaylovsky Gardens (20)**. Walk south along Griboedova Canal until you reach the sweet footbridge that crosses it. Called the **Italyansky most (21)**, it dates from 1896, but was redesigned in 1955. Its main

purpose seems to be to afford photographers a postcard-perfect view of the Church of the Saviour on Spilled Blood. Note the amazing building on the west side of the street at No 13. Originally the **House of the Joint Credit Society (22**; not open to the public) and built in 1890, its central cupola was placed to give the appearance of a grand palace.

Continue down to Nevsky pr, where the Style Moderne **Singer Building (23**; p255) stands regally on the corner. Opposite admire the grand sweep of the **Kazan Cathedral (24**; p255), cross Nevsky pr and head south along the Griboedova Canal to the next bridge, no doubt St Petersburg's most picturesque and most photographed, the **Bankovsky most (25)**. The bridge is named after the

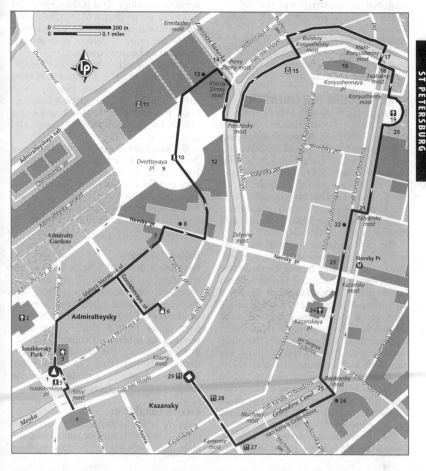

ST PETERSBURG

building behind, formerly the Assignment Bank now the **University of Economics (26)**.

If you're feeling peckish at this point continue along the canal past the wrought-iron footbridge Muchnoy most to the Kamenny most around which there are several great eating or drinking options, including the Armenian restaurant **Kilikia (27**; p282) or, slightly to the northwest along Gorokhovaya ul, **Zoom Café (28**; p282) and **Fasol (29**; p278).

COURSES

See the *St Petersburg Times* for private tutor and language class ads.

Herzen State Pedagogical University (Map pp230-1; ☎ 311 6088; www.herzen.spb.ru; nab reki Moyki 48; Ⓜ Nevsky Prospekt) Runs excellent Russian-language courses, from two weeks to graduate programs several years long, 20 hours per week, from US$4 to US$7 an hour in groups of two to eight.

Liden & Denz (Map pp234-5; ☎ 325 2241; www .lidenz.ru; Transportny per 11; Ⓜ Ligovsky Prospekt) Offers well-structured language courses from US$650 for a two-week intensive program.

ST PETERSBURG FOR CHILDREN

There's heaps to do with kids in St Petersburg – there are even museums your kids will like! For starters, **Museum of Anthropology & Ethnography** (p263) is an all-time favourite with its display of mutants in jars, as is the **Museum of Zoology** (p264) for its stuffed animals. For live animals there's the **Zoo** (p267) and a popular **Dolphinarium** (Map pp238-9; ☎ 235 4631; Konstantinovsky pr 19, Krestovsky Ostrov; admission R50; Ⓨ shows at 3pm, 5pm & 7pm Wed-Fri; extra 11am & 1pm shows Sat & Sun; Ⓜ Krestovsky Ostrov).

The city's parks are first rate and many have kids' playgrounds with swings, roundabouts and climbing frames: check out the **Tauride Gardens** (p260) and the **Mikhaylovsky Gardens** (p252). **Ramses Playground** (Map p229; ul Ziny Portnovoy; Ⓜ Leninsky Prospekt) between houses No 6 and 8 was created by retired circus clown Arkady Kontsepolsky (it's named after his beloved dog Ramses) and is a charming, inventive place that any child will love. For more high-tech amusements there's always the **Divo Ostrov** amusement park (p266) on Krestovsky Island. If you need the little darlings to burn off even more energy check out the boat, bicycle and in-line skate hiring opportunities listed on p269.

Theatres in town catering to kids include a couple offering **puppet shows** and,

of course, the **circus** (p287). And if you're looking for a fun and inexpensive place for a meal, consider **Bushe** (p282), where they decorate bliny in the shape of faces.

TOURS

There's nobody better than Peter Kozyrev or his band of knowledgeable and spritely guides, **Peter's Tours** (www.peterswalk.com), to help show you the city. Their standard walking tour (R400) departs from the HI St Petersburg Hostel (see p275) at 10.30am daily. He also offers lots of cool itineraries, around themes such as Dostoevsky, Rasputin, the Great October Revolution, and food, not to mention the ever-popular White Nights pub crawl, all in English. Customised tours kick off at R800 per hour for up to four people during May to November. Also consider using him for guided tours out to the Imperial Palaces or to arrange transport and airport transfers.

Eclectica (Map pp230-1; ☎ 710 5942; www.eclectica .spb.ru in Russian; Office 4, 5th fl, Nevsky pr 44; Ⓜ Nevsky Prospekt) has booths outside Gostiny Dvor, which sell tickets for English-language tours around the city and to major sights outside the city such as Petrodvorets and Tsarskoe Selo.

Monomex Tours (Map pp234-5; ☎ 445 0159; www .2russia.com; Zanevsky pr 1; Ⓜ Zanevskaya Ploshchad) offers exotic sociological tours, including ones entitled Russian Child Rearing Practices and Police Enforcement, while **Ost-West Kontaktservice** (p243) can arrange more standard tours of the city and surroundings sights.

Helicopter Tours

Baltic Airlines (Map pp230-1; ☎ 704 1676; www.baltic airlines.ru/en/; 2nd fl, Nevsky pr 7/4; 10-15 min R1000; Ⓜ Nevsky Prospekt) offers helicopter flights over the Neva between the Admiralty and Smolny, which take off at regular intervals from in front of the Peter & Paul Fortress every weekend from May to October. They also fly three times a day on weekends to Petrodvorets (p295) and back (R1000 one-way). You can also arrange a tandem parachute jump with the same company for R5000.

River & Canal Trips

Viewing St Petersburg from a boat is an idyllic way to tour the city, and during the main tourist season (May to October) there are no shortage of ways to do this. First up there are four fixed route hourly hop-on, hop-off cruises on large **water buses** (tickets R200; ◷ 11am-7pm). The routes are:

Line A (Map p265; 55 min) Peter & Paul Fortress, Kunstkamera, the Admiralty Pier, Summer Gardens, Mikhaylovsky Gardens, Pushkin Flat Museum on the Moyka, Peter & Paul Fortress.

Line B (Map pp230-1; 90 min) Kazansky most, Mikhaylovsky Gardens, Anichkov Palace, Lomonosova Ploshchad, St Nicholas Cathedral of the Epiphany, Sennaya Ploshchad, Bankovsky most, Kazansky most.

Line C (Map pp230-1; 80 min) Stroganov Palace, Dvortsovaya Ploshchad, Mikhaylovsky Gardens, Lomonosova Ploshchad, Yusupov Palace, St Isaac's Cathedral, Stroganov Palace.

Line D (Map pp230-1; 90 min) Admiralty Pier, Hotel Okhtinskaya, Hotel St Petersburg, Peter & Paul Fortress, Admiralty Pier.

A fifth route runs on weekends only between the Admiralty and Yelagin Island.

In addition there are many private operators of smaller **cruise boats** (from around R150 for 40 minutes) – these boats are typically found at the Anichkov most landing on the Fontanka River, just off Nevsky pr; on the Neva outside the Hermitage and the Admiralty; beside the Kazansky most over the Griboedova Canal; and along the Moyka River at Nevsky pr. At the same places you'll find moored small boats that can be hired as private water taxis. You'll have to haggle over rates: expect to pay around R1500 an hour for a small group.

FESTIVALS & EVENTS

Petersburgers, even more than their famously festive fellow countrymen, love a good knees-up. Whether it be through the carnival atmosphere of those endless summer nights or merrymaking during the freezing, dark winter days, rarely more than a week or two passes without special events taking place. See p707 for general Russian holidays.

February
Mariinsky Ballet Festival (www.mariinksy.ru) The city's principal dance theatre (p287) hosts this week-long international festival, usually in mid- to late-February.

April
Sergei Kuryokhin International Festival (SKIF) Three-day avant-garde festival in late April bringing

together an array of international figures of alternative modern music and performance. Named after the eclectic Russian musician Sergei Kuryokhin, a key part of the Leningrad rock and jazz underground of the 1970s who died in 1996.

Easter (Paskha) Head to Kazan Cathedral (p255) to see Russia's most important religious festival in full Russian Orthodox style.

May
International Labour Day/Spring Festival The vast Soviet era parades down Nevsky pr to Dvortsovaya pl may now be smaller and more subdued, but they still happen and 1 May remains a time for communist demonstrations and merrymaking.

Victory Day (1945) On 9 May St Petersburg celebrates not only the end of WWII but also the breaking of the Nazi blockade. The highlight is a victory parade on Nevsky pr, culminating in soldiers marching on Dvortsovaya pl and fireworks over the Neva in the evening.

City Day Mass celebrations and merrymaking are held throughout St Petersburg on 27 May, the city's official birthday.

June
KlezFest Mid-June music festival celebrating Klezmer, or Eastern European Jewish folk music with a busy programme of concerts, walking tours about Jewish history and lectures.

Beer Festival One of the city's best-attended festivals, for unsurprising reasons, held annually in mid-June in the Peter and Paul Fortress.

Festival of Festivals (www.filmfest.ru) Annual international film festival held in late June that's a noncompetitive showcase of the best Russian and world cinema.

Stars of the White Nights Festival Held at the Mariinsky, the Conservatoire and the Hermitage Theatre, this festival from late May until July has become a huge draw and now lasts far longer than the White Nights (officially the last 10 days of June) after which it is named.

August
Sailing Week Hundreds of competitors take part in a 150km race from Vyborg to St Petersburg in late August, part of a regatta founded by the sailing union of the city on the Neva in 1898.

September & October
Early Music Festival (www.earlymusic.ru) Held from mid-September until early October, this groundbreaking musical festival includes performances of forgotten masterpieces from the age of Catherine the Great, including operas and performances from the Catherine the Great opera.

GAY & LESBIAN ST PETERSBURG

There's a small but reasonably vibrant gay scene in St Petersburg, including Russia's only lesbian club **Tri El** (Map pp234-5; ☎ 710 2016; 5-ya Sovetskaya ul 45; admission R150 Wed, Fri & Sat; ✆ 6pm-midnight Mon & Tue, Wed 9pm-6am Wed, 7pm-midnight Thu, 10pm-6am Fri & Sat; **M** Ploschad Vosstaniya). Tri El allows only men in on Thursday and Fridays; a mixed crowd is welcome at all other gay venues.

The main club remains the sleazy but fun **Greshniki** (Sinners; Map pp230-1; ☎ 570 4291; www .greshniki.ru in Russian; nab kanala Griboedova 29; cover for men free-R200, women R200-500; ✆ 6pm-6am; **M** Nevsky Prospekt), with its leather and chains décor, male strippers and drag queens. Late night male strip shows also feature on the bill at club Ty v Teme?! at **Objekt** (Map pp236-7; ☎ 921 791 3012; nab reki Moyki 82; admission R150; ✆ 10pm-6am Sun & Tue; **M** Sadovaya/Sennaya Ploshchad), which attracts a glam, gay-friendly crowd. For a more intimate bar head to tiny **Mono** (Map pp234-5; ☎ 764 3678; www.monoclub.ru; Kolomenskaya ul 4; cover for men R50-100, women R200; ✆ 10pm-6am), a friendly, pleasantly decorated place with reasonably priced drinks. Thursday is for women when the cover prices are reversed.

Useful sources of information on the gay scene include the rather earnest **Krilija** (Wings; ☎ 312 3180; www.krilija.sp.ru/3eng.htm), Russia's oldest officially registered gay and lesbian community organisation; the website **Excess** (www.xs.gay.ru/english/) which has a link to the gay tour agency **Discover Gay St Petersburg** (www.discovergaypetersburg.com/eng.shtml), who promise, among other things, tours taking in the homoerotic art of the Hermitage!

December
Russian Winter Festival Tourist-oriented troika rides, folklore shows, games held outside of the city from 25 December to 5 January.

Arts Square Winter Festival (www.artsquarewinter-fest.ru) A musical highlight of the year, this festival, held late December to early January at the Philharmonic (p286), takes different themes each year, and stages both classical and contemporary opera and orchestral works.

SLEEPING

In the last few years 'minihotels' (basically small, often family run, B&B operations offering anything from three to 30 rooms) have practically taken over central St Petersburg. Many of these minihotels, pleasant as they are compared to the drab Soviet megahotels of yesteryear, are interchangeable and, frankly, overpriced for what they offer: we list the best ones we found, but there are sure to be more by the time this guide is published.

There are also quite a few new hostels which is great for the budget traveller since St Petersburg remains an expensive city in which to bed down, particularly at the height of the summer. For this reason we've also included brief details of the best out-of-centre and Soviet hotels (ie the ones that have seen some smartening of rooms and management attitudes): when the city gets really packed these may be your only option. Many are also favoured by package

tour operators. Also consider home stays and apartment rentals: the latter can work out as the best deal for groups of travellers sharing or families.

Hotel bills in St Petersburg are always paid in roubles but prices can be listed in roubles, US dollars, euros and sometimes 'units' which is whatever exchange rate the hotel feels like charging. The prices listed here reflect this and are all for highseason (always June, often May and July, too). Note that all the top-end accommodation prices exclude the standard 18% VAT. Out-of-season rates at all hotels can tumble, sometimes by up to half what is quoted here.

The most convenient area to stay for all the major sights is the historic centre, but options around Liteyny pr and the Vladmirskaya and Ploshchad Vostanniya metro stations are also well located. Smolny is a much quieter and less convenient neighbourhood.

West of the historic centre, Mariinsky and Sennaya have some appealing options. Vasilyevsky Island, Vyborg Side and Southern St Petersburg are all less convenient for the main sights but are quieter places to stay if that's what you're looking for.

Homestays & Apartment Rentals
These agencies can arrange apartment rentals:

City Realty (Map pp236-7; ☎ 312 7842; www.city realtyrussia.com; Bolshaya Morskaya ul 35; **M** Nevsky

Prospekt) Has a good range of short- and long-term rental apartments, and can help you buy a place should you really like the city.

Host Families Association (HOFA; Map pp234-5; ☎ /fax 275 1992; http://webcenter.ru/~hofa; ul Tavricheskaya 5/25; M Ploshchad Vosstaniya) The most established and reliable agency for private accommodation. Its homestays start with basic B&B (s/d from US$25/40).

Nevsky Prostor (Map pp240-1; ☎ 325 3838; www .spb-estate.com/eng/; 5th fl Galerny proezd 3, Vasilyevsky Island; M Primorskaya) Has a great website that can help you locate the ideal apartment.

Ost-West Kontaktservice (p243) This agency also arranges homestays and apartment rentals from about US$50 a day.

Budget

HISTORIC CENTRE

Nord Hostel (Map pp230-1; ☎ 571 0342; www.nord hostel.com; Bolshaya Morskaya ul 10; dm/d with breakfast €24/48; 🖳; M Nevsky Prospekt) Located just seconds from Dvortsovaya pl this is an ideal budget base for exploring the city. The spacious dorms in this elegant old building have newish Ikea fittings (one even has a piano!). Other pluses include free Internet and international calls. On the downside they are bad at answering the phone, so best to book in advance via the Web.

Nauka (Map pp230-1; ☎ 315 3368; Millionnaya ul 27; s €20-30, d €25-45, tr/q €20/26; M Nevsky Prospekt) A minute's walk from the Winter Palace, this Soviet hotel is superb value. Rooms are basic with clean, shared facilities (there's a R25 charge for a shower). Enter via the courtyard and take the ancient lift to the 3rd floor. Bookings are recommended and no English is spoken.

Herzen University Hotel (Map pp230-1; ☎ 314 7472; hotel@herzen.spb.ru; Kazanskaya ul 6; s/d R1600/2300; 🖳; M Nevsky Prospekt) This hotel has a great location behind Kazan Cathedral. The old-fashioned rooms, with TV and fridge, are fine, but the hotel cannot register your visa, so you'll have to find an alternative way of doing this. Availability is tight, especially in summer, so make a reservation, for which there will be a 25% extra charge for the first night.

LITEYNY, SMOLNY, VLADIMIRSKAYA & VOSTANNIYA

Russian Room (Map pp234-5; ☎ 900 9928; www.russian room.org; Apt 32, Vilensky per 5; dm/d with breakfast €15/35; 🖳; M Ploshchad Vosstaniya) This branch is the main location of the two belonging to Russian Room (the other, which is open in summer only, is at ul Pestelya 13/15) . Russian Room gives budget travellers a chance to experience life in a cosy Russian apartment. The manager Andrei is very friendly. You'll need to make a booking; they can also arrange visa invitations for €22 and registration for €10.

Sleep Cheap (Map pp234-5; ☎ 715 1304; www .sleepcheap.spb.ru; Mokhovaya ul 18/32; dm €19; 🖳; M Chernyshevskaya) The eight-bed dorms at this minihostel are spotlessly clean and all facilities are modern and in good condition. Airport pick-up is just €10 per person – a great deal if there's one of you, but less so if there's more.

Hotel California (Map pp234-5; ☎ 901 301 6061; www.hotelcalifornia.ru; Apt 36, ul Marata 67/17; dm with breakfast from €16; 🖳; M Vladimirskaya) The entrance to this well-equipped, comfortable new hostel is actually through the courtyard on Sotsialisticheskaya ul. It's run by some of the musicians from local band Dva Samoliota and promises to be a lively place to stay, with visiting musos given preference.

HI St Petersburg International Hostel (Map pp234-5; ☎ 329 8018; www.ryh.ru; 3-ya Sovetskaya ul 28; dm/d with breakfast US$23/56; 🖳; M Ploshchad Vosstaniya) St Petersburg's longest-running hostel remains popular. The clean, simply furnished dorms have three to six beds and there's one double; all rates are slightly cheaper from November to March and for ISIC and HI cardholders. It's just a five-minute walk northeast of Moskovsky vokzal. There's also a kitchen for self-catering and a video room. Note they don't accept credit card payment in the hostel.

St Petersburg Puppet Hostel (Map pp234-5; ☎ 272 5401; www.hostelling-russia.ru; ul Nekrasova 12; dm/d with breakfast US$21/52; 🖳; M Mayakovskaya) This is a great budget option if you can get a bed. It's also an ideal choice if you're travelling with kids because it gives free tickets to the puppet theatre next door.

Zimmer Frei (Map pp234-5; ☎ 273 0867; www .zimmer.ru; Apt 23, Liteyny pr 46; s & d €18; M Mayakovskaya) Enter this curious apartment hotel from the unmarked black door on Liteyny pr. Basic, but very good value, the seven rooms sleep two to four people and share toilet and kitchen facilities. It feels more like an apartment than a hotel.

ST PETERSBURG

Also recommended are these two Soviet old-timers:

Hotel Mercury (Map pp234-5; ☎ 325 6444; fax 576 7977; Tavricheskaya ul 39; s/d with breakfast R1920/2340; M Chernyshevskaya)

Hotel Neva (Map pp234-5; ☎ 278 0500; www .nevahotel.spb.ru; ul Chaykovskogo 17; s/d with breakfast, unmodernised rooms R1700/2400, modernised rooms R2200/3200; M Chernyshevskaya)

MARIINSKY & SENNAYA

Hostel Na Sadovoy (Map pp236-7; ☎ 314 8357; www .budget-travel.spb.ru; Sadovaya ul 53; dm/d with breakfast $22/55; ⌨ ; M Sadovaya/Sennaya Ploshchad) Run by the ex manager of the HI St Petersburg Hostel this new hostel on the 4th floor of the Na Sadovoy Hotel is a welcome addition to the backpacker scene. It has clean four-bed dorms, a good location and clued-up English-speaking staff.

Domik v Kolomne (Map pp236-7; ☎ 710 8351; www .colomna.nm.ru; nab kanala Griboedova 174A; s/d without bathroom €20/25, s/d €40/45; M Sadovaya/Sennaya Ploshchad) Pushkin's family once rented rooms in this house, and the atmosphere of a large flat remains. Rooms, some with lovely views across the canal, have a homely Russian feel.

VASILYEVSKY ISLAND, VYBORG SIDE & SOUTHERN ST PETERSBURG

Petrovskogo College Student Hostel (Map p229; ☎ 252 7563; vassina@mail.wplus.net; Baltiyskaya ul 26; s/d/tr R300/600/900; M Narvskaya) While not close to the centre, this is certainly the cheapest accommodation deal in town. The shared showers and toilets are OK and there's a cafeteria. Reserve in advance though, as it's often full. From the metro walk south down pr Stachek away from the Narva Triumphal Gates to Baltiyskaya ul, where you turn left and continue another 500m.

Midrange

HISTORIC CENTRE

Rachmaninow Antique-Hotel (Map pp230-1; ☎ 327 7466; www.kazansky5.com; Kazanskaya ul 5, 3rd fl; s & d with breakfast from US$170; ⌨ ⌨ ; M Nevsky Prospekt) A boho crowd hang out at this super stylish minihotel, where minimalist décor is offset by antiques. There are contemporary photography and painting displays throughout the premises.

Pushka Inn (Map pp230-1; ☎ 312 0957; www .pushkainn.ru; nab reki Moyki 14; s/d/apt with breakfast from €100/160/200; ⌨ ⌨ ; M Nevsky Prospekt) Modern

furnished rooms and apartments, some overlooking one of the city's prettiest stretches of canal. There's 20% off the menu for guests at its popular café-bar. Their spacious, well-equipped apartments are a great deal.

Polikoff Hotel (Map pp230-1; ☎ 314 7925; www .polikoff.ru; Nevsky pr 64/11; s/d with breakfast from €80/100; ⌨ ⌨ ; M Gostiny Dvor) Tricky to find (the entrance is through the brown door on Karavannaya ul, where you'll need to punch in 26 for reception) the Polikoff Hotel is worth hunting out for its rooms brimming with contemporary cool décor, quiet but central location and pleasant service.

Hotels on Nevsky Association (☎ 703 3860; www .hon.ru; s/d incl breakfast from €120/140; ⌨); Deluxe (Map pp230-1; ☎ 7033860; Bolshaya Konushennaya ul 14; M Nevsky Prospekt); Nevsky pr 22 (Map pp230-1; ☎ 312 1206; M Nevsky Prospekt); Nevsky pr 90 (Map pp234-5; ☎ 273 7314; M Mayakovskaya); Nevsky pr 91 (Map pp234-5; ☎ 277 1888; M Mayakovskaya) This excellent group of minihotels provides decent accommodation spread over four locations. Check out the website for more detailed information on each of the hotels, and apartments also managed by the same group – there are stylish touches to rooms not present in other minihotels and kitchens are available for guest use.

Korona (Map pp230-1; ☎ 571 0086; www.korona-spb .com; 2nd fl, Malaya Konyushennaya ul 7; s/d/apt with breakfast from €134/174/242; ⌨ ⌨ ; M Nevsky Prospekt) The lurid colour scheme of this minihotel is compensated for by its big rooms, good location and helpful staff. The apartments, of which there are three, come with minisaunas.

Turgeniev (Map pp230-1; ☎ 314 4529, fax 571 5180; Bolshaya Konyushennaya ul 13; s & d with breakfast from €90; Ⓜ Nevsky Prospekt) You must book ahead for the four very sweet rooms furnished with antiques (and no modern contraptions such as TV or telephone) at this cosy B&B tucked away in a courtyard off the street; they will meet you at the airport too.

LITEYNY, SMOLNY, VLADIMIRSKAYA & VOSTANNIYA

Arbat Nord Hotel (Map pp234-5; ☎ 703 1899; www .arbat-nord.ru; Artilleriyskaya ul 4; s/d with breakfast €185/195; ⓧ 🖳 ; Ⓜ Chernyshevskaya) This sleek newcomer shows its ugly Soviet neighbour the Hotel Rus, across the road, how to run a good establishment. It offers comfortable rooms, friendly English-speaking staff and a restaurant downstairs.

Brothers Karamazov (Map pp234-5; ☎ 335 1185; www.karamazovhotel.ru; Sotsialisticheskaya ul 11A; s/d with breakfast R3700/4240, prices quoted in units; ⓧ 🖳 ; Ⓜ Vladimirskaya) Even though the 28 uniformly large rooms at this appealing hotel are furnished in a vaguely antiquey way, the overall feel is contemporary. It's professionally run and in a quiet, but handy location.

Marshal Hotel (Map pp234-5; ☎ 279 9955; www .marshal-hotel.spb.ru; Shpalernaya ul 41; d with breakfast from R3980; ⓧ 🖳 ; Ⓜ Chernyshevskaya) Professional service, large, modern rooms and a quiet location on the way to Smolny Cathedral are all in this hotel's favour. Dirty weekenders should request room 9 (R7950), which has a water bed!

Kristoff Hotel (Map pp234-5; ☎ 571 6643; www .kristoff.ru; Zagorodny pr 9; s/d with breakfast €110/130; ⓧ 🖳 ; Ⓜ Dostoevskaya) The 15 good-value rooms here are smart and modern with perks including wi-fi (€10 per day). Downstairs is a popular Russian-European restaurant which is worth a visit in its own right.

Five Corners Hotel (Map pp234-5; ☎ 380 8181; www.5ugol.ru; Zagorodny pr 13; s/d with breakfast from €150/170; ⓧ 🖳 ; Ⓜ Dostoevskaya) This hotel's stylish rooms, decorated in warm colours and with huge beds, overlook the trendy hub of streets at the 'Five Corners' intersection. Staff are polite and efficient, rates include free Internet access and expansion is on the cards.

Vesta Hotel (Map pp234-5; ☎ 272 1322; www.vesta hotel.spb.ru; Nevsky pr 90/92; s/d with breakfast €80/100; Ⓜ Mayakovskaya). Walk right back into the courtyard (which has a kid's playground designed as a pirate ship) to find this mini-hotel. Rooms are nothing flash but they are friendly and clued up and it would be a good place if you have kids.

Oktyabrsky Filial (Map pp234-5; ☎ 718 1515; www .oktober-hotel.spb.ru; Ligovsky pr 43/45; s/d with breakfast R3500/5100; Ⓜ Ploshchad Vosstaniya) Smaller, sister establishment of the Oktyabrskaya Hotel across the square, the Filial has a great location and has improved its service and room décor immeasurably since Soviet days. Book well in advance in summer as it's popular with tour groups.

Also recommended:

Oktyabrskaya Hotel (Map pp234-5; ☎ 718 1515; Ligovsky pr 10; Nevsky section s/d with breakfast from R3200/4800, Oktyabrskaya section s/d with breakfast R3800/5400; 🖳 ⓧ ; Ⓜ Ploshchad Vosstaniya)

MARIINSKY & SENNAYA

Matisov Domik (Map pp236-7; ☎ 318 7051; www .matisov.spb.ru; nab reki Pryazhki 3/1; s/d/apt with breakfast from R2700/3900/6000, prices quoted in units; ⓧ 🖳 Ⓟ ; Ⓜ Sadovaya/Sennaya Ploshchad) There's a good range of rooms available at this comfortable, but somewhat remote, place a short walk west of the Mariinsky Theatre. It's a well run operation and there's also a secure courtyard for parking should you have a vehicle.

VASILYEVSKY ISLAND, VYBORG SIDE & SOUTHERN ST PETERSBURG

Prestige Hotel (Map pp240-1; ☎ 328 5338; www .prestige-hotels.com; 3-aya Linia 52; s/d with breakfast from US$116/141; 🖳 ; Ⓜ Vasileostrovskaya) The single rooms here have double beds making this modern, light-blue-painted minihotel a good deal for a couple. The deluxe rooms have Jacuzzi baths. The English-speaking staff are very welcoming. Look for the flags outside the building.

SPB Vergaz (Map pp240-1; ☎ 327 8883; hotel@ vergaz.spb.ru; 7-aya Linia 70; s/d/apt €90/140/160; Ⓜ Va-sileostrovskaya) Staff here are great and the rooms decent and smart. The apartment is a good deal, and includes an office and kitchen, as well as a bedroom and sitting room. All rooms have cable TV and a mini-bar and breakfast is €6.

Hotel St Petersburg (Map p229; ☎ 380 1919; www.hotel-spb.ru; Pirogovskaya nab 5/2; s/d incl break-fast unrenovated room US$79/104, renovated room US$110/140; Ⓜ Ploshchad Lenina) If you are going to stay in an old Soviet dinosaur, you may as well make it this one as its rooms, both unrenovated and renovated, have glorious views across the Neva towards the Hermitage, and are not badly priced for what they offer.

Top End
HISTORIC CENTRE
Note none of the rates includes breakfast which can cost up to US$34 for the buffet spread at the Grand Hotel Europe.

Grand Hotel Europe (Map pp230-1; ☎ 329 6000; www.grand-hotel-europe.com; Mikhaylovskaya ul 1/7; s/d/ste from US$470/510/690; ⌧ ⌧ ⌧; Ⓜ Nevsky Prospekt) The rooms at this luxurious hotel occupying one of the city's top heritage buildings (p255) uniformly have a refined elegance. Deservedly popular are the 17 terrace rooms which afford spectacular views across the city's rooftops. The beautiful Style Moderne décor of some of its bars and restaurants (particularly *Europe*), are worth a look in their own right.

Hotel Astoria (Map pp230-1; ☎ 313 5757; www.astoria.spb.ru/; Bolshaya Morskaya ul 39; s/d/ste from €340/390/710; ⌧ ⌧ ⌧; Ⓜ Nevsky Prospekt) Right in front of St Isaac's Cathedral, the Astoria is the very essence of old-world class. The pricier rooms and suites are decorated with original period antique furniture. Its easy to see why Hitler wanted to hold his victory celebration here, and why US President George W Bush checked in during his 2002 summit with Putin. If nothing else, drop by for afternoon tea (3-6pm, €16) in the lounge with harp music accompanying cakes, sandwiches and a range of teas.

Hotel D'Angleterre (Map pp230-1; ☎ 313 5787; www.angleterrehotel.com; ul Bolshaya Morskaya 39; s & d/ste from €299/455; ⌧ ⌧ ⌧; Ⓜ Nevsky Prospekt) The cheaper sister establishment to the adjoining Astoria, sports an appealing contemporary design in its rooms with parquet floors; the hotel's *Borsalino* brasserie is a relaxed place with great views of St Isaac's and live jazz in the evenings. The gym has a 7m-long plunge pool, big enough for the kids to splash in.

MARIINSKY & SENNAYA
Alexander House (Map pp236-7; ☎ 259 6877; www.a-house.ru; nab Krukova kanala 27; s/d with breakfast from R4995/5735, prices quoted in units; ⌧ ⌧; Ⓜ Sadovaya/Sennaya Ploshchad) With a prime location for the Mariinsky, this boutique hotel's 14 spacious rooms are each named and tastefully styled

after the world's top cities; try Amsterdam up in the attic or Rome with a view over the canal. There's a comfortable lounge area with an attached kitchen for guests' use, a separate library and a restaurant.

Renaissance St Petersburg Baltic Hotel (Map pp236-7; ☎ 380 4000; www.renaissancehotels.com; Pochtamtskaya ul 4; s & d/ste from US$450/680; ⌧ ⌧ ⌧; Ⓜ Sadovaya/Sennaya Ploshchad) Behind the regal heritage façade lies one of the city's newest five-star establishments which means that its rooms have modern luxuries such as broadband and wi-fi Internet connections. The majority of the rooms look out onto the atrium foyer which rises up eight floors, but the best suites have superb views of St Isaac's cupola.

EATING
Get ready to feast because in terms of range of restaurants, quality and value for money St Petersburg is the best place in Russia to dine. There are places to suit all budgets and while theme restaurants (everything from King Arthur's Camelot to Soviet kitsch) remain popular, we can happily report that the food is now, often as not, very palatable. Telephone numbers are included for places where booking is advisable and opening hours where they differ significantly from the standard, as shown on the inside front cover.

If you want to put together a picnic or get breakfast supplies we list some central supermarkets and markets on p284.

Restaurants
HISTORIC CENTRE
Fasol (Map pp230-1; ☎ 571 0907; Gorokhovaya ul 17; mains R150; Ⓜ Nevsky Prospekt) A few of the modern Russian style dishes at this chic minimalist design café include the namesake beans (*fasol*), but we really love their *forshmak* (chopped herring salad) with freshly fried potato pancakes. The atmosphere is relaxed making it a wonderful place to just hang out.

Spoon Café (Map pp230-1; ☎ 999 9191; Bolshaya Morskaya ul 13; mains R350; ⏰ 8am-midnight; Ⓜ Nevsky Prospekt) This exercise in St Petersburg cool actually delivers well on food, particularly its pasta and salads. Take your pick from the Philippe Starck–style café, good for breakfast, or the more traditional Russian room, perfect for a romantic dinner.

Yerevan (Map pp230-1; ☎ 703 3820; nab reki Fontanki 51; mains R400-500; Ⓜ Gostiny Dvor) This classy Armenian restaurant has appealing ethnic design touches and equally impressive traditional food made with ingredients they promise are from 'ecologically pure' regions of Armenia.

Tandoori Nights (Map pp230-1; ☎ 312 8782; Voznesensky pr 4; mains R300-400, prices in units; Ⓜ Nevsky Prospekt) Certainly the city's most stylish Indian restaurant also arguably serves the tastiest food too, offering a mix of traditional and modern recipes road-tested by a top London-Indian chef. There's a good selection of vegetarian options, too.

Silk (Map pp230-1; ☎ 571 5078; ul Malaya Konyushennaya 4/2; mains R400; Ⓜ Nevsky Prospekt) Dreamy Café-del-Mar-style place, with gauze drapes, soft lighting and lounge-all-night sofas. It also makes a very decent fist of its Japanese dishes, particularly sushi, a set plate of which is R600.

Taverna Olivia (Map pp230-1; ☎ 314 6563; Bolshaya Morskaya ul 31; mains R200; Ⓜ Nevsky Prospekt) A superb addition to the St Petersburg dining scene, there is nothing taverna-like about this cavernous place, subtly painted and decorated in an array of Greek styles. The menu is traditional and the food is both excellent value and extremely good – especially the salad bar.

Sukawati (Map pp230-1; ☎ 312 0540; Kazanskaya ul 8; mains R160; Ⓧ noon-5am; Ⓜ Nevsky Prospekt) The first Indonesian restaurant in Russia has impressed the in-crowd with its stylish ethnic décor and delicious, reasonably authentic fare including plenty of dishes for vegetarians. Their business lunch (R190) is a great deal.

Onegin (Map pp230-1; ☎ 571 8384; Sadovaya ul 11; mains R400-900; Ⓧ 5pm-2am; Ⓜ Gostiny Dvor) Down a small staircase and barely marked at street level Onegin is one of the city's hippest and most OTT-designed spaces, where antiques, purple velvet, plastic chairs and chandeliers all jostle for attention. Even though its predominantly a late night drinking haunt, the food here, ranging from traditional Russian to more modern dishes, is excellent, and their rich Imperial fish soup is a meal in itself.

Park Dzhuzeppe (Map pp230-1; ☎ 318 6289; nab kanala Griboedova 2B; Ⓧ 11am-3am; Ⓜ Nevsky Prospekt) This building was once the toilet block in the Mikhaylovsky Gardens, but has now expanded into an appealing Italian restaurant on two levels, with a pleasant outdoor area in summer. Their pastas and pizzas are authentic.

Yakitoriya pl Ostrovskogo (Map pp230-1; ☎ 315 8343; pl Ostrovskogo; mains R300; Ⓧ 11am-6am; Ⓜ Gostiny Dvor); Petrovskaya nab (Map pp238-9; ☎ 970 4858; Petrovskaya nab 4; Ⓜ Gorkovskaya) The more central of this Japanese restaurant chain's two branches is on pl Ostrovskogo. The other branch is located in Petrograd Side. With its authentic preparation of a huge range of sushi, and all at great value, it's easy to see why it has been so successful.

Tandoor (Map pp230-1; ☎ 312 3886; Voznesensky pr 2; meals R300-600; Ⓜ Nevsky Prospekt) This long-established Indian restaurant has glitzy décor, courteous service and a full, albeit Russianised, menu.

Taleon Club (Map pp230-1; ☎ 312 5373; www .taleon.ru; nab reki Moyki 59; Sunday brunch US$45; Ⓧ noon-4am; Ⓜ Nevsky Prospekt) *The* place to splurge on Sunday brunch, the Taleon Club is a voluptuous affair with as much caviar, oysters and Shampanskoye as you can guzzle. Dress smartly and take along some ID so you can be made a member for entry.

LITEYNY, SMOLNY, VLADIMIRSKAYA & VOSTANNIYA

Gin-No-Taki (Map pp234-5; ☎ 272 0958; pr Chernyshevskogo 17; mains R150-500; Ⓧ 11am-6am; Ⓜ Chernyshevskaya) In a city awash with wannabe Japanese restaurants, this large and lively operation is one of the most authentic with a good range of well-prepared dishes. Should

---

AUTHOR'S CHOICE

There are more elaborate restaurants in St Petersburg and, lord knows, more expensive ones, but when it comes to fine food, service and romantic candlelit ambience few places compare to **Mechta Molokhovets** (Molokhovets' Dream; Map pp234-5; ☎ 279 2247; ul Radisheva 10; mains R900; Ⓜ Ploshchad Vosstaniya). Inspired by the cookbook of Yelena Molokhovets, the Russian Mrs Beeton of the 19th century, the menu covers all the classics from borsch to beef Stroganov. Their speciality is koulibiaca, a golden pastry pie of either fish (R1190) or rabbit and cabbage (R990) – worth every rouble as is their berry kissel, a delicious sweet soup of brambles and wine.

RUSSIA'S MOST EXPENSIVE RESTAURANT

Discretely hidden at the back of the Stroganov Palace is **Russian Empire** (Map pp230–1; ☎ 571 2409; www.concordcatering.com; Nevsky pr 17; mains R1500; Ⓜ Nevsky Prospekt), a place which proclaims itself to be the 'most expensive restaurant in Russia'. Well, if you thrown caution and your platinum credit card to the wind in its outstanding wine cellar, then the bill will undoubtedly mount up, but otherwise its possible to dine here without busting your travel budget. The showily opulent décor of the restaurant's intimate rooms, including Versace-designed plates to match the elaborately painted walls and copies of paintings from the Russian Museum and porcelain candlesticks from Versailles, is matched by the richness of the silver-served food; the excellent deer Stroganov (R1800) with truffle-flecked creamed potatoes was a meal on its own. The atmosphere isn't nearly as snooty as other places in town and management will keep surprising you with little treats. If you really get sloshed, for an extra US$1000 it's possible to bunk down in a handsomely appointed suite in the very cellar where Alexander Stroganov used to hide out.

---

you be inspired by the cooking there's a Japanese grocery shop next door.

Imbir (Map pp234–5; ☎ 713 3215; Zagorodny pr 15; mains R200; ⏰ noon–2am; Ⓜ Dostoevskaya) Coming to you from the same people behind Fasol (p278) the effortlessly cool Imbir inventively combines ornate tsarist décor with contemporary design. It's always full of a trendy local crowd who come here for good coffee and a very reasonably priced menu.

Kafe Kat (Map pp234–5; ☎ 311 3377; Stremyannaya ul 22; mains R200; Ⓜ Mayakovskaya) This cosy restaurant, with fake vines hanging from the ceiling, has been dishing up Georgian favourites for an age. A selection of appetisers plus the cheese bread will fill you up; also sample some of their fine Georgian wines.

Matrosskaya Tishina (Map pp234–5; ☎ 764 4413; ul Marata 54/34; mains R600; Ⓜ Ligovsky Pr) The comic book metallic-maritime design of this seafood restaurant complements the excellent menu of grilled, baked and fried fish. You can even pick which trout or perch you want to end up on your plate.

Trattoria Pompei (Map pp234–5; ☎ 571 2551; ul Ryubinshteina 15/17; mains R400–500 prices in euros; ⏰ 5pm–11pm; Ⓜ Mayakovskaya) Run by an Italian this convivial, unflashy place gets the thumbs up from expats for its great rustic Italian home-cooking plus excellent desserts. Go for the daily specials.

Caravan Saray (Map pp234–5; ☎ 272 7129; ul Nekrasova 1; mains R300; Ⓜ Mayakovskaya) Tasty Uzbek cuisine is served here in an atmospheric Central Asian setting with a side order of belly dancing on some nights.

Bistrot Garçon (Map pp234–5; ☎ 277 2467; Nevsky pr 95; main R800–1000; ⏰ 9am–1am; Ⓜ Ploshchad Vosstaniya) Although this bistro is like stepping into a French film set, it's saved from being too kitsch by professional service and delightful, authentic cuisine. Sometimes the atmosphere is enhanced by an accordion player and a Piaf-wannabe. Breakfast is available too.

Landskrona (Map pp234–5; ☎ 380 2001; 8th fl, Corinthia Nevskij Palace Hotel, Nevsky pr 57; mains from R400; ⏰ 6pm–midnight; Ⓜ Mayakovskaya) Dress smartly for this upmarket Mediterranean restaurant which really comes into its own in summer when its outdoor terrace seats afford panoramic views of the city.

Tres Amigos (Map pp234–5; ☎ 572-2685; ul Rubinshteyna 25; mains R250; Ⓜ Dostoevskaya) Colourfully decorated and fun Mexican joint with all the usual dishes in place such as guacamole (R120) and beef taco salad (R230).

Propaganda Anichov most (Map pp234–5; ☎ 275 3558; nab reki Fontanki 40; mains R300; ⏰ noon–3am; Ⓜ Gostiny Dvor); Petrograd Side (Map pp238–9; ☎ 233 7042; Bolshoy pr 38/40; Ⓜ Chkalovskaya) Constructivism is the theme of Propoganda's main casual restaurant beside the Anichov most. They do a mean burger and fries as well as some Russian dishes such as salmon-filled *pelmeni* (dumplings; R240).

MARIINSKY & SENNAYA

Zov Ilyicha (Map pp236–7; ☎ 717 8641; Kazanskaya ul 34; mains R300–400; ⏰ 1pm–2am; Ⓜ Sadovaya) With its silver busts of Lenin, racy porno videos intercut with Soviet propaganda and waitresses in saucy young Pioneer uniforms, 'Lenin's Mating Call' is hands-down the city's ultimate Soviet kitsch restaurant. Even better, the Russian food is extremely good. No under 18s admitted.

Za Stsenoy (Map pp236-7; ☎ 327 0521; Teatralnaya pl 18/10; meals R400-600; M Sadovaya/Sennaya Ploshchad) The beautifully laid out official restaurant of the Mariinsky Theatre is tastefully decorated with props from past productions. Although there are some fancy modern Russian dishes on offer it's generally best to stick to the simpler ones, which are well executed.

Nikolai (Map pp236-7; ☎ 571 5900; Bolshaya Morskaya ul 52; mains R300; ☽ noon-9pm; M Sadovaya/Sennaya Ploshchad) This traditional Russian restaurant resides in an exquisite wood-panelled room in the House of Architects. It offers good-value, tasty dishes and pleasant service. Cash only.

Lechaim (Map pp236-7; ☎ 972 2774; Lermontovsky pr 2; mains R500; ☽ noon-11pm Sun-Fri; M Sadovaya/Sennaya Ploshchad) Hidden away beneath the Grand Choral Synagogue (p262) it's likely you'll have this classy kosher restaurant to yourself despite it being the city's best place for traditional Jewish cooking, which is served in hearty portions.

Dvoryanskoye Gnezdo (Map pp236-7; ☎ 312 3205; ul Dekabristov 21; mains R1000; M Sadovaya/Sennaya Ploshchad) Set in the summer pavilion of Yusupov Palace, 'The Noble Nest' is the visiting VIP's choice, serving some of the finest Russian and European cuisine in town in an intimate, tsarist setting. Service is a little on the snooty side, though.

Nebo (Map pp236-7; ☎ 449 2488; 5th fl, PIK, Sennaya pl 2; mains R350; M Sennaya Ploshchad) From low grey sofas you gaze out at a splendid panorama towards the Neva. The food? Well, they do sushi of course, and other things, but who cares with a view like this? Well worth the price of an espresso (R70). Did we mention the view?

VASILYEVSKY ISLAND

Restoran (Map pp240-1; ☎ 327 8979; Tamozhenny per 2; meals R400-500; M Vasileostrovskaya) Chic minimalist décor provides an ideal setting for a well-presented range of traditional Russian dishes. There's a good table of appetisers and some salads and some interesting, homemade, flavoured vodkas.

Byblos (Map pp240-1; ☎ 325 8564; Maly pr 5; mains R150-300; M Vasileostrovskaya) The only Lebanese place in town is worth visiting for its excellent value three-course lunch (R159), as well as in the evening for delicious meze, hummus, *kibbeh*, tabbouleh, kofta and of course hookahs (R300) and Lebanese wine.

Russky Kitsch (Map pp240-1; ☎ 325 1122; Universitetskaya nab 25; meals R300; ☽ noon-4am; M Vasileostrovskaya) The self-proclaimed 'period of perestroika café' raises bad taste to an ironic art that, against all odds, works. Check out Brezhnev smooching with Castro on the ceiling of the 'kissing room' and a host of other cheeky touches, including menus secreted in works by Lenin and Stalin. Most dishes (especially the salad bowl) are fine. Come for a drink and a gawp, if nothing else.

Staraya Tamozhnya (Map pp240-1; ☎ 327 8980; Tamozhenny per 1; mains R1000; M Vasileostrovskaya) The 'Old Customs House', one of the most consistently recommended places in town, has a delightful atmosphere with vaulted brick ceilings, live jazz, fantastic service and large portions of very well-prepared Russian and European specialities.

Swagat (Map pp240-1; ☎ 217 2111; Bolshoy pr 91; meals R400-500; M Vasileostrovskaya) Less conveniently located than St Petersburg's other Indian restaurants, but still worth visiting. Its north Indian cuisine, including tandoori, tikka and masala curry dishes, is authentically spicy. There's sometimes sitar music after 8pm.

PETROGRAD SIDE

Na Zdorovye (Map pp238-9; ☎ 232 4039; Bolshoy pr 13; meals R200-300; M Sportivnaya) Fun and colourful; a heady mix of both Soviet and Russian folk culture dictates the décor here. The food, also a combination of traditional Russian and Soviet cuisine, is imaginatively presented and tasty.

Salkhino (Map pp238-9; ☎ 232 7891; Kronverksky pr 25; meals R400-500; M Gorkovskaya) Justly popular Georgian restaurant, serving big portions of delicious food in a convivial, arty setting enlivened by the motherly service of its owners. It's worth splashing out on their quaffable Georgian wines.

TOP FIVE RUSSIAN RESTAURANTS

- Mechta Molokhovets (p279)
- Fasol (p278)
- Restoran (above)
- Na Zdorovye (right)
- Bliny Domik (p283)

Aquarel (Map pp238-9; ☎ 320 8600; Birzhevoy most, Petrograd Side; meals R600-1000; ◷ noon-6am; Ⓜ Sportivnaya) Based on a moored boat with fantastic views across the Neva to the Hermitage, this stylish place has a cheaper café on the top floor serving pasta and pizza, and a DJ in the evenings.

Russkaya Rybalka (Map pp238-9; ☎ 323 9813; 11 Yuzhnaya Doroga, Krestovsky Island; mains R600-800; Ⓜ Krestovsky Ostrov) Worth stopping by if you're exploring Krestovsky Island. The name means Russian fishing and that's exactly what you can do at the pools outside this operation based in a cutely designed wooden building. Its fish include trout, stertlet and other types of sturgeon.

Kafe Tbilisi (Map pp238-9; ☎ 230 9391; Sytninskaya ul 10; meals R300; Ⓜ Gorkovskaya) Behind the Sytny Market this Georgian place is a St Petersburg institution. It may be dark and Soviet-like inside, but nonetheless serves top-class food. Try the home-made cheese, and the *lavash* (flat bread) and *khachapuri* (cheese bread).

Aquarium (Map pp238-9; ☎ 326 8286; Kamennoostrovsky pr 10; meals R600; Ⓜ Gorkovskaya) This slick upmarket Chinese restaurant is worth the expense. It serves a good range of seafood, including abalone, in a Fu Man Chu lair-like setting.

Cafes & Quick Eats

For cheap eats stroll along pedestrianised 6-ya 7-ya linii where you'll find several chain cafés and no-frills restaurants.

HISTORIC CENTRE

Zoom Café (Map pp230-1; Gorokhovaya ul 22; mains R140; ✕ ; Ⓜ Nevsky Prospekt) This literary-styled café has a lot of things going for it. Unfussy tasty European and Russian food (with 20% off all prices up till 4pm), wi-fi access, a very relaxed ambience, and a no-smoking zone. What are you waiting for?

BEST WORLD-CUISINE RESTAURANTS		
Caucasian	Yerevan	(p279)
Chinese	Aquarium	(above)
French	Bistro Garçon	(p280)
Greek	Taverna Olivia	(p279)
Indian	Tandoori Nights	(p279)
Italian	Trattoria Pompei	(p280)
Japanese	Gin-No-Taki	(p279)
Jewish	Lechaim	(p281)

Chaynaya Lozhka (Map pp234-5; www.teaspoon .ru in Russian; Nevsky pr 44; mains R100; ◷ 9am-10pm; Ⓜ Gostiny Dvor) This incredibly brightly decorated, and good, fast-food café is found all over St Petersburg: check their website for a full list of locations. They do excellent bliny and salads and a wide range of loose leaf teas and infusions, hence their name which means 'golden teaspoon'.

Bushe Malaya Morskaya ul (Map pp230-1; Malaya Morskaya ul 7; snacks R20-40; ◷ 9am-10pm, Mon-Fri, 10am-10pm Sat & Sun); ul Razyezzhaya (Map pp234-5; ul Razyezzhaya 13; snacks R20-40; ◷ 9am-10pm, 10am-10pm Sat & Sun; Ⓜ Vladimirskaya) A baked-goods paradise that's great for breakfast or a snack. At the Malaya Morskaya branch they also prepare bliny with funny face designs that the kids will love.

Kilikia (Map pp230-1; ☎ 327 2208; Gorokhovaya ul 26/40; mains R200-300; ◷ noon-3am; Ⓜ Nevsky Prospekt) This large yet cosy Armenian place is excellent value and serves up well-presented, delicious Caucasian and Russian dishes. It's especially popular with the large Armenian community in St Petersburg and has live music most evenings.

Herzen Institute Canteen (Map pp230-1; Herzen Institute courtyard, nab reki Moyki 48; mains R50-100; ◷ noon-6pm Mon-Sat; Ⓜ Nevsky Prospekt) This outlet caters to the students of the Herzen Institute who come here in droves at lunch. Things are basic – plastic plates and cutlery, but you'll not eat better at these prices.

Kharbin (Map pp230-1; ☎ 311 1732; nab reki Moyki 48; mains R400) This excellent Chinese restaurant shares the kitchen with the Herzen Institute Canteen next door.

Teremok (Map pp230-1; cnr Malaya Sadovaya & Italiyanskaya ul; bliny R30-100; ◷ 10am-10pm; Ⓜ Gostiny Dvor) Sprinkled all over the city, these bliny kiosks are superb value and serve up great treats to which the crowds of satisfied customers milling about in the immediate vicinity can attest. You can make up your own pancake by just pointing to the fillings you want.

Ili (Map pp230-1; Nevsky pr 52; mains R100-200; ◷ 24hrs; Ⓜ Gostiny Dvor) With round the clock hours, a DJ playing at night, Internet access and a prime position on Nevsky pr, this café/bistro/bar is more of a hang out than a food destination per se. But it's all done quite stylishly and the food is OK.

Sever (Map pp230-1; Nevsky pr 44; ◷ 10am-9pm Mon-Sat, to 8pm Sun; Ⓜ Gostiny Dvor) This legendary cake shop, chock-full of cookies and oddly coloured pastries and cakes, also has an area for stand-up eating and drinking.

LITEYNY, SMOLNY, VLADIMIRSKAYA & VOSTANNIYA

Bliny Domik (Map pp234-5; ☎ 315 9915; Kolokolnaya ul; meals R100-200; 🕑 8am-11pm; Ⓜ Vladimirskaya) There's more than bliny on the menu at Bliny Domik and it's all pretty good. This long-running favourite (it can get very busy – try breakfast or a late lunch to avoid the crowds) is set up like a country home but isn't too kitsch like other places and live piano music adds to the atmosphere in the evenings.

Bufet (Map pp234-5; ☎ 764 7888; Pushinskaya ul 7; meals R200-300; Ⓜ Ploshchad Vosstaniya) This cosy café-bar charms with its eclectic mix of antiques and whatnots, from Indian puppets to a retro radio. They prepare loose leaf tea properly, the English-speaking owner will translate the menu for you and the food is also very tasty; try the chicken stuffed with apricot (R250).

Baltic Bread (Map pp234-5; www.baltic-bread.ru /eng/; Vladimirsky pr 19; sandwiches R40; 🕑 10am-9pm; Ⓜ Dostoevskaya) This outstanding bakery/café has a new ritzy branch in the Vladimirsky Passazh shopping mall serving some 80 different types of baked goods; come here for an espresso (R50), cake (R30) or sandwich. Their original branch is at Grechesky pr 25 (Map pp234-5).

Olyushka & Russkye Bliny (Map pp234-5; Gagarinskaya ul 13; mains R55-75; 🕑 11am-6pm Mon-Fri; Ⓜ Chernyshevskaya) The students at the nearby university quite rightly swear by these authentic canteens that hark back to the simplicity of Soviet times. Olyushka serves only *pelmeni*, all handmade, while Russkye Bliny does a fine line in melt-in-the-mouth pancakes.

Troitsky Most Zagorodny pr (Map pp234-5; Zagorodny pr 38; mains R100; 🕑 9am-11pm; Ⓜ Dostoevskaya); Kamennoostrovsky pr (Map pp238-9; Kamennoostrovsky pr 9/2; Ⓜ Gorkovskaya) The Zagorodny pr branch is by far the nicest of this chain of vegetarian cafés, with the Indian spiritual-style Trang Café attached and overlooking a small park. The Petrograd Side branch on Kamennoostrovsky pr, facing the bridge after which it is named, is the original (with another branch a couple of blocks away). The mushroom lasagne is legendary.

Gauranga (Map pp234-5; Ligovsky pr 17; mains R100; 🕑 noon-9pm; Ⓜ Ploshchad Vosstaniya) The cheap and decent vegetarian food at this Hare Krishna–ish place is largely inspired by Indian cooking, although there are several Russian dishes too, and Central Asian favourites such as *plov* (rice pilaf).

Marius Pub (Map pp234-5; ☎ 315 4880; ul Marata 11; mains R300; 🕑 24hr; Ⓜ Mayakovskaya) Reliable and rightly popular, Marius Pub serves hearty Russian and European pub grub at all hours, and also does a mean breakfast buffet (R300) and good value business lunch (R160).

U Tyoshchi na Blinakh Zagorodny pr (Map pp234-5; Zagorodny pr 18; mains R150; 🕑 10am-8pm; Ⓜ Vladimirskaya); Sytninskaya ul (Map pp238-9; Sytninskaya ul 16; Ⓜ Gorkovskaya); Ligovsky pr (Map pp234-5; Ligovsky pr 25; Ⓜ Ploshchad Vosstaniya) 'Mother-in Law's pancakes' are being served up in so many locations that it's a wonder she's not dropped dead from exhaustion yet. The cafeteria-style chain is a great place to fill up quickly and cheaply.

MARIINSKY & SENNAYA

Stolle (pies R50; 🕑 8am-10pm); ul Dekabristov 33 (Map pp236-7; ul Dekabristov 33; Ⓜ Sadovaya/Sennaya Ploshchad); ul Dekabristov 19 (Map pp236-7; ul Dekabristov 19; Ⓜ Sadovaya/Sennaya Ploshchad); Vasilyevsky Island (Map pp240-1; Syezdovskaya & 1-ya linii 50; Ⓜ Vasileostrovskaya); Konyushennaya per (Map pp230-1; Konyushennaya per 1/6; Ⓜ Nevsky Prospekt) This minichain of cafés bakes traditional Russian savoury and sweet pies that are so yummy we guarantee you'll be back for more. Both the ul Dekabristov branches are close to the Mariinsky, although the former is the more appealing.

Café Idiot (Map pp236-7; ☎ 315 1675; nab reki Moyki 82; meals R300; 🕑 11am-1am; ✗; Ⓜ Sennaya Ploshchad) This long-running vegetarian café popular with expats is a little overpriced, but the atmosphere is excellent – funky lamps and tables, couches to lounge on and several rooms with different ambiences (including one that's nonsmoking). An ideal place to visit for a nightcap or supper after attending the Mariinksy, as its kitchen stays open late.

Russian Vodka Museum Traktir (Map pp236-7; ☎ 312 9178; Konnogvardeysky bul 5; meals R200; 🕑 11am-10pm; Ⓜ Sadovaya/Sennaya Ploshchad) You don't need to be visiting the museum (p262) to eat at its simple *traktir* (tavern), which serves appetising Russian soups and dishes.

A couple of good, inexpensive Caucasian places near Sennaya pl:

Kafe Adzhika (Map pp236-7; Moskovsky pr 7; meals R150; 🕑 24hr; M Sadovaya/Sennaya Ploshchad)

Sumeta (Map pp236-7; ☎ 310 2411; ul Yefimova 5; mains R100; M Sadovaya/Sennaya Ploshchad) Try their meat or pumpkin-filled *chudu* (large pancake; R150).

PETROGRAD SIDE

Butik (Map pp238-9; Kamennoostrovsky pr 40; meal R90; 🕑 9am-11pm; M Petrogradskaya) A great place for a quick snack of lunch, this appealing Subway-style sandwich operation is crying out to be franchised across the city.

Self-Catering

SUPERMARKETS

There are dozens of western-style supermarkets dotted all over the city. Some of the more central ones, all located in the basement of their respective buildings:

Lend (Map pp234-5; Vladimirsky Passazh, Vladimirsky pr 19; 🕑 24hr; M Dostoevskaya)

Passazh (Map pp230-1; Nevsky pr 48; 🕑 10am-10pm; M Gostiny Dvor)

Perekrestok (Map pp236-7; PIK, Sennaya pl 2; 🕑 24hr; M Sennaya Ploshchad)

MARKETS

These are fascinating venues to visit, and not only for the choice of exotic and fresh produce (the meat is so fresh that in some cases it's still being hacked off the carcass). Bargaining, even if the price is marked, is encouraged, and you'll often be beckoned to try samples of honey, cream products and pickles, with no obligation to buy. Try the following:

Kuznechny (Map pp234-5; Kuznechny per; 🕑 8am-8pm; M Vladimirskaya) Best and most expensive market in town.

Maltsevsky (Map pp234-5; ul Nekrasova 52; 🕑 8am-8pm; M Ploshchad Vosstaniya)

Sennoy (Map pp236-7; Moskovsky pr 4-6; 🕑 8am-8pm; M Sadovaya/Sennaya Ploshchad)

Sytny (Map pp238-9; Sytninskaya pl 3/5; 🕑 8am-6pm; M Gorkovskaya)

DRINKING

St Petersburg is certainly not short of bars, with several of the live music venues (p286) being good places for a drink or a bite to eat earlier in the evening. If you're looking for a café, there are also plenty of appealing modern places to choose from, among them the

St Petersburg equivalent of Starbucks **Idealnaya Chashka** (www.chashka.ru; Map pp234-5; Nevsky pr 112 & 130; 🕑 9am-11pm) which has 11 other outlets around town, and the similar **Kofe Haus** (Map pp230-1; Nevsky pr 7 & Bolshaya Konyushennaya ul 13; 🕑 24hr; M Nevsky Prospekt). Chaynaya Lozhka (p282) serves a wonderful range of teas, while Stolle (p283) is also a convivial place for a drink, both soft and alcoholic.

Coffee & Tea Houses

The following are some of the more unique places you can get your caffeine or tea fix and several of them serve alcohol, too.

Le Goga (Map pp234-5; ul Razyezzhaya 6; 🕑 11am-6am; M Vladimirskaya) At the heart of the trendy 'five corners' area, this contemporary designed café-bar, does a nice line in creamy cakes and fortifying drinks with a side order of groovy atmosphere.

Café Rico (Map pp234-5; Nevsky pr 77/1, enter on Pushkinskaya ul; M Ploshchad Vosstaniya) The coffee is well made at this laid back café with South American-influenced décor. They also offer a wide range of coffee cocktails and snacks.

Coffee Break (Map pp230-1; nab kanala Griboedova 22; 🕑 7.30am-11pm; M Nevsky Prospekt) Not just a good modern café, but also an interesting art gallery infused with chill-out music. The choice of coffees, teas and other drinks is impressive.

El Barrio (Map pp230-1; Inzhenernaya ul 7; M Gostiny Dvor) The artfully minimalist décor and a good range of drinks, including some wines from R70 a glass, make this a pleasant place to revive or while away the evening.

James Cook Pub (Map pp230-1; Shvedsky per 2; 🕑 café from 9am, pub from noon-last customer; M Nevsky Prospekt) There's a convivial expat-ish pub here, but the best reason for showing up is to sample their fantastic range of coffees, teas and home-baked pastries.

Untsiya (Ounce; Map pp234-5; Nevsky pr 63; 🕑 10am-10pm; M Mayakovskaya) Hiding behind this tea shop there's a very chic tea salon looking on to a quiet courtyard. Sample from among 100 different teas from R75 to R175 a pot.

Chayny Dom (Map pp234-5; ul Rubinshteina 24; M Dostoevskaya) Laid back Oriental-style place with many teas on offer (from R80 a pot), as well as Turkish coffee, nice desserts, alcohol and hookah pipes (from R300); try one with absinthe (R1200) for a real head trip!

Tsely Mir (Whole World; Map pp240-1; 3-ya liniya 48; Ⓜ Vasileostrovskaya) On Vasilyevsky Island, this is a tranquil place where you can lounge on cushions on the floor and choose from 120 different types of tea; a pot for two starts from R75.

Bars

Tsinik (Cynic; Map pp236-7; ☎ 312 8779; per Antonenko 4; ⏰ 11am-3am Sun-Thu, 11am-6am Fri & Sat; Ⓜ Sadovaya/Sennaya Ploshchad) Laid-back, no-frills cellar bar with a cool, student-slacker/arty crowd nursing cheap beer and famously delicious *grenki* (black bread fried in garlic). It also has the only men's toilets in the world with the walls entirely covered with Pushkin's poem *Eugene Onegin*.

Red Lion (Map pp236-7; ☎ 571 4526; pl Dekabristov 1; ⏰ 24hr; Ⓜ Sadovaya/Sennaya Ploshchad) Occupying a huge basement space in the Senat building, this long-running bar nonetheless pounds with atmosphere, offering a wide range of beers, big screen TVs, a dance floor and standard British pub grub, such as fish and chips, and Irish stew. Women get free Shampanskoye every Tuesday from 7.30pm to 10pm.

City Bar (Map pp230-1; ☎ 314 1037; Millionnaya ul 10; ⏰ 11am-last client; Ⓜ Nevsky Prospekt) Fabulous St Petersburg identity Aileen presides over this popular expat place, busy every night of the week with foreigners, travellers and Russians who enjoy their company. There's a wi-fi connection for web surfers here, and a free book, DVD and video lending library.

Tinkoff (Map pp230-1; ☎ 718 55 66; www.tinkoff.ru; Kazanskaya ul 7; ⏰ noon-2am; Ⓜ Nevsky Prospekt) Set inside a gigantic, contemporary brewery, come here to sample one of eight freshly microbrewed beers, including the delicious White Unfiltered. There's also good, pricey food, including a sushi bar.

Sunduk (Map pp234-5; ☎ 272 6633; Furshtadskaya ul 42; ⏰ 10am-11pm; Ⓜ Chernyshevskaya) Cosy grotto space with good food, great atmosphere and the funkiest bathrooms in the city. There's an R80 charge for the live music (mainly jazz), which is performed nightly after 8.30pm.

Sakvoyazh Beremennoi Shpionki (Map pp230-1; ☎ 571 7819 Bolshaya Konyushennaya ul 13; ⏰ noon-2am; Ⓜ Nevsky Prospekt) In a city of bizarrely designed drinking and dining halls the 'Pregnant Spy's Suitcase' is one of the wack-

iest. The food is notionally Mexican and European but you don't come here for that, more for the outlandish décor ranging from Kamasutra room to torture chamber.

Che (Map pp234-5; ☎ 277 7600; www.caféclubche.ru; Poltavskaya ul 3; ⏰ 24hr; Ⓜ Ploshchad Vosstaniya) This is where you'll find the smart set, slumped in the comfy sofas. It's one of the most Euro-trendy spaces in the city, serving good coffee, wine and snacks; there's often live jazz in the evenings and they also do a good breakfast.

Novus (Map pp230-1; Bolshaya Morskaya ul 8; Ⓜ Nevsky Prospekt) The latest hit DJ bar is found on the 2nd floor of an otherwise anonymous bistro. Students and arty types gather to sink beers and play the Latvian table game the bar is named after.

Probka (Map pp234-5; ☎ 273 4904; ul Belingskogo 5; Ⓜ Gostiny Dvor) Small, romantic and sophisticated – what more could you ask of a wine bar that features a choice selection from around the world? Several wines are available by the glass and there's a menu of light snacks, or a more expensive Italian restaurant upstairs.

Time Out (Map pp234-5; ☎ 713 2442; ul Marata 36; ⏰ 1pm-5am; Ⓜ Vladimirskaya) Your average sports bar, with pool table and satellite TV, but there's also a foreign book exchange, good pizza and happy hour from 5pm to 8pm.

A couple of lively, long-established Irish bars in town:

Mollie's Irish Bar (Map pp234-5; ☎ 319 9768; ul Rubinshteyna 36; Ⓜ Dostoevskaya)

Shamrock (Map pp236-7; ☎ 570 4628; ul Dekabristov 27; ⏱ 9am-2am; Ⓜ Sadovaya/Sennaya Ploshchad)

ENTERTAINMENT

Check Friday's *St Petersburg Times* for up-to-date listings.

Tickets

The box offices at some of the city's largest venues, including the Mariinsky, Mussorgsky, Hermitage and Maly Theatres, charge higher foreigner's prices. It's still cheaper than what you'd pay for the same tickets purchased through a top hotel's concierge or travel agency. If you can prove that you're working or studying in Russia, you'll pay the Russian price.

If you purchase a Russian ticket and your cover is blown inside the theatre (an embarrassing experience), you'll be made to pay the difference by rabid babushkas. Scalpers usually sell last-minute tickets outside the theatre an hour before the show. These will be Russian tickets, and if they're for a sold-out show, they can go for anything up to and beyond US$50 each. Check the ticket carefully and see that the date and seat position promised are correct – there are fakes around. See p85 for useful words to help you when buying tickets.

There are ticket-booking kiosks and offices all over the city; one of the handiest for all types of performances is the **Theatre Ticket Office** (Map pp230-1; ☎ 314 9385; Nevsky pr 42; ⏱ 10am-9pm; Ⓜ Gostiny Dvor).

Cinemas

Check out Friday's *St Petersburg Times* for full cinema listings. Movie theatres line Nevsky pr, but all of the Western films played at them are dubbed. Check out the following:

Avrora (Map pp230-1; ☎ 315 5254; www.avrora .spb.ru; Nevsky pr 60; Ⓜ Gostiny Dvor) Young Dmitry Shostakovich once played piano accompaniment to silent movies here.

Dom Kino (Map pp230-1; ☎ 314 0638; www.domkino .spb.ru; Karavannaya ul 12; Ⓜ Gostiny Dvor) Arty Russian and foreign films, as well as some higher brow Hollywood productions screen here. This is also where the British Council holds its British Film Festival.

Mirage (Map pp238-9; ☎ 974 7448; www.mirage.ru; Bolshoy pr 35; Ⓜ Petrogradskaya) Modern multiplex cinema, with restaurant and Internet café. Sometimes screens English-language movies. Watch out for pickpockets here.

Live Music

BANDS

Check the websites of the following (all in Russian) for details on current gigs.

Platforma (Map pp234-5; ☎ 719 6123; www.plat formaclub.ru; ul Nekrasova 40; cover R100-200; ⏱ 24hr; Ⓜ Ploshchad Vosstaniya) Some of St Petersburg's most interesting bands and coolest DJs play at this convivial space most evenings. Open round the clock it's also a fine place to eat or for a drink earlier in the evening when you can browse their bookstore.

Red Club (Map pp234-5; ☎ 277 1366; www.club red.ru; Poltavskaya ul 7; cover R100-400; ⏱ 7pm-6am; Ⓜ Ploshchad Vosstaniya) This is a great warehouse venue, behind Moskovsky vokzal, that is a mainstay for local groups and is usually packed out for gigs.

Moloko (Map pp234-5; ☎ 274 9467; www .molokoclub.ru; Perekupnoy per 12; cover R50-100; ⏱ 7pm-midnight Wed-Sun; Ⓜ Ploshchad Vosstaniya) Everything an underground club should be – dimly lit, modestly decorated and bubbling with promise. Great bands running the gamut of genres play here, and it's one of the few places to get going earlier in the evening.

Fish Fabrique (Map pp234-5; ☎ 764 4857; www .fishfabrique.spb.ru; Pushkinskaya ul 1; cover R70-150; ⏱ 3pm-late; Ⓜ Ploshchad Vosstaniya) Legendary bar set in the building that's the focus of the avant-garde art scene, thus attracting an interesting crowd, who give this cramped space its edge. Live bands kick up a storm at 10pm nightly. Enter through the arch at Ligovsky pr 53

Manhattan (Map pp236-7; ☎ 713 1945; www.man hattanclub.ru; nab reki Fontanki 90; cover R100-130; ⏱ 2pm-5am; Ⓜ Sennaya Ploshchad) Frequented by a sociable, studenty crowd, this basement space has a relaxed atmosphere, and often ear-splitting music sets from 8pm onwards.

Money Honey Saloon & City Club (Map pp230-1; ☎ 310 0549; Sadovaya ul 28-30, Apraksin Dvor 13; cover R100; ⏱ 10am-5am; Ⓜ Gostiny Dvor) Downstairs the Money Honey Saloon has great live rockabilly and country bands; the crowds' raucousness sometimes spills over into rowdiness later on. Upstairs at the more salubrious City Club is a dance floor and pool tables, and lots of space to mingle. Enter via the courtyard off Sadovaya ul.

CLASSICAL, BALLET & OPERA

September to the end of June is the main performing season – in summer many companies are away on tour, but plenty of performances are still staged. Ticket prices range from R150 to R4000.

Mariinsky Theatre (Map pp236-7; ☎ 326 4141; www.mariinsky.ru/en; Teatralnaya pl 1; box office ✆ 11am-7pm; Ⓜ Sadovaya/Sennaya Ploshchad) Home to the world-famous Kirov Ballet and Opera company, a visit here is a must, if only to wallow in the sparkling glory of the interior. See p262 for a brief history of this famous theatre. Use the website to book and pay for tickets in advance of your visit.

Shostakovich Philharmonia Bolshoy Zal (Big Hall; Map pp230-1; ☎ 710 4257; www.philharmonia.spb.ru /eng/indexi.html; Mikhailovskaya ul 2; Ⓜ Gostiny Dvor) The St Petersburg Philharmonica's Symphony Orchestra is particularly renowned, and this grand venue is one of its two concert halls, the other being the **Maly Zal imeni Glinki** (Small Philharmonia; Map pp230-1; ☎ 571 8333; Nevsky pr 30; Ⓜ Nevsky Prospekt).

Glinka Capella (Map pp230-1; ☎ 314 1058; nab reki Moyki 20; Ⓜ Nevsky Prospekt) This venue also has high standards, focusing on choral, chamber and organ concerts.

Mussorgsky Opera & Ballet Theatre (Map pp230-1; ☎ 585 4305; www.mikhailovsky.ru; pl Iskusstv 1; Ⓜ Nevsky Prospekt) It's generally cheaper and easier to get tickets to the ballet and opera performances staged here. More contemporary works are also performed here than by the Kirov and standards are respectable.

Imperial Hermitage Theatre (Map pp230-1; ☎ 279 0226; www.hermitagemuseum.com/html_En/02 /hm2_72.html; Dvortsovaya nab 34; Ⓜ Nevsky Prospekt). Check the website to see what is being performed at this beautiful venue that's part of the Hermitage.

Rimsky-Korsakov Conservatory (Map pp236-7; ☎ 314 9693; www.conservatory.ru/eng/eng.shtml; Teatralnaya pl 3; Ⓜ Sadovaya/Sennaya Ploshchad) This illustrious music school opposite the Mariinsky is worth checking out for its student performances.

JAZZ
Petersburgers have a particular love of jazz music. Cover charges range from R60 to R150 depending on the night and acts. Live jazz is also played at the café-bars Che (p285) and Sunduk (p285).

JFC Jazz Club (Map pp234-5; ☎ 272 9850; www .jfc.sp.ru; Shpalernaya ul 33; ✆ from 7pm; Ⓜ Chernyshevskaya) Small and New York–styled, this is the best of its kind in the city and features

jazz, blues and improv bands from Russia and around the world.

Jazz Philharmonic Hall (Map pp234-5; ☎ 764 8565; www.jazz-hall.spb.ru; Zagorodny pr 27; ✆ concerts from 8pm; Ⓜ Sadovaya/Sennaya Ploshchad) Representing the traditional side of jazz. It has two resident bands performing straight jazz and Dixieland. Foreign guests appear doing mainstream and modern jazz.

Jimi Hendrix Blues Club (Map pp234-5; ☎ 279 8813; Liteyny pr 33; ✆ from 7.30pm; Ⓜ Chernyshevskaya) This intimate 15-seater bar-restaurant has good concerts from time to time.

Neo Jazz Club (Map pp234-5; ☎ 273 3830; Solyanoy per 14; ✆ 8pm-midnight; Ⓜ Chernyshevskaya) This is a laid-back place with more mellow live jazz music. Most people come here for supper too (very good Armenian specialities at reasonable prices) and to just chill.

Jazz Time Bar (Map pp234-5; ☎ 273 5379; Mokhovaya ul 41; ✆ noon-2am; Ⓜ Gostiny Dvor) Charmingly unpretentious, this bar has live music every night ranging from jazz-funk, swing and country.

Circus & Puppets
Contact the theatres to check on performance times.

St Petersburg State Circus (Map pp230-1; ☎ 314 8478; www.reserve.sp.ru/circus/index_e.htm; nab reki Fontanki 3; tickets R300; Ⓜ Gostiny Dvor) One of Russia's leading circus companies has had a permanent home here since 1877.

Bolshoy Puppet Theatre (Map pp234-5; ☎ 273 6672; ul Nekrasova 10; tickets R50-60; Ⓜ Gostiny Dvor) This is the main venue for puppets; there are 16 different shows in the repertoire, including two for adults.

Demmeni Marionette Theatre (Map pp230-1; ☎ 571 2156; Nevsky pr 52; tickets R50-60; Ⓜ Gostiny Dvor) This is the oldest professional puppet theatre in Russia, in business since 1917.

Nightclubs
The city's nightclub scene is varied, inventive and perpetually changing – you're bound to find somewhere you like. Cover charges range from R100 to R1000 depending on the venue and night; In the summer, dance parties are often held out on the Gulf of Finland islands around Kronshtadt (p303).

Griboedov (Map pp234-5; ☎ 764 4355; www.grib oedovclub.ru; Voronezhskaya ul 2A; cover R200, free 5-8pm; ✆ 5pm-6am; Ⓜ Ligovsky Prospekt) Run by ska band Dva Samoliota (the same guys behind the Hotel California hostel, p275), this hip club in an artfully converted bomb shelter is a fun place most nights. Weekends are stiflingly crowded; for something different try Wednesday nights for 1970s and '80s Russian disco.

Tunnel (Map pp238-9; ☎ 233 4015; www.tunnel club.ru; cnr Lyubansky per & Zverinskaya ul; cover R250-350; ☷ midnight-6am Fri & Sat; Ⓜ Gorkovskaya) The original 'underground' club, quite literally since it occupies a sprawling bomb shelter. Come here for hard core electronic dance music.

Par.spb (Map pp238-9; ☎ 233 3374; www.par.spb .ru; Aleksandrovsky Park 5B; cover R400; ☷ 11am-6am Fri-Sun; Ⓜ Gorkovskaya) This stripped-back, arty club, with two dance spaces and a chill-out area, offers different music each night and has a strict door policy.

Jet Set (Map pp234-5; ☎ 275 9288; www.jetset .spb.ru; Furshtatskaya ul 58B; cover R500-1000; ☷ 10pm-6am Fri & Sat; Ⓜ Chernyshevskaya) Attracting top DJs and musicians, Jet Set is the kind of VIP club that many Petersburgers claim to loathe, although quite a few seem to want to be on the guest list. Make the grade with face control and you'll discover a sumptuous space, with an oriental theme upstairs.

Second Floor (Vtori Etazh; Map pp230-1; Dumskaya ul 9; Ⓜ Nevsky Prospekt) Above Dacha (see boxed text, p285) is this relaxed club with substantially more room for dancing, plus a chill-out room. The music policy and clientele are similar to Dacha. The weekend R50 entrance charge goes towards your first drink.

Opium (Map pp230-1; ☎ 312 0148; Sadovaya ul 12; cover R500; ☷ 10pm-6am; Ⓜ Gostiny Dvor) It's a similar story at Opium, which is expensive, elitist and glitzy but with excellent music and the in-crowd clawing at the door.

Havana (Map pp236-7; ☎ 259 1155; www.havana -club.ru; Moskovsky pr 21; cover R100-200; ☷ 9pm-6am; Ⓜ Tekhnologichesky Institut) Work on those Ricky Martin moves as this is a real salsa and Latin club with a Cuban theme and imported dancers. It's big and fun, and fills up on the weekends.

Sports

Petrovsky Stadium (Map pp238-9; ☎ 328 8903; Petrovsky ostrov 2; Ⓜ Sportivnaya) Petersburgers are fanatical about the fortunes of local soccer team **Zenit** (www.fc-zenit.ru) who usually play here. Tickets (R60 to R800) can be pur-

chased at theatre ticket booths or at the stadium, three days before a game. Be sure to be wearing Zenit's light blue colours if you want to avoid getting into any bothersome situations.

Theatre, Cabaret & Dance Shows

Drama is taken very seriously in St Petersburg and there are dozens of theatrical performances each night, practically all in Russian. Even if you don't speak the language, some of the theatres are visual treats in themselves. There is also a cabaret and a dance show that require little in the way of language skills for appreciation.

Feel Yourself Russian Folkshow (Map pp236-7; ☎ 312 5500; www.folkshow.ru; Nikolayevsky Palace, ul Truda 4; ticket incl drinks & snacks R1280; ☷ show 6.30pm; Ⓜ Nevsky Prospekt) Terrible title, but not a bad show of traditional Russian folk dancing and music. Worth attending to get a look at the spectacular interior of the Nikolayevsky Palace, if nothing else.

Aleksandrinsky Theatre (Map pp230-1; ☎ 710 4103; pl Ostrovskogo 2; Ⓜ Gostiny Dvor) Also known as the Pushkin, this is the city's premier drama theatre, where Chekhov's *The Seagull* saw its premier. It's an architectural treat.

Bolshoy Drama Theatre (Map pp230-1; ☎ 310 0401; nab reki Fontanki 65; Ⓜ Sennaya Ploshchad) This is another top mainstream theatre, showcasing innovative productions.

Lensoveta Theatre (Map pp234-5; ☎ 713 2191; Vladimirsky pr 12; Ⓜ Mayakovskaya) Even if your Russian isn't great, the plays here are so good that you can't go wrong. Beckett's *Waiting for Godot* (B Ozhidaniy Godo) and Pinter's *The Lover* (Lyubovnik) are in the repertoire.

Maly Drama Theatre (Map pp234-5; ☎ 713 2049; ul Rubinshteyna 18; Ⓜ Dostoevskaya) The theatre with the best international reputation, built up under the directorship of Lev Dodin whose productions of Dostoevsky's *The Devils* and Chekhov's *Play Without a Name* have been widely acclaimed.

Hulli Gulli (Map p229; ☎ 246 3827; Lanskoe sh 23; cover R500; ☷ 9pm-4am; Ⓜ Chyornaya Rechka) Infamous cabaret show with a wild and foulmouthed MC orchestrating the night's strip shows, saucy comedy and magic acts, and penis-measuring contests (for each of your centimetres you get 1% discount off the price of drinks). Get there by 10pm – staff may not let you in after the show has begun. From the metro, head north along nab Chyornoy Rechki one block, turn right onto Lanskoe sh, and try to lose your inhibitions along the way.

SHOPPING

You can find pretty much everything along Nevsky pr. If you're feeling homesick for a Western shopping environment there are also the malls **PIK** (Map pp236-7; Sennaya pl; **M** Sennaya Ploshchad), **Sennaya** (Map pp236-7; ul Yefimova 3; **M** Sennaya Ploshchad) and **Vladimirsky Passazh** (Map pp234-5; Vladimirsky pr 19; **M** Dostoevskaya).

Art

St Petersburg's art scene, fuelled by several illustrious art schools, is a great one to check out.

Free Arts Foundation (Map pp234-5; ☎ 764 5371; www.p10.nonmuseum.ru/index_e.html; Pushkinskaya ul 10, enter through arch at Ligovsky pr 53; ☺ 3-7pm Wed-Sun; **M** Ploshchad Vosstaniya) Often referred to simply by its address, Pushkinskaya 10, this contemporary art mecca is guaranteed to turn up something weird and wonderful. There are lots of separate galleries, all with different opening times, spread throughout the complex; most are open on Saturday. You'll find anything from paintings and sculpture to digital works. Occasionally performance pieces take place, such as poets firing live rounds of ammunition at bottles of Baltika beer. Check out The John Lennon Temple of Love, Peace and Music, in Wing C on the 1st floor, and the Gallery of Experimental Sound for artfully remodelled vintage clothes.

Artists' Union of Russia Exhibition Centre of Graphic Arts (Map pp230-1; ☎ 315 7474; Bolshaya Morskaya ul 38; ☺ 1-7pm Tue-Sun; **M** Nevsky Prospekt) Displays the more establishment side of the St Petersburg arts scene. Check out the lovely carved wooden doors on the 3rd floor. Some exhibitions here have an entrance fee.

Pechatnya (Map p265; ☎ 238 0742; Peter & Paul Fortress; ☺ 11am-5pm; **M** Gorkovskaya) Yet another reason for visiting the Fortress is this great shop making and selling unique prints.

A couple more good galleries with both paintings and souvenir arts and crafts available for sale:

Art Gallery Borey (Map pp234-5; ☎ 273 3693; Liteyny pr 58; ☺ noon-8pm Tue-Sat; **M** Mayakovskaya)

Sol-Art (Map pp234-5; ☎ 327 3082; Museum of Decorative & Applied Arts, Solyanoy per 15; ☺ 10am-6pm; **M** Chernyshevskaya)

Music & DVDs

The kiosks lining the underground passage from Nevsky pr beneath Sadovaya ul sell pretty much any bootleg CD or DVD you could wish for. Law-abiding citizens will avert their gaze and continue to **505** (Map pp234-5; Nevsky pr 72; **M** Mayakovskaya) which has an excellent range of legal CDs, DVDs and computer games at reasonable prices.

Photography

One-hour drop-off places for prints are common. For digital photo needs, slide film, professional rolls, equipment and development, your best option is **Yarky Mir** (Map pp234-5; ul Nekrasova 1; **M** Gostiny Dvor) and (Map pp230-1; Nevsky prospekt 6; **M** Nevsky Prospekt); it has several other branches around the city, too.

Souvenirs & Soviet Memorabilia

There's a well-stocked **souvenir market** (Map pp230-1; ☺ 10am-dusk; **M** Nevsky Prospekt), diagonally across the canal from the Church of the Saviour on Spilled Blood (p252) as well as stalls selling *matryoshka* dolls and the like outside other major tourist sights, such as the Hermitage. At each of these places, a certain amount of bartering is perfectly acceptable.

Tovar dlya Voennikh (Map pp230-1; Sadovaya ul 26; ☺ 10am-7pm Mon-Sat; **M** Gostiny Dvor) In a city with men in uniform on every street corner, this is where you get yours (the uniform that is!). Buy cool stripy sailors tops, embroidered badges, boots, camouflage jackets and caps at decent prices. Look for the circular green and gold sign with Military Shop written in English; the entrance is inside the courtyard.

La Russe (Map pp234-5; ☎ 572 2043; www.larusse .ru; Stremyannaya ul 3; ☺ 11am-8pm; **M** Mayakovskaya) Lots of rustic old whatnots and genuine antiques at this quirky, arty store where you can unearth everything from a battered samovar to beautifully decorated sleighs and traditional wool spinning devices. Enquire about their occasional excursions into the countryside.

Lomonosova China Factory (Map p229; ☎ 560 8544; pr Obukhovskoy Oborony 151; ☺ 10am-7pm Mon-Sat, 10am-5pm Sun; **M** Lomonosovskaya) This famous

ST PETERSBURG

factory has an outlet shop on site, where you get anything from the company catalogue at prices lower than in the department stores. You'll also find a branch of the Hermitage here. From the metro, turn left (east), walk under the bridge to the embankment then left – the factory's ahead. If you don't want to drag this far out, go to its **city centre shop** (Map pp234-5; Nevsky pr 160; 10am-8pm; **M** Ploshchad Alexandra Nevskogo) where prices are only a bit more expensive.

Sekunda (Map pp234-5; ☎ 275 7524; Liteyny pr 61; 11am-7pm Mon-Sat; **M** Mayakovskaya) This small antique and bric-a-brac place sometimes has unusual souvenirs from old postcards to stuffed moose heads. Enter through the courtyard.

Speciality Shops

Pchelovodstvo (Map pp234-5; ☎ 273 7262; Liteyny pr 46; 10am-8pm Mon-Sat; **M** Mayakovskaya) This is where you'll find many types of fresh honey from Russia's Rostov region, dozens of products, remedies and creams made from bee pollen, as well as unique teas, which make nice gifts.

Soldat Udachi ul Nekrasova (Map pp234-5; ☎ 279 1850; ul Nekrasova 37; 10am-9pm; **M** Ploshchad Vosstaniya); Bolshoy pr (Map pp238-9; ☎ 232 2003; Bolshoy pr 17, Petrograd Side; 10am-9pm; **M** Sportivnaya) This weaponry store has everything a modern-day Rambo could wish for, including GPS devices, Swiss army knives and camping gizmos.

Intendant (Map pp230-1; ☎ 311 1510; Karavannaya ul 18/37; 11am-11pm; **M** Gostiny Dvor) St Petersburg's finest wine shop stocks a fantastic range of local and imported bottles. Try some Georgian wine, either the dry white Gyrozhani (R300) or the dry red Mukuzani (R450).

GETTING THERE & AWAY
Air

Pulkovo-1 and **Pulkovo-2** (Map pp229; Pulkovo-1 ☎ 704 3822, Pulkovo-2 ☎ 704 3444; eng.pulkovo.ru/) are, respectively, the domestic and international terminals that serve St Petersburg.

St Petersburg has direct air links with most of the major European capitals. Airline offices, generally open from 9.30am to 5.30pm Monday to Friday, in St Petersburg include:

Aeroflot (Map pp230-1; ☎ 327 3872; Kazanskaya ul 5; **M** Nevsky Prospekt)

DOMESTIC FLIGHTS FROM ST PETERSBURG

Destination	Flights per day	Duration	One-way fare
Arkhangelsk	1	1½hr	R4243
Kaliningrad	2	1½hr	R3293
Irkutsk	1	5½hr	R7943
Moscow	10	50 mins	R2243
Murmansk	1	2hr	R4643
Novosibirsk	2	4hr	R6243
Sochi	1	3hr	R6023
Vladivostok	1	11hr	R12,743
Yekaterinburg	1	2½hr	R6143

Air France (Map pp230-1; ☎ 336 2900; Bolshaya Morskaya ul 35; **M** Nevsky Prospekt)

British Airways (Map pp230-1; ☎ 380 0626; Malaya Konyushennaya ul 1/3A; **M** Nevsky Prospekt)

Delta (Map pp230-1; ☎ 571 5820; Bolshaya Morskaya ul 36; **M** Nevsky Prospekt)

Finnair (Map pp230-1; ☎ 303 9898; Malaya Konyushennaya ul 1/3A; **M** Nevsky Prospekt)

KLM (Map pp230-1; ☎ 346 6868; Malaya Morskaya ul 23; **M** Nevsky Prospekt)

Lufthansa (Map pp230-1; ☎ 320 1000; Nevsky pr 32; **M** Nevsky Prospekt)

Pulkovo Express (Map pp236-7; ☎ 303 9268; 1-aya Krasnoarmeyskaya ul 6; **M** Tekhnologichesky Institut)

Scandinavian Airlines System (SAS; Map pp230-1; ☎ 326 2600; Nevsky pr 25; **M** Nevsky Prospekt)

Transaero (Map pp234-5; ☎ 279 6463; Liteyny pr 48; **M** Mayakovskaya)

Tickets for all airlines can be purchased from travel agencies (p243) and from the **Central Airline Ticket Office** (Map pp230-1; ☎ 315 0072; Nevsky pr 7; 8am-8pm Mon-Fri, 8am-6pm Sat & Sun; **M** Nevsky Prospekt), which also has counters for train and international bus tickets.

If you have time and want to save money, consider flying part way to St Petersburg by one of the budget airlines such as Easyjet who have services both to Tallinn and Riga out of London and Berlin, or to Helsinki, then connect with trains or buses from there. See www.waytorussia.net/transport /international/budget.html for some detailed itineraries on how best to do this.

Boat

Between early April and late September international passenger ferries leave from the

Morskoy vokzal (Map pp240-1; ☎ 322 6052; pl Morskoy Slavy 1; Ⓜ Primorskaya). It's a long way from the metro, so take either bus 7 or trolley bus 10 from outside the Hermitage.

From here St Petersburg is regularly connected by **Silja Line** (www.silja.fi) cruises with Helsinki in Finland (from €120, 15 hours) and less frequently by ferry with Tallinn in Estonia (€20, 14½ hours) and Rostock in Germany (€90, 42hrs). **Baltfinn** (www.baltfinn .ru) offers a weekly ferry service on the *George Ots* (4-berth cabin from R2450, 18 hours), travelling between Baltiysk (the port near the Russian enclave of Kaliningrad) and St Petersburg. **Baltic Line** (www.baltics.ru/bl/eng/) and **Trans Russia Express** (www.tre.de) both run weekly ferries to Lubeck in Germany which also go via Baltiysk, check their websites for current details. You can buy tickets direct from the ferry companies at the sea port or at several central travel agencies, such as **Baltic Tours** (Map pp230-1; ☎ 320 6663; www.baltic tours.ru; Sergei Tyulenina per 4-13; ⏱ 10am-6pm Mon-Fri; Ⓜ Nevsky Prospekt).

From June to the end of August regular **river cruises** go along the Neva to inland Russia, including to Valaam, Kizhi and Moscow. Prices and schedules vary, so book through a specialist travel agency, such as **Cruise Russia** (Map pp234-5; ☎ 764 6947; www.cruise -ru.com; Ligovsky pr 87; ⏱ 10am-6pm Mon-Fri; Ⓜ Ligovsky Prospekt) or at the **River Passenger Terminal** (Map p229; ☎ 262 0239; pr Obukhovskoy Oborony 195; Ⓜ Proletarskaya).

Bus

St Petersburg's main bus station, **Avtovokzal No 2** (Map pp234-5; ☎ 766 5777; nab Obvodnogo kanala 36; Ⓜ Ligovsky Prospekt) – there isn't a No 1 – has both international and European Russia services.

Other international buses are offered by a number of companies:

Ardis Finnord (Map pp230-1; ☎ 314 8951; Italiyan-skaya ul 37; Ⓜ Gostiny Dvor) Two buses daily run from its offices to Helsinki (R1700).

Ecolines (Map pp236-7; ☎ 315 2550; www.ecolines.ru; Podyezdny per 3; Ⓜ Pushkinskaya) Daily overnight bus from the Vitebsky vokzal to Riga (R500) and three times a week to Kyiv (R600) and Odesa (R840) in Ukraine.

Eurolines (Map p229; ☎ 449 8370; www.eurolines.ru; ul Shkapina 10; Ⓜ Baltiyskaya) From outside the Baltisky vokzal, its buses run to Tallinn (five daily, R450 to R650) and Tartu (daily, R650) in Estonia, and Riga (daily, R400) in Latvia. The head office is 50m west of Baltisky vokzal,

Destination	Buses per day	Duration	One-way fare
Helsinki	2	8hr	R1700
Moscow	1	12hr	R480
Novgorod	14	3½hr	R179
Petrozavodsk	1	9hr	R270
Pskov	2	5½hr	R302
Rīga	2	11hr	R500
Tallinn	7	7½hr	R550-650

BUSES FROM ST PETERSBURG

but you can also buy tickets at its kiosk inside the Central Airline Ticket Office (opposite).

Neofahrt Tour (Map pp234-5; ☎ 718 2189; Oktyabr-skaya Hotel, Ligovsky pr 43/45; Ⓜ Ploshchad Vosstaniya) Overnight bus to Helsinki leaves from outside the main building of the Oktyabrskaya Hotel at around 9pm.

Saimaan Liikenne (Map pp238-9; ☎ 332 0833; www .savonlinja.spb.ru; ul Chapayeva 5; Ⓜ Gorkovskaya) Daily buses to Helsinki and Lappeeranta (departing from the Grand Hotel Europe).

Car & Motorcycle

See p734 for general driving information. Always remember to take it slowly; not only are there numerous speed traps (towards Vyborg, there's one just outside the city limits, where the speed limit becomes 60km/h), but the state of some roads can easily lead you to the repair shop in no time.

RENTAL

Agencies offering self-drive and chauffeured vehicles include:

Astoria Service (Map pp234-5; ☎ 712 1583; www .astoriaservice.ru; Borovaya ul 11/13; Ⓜ Ligovsky Prospekt)

Europcar (Map pp234-5; ☎ 380 1662; www.europcar .ru; nab reki Fontanki 38/4; Ⓜ Gostiny Dvor)

Hertz Malaya Morskaya ul (Map pp230-1; ☎ 272 5045; www.hertz.com.ru; Malaya Morskaya ul 23; Ⓜ Nevsky Prospekt); Pulkovo-2 airport (Map p229; ☎ 324 3242)

Train

The three major long-distance train stations are: **Ladozhsky vokzal** (Ladoga station; Map p229; ☎ 768 5304; Zhanevsky pr 73; Ⓜ Ladozhskaya) for services to/from Helsinki and the far north of Russia; **Moskovsky vokzal** (Moscow station; Map pp234-5; ☎ 768 4597; pl Vosstaniya; Ⓜ Ploshchad Vosstaniya) for Moscow, the Urals, Siberia, Crimea and the Caucasus; and **Vitebsky vokzal** (Vitebsk station; Map pp234-5; ☎ 768 5807; Zagorodny pr

52; Ⓜ Pushkinskaya) for the Baltic states, Eastern Europe, Ukraine and Belarus. Some suburban services also run from these stations as they do from **Baltisky vokzal** (Baltic; Map p229; ☎ 768 2859; Obvedny Kanal 120; Ⓜ Baltiyskaya)

and **Finlyandsky vokzal** (Finland; Map p229; ☎ 768 7687; pl Lenina 6; Ⓜ Ploshchad Lenina).

Tickets can be purchased at the train stations, the **Central Train Ticket Office** (Map pp230-1; ☎ 762 33 44; nab kanala Griboedova 24; ☺ 8am-8pm

RAIL ROUTES FROM ST PETERSBURG

Trains from St Petersburg to Moscow

Train no & name	Departure	Duration	Fare
1 *Krasnya Strela*	11.55pm	8hr	R1700
3 *Ekspress*	11.59pm	8hr	R1700
5 *Nikolaevsk Ekspress*	11.35pm	8hr	R1700
23 *Yunost*	1.10pm	8hr	R1300
53 *Grand Express*	11.47pm	9hr	R3000-13,000
159 *Avrora*	4.00pm	5½hr	R1300
163 *ER200*	6.30pm	4½hr	R1700
165 *Nevsky Ekspress*	6.30pm*	4½hr	R1700

Notes: *Mon, Thu & Fri only

Domestic Trains from St Petersburg

Destination	Train no	Departure	Duration	Fare
Arkhangelsk	390A	8pm LS*	25½hr	R1229
Kazan	103	4.36pm MS†	27½hr	R1482
Murmansk	022	5.50pm LS	28½hr	R1400
Nizhny Novgorod (Gorky)	59	5.24pm MS	15½hr	R1600
Novgorod	81	5.00pm MS	3hr	R158
Omsk	13	8.40pm MS=	53½hr	R3037
Petrozavodsk	658	22.13 LS	8½hr	R457
Pskov	677	5.24 VS	5¼hr	R677

Notes: MS – Moskovsky vokzal   LS – Ladozhsky vokzal   VS – Vitebsky vokzal
       * Mon, Tue, Thu & Fri   † odd days

International Trains from St Petersburg

Destination	Train no & name	Departure	Duration	Fare
Brest	49	3.01pm VS	19hr	R932
The Brest train No 49 has carriages that are detached there and go on to Budapest and Prague:				
Budapest	49	3.01pm VS*	45hr	R5330
Prague	49	3.01pm VS†	40½hr	R3790
Helsinki	034 *Repin*	7.28am LS	6hr	R1856
Helsinki	036 *Sibelius*	4.28pm LS	6hr	R1856
Kaliningrad	079	6.16pm VS	27½hr	R1247
Kyiv	053	9.11pm VS	24hr	R961/1102‡
Minsk	051	7.03pm VS	15hr	R1166
Odesa	19	11.40pm VS	35hr	R1260
The Odesa train has carriages that are detached along the way and go on to Berlin and Warsaw:				
Berlin	19	11.40pm VS§	31hr	R4670
Warsaw	19	11.40pm VS§	29hr	R2240
Riga	037	9.46pm	13hr	R1812
Vilnius	391	8.28pm||	15¼hr	R1387/1499#

Notes: LS – Ladozhsky vokzal   VS – Vitebsky vokzal   *Russian/Ukrainian train   † Mon, Wed, Thu, Sun
       ‡Tue & Sun   § daily except Thu ||odd days   # Russian/Lithuanian train

Mon-Sat, 8am-4pm Sun; Ⓜ Nevsky Prospekt) and the
Central Airline Ticket Office (p290).

MOSCOW
There are 12 to 14 daily trains to Moscow, all departing from Moskovsky vokzal:
the table lists the best services. The overnight sleepers will save a night's accommodation costs (and for a small extra
charge you'll also get breakfast or a light
meal thrown in). If you really want to save
money, four services (19, 27, 29 and 55) have
platskartny (dorm) carriages with tickets
for R350.

FINLAND & OTHER INTERNATIONAL DESTINATIONS
There are two daily trains between St Petersburg and Helsinki: the Russian-operated
Repin, and the *Sibelius* run by **Finnish Railways** (www.vr.fi). For details on services going
to Helsinki see the table, opposite. From
Helsinki to St Petersburg the *Repin* leaves
at 3.42pm and arrives at 10.25pm, while
the *Sibelius* leaves at 7.42am and arrives in
St Petersburg at 2.23pm. Services in both
directions stop at Vyborg (p303), so you
can save yourself some money if you take a
bus or local train there and then catch the
train to Helsinki.

Note services to Berlin, Budapest, Kaliningrad, Kyiv, Prague and Warsaw pass
through Belarus, for which you're required
to hold a transit visa (see p720). The train
to Smolensk in Russia also passes through
Belarus. Border guards have been known to
force people off trains and back to where
they came from if they don't have a visa.

GETTING AROUND
St Petersburg's excellent public transport
system makes getting around simple and
inexpensive. Pack a good pair of walking
shoes: the centre is best seen on foot.

To/From the Airport
St Petersburg's airport is at Pulkovo, about
17km south of the centre. This is easily and
(very) cheaply accessed by metro and bus.
From Moskovskaya metro, bus 39 runs to
Pulkovo-1, the domestic terminal, and bus
13 runs to Pulkovo-2, the international terminal. There are also plenty of *marshrutky*.
The trip takes about 15 minutes and costs
just R15 (R20 for a metro/bus combination),
or you can take the buses and *marshrutky*
K3 all the way from the airport to Sennaya
pl in the city centre or K39 to pl Vosstaniya. Buses stop directly outside each of
the terminals.

If you do opt for a taxi you should be
looking at around R600 to get to the city
(R400 is the price from the city to the airport). Expect that most taxi drivers will
request more once they realise you're a foreigner and be prepared to haggle or take the
bus. Practically all hotels and hostels can
arrange transfers, generally for a slightly
more expensive fee than a regular taxi.

Bus, Marshrutka, Trolleybus & Tram
Tickets (R10 to R15 depending on the
service) are bought inside the vehicle. Bus
stops are marked by roadside 'A' signs (for
avtobus), trolleybus stops by 'Ⅲ' (representing a handwritten Russian 'T'), tram
stops by a 'T', all usually indicating the line

RAISING THE BRIDGES

Many of St Petersburg's main bridges are raised nightly when the Neva isn't frozen (from the end
of April to the end of September) to let seagoing ships through. The following schedule (which
every year changes by five minutes here or there; double-check at www.cityspb.ru/bridges.html)
governs the lives of the city's motorists and nighthawks trying to get from one area to another.
Watching the bridges rise is also a favourite romantic activity of locals and foreigners alike.

Aleksandra Nevskogo most (Map pp234-5) 2.20am-5.05am
Birzhevoy most (Map pp238-9) 2.10am-4.50am
Bolsheokhtinsky most (Map pp234-5) 2.00am-5.00am
Dvortsovy most (Map pp240-1) 1.35am-2.55am & 3.15am-4.50am
Leytenanta Shmidta most (Map pp240-1) 1.40am-4.55am
Liteyny most (Map pp234-5) 1.50am-4.40am
Troitsky most (Map pp238-9) 1.50am-4.40am
Tuchkov most (Map pp238-9) 2.10am-3.35am & 3.55am-4.45am

numbers too. Stops may also have roadside signs with little pictures of a bus, trolley-bus or tram. *Marshrutky* stop anywhere you hail them. Most transport runs from 6am to 1am.

The following are some important long routes across the city:

Along Nevsky pr between the Admiralty and Moskovsky vokzal Station Buses 7 and 22; trolleybuses 1, 5, 7, 10 and 22. Trolleybuses 1 and 22 continue out to Hotel Moskva and Alexander Nevsky Monastery. Trolleybuses 5 and 7 continue to Smolny.

Around the Sadovaya ul ring road south of Nevsky pr Trams 3, 13 and 14. Tram 3 continues north of Nevsky prospekt and then crosses the Troitsky most into Petrograd Side.

From the Hermitage to the Pribaltiyskaya Hotel on Vasilyevsky Island Bus 7; trolleybus 10.

To the Kamenny Islands Tram 34 from the Baltisky vokzal or Liteyny pr just north of Nevsky prospekt goes along Kamennoostrovsky pr and ends up on Krestovsky Island. Bus 10 from the corner of Bolshaya Morskaya ul and Nevsky pr will also get you there.

To the Petrograd Side at the Botanical Gardens Bus 128 runs from near Primorskaya metro station along both Bolshoy prs.

Metro

The **metro** (R10; ⏲ 5.30am-midnight) is usually the quickest way around the city and you'll rarely wait more than three minutes for a train; the clock at the end of the platform shows time elapsed since the last train departed. The grandest stations are on Line 1 (see below).

Zhetony (tokens) can be bought from the booths in the stations. More convenient and better value are the magnetic-strip multiride pass-cards (for seven, 15 or 30 days with various multiples of rides), known locally as a *karta*. All metro stations have card-reading turnstiles – place your card in the slot and when it comes back out you'll have a green light to proceed if there's sufficient credit left on the card.

Taxi

Official taxis (four-door Volga sedans with a chequerboard strip down the side and a green light in the front window) have a meter that drivers sometimes use, though you most often pay a negotiated price. If you want to book a taxi in advance try **Peterburgskoe taksi 068** (Petersburg Taxi; ☎ 068, 324 7777; www.taxi068.spb.ru in Russian; ⏲ 24hr), **Taxi Blues** (☎ 271 8888) or **Taxi-Million** (☎ 700 0000; ⏲ 24hr).

Most often though, people use unofficial taxis; ie any car you can stop. Negotiate the price for your destination before getting in; most short rides around the city centre

---

TOURING LINE 1

If you've had your fill of museums and palaces in St Petersburg, an ideal way to spend a rainy or cold day is to take a tour of metro Line 1 – that's the red line on the official metro map. Along the section between pl Vosstaniya and Avtovo, opened in 1955, you'll find a striking selection of station designs. Here are the things to look out for:

Ploshchad Vosstanniya (Map pp234–5) Lenin and Stalin are depicted together in the rondels at either end of the platform, as well as Lenin on a tank, Lenin alone and the Kronshtadt sailors.

Pushkinskaya (Map pp234–5) A statue of the poet rests at the end of the platform and a moulding of his head is above the escalators. Nip out the station to the view the nearby Style Moderne Vitebsky vokzal (p261).

Tekhnologichesky Institut (Map pp234–5) On the platform heading south are reliefs of famous Russian scientists, while on the northbound platform read the dates of Russia's major scientific achievements along the columns.

Baltiyskaya (Map p229) A naval theme here with a wavy motif on the mouldings along the platform ceiling and a vivid marble mosaic at the end of the platform depicting the volley from the Aurora in 1917.

Narvskaya (Map p229) One of the best stations, with a fantastic sculptured relief of Lenin and rejoicing proletariat over the escalators and lovely carvings of miners, engineers, sailors, artists and teachers on the platform columns.

Kirovsky Zavod (Map p229) Named after the nearby heavy engineering plant, the decoration along the platform also takes its inspiration from oil wells and industry. A scowling bust of Lenin can just be seen at the platform's end, half hidden by scaffolding.

Avtovo (Map p229) Scaffolding also unfortunately obscures the red and gold mosaic at the end of this station's platform, but it doesn't distract from the otherwise Babylonian lavishness of the marble and cut-glass clad columns holding up the roof, the relief of soldiers in the ticket hall and the temple-like entrance.

shouldn't cost more than R100. See p737 for safety rules on taking unofficial taxis.

AROUND ST PETERSBURG

Several grand imperial palaces and estates surround St Petersburg of which Petrodvorets and the palace-park ensembles at Tsarskoe Selo and Pavlovsk are the best. A visit to St Petersburg isn't really complete without a trip to at least one of these palaces, but be warned that at the height of the summer the crowds and lines to get into the palaces themselves are horrific (p296).

Other good day trips include Kronshtadt, a once-closed naval base on an island in the Finnish Gulf, where you'll find one of the most striking cathedrals in northern Russia. Further northwest is the charming old Finnish town of Vyborg, and eastwards, near Lake Ladoga, is what very well could have been Russia's first capital, the sleepy village of Staraya Ladoga. If you have a bit more time, spending a night in a monastery on an island in Lake Ladoga is also possible.

Longer excursions from St Petersburg, include Novgorod (p327), Pskov (p334), Valaam (p362) and Kizhi (p361).

PETRODVORETS ПЕТРОДВОРЕЦ

Looking especially stunning now the Grand Cascade fountains have been regilded, **Petrodvorets** (Map p297; ☎ 427 7425; www.peterhof.org; ul Razvodnaya 2), 29km west of St Petersburg on the Gulf of Finland, is arguably the most impressive of St Petersburg's suburban palaces.

This 'Russian Versailles' is a far cry from the original cabin Peter the Great had built here to oversee construction of Kronshtadt naval base. He liked the place so much he built a villa, Monplaisir, and then a whole series of palaces across an estate originally called Peterhof (pronounced Petergof), which has been called Petrodvorets (Peter's Palace) since 1944. All are set within a spectacular ensemble of gravity-powered fountains that are now the site's main attraction.

While Petrodvorets was trashed by the Germans in WWII (what you see today is

ST PETERSBURG

AROUND ST PETERSBURG

0 _____ 40 km
0 _____ 20 miles

FINLAND

Svetogorsk
Priozyersk
Kamennogorsk
Konevets Island
Vladimirovka
Seleznevo
To Helsinki
Vyborg
Sapernoe
LAKE LADOGA
Vysotsk
Sosnovo
Zaporozhskoe
Kirilovskoye
Primorsk
Pervomayskoe
To Nizhnesvirsky Nature Reserve (50km)
Ryabovo
Roshchino
Zelenogorsk
Repino
Toksovo
Ladozhskoe Ozero
Novaya Ladoga
GULF OF FINLAND
Sestroretsk
Vsevolozhsk
Staraya Ladoga
Kotlin Island
Volkhov
Kronshtadt
Shlisselburg
Sosnovy Bor
Oranienbaum
Petrodvorets
Strelna
ST PETERSBURG
Kirovsk
Naziya
Neva
Ropsha
Kolpino
Mga
Tsarskoe Selo
Ust-Luga
Kolly
Begunitsy
Pavlovsk
Ulyanovka
Shapki
Gatchina
Tosno
Kirishi
To Tallinn
To Moscow

TICKETS FOR THE PALACES

There's no avoiding the mammoth summertime queues to enter the main imperial palaces at Petrodvorets and Tsarskoe Selo. It's not unusual to stand in line for hours and in some cases not get in at all (for example when huge cruise ship tour groups are in town). Fights have even broken out in the queues! Avoiding some of this hassle is possible – at a price, of course. The simplest solution is to book yourself on a guided tour of either palace with a travel agency and make sure that they prebook your entry ticket; Peter's Walking Tours (p272) can do this for you. At Tsarskoe Selo it's also possible to buy a VIP ticket (€33) which gains you express entry.

largely a reconstruction), according to recent historians it suffered heaviest damage under Soviet bombing raids in December 1941 and January 1942. This was because Stalin was determined to stop Hitler from his plan of hosting a New Year's victory celebration inside the palace.

While a visit here is highly recommended, if you plan to see all the various museums in the estate it can also be an expensive and frustrating affair. The total cost for entering the lower park and all the palaces and museums is R1900. Plus many of the museums have different closing days, and some are closed or only open for weekends from October to May.

The Upper Park is free – the gardens here are lovely. Admission to the Lower Park is payable at the cash booths on the jetty and outside the gates leading to the Grand Cascade; hold on to your ticket when exiting this area so you can go back in later if you need to.

Sights
GRAND CASCADE, LOWER PARK & GROTTO

Petrodvorets' uncontested centrepiece is the **Grand Cascade**, a symphony of over 140 fountains and canals partly engineered by Peter himself. To see the fountains you have to pay to enter the **Lower Park** (adult/student R300/150; 9am-8pm Mon-Fri, to 9pm Sat & Sun) and they only work from mid-May to early October (11am–5pm Monday to Friday

and 11am–6pm Saturday and Sunday), but the gilded ensemble looks marvellous any time of year. The central statue of Samson tearing open a lion's jaws celebrates – as so many things in St Petersburg do – Peter's victory over the Swedes. If you're interested in knowing how the fountains work, pay a visit to the **Grotto** (R110; same as Grand Cascade) beneath the Grand Cascade, where there are also some trick fountains.

GRAND PALACE

Between the cascade and the formal Upper Garden is the appropriately named **Grand Palace** (adult/student R430/215; 10.30am-6pm Tue-Sun, closed last Tue of month). Be warned: it's almost always packed with tour groups in summer.

Peter's modest project, finished just before his death, was grossly enlarged by Rastrelli for Empress Elizabeth and later redecorated in lavish style for Catherine the Great. It's now a vast museum and a monument to the craft of reconstruction (which is still going on). Anything not nailed down was removed before the Germans arrived, so the paintings, furniture and chandeliers are original.

Highlights include the **Chesma Hall**, full of huge paintings of Russia's destruction of the Turkish fleet at Çesme in 1770. Of some 20 rooms, the last, without a trace of Catherine, is the finest – Peter's simple, beautiful study, was apparently the only room to survive the Germans. The study has 14 fantastic carved-wood panels, of which six reconstructions (in lighter wood) are no less impressive; each took 1½ years to do. Peter the Great still looks like the tsar with the best taste.

MONPLAISIR

Peter's outwardly more humble, sea-facing villa **Monplaisir** (adult/student R290/145; 10.30am-6pm Thu-Tue May-Oct, closed last Thu of the month) remained his favourite. It's easy to see why: it's wood-panelled, snug and elegant, peaceful even when there's a crowd – which there used to be all the time, what with Peter's mandatory partying ('misbehaving' guests were required to gulp down huge quantities of wine).

The Rastrelli-designed **Catherine Wing** (adult/student R110/55; 10.30am-6pm Fri-Wed May-Oct, 10.30am-5pm Sat & Sun Oct-May, closed last Tue of month) was added on the west side of Mon-

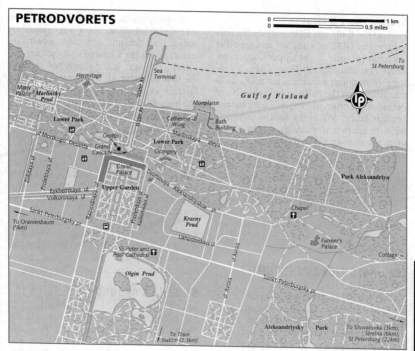

PETRODVORETS

plaisir by Empress Elizabeth in the 1740s; Catherine the Great was living here (conveniently) when her husband Peter III was overthrown. It has some pleasant period interiors. On Monplaisir's east side is Quarenghi's 1800 **Bath Building** (adult/student R150/75; 10.30am-6pm Thu-Tue, closed last Tue of the month), which is nothing special inside. In the garden in front of the buildings look out for some more trick fountains.

HERMITAGE & MARLY PALACE
On the west side of the Lower Park, near the shore, the **Hermitage** (adult/student R110/55; 10.30am-6pm Tue-Sun) is a two-storey pink-and-white box featuring the ultimate in private dining: special elevators hoist a fully laid table into the imperial presence on the 2nd floor, thereby eliminating any hindrance by servants. The elevators are circular and directly in front of each diner, whose plate would be lowered, replenished and replaced. The entry ticket here also includes admission to the modest **Marly Palace** (10.30am-6pm Tue-Sun), further to the west, inspired by a French hunting lodge.

PARK ALEKSANDRIYA & SS PETER & PAUL CATHEDRAL
To escape the crowds, even on summer weekends, wander through rambling **Park Aleksandriya** (admission free), immediately east of the Lower Park. Built for Tsar Nicholas I (and named for his tsarina), it features a neo-Gothic chapel, the ruined **Farmer's Palace** (1831), which vaguely resembles a stone farmstead, and the **Cottage** (adult/student R180/90; 10.30am-6pm Tue-Sun), a small palace dating from 1829 and modelled on an English country cottage, also with neo-Gothic interiors.

The eye-catching five-domed **SS Peter & Paul Cathedral**, across the road and east of Petrodvorets' Upper Park, is built in neo-Byzantine style but dates only from the turn of the 20th century.

Eating
There are tourist-orientated cafés and restaurants scattered around the Lower Park, none particularly outstanding and all over-priced. Bring a picnic, or consider visiting the good restaurant at Shuvalovka (p299), 3km back towards St Petersburg.

Getting There & Away

Hop on the K404 bus from outside the Baltisky vokzal (R30, 40 minutes) and get off at the main entrance to the Upper Garden, on Sankt Peterburgsky pr. There's also a reasonably frequent suburban train (R20, 30 minutes) from the Baltisky vokzal to Novy Petrodvorets, from where you'll have to take any bus except 357 to the fifth stop, which will take another 10 minutes. Alternatively, there are *marshrutky* to Petrodvorets from outside metro Avtovo.

From May to September, a fine alternative is the *Meteor* **hydrofoil** (one-way/return R250/450, 30 min) from the jetty in front of St Petersburg's Hermitage, which goes every 20 to 30 minutes from 9.30am to at least 7pm. If you're really in a hurry there are also helicopter flights from the Peter & Paul Fortress (p272).

LOMONOSOV (ORANIENBAUM) ЛОМОНОСОВ

While Peter was building Monplaisir, his right-hand man, Alexander Menshikov, began his own palace, **Oranienbaum**, 12km down the coast, a grand enterprise that eventually bankrupted him. Following Peter's death and Menshikov's exile, the estate served briefly as a hospital and then passed to Tsar Peter III, who didn't much like ruling Russia and spent a lot of time there before he was dispatched in a coup led by his wife Catherine (the Great).

Spared Nazi occupation, after WWII Oranienbaum was renamed after the scientist-poet Mikhail Lomonosov and now doubles as a **museum** and **public park** (☎ 423 1627; park admission free; 🕑 9am-10pm). Sadly most of Menshikov's impressively large **Great Palace** (Bolshoy dvorets; adult/student R185/92; 🕑 11am-4pm Mon & 11am-5pm Wed-Sun), the first building you come to from the park's entrance, is in a shocking state and many of its decrepit rooms are still under renovation. Instead head straight south through the park to the extravagantly rococo **Chinese Palace** (Kitaysky dvorets; adult/student R370/185; open 29 May-1 Oct; 🕑 11am-4pm Mon & 11am-5pm Wed-Sun). Designed by Antonio Rinaldi, Catherine the Great called it her 'dacha', albeit one including painted ceilings and fine inlaid-wood floors and walls. Check out the sumptuous **Large Chinese Room**, done up in the 'Oriental' style of the day.

Also in good shape is **Peter III's Palace** (Dvorets Petra III; adult/student R260/130), a boxy miniature palace, with rich, uncomfortable-looking interiors and some Chinese-style lacquer-on-wood paintings. It is approached through the **Gate of Honour**, all that remains of a toy fortress where Peter amused himself drilling his soldiers.

Perhaps Oranienbaum's best feature is the quiet and somewhat sombre park – it's a great place for a picnic or a tranquil walk away from the crowds.

The suburban train from St Petersburg's Baltisky vokzal to Petrodvorets continues to Lomonosov (R32). Get off at Oranienbaum-I (not II) train station, an hour from St Petersburg. From the station it's a short walk south, then west at the Archangel Michael Cathedral (Sobor Arkhangela Mikhaila) along Dvortsovy pr until you reach the palace entrance. *Marshrutka* to Lomonosov also run from outside metro Avtovo.

STRELNA & AROUND СТРЕЛЬНА И ОКРЕСТНОСТИ СТРЕЛЬНЫ

Six kilometres east of Petrodvorets is the town of Strelna, where you'll find two more palaces originally built for Peter. The butterscotch-painted Konstantinovsky Palace was chosen by Vladimir Putin as his St Petersburg residence, renovated to host 2003's Russia-EU summit and reopened as the **Palace of Congress** (Dvorets Kongressov; ☎ 438 5360; www.konstantinpalace.ru; Beryozovaya alleya 3; adult/student R200/100, plus R200 for Russian language tour, R2500 for English-language tour; 🕑 10am-5pm Thu-Tue). Visits here are by appointment only, and although the palace is not a must-see sight, it nonetheless provides a fascinating glimpse of how a modern-day tsar (sorry, president) likes to entertain his guests. There's a small collection of medals from the Hermitage's collection here and some reconstructed rooms from the time of Grand Duke Konstantin Konstanovich, the palace's last Imperial owner and something of a poet and musician. As you'd expect, security is tight; you must bring your passport and it will be checked at regular intervals on the tour.

The compact, and infinitely more charming **Peter I's Palace at Strelna** (☎ 427 7425; www.peterhof.org/museums/strelny/; adult/student R100/50; 🕑 10am-4pm Tue-Sun) lies a short walk to the west of the Palace of Congress. This is one of the first palaces that Peter the Great built out this way while supervising his far grander enterprise down the road. It has some well-furnished interiors with interesting exhibits, most notably a combined travelling chest and camp bed belonging to Alexander III.

Midway between Strelna and Petrodvorets is the tourist 'village' **Shuvalovka** (☎ 331 9999; www.shuvalovka.ru/english.htm; Sankt-Peterburgskoe sh 111; ☺ 10am-10pm). This complex of traditional-style wooden buildings is both quaint and kitsch but it does have plus points, namely an excellent restaurant and the opportunity to see Russian craftspeople in action.

Sleeping & Eating

All those visiting VIPs need somewhere to stay, so next to the Palace of Congress is the luxurious **Baltic Star Hotel** (☎ 438 5700; www .balticstar-hotel.ru; Berlozovaya alleya 3; s/d from R9280/9920 prices in units; 🛇 🖵 ⊠ 🅿). It's a fancy enough place, but there's no really compelling reason for staying this far out of St Petersburg. Its elegant European restaurant **Northern Venice** is worth a look if you're hungry. Otherwise beneath the Palace of Congress there's the **Rákóczi Wine Cellar** (☎ 320 6237; ☺ same as palace), specialising in Hungarian wines, where you can taste four wines for R100.

Also well worth checking out if you're really hungry is the traditional Russian restaurant **Sobraniye** at Shuvalovka, which serves a great four-course lunch for R200 as well as a full à la carte menu and many flavoured vodkas. If you get really sloshed the complex also includes the cute **Hotel Koshel** (s/d incl breakfast from €80/90).

Getting There & Away

Strelna is reached by the same trains and buses serving Petrodvorets (opposite).

TSARSKOE SELO & PAVLOVSK
ЦАРСКОЕ СЕЛО И ПАВЛОВСК

The grand imperial estate of **Tsarskoe Selo** (Tsar's Village; Map p300; ☎ 465 2281; eng.tzar.ru; Sadovaya ul 7) in the town of Pushkin, 25km south of St Petersburg, is often combined on a day trip with the palace and sprawling park at Pavlovsk (p301), 4km further south. This is a pity because both are gorgeous places that deserve a day each to be fully appreciated; if you have the time it's best to see them separately.

The railway that connects Pushkin and Pavlovsk with St Petersburg was Russia's first opened in 1837 to carry the royal family between here and the then capital. The town changed its name to Pushkin in 1937 after Russia's favourite poet, who studied here and whose school and dacha you can also visit.

Sights
CATHERINE PALACE

The centrepiece of Tsarskoe Selo, created under Empresses Elizabeth and Catherine the Great between 1744 and 1796, is the vast baroque **Catherine Palace** (Yekaterininsky dvorets; adult/student R500/250; ☺ 10am-6pm Wed-Mon, closed last Mon of the month), designed by Rastrelli and named after Elizabeth's mother, Peter the Great's second wife. As at the Winter Palace, Catherine the Great had many of Rastrelli's original interiors remodelled in classical style. Most of the gaudy exterior and 20-odd rooms of the palace have been beautifully restored – compare them to the photographs of the devastation left by the Germans.

Everyone has to go on a guided tour here but it's easy to slip away once you're inside the palace; getting in is another matter, especially in the summer (see p296). Tours start with the white **State Staircase** (1860). South of here, only three rooms have been restored: the **Gentlemen-in-Waiting's Dining**

THE MYSTERY OF THE AMBER ROOM

The original Amber Room was created from exquisitely engraved amber panels given to Peter the Great by the King of Prussia in 1716. Rastrelli later combined it with gilded woodcarvings, mirrors, agate and jasper mosaics to become the knockout highlight of Catherine Palace. Plundered by the Nazis during WWII, the room's decorative panels went missing in Kaliningrad in 1945, becoming one of the art world's great mysteries. It's believed, but is yet to be confirmed, that the panels were destroyed in a fire in Kaliningrad while under Red Army occupation. In 2004, as Putin and German Chancellor Gerhardt Schröder presided over the opening of the new Amber Room, restored largely with German funds, another rumour started doing the rounds: that this is in fact the original Amber Room, surreptitiously returned by the Germans.

Room, the dazzling **Great Hall**, the largest in the palace, and an **antechamber** with some huge blue-and-white Dutch ovens.

The rooms north of the State Staircase on the courtyard side include the **State Dining Room**, **Crimson** and **Green Pilaster Rooms**, **Portrait Room** and the famous **Amber Room** recently restored to its former glory (see p299) and much smaller than you may have thought from its publicity photos. This is the only room of the palace where photography is forbidden.

Most of the palace's north end is the early classical work of architect Charles Cameron, including the elegant **Green Dining Room**, the **Blue Drawing Room**, **Chinese Blue Drawing Room** and **Choir Anteroom**, whose gold

silk, woven with swans and pheasants, is the original from the 18th century.

CATHERINE PARK

Around Catherine Palace extends the lovely **Catherine Park** (Yekaterininsky Park; adult/student R100/50; ⏲ 6am-11pm). The main entrance is on Sadovaya ul, next to the palace chapel. On the edge of the park is the **Cameron Gallery** (adult/student R160/80; ⏲ 10am-5pm Wed-Mon) which has changing exhibitions. Between the gallery and the palace, notice the south-pointing ramp which Cameron added for the ageing empress to walk down into the park.

The park's outer section focuses on the **Great Pond**, where you can rent boats in summer. This section is dotted with intriguing

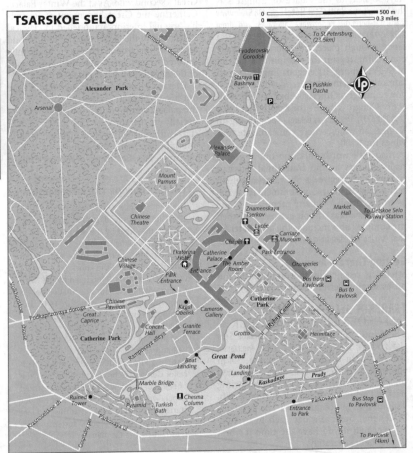

structures ranging from the **Pyramid**, where Catherine the Great buried her favourite dogs, to the **Chinese Pavilion** (or Creaking Summerhouse), **Marble Bridge** (copied from one in Wilton, England) and **Ruined Tower**, which was built 'ready-ruined' in keeping with a 1770s romantic fashion – an 18th-century empress's equivalent of prefaded denim.

ALEXANDER PALACE & PARK
A short distance north of the Catherine Palace, and surrounded by the overgrown and tranquil **Alexander Park** (admission free) is the classical **Alexander Palace** (☎ 466 6071; www.alexanderpalace.org; Dvortsovaya ul 2; adult/student R260/130; ☼ 10am-5pm Wed-Mon, closed last Wed of the month). It was built by Quarenghi between

1792 and 1796 for the future Alexander I, but Nicholas II, the last tsar, was its main tenant. It's a poignant place that doesn't get many tourists and is a welcome contrast to the Catherine Palace.

PAVLOVSK PARK & GREAT PALACE
Pavlovsk's beautifully landscaped **park** (Map p301; adult/student R80/40; ☼ 9am-9pm) of woodland, rivers, lakes, tree-lined avenues, classical statues and temples is one of the most exquisite in Russia; it's a delightful place to wander around and swallows crowds easily compared to Tsarskoe Selo.

Although designed by Charles Cameron between 1781 and 1786, on Catherine the Great's orders for her son, the future Paul I,

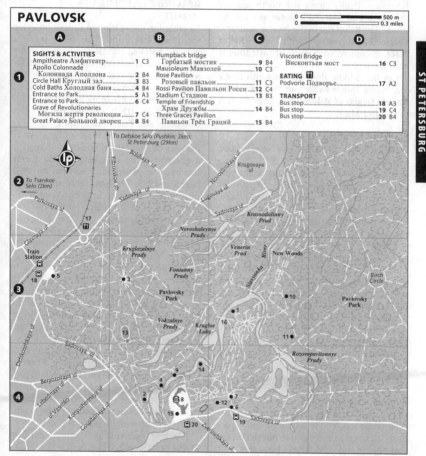

PAVLOVSK

0 — 500 m
0 — 0.3 miles

SIGHTS & ACTIVITIES		
Ampitheatre Амфитеатр	1	C3
Apollo Colonnade		
Колоннада Аполлона	2	B4
Circle Hall Круглый зал	3	B3
Cold Baths Холодная баня	4	B4
Entrance to Park	5	A3
Entrance to Park	6	C4
Grave of Revolutionaries		
Могила жертв революции	7	C4
Great Palace Большой дворец	8	B4

Humpback bridge		
Горбатый мостик	9	B4
Mausoleum Мавзолей	10	C3
Rose Pavilion		
Розовый павльон	11	C3
Rossi Pavilion Павильон Росси	12	C4
Stadium Стадион	13	B3
Temple of Friendship		
Храм Дружбы	14	B4
Three Graces Pavilion		
Павильон Трёх Граций	15	B4

Visconti Bridge		
Висконтьев мост	16	C3
EATING 🍴		
Podvorie Подворье	17	A2
TRANSPORT		
Bus stop	18	A3
Bus stop	19	C4
Bus stop	20	B4

To Detskoe Selo (Pushkin; 2km); St Petersburg (29km)

To Tsarskoe Selo (2km)

Bolshaya ul

Filtrovskoe sh

Parkovaya ul

Sadovaya ul

Lugovaya ul

Novofriadskaya ul

Krugovaya ul

Sadovaya ul

Krasnodolinny Prud

Slavyanka ul

Novoshaleynye Prudy

Glavnaya ul

Train Station

Kruglozalnye Prudy

Fontanny Prudy

Pavlovsky Park

Venerin Prud

Slavyanka River

New Woods

Birch Circle

Pavlovsky Park

Derzhoedskaya ul

Sadovaya ul

Vokzalnye Prudy

Krugloe Lake

Rozovopavilonnye Prudy

Beryozovaya ul

Lebedeva ul

ul'Vasenko

Cogata naya ul

Komushernaya ul

Sadovaya ul

Zvenneelskaya ul

the interiors of Pavlovsk's **Great Palace** (☎ 470 2155; www.pavlovskart.spb.ru; ul Revolyutsii; adult/student R370/185; 10am-6pm Sat-Thu, closed 1st Fri of the month) were largely orchestrated by Paul's second wife Maria Fyodorovna. The original palace was burnt down two weeks after liberation in WWII by a careless Soviet soldier's cigarette which set off German mines (the Soviets blamed the Germans). As at Tsarskoe Selo its restoration is remarkable.

The finest rooms are on the middle floor of the central block. Cameron designed the round **Italian Hall** beneath the dome, and the **Grecian Hall** to its west, though the lovely green fluted columns were added by his assistant Vincenzo Brenna. Flanking these are two private suites mainly designed by Brenna – Paul's along the north side of the block and Maria Fyodorovna's on the south. The **Hall of War** of the insane, military-obsessed Paul contrasts with Maria's **Hall of Peace**, decorated with musical instruments and flowers.

On the middle floor of the south block are Paul's **Throne Room** and the **Hall of the Maltese Knights of St John**, of whom he was the Grand Master.

Sleeping & Eating

Ekaterina Hotel (☎ 446 8042; www.hotelekaterina.ru; ul Sadovaya 5; s & d with breakfast €120;) Staying at this small, midrange hotel inside the palace's old servants' block not only provides great views on the building's gilded façade, but also is about your best chance of being first in the queue to get into the palace. The rooms are modern and reasonably spacious.

Podvorye (☎ 465 1399; Filtrovskoye sh 16, Pavlovsk; mains R500-800, prices in units; noon-11pm) Run by the same company as the Ekaterina Hotel, this traditional Russian log house on steroids, a short walk northeast of Pavlovsk station, dishes up huge portions of delicious Russian food, with a side-order of live Russian music and dancing. It's one of Putin's favourite restaurants.

Staraya Bashnya (☎ 466 6698; Akademichesky pr 14, Pushkin; mains R600-800, prices in units; noon-11pm) There are just four tables shoehorned into an old watchtower at this darling restaurant five minutes' walk north of the Alexander Palace, so you must book. In summer they have outdoor tables too. You're bound to find something on its extensive menu to please and the atmosphere and service can't be beaten.

Getting There & Away

Marshrutky (R25, 30 minutes) regularly shuttle to both Pushkin and Pavlovsk from outside metro Moskovskaya.

Infrequent suburban trains run from St Petersburg's Vitebsk station. For Tsarskoe Selo get off at Detskoe Selo station (R21), and for Pavlovsk (R28) at Pavlovsk station. It's about half an hour to either place.

From Detskoe Selo station *marshrutky* (R10, 5 minutes) frequently run the couple of kilometres to Tsarskoe Selo; many continue on to Pavlovsk station (for entry to the park) and to the front of Pavlovsk's palace. Walking at least one way across the park at Pavlovsk is recommended.

GATCHINA ГАТЧИНА
☎ 81371

Notable for its weathered limestone exterior, much less florid than other imperial palaces, **Gatchina** (☎ 13492; www.alexanderpalace.org/gatchina; adult/child R200/100; 10am-6pm Tue-Sun), 45km southwest of St Petersburg, was a gift from Catherine the Great to her lover Grigory Orlov for helping her get rid of her husband Peter III. It was later passed on to Catherine and Peter's son Paul I.

Gutted during WWII, only a small portion of the palace, which is shaped in a graceful curve around a central turret, has been reopened since restoration work began in 1985. The handful of state rooms on the first floor are impressive, as is the small chapel still under restoration. The most interesting feature is a 135m-long tunnel running from the palace cellar to the ornamental lake; the entrance is beside the small exhibition of antique firearms.

The best reason for coming here is to wander around the attractive **park** which has many winding paths through birch groves and across bridges to islands in the lake. Look out for the **Birch House** (Beriozoy Dom), with a façade made of birch logs, and the ruined **Eagle Pavilion** (Pavilion Orla).

In the nearby town there are a couple of interesting churches. The baroque **Pavlovsky Sobor** (ul Sobornaya), at the end of the main pedestrianised shopping street, has a grandly restored interior with a soaring central dome. A short walk west is the **Pokrovsky Sobor**, a red-brick building with bright blue domes.

Hungry? Take your pick from either **Dom Khleba** (ul Sobornaya 2; 8am-8pm), a good bakery and café that's handy for a snack or for picnic supplies, or **Kafe Piramida** (ul Sobornaya 3A; mains R80; ☯ 10am-11pm), a publike place serving simple Russian meals with some outdoor seats on the pedestrian street.

Infrequent suburban trains run to Gatchina (R30, one hour) from Baltisky vokzal. The palace is a couple of hundred meters directly east of the station. It is easier to take the metro to Moskovskaya vokzal and then hop on express bus K18 (R25, 40 mins) which runs roughly every half-hour to the palace entrance. Alternatively there are several *marshrutky* (R30, 40 mins) shuttling between Moskovskaya vokzal and Gatchina, stopping along pr 25 Oktyabrya from where the park and palace are immediately to the west.

KRONSHTADT КРОНШТАДТ

☎ 812 / pop 45,100

Within a year of founding St Petersburg, Peter – desirous of protecting his new Baltic toehold – started work on the fortress of Kronshtadt on Kotlin Island, 29km out in the Gulf of Finland. It's been a pivotal Soviet and Russian naval base ever since, and was closed to foreigners until 1996.

The main reason to visit here is to see the unusual and beautiful **Naval Cathedral** (Morskoy Sobor). Built between 1903 and 1913 to honour Russian naval muscle, this neo-Byzantine-styled wonder stands on Yakornaya pl (Anchor sq), where you'll also find an eternal flame for all of Kronshtadt's sailors, and the florid Art Nouveau monument of Admiral Makarov. The intricately detailed façade (anchors and all) repays close inspection, while inside a section of the cathedral houses the mildly interesting **Central Naval Museum** (☎ 236 4713; admission R300/100; ☯ 11am-5.15pm Wed-Sun).

Otherwise, Kronshtadt is pleasant to stroll around. In the harbourside **Petrovsky Park**, 700m southwest of the cathedral, there's a statue of Peter the Great and you can glimpse Russian warships and even some submarines: be careful about taking photographs though. For a drink or snack try **Skazka** (pr Lenina 31; ☯ 10am-11pm), a cute café on the main drag decorated with Disney characters.

In recent summers, Kronshtadt and some of the surrounding sea forts have been the scene of big dance parties – check the

---

THE KRONSHTADT MUTINY

In 1921 Kronshtadt was the scene of a short-lived mutiny against the Bolsheviks, one of the last overt signs of opposition to the revolution until *perestroika* (restructure). The Red Army sailors stationed there, ironically, were the most revolutionary, pro-Bolshevik element in 1917; Trotsky called them 'the pride and glory of the Russian Revolution'.

Four years later, hungry and poor, the sailors set up a Provisional Revolutionary Committee and drafted a resolution demanding, among other things, an end to Lenin's harsh War Communism. Red Army attempts to stifle the mutiny were at first repulsed, but on 16 March 1921 the mutineers were defeated when 50,000 troops crossed the ice from Petrograd and massacred nearly the entire naval force. Though bloodily suppressed, the event did cause Lenin to relax state pressure and scrap War Communism, marking the end of the Russian revolutionary movement.

St Petersburg media (p228) for details of events here.

Catch bus 510 to Kronshtadt from metro Staraya Derevnya (R20, 30 minutes) or take a *marshrutka* from metro Chyornaya Rechka; exit the station to your left and cross the street to find the stop. In Kronshtadt, the bus stop is on the corner of ul Grazhdanskaya and pr Lenina. From there it's about a 1km walk southeast to the Naval Cathedral.

VYBORG ВЫБОРГ

☎ 81378 / pop 81,000

Pronounced Vih-bork, this Gulf of Finland port and rail junction, 174km northwest of St Petersburg and just 30km from the Finnish border, is an appealing provincial town dominated by a medieval castle and peppered with decaying Finnish Art Nouveau buildings and romantic cobblestone streets.

The border has jumped back and forth around Vyborg for most of its history. Peter the Great added it to Russia in 1710. A century later it fell within autonomous Finland, and after the revolution it remained part of independent Finland. Since then the Finns have called it Viipuri. Stalin took

Vyborg in 1939, lost it to the Finns during WWII, and on getting it back deported all the Finns.

Today it remains resolutely a Russian town but the Finns are back by the coachloads, coming to shop and drink the town's cheap booze. With the exception of Park Monrepo all Vyborg's main sights are neatly arranged around a compact peninsula, making it an ideal town to explore on foot.

Information

You can change money at the Druzhba Hotel and there are plenty of ATMs around town including one in the **Telephone office** (cnr ul Mira & Moskovsky pr; ☻ 8am-10pm).

You can buy town maps (R7) at the **bookshop** (pr Lenina 6; ☻ 10am-6pm Mon-Sat, 11am-5pm Sun).

Sights & Activities

VYBORG CASTLE

Rising stoutly from a rock in Vyborg Bay, **Viborg Castle** (Vyborgsky zamok; ☎ 21515; admission museum & tower adults/students R150/100; ☻ museum 11am-6pm Tue-Sun, tower 11am-6pm daily) is the city's oldest building, built by the Swedes in 1293 when they first captured Karelia from Novgorod. Most of it now consists of 16th-century alterations. Inside the castle is a mildly diverting small **museum** on local history, including a tacky set-up of a border post; skip this and climb the many steps

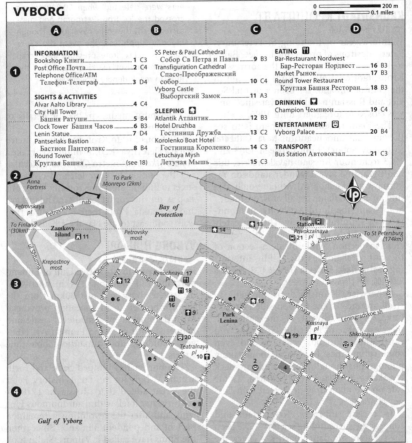

VYBORG

| | | 0 ———— 200 m |
| | | 0 ———— 0.1 miles |

INFORMATION
Bookshop Книги................................**1** C3
Post Office Почта...............................**2** C4
Telephone Office/ATM
  Телефон-Телеграф......................**3** D4

SIGHTS & ACTIVITIES
Alvar Aalto Library............................**4** C4
City Hall Tower
  Башня Ратуши..............................**5** B4
Clock Tower Башня Часов.............**6** B3
Lenin Statue......................................**7** D4
Pantserlaks Bastion
  Бастион Пантерлакс...................**8** B4
Round Tower
  Круглая Башня.........................(see 18)

SS Peter & Paul Cathedral
  Собор Св Петра и Павла..........**9** B3
Transfiguration Cathedral
  Спасо-Преображенский
  собор..**10** C4
Vyborg Castle
  Выборгский Замок....................**11** A3

SLEEPING 🛏
Atlantik Атлантик.........................**12** B3
Hotel Druzhba
  Гостиница Дружба.....................**13** C2
Korolenko Boat Hotel
  Гостиница Короленко..............**14** C3
Letuchaya Mysh
  Летучая Мышь..........................**15** C3

EATING 🍴
Bar-Restaurant Nordwest
  Бар-Ресторан Нордвест..........**16** B3
Market Рынок..................................**17** B3
Round Tower Restaurant
  Круглая Башня Ресторан........**18** B3

DRINKING 🍸
Champion Чемпион........................**19** C4

ENTERTAINMENT 🎭
Vyborg Palace................................**20** B4

TRANSPORT
Bus Station Автовокзал...............**21** C3

Anna Fortress

To Park Monrepo (2km)

Petrovskaya pl
Petrovskaya nab

Bay of Protection

To Finland (30km)

Zamkovy Island 🏰 11

Petrovsky most

Train Station 🚆

Privokzalnaya pl
🚌 21 Zheleznodorozhnaya

To St Petersburg (174km)

ul Shturma

Krepostnoy most

Xenia Val

ul Podgornaya

🏨 12

🏨 14

🏨 13

ul Progonnaya

Rynochnaya pl 17 🍴

🍴 18

nab 40-letiya Komsomola

ul Vokzalnaya

ul Avilova

ul Onezhskaya

• 6

🍴 16

🏨 9

ul Krepostnaya

pr Lenina ● 1

🏨 15

ul Severnaya

ul Dmitrova

Park Lenina

Krasnaya pl

Leningradskoe sh

Vyborgskaya ul

ul Storozhevoy Bashni

🎭 20

Teatralnaya pl

🛏 10

Leningradsky pr

🍸 19

🏛 7

2

ul Severnaya

Shkolnaya pl

☎ 3

ul Yuzhny Val

● 5

4

● 8

ul Sovetskaya

ul Pushkina

ul Leningradsky

ul Krepostnaya

pr Lenina

ul Keppa

Moskovsky pr Lenina

ul Mira

ul Kirova

Gulf of Vyborg

of the whitewashed tower for great views over the town. A great website with history of the castle and other fortifications across northern Russia is www.nortfort.ru.

PARK MONREPO
A lovely place to escape the world for a few hours if not most of the day is this sprawling **reserve** (☎ 20539; www.oblmuseums.spb.ru/eng /museums/20/info.html; ⏱ 10am-6pm) around 3km west of the train station. Laid out in a classical style, with curved bridges, arbours and sculptures, the park is as pretty as the grounds at Pavlovsk, only wilder. Read about the park's interesting history on the website.

OTHER SIGHTS
All of the other sights are located in the small heart of town. From the train and bus stations follow Leningradsky pr to **Park Lenina**. Turn left on pr Lenina and continue to pl Krasnaya where a portly **Lenin statue** still surveys the square. Opposite in the park is the **Alvar Aalto Library**, designed by the famous Finnish architect in 1935; he disowned it when the Russians renovated it with a granite façade.

Walk south down Leningradsky pr until you reach the **Pantserlaks Bastion** (1574), once part of a Swedish fortress and now containing a gallery. Return to Vyborgskaya ul and walk northwest past the blue-domed **Transfiguration Cathedral** built in 1787. Continuing in the same direction, zigzag through the streets, lined with picturesquely crumbling buildings, to the 17th century **Clock Tower** on ul Storozhevoy Bashni, then continue downhill and cross the Krepostnoy most to reach **Vyborg Castle**. On the far side of the bridge are the walls of **Anna Fortress** built in the 18th century as protection against the Swedes and named after Empress Anna Ioanovna.

Return to the town centre via Krepostnaya ul, checking out the Lutheran **SS Peter & Paul Cathedral** on the way. In pl Rynochnaya near here, the 16th century **Round Tower** now houses a good restaurant.

Sleeping
Vyborg is only a couple of hours' journey from St Petersburg, but there are several decent accommodation options, if you should wish to stay over. Note that rates are often higher on Friday and Saturday when the carousing Finns hit town; come during the week if you're looking for a quieter time.

Korolenko Boat Hostel (☎ /fax 34478; cabins per person R450) This hostel on a well-maintained 1957 Volga River cruise boat, is berthed opposite Hotel Druzhba just beyond the Viking boats. The cabins are tiny with just a sink and shared showers and toilets, but they're nicely furnished and the staff are friendly. The 24-hour bar can get rowdy.

Letuchaya Mysh (☎ 34537; www.bathotel.ru; ul Nikolaeva 3; s/d incl breakfast from R1600/2000) Also known as the Bat Hotel, this charming, modern and bright B&B occupies the attic of a small heritage building just off pr Lenina. All rooms have attached bathroom and TV and they promise Internet access will soon be available.

Hotel Druzhba (☎ 22383; booking@lens.spb.ru; ul Zheleznodorozhnaya 5; s/d with breakfast from R2200/2600) For views across the bay to the castle this ugly place next to the bus station can't be beaten. The old-fashioned rooms are due for an upgrade, and rates include a morning sauna.

Atlantik (☎ 24776; ul Podgornaya 9; s/d without bathroom €20/35; s/d with bathroom €25/45) Close to the castle, this is another new hotel in an old, decrepit building. The rooms are freshly painted and clean though, and rates include breakfast.

Eating & Entertainment
Round Tower Restaurant (☎ 31729; pl Rynochnaya 1; mains R200; ⏱ 10am-midnight) On the top floor of the tower this is the most atmospheric place in town to eat. The borsch is good and hot and the deep-fried pike-perch stuffed with mushrooms is interesting!

Champion (☎ 20247; pr Lenina; ⏱ noon-2am) The coolest Western-style bar in town is supposed to be Irish and yet it also serves several Japanese-style dishes, draft Asahi beer, and has an English menu.

Bar-Restaurant Nordwest (☎ 25893; ul Krasnoarmeiskaya 17; ⏱ 24hr) A little bit tacky looking but with a long menu (in English) and a decent range of wines.

Vyborg Palace (☎ 20560; ul Krepostnaya; mains R150-200; cinema from R80) This one-stop entertainment venue includes a restaurant, a cinema and a club! The jolly restaurant serves more mock-Japanese and European dishes and the **club** (cover R100; ⏱ 10pm-6am Fri & Sat) pumps out a mix of house and pop.

Market (⏰ 8am-6pm) Just north of the Round Tower, this market has fresh produce for a picnic.

Getting There & Away

Suburban trains for Vyborg leave from St Petersburg's Finlyandsky vokzal (R98, 2½ hours), usually early in the morning and in the late afternoon. The best service is the 87 *Baltika* leaving at around 7.50am (R128). It has comfy seats and a buffet. Returning from Vyborg, good trains include the 88 at 10am, 96 at 3.15pm and 98 at 8.13pm.

All buses between St Petersburg and Helsinki stop at Vyborg. There are also several buses a day to/from Vyborg (R130, 2½ hours). From St Petersburg, they leave Avtovokzal No 2 and stop in front of metro pl Lenina, on ul Botkinskaya.

STARAYA LADOGA СТАРАЯ ЛАДОГА

☎ 81363 / pop 3000

Although you'd hardly guess it now the tranquil village of Staraya (Old) Ladoga, 125km east of St Petersburg on the winding banks of the Volkhov River, was once an active participant in the very birth of the Russian nation (see boxed text, below). Today there's little to see along its quiet streets other than an ancient fortress, several churches and some prettily painted wooden cottages. It makes for a pleasant escape from St Petersburg, particularly in summer when a swim in the river adds to the charm.

Dating from around the 8th century, the town was known only as Ladoga until 1704 when Peter the Great founded Novaya (New) Ladoga to the north, as a transfer point for the materials arriving to build St Petersburg. Protected as a national reserve, the town's basic structure and street patterns have remained virtually unchanged since the 12th century, give or take a few ugly Soviet blocks.

Sights

Everything of interest lies along the main street Volkhovsky pr. The highlight is the **fortress** (☎ 49331; free; ⏰ 9.30am-6pm Tue-Sun May-Aug, 9.30am-4.30pm Tue-Sun Sep-Apr) at the southern end of the village and with an excellent view along the river. Within its partially ruined 7m-thick walls you'll find the stone **St George's Church** (admission R30), only open May to October, to protect the delicate 12th-century frescoes still visible on its walls, and the cute wooden **Church of Dimitri Solun**. Inside the fortress' main tower is the **Historical-Architectural & Archaeological Museum** (admission R25) housing an interesting retrospective of the area's history including a scale model of how the fortress once looked, items found on archaeological digs and English explanations.

At one time, six monasteries worked in this small region. Now only the **Nikolisky Monastery** (⏰ 9am-7pm), 500m south of the fortress, remains; it's in the process of being rebuilt, the main church and bell tower now looking quite handsome.

Atop the hill at the north end of the village the striking blue, onion-domed **John the Baptist Church** (⏰ 9am-6pm), dating from 1694, is in much better repair, the frescos and iconostasis inside being particularly colourful. Nearby, beside the river banks, is an ancient burial mound and, beneath the church, caves where glass was once made.

RUSSIA'S ANCIENT CAPITAL

Just as the origins of Rus are continually debated, so will Staraya Ladoga's status as 'Russia's first capital'. Nevertheless, its age (historians have given 753 as the village's birthdate) and significance remain uncontested.

When the Scandinavian Viking Rurik, along with his relatives Truvor and Sineus, swept into ancient Russia in 862, he built a wooden fortress at present-day Staraya Ladoga and made this his base. You can see Rurik in a colourful mosaic on the side of the village school. Locals even claim the tumulous on the banks of the Volkhov River at the northern end of the village is the grave of Oleg, Rurik's successor.

Archaeological expeditions continue to uncover a wealth of information about the town's past. In 1997, a second 9th-century fortress was discovered 2km outside the village. Evidence of Byzantine cultural influences in the frescoes of the village's 12th-century churches point to the town as a cultural as well as historical and commercial crossroad.

Eating

There are no hotels in Staraya Ladoga and just a handful of eating options. In the past the food and ambience at Ladya, above the village's general store, was good but it was closed for repairs at the time or research.

An alternative is the café-bar **Nochnaya Ptitsa** (Volkhovsky pr; mains R30; ☺ 3pm-3am Mon-Thu, noon-3am Fri-Sun), a 100m north of the fortress. The food is nothing to write home about but its nicely decorated inside and has an outdoor seating area in summer.

Getting There & Away

Take one of the frequent *elektrichka* (suburban train) to Volkhov (the Volkhovstroy I station) from Moscow station in St Petersburg (R70, 2½ hours). From Volkhov, take the hourly bus or minibus 23 (R13, 20 minutes) headed towards Novaya Ladoga from the main bus stop outside the station, just across the square. Get off when you see the fortress.

NIZHNESVIRSKY NATURE RESERVE НИЖНЕСВИРСКИЙ ГОСУДАРСТВЕННЫЙ ЗАПОВЕДНИК

On the southeastern shore of Lake Ladoga, the 414 sq km **Nizhnesvirsky Nature Reserve** (☎ 8126-420 5201; orlan@orlan.spb.su), 175km from St Petersburg, is an important stopover for migratory birds and home to a variety of animals, among them the Lake Ladoga ringed seal, a freshwater subspecies particular to the area. Arrangements to visit the reserve can be made directly, or through the American Association for the Support of Ecological Initiatives (AASEI). In St Petersburg call the AASEI's local branch **ADONIS** (☎ 812-307 0918; alexk@aasei.spb.su), or contact director Bill Wasch at its **US headquarters** (☎ 860-346 2967; www.wesleyan.edu/aasei).

KONEVETS ISLAND ОСТРОВ КОНЕВЕЦ

An unusual overnight excursion is to Konevets Island, around 100km north of St Petersburg, close to the western shore of Lake Ladoga. The beautiful sky-blue domed monastery here was founded in 1393 by Arseny Konevetsky. The island was part of Finland between world wars, while in Soviet times, it became an off-limits military base (the base is still there). The monastery reopened in the early 1990s and has since undergone massive restoration with Finnish funding.

As well as the main Kremlin grounds there are several charmingly decorated wooden chapels in nearby forests, including one on a huge boulder; this was the site of pagan horse-slaughtering rituals. The rest of the island is very peaceful, with clean beaches and lots of forests to wander through.

The easiest way to the island is on a one-day tour (R580), held most Sundays, and organised by the monastery's St Petersburg office (Map pp234-5; ☎ 571 8079; www.konevets.spb .ru, in Russian; Zagorodny pr 7; Ⓜ Vladimirskaya). The tours depart around 9am from the metro station Ozerki. Two-day tours are scheduled once a month or during festivals and include accommodation. You can also contact the monastery about overnight accommodation on the island; they run a couple of simple guesthouses for pilgrims (R200 per night).

By public transport take a suburban train from Finlyandsky vokzal to Sosnovo, then a bus to Vladimirovka, then try to hire a boat to sail the 5km to the island, a total trip of around seven hours.

The monastery's website has a good map of the island and check the Wandering Camera website (www.enlight.ru/camera /290/index_e.html) for a visual preview of what you'll see there.

ST PETERSBURG

Western European Russia
Западно-Европейская Россия

With its birch forests, idyllic rivers and endless rolling steppe, Western European Russia is an enticing vision straight out of Russian folklore. Those seeking the soul of Old Rus would do well to explore this historically rich region, as the charming old villages, photogenic fortress towns and gold-domed monasteries are just part of the lure.

Novgorod, founded over 1000 years ago, occupies a pivotal place here. Its claim as the birthplace of modern Russia can be experienced in its red-brick ramparts, ancient churches and inspiring vistas along the meandering Volkhov River. Other striking kremlin towns include Pskov and Smolensk, both set along scenic rivers and with a colourful past that began well before the Mongols swept through the land. Smolensk is also famed for its well-known native son, Mikhail Glinka, widely regarded as the founder of Russian orchestral music. The symphony hall where he conducted is still a fantastic place to hear live concerts throughout the year.

Some of Russia's greatest writers hail from this region. In Mikhailovskoe, Pushkin's ancestral home, travellers can stroll the serene lake shore that inspired one of Russia's greatest poets. For an equally bucolic experience, step back into the 19th century at Staraya Russa, a sleepy town of blue- and green-painted wooden houses, an ambling river and the house of Dostoevsky, who set *The Brothers Karamazov* there.

This chapter also includes Kaliningrad, one of Russia's more elusive destinations, with six centuries of Prussian history. Geographically isolated from the rest of Russia, this small wedge facing the Baltic makes for some fascinating exploration. It boasts a lively, youthful city and some lovely countryside that includes the Curonian Spit, a long, narrow strip of land backed with sand dunes and lined with wildlife-filled forests. In addition to Kaliningrad, this region comprises the areas between Moscow and St Petersburg up to the borders of Estonia, Latvia, Belarus and Ukraine.

HIGHLIGHTS

- Gaze at the idyllic landscape that inspired one of Russia's greatest poets at **Mikhailovskoe** (p339)
- Delve into centuries of Russian history at the striking kremlin town of **Novgorod** (p327)
- Witness Russia's great orchestral legacy in the **Glinka Concert Hall** (p326) in Smolensk
- Follow the winding river Polist through **Staraya Russa** (p333), the village where Dostoevsky once lived
- Explore old Prussian ruins and the breathtaking coastline in the **Kaliningrad region** (p341)

History

Slavs, migrating from the west, first settled in the region between the 6th and 8th centuries AD. At the same time Varangians (Vikings) from Scandinavia began trading and raiding across the region en route to the Black Sea. In 862, apparently at the invitation of local Slavs, Varangians under Prince Rurik came to rule, establishing order in the land of 'Rus'. Their first permanent settlement, Novgorod, is seen by many as the birthplace of Russia. Rurik's successor Oleg founded the Kyivan Rus state, and the upstart principalities of Vladimir and Muscovy are descended from the same line.

By the 12th century Novgorod was a European political and commercial centre, expanding aggressively and increasingly attracting the attention of the Swedes, who held sway in most of present-day northwest Russia. The friction, at first economic, took on a religious tenor as Swedish crusaders tried to push back the Orthodox 'heathens'. Novgorod's Prince Alexander Nevsky is considered a Russian hero for thrashing both the Swedish and Teutonic crusaders in the 1240s (the latter fantastically imagined in Eisenstein's 1938 film *Alexander Nevsky*), putting an end to Christian intentions in Russia.

Though the Mongol Tatars got only as far as the swamps outside Novgorod, the city's princes sensibly accepted the Tatars as rulers. By 1480 Ivan III had driven them out and annexed Novgorod and all its northern lands for Moscow. South of Moscow, towns such as Oryol and Voronezh were founded to serve as fortifications against the Tatars.

From 1558 to 1583, Ivan IV (the Terrible) fought Poles, Lithuanians and Swedes in an unsuccessful grab for Baltic real estate. Soon afterwards, with Russia in a shambles during the Time of Troubles (p39), Sweden and Poland took bits of western Russian territory, including Smolensk and the eastern end of the Gulf of Finland. Under the early Romanov tsars (1613–82), Russia gradually expanded its territories west and south of Moscow, but experienced revolts from Cossack communities, including those from Voronezh, near the Don River.

Determined to defeat the Swedes and reach the Baltic, Peter the Great made an

WESTERN EUROPEAN RUSSIA

alliance with Poland and Denmark, and forced his way to the Gulf of Finland, pausing only to lay the foundations of St Petersburg. With his new navy he won the Great Northern War (1700–21), regaining everything from Sweden, plus the Baltic coastline down to Riga in Latvia. With the Partitions of Poland between 1772 and 1795, Russia's western territories expanded further to include Lithuania, Belarus and much of Poland.

In 1920 Soviet Russia recognised the independence of Estonia, Latvia and Lithuania. During the early stages of WWII secret deals that had been struck with Nazi Germany allowed the USSR's western European border to expand again. Hitler subsequently invaded the western USSR, including the Baltic States, and the German war machine devastated many cities in this region. Towns in the south such as Oryol, Bryansk and Smolensk saw the heaviest fighting, with cities like Kursk and Voronezh almost completely destroyed. For the most part they have been thoroughly rebuilt, with the sad loss of many of their historic neighbourhoods (not to mention the millions of casualties).

After the German army was driven out of Russia, the Red Army also seized Kaliningrad, a previously German city, and Russianised it over the subsequent 60 years. The tumultuous events of 1990–91 saw the new independence of the Baltic States, Belarus and Ukraine, and Russia's western boundaries became borders between countries, rather than just between republics of the Soviet Union.

SOUTH & WEST OF MOSCOW

Set on rolling, ever-changing steppe, this region has small, attractive towns and ragged, industrial cities. Among the highlights are the sleepy village Yelets, the revitalised old streets of Smolensk, the literary-minded town Oryol and nearby Spasskoe-Lutovinovo, Turgenev's lushly landscaped estate. The rather Soviet cities of Voronezh and Kursk, while omitted from many itineraries, have some worthwhile sights. Towns in this region are generally poor, with large portions of the populace unemployed and given to loitering on street corners, often in Adidas sweatclothes, for some reason.

> ## TELEPHONE CODE CHANGES
>
> In late 2005, the Russian Communications Ministry announced plans to change the area codes for 19 regions across Russia, including many towns in western European Russia. All codes that used to start with '0' should now start with a '4' instead, although be aware that there may be teething problems with this change. The new numbers are reflected here.

Keeping a low profile will help you to avoid offence or threats, though for the most part the residents aren't antiforeigner or aggressive, just bored.

The major towns listed here are easily accessible by train. The main routes from Moscow are the eastern route to Yelets and Voronezh; the central route through Oryol, Kursk and Belgorod en route to Kharkiv in Ukraine; and the western route, through Smolensk heading towards Minsk (Belarus).

YELETS ЕЛЕЦ
☎ 47416 / pop 118,000 / ⊗ Moscow

Amid lovely countryside, Yelets is a relaxing town that looks like a slice of mid-19th-century Russia. Streets are lined with colonnaded buildings and wood and brick houses, while the town's showpiece, beautiful Ascension Cathedral, is visible from kilometres around. Tucked into the town's tidy streets are another half-dozen working churches and cathedrals, as well as ruins of several more. There's also a well-stocked regional museum and a museum devoted to Soviet composer Tikhon Khrennikov.

Yelets was founded on the Sosna River in 1146 as a fortification against the Polovtsy, invaders from the east. It was sacked by Tatars three times and rebuilt in the 1500s.

If you do not require much in the way of nightlife or hotel amenities, you might consider staying here and visiting the far larger and gruffer Voronezh on a day trip.

Orientation
Yelets' centre is laid out in a grid, with ul Kommunarov connecting City Park in the east with Ascension Cathedral in the west. Further west (downhill) lies the Sosna River. The train station and long-distance bus stop are about 3km southeast of the centre.

Horse-drawn carts would look perfectly appropriate on ul Mira, perhaps the most picturesque street in town; it's also the main shopping street, filled with pedestrians throughout the day. At the southern end is the main square, pl Lenina, which looks like a movie set for an Ostrovsky drama. Near the square is a bare-bones **souvenir shop** (ul Mira; ✆ 9am-6pm Mon-Fri, 9am-3pm Sat). Excellent Russian-language maps (R20) are available from kiosks or the Hotel Yelets.

Information

Bagira Plyus (ul Mira 96; per hr R50) Attracting a gaggle of eager young schoolchildren, this Internet café keeps irregular hours.

Sberbank (ul Mira) Best place in town to change money (US dollars and euros only).

Yelets Travel Bureau (✆ 20618; ul Mira 121; ✆ 8.30am-5pm Mon-Fri) This office can arrange tours around town and to Znamensky Monastery (in Russian only) for around R300 per person.

Sights

CHURCHES

Beneath the gleaming dome of **Ascension Cathedral** (foot of ul Kommunarov; ✆ services 8-11am & 5-7pm) you'll find a fantastical, multicoloured interior, with gilt-framed iconography stacked high on each wall. It was designed by Konstantin Ton (1794–1881), the architect who designed both St Petersburg's Moscow and Moscow's Leningrad train stations. There's a great view of the cathedral from the bridge crossing the Sosna, just east of town.

Vvedenskaya Church (Vvedensky spusk), a tiny jewel box of a church, stands near a cluster of photogenic late-17th- and early-18th-century wooden houses. At the bottom of the hill, a path under the trees bearing right leads to a floating footbridge over the river to the local **beach**. Built during the early 1900s, **Great Count's Church** (ul Sovetskaya) has a distinctly modernist, even Art Nouveau flair, with an exotically tiled interior of metallic hues. The cross on the top is made of crystal, supposedly donated from the local glassware factory.

OTHER SIGHTS

The town's **City Park** (Gorodskoy Park) is quite relaxing, with a Ferris wheel that spins during summer. There's a small **Children's Park** (Detsky Park) across the street, with basic playground equipment, the chassis of a MiG fighter jet and a café.

For a fine view of the town's gilded cupolas, ask the firefighters at the antique red-brick fire house to let you climb up their **fire observation tower** (ul Kommunarov).

Yelets' **Regional Museum** (ul Lenina 99; admission R10; ✆ 9am-5pm Tue-Sat) houses artefacts from its colourful past. Particularly interesting are the model of ancient Yelets and the collection of Russian coins from the 4th century BC to the Soviet era. Upstairs is a collection of paintings by local 19th-century artist Meshchkov and information on Yelets' devastating WWII experience.

The crisp **Khrennikov Museum** (✆ 49476; ul Mayakovskogo 16; admission R10; ✆ 9.30am-4.30pm Tue-Sat) pays homage to the successful Soviet composer on the site where he grew up and first studied music. Original furniture, photos and artefacts fill the small house; because Khrennikov was favoured by the Soviet state, the documentation is also interesting in terms of the history of Soviet aesthetics. Writer Ivan Bunin spent some of his childhood in Yelets, studying at the town's gymnasium. A small **museum** (✆ 24329; ul Gorkogo 16) chronicles his life and works.

The crumbling tower visible over the town's north end is the early-19th-century **Znamensky Monastery**. For a nice hour-long hike, follow ul Sovetskaya towards the monastery. At the fork in the road, veer right downhill to the water and cross the handmade footbridge. A bit to your left will be the base of a stone stairway leading up to the monastery. All that's left today are remnants of the old wall, the shell of a tower and an unsurpassed view over all Yelets. The large blue cupolas off to the right, as you look out from the monastery, belong to the now-abandoned **Church of the Nativity** (Tserkov Khristorozhdestvenskaya).

Sleeping & Eating

Hotel Yelets (✆ 22235; ul Kommunarov 14; s/d from R405/680) This nine-storey monstrosity is the only hotel in town. It's well worn, with ageing wallpaper and dated fixtures, but rooms have nice views of the cupolas and the staff are grateful, if somewhat astonished, to see tourists. If by some quirk the hotel is full, you could try walking along the surrounding streets and asking for a room to rent.

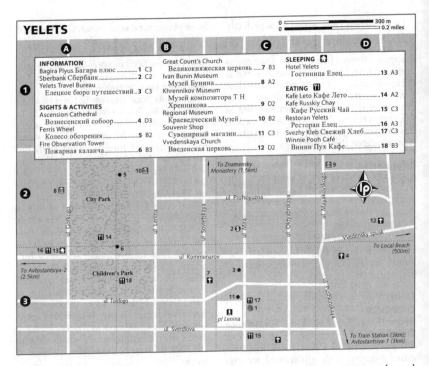

YELETS

0 _____ 300 m
0 _____ 0.2 miles

INFORMATION
Bagira Plyus Багира плюс 1 C3
Sberbank Сбербанк 2 C2
Yelets Travel Bureau
　Елецкое бюро путешествий ..3 C3

SIGHTS & ACTIVITIES
Ascension Cathedral
　Вознесенский собоор..............4 D3
Ferris Wheel
　Колесо обозрения 5 B2
Fire Observation Tower
　Пожарная каланча....................6 B3

Great Count's Church
　Великокняжеская церковь 7 B3
Ivan Bunin Museum
　Музей Бунина............................8 A2
Khrennikov Museum
　Музей композитора Т Н
　Хренникова................................9 D2
Regional Museum
　Краеведческий Музей 10 B2
Souvenir Shop
　Сувенирный магазин 11 C3
Vvedenskaya Church
　Введенская церковь................12 D2

SLEEPING 🛏
Hotel Yelets
　Гостиница Елец.........................13 A3

EATING 🍴
Kafe Leto Кафе Лето 14 A2
Kafe Russkiy Chay
　Кафе Русский Чай....................15 C3
Restoran Yelets
　Ресторан Елец...........................16 A3
Svezhy Kleb Свежий Хлеб..........17 C3
Winnie Pooh Café
　Винни Пух Кафе........................18 B3

Restoran Yelets (☎ 22296; ul Kommunarov 18; meals R100-250) Located in the same building as the hotel (go outside and turn left), this is a red-velvet, disco-light extravaganza. The live music – synchroniser, drum box and schmaltzy vocalist – starts at 8pm. The food, on the other hand, is pretty decent. The *firmenniye blyuda* (house specials) are good bets. Listed on the first page of the menu and changed periodically, they always include some tasty meat dishes and bliny.

Kafe Russkiy Chay (pl Lenina; meals R10-30; 🕙 8am-8pm) Set with long wooden tables and benches, this simple eatery remains a bastion of communal dining, its popularity persisting despite the basic, almost tasteless fare. *Pelmeni* (small dumplings usually filled with meat), bliny, soup and salads are among the options. Order at the counter.

Svezhy Khleb (ul Mira at pl Lenina; 🕙 7.30am-7pm) This no-frills bakery serves dark bread, croissants and jam-filled *bulochki* (buns).

Winnie Pooh Café (Children's Park; snacks R20-35; 🕙 10am-8pm) Popular with the six- to 10-year-old set, this brightly hued eatery makes a fine pit stop for pizza, ice cream, cake and pots of tea.

Kafe Leto (🕙 11am-11pm Jun-Sep) Just inside the City Park, off ul Kommunarov, this open-air spot serves standard *pelmeni*, shashlyk, salads and soup. It's also a fine place for a drink in the afternoon.

Getting There & Away

On the Moscow–Donetsk railway, Yelets has several services each day to Moscow (R565, eight to 10 hours) and Oryol (R105 to R200, four hours by train and six hours by *elektrichka*, a slower suburban train). The **train station** (☎ 33109) has lockers (R40 per day) and a banner-waving collection of Soviet socialist realist oil paintings in the main hall.

There are several buses a day to/from Voronezh (R85). Buses to/from Tula and Oryol take about six hours. There are two long-distance bus stops in Yelets: one is near the train station on the main highway; the other is 2.5km west of City Park off ul Kommunarov. From here to town, bus 1 runs every 15 minutes and stops just past Hotel Yelets on ul Kommunarov; it's a 10-minute ride. From the train station to the centre, walk to the west end of the platform and cross the tracks to the bus stop. Buses to local destinations as well as some buses to Voronezh leave from bus stop No 1 (Avtostantsiya-1) next to the train station. For other destinations, head to bus stop No 2 (Avtostantsiya-2). A taxi to Hotel Yelets should cost about R50.

VORONEZH ВОРОНЕЖ
☎ 483 / pop 841,000 / ☺ Moscow

Upon reaching the industrial shores of Voronezh, your first reaction may be to swallow in dread. Black, belching smokestacks line the riverbank, and in addition to the smog, an opaque gritty pessimism hangs over the town. Indeed, Voronezh is a city scraping and clawing its way out of the Soviet era, with few immediate signs of success. Construction is rampant in this large city, giving rise to everything from gleaming new churches to cookie-cutter apartment buildings – but all the scaffolding cannot conceal the poverty that afflicts most citizens here.

The sullen Adidas-clad young men who seem to lurk on every corner of provincial European Russia are particularly numerous in Voronezh. Unfortunately, there have been attacks on foreign visitors in recent years, and travellers should be particularly cautious when visiting this city.

Though Voronezh lacks the charm and accessibility of smaller towns in the region, it does contain some interesting sights, and the growing number of cafés and restaurants suggest Voronezh may be on the up and up. The city and the surrounding district are fondly remembered by many Russians for their rich history, which you can uncover at a handful of small museums, as well at the beautiful St Alexey monastery.

History
Voronezh was first mentioned in 12th-century chronicles, but it was officially founded in 1585 as a fortress against invading Tatars. Some *stanitsi* (Cossack villages) were established in this frontier region, and uprisings against Russian domination were common. Some of the more legendary uprisings were led by Stepan (Stenka) Razin in 1670–71 and Kondraty Bulavin in 1707–08.

During the reign of Peter the Great, the first Russian warship, the *Predestinatia,* was built here in 1696; more than 200 warships

from the Voronezh dockyards followed to form the new Russian fleet.

During WWII the city suffered frontline fighting for 200 days, with over 90% of its buildings destroyed (especially during intense skirmishes in July and August 1942).

Orientation
The main street is pr Revolyutsii; its northern tip is connected to the train station by ul Koltsovskaya, while the southern tip passes through pl Lenina before becoming ul Kirova. The other main street is ul Plekhanovskaya, intersecting at pl Lenina. The eastern bank of Voronezh across the reservoir was founded in 1928. In fact the view across the river is a Soviet dream: factories and smokestacks piled one upon the other and all becloaked in the smog of productivity. Usable Russian-language maps of the city are available from kiosks at the train station and at bookshops in town.

Information
Kamelot Programma For information on goings-on around town, as well as current museum exhibitions, pick up a copy of this Russian-language publication, out each Wednesday, at any newsstand.

Knizhny Magazin Masko (pl Lenina 15) On the southeast corner of pl Lenina, this bookshop sells Russian-language maps of the city.

Main post office (pr Revolyutsii 23; per hr R60) Provides Internet service.

Public library (pl Lenina 2; per hr R40) The library's ground-level computer centre provides Internet access.

Sberbank (ul Plekhanovskaya 12; pr Revolyutsii 52) One of several places to change US dollars, Sberbank has two convenient locations with 24-hour ATMs.

Voronezh Office of Travel & Excursions (☎ 552 570; ul Plekhanovskaya 2) Excursions around town can be booked through this agency. English-language tours are unlikely, but not impossible; call in advance.

Sights
MUSEUMS
The **IN Kramskoy Regional Fine Arts Museum** (Khudozhestvenny muzey IN Kramskogo; ☎ 553 867; pr Revolyutsii 18; admission R20; ☺ 10am-6pm Tue-Sun) is reached through a passage leading into a courtyard; look for the large green structure. Russian painting and sculpture, Greek and Roman sculpture and an Egyptian sarcophagus form the bulk of the collection, with exhibitions of modern local artists behind the main building.

Well stocked if not well lit, the **Regional Museum** (Kraevedchesky muzey; ☎ 523 892; ul Plekhanovskaya 29; admission R10; ☻ 10am-6pm Wed-Sun) has permanent exhibits on Peter the Great and the history of the region from the pre-Bronze Age to the Soviet era. The museum is closed on the first Wednesday of each month. Postcards of old Voronezh are on sale at the ticket office.

The large, two-storey **Museum of the Great Patriotic War 1941–1945/Arsenal** (Muzey Velikoy Otechestvennoy voyny 1941–1945/Arsenal; ☎ 552 421; ul Stepana Razina 43; admission R20; ☻ 11am-6pm Tue-Sun) has the usual photos and weapons found in WWII museums. One of the most interesting exhibits is an *obyavlenie* (a handwritten bulletin) ordering residents to evacuate and leave everything behind except their cows and goats. Outside the museum, about 50m towards the reservoir, are a few tanks and a rocket-launching truck.

IS Nikitin Literary Museum (Oblastnoy Literaturny muzey imeni IS Nikitina; ul Plekhanovskaya 3; admission R20; ☻ 10am-6pm Tue-Sat) includes exhibits on writers Alexey Koltsov, Ivan Bunin and Andrei Platonov in the former home of Ivan Nikitin, a second-rate realist poet born in Voronezh in the early 19th century.

You'll have to delve deep into the back-streets of Voronezh to reach the quirky collection at the **AL Durov House-Museum** (Dom-muzey AL Durova; ☎ 530 387; ul Durova 2; admission R40; ☻ 10am-6pm Tue-Sat), near the reservoir. The Durovs were Russia's most famous circus stars, and the museum is situated on what were once the grounds of their home-base circus. It showcases photos and costumes. Even if it is closed, you can still admire the grounds, including Durov's grave.

CHURCHES & MONASTERY

There are a dozen churches, cathedrals and monasteries in town, with more appearing all the time. The large green-domed church in the centre, visible from many points in town, is the brand-new **Voskresevesky Khram** (ul Ordzhonikidze 15). It boasts a colourful fresco-covered interior that now hosts regular choral services.

The recently restored **St Alexey of Akatov women's monastery** (Svyato Alekseevo-Akatov zhensky monastyr; ul Osvobozhdeniya Truda 1) is worth visiting. The interior of the monastery church is covered entirely with frescoes; if you come at 7.30am or 5pm you'll hear the intensely beautiful service. The monastery, founded in 1674, is near the river on lovely grounds, which include a tiny graveyard, and surrounded by colourful, lopsided cottages.

In a downtrodden part of town, the small 1720 **Nicholas Church** (Nikolskaya tserkov; ul Taranchenko 19-a) has a fresco-covered entryway and an 18th-century iconostasis. In spite of the many icons and ornamentation, it has the feel of a country church and holds frequent Orthodox services.

Sleeping

Voronezh has a limited range of sleeping options. Both hotels listed below are convenient, just off pl Lenina.

Hotel Don (☎ 555 315; ul Plekhanovskaya 8; s/d from R1300/1400) With large, pleasant rooms and well-maintained facilities, the Hotel Don is the city's best. It is often booked with groups or conferences; best to call ahead.

Hotel Brno (☎ 509 249; ul Plekhanovskaya 9; s/d from R750/1000) This giant, unattractive building looming over the city hides smallish but fairly clean rooms. Outside the hotel, you

WALKING TOUR

For a stroll through Voronezh's past, start at the **Arsenal** (take any minibus from ul Plekhanovskaya to the stop just before Chernyavsky bridge), cross ul Stepana Razina and take the narrow, dusty Sacco and Vanzetti ul north. The streets that cross Sacco and Vanzetti ul are named after Russian artists (notice dilapidated ul Dostoyevskogo). Turn right onto ul Durova and follow the dirt road to the **AL Durov House-Museum**. Next, go towards the reservoir then turn right and continue about 100m to an overgrown stone staircase. This leads to the **St Alexey monastery**, which will emerge on your left. Leaving the monastery, follow the street away from the reservoir, past the 18th-century **Vvedenskaya Church** (Vvedenskaya tserkov; ul Osvobozhdeniya Truda 18) and back to ul Stepana Razina. From the bridge at the foot of Razina, you can see the gold dome of the **Intercession Cathedral**, from where it's a short walk to the café- and store-lined pr Revolyutsii.

can often find locals renting private rooms for around R500 a night.

Eating

Restoran Pushkin (☎ 533 305; ul Pushkinskaya 1; meals R200-900) The elegant green-toned dining room makes a fine setting for an indulgent meal. Among the selections on the English-language menu are salmon with caviar, rack of lamb and roast duck. The three-course business lunch (R315) is good value. At night, Pushkin's excellent dishes are marred only by the live music.

Sinyor Pomidor (ul Plekhanovskaya 4; pizzas R140-200) A block south of Hotel Don, this pleasant café serves decent pizzas for two (half pizzas available), with friendly service and Italianesque décor.

Kofeynya Cappuccino (☎ 208 792; ul Plekhanovskaya 2; meals R50-150; ☽ 10am-11pm) This colourfully painted coffee house boasts electronic music and a range of caffeinated beverages, tasty desserts and snacks.

Paladin (☎ 551 862; ul Pushkinskaya 7; mains R100-250) Down the road from Restoran Pushkin, Paladin specialises in shashlyk and other meat dishes – not surprising given the medieval-inspired setting.

Po Shchuchyemu Velenyu (☎ 550 479; pr Revolyutsii 47; meals R90-150) This decent restaurant is easily spotted by its unusual log-cabin façade. Inside, you'll find a good buffet, subdued conversation and a splash of style.

Entertainment

In addition to the **Regional Philharmonia** (Oblastnaya filarmoniya; ☎ 554 877; pl Lenina 11), the **State Theatre of Opera & Ballet** (Gosudarstvenny teatr opery i baleta; ☎ 553 927; pl Lenina 7) hosts regional productions, some youth productions and the occasional touring show. Puppet theatre, one of the few arts truly embraced by the Soviets, can be admired at the **Regional Puppet Theatre** (Oblastnoy teatr kukol; pr Revolyutsii 50). Tickets for all venues can usually be had for R60 to R120.

Getting There & Away

Voronezh is well connected by rail and bus, but there are several daily flights to/from Moscow (Domodedovo).

Several trains run daily to Moscow (R675, 10 hours). Trains to other destinations include Saratov (18 hours), Kislovodsk (25 hours), St Petersburg (24 hours) and Yelets (R400, 4½ hours).

Sample destinations from **Voronezh bus station** (☎ 161 378) are Moscow (R540, eight hours), Saratov (R650, 12 hours), Volgograd (R675, 12 hours), Oryol (R480, seven hours) and Yelets (R90, three hours). You may have to pay a small fee (R10 to R50) for your luggage.

Getting Around

Buses to the airport (40 minutes) depart from the train station or near Hotel Brno.

Outside the **train station** (pl Chernyakhovskogo) you'll encounter a mess of buses, *marshrutky* (dedicated minibuses) and trams. Most have major destination points pasted to the window; to reach the centre, look for pl Lenina. Some trains may stop at **Pridacha**, a few kilometres outside the city. If you arrive there, follow the other arrivals 300m out of the station, where you'll find a parking lot full of *marshrutky* to whisk you into town.

To get to the **main bus station** (Moskovsky pr 17) take tram 12. To reach the centre from the bus station, exit the station and catch a bus heading right; buses 6 and 7 are among those that run along ul Plekhanovskaya.

ORYOL ОРЁЛ

☎ 4862 / pop 345,000 / ☽ Moscow

Once the winter snows have melted, Oryol can seem like a magical place. Afternoon boaters float idly along the Oka River as the glow of sunlight illuminates the golden domes of Orthodox churches about town. Couples and friends stroll along the blossom-lined riverbanks, and fill the parks and plazas until late in the evening, when red-and-yellow trams are still rattling through town.

In sharp contrast to nearby industrial cities, Oryol is a visibly wealthy place, with a distinctly European capitalist flavour. Founded in 1566 as a fortress against the Tatars, Oryol (arr-*yol*, meaning eagle) reached its peak during the 19th century, when a surprising number of gentry lived here (19,000 out of a population of 32,000 in 1853). The writer Ivan Turgenev was one of 12 writers who thrived here; their work is remembered at the several museums about town.

For lovers of 19th-century Russian literature, Oryol is bound to be rewarding. To others, the town may seem to be in something of a time warp, with capitalism and communism rather awkwardly commingled.

WESTERN EUROPEAN RUSSIA

Orientation

Though the main streets are freshly cobbled and the cupolas newly gilded, most activity still hovers around the less-polished, inner areas of the city. The train station is 3.5km northeast, and the bus station is 3km south of pl Lenina. The pedestrian ul Lenina runs between pl Karla Marksa and pl Lenina, connecting the old city centre to Moskovskaya ul, the main commercial strip today. Both areas are of interest to the visitor, and pleasant footbridges make crossing back and forth between them easy.

Pick up a map at the train station or from one of the kiosks in town.

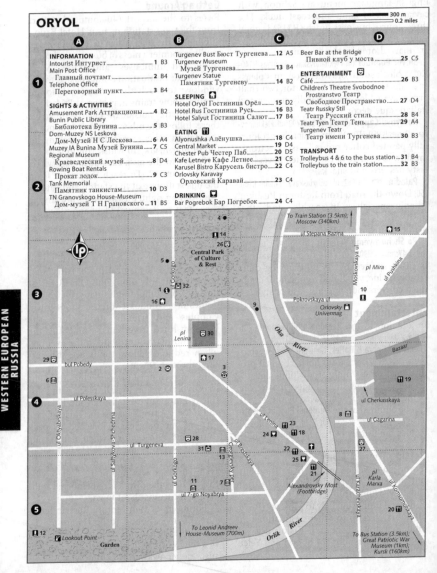

ORYOL

0 .... 300 m
0 .... 0.2 miles

INFORMATION
Intourist Интурист 1 B3
Main Post Office
    Главный почтамт 2 B4
Telephone Office
    Переговорный пункт 3 B4

SIGHTS & ACTIVITIES
Amusement Park Аттракционы 4 B2
Bunin Public Library
    Библиотека Бунина 5 B3
Dom-Muzey NS Leskova
    Дом-Музей Н С Лескова 6 A4
Muzey IA Bunina Музей Бунина 7 C5
Regional Museum
    Краеведческий музей............8 D4
Rowing Boat Rentals
    Прокат лодок 9 C3
Tank Memorial
    Памятник танкистам........... 10 D3
TN Granovskogo House-Museum
    Дом-музей Т Н Грановского ... 11 B5

Turgenev Bust Бюст Тургенева 12 A5
Turgenev Museum
    Музей Тургенева 13 B4
Turgenev Statue
    Памятник Тургеневу............ 14 B2

SLEEPING
Hotel Oryol Гостиница Орёл.........15 D2
Hotel Rus Гостиница Русь...........16 B3
Hotel Salyut Гостиница Салют.....17 B3

EATING
Alyonushka Алёнушка...............18 C4
Central Market 19 D4
Chester Pub Честер Паб.............20 D5
Kafe Letneye Кафе Летнее........... 21 C5
Karusel Bistro Карусель бистро....22 C4
Orlovsky Karavay
    Орловский Каравай..............23 C4

DRINKING
Bar Pogrebok Бар Погребок 24 C4

Beer Bar at the Bridge
    Пивной клуб у моста............25 C5

ENTERTAINMENT
Café 26 B3
Children's Theatre Svobodnoe
    Prostranstvo Театр
    Свободное Пространство........27 D4
Teatr Russky Stil
    Театр Русский стиль.............28 B4
Teatr Tyen Театр Тень.............29 A4
Turgenev Teatr
    Театр имени Тургенева 30 B3

TRANSPORT
Trolleybus 4 & 6 to the bus station ...31 B4
Trolleybus to the train station........32 B3

To Train Station (3.5km);
Moscow (340km)
ul Stepana Razina

Central Park
of Culture
& Rest

ul Gorkogo

pl Mira
Moskovskaya ul
pl Pushkina

Pokrovskaya ul

Orlovsky
Univermag

Oka River

Bazaar

pl
Lenina

bul Pobedy

ul Poleskaya

ul Oktyabrskaya
ul Saltykova-Shchedrina

ul Turgeneva

ul Gorkogo

ul Cherkasskaya

ul Gagarina

ul Lenina

Georgievsky per

Bryenskaya

ul 7-go Noyabrya

pl
Karla
Marxa

ul Kaladnechnaya
ul Komsomolskaya

Alexandrovsky Most
(Footbridge)

To Leonid Andreev
House-Museum (700m)

Orlik River

Lookout Point

Garden

To Bus Station (3.5km);
Great Patriotic War
Museum (1km);
Kursk (160km)

Information

You can change money at Hotel Salyut or at a number of banks, especially on the east side of the river.

Intourist (☎ 761 038; intourist@orel.ru; ul Gorkogo 39; 🕒 9am-6pm Mon-Fri) Several English speakers on staff; English-language town tours should be arranged in advance.

Main post office (ul Lenina 43, per hr R42) Two computers with Internet on 1st floor.

Telephone office (ul Lenina 34; 🕒 8am-8pm) ATM inside. There's also an ATM inside the Hotel Salyut.

Sights

LITERARY ATTRACTIONS

A cluster of **literary museums** (🕒 10am-5pm Sat-Thu) cover an awkward block off the unwieldy Georgievskiy per; a central organisational **office** (☎ 765 520) manages all six. Admission to each is R35.

Short-story writer Nikolai Leskov (1831–95), who immortalised an English jumping flea, is honoured at the **Dom-muzey NS Leskova** (☎ 763 304; ul Oktyabrskaya 9), a few blocks from the main cluster. Also set a bit apart, across the river, the birthplace of writer and dramatist Leonid Andreev is a sweet, late-19th-century cottage, now the **Leonid Andreev House-Museum** (☎ 764 824; 2-ya Pushkarnaya ul 41). The **TN Granovskogo House-Museum** (☎ 763 465; ul 7-go Noyabrya 24) presents materials and memorabilia relating to the historian as well as other 19th-century writers and thinkers.

Though materials on the writer, poet and 1933 Nobel laureate Ivan Bunin (1870–1953) are spread thin through provincial Russia, Oryol's **Muzey IA Bunina** (☎ 760 774; per Georgievskiy 1) has a good collection of photos and other documents, plus a 'Paris Room' devoted to his years as an emigrant, including the bed in which he died. At the end of the one-hour excursion (the only way you're going to make sense of all the curious photos and yellowed books), the guide flips on a tape player and the man himself reads one of his last poems, a typed copy of which lies near his typewriter. Still not sated? There's a statue of Bunin (apparently it bears no resemblance to him) in front of the **Bunin Public Library** (ul Gorkogo 43; 🕒 10am-8pm Mon-Thu, 10am-6pm Sat & Sun), opposite the Park of Culture and Rest. The Greek Revival library itself is in beautiful condition and sees a good deal of scholarly activity. It is a good place for a few warm moments with a book during the chilly months.

Turgenev's estate, Spasskoe-Lutovinovo (p319), is the literary mecca. Not to be outdone, Oryol has its own **Turgenev Museum** (☎ 762 737; ul Turgeneva 11). You will find tributes to Turgenev throughout town, including a big statue of him overlooking the Oka on Turgenevsky spusk, the sloping street off pl Lenina, and a bust in the public garden.

OTHER SIGHTS

The **Park of Culture and Rest** (Park Kultury i Otdykha) is a typical small-city park, with an amusement park at the northeastern end. A walk down the steep embankment to the Oka, between the park and junction of the Oka and Orlik Rivers, brings you to the rental stand where you can rent **rowing boats** (9am-9pm) during the warmer months. The banks of the Oka draw huge crowds of bathers and carpet washers on sunny days.

The nonliterary museums in Oryol are decidedly less interesting than the literary ones. The **Regional Museum** (☎ 766 791; ul Gostinaya 2; 🕒 10am-6pm Tue-Sun) on Oryol's fashionable shopping strip holds some good temporary exhibitions. The **Great Patriotic War Museum** (☎ 766 794; cnr uls Komsomolskaya & Normandiya Neman; 🕒 10am-6pm Tue-Sun) has a rather paltry collection of weaponry, recruitment and propaganda posters and a panorama depicting the liberation of Oryol

Ploshchad Mira (Peace Square) is easily identified by its **WWII tank**. The fighting machine, perched atop a granite base, is a time-honoured spot for newlyweds to pose for photos on the big day. It's also the site for city residents to pay their respects to those who fought and died in battle.

Sleeping

Hotel Rus (☎ 475 550; ul Gorkogo 37; s/d with bathroom from R340/670) Oryol's best option features small but clean, comfortable rooms, helpful staff and a good location on pl Lenina near the park.

Hotel Salyut (☎ 764 207; ul Lenina 36; s/d from R750/900) A rung down on the value ladder, this unattractive hotel, also on pl Lenina, has decent rooms – some in dire need of renovation. At night the loud disco on the 2nd floor pumps techno until late.

Hotel Oryol (☎ 550 525; pl Mira 4; s/d from R600/900) Overlooking pl Mira, this solid, attractive hotel offers bright, airy rooms – though the dim lobby may send you back into the street. Foreigners are a rarity here; it's best to book ahead.

Eating & Drinking

Dining options are fairly limited in Oryol. Your best bet is to stroll along ul Lenina, which has the old town's best selection of restaurants and bars.

Chester Pub (☎ 543 054; ul Komsomolskaya 36; meals R150-300) An Oryolian dream of English pubdom, this handsome three-storey restaurant serves tasty, eclectic dishes like French quail with baked apples, prunes and walnuts; river trout with almonds; chilli con carne; and other surprising choices. For dessert, try the tiramisu or apple puff pastry. English menu.

Karusel Bistro (☎ 760 396; ul Lenina 19; meals R60-120) Good, inexpensive food and beer on tap draw a young student crowd to this sleek diner. Popular dishes include pizza, hamburgers, lasagne, salads and milkshakes.

Beer Bar at the Bridge (Pivnoy Bar 'U Mosta'; ☎ 435 602; ul Lenina 13; dishes R80-150) This mellow basement grotto has a handful of wooden tables and unobtrusive music. Appetisers include fried cheese, fried calamari and other tasty bites to go with the alcohol. The speciality is locally brewed 'English ale', which tastes surprisingly similar to dark Baltika.

Bar Pogrebok (☎ 762 808; ul Lenina 25; meals around R100) Another underground watering hole, Pogrebok sits a few doors down from Pivnoy Bar, and prepares decent traditional Russian main courses. It's low-key during the week, while young crowds fill the place on weekends.

Alyonushka (☎ 760 160; ul Lenina 20; meals R45-150; ☽ 10am-10pm) A large pit filled with soft rubber balls and a continuous loop of cartoons playing on the giant screen set the stage for this very kid-friendly restaurant. The front room is a little less chaotic and serves stiff drinks as well as traditional dishes like *pelmeni* and *solyanka* (a pickled vegetable and potato soup). The younger crowd opt for pizza and French fries.

Orlovsky Karavay (ul Lenina 26; meals R15-45; ☽ 8am-8pm) This bakery and lunch counter offers quick, cheap bites.

Kafe Letneye (ul Lenina 9; ☽ 10am-10pm) Overlooking the footbridge and riverside park, this snack bar has outdoor seating only.

Inside the Park of Culture and Rest there's a **café** (☽ 6-11pm; admission around R20)

where a young, energetic crowd transforms this small space into a dance haven.

There's a teeming daily central market on the south bank of the Oka River just to the east of Moskovskaya ul, along with a bazaar that sells just about everything you could want, from toothpaste and TVs to a large selection of fresh produce from the Caucasus.

Entertainment

Given the literary bent of Oryol, it's no surprise to find a number of quality theatres paying tribute to the works of local luminaries. All tickets cost under R100.

Turgenev Teatr (☎ 761 639; pl Lenina) Hosts good Russian theatre several times a week. It is a clever modernist building, the façade mimicking the effect of a stage with the curtains drawn.

Teatr Russky Stil (☎ 762 024; ul Turgeneva 18) A fun, small-scale, occasionally experimental theatre. Most of the offerings are comedies, often with local colour.

Children's Theatre Svobodnoe Prostraystvo (☎ 764 846; pl Karla Marksa) This excellent children's theatre is both entertaining and good for practising your Russian.

Teatr Ten (☎ 813 570; ul Oktyabrskaya 5) Hosts both opera and theatre.

Getting There & Away

Oryol is on the Moscow–Kharkiv railway, with numerous daily services to the capital (R550, 4½ hours). Backed by neoclassical colonnades, the **train station** (☎ 762 121) is your first clue to the upmarket character of Oryol. Left luggage costs R40 per day, per bag.

All buses, including Moscow-bound buses (several daily, six hours), leave from the less pleasant **bus station** (☎ 721 111), several kilometres south of town, at the opposite end of the Moskovskaya ul and ul Komsomolskaya axis.

Only *prigorodny* trains run from Yelets (R105, 6½ hours). To Kursk there is a fast train (R340, two hours), the *elektrichka* (R160, 3½ hours) and bus service (R90, 2½ hours). There is no direct rail service to Smolensk, but there is one daily bus (R305, eight hours).

Getting Around

The best way to see the city is on foot. From the train station, trams 1 and 2 and trolleybus 3 (all R4) stop at ul Karla Marksa, on the southeastern end of the Alexandrovsky bridge leading to ul Lenina, before continuing on to the bus station. Trolleybuses 4 and 6, which run along ul Turgeneva, also provide convenient access to the bus station.

Taxis to the train or bus station from pl Lenina charge about R80.

SPASSKOE-LUTOVINOVO
СПАССКОЕ-ЛУТОВИНОВО

> Here is the forest. Shadow and silence. Stately poplars whisper high above your head; the long, hanging birch-branches hardly stir…The small golden voice of the robin rings out in its innocent, prattling joy…
>
> *Ivan Turgenev, from*
> A Sportsman's Sketches

Surrounded by lovely countryside, the manor of 19th-century novelist Ivan Turgenev is a splendid place to pay homage to one of Russia's great writers. In addition to the **museum** (☎ 48646-57 214; guided tour R50; grounds only R15; ☉ 10am-6pm), you'll also get a chance to absorb the bucolic setting that inspired the master himself.

Turgenev, born in Oryol in 1818, grew up at his family's estate here, which was originally given to the family by Ivan the Terrible. Though he spent much of his life in Moscow, St Petersburg, Germany and France, Turgenev thought of Spasskoe-Lutovinovo as his home and returned here many times. The beauty of the estate makes this easy to understand. Turgenev was exiled here from St Petersburg in 1852–53 as a result of his work *A Sportsman's Sketches*. He completed his most famous novel, *Fathers and Sons*, at Spasskoe-Lutovinovo.

The main house, restored in the 1970s, contains a good bit of original furniture, some of the writer's personal items and a substantial percentage of his books, which will give you an idea of his astonishing linguistic abilities. There's an icon hanging in Turgenev's study that was given to the family by Ivan the Terrible, and the chessboard is set ready to play (Turgenev was a masterful player). The entrance to the house was formerly the kitchen.

Also on the grounds is the family church, which has been restored and holds regular services. The big oak tree planted as a

sapling by Turgenev and the writer's 'exile house', where he lived in 1852–53, are just away from the main house. Behind the house are paths through the idyllic forest that skirt several lakes – where Turgenev set out on his long hunting expeditions.

Outside the estate, descendants of the peasant serfs who once belonged to the Turgenevs still live and work on tiny farms. There is a flower-bedecked WWII memorial among their homes, a five-minute walk to the right as you exit the estate.

Getting There & Away
The estate is 6km west of the Moscow–Oryol road from a turn-off 65km north of Oryol. To get there, take one of the dozen or so daily *marshrutky* that travel from Oryol to Mtsensk (R50, one hour, 6am to 9pm), then switch at Mtsensk's bus station for an hourly Spasskoe-Lutovinovo bus (R15, 30 minutes). To save time, you can hire a taxi from Mtsensk to the estate for about R120. On the way back, try hopping onto one of the air-conditioned excursion buses.

If you prefer the train, *elektrichka* leave from Oryol at 9am for Bastyevo (R50, 1½ hours), returning at around 4pm. From the northern end of the train station, cross the tracks and walk west 5km (to the left), or catch the bus that runs from Mtsensk via Bastyevo to the estate about once an hour. The bus stop is to your right (east) from the front of the train station.

KURSK КУРСК
☎ 47100 / pop 412,000 / ☉ Moscow

Set along the Tuskar River, Kursk is a working-class city that's seen more than its fair share of destruction over its 1000-year history. Much of the city has been rebuilt since WWII and stands as an unsightly monument to Soviet urban planning, c 1967. Its importance in WWII is well documented in its museums, and the pride of its stolid residents lives on. Aside from this – and a few attractive churches – Kursk doesn't draw many visitors.

Founded (most likely) in the 9th century, Kursk was destroyed by the Tatars in 1240. It then lay in Lithuanian territory for several centuries before being annexed by Moscow and later emerging as a southern frontier fort in the late 16th century. In the 18th and 19th centuries it became a grain-trade and industrial centre and an important railway junction. But its real fame rests on the nearby Battle of the Kursk Bulge (5 July to 5 August 1943), which was one of the Red Army's most important victories in WWII. German tanks attempting a pincer movement on Kursk – at the time the most forward Soviet-held town on this front – were halted by minefields and then driven back, turning Germany's 1943 counteroffensive into a retreat that saw the Red Army pass the Dnepr River by the end of September.

The Kursk battle sprawled over a wide area, liberating places as far apart as Oryol and Belgorod. A memorial stands beside the Kursk–Belgorod highway, 115km from Kursk and 40km south of Oboyan.

Orientation

Kursk's centre is divided by the north–south running ul Lenina, with Krasnaya pl at the southern end. Ul Dzerzhinskogo heads quite steeply downhill from the western side of Krasnaya pl to the valley of a now invisible river, where you'll find the busy central market.

Information

Dom Knigi (☎ 24234; ul Lenina 11) Detailed city maps available here in hard-cover format for R122.

Post office & 24-hour telephone office (☎ 25159, 24873; Krasnaya pl; per min R0.60) Three computers available for Internet access.

Sberbank (ul Lenina 19) Good for changing money. ATMs also lie along ul Lenina north of Krasnaya pl.

Sights

The foot of ul Lenina opens into Krasnaya pl, surrounded by imposing Stalinist buildings – the House of Soviets on the east side, the post office on the west, the Hotel Tsentralnaya on the northwest and the matching city council building on the northeast. At the south end of the square is Kursk's most distinctive building, the domed 1816–28 **Assumption Cathedral**. The Soviets converted the cathedral into a cinema, but it's recently been restored to its former glory. Behind the greenish-blue walls, you'll find a mix of the lavishly ornate (gilded columns, an enormous chandelier) coupled with even larger paintings depicting scenes from Christ's life.

Around ul Sonina from the cathedral is the two-room **Kursk Battle Museum** (☎ 566 290; ul Sonina; admission R50; ⏱ 9am-4pm Wed-Sun), up-

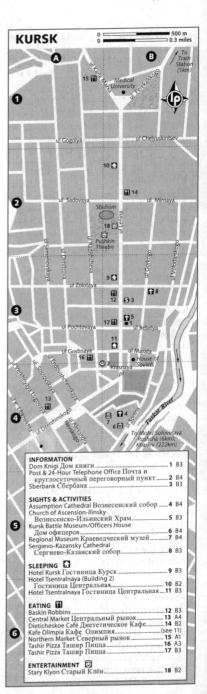

KURSK

0 — 500 m
0 — 0.3 miles

stairs in the ornate red-and-white former House of the Nobles, now the **Officers House** (Dom Ofitserov). Admission buys you good views over town, documentation and artefacts from the battle, and an enthusiastic former Red Army soldier who will tell you all about it and then some. Downstairs, you might be able to stir up a game of billiards with a military man. The tables are available to the public from 1pm to 9pm daily.

Nearby is the small **Regional Museum** (☎ 26275; ul Lunacharskovo 6; admission R16; ☒ 10am-5.30pm Sat-Thu), which houses exhibits on the region's natural and archaeological history, period furnishings from the 19th century and – beyond the red curtains – socialist artwork from the Soviet era.

A block east of ul Lenina, on a pleasant, tree-lined street, is the fine baroque **Sergievo-Kazansky Cathedral** (cnr uls Gorkogo & Zolotaya), built in 1752–58 and designed by Elizabeth I's court architect, Rastrelli. The construction was ordered by a wealthy merchant who sought repentance for a murder he committed (more or less in self-defence so the story goes).

The 1786 **Church of Ascension-Ilinsky** (ul Lenina) was used during the Soviet era as a warehouse for the Dom Knigi bookshop, a hulking neoclassical structure placed smack in front of the strawberry-milk-hued, 18th-century church. With the fall of communism in Russia, the books were moved out and the church reopened. When a regional bank was constructed next door in 1997, tinted glass was used to reflect the church, creating the illusion that it is once again part of the main street. Inside, you can see original frescoes by famous icon painter Vasnetsov.

Sleeping

Hotel Tsentralnaya (☎ 569 048; Krasnaya pl; s/d without bathroom R200/300) The best option in town, this grand old place has high ceilings and tiled bathrooms in some rooms. It's a charming place overall, though they sometimes turn foreigners away so call ahead.

Hotel Kursk (☎ 26980; ul Lenina 24; s/d from R700/980) Inside this uninspiring high-rise, you'll find fairly clean rooms and typical Russian service. The whole place needs an update and seems rather stark, but if the Tsentralnaya turns you down, the Kursk is your best bet.

Hotel Tsentralnaya building 2 (☎ 566 521; ul Lenina 72; s/d without bathroom from R200/300, s/d with bathroom R300/350) Yet another eyesore on Kursk's skyline, the Tsentralnaya 2 is about as original as its name: it has bland but functional rooms and no-nonsense staff.

Motel Solovinaya Roshcha (☎ 504 000; fax 504 050; ul Engelsa 142a; s/d incl breakfast from R1100/1500) Situated in a park some kilometres from the centre, this motel has simple but excellent facilities, including sparkling renovated bathrooms. The breakfast is hearty. From the centre take a taxi (about R100) or one of a number of buses, including bus 10, 21 or 61, or tram 4 or 5. Ask for notice when nearing the hotel; you will have to walk a few minutes off the road to your left. A shady, pine-filled park lines one side of the hotel, lending an almost rural feel.

Eating

Dieteticheskoe Cafe (ul Lenina 61; meals R100-250; ☒ 10am-10pm) This cosy café and restaurant makes a lovely spot for a light meal or a drink in the evenings.

Kafe Olimpiya (☎ 569 227; Krasnaya pl; meals R60-130) Inside the Hotel Tsentralnaya, this somewhat stately dining room serves big plates of Russian fare. Steaks, salads and calamari are among the popular choices. Friendly wait staff.

Tashir Pizza (☎ 521 414; ul Radishcheva 14; slices R35; ☒ 10.30am-10pm) Dramatic curtains adorn this casual pizzeria near the main post office. Slices of pizza are served with mayonnaise (instead of tomato sauce) and are sometimes undercooked. In spite of this, it's not a bad place for a bite. Second location on ul Lenina.

Baskin Robbins (ul Lenina 12; ☒ 10am-11pm) For a cold treat on a muggy day (or a frigid one), stop at this well-known ice-cream chain.

The town's two main markets, the **central market** (Tsentralny; ul Dzerzhinskogo) and the **northern market** (Severny; ul Karla Marksa), sell food, produce and clothes (the sort that will make you say, 'So *that's* where they get it!').

Entertainment

Stary Klyon (☎ 512 635; ul Lenina 58; cover around R50-100; ☒ 6pm until late) This pyramid-shaped building houses a disco and bar plus a few billiard tables. Youthful crowds arrive on weekends for the live music/DJ combo. Nearby are a handful of open-air bars that make for fine people-watching in summer.

Getting There & Away

Kursk is well connected by bus and rail, and there are flights to/from Moscow and St Petersburg.

Like Oryol, Kursk is on the Moscow–Kharkiv railway with trains to Moscow (R420, eight hours) every half-hour, sometimes more. There are also trains to Kharkiv (R225, three hours) and to/from the Caucasus and Crimea daily. To Oryol you can go by train (R170, two hours) or *elektrichka* (R94, three hours). The **station** (ul Internatsionalnaya) is about 3km northeast of Krasnaya pl.

Kursk is also accessible by frequent bus services from Oryol, Belgorod, Moscow and Kharkiv. If you're arriving in Kursk by bus from the south, have the driver let you off at the Motel Solovinaya Roshcha, from where you can get a tram or trolleybus to the centre, saving an hour of doubling back.

Getting Around

Numerous buses, trams, and *marshrutky* ply the route between the train station and Krasnaya pl for R4 to R5. Bus 1 and tram 2 go between the train station, past the corner of uls Karla Marksa and Perekalskogo (in front of the Medical University), and the bus station, northwest of the centre. Taxis charge around R80 from the station to Krasnaya pl.

SMOLENSK СМОЛЕНСК

☎ 4812 / pop 325,000 / ⏲ Moscow

Behind the walls of this old city you'll find well-landscaped parks, a magnificent old cathedral, a smattering of museums and a youthful population breathing new life into this historic town. Its elegant music hall is the jewel of the town, and the regular concerts held here as well as its annual music festival keep Smolensk well connected to flourishing musical traditions of centuries past.

Set on the upper Dnepr River, 390km southwest of Moscow, Smolensk was first mentioned in 863 as the capital of the Slavic Krivichi tribes. The town's auspicious setting gave it early control over trade routes between Moscow and the west and between the Baltic and Black Seas – or in other words 'from the Varangians to the Greeks'. Smolensk became part of Kyivan Rus, but after being sacked by the Tatars in about 1237 it passed to Lithuania. Moscow captured Smolensk in 1340, Lithuania in 1408, Moscow again in 1514, Poland in 1611 after a 20-month siege, and Russia in 1654.

There was a big battle between the Russians and Napoleon's army outside Smolensk in 1812 and more heavy fighting in 1941 and 1943. In a sign of Soviet favour, much of the devastated centre was quickly rebuilt, often along original plans, resulting in the very complete feeling of the central area today. Long sections of the restored city walls boast fine towers reminiscent of the Moscow Kremlin.

Other areas of interest for the visitor include flax production and music. Smolensk was the regional hub of flax production during the Middle Ages, and you can still find fine locally made flax products. Meanwhile, composer Mikhail Glinka, regarded as the founder of Russian art music, grew up near Smolensk and performed frequently in the Nobles' Hall, facing what is now the Glinka Garden. The statue of Glinka, installed in 1885, is surrounded by a fence with excerpts from his opera *A Life for the Tsar* wrought into the iron. Music aficionados will want to make the trip out to Glinka's family home, now a museum. Inquire at the Intourist office.

Orientation

Central Smolensk, surrounded by lengths of ancient wall, stands on a hill on the south bank of the Dnepr. The formal city centre is pl Lenina with the Glinka Garden (Gorodskoy sad imeni MI Glinki) on its south side and the House of Soviets, Drama Theatre and Hotel Tsentralnaya on the north side. Pedestrian-only areas skirt the perimeters of the park. Venture beyond the walled centre to the south to find the art gallery and a bustling commercial and residential area, with more than a little Soviet residue. The train station and Kolkhoznaya pl, site of the main market, are north of the river. Ul Bolshaya Sovetskaya leads across the river and up the hill from Kolkhoznaya pl to the centre. The Moscow–Minsk highway passes about 13km north of Smolensk.

Information

Central post, telegraph & telephone office (ul Oktyabrskoy Revolyutsii 6; per hr R34; ⏲ 8am-8pm Mon-Sat) Internet access available.

Intourist office (☎ 381 492; ul Konenkova 3; ☼ 9am-6pm Mon-Fri) Near Hotel Tsentralnaya, this tourist office is unusually helpful. Staff can arrange a two-to three-hour English-language city tour (R500 per person) and excursions to Novospasskaya (Glinka's birthplace), about 150km away. You'll need to arrange things a day in advance for the city tour and several days in advance for Novospasskaya, for which you'll also need to rent a car or hire a taxi. English-language city map (R15) available.

Knizhny Mir (ul Bolshaya Sovetskaya 22; ☼ 10am-7pm Mon-Sat, 11am-6pm Sun) One of several bookshops on this street (others are at No 12 and No 17), Knizhny Mir sells Russian-language maps (R40).

Sberbank (cnr uls Glinki & Kommunisticheskaya) Money exchange. A 24-hour ATM sits across the street at No 33.

SKA bank (ul Lenina 13a; ☼ 9.30am-5.30pm) Another money exchange.

Sights

FORTRESS WALLS

Built between 1596 and 1602, the impressive 6.5km-long, 5.5m-thick, 15m-high walls originally had 38 towers, with 17 still standing. The pleasant **Central Park of Culture and Rest** (Tsentralny Park Kultury i Otdykha) backs onto a longish southwest stretch of the walls. Overlooking the Spartak Stadium just outside the line of the walls on the west side of the park, the Korolevsky Bastion is a high earth rampart built by the Poles who captured Smolensk in 1611. It saw heavy fighting in 1654 and 1812. The park has a 26m-high cast-iron monument to the 1812 defenders.

At the foot of the walls southeast of the Glinka Garden you'll find an eternal flame memorial to the dead of WWII and the graves of some of the Soviet soldiers who died in Smolensk's defence, plus another monument to the heroes of 1812. A **WWII museum** (☎ 383 265; ul Dzerzhinskogo 4a; admission R10; ☼ 10am-5pm Tue-Sat) within the fortress walls nearby documents the invasion and widespread devastation; it is incredible to realise just how much of old Smolensk is actually reconstruction. A collection of tanks, artillery and a MiG fighter jet are parked behind the museum.

ASSUMPTION CATHEDRAL

Smolensk's big green-and-white working **Assumption Cathedral** rises at the top of a flight of steps off ul Bolshaya Sovetskaya. A cathedral has stood here since 1101 but this one was built in the late 17th and early 18th centuries; it is one of the earliest examples of the Russo-Greek revival in architecture following the Europeanisation trends of Peter the Great's reign. Topped by five domes, it has a spectacular gilded interior, which was partially damaged by fire during WWII. According to legend, Napoleon was so impressed that he set a guard to stop his own men from vandalising the cathedral.

Immediately on your left as you enter, an icon of the Virgin is richly encrusted with pearls drawn from the Dnepr around Smolensk. Further on, a cluster of candles marks a supposedly wonder-working icon of the Virgin. This is a 16th-century copy of the original, said to be by St Luke, which had been on this site since 1103 and was stolen in 1923. The cathedral bell tower is to the left of the cathedral. There's a good view of the fortress walls and two towers from the terrace at the eastern end of the cathedral. Outside the cathedral entrance, you can buy a loaf of tasty (and blessed!) fresh bread.

MUSEUMS

The wealth of Smolensk museums is a blessing for the traveller; they are all closed on Monday.

The pink former Church of Trinity Monastery now houses a small **Flax Museum** (☎ 383 611; ul Bolshaya Sovetskaya 11; admission R10; ☼ 10am-5.30pm Tue-Sun). Historically, flax production has been one of Smolensk's main industries as the moderate climate sustains soil ideal for growing flax. Exhibits here are spare, but you'll get an idea of how the process works. To get a souvenir of the distinctive local style, visit the unsigned **flax shop** (☎ 383 611; ul Przhevalskogo 6/25; ☼ 10am-6pm Mon-Sat) near the Central Park of Culture and Rest.

Smolensk's **History Museum** (☎ 656 871; ul Lenina 8; admission R10; ☼ 10am-6pm Tue-Sun) doubles as a fine-arts museum, displaying a hodge-podge of 18th- and 19th-century portraiture and 13th-century iconography and graffiti, along with battle maps and Soviet paraphernalia. Particularly interesting are the fragments from the 1812 war, including a French uniform from one of Napoleon's soldiers.

The town's main **art gallery** (☎ 381 591; ul Tenishevoy 7/1; admission R10), south of the fortress walls, has paintings by famous artists such as Rerikh and Ivanov, a good sampling of socialist realism, 14th- to 18th-century icons and works by Smolensk artists patronised by Princess Maria Tenisheva (see p326).

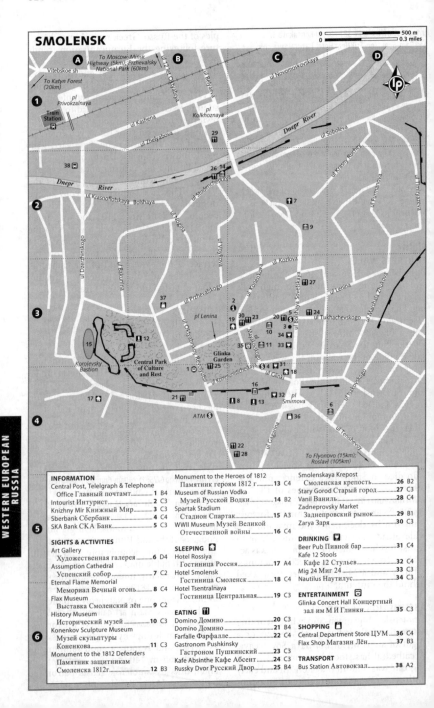

SMOLENSK

INFORMATION

Central Post, Telelgraph & Telephone
Office Главный почтамт.............. **1** B4
Intourist Интурист **2** C3
Knizhny Mir Книжный Мир........... **3** C3
Sberbank Сбербанк **4** C4
SKA Bank СКА Банк **5** C3

SIGHTS & ACTIVITIES

Art Gallery
Художественная галерея **6** D4
Assumption Cathedral
Успенский собор **7** C2
Eternal Flame Memorial
Мемориал Вечный огонь......... **8** C4
Flax Museum
Выставка Смоленский лён **9** C2
History Museum
Исторический музей **10** C3
Konenkov Sculpture Museum
Музей скульптуры
Коненкова **11** C3
Monument to the 1812 Defenders
Памятник защитникам
Смоленска 1812г. **12** B3

Monument to the Heroes of 1812
Памятник героям 1812 г. **13** C4
Museum of Russian Vodka
Музей Русской Водки **14** B2
Spartak Stadium
Стадион Спартак **15** A3
WWII Museum Музей Великой
Отечественной войны **16** C4

SLEEPING

Hotel Rossiya
Гостиница Россия **17** A4
Hotel Smolensk
Гостиница Смоленск **18** C3
Hotel Tsentralnaya
Гостиница Центральная........ **19** C3

EATING

Domino Домино **20** C3
Domino Домино **21** B4
Farfalle Фарфалле....................... **22** C4
Gastronom Pushkinsky
Гастроном Пушкинский **23** C3
Kafe Absinthe Кафе Абсент **24** C3
Russky Dvor Русский Двор....... **25** B4

Smolenskaya Krepost
Смоленская крепость............ **26** B2
Stary Gorod Старый город....... **27** C3
Vanil Ваниль **28** C4
Zadneprovsky Market
Заднепровский рынок........... **29** B1
Zarya Заря **30** C3

DRINKING

Beer Pub Пивной бар **31** C3
Kafe 12 Stools
Кафе 12 Стульев **32** C3
Mig 24 Миг 24 .... **33** C4
Nautilus Наутилус **34** C3

ENTERTAINMENT

Glinka Concert Hall Концертный
зал им М И Глинки.................. **35** C3

SHOPPING

Central Department Store ЦУМ ... **36** C4
Flax Shop Магазин Лён.............. **37** B3

TRANSPORT

Bus Station Автовокзал.............. **38** A2

The one-room **Museum of Russian Vodka** (☎ 381 318; ul Studencheskaya 4; admission R20; ☉ 9am-5pm Tue-Sat) gives visitors a brief overview of the drink's colourful history. Fifteen-minute guided tours (in English or Russian) end at the makeshift bar where you can purchase a glass (or better yet a bottle) of some noteworthy Smolenskiy brands. There's a good restaurant next door.

The **Konenkov Sculpture Museum** (☎ 382 029; ul Mayakovskogo 7; ☉ 10am-6pm Tue-Sun) was closed for renovation at the time of research. When it reopens in 2006, you can expect playful woodworks by Sergei Konenkov, as well as works in steel, bronze and aluminium from some of the other noted artists who hail from Smolensk.

Festivals & Events

The **Glinka Festival**, which runs from 1 to 10 June, showcases Russian music and attracts a wide range of classical talent. Symphony orchestras, choral groups and string quartets perform nightly in various venues with free concerts held beside Glinka Park. Stop by the Intourist office for details.

Sleeping

Hotel Tsentralnaya (☎ 383 604; nr pl Lenina & ul Konenkova; s/d without bathroom from R400/600, s/d with bathroom from R650/800) Set on the edge of the Glinka Garden, this centrally located hotel has clean, bright rooms – though modest in size. Ask for a 'renovated' room to score fresh paint and fixtures.

Hotel Smolensk (☎ 326 866; ul Glinka 11/30; s/d without bathroom from R265/500, s/d with bathroom from R775/1570) Near pl Smirnova, this ageing Soviet hotel has a mix of rooms, the best of which are nicely renovated with OK furnishings. Overall it's a clean, well-run place.

Hotel Rossiya (☎ 655 610; ul Dzerzhinskogo 23/2; s/d from R910/1460) A relic from the Brezhnev era, this hulking hotel has unintended style in its functional but overpriced rooms. There's a bar-restaurant on the 2nd floor and a cinema next door.

Eating

Smolenskaya Krepost (☎ 327 690; ul Studencheskaya 4; meals R120-200) Set in the old castle walls, this charming restaurant has plenty of character – from the stained-glass windows to the tiny fireplace and exposed brick walls – with lovely views of the Dnepr. The menu

features well-prepared traditional Russian dishes.

Russky Dvor (☎ 683 499; Glinka Garden; meals R80-250; ☉ 9am-11pm) This colourful gem boasts a fine location in the middle of Glinka Garden. The exquisitely wrought woodwork covering its several dining rooms make a fine setting for its classic Russian cuisine.

Zarya (☎ 380 239; ul Konenkova 2/12; meals R110-180) Facing the Hotel Tsentralnaya, Zarya is an old favourite for its elegant dining room and decent Russian dishes. Shashlyk, steak, salads, *pelmeni*, open caviar sandwiches and soups round out the menu.

Farfalle (ul Oktyabrskoy Revolyutsii 7; meals R75-130) A few blocks south of the Glinka Garden, this Italian restaurant strives to play the part, with a painting of Venice along one wall and the occasional aria playing overhead. Though far from authentic (no pasta on the menu!), the decent pizzas and salads provide a nice respite from eggs, mushrooms and bliny. Carlsberg on tap.

Domino (ul Dzerzhinskogo 16; meals R30-90; ☉ 24hr) Though the log-cabin interior borders on kitsch, the food at this popular restaurant is actually quite good. In addition to Russian faves, Domino serves pizzas and salads, and the small front patio that opens in summer is good for a drink. English menu available. A smaller branch on ul Lenina, open 10am to 11pm, serves mostly bliny and pizza.

Kafe Absinthe (☎ 385 100; Tukhachevskogo 1; meals R80-120) Below street level, this multiroom restaurant serves Russian fare in a medieval-inspired setting. Perch, beef stroganoff, caviar and, yes, absinthe are among the offerings.

Vanil (☎ 382 224; Oktyabrskoy Revolyutsii; ☉ 9am-11pm) The deep-red walls and wood furnishings of this charming café make a fine setting for conversation, cappuccino and, most importantly, Vanil's desserts. The apple strudel is served warm with vanilla ice cream and drizzled with pine nuts.

Stary Gorod (☎ 386 675; ul Bolshaya Sovetskaya 21; meals R25-80) If the Brady Bunch were Russian, this is what their basement would look like. Lights fancifully strung along the walls of the various dining rooms don't improve the 1960s den interior, but the cheeseburgers, omelettes and *buterbrod* (open sandwiches) are passable. Enter through the courtyard.

Gastronom Pushkinsky (ul Lenina 7; ☉ 24hr) Near the Glinka Garden, this grocery store stocks fresh bread, cheese, beer, wine and all the other items needed to put together a decent picnic.

Smolensk's main market is the **Zadneprovsky** (Kolkhoznaya pl), north of the river. Pick up fresh veggies or colourful undergarments here.

Entertainment

Glinka Concert Hall (☎ 32984; ul Glinki 3; box office ⏲ 9am-7pm Mon-Fri, 1-7pm Sat & Sun) Attending a concert is the best way to get a look at the reconstructed hall where Glinka once entertained Russian nobility and launched the history of secular art music in Russia. The local orchestra uses balalaikas in lieu of violins and is quite good. Tickets run from R50 to R800, depending on who's in town; some shows are free.

Drinking in Smolensk is easier still than eating; there is at least one bar per block in the centre, though the ambience isn't much to speak of.

Mig 24 (ul Bolshaya Sovetskaya 20) A young crowd of beer drinkers and chain smokers congregate nightly at this pleasant café's tables; it is one of the few bars in town with a good view of the street scene.

Nautilis (ul Bolshaya Sovetskaya 18) Next door, a similar crowd gathers at this nautically-inspired bar with a blue-tiled floor, fish tanks along the walls and a gloomy, cavernous feel to the place.

Beer pub (Pivnoi bar; ul Glinka 11) Around the corner from Mig 24, this watering hole is as no-nonsense as its name, serving only beer at two tables and two stools in the former gatehouse to the building beyond.

Kafe 12 Stools (Dvenadtsat stulyev; ul Dzerzhinskogo 2) Near pl Smirnova, this is another tiny spot for a drink or a light bite, with a friendly bartender and Baltika on tap.

Getting There & Away

Smolensk is on the Moscow–Minsk–Warsaw railway with several daily trains to/from Moscow (R500, six hours), Minsk (R400, four hours) and Brest (R1970, eight hours); as well as regular trains to Warsaw (R2136, nine hours), Prague (R3130, 24 hours) and Berlin (R3740, 41 hours). International rail tickets are sold from window 12 at the **train station** (☎ 395 268; ⏲ 9am-6pm Mon-Thu, 9am-5pm Fri).

Smolensk's **bus station** (☎ 218 574; ⏲ 10am-5pm Mon-Fri, 3-6pm Sat), just south of the train station, serves most of the region's smaller towns and offers frequent daily services to Moscow. International bus tickets are available from window No 7. Buses to Moscow also leave from the train station across the footbridge.

Getting Around

From the train station, you can take the bus or tram (R4) to the centre of town. Many buses and trams stop in front of the station; choose one that stops by the green structure to the right beyond the parking lot. Some buses stop at the bus station, across the footbridge from the train station. Taxis to town cost around R50.

AROUND SMOLENSK

Flyonovo Флёново

In the late 19th and early 20th centuries, top Russian art and music names such as Stravinsky, Chaliapin, Vrubel and Serov visited the Flyonovo estate of singer Princess Maria Tenisheva, near Talashkino, 15km southeast of Smolensk on the Roslavl road. The visitors joined in applied-art workshops, which the princess organised for her peasants, and helped in building projects.

The most striking result is the dramatic, almost psychedelic murals and mosaics on the brick Holy Spirit Church – particularly the one of Christ over the entrance. Much of the painting is by well-known landscape painter Rerikh. One house called Teremok, decorated with ornate peasant-style carving, is now a **folk-art museum** (☎ 72106, 371 505; ⏲ 10am-6pm Tue-Sun, closed last Thu of month). Take bus 104 or 130 from Smolensk's bus station to Talashkino. You can also catch a *marshrutka* to Talashkino from pl Smirnova.

Katyn Forest Катынский Лес

In 1990 the Soviet authorities finally admitted that the NKVD (predecessor of the KGB) had shot more than 6000 Polish officers in the back of the head in the Katyn Forest near Smolensk in 1940. The bodies of the officers, who had been imprisoned by the Soviet occupying troops in Poland in 1939, were left in four mass graves.

Until 1990, Soviet authorities had blamed it on the Nazis. Victims were trucked from Gnezdovo, a country station, to Kozyi Gory, site of the graves. The graves have not been disturbed and are now marked by memorials. About 11,000 other Polish officers almost certainly suffered similar fates elsewhere in the USSR.

Less well known is the fact that, according to a 1989 *Moscow News* report, the Katyn Forest was also the site of massacres of 135,000 Soviet prisoners of war by the Nazis (out of an estimated one million Soviet POWs shot by the Germans in WWII) and of thousands of Soviet 'enemies of the state' exterminated by the NKVD in the 1930s.

GETTING THERE & AWAY

Getting there on your own is simple; take bus 101 (direction Smolensk Smetanino) from the Smolensk bus station to Kozyi Gory. It's easy to miss, so look for the sign saying 'Memorial Polskim ofitseram pogibshim v Katyni' about 1km past the highway flyover. If you get to Katyn, you've gone too far. The memorial is marked in two places: the first designated by a simple wooden cross and a marble headstone dedicated to the Russian dead, while the more impressive Polish memorial lies further up the path.

Przhevalsky National Park

Национальный парк имени Пржевальского

Lying 60km north of Smolensk, the birthplace of adventurer Nikolai Przhevalsky is a beautiful national park, a favourite spot for locals to spend a long weekend camping by one of the many lakes. The road to the park is asphalt and after that there are dirt roads and footpaths. A park ranger might be at the post at the entrance to the park, where you may have to pay a small fee. If no one is there, don't be surprised if one of the rangers stops by your campfire to collect the fee.

SOUTH OF ST PETERSBURG

NOVGOROD НОВГОРОД

☎ 8162 / pop 240,000 / ⌚ Moscow

One of Russia's gems, Novgorod is a beautiful town of solid old churches, peaceful tree-lined streets and a magnificent kremlin full of historic treasures. These attributes, coupled with the town's friendly, laid-back residents and its access to lovely countryside, make Novgorod a highly rewarding destination.

The name means 'new town', but Novgorod was here by the 9th century and for 600 years was Russia's most pioneering artistic and political centre. Methodically trashed by the Nazis, it's a sign of the city's historical importance that its old kremlin was one of the Soviet government's first reconstruction projects.

In a sense, Russian history began here. This was the first permanent settlement of the Varangian Norsemen who established the embryonic Russian state. By the 12th century the city, called 'Lord Novgorod the Great', was Russia's biggest: an independent quasidemocracy whose princes were hired and fired by an assembly of citizens, and whose strong, spare style of church architecture, icon painting and down-to-earth *byliny* (epic songs) would become distinct idioms.

Spared from the Mongol Tatars, who got bogged down in the surrounding swamps, Novgorod suffered most at the hands of other Russians. Ivan III of Moscow attacked and annexed it in 1477, and Ivan the Terrible, whose storm troopers razed the city and slaughtered 60,000 people in a savage pogrom, broke its back. The founding of St Petersburg finished it off as a trading centre.

Orientation

Novgorod is only three hours by road from St Petersburg and is just off the M10 highway connecting Moscow and St Petersburg. The town has two main centres: the kremlin on the west bank of the Volkhov River; and the old market district, Yaroslav's Court, on the east bank. The kremlin side fans outward like a pheasant's tail, while the east side is gridlike.

Though the Soviet street names were officially scrapped long ago, some locals still use them, so we've left the more prominent ones in parentheses. City maps in Russian and English are available at the tourist office behind the Novgorod Fine Arts Museum, or at bookshops, hotels and museums.

Information

Novgorod is ready and waiting for visitors. You will find English-language menus, hotels that welcome foreigners and plenty of ATMs. You can change money at hotels.

Main telegraph & telephone office (cnr ul Lyudogoshchaya/Sovetskaya & ul Gazon/Gorkogo; ⌚ 24hr) Conveniently located.

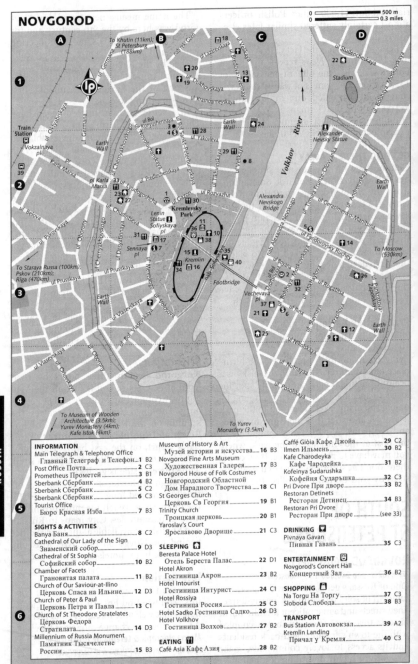

INFORMATION
Main Telegraph & Telephone Office
Главный Телеграф и Телефон...**1** B2
Post Office Почта....................................**2** C3
Prometheus Прометей.........................**3** B1
Sberbank Сбербанк..............................**4** B1
Sberbank Сбербанк..............................**5** C2
Sberbank Сбербанк..............................**6** C3
Tourist Office
Бюро Красная Изба..........................**7** B3

SIGHTS & ACTIVITIES
Banya Баня...**8** B2
Cathedral of Our Lady of the Sign
Знаменский собор.............................**9** D3
Cathedral of St Sophia
Софийский собор...........................**10** B2
Chamber of Facets
Грановитая палата..........................**11** B2
Church of Our Saviour-at-Ilino
Церковь Спаса на Ильине...........**12** D3
Church of Peter & Paul
Церковь Петра и Павла.................**13** C1
Church of St Theodore Stratelates
Церковь Федора
Стратилата...**14** D3
Millennium of Russia Monument
Памятник Тысячелетие
России..**15** B3

EATING
Café Asia Кафе Азия............................**28** B2

Museum of History & Art
Музей истории и искусства.....**16** B3
Novgorod Fine Arts Museum
Художественная Галерея...........**17** B3
Novgorod House of Folk Costumes
Новгородский Областной
Дом Нарядного Творчества....**18** C1
St Georges Church
Церковь Св Георгия......................**19** B1
Trinity Church
Троицкая церковь..........................**20** B1
Yaroslav's Court
Ярославово Дворище...................**21** B3

SLEEPING
Beresta Palace Hotel
Отель Береста Палас.....................**22** D1
Hotel Akron
Гостиница Акрон............................**23** B2
Hotel Intourist
Гостиница Интурист......................**24** C1
Hotel Rossiya
Гостиница Россия............................**25** D3
Hotel Sadko Гостиница Садко......**26** D3
Hotel Volkhov
Гостиница Волхов...........................**27** B2

Caffé Gìòia Кафе Джойа.....................**29** C2
Ilmen Ильмень......................................**30** B2
Kafe Charodeyka
Кафе Чародейка...............................**31** B2
Kofeinya Sudarushka
Кофейня Сударышка....................**32** C3
Pri Dvore При дворе...........................**33** B2
Restoran Detinets
Ресторан Детинец.........................**34** B3
Restoran Pri Dvore
Ресторан При дворе.............(see **33**)

DRINKING
Pivnaya Gavan
Пивная Гавань.................................**35** C3

ENTERTAINMENT
Novgorod's Concert Hall
Концертный Зал..............................**36** B2

SHOPPING
Na Torgu На Торгу...............................**37** C3
Sloboda Слобода...................................**38** B3

TRANSPORT
Bus Station Автовокзал.....................**39** A2
Kremlin Landing
Причал у Кремля.............................**40** D3

Post offices (ul Bolshaya Dvortsovaya 2; 🕑 8am-8pm Mon-Sat, 10am-4pm Sun) There are many around town; this branch, just east of the bridge, has a small Internet salon (per hr R20; 🕑 9am-7pm Mon-Sat).

Prometheus (ul Bolshaya St Peterburgskaya 13; 🕑 10am-7pm Mon-Fri, 10am-5pm Sat) This bookshop sells Russian-language maps.

Sberbank (ul Bolshaya St Peterburgskaya 13; ul Bolshaya Moskovskaya 20) With several branches, including north-west of the kremlin and across from Yaroslav's Court.

Tourist office (☎ 773 074; www.tourism.velikiy novgorod.ru in Russian; Sennaya pl 5; 🕑 10am-6pm) Travellers who have been to other Russian towns will not believe their good luck in encountering this central tourist office, behind the Fine Arts Museum. Staff hand out Russian- and English-language maps (extensive maps available for R50) and other literature, but the real treat here is the friendly, thorough, English-language advice. Staff can arrange a variety of excellent English-language tours around town. Sample tours and prices per person are kremlin (€11), Chamber of Facets (€8) and Yurev Monastery and Vitoslavlitsy (€13). Another worthwhile website is www.novgorod.ru/english.

Sights & Activities
KREMLIN

Overlooking the smooth Volkhov River, the **kremlin** (☎ 73608, information ☎ 77187; 🕑 6am-midnight) is one of Russia's oldest. Formerly known as the Detinets, the fortification was first built in the 9th century, though it was later rebuilt with brick in the 14th century (which still stands today). It houses the city's most famous sites, and is surrounded by a pleasant wooded park. It's worth see-ing with a guide. English-language tours can be arranged, usually a day or two in advance, through the tourist office.

Cathedral of St Sophia

Finished in 1052, the handsome, Byzantine **Cathedral of St Sophia** (🕑 8am-8pm) is the town's centrepiece and one of the oldest buildings in Russia. The simple, fortresslike exterior was designed to withstand attack or fire (flames had taken out an earlier, wooden church on the site); ornamentation was reserved for the interior. The onion domes were probably added during the 14th century – even so, they are perhaps the first example of this most Russian architectural detail. The west doors, dating from the 12th century, have tiny cast-bronze biblical scenes and even portraits of the artists. The icons inside date from the 14th century, and older ones are in the museum. In comparison, the interior frescoes are barely dry, being less than a century old. During the Soviet days, the church was turned into a museum of religion and atheism. Today, services are once again held in the church, usually taking place between 6pm and 8pm daily. Nearby are the 15th-century belfry and a leaning 17th-century clock tower.

Millennium of Russia Monument

One of Novgorod's most famous landmarks, this massive, 300-tonne sculpture was unveiled in 1862 on the 1000th

---

THE SAVIOUR OF NOVGOROD

The most important icon in the Cathedral of St Sophia is that of the patron saint of Novgorod, Our Lady of the Sign (Znameniya Bozhyey Materi), which, according to legend, saved the city from destruction in 1170. Accounts vary, but one colourful story goes something like this…

The Prince of Suzdal and his large army were preparing to attack Novgorod. Things looked pretty bleak for the Novgorodians, and the bishop desperately prayed for the city's salvation. The night before the attack, he had a vision that an icon of the Virgin could save Novgorod, so he had the icon moved from the church to a pillar of the fortress. The next day Suzdal began the siege and, not surprisingly, the icon was hit with an arrow. It then turned back to face Novgorod; tears were in the virgin's eyes. Darkness fell upon the land, and the army from Suzdal began attacking one another in confusion. The Novgorodians then rode out from the city and attacked, quickly dispatching their enemies.

If it all sounds a little far-fetched, take a close look at the icon while you're in the church. You can still see a notch over the saint's left eye, said to be where the original arrow hit. If you visit the Museum of History and Art, you should also check out the 15th-century painting from the Novgorod School depicting three scenes from the battle. It's one of the first icons ever painted to depict an event strictly from Russian history.

anniversary of the Varangian Prince Rurik's arrival. A veritable who's who of Russian history over the last millennium, it depicts some 127 figures – rulers, statesmen, artists, scholars and a few fortunate hangers-on as well.

The women at the top are Mother Russia and the Russian Orthodox Church. Around the middle, clockwise from the south, are Rurik, Prince Vladimir of Kyiv (who introduced Christianity), tsars Mikhail Romanov, Peter the Great and Ivan III, and Dmitry Donskoy trampling a Mongol Tatar. In the bottom band on the east side are nobles and rulers, including Catherine the Great with an armload of laurels for all her lovers. Alexander Nevsky and other military heroes are on the north side, and literary and artistic figures are on the west.

The 16-metre-high statue is fortunate to have survived WWII. The Nazis cut it up, intending to ship it to Germany, but fled before realising their plan.

Chamber of Facets
The Gothic **Chamber of Facets** (adult/student R40/20; 10am-6pm Thu-Tue, closed last Fri of month), part of a palace built in 1433, has a collection of icons and lavish church booty from the region, including some beautiful illuminated manuscripts.

Museum of History & Art
Undergoing renovation at the time of research, the **Museum of History & Art** (adult/student R60/30; 10am-6pm Wed-Mon) is said to be one of the best research museums of its kind in Russia, with a huge collection of early icons, birch-bark manuscripts, paintings, early wooden sculpture and applied art. It's located just south of the Millennium of Russia Monument.

YAROSLAV'S COURT
Across a footbridge from the kremlin is old Novgorod's market, with the remnants of a 17th-century arcade facing the river. Beyond that is the market gatehouse, an array of churches sponsored by 13th- to 16th-century merchant guilds, and a 'road palace' built in the 18th century as a rest stop for Catherine the Great.

The 12th-century Kyiv-style **Court Cathedral of St Nicholas** (Nikolo-Dvorishchensky sobor;

636 187; adult/student R40/22; 10am-6pm Wed-Sun, closed last Fri of month) is all that remains of the early palace complex of the Novgorod princes, from which Yaroslav's Court (Yaroslavovo dvorishche) gets its name. The cathedral, which is still undergoing restoration, holds church artefacts and temporary exhibitions of local interest. Downstairs you can see fragments from the church's original frescoes.

CHURCH OF OUR SAVIOUR-AT-ILINO
On the outside, the 14th-century **Church of Our Saviour-at-Ilino** (ul Ilina; adult/student R60/30; 10am-5pm Wed-Sun) has graffiti-like ornaments and lopsided gables that are almost playful. Inside are the only surviving frescoes by legendary Byzantine painter Theophanes the Greek (and they came close to extinction when the church served as a Nazi machine-gun nest). Recent restoration has exposed as much of the frescoes as possible, though they are still faint. A small exhibit upstairs includes reproductions with explanations in Russian. Note Theophanes' signature use of white warlike paint around the eyes and noses of his figures, and their piercing expressions. The church itself, east of Yaroslav's Court, is pure Novgorod style.

OTHER CHURCHES & SIGHTS
In contrast to the Church of Our Saviour-at-Ilino, the 17th-century Moscow-style **Cathedral of Our Lady of the Sign** (adult/student R40/22; 10am-5pm Thu-Tue) across the street is more complex.

Another interesting study in contrasting styles, the 1557 Muscovite **Trinity Church** (ul Dukhovskaya 20) and Novgorod-style **St George's Church** (ul Dukhovskaya 31) sit directly across the street from one another. Trinity Church, a dark brick edifice with silver-hued cupolas, is still closed and in rather bad shape; St George's opens erratically during the week. Other churches in Novgorod style include the 1406 **Church of Peter & Paul** on ul Bredova-Zverinaya near Hotel Intourist. It's a small, crumbling brick structure occupying its own little field amid a neighbourhood in the process of Euro-transformation. Nearby, the former Zverin Monastery, built in 1468, now houses the **Novgorod House of Folk Costumes** (739 607; ul Bredova-Zverinnaya 14; noon-6pm), which contains exhibits on Novgorod costume production. The craft shop sells some exquisitely woven dresses, dolls, hats and the like.

Across the river, the 1361 **Church of St Theodore Stratelates** (ul Fyodorovsky Ruchey 19/pr Yuriya Gagarina; adult/student R40/22; 🕙 10am-6pm Thu-Tue) has some faded frescoes and displays on the church's history.

YUREV MONASTERY & MUSEUM OF WOODEN ARCHITECTURE

Set amid peaceful marshlands just outside of town, these two sights feel worlds away from the city, and make for a splendid excursion. The 12th-century **Yurev Monastery** (🕙 10am-8pm) still functions as a working Orthodox monastery. It features the heavily reconstructed Cathedral of St George and a clutch of 19th-century add-ons. Services are held in the Church of Exaltation of the Cross (1761), which is attached to the monks' dorms. The monastery grounds are worth a visit, but what really warrants the trip out here is the windswept river setting, with gorgeous views out across the marshes and towards the centre of Novgorod.

Roughly 1km up the road is the beautiful **Vitoslavlitsy Museum of Wooden Architecture** (adult/student R60/30; 🕙 park 10am-6pm, houses close at 4.30pm), an open-air museum of peasant houses and beautiful, intricate wooden churches from around the region. There's a café and souvenir shop on the grounds.

To get to either place, take bus 7 (R4, 15 minutes). The bus back into town stops just outside the Vitoslavlitsy gates; the bus makes a loop out to these sights, so you will be re-boarding a bus continuing in the same direction you were heading when you arrived.

NOVGOROD FINE ARTS MUSEUM

The cool halls of Novgorod's **Fine Arts Museum** (🕿 73763; Sofiyskaya pl 2; adult/student R60/30; 🕙 10am-6pm Tue-Sun) showcase paintings by 18th- and 19th-century Russian artists, including Andropov, Bryullov and Ivanov. The 3rd floor features Novgorod artists. The collection is a strong provincial one, though not spectacular. Local crafts are among the offerings at the art shop in the lobby.

RIVER TRIPS

The Volkhov River flows out of Lake Ilmen, about 10km south. On a good day, the surrounding marshes are lovely, with churches

rising up majestically from the countryside. From May to September, you can catch a boat for a one-hour cruise (R100) at the dock below the kremlin.

BANYA

For a good sweat with a proletarian price tag, visit the public **banya** (🕿 72019; ul Velikaya 4; admission R75; 🕙 4-9pm Wed-Fri, 12.30-9pm Sat & Sun). In addition to just joining the fray, you can rent a four-person private cabin for R220 for three hours. The cabin provides privacy and comfort, and you can order in food and drinks. There is an extra charge to rent a *venik* (birch branch, R25) with which to whip yourself, if so inclined.

Sleeping

Hotel Akron (🕿 136 918; fax 136 934; ul Predtechenskaya 24; s/d from R700/900) This old favourite should be completely renovated by the time you read this. Rooms, though small and uninspiring, get good light from the windows (the fluorescents are unfortunate) and have modern bathrooms, shiny new wallpaper, cable TV and minifridge. Other pluses include friendly service, decent prices and a good location.

Hotel Volkhov (🕿 115 505; fax 115 526; www .novgorod-hotels.com/volkhov-hotel; ul Predtechenskaya 24; s/d with breakfast from R1200/1800) Catering mostly to business travellers, the Hotel Volkhov has modern, nicely furnished rooms with lots of amenities. A sauna is available to guests.

Beresta Palace Hotel (🕿 186 914; www.beresta palace.com; ul Studencheskaya 2; s/d with breakfast from US$85/100; 🏊) On the east bank of the Volkhov, the Beresta is Novgorod's best hotel, with comfortable rooms and good service. It has a health club, sauna and tennis courts. The biggest drawback is the location, which is a bus or taxi ride from the centre.

Hotel Rossiya (🕿 634 185; nab Aleksandra Nevskogo 19/1; s/d from R610/800) On the edge of the River Velikaya, the battered Rossiya looks abandoned at first glance (entry around the back), but inside things are still holding together. Although the hallways are smelly and the bathrooms are cramped and dark, the rooms themselves have been renovated, and boast fine views of the kremlin. Table tennis on 1st floor.

Hotel Sadko (🕿 663 004; sadko@novline.ru; ul Fyodorovsky Ruchey 16; s/d with breakfast from R650/1300) Along a busy street a bit outside the centre, the Sadko has bright, spacious rooms with modern furnishings and welcoming staff. The bathrooms are small, but overall the place is decent value if you don't mind the location. German spoken.

Hotel Intourist (☎ 775 089; www.intourist.natm.ru; ul Velikaya 16; s/d R900/1200) Easily spotted by the fascinating but rather tacky mural of Mother Russia above the entranceway, this old Soviet stalwart is literally crumbling to the ground. Fortunately for guests, the rooms are in better shape. Each boasts USSR-issued red curtains and red comforters, and is clean if not terribly charming. The biggest minus is the state of the ageing, cramped bathrooms (bring your own shower curtain).

Eating & Drinking

No longer the culinary desert it was a few years ago, Novgorod has a handful of decent restaurants. During summertime, several open-air cafés facing the kremlin's west side make pleasant spots for a drink.

Ilmen (☎ 176 310; ul Gazon 2; meals from R50; bistro ☷ 10am-10pm, restaurant ☷ noon-midnight) This polished, new complex has a casual bistro on the 1st floor where you can enjoy sandwiches, salads and drinks on the back terrace. Upstairs, the more formal restaurant has fresh-roasted meats, a good wine selection and a menu packed with Russian and Scandinavian dishes. English menu.

Kafe Charodeyka (☎ 730 879; ul Volosova-Meretskova 1/1; meals R60-180; ☷ 11am-5pm & 6-11pm) A favourite with homesick foreigners and Novgorodians alike, this café has Tuborg on tap and features an eclectic menu with dishes like fresh salmon, breaded pork with vegetables, salad Rosalina (with king prawns) and chicken fingers (stuffed with prunes and dried apricots and baked in cream). In warmer weather, enjoy one of many cocktails at the open-air seating in front. English menu.

Restoran Pri Dvore (☎ 774 343; ul Lyudogoshchaya 3; meals R120-275) A nicely set dining room and professional service await guests at this somewhat formal restaurant near the Hotel Akron. The eclectic menu includes selections such as chicken salad with fruit, French onion soup, chicken Creole (served with tomatoes, white wine and smoked bacon) and salmon steak. An English menu is available, but it doesn't list all the dishes.

> **AUTHOR'S CHOICE**
>
> The medieval seems downright glamorous at the handsome **Restoran Detinets** (☎ 774 624; dishes R50-250; ☷ noon-5pm & 7-11pm) inside the kremlin's Pokrovskaya Tower. Amid castle walls lit by iron chandeliers, sample the city's best Russian cuisine. Delicious fish soups, rich sweet borsch and plates of grilled perch come expertly prepared. Down a winding staircase, the bar serves strong coffee, cocktails and *medovukha*, a honey-brewed mead. The tables are tucked in the brick alcoves of what was the kremlin's Intercession Church. English menu available.

Caffé Gìoia (☎ 731 722; ul Velikaya 11; pizzas R80-180; ☷ 11am-11pm Tue-Sun) This simple, welcoming café serves tasty, thin-crust pizzas, nicely suited to the Russian and imported beers. The capriccioso pizza is a good prelude to cappuccino and tiramisu. English spoken.

Pri Dvore (ul Lyudogoshchaya 3; meals around R75; ☷ 10am-9pm) This popular, cheery little cafeteria serves good prepared salads and hot dishes by the kilogram. Try the tasty pastries or fruit ice creams for dessert.

Café Asia (☎ 772 227; ul Yakovleva 22; meals R100-300) Aiming for Eastern exoticism, this downstairs restaurant is divided into private rooms with rice-paper screens, silky red walls and gauzy curtains. The food is hit-or-miss and includes Korean, Uzbek and Japanese fare. The outdoor terrace opens during summer.

Kofeinya Sudarushka (☎ 679 202; ul Bolshaya Moskovskaya 32) This small restaurant on the east side of town is set with pleasant light wood furnishings and rustic country touches. The menu (English available) features the usual Russian standards (steak, salmon, bliny) as well as fresh juices and coffees.

Kafe Istok (☷ 11am-midnight) This small café behind the monastery serves simple fare and overlooks a nice little beach.

Outside the kremlin's east entrance you'll find the small open-sided bar Pivnaya Gavan, a popular place for a beer and people watching.

Entertainment

Concert Hall (☎ 634 232; Kremlin 6; tickets from R60) Novgorod's Concert Hall is an excellent place to catch live symphony or opera.

Shopping

Souvenirs are plentiful around Novgorod. A row of vendors near the tourist office sell woven birch boxes, mini wooden churches, *matryoshka* dolls and lacquer boxes. You can find a wider assortment of souvenirs at **Sloboda** (☎ 730 793; Kremlin 8; ☼ 10am-6pm) inside the kremlin and at **Na Torgu** (☎ 664 472; ul Ilina 2; ☼ 10am-7pm) near Yaroslav's Court.

Getting There & Away

The **train station** (☎ 739 380) is 1.5km west of the kremlin, at the end of pr Karla Marksa. A fast train runs daily to St Petersburg's Moscow Station (R210, three hours); a slower *elektrichka* runs to/from St Petersburg's Vitebsk Station (R105, four hours). There are also trains twice a week to Kyiv and three times a week to Murmansk.

The modern **bus station** (☎ 739 979), next to the train station, serves St Petersburg half a dozen times daily (R190, four hours). There's also direct bus service to/from Pskov twice daily (R206, 4½ hours).

Getting Around

From the bus and train stations, buses 4 and 20 (R4) pass in range of the Hotel Volkhov (in between the first and second stops from the stations, or a 15-minute walk), Intourist (Universam Kremlyovsky/Kremlyovsky Park stop, about 500m from the hotel), Sadko (the stop on the corner of ul Bolshaya Moskovskaya and pr Fyodorovsky Ruchey right after the bus crosses the river; the hotel is 200m further along Fyodorovsky Ruchey) and Beresta Palace. For the Beresta, get off at the stadium and cut through the park. Returning to the stations, you'll need to catch bus 4 or 19 instead of bus 20. A taxi from the train station to the Beresta or Sadko should cost about R80.

AROUND NOVGOROD
Khutin Monastery

The working **Orthodox convent** (☼ 9am-8pm) at Khutin was founded in the 12th century on sinful land. Early nuns prayed long and hard to exorcise evil spirits abiding here, and were so successful the site is now known for miracles and its holy water springs. Buses from Novgorod station (R4, 30 minutes) run from 9am to 2.30pm daily.

STARAYA RUSSA СТАРАЯ РУССА
☎ 81652 / pop 40,000 / ☼ Moscow

Set along the banks of the tranquil Polist River, Staraya Russa has the idyllic charm of a 19th-century village. Here, Dostoevsky spent summers and wrote much of *The Brothers Karamazov*, and the town is still today something of a mecca for literary enthusiasts.

You can pick up a map at the **Magazin Kniga** (ul Lenina 6; ☼ 9am-6pm Mon-Fri, 10am-5pm Sat & Sun) bookshop, near the main square.

The simple, two-storey **Dostoevsky House** (☎ 21477; ul Dostoyevskogo 42; adult/student R40/20; ☼ 10am-5.30pm Tue-Sun) on the small Pereritsa River is now open as a museum. The house never left the family's possession before becoming a museum, and some original pieces remain. Dostoevsky's desk has copies from his mazelike drafts, and you can see his doodlings on the pages. His bookcase holds books from the period, and his wife's bedroom still contains her bed and chest. A keyboard instrument that Dostoevsky supposedly tinkered with sits by a window overlooking the river. Russian-language guides lead you through, pointing out every detail in a half-hour tour. In summer you might be able to arrange an English-language tour (R50) ahead of time by contacting the **Dostoevsky cultural centre** (☎ 37285; ul Dostoyevskogo 8; ☼ 10am-6pm Tue-Fri & Sun). The centre also offers tours of the town (R300, two hours) and hosts temporary exhibitions (R40). Staraya Russa was the setting for *The Brothers Karamazov*, so fans will want to visit the streets and churches that the characters frequented.

Other attractions in Staraya Russa include the **Local Lore Museum** (Kraevedchesky muzey; ☎ 35866; pl Timura Frunze 6; adult/student R40/22; ☼ 10am-5pm Wed-Mon), which is housed in a 12th-century church and displays old religious relics; you can also see fragments from the church's original frescoes.

Next door to the museum is a **picture gallery** (Kartinnaya gallereya; ☎ 35989; adult/student R40/22; ☼ 10am-5pm Wed-Mon), with a small but noteworthy selection of paintings (and also a few sculptures) of artists who spent time in Staraya Russa. On the same street, ardent war buffs can check out the small but earnest **Museum of the Northwest Front** (☎ 35285; ul Volodarskogo 20; adult/student R40/22; ☼ 10am-5pm Wed-Mon).

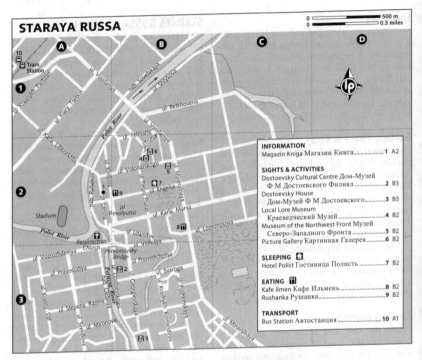

STARAYA RUSSA

INFORMATION
Magazin Kniga Магазин Книга.................1 A2

SIGHTS & ACTIVITIES
Dostoevsky Cultural Centre Дом-Музей
Ф М Достоевского Филиал...................2 B3
Dostoevsky House
Дом-Музей Ф М Достоевского.............3 B3
Local Lore Museum
Краеведческий Музей............................4 B2
Museum of the Northwest Front Музей
Северо-Западного Фронта.....................5 B2
Picture Gallery Картинная Галерея.........6 B2

SLEEPING
Hotel Polist Гостиница Полисть...............7 B2

EATING
Kafe Ilmen Кафе Ильмень........................8 B2
Rushanka Рушанка....................................9 B2

TRANSPORT
Bus Station Автостанция.........................10 A1

Sleeping & Eating

For those who must wake up to the morning air that inspired the master, **Hotel Polist** (☎ 37547; ul Engelsa 20; s/d from R430/520) is an option. Rooms are a bit shabby and in serious need of modernising, but the view of the park across the street is pleasant.

Dining options are scarce. Near the sanatorium, the **Kafe Ilmen** (☎ 31968; ul Mineralnaya 43; meals around R120; ⏱1pm-2am) is your best bet, with basic Russian fare. If you're desperate, there's always the Soviet-era cafeteria **Rushanka** (ul Filipova; meals R20-30; ⏱8am-8pm) near the main square.

Getting There & Away

Buses leave from Novgorod's bus station (R92, two hours, six daily), returning about every 90 minutes. From Staraya Russa bus station, buses 1, 4, 6 and 11 head to the centre, though expect long waits between buses. On foot, it takes about 30 minutes to walk to the main square. Once there, follow the river south to reach Dostoevsky's house. A taxi from the bus station straight to the museum is far simpler and should cost about R50.

PSKOV ПСКОВ

☎ 8112 / pop 200,000 / ⏱ Moscow

Situated 265km southwest of St Petersburg and close to both the Latvian and Estonian borders, Pskov is a pretty town with a long, proud history, which you'll be confronted with at nearly every turn. At the heart of Pskov lies a riverside kremlin with a beautiful cathedral inside, and from the old walls that still encircle the original settlement you can spot dozens of great-domed churches, most designed by Pskov's own school of architects and icon painters. Unfortunately, many of the churches are closed, with few marked for renovation. However, there is an excellent museum, the Pogankin Chambers, where a great deal of the iconographic art from these churches has been collected and displayed.

In addition to its cultural treasures, Pskov has some lovely parks and a riverside promenade along the Velikaya's east bank. These offer respite from the city's traffic-choked main streets.

As a border town (30km from Estonia), Pskov's history is saturated with 700 years of war for control of the Baltic coast. German Teutonic knights captured it in 1240, but Alexander Nevsky routed them two years later in a famous battle on the ice of Lake Peipus. The Poles laid siege to it in the 16th century and the Swedes wrecked it the following century. Peter the Great used it as a base for his drive to the sea, and the Red Army fought its first serious battle against Nazi troops nearby.

This is also Pushkin country. The poet's grave and Mikhailovskoe, his family's estate, are a two-hour drive away.

Orientation

Hotel Rizhskaya is three long blocks west of the Velikaya River, while almost everything else is on the east side. The town's axis is Oktyabrsky pr, ending at Oktyabrskaya pl.

Information

Most hotels in town have travel agencies offering city excursions or day trips to Izborsk and Pushkin's house at Mikhailovskoe. Purchase maps at bookshops or the train station.

Baltiysky Bank (ul Yana Fabritsiusa 27) Near the train station, this bank with ATM changes money.

Books for You (Knigi dlya vas; Oktyabrsky pr 22) One of several bookshops on Oktyabrsky pr that sell maps of town (R25).

Internet Café (pl Lenina; per hr R35; ⏱ 10am-11pm) A youth-filled Internet café below the Oktyabr theatre.

Main post office (Oktyabrskaya pl; ⏱ 10am-7pm Mon-Fri, 10am-4pm Sat & Sun) In addition to postal services, you can change money here.

Sberbank (Oktyabrsky pr 23) With money exchange and 24-hour ATM.

Telephone office (Oktyabrsky pr 17; per hr R35; ⏱ 8am-10pm Mon-Fri, 11am-9pm Sat) Two blocks from the main post office, this telephone office is also a pleasant place to get online. ATM inside.

Tourist information (☎ 724 568; www.tourism.pskov .ru) Pskov recently lost its tourist office; in the meantime, you can phone the director or obtain city info from travel agencies.

Sights
OLD CITY

Pskov's walls formerly had four layers. The kremlin (krom) was the religious and ceremonial centre. Its stone walls and the southern annexe, Dovmont Town (Dovmontov gorod), date from the 13th century. The Central Town (Sredny gorod), around ul Pushkina, was the commercial centre, though little remains of it or its 14th-century walls. The walls and towers of the 15th- to 16th-century Outer Town (Okolny gorod) can still be seen along ul Sverdlova, the Velikaya River embankment and across the tributary Pskova River. You can walk along portions of the ramparts, including behind the kremlin.

Two new museums have opened in the Old Town, though they're both modest affairs and non-Russian speakers will find them rather impenetrable. The **Pskov State Museum** (Pskovskyy Gosudarstveny muzey; admission R30; ☎ 722 563; ⏱ 11am-6pm) shows fragments from the settlement's earliest days when Scandinavian Vikings lived in the area. There are a few displays of knives, jewellery and old keys as well as information on burial methods.

In the same area, but up the stairs, is the fairly dry **Chancery Chamber** (Prikaznaya Palata; admission R15; ⏱ 11am-6pm), which presents old documents on the administration of Pskov during the 17th century.

Kremlin & Dovmont Town

In **Dovmont Town** (named after an early prince), the foundations of a dozen 12th- to 15th-century churches are scattered around. Through a passage is the kremlin, where the veche (citizens' assembly) elected its princes and sent them off to war, and Trinity Cathedral where many of the princes are buried.

You can book guided tours next to the Pskov State Museum (tours in Russian/English R400/850). There's also a small **gift shop** (⏱ 11am-6pm) in the grounds. A budget **excursion office** (☎ 21906; ⏱ 10am-6pm) next door offers Russian-language kremlin tours (R200), city tours (R400) and guided excursions further afield to Pechory Monastery (see p340) and Izborsk (see p338).

Trinity Cathedral

The grandeur of the 1699 **Trinity Cathedral**, Pskov's principal sight, is heightened by the simplicity of the skeletal kremlin surrounding it. The gilded centre dome, as high as a 28-storey building, can be seen from 30km away on a clear day. The interior, with a large collection of bejewelled icons of the Madonna, is still undergoing restoration, though services have returned.

POGANKIN CHAMBERS & MUSEUM
A very rich 17th-century merchant built his fortress-like house and treasury here in the heart of Pskov, with walls 2m thick. The original building and a newer addition now house the **Pskov National Museum of History, Architecture & Art** (☎ 163 311; ul Nekrasova 7; combination ticket adult/student R100/60; ☼ 11am-6pm Tue-Sun, closed last Tue of month), which comprises three separate museums and a wide range of displays. The 2nd floor of the new building houses the war collection, with photos and artefacts from WWII, as well as information on more recent conflicts like Afghanistan and Chechnya. More interesting is the 1st-floor picture gallery, which has works from the 18th, 19th and 20th centuries, including paintings by Nikitin, Tropinin and Zhukovsky, as well as representations from the Russian avant-garde, including a couple of Petrov-Vodkins.

The original house showcases the real gems of the collection. The maze of galleries holds 13th- to 18th-century pottery, weaving and weaponry – including the original 15th-century sword of one of Pskov's princes. A series of icons depicts the life of Christ, most from Pskov churches that have closed. It is a rare chance to thoroughly examine one particular style of iconography at close range. Note, for instance, the bulbous noses and otherwise harsh realism that characterises the Pskov school, as well as a predominance of subdued earth tones. One impressive 17th-century icon on display relates the history of Pskov's development. The museum entrance is on Komsomolsky per.

MIROZHSKY MONASTERY
The attraction here is the Unesco-protected, nonworking **Cathedral of the Transfiguration of the Saviour** (Spaso-Preobrazhensky sobor; ☎ 46702; adult/student R100/80; ☼ 11am-5.30pm Tue-Sun), whose 12th-century frescoes are considered to be one of the most complete representations of the biblical narrative to have survived the Mongols. The frescoes have been beautifully restored after centuries of damage from flooding, whitewashing and scrubbing; 80% of what you see today is original. The artists are unknown but were almost certainly from Greece, based on the style of the frescoes. The guided tour takes 1½ hours and will fascinate art-lovers and historians. The cathedral itself was based on a 12th-century

Greek model, formed around a symmetrical cross. Later additions and demolitions have altered the footprint, but you can still see traces of the original structure along exterior walls. The church closes often due to inclement weather: too hot, too cold or too wet; it's best to call in advance.

The monastery is also a working iconography school; ask to see any current activity. The whole complex is across the Velikaya River from the centre; take bus 2 from the vicinity of Hotel Rizhskaya.

PARKS
Along the Pskova tributary, near a small spillway and the Epiphany Cathedral, is a lovely stretch of park, nice for strolling, picnicking or short hikes. **Gremyachaya Tower**, a decaying 16th-century fortress tower on the north bank, is open to explorers. **Detsky Park**, right in the centre of town, is less bucolic but still pleasant. During summer, children enjoy the park's mechanised rides – and pony rides, no less.

Sleeping
Hotel Rizhskaya (☎ 462 223; Rizhsky pr 25; s/d R700/1200) Overlooking a small square a few blocks west of the Velikaya River, this old Intourist has Pskov's best rooms, with decent furnishings, wood floors, good lighting and modern bathrooms. You'll also find friendly staff (some speak English), a laundry and ATM. The hotel is 15-minute's walk to pl Lenina, though bus 17 whisks you there in minutes.

Hotel Oktyabrskaya (☎ 164 246; fax 164 254; Oktyabrsky pr 36; s/d without bathroom R380/760, s/d with bathroom R650/1300) More convenient, this tired hotel has unrenovated rooms that are pretty shabby, while at the higher end you'll have more comfortable quarters with better lighting and more space. It's located halfway between the train station and the centre.

Hotel Krom (☎ 39007; ul Metallistov 5; dorm per person from R200, s/d with bathroom R880/1760) Housed in a former dormitory, the bare-bones Hotel Krom is still a student-favourite for the cheap, shared rooms and a quiet location near the banks of the Pskova River. There's a café/bar on the 1st floor.

Eating & Drinking
Restaurant Rus (☎ 720 090; meals R150-300) Set in the old kremlin tower overlooking Dovmont

Town, this elegant restaurant exudes atmosphere (from the tables in the tower's alcoves, you can peek out at the river through crossbow slits). Dishes are unspectacular but fresh: marinated mushrooms and potatoes; crab and tomato salad; and salmon with tomatoes and mushrooms. The ambience is marred only by the cheesy lighting and obtrusive Russian pop. Downstairs from the restaurant is a cosy bar. English menu.

Kafe Cherskaya (☎ 723 829; Oktyabrsky pr 40) One of several restaurants along this stretch of Oktyabrsky, Cherskaya has a casual vibe and boasts a cocktail menu as extensive as the food list. Cabbage soup, schnitzel and all the Russian favourites are on hand.

PSKOV

Bavaria (☎ 163 782; ul Sovetskaya 83; meals R70-160) Although the ambience is lacking, Bavaria's eclectic menu (English available) and friendly service make it a good find. Dishes include perch in cabbage, stewed with beer; omelette with ham and mushrooms; and pork stuffed with plums, walnuts and cheese. The only drawback is Bavaria's location; it's about 200m south of pl Pobedy.

Kafe Frigate (☎ 121 317; ul Karla Libknekhta 9, 2nd fl; meals R50-180; ☾ 9am-6am) Overlooking the Velikaya River, Kafe Frigate specialises in seafood and the usual Russian favourites (bliny, borsch, chicken Kiev). The almost elegant, red-hued dining room is strung with rigging ropes and other nautical devices, although the real kitsch arrives in the evening when the ballad-singing band takes the stage.

Club Jaguar (☎ 445 142; Rizhsky pr 16; mains R100-375) Featuring an eclectic menu and friendly service, Club Jaguar is a fine place for a meal. In addition to a good three-course business lunch for R95, you can order sushi, salads, seafood and bliny.

Kafe Snezhinka (☎ 723 086; Oktyabrsky pr 14; meals R60-100; ☾ 24hr) A rather minimalist affair, this music-filled café attracts Pskov's youth, who gather for coffee, beer and light Russian meals. Picture windows look out across Oktyabrsky pr onto Detsky Park.

Noev Kovcheg (☎ 23829; ul Sovetskaya 62; meals R75-150) This smoky, underground restaurant is worth going to on Friday through to Sunday when the chef serves *khash*, a hearty Armenian dish made of meat (from cow's feet), chilli peppers, garlic and vodka, and served with lavash. If shin meat doesn't entice, you can always opt for shashlyk or dolmas.

Café Gorenka (☎ 121 537; Oktyabrsky pr 22; meals around R40; ☾ 9am-10pm) A good place for a snack or coffee, Gorenka has desserts displayed in the front counter; you can also order pizza, sandwiches, salads and ice cream.

Next door to the bus station is a simple **restaurant** (meals R30-60; ☾ 24hr) where you can grab a bite (eggs, bliny, open sandwiches) before catching your bus out of town.

Entertainment

Pskov has a small but friendly nightlife scene. The popular entertainment area at the moment is on Rizhsky pr, a few blocks west of the bridge.

Platforma (☎ 445 142; Rizhsky pr 16; ☾ noon-6am) This complex has a bowling alley (per hour R300–800), billiard tables (per hour R60-120), an Internet café (per hour R80) and a tiny sports bar. It's on the 4th floor.

Club Jaguar (☎ 449 647; Rizhsky pr 16; admission R50-150; ☾ 10pm-6am) You'll find an equally young crowd a few doors down at this disco, located atop the restaurant of the same name.

Bolshoy Kontsertny Zal (☎ 62737; ul Nekrasova 22; tickets from R50; box office ☾ 1-7pm Mon-Sat) This venue stages musical theatre, comedy acts and concerts.

Shopping

Menshikovikh (☎ 161 575; ul Sovetskaya 50) This souvenir shop has a good selection of pottery (particularly teapots and teacups), photos of Pskov's churches and the odd frog figurine. There's also an unsigned **shop** (Oktyabrsky pr 32) with scarves, linen tablecloths, so-so lacquer boxes, teaware and enamelled jewellery.

Getting There & Away

The **train station** (☎ 536 237) has limited amenities, although you can check a bag here (per bag, per day R40). The only direct trains to St Petersburg are night trains (R450, six hours) to the Vitebsk Station; during the day you have to travel to Luga and transfer. One night train goes to Moscow (R1130, 12 hours), Rīga (R1265, eight hours) and Vilnius (R1130, 10 hours).

There are no easy train connections to Novgorod, but two buses daily (R206, 4½ hours) leave from the **central bus station** (☎ 24002). Buses for Pushkinskie Gory via Izborsk leave regularly (R94, two hours). Buses to Pechory (R44, 1½ hours) also leave every three hours. There's one daily bus to Smolensk (R370, seven hours), two to Rīga and one to Tallinn.

Getting Around

Buses 1, 11 and 17 run from the train station past Hotel Oktyabrskaya and through the centre (R5). Bus No 2 or 17 takes you to Hotel Rizhskaya from the station (taxis charge about R80).

AROUND PSKOV
Izborsk Изборск

On a ridge with wide views over the countryside, Izborsk was once the equal of Pskov, chosen as a base by one of the original Varangian princes who ruled over early Russia. Now it's a sleepy village by the ruins of the oldest stone fortress in Russia. Inside the old walls is the 14th-century **Church of St Nicholas**, a small green-trimmed building that was undergoing restoration at the time of research. There's also a stone tower (Bashnya Lukovka), older than the walls, which has a **viewing platform** (R15; ✆ 10am-6pm) at the top. A path around the back of the fortress walls leads down to a lake. The locals you'll pass toting water bottles are coming from the 12 Springs of Happiness, Love, Health and nine other virtues.

Outside the fortress the 17th-century **Church of St Sergius** has a tiny exhibit on local archaeology; some pieces date from the 8th century. A second museum in town, the **State Historic-Archaeological Museum 'Izborsk'** (✆ 96696; ul Pechorskaya 39; admission R5; ✆ 10am-6pm Tue-Sun), houses archaeological finds from Izborsk and contains written explanations, in Russian, of the town's extremely rich history.

SLEEPING & EATING

A crisp, modern cabin behind the fortress harbours an unlikely **guesthouse** (Gostevoy dom; ✆ 96612; s/d with shared bathroom R400/800, ste with bathroom R1200) overlooking the valley. Six of the rooms share a very nice bathroom, while the two-room 'lux' suite has a broad private balcony. It's a good find, though you'll want to call in advance.

Beyond the kremlin walls, near the Church of St Sergius, is **Blinnaya** (✆ 96713; bliny around R35; ✆ 9am-6pm), a sweet little bliny restaurant boasting 'Izborskian' bliny. You can order them with butter, jam, condensed milk or ham. Outdoor tables and benches are a good spot for an afternoon beer.

GETTING THERE & AWAY

It's 32km from Pskov to Izborsk on the Rīga road. Buses run regularly from Pskov's bus station (R27, 45 minutes); be sure to take the bus towards Stary (Old) Izborsk, not Noviy (New) Izborsk.

Mikhailovskoe Михайловское

✆ 246 (within Pskov region), ✆ 81146 (from elsewhere)

Walking around Pushkin's inspiring estate at daybreak, it's easy to see where Russia's greatest poet received his inspiration. As you pass through the moist forest air, you soon reach the edge of a lake, offering magnificent views of tall, regal pines lining the

far shore. A silvery mist rises off the smooth surface of the water as a lone fisherman casts his line out across the reeds.

The family house of Russia's most loved writer is open as part of the **Pushkin Museum Reserve** (✆ 22321; admission R150; ✆ 10am-5pm Tue-Sun Dec-Mar, 9am-8pm Tue-Sun May-Oct, closed Apr & Nov), a 2½-hour bus ride from Pskov. Alexander Pushkin spent two phenomenally productive years in exile at Mikhailovskoe, his family's estate near the settlement of Pushkinskie Gory (Pushkin Hills), 130km south of Pskov. The family first came to the area in the late 1700s, when Pushkin's great-grandfather Abram Hannibal was given the land by Empress Elizabeth. The family house was destroyed during WWII and has since been rebuilt.

The 20-hectare park is closed on the last Tuesday of the month. The attraction is Pushkin's writing room with his comfy leather chair, portraits of Byron and Zhukovsky (Pushkin's mentor, also a poet) and a small statue of Napoleon. The thick religious book on his writing table is the one he supposedly grabbed from the family bookcase and pretended to be reading whenever he saw the local priest coming for a visit.

At Pushkinskie Gory, about 800m north of the bus stop, is the **Svyatagorsky Monastery**, where Pushkin is buried. Not far from the monastery is **Hotel Druzhba** (✆ 21651; ul Lenina 8; s/d from R420/600), which has simple but nice rooms with bath and shower. Odd-numbered rooms boast pleasant views of the forest. To get to the hotel, walk from the bus stop along the road away from the monastery and bear right.

This is lovely countryside and can be seen as part of a day trip.

GETTING THERE & AWAY

Most agencies run excursions from Pskov; check at the hotel where you're staying or contact the tourist office (p335) to find one that matches your schedule. Alternatively, you can do it yourself by catching a bus to Pushkinskie Gory from the Pskov bus station. There are several buses a day (R95, 2½ hours).

The Pushkinskie Gory bus station is about 8km from the Pushkin house; there may or may not be a short-distance bus to cover the last leg. You could also hire a taxi (R80 one way) and return on foot as the walk

PASSION & TRAGEDY: THE SHORT BUT FEBRILE LIFE OF RUSSIA'S GREATEST POET

Born in 1799, the son of nobility with a dollop of African blood in his lineage, Alexander Pushkin grew up in the French-speaking high society of St Petersburg. He went to school at the Lyceum in the shadow of the royal family's summer palace. Before he reached puberty, this precocious youth was using his perfect pitch, sharp wit and flawless sense of timing to hit on court women, diplomats' wives, peasant girls and the like. He and his school friends, many of them also poets, would spend their idle hours, between balls, composing odes and love poems. A child of his time, the Romantic Age, Pushkin was obsessed with obsessions – war, male honour, and beautiful and unattainable women – and he is said to have had a foot fetish. His heroes were Lord Byron and Napoleon.

Pushkin wrote everything from classical odes and sonnets to short stories, plays and fairy tales. He is best loved for his poems in verse, *The Bronze Horsemen* and *Eugene Onegin,* in which he nearly answered that eternal question – why do Russians (like to) suffer so much? Politically, he was a hot potato and the tsars exiled him from St Petersburg thrice, once to his home estate in Mikhailovskoe and twice to the Caucasus, where his romping with the local beauties and war-loving men added more fuel to his poetic fire. At home in Mikhailovskoe, he is said to have spent long evenings drinking with his childhood nanny. Pushkin himself admitted she told him many of the tales which he then turned into national legends. While on long walks, he would compose aloud. To keep his arm in good shape for duelling, he carried a cane filled with rocks.

It did not help. In 1837, Pushkin was mortally wounded in a duel over his wife, the Russian beauty Natalia Goncharova. He lay dying for two days while all of St Petersburg came to pay homage, dramatically directing taxi drivers, 'To Pushkin!' Even today the Russian rumour mills are producing versions of this 166-year-old scandal; only the theories about JFK's assassination come close in weirdness and speculation. During the night, Pushkin's body was carried from Chyornaya Rechka in St Petersburg and buried at the monastery near his home estate. For a riveting account of the duel and the events that preceded it, read Serena Vitale's *Pushkin's Button.*

is pleasant. To get there, take a left out of the bus station and walk for 1km along the road where you'll see the Svyatagorsk Monastery on your left. From there a road leads off to the right, which leads to Mikhailovskoe – keep following the signs from here.

Another option is hitching a ride on an excursion bus leaving from Hotel Druzhba in Pushkinskie Gory or asking a local driver. Be sure to find out when the last bus back to Pskov departs from Pushkinskie Gory. At research time, the last bus back left at around 3.25pm Monday to Thursday. On weekends, the last bus departs at 6.40pm.

Pechory Monastery Печорский Монастырь

Founded in 1473 in a ravine full of hermits' caves, this monastery has been a working cloister ever since. With all the high ground outside, it's an improbable stronghold, but several tsars fortified it and depended on it. A path descends under the 1564 **St Nicholas Church** (Nikolskaya tserkov) into a sea of colours and architectural styles, where several dozen monks still live and study.

Taking photos of the buildings is acceptable if you make a contribution at the front gate; photographing the monks is taboo.

The central yellow church comprises two buildings. At ground level is the original **Assumption Cathedral** (Uspensky sobor), built into the caves; upstairs is the 18th-century baroque **Intercession Church** (Pokrovskaya tserkov). Below the belfry on the left is the entrance to the caves, where some 10,000 bodies – monks, benefactors and others – are bricked up in vaults, with more dying to get in.

You can wander the monastery grounds and visit most of the churches on your own, but to visit the caves you'll have to find a monk willing to lead you down through the spiderweb of dark, spooky, nearly freezing sand tunnels. Everyone carries a candle, which in places you can thrust through holes in the tunnel walls to see the wooden coffins lying lopsided on top of each other. The monks insist that there has never been the smell of decay. At the exit to the caves, you'll be shown an ancient coffin burned around the edge (supposedly this happened when some evil-doer tried to open it).

On the grounds is the summer carriage of Peter the Great's daughter, the licentious Anna Ioanovna, who – as the story goes – came to have some fun with the monks and didn't leave until winter, on a sleigh. Before WWII, this area was in independent Estonia, thereby avoiding the frequent stripping or destruction of churches during that time; the 16th-century bells in St Nicholas Church are original, a rarity in Russia.

There's a booth outside the monastery gates housing an **excursion office** (☎ 81148-21 493; ⏰ 9am-1pm & 2-6pm). The office offers tours in Russian for about R200, depending on the number of people. On the monastery grounds, women must wear skirts and cover their heads; you can borrow wraparound skirts and shawls at the entrance. Men should wear long pants, and both men and women should cover their shoulders. It's possible for men to stay at the monastery and eat with the monks in their modest cafeteria, with special permission. Ask at the front gate, and explain why you are interested in staying.

There are several buses a day from Pskov to Pechory (R33, 1½ hours). In addition, one early morning and one evening train run here.

KALININGRAD REGION
КАЛИНИНГРАДСКАЯ ОБЛАСТЬ

Overlooking the Baltic Sea, the Kaliningrad region boasts some striking scenery. Among the region's attractions, you'll find a vibrant city with 700 years of Prussian history, pleasant coastal towns facing the sea, and the wild Curonian spit, a narrow landmass lined with some of Europe's highest sand dunes, deserted beaches and verdant marshland. You'll also find a colourful array of wildlife hidden in the region's thick forests.

Yet more than its natural wonders, Kaliningrad is known for its history, which differs markedly from the rest of Russia. From the 13th century until 1945, the entire region was German, part of the core territory of the Teutonic knights and their successors, the dukes and kings of Prussia.

Its capital, now named Kaliningrad, was the famous German city of Königsberg, capital of East Prussia, where Prussian kings were crowned. Scant Prussian legacy remains in the city of Kaliningrad, but the countryside is sprinkled with picturesque, moss-covered ruins of Prussian castles. After WWI, East Prussia was separated from the rest of Germany when Poland regained statehood. The three-month campaign by which the Red Army took it in 1945 was one of the fiercest of the war, with hundreds of thousands of casualties on both sides.

Kaliningrad is also Russia's smallest, newest and most westerly province, and its connection to Mother Russia is a complicated one. It often gets left off maps of Russia altogether, which is not an entirely inappropriate omission as Kaliningrad, now surrounded by EU countries, has a strong pull to the west. A different air pervades this region – while its citizens are not quite European in outlook, they seem more Westernised and open than in other parts of Russia. There's still talk of turning Kaliningrad into a fourth 'Baltic state', yet this is far from likely, as Russia would have much to lose by granting autonomy to this prosperous region. The world's largest amber mine, which still produces 90% of the world's amber, lies in Kaliningrad (in Yantarny). The Baltic fleet is still headquartered in the heavily militarised region of Baltiysk, and the area has always been of strategic importance, particularly in light of recent EU expansion east. In fact, foreigners were forbidden to enter the region until 1991.

Visas

Unless you're flying, to reach the Kaliningrad region from anywhere else means you must be in possession of either a double or multiple-entry Russian visa, and/or visas for its neighbouring countries. These must be arranged in advance. This can be done at the main **PVU office** (☎ 228 274, 228 282; Sovetsky pr 13, room 9) in Kaliningrad.

Disabled Travellers

Inaccessible transport, lack of ramps and lifts and no centralised policy for people with physical limitations make the region challenging for wheelchair-bound travellers. In Kaliningrad, Hotel Kaliningrad and several restaurants are wheelchair-accessible.

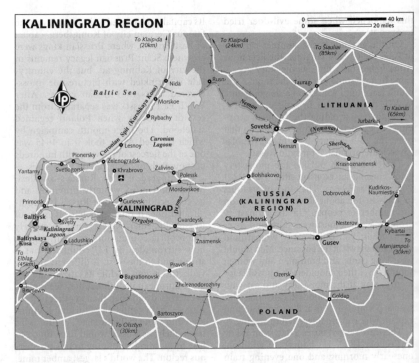

KALININGRAD REGION

0 |————| 40 km
0 |————| 20 miles

To Klaipėda (20km)
To Klaipėda (24km)
To Šiauliai (85km)

Baltic Sea

Nida
Rusnė
Tauragė

Morskoe

Rybachy

Curonian Spit (Kurshskaya Kosa)

Neman

LITHUANIA
To Kaunas (65km)

Curonian Lagoon

Lesnoy

Sovetsk
(Nemunas)

Jurbarkas

Pionersky
Zelenogradsk

Slavsk
Neman

Sheshupe

Yantarny
Svetlogorsk
Zalivino

Khrabrovo
Polessk

Bolshakovo

Krasnoznamensk

Primorsk
Gurievsk
Mordovskoe

Dobrovolsk
Kudirkos-Naumiestis

KALININGRAD

RUSSIA
(KALININGRAD
REGION)

Balga
Svetly
Gvardeysk
Chernyakhovsk

Baltiysk
Kaliningrad Lagoon

Pregolya

Nesterov
Kybartai
To Marijampolė (30km)

Baltiyskaya Kosa
Ladushkin

Deyma

Znamensk

Gusev

To Elbląg (45km)
Mamonovo

Pravdinsk

Braniewo
Bagrationovsk
Zheleznodorozhny

Ozersk

Bartoszyce
POLAND
Goldap

To Olsztyn (30km)

Baltma Tours offers further information or assistance for disabled tourists.

KALININGRAD КАЛИНИНГРАД

☎ 22 (within the region), ☎ 4112 (from elsewhere) / pop 423,000 / ◷ Moscow −1hr

Old photos attest that until 1945 Königsberg was one of Europe's finest-looking cities: regal, vibrant, cultured and an architectural gem. But WWII, later Soviet destruction of German-era constructions and misguided building projects saw to it that today's Kaliningrad is not exactly eye-candy.

However, there are lovely residential corners of the city that predate the war, a forestlike park and a few large ponds which work as effective antidotes to all the concrete. A number of central areas have been given a recent and friendly face-lift. It's also a vibrant, fun-loving city that feels larger than its population would suggest.

Founded as a Teutonic fort in 1255, Königsberg joined the Hanseatic League in 1340, and from 1457 to 1618 was the residence of the grand masters of the Teutonic order and their successors, the dukes of Prussia. The first king of Prussia was crowned here in 1701. The city centre was flattened by British air raids in August 1944 and the Red Army assault from 6 to 9 April 1945. Many of the surviving Germans were killed or sent to Siberia – the last 25,000 were deported to Germany in 1947–8, one of the most effective ethnic cleansing campaigns in European history.

The city was renamed on 4 July 1946 (City Day celebrations are thus held on the first weekend in July) after Mikhail Kalinin, one of Stalin's henchmen who had conveniently died just as a new city name was needed. After opening up in 1991, it struggled through extreme economic difficulties. A wave of elderly German tourists revisiting their *Heimat* (Homeland), often weeping upon seeing what it had become, resulted in a complete reconstruction of Königsberg's cathedral thanks to their donations. Slowly, Kaliningrad has emerged as one of Russia's most Western-minded cities and, due to its mix of historical legacies, one of its most intriguing.

Orientation

Leninsky pr, a north–south avenue, is the city's main artery, running over 3km from the bus and main train station, Yuzhny vokzal (South Station), to Severny vokzal (North Station). About halfway it crosses the Pregolya River and passes the cathedral, the city's major landmark. The real heart is further north, around sprawling pl Pobedy.

Information

INTERNET ACCESS

E-Type (Sovetsky pr 1; per hr R30; ☺ 9am-9pm Mon-Fri, 9am-7pm Sun) In room 155 of the State Technical University.

Internet Café (pr Mira; per hr about R80; ☺ 11am-11pm) This popular, new Internet café serves drinks; frustratingly, they charge by the MB, rather than by time.

Kiberda (☎ 511 830; ul Komsomolskaya 87; per hr R32; ☺ noon-11pm) A funky, grotto-like Internet café that also serves decent meals.

Post offices (ul Chernyakhovskogo 74; per hr R30; ☺ 9am-9pm Mon-Sat; ul Chernyakhovskogo 56; per hr R30; ☺ 10am-10pm Mon-Sat) Many post offices in the city now provide Internet access, including these branches.

MAPS

You can purchase good city maps from any kiosk in town for around R35.

MONEY

There are exchange bureaus at most hotels, often with 24-hour service. Many shops along Leninsky pr and elsewhere have ATMs.

Sberbank (ul Chernyakhovskogo 38 & Leninsky pr 2) This ubiquitous bank has locations throughout the city.

Stroivestbank (ul Gendelya 10) Gives good rates on credit-card advances and exchange.

POST

Main post office (ul Kosmonavta Leonova 22) Located about 600m north of pr Mira.

Post office branch (ul Chernyakhovskogo 32) A smaller, more convenient branch, opposite the central market.

TELEPHONE

International phone calls can be made from card-operated public phone booths (St Petersburg cards work in these). Cards are available from post offices, kiosks and most major hotels.

Hotel Kaliningrad (☎ 469 440; www.hotel.kalinin grad.ru; Leninsky pr 81) Has a handy phone-fax office that's open 24 hours.

Telephone & fax centre (Teatralnaya ul 13/19; ☺ 24hr) Get better rates by ordering calls here. Self-dial long-distance calls can be made one block south at its second office.

TOURIST INFORMATION

A free Russian/English guide to the region and city called *Welcome to Kaliningrad* is available in hotel lobbies. In Your Pocket guide (available only online) has the latest city listings at www.inyourpocket.com /russia/kaliningrad/en.

TRAVEL AGENCIES

Baltma Tours (☎ 211 880; www.baltmatours.com; pr Mira 49; ☺ 9.30am-6.30pm Mon-Fri, 11am-3pm Sat) This is the best travel agency in town and by far the best source of regional information. There's nothing it can't do – from arranging visa support and accommodation to any kind of tour. It offers boat cruises throughout the region and excursions with friendly, knowledgeable guides to every corner of Kaliningrad. Car rental with a driver is typically US$10 per hour, guides cost about US$40 a day extra. Pick up a copy of Batma's regional guide at the office.

Golden Orchid (☎ 538 553, 01145-21 098; www.enet .ru/~goldorch not in English; ul Frunze 6) Specialises in arranging extremely interesting trips to nearby military port Baltiysk (formerly Pillau), with permission, transport, guide and overnight accommodation costing about US$50, or around US$15 for six-hour excursions.

Sights

CATHEDRAL & AROUND

A Unesco World Heritage site, the red-brick Gothic **cathedral** (☎ 446 868; adult/student R70/35; ☺ 9am-5pm) is an outstanding remnant from the German past. Founded in 1333, it was severely damaged during WWII and, since 1992, has been undergoing total reconstruction. On the 1st floor are small Lutheran and Orthodox chapels; upstairs are displays of old Königsberg and objects from archaeological digs. On the top floor is an austere room with the death mask of Emanuel Kant, whose rose-marble **tomb** lies outside on the outer north side. The 18th-century philosopher was born, studied and taught in Königsberg.

The fine blue Renaissance-style building, just across the river to the south of the cathedral, is the **Former Stock Exchange** (Leninsky pr 83), built in the 1870s and now a 'Sailors' Culture Palace'.

North of the cathedral is Tsentralnaya ploshchad (Central Square) on which sits one of the dourest, ugliest of Soviet creations, the upright H-shaped **Dom Sovietov** (House of Soviets). On this site stood a magnificent 1255 castle, damaged during WWII but dynamited out of existence by narrow-minded Soviet planners in 1967–68 to rid the city of a flagrant reminder of its Germanic past. Over 10 long years this eyesore was built in its place, but it has never even been used. Money ran out, and it was discovered that the land below it was hollow, with a (now flooded) four-level underground passage connecting to the cathedral.

Further north, near the university, is the popular **Bunker Museum** (☎ 536 593; Universitetskaya ul 2; adult/student R40/30; ☼ 10am-6pm), the German command post in 1945, where the city's last German commander, Otto van Lasch, signed capitulation to the Soviets.

WORLD OCEAN MUSEUM

Another of Kaliningrad's star attractions, this four-section **museum** (☎ 340 244; nab Petra Velikogo 1; each section adult/student R50/25; ☼ 10am-6pm Wed-Sun Apr-Oct, 11am-5pm Wed-Sun Nov-Mar) has some fascinating exhibits hidden among the three ships docked in the river. *Vityaz*, a former expedition vessel, has displays on its past scientific life as well as on other Russian research expeditions. The *Viktor Patsaev*, named after one of Kaliningrad's famous cosmonauts, was once part of the 'space flotilla' and its exhibits relate to space research. The B-413 submarine gives a glimpse of life for the 300 seamen who served aboard the ship. There's also a pavilion with the skeleton of a 16.8m-long sperm whale, and the fairly uninteresting main hall, with a row of small aquariums and general information about the ocean. Visits to the *Vityaz* and *Viktor Patsaev* are by guided tour (every 45 minutes or so); you can wander freely through the sub.

OTHER SIGHTS

Kaliningrad's outstanding **History & Art Museum** (☎ 453 844; ul Klinicheskaya 21; adult/student R40/30; ☼ 10am-6pm Tue-Sun) is housed in a re-constructed 1912 concert hall by the banks of the pretty Prud Nizhny (Schlossteich, Lower Pond), a favourite recreation spot. The museum displays a fairly open history of the city. Though it mainly focuses on Soviet rule, the German past comes through as the city's spine. There are chilling posters of the castle's destruction.

On the edge of the shimmering Prud Verkny (Upper Pond), the **Amber Museum** (☎ 461 563; pl Vasilevskogo 1; admission R60; ☼ 10am-5pm Tue-Sun) has some 6000 examples of amber artworks, the most impressive being from the Soviet period. In addition to enormous pieces of jewellery containing prehistoric insects suspended within, some of the more fascinating works include an amber flute and a four-panelled amber and ivory chalice depicting Columbus, the *Niña*, the *Pinta* and

RENAMING THE PAST

When Soviet authorities decided to rename the German city of Königsberg, 'Kaliningrad' was decided upon purely by chance. Mikhail Kalinin, the former president of the Supreme Soviet, had never even visited the region. He was, however, a great pal of Stalin's, and when he died in June 1946, Stalin immortalised him by plastering his name upon the town. Not surprisingly, few residents have any association with Kalinin; and those who do know his deeds would rather forget him. While less infamous than Stalin, Kalinin was pretty rotten: he turned his back on the famine in Ukraine in 1932 when millions starved; he also authorised the massacre of thousands of Polish officers in Katyn forest, which was later blamed on the Nazis (see the boxed text, p326).

Given the spate of renaming that has happened elsewhere in Russia, one might wonder why Kaliningrad has been so slow to follow suit. The problem is that there is no past to return to – at least no Russian one. For some, Königsberg, which means 'king's mountain', still conjures unpleasant associations of German conquest. This has given rise to the search for a new name, free of any past associations. Baltiysk – city of the Baltics – has been put forward, and would be an excellent idea, if only there weren't already a Baltiysk. Others are lobbying for Kantgrad, or city of Kant, which would be a fitting, if rather unpoetic, tribute to a man admired by Russians and Germans alike.

While the search for a new name seems like trivia to some residents, others see it as an apt metaphor as Kaliningrad searches for a new identity in a rapidly changing region.

the *Santa Maria*. You can buy amber jewellery in the museum or from the vendors outside. The museum is housed in the attractive **Dohna Tower**, a bastion of the city's old defensive ring sitting at the lower end of a small lake surrounded by parkland. The adjacent **Rossgarten Gate**, one of the old German city gates, contains a decent restaurant.

At the city's northern border, along Sovietsky pr, is the **Fifth Fort** (Pyaty Fort). One of the city's 15 forts constructed between 1872 and 1892 as a second line of defence, and the only one open to the public, it's a heavily wooded ruin that's fun to explore for hidden passages. Take trolleybus 1 to the Pyaty Fort stop.

The **Kaliningrad Art Gallery** (☎ 467 166; Moskovsky pr 62; ☺ 11am-7pm Tue-Sun) features exhibitions by local artists.

PROSPEKT MIRA

Pl Pobedy is the current city centre, which is the site of a massive cathedral that should be complete by the time you read this. The gold domes of the **Cathedral of Christ the Saviour** will be visible from many points in the city.

Extending west of the square is pr Mira, a pleasant artery lined with shops and cafés leading to some of the city's prettiest areas. Some 300m from pl Pobedy is the 1927 **Kaliningrad Drama & Comedy Theatre** (☎ 212 422; pr Mira 4) which was restored in 1980.

Another 200m further on is the **zoo** (☎ 218 924; pr Mira 26; adult/student R100/40; ☺ 9am-9pm Jun-Aug, 10am-5pm Sep-May), which before WWII was considered the third best in the world, but is now in a sorry state (donations accepted – and needed!). Some animals have been sold for funding, and while signs discourage feeding, zoo keepers actually encourage the public to feed the hungry bears, monkeys and other animals on display.

Further west is the splendid **Cosmonaut Monument**, a gem of Soviet iconography. This honours the several cosmonauts who hail from the region. Just west, as pr Pobedy branches out from pr Mira, is the entrance to **Kalinin Park**, an amusement ground and splendid, forestlike park on the grounds of an old German cemetery.

Walks through the linden-scented, tree-lined German neighbourhoods are the best way to experience old Königsberg. The entire area between prs Pobedy and Mira is particularly enchanting (ul Kutuzova especially), despite looking somewhat dishevelled.

AUTHOR'S CHOICE

Kaliningrad's most stylish hotel, the **Dona Hotel** (☎ 351 650; www.dona.kaliningrad .ru; pl Vasilevskogo 2; s/d from R1920/2480) has handsomely furnished rooms with ultramodern design touches worthy of a Philippe Starck protégé. Top-end rooms are pricier but offer spacious digs, with globe lighting, huge windows and flat-screen TVs. The hallways, with Miro-esque carpeting, are a tribute to sleek modernism. You'll also find friendly English-speaking staff, pleasant buffet breakfasts, and one of the city's best restaurants – Dolce Vita.

Sleeping

Kaliningrad's hotels are often booked solid during the week by business travellers. To avoid disappointment, call ahead.

Chayka (☎ 210 729; ul Pugacheva 13; s/d from R1000/1200) One of the most pleasant hotels in town, the 24-room Chaika is set in an old German home, in a leafy, residential area. Rooms are cosy with some nice old touches.

Cherepakha (☎ 957 500; www.turtle-hotel.ru; Zoologichesky Tupik 10; s/d from R2200/2900) This charming guesthouse has 11 snug rooms, each with darkwood furniture, artwork on the walls and views of the park across the street. It's in a peaceful, tree-lined neighbourhood behind the zoo.

Hotel Moskva (☎ 352 300; pr Mira 19; s/d from R1800/2000) This 171-room hotel has been reborn after extensive renovations and boasts bright spacious rooms, friendly atmosphere and a good location.

Hotel Kaliningrad (☎ 350 500; www.hotel.kalin ingrad.ru; Leninsky pr 81; s/d from R1000/1200) The town's principal hotel is conveniently placed and offers many services. The renovated rooms are clean and comfortable, but pretty charmless. Try to avoid rooms facing the city centre, which are noisy due to the traffic.

Gostivoy Dom Okhota (☎ 226 994; Petrovo village; s/d R600/800) For those who don't mind staying out of the city, this wooden chalet is a small slice of paradise. Rooms are modern, bright and clean, and the surroundings peaceful. There's horse riding nearby

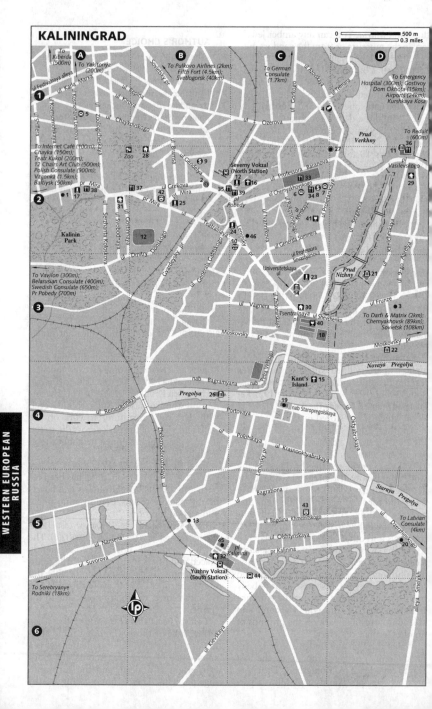

KALININGRAD

0 ____ 500 m
0 ____ 0.3 miles

To Kiberda (500m)
To Yakitonya (200m)
ul Festivalnaya alleya
ul Karla Marxa
ul Komsomolskaya
ul Kosmonavta Leonova
ul Repina
Sovietsky pr
ul Kirova
ul Chaykovskogo
Zoologicheskaya
ul Shmira
To Pulkovo Airlines (2km); Fifth Fort (4.5km); Svetlogorsk (40km)
To German Consulate (1.7km)
ul Gorkogo
ul Azovska
ul Tenana
To Emergency Hospital (300m); Gostivoy Dom Okhota (15km); Airports (24km); Kurshkaya Kosa
ul Ozerova
Prud Verkhny
To Reduit (600m)
pl Vasilevskogo
Severny Vokzal (North Station)
ul Professora Baranova
ul Chernyakhovkogo
ul Professora
ul Grekova
ul Brama
ul Gendelya
Zoo
To Internet Café (100m); Chayka (150m); Teatr Kukol (200m); 12 Chairs Art Club (500m); Polish Consulate (900m); Vagonka (1.5km); Baltiysk (50km)
pr Mira
ul Serzhanta Kolosova
ul Svobodnaya
pr Mira
pl Pobedy
ul Chernyakhovskogo
ul Proletarskaya
ul Sergeeva
Kalinin Park
ul Dmitry Donskogo
Teatralnaya
Gvardeysky pr
Leninsky pr
ul Ivannkova
ul Generala Sommera
ul Klinicheskaya
To Vavilon (300m); Belarusian Consulate (400m); Swedish Consulate (650m); Pr Pobedy (700m)
ul Vagnera
ul Generala Chistakova
ul Professora Sevastyanova
Universitetskaya ul
Prud Nizhny
ul 9-go Aprelya
ul Frunze
To Darfi & Matrix (2km); Chernyakhovsk (89km); Sovietsk (108km)
ul Zhitomirskaya
Moskovsky pr
Tsentralnaya pl
ul Shevchenko
Moskovsky pr
Novaya Pregolya
nab Bagramyana
Petra Velikogo
nab
Pregolya
ul Remeslennaya
Kant's Island
ul Portovaya
nab Staropregolskaya
Staraya Pregolya
ul Oktyabrskaya
ul Zheleznodorozhnaya
ul Polotskaya
ul Krasnooktyabrskaya
Leninsky pr
To Latvian Consulate (4km)
Bagrationa
ul Bogdana Khmelnitskogo
ul Olshtynskaya
pr Kalinina
ul Narsena
ul Suvorova
pl Kalinina
Yuzhny Vokzal (South Station)
alleya Smelykh
ul Dzerzhinskogo
To Serebryanye Rodniki (18km)
ul Kievskaya

1 5 28 37 42 38 17 1 31 25 9 2 @ 35 12 16 39 24 10 46 23 14 30 40 18 13 45 32 44 26 19 15 22 41 6 34 8 7 27 4 11 36 29 21 3 20 43

WESTERN EUROPEAN RUSSIA

and meals can be ordered. It's on the main road to Zelenogradsk, 15km north along Sovetsky pr.

Komnaty Otdykha (☎ 586 447; pl Kalinina; s/d R280/560) Considering it's inside the south train station, the rooms here are surprisingly quiet and clean, and the shared bathrooms are OK.

Eating

12 Chairs Art Club (☎ 955 900; pr Mira 67; mains R200-300; ☻ noon-1am Mon-Sat, 1pm-1am Sun) Dark and atmospheric, this antique-filled cellar in an old German house serves tasty dishes like shrimp with kiwi sauce, trout with almonds, chocolate fondue and a wide range of cocktails, coffees and teas. On cold days you can warm yourself by the fire.

Dolce Vita (☎ 351 612; Vasilevskogo pl 2; meals R400-600; ☻ 1pm-1am Tue-Sun, 3pm-1am Mon) Next to the Dona Hotel, this lovely restaurant is a good place for a splurge. The European-influenced menu includes lobster cream bisque with crayfish, prosciutto with melon, roasted citrus turbot with eggplant chips and many other delectable temptations. The outdoor terrace opens during the summer.

Universal (☎ 216 931; pr Mira 43; meals R100-350; ☻ 10am-3am) This stylish complex comprises a café, restaurant (mains R100 to R150), cinema and nightclub. The restaurant is considered one of the city's top three; if you just want a casual meal, the café, with its various rooms of antique furnishings, makes a fine spot for dishes like French onion soup, vegetable risotto with mushrooms and chocolate truffle tart. English menu.

Valencia (☎ 433 820; pl Pobedy 1; meals R300-600) One of the city's best restaurants, Valencia has an elegantly set dining room, with good Spanish dishes (the paella is a favourite), an extensive wine list and a stately front parlour well-suited for afternoon tea or an apéritif.

Razgulyay (☎ 716 753; pl Pobedy 1; meals R50-180; ☻ 10am-2am Mon-Sat, noon-2am Sun) The extensive buffet features roasted meats, salads, fresh juices and many other tasty selections in a cheery, folk-style setting.

Solyanka (☎ 279 203; pr Mira 24; meals R65-90; ☻ 9am-11pm) There may be a doorman here, but this setup is basically cafeteria-style (non-Russian speakers can point to what they like), serving tasty dishes at great prices.

Yakitoriya (☎ 563 156; ul Leonova 59; meals R200-400) This late-night Japanese restaurant is a welcome addition to the Kaliningrad dining scene. Although the food is far from authentic, the *gyoza*, sashimi and other dishes aren't bad, and the lively, mixed crowd adds to the fun. English picture menu.

Planeta (☎ 465 235; ul Chernyakhovskogo 26; pizzas R60-180) The adjoining arcade, the loud music and the cheap pizzas draw a youthful crowd to this popular hang-out near the market. In addition to beer and pizzas, you can order soups, salads and desserts. In the same building is one of Kaliningrad's more popular nightclubs. Across from Planeta, you can stock up on fresh produce at the city's main market.

Taverna Diky Dyouk (☎ 465 235; ul Chernya-khovskogo 26; meals R190-500) Generous portions of scrumptious Russian, French and Lithuanian dishes are served at this medieval-themed restaurant.

Solnechny Kamen (☎ 539 106; pl Vasilievskogo 3; meals R150-300) In the old Rossgarten Gate, this atmospheric restaurant specialises in seafood, with Russian dishes also well represented. In addition to the brick walls, stained glass and Teutonic touches in the main dining room, there's a pleasant outdoor terrace at the back.

Drinking

Redut (☎ 461 951; Litovsky Val 27; meals R100-300) Although there's lots of food on the menu, the main reason to come to this lively pub is the decent selection of beer brewed on the premises. Try the delicious unfiltered brew. Simple beer-hall atmosphere prevails.

V Teni Zamka (Tsentralnaya pl, kiosk No 63; cappuccino R40-56) The city's best espresso, coffee cocktails and ice cream are served in this tiny but charming space, seating only 20, inside the aptly named kiosk village.

Vostochniy Kafe (☎ 147 121; ul Proletarskaya 3a; meals R150-300) The sounds of gurgling water pipes greet visitors upon entering this basement-level tea salon. Gauzy curtains, strings of Christmas lights and New Age music set the scene for lounging over pipefuls of flavoured tobacco and potfuls of green tea. Waiters are summoned via the red button dangling from the paper lanterns.

Entertainment
NIGHTCLUBS

The city is full of discos and upscale nightclubs. Most charge a cover of around R150-300, though women typically get in free. Both **Planeta** (p347) and **Universal** (p347) are among the city's more popular nightclubs. Universal also has a cinema.

Vagonka (☎ 556 677; Stanochnaya ul 12; ⏰ 11pm-4am) A lively, slightly alternative crowd fills this stylish nightclub west of Kalinin Park. Good DJs and elaborate dance shows make Vagonka a good pick. It's tricky to find, so it's best to take a taxi there.

Darfi & Matrix (☎ 457 777; Yaltinskaya ul 66) Darfi is a bowling and billiards emporium, that's a fun place for a game. Matrix is a house-music club with a young attractive crowd sweating it out on weekends. Both places are east of Dom Sovietov.

THEATRE, MUSIC & PUPPETS
Drama & Comedy Theatre (☎ 212 422; pr Mira 4; admission R100-180) Plays, ballets and classical concerts are staged here throughout the year. Stop by the box office to see what's on.

Philharmonic Hall (☎ 448 890; ul Bogdana Khmelnitskogo 61a; admission from R30) This beautifully restored neo-Gothic church, which boasts excellent acoustics, hosts organ concerts, chamber music recitals and the occasional symphony orchestra.

Teatr Kukol (☎ 214 335; pr Pobedy 1; admission R50) Housed in a 19th-century Lutheran church, this puppet theatre is a big hit with young and old alike. Performances take place on Saturdays and Sundays at noon.

Plans have been made to hold classical concerts in the cathedral in the near future.

Getting There & Away
AIR

Kaliningrad's **domestic airport** (☎ 459 426) and **international airport** (☎ 446 666) are 16km north of the city, near Khrabrovo village.

Pulkova Airlines (☎ 716 663; pl Pobedy 4) flies two to three times daily to St Petersburg; **Aeroflot** (☎ 954 805; pl Kalinina 1) flies four times daily to Moscow. **Kaliningrad Airlines** (☎ 355 095; pl Kalinina 1) flies twice daily to Moscow, thrice weekly to St Petersburg. There is also a daily flight to Warsaw on **LOT** (☎ 342 707; www.lot.com; Leninsky pr 5). In the future, there may be flights connecting Kaliningrad with Copenhagen. Contact Baltma Tours to find out if other international routes have been added.

BUS

The **bus station** (☎ 443 635; international tickets ☎ 446 261; pl Kalinina) is next to Yuzhny vokzal. Buses depart from here to every corner of the region, including one or two per hour to Svetlogorsk, eight daily to Chernyakhovsk and four daily to Smiltyne, Lithuania, along the Kurshkaya Kosa. One bus daily goes to Klaipeda (R135) via Sovetsk, and there are two daily each to Kaunas (R255) and Vilnius (R360). Daily buses go to Rīga (R360), Tallinn (R670) and Warsaw. There are two buses daily to Gdansk and Olshtyn, three weekly to Berlin, Hamburg and Bremen, and weekly buses to Hanover, Essen and Stuttgart. Buses to Poland and Germany are operated by **König Auto** (☎ 430 480).

CAR & MOTORCYCLE

From the south it is possible to enter Kaliningrad from Poland although the lines at the Lithuanian borders at Kybartai or on the Kurshkaya Kosa at Nida are not as monstrous. Petrol is widely available.

SEA

Baltfinn (☎ 728 401; www.baltfinn.ru; ul Suvorova 45) offers a weekly ferry service on the *George Ots*, travelling between Baltiysk and St Petersburg. Passengers can also travel on **Baltic Line** (www.baltics.ru/bl/eng) and **Trans Russia Express** (www.tre.de); both travel weekly between Lubeck, Germany, and St Petersburg, stopping at Baltiysk en route. Check their websites for the latest prices and schedules.

TRAIN

There are two stations in the city: **Severny vokzal** (North Station; ☎ 499 991) and the larger **Yuzhny vokzal** (South Station; ☎ 492 675). All long-distance and many local trains go from Yuzhny vokzal, passing through but not always stopping at Severny vokzal.

Local trains include nine a day to Svetlogorsk (R42), six to Zelenogradsk (R35) and two to Chernyakhovsk (R70). There are four to Vilnius (R1000, six hours), one daily to Berlin (R2400, 14 hours), at least one daily to Moscow (R1400, 23 hours) and St Petersburg (R1400, 26 hours), and every other day to Kyiv (R1180, 25 hours).

Getting Around

At research time, many of the city's streets were being repaired and transit routes were in flux. By the time you read this, routes should be back in operation. Tickets for trams, trolleybuses, buses and minibuses are sold only on board (R10). To get to the domestic airport, take bus 128 from the bus station (R30). Taxis ask at least R400 from the airport, and less to the airport.

SVETLOGORSK СВЕТЛОГОРСК

☎ 253 (within the region), ☎ 41153 (from elsewhere) / pop 13,000 / ⏲ Moscow −1hr

A pleasant but sleepy town on the edge of the sea, Svetlogorsk (formerly Rauschen, founded in 1228) lies just 35km northwest of Kaliningrad and makes for a quick and pleasant getaway from the city. The narrow beach is backed by steep sandy slopes, and pretty wooden houses set among tree-lined streets dot the little town. Avid sunbathers head to Zelenogradsk or the Kurshkaya Kosa for heavier beach action.

The city was fairly untouched by WWII. On Oktyabrskaya ul is a 25m **water tower** and the curious red-tile-domed Jugendstil (Art Nouveau) **bathhouse**. About 200m east of the main beach promenade is an impressive, colourful **sundial**, believed to be the largest in Europe.

At the eastern end of ul Lenina there is a **Commemorative Chapel**, opened in 1994 on the former site of a kindergarten. It is a memorial to the 23 children and 11 adults who died after an A-26 Soviet military transport plane crashed into the building. The tragedy was hushed up for almost 20 years and only came to light when the Orthodox Church built the chapel.

On ul Lenina, by turning right at the soccer fields, you'll soon reach an **Organ Hall** (☎ 21761; ul Kurortnaya), where you can hear concerts of Bach, Handel and others throughout the week. Most begin at 5pm.

Sleeping & Eating

There are several hotel options in town, including inexpensive ex-sanatoriums and a camping ground, all on Kaliningradsky pr, about 500m west of the Svetlogorsk II train station. One block east of the train station you'll find open-air drinking and eating options in the summer, with a sizzling grill selling shashlyk for R150.

Stary Doktor (☎ 21362; www.alter-doctor.ru not in English; ul Gagarina 12; s/d R1550/1850) One of the more charming options in town, Stary Doktor has warm and cosy rooms in an old German home. One of the town's best restaurants and souvenir shops are also at this address.

Dom Ryaka (per Beregovoi 1; meals R200-500) Overlooking the waterfront promenade, this restaurant is a popular but pricey place for a meal. The selection of fresh fish and seafood is decent, but it's the sea views that draw most diners.

Kuk-Si (☎ 21364; Oktyabrskaya ul 3; mains R90-180) One of Svetlogorsk's more surprising options, this nicely appointed Korean restaurant serves tasty dishes, made with fresh ingredients.

Kafe Blinnaya (Oktyabrskaya ul 22; bliny R10-20; ⏲ 10am-6pm) This simple café serves a variety of inexpensive bliny.

WESTERN EUROPEAN RUSSIA

Max (☎ 22040; Oktyabrskaya ul 36) This night-club and bar attracts buzzing crowds of 20-somethings that come from Kaliningrad just to party for the evening.

Getting There & Away

Nine trains a day make the trip from Kaliningrad (R42, 1¼ hours). Be sure to get off at Svetlogorsk II, not I. More convenient and faster (45 to 60 minutes) are more than 20 buses and taxi buses which make the trip daily, leaving from the bus station and stopping outside the Severny vokzal on Sovetsky pr (timetables are posted on the street at the bus stop). Svetlogorsk's bus station is 500m west of the train station, at the corner of ul Lenina and Kaliningradsky pr.

KURSHKAYA KOSA КУРШКАЯ КОСА

☎ 250 (within the region), ☎ 41150 (from elsewhere) / 🕑 Moscow −1hr

Tall, windswept sand dunes and dense pine forests full of wildlife lie along this dramatic strip of land dividing the tranquil Curonian lagoon from the Baltic Sea. A paradise for both migratory birds and those interested in one of Russia's most fascinating – and least visited – sites, the Kurshkaya Kosa is the Russian half of the narrow, 98km-long Curonian Spit. It's a Unesco World Heritage Site, and a lovely place for exploring.

Fishing and holiday villages dot the eastern coast. The main ones, from south to north, are: Lesnoy (formerly Sarkau); Rybachy (formerly Rossitten), the largest with a population of 1200; and Morskoe (formerly Pillkoppen). Highlights include admiring the dunes (the most magnificent are just south of Morskoe) and quiet walks by the sea or lagoon and through the pine forests.

The **Kurshkaya Kosa National Park** (☎ 21346; Lesnaya ul 7; 🕑 9am-6pm), the first national park in Russia, is headquartered in Rybachy, but runs a fascinating bird-ringing centre 7km north of Lesnoy, on the site of what was the world's first ornithological station. Some 25,000 visitors a year come by to see some of the world's largest bird-trapping nets (one is 15m high, 30m wide and 70m long), which trap an average of 1000 birds a day. A highly worthwhile, by-donation tour of the facilities (best pre-arranged) will show you how they catch and ring hundreds of birds, including the blue-tit, scarlet chaffinch and middle spotted woodpecker, before releasing them. There is also a museum at the headquarters in Rybachy.

In Rybachy, also worth a visit is the red-brick church **Temple of Sergei Radonezhsky** (1873), reopened in 1990 after being used as a storage room for fishing equipment. The simple interiors are charming.

The **Ecotourism Information Centre** (☎ 28275; Tsentralnaya ul) in Lesnoy works in collaboration with the national park and organises excursions, transport and accommodation. You can also rent bikes there – the perfect way to explore the spit.

Sleeping & Eating

Kurshkaya Kosa (☎ 28242; Tsentralnaya ul 17; s/d/ste 15 Jun-25 Aug US$60/65/70, other times US$25/30/40) Located in Lesnoy, this is one of the best choices – cheery, modern and steps from the beach. The suites fit four people and are great deals. There's also an excellent res-taurant here.

Postoyaly Dvor (☎ 41296; s/d with breakfast €51/65) On the main road at the turn-off to Rybachy, this popular motel has small but pleasant rooms with nice wood furnishings. In the summer, the idyllic charm wanes as crowds descend on the adjoining restaurant's outdoor terrace. The restaurant (open 10am to midnight), which has the feel of a hunting lodge, has a solid reputation throughout the region – particularly for its seafood – though its dishes are good but not spectacular (meals R200 to R300). Some English spoken.

Dom Otdykha (☎ 21244; Pogranichnaya ul 11; s/d R250/350) This hotel in Rybachy has sparse, recently renovated rooms, some overlooking the lagoon.

Morskaya vezda (☎ 41330; Dachnaya ul 6; s/d from R2500/3500) Also near the beach, this handsome new guesthouse in Morskoe has 13 nicely furnished rooms, a sauna and billiard table. Guests can rent bicycles or beach gear.

Getting There & Away

Four buses a day from Kaliningrad (via Zelenogradsk) take the road to Smiltyne in Lithuania on the northern tip of the peninsula. There are about three others that run daily between Zelenogradsk and Morskoe.

CHERNYAKHOVSK ЧЕРНЯХОВСК

☎ 241 (within the region), ☎ 41141 (from elsewhere) / pop 43,000 / ☽ Moscow −1hr

On the shady banks of the Inster River stands the old Georgenburg castle, its striking brickwork hearkening back to the days when Teutonic knights ruled the land. Although its best days are behind it, much of the Georgenburg remains, making it one of the region's best-preserved castles. Aside from this, few visitors make the trip to Chernyakhovsk, the second-largest city and former Prussian city of Insterburg. First mentioned in 1390, when the Teutonic knights built the Georgenburg castle here, the city has been trampled by war several times and remains run down compared to the capital.

In castle ruins is a small **museum** (☎ 32424; Zamkovaya ul 1; admission by donation), open by appointment. The castle was damaged but not ruined in WWII, but the Soviets subsequently destroyed parts of it and turned the rest into a town dump. Volunteers continue the endless renovations to this day. Every Sunday at noon, the local Knight's club meet and engage in medieval fencing matches, using handmade armour and weapons.

Nearby is one of Prussia's most famous horse-breeding sites, the **Georgenburg Stud Farm** (☎ 32301; www.georgenburg.com in Russian; ul Tsentralnaya 18), a tradition resurrected in the 1990s. Equestrian-lovers shouldn't miss the Georgenburg Cup, the international show-jumping tournament with entrants from some 20 different countries. It is typically held on the second weekend in September.

At least eight buses and minibuses a day make the 110-km, 1¾-hour trip from Kaliningrad. There are at least as many trains a day – all eastbound trains stop there.

Northern European Russia
Северно-Европейская Россия

In St Petersburg or Moscow it's oddly easy to be unaware of the great expanses of Russia that stretch north. Indeed, probably as many foreign travellers enter northern European Russia from neighbouring Finland and Norway as venture north from the 'Russian heartland'. But the gradually growing number of travellers here are discovering a land of constant surprises, profound beauty and even a spot of urban sophistication.

This is a territory of midnight sun and polar night, frozen tundra, frozen seas, thousands of islands, hundreds of thousands of lakes, four sizable cities fully adapted to the most extreme of climates, and some barely believable masterworks of old Russian architecture in the most isolated of locations (Varzuga, Kizhi, Solovetsky…), testifying to rare depths of resilience and spirituality. The Russian north is a place you might even find yourself falling in love with.

For many visitors the deepest impact is made by the Solovetsky Islands, a hauntingly beautiful White Sea archipelago that is home to a fabled, historic monastery and also housed one of Stalin's most brutal Gulag camps. The hills, rivers and pristine southern coast of the Kola Peninsula and the forests and lakes of Karelia provide lovers of the outdoors with marvellous hiking, boating, skiing, rock-hunting and off-road tours, and world-class fishing.

Northern European Russia has good transport links with the rest of the country, especially by rail, but you can also fly or drive here. Nowhere else in Russia are Arctic regions so easily accessible.

The short summer (June to August) is obviously the best time to come to the north: temperatures are more comfortable, the seas, lakes and rivers unfreeze, allowing boats to travel to the islands – and it never goes dark!

HIGHLIGHTS

- Be awed by the **Solovetsky Islands'** (p391) haunting beauty and horrific history
- Venture along the Kola Peninsula's isolated **White Sea coast** (p385)
- Stay up late with **white nights** and **northern lights** (p364)
- Tune into the Arctic urban buzz of **Murmansk** (p364) and **Arkhangelsk** (p386)
- Revel in Kizhi's glorious **wooden architecture** (p361)

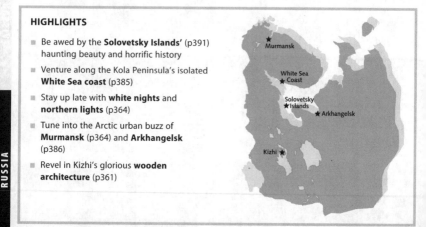

Murmansk

White Sea Coast

Solovetsky Islands

Arkhangelsk

Kizhi

History

The first hardy inhabitants settled in the north by the 6th millennium BC, after the retreat of the last ice age. Petroglyphs and mysterious stone labyrinths dotted around the Kola Peninsula, Solovetsky Islands and elsewhere attest to the religious life of the inhabitants from the 3rd to the 1st millennium BC.

Russians from Novgorod started to head north on hunting, fishing and trapping expeditions to the area around the White Sea in the 11th century. Eventually some of their seasonal camps developed into permanent settlements, the origin of towns such as Kandalaksha, Umba and Varzuga. These settlers became known as Pomors (Pomory

in Russian, meaning Coast-dwellers), and they developed a distinct material culture and a unique and lively dialect of Russian which still survives here and there (just).

The Vologda area came under Moscow's aegis in the early 15th century; the rest of the northwest followed with Ivan III's annexation of Novgorod's territories in 1478. What gave an impulse to the region's development was the arrival of English sailors, in search of a northeast passage to China, at the mouth of the Severnaya Dvina River in 1553. Ivan the Terrible founded Arkhangelsk on the spot in 1584: it was Muscovy's first seaport and the initial key to Russian trade with the west.

Arkhangelsk's light was dimmed by Peter the Great's obsession with crushing the

NORTHERN EUROPEAN RUSSIA

challenge of Sweden, which ruled Finland and had designs on bits of Russia. This led Peter to found the much more important port of St Petersburg in 1702. Another of the northwest's major cities, Petrozavodsk, was founded in 1703 as an armaments factory for Peter's Swedish campaigns.

It was war that gave birth to the northwest's fourth big city, too. Come WWI, with its other ports under threat, Russia needed a new supply port where its Western allies could unload military hardware. Murmansk on the Kola Peninsula, on an ice-free inlet from the Barents Sea, was chosen as the site, and a new railway was rapidly built to connect it with St Petersburg and Moscow.

After the October Revolution, the Western allies (who opposed it) occupied Murmansk and Arkhangelsk for two years, at one point advancing south almost to Petrozavodsk. This episode is known in Russia as the Intervention.

The Murmansk railway helped Soviet governments unlock the Kola Peninsula's mineral resources from the late 1920s on, bringing new towns such as Monchegorsk and Kirovsk into existence. Prisoners from the northwest's many Gulag camps helped to build new factories and also the White Sea-Baltic Canal in Karelia in the 1920s and 30s. Many of today's inhabitants are descended from those who worked on these projects.

Stalin invaded Finland in 1939–40, but Finland, having obtained independence from Russia only in 1917, fought the Red Army to a standstill. In 1941 Finland allied with Germany, hoping to regain territory it had lost to the Red Army. Hitler launched attacks along the entire Soviet-Finnish border and the Finns occupied Petrozavodsk. The Germans were held back from Murmansk, which along with Arkhangelsk was a key port where Allied convoys could land supplies for the Soviet Union, but Murmansk was bombed to rubble. The Red Army pushed the enemy back in 1944, establishing by the end of the war its current borders with Finland and Norway.

The northwest, especially the Kola Peninsula with its many military installations, was hit hard by the collapse of the Soviet command economy in the 1990s, and suffered a big population decline. But the benefits of Russia's transition are at last being felt here and the major cities have a palpably progressive air about them.

Climate

Petrozavodsk is about 5°C cooler than St Petersburg in any season, while Murmansk and Arkhangelsk can be decidedly winterlike as early as the first week in September and as late as the end of May.

Full snow cover in the region lasts from around December to April, but the effect of the Gulf Stream takes a little of the edge off the bitter winters in Murmansk and around the Kola Peninsula's coast and even down in the Solovetsky Islands. So while these places will be several degrees cooler than St Petersburg in summer they have similar temperatures in winter. Murmansk temperatures range from –10°C to –15°C in January and February, and from 8°C to 14°C in July. Arkhangelsk, with less Gulf Stream effect, experiences temperatures between –12°C and –20°C in January.

As well as higher temperatures, summer also brings many more hours of daylight – two months without sunsets in Murmansk. While there's still fun to be had in winter, most of it has to be had by electric light!

Getting There & Away

Foreign visitors coming direct into the region from Scandinavia probably at least equal in number those who push up from St Petersburg or Moscow. Note that it is not permitted to cross the land borders into Russia from Norway or Finland by foot or bicycle. Also note that information on air services in this chapter is particularly volatile: schedules, destinations and airlines change frequently.

FINLAND

The Russian airline **Severstal** (☎ 968-138 370 in Helsinki; airport.cpv.ru) has flights three times a week between Helsinki and Petrozavodsk. Aeroflot-Nord's Luleå (Sweden)–Rovaniemi (Finland)–Murmansk–Arkhangelsk route was not operating at research time.

There are land crossings between Finland and Russia at Raja-Jooseppi/Lotta (between Ivalo and Murmansk; 8am to 10pm daily), Salla/Alakurtti (between Kemijärvi and Kandalaksha; 8am to 8pm Monday to Friday), Vartius/Kostomuksha (8am to 10pm daily), and Värtsilä/Vyartsilya (between

Joensuu and Sortavala; 8am to 9pm daily) –
all hours given are in Russian time.

Gold Line (☎ 016-334 5540, 016-334 5500; www
.goldline.fi) based in Rovaniemi, Finland, runs
a bus service between Ivalo and Murmansk
(€50, 6½ hours one-way) via the Raja-
Jooseppi crossing, on Monday, Wednesday and Friday only at the time of writing.
Departure from Ivalo is at 3.30pm. Gold
Line also runs a bus Monday and Thursday
between Kemijärvi and Kandalaksha (Kan-
talahti in Finnish; €35, 4½ hours one-way)
Departure from Kemijärvi is at 3.30pm.

Savo-Karjalan Linja (☎ Joensuu 013-122324; www
.savokarjalanlinja.fi) runs a bus between Joensuu
and Sortavala (€19, three hours one-way)
via the Värtsilä crossing, daily from June to
September, and on Monday, Wednesday,
Friday and Saturday in other months. Departure from Joensuu bus station is at 9am.

NORWAY

Arkhangelsk-based **Aeroflot-Nord** (www.avl
.aero) flies three times a week from Tromsø
to Murmansk and Arkhangelsk.

A road runs to Murmansk from the
northern Norwegian town of Kirkenes via
the Storskog/Borisoglebsk border crossing
(9am to 11pm in Russian time). Two established Kirkenes travel agencies, **Grenseland/
Sovjetreiser** (☎ 7899 2501; www.grenseland.no;
Hotel Rica Artic, Kongensgate 1) and **Pasvikturist**
(☎ 7899 5080; www.pasvikturist.no; Dr Wesselsgate
9) run minibus or bus services along this
route daily (NKr300 to NKr400 one-way,
five to seven hours, daily). Both companies
also offer a Russian visa service (contact
them a month in advance for this) and
tours to the Murmansk area and the Solovetsky Islands.

The ride from Kirkenes to Murmansk
takes you through the dreary Russian town
of Nikel and across a rather bleak landscape
dotted with lakes and military camps. Past
sulphur emissions from Nikel's huge, antiquated, nickel-processing plant are responsible for a 15km stretch of badly stunted
vegetation east of Nikel.

ST PETERSBURG & MOSCOW

A small squadron of airlines flies from
Moscow and St Petersburg to Murmansk,
Arkhangelsk and Khibiny airport near
Apatity. You can also fly from Moscow to
Vologda; see each city for details.

Trains – on some routes several a day
– run from Moscow and St Petersburg to all
four major cities, but the only significant bus
service into the northwest from Russia's big
two cities is St Petersburg–Petrozavodsk.

River cruises from Moscow and St Petersburg visit Valaam and Kizhi Islands.

Getting Around

Unless you're driving, trains are generally
the way to go. Summer journeys can be
beautiful: the track is never far from a river
or lake. From Petrozavodsk, the Murmansk
line heads north via Kem, Kandalaksha and
Apatity. From Vologda it's a straight 650km
or so north to Arkhangelsk.

Buses provide inexpensive transport
within limited areas but there are few long-
distance services.

Intercity flights come and go. At the time
of research the main regional routes were
Murmansk–Arkhangelsk, Arkhangelsk–
Kotlas, Arkhangelsk–Solovetsky Islands
and (summer only) Murmansk–Solovetsky
Islands and Arkhangelsk–Petrozavodsk.

Driving a car can be convenient. Main
intercity roads are mostly in decent condition, though some stretches of the St
Petersburg–Murmansk highway in northern Karelia spring to mind as exceptions.

If you're in a hurry and not pinching
kopecks, hiring someone to drive you to a
nearby city is a common alternative. You
can usually negotiate a fair price, and the
driver is bound to have some interesting
stories to tell. See p735 for tips on hiring a
private driver.

The Solovetsky Islands, Kizhi and Valaam are commonly reached by boat (from
Kem, Petrozavodsk and Sortavala, respectively). These services are restricted to the
ice-free summer months (usually late May/
early June to some time in September or
October).

KARELIA КАРЕЛИЯ

The Republic of Karelia stretches from not
far north of St Petersburg to the Arctic
Circle – more than half of it is forest, and
fully a quarter is water, including nearly
all of Lake Onega and half of Lake Ladoga,
the two largest lakes in Europe. Apart
from the lovely capital, Petrozavodsk, it's

the rivers, lakes and islands that provide Karelia's main appeal – and Kizhi island in Lake Onega, with its fairy-tale wooden architecture, is not to be missed.

The region known historically as Karelia, which also includes parts of southeastern Finland, has long been contested by Russia, Finland and Sweden. Between WWI and WWII the southwest of the Republic of Karelia was in Finland, and during WWII Nazi-supported Finland occupied much of the Republic including Petrozavodsk. Many ethnic Karelians (a Finno-Ugric people related to the Finns, Estonians and others) fled to Finland when the Soviet Union recaptured this territory in 1944, and Karelians form only about 10% of the Republic of Karelia's population of 720,000 today.

PETROZAVODSK ПЕТРОЗАВОДСК
☎ 8142 / pop 282,000 / ⊗ Moscow

Petrozavodsk, 420km northeast of St Petersburg, is one of the Russia's loveliest cities, set on the shore of Lake Onega with countless green parks and pretty squares flanking its broad, tree-lined avenues. With two universities, the city has a large student population and its proximity to Finland lends a markedly European atmosphere. Petrozavodsk is a place to enjoy hanging out as well as a springboard for trips to Kizhi and Valaam and a starting point for journeys further north.

Known to Finns as Petroskoi, the city was founded by Peter the Great in 1703 as an armaments plant to help his Great Northern War effort against Sweden. Its name means 'Peter's factory'. The town was subsequently used by both the tsars and the Bolsheviks as a place of exile for St Petersburg's troublemakers.

Orientation
The city straddles the little Lososinka River but most of what's important is north of the river. The key streets are pr Lenina, running from the train station to the lake, and pr Marksa, running from pl Lenina to the hydrofoil terminal and flanked by parks nearly all the way.

City and regional maps are sold at **ExLibris** (☎ 763 376; ul Engelsa 13; ⊗ 10am-7pm Mon-Fri, 10am-5pm Sat, noon-5pm Sun) and **Knizhny Dom** (☎ 761 420; pr Marksa 14; ⊗ 9am-8pm).

Information

INTERNET ACCESS
Internet Tsentr (☎ 711 888; ul Anokhina 20; per hr R30; ⊗ 8am-11pm) Plenty of speedy computers.

INTERNET RESOURCES
Karelia Cultural Tourism (culture.karelia.ru)
Karelia Tourism Portal (ticrk.ru/eng)
Komart (www.komart.karelia.ru) What's on in Karelia.

MONEY
You'll find 24-hour ATMs at the Severnaya and Karelia hotels and Sberbank. The following have exchange counters:
Karelia-Market (ul Kirova 2; ⊗ 10am-8pm Mon-Sat, 11am-6pm Sun)
Sberbank (ul Kuybysheva 17 & ul Sverdlova 33; ⊗ 9am-2pm & 3-7.30pm Mon-Fri, 9am-2pm & 3-6pm Sat)

POST
Post office (☎ 782 425; ul Dzerzhinskogo 5; ⊗ 8am-9pm)

TELEPHONE
Severo-Zapadny Telekom (ul Sverdlova 31; ⊗ 24hr) Public phone office.

TOURIST INFORMATION
Tourism information centre (☎ 764 835; tic@ticrk .ru; ul Kuybysheva 5; ⊗ 9am-5pm Mon-Sat Jun-Aug, 9am-5pm Mon-Fri Sep-May) Helpful English-speaking staff and plenty of information.

TRAVEL AGENCIES
Intourist (☎ 781 378, 781 549; intourist.onego.ru; pr Lenina 21; ⊗ 9.30am-7pm Mon-Fri, 11am-4pm Sat) Has friendly, English- and Finnish-speaking staff who can help with organising accommodation bookings or any kind of individual or group tour in Karelia.
Lukomorie (☎ 714 547; www.lukomorie.ru; train station; ⊗ 7am-7pm) Specialises in group tours, especially to Valaam, Kizhi and the Solovetsky Islands, and helicopter trips all over Karelia.
North-West Travel Bureau (☎ 764 718; www.nwtb .ru; Titova ul 11) Specialist in adventure and ecotours.

Sights & Activities
Really the nicest thing to do in Petrozavodsk is to stroll its many parks and gardens, especially those along the lakeside and flanking the Lososinka River. The lakeside promenade, **Onezhskaya nab**, is dotted with large sculptures, many of them gifts from Petrozavodsk's international twin cities. One of the most eye-catching is **The Fishermen**, a kind

of *Old-Man-and-the-Sea*-meets-*The-Scream* affair commissioned by Rafael Consuegra from Duluth, Minnesota, USA. There's a summertime **amusement park** (☎ approx noon-10pm Jun-Aug) next to the ferry terminal.

The pretty crescents of neoclassical buildings on pl Lenina were built in 1775 as headquarters for Petrozavodsk's armaments plants. One of them houses the good **Museum of Local Studies** (☎ 780 240; pl Lenina 1; admission R50; ☽ 10am-5.30pm Tue-Sun), with nicely laid-out displays on the founding of the city and history of Karelia (though little is in English) – plus everything you need to know about the *Kalevala*, Finland's national epic which was pieced together in the 19th century from northern Karelian song-poems.

Petrozavodsk's best museum is the recently modernised **Fine Arts Museum** (☎ 773 723; pr Marksa 8; admission R100; ☽ 10am-6pm Tue-Sun). It has good collections of 15th- to 17th-century Karelian icons, Karelian folk art, 20th century Karelian art, art inspired by the *Kalevala*, assorted Russian and western European art and a busy programme of temporary exhibitions.

Geologists rave about the **Pre-Cambrian Geology Museum** (☎ 783 471; geology@krc.karelia.ru; Pushkinskaya ul 11; admission free; ☽ 9am-5pm Mon-Fri) in the Russian Academy of Sciences. It houses rocks and minerals up to three billion years old, including some unique to Karelia. Prior appointments are preferred, but if you just go in and explain that you'd like to see the museum, chances are someone will accompany you up to the 5th floor.

Akvatika (☎ 765 005; Pushkinskaya ul 7; per 1½hr R200; ☽ 8am-10.30pm) is an excellent indoor swimming facility with a large, clean, four-lane pool, Jacuzzis, a kids' pool, Turkish bath, sauna and a waterslide! In summer you may find it doesn't open till about 2pm.

Petrozavodsk's most important and striking church is the **Alexander Nevsky Cathedral** (☎ 553 371; pr A Nevskogo; ☽ 8am-8pm). Built in the 1820s, it became a museum in Communist times, then reopened as a church in 2000. The interior has been completely renovated with many shining new icons.

An **Afghan War Memorial** lists locals who died in the conflict. It's hard to track down though: if you can find ul Leningradskaya 19 (behind which is an awesome view of the parks and lake), it's just south of that, on a hill above the river. The adjacent dirt

> **BLAST FROM THE PAST**
>
> A statue of Yury Andropov, the second-last old-guard Communist ruler of the Soviet Union (1982–84), was unveiled (to protests and arrests) on Petrozavodsk's ul Andropova in 2005. Andropov spent some time as chief of the local Komsomol (Communist Party youth wing) in the 1930s. He also headed the Soviet secret police, the KGB, from 1967 to 1982 and organised the Soviet crushing of the 1956 Hungarian rebellion. The new statue was part of what appeared to be a campaign by President Putin to rehabilitate his former boss.

road, Volnaya ul, leads to two interesting side-by-side **cemeteries**, one Jewish and one Russian Orthodox.

Sleeping

Hotel Severnaya (☎ 762 080, 780 703; severnaja.onego.ru; pr Lenina 21; s/d with shared bathroom R380/600, s with private bathroom R860-1400, d with private bathroom R1400-1800, lyux R3000-5280; ☐) Clean and smack in the centre, with helpful, English- and Finnish-speaking desk staff, the Severnaya isn't flashy but it's comfortable. Facilities include restaurant, café (serving breakfast for R120) and business centre with Internet. Reservations cost 15% of your room rate but are worthwhile.

Hotel Prionezhsky (☎ 765 281; www.nikolaevskie-oteli.ru; ul Fedosovoy 46; s/d standard US$71/95, superior US$95/131, ste from US$196; P ☒ ☐) Petro's classiest hotel, on the lakeside 700m northwest of the ferry terminal, claims, probably with justification, to be the only hotel in Karelia built to modern European standards. It has just a dozen modern, bright and cosy rooms and suites, allowing for attentive service. Restaurant, bar, sauna and business centre complete the equation.

Hotel Karelia (☎ 560 897; office_karelia@hotel.karelia.ru; nab Gyullinga 2; s R2450-2950, d R3450-3950, superior rooms R3950-4950, all incl breakfast; P ☐ ☒) Architecturally a multistorey monstrosity, the Karelia has been completely modernised and now offers spick-and-span rooms with wood furniture and glassed-in showers. Rooms facing the lake have fabulous views. The helpful desk staff speak English and the hotel has an ATM, business centre, restaurant and 24-hour bar.

NORTHERN EUROPEAN RUSSIA

NORTHERN EUROPEAN
RUSSIA

PETROZAVODSK

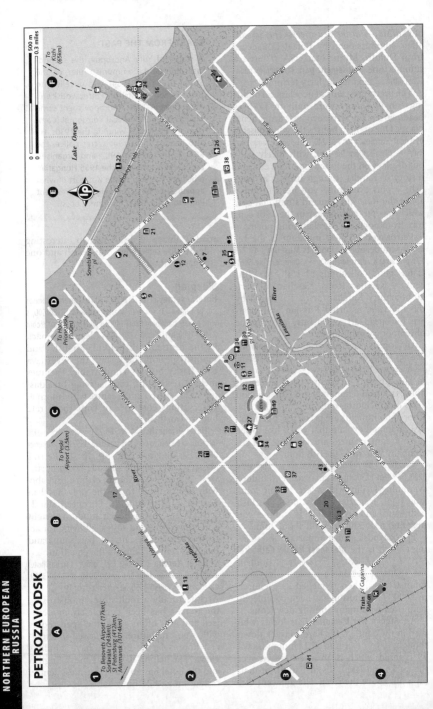

Hotel Maski (☎/fax 761 478; maski.onego.ru; pr Marksa 3; s/d R1800/1900, semi-lyux R2800, lyux R3500-3800; P 🖳) In an unusual circular building with a domed dining room at its centre, the Maski provides good, modern, pine-furnished rooms. There's a sauna too (R500 per hr).

Hotel Fregat (☎ 796 263; fax 764 162; Onezhskaya nab 1; s/d R1600/1800, lyux R2200) The Fregat looks like a rundown dump from the outside, but the rooms are modernised and bright with wood floors and good bathrooms. One facing the lake would be fine.

Eating

Petrozavodsk has a good café scene but outstanding restaurants are thinner on the ground.

Restoran Petrovsky (☎ 780 992; ul Andropova 1; meals R200-350; ⏲ noon-5pm & 6pm-2am) Waiters in traditional Karelian dress serve some Karelian dishes in among a mainly Russian menu. The food is satisfying and the setting – several vaultlike dining areas with four to six tables each – has some atmosphere.

Saloon Sanches (☎ 763 977; pr Lenina 26; meals R250-450; ⏲ 10am-1am) Sanches hasn't quite decided whether it's Mexican or American (guess that makes it Tex-Mex), but with quick, friendly service and big, tasty burritos, it's a good bet.

Restoran Karelia (☎ 560 897; Hotel Karelia, nab Gyullinga 2; meals R300-700) This hotel restaurant tries hard with a fairly international menu including some vegetarian main dishes. It's

spacious and bright and the live music is low-key.

Amerikanskoe Morozhenoe (American Ice Cream; ☎ 784 108; Krasnaya ul 8; ice cream R12-100; ⏲ 10am-8pm) Serves up locally produced versions of Cherry Garcia, Chunky Monkey and other favourites. Sundaes, milkshakes and fudge bars – is this heaven? Three scoops for R36 – it is!

Bar Neubrandenburg (☎ 785 038; ul Engelsa 13; coffee & cake R70-150; ⏲ 10am-1am Sun-Thu, 10am-2am Fri & Sat) The Neubrandenburg's coffee-house section has some of the best cakes, pastries (and coffee) in town. Note that despite the address, the entrance is actually on pr Lenina.

Kafe Maski (☎ 761 478; pr Marksa 3; meals R200-600; ⏲ 8am-11pm) The Hotel Maski's circular, domed dining room is good for a tranquil Russian meal with attentive service, though an obligatory 10% service charge is added to your bill.

Bistro Dezhavyu (☎ 782 085; pr Lenina 20; meals R100-175) One of the most popular of pr Lenina's many cafés, the Dezhavyu (get the name?) is OK for a cheap meal as well as a drink or snack.

Gostiny Dvor (☎ 781 369; pr Marksa 22; meals R60-130; ⏲ 10am-9pm) A cheap, clean and reliable *stolovaya* (canteen) option.

Lotos (☎ 781 558; ul Anokhina 37; ⏲ 24hr) The best-stocked supermarket in town.

Drinking & Entertainment

If you're under the weather, the local firewater Karelskoe Balzam, made from 20 herbs,

NORTHERN EUROPEAN RUSSIA

is said to have tremendous healing powers. At 45% alcohol, so it should!

Bar Neubrandenburg (☎ 785 038; ul Engelsa 13; ½ litre beer R30-60; ☺ 10am-1am Sun-Thu, 10am-2am Fri & Sat) The outdoor tables at this sociable German-style beer bar are a fine spot on a summer evening.

Karelia (☎ 767 278; pr Lenina 27; men R50-100, women R0-70; ☺ 11pm-6am) A palatial, silver-pillared, two-level disco/nightclub enlivened by Petrozavodsk's large student population.

Restoran & Bar Fregat (☎ 796 498; nab Onezhskaya 1; meals R150-300; ☺ noon-2am Mon-Thu, noon-3am Fri-Sun) The Fregat has a good and versatile band playing nightly, and attracts a fairly young and cool crowd, especially in the up-stairs bar. An erotic dance show happens at 11pm on Friday and Saturday.

Restoran Severny (☎ 765 574; Hotel Severnaya, pr Lenina 21; meals R250-600; ☺ noon-3am) This glitzy hotel restaurant features dance shows, folk shows and varied live or DJ music on dif-ferent nights of the week. The Russian and international food is pretty good too.

Spartak(☎ 773 113; ul Dzerzhinskogo 3; ☺ noon-4am Mon-Tue, noon-6am Wed-Sun) A mainly students-and-20s crowd fills this large bar, dedicated to Spartak Moscow football team, for fairly tranquil drinks. There's a dance area (ad-mission R50 to R100) upstairs.

Kafe Randevu (☎ 782 818; ul Kirova 2; ☺ 10am-midnight Mon-Thu, 11am-2am Fri & Sat, 11am-midnight Sun) Good for a nightcap, the 'Rendezvous' has large glass windows, indoor street lamps, and a uniquely relaxed atmosphere. Occasional DJ nights are staged. The en-trance is actually on pr Marksa.

Musical Theatre & Russian Drama Theatre (☎ 784 364; pl Kirova 1; admission R50-150; ☺ shows 7pm Tue-Fri, 6pm Sat & Sun) Stages light op-eras, plays, ballets and folk-group shows. Check out the wild interior décor: a mix of Ancient Greek, Roman and Soviet styles, with Russian maidens dancing on the ceiling around an enormous chandelier. Keep an eye open for shows by Kantele, Karelia's entertaining state dance and song ensemble.

Shopping
Khudozhestvenny Salon (☎ 761 112; ul Gertsena 41; ☺ 10am-7pm Mon-Fri, 10am-6pm Sat, 11am-5pm Sun) Good for folk art, jewellery and paintings.

The Severnaya, Karelia and Maski hotels have worthwhile gift shops.

Getting There & Away
AIR
From **Besovets airport** (☎ 764 566), 19km northwest of the centre, Severstal flies to/from Helsinki (R8515, 1½ hours one-way) on Monday, Wednesday and Friday, and Aeroflot-Nord flies to/from Arkhangelsk (R3600, one hour) on Sunday from about June to September.

You can buy tickets at the **Petrozavodskoe Agentstvo Vozdushnykh Soobshcheny** (PAVS; ☎ 780 044, international flights ☎ 765 901; ul Antikaynena 20; ☺ 8am-8pm Mon-Sat, 8am-6pm Sun).

BUS
From the **bus station** (☎ 722 013; ul Chapaeva 3) buses leave for St Petersburg (R270, nine hours, once or twice daily) and Vologda (R469, 12 hours, four days a week). To Sortavala there are *marshrutky* (R250, four hours, 8am and 3.45pm) and a bus (R178, five hours, 3pm) via Kolatselga, and a *marshrutka* (R300, 6.30am) and a bus (R241, 4.30pm) on the longer, seven-hour route via Olo-nets, all leaving from the bus station. For the *marshrutky* it's advisable to book ahead and this may need to be done by phone: if neces-sary get your hotel to call the bus station.

TRAIN
Ticket windows at the **station** (☎ 765 743; pl Gagarina 1) are open 24 hours. At least four trains run daily to/from St Petersburg (R470 to R625, seven to 8½ hours) and Moscow (R900 to R1140, 15 to 20 hours), and at least six to/from Murmansk (R925 to R1235, 20 to 24 hours) via Kem (R510 to R625, nine hours) and Kandalaksha (R770 to R940, 14 hours).

Getting Around
A *marshrutka* from pl Gagarina outside the train station runs to/from Besovets airport (R15, 30 minutes, 11.30am and 4.10pm, Monday, Wednesday and Friday) for the Helsinki flights.

Marshrutky 1 and 4 run from the bus station to the train station and along pr Lenina. Trolleybus 2 and buses 4 and 5 also run along pr Lenina from the train station. Taxis in town cost R60 to R100.

AROUND PETROZAVODSK
To the north and west of the city lies one of the most beautiful and accessible regions

for hunting, fishing, hiking and camping in Russia. Finnish tourists in particular can be found all over Karelia.

Camping and campfires are permitted almost anywhere, except where posted: Не разбивать палатку (No putting up of tents) and/or Не разжигать костры (No campfires). Check with locals if you're in doubt.

The region's rivers (such as the Shuya, Okhta, Suna and Tumcha) and lakes make for some great rafting and canoeing, although there aren't many rapids.

Popular day-trip destinations from Petrozavodsk – apart from Kizhi (below) and Valaam (p362) – are Martsialnye Vody (55km north from Petrozavodsk), Russia's first mineral spa, founded by Peter the Great, and the 10.7m Kivach Waterfall (Vodopad Kivach), on the Suna River about 10km northeast of Martsialnye Vody as the crow flies (but a drive of some 50km).

Unless you have your own vehicle, it's difficult to get out and about in Karelia without the help of a tourism firm. Contact the travel agencies mentioned on p356. Intourist does day-trips to Martsialnye Vody, Kivach and the nearby town of Kondopoga for up to three people at a price of R190 for the group, plus an additional R15 per person.

Kizhi Кижи

An old pagan ritual site, Kizhi – one of at least 1600 islands in Lake Onega – made a natural 'parish' for 12th-century Russian colonists. None of the early churches remain, but the churches built in this remote spot in the 18th century make Kizhi a not-to-be-missed pilgrimage site for anyone touched by the magic of old Russian architecture. Since the 1950s other wooden buildings have been gathered from around Lake Onega to make the 6km-long island the centrepiece of the **Kizhi Museum-Reserve** (☎ 8142-519 825, in Petrozavodsk 8142-767 091; kizhi .karelia.ru; Russians/others R55/418; ☼ 8am-8pm Jun-Aug, 9am-4pm Sep–mid-Oct & 15-31 May, 10am-3pm mid-Oct–mid-May). With an ISIC card you may secure a discount on the steep admission price.

The big highlight is the fairy-tale **Transfiguration Church**, built in 1714. With its chorus of 23 domes plus gables and ingenious decorations to keep water off the walls, it is the gem of Russian wooden architecture. Next door is the nine-domed **Church of the Intercession** (1764) with a rich collection of 16th- to 18th-

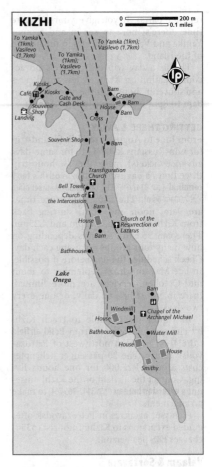

century icons. Between the two churches stands an 1862 **belltower**. These three buildings constitute the World Heritage-listed **Kizhsky pogost** (Kizhi Enclosure).

In summer, music students regularly play the bells of the **Chapel of the Archangel Michael** and leave a hat for your donations outside – an unusual form of busking! The little **Church of the Resurrection of Lazarus**, constructed in the 14th century at Murom monastery, may be the oldest wooden building in Russia.

Most visitors content themselves with a look round the southern part of the island (south of the main pier), which takes a couple of hours, and the fresh air and views on a sunny day are reason enough to come here (but beware of poisonous snakes in the remoter parts). If you give yourself more time, there's more to see in and around Yamka and Vasilyevo villages in the middle of the island.

This is a day trip only; there's no accommodation on Kizhi. A few small cafés and souvenir shops near the pier open from 8am to 8pm from about June to August.

GETTING THERE & AWAY

From June to August, **hydrofoils** (round-trip for non-Russians R900/1140 for same-day/advance tickets) make the 1¼-hour trip three times a day from Petrozavodsk's **ferry terminal** (☎ 8142-796 315; pr Marksa 1A; ticket office ⏰ 7.30am-6pm). The usual departure times are 9am, noon and 1pm, starting back from Kizhi at 1.25pm, 4.15pm and 4.25pm. There can be extra services depending on how many tour groups are going each day. Check schedules the day before if possible. In late May and from September to about mid-October, services are more limited: there may just be one daily, or one every two days.

In winter it's possible to reach Kizhi by chartered helicopter from **Peski airfield** (☎ 8142-747 566) 5km northwest of Petrozavodsk centre. The 20-passenger helicopter costs around R25,000 for one hour's flying. Contact the airfield or the Kizhi museum's **excursion bureau** (☎ 8142-765 764) to make arrangements.

Plenty of agencies in Petrozavodsk offer guided excursions to Kizhi: Intourist (p356) charges €85 per person.

Valaam & Sortavala
Валаам и Сортавала
☎ 81430 / pop (Sortavala) 28,000 / ⏰ Moscow
The Valaam Archipelago, consisting of Valaam Island and about 50 smaller islands, sits in northern Lake Ladoga. The main attractions here are the 14th-century **Valaam Transfiguration Monastery** (Valaamsky Spaso-Preobrazhensky monastyr; ☎ 38182, 38233; www.valaam.ru) and the beautiful tree-covered island on which it stands, with its many bays and headlands. The island can be reached by boat or hydrofoil, mid-May to mid-October (opposite).

Most agree that the monastery was founded in the late 14th century in part as a fortress against Swedish invaders, who managed to destroy it completely in 1611. Rebuilt in the 18th century with money

from Peter the Great, the monastery burned down in 1754 and was rebuilt again in the 19th century. When the Soviet Union took northern Lake Ladoga from Finland in WWII many of the monks and much of the monastery's treasure were moved to Finland. The Soviet authorities turned the monastery into a home for war invalids.

Monks started returning to Valaam in 1989 and today it has a community of about 200 monks. Restoration work at the main monastery complex and the outlying minor monasteries known as *skity* is ongoing.

The usual jumping-off point for Valaam is the sleepy town of Sortavala, on the northern shore of Lake Ladoga. Just off Sortavala's central pl Kirova, Sberbank (ul Komsomolskaya 8) has a 24-hour ATM.

On the island, the centrepiece is the monastery's Transfiguration Cathedral with its five blue domes. The island has a unique microclimate which in the past even allowed monks to grow large watermelons. From the small pier near the monastery where you arrive from Sortavala, it's a blissful walk of about 5km through forests and meadows to the bigger harbour where boats from St Petersburg tie up.

TOURS

Excursions from Sortavala include a one-hour trip each way plus a two-hour guided tour of parts of the main monastery complex plus other places of interest such as the monastery's fish farm and system of canals and wells. Trips cost around R900/1400 with a total of three/five hours on the island, and are sometimes available in English.

A leading agency on the main street in Sortavala is **Ladoga Tours** (☎ 23184; www.ladoga tours.ru; ul Karelskaya 27). Agencies in Petrozavodsk (p356) will also organise things for you.

SLEEPING

Hotel Zimnyaya (☎ 38248; www.valaam.twell.ru; ul Tsentralnaya 4; s R1100-2250, d R1200-2500, tr R1500-2100; 3 meals R750) On the island close to the monastery, the Zimnyaya occupies the 2nd floor of a 19th-century building. Rooms are bare but clean. Only a handful have private bathrooms. It can get full, so try to book ahead, even though this adds 25% to your room price.

Hotel Seurakhuone (Dom Ofitserov; ☎ 22338; ul Karelskaya 22; s/d R600/800, lyux R850/1100; ⓟ) Centrally placed by the bridge near the dock. This hotel in Sortavala has comfy rooms, many of them overlooking the lake.

Hotel Piypun Pikha (☎ /fax 23240; www.ladoga tours.ru; ul Promyshlennaya 44; s/d/tr incl breakfast R1000/1840/1700; Ⓟ) Lovely lakeside location on the east edge of Sortavala. The restaurant, foyer and nightclub are spiffier than the rooms but it's still the most comfortable place in town, with its own excursions to Valaam.

GETTING THERE & AWAY
Boat

During the main tourist season (mid-June to late August), hydrofoils (45 minutes one-way) and boats (up to three hours) to Valaam leave the Sortavala dock, 300m from pl Kirova, at variable times between 9am and 3pm. You can make your own arrangements at the dock, returning on a different day if you wish, but it's easy to take a day-trip with a tour firm (see opposite). Earlier and later in the season, don't count on being able to get to the island every day.

Overnight river cruises to Valaam leave St Petersburg's river terminal (see p290) every day or two from late May to mid-September. Double cabins to Valaam and back cost from R5000 to R15,000, including meals and excursions. A reliable cruise agent in St Petersburg is **Solnechny Parus** (☎ 812-327 3525; www.solpar.ru; ul Vosstania 55).

Bus

Sortavala's **bus station** is on ul Kirova, just off pl Kirova. *Marshrutky* heading to Petrozavodsk via Kolatselga (R250, four hours) leave at 4.30am and 3pm, with a bus at 5.30am (R178, five hours). There's also a *marshrutka* (R300, seven hours) at 6.30am and a bus (R241, 7½ hours) at 4.30am on the longer route via Olenets.

The Finnish **Savo-Karjalan Linja** (☎ 42300; www.savokarjalanlinja.fi) departs for Joensuu, Finland (€19, three hours) at 3.45pm daily from June to September, and on Monday, Wednesday, Friday and Saturday in other months.

Train

Train 349/679 leaves from St Petersburg's Ladozhsky vokzal for Sortavala (R362 to R443, six hours) at 4.11pm on odd-numbered dates (except the 1st of some

months), with some carriages bound for Petrozavodsk (R360 to R445, 9½ hours from Sortavala). In the opposite direction train 680/350 from Petrozavodsk to St Petersburg stops at Sortavala at a drowsy 3.41am on odd dates. Sortavala station is 1km south of pl Kirova.

KEM КЕМЬ
☎ 81458 / pop 17,000 / ◷ Moscow

Kem, 470km north of Petrozavodsk, has a picturesque setting where the Kem River empties into the Kemskaya Bay, but the only real reason to stop here is the daily boats to the Solovetsky Islands (p391) from Rabocheostrovsk, 10km northeast of Kem, from at least early June to late August.

Kem used to belong to the Solovetsky monastery and has always had a close connection with the islands. During the 1920s and 1930s, the Solovetsky camps' administration was based in Kem and prisoners bound for the islands would be herded through the transit camp here.

Today, Kem is a relaxed low-rise town of mainly wooden houses, with plenty of open spaces (and greenery in summer). Logging and sawmills are the area's main industries.

Orientation & Information

Pr Proletarsky, the main street, runs 1.5km east from the train station to the central square, then continues 600m east to a T-junction with ul Lenina (where you turn left for Rabocheostrovsk).

Post office (☎ 21733; pr Proletarsky 27; Internet per hr R40; ◷ 9am-6pm Mon-Fri, 9am-2pm Sat) Facing the main square; the Internet room is upstairs.

Sberbank (pr Proletarsky; ◷ 9am-2pm & 3-6pm Mon-Fri, 9am-3pm Sat) East of the main square, with currency exchange but no ATM.

Sights

If you're in Kem for a few hours, head to the east end of pr Proletarsky then go right (south) down ul Lenina and left along the causeway. The highlight here (1km from the end of pr Proletarsky) is the lovely wooden **Assumption Cathedral** (Uspensky sobor; ul Vitsupa) dating from 1711. It was closed for long-term repairs at research time, but it's worth a look in any case, as is the main channel of the Kem River just beyond it.

Sleeping & Eating

Hotel Prichal (☎ 35360; prichal@onego.ru; Naberezhnaya ul 1, Rabocheostrovsk; s R970-1080, d R1530-1950, tr R2160-2700, all incl breakfast; **P**) Right by the port at Rabocheostrovsk, the Prichal has clean, modern, pine-furnished rooms in attractive wooden cottages. A great sauna (€20 for 1½ hours for up to five people) is on the premises, as are a good restaurant-bar-disco, and the staff are amiable.

Hotel Kem (☎ 20833; ul Energetikov 17; s/d R500/700; **P**) Reasonable but atmosphere-less hotel 400m from the central square. Each bathroom and toilet is shared by two rooms. No food or drinks are available.

Kafe-Bar (☎ 28364; ul Mosorina 6; meals R60-140; ⏲ 10am-midnight Sun-Thu, 10am-2am Fri & Sat) Just 200m off the central square and with minor pretensions to style, this spot serves a fair range of starters and soups, plus inexpensive main dishes from pizza to trout.

Getting There & Around

Kem is a stop along the Petrozavodsk–Murmansk railway, with six to eight daily trains to Murmansk (R650 to R800, 12 hours) and Petrozavodsk (R510 to R625, nine hours) and two or three each day to St Petersburg (R1050 to R1300, 17 hours) and Moscow (R1230 to R1500, 23 to 27 hours). Station ticket windows are open 24 hours.

For information on boats to the Solovetsky Islands, see p395.

'Vokzal-Port' *marshrutky* and bus 1 (both R10, 30 minutes) run every 20 to 30 minutes between pr Proletarsky (in front of the train station) and Rabocheostrovsk. *Marshrutky* charge R20 after 9pm. A taxi to Rabocheostrovsk is R150.

KOLA PENINSULA
КОЛЬСКИЙ ПОЛУОСТРОВ

The Kola Peninsula is a 100,000-sq-km knob of tundra, forest, lakes, bogs, rivers and low mountains between the White Sea and the Barents Sea, making up most of the Murmansk *oblast* (region).

While the centre of the peninsula, near the main road and railway, is relatively developed and populated, the east is virtually devoid of human habitation, except for a few villages and small coastal towns accessible only by sea.

The region endured a rough time in the 1990s with the dismantling of the Soviet command economy and the shrinking of the armed forces, its population fell from over 1.1 million in 1989 to an estimated 842,000 in 2005. But things are on the mend, and average wages here are now above national levels.

The Kola Peninsula is a place of amazing, if stark, beauty, and apart from the liveliness of Murmansk and other towns, it's the fresh-air attractions that make it exciting – skiing and snowboarding at Kirovsk, hiking in the Khibiny mountains, fishing some of the world's best salmon rivers, snowmobile safaris in winter, swimming in the White Sea in summer. The Kola Peninsula is also extraordinarily rich in rare minerals and semiprecious stones, and hunting for these is another special pastime here.

Since most of the Kola Peninsula is north of the Arctic Circle, here you can experience to the full those two wonderful natural phenomena, the midnight sun and the northern lights. In Murmansk the sun never sets from late May to late July, then from 29 November to 15 January it doesn't peep above the horizon. But even in midwinter you still get a few hours of murky daylight, and the northern lights and the shine of the moon and stars on the snow-covered landscape can be quite magical.

In summer, bring sunscreen and sunglasses – Arctic sunburn can really sneak up on you!

MURMANSK МУРМАНСК
☎ 8152 / pop 370,000 / ⏲ Moscow

Midway between Moscow and the North Pole, Murmansk is the largest city north of the Arctic Circle. It's also the most easily-visited northerly city in Russia, perfect for experiencing the midnight sun and polar night.

Murmansk endured a pretty bleak 1990s when its population (previously approaching 450,000) shrank drastically. But with a profitable fishing industry and a dose of cooperation from Scandinavian neighbours and other Western countries, Murmansk is now well on the way back up. Its many shops are full not only of bright, attractive goods but also of people buying them, and the restaurant, bar and nightclub scene has entered a whole exciting new dimension just within the last handful of years.

Orientation

Murmansk lies about 45km from the open sea, on the east bank of the Kola Inlet. The main street is pr Lenina, and the central hub is pl Pyat Uglov (Five Corners Sq, formerly pl Sovetskoy Konstitutsii).

Information

INTERNET ACCESS

Hotel Arktika (pr Lenina 82; per hr R20 plus R1 per MB; ☑ 9am-9pm) Business centre is on the 13th floor.
Russlandia Polyarnye Zori Hotel (ul Knipovicha 17; per hr R60 plus R5 per MB; ☑ 9am-1pm & 2-9pm Mon-Fri, 10am-1pm & 2-6pm Sat & Sun) Efficient 2nd-floor business centre.

INTERNET RESOURCES

Murman.ru (www.murman.ru) Eclectic portal for all things Kola.
Murmanout (http://murmanout.ru) City leisure guide.
Murmansk Tourism Portal (www.murmantourism.ru) Huge amount of useful stuff in Russian and some in English.

MONEY

Hotel Arktika (pr Lenina 82; ☑ 9am-2pm & 3-4.30pm Mon-Fri) Exchange office. Also 24-hour ATM in foyer.
Hotel Meridian (ul Vorovskogo 5/23) ATM.
Russlandia Polyarnye Zori Hotel (ul Knipovicha 17; ☑ 3.30-7pm Mon, 10am-1pm & 3-6.30pm Tue-Fri, 12.30-4pm Sat) Exchange office on 1st floor. Also 24-hour ATMs in foyer.

POST

Main post office (pr Lenina 82A; ☑ 9am-2pm & 3-7pm Mon-Sat, 11am-2pm & 3-6pm Sun) Long queues.

FISHING ON THE KOLA PENINSULA

The swift rivers of the Kola Peninsula provide some world-class fly-fishing, especially for that ultimate fly-fisher's challenge, the Atlantic salmon. The Varzuga River in the southeast is renowned for the huge numbers of salmon it yields. Shorter, steeper rivers in the northeast such as the Iokanga and Varzina are the places for *really* big fish: 40lb (18kg) salmon *are* caught here (occasionally). Between the Varzuga and Iokanga is the marvellous Ponoy, a halfway house in quantity and size of fish, with a particularly long season (May to October).

The fishing is controlled by local companies and organisations which maintain comfortable lodges and camps on the best rivers. Helicopters are used for transport to some of the camps and fishing spots. Catch-and-release fishing is the norm.

The privilege of a week's fishing can command huge prices and Western fishing-travel agencies have exclusive contracts for some camps, especially during the best weeks of the season:

Frontiers (☎ 020 7493 0798 in UK, ☎ 800-245-1950 in USA; www.frontierstravel.com) Books the superb Ryabaga camp on the Ponoy and the main lodge on the Iokanga, with prices from around US$4000 to US$10,000 a week, plus international flights.
Loop Tackle (☎ 08-5441 0192 in Sweden; www.looptackle.se/travel) Books good new camps on the Ponoy system.
Roxton Bailey Robinson (☎ 01488-689 701 in UK; www.rbrww.com) Charges around £4000 a week for the prime weeks on the Varzuga from mid-May to late June, including flights from Britain; their guests catch an average of nearly 50 salmon each.

Some Russian operators are worth contacting for possibly lower prices, though the best weeks of the season may not be available:

Reka Ponoy (River Ponoy; ☎ 8152-230 070 in Murmansk; info@ponoiriver.murmansk.ru) Runs the Ryabaga camp.
Serebro Ponoya (Silver of the Ponoy; ☎ 8152-424 545 in Murmansk; serebrop@rol.ru) Three camps on the Ponoy.
Vskhody Kommunizma (www.vktour.ru) Murmansk (☎ 8152-288 931/265 533; office 507, Hotel Meridian, ul Vorovskogo 5/23) Varzuga (☎ 81559-62424/62437) Several comfortable small camps on the Varzuga.

Many general travel agencies can set you up with fishing on local rivers that can be just as much fun as the hardcore salmon stuff.

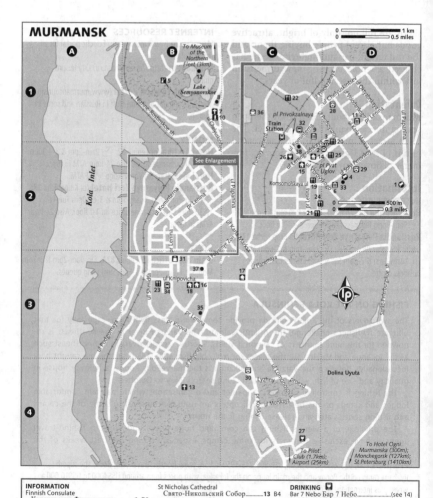

MURMANSK

INFORMATION
Finnish Consulate
  Консульство Финляндии **1** D2
Flait Флайт..(see 18)
Main post office Почтамт............... **2** D2
Murmanelektrosvaz
  Мурманэлектросвязь.................... **3** D1
Norwegian Consulate
  Консульство Норвегии.................. **4** D2
Swedish Consulate
  Консульство Швеции..................(see 4)

SIGHTS & ACTIVITIES
'Alyosha' Monument & Lookout
  Памятник Алёша и
  панорама **5** B1
Artistic Craftsmanship Centre
  Центр художественных
  ремесел..................................... **6** D2
Church of the Saviour on the Waters
  Храм Спас-на-Водах................... **7** B1
Detsky Gorodok
  Детский городок......................... **8** B1
Fine Arts Museum
  Художественный музей.............. **9** C1
Lighthouse Monument
  Памятник Маяк.......................... **10** B1
Museum of Regional Studies
  Краеведческий музей................. **11** D1
Oceanarium Океанарум............... **12** B1

St Nicholas Cathedral
  Свято-Никольский Собор............ **13** B4

SLEEPING
Hotel Arktika
  Гостиница Арктика...................... **14** C2
Hotel Meridian Отель Меридиан... **15** C2
Hotel Moryak Гостиница Моряк... **16** B3
Hotel Valgalla Отель Валгалла....... **17** C3
Russlandia Polyarnye Zori Hotel
  Руссландия Полярные
  Зори Отель.................................. **18** B3

EATING
Alan Алан **19** C2
Dnyom i Nochyu Днём и
  Ночью..(see 14)
Kafe Yunost Кафе Юность............ **20** D1
M-Klub М-Клуб..........................(see 15)
Mama Mia Мама Миа.................. **21** C2
Restoran Polyarnye Zori
  Ресторан Полярные Зори........(see 18)
Restoran Spasatelny Krug
  Ресторан Спасательный Круг... **22** C1
Russky Klondayk Supermarket
  Супермаркет
  Русский Клондайк....................... **23** B3
Rvanye Parusa Рваные Паруса..... **24** C2
Yevroros Supermarket
  Супермаркет Евророс................ **25** D2

DRINKING
Bar 7 Nebo Бар 7 Небо..............(see 14)
Barents Var Баренц Бар ....(see 18)
Guten Morgen Гутен Морген...... **26** C2
Red Pub Ред Паб......................... **27** C4

ENTERTAINMENT
7 Kontinent 7 Континент............. **28** D1
Klub Ledokol Клуб Ледокол......(see 18)
Puppet Theatre Театр кукол........ **29** D2
Sfera Сфера................................. **30** C4

SHOPPING
City Exhibition Hall
  Городской выставочный зал **31** B3

TRANSPORT
Bus Station Автовокзал............... **32** C1
Gulliverrus Гулливеррус.............. **33** D2
Knipovicha Bus Stop
  Остановка Книповича................. **34** B3
Kola TAVS Кола ТАВС.................. **35** B3
Passenger Port Морской вокзал... **36** C1
Pulkovo Airline
  Пулково Авиапредприятие.......(see 18)
Siberian Airlines Сибирь.............(see 23)
Sputnik Murmansk
  Спутник Мурманск..................... **37** B3
Train Ticket Windows
  Железнодорожные кассы........... **38** C2

ZATOS

During the Cold War the Kola Peninsula bristled with nuclear and other hardware, especially its northwestern area around Murmansk, and had the dubious distinction of housing the world's greatest concentration of military and naval forces. Today, Russia's armed forces have been drastically scaled back and foreign money is assisting with the safe decommissioning of nuclear weaponry here. Nevertheless the Murmansk area is still the home of Russia's Northern Fleet and there are still plenty of soldiers, sailors and closed military zones on and near the Kola coast.

The closed zones, known as ZATOs (Zakrytye Administrativo-Territorialnye Obrazovania, Closed Administrative-Territorial Formations) include the Kola Inlet ports of Severomorsk (head-quarters of the Northern Fleet); Polyarny and Gadzhievo (nuclear submarine bases), with over 50 decommissioned reactor compartments stored at nearby Sayda-Guba; Vidyaevo and Zaozersk nuclear submarine bases west of the Kola Inlet (Vidyaevo was the home port of the ill-fated *Kursk*); and Ostrovnoy on the peninsula's eastern coast, a former submarine base that's now a dumping and recycling centre for dismantled submarines and radioactive waste.

Entering any closed city or zone requires special permission, which usually involves an invita-tion from a resident. You would face a rash of trouble, possibly a huge fine or even time in jail if you were caught without the right paperwork. Determined folks can do online research to obtain information on visiting.

TELEPHONE

Murmanelektrosvyaz (☎ 455 819; ul Leningradskaya 27; ☒ 9am-11pm) Public call office.

TRAVEL AGENCIES

Flait (☎ 289 551; www.russland.ru/murmansk; office 222, Russlandia Polyarnye Zori Hotel; ☒ 10am-6pm Mon-Fri, 10am-2pm Mon) Professional, multilingual agency offering services in the Kola Peninsula and Arkhan-gelsk Region including reasonably priced hotel bookings, visa support, transport tickets, tours and fishing day-trips.

Sights

MUSEUMS & GALLERIES

Overall the city's most interesting museum, the **Museum of Regional Studies** (☎ 422 617; pr Lenina 90; admission R15; ☒ 11am-6pm Sat-Wed) fea-tures geology, natural history and oceanog-raphy on the 2nd floor, and Kola Peninsula history on the 3rd floor, from prehistoric rock art through the Sami (Lapps) and Po-mors to the founding of Murmansk, two world wars and the Soviet era. There's a reasonable souvenir shop here, and tours in English cost R450 for up to 15 people.

The **Museum of the Northern Fleet** (Voenno-morskoy muzey Severnogo flota; ☎ 221 445; ul Tortseva 15; admission R50; ☒ 9am-1pm & 2-4.30pm Thu-Mon) is a must if you're a WWII or naval buff. Its displays run from the founding of Rus-sia's first navy in Arkhangelsk by Peter the Great through to the Murmansk convoys of WWII, the Cold War and the modern fleet. The museum is about 5km north

of the centre: you can get there by taking trolleybus 2 or 4 north on pr Lenina to their last stop (Ivchenko), then take bus 10 for four stops to the Nakhimova stop on ul Admirala Lobova. Walk 300m on from the Nakhimova stop then turn left at the new Church of St Vladimir (khram svyatogo knyazya Vladimira), which was built in 2000. The museum is in a large blue build-ing 150m along this street (ul Tortseva).

Located in Murmansk's oldest stone build-ing (1927), the **Fine Arts Museum** (☎ 450 385; ul Kominterna 13; admission per exhibit R20; ☒ 11am-6pm Wed-Sun) houses only temporary exhibitions, usually three or four at a time, and it's pot luck whether any of them are worth visiting. There's a good souvenir shop downstairs.

The **Artistic Craftsmanship Centre** (☎ 450 838; ul Sofyi Perovskoy 3; admission free; ☒ 10am-5pm Sat & Sun, 10am-6pm Mon-Wed) hosts about 30 exhib-itions a year of regional crafts. You might come across anything from lacework or Pomor costumes to amulets made from rye dough or items of braided birch bark.

LAKE SEMYONOVSKOE & AROUND

Atop the hill 2km north of pl Pyat Uglov, **Lake Semyonovskoe** is the focus of the largest open space near the centre and a favourite play-ground for Murmansk. The lake is named after the would-be hermit Semyon Korzhnev, an old tsarist soldier who retired at the turn of the 20th century to a cabin on the shore and was the only resident for miles around.

Imagine his disappointment when Murmansk appeared on his utopian horizon!

The lake and indeed much of Murmansk are overlooked by **Alyosha**, a truly gigantic concrete Great Patriotic War soldier from whose feet you can enjoy spectacular views over the city. The lake is frozen for much of the year but in summer people swim and boat here. The lakeshore **Oceanarium** (☎ 315 884; pr Geroev-Severomortsev 2; adult/child R130/100; ☿ shows 11am, 3pm & 5pm Wed-Sun) hosts splashy seal shows all year.

Across pr Geroev-Severomortsev you'll find the gleaming new gold-domed **Church of the Saviour on the Waters** (☿ 11am-7pm), built in 2002 from public donations. Below the church is the **Lighthouse monument** (admission free; ☿ 11am-5pm Wed-Sun), a memorial to sailors lost at sea during peacetime, also built in 2002. Inside, sound effects of wind and sea play and there's a book containing the names of the lost sailors. These include the crew of the nuclear submarine *Kursk*, pride of the Northern Fleet, which sank with the loss of all 118 on board in the Barents Sea in 2000 – Russia's worst peacetime naval disaster and a tremendous blow to national pride.

Just up the street from the church, **Detsky Gorodok** (☎ 781 308; admission free; ☿ 24hr) is a children's attraction consisting of a fake fort with swings, tunnels and climbing frames – plus a café (snacks R20-60; ☿ 1-11pm Mon-Thu, noon-1am Fri-Sun) where all ages can get a warming drink or snack.

You can get to the lake on trolleybuses 2 or 4 up pr Lenina.

ST NICHOLAS CATHEDRAL

St Nicholas Cathedral (☎ 562 644; ul Zelyonaya) is the Orthodox Church's Kola Peninsula headquarters and has a colourful history. From 1924 to 1946 Murmansk was a city completely without churches. Then a small wooden house on ul Zelyonaya was converted into a church. In 1984 the congregation decided to build a larger, grey-brick church around the wooden building. When the Soviet government learned of the effort in 1985, it sent in miners with dynamite. Demonstrators descended upon the site, blocking the miners, and the government eventually permitted what existed of the building to stand, while forbidding any further work. In 1987, with perestroika, construction resumed, and over the next

---

CRUISING THE ARCTIC

Murmansk is the starting point for July and August cruises to the North Pole and Arctic islands on Russian icebreakers, an exotic and expensive experience on which passengers see not only dramatic seascapes and scenery but also, with luck, a good deal of Arctic wildlife. You need to book well in advance and many agencies include flights from Helsinki or Moscow to Murmansk in the package. The voyages last around two weeks and you're looking at about US$16,000 for a cruise to the North Pole itself in one of Russia's nuclear icebreakers, or US$7000 to US$11,000 for a trip to dramatic Franz Josef Land or Novaya Zemlya and Severnaya Zemlya in non-nuclear icebreakers. Agencies selling these trips include **Quark Expeditions** (www .quarkexpeditions.com), **Blue Water Holidays** (www.cruisingholidays.co.uk), **Arcturus** (www .arcturusexpeditions.co.uk) and **Poseidon** (www .northpolevoyages.com). The ships are comfortably fitted out for passengers and at least some of the profits go towards the upkeep of Russia's icebreaker fleet.

---

few years the St Nicholas Church and the adjacent Church of St Trifon Pechengsky were completed. The two together make up the St Nicholas Cathedral. Their architecture isn't breathtaking, but if you'd like to visit, you can get there on trolleybus 2 or 4 from the train station. From the fourth stop (Marata), walk 150m ahead up pr Kirova then go 900m to the right along ul Zelyonaya. You should find at least one of the churches open from about 8am to 7pm.

NUCLEAR ICEBREAKERS

You might see one of the four Murmansk-based nuclear-powered icebreakers in the port (most likely in summer). They have what looks like a block of flats forward of their midships.

Festivals & Events

The annual 10-day Festival of the North (Prazdnik Severa) or 'Polar Olympics', held since 1934, takes place at the end of March

(Continued on page 377)

Catherine Palace (p299), Tsarskoe Selo

Bronze Horseman (p257), St Petersburg

Mikhaylovsky Castle (p256), St Petersburg

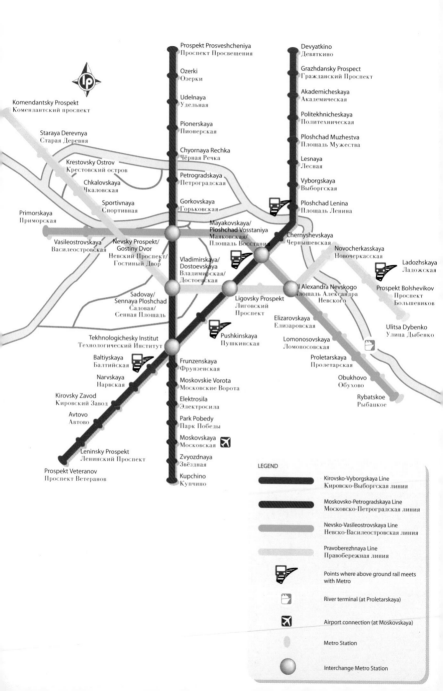

Prospekt Prosveshcheniya
Проспект Просвещения

Devyatkino
Девяткино

Ozerki
Озерки

Grazhdansky Prospect
Гражданский Проспект

Komendantsky Prospekt
Коменлантский проспект

Udelnaya
Удельная

Akademicheskaya
Академическая

Staraya Derevnya
Старая Деревня

Pionerskaya
Пионерская

Politekhnicheskaya
Политехническая

Krestovsky Ostrov
Крестовский остров

Chyornaya Rechka
Чёрная Речка

Ploshchad Muzhestva
Площадь Мужества

Chkalovskaya
Чкаловская

Petrogradskaya
Петроградская

Lesnaya
Лесная

Sportivnaya
Спортивная

Vyborgskaya
Выборгская

Primorskaya
Приморская

Gorkovskaya
Горьковская

Ploshchad Lenina
Площадь Ленина

Vasileostrovskaya
Василеостровская

Mayakovskaya/
Ploshchad Vosstaniya
Маяковская/
Площадь Восстания

Chernyshevskaya
Чернышевская

Nevsky Prospekt/
Gostiny Dvor
Невский Проспект/
Гостиный Двор

Novocherkasskaya
Новочеркасская

Ladozhskaya
Ладожская

Vladimirskaya/
Dostoevskaya
Владимирская/
Достоевская

Prospekt Bolshevikov
Проспект
Большевиков

Sadovay/
Sennaya Ploshchad
Садовая/
Сенная Площадь

Ligovsky Prospekt
Лиговский
Проспект

Pl Alexandra Nevskogo
Площадь Александра
Невского

Ulitsa Dybenko
Улица Дыбенко

Elizarovskaya
Елизаровская

Tekhnologichesky Institut
Технологический Институт

Pushkinskaya
Пушкинская

Lomonosovskaya
Ломоносовская

Baltiyskaya
Балтийская

Frunzenskaya
Фрунзенская

Proletarskaya
Пролетарская

Narvskaya
Нарвская

Moskovskie Vorota
Московские Ворота

Obukhovo
Обухово

Kirovsky Zavod
Кировский Завод

Elektrosila
Электросила

Rybatskoe
Рыбацкое

Avtovo
Автово

Park Pobedy
Парк Победы

Leninsky Prospekt
Ленинский Проспект

Moskovskaya
Московская

Prospekt Veteranov
Проспект Ветеранов

Zvyozdnaya
Звёздная

Kupchino
Купчино

LEGEND

Kirovsko-Vyborgskaya Line
Кировско-Выборгская линия

Moskovsko-Petrogradskaya Line
Московско-Петроградская линия

Nevsko-Vasileostrovskaya Line
Невско-Василеостровская линия

Pravoberezhnaya Line
Правобережная линия

Points where above ground rail meets
with Metro

River terminal (at Proletarskaya)

Airport connection (at Moskovskaya)

Metro Station

Interchange Metro Station

JONATHAN SMITH

Winter Palace, home to much of the Hermitage (p244), St Petersburg

Peter and Paul Fortress (p264),
St Petersburg

JONATHAN SMITH

LEE FOSTER

Summer Palace (p256), St Petersburg

372

Women in embroidered costume at the Vitoslavlitsy Museum of Wooden Architecture (p331)

GEORGI G SHABLOVSKY

GRAHAM BELL

Monastery of the Resurrection in Uglich (p217)

Transfiguration Church (left) and Church of the Intercession (right), Kizhi Island (p361)

GRAHAM BELL

GEORGI S SHABLOVSKY

Ordzhonikidze Sanatorium, Sochi (p463)

RICHARD NEBESKY

Volga River, Volgograd (p422)

PATRICK HORTON

Traditional felt hats for sale in Azau, at the base of Mt Elbrus (p487)

PETER SOLNESS

Horses, Buryatiya (p589)

Olkhon Island (p578), Lake Baikal

PETER

MARK NEWMAN

Volcanic crater lake, Kamchatka Peninsula (p642)

Statue of Lenin on ploshchad Lenina, Khabarovsk (p607)

SIMON RICHMOND

PETER SOLNESS

Horseman on the steppe of Khakassia (p537)

Reconstruction of a 10th-century church, Vitsebsk (p691)

WWII Memorial, Vitsebsk (p691)

National Academic Opera and Ballet Theatre (p677), Minsk

(Continued from page 368)

or beginning of April. Events include reindeer-sled races, reindeer-plus-ski races (in which the deer pulls a contestant on skis), an international ski marathon, ice hockey and snowmobile races and there is a general carnival atmosphere. Hotels are heavily booked during this time. Most events in Murmansk are held at the Dolina Uyuta (Cosy Valley), a 25-minute ride south from the train station on bus 1.

Sleeping

Russlandia Polyarnye Zori Hotel (☎ 289 500; www .russlandia.ru; ul Knipovicha 17; s/d economy R945/1505, standard R2275/2835, business R3185/3745, lyux from R3675/4235, all incl breakfast; P ✗ 🖳) With efficient English-speaking staff, and facilities from travel agencies and business centre to restaurant, nightclub and two saunas, the Polyarnye Zori is understandably popular, especially with Westerners. Rooms are large, clean and comfortable, all with cable TV. Economy rooms are identical in size and layout to the others, but unmodernised – still perfectly fine.

Hotel Meridian (☎ 288 900; www.meridian-hotel .ru; ul Vorovskogo 5/23; s R1300-2400, d R3380, s/d ste from R3900/4080, all incl breakfast; ✗ 🖳) The Meridian is a comfortable, fully modernised and professionally run hotel with a great location facing pl Pyat Uglov. Rooms are attractively decorated, all with Internet connections, satellite TV and heated bathroom floors. And there's a gleaming bowling centre and disco in-house.

Hotel Arktika (☎ 457 988; www.hotel.an.ru; pr Lenina 82; s R790-1690, d R1100-2190, ste R1750-3700; P 🖳 🖳) This three-winged 1980s giant overlooks pl Pyat Uglov. Despite the Soviet-era design, staff are agreeable and the standard rooms have been modernised to an approximation of Western standards, with modern shower cubicles and a touch of art. Economy rooms have similar amenities but are more jaded.

Hotel Valgalla (☎ 441 414; www.valgalla.net; ul Rogozerskaya 14; r R6000, ste R8300-9500, all incl breakfast; P) The small, modern, luxurious Valgalla is a fine choice if you have roubles to spare. With spacious, well-equipped rooms and a restaurant, bar with billiards and excellent modern sauna, it's a small world unto itself in a two-storey building surrounded by tall apartment blocks.

Hotel Moryak (☎ 455 527; fax 452 383; ul Knipovicha 23; s R590-750, d R600-1900) Clean if dowdy, the Moryak is a good bet for budget travellers. The more expensive doubles aren't really worth the money. Lock up well: security isn't the greatest here.

Hotel Ogni Murmanska (☎ 526 000; fax 521 989; www.ognimurmanska.ru; Sankt-Peterburgskoe sh Km 8; s R1450-3200, d R2925, all incl breakfast; P 🖳 🖳) This classy hotel overlooking the city from the eastern hills offers luxurious rooms (some are bilevel, some have sauna), a rather formal restaurant, a bar, its own ski slopes and (coming soon) tropical baths!

Eating

Mama Mia (☎ 450 060; ul Yegorova 14; meals R200-400) Cosy, unpretentious and popular with everyone, Mama Mia specialises in large and good pizzas (at R130 to R200 they're enough for two), but also offers a wide choice of pasta, meat (including reindeer), fish and starters. There's an English-language menu.

Alan (☎ 453 011; Komsomolskaya ul 2; meals R200-350) Curiously ornate but with friendly service, the Alan serves tasty Caucasian fare. Servings are not the hugest so order some delicious *khichiny* (cheese-filled flatbreads) to round things out.

Rvanye Parusa (☎ 478 034; ul Yegorova 13A; meals R500-1000) This fun two-level eatery is done up as a sailing ship (the name means Ragged Sails), and features a cosy Italian trattoria downstairs and a larger Russian/ international restaurant (with sushi) upstairs. Good for that meal where you can loosen the purse strings a little. There's a microbrewery here too, with 12%-plus beers.

Restoran Spasatelny Krug (☎ 480 080; Portovy proezd 34; meals R500-1000; 🕒 noon-2am Mon-Fri, 2pm-2am Sat & Sun) Classy but friendly, this stonewalled restaurant in the Seamen's Club serves lots of good fish, seafood and meat, and has a fine list of European wines. Service can be a bit slow as many dishes are prepared to order, but they're worth the wait.

Dnyom i Nochyu (☎ 481 609; Hotel Arktika, pr Lenina 82; meals R150-250; 🕒 24hr) Good-quality self-service café serving Russian standards.

Kafe Yunost (☎ 457 434; pr Lenina 86; desserts R10-50; 🕒 9am-8pm) A bright place for cakes, pastries, ice cream, coffee and tea.

Restoran Polyarnye Zori (☎ 289 500; Russlandia Polyarnye Zori Hotel, ul Knipovicha 17; meals R400-1100) Best value at this large hotel restaurant is the R220 buffet lunch, served from noon to 4pm Monday to Friday.

M-Klub (☎ 288 900; Hotel Meridian, ul Vorovskogo 5/23; meals R300-700; ☯ 7.30-11am & noon-3am) Good hotel restaurant on a more intimate scale than the Polyarnye Zori, with a vast range of wines.

Murmansk has heaps of supermarkets. Two of the best stocked and most convenient are **Yevroros** (☎ 456 519; pr Lenina 71; ☯ 11am-8pm Mon-Sat, 11am-6pm Sun) and **Russky Klondayk** (☎ 685 466; ul Knipovicha 5; ☯ 8am-1am).

Drinking

Bar 7 Nebo (☎ 457 988; Hotel Arktika, pr Lenina 82; ☯ 9am-6am) Take the lift to the hotel's 16th floor for the best panoramas of Murmansk.

Red Pub (☎ 246 223; Molodyozhny proezd 12; ☯ noon-2am Sun-Thu, noon-4am Fri & Sat) This fun Soviet-nostalgia pub is worth the hike from the centre. Revolutionary posters and art deck the walls and the food menu includes 'Gifts from Mexican Revolutionists' such as guacamole. Take a taxi or trolleybus 6 south on pr Lenina, to the Avtopark stop. Once within sight of the pub you won't mistake it: it's red all over.

Guten Morgen (☎ 455 935; ul Kominterna 7; ☯ noon-2am) Just the ticket for a *pivo* or two in German beer-bar ambience.

Barents Bar (☎ 289 500; Russlandia Polyarnye Zori Hotel, ul Knipovicha 17; ☯ 8am-6am Mon-Sat, 2pm-6am Sun) Convivial hotel bar, a favourite with Westerners.

In summer, beer-and-shashlyk tents spring up around the city and are great places to while away an hour or two.

Entertainment

Pilot Club (☎ 527 474; pr Kolsky 154; admission from R100 Thu-Sun; ☯ 10pm-5am Wed & Sun, 10pm-6am Thu, 10pm-8am Fri & Sat) Huge and hugely popular industrial-design techno/house/pop club south of the centre. Most of the crowd is under 25 but there are no rules against enjoying yourself above that age!

Sfera (☎ 232 387; pr Kolsky 27; bowling lane per hr R300-800; nightclub women R50-120, men R100-170; ☯ noon-6am, nightclub 9pm-6am Wed-Sun) The Sfera is a complete entertainment complex with six lanes of Brunswick bowling, billiards, big-screen sports room, bar, restaurant and a popular nightclub with a 20s crowd enjoying two large dance areas: the Tropic and the cooler, industrial-design Fabric (open Friday and Saturday only). Worth a visit almost any minute of the week! You can get there by trolleybus 6 south on pr Lenina.

Klub Ledokol (☎ 289 550; Russlandia Polyarnye Zori Hotel, ul Knipovicha 17; admission free-R200; ☯ 4pm-5am) The Polyarnye Zori's nightclub attracts a 30-ish, moderately well-heeled crowd for mainly pop music, billiards, and some nights even striptease. Sometimes jazz bands play midweek.

7 Kontinent (☎ 451 769; ul Karla Marksa 1; admission women/men R70/100; ☯ 11pm-6am Fri & Sat) Popular with students, this disco has a smallish dance floor and bigger, relaxed bar.

Puppet Theatre (☎ 458 178; ul Sofyi Perovskoy 21A; admission R25-40; ☯ shows usually 11.30am & 2pm Sat & Sun Sep-Jun) Murmansk's puppet theatre was the first in the USSR (founded in 1933) and is still one of the best.

Shopping

Pr Lenina is strung with well-stocked shops of many kinds. Best for arts and crafts is the **City Exhibition Hall** (☎ 472 834; ul Kommuny 18; ☯ 10am-7pm Mon-Fri, 11am-5pm Sat) with enamelled boxes and bowls, semiprecious stones, clocks, minerals, *matryoshki* and more, at good prices.

Getting There & Away

AIR

Flights from Murmansk's **airport** (MMK; ☎ 583 254, 583 331) go to Moscow Sheremetyevo daily by Aeroflot-Don (R5600), and five days a week by Aeroflot Russian Airlines (R4000); to Moscow Domodedovo (R4000, 2¼ hours) five days a week by Siberia Airlines. Pulkovo goes to St Petersburg (R5750, 1¾ hours), and Arkhangelsk (R3950, two hours) can be reached by Aeroflot-Nord six days a week. Aeroflot-Nord also goes to the Solovetsky Islands (R2600, 1¼ hours) on Tuesday and Thursday, early June to early September, and to Tromsø, Norway (US$185, 2½ hours) three days a week.

You can buy tickets at **Kola TAVS** (☎ 256 043; www.kolatavs.ru; pr Lenina 19; ☯ 8am-7pm Mon-Sat, 10am-5pm Sun & holidays) and the Hotel Arktika's **aviakassa** (pr Lenina 82; ☯ 9am-4pm Mon-Sat). Airlines' own ticket offices include **Pulkovo** (☎ 289 564; Russlandia Polyarnye Zori Hotel, ul Knipovicha 17; ☯ 9am-7pm Mon-Fri, 10am-6pm Sat) and **Siberia Airlines** (☎ 685 520; Torgovy Tsentr Rus, ul Knipovicha 5; ☯ 11am-7pm Mon-Fri).

BUS

From Murmansk's **bus station** (☎ 454 884; ul Kominterna 16) buses go to Monchegorsk (R149, 3½ hours, seven daily), Apatity (R221, five hours, four daily), Kirovsk (R238, 5½ hours, four daily), Kandalaksha (R270, 6½ hours, 5.15pm daily except Sunday) and Ivalo, Finland (R1850, 6½ hours, 8.30am Monday, Wednesday and Friday). Buses leave from the yard between the bus ticket building and the train station.

At least two daily minibus services run to Kirkenes, Norway (five to seven hours). **Sputnik Murmansk** (☎ 440 045; sputnikmur@an.ru; ul Polyarnye Zori 12), in cooperation with Kirkenes' Grenseland travel agency, leaves from the Russlandia Polyarnye Zori Hotel at 8am Monday to Saturday and noon on Sunday, also picking up passengers at the Hotel Arktika. You can get tickets (R600 one-way) on the bus if places are available, or in advance at Flait travel agency (see p367). **Gulliverrus** (☎ 453 000, 459 000; www.gulliverrus.ru; ul Sofyi Perovskoy 17A; ☼ 10am-6pm Mon-Fri, 1-5pm Sat & Sun), in co-operation with Kirkenes' Pasvikturist, has a minibus leaving from the **Norwegian consulate** (ul Sofyi Perovskoy 5) at 7am daily, charging R650.

TRAIN

From the **train station** (☎ 484 600; ul Kominterna 14) at least six trains daily run to Apatity (R250 to R390, four to five hours), Kandalaksha (R300 to R480, six hours), Kem (R650 to R800, 12 hours) and Petrozavodsk (R925 to R1235, 20 to 24 hours), with two or three each continuing to St Petersburg (R1325 to R1620, 28 to 29 hours) and Moscow (R1615 to R2160, 36 to 40 hours). A train leaves for Vologda (R1290 to R1580, 37 hours) on even dates (daily during some summer periods), with some coaches bound for Arkhangelsk (R1000 to R1225, 31 hours).

The main **ticket windows** (☼ 8am-6pm Mon-Fri, 8am-5pm Sat) are in a separate building across the street from the station. You can also buy tickets at **Kola TAVS** (☎ 256 043; www.kolatavs.ru; pr Lenina 19; ☼ 8am-noon & 1-3.30pm Mon-Fri, closed last day of month) and at a **counter** (☼ 8am-6pm) in the Hotel Arktika.

Getting Around

Murmansk airport is 30km southwest of the city at Murmashi. Bus and *marshrutka* 106 run between the airport and the city bus station (30 to 40 minutes) a few times an hour. For the Russlandia Polyarnye Zori or Moryak hotels, get off at the Knipovicha stop (by Detsky Mir department store). A taxi from the city to the airport costs about R400, but you may have to pay R600 in the opposite direction.

Taxis within the city cost R50 to R150.

Buses (R8 per ride) and trolleybuses (R7 per ride) connect the city centre with most outlying areas.

MONCHEGORSK МОНЧЕГОРСК

☎ 81536 / pop 63,000 / ☼ Moscow

A neat, fairly prosperous town set between several lakes, Monchegorsk makes a good base for exploring the centre and south of the Kola Peninsula – although the approach from the south is hardly encouraging as you pass through expanses of stunted or non-existent vegetation, and then encounter the enormous Severonikel Kombinat factory whose past sulphur emissions are responsible for the ecological devastation. Nickel smelting here ceased in the late 1990s but it will be a while before the environment recovers.

Orientation & Information

The 3km main street, pr Metallurgov, runs east to an inlet of Bolshaya Imandra Lake. Broad pl Lenina interrupts pr Metallurgov's trajectory after 2km.

ATM (Galereya shopping centre, pl Lenina; ☼ 10am-8pm Mon-Sat, noon-6pm Sun)

Kola Travel (☎ 57099, mobile 921 287 1311; www .kolatravel.com; pr Lenina 15/2-11) Experienced, enthusiastic, multilingual Dutch- and Russian-run travel firm, offering guided and independent trips covering just about every activity the Kola Peninsula can offer: hiking, biking, 4WD trips, rock-hunting, snowmobile safaris, skiing, self-drive car trips, train and bus tours. Many trips get to remote areas in the centre and east of the peninsula, and prices are pretty reasonable.

Library (pr Metallurgov 27; Internet per hr R36; ☼ noon-7pm Mon-Thu, 11am-6pm Sat & Sun)

Sberbank (pr Metallurgov 7; ☼ 10am-2pm & 3-7pm Mon-Fri, 10am-5pm Sat) Currency exchange and 24-hour ATM, almost opposite the Hotel Sever.

Sights

Ascension Cathedral (kafedralny sobor Vozneseniya; ☎ 52043; Krasnoarmeyskaya ul 15), paid for by the Severonikel plant and consecrated in 1997, stands in the southeastern Moncha district overlooking Bolshaya Imandra Lake. It's impressive both outside and in, with four gold domes and colourful interior murals. Services are usually held at 8am or 8.30am, 9am and 5pm Wednesday to Sunday, and 5pm Tuesday. It's a 3km walk (or a R6 ride on bus or *marshrutka* 10) from pl Lenina.

The **Museum of Coloured Stones** (Muzey tsvetnogo kamnya; ☎ 55338; Leningradskaya nab 6; admission R20; ☒ 10am-1pm & 2-5pm Fri-Tue) is worth a stop if you like rocks or gems.

Sleeping & Eating

Hotel & Kafe Metallurg (☎ 74533; pr Metallurgov 45A; s/d R700/1200, semi-lyux r R2400) A well-run hotel towards the lake end of pr Metallurgov, with neat, bright rooms. It's essential to phone ahead. The adjoining café has an English-language menu offering a good range of salads plus meat and fish dishes (meals R120 to R250) – and live music and dancing Friday and Saturday.

Hotel Sever (☎ /fax 72655; pr Metallurgov 4; s R320-700, d R540-1400) The best rooms have been recently remodelled and quite acceptable, with green paint jobs, new pine doors and tiled bathrooms.

Kafe Bar Ani (meals R80-180; ☒ noon-2am; ☒) Next door to the Hotel Sever, Ani is clean, inexpensive and especially good on Caucasian fare such as kebabs, *chanakhi* (meat-and-veg hotpots) and delicious *khachapuri* (cheese-filled pastries).

Kafeynya (☎ 72136; pr Metallurgov 3; meals R120-350; ☒ 7.30am-11pm) Opposite the Hotel Sever, this spot has the most imaginative décor in town (bamboo with rough-hewn orange plaster and red brickwork). Unfortunately the menu is largely a work of imagination too, so ask what they recommend. It's a popular place.

Getting There & Around

From the shiny new **bus station** (☎ 72150; ul Komsomolskaya 25B), one block off pr Metallurgov, buses head to Murmansk (R149, 3½ hours, seven daily), Olenegorsk (R38, 45 minutes, up to 11 daily), Apatity (R74, one hour, four or five daily), Kirovsk (R91, 1½ hours, four daily) and Kandalaksha (R123, two hours, 8.30pm daily except Sunday). Here you can also buy tickets for trains from Olenegorsk (28km northeast of Monchegorsk, on the Murmansk–Petrozavodsk line) and for flights from Murmansk or Khibiny airport near Apatity.

Taxis in town cost R40.

AROUND MONCHEGORSK
Lapland Biosphere Reserve
Лапландский Биосферный Заповедник
The Unesco-listed Lapland Biosphere Reserve, which covers some 2784 sq km west of Monchegorsk, is a beautiful and pristine zone of forests, lakes, rivers, alpine tundra and mountains up to 1114m that is home to herds of wild reindeer, lemmings, beavers, brown bears and moose. Tourist access is limited to a visitors' centre, museum and two walking trails (a 2km winter trail and a 3km summer trail) beside Chunozero Lake at the reserve's southeast corner. These facilities, reached by a 4km approach road from the M-18 highway, were due to reopen after reconstruction work by 2006. The reserve's **headquarters** (☎ 81536-58018; www.lapland.ru; per Zelyony 8; ☒ 8am-12.30pm & 1.30-5pm Mon-Fri) is in the Moncha district of Monchegorsk.

Lovozero Ловозеро
☎ 81538 / pop 3500 / ☒ Moscow
The village of Lovozero, a 110km drive northeast of Monchegorsk, is the main Sami centre on the Kola Peninsula (and in Russia). About 900 of the 2000 Russian Sami live here, though some 300 of those are away much of the year following reindeer herds. Russian Sami were forcibly collectivised and brutally suppressed here under Stalin. Today Sami culture is reviving, in part thanks to contacts with the more numerous Sami in Scandinavia. Reindeer herders and reindeer can generally only be seen in Lovozero from December till March.

Sberbank (ul Sovetskaya; ☒ 10am-1pm & 2.45-6pm Mon-Fri) changes currency and will give cash advances on Visa, Cirrus, MasterCard and Maestro cards.

SIGHTS & ACTIVITIES
The **Kola Sami History & Culture Museum** (☎ 31477, 30282; ul Sovetskaya; admission R15; ☒ 10am-1pm & 2-5pm Tue-Fri, 10am-4pm Sat) has interesting displays on the Sami and area history, including an amazing rock from Chalmny-Varre village that's covered in petroglyphs 2000 to 3000 years old. The museum shop sells Sami crafts including reindeer-fur slippers and boots (from R900).

The beautiful and rather spooky 8km-long **Lake Seydozero** is 22km south of Lovozero. If you believe that some places have special spiritual vibes this is definitely one of them, and it's a holy place for the Sami. You can get there by boat from Lovozero followed by a minimum 2km walk each way. Ask for a guide at the Hotel Koavas. Kola Travel (p379) also does Seydozero day-trips from Monchegorsk, with a visit to the Lovozero museum, for around €180/200 for one/two people, plus enticing trekking and camping expeditions.

SLEEPING & EATING

Hotel Koavas (Hotel Virma; ☎ 31515; www.covas.ru; ul Pionerskaya 13; s/d/tr incl breakfast R700/1200/1500) This dowdy 1980s hotel, just off the main street, is being upgraded with Sami-style design under Norwegian management. All rooms are getting private bathrooms, and a restaurant, café, shop and sauna are being installed (due to be ready by mid-2006).

GETTING THERE & AWAY

From Olenegorsk **bus station** (☎ 81552-58674), beside Olenegorsk train station on the Murmansk–Petrozavodsk line, buses run to Revda (R74, 1½ hours), 27km west of Lovozero, departing at 11am daily and at 6.20pm daily except Wednesday and Sun-

day. Buses run from Revda to Lovozero (R25, 45 minutes) at 1.20pm, 4.40pm and 7.40pm daily. A taxi or car to Lovozero costs around R100 from Revda, R600 from Olenegorsk or R2000 from Murmansk.

APATITY АПАТИТЫ
☎ 81555 / pop 70,000 / ⏱ Moscow

The Kola Peninsula's second-largest city has grown from almost nothing in the 1960s to become a processing and transport centre for the apatite mines at nearby Kirovsk and has also become the largest scientific centre in northern Russia. Nine separate research institutes of the Russian Academy of Sciences are here. The nearby Khibiny and Lovozero mountains are a dreamland for rock collectors, with over 500 mineral types catalogued.

Orientation & Information

The main streets are uls Fersmana and Lenina. The train station is a 3km bus or taxi ride west of the centre.

Agentstvo Svyaz-servis (pl Lenina 4A; ⏱ 11am-6pm Mon-Fri, 11am-5pm Sat) Public phone office.

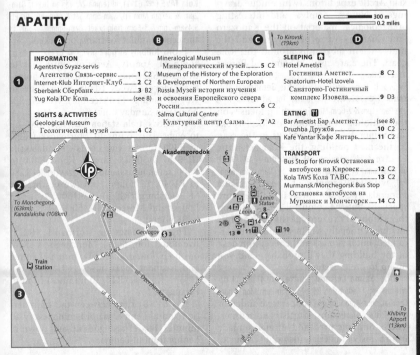

APATITY

0 _____ 300 m
0 _____ 0.2 miles

To Kirovsk (19km)

| INFORMATION |
| Agentstvo Svyaz-servis Агентство Связь-сервис .... 1 C2 |
| Internet-Klub Интернет-Клуб ..... 2 C2 |
| Sberbank Сбербанк .... 3 B2 |
| Yug Kola Юг Кола .... (see 8) |

| SIGHTS & ACTIVITIES |
| Geological Museum Геологический музей .... 4 C2 |

Mineralogical Museum Минералогический музей 5 C2
Museum of the History of the Exploration & Development of Northern European Russia Музей истории изучения и освоения Европейского севера России 6 C2
Salma Cultural Centre Культурный центр Салма 7 A2

| SLEEPING |
| Hotel Ametist Гостиница Аметист .... 8 C2 |
| Sanatorium-Hotel Izovela Санаторно-Гостиничный комплекс Изовела .... 9 D3 |

| EATING |
| Bar Ametist Бар Аметист .... (see 8) |
| Druzhba Дружба .... 10 C2 |
| Kafe Yantar Кафе Янтарь .... 11 C2 |

| TRANSPORT |
| Bus Stop for Kirovsk Остановка автобусов на Кировск .... 12 C2 |
| Kola TAVS Кола ТАВС .... 13 C2 |
| Murmansk/Monchegorsk Bus Stop Остановка автобусов на Мурманск и Мончегорск ...... 14 C2 |

To Monchegorsk (63km); Kandalaksha (108km)

Akademgorodok

Lenin Statue

pl Geologov

To Train Station

To Khibiny Airport (13km)

ATM (ul Lenina 3; 24hr) Inside Hotel Ametist.

Internet-Klub (ul Fersmana 11; per hr R30; 10am-10pm Mon-Sat, noon-6pm Sun)

Sberbank (pl Geologov 1; 10am-2pm & 3-7pm Mon-Fri, 10am-2pm & 3-5pm Sat, 11am-5pm Sun) Currency exchange, cash advances on Visa and MasterCard, and an ATM around the side on ul Bredova.

Yug Kola (South Kola) Apatity (/fax 74178; www .kolaklub.com/southkola, www.kola.biz; Room 114, Hotel Ametist, ul Lenina 3; 10am-6pm Mon-Fri, 11am-5pm Sat); US branch (775-527-1370; southkolareno@sbcglobal.net; Reno, Nevada) Experienced firm offering tours and itineraries of many kinds including mineralogical tours, snowmobile tours and fishing trips at a very comfortable lodge near Lake Kanozero. The amiable, English-speaking director, Sergei Burenin, will take care of the paperwork for getting mineral samples out of the country.

Sights & Activities

To the nongeologist, Apatity's most interesting museum is the **Museum of the History of the Exploration & Development of Northern European Russia** (79255; Akademgorodok 40A; admission R50; 10am-6pm Mon-Fri), which has explanations in English. It features Russian Arctic expeditions (with unique drawings of Novaya Zemlya) and interesting archaeological material on the Kanozero and Chalmny-Varre petroglyphs and the nine ancient labyrinths around the Kola coast. There are also old Sami and Pomor artefacts.

Rock fans will enjoy the **Geological Museum** (79274; ul Fersmana 16; admission R15; 9am-1pm & 2-6pm Mon-Fri), which focuses on the 'rational exploitation' of local rocks and minerals; the entrance is in the rear. In the next building, the Kola Scientific Centre's **Mineralogical Museum** (79739; ul Fersmana 14; admission free; 9am-5pm Mon-Fri), with 900 samples of Kola Peninsula minerals, rocks and ores, is a little more specialist but the colourful minerals from the Khibiny-Lovozero massif will impress anyone. Officially, visits should be prearranged, but if you ask at the reception desk of the building they'll probably send you on up to the museum.

The **Salma Cultural Centre** (41183; ul Dzerzhinskogo 1; admission R5; noon-7pm Mon, noon-6pm Sat, noon-4pm Sun) is a cooperative outlet for over 200 Kola Peninsula artists and artisans. You'll find pictures and artefacts made from a host of materials including colourful

sand/dust from local minerals, birch bark, stone, wood and ceramics. Prices are low.

Sleeping & Eating

Hotel & Bar Ametist (74501; fax 74118; ul Lenina 3; s/d R600/900, polu-lyux d R1220) The Ametist is conveniently central and has plain but quite acceptable rooms, with bathtub, carpet, TV and in some cases mountain views. The sparkling bar (meals R70-200) on the 2nd floor does fine food and has a real Italian coffee machine.

Sanatorium-Hotel Izovela (62666; ul Pobedy 29A; s/d R700/720, lyux d R1800;) At the southeast edge of town, the Izovela is primarily a sanatorium but also has some reasonable pine-furnished hotel rooms, plus a *banya* and *stolovaya*.

Kafe Yantar (77028; ul Kosmonavtov 8; meals R150-300;) A neat little restaurant and café with good Russian dishes, efficient service and a huge range of teas.

Druzhba (ul Lenina 5; 24hr) Amazingly well stocked supermarket.

Getting There & Around

Kola TAVS (61111; ul Lenina 2A; air tickets 8am-2pm & 3-7pm Mon-Fri, 8am-6pm Sat & Sun, bus tickets 5.45am-2pm & 3-6pm, train tickets 8am-6pm Mon-Sat) is the central outlet for transport tickets.

From **Khibiny airport** (KVK; 62132), 14km south of Apatity, Aeroflot-Nord flies to Moscow Sheremetyevo (R4000, 2¼ hours) three days a week (daily from June to August) and to St Petersburg (R3150, 1¾ hours) on Sunday only.

Apatity's **train station** (71200) has up to eight daily trains to Murmansk (R250 to R390, four to five hours), Kandalaksha (R80 to R130, 1½ hours), Kem (R400 to R500, seven hours) and Petrozavodsk (R780 to R1040, 16 hours), and two or three to St Petersburg (R1150 to R1500, 24 to 25 hours) and Moscow (R1450 to R1850, 31 to 35 hours).

There are **buses** to Murmansk (R221, five hours, four daily), Monchegorsk (R74, one hour, four or five daily) from pl Lenina, and frequent local buses (101, 102 and 105) to Kirovsk (R16, 30 minutes) from ul Fersmana.

Bus 8 (R8) runs between the train station and ul Lenina, via pl Lenina, every 40 minutes. Bus 11 also goes up and down ul Lenina from pl Lenina.

KIROVSK КИРОВСК

☎ 81531 / pop 30,000 / 🕒 Moscow

Surrounded by the Khibiny mountains and with 2km-wide Lake Bolshoy Vudyavr spread at its feet, Kirovsk is almost an attractive town. If you throw back a couple of shots, squint and look in the right direction, you might just believe you're in a Swiss alpine village. But Kirovsk was founded in 1929 for mining the world's deposits of apatite, the raw material of phosphate fertilisers, and the lake is fronted by rail tracks and decaying industrial plants. Still, it has the best skiing and snowboarding in northwestern Russia, with a season that can last into June and prices that will make you want to stay all year.

Information

Bank Menatep (☎ 96328; pr Lenina 12A; 🕒 9am-4pm Mon-Fri) Situated just off pr Lenina, this bank has an exchange booth and a 24-hour multicard ATM.

Svyaz-servis (☎ 55506; pr Lenina 9; 🕒 10am-9pm) Public phone office.

Sights

The crumbling Kirovsk **train station**, off Apatitskoe sh down near the lake, is, like many of Russia's 'Potyomkin villages' (constructed only to impress visiting officials), a monument to Soviet antilogic. Locals joke that its first and last passenger was Josef Stalin. Now it looks like a bomb was dropped on it. It's fun to gingerly climb staircases that drop off into the garbage and ruins below – just be careful, and don't trust the handrails.

There are a couple of things to visit northeast of town, off the road to the Kukisvumchorr *mikrorayon* (microdistrict), nicknamed 25 Km. The **Kazan Church** (Kazanskaya tserkov; 🕒 8am-6pm), about 2.5km from central Kirovsk, was converted from a typical northern Russian wooden house. The inside is lovely, with an impressive iconostasis and the allegedly miraculous Icon of St Nicholas, which reportedly miraculously restored itself to good condition (having previously been in a rather tatty state) on the night of 21 May 1994. Ask the bus conductor for the church and from the stop, start back towards Kirovsk, turn left, then left again and the church is 200m on the right-hand side of the road.

A turnoff to the left, 1.5km beyond the church turnoff, brings you in a further 1.7km to the lovely **Polar-Alpine Botanical Gardens** (Botanichesky sad; ☎ 51436; 🕒 8.30am-4pm Mon-Fri), devoted primarily to Kola Peninsula flora but also with hothouses of tropical and semitropical plants. From June to September it's possible to visit the extensive parklands and, by prior arrangement, walk a 2km trail that climbs to the alpine tundra at an altitude of 700m. The rest of the year only the hothouses are open.

Buses 1, 12, 16 or 105 (R10) run from pr Lenina in Kirovsk to Kukisvumchorr, passing the turnoffs for the church and botanical gardens. A taxi to the gardens with a stop at the church will cost about R100.

Activities

The ski season in Kirovsk is delightfully lengthy – from November to May, even June some years, with the best snow from January to April. There are two main ski stations, on the north and south slopes of Aykuayvenchorr mountain at the foot of which the town stands. The lengths and steepness of the runs are comparable at both – good for both beginners and experienced skiers – but the **Bolshoy Vudyavr station** (☎ 34614), opened in 2001 on the southern side of the mountain, 12km from the town centre, has more modern facilities. Take your passport to either station as ID to rent equipment.

At the new station you'll find half a dozen downhill routes of up to 3km. Lift fees for 1/5/10/20 rides are R40/180/350/700; boots and poles cost R150 to R220 per hour or R600 to R850 per day; snowboards are R200/700 per hour/day. A taxi from the city centre is R200.

The **old station** (☎ 95474), on Aykuayvenchorr's northern slopes immediately above the town, is a little cheaper, with a full-day lift pass at R400. A taxi from the centre costs R60/40 with/without skis.

In summer (about mid-June to mid-September) the Khibiny mountains provide the best **hiking** in northwestern Russia, in an expanse of flat-topped mountains divided by deep valleys, swift rivers and lakes. The highest point, Yudychvumchorr, rises 1200m above sea level. Don't treat these hills lightly: avalanches happen and the weather can be extreme, even in summer, so don't wander off without a guide. Kola Travel (p379) in Monchegorsk and the St Petersburg-based **Geographic Bureau** (www.geographicbureau.com) offer guided treks. The Khibiny are also a very happy hunting

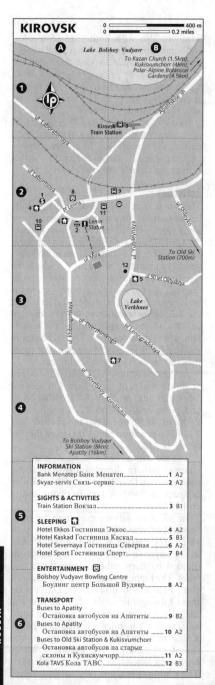

KIROVSK

0 ___ 400 m
0 ___ 0.2 miles

To Kazan Church (1.5km);
Kukisvumchorr (4km);
Polar-Alpine Botanical
Gardens (4.5km)

Lake Bolshoy Vudyavr

Kirovsk
Train Station

ul Laboratornaya

Apatitskoe sh

ul Labuntsova

pr Lenina

ul Shirko

Lenin
Statue

ul Yubileynaya

To Old Ski
Station (700m)

ul Mira

ul 50 let Oktyabrya

Lake
Verkhnee

ul Khibinogorskaya

ul Dzerzhinskogo

ul Leningradskaya

ul Sovetskoy Konstitutsii

To Bolshoy Vudyavr
Ski Station (8km);
Apatity (16km)

INFORMATION
Bank Menatep Банк Менатеп 1 A2
Svyaz-servis Связь-сервис 2 A2

SIGHTS & ACTIVITIES
Train Station Вокзал 3 B1

SLEEPING 🛏
Hotel Ekkos Гостиница Эккос 4 A2
Hotel Kaskad Гостиница Каскад 5 B3
Hotel Severnaya Гостиница Северная 6 A2
Hotel Sport Гостиница Спорт 7 B4

ENTERTAINMENT 🎭
Bolshoy Vudyavr Bowling Centre
   Боулинг центр Большой Вудявр 8 A2

TRANSPORT
Buses to Apatity
   Остановка автобусов на Апатиты 9 B2
Buses to Apatity
   Остановка автобусов на Апатиты 10 A2
Buses to Old Ski Station & Kukisvumchorr
   Остановка автобусов на старые
   склоны и Кукисвумчорр 11 A2
Kola TAVS Кола ТАВС 12 B3

ground for rockhounds and Kola Travel and Apatity's Yug Kola (p382) offer mineralogical expeditions.

Sleeping & Eating

Hotel Severnaya (☎ 54442; pr Lenina 11; r R1400, lyux R2400, all incl breakfast) This large Hungarian-built hotel is the best choice for its central location and solidly comfortable, good-sized rooms with great big bathtubs, though the atmosphere is a bit stiff and formal. The restaurant (meals R160-400) has good, standard Russian food but some nights also deafening music for the large banqueting groups.

Hotel Kaskad (☎ 95603; www.kaskad.kirovsk.net in Russian; ul Yubileynaya 14B; s/d R550/800) This little hotel is the homeliest place in town, with individually decorated, carefully furnished rooms, all equipped with bathroom, phone and TV. Breakfast is available on request.

Hotel Ekkos (☎ 32716; pr Lenina 12B; s R1000, d or tr R1500, lyux R2100) Housed on the 4th floor (no lift) of a cute castlelike building just off pr Lenina, the Ekkos provides good rooms with bathrooms and small kitchen. Some are bilevel. There's also a café looking out to the mountains, but you need to book ahead to eat there.

Hotel Sport (☎ 92650; ul Dzerzhinskogo 7A; s/d/tr R360/520/750, polu-lyux D R920-1000) The rooms at this hotel, on a lane just off ul Dzerzhin-skogo, are basic, lino-floored affairs, each sharing a bathroom with one other, but they're clean. There's a free daily shuttle to the old ski station.

Bolshoy Vudyavr Bowling Centre (☎ 32930; pr Lenina 8; meals R120-400; bowling per hr R400-600; 🕒 1-3pm Mon & Tue, 1pm-1am Wed, Thu & Sun, 1pm-6am Fri & Sat, bowling closed Mon & Tue) The swish four-lane bowling centre and its attached café/bar and billiard tables are the place to be. The café does some of the best meals in town, including a good-value 'business lunch' from 1pm to 3pm, Monday to Friday, for only R120. Friday and Saturday nights there's a disco here (9pm to 6am).

Getting There & Away

Frequent local buses (101, 102 and 105) run to Apatity (R16, 30 minutes). There are also four daily buses to Monchegorsk (R91, 1½ hours) and Murmansk (R238, 5½ hours), leaving from pr Lenina in the centre.

Kola TAVS (☎ 94160; ul Yubileynaya 13; ☒ air & bus tickets 8.30am-2pm & 3-6pm, train tickets 8am-2pm & 3-5pm Mon-Fri, 8am-2pm Sat) sells tickets for buses from Kirovsk, trains from Apatity and planes from Khibiny airport.

KANDALAKSHA КАНДАЛАКША
☎ 81533 / pop 38,000 / ☒ Moscow

The port of Kandalaksha, 232km south of Murmansk, dates back to the 15th century but there's nothing much to keep you here longer than you need to wait for your bus or train. Stations for these are adjacent in the north of town, 1km from the central square (to head towards the centre, cross the footbridge over the railway). **Hotel Belomorie** (☎ 93100; ul Pervomayskaya 31; s/d R800/1000, polu-lyux R1500), on the central square, has drab but serviceable rooms with private bathrooms.

The **train station** (☎ 30425; ul Murmanskaya 24) is on the Petrozavodsk–Murmansk line and is served by the same trains as Apatity (p382), which is 1½ hours north. From the **bus station** (☎ 31730; ul Kirovskaya 24A; ☒ 4.30-11am & 2-5.30pm Mon-Sat, 7am-12.30pm & 1.30-6pm Sun) small buses leave for Umba (R119, two hours) at 8.05am and 5.10pm daily, and there's a bus to Kemijärvi, Finland (R1295, 4½ hours), at 8am Monday and Thursday.

WHITE SEA COAST
The Kola Peninsula's southern shore, on the White Sea, is a beautiful, pristine and completely unspoilt coastline with some fascinating architectural, archaeological and geological sites – still largely undiscovered by the outside world. The Varzuga River provides some of the very best salmon fishing in the world.

Umba Умба
☎ 81559 / pop 6500 / ☒ Moscow

The largest settlement on this coast, Umba is still a wonderfully tranquil place to hang out and explore on foot. The 103km paved road from Kandalaksha runs through forest, with glimpses of lakes and the island-strewn Kandalaksha Bay.

Umba has three parts, linked by bridges. The two newer (19th-century) parts of town occupy south-pointing promontories formed by inlets of the White Sea, with the main bus stop and town centre on the

eastern promontory. The third and westernmost part of town, Staraya (Old) Umba, founded by Pomor settlers in the 15th century, sits on the west bank of the rushing River Umba.

Hundreds of petroglyphs from the 2nd or 1st millennium BC have been discovered since 1998 at Lake Kanozero, 30km northwest of Umba.

Sberbank (☎ 52583; ul Belomorskaya 6; ☒ 11am-1pm & 3-7pm Mon-Fri), near the bus stop, changes currency.

Umba Discovery Umba (☎ 51629, mobile 921 156 6412, irinaumba@com.mels.ru); St Petersburg (☎ 812-380 3087, fax 812-327 5112; ul Petrozavodskaya 11), with an energetic local representative who speaks reasonable English, can provide accommodation in Umba and Varzuga, fishing trips and a variety of tours.

SIGHTS & ACTIVITIES
The **Museum of the Tersky Pomors** (☎ 53532; ul Dzerzhinskogo 78; admission R15; ☒ 9am-5pm Mon-Fri, 10am-5pm Sun) has an excellent collection of Pomor crafts and items of everyday use – fishing and hunting gear, clothes, toys, lacework. A guide and translator costs R450 for up to 15 people. If you can afford this, it's well worth it.

The Umba River and its tributaries are not quite the angler's paradise that the Varzuga River is but they still offer good **fishing** for salmon, trout and grayling. The comfortable Umba Lodge, 12km upriver from Umba, can be booked through agencies such as Kola Travel in Monchegorsk (p379), Yug Kola in Apatity (p381) or Umba Discovery. Packages start from around €2000 a week, including transfers to and from Murmansk.

SLEEPING & EATING
Umba Discovery has a lovely **seaside lodge** here, open all year. Its three cosy wooden houses (R3600 per night for up to four people) are set beside a beautiful bay. Meals are available at the lodge (breakfast/lunch/dinner R150/250/350) and there's also a *banya* on site (R600 per session). Umba Discovery also rents out good, clean apartments and houses in town (from R450 per person).

Kola Travel (p379) in Monchegorsk is building a hotel in Umba, due to open in 2006.

SHOPPING

Ametistovy Bereg (ul Dzerzhinskogo 57) sells lovely jewellery and decorative pieces made from local minerals and semiprecious stones.

GETTING THERE & AWAY

Buses (☎ 52385 for bookings) to Kandalaksha (R119, two hours) leave at 11am and 7.40pm from the ul Belomorskaya bus stop. Private-car drivers wait for passengers here and outside Kandalaksha train station, charging around R1000 per vehicle.

Tersky Coast Терский берег

The coast east of Umba is known as the Tersky coast, from an old Sami name, Ter, for the Kola Peninsula. The main destination here is Varzuga, at the end of the road 140km beyond Umba, and there are a few interesting stops en route. The road from Umba is paved for 29km, then it's a reasonable-condition gravel road the rest of the way. There's no regular public transport along this road. Umba Discovery (p385) charges about R4000 for up to four people for a guided daytrip from Umba to Varzuga and back.

Keep a look out for a sign at the 108km mark pointing to 'Rodnik' (a holy spring) inland and to 'Chasovnya' (chapel) towards the seashore. Both are a couple of hundred metres off the road. The **Chapel of the Unknown Monk** (Chasovnya bezymyannogo inoka) contains the tomb of an unidentified monk whose body was washed up here in the 17th century. According to legend, bounteous fishing catches and miraculous healings started to occur nearby. The tomb is still a holy place where people come to pray.

From the road's 117km point a track runs about 1km down to a spot on the shore where it's easy to find **amethyst-bearing stones**. Find what looks like minor earthworks by the shore then look for clumps of the purple crystals among the rocks facing the sea there. Another purple mineral, fluorite, is also common here.

Shortly beyond this point the road turns inland for its final 16km to Varzuga.

VARZUGA ВАРЗУГА

☎ 81559 / pop 500 / ✹ Moscow

Straddling the broad Varzuga River, Varzuga is the only village set inland from the Tersky coast, and is the site of the Kola Peninsula's loveliest building, the Dormition

Church. Its Pomor people have long based their livelihood on the salmon and fresh-water pearls found in their river.

The slender, single-towered, perfectly proportioned **Dormition Church** (Uspenskaya tserkov) is a masterpiece of wooden architecture built in 1674 – without, it's said, a single nail. Legend has it that on completion of the building, the master carpenter, Kliment, tossed his tools into the river, declaring that he could never surpass what he had just created. For the moment you can admire his achievement from outside only, as it's closed for conservation work. The **Church of St Afanasy the Great** (Tserkov Svyatitelya Afanasiya Velikogo; ✹ 9am-9pm) next door, built in 1852, is open. Many of the icons here were kept in hiding by locals during the Soviet years. Also nearby is a neat wooden bell tower, built in 2001 to replace the 1674 original which was wrecked in 1939.

The Atlantic **salmon season** on the Varzuga River lasts from mid-May to mid-October, with the very best fishing at the start and end of that period. One-day catch-and-release permits are available at kiosks near the Dormition Church for around R1000 (though the price was subject to litigation at the time of writing). For information on fishing holidays on the Varzuga see p365.

Umba Discovery (p385) offers accommodation with families in two-storey houses in Varzuga (R700 to R800 per person including breakfast and dinner).

ARKHANGELSK REGION АРХАНГЕЛЬСКАЯ ОБЛАСТЬ

The Solovetsky Islands are, for one reason or another, the most amazing part of many people's visit to northwest Russia. Few visitors have much time for anywhere else in Arkhangelsk Region except the historic capital city. But Arkhangelsk's excellent tourist information office has plenty of suggestions if you're tempted to explore further.

ARKHANGELSK АРХАНГЕЛЬСК

☎ 8182 / pop 345,000 / ✹ Moscow

Arkhangelsk – once Russia's only port – is a historic though not exactly pretty city.

It does have an insidious kind of beauty, however, especially on its waterfront along the 2km-wide Severnaya (Northern) Dvina River. The rest of the city is chiefly an expanse of concrete, but it's one with broad, tree-lined streets, interspersed with surprising enclaves of old wooden houses (notably along pr Chumbarova-Luchinskogo).

Arkhangelsk is also blessed with a populace that is surely among the friendliest in Russia and is relatively well connected with the world at large. There's a real sense of Arkhangelsk as a 'happening' city if you meet the right people.

History
The construction of Arkhangelsk was decreed by Ivan the Terrible in 1583, 30 years after the English *Edward Bonaventure*, captained by Richard Chancellor, had arrived at what was then a remote fishing settlement while searching for the northeast passage to China. Chancellor headed overland to Moscow where Ivan (still in his pre-Terrible period) proved keen to establish trade ties with England.

Arkhangelsk was Muscovy's first seaport and between 1668 and 1684 a large fortified trading centre, the Gostiny Dvor, was constructed on its riverbank. Luxurious European textiles such as satin and velvet arrived here and flax, hemp, wax and timber for ships' masts were exported. In 1693 Peter the Great began shipbuilding operations here, launching the Russian navy's tiny first ship, the *Svyatoy Pavel*, the following year.

The founding of St Petersburg in 1702 pushed Arkhangelsk out of the limelight but it later became a centre for Arctic exploration and a focus of the huge northern lumber industry.

Orientation
Arkhangelsk sits on the east bank of a bend in the Severnaya Dvina River. The main axis, Voskresenskaya ul, runs northeast from the sharpest point of the bend all the way to the train station, 3km away. Troitsky pr, which runs parallel to the river one block inland from it, is the other key thoroughfare. Voskresenskaya ul and Troitsky pr intersect at pl Lenina, whose towering 22-storey skyscraper is visible from most places in the city.

For maps, try **Dom Knigi** (ul Lenina 3; ⏱ 10am-8pm Mon-Fri, 10am-6pm Sat & Sun).

Information
You'll find ATMs (among other places) at the Pur-Navolok and Dvina hotels.

Exchange office (1st fl, pl Lenina 4; ⏱ 9.30am-1pm & 2-4.30pm Mon-Fri) In the skyscraper on pl Lenina.

Hotel Dvina (☎ 288 888; www.hoteldvina.ru; Troitsky pr 52) ATM.

Internet-Klub (☎ 652 081; Office 1405, pl Lenina 4; per hr R40; ⏱ 9am-9pm Mon-Fri, 10am-10pm Sat) On the 14th floor of the pl Lenina skyscraper.

Pomor Land (www.pomorland.info) Arkhangelsk Region official tourism site, with a lot of useful info.

Pomor Tur (☎ 204 600, 214 040; www.pomortur.atnet .ru; ul Svobody 3; ⏱ 10am-6pm Mon- Fri) A leading local tour agency, Pomor Tur offers city and regional excursions and tours, trips to the Solovetsky Islands, and visits to some lesser-known destinations.

Post office (Troitsky pr 45; ⏱ 8am-7pm Mon-Fri, 9am-5pm Sat, 10am-5pm Sun)

Premier supermarket (Troitsky pr 52; ⏱ exchange office 9.20am-2pm & 2.40-8.30pm, ATM 9am-10pm) Has exchage office and ATM.

Pur Navolok Hotel (☎ 217 200; www.purnavolok.ru; nab Severnoy Dviny 88; ⏱ exchange office 9.30am-1pm & 2-5pm Mon-Fri) Exchange office and ATM.

Tourist information office (☎ 214 082; www.pomor land.info; ul Svobody 8; ⏱ 9am-1pm & 2-5.30pm Mon-Thu, 9am-1pm & 2-4pm Fri) Enthusiastic, well-informed, English-speaking staff have good city maps and plenty of other material to give you on the city and the rest of Arkhangelsk Region, and are keen to answer questions. Wow!

Sberbank (Voskresenskaya ul; ⏱ 24hr).

Sights
NABEREZHNAYA SEVERNOY DVINY
The **Severnaya Dvina embankment** is where the city began and it makes for a pleasant stroll at any time of year if the weather is half-decent (see p389).

The **Gostiny Dvor** (Merchants' Yard; nab Severnoy Dviny 85/86) was built as a trading centre between 1668 and 1684 – originally a large turreted structure stretching all the way from ul Svobody to ul Engelsa – and Arkhangelsk grew up around it in the 17th and 18th centuries. Its **exhibition rooms** (☎ 209 215; per exhibition R20; ⏱ 10am-6pm Tue-Sun) usually house at least a couple of worthwhile historical, art or other displays.

Arkhangelsk is not a city of great churches but there are a few small, pretty ones along the riverbank. The **Nikolsky Church** (Teatralny per 3), dating from 1904, is still being rebuilt following Soviet-era desecration, but is quite

ARKHANGELSK

0 ——————————— 1 km
0 ——————————— 0.5 miles

INFORMATION
Dom Knigi Дом Книги **1** B5
Exchange Office Обмен валют ...... (see 2)
Internet-Klub Интернет-Клуб **2** B6
Pomor Tur Помор Тур **3** A5
Post Office Почтамт **4** A6
Sberbank Сбербанк **5** C4
Solovki Travel
 Соловки Трэвэл .... (see 18)
Tourist Information Office
 Туристский
 информационный центр **6** A5
Turistichesky Kompleks Solovki
 Office **7** B6

SIGHTS & ACTIVITIES
AA Borisov Museum
 Музей имени АА Борисова **8** B6
Church of SS Zosima, Savvaty & German
 Храм Преподобных Зосимы,
 Савватия и Германа **9** B6
Fine Arts Museum Музей
 изобразительных искусств ... **10** A5
Gostiny Dvor Гостиный Двор **11** A6
Lenin Statue
 Памятник ВИ Ленину **12** A5
Nikolsky Church
 Никольский храм **13** B6

Northern Seafaring Museum
 Северный морской музей **14** B6
Regional Studies Museum
 Краеведческий Музей **15** A5

SLEEPING
Business Centre Hotel
 Бизнес-Центр Отель **16** B5
Hotel Belomorskaya
 Гостиница Беломорская **17** D5
Hotel Dvina Гостиница Двина **18** B6
Hotel Polina Гостиница Полина .. **19** B6
Pur Navolok Hotel
 Пур Наволок Отель **20** A5

EATING
Kafe U Tyoshchi Кафе у Тёщи ..... (see 23)
Kofeynya U Poliny
 Кофейня у Полины .... (see 25)
La Forchetta d'Oro
 Пиццерия Золотая Вилка **21** B6
Le Petit Restaurant .... (see 18)
Paratov Паратов **22** C6
Premier Supermarket
 Торговый Центр Премьер **23** B6
Restoran Bobroff
 Ресторан Бобpофф **24** A5
Restoran Dvina Ресторан Двина .. **25** B6

Restoran Na Voskresenskoy
 Ресторан
 На Воскресенской .... (see 16)
Restoran Pomorsky
 Ресторан Поморский .... (see 25)
Solovetskoe Podvorie
 Соловецкое Подворье **26** B6

DRINKING
Bar Dva Piva Бар Два Пива **27** A3

ENTERTAINMENT
Modern Модерн **28** A3
Pelikan Пеликан **29** A6
Restoran Amadey
 Ресторан Амадей **30** B5
Trud Stadium Стадион Труд **31** B3

TRANSPORT
Aeroflot-Nord Аэрофлот-Норд .. **32** B6
Bus Station Автовокзал **33** D4
Pulkovo Airline
 Пулково Авиапредприятие ... (see 2)
Sea & River Terminal
 Морской-речной вокзал **34** C6
TsAVS ЦАВС **35** D4

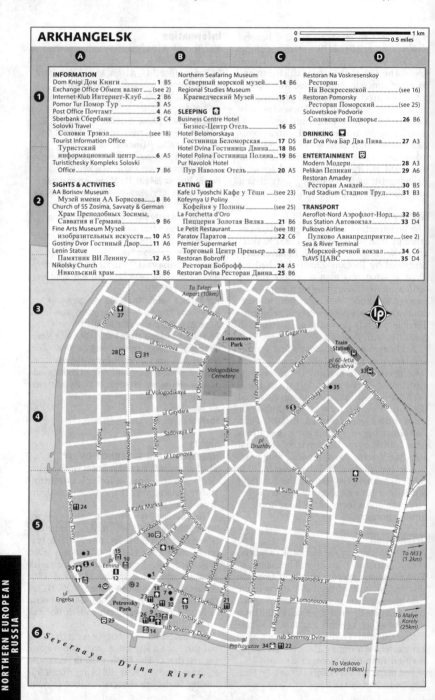

PROMENADE OF DREAMS

The soul of Arkhangelsk dwells along the Severnaya Dvina embankment. When a north wind is blowing this is a place to avoid, but given even a hint of mild summer weather Arkhangelskians emerge from their burrows to stroll along the broad riverside promenade, by day and by what passes for night. As the summer sun slowly declines in the north-northwest people gather in knots of three or four on the embankment, or drop into one of the many beer-and-shashlyk tents, or simply wander along communing with their inner selves, while the colours of the sky, reflected in the 2km-wide river, grow ever less believable.

richly decorated and some of the unusual original ceiling frescoes survive. The green-and-white **Church of SS Zosima, Savvaty & German** (nab Severnoy Dviny 77/1), just along the street, is an outpost of the Solovetsky Monastery (p391) with recently carved wooden sculptures and an iconostasis that's still a work in progress.

MUSEUMS

The **Fine Arts Museum** (☎ 653 616; pl Lenina 2; admission R50; ☼ 10am-5pm Wed-Mon) is surprisingly good. It boasts an impressive selection of 14th- to 18th-century icons and a good selection of 18th-to-early-20th-century Russian painting, with work by nearly all the leading names – look for Stanislav Khlebovsky's *Death of Prince Oranskogo* (1861) and IB Lampi's portrait of Catherine the Great (1790s). On the 2nd floor, don't overlook the 19th- and early-20th-century textiles and decorative art.

The **Regional Studies Museum** (☎ 653 308; pl Lenina 2; per exhibit R20; ☼ 10am-6pm Tue-Sun), a couple of doors from the Fine Arts Museum, holds a sobering 2nd-floor exhibition dedicated to local soldiers who died in the war with Afghanistan, plus a lumpy taxidermy collection of local sea and land life that's interesting in a ghoulish sort of way.

The **AA Borisov Museum** (☎ 205 647; Pomorskaya ul 3; admission R30; ☼ 10am-5pm Wed-Mon) is devoted to Alexander Alekseevich Borisov (1866–1934), the first artist ever to dedicate himself to the Arctic. You'll feel chilly just looking at his land- sea- and icescapes and the recreation of the quarters Borisov occupied on

Novaya Zemlya in 1900–01, complete with polar-bear-pelt-covered rocking chair.

The **Northern Seafaring Museum** (nab Severnoy Dviny 80) was closed for long-term renovations at research time. It's worth checking on progress as the museum has interesting collections on subjects like Novaya Zemlya, polar expeditions and Arkhangelsk's shipbuilding history.

Sleeping

Pur Navolok Hotel (☎ 217 200; www.purnavolok.ru; nab Severnoy Dviny 88; s R750-2300, d R1300-3450, polu-lyux R2450, lyux R3000-8100, all incl breakfast; 🖳) The city's top hotel has a prime location overlooking the river. Rooms in the unmodernised Korpus (Building) 2 are generally cheaper but they have much the same facilities as those in the glitzy new Korpus 1. The very professional desk staff speak English and the hotel boasts a host of amenities including fine restaurant, bar, business centre (Internet per hr R60) and excursions service.

Hotel Dvina (☎ 288 888; www.hoteldvina.ru; Troitsky pr 52; s R800-1600, d R1100, lyux R2000-2800; P X) After a full interior renovation the large Dvina provides tasteful and decent-sized rooms, plus friendly staff and a convenient travel desk. With a variety of good eating options close by, this is a fine place to base yourself.

Business Centre Hotel (☎ /fax 210 130; greentel@atknet.ru; Voskresenskaya ul 8; s/d incl breakfast R2726/2871, with sitting room R3915/4060; X 🖳) This very comfortable, small, business-oriented hotel has multilingual desk staff and high-class service. All rooms are of Western standard and individually decorated.

Hotel Polina (☎ 201 860; fax 201 877; pr Chumbarova-Luchinskogo 37; r R2400, apt R3200, all incl breakfast) In a pastel-green wooden building, the Polina has just half a dozen beautiful rooms and apartments, all with double beds, and spacious sitting areas with fireplaces. There's billiards and a sauna (R400 per hour) too.

Hotel Belomorskaya (☎ 661 600; fax 465 327; www.belhotel.ru; ul Timme 3; s/d R830/1160, ste R1330-1600; P) The concrete-slab architecture and soulless foyer don't inspire confidence but the rooms are good-sized and in good condition. The location is reasonably convenient for the bus and train stations (a short ride away by bus 64) but not for anything else. The large restaurant has loud music to dine by.

AUTHOR'S CHOICE

Semibistro, semitavern, **Restoran Bobroff** (☎ 285 813; nab Severnoy Dviny; meals R250-700; ⏳ 11.30am-2am) is refreshingly different and serves great food in a great location facing the river. Try some of the seafood and meat appetisers and save room for the *blinchiki lakomka* ('gourmand pancakes' – with cream and forest fruits) at the end. The menu is in English and Russian.

Eating

Kofeynya U Poliny (☎ 653 997; Troitsky pr; cakes & desserts R35-65; ⏳ 9am-11pm) U Poliny has everything a good café should – cheesecake, glacé fruit tarts, busy young staff bustling about, and a big choice of coffee and tea. Easily the best café north of St Petersburg.

Restoran Dvina (☎ 207 323; Troitsky pr; meals R300-800; ⏳ noon-5pm & 6.30pm-midnight) A bright European atmosphere and good seafood and Italian dishes make the Dvina a sure-fire success.

Restoran Pomorsky (☎ 201 858; Troitsky pr; meals R250-1000; ⏳ noon-5pm & 6.30pm-midnight) Upstairs from the Dvina restaurant, the Pomorsky serves top-class fish and seafood, accented by maritime décor and relaxed background music.

Paratov (☎ 214 141; Berth 152, Morskoy-Rechnoy Vokzal, nab Severnoy Dviny 26; meals R300-900; ⏳ 24hr) This floating restaurant behind the Sea & River Terminal serves delicious sushi and other Japanese food in a spick-and-span stainless steel environment. A pictorial menu saves you having to grapple with Japanese in Cyrillic.

Le Petit Restaurant (☎ 211 304; Hotel Dvina, Troitsky pr 52; meals R250-700) The Hotel Dvina's neat little restaurant provides good French and Russian dishes in a relaxed European café atmosphere.

Restoran Na Voskresenskoy (☎ /fax 210 130; Business Centre Hotel, Voskrensenskaya ul 8; meals R250-550; ⏳ 8am-10am & noon-midnight) This classy little restaurant is very reasonably priced (especially the R170 weekday buffet lunch).

Also recommended:

Kafe U Tyoshchi (☎ 205 231; Troitsky pr 52; ⏳ 9am-9pm; desserts & salads R25-40; ✗) Fine café haven, next to the Premier supermarket.

La Forchetta d'Oro (☎ 209 999; pr Chumbarova-Luchinskogo 8; pizzas R100-150; ⏳ 11am-11pm)

Premier (Troitsky pr 52; ⏳ 9am-10pm) Very well-stocked supermarket/department store next to Hotel Dvina.

Solovetskoe Podvorie (☎ 652 418; nab Severnoy Dviny 78; meals R300-700; ⏳ noon-2am) Has a Russian *izba* (cottage)-style room, serving national dishes, and a more satisfying European-style menu in the other room.

Drinking & Entertainment

Pelikan (☎ 652 449; nab Severnoy Dviny; admission varies; ⏳ 7pm-8am) This floating nightclub with middle-of-the-road dance music can be a lot of fun. The bar is perfectly positioned for watching the sun go down, and then come up again, over the Severnaya Dvina.

Bar Dva Piva (cnr Troitsky pr & ul Komsomolskaya; admission after 8pm Fri & Sat upstairs/downstairs R30/60; ⏳ noon-2am) Dva Piva (Two Beers) is like a cosy pub with seats in booths and a mid-20s-plus clientele enjoying – yes – a couple of beers with friends. The downstairs bar has a similar arrangement around a dance floor – lively but equally unpretentious.

Restoran Amadey (☎ 655 051; Voskresenskaya ul 17; meals R300-600; ⏳ noon-2am) Jazz lovers head here for the excellent live sessions from Thursday to Saturday nights.

Trud Stadium (☎ 285 440; www.vodnikbc.ru; pr Lomonosova 252) Arkhangelsk is proud of its bandy team Vodnik, several times European and world champions. Bandy? It's like field hockey on skates, with a red ball and 11 players per side on an ice-covered, soccer-size arena. Vodnik's season is from November to March.

Modern (☎ 657 559; pr Lomonosova 269; admission R200-250; ⏳ 11pm-5am Fri & Sat) This weekend nightclub is popular with a mid-20s-plus crowd; sometimes hosts live bands.

Getting There & Away

AIR

Talagi airport (ARH; ☎ 211 560), 12km northeast of the centre, has flights by **Aeroflot-Nord** (☎ 655 776; Pomorskaya ul 7; ⏳ 9am-7pm Mon-Fri, 10am-5pm Sat & Sun) to/from Moscow Sheremetyevo (R4900 one-way, 1¾ hours, two or three daily), Murmansk (R3950, two hours, five or six a week), Kotlas (R2300, 1½ hours, Monday to Friday), the Solovetsky Islands (R1860, one hour, Monday and Friday, plus Sunday from mid-June to mid-September), Petrozavodsk (R3600, one hour, Sundays from about June to September) and Tromsø, Norway (US$230, five hours,

Monday, Wednesday and Friday), via Murmansk. **Pulkovo** (☎ 635 898; ground fl, pl Lenina 4; ☺ 10am-3pm Mon-Fri) flies to/from St Petersburg (R4200, 1½ hours, one or two daily).

Further Solovetsky Islands flights (R1860, one hour) go on Wednesday, plus Monday and Friday from June to October, in small planes from **Vaskovo airport** (☎ 450 926), 20km south of the city centre.

You can also buy air tickets at the helpful **ticket desk** (☺ 9am-2pm & 3-5pm Mon-Fri) in the foyer of the Hotel Dvina and at **TsAVS** (☎ 238 098; Voskresenskaya ul 116; ☺ 9am-7pm Mon-Fri, 10am-5pm Sat & Sun).

BUS

From the **bus station** (☎ 238 771; ul 23-y Gvardeyskoy Divizii 13) there's a bus to Veliky Ustyug (R460, 11½ hours) at 8am daily.

TRAIN

From the **station** (☎ 237 241; pl 60-letia Oktyabrya 2), two or three trains daily run to Moscow (R1087 to R1331, 21 to 24 hours) via Vologda (R615 to R820, 14 to 15 hours) and Yaroslavl (R778 to R1038, 18 to 20 hours). There's one train daily each to St Petersburg (R1071 to R1312, 26 hours) and Kotlas (R707 to R866, 19 hours), and a train on odd dates (daily during some summer periods) to Murmansk (R997 to R1222, 30 hours) via Kem (R510 to R655, 16 hours).

There's a convenient **train ticket desk** (☺ 9am-2pm & 3-5pm Mon-Fri) in the Hotel Dvina.

Getting Around

The **Sea & River Terminal** (nab Severnoy Dviny 26) is the main terminus for city buses and *marshrutky*, appearing as 'MR Vokzal' on destination boards.

Bus and *marshrutka* 12 run every few minutes between Talagi airport and the Sea & River Terminal, via pl Lenina and Troitsky pr (passing close to most hotels). Bus 110 runs between Vaskovo Airport and the Sea & River Terminal. A taxi between Talagi and the centre costs R200 to R250.

Bus 54 and *marshrutka* 1 run between the train station and the Sea & River Terminal every few minutes via Voznesenskaya ul, pl Lenina and Troitsky pr.

Buses cost R6 per ride, *marshrutky* R8. Normal taxi rides in town are R40 to R50.

MALYE KARELY МАЛЫЕ КАРЕЛЫ
☎ 8182

This open-air **Wooden Architecture Museum** (☎ 204 164; admission R50; ☺ 10am-pm Wed-Sun Jun-Sep, 10am-3pm Wed-Sun Oct-May), 25km east of Arkhangelsk, features a large collection of 16th- to 19th-century wooden churches, windmills, watermills, bell towers, *chyornye izby* ('black cottages', so called because their lack of a full chimney resulted in smoke-stained outside walls) and more, gathered from around the Arkhangelsk Region. Don't miss **St George's Church** (Georgiyevskaya tserkov) from Vershina, dating from 1672, or the five-domed **Ascension Church** (Voznesenskaya tserkov) from Kushereka village, built in 1669. The natural scenery around the reserve is quite pleasant – bringing a picnic would be a splendid idea. The Mezensky section of the grounds features some of the most interesting structures and the nicest views of the surrounding valleys.

Sleeping & Eating

You'll find a restaurant and shop just outside the museum grounds, as well as shashlyk and hot-dog stands around the entrance. About 500m from the entrance is the **Turisticheskaya Derevnya Malye Karely** (☎ 448 990; www.karely.ru; s R900-1300, d R1500-1900; ⓟ), a 'holiday village' that makes a fine place to stay if you're not in a hurry to get back to Arkhangelsk. As well as modern, wood-built, European-standard rooms and family cottages, there's a good Russian/European restaurant, and you can enjoy bowling and billiards in your spare moments.

Getting There & Away

Bus and *marshrutka* 104 go from Arkhangelsk inner-city bus station, via Troitsky pr, to Malye Karely (R10, 45 minutes) about every 20 to 30 minutes. A taxi from the city should cost about R150.

SOLOVETSKY ISLANDS СОЛОВЕЦКИЕ ОСТРОВА
☎ 8183590 / pop 1000 / ☺ Moscow

Perched in the icy waters of the southern White Sea, the Solovetsky Islands (often referred to as Solovki) have for centuries been the scene of amazing extremes of human heroism, endurance, suffering and cruelty. The islands were home to one of the most famous and powerful monasteries in the Russian Empire (today much revived), a tsarist-era penal colony, and one of the cruellest Soviet prison camps. They are also places of unique and haunting natural beauty, with countless bays, headlands and lakes, extensive forests and hardly any human inhabitants. Try to give yourself at

least two days, preferably more, to explore Solovki. You're unlikely to regret it.

Most people come between June and August, when navigation is open and it's not so cold. Vicious mosquitoes and swarms of midges (worst in July and August) can make you miserable at these times, so bring bug spray and clothing to cover all of your body.

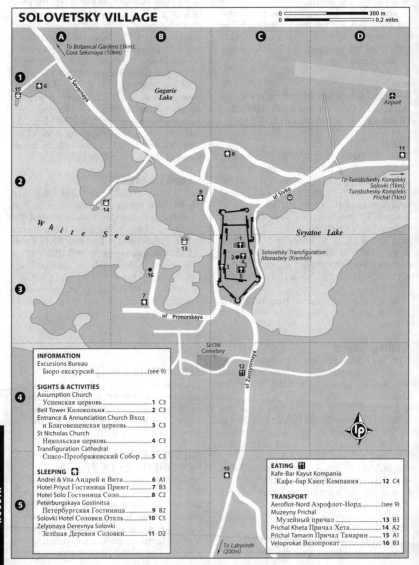

SOLOVETSKY VILLAGE

INFORMATION
Excursions Bureau
　Бюро екскурсій ....(see 9)

SIGHTS & ACTIVITIES
Assumption Church
　Успенская церковь **1** C3
Bell Tower Колокольня **2** C3
Entrance & Annunciation Church Вход
　и Благовещенская церковь.......................**3** C3
St Nicholas Church
　Никольская церковь.......................**4** C3
Transfiguration Cathedral
　Спасо-Преображенский Собор **5** C3

SLEEPING
Andrei & Vita Андрей и Вита.......................**6** A1
Hotel Priyut Гостиница Приют **7** B3
Hotel Solo Гостиница Соло.......................**8** C2
Peterburgskaya Gostinitsa
　Петербургская Гостиница.......................**9** B2
Solovki Hotel Соловки Отель **10** C5
Zelyonaya Derevnya Solovki
　Зелёная Деревня Соловки.......................**11** D2

EATING
Kafe-Bar Kayut Kompania
　Кафе-бар Кают Компания **12** C4

TRANSPORT
Aeroflot-Nord Аэрофлот-Норд.......................(see 9)
Muzeyny Prichal
　Музейный причал **13** B3
Prichal Kheta Причал Хета.......................**14** A2
Prichal Tamarin Причал Тамарин **15** A1
Veloprokat Велопрокат **16** B3

July temperatures average 13°C, but the weather here is notoriously fickle: you must always be ready for cool to cold temperatures.

History
Stone labyrinths and burial mounds from the 3rd to 1st millennia BC prove that the islands had a human presence in ancient times. Some writers posit that the islands were considered a gateway to another world and were only visited for ritual purposes.

In 1429 Savvaty and German, monks from the Kirillo-Belozersky Monastery (p400), founded a wooden monastery in the area now called Savvatevo. They and a third monk who came in 1436, Zosima, are considered the founders of the monastery which grew fairly quickly into a rich and powerful monastery that owned vast amounts of land around the White Sea. Its mid-16th-century father superior, Philip Kolychov, founded the large stone churches and thick fortress walls that still characterise its architecture. The monastery suffered a seven-year siege and plunder by tsarist troops in the 17th century for its opposition to Patriarch Nikon's reforms, but remained important until the Soviet government closed it in 1921.

In 1923 a work camp for 'enemies of the people' called the SLON (Solovetsky Lager Osobogo Naznachenia – Solovetsky Special Purpose Camp) was opened. At first, prisoners worked fairly freely, keeping up the botanical garden and libraries. Many of them were scientists, writers, artists or priests. In 1937 Stalin reorganised the SLON into one of his severest Gulag camps, where prisoners were kept in intolerable conditions and tortured or killed at will. The prison was closed in 1939.

Restoration work on the badly damaged monastery began in the 1960s and monks began to return in the late 1980s. The islands acquired Unesco World Heritage listing in 1992. Today there's a flourishing monastic community but reconstruction of the main monastery and the numerous minor ones is a long-term task. Following in the monks' footsteps has come an ever-growing stream of pilgrims and tourists.

Orientation
The Solovetsky Islands are six separate main islands and dozens of lesser ones, with a combined land mass of 300 sq km and over 500 lakes. Solovetsky Island (sometimes called Bolshoy Solovetsky Island) is by far the largest (24km north–south and 16km east–west) and home to Solovetsky village (the only one), surrounding the monastery.

Information
The islands have no ATMs, hardly anywhere accepts credit cards and the only bank doesn't do foreign currency exchange. Some businesses will be able to change money, but it's best to bring plenty of roubles with you.

Solovki International Tourist Association (www.solovky.net, www.solovky.com) is a good web source on history, accommodation, tours and mysticism.

Sights & Activities
MONASTERY
The **Solovetsky Transfiguration Monastery** (☎ 240, museum ☎ 281; admission free, museum R130; ☼ 8am-8pm, museum 9am-7pm), also known as the kremlin for its heavily fortified aspect, stands at the heart of the village. You can wander round the courtyard and visit such churches as are open (their hours are variable) for no charge.

The most fully restored and most used church is the **Annunciation Church**, above the entrance, built between 1596 and 1601. The church contains the tombs of SS Zosima, German and Savvaty, whose remains were recently returned from Soviet-era storage in the Lubyanka, the KGB headquarters in Moscow. The other main churches in the monastery – in various stages of restoration – are the **Transfiguration Cathedral** (1558–66), which has a beautiful, brand-new six-tier iconostasis; the majestic **St Nicholas Church** (1832–34), with an adjoining **belltower** (1777) that provides the greatest view of the island when it's open; and the **Assumption Church** (1552–57), adjoined by an enormous refectory (monks' dining room).

The museum displays in the monastery cover the monastery's history, the SLON and the story of the later naval training base here. The photos, documentation and artefacts in the Gulag section add up to a revealing portrayal of the suffering and inhumanity that went on here.

SLON CEMETERY

In the southern part of the village, off ul Zaozyornaya, is an area where dead prisoners were buried. It's now a small, treed park with a simple monument bearing the two-word inscription *Solovetskim Zaklyuchyonnym* – 'To the Solovetsky Prisoners'.

LABYRINTH

Though none of the islands' ancient stone labyrinths is close to the village, there's an artificial one (constructed in the 1960s) about 1km south. Follow the track along the Solovki Hotel's perimeter fence until you reach the shore, then go about 100m to the right. To the untutored eye, it's as good as the real thing!

ABANDONED PRISON

At the back of the Turistichesky Kompleks Solovki (see opposite), about 1.5km east of the monastery, is an abandoned prison, built in 1939. Roaming freely inside the empty brick building is an even creepier experience than visiting the Peter & Paul Fortress in St Petersburg.

BOTANICAL GARDEN

Three kilometres northwest of the village, Solovki's **botanical garden** (botanichesky sad; admission R100; ☙8am-8pm) is one of the most northerly in the world. Nestled in a warmth-trapping valley, the gardens boast many trees and plants usually found in more southerly climates. On Alexander Hill is the adorably miniature **Alexander Nevsky Chapel** (1854); find the nearby bench for the most beautiful view – the wind magically seems to ignore this tranquil spot.

GORA SEKIRNAYA

Literally **'Hatchet Mountain'**, Gora Sekirnaya is 10km northwest of the village and is infamous thanks to the torture Alexander Solzhenitsyn alleged took place there in his *Gulag Archipelago* (though scholars now dispute many of his claims). The unassuming **Ascension Church** (1857–62) at the top of the steep hill was used for solitary confinement; there are spectacular views from here. The church is now back in monastic hands and its faded frescoes have been joined by new icons. If you want to look inside without being on a group tour, you need to buy a ticket (R150) at the Excursions Bureau in Solovetsky village.

Many prisoners died from cold and starvation at Gora Sekirnaya, and their bodies were thrown down the steep stairs nearby, at the foot of which stands a cross in memory of all who died on Solovki, placed there in 1992 by Patriarch Aleksey.

You can make a circuit from here via Savvatyevsky minor monastery and the tiny settlement of Isakovo, to rejoin the main road 8km from the village. With the Botanical Garden thrown in, this makes a round trip of some 28km from the village. Allow five or six hours to do this by bicycle.

WILDLIFE SPOTTING

Belugas (white whales; *belukha* in Russian) gather to breed off Cape Beluzhy on the west coast of Solovetsky Island from about late June to mid-August. Seals can most often be seen in the channel between Solovetsky Island and Bolshaya Muksalma Island in the summer months. You're also likely to spot some on the crossing from Kem.

OUTLYING ISLANDS

The Solovetsky Islands are home to 35 mysterious stone labyrinths from the 3rd to 1st millennia BC and 13 of them are on little **Bolshoy Zayatsky Island** off the southwest coast of Solovetsky Island. **Anzer Island**, to the northeast, has two of the larger minor monasteries, and many visitors consider it to have a specially spiritual aura.

Tours

A guide is a big help to understanding many of the islands' sights. The Solovetsky Museum-Reserve's **Excursions Bureau** (☎ 321; scg@solovky.ru; Peterburgskaya Gostinitsa; ☙9am-8pm mid-May–mid-Oct) offers tours on many monastery, island and Gulag themes. They last from 1½ hours to a whole day, with prices from R110 to around R600 per person, in groups of 15. If there are less than 15 people, those who take part have to share the full cost. In July and August the chances are fairly good of being able to join existing groups, and tours in English are more readily available.

A number of agencies offer tour packages from the mainland to the Solovetsky Islands:

Pomor Tur (see p387) Packages by air or sea from Arkhangelsk – around R14,000 to R15,000 per person for a three-night trip.

Solovki Tour (http://solovky.com) Three- to eight-day tours on ecological, religious, Gulag or general themes.

Solovki Travel Arkhangelsk (☎ 8182-657 718; www .solovki.ru; Room 1031, Hotel Dvina, Troitsky pr 52) Moscow (☎ 495-544 5153; ul Novoslobodskaya 20) Charter flights from Moscow and a range of tour packages up to eight days.

Sleeping & Eating

Most places open only from early June to early September. If the weather is bad in late August, some may close early.

Zelyonaya Derevnya Solovki (Solovki Green Village; ☎ 283, ☎ /fax in St Petersburg 812-115 1491; info@solovky.com; ul Sivko 20; d/polu-lyux/lyux incl breakfast R3600/4200/6600; meals around R300) This excellent little log-built hotel, with views across Svyatoe Lake to the monastery, opened in 2005. The comfortable rooms have log-cabin walls and bright modern bathrooms, and there's also an inexpensive restaurant. Bikes, fishing gear, tents and antimosquito hats are available to guests.

Hotel Solo (☎ 246; avos@severodvinsk.ru; ul Kovalyova 8; s R595-980, d R1260-1750; meals R120-500) The Solo is quite cosy despite its dour exterior. Most rooms have private bathrooms. There's also a café-bar open to all and a TV room with a big fireplace.

Andrei & Vita (☎ 921 245 8022; ul Severnaya 19; s/d R300/600) Simple but clean rooms in this wooden family house, just off the Tamarin Pier, are available all year. Andrei and Vita don't speak English but are welcoming and a lot of fun. No meals available.

Solovki Hotel (☎ 331; s/d standard R3900/4200, junior ste R4500/4800, ste R7200/7500, all incl breakfast; meals R300-600) The island's fanciest hotel has cosy rooms in wooden houses – nicely designed but service is on the dreamy side. You can book through Solovki Destination Service (www.solovki-tour.ru).

Turistichesky Kompleks Solovki (☎ 221; Arkhangelsk office ☎ 8182-655 008, pr Chumbarova-Luchinskogo 43; www.solovkibp.ru in Russian; s R810-3000, d R1140-4800, tr R1800; meals R120-180) On the shore of the little Lake Varyazhskoe, 1km east of the village, this place is smaller and friendlier than its name might suggest. Most rooms are in basic cottages with shared bathrooms, but there are also a few very comfy rooms with private bathroom. A café serves inexpensive set meals.

Turistichesky Kompleks Prichal (☎ 283, ☎ /fax in St Petersburg 8182-115 1491; info@solovky.com; r R1500,

tr R2100) Also beside Lake Varyazhskoe, the Prichal has plain but quite spacious rooms with private bathrooms in two long wooden buildings.

Peterburgskaya Gostinitsa (☎ 321; s/d/tr/q R900/1200/1500/1600) This hostel, inside a renovated 19th-century monastery inn (just outside the monastery walls) has plain, clean rooms with shared bathrooms. You might find it's fully booked.

Kafe-Bar Kayut Kompania (ul Zaozyornaya 4; meals R60-100; ⏰ 8am-9pm; ✗) Simple meals are served in this *stolovaya*.

Getting There & Away

AIR

There are at least three flights a week to and from Arkhangelsk year-round. See p390 for more information. In 2005 Aeroflot-Nord also began summer flights to/from Murmansk (see p378). Book summer flights as far ahead as you can: they are very popular. It's also important to remember that flights can be delayed by anything up to a couple of days if the wind is severe, which happens quite often!

If you're coming straight from Moscow, look into the inexpensive return flights offered for around R7800 by Solovki Travel and Solovki Tour (see opposite).

Aeroflot-Nord has an office in the Peterburgskaya Gostinitsa.

BOAT

The only dependable (more or less) boat services to the Solovetsky Islands go from

Rabocheostrovsk, 10km from Kem, from the beginning of June to the end of August. Before June, ice around the islands usually makes passage impossible. During this summer season a daily service is scheduled to leave Rabocheostrovsk at 8am, and start back from Solovki at 5.30pm. The 2½-hour crossing costs R700 one-way for foreigners. Hotel Prichal at Rabocheostrovsk (p364) can confirm schedule information (in Russian). At least one other boat is likely to cross between Kem and Solovetsky every day during the navigation season – ask at the ports – and if you're lucky they'll only charge you the Russian fare (R350). Some sailings may continue as late as October.

Solovetsky village has several docks (prichaly). The main boat from Rabocheostrovsk normally puts in at Prichal Tamarin at the north end of the village.

Getting Around

Exploring by bicycle is fun, although the island roads are completely unpaved, pretty bumpy and can be either sandy or muddy depending on the weather. If you're going any distance, you need a bike with gears. Most places to stay can arrange bikes to rent, and **Veloprokat** (ul Primorskaya 15; 🕑 24hr) rents bikes for R50 per hour.

VOLOGDA REGION
ВОЛОГОДСКАЯ ОБЛАСТЬ

Due to its prominence up until the 17th century, the Vologda region has a rich history and plenty of lovely old churches. Its capital, Vologda, is especially worth the trip from Moscow or Yaroslavl, but also in this region are the World Heritage–listed frescoes of Ferapontovo and the official home town of Father Frost, Russia's equivalent of Father Christmas.

VOLOGDA ВОЛОГДА

🕿 8172 / pop 295,000 / 🕑 Moscow
About 450km northeast of Moscow, Vologda is a pleasant provincial city with a high concentration of churches and monasteries, many lovely parks and wide avenues, and a low-rise city centre with a good

number of 18th- and 19th-century wooden houses. The tranquillity in summer is disturbed only by Vologda's large, but fortunately slow and clumsy, mosquitoes.

Having taken Moscow's side against all comers seemingly from its inception, Vologda was rewarded by Ivan the Terrible, who deemed the quaint city perhaps worthy of his living there (Vologdians are steadfast in their belief that the city was a contender for Russian capital), and a perfect site for a grand cathedral.

Up to the 17th century Vologda was an important centre of industry, commerce and arts – Vologda lace is still a coveted luxury item – but with the development of Arkhangelsk and then St Petersburg, Vologda was pushed into the background. At the start of the 20th century, many political undesirables (like Josef Stalin and religious philosopher Nikolai Berdyaev) were exiled here. And, for a few months in 1918, Vologda became the diplomatic capital of Russia.

Orientation

Vologda straddles the Vologda River, with the city centre on the southern side. The Kremlin and St Sofia's Cathedral, the major landmarks and historic sites, stand together on the south bank, west of the main bridge. The main street axis is ul Mira, running north from the train and bus stations.

Dom Knigi (🕿 723 223; ul Mira 38; 🕑 10am-7pm Mon-Fri, 10am-5pm Sat & Sun) sells some regional and detailed city maps.

Information

Central library (🕿 251 867; ul Ulyanovoy 1; Internet per hr R40; 🕑 10am-8pm Mon-Thu, 10am-6pm Sat & Sun)
Post office (Sovetsky pr 4; 🕑 8am-2pm & 3-7pm Mon-Fri, 10am-5pm Sat)
Sberbank Lenina (ul Lenina 1; 🕑 8am-8pm Mon-Sat); Mira (ul Mira 74; h9am-2pm & 3-7pm Mon-Sat) Money exchange and 24-hour ATMs.
Severgazbank (ul Blagoveshchenskaya 3; 🕑 9am-1pm & 2-4pm Mon-Fri) Currency exchange & 24hr ATM.
Severo-Zapadny Telekom (ul Ulyanovoy 8; per hr R54; 🕑 8am-10pm) Internet, ATM & public phone office.

Sights & Activities
KREMLIN
Vologda's **kremlin** (Arkhiyereysky dvor, Archbishop's Courtyard; admission free; 🕑 9am-5.30pm) is the city's historical centrepiece, a 17th-century forti-

fied enclosure of churches, archbishop's chambers and other handsome buildings. It was built as a church administrative centre to accompany St Sofia's Cathedral next door, whose domes and bell tower greatly enhance the beauty of the kremlin's courtyards. Today the kremlin houses the main exhibits of the city's **History, Architecture & Art**

Museum (☎ 722 283; exhibits R20-30 each; ✆ 10am-5pm Wed-Sun).

Forty-minute kremlin tours in English are available for R500 from the excursions department (☎ 722 511) in the Gavriilovsky Korpus. The museum's history and natural history section, in the same building, ranges from stuffed wildlife to stuff on

VOLOGDA

| | | 0 — 600 m |
| | | 0 — 0.4 miles |

A   **B**   **C**   **D**

To Spaso-Prilutsky Monastery (3.5km); Airport (7km)

ul Karla Marksa

ul Nekrasova

ul Chernyshevskovo

Summer Footbridge

ul Mayakovskogo

ul Orlova

Vologda   **River**   *Footbridge*

Prechistenskaya nab

Kremlyovskaya pl

pr Pobedy

To Ferapontovo (121km); Kirillov (131km)

ul Blagoveshchenskaya

ul Batyushkova

ul Mira

Kamenny Most

pl Revolyutsii

ul Lermontova

ul Lenina

To Nikolaevskiy Hotel Club (3.8km)

Oktyabrskaya ul

ul Lev Tolstovo

Sovetsky pr

Pushkinskaya ul

Kozlenskaya ul

To Peter the Great House-Museum (500m)

ul Maltseva

ul Chelyuskintsev

ul Chekhova

Predtechenskaya ul

Galkinskaya

ul Gertsen

Zosimovskaya ul

Sodima Zolotukha

Puteyskaya ul

pl Babushkina

Train Station

INFORMATION
Central Library Библиотека	**1** B3
Dom Knigi Дом книги	**2** A4
Otel-Tur Отель-Тур	(see 17)
Post Office Почтамт	**3** B3
Sberbank Сбербанк	**4** A4
Sberbank Сбербанк	**5** B3
Severgazbank Севергазбанк	**6** B3
Severo-Zapadny Telekom Северо-Западный Телеком	**7** B3

SIGHTS & ACTIVITIES
Afghanistan Hall Афганский зал	**8** B3
Church of St John the Baptist Церковь Иоанна Предтечи	**9** B3
Kremlin Кремль	**10** A3
Lenin Statue Памятник В И Ленину	**11** B3
Museum of Diplomatic Corps Музей дипломатического корпуса	**12** B4
Museum of Forgotten Things Музей забытых вещей	**13** A2
St Sofia's Cathedral Софийский Собор	**14** A2

SLEEPING
Hotel Spasskaya Гостиница Спасская	**15** A3
Hotel Sputnik Гостиница Спутник	**16** A5
Hotel Vologda Гостиница Вологда	**17** B5

EATING
Akvarium Pizzeria Пиццерия Аквариум	**18** B2
Central Market Центральный рынок	**19** A3
Kafe Ars Кафе Арс	**20** A3
Kafe Lesnaya Skazka Кафе Лесная Сказка	**21** B3
Kaffa Каффа	**22** B3
Restaurant Mercury Ресторан Меркурий	**23** B3
Restoran Spassky Ресторан Спасский	(see 15)

ENTERTAINMENT
Pivnoy Bar Bochka Пивной бар Бочка	(see 15)
TNT	(see 15)
X-Stream Bowling Centre	(see 15)

SHOPPING
Vologodskie Suveniry Вологодские Сувениры	**24** A4

TRANSPORT
Bus Station Автовокзал	**25** B5
Buses to Spaso-Prilutsky Monastery & Airport Остановка автобусов на Спасо-Прилуцкий Монастырь и Аэропорт	**26** B2
Intra Интра	**27** B3

NORTHERN EUROPEAN RUSSIA

Stalin's periods of exile in Vologda. Those with a morbid streak will appreciate the female skeleton from the 2nd century BC and the astounding, Hieronymus Bosch–like anonymous painting from 1721, *Strashny Sud* (Frightful Trial).

The museum's art section on the east side of the main courtyard includes some astounding examples of Vologda lace and embroidery, and a host of 15th- to 17th-century icons including one of St Dmitry Prilutsky painted for Vologda's Spaso-Prilutsky Monastery by the great Dionysius in 1503. More recent art is housed in the Picture Gallery (Kartinnaya Galyeryeya) entered from the outside of the Kremlin's east wall.

ST SOFIA'S CATHEDRAL & BELL TOWER
Five-domed St Sofia's is said to have been built on the direct orders of Ivan the Terrible. Ivan's ruthlessness at Novgorod – where he sacked his own city and fried citizens alive in enormous pans made specially for the occasion – was well known throughout Russia. So the Vologda workers jumped: the massive stone cathedral Ivan wanted was erected in just two years (1568–70) – and they only worked in summer.

But haste, of course, makes waste. Local legend has it that Ivan, upon walking into St Sofia's for the first time, was struck on the head by a 'red tile' that had been grouted to the ceiling without due care. Ivan stormed out of the cathedral and never returned. The cathedral was finally consecrated after the feisty tsar's death. Its beautiful frescoes, painted in the 1680s, were restored between 1962 and 1978.

Next to the kremlin gate, St Sofia's lovely 78.5m gold-topped **bell tower** (Kolokolnya) was built in 1869–70, replacing an earlier one built in 1659.

It's possible to visit the cathedral and bell tower by arrangement with the museum administration in the kremlin.

MUSEUM OF FORGOTTEN THINGS
Housed in a restored home with period furniture, this interactive **museum** (☎ 251 417; ul Leningradskaya 6; admission R15, with tour in Russian R40; ☼ 10am-5pm Wed-Sun) aims to impart an understanding of Russian life in the 19th century. Guests are encouraged to attempt to set the dining-room table with imperial

china, play period music on a gramophone and learn the complicated norms of receiving guests.

PETER THE GREAT HOUSE-MUSEUM
Opened in 1885, this is Vologda's oldest **museum** (☎ 752 759; Sovietsky pr 47). Peter I stayed in this late-17th-century stone building during his visits to Vologda, and some interesting personal effects of the tsar are exhibited. The museum was closed for repairs at research time.

CHURCH OF ST JOHN THE BAPTIST
Before the revolution, on pl Revolyutsii there were three churches and one grand cathedral. Only the **Church of St John the Baptist** (1710–17) survived. The church makes an ironic backdrop for the very first **Lenin statue** ever erected in the USSR, back in 1924, and possibly the only one that's life-size.

MUSEUM OF DIPLOMATIC CORPS
This unusual **museum** (☎ 722 002; ul Gertsena 35; admission R30; ☼ 8.30am-5.30pm Mon-Fri) chronicles a little-known blip in WWI history. In February 1918, when Allied ambassadors in Petrograd were ordered to evacuate (Germans were approaching), US ambassador David Francis suggested simply relocating; he studied a map and chose Vologda. The British, Japanese, Chinese, Siamese, Brazilian, Belgian, French, Italian and Serbian embassies followed his lead and set up shop here until July (when they decamped again to Arkhangelsk). The eclectic and impressively researched exhibit, housed in the former US 'embassy', is full of surprises.

AFGHANISTAN HALL
The moving **Afghanistan Hall** (☎ 720 761; Dom Ofitserov, ul Ulyanovoy 6, 2nd fl; admission free; ☼ 10am-6pm) commemorates locals who died in the war in that country. Many of them were teenagers.

SPASO-PRILUTSKY MONASTERY
This working **monastery** (☎ 549 275; Priluki village; admission free; ☼ 9am-5pm Mon-Sat, 11am-5pm Sun), dating from the 14th century, rises beside the Vologda River on the northern outskirts of the city. It's a beautiful place even though visitors are restricted to limited areas inside. Standard modest dress and

covered heads for women are required. The upper church of the five-domed Transfiguration Cathedral (Spaso-Preobrazhensky sobor), built in the 16th century, is still in the early stages of restoration, but the lower church is full of icons and holds services. Behind is the beautiful, wooden Dormition Church (Uspenskaya tserkov), built in 1519 with a single spire and an equal-armed cross plan.

Get there by bus 101, 102, 103 or 133 or *marshrutka* 52, 70 or 75 (all R6) from town (you can catch them just east of the north end of ul Mira). If you walk across the railway bridge over the river (mind the gaps in the concrete) you can get a great photo of the monastery from the far bank.

Tours

Marina Barandina (☎ 757 040 evenings & weekends) speaks English extremely well and is an expert on Vologda's history and places of interest. At weekends (only) she conducts excellent general city tours, tours to Spaso-Prilutsky Monastery (both R250 per hour) and trips to Kirillov and Ferapontovo (around R5000 for an eight-hour trip including transport).

Otel-Tur (☎ 760 530; hotel_tour@rbcmail.ru; Hotel Spasskaya, Oktyabrskaya ul 25; ⏰ 9am-noon & 1-6pm Mon-Fri) is one of the better agencies for tours in and around Vologda.

Sleeping

Hotel Spasskaya (☎ 720 145; Oktyabrskaya ul 25; www .spasskaya.ru; s R1400-2100, d R1500-2100, lyux s/d from R4500/4800, all incl breakfast; P 🖳) With a central location, large, bright rooms and efficient staff, the peach-coloured Spasskaya makes a fine place to stay. In-house amenities include restaurant, bowling centre, nightclub, train-ticket office, shop and a café in the foyer, which serves a real rarity in the mornings: fresh fruit juices!

Nikolaevskiy Hotel Club (☎ 765 888; www.nik -hotel.ru; Kostromskaya ul 14; s/d R1500/1650, ste from R2500, all incl breakfast; P 🖳) This new hotel in the south of town provides Vologda's most luxurious lodgings. Staff are both friendly and professional (and they speak good English at the desk), the rooms are comfortably modern and the hotel boasts an array of amenities from a gym, business centre and a beautiful sauna to a bar with billiards and a semiformal restaurant (meals R400 to

R1000) with relaxed jazz. A taxi from the centre costs R60.

Hotel Vologda (☎ 723 079; ul Mira 92; s R560-1000, d R1000-1500, ste €100, all incl breakfast) Within walking distance of the train and bus stations, the Vologda has a range of decent to excellent rooms, all with bathroom, TV and phone. Staff are rather unenthused.

Hotel Sputnik (☎ 722 752; Puteyskaya ul 14; s/d R520/840, polu-lyux R860/1250) Also walkable from the train and bus stations, the Sputnik has good-sized, clean, renovated *polu-lyux* rooms with sitting room. The cheaper rooms are unrenovated but still have shower and TV. A small café (meals R270 to R350) serves meals and drinks.

Eating

Restoran Spassky (☎ 726 224; Hotel Spasskaya, Oktyabrskaya ul 25; meals R500-800) This hotel restaurant is the fanciest and most expensive restaurant in the centre. With luck you'll be able to enjoy a relaxed dinner with some smooth jazz.

Kafe Ars (☎ 720 575; Oktyabrskaya ul 38; meals R150-400; ⏰ 11am-10pm) The Ars is a neat, efficient and even stylish place, serving good Russian meals (outdoors as well as inside in summer), with a menu in English and Russian.

Kaffa (ul Lenina 3; cakes & pastries R20-40; ⏰ 9am-10pm Mon-Fri, 10am-10pm Sat & Sun) Take a break at this little African-themed café for great strudel, cheesecake, coffee and tea.

Kafe Lesnaya Skazka (☎ 769 205; Sovietsky pr 10; meals R120-350; ⏰ 11am-3am) You can go for a light snack or a full meal at this dependably good café. The more modern section (through the right-hand entrance) is more cheerful than the original part which occupies the converted Chapel of the Laying of the White Robes (1911).

Restaurant Mercury (☎ 723 693; ul Mira 6; meals R250-400) Can be a blast with the right company. Effusive women will guide you to heavily laid-out tables and lavish you with attention while a band plays gypsy tunes (Vologda has a sizable Roma population).

Akvarium Pizzeria (☎ 769 176; ul Orlova 6; pizzas R45-70, other main dishes R70-140; ⏰ 11am-5pm & 6-11pm Sun-Thu, 11am-5pm & 6pm-2am Fri & Sat) Dark with nightclub-type lighting and house music even at midday, the Akvarium also prepares quite tasty pizzas.

Central Market (☎ 728 057; ul Batyushkova 3A; ⏰ 7.15am-7pm Tue-Sun, 7.15am-4pm Mon) Wide selection of all types of food.

Drinking & Entertainment

The **Hotel Spasskaya** (Oktyabrskaya ul 25; www
.spasskaya.ru) takes care of most of downtown
Vologda's leisure needs. Its **X-Stream Bowling Centre** (☎ 790 059; per lane per hr R300-700;
☺ 11am-5am) is popular night and day, and
has billiards too; you can down a few beers
at the rustically wood-furnished **Pivnoy Bar
Bochka** (☎ 790 070) and then move on, still
within the same building, to the **TNT nightclub** (☎ 790 050; ☺ 8pm-6am) which provides
different ambiences for different nights.
Friday and Saturday (when there's a R200
admission charge) feature a floor show with
erotic dancing; Sunday is students' night
with karaoke.

Shopping

The best place for artisanry is the excellent **Vologodskie Suveniry** (☎ 251 481; ul Chekova
12; ☺ 10am-7pm Mon-Sat). *Kruzhevo* (Vologda
lace) is the big local speciality but here
you'll also find colourful Vologda lacquer
ware, painted wooden trays and bowls
from Severodvinsk, and delicately carved
birchwood items from Veliky Ustyug and
Omsk. There's also a good crafts shop in
the Kremlin.

Getting There & Away

You can buy air and train tickets at **Intra**
(☎ 724 611; ul Ulyanovoy 9; ☺ 8am-1pm & 2-7pm).
There's another train ticket office in the
Hotel Spasskaya.

The **Vologda airline** (☎ 790 733, 793 232; at airport; www.vologda.ru/~avia) flies to/from Moscow
Vnukovo (R2040, 1¼ hours) on Tuesday and
Thursday, and to/from Veliky Ustyug (R890,
one hour) about four times a month.

From the **train station** (☎ 720 643; pl Babushkina 8) there are at least seven daily trains
to Moscow (R560 to R1080, seven to nine
hours), three or more to St Petersburg (R630
to R1220, 12 to 13 hours), two or more to
Arkhangelsk (R615 to R820, 14 to 15 hours)
and four or more to Kotlas (R800 to R1000,
12 to 13 hours). A train to Murmansk
(R1290 to R1580, 37 hours) leaves on even
dates (daily during some summer periods).

The **bus station** (☎ 750 452; pl Babushkina 10) has
services to Petrozavodsk (R469, 12 hours)
at 8.10am four days a week, Veliky Ustyug
(R391, 10 hours) at 9.15am daily and 7am
Wednesday and Thursday, and Yaroslavl
(R183, five hours) at 2.20pm daily.

Getting Around

Bus 133 runs to the airport (R11, 30 minutes) six times daily from outside the bus
station. A taxi is R100 to R150.

Taxis from the train or bus station to the
centre should be R50 to R60.

KIRILLOV & FERAPONTOVO
КИРИЛЛОВ И ФЕРАПОНТОВО
☎ 81757

The **Kirillo-Belozersky Museum of History, Architecture & Fine Arts** (☎ 31735; Sobornaya pl 1; admission R50; ☺ 9am-5pm Tue-Sun), occupying a
nonworking 14th-century monastery of
the same name, is the reason to visit the
small town of Kirillov, 130km northwest of
Vologda. Legend has it that the monastery's
founder, Kirill, was living at Moscow's Si-
monovsky monastery when he had a vision
of the Virgin Mary showing him the towers
of a new monastery. One of Kirillov's many
marvellous icons depicts this vision.

Massive walls surround four main areas:
the large **Assumption Monastery**, the small
Ivanov Monastery, the **Stockaded Town** and
the **New Town**. The regular admission ticket
includes the churches and cathedrals and
exhibits on regional history and the history
of the monastery.

In the tranquil village of **Ferapontovo**,
20km northeast of Kirillov, is another well-
preserved **monastery** (☎ 49161; admission R60;
☺ 9.30am-5pm). The great Dionysius came
here in 1502 to paint frescoes on the church's
interior (he did it in an amazing 34 days) and
Ivan the Terrible is said to have frequented
and enjoyed this church. The frescoes are a
highpoint of Russian mural art and were the
main reason Ferapontovo received World
Heritage listing in 2000. Don't come on wet
or very humid days as the museum may be
closed to protect the artworks.

Getting There & Away

Buses to Kirillov (R120, three hours)
leave Vologda bus station at 7am, 8.30am,
10.50am and 1pm. Buses back to Vologda
leave Kirillov at 11.55am, 2.25pm and
6.50pm. To reach Ferapontovo direct from
Vologda, take an early bus heading to Lipin
Bor, Petrozavodsk or Vytegra and get off
at the Ferapontovo turnoff (R101 to R119,
2½ hours), a 2km walk from the village.
Between Kirillov and Ferapontovo you'll
need a taxi (around R250).

A taxi from Vologda to Kirillov and back, with two hours' waiting time, costs around R1500. Add another R500 or so for Ferapontovo.

VELIKY USTYUG ВЕЛИКИЙ УСТЮГ
☎ 81738 / pop 33,000 / ☺ Moscow

The fate of this provincial town 350km east of Vologda changed forever in 1998, when (for obscure reasons) Moscow Mayor Yury Luzhkov declared Veliky Ustyug to be the official home of Ded Moroz, gave the town a large sum of money, and said 'Make it so'. Ded Moroz translates as Father Frost, and he's the Russian equivalent of Santa Claus.

The town itself does often look like a children's storybook, especially when covered in snow. It's a trek from Vologda, but if you have a couple of days spare and would like to experience an old-fashioned Russian country town, laced with a shot of Father Frost kitsch, it will be fun.

Veliky Ustyug is set on the northeast bank of the Sukhona River, which meets the Yug at the southeast end of town to form the Severnaya Dvina. The town has a history of terrible springtime floods, when the frozen rivers start to melt and large chunks of ice coagulate at the confluence, forming a natural and disastrous dam.

Orientation & Information

Sovietsky pr, also called ul Uspenskaya, is the main street, one block back from the Sukhona River. One block further back is ul Krasnaya.

The high season here is the weeks leading up to Christmas and New Year. Book ahead if you plan to visit during this time, or during other Russian holidays. But note that Father Frost himself may be away travelling from before Christmas until March.

Agencies such as **Ded Moroz** (☎ /fax 20432; www.ded_moroz.ru; Sovietsky pr 85) offer packages.

There are **ATMs** in the Hotel Sukhona and **Prestizh supermarket** (ul Krasnaya 110, ☺ 24hr).

Sights & Activities
MUSEUMS & CHURCHES

The **State Historical, Architectural & Art Museum-Reserve** (☎ 23576; Dom Usova, ul Naberezhnaya 64; admission per exhibit R15-25; ☺ 10am-5pm Tue-Sun), headquartered in an 18th-century riverside mansion, is truly excellent for a small town. Good guided tours of its displays on local history, art, crafts and nature are available, but only in Russian.

Views along the church-speckled riverfront are among the most epic in northern Russia. Several of the finest churches are also part of the museum-reserve, with tickets available at Dom Usova. The **Ascension Church** (Tserkov Vozneseniya; ☎ 23405; Sovietsky pr 84; ☺ 10am-noon & 1-5pm Tue-Sat) was built in 1648 and is the town's oldest building. Externally it's a riot of small white gables and black domes, and inside, the iconostasis is glorious. In the opposite direction along the riverfront, outside **St Procopio's Cathedral** (Tserkov Prokopiya Pravednogo; ul Naberezhnaya 57) is a wishing stone purported to grant your wish if you sit on it, clear your mind, and look at the large fresco on the church across the river. The bell tower of the 1658 **Dormition Cathedral** (Uspensky sobor; Sovietsky pr 84; admission R20; ☺ 10am-5pm Tue-Sun) behind St Procopio's provides terrific views.

FATHER FROST

Ded Moroz has a **residence** (☎ 20432; Sovietsky pr 85; ☺ 9am-6pm) in Veliky Ustyug, with a souvenir shop and 'throne room' (admission R20), where he shows up at festival times when plenty of tourists are in town. Next door is the cute **Pochta Deda Moroza** (Father Frost Post office; per Oktyabrsky 8; ☺ 10am-6pm Mon-Fri, 10am-5pm Sat, 10am-3pm Sun), where boxes and boxes of letters from children all over Russia are sorted and dutifully answered – probably the most efficient post office in the country!

Father Frost's actual estate, **Votchina Deda Moroza** (☎ 20595; admission R40; ☺ 10am-5.30pm) is out among the forests 15km west of Veliky Ustyug (R100 by taxi). Votchina comprises various attractions for small children, several places to eat and drink, another souvenir shop, a small hotel and…the **Dom Deda Moroza** (House of Father Frost; tours per person R50 every 30 min). Inside this large wooden fairy-tale-type structure, you'll encounter the very tall, red-clad, white-bearded Ded Moroz who booms easy questions in a deep and friendly voice at the assembled visitors. For an extra R25, you can have your photo taken with him.

Sleeping & Eating

Hotel and Kafe Sukhona (☎ 22552; fax 21025; Krasny per 12; s/d with private bathroom R834-1200/R1216-2400). This hotel just off ul Krasnaya in the middle of town, has good, modernised rooms with flowery wallpaper and TV. the café (meals R150 to R200) is straightforwardly fine.

Hotel Dvina (☎ 20348; fax 20443; ul Krasnaya 104; s R600-750, d/tr R1000/1350) Just round the corner from the Sukhona, this friendlier, smaller place recently reopened after modernisation. Rooms are carpeted and most have private bathrooms.

Kafe Vodoley (☎ 23478; Krasny per 13; R140-350; ☼ 10am-3am) Done out like some corner of Jurassic Park with a smiling tyrannosaurus looming in one corner, the Vodoley delights the kids. There's also good Russian food with friendly, efficient service. Oh yes, and karaoke in the evenings.

Russkoe Kukhnya (Sovietsky pr 72; baked goods R10-40; ☼ 9am-2pm & 3-5pm Mon-Sat) Great bakery with fresh pastries.

Shopping

Souvenirs in Veliky Ustyug are unique, lovely and affordable. **Silverwork** is a speciality, and shops sell everything from rings to silverware collections. **Niello metalwork** on silver is especially popular. Carved birch crafts are another local speciality. **Severnaya Chern** (Sovietsky pr 113; ☼ 10am-1pm & 2-6pm Mon-Fri, 10am-3pm Sat) is the best place to go for nielloware.

Getting There & Away

AIR

Veliky Ustyug's **airport** (☎ 22110), about 5km west of town, has flights to/from Vologda (R890, one hour) by the Vologda airline about four times a month. Kotlas airport, 65km north of Veliky Ustyug (R550, one hour by taxi), has flights to Arkhangelsk (R2300, 1½ hours) by Aeroflot-Nord at 8am Monday to Friday.

BOAT

From mid-May to mid-August occasional passenger boats run along the Severnaya Dvina River between Veliky Ustyug's **river port** (ul Naberezhnaya 72) and Arkhangelsk, a 2½-day trip. The passage costs from R455 to R2124 per person depending on your accommodation; tickets are sold at the river port.

BUS

From the **bus station** (☎ 29897, ul Transportnaya), in the north of town, buses leave for Vo-

> ### MEN IN RED COATS
>
> There's no doubt about it – Father Frost has a lot in common with Santa Claus. Indeed, the Russian and Finnish authorities occasionally arrange for the two to get together in much-publicised fraternisations. Both are white-bearded old men in red suits who bring gifts to children in midwinter. There are some differences, however, beyond the fact that Father Frost arrives in a horse-drawn troika on New Year's Eve, while Santa delivers on Christmas Eve in a sleigh pulled by flying reindeer. In personality and appearance, Father Frost is taller, mightier and much gruffer than jolly, kind, rotund Santa – but he's still fair. While Santa is assisted by lots of elves, Father Frost has just one chief helper, Snegurochka (the Snow Maiden). Nor does Father Frost feel any need of a sack to carry his gifts in: his only prop is a big stick. And while Santa happily relaxes with his pipe by the fireside in his spare time, Father Frost likes to keep busy with his hobby of freezing lakes and rivers.

logda (R391, 10 hours) at 7.30am daily and 10am Thursday, Friday and Sunday, Yadrikha (R44, one hour) and Kotlas (R60, 1¼ hours) 12 times daily, and Arkhangelsk (R460, 11 hours) at 4am.

TRAIN

Veliky Ustyug **station** (☎ 29920) had no services at research time. The nearest operative station is Yadrikha, 50km north on the Vologda–Kotlas line, connected to Veliky Ustyug by bus and taxi or car (around R400). At least five daily trains run to Vologda (R800 to R1000, 12 to 13 hours), four to Moscow (R1000 to R1240, 19 to 21 hours), one to Arkhangelsk (R700 to R860, 19 hours) and about four a week to St Petersburg (R1000 to R1230, 25 hours).

Train tickets are sold in Veliky Ustyug at the **Zh/D Kassy** (ul Krasnaya 110A; ☼ 10am-7pm Mon-Fri, 9am-4pm Sat & Sun).

Getting Around

Taxis in town cost R30. Bus 1 (R6) from the bus station runs to ul Krasnaya.

Volga Region
Поволжье

The Volga region (Povolzhye – literally 'Along the Volga River') is the heartland of Russia. 'Mother Volga', the majestic river that dominates the region, is one of the nation's most enduring and endearing symbols. The cultural legacies of Russian merchants, Tatar tribes and German colonists are displayed in the ancient kremlins, spire-topped mosques and Lutheran churches along the river banks. The Volga was the site of WWII's fiercest battle, now marked by a jaw-dropping monument.

The Volga River is immortalised in the *Song of the Volga Boatmen*: 'Mighty stream so deep and wide. Volga, Volga our pride.' Today the river's lush environs attract boaters, bathers, hikers, birders and fishermen.

The Volga is Europe's longest river at 3700km. Its headwaters lie in the Valdai Hills north-west of Moscow. The river flows eastwards to Kazan, from where it bends southwards, making its way unhurriedly to the brackish delta of the Caspian Sea.

Bisecting the Eurasian continent, the Volga has brought together different peoples and cultures throughout the centuries. It now almost resembles a chain of ethnic republics, a political legacy of Soviet federalism. After the Russians, the most prominent group is the Volga Tatars (6.6 million). The Volga Germans remain widely dispersed, although a small enclave still exists near Saratov.

HIGHLIGHTS

- Cruising **'Mother Volga'** (p406), Europe's longest river and Russia's lifeline
- Visiting the Tatar mosques and markets in **Kazan** (p411)
- Snacking on *oblyoma* (dried, salty fish) and fresh, cold beer along the river banks of **Astrakhan** (p426)
- Remembering Stalingrad's horrors and heroics at **Mamaev Kurgan** (p423)
- Scoping out the scene and soaking up the sun on Samara's sand-swept **beaches** (p417)

History

Since ancient times, the Volga has supported agricultural settlements and served as a main link in transcontinental commerce. More than a thousand years ago, the Vikings plied its waters, establishing a trade route between Baghdad and the Baltic.

MEDIEVAL VOLGA

In the Middle Ages, the Lower Volga was dominated by the Khazars, notable among the Turkic tribes for religious tolerance. The Khazar capital stood at Itil (present-day Astrakhan). The Middle Volga was the domain of another Turkic tribe, the Bulgars. Descendants of the Huns and distant relatives of the Balkan Bulgarians, they migrated eastwards, mixed with local tribes and adopted Islam in the 10th century. Their feudal state was northeastern Europe's most advanced economic and cultural centre at that time. The forests of the Upper Volga were originally settled by Ugro-Finnic tribes, who were eventually displaced by the migrating Slavs. The river was also a vital conduit in the lucrative fur trade for Novgorod's merchants.

THE GOLDEN HORDE

In the 13th century, the entire Volga region was conquered by the heirs of Chinggis (Genghis) Khaan, the Mongol-led Golden Horde, who made Sarai (near present-day Volgograd) their capital. For the next 200 years, the Volga's Slavic and Turkic commu-

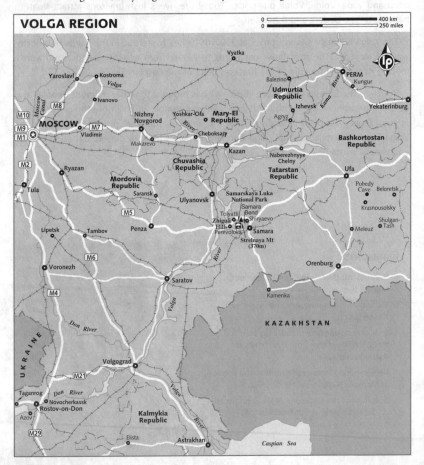

nities swore allegiance and paid tribute to the great khan, or suffered his wrath. Challenged by Tamerlane's marauder armies in the south and upstart Muscovite princes in the north, the Golden Horde eventually fragmented into separate khanates: Kazan, Astrakhan, Crimea and Sibir. In the 1550s Ivan the Terrible razed Kazan and Astrakhan, and claimed the Middle and Lower Volga for Muscovy (modern-day Moscow), the capital of the new Russian state.

COSSACKS
While the river trade was a rich source of income for Muscovy, it also supported gainful bandit and smuggling ventures. Hostile steppe tribes continued to harass Russian traders and settlers and the region remained an untamed frontier for many years.

In response, the tsar ordered the construction of fortified outposts at strategic points On the river. Serfs, paupers and dropouts fled to the region, organising semiautonomous Cossack communities (p37). The Cossacks elected their own atamans (leaders) and pledged their swords in service to tsar and Church. The Cossacks not only defended the frontier for the tsar, but also operated protection rackets, plundered locals, and raided Russia's southern neighbours.

Cossacks conducted large-scale peasant uprisings. In 1670 Stepan Razin led a 7000-strong army of the disaffected, which moved up the Lower Volga before meeting defeat at Simbirsk (Ulyanovsk). In 1773 Yemelyan Pugachev declared himself tsar and led an even larger contingent of Cossacks and runaway serfs on a riotous march through the Middle Volga region. The bloody revolt was forever romanticised by Alexander Pushkin in his novel *The Captain's Daughter*.

GERMANS IN THE VOLGA REGION
Astounded by the scale of rebellion, Catherine the Great responded with a plan for economic development in the region, particularly cultivation of the fertile southern river basin. In 1763 she issued an invitation to Germany's peasants to colonise the region. Eager to escape economic hardship and religious persecution, German Lutherans relocated to settlements along the Volga, with the largest concentration near Saratov. By end of the 19th century, the population had reached over 1.5 million ethnic Germans.

In the 1920s a German autonomous republic was established along the Lower Volga. Hitler's 1941 blitzkrieg across the USSR's western border prompted a wave of persecution against the Volga Germans, who were branded 'enemies of the state'. The German autonomous republic was eliminated, residents were forced into exile and their citizenship was revoked. After Stalin's death, nearly a million survivors were liberated from Siberian labour camps, but were not allowed to return to their old villages.

SOVIET DEVELOPMENT
The USSR harnessed the mighty Volga for its ambitious development plans. Eight complexes of dams, reservoirs and hydroelectric stations were constructed between the 1930s and 1960s. A network of canals connected Russia's heartland to Moscow, and the Baltic and Black Seas. Smoke-stacked factories, sulphurous petrochemical plants, sprawling collective farms and secret military complexes sprang up along its shores. Provincial trading towns, such as Nizhny Novgorod and Samara, grew into urban industrial centres and were closed to outsiders.

The river continues to convey as much as two-thirds of all Russia's overland cargo freight. The Volga Basin supplies one-quarter of all Russia's agricultural output and one-fifth of its total fish catch; however, the accumulated effects of Soviet-era development inflicted severe harm on the river's fish stocks and posed serious health risks to adjacent communities (p428).

THE VOLGA TODAY
Fundamentally transformed by communism, the Volga has recently reclaimed some of its historic identity. Closed cities have reopened and river trade has resurfaced. The frontier images of yore have reappeared in contemporary guise with organised crime and regional separatists; local khans have revived tribal customs and even the Cossacks have suited up in traditional regalia. Tatarstan, heir to the Kazan khanate, declared sovereignty and challenged Moscow's authority along the Middle Volga (p411).

Climate
The climate of the Volga region is still Continental, with slightly milder winters than other parts of the country. Summers

are very hot and humid, especially further south.

Getting There & Around

Trains run regularly between the Volga towns. In summer months, another, more romantic, option is available. From May to September cruise ships ply the Volga River from Moscow to Astrakhan or Rostov-on-Don. If you wish to follow in the wake of the merchants, the Cossacks and Donald Tyson (right), you have several options.

Similar to trains, transit ship cabins have two or four bunks, shared toilets and bland, cheap food. Stops along the way are too brief for sightseeing, but if your schedule is flexible, you can purchase tickets for individual segments of your route from river stations at each port of call.

Journey times vary depending on weather and currents, and prices vary according to class of service. Average times, distances and prices based on 'Middle class' (1B) quoted by Volga Flot are listed below.

Route	Duration	Distance	Price
Moscow– Nizhny Novgorod	65hr	860km	R2700
Nizhny Novgorod– Kazan	20hr	408km	R1560
Kazan–Ulyanovsk	10hr	228km	R1140
Ulyanovsk–Samara	12hr	216km	R1140
Samara–Saratov	24hr	429km	R1640
Saratov–Volgograd	18hr	385km	R1560
Volgograd–Astrakhan	20hr	494km	R1780

Companies also organise affordable, all-inclusive cruises targeted to Russians, like the one Donald Tyson undertook (see the boxed text, right). While the quality of accommodation varies, the cruises eliminate a lot of hassle and provide an opportunity to call at various ports along the way.

Cruise companies:

Capital Shipping Company (Map pp126-7; ☎ 495-458 9624; www.cck-ship.ru in Russian; Rechnoy Vokzal, Leningradsky sh 51; Ⓜ Rechnoy Vokzal) Operates transit boats departing regularly from Moscow's Northern River Station, as well as comprehensive cruise packages.

Cruise Company Orthodox (Map pp126-7; ☎ 495-943 8560; www.cruise.ru; ul Alabyana 5; Ⓜ Sokol) A Russian company that also caters to foreigners, meaning English-speaking staff and upgraded accommodation. Cruises go all the way to Rostov-on-Don, through the locks

ABOARD THE ENGINEER PTASHNIKOV

I risked a minicruise (46 hours) from Kazan to Nizhny to Kazan on the *Engineer Ptashnikov*, built in East Germany in the 1950s, and was extremely glad that I did. I rather liked the ship's décor. I had a smallish single cabin with a washbasin with hot and cold water; shower and loo were in the corridor…. Loo paper supply was intermittent – bring your own! Cabin linen consisted of two rather small sheets, a pillow but no pillowcase, a very tiny towel (bring a bath towel if you want a shower!) and a sort of quilt.

There were a few oldish people on the ship and a few family groups but the majority of the passengers were in their late teens or 20s. There was various optional entertainment, discos etc, and good sunbathing opportunities. The ship had two restaurants, one on each main deck, and meals were taken on a two-shift system in each. Food was OK, through unexciting.

The cruise provided a marvellous chance to speak a lot of Russian, though anybody with no Russian would be rather lost.

Donald Tyson, June 2004

of the Rostov-Don Canal. Cruise Company Orthodox also has a **Rostov-on-Don office** (☎ 8632-654 364; fax 8632-651 486; Bolshaya Sadovaya ul 87).

Cruise Marketing International (☎ 800-578 7742; www.cruiserussia.com in US; 3401 Investment Blvd, Ste 3, Hayward CA USA) Offers a series of 11- and 15-day cruises between Moscow and St Petersburg, with stops in little villages and Golden Ring towns.

Volga Flot (Volzhskoe Parokhodstvo; Map p408; ☎ 8312-313 449, fax 8312-303 660; www.volgaflot .com; Rechnoy Vokzal, Nizhny Novgorod) A Nizhny Novgorod–based shipping company that also provides transit passenger services.

NIZHNY NOVGOROD
НИЖНИЙ НОВГОРОД

☎ 8312 / pop 1.31 million / ⊙ Moscow

Sometimes called Russia's 'third capital', Nizhny Novgorod is markedly less cosmopolitan than Moscow and St Petersburg. But its ancient kremlin on the banks of the Volga and its pleasant pedestrian promenade make it an appealing place to spend a few days.

During Soviet times the city was named Gorky, after the writer Maxim Gorky, born here in 1868. Literature connoisseurs will find several museums in his memory. Everyone else will find one of Russia's most dynamic provincial capitals, replete with eating and entertainment opportunities.

History
Founded in 1221, Nizhny Novgorod has long been an important trading centre. Barges used to dock on the river and exchange goods; the floating market later became a huge trade fair, the Yarmarka, a tradition that continues to this day. In the 19th century it was said, 'St Petersburg is Russia's head; Moscow its heart; and Nizhny Novgorod, its wallet'.

The presence of many industries connected with the military (submarine construction, for example) meant that Nizhny Novgorod was closed to foreigners for many decades; this is one reason why the late Andrei Sakharov, physicist, dissident and Nobel laureate, was exiled here in the 1980s.

Orientation
Nizhny Novgorod, lying on the southern bank of the Volga River, is split by the Oka River. The kremlin sits on the high eastern bank overlooking the Volga. Outside its southern wall, the city's main streets spoke out from pl Minina i Pozharskogo. From here the pleasant and pedestrian Bolshaya Pokrovskaya ul heads south to pl Gorkogo. The train and bus stations are side by side on the western side of the Oka.

Information
Central post office (pl Gorkogo; ☯ 24hr)
Dom Knigi (☎ 442 273; pl Lenina; ☯ 10am-7pm Mon-Fri, 10am-6pm Sat, 11am-4pm Sun) Carries maps with local transport routes, and some English-language books.
Pauteen.ru (ul Sergievskaya 1; per hr R40; ☯ 11am-5am) Internet café.
Post office (Bolshaya Pokrovskaya ul 7; ☯ 8am-7pm Mon-Sat, to 3pm Sun) Near the kremlin.
Sberbank (Bolshaya Pokrovskaya ul 3; ☯ 8am-6pm Mon-Fri, 9am-2pm Sun) ATM and currency exchange.
Team Gorky (☎ 651 999; www.teamgorky.ru; ul 40 let Oktyabrya 1a) Organises adventure tours in the Volga region and beyond, including several three-day trips in the region (from €85 per person) and a 10-day bike tour of the Golden Ring (€560 per person).

Volga Telecom (☎ 301 270; pl Gorkogo; per hr R40; ☯ 24hr) A convenient Internet facility with plenty of computers.

Sights
KREMLIN
The mighty walls of the kremlin and its 11 towers date from the 16th century. Sometimes the ramparts are open for a sweeping view of the kremlin grounds and beyond; climb up through the restaurant in the Kladovaya Bashnya gate.

Inside, most of the buildings are government offices. The small, 17th-century **Cathedral of the Archangel Michael** (☯ 9am-2pm) is a functioning church. Behind it, an eternal flame burns near a striking **monument** to the heroes of WWII. At the northeast end of the grounds, the former governor's house is now the **Nizhegorodsky State Art Museum** (☎ 391 373; admission R30; ☯ 10am-5pm Wed-Mon). Exhibits range from 14th-century icons to 20th-century paintings by artists including Nikolai Rerikh and Vasily Surikov.

SAKHAROV MUSEUM
A reminder of more repressive times, the **Sakharov Museum** (☎ 668 623; pr Gagarina 214; admission R30; ☯ 10am-5pm) provides a sobering but fascinating view of Andrei Sakharov's life.

Sakharov was a nuclear physicist who was involved in developing the Soviet Union's first hydrogen bomb. Over the years he became one of the main figures opposing the Soviet regime from within. In 1975 Sakharov was awarded the Nobel Peace Prize but never dared to go and pick it up.

Sakharov was exiled to Gorky in 1980, and his wife Yelena Bonner joined him in 1984. Located in the actual flat in which they lived, the museum documents their lives before and after their exile. You can see the telephone that was installed in 1986, expressly so that Mikhail Gorbachev could call to inform Sakharov of his pending release. To get here catch *marshrutka* (fixed-route minibus) 104 or 4 from pl Minina i Pozharskogo.

GORKY MUSEUMS
Fans of Maxim Gorky can visit the historic wooden houses in which the writer lived and worked. The best is the **Gorky Museum** (☎ 361 651; ul Semashko 19; ☯ 9am-5pm Tue-Wed & Fri-Sun), where he lived during his 30s. **Gorky**

VOLGA REGION

NIZHNY NOVGOROD

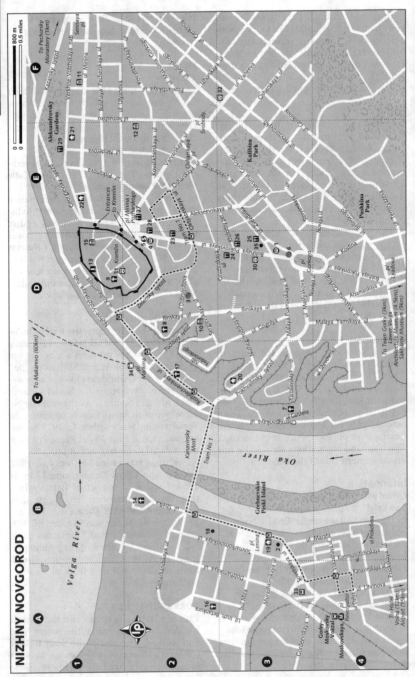

Volga River

Oka River

0   800 m
0   0.5 miles

INFORMATION
Central Post Office Центральный
почтамт...1 D3
Dom Knigi Дом Книги 2 B3
Pauteen.ru...3 D2
Post Office Почтамт..................................4 D2
Sberbank Сбербанк...................................5 D2
Volga Telecom Волга Телеком 6 D3

SIGHTS & ACTIVITIES
Annunciation Monastery
Благовещенский монастырь 7 C3
Assumption Church
Успенская церковь...........................8 D2
Cathedral of the Archangel Michael
Собор Михаила Архангела...........9 D1
Gorky House Дом Горького 10 D2
Gorky Literary Museum Литературный
Музей Горького..................................11 F1
Gorky Museum Музей Горького 12 E2
Monument to Heroes of WWII
Памятник Отечественной
войны...13 D1

Nevsky Cathedral Невский собор......14 B2
Nizhegorodsky State Art Museum
Художественный музей...............15 D1
Saviour Old Market Cathedral
Спасский староярмарочный
собор...16 A2
Stroganov Church Строгановская
церковь..17 C2
Yarmarka Ярмарка...................................18 B2

SLEEPING
Central Hotel
Гостиница Центральная.................19 B3
Nizhegorodsky Hotel Complex
Нижегородский Гостиничный
Комплекс...20 C3
October Hotel
Гостиница Октябрьская..................21 E1
Volga Slope Hotel
Гостиница Волжский Откос 22 E1

EATING
Bar Bochka Бар Бочка............................23 D2

Broadway Pizza Бродвей пицца......24 D3
English Embassy
Английское Посольство 25 D3
Gorod Gorky Город Горький............26 D3
Mexican Studies
Мексиканские Этюды.....................27 E2
Michelle Мишель.......................................28 E2
Potato Papa Картофельный Папа...29 E1

ENTERTAINMENT
Jam Prestige
Джем Престиж джаз клуб..............30 D3
Kremlin Concert Hall Кремлевский
Концертный Зал...............................31 D1
Pushkin Theatre of Opera & Ballet Театр
оперы и балета..................................32 F3

TRANSPORT
Bus Station Автостанция 33 A3
River Station Речной вокзал 34 C2
Turbyuro Турбюро 35 D2
Volga Flot Волжский флот..........(see 24)

House (☎ 340 670; Pochtovy syezd 21; ☽ 10am-5pm Thu-Tue), accessible by tram 2, is where he spent his childhood years. For a more in-depth look at the events and personalities that influenced Gorky's work, visit the **Gorky Literary Museum** (☎ 338 589; ul Minina 26; ☽ 9am-5pm Wed-Sun).

LOWER VOLGA ARCHITECTURE MUSEUM
This open-air **museum** (☎ 651 598; Gorbatovskaya ul 39; admission R50; ☽ 10am-4pm Sat-Thu) has a pleasant woodland site and a collection of traditional wooden buildings, some of which are open for visitors. The highlight is the **Pokrovskaya church**, a beautiful wooden church dating from 1731.

CHURCHES & MONASTERIES
The proliferation of onion domes and golden spires is a ubiquitous reminder of the city's rich history. The 13th-century **Annunciation Monastery**, above Chernigovskaya ul, is the oldest church, but it is not open to the public. Nor is the prominent **Pechorsky Monastery**, overlooking the Volga, which dates from the 17th century.

The stone **Assumption Church** (Ilinskaya ul), also from the 17th century, is unique in that its design was normally exclusive to wooden churches. The baroque **Stroganov** (Rozhdestvenskaya ul) or Nativity Church has retained its magnificent stone carvings.

On the west bank of the Oka River is the eye-catching **Nevsky Cathedral** (ul Strelka). The **Saviour Old Market Cathedral** (ul Inzhenera Betankura) sits behind the **Yarmarka**, the handsomely restored exhibition hall on pl Lenina.

Sleeping
October Hotel (☎ 320 670; www.oktyabrskaya.ru; Verkhne-Volzhskaya nab 9A; s/d with breakfast from R2900/4500; 🖳) This business hotel has a prime location overlooking the Volga. All of the rooms are renovated with new furniture, modern bathrooms and a hint of post-Soviet kitsch.

Volga Slope Hotel (☎ 390 530; fax 194 894; Verkhne-Volzhskaya nab 2a; s/d R800/1200) This Soviet relic has friendly staff and decent rooms for the price. Nicer, renovated rooms overlooking the Volga cost around R2500, while budget travellers may appreciate the cheapies (from R300) with shared facilities.

Nizhegorodsky Hotel Complex (☎ 305 387; www.hotel.r52.ru; ul Zalomova 2; s/d with breakfast from R900/1200) A 15-minute walk from Nizhny's main drag, this old-style place is good value. The facility is not the most attractive, but rooms are adequate and service is friendly.

Hotel Volna (☎ 961 900; www.volnahotel.ru; ul Lenina 98; s/d with breakfast from R4480/6700; ✕ ✗ 🖳 ☎) Nizhny's top hotel offers all the expected facilities, including tastefully decorated rooms, a well-equipped gym and a couple of upscale restaurants. The location, 9km south of the station (but near the end of the metro), is not in its favour.

Central Hotel (☎ 775 500; www.hotel-central.ru; Sovetskaya ul 12; s/d from R1100/1700) The location near the station is convenient, but it attracts a rough and tumble crowd (as does the casino in the lobby). Nonetheless, service and security are satisfactory. Upgraded rooms are R1700/2200 with breakfast, but the difference in comfort level is negligible.

Eating & Drinking

English Embassy (☎ 336 165; ul Zvezdinka 12; meals R300-500, business lunch R150; ◷ 8am-midnight Sun-Thu, 8am-2am Fri & Sat) This convivial British pub offers all your favourites, from steak and eggs for breakfast, to roast beef and pudding for dinner, to fish and chips for the late-night munchies. A good selection of draught beers is available from the wood and brass bar.

Gorod Gorky (☎ 332 017; Bolshaya Pokrovskaya ul 30; meals R150-400; ◷ 11am-midnight) Of several Soviet nostalgia places, this quietly upmarket choice is the most entertaining. Enter through the archway to Dom Ofitserov (look for the 'Muzey CCCP' sign). Walk through a waxwork Leonid Brezhnev's office into the dining room, littered with Soviet memorabilia and Beatles photos. The food is surprisingly good, and you can compare how much it costs today with how little it cost in 1974.

Michelle (☎ 192 914; Bolshaya Pokrovskaya ul 6; meals R150-300; ◷ 10am-11pm) This place is – first and foremost – a coffee bar, offering several varieties of aromatic brew in a simple café setting. The menu also features soups and sandwiches and dishes with French nuances – innovative fare for the price.

Bar Bochka (☎ 335 561; Bolshaya Pokrovskaya ul 14; meals R200-400) An old-school Georgian place. The dark, basement location has a bar-like atmosphere, live crooners and shashlyk for every palate.

Mexican Studies (☎ 391 460; pl Minina i Pozharskogo 2; meals R300-600) This place takes Mexican seriously. See if you can pass the test by finishing off plates piled high with rice and beans, burritos, fajitas and *empanadas* (meat-filled pastries). Conveniently located opposite the kremlin, it is the place to go for something spicy.

Recommended for cheap eats:

Potato Papa (☎ 194 101; Verkhne-Volzhskaya nab; meals R60-100; ◷ 11am-9pm) Cafeteria with lovely river views.

Broadway Pizza (☎ 917 916; Bolshaya Pokrovskaya ul 31; pizza from R45; ◷ 8am-4am) A great stop for a late-night snack.

Entertainment

Jam-Prestige (☎ 333 246; Bolshaya Pokrovskaya ul 49A; admission R50-200; ◷ shows 8-9pm) For jazz, blues and rock and roll, this small basement dive is a great venue. The place also hosts swing dancing on Monday and Saturday, so bring along your dancing shoes.

The **Kremlin Concert Hall** (Kremlevsky Kontsertny zal; ☎ 391 187; ◷ shows 6pm) at the west end of the kremlin is the home of the philharmonic, playing a full schedule of classical concerts. For Russian classics, the beautifully renovated **Pushkin Theatre of Opera & Ballet** (☎ 351 640; ul Belinskogo 59) is also recommended.

Getting There & Away

AIR

The Nizhny Novgorod International Airport is 15km southwest of the city centre. Several flights go daily to Moscow (R1000 to R3000, one hour). **Lufthansa** (☎ 759 085) flies directly to/from Frankfurt three times a week. Airline tickets are available at agencies around the city, including the **Turbyuro** (☎ 104 503; ul Zvezdinka 10; ◷ 10am-7pm Mon-Sat).

BOAT

The **river station** (☎ 303 666) is on Nizhne-Volzhskaya nab, below the kremlin. Apart from short trips along the Volga (see opposite), this is where you can find out about the summer cruises linking Nizhny Novgorod with St Petersburg, Moscow and cities further down the Volga.

BUS

Buses go to/from Moscow's Shchyolkovsky station (R300, nine hours, five daily), as well as Vladimir (R180, 4½ hours, four daily) and Kostroma (R325, daily, eight hours).

TRAIN

The Nizhny Novgorod train station still goes by its old name of Gorky-Moskovsky vokzal (station), so 'Gorky' appears on most timetables. It is on the western bank of the Oka River, at pl Revolyutsii. Several trains go to Moscow (seven hours), including one fast train (R300, 4½ hours), which departs every morning at 6.30am. All of these stop at Vladimir (R240, two to three hours). One train also continues all the way to St Petersburg (R1500, 16 hours).

Heading east, trains stop at all routes along the trans-Siberian route – the next stop is Perm (R1700, 14 hours). Trains also depart to Samara (R710, 17 hours, every other day) and Kazan (R640, nine hours, daily).

The **service centre** (☎ 483 470) at the train station is helpful for buying tickets, and also offers other services like Internet access.

Getting Around

Tram 1 is convenient, starting from the train station, crossing the Kanavinsky Most and climbing the hill to the kremlin.

There are plans to extend the metro across the river but it's unlikely to happen in the life of this book. Currently the metro is only useful to get to Hotel Volna.

AROUND NIZHNY NOVGOROD
Makarevo Макарево

The sleepy village of Makarevo is around 60km east of Nizhny Novgorod along the Volga. The fortified stone walls and church domes of its **Makarev Monastery** (☎ 249-26967; admission R150; ☺ 9am-5pm) look magnificent on the approach from the river. The monastery and surrounding village, founded in 1453, thrived on vibrant river trade through the 19th century. The monastery was closed during the Soviet period, but a few nuns returned in 1991 to help restore the churches. Today four churches are working, but only 20 nuns live here. The village of 180 people is made up of rustic wooden cottages, as well as a small **museum** in the old school house. Most locals come here for a day of sunbathing by the river; bring a picnic because there are only a few small shops.

From Nizhny Novgorod, boats depart for Makarevo (R125, 3½ hours) in the morning from near the river station, and return in the evening.

KAZAN КАЗАНЬ

☎ 8432 / pop 1.1 million / ☺ Moscow

Kazan is the capital of Tatarstan, home to the descendants of the nomadic Turkic tribe that wreaked particular havoc in ancient Rus. The atmosphere of this intriguing autonomous republic is redolent of Central Asia. The spires of many mosques dot the skyline – including the grand Kul Sharif Mosque inside the historic kremlin.

Nationalism is strong here – as evidenced by the bilingual signposts and the ubiquitous green, white and red of the Tatar flag. Ethnic pride was particularly passionate in 2005, when the city celebrated 1000 years since its founding. Many parks and buildings received a massive makeover in anticipation of the celebration, so the city centre is looking better than ever.

History

Kazan, one of Russia's oldest Tatar cities, dates back to 1005. Capital of the Kazan khanate in the 15th and 16th centuries, it was famously ravaged in 1552 by Ivan the Terrible, who forced the Muslim khan to become Christian. St Basil's Cathedral in Moscow was built to celebrate Kazan's downfall. The city later flourished as a gateway to Siberia.

During Soviet times, Kazan became the capital of the Tatar Autonomous Republic. In autumn 1990, this oil-rich region (now renamed Tatarstan) declared its autonomy from the rest of Russia, launching several years of political warfare with Moscow. But full independence remains unlikely given that 43% of the population is Russian.

Orientation

Kazan's city centre is flanked in the north by the Kazanka River and in the west by the Volga; the train station is on the east bank of the Volga. About 500m east of the Volga shore, a canal bisects the town centre, separating the train station and surrounding gritty residential area from the principle commercial area. The main drag, ul Baumana, is just east of the canal, running from the kremlin in the northwest down to busy ul Pushkina. South of the canal, ul Pushkina changes name to ul Tatarstan and continues south to the bus and river stations.

Information

Bookstore No 1 (☎ 924 510; ul Baumana 19; ☺ 9am-6pm) A centrally located bookshop with a good selection of maps, and books about Tatar history and culture.

Main post & telephone office (Kremlyovskaya ul 8; per hr R30; ☺ 8am-7pm Mon-Fri, 9am-6pm Sat & Sun) Has Internet facilities.

Telephone office (cnr ul Pushkina & Profsoyuznaya; per hr R30; ☺ 8am-9pm Mon-Fri, 10.30am-6pm Sat & Sun) Has Internet facilities.

Unix (cnr Kremlyovskaya & Universitetskaya uls, 2nd fl; per hr R40; ☺ Mon-Sat) A student computer centre that is open to the public for Internet services.

Sights
KREMLIN

Declared a Unesco World Heritage site in 2000, Kazan's striking kremlin is the focal point of the city's historic centre. It is home to government offices, pleasant parks and a few religious buildings that are usually open and operating. Some of the white limestone walls date from the 16th and 17th centuries.

Completely renovated for the 2005 celebrations, the **Annunciation Cathedral** was designed by the same architect responsible for St Basil's Cathedral in Moscow. The new iconostasis – designed in the Pskov style – is similar to that of the Assumption Cathedral inside the Moscow Kremlin.

Nearby, the slightly leaning 59m-high **Syuyumbike Tower** is named after a long-suffering princess who was married to three successive khans. Ivan the Terrible launched his siege of Kazan as a result of Syuyumbike's refusal to marry him – according to legend. To save her city, the princess agreed to marry the tsar, but only if he could build a tower higher than any other mosque in Kazan in a week. Unfortunately for Syuyumbike, the tower was completed, driving her to jump to her death from its upper terrace shortly thereafter.

Today, the tower competes with a rival landmark inside the kremlin. The enormous **Kul Sharif Mosque** was constructed on the site of a mosque by the same name, which was burnt and destroyed after Ivan the Terrible captured the city in 1552.

OTHER SIGHTS

Opposite the kremlin's main entrance, the **National Museum of the Republic of Tatarstan** (☎ 928 984; Kremlyovskaya ul 2; admission R15-100; ❧ 10am-5pm Tue-Sun) is in an ornate 1770 building. The museum has a range of exhibits, from Tatar history to water and wildlife to local artists. The Gallery of Zarif is a unique exhibit by a local artist-philosopher.

Of Kazan's several Orthodox churches, the most attractive is the **SS Peter & Paul Cathedral** (ul Musy Dzhalilya 21; ❧ 1-3pm). Built between 1723 and 1726, this baroque cathedral, with its heavily decorated façade and soaring iconostasis, commemorates the visit of Tsar Peter I to the city in 1722.

At the foot of Kremlyovskaya ul, you can't miss the overbearing classical façade of the main building of **Lenin State University**, where Vlad Ilych himself was a student. Across the street, the statue of a young Lenin looks like he's on his way to class. However, the plaques don't tell us that he was actually expelled from the university for revolutionary activity and questionable connections. The

university library (cnr uls Astronomicheskaya & Kremlyovskaya) has an exquisite decorated exterior.

Many of the mosques are clustered in the rather dumpy southwest corner of town. Near the central market is the **Soltanov mosque** (ul Gabdull Tukaya 14), dating from 1867, and the **Nurullah mosque** (ul Kirova 74), which has been rebuilt several times since 1849.

Sleeping

Visa registration is tricky in Tatarstan, and cheaper hotels may be hesitant to accept foreign guests, especially those with tourist visas or those staying more than two nights

Hotel Fatima (☎ 924 636; ul Karla Marksa 2; s/tw R600/900) Spitting distance from the kremlin, this new hotel is a great bargain. Bathrooms are shared, but the whole place is modern and clean. You can't beat it, for the price.

Hotel Volga (☎ 316 349; fax 921 469; ul Said-Galeeva 1A; s/d with breakfast & without bathroom R500/820, s/d with breakfast & bathroom from R900/1500) Convenient to the train station, this nicely revamped hotel has rooms for every budget (although the midrange rooms get booked early). Rooms facing the street can be noisy, but the place is clean and welcoming.

Hotel Giuseppe (☎ 926 934; hotelgiuseppe@mi.ru; Kremlyovskaya ul 15/25; s/d with breakfast from R3040/5700; ⊗) Inside the restaurant of the same name, this friendly place has spacious, comfortable rooms – even plush, by Kazan standards. Weekdays they are often booked by business travellers, so reserve in advance. Cash only.

Hotel Mirage (☎ 780 505; www.summithotels.com; Kirova 1a; r from R6000; ⊗ ⊗ ⌨ ⊠) This new, international-standard hotel is ideally located between the train station and the kremlin. With a luxurious, modern décor, it somehow seems out of place in this ancient city, but it is still a welcome addition for business travellers and luxury minded guests.

Hotel Tatarstan (☎ 388 379; fax 316 704; ul Pushkina 4; s/d from R1400/1600) Location is the primary advantage of this concrete slab of a hotel. Rooms are Soviet standards – not exactly stylish nor particularly comfortable, but clean and functional.

Hotel Duslik (☎ /fax 923 320; Pravobulachnaya ul 49; s/d R1200/1800) Despite the stark lobby, this place has simple but nicely renovated rooms that are good value for the price. Unfortunately, the quality of the service – and the consistency of the prices – does not match the quality of the rooms.

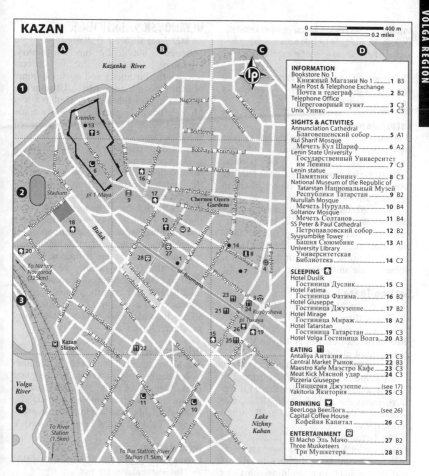

KAZAN

0 — 400 m
0 — 0.2 miles

INFORMATION
Bookstore No 1
Книжный Магазин No 1 ....**1** B3
Main Post & Telephone Exchange
Почта и телеграф **2** B2
Telephone Office
Переговорный пункт **3** C3
Unix Уникс **4** C3

SIGHTS & ACTIVITIES
Annunciation Cathedral
Благовещенский собор **5** A1
Kul Sharif Mosque
Мечеть Кул Шариф **6** A2
Lenin State University
Государственный Университет
им Ленина **7** C3
Lenin statue
Памятник Ленину **8** C3
National Museum of the Republic of
Tatarstan Национальный Музей
Республики Татарстан **9** C3
Nurullah Mosque
Мечеть Нурулла **10** B4
Soltanov Mosque
Мечеть Солтанов **11** B4
SS Peter & Paul Cathedral
Петропавловский собор **12** B2
Syuyumbike Tower
Башня Сююмбике **13** A1
University Library
Университетская
Библиотека **14** C2

SLEEPING
Hotel Duslik
Гостиница Дуслик **15** C3
Hotel Fatima
Гостиница Фатима **16** C3
Hotel Giuseppe
Гостиница Джузеппе **17** B2
Hotel Mirage
Гостиница Мираж **18** A2
Hotel Tatarstan
Гостиница Татарстан **19** C3
Hotel Volga Гостиница Волга **20** A3

EATING
Antaliya Анталия **21** C3
Central Market Рынок **22** B3
Maestro Kafe Маэстро Кафе **23** C3
Meat Kick Мясной удар **24** C3
Pizzeria Giuseppe
Пищерия Джузеппе ....(see 17)
Yakitoria Якитория **25** C3

DRINKING
BeerLoga BeerЛога ....(see 26)
Capital Coffee House
Кофейня Капитал **26** C3

ENTERTAINMENT
El Macho Эль Мачо **27** B2
Three Musketeers
Три Мушкетера **28** B3

Eating & Drinking

Pizzeria Giuseppe (☎ 326 934; Kremlyovskaya ul 15; pizza R50-100) A lively place for pizza and pastas, cappuccinos and *cannoli* (sweet pastry tubes with a rich, creamy filling). The place is not big on atmosphere, but it still attracts young couples and families, who fill up on tasty, inexpensive Italian treats.

BeerLoga (☎ 922 436; ul Pushkina 5; meals R300-500; noon-2am) Ten beers on tap and a whole range of spicy sausages feature at this Bavarian beer bar. The rustic décor and convenient location make it a popular spot.

Capital Coffee House (☎ 926 390; ul Pushkina 5; breakfast R50; 8am-midnight Mon-Fri, noon-midnight Sat & Sun) Next door to Kazan's trendiest brewpub is the city's trendiest coffee house.

Come for the wide range of coffee drinks or for free wi-fi access.

Yakitoria (☎ 922 713; ul Pushkina 3; sushi R40-60, meals R200-400; 11am-6am) Moscow's favourite sushi bar has gone national, with its popular outlet on Kazan's main square. Service is pleasant and efficient, turning over tables at this bustling place.

Meat Kick (☎ 929 332; Profsoyuznaya ul 9; meals R400-600) Besides the sought-after salad bar, this place offers Western-style steakhouse fare. To sample the Volga's riches, try the upscale seafood restaurant in the same building.

Other recommendations on ul Baumana:
Maestro Kafe (☎ 921 338; ul Baumana 47; breakfast R50; 24hr) Specialises in bliny and coffee; a great place for breakfast or a late-night snack.

Antaliya (☎ 383 803; ul Baumana 74; mains R100-150; ☻ 10am-10pm) Popular for Turkish treats, including *shawarma* (grilled meat and salad in flat bread) and Efes beer.

The colourful, sprawling **central market** (ul Mezhlauka) is good for stocking up on snacks or just for browsing.

Entertainment

El Macho (☎ 925 883; ul Musy Dzhalilya; admission R50-150; ☻ noon-5am) Mexican food and Latin music are the attractions of this popular club. It varies from day to day, but live music and free salsa lessons are often on the programme.

Three Musketeers (☎ 923 711; ul Baumana 42/9; admission R100; ☻ noon-5am) This stylish basement club has a wide range of entertainment options, including pool tables, dance floor, live music and – for better or for worse – male and female striptease.

Getting There & Away

Flights go to Moscow (R1800 to R2300, 1½ hours, three daily), and Lufthansa has twice-weekly flights to/from Frankfurt. The river station for cruises along the Volga is at the end of ul Tatarstan.

The **long-distance bus station** (☎ 930 400) is at the intersection of uls Tatarstan and Portovaya (take tram 7 from the train station). Buses go to Ulyanovsk (R230, five hours, five daily) and Samara (R290, 10 hours, daily).

The beautifully restored original train station on ul Said Galeeva now serves as a waiting room. Long-distance tickets are sold in the sleek new building, north of the tatty, suburban train station. The 2nd floor has a service centre that is useful if the ground-floor ticket counters are crowded. Frequent trains link Kazan to Moscow (R1150, 13 hours), Nizhny Novgorod (R640, nine hours) and Yekaterinburg (R1275, 15 hours). Trains going to Perm (R706, 16 hours) travel along a winding, scenic route through the mountains. They run every second day, daily in summer.

Getting Around

A bus to the airport departs from the train station every hour from 4am to 10.30pm. Tram 7 links the train and river stations. Tram 2 goes from the station to the bottom of ul Baumana near Hotel Tatarstan.

ULYANOVSK УЛЬЯНОВСК

☎ 8422 / pop 636,000 / ☻ Moscow

Founded as Simbirsk in the 17th century, Ulyanovsk is a tourist stop for only one reason: it's the birthplace and boyhood home of Lenin (born Vladimir Ilych Ulyanov).

Initially a fortified town, Simbirsk was Moscow's border guard post and a trade centre. During the 18th century it earned the nickname 'Nobles' Nest', as Russia's rich used to retire here for their holidays.

Despite taking its new name upon Lenin's death, the city stayed a backwater until the centenary of his birth in 1970. Then, in a Brezhnevian orgy of development, the city centre became a 'memorial zone', with the construction of a vast museum complex and yawning plaza, and the restoration of an entire neighbourhood, including no less than seven Ulyanov family houses.

Now the city is cleverly repackaging itself as 'Old Simbirsk'. The quiet, tree-lined streets and brightly painted wooden houses contain a bevy of little museums, all of which hark back to late-19th-century provincial Russia.

Orientation

The main memorial zone occupies the high Volga banks from pl Lenina to the giant Lenin Memorial Centre. Two blocks east is ul Goncharova, the shopping district. The restored neighbourhood is further east, occupying ul Tolstogo and ul Lenina (of course).

Information

Internet Salon (☎ 420 911; ul Bebelya 22; per hr R35; ☻ 24hr) Enter through the courtyard.

Main post office & telephone exchange (cnr uls Tolstogo & Goncharova)

Svyaz-Bank (☎ 394 385; ul Sovetskaya 19; ☻ 9am-1pm & 2-4pm Mon-Fri) Has a foreign-exchange office in Hotel Venets' lobby.

Sights

LENIN MEMORIAL CENTRE

The sprawling Memorial Centre is built around two Ulyanov family houses. The **Lenin Flat-Museum** (☎ 394 970; ☻ 9am-4.45pm Sun-Wed & Fri) has the expected collection of personal items in the flat where the Ulyanovs lived for several years. The house where Lenin was born is now a **Museum of Folk Art** (☎ 441 975; admission R10; ☻ 9am-5pm Sat-Thu), with a small collection of local paintings

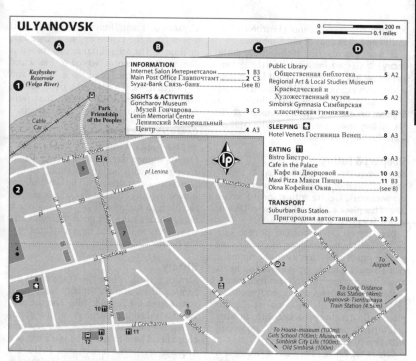

ULYANOVSK

and crafts. The gigantic cement **Historical Cultural Centre** (☎ 394 904; admission R15, special exhibits R35; 10am-4.30pm Tue-Sun) contains another museum; enter from pl 99 VI Lenin. Upstairs are a zillion Lenin portraits and glossy depictions of the revolution.

Down the river banks behind the centre is the **Park of Friendship of the Peoples** built by the Soviet republics in 1970. A sometimes-functioning cable car descends to the river.

OLD SIMBIRSK

In 1875 the Ulyanov family moved to Moskovskaya ul (now ul Lenina), at the time a rather prestigious street with a cobbled roadway and wooden pavements. These have since been updated, but the leafy trees and cosy wooden houses still evoke the atmosphere of the 19th century. The whole district is dotted with tiny museums depicting Old Simbirsk.

The pleasant ul Lenina and neighbouring ul Tolstogo contain four more houses where the Ulyanovs resided (two of which are now museums). The too-perfect **house-museum** (☎ 312 222; ul Lenina 68; 9am-4.30pm

Wed-Mon) is worth a visit for its detailed look at upper-middle-class life of that time. The other house hosts the **Museum of Simbirsk City Life** (☎ 326 319; ul Lenina 90; 10am-4pm Tue-Sun), with rotating exhibits.

Several other buildings from the era have small museums, such as the first **girls' school** (☎ 420 072; ul En gelsa 6; 10am-4.30pm Tue-Sun). Other buildings include the old Simbirsk police and fire stations (Nos 43 and 47).

For a break from Lenin idolatry, you could peek in the **Goncharov Museum** (☎ 417 966; ul Lenina 134; admission R30; 10am-6pm Tue-Sat) in the two-storey house where the writer Ivan Goncharov grew up. His most famous work is *Oblomov*, the story of a wealthy nobleman who spent most of his life in bed.

OTHER MUSEUMS

Lenin's former high school now houses the classic **Simbirsk Gymnasia** (☎ 443 019; ul Sovetskaya 18; 9am-4.30pm Tue-Sun). When young Vlad finished school (with a gold medal, of course), his report card said he was 'highly capable, hard-working and painstaking… a top scholar in all forms'. Today, the

VOLGA REGION

museum shows old-school classrooms (literally) and dioramas of old Simbirsk.

In a similar vein, the 19th-century **public library** (☎ 313 686; Kommunisticheskaya ul 3; ☺ 9am-5pm Tue-Sat) has also been turned into a museum, with exhibits of old books, maps and other documents from the archives. The **Regional Art and Local Studies Museum** (☎ 313 784; bul Novy Venets 3; art/regional R20/15; ☺ 10am-5.30pm Tue-Sun) is opposite.

Sleeping & Eating

Hotel Venets (☎ 394 576; ul Sovetskaya 15; s/d with breakfast R1550/1850) A towering block opposite the Memorial Centre with standard Soviet fare. This place evokes 1970s Soviet Union, which is exactly when it was built.

Okna (☎ 427 877; ul Sovetskaya 15; meals R200; ☺ noon-2am) On the 2nd floor, this trendy café lends a touch of modernity to the dinosaur Hotel Venets. Trendy types are drawn by its bright atmosphere and Internet computers.

Maxi Pizza (☎ 421 465; ul Goncharova 21; meals R150; ☺ 10am-midnight) This cafeteria-style pizza place is almost always packed with students and other young folks. You can't go wrong with cheap, tasty pizza and beer.

Cafe in the Palace (☎ 416 698; ul Karla Marxa 9; meals R200-400; ☺ 11am-11pm) Decorated with heavy drapes and rich colours, reminiscent of the namesake palace, this upscale café serves classic Russian fare. The space is small, but it still squeezes in a dance floor for the romantics.

Bistro (☎ 318 634; ul Goncharova; meals R50-100; ☺ 9am-9pm) A sparkling Russian fast-food place next to the suburban bus station. There's a well-stocked food store next door.

Getting There & Away

Flights go once or twice a day to/from Moscow (R3100 to R3600, two hours); there's an **Aeroflot office** (☎ 394 750; ul Sovetskaya 15; ☺ 8am-noon & 1-4pm Mon-Sat) in the foyer of Hotel Venets. Several morning buses make the journey to Kazan (R230, five hours) and Samara (R230, five hours). Trains go to Moscow (R1100, 15 hours), Kazan (R320, six hours), Ufa (R650, 15 hours), Saratov (R520, 11 hours), Samara (R360, five hours) and Volgograd (R780, 15 hours).

Getting Around

For the airport, take bus 6 from the stop on ul Goncharova behind Hotel Venets.

Ulyanovsk-Tsentralnaya train station is 4.5km from the centre by bus 1, 2 or 117, or tram 4. The long-distance bus station is 4km from the centre, served by bus 9 and 20 from the corner of ul Karla Marxa and ul Goncharova. To get to the river station, take tram 4 from Hotel Venets, then walk down a lane to the Kuybyshev Reservoir.

SAMARA САМАРА

☎ 8462 / pop 1.16 million / ☺ Moscow + 1hr

On a summer day, Samara's river banks are packed with bathing beauties, in-line skaters and beer drinkers. The lazy Volga is indeed inviting on a hot day, and Samara is the place to jump in. If you're not a beach bum, Samara has a few good museums and also serves as the base for excursions into the nearby Zhiguli Hills.

History

Samara grew up where the Volga meets the Samara River, at a particularly sharp bend across from the Zhiguli Hills. The site provided a valuable vantage point for monitoring river activity; in 1568 a fortress was constructed here to guard the tsar's recently acquired territorial possessions. In 1606 a customs house was built that enabled the tsar to take a cut of the profitable river trade.

In 1670 Stepan Razin's rebel band came through, pausing to torch the town and drown the military governor. A hundred years later, Pugachev's peasant army also paid a call on Samara. The military governor, apparently a student of history, thought it best to flee on that occasion, leaving the town to the whims of the angry throng.

The Russian Civil War began in Samara, when a unit of Czechoslovakian prisoners of war commandeered their train and seized control of the city. They were quickly joined by a contingent of old regime officers, who formed the restorationist White Army.

The name of the city and province was changed in 1935 to Kuybyshev, in honour of a local Bolshevik hero who made it big in Moscow. In WWII, Kuybyshev became the 'second capital', housing much of the relocated central government, including Stalin's bunker. Industry developed along the river, oil was discovered in the province and the city was closed. With the fall of Soviet communism, the city was reopened and its original name restored.

Orientation

The centre of Samara is on the eastern bank of the Volga at its junction with the Samara River. The main street, ul Kuybysheva, runs from pl Revolyutsii in the west (a few blocks south of the river station), then changes name to Volzhsky pr as it continues east along the Volga.

Information

Alfa-Bank (☎ 420 624; ul Molodogvardeyskaya 151; 🕙 noon-8.30pm Tue-Fri, noon-7.30pm Sat) Has an ATM.

Chakona (☎ 784 234; www.chaconne.ru; Ulyanovskaya ul 18; 🕙 10am-9pm) Packed with books and maps, and often packed with people. Located on the top floor of the Vavilon shopping centre.

Post office (ul Kuybysheva 82; 🕙 8am-8pm Mon-Fri, 9am-6pm Sat & Sun) Conveniently located and has a 24-hour telephone centre.

Samara Intour (☎ 792 060; www.samaraintour.ru in Russian; Samarskaya ul 51/53; 🕙 9am-6pm Mon-Fri, 10am-3pm Sat) City tours, river cruises and excursions in the region, including rafting trips along Samarskaya Luka.

Vizit Internet Centre (☎ 704 391; Samarskaya ul 199; per hr R36-48; 🕙 9am-10pm) A crowded basement place with plenty of computers.

Sights

ALONG THE NABEREZHNAYA

The Volga River is banked by a wide swath of lush parks and the city's main attraction: sandy beaches. Swimming, sunbathing and strolling along the naberezhnaya (embankment) are the locals' favourite pastimes.

Ploshchad Slavy is a memorial to Samara's role in WWII. The 53m-high statue of a worker holding a pair of wings symbolises the city's aviation-related contributions: local factories produced the IL-2, known as the 'flying tank', during WWII. On the east side of the square, the **St George Cathedral** honours the heroes of the Great Patriotic War.

The **Iversky Women's Monastery** (Vilonovskaya ul), founded in 1850, was home to 360 nuns, mostly daughters of local merchants.

Walk through **Strukovsky Garden** and up the steps to Teatralnaya pl, with its striking monument to Bolshevik hero Vasily Chapaev, and the ornate 1888 **Drama Theatre**.

A slow walk from one end of the naberezhnaya to the other takes a few hours, longer if you stop for a cold drink at one of the *letny kafe* (summer cafés). Even better, head to the eastern side of the **Zhiguli Brewery** (☎ 642 116; Volzhsky pr 4) and fill your bottle with fresh local beer for R15 per litre.

MUSEUMS

Stalin's Bunker (☎ 333 571; ul Frunze 167; 🕙 11am-1pm & 2-3pm Mon-Fri), built nine storeys below the Academy of Culture and Art, never actually served its intended purpose, as Stalin decided to stay in Moscow to direct events. The secret hideaway is nonetheless fascinating. Only guided groups can visit, so call in advance to make arrangements.

The massive **Alabin Museum** (☎ 322 889; www.alabin.ru in Russian; Leninskaya ul 142; admission R30; 🕙 10am-5pm Tue-Sun) has exhibits on regional palaeontology and archaeology, including dinosaur fossils found in the Zhiguli Hills. The affiliated **Ulyanov family house-museum** (☎ 323 668; Leninskaya ul 131 & 135; admission R15; 🕙 9am-5pm Mon-Sat) is where Vladimir Ilych and his family lived for three years from 1890 to 1893.

The **Samara Art Museum** (☎ 333 209; ul Kuybysheva 92; admission R50; 🕙 10am-6pm Wed-Mon) exhibits mainly Russian art, including works by artists who came to the region to paint. Look for *Boyarishina,* gifted by Surikov to a local doctor who treated him when he fell ill. The museum also holds an impressive collection of over 100 avant-garde paintings.

CHURCHES & SYNAGOGUES

The **Pokrovsky Cathedral** (Leninskaya ul 75A), built in 1860, was once resplendent in gold, marble and artistry. Apparently these riches proved their value during the 1920s famine, when they were sold to Finland for 32 wagons of bread for Samara residents to eat.

After the suppression of Polish uprisings in the Russian empire in 1830, a small group of Polish exiles settled in Samara. In 1902 this community built the Gothic **Catholic Church** (☎ 334 188; ul Frunze 157; 🕙 9am-12.30pm & 3-6pm). Reminiscent of a medieval German basilica, the **Lutheran Church** (ul Kuybysheva 115; 🕙 service 10am Sun) was built by a growing German population, who settled here from the 1860s under Catherine the Great's agricultural development programme. This church often hosts concerts on Sunday afternoons.

When the **synagogue** (ul Sadovaya 49) was built in 1903, it served over 1000 people, the largest Jewish community in the Volga region. The building served as a bread factory during Soviet times.

Sleeping

BUDGET

Volga Hotel (☎ 421 196, 421 321; fax 423 881; Volzhsky pr 29; s/d from R700/1000) Located at the naberezhnaya's northern end, this hotel has the cheapest rooms in town. It maintains its unwelcoming Soviet ambience, but it's not a bad option. Upgraded rooms with river views go for R1800/2500 with breakfast. Watch out for the 50% reservation fee.

MIDRANGE

National Hotel (☎ 337 695; ul Frunze 91/37; r with breakfast from R1500) This historic hotel (once called the Metropol) has been nicely updated. Simple rooms – all with modern

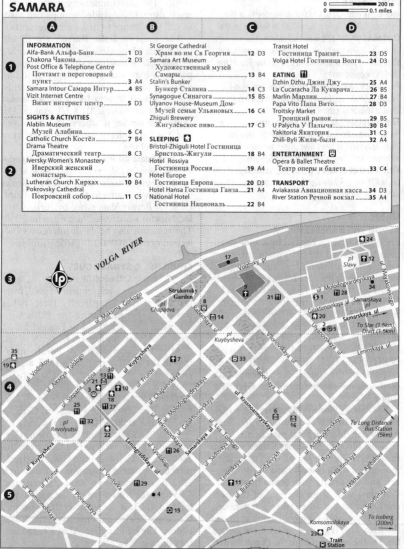

SAMARA

0 —————— 200 m
0 —————— 0.1 miles

INFORMATION
Alfa-Bank Альфа-Банк 1 D3
Chakona Чакона 2 D3
Post Office & Telephone Centre
  Почтамт и переговорный
  пункт 3 A4
Samara Intour Самара Интур 4 B5
Vizit Internet Centre
  Визит интернет центр 5 D3

SIGHTS & ACTIVITIES
Alabin Museum
  Музей Алабина 6 C4
Catholic Church Костёл 7 B4
Drama Theatre
  Драматический театр 8 C3
Iversky Women's Monastery
  Иверский женский
  монастырь 9 C3
Lutheran Church Кирхах 10 B4
Pokrovsky Cathedral
  Покровский собор 11 C5

St George Cathedral
  Храм во им Св Георгия 12 D3
Samara Art Museum
  Художественный музей
  Самары 13 B4
Stalin's Bunker
  Бункер Сталина 14 C3
Synagogue Синагога 15 B5
Ulyanov House-Museum Дом-
  Музей семьи Ульяновых 16 C4
Zhiguli Brewery
  Жигулёвское пиво 17 C3

SLEEPING 🛏
Bristol-Zhiguli Hotel Гостиница
  Бристоль-Жигули 18 B4
Hotel Rossiya
  Гостиница Россия 19 A4
Hotel Europe
  Гостиница Европа 20 D3
Hotel Hansa Гостиница Ганза 21 A4
National Hotel
  Гостиница Националь 22 B4

Transit Hotel
  Гостиница Транзит 23 D5
Volga Hotel Гостиница Волга 24 D3

EATING 🍴
Dzhin Dzhu Джин Джу 25 A4
La Cucaracha Ла Кукарача 26 B5
Marlin Марлин 27 B4
Papa Vito Папа Вито 28 D3
Troitsky Market
  Троицкий рынок 29 B5
U Palycha У Палыча 30 B4
Yakitoria Якитория 31 C3
Zhili-Byli Жили-были 32 A4

ENTERTAINMENT 🎭
Opera & Ballet Theatre
  Театр оперы и балета 33 C4

TRANSPORT
Aviakassa Авиационная касса ... 34 D3
River Station Речной вокзал 35 A4

furniture and renovated bathrooms – are
good value. The attached café serves excellent Russian food and live jazz music.

Hotel Rossiya (☎ 390 311; www.hotel-rossia.ru; ul
Maksima Gorkogo 82; s/d with breakfast from R1150/1780)
Rooms are not exactly stylish, but they are
functional, and some have views over the
Volga. This place offers good value, espe-
cially for solo travellers.

Bristol-Zhiguli Hotel (☎ 320 673; bristol@samara
mail.ru; ul Kuybysheva 111; r with breakfast from R2200)
Housed in an ornate 19th-century building,
this hotel is undergoing massive renovation,
which promises to remedy its dilapidated and
dingy condition. Cheaper rooms (R1000) are
available in the hotel's second building at ul
Kuybysheva 78, but it's a last-resort option.

Recommended near the train station:

Transit Hotel (☎ 393 000; fax 394 187; Komsomolskaya pl 2/1; r from R2300) A sleek modern place located
on the 1st floor of the train station.

Iceberg (☎ 702 289; www.icegroup.ru in Russian;
Dachnaya ul 2; r with breakfast from R2800; 🞲 💻) A
small place that is comfortable, if not super stylish. Cool,
artsy, Italian restaurant (Vincent) on site.

TOP END

Hotel Europe (☎ 708 631; www.hoteleurope.ru; Galaktionovskaya ul 171; s/d with breakfast from R2625/3412;
🞲 🞲 💻 🞲) Housed in a lovely 1902 man-
sion, this newish hotel has 20 simple guest
rooms and a highly rated restaurant. The
décor is comfortable and modern – if nondescript – but all the amenities are available.

Eating & Drinking

U Palycha (☎ 323 605; ul Kuybysheva 100; meals R500-
800) Highly recommended for Russian cuis-
ine. This fashionable, pricey restaurant has
over 250 dishes and live Russian folk music
every night.

Marlin (☎ 324 051; Leningradskaya ul 32; meals
R500-800; ◔ 24hr) If you didn't guess from the

name, the fish tanks inside are a dead givea-
way to this restaurant's speciality. The menu
offers such delicacies as steamed lobster and
sashimi, but we recommend tried and true
Russian faves straight from the Volga.

Zhili-Byli (☎ 704 132; ul Kuybysheva 81; meals R200-
300, salad bar R150; ◔ 11am-midnight) Recreates a
Russian country inn, complete with convivial atmosphere, reasonable prices and
abundant soups and salads.

Papa Vito (☎ 704 360; ul Molodogvardeyskaya 153;
pizzas R150) High ceilings and tall windows
overlooking pl Slavy make this pleasant
Italian restaurant a popular lunch spot. The
menu features salads, pastas and pizza.

La Cucaracha (☎ 324 878; ul Galaktionovskaya 39/8;
meals R300) Claims the best Mexican food east of
Moscow. Although some dishes have funny
Russian nuances, the guacamole doesn't dis-
appoint. Live Latin music most nights.

Dzhin Dzhu (☎ 329 956; ul Kuybysheva 72; meals
R500-1000; ◔ 24hr) The stylish Chinese décor
here is complete with bamboo furniture
and goldfish ponds. The food is tasty and
authentic, if expensive.

Yakitoria (☎ 700 767; ul Molodogvardeyskaya 182;
meals R200-300; ◔ 11am-6am) This Moscow
chain is spreading the love of sushi, with
outlets popping up all over Russia. If you
must eat raw fish in the middle of Russia in
the middle of the night, you can.

Troitsky market (ul Galaktionovskaya; ◔ 7am-6pm)
Great for self-caterers, the market has tables
piled high with fresh fruit and veggies, as
well as breads, meats and cheeses.

Entertainment

Opera & Ballet Theatre (☎ 322 509; pl Kuybysheva 1)
The main venue for classical dance and musical performances.

Draft (Skvoznyak; ☎ 343 402; cnr ul Novo-Sadovaya
& pr Maslenikova; ◔ 5pm-3am) Across the street
from Zvezda, this place has live music by
local rock and blues groups. You can also
play pool or watch extreme sports on TV.

Star (Zvezda; ☎ 703 447; www.zvezda.v63.ru in Russian; ul Novo-Sadovaya 106) A huge entertainment
complex with cinemas, bowling and billiards, plus a pumping nightclub and bar.

Getting There & Away

Air and rail tickets are available without
queues at the convenient **Aviakassa** (☎ 421 085;
ul Molodogvardeyskaya 221). Lufthansa operates a
direct flight from Samara to Frankfurt (four

GRUSHINSKY FESTIVAL

Every summer, the first Saturday in July kicks off one of Samara's most anticipated events, the Grushinsky Festival. The event has its roots in the 1960s, when the musical poetry known as 'Author's Song' gained popularity among intellectuals and hippy types. Simple melodies, acoustic guitar and poetic lyrics characterise this folksy music, making it difficult for non-Russian speakers to really appreciate it.

Since the 1960s, musicians from all over Russia and the former Soviet bloc collect in the Samara Bend National Park to perform their Authors' Songs, with as many as 200,000 gathering on 'spectator hill'. A stage in the shape of a guitar is set up on the lake below. Besides performances by better-known musicians, there is also a sort of 'open mike' competition, plus campfires, football and general merrymaking.

The festival is named after Valery Grushin, outdoorsman and hiker, student at the local aviation institute, and member of the trio 'Singing Beavers'. Grushin perished in 1967 while saving drowning children from the Uda river in Siberia.

hours, daily). Flights throughout the day go to Moscow (R2800 to R3500, 2½ hours) and St Petersburg (R5600, three hours). There are seasonal flights to Irkutsk, Novosibirsk and Baku.

The river station is at the west end of the naberezhnaya, in front of Hotel Rossiya. Long-distance cruises go to destinations along the Volga. There are also boats to regional destinations including Shiryaevo.

The central bus station is 6km southeast of the centre. Buses go to Ulyanovsk (R230, five hours, eight daily), Saratov (R325, twice daily) and Kazan (R290, daily). It is worth leaving Samara by train if only to wait in the ultramodern, clean and efficient station. In addition to several trains to Moscow (R1500, 18 to 20 hours), there are daily trains to Saratov (R570, eight hours), Kazan (R560, 13 hours), Astrakhan (R1100, 23 hours) and Ufa (R580, nine hours). Trains to St Petersburg and Volgograd go a few times a week.

Getting Around
Trolleybus 2 runs between the train and bus stations. From ul Kuybysheva, take bus 37, 46, 47 or 57 to the central bus station. Bus 24 runs from pl Revolyutsii to pl Slavy.

AROUND SAMARA
Shiryaevo Ширяево
In the 1870s, Ilya Repin spent two years in this village just north of Samara on the west bank of the Volga. Here he completed sketches for his famous painting, the *Barge Haulers on the Volga*, which is now in St Petersburg's Russian Museum (p252). Apparently Repin created somewhat of a scandal

when he was here, as local villagers felt objectified when used as models for the artist.

Today, the pleasant village is more welcoming to art lovers. The **Repin museum** (☎ 848-626 8257; ul Sovetskaya 14; ☯ 11am-4pm Tue-Sun) has a nice selection of Volga River paintings, including some Repin reproductions. The appeal lies less in seeing the art, however, and more in experiencing this quintessential Volga village.

The three-hour trip from Samara to Shiryaevo by hydrofoil makes for a pleasant day trip in summer months. In other seasons, the village is more difficult to reach, as only one bus per day makes the long journey.

Samara Bend Самарская Лука
While Samara sits on the left bank of the Volga, the right bank is dominated by the rocky Zhiguli Hills. The river loops around the hills creating a peninsula, encompassing 32,000 hectares of national forest reserve. The Samara Bend National Park (or Samarskaya Luka in Russia) is a prime area for hikes along rocky ledges and grand Volga vistas. The peaks – the highest being Strelnaya mountain at 370m – are in the northwest corner of the reserve.

These hills were the hide-out of peasant rebel Stepan Razin in the 17th century. He supposedly hid his loot in a large 20-sq-metre cave near the village of Perevoloka, in the southwest corner.

The traditional way to experience the Samara Bend is by boat. Every year, thousands of locals raft *zhigulyovskaya kruglosvetka* (around the world). The route follows the loop in the river, then cuts back up north via a channel on the west side of the park. Samara Intour (p417) organises these trips for around R5000 for a 10-day trip.

Otherwise, the easiest way to reach the reserve is to take a riverboat to any of the villages on the right bank, such as Shiryaevo or Polyana, or just across the river to Rozhdestveno.

SARATOV САРАТОВ

☎ 8452 / pop 873,000 / ☺ Moscow

Although it lacks major tourist attractions, Saratov is a pleasant city with a thriving commercial centre and an attractive green river embankment. Founded in 1590, Saratov was initially a fortress forming a line of defence for the trade route along the Volga.

A large community of ethnic Germans, mostly farmers, settled along the Volga around Saratov in the 18th and 19th centuries and even got their own autonomous republic within Russia in 1924. However, this was abolished during WWII when Saratov was actually occupied by the Nazis. Emigration and deportation have since decreased their numbers.

The first man in space, cosmonaut Yury Gagarin, lived in Saratov and studied at the local university, which now bears his name. The lively café scene on pr Kirova and the town's distinctive German flavour (due mainly to the tourists it attracts) make Saratov an enjoyable place to spend a day.

Orientation

The centre of town is the pedestrian mall on pr Kirova, stretching 1km from the market at ul Chapaeva to ul Radishcheva. Three blocks north, busy Moskovsky pr links the train station to the river station.

Information

Crazy Mouse (☎ 277 450; pr Kirova 25; ☺ 24hr) This Internet café is located downstairs from the Fortuna casino.

Dom Knigi (☎ 243 292; ul Volskaya 81; ☺ 9am-7pm) Has a fine collection of maps and reference books.

Post office (cnr pr Moskovsky & ul Chapaeva; ☺ 9am-6pm) Near the market.

Sberbank (☎ 503 295; pr Kirova 7; ☺ 9am-2pm & 3-7pm Mon-Fri) Has foreign-exchange services and an ATM.

Volga-Heritage Ltd (☎ 280 975; volga-heritage@inbox.ru; nab Kosmonavtov 7a) Highly recommended for tours investigating German heritage in the Volga region.

SARATOV

| | 0 | 400 m |
| 0 | | 0.2 miles |

INFORMATION
Crazy Mouse Бешенная Мышь 1 A4
Dom Knigi Дом Книги 2 A4
Post Office Почтампт.............................3 A3
Sberbank Сбербанк................................4 B4

SIGHTS & ACTIVITIES
Gagarin Museum Музей Гагарина 5 B4
Radishchev Museum Музей Радищева ...6 B4

SLEEPING 🏠
Hotel Volga Гостиница Волга 7 A4

EATING 🍴
Buratino Буратино.................................8 B4
Cafe et Chocolat Кафе и Шоколад.........9 A4
Restaurant Bavaria Бавария 10 A3

DRINKING 🍷
East West Восток Запад 11 A4
Papa's Irish Bar...................................12 A4
Seahorse Морской Конёк 13 A4

ENTERTAINMENT 🎭
Grand Michel Гранд Мишель 14 A4
Opera & Ballet Theatre
   Театр оперы и балета.....................15 B4
Philharmonic Theatre Филармония 16 B4
Sobinov Conservatory
   Консерватория Собинова...............17 B4

Sights

River views and shady walks are the highlights of the **Naberezhnaya Kosmonavtov** (Cosmonaut's Embankment) along the Volga, surveyed by a resolute Yury Gagarin from the river's shore. The **Regional Museum** (Muzey Kraevedeniya; ☎ 282 491; ul Lermontova 34; admission R40; ☺ 10am-5pm Tue-Sun) has many news clips and photos from Gagarin's life, as well as the airplane in which he learnt to fly. The typical local nature and history displays are also here. Across the street, the 17th-century **Trinity Cathedral** is a heavily decorated church that was undergoing renovation at the time of research.

For the full story on Gagarin in Saratov, check out the **Gagarin Museum** (☎ 237 666; ul

Sakko i Vanzetti 15; 9am-4pm Mon-Fri). Not only did the cosmonaut live and study in Saratov, he also landed (crashed?) his rocket nearby after his much-lauded flight. The landing site, 40km out of town near the village of Kvasnikovka, is marked by a commemorative monument.

The **Radishchev Museum** (263 627; ul Pervomayskaya 75; admission R30, special exhibits R120; 10am-6pm Tue-Sun) is the main branch of the Fine Arts Museum, with a good selection of art from the 18th to the 20th centuries.

Sleeping

Hotel Volga (243 645; fax 240 235; pr Kirova 34; s/d with breakfast from R960/1040) This early-20th-century mansion is the most atmospheric accommodation option. Rooms with high ceilings and an impressive art collection give the hotel a glorious, prerevolutionary air. Upgraded rooms are also available for about twice the price.

Hotel Slovakia (289 501; slovakia@mail.saratov .ru; ul Lermontova 30; s/d from R1000/1500) A towering Soviet block on the waterfront, Hotel Slovakia is the most common option for visiting business types. The cheapest rooms are adequate but not particularly appealing. Nicer, renovated rooms with river views start at R2500 with breakfast.

Eating & Drinking

Papa's Irish Pub (263 506; pr Kirova 20; meals R200-300, business lunch R150) Papa's has everything you need in your local Irish pub, including sports on the big screen, happy hour specials on weekday afternoons and Guinness on tap.

Bavaria (279 947; ul Volskaya 58; meals R300-400; 11am-midnight) The place to go for Wiener schnitzel and ale, Volga-style.

Buratino (277 479; pr Kirova 10; meals R200-300; 11am-midnight) If you want to do the café scene, head directly here, a favourite of expats. A funky retro-Soviet place is in the basement.

Seahorse (238 232; ul Maksima Gorkogo 16/20; noon-3am) This stylish place offers a restaurant, bar and nightclub bordering on swanky.

Recommended cafés:

Cafe et Chocolat (734 313; Volskaya ul 57; coffee R50-100; 9am-11pm) A Parisian café, lovely for breakfast or for an afternoon pick-me-up.

East West (436 272; Volskaya ul 48; drinks from R60; 9am-11pm) A travel-themed coffee shop where, appropriately enough, the walls and ceilings are covered with maps.

Entertainment

Sobinov Conservatory (230 652; pr Kirova 1) One of the best in Russia, holding frequent performances by resident and visiting musicians.

Philharmonic Theatre (224 872; Sobornaya pl 9) This is also a classical-music venue.

Opera & Ballet Theatre (263 164; Teatralnaya pl; shows at 6pm) Has opera and ballet performances.

Grand Michel (243 640; pr Kirova 22; 1pm-6am) A lively entertainment complex with bowling for about R600 an hour and billiards for R100 to R150 an hour.

Getting There & Around

The **train station** (Privokzalnaya pl) is at the western end of Moskovsky pr. Daily trains go to/from Moscow's Paveletsky vokzal (R1340, 15 hours), as well as Samara (R570, eight hours), Volgograd (R620, eight hours) and Astrakhan (R750, 12 hours).

The **river station** (269 324; Kosmonavtov nab) is at the eastern end of Moskovsky pr. The friendly port office has schedule details for long-distance and local tour boats.

Trolleybuses 2 and 2A stop at the market at the western end of pr Kirova. Trolleybuses 1 and 9 ply pr Moskovsky from the train station to the river station.

VOLGOGRAD ВОЛГОГРАД

8442 / pop 1.01 million / Moscow

Volgograd was founded in 1589 as Tsaritsyn, a mighty fortress at the convergence of the Volga and Don rivers. Nothing is left of ancient Tsaritsyn, however, due to events in more recent history.

During the Soviet period, the city was renamed Stalingrad to honour the leader who took credit for organising its defences during the Civil War. As the locale of WWII's most decisive battle, the old city was levelled and hundreds of thousands died. See the boxed text, p424.

In 1952 the Lenin Ship Canal (also known as the Volga-Don Canal) was finished, connecting the two rivers and completing an intricate network of waterways from the Arctic to the Mediterranean. After Stalin's

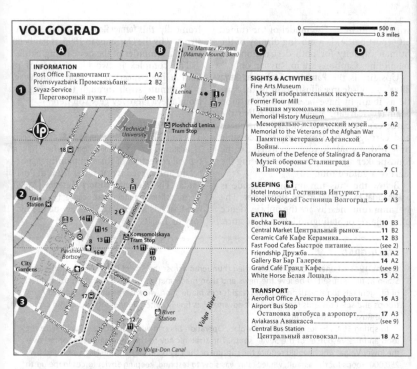

VOLGOGRAD

INFORMATION	
Post Office Главпочтамп 1 A2	
Promsvyazbank Промсвязьбанк..............2 B2	
Svyaz-Service	
Переговорный пункт......................(see 1)	

SIGHTS & ACTIVITIES	
Fine Arts Museum	
Музей изобразительных искусств............3 B2	
Former Flour Mill	
Бывшая мукомольная мельница 4 B1	
Memorial History Museum	
Мемориально-исторический музей 5 A2	
Memorial to the Veterans of the Afghan War	
Памятник ветеранам Афганской	
Войны..6 C1	
Museum of the Defence of Stalingrad & Panorama	
Музей обороны Сталинграда	
и Панорама..7 C1	

SLEEPING	
Hotel Intourist Гостиница Интурист...............8 A2	
Hotel Volgograd Гостиница Волгоград..........9 A3	

EATING	
Bochka Бочка...10 B3	
Central Market Центральный рынок..........11 B2	
Ceramic Café Кафе Керамика.....................12 B3	
Fast Food Cafes Быстрое питание..................(see 2)	
Friendship Дружба..13 A2	
Gallery Bar Бар Галерея..............................14 A2	
Grand Café Гранд Кафе..............................(see 9)	
White Horse Белая Лошадь........................15 A2	

TRANSPORT	
Aeroflot Office Агенство Аэрофлота 16 A3	
Airport Bus Stop	
Остановка автобуса в аэропорт..............17 A3	
Aviakassa Авиакасса.....................................(see 9)	
Central Bus Station	
Центральный автовокзал........................18 A2	

fall from grace, the city was renamed once again in 1961, this time to pay tribute to the river that dominates its geography, economy and culture.

Rebuilt from scratch since WWII, Volgograd is a bit sterile, although memories of the 'Great Patriotic War' are still fresh. Even today Volgograd bears witness to the simultaneously most triumphant and tragic event in Soviet history, the Battle of Stalingrad.

Orientation

Volgograd's main north–south artery is pr Lenina. From the central pl Pavshikh Bortsov (Fallen Warriors' Square), the promenade alleya Geroyev (Avenue of Heroes) crosses pr Lenina to the river station on the Volga's west bank.

Information

Post office (pl Pavshikh Bortsov; ☽ 24hr)
Promsvyazbank (☎ 236 623; pr Lenina 17; ☽ 9am-4pm Mon-Sat) ATM available around the clock.
Svyaz-Service (☎ 331 660; per hr R30-60; ☽ 24hr)
Fax and Internet facilities, adjacent to the post office.

Sights & Activities

MAMAEV KURGAN (MAMAY MOUND)

Known as Hill 102 during the Battle of Stalingrad, Mamaev Kurgan was the site of four months of fierce fighting. It's now a moving memorial to all who died in this bloody but victorious fight.

The complex's centrepiece is an evocative 72m statue of Mother Russia wielding a sword extending another 11m above her head. The area is covered with statues, memorials and ruined fortifications. The Pantheon is inscribed with the names of 7200 soldiers who died here. These names are meant to represent just a handful of the estimated one million Russian soldiers who were killed in this tragic battle. Take the high-speed tram to the Mamaev Kurgan stop, 3km north of the centre.

MUSEUM OF THE DEFENCE OF STALINGRAD & PANORAMA

This exhaustive **museum** (☎ 346 723; ul 13-y Gvardeyskoy Divizii; admission R70, guided tours R500; ☽ 10am-5pm Tue-Sun) has dozens of exhibits on the Battle of Stalingrad and the soldiers who fought in it. The model of the ruined city (post battle) is a moving display of the human capacity for both destruction and rebuilding. Captions are in Russian only.

Upstairs is the **Panorama 'Stalingradskaya Bitva'**, a 360-degree illustration of the battle as it might have been seen from atop Mamaev Kurgan. Viewers can relive the battle experience in the midst of the chaos and carnage. The Panorama is accessible only with a guided group, so listen for the loudspeaker announcements indicating the start of a guided tour.

Below the museum on the riverside is a **Memorial to Veterans of the Afghan War**. The startling ruins nearby are the only evidence of the Battle of Stalingrad left in the centre.

Ironically, this **former flour mill** had been constructed by the Germans in 1893. It has been left as a reminder of the devastating battle.

The complex is two blocks east of pl Lenina high-speed tram stop; otherwise, a 20-minute stroll through the river park from alleya Geroyev gets you here.

OTHER MUSEUMS

The small **Fine Arts Museum** (☎ 382 444; pr Lenina 21; admission R30; ☒ 10am-5.30pm Thu-Tue) has a typical collection of Russian paintings, porcelain and carved ivory. Enter from ul Port-Saida. The **Memorial History Museum** (☎ 361 705; cnr uls Kommunisticheskaya & Gogolya; ☒ 10am-5pm Wed-Mon) has several exhibits about the history of Tsaritsyn.

STALINGRAD

In June 1941 an unexpected Nazi blitzkrieg thundered across the Soviet Union. Caught off guard, Stalin at first refused to believe the news and then made matters worse by refusing the request of his generals to retreat and regroup. Nazi forces made short work of the unprepared Red Army troops and sped towards Moscow. Their advance was finally halted on the outskirts of the capital as the Russian winter set in.

In spring 1942, Hitler devised a new plan, Operation Blue, in which his forces would seize the food and fuel resources of the Soviet south. The strategic key to this campaign was control over the lower Volga, which would require the capture of the city of Stalingrad. The Nazis amassed over 250,000 troops for the assault, while Stalin was slow to respond, keeping Soviet forces in the north in fear of another attack on Moscow. In August, German Field Marshal Paulus launched the offensive; his troops quickly reached the river and entered the city. Victory seemed all but certain.

The Red Army's brilliant tactician, Marshal Zhukov, was dispatched to organise a desperate defence. For the next two months, the Battle of Stalingrad raged. Street by street, house by house, hand to hand. Neither side flinched, and a flood of reinforcements sustained the bloodletting.

By November threadbare Soviet forces somehow still held the city. The German armies were overextended and demoralised. Zhukov launched Operation Uranus, a one-million-man counter-offensive that severed German supply lines and isolated the 300,000 Nazi troops.

An embittered Hitler insisted there be no surrender. German efforts to break out of Zhukov's closing snare continued into winter. By the end of January, most of them were killed or taken prisoner. The fight for the Volga was over. The Nazis were finally stopped, and the Red Army's excruciatingly slow and devastating push westward towards Berlin had begun.

Stalingrad was the longest, deadliest and strategically most decisive battle of WWII. The level of physical destruction was immeasurable. The surrounding countryside lay in waste, the city a lifeless, smouldering shell. An estimated 750,000 German soldiers died; the number of Soviet deaths was never officially calculated, but estimates range upwards of one million. A few hundred thousand prisoners of war were sent off to perish in slave labour camps.

Stalingrad marked arguably the greatest triumph of the Soviet regime. The formidable Nazi war machine was defeated and the Soviet empire soon spread across Eastern Europe. The wartime experience brought together Soviet communism and Russian nationalism in a way that legitimised Stalin's rule. With more than 25 million deaths, the war touched virtually every family.

The cult of WWII, celebrating the ageing veterans and honouring the deceased, is still strong in Russia today, long after it has faded in much of the rest of Europe. After the Generalissimo's death, the city was renamed Volgograd. But the notion of Stalingrad would never die. It was, and remains, embedded in the collective memory of the Russian nation.

Sleeping

Hotel Intourist (☎ 364 553; fax 361 648; ul Mira 14; s/d from R1900/2270;) After recent renovations, this vast place no longer feels faded. The level of service matches the bright, welcoming lobby. Rooms are light and comfortable, if slightly overpriced.

Hotel Volgograd (☎ 408 030; www.hotelvolgograd .ru; ul Mira 12; s/d R1350/1900;) South across pl Pavshikh Bortsov, this is another vintage gem, with a wide range of rooms and prices. The cheapest rooms start at R800 per person. The ground floor Grand Cafe is among Volgograd's hottest spots to sip a cappuccino and scope out the scene (below).

Eating

Gallery Bar (☎ 331 458; ul Mira 11; meals R200-300; noon-11pm) A popular – if pricey – bar with tasty food and cold Guinness. If you come for dinner, head to the more convivial upstairs seating area.

Bochka (☎ 919 319; Sovetskaya ul 16; meals R200-400; 11am-midnight) This dark and cosy basement place has a good selection of beer and European cuisine. It draws a business lunch crowd, but it's more fun in the evening, when live music plays.

Ceramic Café (☎ 362 241; ul Chuykova 9; meals around R100; 10am-10pm) This cheerful and cheap place is always busy with Russian families and couples on dates. The decoration, provided by local artists, is for sale.

Friendship (☎ 383 348; pr Lenina 15; meals R500-800) Calls itself an English bar, for some reason. Despite the misnomer, this upscale restaurant has a decent reputation for food. The atmosphere is a bit stuffy with its ruffled violet curtains, but there is live music most nights.

White Horse (☎ 331 739; ul Ostrovskogo 5; meals R200; noon-2am) One of several divey places in this residential courtyard – all of which seem to be better for drinking than for eating. Local rock bands play on Fridays and Saturdays.

A few friendly fast-food cafés populate the square opposite the Fine Arts Museum. Stocked with typical fruit, veggies and cheeses, the **central market** (cnr uls Komsomolskaya & Sovetskaya) is the best place for self-caterers.

Getting There & Away

Buy airline tickets at the **Aviakassa** (☎ 408 066; Hotel Volgograd, ul Mira 12; 9am-5pm Mon-Fri, 9am-3pm Sat) or at the **Aeroflot office** (☎ 300 515; alleya Geroyev 6; 9am-6pm) for flights to/from Moscow (R4300, seven daily). Flights go once or twice a week to/from Baku and Yerevan.

The river station, just south of the foot of alleya Geroyev, was once one of the grandest on the river. Now, however, it shares the fate of many other public buildings and has much of its space given over to businesses peddling a variety of wares. Go around to the back on the ground level for ticket sales.

The Central Bus Station is a 10-minute walk across the tracks from the train station. Train services run daily to/from Moscow's Paveletsky vokzal (R1670, 20 hours), as well as to Astrakhan (nine hours), Volgograd (R620, eight hours) and Rostov-on-Don (R520, nine hours). A train to Ulyanovsk (R750, 20 hours) departs every second day.

Getting Around

The city centre is accessible on foot. To get to Mamaev Kurgan or the Stalingrad museum you can take the *skorostnoy tramvay* (high-speed tram), which is basically a single metro line that runs along or under pr Lenina. To get to the airport, catch a *marshrutka* from the stop in front of the TABC Volga Airlines office, at the corner of ul Volodarskogo and pr Lenina. Buses run every 30 minutes or so.

ASTRAKHAN АСТРАХАНЬ

☎ 8512 / pop 500,000 / Moscow

Situated at the upper end of the Volga River delta, about 100km from the Caspian Sea, Astrakhan is both a river and a sea port. The Golden Horde controlled this area in the 13th century and founded a city on the west bank of the Volga River. After Kazan fell to Ivan the Terrible, however, his troops took over the rest of the Volga River region and destroyed the original Tatar city. In 1558 the Russian troops built the kremlin on the east bank of the river and founded the modern city of Astrakhan.

As a trading centre between Europe, Central Asia and the Caucasus, Astrakhan has always been prosperous. Today its economic role hinges on its dwindling sturgeon population for caviar production (see boxed text, p428) and its disputed access to the Caspian Sea for oil production.

Astrakhan serves as a gateway to the beautiful Volga Delta and the carefully preserved area of waterways and wetlands leading south to the Caspian. Marked by canals and bridges, an impressive kremlin and lively markets, Astrakhan is pleasant for whiling away a day.

Orientation

Astrakhan's centre is on an island surrounded by the Volga River, the Kutum Canal and the May 1st Canal. Ul Pobedy, the major thoroughfare, cuts across the eastern end of the island and goes north to the train station. The naberezhnaya, west of the kremlin, is where locals go to have a drink, or stroll and watch the sun set over the Volga. Maps of Astrakhan exist but they are not widely sold.

Information

Business Centre (☎ 391 203; business@asranet.ru; Sovetskaya ul 5; ☺ 8am-6pm Mon-Fri, 9am-4pm Sat & Sun) Has Internet facilities.

Dair (☎ 369 516; Boevaya ul 2; per hr R60; ☺ 24hr) An entertainment complex with an Internet café

Intourist Delta Volga (☎ 244 576; www.deltavolgy .narod.ru; ul Zhelyabova 33) Offers a wide range of excursions into the Volga Delta, including bird-watching and fishing. Staff can also arrange a 'Delicacy Tour', visiting local fisheries and sampling caviar and other local treats.

Post office (cnr uls Kirova & Chernyshevskogo; ☺ 8am-7pm)

Sberbank (☎ 229 381; ul Trusova 11; ☺ 8.30am-6pm Mon-Sat) Foreign-exchange and cash-advance services.

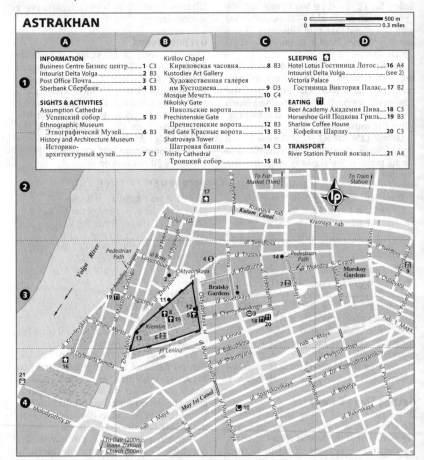

Sights
KREMLIN
The large 16th-century fortress on top of Zayachy Hill is a peaceful green haven in what can be a hot, dusty city. Enter through the main, eastern **Prechistenskie Belfry Gate** (1908–12), with its impressive bell tower.

Inside, the main churches are the magnificent **Assumption Cathedral** (1698–1710) and the lovely but fading 18th-century **Trinity Cathedral**. At the time of research, only **Kirillov Chapel** was open for visitors.

Other buildings, including the **Nikolsky Gate** in the north wall, house rather mundane cultural and historical exhibits. The most interesting is in the **Red Gate**, in the kremlin's western corner, which also provides a panoramic view of city and river. The **Ethnographic Museum** (☎ 225 444; ☺ 10am-5pm Tue-Sun) is also on the grounds of the kremlin.

OTHER SIGHTS
The **Kustodiev Art Gallery** (☎ 226 409; ul Sverdlova 81; admission R15; ☺ 10am-6pm) has an extensive collection of sculptures and paintings by artists including Mikhail Nesterov, Boris Kustodiev and Isaac Levitan.

The **History and Architecture Museum** (☎ 221 429; Sovetskaya ul 15; admission R30; ☺ 10am-5pm Sat-Thu) holds special exhibitions on local palaeontology and archaeology, with treasures excavated from around the region. Nearby, **Shatrovaya Tower** (cnr uls Trusova & Kommunisticheskaya) is all that remains of the 16th-century Saviour-Transfiguration Monastery (Spaso-preobrazhensky monastyr).

The **Ioann Zlatoust Church** (Magnitogorskaya ul), dating from 1763, is one of the city's few churches that has managed to survive the ravages of time and revolution. It used to house the bus station during Soviet times, but it has since been fully and beautifully restored, including the frescoes. The **mosque** (ul Spartakovskaya), just south of the centre, is evidence of Astrakhan's diverse population.

Sleeping
Victoria Palace (☎ 394 801; Krasnaya nab; r from R4300) A shiny, new four-star hotel with fancy rooms and prices to match.

Hotel Lotus (☎ 229 500; www.hotellotus.ru; Kremlevskaya ul 4; s/d with breakfast R1000/1600) At the southern end of the naberezhnaya, this

hulking hotel is ugly on the outside, but OK inside. Rooms are Soviet standards – some with river views. *Polu-lyux* (small suites) for R2600 provide extra space, but not extra comfort, so don't bother to upgrade.

Intourist Delta Volga (☎ 244 576; www.delta volgy.narod.ru; ul Zhelyabova 33; r R1200) Operates a tiny hotel with three modern rooms from its centrally located office.

Eating & Drinking
The best meal in town is a hot shashlyk and cold beer from a café on the naberezhnaya.

Horseshoe Grill (☎ 395 005; ul Anatoliya Sergeyeva 7; mains from R300) If the weather drives you inside, try this place, which is also along the naberezhnaya. The atmosphere is pleasant (although a bit dark in summer) and the menu is more varied than its outdoor counterparts.

Beer Academy (☎ 227 750; ul Lenina 7; meals R300-500; ☺ noon-2am) This place is serious about beer – as is evident by the beer fountain that stands in the entry. It's a convivial place with a great selection of draught beers and an extensive food menu, too.

Sharlow Coffee House (cnr uls Volodarkogo & Lenina; coffee from R60; ☺ 10am-10pm) Another popular spot for those seeking a caffeine fix. The colourful ceiling and gigantic coffee-themed murals lend an artsy atmosphere to this cheery place. A few soups and sandwiches are available, in addition to the sweet stuff.

The lively **fish market** (Pokrovskaya pl) is worth a visit to pick up some snacks or to witness the vibrant trade in produce and fish. Try *oblyoma*, the local speciality, a salty fish complemented by beer (or vice versa). Head north of Kommunisticheskaya ul until it becomes Pokrovskaya pl.

Getting There & Away
Flights go to/from Moscow (R4850, 2½ hours, three daily). Daily trains go to Moscow

---

ROE TO RUIN

Caviar: the very word evokes glamorous lifestyles, exotic travel and glittering festivities. But the sturgeon, the source of this luxury item, is in grave danger. Although it has survived since dinosaurs roamed the Earth, the question now is whether this 'living fossil' can withstand the relentless fishing pressure, pollution and habitat destruction that have brought many sturgeon species to the brink of extinction.

Sturgeon are remarkable fish: clad in bony plates and equipped with broad snouts, some species live to be more than 100 years old and can grow to be 1125kg and 4.5m long, although the very largest fish are extremely rare today, following decades of overfishing. Like humans, many sturgeon species reproduce relatively late in life; some do not reach sexual maturity until the ages of 15 to 25. A single sturgeon can produce hundreds of pounds of fish eggs, or roe.

Sturgeon today face several major obstacles to survival. Primarily, the global caviar market has placed a premium on sturgeon, prompting overfishing and poaching. Political turmoil in sturgeon-producing countries, including Russia, has resulted in a flourishing black-market trade. Many sturgeon migrate through the waters of different states and countries, resulting in a lack of effective management of their populations. Coupled with an ongoing loss of habitat and a slow pace of reproduction, the sturgeon are facing an upstream swim.

If you're thinking of buying caviar, read the box, p107, first.

(R1500, 30 hours), Volgograd (R620, eight hours) and Rostov-on-Don (R950, 24 hours). Trains also head south to Makhachkala in Dagestan (R550, 12 hours) and to Baku in Azerbaijan (R950, 24 hours).

Astrakhan is the end point of cruises on the Volga; the **river station** (ul Kremlevskaya 1) is located on the naberezhnaya. There are no regular passenger boats to the other Caspian Sea ports.

Getting Around

Bus 5 and trolleybus 3 go to/from the airport, train station and pl Lenina. Catch the bus from any stop along ul Pobedy, ul Sverdlova or ul Zhelyabova. Trolleybus 1, 2, 3 and 4 run to/from the train station and pl Lenina.

AROUND ASTRAKHAN

Volga Delta Дельта Волгы

The delta of the lower Volga River, where the river divides into thousands of branches, is home to an immense treasure of flora and fauna. Among the reeds here are beavers, racoons, muskrats, foxes and otters. The waterways and marshes are also home to flocks of waterfowl and other birds, including herons, swans, cormorants and mag-

nificent bald eagles. Over 100 species of fish inhabit these waters, including carp, pike perch, shoot fish, bream, chub, roach and perch, not to mention the mighty sturgeon (see the boxed text, above).

About 90% of Volga Delta territory is uninhabited by humans and accessible only by boat. Whether fishing, bird-watching or sunbathing, a cruise through the delta's winding waterways is among the best ways to spend a day in the Volga region.

Fishing season is from April to November. In most cases, anglers will not be allowed to keep their prizes, but should throw the fish back after securing photographic evidence. (Birds abound during these months as they follow the fish.) April can be chilly, but still enjoyable. May and June are apparently unbearable in the delta due to the inescapable swarms of mosquitoes. In August, the area is abloom with floating lotus flowers, often growing over 2m high and featuring blossoms larger than your head. September and October are also pleasant.

Access to the delta is restricted to tour agencies and fisheries with special permission, so the only way to visit the area is to book a tour with a local agency such as Intourist Delta Volga (see p426).

The Urals Урал

The Ural Mountains – the celebrated division between Europe and Asia – stretch 2000km from the arctic Kara Sea in the north to Kazakhstan in the south.

The physical reality of the Urals is not as dramatic as it sounds. The Urals are as low as famous mountain ranges go, failing to top 2000m anywhere. Nonetheless, for outdoorsy types the mountains provide endless opportunities – from hiking and biking to skiing and spelunking. Rafting in the Urals is a spring tradition, when the melting snow augments the river waters. Adventurers will appreciate the undulating hills covered with birch and pine forest, and vast stretches of taiga dotted with mountain lakes and rocky outcrops.

While the Urals are a goldmine for outdoor adventurers, it is difficult to organise such expeditions independently, which explains why the region is still relatively undiscovered by foreign travellers. A few agencies in Yekaterinburg offer active excursions.

The Urals have been vital to Russia for centuries as a major source of metals and minerals, which gave rise to industrial cities such as Perm, Yekaterinburg and Chelyabinsk. Today, these cities are vibrant economic and cultural centres, each with its own intriguing – and sometimes dark – history.

Yekaterinburg is on the east side of the Middle Urals – the lowest part of the mountains – which is why many travellers miss the mountains entirely. The highest peaks are in the far north, culminating at Mt Narodnaya (1894m).

HIGHLIGHTS

- Hiking or biking the Urals in **Taganay National Park** (p447)
- Shivering in the darkness of a cell at **Perm-36** (p436)
- Following the pilgrims from the Romanovs' execution site at the **Church of Blood** (p438) to their original burial site at **Ganina Yama** (p444)
- Speeding down the snowy slopes at **Abzakovo** (p447)
- Straddling continents at the **Europe–Asia border** (p444)

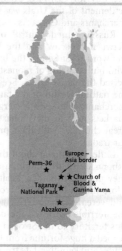

Perm-36 ★

Europe – Asia border ★

★ ★ Church of Blood & Ganina Yama

Taganay ★ National Park

★ Abzakovo

THE URALS

History

Russia's medieval princes and merchants liked to speculate on the store of riches that lay within the dense forests east of the Volga. But the mountainous terrain and murderous tribesmen of the Urals region long kept their ambitions in check.

BEFORE THE SLAVS

The Urals are one of the world's oldest mountain chains, the geological consequence of a colossal continental collision that occurred over 300 million years ago. The Urals still mark the borderline of the more-recent geographical heirs to these once separate landmasses – Europe and Asia. The mountains run north to south, stretching from the Arctic ice to the Central Asian steppe. Because of their advanced age, the mountains have been worn down over time by wind, rain and snow.

Before the Slavs moved in, the region was populated by various Uralic tribes, whose contemporary descendants include the Khanty and Mansi peoples of western Siberia as well as the Finns and Hungarians of central Europe.

SLAVIC EXPANSION

In the 16th century, the rising Muscovite principality won a series of strategic battles against their tribal foes that finally opened the way for eastward expansion. Russian settlement of the Urals was led by monks, merchants and Cossacks.

Russia gained control over the lands between Moscow and the Urals through the work of St Sergei, the bishop of Perm, who built a string of monasteries and converted the native tribes. Seeking to exploit the natural wealth of the taiga, pioneering merchants followed the clergy. They set up markets next to the monasteries, erecting great churches with their profits from the fur trade.

Little was known about the lands on the other side of the mountains, except that they possessed hidden wealth and danger. More than a few traders crossed the Urals and were never heard from again. Tsar Ivan the Terrible entrusted the development of this territory to the Stroganov family, who reaped a huge fortune from the salt and fur trades and kept the state treasury filled with tax revenues.

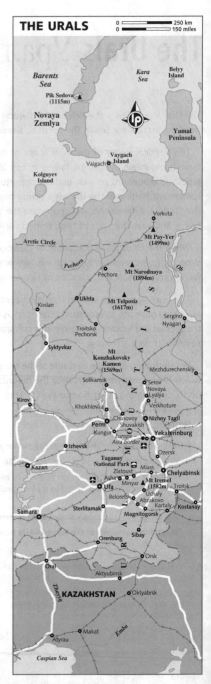

INDUSTRIAL EXPANSION

The discovery of mineral wealth in the Urals during the reign of Peter the Great led to the first large-scale Russian settlements. Yekaterinburg, founded in 1723 and named for the Empress Yekaterina (Catherine I), wife of Peter the Great, emerged as the economic centre of the Urals. Rich deposits of coal, iron ore and precious stones gave rise to a mining industry, including science and engineering institutes. By the early 19th century, the Urals metals industry supplied nearly all the iron produced in Russia and exported to European markets. The Statue of Liberty in New York and the roof on the Houses of Parliament in London were made from copper and iron from the Urals region.

In 1917 the Russian empire was consumed by the outbreak of revolution and civil war. Red radicals and White loyalists fought back-and-forth battles across the Urals. Yekaterinburg became the site of one of history's most notorious political murders, when Tsar Nicholas, Tsaritsa Alexandra and their children were shot in middle of the night and disposed of in an abandoned mine.

The Urals region figured prominently in the Soviet Union's rapid industrialisation drive in the 1930s. Some of the world's largest steelworks and industrial complexes were built there, including Uralmash in Sverdlovsk (modern-day Yekaterinburg) and Magnitogorsk in Chelyabinsk.

During WWII more than 700 factories were relocated to the Urals, beyond the reach of the advancing Nazis. The Urals became a centre of Soviet weapons manufacturing: Kalashnikov rifles from Izhevsk, T-34 tanks from Nizhny Tagil, and Katyusha rockets from Chelyabinsk. During the Cold War, secret cities, identified only by number, were constructed in the Urals to house the military nuclear and biochemical industries.

THE URALS AFTER COMMUNISM

In the late Soviet period, a Urals-bred construction engineer turned anticommunist crusader toppled the Soviet dictatorship. Boris Yeltsin had gained a reputation as the energetic and populist-leaning communist governor of Sverdlovsk when the reform-minded Mikhail Gorbachev first introduced him to the national political stage, a move that Gorbachev would soon regret.

In his political fights against the old Soviet order and the neocommunists of the post-Soviet transition, the Urals provided Yeltsin with strong support. Despite the hardships that radical economic reform inflicted on the heavily subsidised industrial sector, Yeltsin scored big election victories in the Urals cities in the 1991 and 1996 Russian presidential campaigns.

As elsewhere in Russia, the postcommunist transition in the Urals did not go according to the early optimistic plans. The region suffered the severe collapse of its manufacturing and agricultural sectors. Public employees went without wages. Rocket scientists became taxi drivers. Mafia turf wars were waged over the right to 'protect' the nascent private business sector. A regional autonomy movement, the short-lived Urals Republic, was not able to forestall a recentralisation by the Kremlin. Meanwhile, former communist political bosses entrenched themselves in elected office.

But after this harsh first decade, signs of economic recovery are now visible, at least in the larger cities. The region's rich export commodities, especially metals, and the revival of the military industrial sector have helped sustain the region.

National Parks

Founded in 1991, Taganay is the first national park in the Urals. The park covers 564 sq km in the western part of the Chelyabinsk Oblast, adjoining the northern suburbs of Zlatoust. It is a long narrow band, 52km long and 10km to 15km wide. Taganay contains a wide variety of landscapes, from flower-filled meadows to mountain tundra, as well as some of the southern Urals' notable ridges (Small, Middle and Big Taganay and Itsyl). It is also well known for its mineral reserves, including Russia's largest deposit of aventurine (known locally as taganit). The park is a popular destination for hiking, mountain biking and rafting.

In the far northern Komi Republic, the Virgin Komi Forests are designated as a World Heritage Site by Unesco. Its three million hectares are mostly tundra and mountain tundra, as well as an extensive area of virgin boreal forest (one of the largest expanses remaining in Europe). This vast area of conifers, aspens, birches, peat bogs, rivers

THE URALS

LIZARD QUEENS AND STONY CULTS

Legend attributes the mineral wealth of the Urals to the workings of a mysterious queen, who lived within a copper-lined mountain. She was a black-haired beauty with magical powers, appearing at times endearing and at other times wrathful towards the mortals she encountered in the hills, doting on shepherd boys and dropping boulders on mining bosses. The queen often took the form of a lizard.

The Lizard Queen is an enduring Russian myth about the Ural Mountains. Her story was passed down generations of Urals inhabitants by oral tradition. The adventures of the reptilian heroine were finally put to pen by writer Pavel Bazhov. Born in Perm in 1879, Bazhov learned the stories as a boy from old miners. His collection of 52 interconnected fairy tales, *The Malachite Box*, was published in 1939 and quickly became a standard of Soviet children's literature.

Perhaps the most popular Bazhov tale is *The Stone Flower*, which concerns a young man, Danil, who left home to learn the art of stone cutting. He journeyed into the mountains and was enticed into the cave of the queen, where she taught him the craft, but then refused to allow him to leave. The story is the subject of a famous ballet by the composer Sergei Prokofiev.

The magic of minerals is not confined to the lizard people of yore. New Age mystics tout the hidden powers of Urals stone. Malachite is said to strengthen spirituality, while jasper increases intellectual capabilities. The pink-coloured rhodonite is supposed to increase self-reliance. Dreamy green amazonite brings a sense of calm or – if used to excess – laziness. Agate leads to well-being and longevity.

After decades of communist-imposed atheism, some Russians, looking to fill a spiritual void, have formed a Bazhov-inspired pagan cult. The followers meet in the woods of the Urals each summer to worship the Lizard Queen of Copper Mountain. After paying homage to a wooden effigy of Her Scaliness, they set the figure ablaze. This Bazhov Academy of Secret Knowledge has been officially deemed an unworthy and destructive sect by the Russian Orthodox Church.

and natural lakes is a valuable resource for scientists studying biodiversity.

Getting There & Around

The major cities of the Urals are all accessible by train: in the Middle Urals, Perm and Yekaterinburg are on the main line of the trans-Siberian route; while the southern Urals cities, Chelyabinsk and Ufa, also have direct routes from the west. The trickier part is travelling from north to south within the Urals, where the mountains tend to make train routes winding and slow. In these cases, travelling by bus is often the better option.

PERM ПЕРМЬ

☎ 3422 / pop 1 million / ☽ Moscow + 2hr

Dominated by heavily trafficked avenues and concrete blocks, Perm is a modern, industrial city that most travellers could bear to miss. Its chequered history, however, draws them in to bear witness to the combined thousands of years that were lost by prisoners at the notorious labour camp Perm-36. and to discover what has become of the once-secret city of Molotov (named

during the Soviet period for the foreign minister who was also the namesake of the explosive cocktail).

Today, Perm is not as menacing, but its reputation as a bland, provincial capital persists. (Chekhov used Perm as inspiration for the city his Three Sisters were so desperate to leave.) It is unfortunate, as the city boasts its fair share of cultural attractions, from a championship basketball team to the one-of-a-kind Prikamye art collection

Economically, the city is thriving. Evidence of its military history is everywhere, but so are signs of ongoing economic development, from shiny new bank buildings to sushi bars.

Orientation

Perm sprawls along the south bank of the Kama River. The city centre is at the intersection of ul Lenina and Komsomolsky pr, and Perm-II station is about 2.5km southwest of here.

Information

Internet Centre (☎ 373 605; ul Kommunisticheskaya 77; per hr R30; ☽ 24hr) Often crowded with young boys playing video games, but the large, dark hall has plenty of computers.

Main post office (ul Lenina 29; per hr R30; ☪ 24hr) Also offers Internet access.

Permtourist (☎ 906 237; www.permtourist.ru in Russian; ul Lenina 58) Arranges local excursions as well as cruises along the Kama River and further to the Volga.

Sberbank (ul Lenina 31; ☪ 10am-8pm Mon-Sat) Cashes travellers cheques and gives credit card advances.

Sights

Housed in the grand Cathedral of Christ Transfiguration on the banks of the Kama, the **Perm State Art Gallery** (☎ 129 524, 122 395; www.sculpture.permonline.ru; Komsomolsky pr 4; admission R30; ☪ 10am-6pm Tue-Fri, 11am-7pm Sat, noon-6pm Sun) is renowned for its collection of

Prikamye wooden sculpture. Dating back to the 17th century, the religious figures are examples of a primitive style that is unique to the Perm region. The museum also contains a large collection of icons, some works by the Peredvizhniki ('the Wanderers', a group of 19th-century Russian artists) and temporary exhibits by contemporary artists.

Next door, the **Ethnographic Museum** (☎ 122 456; Komsomolsky pr 6; admission R10; ☪ 10am-6pm Sat-Thu) features mainly stuffed animals but houses some exhibits on local history.

The **Sergei Diaghilev Museum** (☎ 120 610; Sibirskaya ul 33; admission free; ☪ 9am-6pm Mon-Fri) is a small, lovingly curated exhibition on this world-famous ballet and opera impresario

THE URALS

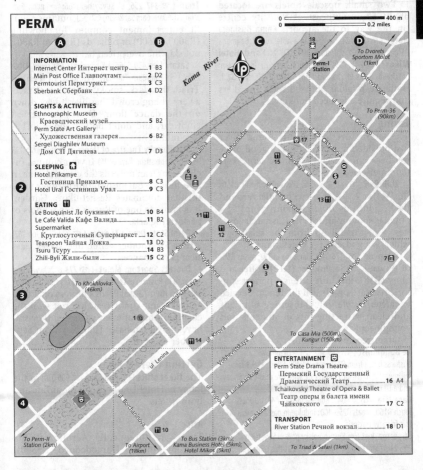

PERM

0   400 m
0   0.2 miles

Kama River

To Dvorets Sportom Molot (1km)

Perm-I Station

To Perm-36 (90km)

INFORMATION
Internet Center Интернет центр **1** B3
Main Post Office Главпочтамт **2** D2
Permtourist Пермтурист **3** C3
Sberbank Сбербанк **4** D2

SIGHTS & ACTIVITIES
Ethnographic Museum
    Краеведческий музей **5** B2
Perm State Art Gallery
    Художественная галерея **6** B2
Sergei Diaghilev Museum
    Дом СП Дягилева **7** D3

SLEEPING 🛏
Hotel Prikamye
    Гостиница Прикамье **8** C3
Hotel Ural Гостиница Урал **9** C3

EATING 🍴
Le Bouquinist Ле букинист **10** B4
Le Café Valida Кафе Валида **11** B2
Supermarket
    Круглосуточный Супермаркет **12** C2
Teaspoon Чайная Ложка **13** D2
Tsuru Цуру **14** B3
Zhili-Byli Жили-были **15** C2

To Khokhlovka (46km)

To Casa Mia (500m); Kungur (150km)

ENTERTAINMENT 🎭
Perm State Drama Theatre
    Пермский Государственный
    Драматический Театр **16** A4
Tchaikovsky Theatre of Opera & Ballet
    Театр оперы и балета имени
    Чайковского **17** C2

TRANSPORT
River Station Речной вокзал **18** D1

To Perm-II Station (2km)

To Airport (18km)

To Bus Station (3km); Kama Business Hotel (5km); Hotel Mikos (5km)

To Triad & Safari (1km)

(1872–1929), whose family came from the
Perm region.

Sleeping

Hotel Ural (☎ 906 258, 906 220; ural-hotel@permtourist
.ru; ul Lenina 58; s/d from R720/1000, 25% reservation
fee) Average distance from front desk to
drab room is about 1km. This monolith
has the charm of a Soviet apparatchik,
but the central location is convenient. For
R1500/1800, you'll get a slightly upgraded
room with telephone and TV, as well as
breakfast.

Hotel Prikamye (☎ /fax 348 662; Komsomolsky
pr 27; s without bathroom R700, s/d with bathroom from
R1200/1600) If Hotel Ural is full, another decent option is right around the corner.

Two small, upscale hotels are located
about 5km southeast of the city centre
on the way to the airport. **Kama Business
Hotel** (☎ 280 248; www.kama-hotel.ru; ul Baumana
25b; s with breakfast from R2900; ▨ ▧) and **Hotel
Mikos** (☎ 241 999; www.micos.perm.ru in Russian;
Stakhanovskaya ul 10a; s/d from R2400/2900; ▧ ▨).
Both are popular with business travellers
and require advanced booking.

Eating

The terrace overlooking the Kama River
just outside the Art Gallery is a good place
for beer and shashlyk from a *letny kafe*
(summer café).

Zhili-Byli (☎ 125 771; Sibirskaya ul 9; meals R150-
200; ☺ 11am-2am) A chain with outlets around
the region, this *traktir* (country inn) is a
popular spot for affordable Russian favourites. You can fill up from the salad bar,
which is a godsend for vegetarians.

Teaspoon (☎ 126 048; Sibirskaya ul 19a; meals R30-
60; ☺ 9am-10pm) Serving tea (R12), coffee and
bliny (R18), this little café is a perfect stop
for breakfast or for a light lunch. Service
is cafeteria-style, but the setting is bright
and clean, attracting lots of students and
young people.

Other recommendations:

Le Bouquinist (☎ 449 582; ul Borchaninova 12;
business lunch from R150, meals R400-500; ☺ 9.30am-
midnight) A romantic French café with live music on Friday
and a DJ on Thursday and Saturday.

Casa Mia (☎ 377 647; Komsomolsky pr 47; business
lunch R160, meals R250-400) Indulge in pasta or pizza at
this friendly trattoria.

Supermarket (cnr Komsomolsky pr & ul Sovetskaya;
☺ 24hr) Stock up for your train ride at this central shop.

Tsuru (☎ 363 460; ul Lenina 66a; business lunch R120,
meals R200-400) Evidence that the sushi craze has not
bypassed Perm.

Entertainment

Triad (☎ 347 256; ul Kuybysheva 66; ☺ noon-6pm
Mon-Fri, 10am-6am Sat & Sun) Check out this neon-
lit entertainment complex for bowling
(R300 to R600) or billiards (R100 to R200),
but skip the overpriced bar.

Safari (☎ 450 556; ul Kuybysheva 66; cover R100-
250; ☺ 11pm-8am Thu-Sat) Tucked in behind
Triad, this dark, smoky nightclub attracts
a very young crowd that likes to get down
on the dance floor. Don your sexiest
clubwear, and don't bother show up before midnight.

Tchaikovsky Theatre of Opera & Ballet (☎ 123
087; Kommunisticheskaya ul 25) If your cultural in-
clinations lean towards the classical, take in
a performance at the beautiful baroque theatre that dominates Reshetnikova Garden.
It is home to one of Russia's top schools of
performing arts.

Perm State Drama Theatre (☎ 361 092, 360 767;
ul Lenina 53) Another venue that stages classical performances.

Dvorets Sportom Molot (☎ 773 897; www.ural
-great.ru in Russian; ul Lebedeva 13; tickets from R50; box
office ☺ 10am-7.30pm) Perm's professional basketball team, Ural Great, has not won the
championship for a few years, but they still
have a loyal fan base. They play from September to April.

Getting There & Away

The **ticket office** (☺ 9am-8pm; ☎ 906 030) in the
lobby of Hotel Ural is useful for airline and
train tickets.

AIR

There are three daily Aeroflot flights
to/from Moscow Domodedovo (R3500),

with additional flights to Yekaterinburg (R2500, four weekly), Samara (R3300, three weekly) and St Petersburg (R5100, two weekly). Weekly flights go to Novosibirsk, Baku and Tashkent. **Lufthansa** (☎ 284 442) flies to/from Frankfurt twice a week.

BOAT

The **river station** (☎ 199 304) is at the eastern end of ul Ordzhonikidze, opposite Perm-I station. Boats depart here for cruises down the Kama River to the Volga.

BUS

Plans for a new bus station near Perm-II train station will probably not be realised until 2007. In the meantime, use the old station at the southern end of ul Popova for buses to Khokhlovka and Chusovoy.

TRAIN

Perm-II, the city's major train station, is on the trans-Siberian route. Many trains travel the route from Moscow, including the *firmeny* train (a nicer, long-distance train) called the *Kama* (20 hours, R1950). Heading east, the next major stop is Yekaterinburg (R650, six hours). Trains also travel every second day, more frequently in summer, to Chelyabinsk (R1050, 12 hours) and Kazan (R706, 16 hours). Note that some trains to Kazan depart from the *gorny trakt* (mountain track) on the north side of Perm-II, as opposed to the *glavny trakt* (main track).

The crumbling Perm-I station, 1km northeast of the centre, is used only for suburban trains, such as those to Kungur.

Getting Around

Buses 110, 119 and 120 serve the airport (35 minutes), or take a taxi for about R250. Take tram 7 or any bus or trolleybus between Perm-II station and Hotel Ural.

AROUND PERM

Khokhlovka Хохловка

The **Architecture-Ethnography Museum** (☎ 997 182; admission R35; ⌚ 9am-6pm Mon-Sun late-May – mid-Oct) is set in the rolling countryside near the village of Khokhlovka, about 45km north of Perm. Its impressive collection of wooden buildings includes two churches dating from the turn of the 18th century. Most of the structures are from the 19th or early 20th centuries, including an old firehouse, a salt production facility and a Khanty *izba* (traditional wooden cottage). A few buses a day serve Khokhlovka from Perm (one hour, R50).

EVEN WALLS HAVE EARS *Yakov L Klots*

'Even walls have ears,' goes the Russian saying. At Perm-36, the former camp for political prisoners, the walls have survived…unlike most of those who were kept behind them. Dissidents, poets, intelligentsia. Ordinary people whose lives had been taken away and silenced. Concrete floors, barred windows, plank beds, aluminium bowls, spoons and mugs, and the barbed wire coiling along the borders of the restricted areas: all outlived the inmates.

Nowadays, representing the camp's daily routine with an existential accuracy, the walls keep the memory of bygone times – of prisoners who were not fated to see their place of detention become a museum, of halls walked by prison guards instead of high-school students.

Before the first prisoners were brought to Perm-36, all of the trees around the grounds were destroyed. The purpose was to prevent convicts from determining in which part of our vast country they had landed. Prisoners were not allowed to leave their cells, so they could not hear the gush of the Chusovaya river, which flowed a few hundred metres from the camp's gate. And now the rich local landscape that they might spy through narrow window slits was wiped out.

But the guards were powerless to prevent local birds from flying and singing above the camp barracks. So an inmate – a biologist sentenced to 25 years of 'special regime imprisonment' – identified the bird species by their songs, and determined he was in the Urals.

One can never know for sure what tomorrow is going to be like. Perhaps the darkest side of life in imprisonment is the constant awareness that tomorrow is *not* going to be different from yesterday. The deathly silence that resounds in the damp, dark cells at Perm-36 reminds us of what this place was like yesterday.

Perm-36 Пермь-36

Once an ominous island in the Gulag Archipelago, **Perm-36** (☎ 120 030; www.perm36.ru in Russian; admission R60, ☺ by appointment) is now a fascinating museum and moving memorial to the victims of political repression.

For most of its history since 1946, Perm-36 was a labour camp for political prisoners, in other words, dissidents. Countless artists, scientists and intellectuals spent years in the cold, damp cells, many in solitary confinement. They worked at mundane tasks like assembling fasteners and survived on measly portions of bread and gruel.

Much of the evidence of this history was destroyed when the camp closed in 1988, but the museum staff is dedicated to recreating the camp as it was. Windowless cells and barbed wire are eerie reminders that this history is not so distant. The exhibits make the reality of prison life all too clear.

The memorial centre is about 10km from the town of Chusovoy, which is 100km east of Perm. A new road makes the museum accessible by bus from Perm. Alternatively, museum staff can make arrangements for a taxi for about R3000. A guided tour costs R600. Museum management plans to build a small on-site hotel and conference facility, expected to open in 2007.

Kungur Кунгур

Founded in 1663, the town of Kungur was a copper-smelting centre during the 17th and 18th centuries. Many notable (though dilapidated) buildings remain from this heyday, including **All Saints Church**, a 17th-century **governor's house** and the 19th-century arcade, **Gostiny Dvor**. Get the full story at the **Regional Local Studies Museum** (ul Gogolya 36; admission R20; ☺ 11am-5pm).

Kungur was long a popular destination for potential spelunkers investigating the **Kungur Ice Cave** (Ledyanaya peshchera; admission R350; ☺ 10am-5pm), about 5km out of town. The extensive network of caves stretches for more than 5km, although only about 1.5km are open to explore. The grottos are adorned with unique ice formations, frozen waterfalls and underground lakes. Permtourist (see p433) arranges tours here, as well as accommodation in the adjacent **Stalagmit Hotel** (☎ /fax 34271-39 723; r R600, upgraded r from R1200).

Trains from Perm (R60, 2½ hours, eight daily) arrive at the station on ul Bachurina in Kungur. A day trip is possible if you start early but check the train schedule in advance.

YEKATERINBURG ЕКАТЕРИНБУРГ

☎ 343 / pop 1.29 million / ☺ Moscow +2hr

From the execution of Tsar Nicholas II and his family in 1918 to the high-profile Mafia killings in the 1990s, Yekaterinburg is notorious for its bloody history. Contemporary Yekaterinburg remembers these events, attracting pilgrims and tourists alike to the sites associated with the Romanov deaths.

As the economic and cultural capital of the Urals region, however, the city offers visitors much more than a dramatic history. The Urals' mineral wealth is on display in the city's many museums, while the ongoing economic boom is evident in the crowded cafés and clubs around the centre. Yekaterinburg also has the accommodation options and facilities to serve as a convenient base for adventure activities and winter sports in the Urals.

History

Yekaterinburg was founded as a factory-fort in 1723 as part of Peter the Great's push to exploit the Ural region's mineral riches. The city was named after two Yekaterinas: Peter's wife (later Empress Catherine I), and the Russian patron saint of mining.

Yekaterinburg is most famous as the place where the Bolsheviks murdered Tsar Nicholas II and his family in July 1918. Six years later, the town was renamed Sverdlovsk, after Yakov Sverdlov, a leading Bolshevik who was Vladimir Lenin's right-hand man until his death in the flu epidemic of 1919.

WWII turned Sverdlovsk into a major industrial centre, as hundreds of factories were transferred here from vulnerable areas west of the Urals. The city was closed to foreigners until 1990 because of its many defence plants. Remnants of this era still litter the city, with fighter planes proudly displayed in schoolyards and missiles arranged outside the city's Military History Museum.

It was one such missile that in 1960 brought down US pilot Gary Powers and his U2 spy plane in this area. Powers, who bailed out successfully, was exchanged for a Soviet spy in 1962.

During the late 1970s a civil engineering graduate of the local university, Boris Yeltsin, began to make his political mark, rising to become regional Communist Party boss before being promoted to Moscow in 1985.

In 1991 Yekaterinburg took back its original name. After suffering economic depression and Mafia lawlessness in the early 1990s, business has been on the upswing for the past decade.

Orientation

The city centre lies between the main boulevards, pr Lenina and ul Malysheva, and runs from pl 1905 goda in the west to ul Lunacharskogo in the east. The train station is 2km north of the centre on ul Sverdlova, which changes its name to ul Karla Libknekhta closer to the centre.

Information

Alfa Bank (☎ 371 4226; ul Malysheva 33a) Has a 24-hour ATM that dispenses roubles or US dollars.

Coffee.IN (☎ 277 6873; ul 8 Marta 8; per hr R50; ☺ 24hr) Internet café located in the shopping centre Mytny Dvor. Enter from the back.

Dom Knigi (☎ 358 1898; ul Antona Valeka 12; ☺ 9am-7pm) Best for foreign-language and local-interest books.

Ekaterinburg Guide Center (☎ 268 1604; www .ekaterinburg-guide.com; ul Krasnoarmeyskaya 1) An enthusiastic group that organises English-language tours of

THE URALS

BONES OF CONTENTION

What happened to the Romanovs – even after their 1918 execution – is a mixture of the macabre, the mysterious and the just plain messy.

The Romanov remains resurfaced back in 1976, when a group of local scientists discovered them near Porosinkov Log, about 3km from Ganina Yama. So politically sensitive was this issue during Soviet times that the discovery was kept secret until the remains were finally fully excavated in 1991. The bones of nine people were tentatively identified as Tsar Nicholas II, his wife Tsaritsa Alexandra, three of their four daughters, the royal doctor and three servants.

Absent were any remains of the royal couple's only son, Tsarevitch Alexey. Also notably absent was the fourth daughter, which gave a new lease of life to theories that the youngest daughter, Anastasia, had somehow escaped.

In 1992 bone samples from the excavated skeletons were sent to the British government's Forensic Science Service, to be tested by DNA identification techniques. Using blood and hair samples from distant descendants of the tsar and tsarina, the scientists established with 'more than 98.5%' certainty that the bones were those of the royal family.

In 1994, an official Russian inquiry team in Yekaterinburg managed to piece together the skulls found in the pit, badly damaged by rifle butts, hand grenades and acid. Using plaster models of the faces, DNA tests and dental records, they determined that the three daughters found were Olga, Tatyana – and Anastasia. The missing daughter was Maria.

Maria and Alexey's bodies have never been discovered. But the now-official story of the Romanov execution explains their absence. And what a tale of ghoulish bungling it is.

According to the Russian team, all five children died with their parents in the cellar of Dom Ipatyeva. The bodies were dumped at Ganina Yama, an abandoned mine 16km away, followed by several grenades intended to collapse the mine shaft. The mine, however, did not collapse. It was then decided to distribute the bodies among various smaller mines and pour acid on them. But the expert in charge of the acid fell off his horse and broke his leg; and the truck carrying the bodies became bogged in a swamp.

By now understandably desperate, the disposal team opted to bury the corpses. They tried burning Alexey and Maria in preparation, but realised it would take days to burn all the bodies properly, so the others were just put in a pit and doused with acid. Even then, most of the acid soaked away into the ground – leaving the bones to be uncovered 73 years later.

In mid-1998 the royal remains were finally buried at St Petersburg's SS Peter & Paul Cathedral, alongside their predecessors dating back to Peter the Great. The Orthodox Church, however, has never recognised that the royal remains were removed from Ganina Yama, and church officials were not in attendance at the burial in St Petersburg.

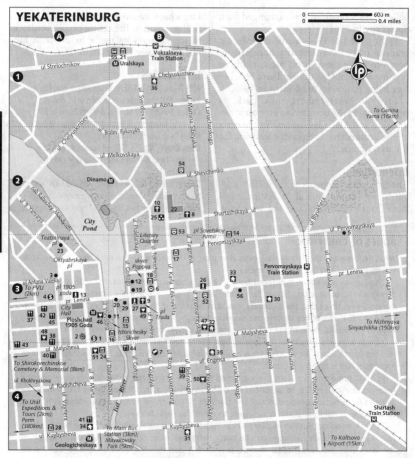

YEKATERINBURG

0 —————— 600 m
0 —————— 0.4 miles

the city and trips into the countryside. Popular excursions include rafting, hiking and biking trips in the Urals (€40 to €52 per person), as well as Ganina Yama and the Europe-Asia border (see p444). Enter through the side entrance of Bolshoy Ural Hotel. Also arranges discounted accommodation and home stays.

Gutabank (☎ 359 2621; pr Lenina 27; ⏰ 9am-4.30pm Mon-Fri) One of the few places in the city that accepts travellers cheques.

Karta (☎ 375 6290; ul Pervomayskaya 74; ⏰ 9am-1pm & 2-6pm Mon-Fri, 9am-2pm Sat) An extensive selection of maps of Yekaterinburg and Sverdlovsk Oblast, as well as other cities and regions.

Main post office (pr Lenina 39; ⏰ 10am-7pm Mon-Fri) Offers Internet and international telephone connections.

Ural Expeditions & Tours (☎ 376 2800; http://welcome-ural.ru; 23 Posadskaya ul) This group of geologists

from the Sverdlovsk Mining Institute has found a unique way to market their skills and knowledge – leading trekking, rafting and horse-riding trips to all parts of the Urals, including Taganay National Park. English-speaking guides.

Sights & Activities
ROMANOV DEATH SITE
On the night of 16 July 1918, Tsar Nicholas II, his wife and children were murdered in the basement of a local merchant's house, known as Dom Ipatyeva (named for its owner, Nikolay Ipatyev). During the Soviet period, the building housed a local museum of atheism, but it was demolished in 1977 by then-governor Boris Yeltsin, who feared it would attract monarchist sympathisers.

INFORMATION
Alfa-Bank Альфа-Банк **1** A3
Coffee.IN **2** A3
Dom Knigi Дом книги **3** A3
Ekaterinburg Guide Centre
   Екатеринбургский центр
   гидов ....(see 32)
German Consulate ....(see 31)
Gutabank Гутабанк **4** A3
Karta Карта магазин **5** D2
Main Post Office Почтамт **6** B3
US & UK Consulates General
   Генеральные консульства
   Великобритании и США **7** B4

SIGHTS & ACTIVITIES
Ascension Church
   Вознесенская церковь **8** B2
Chapel of St Catherine
   Часовня Святой Екатерины **9** B3
Chapel of the Revered Martyr Grand
   Princess Yelizaveta Fyodorovna .....(see 25)
Church of the Blood
   Церковь на Крови **10** B2
Geological Alley
   Геологическая аллея **11** B3
Governor's Mansion
   Резиденция Губернатора **12** B3
Lenin Statue Памятник Ленину **13** B4
Military History Museum
   Военно-Исторический
   музей **14** C2
Museum of Architecture & Industry
   Музей истории архитектуры
   города и промышленной
   техники Урала **15** B3
Museum of Fine Arts Музей
   изобразительных искусств **16** B3
Museum of Photography
   Музей Фотографии **17** B3

Nevyansk Icon Museum
   Музей Невянская икона **18** B3
Nikolai Sevastianof Mansion
   Дом Николая Севастьянова **19** B3
Order of Lenin Орден Ленина **20** B3
Railway Museum
   Железнодорожный музей **21** B1
Rastoguev-Kharitonov Mansion
   Усадьба
   Расторгуев-Харитонова **22** B2
Regional Government Building
   Дом областной
   администрации **23** A3
Regional Studies Museum **24** A4
Romanov Death Site
   Место убийства Романовых **25** B2
Sverdlov Statue
   Памятник Свердлову **26** B3
Tatishchev & de Gennin Statue
   Памятник Татищеву и дэ
   Геннин **27** B3
Ural Geology Museum
   Уральский геологический
   музей **28** A4
Urals Mineralogical Museum
   Уральский минералогический музей
   (see 32)
Water Tower
   Водонапорная башня **29** B3

SLEEPING 🛏
Academy of Geology Hotel
   Гостиница Академии
   геологии **30** C3
Atrium Palace Hotel
   Атриум палас отель.............................**31** B4
Bolshoy Ural Hotel
   Гостиница Большой Урал **32** C3
Country Inn ....(see 32)
Hotel Iset Гостиница Исеть **33** C3

Hotel Magister
   Гостиница Магистр.............................**34** A4
Hotel Premier
   Гостиница Премьер **35** C4
Hotel Sverdlovsk
   Гостиница Свердловск **36** B1

EATING 🍴
Dacha Дача **37** A3
Em Sam Ем сам **38** A3
Georgian Kitchen
   Грузинская кухня **39** B4
Grand Buffet Гранд-буфет **40** A4
Kupets Купец..**41** A4
Mak Pik Мак Пик **42** A4
Nigora Нигора **43** A4
Port Stanley Порт Стенли **44** B4
Uspensky Shopping Center (Food Court)
   Успенский торговый центр........**45** A3

DRINKING 🍸
Coffee Shop No 7 Кофейня No 7 ....**46** A3
Gordon's Гордонс...................................**47** B3
Old Dublin Старый Дублин **48** A3
Rosy Jane Рози Джейн **49** B3
Tinkoff Тинкофф **50** B4
Zebra Зебра **51** A4

ENTERTAINMENT 🎭
Opera & Ballet Theatre
   Театр оперы и балета........................**52** B3
Philharmonic Филармония **53** B2
Vodoley Водолей **54** B2

TRANSPORT
Bus Station Автовокзал..........................**55** B1
Railway & Air Kassa
   Железнодорожные и Авиа
   кассы ....(see 1)
Transaero City Centre Трансаэро......**56** C3

THE URALS

Today, the site is marked by an iron cross dating from 1991, and a second marble cross from 1998 when the Romanovs' remains were sent to St Petersburg for burial in the family vault.

The massive Byzantine-style **Church of the Blood** (☎ 371 6168; ul Tolmachyova 34) now dominates this site. While many believe these funds might have been better spent, this new church was built to honour the Romanov family, now elevated to the status of saints. Rumour has it that this controversial church contains the most expensively commissioned icon in all of Russia.

Nearby, the pretty wooden **Chapel of the Revered Martyr Grand Princess Yelizaveta Fyodorovna** (⏰ 9am-5.30pm) honours the royal family's great-aunt and faithful friend. After her relatives' murders, this pious nun met an even worse end, when she was thrown down a mineshaft, poisoned with gas and buried. You can visit this spot, where a monastery has recently been built, on a trip to Nizhnyaya Sinyachikha.

MUSEUMS

The city of Yekaterinburg grew up around Istorichesky skver (Historical Sq), where today you'll find a clutch of tiny museums housed in the historic buildings. Peek into the old **water tower**, one of the city's oldest

structures, then head over to the old mining-equipment factory and mint buildings. These contain the **Museum of Architecture & Industry** (☎ 371 4045; ul Gorkogo 4 & 5; ⏰ 11am-6pm Tue-Sat), which displays the machinery used in the mining industry from the 18th and 19th centuries up through WWII.

On the opposite side of the river, the star exhibit of the **Museum of Fine Arts** (☎ 371 0626; ul Voevodina 5; admission R50; ⏰ 11am-6pm Wed-Sun) is the elaborate Kasli Iron Pavilion that won prizes in the 1900 Paris Expo.

The **Regional Studies Museum** (☎ 376 4762; ul Malysheva 46; admission R30; ⏰ 11am-5pm Mon-Fri) has some interesting exhibits on the Romanovs and the Old Believers in the Ural region.

For a stunning introduction to the Urals semiprecious stones, visit Vladimir Pelepenko's private collection, also known as the **Urals Mineralogical Museum** (☎ 350 6019; ul Krasnoarmeyskaya 1A; admission R50; ⏰ 10am-7pm Mon-Fri, 10am-5pm Sat & Sun), in Bolshoy Ural Hotel. This impressive collection contains thousands of examples of minerals, stones and crystals from the region, many crafted into mosaics, jewellery and other artistic pieces.

More-serious geologists will appreciate the **Ural Geology Museum** (☎ 251 4938; ul Kuybysheva 39; admission R50; ⏰ 11am-5pm Mon-Sat), which has over 500 carefully catalogued Ural region minerals and a collection of meteorites.

The **Military History Museum** (☎ 350 1742; ul Pervomayskaya 27; admission R30; ⊙ 9am-4pm Tue-Sat) is a must for military buffs.

Other unique museums:

Museum of Photography (☎ 371 0637; ul Karla Libknekhta 36; admission R20; ⊙ 11am-5.30pm Wed-Mon) Features evocative photos of old Yekaterinburg.

Nevyansk Icon Museum (☎ 365 9840; ul Tolmachyova 21; admission free; ⊙ noon-8pm Wed-Sun) Icons from the 17th to the 20th century, from the local Nevyansk school.

Railway Museum (☎ 358 4222; ul Chelyuskintsev; ⊙ noon-6pm Tue-Sat) Housed in the old train station, dating from 1881. Exhibits highlight the history of the railroad in the Urals, including a re-creation of the office of the Stalin-era railway director.

WINTER SPORTS

Winter in the Urals lasts a long time, making this a terrific place for winter sports. The rolling hills that surround Yekaterinburg are breathtaking when covered with a fresh layer of snow. Urals Expeditions & Tours (p438) can arrange dogsledding excursions (per person €65), as well as winter hikes and snowmobile trips.

If there's no time to leave the city, head to **Mayakovsky Park**, 5km south of town, for cross-country skiing. Take tram 3 from the train station or tram 29 from ul Lenina. Equipment is available to rent.

Walking Tour

A walking tour is the ideal way to take in the scope of the city's tumultuous history. Start at Istorichesky skver where pr

Lenina crosses a small dam forming the Gorodskoy prud (City Pond) on its north side. This area, better known as the *plotinka* (little dam), was where Yekaterinburg began back in 1723. Water from the dam powered an iron forge for mining equipment and a mint; these historic buildings now house the **Museum of Architecture & Industry (1**; p439).

The bridge on ul Lenina holds the striking, red, sculpted **Order of Lenin (2)** given to the city for honourable service during WWII. On the west side of the *plotinka* is **Geological Alley (3)**, a small park dotted with rocks from the Ural region.

About 100m west along pr Lenina is **ploshchad 1905 goda (4)**. The impressive Stalinist building with the clock tower is the **town hall (5)**. The looming **statue of Lenin (6)** occupies the spot where once stood one of Yekaterinburg's main cathedrals and a statue of Tsar Alexander II Romanov, both destroyed in 1930 by Bolshevik radicals. Further west, artists sell their wares along the tree-lined strip in the centre of pr Lenina.

Cross the bridge heading east on pr Lenina, where the founders of Yekaterin-

---

WALK FACTS

Start Istorichesky Skver
Finish Istorichesky Skver
Distance 3½km
Duration 2 hours

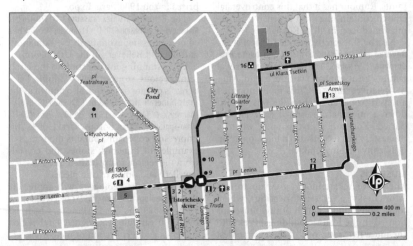

burg – Tatishchev and de Gennin – proudly hold the tsar's decree. This **monument to the founders of the city (7)** was unveiled on the city's 275th anniversary in 1998. The nearby **Chapel of St Catherine (8)** was erected in the same year on the site of a former cathedral honouring the patron saint of mining.

Across the street, the architecture demonstrates the radical changes of the 19th and 20th centuries. The eclectic 19th-century **Nikolai Sevastianof mansion (9)**, which is now a trade union's headquarters, was a rich merchant's attempt to outshine the **governor's mansion (10)**, which stands next door. In total contrast are the clean lines of the **regional government building (11)** across the pond, a prime example of 1930s constructivism. Further east, a **statue of Yakov Sverdlov (12)** stands in front of the Opera & Ballet Theatre (p443).

At the roundabout, head north on ul Lunacharskogo towards **ploshchad Sovetskoy Armii (13)**, dominated by a powerful monument. The giant soldier with downcast head commemorates primarily losses in Russia's Afghanistan War (1979–89), but plaques around the statue also note those lost in other conflicts during the Cold War years.

Continue north from the square along ul Mamina-Sibiryaka. A pretty park climbs up the hill known locally as the Yekaterinburg Acropolis. At the top is the ostentatious **Rastorguev-Kharitonov mansion (14)** and the restored **Ascension Church (15**; ul Karla Tsetkin 11). Immediately ahead of the church is the **Romanov execution site (16**; p438).

Walk a few blocks west along ul Pervomayskaya. The block north of here on ul Proletarskaya is known as the **Literary Quarter (17)**. Several of these wooden houses are museums dedicated to local writers. Once

you reach the City Pond, follow the shoreline south back to Istorichesky skver.

Sleeping
BUDGET
Ekaterinburg Guide Center (☎ 268 1604; www .ekaterinburg-guide.com; ul Krasnoarmeyskaya 1, 1-/2-/3-person home stays with breakfast €22/36/52) Experience real Russian living by staying with a local family. The agency also rents apartments for €40 to €50 per night – a bargain if you are travelling in a group.

Bolshoy Ural Hotel (☎ 350 6695; fax 355 0583; ul Krasnoarmeyskaya 1; s with/without bathroom R1450/500) This place lives up to its name: if nothing else, it is indeed *bolshoy* (large), occupying an entire city block. The somewhat seedy atmosphere is buffered by the prime location – steps from the Opera Theatre and the all-important Gordon's Scottish pub.

MIDRANGE
Academy of Geology Hotel (☎ 350 0508, 350 0510; pr Lenina 54, Bldg 6; r with breakfast R1200) This decent budget option offers attentive service and four smart, spacious rooms. Located in a quiet complex off the main road, it is difficult to find. Enter the courtyard from ul Bazhova and look for the marble entrance with the unmarked metal door. Unfortunately, this place does not register visas, so it is not a good option for visitors staying more than a day or two.

Hotel Sverdlovsk (☎ 353 6574; fax 353 6248; ul Chelyuskintsev 106; s/d from R1200/1500) Gives a choice between cheap and dilapidated rooms or upgraded and overpriced. In its favour is its location opposite the station.

Country Inn (ul Malysheva) Under construction at the time of research, this hotel is expected to be a Western-managed three-star tourist hotel, filling a void of midrange options. It is due to open in 2006; contact the Ekaterinburg Guide Center for information.

TOP END
Hotel Premier (☎ 563 897; fax 563 880; www.premier -hotel.ru; ul Krasnoarmeyskaya 23; s/d with breakfast R4000/5300; ✷ ▯) Another small and personable European-style hotel. Rooms can be a bit stuffy in winter when air-con is not working, but otherwise they are spacious and stylish. The location offers the best of both worlds: a quiet residential street, just a few steps from the main drag.

AUTHOR'S CHOICE

If **Hotel Iset** (☎ 350 0128; hotel_resr@etel.ru; pr Lenina 69; s/d with breakfast from R2900/3600) looks funky from the street, it is because it's shaped like a hammer and sickle when seen from the sky. All of the rooms at this retro Soviet-style hotel have been upgraded, featuring hardwood floors, new bathrooms and odd furniture ensembles. It's all part of the charm.

Hotel Magister (☎ 229 7044, 257 4206; magister1@ etel.ru; ul 8 Marta 50; s/d with breakfast R4100/4600; ☒ ▢) Quaint, comfortable rooms and accommodating staff make the Magister a long-standing favourite with visitors to Yekaterinburg. New windows block out the noise from the busy street below. This small, private hotel is 'home' for many long-term business travellers, so book well in advance.

Atrium Palace Hotel (☎ 359 6000; www.atrium hotel.ru; ul Kuybysheva 44; s/d incl breakfast €210/260; ☒ ☒ ▢ ☒) Atrium Palace once claimed to be the only five-star hotel east of Moscow. This snazzy place has several pricey restaurants, a popular bar and nightclub, plus a fitness centre and sauna. Rack rates are quoted, but discounts are usually available, especially if you make your reservation through the Ekaterinburg Guide Center.

Eating
RESTAURANTS
Dacha (☎ 379 3569; pr Lenina 20a; meals R200-300) Each room in this restaurant is decorated as a room in a Russian country house, from the casual garden to the more formal dining room. It's a great place to enjoy unbeatable Russian cuisine and hospitality.

Port Stanley (☎ 355 1955; ul Gorkogo 10; meals R600-1000) The sunny terrace on the banks of the Iset makes this a top spot for dining in summer, while the modern interior is also pleasant. The menu is seafood – not from the Iset, we hope. Sample Russian favourites, like grilled sturgeon or herring salad, or more-exotic fare, like sea bass or lobster.

Nigora (☎ 376 3941; ul Malysheva 19; meals R200-300) Nigora offers spicy, filling Uzbek food – soup and *plov* (rice with lamb and carrot) to fill the belly and warm the soul. Heavy wooden tables and a low, painted ceiling add to the cosy, welcoming atmosphere.

Georgian Kitchen (☎ 350 0541; ul Belinskogo 20; meals with wine R300-500; ☻ 24hr) This is a classic Georgian place, complete with kitschy art and Christmas lights. But the shashlyk, *kharcho* (rice with beef or lamb soup) and *khachapuri* (cheese bread) are spicy and delicious. The keyboardist-crooner belting out the ballads never fails to inspire some dancing (or perhaps that's the Georgian wine).

Grand Buffet (☎ 359 8366; ul Malysheva 36; meals R250-350) All-you-can-eat buffet with Russian fare. You'll find nearly anything you are

craving, as the basement saloon serves Tex-Mex and there's an Italian place next door.

Em Sam (☎ 376 6066; Malysheva 27; meals R150-300; ☻ 11am-midnight) Sushi is the rage all over Russia, and Yekaterinburg is no exception. Nice lunch specials and a convenient location make this place particularly popular. There is another outlet in Bolshoy Ural Hotel.

QUICK EATS & SELF-CATERING
Uspensky Food Court (☎ 371 6744; ul Vainera 10; meals R30-100; ☻ 10am-8pm) On the top floor of the Uspensky shopping centre, this food court offers burgers, pizza, sandwiches, sushi and more. Floor-to-ceiling windows provide a sweeping view of the city centre and a new perspective on the activity below.

Mak Pik (☎ 371 6898; pr Lenina 24/8; meals R100; ☻ 9am-10pm) Now in several locations around the city, Yekaterinburg's original fast-food restaurant specialises in burgers like the 'Big Mak Pik'; it also has pizza, *pelmeni* (Russian-style ravioli) and, of all things, sushi.

Kupets (ul 8 Marta 48; ☻ 24hr) If you're looking for a large, Western-style supermarket with a wide selection of Russian and imported food items, head here.

Drinking
Coffee Shop No 7 (☎ 378 9370; ul Voevodina 4; breakfast R100-200; ☻ 8am-midnight) A pleasant location on the *plotinka*, smooth jazz and frothy cappuccinos. What more can you ask from your local coffee shop?

Old Dublin Pub (☎ 376 5173; ul Khokhryakova 23; meals R400-600, ½L Guinness R140; ☻ noon-2am) A long-standing favourite among expats in Yekaterinburg, this place is actually owned – partially – by an Irish bloke.

Gordon's (☎ 355 4535; Krasnoarmeyskaya ul 1; business lunch R180, meals R400-600; ☻ noon-2am) The aforementioned Irish bloke opened this Scottish pub in 2005, and it promises to be a popular spot, thanks to the excellent food and 12 beers on tap. Bartenders in kilts don't hurt, either.

Rosy Jane (☎ 371 0607; ul Lenina 34; ☻ 24hr) An English pub – not to be confused with the Scottish pub down the street and the Irish pub around the corner. The dark wood bar features seven different draught beers and more than 150 kinds of whisky.

Tinkoff (☎ 378 4008; Krasnoarmeyskaya 64; ½L beer R120; ☻ noon-2am) This microbrewery features seven home-grown brews as well as some

seasonal specialities, plus a menu of sausages, sandwiches and other tasty snacks.
You will recognise the restaurant's open
layout and industrial décor if you have been
to Tinkoff outlets in other cities.

Entertainment

Vodoley (☎ 377 7277; ul Shevchenko 9; ☒ 1pm-6am)
There is something for everyone at this entertainment complex – from bowling to billiards
to dining to dancing. There is strict control at
the door, so be sure to dress the part.

Zebra (☎ 377 6891; ul Malysheva 44; ☒ 10pm-
10am) If you are serious about dancing, this
is the place to strut your stuff. Progressive,
house and techno play all night long.

Philharmonic (☎ 371 4682; www.filarmonia.e-burg
.ru in Russian; ul Karla Libknekhta 38) Yekaterinburg's
top venue for the classical performing arts
often hosts visiting directors and soloists,
as well as the regular performances of the
acclaimed Urals academic orchestra.

Opera & Ballet Theatre (☎ 350 8057; pr Lenina 45A;
tickets from R100) The level of professionalism is
not quite on par with the Philharmonic, but
the ornate baroque theatre is still a lovely
place to see the Russian classics.

Getting There & Away

AIR

The main airport is **Koltsovo** (☎ 226 8909, 264
4202), 15km southeast of the city centre.
Flights go three times a day to/from Moscow (R6000, 2½ hours).

Flights leave almost daily for Irkutsk
(R7500, four hours), Novosibirsk (R5200,
two hours), Samara (R4000, two hours), St
Petersburg (R6000, 2½ hours) and Vladivostok (R13,000, 11 hours). Flights go less
frequently to Baku, Khabarovsk, Krasnodar,
Mineralnye Vody, Odesa, Rostov, Saratov,
Sochi, Tashkent, Volgograd and Yerevan.
Note that some of these flights are operated
by Urals Airlines, which has a poor record
for safety violations (including seven emergency landings in 2004!). A US consulate
advisory warns against flying on any Urals
Airlines flights until this record improves.

Several airlines operate direct flights to
Europe, two or three times a week: **Lufthansa**
(☎ 264 7771; €400 return) flies to Frankfurt; **British Airways** (☎ 264 4216; €500 return) to London;
and **Czech Airlines** (☎ 264 4214) flies directly
to Prague. **Transaero City Centre** (☎ 365 9165; pr
Lenina 50) handles bookings for all airlines.

BUS

The main **bus station** (☎ 229 9518, 229 4881; ul
8 Marta 145) is 3km south of the city centre.
This is the place to catch buses to Chelyabinsk (R160, three hours, 10 daily). Buses to
Alapaevsk (R110, three hours, three daily)
and Verkhoturie (R216, five hours, daily)
are more likely to leave from the **northern
bus station** (☎ 353 8166, Vokzalnaya ul 15) near the
train station.

TRAIN

Yekaterinburg – sometimes still 'Sverdlovsk'
on timetables – is a major rail junction
with connections to all stops on the trans-
Siberian route. Trains to/from Moscow go
frequently, but the most comfortable one is
the *Ural* (R2050, 26 hours, daily). All trains
to Moscow stop at either Perm (R650, seven
hours) or Kazan (R1275, 15 hours). Heading east, the next major stops are Omsk
(R1200, 12 hours) and Novosibirsk (R1280,
21 hours). You can buy tickets at outlets
throughout the city, including the convenient **Railway and Air Kassa** (☎ 371 0400; ul Malysheva 31; ☒ 7am-9pm).

Getting Around

Bus 1 links the train station and Koltsovo
airport (45 minutes) from 5.30am to 11pm.

Many trolleybuses (pay on board) run
along ul Sverdlova/ul Karla Libknekhta
between the train station and pr Lenina.
Trams 4, 13, 15 and 18 and bus 28 cover long
stretches of pr Lenina, with bus 4 continuing
to the main bus station. The smaller northern bus station, primarily serving regional
destinations, is near the train station.

A single metro line runs between the
northeastern suburbs and the city centre,
with stops at the train station (Uralskaya),
pl 1905 goda and ul Kuybysheva near the
Magister hotel (Geologicheskaya).

AROUND YEKATERINBURG
Shirokorechinskoe Cemetery & Memorial to the Victims of Political Repression Широкоречинское кладбище и Мемориальный комплекс Жертв Политических Репрессий

A trip out to Shirokorechinskoe cemetery,
8km west of the city centre along the
Moskovsky Trakt, reveals Yekaterinburg's
more recent history. At the entrance are the
monumental graves of the victims of 1990s

gang warfare. They are hard to miss: look for the life-sized engraving of the 35-year-old gangster, his hand dangling Mercedes car keys as a symbol of his wealth.

Across the road is a vast memorial, opened in 1992 and dedicated to victims of the political repression of the 1930s. Some 25,000 people were killed in Yekaterinburg during Stalin's rule, and many of their bodies were later discovered here.

Bus 9 and 24 go from the west end of ul Lenina to nearby pl Kommunarov. Alternatively, catch a taxi from the city to the cemetery for R150 per hour.

Ganina Yama Ганина Яма

After the Romanov family was shot in the cellar of Dom Ipatyeva, their bodies were discarded in the depths of the forests of Ganina Yama, 16km northeast of Yekaterinburg. In their honour, the Orthodox Church has built the exquisite **Monastery of the Holy Martyrs** (☎ 343-217 9146) at this pilgrimage site. Set deep in the peaceful birch forest, the wooden buildings were constructed using ancient methods, which preclude the use of nails. An observation platform overlooks the mine shaft where the remains were deposited and burned. According to the Orthodox Church, this is the final resting place of the Romanov family and is therefore sacred ground (see the boxed text, p437).

To reach Ganina Yama by public transport, take the *elektrichka* (suburban train) to Shuvakish. Be sure to check the return train schedule in advance. If you hire a taxi from Yekaterinburg, take the road to Nizhny Tagil and look for the wooden signpost in the median strip 16km out of the city. Follow the signs to the monastery. Alternatively, Ekaterinburg Guide Center (p437) offers a three-hour tour for €20 to €27 per person.

Nizhnyaya Sinyachikha & Around
Нижняя Синячиха

The pretty village of Nizhnyaya Sinyachikha, about 150km northeast of Yekaterinburg and 12km north of the town of Alapaevsk, is home to an open-air **Architecture Museum** (☎ 246-75118; admission R20, guided tour R50; ☼ 10am-4pm). Here there are 15 traditional Siberian log buildings, featuring displays of period furniture, tools and domestic articles. The stone cathedral houses a collection of regional folk art, which is one of the best of its kind. This impressive grouping of art and architecture was gathered from around the Urals and recompiled by the single-handed efforts of Ivan Samoylov, an enthusiastic local historian.

About 2km west of Nizhnyaya Sinyachikha is a new monastery dedicated to Grand Princess Yelizaveta (see p438), on the spot where she died. Three buses a day go to Alapaevsk (R110, 3½ hours).

Verkhoturie Верхотурье
This small town on the Tura River, about 310km north of Yekaterinburg, is the site of the 400-year-old **St Nicholas Monastery**, one of the region's oldest and most important religious centres.

STRADDLING THE CONTINENTS

If you wish to have one foot in Europe and one in Asia, you can head 40km west of Yekaterinburg on the Moskovsky Trakt to the **Europe–Asia border**. Erected in 1837 at a 413m high point in the local Ural Mountains, the marker is a popular spot for wedding parties on their postnuptial video and photo jaunts.

In an attempt to make this geographic landmark more accessible to intercontinental travellers, city officials are in the process of erecting a new, more prominent marker at a new spot along the border. Conveniently, the new marker will be just 17km out of Yekaterinburg. The city has grand plans for monuments, museums, parks and gift shops, as well as European and Asian restaurants on their respective sides of the border.

Sceptics should be assured that this is more than a symbolic meeting of east and west. The site – on the watershed of the Iset and Chusovaya Rivers – was confirmed by scientists who examined geological records and studied the patterns of water flow. This clash of continents is the real deal.

Hire a taxi from Yekaterinburg for R150 per hour or make arrangements for this excursion through Ekaterinburg Guide Centre (p437) for €20 to €27 per person.

As the story goes, a mysterious peasant known as Simeon lived in a nearby village in the 17th century. For years, he lived simply, earning his keep by making clothes for local residents. When he died, nobody thought too much about it; but years later his grave was inexplicably unearthed and his body had not decayed – a sure sign of sainthood. The holy relic was brought to the monastery in the early 20th century, when the impressive Krestovozdvizhensky Cathedral was built to accommodate the pilgrims.

Although the cathedral was used as a garbage dump during the Soviet period, it is gradually being restored to its former grandeur. The unusual ceramic iconostasis has been replaced, as has the elaborate coffin of St Simeon. Today, pilgrims still come to kiss the coffin of this saint to absorb his healing powers.

Grigory Rasputin lived here for three years and – in fact – learned to read and write here. He long intended to bring the tsarevitch to cure his haemophilia, but this pilgrimage was never undertaken.

Today, the monastery is home to about 30 monks, and 20 students aged 14 to 16. Besides the two large cathedrals, it contains a small **museum** (☎ 219-22604; admission R10; ☼ 9am-5pm Wed-Sun) with some exhibits about the history of the monastery and its interactions with the royal family. Pilgrims are welcome to stay at the simple **hostel** (☎ 219-21826; three nights free of charge) that is on the monastery grounds.

Trains run from Yekaterinburg to the nearby town of Karpinsk. Alternatively, take the bus (R216, five hours, daily).

CHELYABINSK ЧЕЛЯБИНСК
☎ 3512 / pop 1.08 million / ☼ Moscow + 2hr
Chelyabinsk, 200km south of Yekaterinburg, is another city of contrasts – a sprawling industrial town set amid the gentle hills and inviting lakes of the Urals.

Founded in 1736, Chelyabinsk prospered as a tea trading city and expanded after 1892 with the completion of the railway from Moscow. Eventually, the trans-Siberian main line was to bypass the city. But expansion continued as its arms factories turned out Katyusha rockets and legendary, WWII-winning T-34s, for which it was nicknamed 'Tank City'.

Despite a heavy mantle of industrial sprawl, Chelyabinsk retains odd hints of

architectural appeal and is a useful transport hub for excursions into the southern Urals.

Orientation
The centre of this amorphous sprawl is pl Revolyutsii on pr Lenina, where a harried-looking Vladimir Ilych heads resolutely 'forward to communism'. North of here, the streets lie in a navigable grid pattern, with the pleasant pedestrian ul Kirova heading north to the Miass River. The bus and train stations are side by side on ul Svobody, 2km south of pl Revolyutsii.

Information
Alfa Bank (☎ 665 101; ul Kirova 108; ☼ 9am-6pm Mon-Fri)
AlfaNet.ru (☎ 642 430; pr Lenina 49; per hr R10-12 plus R4 per Mb; ☼ 24hr) Small café with Internet access.
Book World (☎ 632 359; ul Kirova 90; ☼ 10am-8pm) One of many bookshops around the city centre.

Sights
The highlight of Chelyabinsk is strolling down ul Kirova, paved with cobblestones and closed to car traffic. Life-sized bronze statues of local personages dot the street, which is lined with boutiques and cafés. An outdoor **book market** crowds the corners at ul Karla Marksa. The surrounding streets are worth a wander to discover some late-19th- and early-20th-century mansions. Some of the best are at ul Karla Marksa 68, ul Vasenko 41, ul Pushkina 1, and ul Tsvillinga 15.

At the northern end of ul Kirova, the **Fine Arts Gallery** (☎ 630 934; ul Truda 92; admission R30; ☼ 10am-5pm Tue-Sun) has a permanent collection of European and Russian paintings and china, as well as rotating exhibits that usually feature local artists. The **Geology Museum** (ul Truda 98; ☼ 10am-3pm Tue-Sun) is housed in an attractive brick building nearby.

Active religious buildings include an early-20th-century **synagogue** (ul Pushkina 6a) and the 1899 **mosque** (ul Yelkina 20), its lighthouse of a minaret topped with a golden spire. The 1883 **St Simeon Cathedral** (Kyshtymskaya ul 32) has a curious exterior featuring lion and dragon ceramics and a lovely interior. It's beside the north bus station; take tram 6 to ul Kalinina then walk a block east, then south.

Sleeping
Meridian (☎ 750 000; www.hotel-meridian.ru; pr Lenina 21; s/d with breakfast R2300/2900; ⊠) The latest

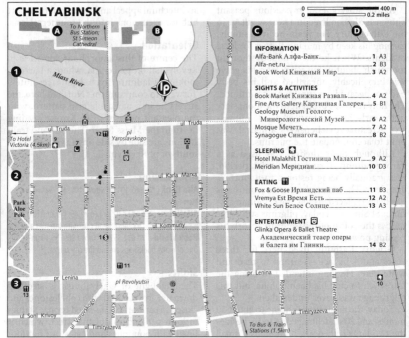

CHELYABINSK

INFORMATION
Alfa-Bank Алфа-Банк.....................................1 A3
Alfa-net.ru..2 B3
Book World Книжный Мир............................3 A2

SIGHTS & ACTIVITIES
Book Market Книжный Развал......................4 A2
Fine Arts Gallery Картинная Галерея..........5 B1
Geology Museum Геолого-
    Минерологический Музей........................6 A2
Mosque Мечеть..7 A2
Synagogue Синагога......................................8 B2

SLEEPING
Hotel Malakhit Гостиница Малахит..............9 A2
Meridian Меридиан.......................................10 D3

EATING
Fox & Goose Ирландский паб......................11 B3
Vremya Est Время Есть.................................12 A2
White Sun Белое Солнце.............................13 A3

ENTERTAINMENT
Glinka Opera & Ballet Theatre
    Академический теаер оперы
    и балета им Глинки...................................14 B2

addition to travellers' Chelyabinsk is this shiny glass and marble skyscraper, just over 1km east of pl Revolyutsii. Rooms are plain, modern and new. It's not much for atmosphere but the location is convenient.

Hotel Malakhit (☎ 630 948; ul Truda 153; s/d from R900/1400) This typical Soviet block is pretty dreary, from the cavernous lobby to the cramped rooms. The completely renovated rooms (with breakfast R1500/2000), located in a separate wing, offer an escape.

Victoria (☎ 989 820; www.victoria.ru; ul Molodogvardeytsev 34; s/ste with breakfast from R3240/4680; ⊠ ▯) The town's original business hotel is a smaller, more personable affair, 4km northwest of the centre. Guests can enjoy a gourmet restaurant and a happening nightclub, as well as modern, tastefully decorated rooms and suites.

Eating & Drinking

Vremya Est (☎ 637 852; ul Kirova 82; buffet R140-250, meals R200-400; ☽ 11am-2am) A trendy café with modern, industrial décor and a spacious dance floor. The menu features a vast smorgasbord (in Russian *Shvedsky stol,* literally

'Swedish table'), as well as other Russian standards. Live music plays nightly.

Fox & Goose (☎ 643 790; ul Kirova 177; business lunch R145, meals R300-500; ☽ 11am-midnight) Another town, another amiable Irish pub. This one features a dark wood bar and forest green complements, creating an appropriately cosy atmosphere. It's an ideal place to meet travellers, business people and other friendly folk.

White Sun (☎ 630 744; pr Lenina 63; meals R300-400; ☽ 11am-midnight) This pseudo-desert 'outpost' serves Central Asian cuisine – spicy soups, shashlyk and *plov.* Servers and staff are appropriately costumed, adding to the exotic ambience.

Entertainment

The majestic building at the end of ul Kirova, which fronts pl Yaroslav, is the **Glinka Opera & Ballet Theatre** (☎ 638 763; pl Yaroslavskogo 1; tickets R30-150). Russian classics show most nights.

Getting There & Away

Trains go daily to Moscow (R3100, 33 hours). Slow trains wind their way through the mountains north to Yekaterinburg (R300, 5½ hours), and south to Ufa (R510, 9½ hours) and further to Samara (R930, 18 hours). Heading east, most trains cut through Kazakhstan (visa required). You'll have a much greater choice out of Yekaterinburg.

The most efficient way to reach Yekaterinburg is by bus (R160, three hours, 10 daily). The bus is also more useful for Magnitogorsk (R285, five to six hours, 10 daily) and Miass (R90, two hours, 14 daily).

Getting Around

The bus and train stations are side by side on ul Svobody, 1.5km south of the centre. Bus 18 runs up ul Svobody to pr Lenina, then continues north on ul Tsvillinga. Trams 17, 30 and 40 ply the same route.

AROUND CHELYABINSK
Lakes District Край Озер

Locals rave (somewhat overenthusiastically) about the pleasant lakes around Chelyabinsk and Miass, notably Ilmenskoe and Turgoyak. Crowded with *turbazy* (holiday camps) and sanatoriums, which serve as bases for travellers wishing to escape the city, the region is ideal for boating, swimming, skiing and otherwise exploring the Urals countryside.

On the shores of Lake Turgoyak, known locally as the 'Blue Pearl', the resort **Golden Beach** (☎ 3513-560 093; www.goldenbeach.ru in Russian; Miass; r R1800-2300) receives rave reviews. Nicely renovated rooms are in two-storey *izby*. The highlight is the floating *banya* (a hot sauna-like bath), allowing steamers to cool off with a dip in the lake's clear waters.

Shiny lake Yelovoe is 80km southwest of Chelyabinsk on the road to Ufa. At **Uralskye Zori** (☎ 35168-782 170, 654 987; Chebarkul) you can rent equipment for winter sports like skiing, skating and snowmobiling, while summer activities include swimming, surfing and lake lounging.

Taganay National Park Таганай Национальный Парк

Descriptions of Taganay as the 'Russian Switzerland' are – again – a bit exaggerated, but the park's forested mountains and rocky protrusions are nonetheless splendid (see p431). The most convenient starting point for walking in Taganay is the steel town **Zlatoust**. If you need to stay in town, the lakeside **Hotel Taganay** (☎ 3513-651 225; pr 30 let Pobedy 7; r R700-900; 🖳 🐾) is accessible by bus 14.

The national park is dangerous to explore without a guide, as it is not well marked. Ural Expeditions & Tours (p438) offers English-language guided hiking trips in the park, ranging from one day to one week. Otherwise, contact the **park rangers' office** (☎ 3153-637 688) in advance.

MAGNITOGORSK МАГНИТОГОРСК
☎ 3511 / pop 439,000 / ☿ Moscow + 2hr

Like Frankenstein's monster, memorable Magnitogorsk is a city brought back from the dead, with pr Lenina as its reanimated Stalinist spine. Across the Ural River, the steel mills of the Ordzhonikidze district are magnificently ugly, with snarling, densely packed gangs of chimneys belching dense curtains of smoke in fearfully multifarious colours. This is most photogenically viewed from Park Pobedy, behind the gigantic, 83-tonne, square-jawed colossus of the **Tyl Frontu** memorial. Over 15m tall, this pair of Soviet archetypes hold aloft an enormous sword, symbolic of the city's industrial support for the WWII patriotic effort.

The new gold-domed **Ascension Cathedral** and the gold-spired **mosque** are anomalies on the otherwise industrial skyline.

Magnitogorsk is a fascinating stop, but it's best to keep it brief. If you find yourself stuck here for a night, the **Hotel Valentino** (☎ 376 766; ul Gryaznova 24; d/tw incl breakfast R1760/1960) is an acceptable new business hotel just southwest of pl Mira.

Getting There & Around

Besides the daily train to Moscow, there's an overnight service to Ufa (R560, 10 hours) via Abzakovo (one hour). Buses are more practical for journeys to Chelyabinsk (R285, six hours, 10 daily).

The bus and train stations are both located at the north end of ul Lenina. Bus 21 runs down ul Lenina past the Tyl Frontu memorial all the way to the Ascension Cathedral. Bus 7 and tram 17 go down the parallel pr Karla Marksa past Hotel Valentina.

AROUND MAGNITOGORSK
Abzakovo Абзаково

In an attractive spot in the wooded mountains between Magnitogorsk and Beloretsk, this quaint village is best known for the **Abzakovo Resort** (☎ 3519-259 300; www.abzakovo .ru in Russian), where President Vladimir Putin

THE URALS

comes to ski. (You can thank him for the wide new road from Magnitogorsk.)

As a downhill ski destination, it is among the best in Russia, with 15km of trails ranging from bunny slopes to black diamonds. Lift tickets are R350 to R500 per day or R50 to R60 per ride, and decent equipment is available for rental. The ski season usually runs from November to April.

In summer, the resort is open for horse riding (per hour R250) and cycling (per hour R40), as well as tennis, basketball and other sports. The giant indoor aqua park (two hours R70 to R90) and the small, sad zoo (admission R30) are also open year-round.

SLEEPING & EATING

Abzakovo Resort (☎ 3519-259 300; www.abzakovo .ru; s/d from R750/1400 Mon-Thu, R1200/2200 Sat & Sun; 🍴) The bulk of the lodgings – as well as restaurants, aqua park and other facilities – is at the hotel complex 2km from the mountain (accessible by shuttle bus). Rates vary widely, depending on the season and standard of rooms. There are also five cottages right on the mountain, but they are not as convenient for the rest of the resort's facilities.

Tautash (☎ 3519-259 267; www.tautash.ru; r R1300 Mon-Thu, R900 Fri-Sun; 🍴 🍴) On the road from the train station to the ski resort, this new hotel is a good alternative to the resort itself. Facilities include a restaurant, nightclub and sauna. The expensive, exotic 'VIP' rooms are reminiscent of the honeymoon suite at a cheesy motel, with themes such as 'Old Castle' and 'Egypt'. Rates quoted are for summer months and are likely to rise sharply during the ski season.

GETTING THERE & AROUND

To reach the resort, get off the bus or train at the Novoabzakovo station (where the Magnitogorsk–Ufa train stops) and stroll 15 minutes towards the mountains, keeping straight ahead after the river bridge.

UFA УФА

☎ 3472 / pop 1.04 million / 🕐 Moscow +2hr
Ufa is capital of the self-consciously autonomous Bashkortostan Republic. Although the Muslim, Turkic Bashkir people now make up barely one-third of Bashkortostan's population of four million, you will hear their lispy language spoken widely in rural areas and on many city radio programmes, along with their curious style of singing. Written Bashkir requires nine extra Cyrillic letters that are absent from standard Russian. 'Hello' in Bashkir is *hau-ma*; 'thank you very much' is *zur rakhmat*.

Orientation

Ufa fills a 20km-long dumbbell-shaped area of land between the Belaya and Ufa Rivers. The southern lobe contains the city's dynamic centre. Ufa's main thoroughfare is ul Lenina, which runs from the centre north to the river station. The train station is at the northern end of ul Karla Marksa, which runs parallel to ul Lenina two blocks west.

Information

Alfa Bank (☎ 765 696; ul Lenina 32; 🕐 9am-7pm Mon-Fri, 10am-6pm Sat) Changes money and has an ATM.
Poligon (☎ 230 354; Sovietskaya ul 11; per hr R30; 🕐 24hr) Convenient Internet facilities.
Post office (ul Lenina 28) Near Alfa bank.

Sights

The focus of appealing ul Lenina is the 19th-century **Trading Arcade**, set on a fountain-cooled piazza. Behind the renovated façade is a luxuriously marble-lined shopping mall full of boutiques, cafés and carts selling freshly squeezed orange juice.

The **National Museum** (☎ 221 250; Sovetskaya ul 14; admission R150; 🕐 10am-6pm Tue-Sat) is housed in a fantastically renovated Art Nouveau building. Despite the fancy name, most of the exhibits are standard Soviet history and stuffed animals, typical of a regional museum. The interesting exhibits on Bashkir history and current events are the exception.

The **Nesterov Art Gallery** (☎ 234 236; ul Gogolya 27; admission R50; 🕐 10am-4pm Tue-Sun), also recently renovated, contains a fabulous collection of artwork by namesake (and Ufa native) Mikhail Nesterov, as well as many other Russian artists. Avant-garde and futurism are also well represented.

Ul Krupskoy is named for Lenin's wife Nadezhda Krupskaya, who lived here for several years while Vladimir Ilych was abroad. Only one house remains from that period: it is the grey, clapboard cottage where Lenin stayed for three weeks in 1900 awaiting a boat to Pskov. The cottage is now a small **Lenin Museum** (☎ 232 439; Krupskoy ul 45; admission R10; ☼ 10am-6pm Tue-Sat). It contains many depictions of Lenin and Krupskaya during their time in Ufa, including an unusually human statue of Vladimir Ilych holding hands with his wife.

Ufa's most photogenic spot is the equestrian **statue** of 18th-century Bashkir hero Sal-

avat Yulaev, who appears ready to leap the wide Belaya river into the forest beyond.

From here, a mostly downhill stroll takes you via the imposing university buildings, past the giant Bashkortostan drama theatre and through remnant wooden cottages of ul Salavata Yulaeva for the best available view of the city's historic **mosque** (ul Tukaeva 52).

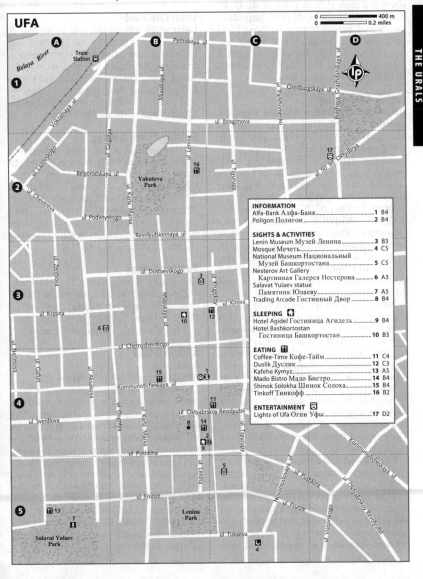

UFA

0   400 m
0   0.2 miles

INFORMATION
Alfa-Bank Альфа-Банк................................1 B4
Poligon Полигон..2 B4

SIGHTS & ACTIVITIES
Lenin Museum Музей Ленина.....................3 B3
Mosque Мечеть..4 C5
National Museum Национальный
    Музей Башкортостана............................5 C5
Nesterov Art Gallery
    Картинная Галерея Нестерова................6 A3
Salavat Yulaev statue
    Памятник Юлаеву...................................7 A5
Trading Arcade Гостинный Двор................8 B4

SLEEPING 🛏
Hotel Agidel Гостиница Агидель.................9 B4
Hotel Bashkortostan
    Гостиница Башкортостан......................10 B3

EATING 🍴
Coffee-Time Кофе-Тайм...........................11 C4
Duslik Дуслик...12 C3
Kafehe Kymyz..13 A5
Mado Bistro Мадо Бистро........................14 B4
Shinok Solokha Шинок Солоха.................15 B4
Tinkoff Тинкофф......................................16 B2

ENTERTAINMENT 🎭
Lights of Ufa Огни Уфы............................17 D2

THE URALS

Sleeping

Hotel Agidel (☎ 225 680; ul Lenina 14; r per person with breakfast from R700) The selling point here is the superbly central location opposite the trading arcades. The cheapest rooms do not include a shower (R15), so the upgraded rooms (from R950) are worth the extra cash.

Hotel Bashkortostan (☎ 790 000; gkbashkiria@ ufacom.ru; ul Lenina 25-29; s/d 2600/4540; ❄ 🖳 🖳) This modern complex offers all the facilities you would expect from a business hotel, including bar, restaurant and fitness centre, not to mention the efficient service. Considering this, the small single rooms (R1900) offer excellent value.

Eating & Drinking

Coffee-Time (☎ 220 435; ul Oktyabrskoy Revolyutsii 3; breakfast R100; ☺ 24hr) One of Ufa's most popular spots for a coffee break. Jazz music, B&W photos and a menu featuring crepes instead of bliny give this place a European flair. In the evening, the café is often crowded with couples on dates and other fashionable young folk.

Shinok Solokha (☎ 225 333; Kommunisticheskaya ul 47; meals R200-300; ☺ noon-11pm) A homey Ukrainian cottage, complete with curtains on the windows and servers in traditional garb. The menu features Ukrainian specialities like borsch and *vareniki* (boiled filled dumplings). One in a row of themed restaurants, including a Czech beer pub.

Duslik (☎ 502 280; ul Krupskoy 9; meals R500-800) Ufa meets Samarkand in this elaborate Uzbek palace. The interior, over the top by some estimates, re-creates a sumptuous terrace, complete with bamboo ceiling, greenery and flowing fountain. It is a popular spot with businesspeople, especially for the tasty *plov*.

Tinkoff (☎ 231 909; ul Lenina 100; ½L beer R120; ☺ noon-2am) The newest outlet of this national microbrewery has the same industrial style and delicious draughts as the other outlets. The extensive menu complements the beer, as does the occasional live music or DJ act.

Kafehe Kymyz (Salavat Yulaev park; meals R100-200; ☺ 11am-10pm) Located in the park near the Yulaev horseman statue, this café has outdoor seating – a perfect place in summer to sample some classic Bashkir snacks. Try *vak-belyash* (a delicious pastry filled with ground beef and potato) or *lulya* kebab (minced-meat sausage cooked on an open

flame and served in a pita). Wash down with some kumiss (fermented mares' milk).

Mado Bistro (☎ 227 030; ul Lenina 16; meals R100; ☺ 9am-9pm) This bustling cafeteria is conveniently located opposite the trading arcades. It is always busy with students and families filling up on Russian classics and not-so-classics like burgers and pasta.

Entertainment

Lights of Ufa (☎ 908 690; ul 50 let Oktyabrya 19; ☺ 11am-2am) This shiny modern building includes a host of entertainment options, including a concert hall and your traditional disco. The microbrewery Brau Haus is the most fun, featuring live jazz, dancing and fresh-brewed lager. From ul Lenina, take any bus north to 'Dom Pechati'.

Getting There & Away

The train station is 2km north of the centre at the end of ul Karla Marksa. Overnight trains serve Samara (R580, nine hours), Ulyanovsk (R900, 14 hours), Chelyabinsk (R510, 8½ hours) and Magnitogorsk (R560, 10 hours) via Abzakovo (nine hours). There are several daily services to Moscow (at least 30 hours), as well as a daily train to Astana (R1540, 32 hours), in Kazakhstan.

Getting Around

The handy if convoluted bus 101 route snakes between the train station and the airport, via the main bus station and ul Lenina. Bus 2 links the Salavat Yulaev monument and the north bus station via ul Lenina.

AROUND UFA

Asha Аша

☎ 35139 / pop 37,000 / ☺ Moscow + 2hr

This small, drab mineralogical factory town seems an odd place to visit, but it attracts ski bunnies from November to April. The downhill ski centre **Adzhigardak** (☎ 3512-322 499 in Chelyabinsk; lift tickets per day R400-550, per ride R60) is a 10-minute taxi ride out of town – an anomaly in this otherwise depressing place. The 10 ski runs are not as extensive as at Abzakovo, but still respectable. And the birch trees, blue skies and other mountain scenery are equally revitalising. *Elektrichki* make the trip from Ufa (R65, 2½ hours, four daily) often enough to make this an easy day trip, but check the schedule before you hit the slopes.

Russian Caucasus
Кавказ

This beautiful and many-faceted part of Russia receives few travellers, despite being only a plane or train journey from Moscow, and that's a pity. The colossal Caucasus mountains, 1100km of soaring peaks and deep valleys, stride from the Caspian to the Black Sea. Between the mountain range and the Black Sea is a coastal strip that endows Russia with its most southerly seaside resorts. The pearl is Sochi, with glorious summer sun, warm sea, plenty of classy bars and restaurants, and performances by Russia's top entertainers. In the mountains near Sochi lies Krasnaya Polyana, on the way to being another big European ski resort. Here, in this 'Switzerland by the sea', you can easily ski and swim in the sea on the same day.

This region, one of the last to be added to the tsarist Russian Empire, was won and controlled with the help of Cossack warriors. Their homeland lies in the Kuban Steppe, around Rostov-on-Don, where Cossack culture remains undiminished; their old capital, Starocherkassk, is where to find it. Wander east and the central Caucasus mountains rise from the vast steppe in a land of dead volcanoes and gushing mineral springs. Their curative powers attracted mid-19th-century society, which transformed Pyatigorsk and Kislovodsk into elegant spa towns. Visitors to the sanatoriums can roam the parks and take day trips to Dombay and Mt Elbrus. Threaded into this landscape is the drama of writer Lermontov's death echoing the plot of his novel *A Hero of Our Time,* also set here.

Even if you're no skier, hiker or climber, do venture into the mountains by visiting Dombay or Mt Elbrus and ride cable cars and chairlifts part of the way up to view the savage beauty of this lofty range. At the eastern end lies unsafe-to-visit Chechnya and Dagestan, a complicated and fractious ethnic jigsaw with an Asiatic atmosphere, extending from the mountains to the Caspian Sea.

RUSSIAN CAUCASUS

HIGHLIGHTS

- Sleep in Stalin's bedroom in his Black Sea hideaway, the **Green Grove dacha** (p469)
- Catch cable cars and text your friends that you're up **Mt Elbrus** (p487), Europe's highest mountain
- Lounge about in sunny **Sochi** (p463) and have your photo taken with Lenin
- Sample superb Russian champagne at **Abrau-Dyurso** (p462)
- Ride Dombay's **chairlifts** (p482) to survey waterfalls, glaciers and sharks-teeth mountain summits

★ Abrau-Dyurso

Sochi ★ ★ Stalin's dacha
★ ★ Elbrus
Dombay

History

The Caucasus has stood at the crossroads of Mediterranean, Central Asian, West Asian and Eastern European cultures since the Bronze Age. The result is an extraordinary mix of races with three main linguistic groups: Caucasian, Indo-European and Turkic. Most people are either Orthodox Christians or Muslims. The Caucasus has suffered many invasions and occupations, having been squeezed between rival Roman, Byzantine, Persian, Arab, Ottoman and Russian empires.

LIFE BEFORE THE RUSSIANS

Little is known of the area's prehistory. Earliest human traces date from Neolithic times when farming was replacing hunting and gathering. The first communities evolved in Dagestan's valleys around the same time as agriculture developed in West Asia and China, establishing this region as an early cradle of civilisation.

Significant post-Neolithic remains are the 3000-plus dolmens scattered across the coastal foothills from Novorossiysk to Sochi. These funeral memorials of huge flat stones date from the 4th to the 2nd century BC.

Mass migrations brought in many different peoples, including Scythians in the 8th century BC followed by Sarmatians five centuries later. In the 1st millennium AD, groups including Kipchaks (ancestors of the present-day Balkar), Huns, Pechenegs and Khazars all left their mark, some settling and mixing with existing inhabitants.

The first dominant state created by the Alans, ancestors of modern Ossetians, blossomed during the 10th century AD and at its peak ruled most of the northern Caucasus. The state was conquered by the Mongol Tatar invasions of the early 13th century and any remnants destroyed by Timur's (Tamerlane) army in 1395.

THE RUSSIANS ARRIVE

Escaping Russian serfs and adventurers had already settled in the lower Terek River region when Russian military power arrived here in the late 1550s. Russian imperial influence grew at the expense of the Ottoman

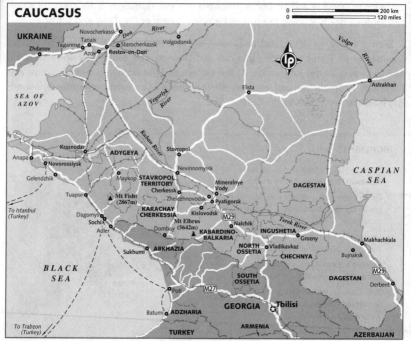

Turks who were gradually edged out. Russian imperial conquests met with fierce resistance from local tribes from the Caspian to the Black Sea. The predominantly Muslim populace resented being ruled by European and Christian Russians and bitter guerrilla-type warfare lasted several decades.

At times of threat the Caucasian tribes have united. In the 19th century, Imam Shamil brought together Dagestani and Chechen tribes and the Cherkess for a 30-year fight against the Russians that ended with Shamil's surrender in 1859 (see p124). This was the last major threat to Russian hegemony until the current Chechen wars. Many with strong Muslim beliefs, who felt they had no future under Russian suzerainty, fled to Turkey and its empire in West Asia. An exception was the Ossetians, who as Christians had never fought the Russians and wanted no part in the Islamic state that was Shamil's intention.

During the October Revolution, many tribes united to form the Mountain Republic. Independence lasted until 1921 when Soviet forces, having consolidated power, conquered the remainder of the Tsarist Empire. The Mountain Republic was given autonomous status while various Dagestani nationalities were combined into a new Dagestan Autonomous Republic. The autonomous Mountain Republic ceased in 1924 after it divided into four new autonomous regions: Adygeya, Chechnya, Kabardino-Balkaria and Karachay-Cherkessia. Soviet policy was to divide and rule by creating small autonomous regions, often combining two totally different nationalities.

In 1944 Stalin ordered the mass deportation of Balkar, Chechen, Ingush and Karachay peoples to Central Asia and Siberia, on the pretext of potential collaboration with German forces. Those left behind took over the property and land of the deported. Khrushchev allowed the exiled groups to return in 1957 but without compensation or repossession of their property. The oppressive and dictatorial nature of the Soviet regime smothered any potential conflict but this changed very quickly after the failed 1991 coup in Moscow.

POST-SOVIET ERA

The political restructuring of Russia transformed the region into the semiautonomous republics of Karachay-Cherkessia, Kabardino-Balkaria, Dagestan, North Ossetia, Adygeya and Checheno-Ingushetia, later separated into Chechnya and Ingushetia.

The slipping of the Soviet leash let loose a host of ethnic-based rivalries, paramount of which has been the Chechnya conflict; see p492. The battleground spilt over into North Ossetia in September 2004 when militants slaughtered hundreds of children, teachers and parents at a school in Beslan. There was also a major conflict between the North Ossetians and the Ingush that preceded the Chechen conflict and remains unresolved, since most Ingush who fled North Ossetia in 1992 still have not returned home. Political unrest has also surfaced in Karachay-Cherkessia. In November 2004 thousands forced the president to flee after the unexplained murder of several prominent citizens. The president's son-in-law had been implicated.

In Kabardino-Balkaria the growth in Islam is being met by heavy-handed police action with people persecuted on ethnic and religious grounds. The fact that Chechen warlord, Shamil Basayev, chose to launch an attack on the state's capital, Nalchik, suggests this policy has backfired. In October 2005, separatist Chechen guerrillas launched multiple attacks on Nalchik police and military posts. A dozen civilians were killed plus between 41 (Basayev figures) and 91 (Russian figures) guerrillas and a number of security personnel. President Putin promises severe retaliation for any future actions which does not bode well for peace in this region.

Climate

In winter, the Black Sea coast relishes being Russia's warmest place – it's rarely freezing.

'CAUCASIAN MALE, HEIGHT...'

Ever wondered why white people are referred to as Caucasian? Well, in 1795 the German ethnologist Johann Blumenbach visited the Caucasus and was impressed by the health and physique of the mountain people. Despite them not being quite white he used the term Caucasian as one of his five great divisions of mankind. In bartending, a Caucasian is a mixed drink also referred to as a White Russian.

In summer (June to September) it's warm and humid, around 25°C. To the north, the continental climate provides three or four freezing winter months from November to February, then temperatures shoot up to about 30°C from June to August.

The higher you go, the cooler it gets – many Caucasus peaks are permanently snow-covered – but on a sunny summer day you'll still be sweating at 3000m. November to April/May is the wettest season, with the coastal strip getting significant rainfall of around 1200mm to 1800mm annually.

National Parks

The most significant is Prielbruse National Park (p487), containing the magnificent Mt Elbrus, glaciers and waterfalls and home to bear, chamois, wild goat and an enormous range of plant life. While not a national park, Teberdinsky Nature Reserve (p481) maintains a near-pristine temperate ecosystem with chamois, bear, lynx, boar and reintroduced bison against a backdrop of majestic mountains.

Language

While Russian is spoken and understood by all, there are a significant number of local languages, especially in eastern mountain areas. In tourist centres on the coast and in the Mineral Waters area there will be some who can speak a little English.

Dangers & Annoyances

Chechnya, Dagestan and Ingushetia are no-go areas; they're just too dangerous. Unfortunately terrorist activity is no longer confined to just those states; the Beslan school massacre has made North Ossetia a place to avoid, and the attacks on military and police posts in Nalchik mean you should also consider avoiding the capital of Kabardino-Balkaria.

Elbrus, the most popular place in the central Caucasus, has remained untouched by recent troubles but a prudent traveller will check on the latest advice before going. The western Caucasus is as safe as the rest of European Russia.

Getting There & Away

AIR

International flights go from Armenia, Turkey, Germany and Belarus to Rostov-on-Don, Sochi and Mineralnye Vody. These

---

ACCOMMODATION

While accommodation is plentiful, many places can't or don't want to be involved in registering foreigners. The places included in this chapter do register foreigners. Seaside accommodation gets a huge price hike starting in May and increasing monthly to August, then prices reduce in September and again in October. Seaside accommodation prices quoted here are for June, which we reckon is the best time to visit. Inland cities don't have seasonal price changes. Places with skiing have high-season prices during their skiing seasons and low season is generally September to early November; see Dombay (p481) and Elbrus (p488) for more details.

---

airports plus Anapa, Krasnodar and Nalchik also receive domestic flights, mostly from Moscow and St Petersburg. Check schedules as they change regularly.

BOAT

See the Novorossiysk (p461) and the Sochi (p468) section for ferries to Georgia and Turkey.

TRAIN

Main lines from the north funnel through Rostov-on-Don and then diverge. One runs to Mineralnye Vody with a line down to Kislovodsk, and another to Vladikavkaz in North Ossetia. The second runs to Krasnodar dividing into a line to Novorossiysk and Anapa, and the other to the coast and Sochi. Unless you have a Ukrainian visa and a multiple-entry Russian one, avoid any northbound Moscow trains that go via Ukraine. Otherwise, some trains travel to Ukraine and Belarus but foreigners are not allowed on the few *elektrichki* from Sochi that cross the Abkhazia border.

Getting Around

Train is easiest and most comfy for travelling between major centres; use bus, *marshrutka* and *elektrichka* for local travel. As schedules and prices fluctuate, check at bus and train stations before making your move. Public transport to the mountains is very limited for Dombay and Elbrus. Given the mountain terrain, the most obvious route on the map may not be practicable. Taxis are plentiful and can even be used between towns and for getting into the mountains.

KUBAN STEPPE
КУБАНСКАЯ СТЕПЬ

From Rostov-on-Don, the overland routes to the Caucasus and the Black Sea coast cross the intensively cultivated Kuban Steppe, named after its river flowing from Elbrus into the Sea of Azov. The trip from Rostov-on-Don to Pyatigorsk or Kislovodsk on the northern fringe of the Caucasus can be made in a day – by road it's just under 500km.

ROSTOV-ON-DON
РОСТОВ-НА-ДОНУ

☎ 863 / pop 1.1 million / ☽ Moscow

Rostov-on-Don is an expansive town with the bustle of a regional capital, but the wide leafy streets and scattered parks take away any notion of crowding. Passing through the city is the Don River, celebrated in Mikhail Sholokhov's novels of the Civil War – *And Quiet Flows the Don* and *The Don Flows Home to the Sea*.

The Don is no longer quiet. In 1952 the Lenin Ship Canal linked the Volga and the Don near Volgograd, creating an immense network of canals, lakes and rivers. Ocean-going ships can now sail across Russia from the Arctic to the Mediterranean.

For those travelling through here, Rostov-on-Don and the Cossack capitals make a pleasant stopover for a couple of days. If possible, take a trip on a ferry along the Don or maybe cruise up to Moscow.

History

When serfs, paupers and dropouts fled to the south in the 15th century they established communities in the Don River basin and their capital at Starocherkassk. Known as Don Cossacks, these communities elected their own ataman (leader), formed armies and gained a degree of autonomy.

Their relationship with the central Russian government was turbulent: they initiated three major uprisings in the 17th and

18th centuries and put up furious resistance to the October Revolution. At other times they formed the backbone of armies securing Russia's southern borders.

Orientation

Rostov-on-Don is mostly on the northern bank of the Don, which flows south of Moscow to the Sea of Azov. The main east–west axis, Bolshaya Sadovaya ul, passes many of the city's hotels and restaurants; the bus and train stations are at its western end.

Information

Agentstvo URDV (☎ 263 1222; Bolshaya Sadovaya ul 113; ☽ 8am-7pm) Plane and train ticketing.

Comfort Internet (☎ 295 0589; Pushkinskaya ul 141; per MB R3, per hr R25; ☽ 9am-11pm)

Post & telegraph office (☎ 240 7776; ul Lermontovskaya 116; ☽ 8am-6pm)

Russian Voyage (Russkii Voyazh; ☎ /fax 244 1066; Temernitskaya ul 83; ☽ 10am-6pm Mon-Fri, 10am-3pm Sat) Agent for Don River cruises.

Sberbank (☎ 240 4715; Bolshaya Sadovaya ul 39; ☽ 8am-1pm & 2-7pm Mon-Fri, 9am-2pm Sat) Changes travellers cheques; ATM.

Sights & Activities

The **Regional Museum** (☎ 240 5213; Bolshaya Sadovaya ul 79; admission R60, with gold exhibition R190, camera R50; ☽ 10am-5.30pm Tue-Sun) has a special section featuring early-AD gold artefacts with some spectacular jewellery and weaponry. Other exhibits effectively cover the region's prehistory, including nearby Tanais and tribes who predated the Cossacks. While there are well-presented Cossack displays, the better exhibits are at Novocherkassk. Upstairs is mainly devoted to revolutionary Russia but our favourite item was a massive 2m long, 1.5m wide 1956 hi-fi and TV system.

The lavish **Nativity of the Virgin Cathedral** (☎ 240 2947; ul Stanislavskogo 58; 7am-7pm) pokes its golden domes above the lively open-air market. Within is a glorious display of Orthodox religious art and decoration.

Central on Bolshaya Sadovaya ul, **Gorky Park** is the summer meeting place among the trees for revelling, with funfair rides, street stalls, karaoke joints and plenty of bars.

Tours

Russian Voyage sells tickets (singles, full board) for Don and Volga cruises, May to September. These sail to Volgograd (from

R7150, five to six days, three cruises in May and June, one in July), Samara (from R13,650, 11 days, one cruise in June), Astrakhan (from R13,650; 11 days, one cruise in July and September) and Moscow (from R1430, 11 to 12 days, two cruises in season).

Sleeping

Being a regional capital, places fill up quickly during the week so book ahead.

Intourist Hotel (☎ 238 4746; fax 232 5427; Bolshaya Sadovaya ul 115; s/d incl breakfast from R800/R1400, lyux R3000, apt from R3000; ⊠ ▢) Renovation has turned this into a modern hotel, both in facilities and quality of service. The buffet breakfast is superb: champagne, salmon caviar and Danish pastries! The cheaper rooms are perfectly good but for river views go for the top floors front side. An alternative to the expensive restaurant is the bar downstairs.

Hotel Rostov (☎ 290 7666; www.rostovhotel.ru; Budyonovsky pr 59; s R1200-1400, d incl breakfast R2000-4000, ste R2700-7000; ⓟ ⊠) Very much a business person's hotel. Luxury climbs with price and a suite provides you with your own bar, dining room plus glass cupboard with fancy crockery. The cheap singles are comfortable but simple. Services include air and train ticketing, currency exchange, translation services and a fitness centre.

Tourist Hotel (☎ 238 4746; hottour@rost.ru; per M. Nagibina 19; r incl breakfast R800-3500; ⊠ ⊠) Sunglasses warning! Loud wallpaper and carpet designs in the cheap rooms. Still they're the best value compared to the crummy two-storey rooms that should be avoided. Facilities include an exchange office and a ticketing counter for train and plane.

Eating & Drinking

Café Salvador (ul Universitetskaya 44; meals R150-360) Scribbly signage makes this a little difficult to find but once inside you'll know you're there. It revels in ultramodern design with blues, oranges and languid shapes formed by light and shadow. Certainly adding to Rostov's street cred, it's a place for a coffee, late drink or snack at any time.

Café Mango (ul Serafimovicha 49; meals R130-240) An intimate little side-street café, Mango does cheap snacks and is the sort of place to sit with a book and sink almost too many beers – the staff wouldn't mind.

Zolotoy Kolos (Bolshaya Sadovaya ul 43; coffee R30, cakes R6-16, pizza R60-100; ⓥ 10am-11pm) The chocolate-

and-cream décor sets the scene for a big cake experience. Every cake and dessert shouts 'lick me'. If you don't want to drool over cakes and coffee there are big pizzas.

Guinness Bar (Bolshaya Sadovaya ul 57; meals R175-400; ⓥ 10am-1am) At R200 for half a litre you need to be cashed up to drink Guinness all night but there's cheaper local beer. The food is good, and there's a menu in English. Give the shrimp black pasta a try.

Central Market (☎ 299 9576; cnr Budyonovsky pr & ul Stanislavskogo; ⓥ 6am-10pm Tue-Sun May-Sep, 7am-8pm Oct-Apr) Stock up here for DIY feeding while checking out the jostling crowds and the array of items on sale.

Entertainment

Club Lila (☎ 262 3819; Sotsialisticheskaya ul 68; cover R150; ⓥ 6pm-2am) Eardrum alert! This club features live music by local groups in an underground cavern that reverberates with an earthquake of sound. There is a quieter area with seating just off the bar.

Rostov Musical Theatre (Musykalny Teatr; ☎ 264 0707; Bolshaya Sadovaya ul 134; ⓥ ticket office 10am-7pm) This modern and notable theatre, in the shape of a white concert piano, presents ballet and opera between September and June.

Getting There & Away
AIR
Flights go to Moscow Domodedovo (R2520 to R4900, daily) and St Petersburg (R6400, Tuesday to Thursday and Saturday).

Aeroflot-Don flies to Istanbul (US$170, Monday and Friday), Vienna (€230, Monday, Wednesday, Friday and Sunday), Dusseldorf

USEFUL BUS & TRAIN ROUTES FROM ROSTOV-ON-DON

Rostov's modern **bus station** (☎ 244 1010; pr Siversa 1) is near the train station.

Destination	Daily departures	Duration	Fare
Anapa	10.40am	10hr	R270
Krasnodar	6.16am, 3.45pm, 5.35pm	5¼hr	R171
Odesa (Ukraine)	4.40pm	18hr	R415
Pyatigorsk	9.30am	10hr	R355
Volgograd	6am-10.30pm	11hr	R370

Some major trains from Rostov's **train station** (☎ 267 0210; pl Privokzalnaya):

Destination	Train	Departures	Frequency	Duration	Fare
Kyiv	17/25	9.16pm	odds/evens	19½hr	R800
Kislovodsk	28	9.28pm	daily	10½hr	R705
Mineralnye Vody	830*	2.07pm	daily	6½h	R236
Minsk	37	6.50am	odds	35hr	R1600
Moscow	27	6.38am	daily	24hr	R2100
Novorossiysk†	44	2am	daily	7½hr	R570
St Petersburg	43	0.48am	daily	35hr	R2400
Sochi	76	8.03pm	daily	14hr	R750

* *elektrichka*   † passes through Krasnodar

(€235, Monday, Wednesday, Friday and Sunday) and Frankfurt (€235, Saturday).

BOAT
Hydrofoils operate May to October from the river station ticket office (☎ 262 0280; Budyonovsky pr), with boarding one hour before departure time. There's a Starocherkassk hydrofoil (R25) which departs at 2pm and returns at 4.20pm from Monday to Friday, 7am and 2pm on Saturday (returning 9.20am and 4.20pm) and 10am on Sunday (returning 9.20am). There is also an Azov hydrofoil (R27) that departs at 10am and returns at 5pm Thursday to Sunday.

Getting Around
Buses 7, 12 and 13 and trolleybuses 1, 9 and 15 ply Bolshaya Sadovaya ul down to the train and bus stations. Avoid taxis loitering outside hotels; they have no concept of reasonable fares. **Romaks Taxi** (☎ 277 9691) is cheap and efficient.

AROUND ROSTOV-ON-DON
Starocherkassk СТАРОЧЕРКАССК
☎ 863
Founded in 1593, Starocherkassk (Old Cherkassk) was the Don Cossack capital for two centuries. Once a fortified town of 20,000, it's now a farming village with a main street restored to near 19th-century appearance.

Allegedly, Peter the Great met a drunken Cossack here sitting on a barrel, wearing only a rifle. This image of a soldier who'd sooner lose his clothes than his gun so impressed the tsar that he commissioned the scene as the Don Cossack army seal.

SIGHTS
Near the main street's northwestern end is the **fortified house** of Kondraty Bulavin, leader of the Peasant War (1707–09). Bulavin lived and died in this solid stone house with 1m-thick walls and iron doors; nowadays it's a Unesco office.

Walk southeast, past the plain **SS Peter & Paul Church** (1751) on the left, and see sturdy **Cossack fort-houses** typically built on a high basement to avoid regular flooding. Further on, within a brick-walled ataman palace compound, there's a **ticket office** (☎ 29749; admission R40, camera/video R15/50 for each of Resurrection Cathedral, bell tower, palace compound, English- or German-speaking guide R150; ⊙9am-5pm) for several sights.

Within the **palace compound**, the kitchen building has a display of Cossack weapons while three floors of the palace are a cultural museum of Cossack Russia. Of particular interest is the bronze relief map of Starocherkassk showing its defensive advantage and a display of nonmilitary uniforms of Soviet Russia. Included are school uniforms, youth movement (Komosol) uniforms and uniforms for various public servants including holiday costumes for coal miners.

Adjacent is the **Church of Our Lady of the Don** (1761), which was the private church of the ataman. Within is a magnificent golden iconostasis with rows of saints in pious poses.

In the square at the main street's eastern end, Stepan Razin rallied his followers in 1670 and was later clapped in chains on the same spot. The **Resurrection Cathedral** (Voskresensky sobor) here contains a soaring golden iconostasis, a baroque chandelier and an unusual floor of metal tiles. Peter the Great provided the design of the church, and sent builders from Moscow as well as bells, ironwork, church utensils and 100 roubles; when he visited in 1709 he helped lay the altar brickwork. The adjacent **bell tower** provides a bird's-eye panorama.

Most summer weekends, Starocherkassk holds a 'Cossack fair', which features music, dancing, crafts and horse riding.

GETTING THERE & AWAY
The hydrofoil is a delightful way to travel for a weekend visit from Rostov-on-Don. Otherwise, it's the frequent *marshrutka* 131 (R20, 45 minutes) from pl Karla Marksa, Rostov; Last return service is 5.45pm. A taxi (about R250) is the only option between Starocherkassk and Novocherkassk.

Novocherkassk Новочеркасск
☎ 86352 / pop 185,000
In 1805 the Don Cossacks moved their capital to Novocherkassk (New Cherkassk), 40km northeast of Rostov; this is said to be the setting for Nobel laureate Mikhail Sholokhov's novel, *And Quiet Flows the Don*.

Ataman Matvey Platov, a Cossack general whose brigade chased Napoleon back to Paris, is a national hero; a monument here commemorates him as do many streets and squares in Russia that bear his name. The **Don Cossacks Museum** (Donskoy muzey; ☎ 41366; ul Atamanskaya 38; admission R100, camera/video R20/100; ✆ 10am-5pm Tue-Sun) has an admirable collec-

tion of memorabilia and paintings depicting Cossack history and culture. Pride of place goes to a sword presented to Platov in England.

The interior of **Ascension Cathedral** (Voznesenskaya sobor; ☎ 27025; pl Ermaka; ✆ 7.30am-7pm) is covered with frescoes. Dark greys, browns and greens echo solemnity and spirituality around a huge narthex that amplifies every whispered prayer.

Catch bus 3 along Bolshaya Sadovaya ul to Rostov's old bus station and transfer to bus 101 (R18, 45 minutes, every 20 minutes); at Novocherkassk catch a *marshrutka* (R5, 20 minutes) into the centre.

Tanais Танаис
☎ 86349
From the 3rd century BC until the 4th century AD, the Greek trading colony of Tanais flourished at the mouth of the Don. The Roman writer Pliny wrote, 'At the mouth of the River Tanais is a city and for everyone who comes here there is Europe on the left and Asia on the right'.

Travel 30km from Rostov towards Taganrog and a turning near Nedvigovka takes you to the Tanais excavations and a **museum** (☎ 20249; admission R25; ✆ 9am-5pm Wed-Sun Apr-Nov). Several hectares reveal a patchwork of foundation walls of what was once an extensive settlement. More parts are continually being uncovered and a typical house has been recreated to give a sense of place. The best way to get there is the Tagangrog bus; get off at the turning and walk the last 2km.

Azov Азов
☎ 242
In the 13th century Genoese merchants established a trading settlement here but in 1471 they were turfed out by the Turks, who built a massive fortress to keep the Russians out of the Black Sea. For 200 years they were successful.

Today it's a sleepy country town but well worth visiting for the comprehensive **museum** (☎ 40771; ul Moskovskaya 38/40; admission adult/child R20/5, camera/video R50/100; ✆ 10am-5pm Tue-Sun). Prime attraction is a complete mammoth skeleton that dwarfs everything else in the room it's crowded into. That apart, there are prehistory exhibits, some Turkish items, a model of Azov Fort defended against Peter the Great in July 1696 and, up the intriguing metal stairs, a section on the Civil and Great Patriotic Wars. Only a renovated stretch and some embankment remains of **Azov Fort** (Azovskaya Krepost). From the top you can sit and watch the busy river port.

Marshrutky (R28, 45 minutes, every 15 minutes) for Azov leave from Rostov's bus station. The return hydrofoil from Rostov departs at 5pm Thursday to Sunday and other ferries on their way to Rostov call in at 7.30am and 6.30pm daily.

KRASNODAR КРАСНОДАР

☎ 861 / pop 650,000 / ⏰ Moscow

When Catherine the Great travelled south to tour the lands conquered from the Turks, her lover Potemkin had cheerful façades erected along her route. These hid the mud-splattered hovels that made up the newly founded city bearing her name, Yekaterin-odar ('Catherine's gift').

Krasnodar no longer needs those façades, as many of the elegant, turn-of-the-20th-century buildings have been externally restored. Modern development has happened elsewhere and single-storey buildings still line the main street. Wander east through the backstreets or better still hop on a rickety tram down ul Kommunarov and enjoy the vista of old houses.

On summer weekends part of Krasnaya ul becomes a pedestrian zone and is quickly populated by those out to promenade, meet friends or slip into party mode at dusk. Street musicians, karaoke stands, artists and vendors compete for pavement space with cafés and bars while clothes shops open their doors to entice a stream of young customers.

Orientation

The road from Rostov-on-Don feeds into the northern end of Krasnaya ul, Krasnodar's 2km-long leafy colonnade of a main street. Train and bus stations are to the southeast and the airport is 15km to the east.

Information

Aerobusiness (☎ 251 6246; Krasnaya ul 75; ⏰ 9am-8pm) Air and rail ticketing.

Alfa Bank (☎ 259 6464; Krasnaya ul 124; ⏰ 9am-5pm Mon-Sat, 9am-3pm Sun) Cashes travellers cheques, ATM.

Hotel Moskva (☎ 253 1807; Krasnaya ul 66; ⏰ 9.30am-5pm Wed-Sun) Changes money and cashes travellers cheques Wednesday to Saturday.

Hotel Moskva air ticket counter (☎ 273 9304; ⏰ 9am-6pm Mon-Sat, 9am-2pm Sun) Domestic flights only.

Main post office (☎ 253 2661; ul Karasunskaya 68; ⏰ 8am-9pm Mon-Sat, 9am-8pm Sun)

Telecommunications Centre (☎ 262 4039; Krasnaya ul 118; ⏰ 24hr) Internet access available until 8.45pm for R30 per hr.

Sights

You'll find Scythian and ancient Greek figures at the **Regional Museum** (Kraevedchesky muzey; ☎ 267 9034; ul Voroshilova 67; admission per exhibit R30, camera R50; ⏰ 10am-5pm Tue-Sun, 10am-4pm Fri). Although the captions are in Russian, there's enough of visual interest – natural history, prehistoric items, Cossack and revolution history and the German occupation – to make a visit worthwhile.

Housed in a stately, newly renovated 1905 building, the **Art Museum** (Khudozhestvenny muzey; ☎ 268 0977; Krasnaya ul 13; admission per exhibition R50-60, camera/video R50/100; ⏰ 10am-5.30pm Sat-Thu, 10am-4.30pm Fri) is well worth a visit, often with good travelling exhibitions – Picasso, Klee, Chagall and Dali drawings during our visit. Upstairs under painted ceilings is the permanent collection including a portrait of Catherine the great, who seems to be concealing a hot-air balloon under her huge dress.

Sleeping

Hotel Intourist (☎ 259 6697; Krasnaya ul 109; r R1300-2600; P ⏰ ⏰) Good rooms but too much furniture – some have seating for eight people. The friendly reception staff speak English and can arrange airport transfers, airline ticketing and excursions.

Hotel Moskva (☎ 273 9304; fax 273 9301; Krasnaya ul 60; r incl breakfast from R1300) Tired basic rooms and indifferent reception staff but the hotel has lots of rooms, is very central and if you arrive late in the evening checkout isn't until 24 hours later.

Hotel Tsentralnaya (☎ /fax 273 9962; cnr uls Mira & Krasnaya 25; s/d without bathroom from R650/740, s/d with bathroom R1300/1700) They've been renovating. Reception pushes the decent doubles in preference to the cheap, ordinary and timeworn ones. Your wallet and powers of persuasion will determine which room you get.

Eating

Khrustalny Restaurant (☎ 259 6697; Hotel Intourist, Krasnaya ul 109; dishes R150-600; ⏰ 7am-midnight)

TRAINS FROM KRASNODAR

Some major trains from the Krasnodar **train station** (☎ 262 0887; pl Privokzalnaya):

Destination	Train	Departures	Frequency	Duration	Fare
Kyiv	18	4.06pm	odds	24hr	R1000
Mineralnye Vody	834*	7.28am	odds	6hr	R500
Minsk	38	1.30am	odds	40hr	R1500
Moscow†	104	10.29pm	daily	23hr	R2700
St Petersburg†	36	1am	odds	36½hr	R2900
Sochi	801*	7am	daily	5hr	R400

* *elektrichka*   † trains pass through Rostov

Quite a surprise for a three-star hotel restaurant. There's a varied menu, reasonable prices, good food and friendly service. For the gourmet, snails, frogs' legs and caviar appear on the menu.

Eastern Fairy Tales (☎ 267 2567; Krasnaya ul 17; meals R150-750; ☺ 9am-11pm) Waitresses in belly-dancing costumes serve up an eclectic mix of Uzbek, Korean and Japanese food in this prettily decorated restaurant painted in cucumber-cool colours and adorned with calligraphic motifs. The food's good, the divans are comfortable and for smokers there are *nargilas* (water pipes) to go with exceptionally good coffee.

Bar Kit (Krasnaya ul 60; business lunches R150, snacks R50-90; ☺ 10am-late) This undercover pavement café is the ideal viewing place for watching Krasnodar at work or play. The menu's fairly standard but the food's good and the beer tastes fine on a hot summer's night.

There's a host of food stalls around the bus and train stations on pl Privokzalnaya.

The **central market** (ul Budyonnogo; ☺ 7am-6pm) is one block to the west of Hotel Intourist. There's also another **market** (cnr uls Kommunarov & Gogolya; ☺ 7am-6pm) that's an excellent source of fresh fruit and spicy pickled Korean food.

Getting There & Away

Siberia Airlines, Aeroflot and Kuban Air have flights to the main Moscow airports daily (R2080 to R4000). Pulkovo Airlines and Kuban Airlines fly to St Petersburg (R5600, daily) and Kuban also flies to Sochi (R950, Wednesday).

Internationally, Kuban Air flies to Frankfurt (€398, Saturday) and Hanover (€398,

Sunday). Belavia flies daily to Minsk via Moscow (US$165 return).

Marshrutka 15 goes to the airport from outside the central market; taxis charge R200 for this trip.

The **bus station** (☎ 262 5144; pl Privokzalnaya) has a handy touch-screen display with bus times and fares. Useful services are Novorossiysk (R87, three hours, frequent), Anapa (R112, 3½ hours, frequent) and Rostov (R184, five hours, seven daily).

BLACK SEA COAST
ПОБЕРЕЖЬЕ
ЧЁРНОГО МОРЯ

A narrow coastal strip edges the Black Sea from where rolling hills ascend fairly rapidly into mountains in the southeast and low uplands in the northwest. This is Russia's seaside playground. A long summer from June to October gives rise to warm to hot weather, plenty of sunshine and a warm sea. Several resort towns dot the sometimes-rugged coast and Sochi is the pearl.

While the sea is unexciting – pebbles all the way to Anapa, which has the only sandy beach – it is safe swimming. Despite pollution of the Black Sea at depth, dolphins can often be seen frolicking off the coast. The interior, slashed by deep valleys, provides some terrific walking through lake and waterfall-filled terrain. Skiing is popular at nearby Krasnaya Polyana and Mt Fisht from about January to April.

NOVOROSSIYSK НОВОРОССИЙСК

☎ 8617 / pop 242,000 / ⊙ Moscow

Novorossiysk is home to the Russian navy and much of the country's cement production comes from dismantling the surrounding hills. For travellers it's a transport hub for the nicer seaside towns of Anapa, Gelendzhik and Sochi, or maybe a boat to Turkey.

The Krasnodar road skirts the south of the port to become Anapskoe sh and then ul Sovietov as it arrives in the CBD.

The **post office** (☎ 251 627; ul Sovietov 36; ⊙ 8am-9pm) has an ATM outside.

Sights & Activities

Novorossiysk is peppered with WWII memorials. In 1943, a small Soviet landing party heroically held out here for 225 days, forming a bridgehead for the counteroffensive against the occupying Germans. The immense memorial at **Malaya Zemlya** celebrates their feats. This huge concrete construction represents a landing ship disgorging a party of soldiers and sailors depicted in chunky bronze.

Inside the 'ship' is an amazing walk-through **gallery** (☎ 233 747; admission R50, camera/video R15/50; ⊙ 9.30am-1pm & 2-5.30pm Jun-Sep, 10.30am-4.30pm Tue-Sun Oct-May), with plaques of heroes and a recording of a solemn, deep-voiced choir singing patriotic songs.

More memorials lie on pr Lenina where the party landed, and further east at **Dolina Smerti** (Death Valley), where the Russians came under the fiercest bombardment.

Novorossiysk's maritime and war history is celebrated in the **Town History Museum** (Muzey istorii goroda; ☎ 610 027; ul Sovietov 58; admission R50, camera/video R30/50; ⊙ 10am-6pm Sat-Wed). A small section deals with Soviet leader Brezhnev's involvement in Novorossiysk's wartime defence.

The **Planetarium Gagarin** (☎ 644 812; ul Sovietov 53; adult/child R30/20; ⊙ 9am-5pm) has heavenly shows every hour.

Sleeping & Eating

Hotel Novorossiysk (☎ 606 505; reserve@hotel-novoros.ru; ul Isayeva; unrenovated s/d from R600/826, renovated s/d from R1715/2014) Best option in town, but choose the rooms at the back that come with a balcony overlooking the sea. However, don't buy breakfast vouchers but pay in the restaurant. As for laundry, read the

boxed text, above. The 3rd-floor restaurant has smiling staff and meals from R125 to R270; try the bliny with strawberries and yogurt for breakfast. The menu is partly in English.

Hotel Brigantine (☎ 216 373; fax 216 446; sh Anapskoe 18; s/d from R550/700, deluxe/lyux from R1800/2200; P ✕) The hotel has rooms ranging from unrenovated basic boxes to more luxurious rooms with TV, fridge and phone. There's an ATM in the lobby decorated with wood carved with maritime motifs.

Dublin (ul Sovietov 44; meals R200-400; ⊙ 24hr) Bar owners the world over must think there's a bit of the Irish in all of us, just desperate to talk the blarney and down pints of Guinness. This underground Irish pub is a good starting place. Decent meals here cross the global divide; salads are good and the Shanghai chicken curry needs that Guinness to put out the fire.

Morskoy Yorsh (☎ 604 940; Sea Terminal; meals R155-460; ⊙ 10am-2am) Ignore the prohibited zone sign at the end of the sea terminal and climb upstairs. This place is a bit posh now so no larking around. Come here during the week as on weekends it heaves. The place is good for fish dishes but definitely not the poisonous puffer fish after which the restaurant is named.

Getting There & Away

BOAT

An infrequent passenger ship (full board in four-berth cabin from R2000, voyage 36 hours) sails to Istanbul on a Tuesday, fortnightly in winter increasing to three or more a month in summer. Boarding is at 2pm for a 6pm sailing. Tickets are bought from helpful **Transflot** (☎ 607 066; fax 254 756;

MONEY LAUNDERING *Patrick Horton*

Laundry is so matter of fact that you often hand it over without regard to the price. Imagine my consternation when charged US$50 for 14 items. I complained to the floor staff and was told that prices were prices. I took the issue up the ladder of command, and all were apologetic but that's what I had to pay. The director wouldn't see me and security staff were loitering around in case I did a runner. What else but pay up and resolve always to look at prices first.

RUSSIAN CAUCASUS

seaport customs area; ⊙ 9am-5.30pm), which has an English-speaking receptionist.

BUS

The **bus station** (☎ 252 245; ul Chekhovskogo) runs bus services to Krasnodar (R87, 3½ hours, seven daily from 6am to 7pm), Sochi (R171, nine hours, 7.50am and 8.30pm) and Gelendzhik (R22, one hour, six daily), plus *marshrutky* to Anapa (R50, 45 minutes, six daily).

TRAIN

From the **train station** (☎ 298 126; ul Zhukovskogo) three daily trains go to Moscow (R2500, 26 to 34 hours) passing through Krasnodar and Rostov-on-Don. For Sochi or Mineralnye Vody change at Krasnodar.

AROUND NOVOROSSIYSK

Abrau-Dyurso Абрау-Дюрсо

This area, 20km from Novorossiysk, has been famous since 1886 when Tsar Alexander II granted land for champagne vineyards. Catch a frequent *marshrutka* from Novorossiysk bus station and join a **tasting tour** (☎ /fax 8617-285 405; admission R250; ⊙ 10am-5pm). You'll get to see the process and be led through dark, musty tunnels where millions of bottles are stored, before sampling some rather nice champagnes.

Anapa Анапа

☎ 8617 / pop 57,000

The pleasant sheltered bay, sandy beach and direct train line north make Anapa a favourite seaside resort for those as far away as Moscow. Compared to quieter Gelendzhik it's brasher and more commercial, but it has the beach, aqua parks, hotels and restaurants to make it attractive for those who want to dip their toes or more in the Black Sea.

INFORMATION

Internet Café (☎ 50025; ul Krasnodaskaya 8; per hr R40; ⊙ 9am-noon & 1-10pm).

Sberbank (☎ 56222; ul Lenina 14; ⊙ 9am-1pm & 2-5pm Mon-Fri) Cashes travellers cheques – or 'road cheques'; Visa and MasterCard ATM.

Sputnik (☎ 50522; sputnik@anapa.kuban.ru; ul Kalanina 27; ⊙ 8am-8pm) Sells plane and train tickets.

SIGHTS & ACTIVITIES

Pavement sellers hawk one-hour around-the-bay sea cruises (R200, daily in summer) and

weekend four-hour cruises (R500) including the dolphinarium down the coast at Utrish.

Roaming Greeks established several dozen trading settlements on the Black Sea coast and Anapa, founded as Gorgipaya in the 4th century BC, was a walled city and significant regional centre. The **Archaeological Museum** (☎ 43154; ul Naberezhnaya 4; adult/child R30/20, camera/video R25/50; ⊙ 9am-6pm Tue-Sun) has items from that period – pottery, weapons, jewellery, coins and household items. Behind the museum are some of the excavated foundations.

Most Russian seaside resorts come with a place like **Aqua Park** (☎ 12262; ul Tsentralnaya Naberezhnaya; adult/child R400/200; ⊙ 10am-6pm May-Oct). These fun parks, filled with swimming pools, water slides and sunbaking areas, are a blessing for families.

SLEEPING & EATING

Expect to be greeted at the bus and train stations by people with rooms (R150 to R300) and apartments (R500 to R1500) for rent; check that they can register you.

Anapa Ocean (☎ 51078; anapaocean@au.ru; ul Pushkina 19; per person full board & treatment Oct-Apr R750-850, May-Sep R1200-1600, lyux r Oct-Apr from R1700, May-Sep from R3200; P ⊠ ⛊) This sanatorium, a tower adorned with golden corrugated panels, overlooks the sea. Standard rooms are a few notches above basic while *lyux* come with a small sitting room, balcony and pretty floral sheets. Rooms at the top front enjoy a sea view and are near the swanky top-floor bar-restaurant with outside patio. Other facilities include a cinema and fitness club.

Ship (ul Naberezhnaya; meals R100-360; ⊙ 9am-late) The embankment comes to a promontory at the Ship, where the restaurant has a commanding view of the bay. The ideal sunset spot to unwind with a beer and snacks.

Laskovy Bereg-2 (Victory Park; meals R125-300; ⊙ 24hr) This outdoor restaurant on the embankment edge of the park has tasty summer specialities such as bliny with shrimps and *okroshka* (a cold soup of cucumbers, vegetables and eggs in sour cream), *kvas* and yogurt.

GETTING THERE & AWAY & AROUND

The **bus station** (☎ 56861; ul Krasnoyazmeyskaya) has services to Krasnodar (R109, 3½ hours, 16 buses daily) and Krasnodar airport (R117, four hours, 12.35pm and 7.30pm).

The **train station** (☎ 33186; ul Krestayanskaya) has three daily trains to Moscow (R1600, 11.28am, 12.15pm and 5.27pm, 31 to 36 hours), passing through Krasnodar and Rostov-on-Don.

Daily Aeroflot flights leave Anapa **airport** (☎ 33218) for Moscow (R2830 to R6000), Sochi (R1602, Saturdays June to September) and St Petersburg (R5925 to R6175, daily June to September).

A taxi to the airport costs R200.

Gelendzhik Геленджик
☎ 86141 / pop 50,000 / ☽ Moscow

The town of Gelendzhik sweeps around a curving bay that provides shelter for this laid-back seaside resort. The beach is pebbly but the calm sea is clean and inviting.

Vneshtorbank (ul Karla Marksa 6) has a MasterCard and Visa ATM.

SIGHTS & ACTIVITIES
With displays of Adygean life and culture, the **Historical Museum** (Istorichesky muzey; ☎ 35287; ul Ostovskogo 1; adult/child R30/15; ☽ 9am-5pm) makes a rare admission that until the Russian invasion in the 1830s this was the land of the Adygeans who left in a diaspora to other countries.

One-hour sea cruises (adult/child R200/ 100) are available from the sea terminal, an obvious jetty jutting out to sea. They allow for 15 minutes swimming out in the bay and tempt you with dolphin sightings.

SLEEPING & EATING
Hotel Kavkaz (☎ 71225; kavkaz@smtp.ru; ul Mayachnaya 3; s/d full board from R2100/2400, lyux from R2640; P ✗ ⊛) A large renovated 1930s holiday resort with sports facilities, private beach and organised excursions. Standard rooms are surprisingly good with pleasant furnishings. As prices rise space increases, armchairs appear and *lyux* rooms gain air-con and sitting rooms.

Pansionat Stroitel (☎ 26100; gelhotelsea@gl .kuban.ru; r per person R490-1200; ✗) Gelendzhik's cheapie but it's closed in winter. There's a big range of rooms, cheaper with shared bathroom while the more expensive have bathrooms and air-con. In the grounds, near the sea, are 12 cottage units with attached bathrooms and air-con.

Golden Orb (☎ 34455; ul Mira 26/2; s R1000, r R1400-1800) The Orb has several good-quality

rooms, some in lurid satin green, with full facilities and large bathrooms; the ground-floor rooms are suitable for people with disabilities. The owners have two other guesthouses.

Bistro Katalpa (ul Mira 16; meals R140-320) A pleasant small café with a street-front courtyard shrouded in vine leaves and shaded by a tree canopy. The crab and mushroom salad with Russian black bread is highly recommended.

GETTING THERE & AWAY
Buses ply to Novorossiysk (R22, one hour, six daily) from the bus stand north of the town on the Novorossiysk road. A taxi from the sea front to the bus stand should be about R50.

SOCHI СОЧИ
☎ 8622 / pop 329,000 / ☽ Moscow

Sochi may not have the best European beaches and there's still an element of tackiness but the city is in makeover mode. Investment money is being pumped in, some by government and some by developers who've gone overseas, seen what they've liked and copied it in Sochi.

Wander the downtown area by the elegant sea terminal and you're in a garden city where the scent of magnolia trees mingles with the tang of salt carried on sea breezes. Follow the sea embankment (naberezhnaya) and you'll cruise by a blur of restaurants, bars, shops and souvenir stalls jostling for attention. The place oozes booze and food and at night resounds to a pumping mix of Russian ballads, rousing Armenian tunes, Western pop and a little dance music.

If crowds are not your scene you can escape into the hills and mountains. If you're a snow bunny then Krasnaya Polyana (Red Valley) is the place; the snow lingers into late spring, allowing you to ski in the morning and swim in the sea in the afternoon.

Summer season is from the end of May to the end of September, with crowds pouring in during July and August when, coincidentally, prices are at their highest. We reckon that June is the best time to come, when the city is at its freshest.

Orientation
Greater Sochi, some 150km long, is the world's second-largest conurbation after

RUSSIAN CAUCASUS

SOCHI

0 ——————— 1 km
0 ——————— 0.5 miles

INFORMATION
Book World Книгомир **1** D2
Bookshop Книжный Магазин **2** D2
Comstar Комстар **3** D1
Kodak .... (see 23)
Main Post Office Главпочтамт **4** C2
Main Telephone Centre
    Переговорный Пункт **5** C2
Moscow Capital Московский Капитал **6** C3
Reinfo Реинфо **7** C3
Service Avia Сервис Авиа **8** C3
Sochi Telecom Сочи Телеком **9** D2
Territorial Aero Communications Agency
    Территориальное Агентство
    Воздушного Сообщения **10** D2
Vneshtorgbank Внешторгбанк **11** D2

SIGHTS & ACTIVITIES
Aquarium Аквариум **12** D1
Art Museum Художественный Музей **13** C3
Church Of Michael the Archangel
    Храм Михаила Архангела **14** C3
Lenin Mosaic Мозаика Ленина **15** C1
Luna Park Луна Парк **16** C2
Mayak Маяк **17** C2
Stadium Стадион **18** C5
Ticket Office Билетные Кассы **19** C4
Town History Museum
    Музей Истории Города **20** D2

SLEEPING
Chermnomorje Sanatorium
    Черноморье Санаторий **21** C3
Hotel Magnolia Гостиница Магноля **22** C3
Hotel Moskva Гостиница Москва **23** C2
Hotel Primorskaya
    Гостиница Приморская **24** C3
Hotel Sochi Гостиница Сочи **25** C3
Hotel Zhemchuzhina
    Гостиница Жемчужина **26** C4
Park Hotel Парк Отель **27** C3
Resort Bureau .... (see 20)

EATING
Cafe Cinzano .... (see 23)
Home Kitchen Домашняя Кухня **28** C2
La Pizzeria Ла Пиццерия **29** C2
Market Рынок **30** D1
Natasha's Наташа **31** C2
Paterson Supermarket
    Супермаркет Патерсон **32** C4
Stolovaya No 17 Столовая 17 .... **33** C3
Yapona Mama Япона Мама **34** C3

DRINKING
Tinkoff Тинькофф **35** C3

ENTERTAINMENT
Circus Цирк **36** C4
Festival Hall Зал Фестивальный **37** C2
Green Theatre Зелёный Театр **38** C1
Malibu .... (see 17)
Park Rivera **39** D1
Saint Tropez Ст Тропез **40** D1
Stereo Стерео **41** C3
Summer Theatre Летний Театр **42** C4
Winter Theatre Зимний Театр **43** C3

SHOPPING
Art Salon Художественный Салон **44** C3

TRANSPORT
Bus Station Автовокзал **45** D2
Cable Car Канатно-Кресельная Дорога ... **46** C4
Information Office .... (see 47)
Sea Terminal Морской Порт **47** C2
Ticket Office .... (see 47)

Map labels

To British Council (500m)

BLACK SEA

To Dagomys Tea Houses (20km)

Park Rivera

ul Yegorova
Sochi River
ul Konstitutsii
ul Vorovskogo
ul Navaginskaya
ul Karla Libknekhta
ul Gorkogo

Train Station

Harbour

ul Nesebskaya

ul Pervomayskaya

ul Voykova

Naberezhnaya

ul Ordzhonikidze
Kurortny pr
ul Sokolova

ul Chernomorskaya
ul Dmitrievoy

Park Frunze

pr Pushkina

Arboretum

Arboretum

Kurortny pr

BLACK SEA

To Hotel Lazurnaya (1km); Aktyor Sanitorium (1km);
Mettalurg Sanitorium (1km); Avangard Sanitorium (1km);
Zelenaya Roscha (3km); Patskha Restaurant (4km);
Matsesta (5km); Agura Valley (6km); Mt Bolshoy
Akhun (17km); Adler & Airport (24km);
Vorontsovskaya Cave (37km); Krasnaya Polyana (66km)

Los Angeles. Sochi itself stretches 7km from the Sochi River to Matsesta. Kurortny pr, a few blocks from the sea, links the northeastern cluster of train and bus stations, harbour and shopping centre, the hotel district and the arboretum in the southeast.

Information

BOOKSHOPS

Bookshop (☎ 923 352; ul Navaginskaya 12; ☻ 9am-8pm) Sells maps and some Russian-language guides to the area.

Book World (Knigo Mir; ☎ 609 159; ul Gorkogo 54; ☻ 9am-6pm) Maps, CDs and a few English fiction titles.

CULTURAL CENTRES

British Council (☎ 605 240; www.britishcouncil.ru; ul Gagarina 10a; ☻ noon-6pm Tue-Sat Oct-Apr, Mon-Fri May-Sep) Free Internet and library.

INTERNET ACCESS

Comstar (☎ 622 695; ul Moskovskaya 5; per hr R30; ☻ 8.30am-11pm)

Sochi Telecom (☎ 624 430; ul Vorovskogo 6; per hr R36; ☻ 9am-8pm)

INTERNET RESOURCES

www.sochiclub.ru A perkily written site on Sochi.

MONEY

Hotel Lazurnaya (Kurortny pr 103) ATM and cashes travellers cheques.

Moscow Capital (☎ 622 729; ul Sokolova 25/14; ☻ 11am-10.30pm) Currency exchange kiosk and ATM.

Vneshtorgbank (☎ 923 319; ul Karl Libknekhta 10; ☻ 9am-5.30pm) Barely competent bank cashes Amex travellers cheques; MasterCard and Visa advances.

PHOTOGRAPHY

Kodak (☎ 608 080; Hotel Moskva foyer; ☻ 9am-7pm) Films and printing. Burning digital photos to CD costs R35.

POST

Main post office (☎ 922 810; cnr Kurortny pr & ul Vorovskogo; ☻ 8am-6pm)

TELEPHONE

Main telephone centre (☎ 920 564; ul Vorovskogo 6; ☻ 8am-noon & 1-7.45pm)

TRAVEL AGENCIES

Reinfo (☎ /fax 622 042; www.heliski.ru, www.reinfo -sochi.ru; Park Hotel Business Centre, room 316; ☻ 9am-6pm Mon-Sat) Well-established tour operator with extensive range of programs: skiing, hiking, sailing, white-water rafting; excursions to Krasnaya Polyana, Mt Fisht, Vorontsovskaya Cave and lesser-known places. Can book sanatoriums and Krasnaya accommodation.

Service Avia (☎ 924 050; Kurortny pr 50; ☻ 9am-5pm Oct-Apr, 9am-8pm May-Sep). Air and rail ticketing, excursion booking.

Territorial Aero Communications Agency (☎ 923 603; ul Navaginskaya 16; ☻ 8am-7pm) Air ticketing.

Sights & Activities

No matter that it's narrow and stony, Sochi's beach is dressed up in season with artificial trees, sunbathing loungers, awnings and private changing pavilions to imitate a South Seas ambience. And the Russians love it.

The snow-capped mountains which lie behind Sochi can only be appreciated from a **sea cruise** (☎ 609 603; Sea Terminal; R250; ☻ 11am-7.30pm), and there may be the bonus of seeing dolphins.

The **Town History Museum** (Gorodskoy Istorichesky muzey; ☎ 929 349; ul Vorovskogo 54; adult/child R30/15, camera/video R40/150; ☻ 9am-6pm) has a superbly presented and impressive collection. What shines is the space display with the *Soyuz 9* capsule that returned to Earth in June 1970 after 18 days in orbit. On board were local lad, engineer Sevastyanov, and his pilot Nikoliev. Space suits, photographs, equipment and food complement the capsule.

Sochi's lovely **arboretum** (Dendrariy; ☎ 975 117; Kurortny pr; admission R30; ☻ 8am-dusk), with more than 1500 species of trees and shrubs from the world over, is attractively laid out and relaxing to wander through. Pay at the ticket office and then take the **cable car** (adult/child one way R80/40; ☻ 8am-dusk) to the top and walk back down.

Try the large **Lenin Mosaic**, opposite Park Rivera, for a backdrop with a difference for your holiday photos.

The **Art Museum** (Khudozhestvenny muzey; ☎ 622 947; Kurortny pr 51; adult/child R30/15; ☻ 10am-6pm) resides in a classical building that's an artwork in itself. There are visiting exhibitions and an expansive permanent collection.

Sochi for Children

Being a family holiday resort there's a lot of fun places for children.

Circus (☎ 920 375; cnr Pushkina & Kurortny prs; tickets R150-300; box office Jun-Sep ☻ 9am-6pm) Sochi's circus presents Russian and international performances.

Luna Park (☎ 623 847; ul Ordzhonikidze 6; rides R30-60; ☉ 10am-5pm winter, 10am-midnight summer) Another summertime place for young children with rides and jumping castles.

Mayak (☎ 623 648; Naberezhnaya; adult/child per day R600/300; ☉ 10am-5pm summer) For a self-contained aqua park, Mayak has most things you could want – pools, water slides, sunbaking couches and cafés and bars for energy top-ups after all that hard enjoyment.

Stereo (☎ 620 070; Kurortny pr 37; adult/child R70/50; shows 3pm & 5pm) In the 1970s Russia produced 3-D movies, some of which can be seen here.

Inside **Park Rivera** (☎ 693 434; Kurortny pr; ☉ 24hr) are several **fun fairs** (rides R20-150, day pass R550; ☉ 10am-midnight) including a rollercoaster and a Ferris wheel. There's an **aquarium** (admission R100; ☉ 10am-10pm) plus a tacky range of art and craft shops, pony rides and an avenue of magnolias with trees planted by cosmonauts, including one planted by an Afghani.

Tours
Pavement sellers, most hotels and many travel agents sell excursion tours that are the easiest way of visiting places around Sochi. Typical tours are Sochi (R150, two hours), Mt Akhun Bolshoy (R180, three hours), Agura Waterfall (R180, three hours) and Krasnaya Polyana (R250, seven hours).

Festivals & Events
The season starts in late May with a weekend **beer festival**. The fizz has gone out of it over the last few years and it's been shifted to a wholesale food market (ul Gorkogo).

A weeklong **film festival** in June attracts the film stars of Russia and the occasional foreign actor. Outdoor screens in Park Rivera have free screenings but for those in the Winter Theatre you have to pay.

The season closes in late September with the Velvet Season **fashion show**, another weeklong extravaganza attracting top names in the fashion industry.

Sleeping
Sochi has many hotels and willing citizens with a room or apartment to rent. Rates can increase by about 25% monthly between May and August.

BUDGET
An option is to rent a **room** (Oct-Apr R250-400, May-Sep R1000-1500) from those offering them

at the train station but check if they can register foreigners.

Alternatively, the booking agency **Resort Bureau** (Kurortnoe byuro; ☎ /fax 922 976; propan@sochi .ru; ☉ 24hr) parks a mobile office outside the train station and has an office at the Town History Museum.

Hotel Sochi (☎ 621 987; www.sochi-magnolia.ru; Kurortny pr 50; s with shared bathroom R370, s/d incl breakfast R596/1092) The city's best-value option. If you can't organise registration then you can be a phantom resident of one of their bare-bones singles. Other rooms are quite adequate. This hotel and the Hotel Magnolia (in the same block) are run by the same outfit so go to the Magnolia to check in and have breakfast.

MIDRANGE
Hotel Primorskaya (☎ 925 743; management@heliopark .ru; ul Sokolova 1; s/d economy R295/395, unrenovated R545/900, budget R550/715, renovated R590/990) This sprawling, pale-yellow hotel, with elements of charm remaining from its 1936 origins, covers a large block around a central patio. Many categories and options of rooms are available to suit thin wallets. Being as near to the sea as geography allows makes it a favourite and it quickly books up in season.

Hotel Zhemchuzhina (☎ 661 188; fax 661 888; ul Chernomorskaya 3; r from R900, lyux from R3500; Ⓟ 🗙 🖳 🖳) This 965-room place by the sea has its own beach and tennis courts, and is serviced by helpful and smiling staff. The cheapest rooms, unrenovated and without sea views, are on the 1st floor while the renovated section is a vast improvement with better furnishings. *Lyux* rooms have the best sea views, with balconies and air-con.

Hotel Moskva (☎ 608 010; reservation@moskva -hotel.ru; Kurortny pr 18; s/d 865/1310, lyux R1505/2140; 🗙) Smack in the town centre the Moskva is a large, noisy and run-down place that's in the throes of restoration. For the budget-minded the standard rooms are quite adequate, doubles have sea views and balconies, and *lyux* rooms boast a lounge and air-con. Breakfast costs R120 to R160 extra.

TOP END
Park Hotel (☎ 693 000; info@radissonpark.ru; per Morskoy 2; s/d Jan-Mar & Nov-Dec R2113/2600, Apr-Jun & Oct R3218/3705, Jul-Sep R3705/4193; Ⓟ 🗙 🗙 🖳 🖳) The resurrection of this old Soviet-era hotel now shines as a beacon of blue-tinted glass. Within are very pleasant rooms, many with

sea views and air-con, cable TV, fridges, bathtubs plus an array of beside-the-washbasin goodies. One floor has nonsmoking rooms. An ATM, bar, restaurant, two types of sauna and a fitness centre complete the picture.

Hotel Lazurnaya (☎ 663 333; fax 663 292; Kurortny pr 103; s/d incl breakfast from US$149/169; P 🞖 🖳 🛉) Oozes luxury. On the edge of Sochi this four-star is set in copious grounds with a private beach. All 300 rooms have sea views, Internet connections and cable TV. Moving up in price gains safes, bigger bathrooms, bidets, Jacuzzis and private balconies. Guest facilities include bars, a top-notch restaurant, a travel agency, saunas, health centre and pool (nonresidents US$25 per day).

Eating

There are so many restaurants and cafés tapping into a world of cuisines that you could eat in a different place every day throughout the summer.

RESTAURANTS

Patskha Restaurant (☎ 308 3388; Cheltenham Alley, Khosta; meals R350-1000; 🕙 9am-late) Heaps of character here. Linger for long, drawn-out meals lubricated with local wine. The delicious cuisine is Georgian and the prime dish is trout or sturgeon which you catch yourself from a pool outside. Keep an eye on what you're ordering as the bill rapidly mounts, leaving you with a hole in your wallet.

Home Kitchen (Domashnyaya Kukhnya; ul Kooperativnaya 4; meals R80-250; 🕙 9am-10pm) Near the sea

terminal this unpretentious eatery comes in two parts served by a central kitchen. Opt for the older more homely part for a cosy meal in company or the modern section for a quicker meal. The Greek salad was one of the best we've ever tasted.

Yapona Mama (☎ 334 111; ul Ordzhonikidze 25; meals R110-700; 🕙 10am-midnight) Russia has discovered Japanese cuisine and this smallish restaurant is one of several in Sochi. The illustrated menu greatly helps in ordering if you don't know the Russian for sushi or tempura. You can order a couple of pieces or mix and match to make a big feast.

La Pizzeria (☎ 926 064; Naberezhnaya; meals R180-400) Down on the seafront this restaurant has a large canopied bar at the front and a rustic Italian interior. A menu in English reveals a large range of pizzas and pasta. The salmon pizza is probably the best but order 'small' unless you have a huge appetite.

CAFÉS

Café Cinzano (meals R160-570; 🕙 9am-midnight) Hanging onto the end of the Hotel Moskva, this café has some of the best food in Sochi. Try the bliny stuffed with mushrooms or salmon caviar, the peach pie or the wide range of salads.

Stolovaya No 17 (per Morskoy 3; meals R40-100; 🕙 8am-7pm) A piece of history. This wonderful canteen is a relic of Soviet days when 30m queues waited patiently for a cheap meal. Now there's a kitchen full of babushkas serving a range of tasty options presented at a pick-and-choose counter. Plastic

RUSSIAN CAUCASUS

tablecloths cover metal tables decorated with plastic flowers and you get to eat with aluminium cutlery.

Natasha's (ul Vorovskogo 3-1; meals R110-200; ⏰ 8am-11pm) If you've never tasted *khachapuri* or are addicted to the snack then this pavement café is the specialist. They create a two-handled bowl of pastry, fill it with a pool of melted cheese and then float an egg in it.

SELF-CATERING
Sochi's market (ul Moskovskaya; ⏰ 6am-6pm) Has fresh fruit and vegetables. Try fresh pomegranate juice in season and for nibbles *churchkhela*, very tasty sticks of nuts coated with fruit jelly.

Paterson Supermarket (cnr Kurortny pr & ul Dmitrievoy; ⏰ 9am-11pm) A large supermarket with everything you might need.

Drinking
Tinkoff (☎ 951 111; ul Primorskaya 19; meals R200-600; ⏰ noon-1am) Below the Winter Theatre this new brewery-restaurant rises up from the sea embankment as a three-storey monument to the new Sochi. They brew decent beer here. In summer live bands play on the top-floor open terrace.

Entertainment
There's no central listing for events; just keep an eye on the billboards.

NIGHTCLUBS
Saint Tropez (☎ 646 350; ul Moskaya 19; cover R200; ⏰ 8pm-5am) Sochi's premier nightspot has two dance floors to suit the mood. One with low-level lighting, cool music and snuggle-up tables and the other lit with hyper-active spots resounding to pulsating techno.

Malibu (Naberezhnaya; cover Mon-Fri R200; ⏰ 10pm-4.30am) An open-air spot that throbs to the sound of DJ-spun music while the moon casts a silvery path over the ocean.

THEATRE
Winter Theatre (Zimny Teatr; ☎ 629 616; pl Teatralnaya; ⏰ 10am-7pm booking office) Built in a majestic, imperial style this massive, colonnaded building would add grace to any world capital. Opera, ballet and drama are presented here.

The following places put on drama performances and concerts in the summer:

Green Theatre (Zelyony Teatr; ☎ 641 014; Park Rivera; ⏰ box office 11am-8pm)

Summer Theatre (Letny Teatr; ☎ 920 795; Park Frunze; ⏰ box office 10am-8pm)

LIVE MUSIC
Festival Hall (☎ 928 670; ul Ordzhonikidze 5; tickets R300-1000) Many of Russia's top music acts play in Sochi in summer and this massive hall, with its open front to the sea embankment below, plays host to most of them.

Shopping
Art Salon (☎ 921 482; Kurortny pr 29; ⏰ 10am-6pm) Sochi has a thriving artistic community and the Art Salon is choc-a-block with paintings, woodcarvings, icons and pottery items.

Getting There & Away
AIR
Sochi's **airport** (☎ 440 888) is at Adler. Aeroflot flies daily to Moscow (R2923) and in summer there's a weekly flight to Mineralnye Vody (R928, Sunday). Pulkovo flies to St Petersburg (R6200, daily). Flights are more frequent during summer.

Belavia flies to Minsk, Belarus (US$130, Monday, Wednesday, Thursday and Friday, May to October), and daily via Moscow (US$130).

BOAT
The sea terminal has an **information office** (☎ 609 603; ⏰ 8am-8pm) and a **ticket office** (☎ 609 617; ⏰ 10am-6pm Wed, Sat & Sun).

Trabzon, Turkey
There's a Thursday and Sunday sailing (Pullman R1650, shared cabin R2300, 11 hours) that boards at 6pm for an 11pm departure. Return journeys are Friday and Monday.

Poti & Batumi, Georgia
A boat sails on Tuesday to Batumi (R1730, 12 hours, 6pm), calling at Poti (R1580), and returns at 6pm on Friday.

A quicker hydrofoil leaves on Friday for Batumi (R1750, six hours, 1pm), also calling at Poti (R1750), and returns at 1pm on Tuesday.

BUS
Services from the **bus station** (☎ 646 435, ul Gorkogo 56a) include those to Krasnodar (R180, eight hours, 10.10am and 1.30pm), Novorossiysk (R172, nine hours, 8.30am and 12.25pm) and Kislovodsk (R445, 17 hours,

4.30pm). Bus 125 goes to Adler (R15, 40 minutes, 12 daily).

TRAIN

The **train station** (☎ 609 009; ul Gorkogo) has a **service centre** (☎ 924 459; ⏰ 9am-1pm & 2-8pm) for inquiries and ticket sales. Four daily trains go to Moscow (R2200, 27 to 37 hours), more in summer. Train 644 goes to Kislovodsk via Mineralnye Vody and Pyatigorsk (R800, 17 hours, 5.11pm, odd dates) and train 642 goes to Rostov via Krasnodar (R1000, 14 hours, 6.31pm daily).

Getting Around

To get to the airport take bus 124C (R15, one hour, 10.10am, 12.50pm, 4.50pm and 7.15pm) from Sochi bus station. A taxi costs about R200.

Much of Sochi is quite walkable; there's no transport along the embankment. *Marshrutky* charge R7.

AROUND SOCHI

☎ 8622

Except for Mt Fisht and Zelenaya Roscha the easiest way to visit the following places is on an excursion.

Zelenaya Roscha Зелёная Роща

Stalin's dacha, **Zelenaya Roscha** (Green Grove; ☎ 695 600; zelrosha@mail.sochi.ru; Kurortny pr 120; admission R100; ⏰ 9am-4pm Mon-Sat), dates from 1936. Visiting requires prior arrangement with a travel agency (see p465), but this is an amazing place built to accommodate a small, private man who without remorse caused death and misery to millions of Russians. You can also arrange to sleep here.

The depth of the water in Stalin's swimming pool (just 1.5m) and the height of the stair treads, sofas, chairs, tables, bed and even billiard table were fixed to accommodate his small stature (165cm). Security was extremely tight: a guard every 15m around the dacha, a secret lift and tunnel down to the sea, and the painting of the buildings green to camouflage them within the forest.

Visitors can see Stalin's private rooms (some original furniture remains), the movie theatre where he checked every film before public release and his billiards room. Stalin was a lousy player, and he played only those he could beat or were wily enough to lose.

Agura Valley Агурское Ущелье

The Agura Valley cuts a cleft into the rolling foothills with Mt Bolshoy Akhun on its eastern flank and the precipitous **Orlinye Skaly** (Eagle Cliffs) on the west. Within the cleft are three waterfalls, one at 30m, crashing down into water holes.

There are three routes to view the waterfalls. The first is a rough road leading up by the right-hand side of the Matsesta clinic to the top of the Orlinye Skaly escarpment. This reveals fine views over the waterfalls, Mt Bolshoy Akhun and the snow-capped peaks in Abkhazia. Also sharing the view is a golden statue of Prometheus waving his broken chains; see the boxed text, below.

A more strenuous option is a three-hour hike up beside the Agura River from the Sputnik skyscraper on the main Sochi–Adler road.

The remaining option is a downhill ramble from Mt Bolshoy Akhun.

Mt Bolshoy Akhun Гора Большой Ахун

elevation 662m

An 11km-road, just south of the Agura turning, signposted 'Akhun' leads up to a **lookout tower** (admission R35; ⏰ 10am-6pm low season, 10am-9pm high season). The tower gives commanding views of Sochi, Adler and Mt Fisht.

Below the tower is the rustic **Prokhlada Café** (dishes R30-60; ⏰ 10am-late) with outside tables and an inside restaurant. Inside boasts a roaring fire in winter and in summer there's often live music. It serves good shashlyk but try the *lobiyo* (spicy bean stew).

A path by the tower wanders down through the Agura Valley. It's a two-hour descent along the river and waterfalls, longer if you start enjoying homemade wine sold by locals near the water hole (good for swimming). The path ends in a small car park by the Salkhino restaurant.

PROMETHEUS UNCHAINED

In Greek mythology Prometheus stole fire from the gods to give to humankind. As a punishment, Zeus had him chained to a mountain in the Caucasus and had a vulture devour his liver every day. His sentence was meant to run for 30,000 years but he was freed by Hercules after 30.

RUSSIAN CAUCASUS

Catch a *marshrutka* back to Sochi from the main road, a 1.5km walk away.

Vorontsovskaya Cave
Воронцовская Пещера

Usually done on an excursion **Vorontsovskaya Cave** (☎ 643 267; adult/child R110/55, guide R100; ☺ 11am-6pm Tue & Sat winter, 11am-6pm summer), 41km from Sochi, has about 500m of illuminated passage with stalactites and the like.

Mt Fisht Гора Фишт
elevation 2867m

About 100km from Sochi, but reachable only by helicopter or a four-day return trek, Mt Fisht is the start of the Caucasus mountain range. Contact Reinfo (p465) for heliskiing and guided hiking.

Krasnaya Polyana Красная Поляна
elevation 550m

A spectacular road passing through a deep, narrow canyon leads up from Adler to Krasnaya Polyana (Red Valley). At the end, about 70km from Sochi, is a small settlement surrounded by mountains up to 2375m high.

Krasnaya Polyana is a well-developed ski resort with chairlifts for intermediate skiing and snowboarding, and heliskiing for the experienced.

In the last few years there's been an explosion of hotel building aimed at making the place a major European skiing centre. A few shops, bars and cafés are clustered around the chairlift station.

INFORMATION
There is an ATM at the Pyramid restaurant in the Peak Hotel.

Alpika Service (☎ 697 930; ☺ 8.30am-6pm winter, 10am-6pm summer) Ski equipment hire near the chairlift station.

Emergency services (☎ 430 422)

Paraguide (☎ 697 917; ☺ 10am-6pm) Paragliding, rafting, heliskiing and 4WD tours located near the chairlift station.

Weather reports (☎ 697 916)

ACTIVITIES
The main skiing season is November to May. Spring takes over as the snow retreats, blanketing the slopes with a mass of flowers. While Krasnaya Polyana can be 'done' on a day excursion, a few days is needed to gain a real appreciation of this bracing environment.

Easiest access to the mountains is by the four **chairlifts** (sightseeing R500, all-day skiing adult/child R600/300; ☺ 8.30am-4.30pm Nov-May, 10am-5.30pm Wed-Sun Jun-Oct) which take you up in 15-minute stages to 1500m.

Apart from plenty of hiking there are **jeep rides** (per hr R600, 2-day/1-night camping per person US$50) in summer. Contact Paraguide, Reinfo (p465) or local jeep drivers.

Alternatively there's year-round **horse riding** (R500) for a 14km return trip to the mineral springs or mountain biking.

SLEEPING & EATING
Lazurnaya Peak Hotel (☎ 663 600; resp@lazurnaya.ru; ul Zaschitnikov Kavkaza 77; s/d incl breakfast & dinner from €130/170 low season, €170/210 high season; P ☒). Apart from high-class accommodation this hotel provides everything. There's an ATM, bars, restaurant, fitness centre, baths and sauna, ski instructors, equipment hire and transfers. The nightclub will use up any energy left after skiing and there's a big open fire in the foyer to collapse around.

Ibis (☎ 622 042; ul Zaschitnikov Kavkaza; chalets winter/summer R3300/2000) Ibis is a rustic collection of cosy wooden cottages taking five or six people at a squeeze. A café provides full board for an extra R200 per person.

Hotel Tatyania (☎ 918 405 9662; malekon@sochi .ru; r winter/summer from R3000/2000) On the Krasnaya Polyana road, Tatyania is a brand-new midrange hotel with furnishings just out of the wrappers and glistening white bathrooms. The hotel has a restaurant, billiards and bowling. Winter prices include transfers to the chairlift.

Restaurant Pyramid (meals R80-300) One of several clustered around the lowest chairlift station, the Pyramid offers European and Caucasian cuisine. House speciality is trout, kept in a pool outside, and you start your menu choice by going out with a fishing rod.

SHOPPING
Plenty of stalls sell big hairy Caucasian hats, tacky souvenirs, homemade wine, pickles and honey to the swarms of day visitors.

GETTING THERE & AWAY
From Sochi take bus 125 (R15, one hour, 12 buses daily) and change at Adler to bus 135 (R38, 1½ hours, nine daily).

Taxi drivers lurking around Adler bus station will offer a ride to Krasnaya Polyana for R100 per passenger. Alternatively, take a day tour from Sochi (see p466).

DAGOMYS ДАГОМЫС

☎ 8622 / ☽ Moscow

Dagomys resort, 12km from Sochi, stands in its own hilly grounds, between the sea and the Sochi–Dagomys road, 1km away. Built for the peak of foreign tourism in late Soviet times, the resort is not as lively as Sochi. The attraction is for a quiet holiday with everything in one place.

Sleeping & Eating

Hotel Dagomys (☎ 524 053; fax 522 100; ul Leningradskaya 7; s/d incl 2 meals from R940/1250, lyux from R2050/2400; P ✗ ❑ ⬛) A white pyramid hogging the skyline, this four-star, 1800-bed hotel offers everything from basic doubles to two-floor apartments with double bathrooms. The hotel has several bars (including a rooftop one), restaurants, a post office, exchange kiosk, shopping arcade and a service bureau for excursions, car rental, plane and train tickets. There are extensive sanatorium facilities and resort features of beach, indoor and outdoor pools (nonguests R250 per day), sports centre with tennis courts and a concert hall-cum-cinema. Given such services, the unadventurous need go nowhere else.

Olympic (☎ 521 194; fax 524 625; ul Leningradskaya 7a; s/d from R1010/1390) Below Hotel Dagomys, this three-star has well-equipped rooms similar to Dagomys' cheaper options. All rooms face either sea or mountains.

Motel Meridian (r per person from R670) Adjacent to and run by the Olympic. The motel-style rooms range from two beds and a kitchenette to a spacey two-level suite with bedroom, sitting room and kitchenette.

Restoran Dubrava (☎ 521 490; ul Leningradskaya 7; meals R260-800) This roundhouse restaurant with excellent European food is well worth a visit even from Sochi. It's rather an eclectic place with Belgian Trappist beers, Scottish single malt whiskies and *nargilas* (water pipes) on the menu. The courteous and friendly staff can speak some English. Booking would be advisable in season.

Getting There & Around

A free lift from the Dagomys complex (R30 for nonguests) speeds you quickly down to the beach.

Marshrutky leave Sochi bus station for Dagomys (R14, 20 minutes, every 15 minutes) and stop on the main road. A taxi shouldn't cost more than R300.

AROUND DAGOMYS

Dagomys boasts the world's most northerly tea plantations. Performances at **Tea Houses** (☎ 521 955; admission R150; ☽ 11am-5pm summer), a traditional wooden lodge, celebrate Russian culture in song and dance. The upper room has a magnificent tiled fireplace and chimney centrepiece and a collection of decorated samovars; downstairs there are models of the multidomed wooden churches of Kizhi to admire.

A taxi from Dagomys should cost about R200.

MINERAL WATER SPAS МИНЕРАЛЬНЫЕ ВОДЫ

The central Caucasus rises from the steppe in an eerie landscape studded with dead volcanoes and spouting mineral springs. The curative powers of the springs have attracted unhealthy, hypochondriac or just holiday-minded Russians since the late 18th century, when wounded soldiers appeared to heal quicker after bathing in them. The area had already passed from Turkish to Russian hands in 1774 but still came under attack from local tribes. The first settlements were forts that evolved into graceful spa towns.

Today Kavkazskie Mineralnye Vody (Caucasian Mineral Waters) is a holiday resort where the healthy outnumber the ailing. The atmosphere is relaxed, the air fresh and the walks lovely. The parks and elegant spa buildings recall the 19th century, when fashionable society trekked from Moscow and St Petersburg to see, be seen and look for a spouse.

Many of the 130-plus springs have fizzled out for lack of maintenance. Those remaining feed fountains in drinking galleries and provide the elixir for sanatoria treatment

RUSSIAN CAUCASUS

USEFUL BUS & TRAIN ROUTES FROM MINERAL WATER SPAS

The main Mineral Water Spas **bus station** (☎ 86531-56111) is at the airport.

Destination	Departures	Buses daily	Duration	Fare
Kislovodsk	9.40am-8.30pm	7	1hr	R43
Krasnodar	7.10am-9.10pm	12	8hr	R336
Nalchik	6.40am-6.30pm	9	2hr	R90
Pyatigorsk	8am-6pm	14	½hr	R20
Rostov	9.55am-8.55pm	4	10hr	R400
Sochi	6.20pm	1	16hr	R550
Teberda	2.45pm	1	5hr	R182

The **train station** (☎ 86531-46120; ul Pushkina 33) at Mineral Spas picks up trains originating in Kislovodsk (passing through Pyatigorsk), Nalchik and Vladikavkaz. The **Servis Centre** (☎ 86531-56239; ⌚ 8am-noon & 1-7pm) can assist with ticketing.

Destination	Train	Departures	Frequency	Duration	Fare
Kyiv	25	2.02pm	evens	26hr	R1240
Minsk	145	5.38pm	odds	37hr	R1410
St Petersburg	49	7.03pm	daily	44hr	R2570
Moscow*	27/33/41	3 trains	daily	32-34hr	R1940-2800
Moscow†	3	9.17pm	daily	26hr	R2950
Adler (Sochi)	389/643	8.29pm	odds/evens (summer)	12hr	R690
Novorossiysk‡	387	9.27pm	evens	11hr	R690
Nalchik	6810	3.08am	daily	5hr	R74

(*) via Rostov   (†) via Kyiv, Ukraine   (‡) via Krasnodar

of muscle, bone, heart, circulation, nervous system, joints and skin problems. For a fee, at some sanatoria, you can experience being plastered with supposedly curative black mud or being blasted by a shock shower.

Pyatigorsk and Kislovodsk are the main resorts, and Essentuki and Zheleznovodsk the minor resorts.

Getting There & Away
AIR
The regional centre is Mineralnye Vody with the regional airport and train station. Despite being as flash as a country bus stand and, according to a BBC report, one of the worst run in Russia, the **airport** (☎ 86531-58221) is an important air transport hub.

Daily flights (R3590 to R4160) go to Moscow Vnukovo, Domodedovo and Sheremetyevo 1 with KMV Airlines, Aeroflot and Siberia Air. KMV (R5390 to R6500, Thursday and Sunday) and Pulkovo (R6400, Monday, Tuesday, Wednesday and Friday) fly to St Petersburg.

KMV also flies to Baku, Azerbaijan (R4500, Thursday and Saturday), Yerevan, Armenia (R4000, Monday, Tuesday and Friday), and Munich (US$300, Tuesday).

KMV Avia charter flights go to Istanbul (US$220, Sunday) and Antalya (US$270, Thursday and Saturday) in Turkey and to Salonika (€166, Friday) in Greece.

TAXI
Taxi prices from the airport are Pyatigorsk (R300), Kislovodsk (R500) and Dombay or Elbrus (R2000 to R2500). You may be able to negotiate a better price from an arriving rather than a rank taxi.

PYATIGORSK ПЯТИГОРСК
☎ 8793 / pop 141,000 / elevation 510m / ⌚ Moscow

Pyatigorsk, the name being a Russification of Mt Beshtau (Five Peaks), began life as Fort Konstantinovskaya in 1780. It quickly developed into a fashionable resort as it attracted Russian society to its spas and stately buildings. Many of these buildings remain today, making this an attractive town to ramble around and appreciate the bars and restaurants on pr Kirova.

Orientation

Pyatigorsk sprawls around the foot of Mt Mashuk (993m). Tree-lined pr Kirova is the main street, running west from below the Academic Gallery through the town centre to the train station.

To the northwest the town's suburbs stretch towards the jagged crags of Mt Beshtau (1400m). To the south, on a clear day, the twin snow-covered peaks of Mt Elbrus can be seen from several points around town.

Cruising the antiquated tram network is a pleasant way to discover the town. Some trams, imported from Germany, still carry German advertisements.

Information

Book World (Knigo Mir; ☎ 352 766; Upper Market; ☺ 8am-6pm) Some English books and maps.
Hotel Intourist (☎ 363 410; per hr R50; ☺ 9am-1pm & 2-6pm) Offers Internet access.

Main post office (☎ 335 136; cnr pr Kirova & ul Kraynego; ☺ 8am-6.30pm Tue-Sat, 8am-5pm Sun & Mon)
Main telephone centre (☎ 337 838; ul Kraynego; per hr R44; ☺ 6am-11pm) Internet available from 9am to 8pm.
Pyatigorsk Intour (☎ 363 411; tour@infranet.ru; pl Lenina 13; ☺ 10am-6pm) Located inside Hotel Intourist. English-speaking staff, Elbrus and Dombay hikes/climbs, English-, French- and Spanish-speaking guides, hotels and sanatorium bookings, foreigner registration.
Sberbank (☎ 323 606; pr Kirova 59; ☺ 8am-1pm & 2-6pm Mon-Sat, 8-11am Sun) Cashes travellers cheques; ATM.
Tourist Bureau (☎ 350 110; ruse@megalog.ru; pr Kirova 70; ☺ 10am-6pm) Private company with excursions, ticketing, sanatorium bookings, English-speaking staff, foreigner registration.
Tourism Light (☎ 355 025; light@megalog.ru; ul Dzerzhinskogo 41; ☺ 10am-6pm) Airline ticketing, excursions, English-speaking staff, accommodation booking, foreigner registration.

Sights
LERMONTOV SIGHTS

Many attractions revolve around larger-than-life writer, poet, painter, cavalry soldier, society beau and duellist, Mikhail

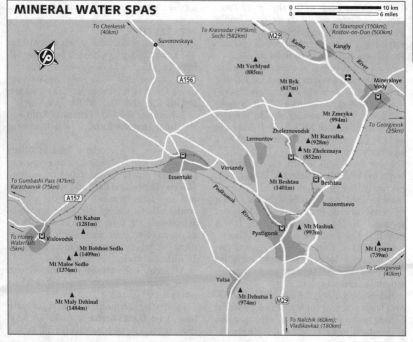

MINERAL WATER SPAS

A HERO OF OUR TIME

The Mineral Waters area is haunted by the Romantic writer Mikhail Lermontov, whose tale *Princess Mary*, from his novel *A Hero of Our Time*, is set here. In an uncanny echo of the novel's plot, Lermontov was killed in a duel at Pyatigorsk in 1841. The book – very short by Russian literary standards – makes a great travelling companion, as does *Lermontov, Tragedy in the Caucasus* by Laurence Kelly, which provides an intriguing background to the man and his society.

Lermontov had been banished twice from St Petersburg to serve in the army in Pyatigorsk: first, after blaming the tsarist authorities for the death in a duel of another 'troublesome' writer, Pushkin; and second, for himself duelling. Lermontov was challenged once again in Pyatigorsk for jesting about the clothes of one Major Martynov. Lermontov, firing first, aimed into the air but was in return shot through the heart. Many saw his death, like Pushkin's, as orchestrated by the authorities.

Many places in Kislovodsk and Pyatigorsk are linked to the man and his fiction, and a visit to the superb Lermontov museum in Pyatigorsk is essential.

Lermontov (see boxed text, above). With the aid of a taxi (about R150) and some walking, these attractions can be strung together as an enjoyable outing.

Take the taxi to the forest clearing that has the monument marking the **Lermontov duel site** (bul Gagarina). The actual duel site is unknown but is thought to be near the needle-point obelisk that even today is bedecked with flowers. Continue by taxi to **Proval**. This is a cave open to the sky where 19th-century couples would dance on a bridge over the pond of light-blue (and smelly) sulphurous water. At the time of research Proval was closed due to flood damage.

Walk from Proval southwest down bul Gagarina to an obvious path on the left that leads through woods to a little domed pavilion, the **Aeolian Harp**, long a favourite lookout point. Early morning should reveal a magnificent view of Mt Elbrus. It was built in 1831 to replace a real harp plucked by a weather vane.

From here walk down via **Lermontov's Grotto** to the **Academic Gallery** (pr Kirova) below. Formerly the Elizabeth Gallery, it was built in 1851 by English architect Upton to house one of Pyatigorsk's best-known springs – No 16 (currently closed). It was here that Lermontov's antihero, Pechorin, first set eyes on Princess Mary. A small gallery houses a **butterfly and insect exhibition** (adult/child R30/20; 11am-8pm) including live tarantulas and scorpions.

Below the gallery, the tree-shaded pr Kirova leads you past some glorious historical houses and various springs squirting out of spouts in walls. Look for the plaque announcing that Tolstoy served his military service here.

Lermontov's thatched cottage where he spent his last two months in 1841 is in the **Lermontov Museum** (Domik Lermontova; ☎ 52710; ul Buachidze 9; admission R100, camera/video R30/50; 10am-5pm Wed-Sun), a group of Lermontov-related buildings in a beautiful garden. The buildings still have some original furniture, copies of Lermontov's poems, sketches and a collection of watercolours of local scenes.

PARK TSVETNIK

Prime attraction is the striking light-blue and beautifully proportioned **Lermontov Gallery** (Lermontovskaya gallereya), built in 1901 in cast iron with stained-glass windows. Once a drinking gallery it's now a **concert hall** (☎ 58350; tickets R90-200; 9am-7pm).

Behind are the 1831 **Lermontov Baths** and the 1880 **Yermolov Baths**, now a treatment centre.

Opposite is a modern **Drinking Gallery** (Pitevaya gallereya; 7am-6pm), where you can take the waters from endlessly gushing faucets. The taste is flat and yucky – diluted bad eggs come to mind. This is the sulphur content that's supposedly good for stomach complaints, probably because it kills off anything in your stomach. Behind, another drinking gallery offers two more from the 16 different underground springs.

Adjacent is the **university** (pr Kirova 36) with some expressive gargoyles and bas-reliefs on its upper façade.

From the Lermontov Gallery, a path leads past **Diana's Grotto**, a small artificial cave, up to Goryachaya (Hot) Hill, with a much-photographed bronze **eagle sculpture** and a Chinese pavilion **lookout**.

MT MASHUK & AROUND

A **cable car** (☎ 974 008; bul Gagarina; per journey R50; ✆ 10am-5pm) whisks you up Mt Mashuk for fresh breezes and a great panorama, weather permitting. The best views of Mt Elbrus are early in the morning; it's a fairly easy 45-minute climb.

OTHER ATTRACTIONS

Pyatigorsk's **Regional Museum** (Kraevedchesky muzey; ☎ 54525; ul Bernardacci 2; adult/child R60/20, camera/video R20/40; ✆ 10am-5pm) marks the development of Pyatigorsk from fortress to

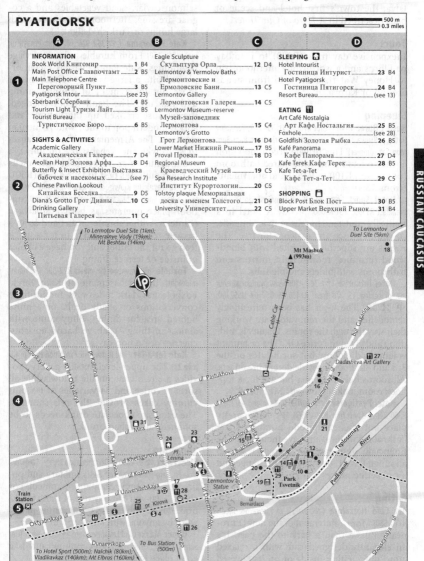

PYATIGORSK

0 — 500 m
0 — 0.3 miles

A	**B**	**C**	**D**

INFORMATION
Book World Книгомир **1** B4
Main Post Office Главпочтамт **2** B5
Main Telephone Centre
 Переговорный Пункт **3** B5
Pyatigorsk Intour ....(see 23)
Sberbank Сбербанк..............................**4** B5
Tourism Light Туризм Лайт............**5** B5
Tourist Bureau
 Туристическое Бюро **6** B5

SIGHTS & ACTIVITIES
Academic Gallery
 Академическая Галерея..........**7** D4
Aeolian Harp Эолова Арфа...........**8** D4
Butterfly & Insect Exhibition Выставка
 бабочек и насекомых .... (see 7)
Chinese Pavilion Lookout
 Китайская Беседка..................**9** D5
Diana's Grotto Грот Дианы...........**10** C5
Drinking Gallery
 Питьевая Галерея **11** C4

Eagle Sculpture
 Скульптура Орла....................**12** D4
Lermontov & Yermolov Baths
 Лермонтовские и
 Ермоловские Бани....................**13** C5
Lermontov Gallery
 Лермонтовская Галерея.........**14** C5
Lermontov Museum-reserve
 Музей-заповедник
 Лермонтова....................................**15** C4
Lermontov's Grotto
 Грот Лермонтова....................**16** D4
Lower Market Нижний Рынок.......**17** B5
Proval Провал...**18** D3
Regional Museum
 Краеведческий Музей **19** C5
Spa Research Institute
 Институт Курортологии.......**20** C5
Tolstoy plaque Мемориальная
 доска с именем Толстого......**21** D4
University Университет **22** C5

SLEEPING 🏠
Hotel Intourist
 Гостиница Интурист.............**23** B4
Hotel Pyatigorsk
 Гостиница Пятигорск............**24** B4
Resort Bureau.....................................(see 13)

EATING 🍴
Art Café Nostalgia
 Арт Кафе Ностальгия............**25** B5
Foxhole ....(see 28)
Goldfish Золотая Рыбка **26** B5
Kafé Panorama
 Кафе Панорама........................**27** D4
Kafe Terek Кафе Терек **28** B5
Kafe Tet-a-Tet
 Кафе Тет-а-Тет........................**29** C5

SHOPPING 🛍
Block Post Блок Пост **30** B5
Upper Market Верхний Рынок.......**31** B4

To Lermotov Duel Site (1km);
Mineralnye Vody (19km);
Mt Beshtau (14km)

To Lermotov
Duel Site (5km)

Mt Mashuk
▲ (993m)

Cable Car

Dadasheva Art Gallery

ul Pastukhova

ul Akademika Pavlova

ul Mira

pl. Lenina

ul Khetagurova

ul Kozlova

ul Universitetskaya

Train
Station

ul Matunina

pr Kirova

Oktyabrskaya ul

Dunaevskogo

To Bus Station
(500m)

ul Kraynego

To Hotel Sport (500m); Nalchik (80km);
Vladikavkaz (140km); Mt Elbras (160km)

Lermontov
Statue

Park
Tsvetnik

ul
Bernardacci

Podkumok River

Teploseraya

Shossepnaya ul

RUSSIAN CAUCASUS

major 19th-century health resort, and its WWII history as a hospital town with a brief period of German occupation.

The striking classical building, the **Spa Research Institute** (Institut Kurortologii; pr Kirova 34), which develops mineral water treatments, was Pyatigorsk's first stone building. Built in 1828 (rebuilt 1955) it was once Restoratsiya, the town's first hotel and scene of balls described in *A Hero of Our Time*.

Tours

Inexpensive day trips (R300) to Dombay or Elbrus and a worthwhile afternoon trip to Honey Waterfalls are sold from stands around pr Kirova.

Sleeping

Resort Bureau (Kurortnoe byuro; ☎ 350 827; Yermolov Baths, pr Kirova 21; ☺ 9am-3pm Mon-Fri winter, 8am-3pm Mon-Sat summer) This private accommodation agency offers rooms with shared bathroom (per person R100 to R150) and apartments (from R350).

Hotel Sport (☎ 390 639; ul Dunaevskogo 5; r incl breakfast R1500, lyux R3000; P ✖) A hotel in a football grandstand but the nonviewing side, so you don't see any matches for free. The rooms are superbly furnished with blond-wood furniture, room-height mirrors and bathrooms with bidets and big tubs.

Hotel Intourist (☎ 363 410; www.pyatigorskintour.ru; pl Lenina 13; s/d from R1400/1500, lyux US$2100; P ✖ 🖳) The foyer has been refreshingly remodelled and the renovators are working their way through the rooms. Quality is middling and given the price OK. The restaurant is large and gloomy but small cafés on the 3rd and 8th floors provide decent breakfasts. All rooms have balconies but ask for a top-floor room looking towards Mt Elbrus.

Hotel Pyatigorsk (☎ 36703; ul Kraynego 43/1; s/d R260-840, s/d lyux from R780/1560; P) Not a pretty place but it is cheap; odd numbers share bathrooms while evens have their own. The financially desperate can sleep on a sofa in a lounge for R130. There are exchange and air ticketing offices.

Eating

Art Café Nostalgia (☎ 57051; pr Kirova 56; meals R110-580) More a statement of the new (European) Russia than a hark to the past. It's an elegantly designed café with a relaxed atmosphere either inside or on its covered terrace. Service is attentive, with maybe an English-speaking waiter, and the food is light but ample and subtle in taste.

Goldfish (Zolotaya Ribka; ul Kraynego 59; meals R70-200) A jungle of rampant vines almost covers this sunken garden leaving hidy-hole shelters containing wonky plastic tables. House speciality is the Goldfish salad – shrimps, salmon caviar, salad vegetables and a cognac dressing; afternoon tea is served with large lumps of Turkish delight.

Kafé Panorama (☎ 352 926; off Teplosernaya ul; meals R60-150) From humble railway carriage beginnings, Kafé Panorama has metamorphosed into a large swanky restaurant for those out for a night of dining, wining and dancing. The band hasn't changed; they've just cranked up the volume and added modern pop to their wild Armenian rhythms. The Armenian cuisine specialises in shashlyks and kebabs; try the *lulya*, a ground mutton or chicken kebab that melts in the mouth. It's best to take a taxi (R50).

Kafe Terek (ul Kraynego 49; meals R50-140; ☺ stolovaya 8am-5pm, restaurant 8am-midnight) This top-floor place operates as both a *stolovaya* (canteen) with a counter buffet and as an à la carte restaurant. If you're in for a quick feed go for the buffet and you have a choice of inside or terrace dining.

Foxhole (ul Kraynego 49; meals R22-50; ☺ 10am-midnight) In the basement of Kafe Terek, Foxhole has dark hideaways for intimate conversations or shady deals, or a more lighted area for dining. Bliny come with almost anything – cabbage, bacon, apricots, cherries or salmon caviar.

Kafe Tet-a-Tet (2nd fl, Tsvetnik Exhibition Hall; pr Kirova 23) The upper-level outside gallery provides a circle view on life below while all sorts of coffee and 34 varieties of tea plus yummy cakes provide the refreshments. The exquisite chocolate drink needs to be spooned rather than drunk.

Shopping

Block Post (☎ 974 090; ul Dzerzhinskogo 37; ☺ 9am-7pm Mon-Fri, 9am-6pm Sat & Sun) Sells military and police gear plus some camping equipment. For about R300 you can buy one of those black-peaked hats with tops as big as dinner plates, worn by anyone with a uniform in Russia.

Upper Market (ul Levanevskogo; ☺ 7am-4pm Tue-Sun). This sells nearly everything and is a good place to look for footwear.

Getting There & Away

Services from the **bus station** (☎ 53432; ul Punimoviche 34) go to Nalchik (R66, two hours, 11 buses daily), Mineralnye Vody (R20, 40 minutes, five buses and five *marshrutky* daily) and Teberda (R162, 3½ hours, 3.35pm).

Marshrutka 113 leaves from Upper Market for Zheleznovodsk (R14, 20 minutes, frequent).

All trains from Kislovodsk stop at Pyatigorsk **train station** (☎ 50291; ul Oktyabrskaya). Add about 45 minutes to Kislovodsk departure times (see p472). The **service bureau** (☎ 351 334; ☻ 8am-1pm & 2-8pm) will book your advance ticket while you sit in comfort.

Getting Around

Tram 4 connects the train station with the town centre through pr Kirova. A taxi to Mineralnye Vody airport should cost R260.

KISLOVODSK КИСЛОВОДСК

☎ 87937 5-digit numbers, 8793 6-digit numbers / pop 133,000 / elevation 822m / ☻ Moscow

Kislovodsk (Sour Waters), the most popular of the resorts, is hillier, greener, prettier but more expensive than Pyatigorsk. 'Love affairs that begin at the foot of Mashuk reach happy endings here', Lermontov wrote. If you're not staying in Kislovodsk then come for a day trip.

Orientation

The train station and Narzan Gallery at the eastern and western ends of ul Karla Marksa, respectively, link the centre with Kurortny Park spreading to the south. The bus station is on the Essentuki road on the northern edge of town.

The Kartinform Kislovodsk map (R40 from any kiosk or bookshop) shows the extensive walking trails.

Information

BOOKSHOPS

Bukinist (☎ 50214; ul Karla Marksa 3; ☻ 9am-6pm) Maps and art albums.

INTERNET ACCESS

Narzan Network (☎ 61000; pl Oktyabrskaya; per hr R44; ☻ 8am-8pm) Upstairs in the post office.

MONEY

APB Bank (bul Kurortny) Opposite Narzan Gallery. MasterCard and Visa ATM.

Sberbank (☎ 61515; ul Kujbisheva 51; ☻ 9am-1pm & 2-5pm) Cashes travellers cheques and currency.

PHOTOGRAPHY

Kavkaz Photo (☎ 20803; bul Kurortny 6; ☻ 10am-8pm) Film, processing, printing digital photos and downloading to CD.

POST

Main post and telephone office (☎ 61000; Oktyabrskaya pl; ☻ post office 8am-8pm, telephone centre 7am-11pm)

TOURIST INFORMATION

Circus ticket office (☎ 59658; ul Karla Marksa 1; tickets R150-200; ☻ 9am-6pm) Next to Bukinist; performances Saturday and Sunday at noon and 4pm.

TRAVEL AGENCIES

KMV (KMB; ☎ 976 047; bul Kurortny 2; ☻ 8am-7pm) Airline ticketing.

Sights

NARZAN BATHS & GALLERY

The main **Narzan Baths** (bul Kurortny 4) are in a 1903 Indian temple–style building. Bathing in Narzan ('Drink of Brave Warriors' in Turkish) is said to prolong life and ease pain but you'll have to wait as the building is closed due to dodgy ceilings.

The rich, carbonic Narzan Spring bubbles up inside a glass dome and feeds 12 drinking fountains in the graceful, well-preserved 1850s **Narzan Gallery** (Narzannaya gallereya; ☎ 50352; Kurortny Park; admission free ☻ 7-9am, 11am-2pm & 4-6pm) designed by English architect S Upton. Visitors who know Bath, England, another mineral springs watering place, will immediately recognise the architectural style executed in the same warm yellow stone.

KURORTNY PARK

From June to August, this flower-covered park is filled with street artists, musicians, chess players and holidaymakers toting water bottles to and from the springs. Numerous stalls selling art and craft make this an open-air art gallery. The central feature is a semicircle **colonnade**, opposite which, up some steps, is a **Lermontov statue**. Caged in a grotto below is the **demon** from Lermontov's famous poem, *The Demon,* believed to be Lermontov's troubled alter ego.

Various forested paths then thread their way along the riverbank and uphill towards

Mt Maloe Sedlo. Most are numbered and signed as they're part of the exercise regime prescribed by the sanatoriums. The Kislovodsk map shows these walks.

The energetic option is to climb Mt Maloe Sedlo and catch the cable car down. The lazier option is to get a taxi to Ordzhonikidze Sanatorium and walk 500m to the **cable car** (kanatnaya doroga; ☎ 65691; adult/child one way R50/30; ⓨ 10am-1pm & 2-5pm winter & 10am-1pm & 2-6pm summer) that will sweep you above tree height to the top of 1376m-high Mt Maloe Sedlo (Little Saddle), with its great panorama of valleys and plateaus. The last cable car leaves 30 minutes before closing.

If walking up, paths lead via a rose garden to the **Krasnye Kamni** (Red Rocks), col-oured by their iron content and topped by an eagle sculpture. Further uphill are the **Serye Kamni** (Grey Rocks), featuring good views. Just past here you can slog up to **Krasnoe Solnyshko Hill** (Red Sun Hill), with possible views of Mt Elbrus.

From the top trails you can walk 5km southeast along the top to Mt Maly Dzhinal (1484m). Mt Bolshoe Sedlo (1409m) is 1km northeast. **Horse rides** (from R200) are possible.

OTHER ATTRACTIONS

To secure Russia's new southern frontier Catherine the Great built a line of forts along the Caucasus mountain range. Kislovodsk was one of them, and the **Regional Museum** (Kraevedchesky muzey; ☎ 37049; per Mira

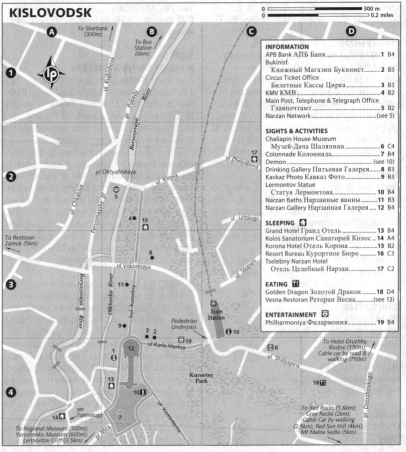

KISLOVODSK

| 0 | 300 m |
| 0 | 0.2 miles |

INFORMATION
APB Bank АПБ Банк.................................1 B4
Bukinist
Книжный Магазин Букинист.............2 B3
Circus Ticket Office
Билетные Кассы Цирка.......................3 B3
KMV КМВ...4 B2
Main Post, Telephone & Telegraph Office
Главпочтамт.......................................5 B4
Narzan Network..................................(see 5)

SIGHTS & ACTIVITIES
Chaliapin House Museum
Музей-Дача Шаляпина.......................6 C4
Colonnade Колоннада..........................7 B4
Demon...(see 10)
Drinking Gallery Питьевая Галерея.....8 B3
Kavkaz Photo Кавказ Фото..................9 B3
Lermontov Statue
Статуя Лермонтова...........................10 B3
Narzan Baths Нарзанные ванны.........11 B3
Narzan Gallery Нарзанная Галерея 12 B4

SLEEPING
Grand Hotel Гранд Отель....................13 B4
Kolos Sanatorium Санаторий Колос ...14 A4
Korona Hotel Отель Корона................15 B2
Resort Bureau Курортное Бюро 16 C3
Tselebny Narzan Hotel
Отель Целебный Нарзан....................17 C2

EATING
Golden Dragon Золотой Дракон.........18 D4
Vesna Restoran Ресторан Весна..........(see 13)

ENTERTAINMENT
Philharmoniya Филармония.................19 B4

To Sberbank
(300m);

To Bus
Station
(6km);

ul Kulibsheva

pl Pobedy

Beryozovaya River

To Restoran
Zamok (5km)

ul Chkalova

Pervomaysky pr

pl Oktyabrskaya

ul Kirova

Beryozovaya pr

ul Vokzalnaya

bul Kurortny

Olkhovka River

River

ul Zhelyabova

ul Uritskogo

ul Stepan

Pedestrian
Underpass

Train
Station

ul Karla Marksa

Kurortny
Park

ul Shalyapina

To Hotel Druzhba
Rostov (150m);
Cable car by road &
walking (750m)

pr Dzerzhinskogo

per Yanovskogo

pr Mira

ul Kominterna

To Regional Museum (500m);
Yaroshenko Museum (600m);
Lermontov Cliff (3.5km)

To Red Rocks (1.6km);
Grey Rocks (2km);
Cable Car by walking
(2.5km); Red Sun Hill (4km);
Mt Maloe Sedlo (5km)

BOY FALLS FOR WRONG GIRL

Local legend tells the story of a girl from a rich family who fell in love with a boy from a poor family. Her father wouldn't let her marry her love as he'd promised her to an old, ugly but rich merchant. She refused the match and ran away with the boy, her family pursuing them to the edge of a cliff just outside Kislovodsk. Faced with a dilemma, the boy suggested jumping off together and ending their lives in love rather than misery. The girl agreed but said she was afraid. Her lover should jump first, she suggested, so he did – and died. Looking down at his splattered body, the girl decided not to join him and ended up marrying the old man.

11; adult/child per exhibition R30/10; ❧ 10am-6pm) is within the remaining walls of that 1803 fort. The first exhibit traces the city's history. Pushkin, Tolstoy and Lermontov were visitors and dissident writer Solzhenitsyn was born here. Disappointingly there's only one display devoted to him. The second exhibit chronicles the Great Patriotic War, Kislovodsk as a hospital city and the six-month German occupation in 1942.

The small **Yaroshenko Museum** (Yaroshenko muzey; ☎ 31111; ul Yaroshenko 1; adult/child R40/15; ❧ 10am-6pm Wed-Mon) houses the works of painter Nikolai Yaroshenko, who lived in this house surrounded by a most pleasant garden-orchard. Yaroshenko was an outstanding late-19th-century Russian artist, an incomparable portraitist and a leading proponent of Russian realism. A second building displays works of his contemporaries. An English-speaking guide is available.

Travel about 4km southeast into the valley of the Olkhovka River and you'll realise how beautiful the surrounding countryside is – a baize-green plateau cut by deep winding valleys with sides of crags and cliffs. One of these crags is Lermontovskaya Skala (Lermontov Cliff), where the climactic duel in *A Hero of Our Time* was set.

Chaliapin House Museum (Dom Shalyapina; ☎ 67560; adult/child R30/10; ❧ 11am-6pm Wed-Mon) is a wood and stained-glass villa near the train station. Chaliapin, the legendary Russian opera singer, lived here in 1917 and his downstairs room is devoted to photo-

graphs of his various roles. One can also admire marvellous plaster ceilings bursting with cherubs and fruit designs, and a lovely glaze-tiled chimney.

Tours
Pavement sellers and hotels sell excursions to Elbrus (R300, 6.30am Wednesday, Saturday and Sunday), Dombay (R300, 6.30am Tuesday, Thursday, Saturday and Sunday) and Honey Waterfalls (R150, 2.30pm daily).

Sleeping
BUDGET
Resort Bureau (Kurortnoe byuro; ☎ 33165; train station; ❧ 7am-7pm) The bureau is an agency for several sanatoriums (accommodation and treatment R705 to R8025) and renters of rooms/apartments (from R100 to R500). A staff member can speak some English. Register your visa with the Tselebny Narzan Hotel.

Hotel Druzhba Rostov (☎ 66600; pr Dzerzhinskogo 22; s/d from R430/680; P) Some rooms have not been renovated so they're the cheapies. Advance booking is essential as the place is often full. There's a bar and restaurant.

MIDRANGE & TOP END
Korona Hotel (☎ 50396; koronabora@list.ru; bul Kurortny 5; r incl breakfast R3100; P ✖) The Korona is a new boutique hotel, tastefully decorated with attention to design. Apart from the usual phone/fridge/cable TV, rooms come with sofa beds for extra guests, safes and bathrobes; some have balconies. With only six rooms it's best to book.

Tselebny Narzan Hotel (☎ 66197; www.intournarzan.kurortinfo.ru; ul Zhelyabova 5; full board/plus treatment

AUTHOR'S CHOICE

Grand Hotel (☎ 33119; grand@narzan.com; bul Kurortny 14; s/d incl breakfast from R980/1400) is definitely the nicest place in town with all those little extras that mark out a classy place – the smile of the receptionist, the grand entrance staircase and the readiness of the burly porter to heft two suitcases at a time up three flights of stairs. The rooms are well-furnished and spacious bathrooms come with bathrobes and hairdryer. The 3rd floor's the best; a lightly tinted blue glass roof makes you feel the sun is always shining when you come out of your room.

RUSSIAN CAUCASUS

TRAIN SERVICES FROM KISLOVODSK

From Kislovodsk's attractive **train station** (☎ 52270; ul Vokzalnaya) there's a frequent weekday *elektrichka* service through Essentuki (R11, 30 minutes) to Pyatigorsk (R16.50, 50 minutes) and Mineralnye Vody (R38.50, 1¾ hours); weekends only have three trains (11am, 4pm and 9.05pm). Major distance trains:

Destination	Train	Departures	Frequency	Duration	Fare
Kyiv	25	11.38am	evens	28½hr	R1250
Minsk	145	3.11pm	odds	40hr	R1430
Moscow	3	7.10pm	daily	27½hr	R1990
Moscow*	27	7.42pm	daily	35hr	R2840
Sochi	642	5.52pm	daily summer	14½hr	R760
St Petersburg	49	4.50pm	daily	46hr	R2660

* via Ukraine

---

s R1950/2300, d R2300/3000, deluxe R5000; (P) (✕) (⌧)) 'Either this wallpaper goes or I do': Oscar Wilde. The wallpaper stayed – they were his dying words – and is now on the walls of this hotel. Unless you have a Wilde temperament you can forgive the hotel's choice. All rooms are more than adequate; deluxe rooms have add-on sitting rooms and Jacuzzis. The hotel is a visa registration agency (R350) with exchange and plane ticketing counters. There's a sauna (nonguests per hour R50).

Kolos Sanatorium (☎ /fax 31112; per Yanovskogo 7; full board s from R895-2500, d from R1320-4160) This is one of the few sanatoriums to accept foreigners. Medically they deal with heart, circulation, joints and nerves through mud baths, hot Narzan baths and shock showers (like being doused with a fire hose).

Eating

Golden Dragon (Zolotoy Drakon; ☎ 67002; ul Shalyapina 12; meals R140-400) Tired of shashlyk? Golden Dragon's menu of Korean and Japanese food might tempt you. Attention to service, endless tea, hot towels, little plates and warmers for different dishes make you feel wanted. Live music and dancing begin after 7pm.

Vesna Restoran (☎ 33119; bul Kurortny 14; meals R80-250) The Grand Hotel's restaurant has first-class food and service. The menu in English offers a 'fragrant salting from the chief' for R85, although we didn't investigate further. On warm summer nights the restaurant spreads its tables outside and a man at a piano entertains the diners.

Restoran Zamok (☎ 34609; Alikonovskoe uschelje; dishes R210-400; ⏲ noon-late; ✕) This modern castle, 7km west of Kislovodsk in the Alikonovka gorge, was built to trade on the local legend of treachery and love (see the boxed text, p479). It's a favoured place for locals, visitors and wedding parties. The restaurant setting is pseudomedieval, the dishes are Georgian and the wine is hellishly expensive. A taxi should cost about R70.

The **café** (⏲ 10am-6pm) on top of Mt Maloe Sedlo provides good shashlyk, salad and *lavash* (flat bread) plus big glasses of homemade wine. Eat on the balcony and look down on Kislovodsk.

Entertainment

Philharmoniya (☎ 20422; ul Karla Marksa 1; tickets R90-1000) Founded in 1895, the Philharmoniya presents concerts, opera, musical and comedy events in a beautiful baroque and neoclassical auditorium.

Getting There & Away

Services from the **bus station** (☎ 41161; ul Promyshlennaya 4) head to Anapa (R510, 13 hours, 6pm), Gelendzhik (R539, 15½ hours, 2pm even dates) and Krasnodar (R381, 10 hours, 12.40pm) via Mineralnye airport. *Marshrutky* leave from the train station for Pyatigorsk (R60, 7.30am to 1pm, frequent service).

A taxi to Dombay costs R1600 to R2500.

ZHELEZNOVODSK ЖЕЛЕЗНОВОДСК

☎ 86532 / pop 29,000 / ⏲ Moscow
The smallest spa town, Zheleznovodsk (Iron Waters) lies at the foot of Mt Zheleznaya (852m) on the northern side of Mt Beshtau.

It's an ideal half-day trip from Pyatigorsk by *marshrutka*. Get off on ul Lenina, where the pleasant park spreads up the mountain towards natural forest. Zheleznovodsk waters are used for digestive, kidney and metabolic problems.

Before walking up, have a nose around the red-and-white-striped 1893 **Ostrovsky Baths** (Ostrovoskiye Vanny). They've been closed for a while but of particular interest is the Islamic influence – pointed arches, a pseudo minaret and decorative Arabic calligraphy.

Another beautiful building is the blue-and-white, iron-and-glass **Pushkin Gallery** (Pushkinskaya gallereya), imported as a prefabricated building from Warsaw and erected in 1901. A companion to Pyatigorsk's Lermontov Gallery, it's a similar exercise in elegance and composition.

Another Islamic-influenced gem nearby is the Emir of Bukhara's blue-and-yellow late-19th-century palace, now part of **Telman Sanatorium** (Sanatory Telmana) complex. Lenin's wife and sister received treatment here.

Of the resort's 54 springs, only four remain, three with the same water. Others have run dry or fallen into disrepair. To see how the place looked in its heyday, visit the **local museum** (Kraevedchesky muzey; ☎ 42602; ul Lermantova 3; adult/child R10/5; ⌚ 10am-5pm Tue-Sun) across from Telmana Sanatorium. It has a good photograph collection.

THE CAUCASUS RANGE

The remarkable 1100km-long Caucasus mountain range is 25 million years old and is a geographical, political and ethnic boundary, its watershed forming Russia's southern frontier with Abkhazia, Georgia and Azerbaijan.

The range is littered with glaciers, about 2000 of them, most edging down the northern side, and some are 13km or 14km long, especially in the middle third of the ranges where they are narrowest and the peaks highest. There are 200 peaks over 4000m, 30 over 4500m and seven over 5000m. Russia is proud of its highest European mountain – Mt Elbrus (5642m); Mont Blanc, highest in Western Europe at 4807m, is exceeded by 15 Caucasus peaks.

CENTRAL CAUCASUS ЦЕНТРАЛЬНЫЙ КАВКАЗ

The two mountain destinations most visited by foreigners for wonderful skiing, hiking and climbing are Dombay and Elbrus, accessible from Pyatigorsk, Kislovodsk and Nalchik.

Anyone considering hiking or climbing in this area should read *Trekking in the Caucasus* by Yury Kolomiets and Alexey Solovyev.

DOMBAY ДОМБАЙ

☎ 87872 / elevation 1600m / ⌚ Moscow

Zooming through a winding narrow and forested valley, visitors to Dombay are suddenly confronted with a sheer wall of mountains crowned with white shark-teeth summits. This is the heart of the Caucasus. Only those blasé about mountains would fail to be knocked off their perches by this stupendous vista.

Not only can you gawk from the bottom but also easily at 3000m, where you can scan snow peaks, glaciers and distant views.

Skiing, walking, hiking, climbing and plain sightseeing are what attract visitors. New hotels and cafés are being built for an increasing number of visitors; during the peak ski season, late December to April, hotels can be full and prices can triple.

Dombay is at the heart of **Teberdinsky Nature Reserve** (admission R20) which is rich in flora and fauna, see the boxed text, p483.

Orientation

Three deep valleys watered by glacier-fed torrents – Alibek from the west, Amanauz from the south and Dombay-Yolgen from the east – meet here to flow north, eventually as the Teberda River. Straddling both sides of the Amanauz River is the village of Dombay. From here a cable car and four chairlifts ascend the Mussa-Achitara (Horse Thief) ridge to the east. Kiosks by the bottom cable car station sell maps.

Information

The closeness of the Abkhazia border means that foreigners require permits for

anywhere other than the village environs and Mussa-Achitara ridge. Come with enough roubles. Hotel Gornye Vershiny has an ATM and exchanges foreign currency.

BARS (BARC; ☎ 58223; bars@dombai.info; ☺ 9am-1pm & 2-6pm) Accommodation booking, excursions, guides, climbing, ski hire and border permit arrangement.

Rescue Post (Spasatelnaya Sluzhba; ☎ 58138; ☺ 24hr) Emergency help, plus advice on more technical hikes and climbs. Summer guide service except mid-July–August.

Tourist Service (☎ 58238; express@dombayinfo.ru; per hr R100 ☺ 8am-11pm) Internet access, foreigner registration, border permit arrangement, excursions, hotel booking, ski hire and lessons, heliskiing, paragliding, rafting and kayaking.

www.dombai.info Infrequently updated but with some nonperishable information and photographs.

Sights & Activities
MUSSA-ACHITARA

Thrusting up the north side of the Dombay-Yolgen Valley, the 3012m-high Mussa-Achitara ridge provides magnificent skiing and views around the Dombay peaks, valleys and glaciers.

Access is by four **chairlifts** (per stage R100; ☺ 9am-5pm Mon-Fri, 8am-6pm Sat & Sun) and a **cable car** (☎ 58238; adult/child R200/100; ☺ 9am-5pm high season, 9am-11am & 3-5pm Mon-Fri, 9am-5pm Sat & Sun low season). An additional cable car should be completed for 2006. Take chairlift 1 (1600–1700m) and 2 (1700–2260m) to the upper cable car station. Alternatively, take the cable car from near Hotel Solnechnaya Dolina. Chairlifts 3 (2260–2500m) and 4 (2500–3000m) complete the ascent.

SKIING

Excellent skiing, similar to the European Alps, is possible from November until late May. There are good long, steep runs for experienced skiers from the Mussa-Achitara ridge down to 1620m. Plenty of terrain exists for ski touring if you have a local guide, but beware of avalanches. Ski equipment and snowboards can be rented at hotels or travel agencies.

WALKS & HIKES

The following routes require a border permit (free), obtainable from one of the

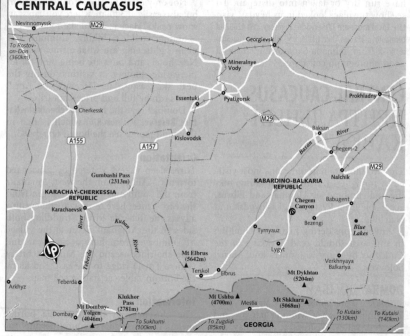

CENTRAL CAUCASUS

Nevinnomyssk

M29

To Rostov-on-Don (360km)

Georgievsk

Mineralnye Vody

Essentuki   Pyatigorsk

Cherkessk

M29

Prokhladny

Baksan   River

A155

A157

Kislovodsk

Baxan

Chegem-2

M29

Gumbashi Pass (2313m)

KARACHAY-CHERKESSIA REPUBLIC

KABARDINO-BALKARIA REPUBLIC

Nalchik

Karachaevsk

River

Kuban

River

Chegem Canyon

Babugent

Bezengi

Blue Lakes

Tyrnyauz

Lygyt

Verkhnyaya Balkariya

Arkhyz

Teberda

Teberda

Klukhor Pass (2781m)

Mt Elbrus (5642m)

Terskol   Elbrus

Mt Ushba (4700m)

Mestia

Mt Dykhtau (5204m)

Mt Shkhara (5068m)

Dombay

Mt Dombay-Yolgen (4046m)

To Sukhumi (100km)

To Zugdidi (85km)

GEORGIA

To Kutaisi (130km)

To Kutaisi (140km)

FLORA AND FAUNA

Altitude, climate ranges and inaccessibility have made the Caucasus extremely rich in flora and fauna. Three progressions of vegetation exist. By the coast and at lower altitudes temperate rainforest dominates with oak, beech and chestnut. Ancient groves of yew remain in places like the Teberdinsky Nature Reserve, along with gigantic 600-year-old beeches and a species of grass higher than a human. Conifer forests dominate with increasing altitude and above the tree line subalpine meadows are home to many flowering species and rhododendron bushes. Higher still, alpine grasslands have many endemic low-growing perennials.

Bear, wolf, wild boar, lynx, jackal, ibex, deer, tur (wild Caucasian goat), chamois and wild sheep populate the Caucasus. European bison, locally once extinct, have been reintroduced into the Teberda Reserve. The casual visitor is unlikely to see any of these except goat and bison, as they inhabit the large, wild, unpopulated tracts of the Caucasus. Birdlife is equally rich, especially with predators, including eagles, hawks and black griffon vultures.

travel agencies. A guide is essential for journeys near the border as some of the most spectacular sights are tricky to get to; you need to cross glaciers and torrential rivers. Plus there's a bear population. The hardy, friendly (somewhat English-speaking) guides at the rescue post know the terrain well and can give advice. Remember, these people are responsible for rescuing you if you get lost.

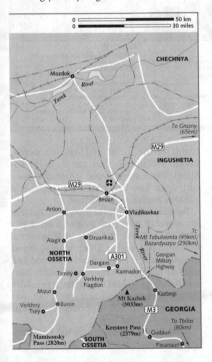

Chuchkhur Waterfalls & Ptysh Valley

It's an easy scenic 6km walk from the start of chairlift 1 to two fine waterfalls on the Chuchkhur River. First, follow the vehicle track and then branch across Russkaya Polyana clearing; it's another two hours (5km) to the first set of waterfalls. Past the waterfalls, a steep path leads towards Chuchkhur Pass. Twenty minutes downstream from the falls, a path forks south for a steady 2km walk up Severny (North) Ptysh Valley and another waterfall, this one over 70m high.

Amanauz Valley

A marked trail, steep in parts, leads south from the Dombay housing area and goes for about 4km, up through two sets of woods to a waterfall and Chyortova Melnitsa (Devil's Mill) viewpoint.

Alibek Glacier

The track behind Hotel Solnechnaya Dolina leads 6km up Alibek Valley to a mountaineers' hostel, passing a climbers' cemetery after 2km. From the hostel a path ascends to little Lake Turie near Alibek Glacier, 9km from Dombay. A strenuous variation is to fork left from the path after the hostel, and head through woods to the dramatic Alibek Falls. If you cross the dodgy bridge at the foot of the falls and then scramble up the left side you can walk on the glacier and up the scree on its right side to Lake Turie.

CLIMBS

Peaks that can be tackled from Dombay include Sofrudzhu (3780m), Dombay-Yolgen (4046m), Sulakhat (3409m) and Semyonovbashi (3602m) above Alibek Valley.

RUSSIAN CAUCASUS

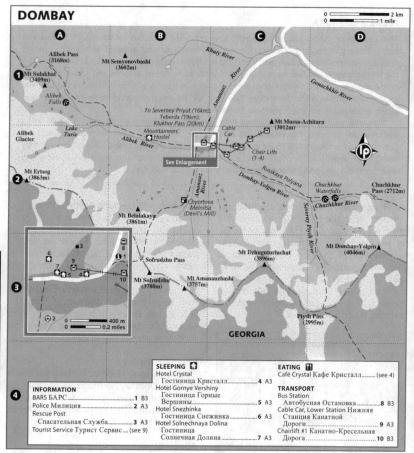

DOMBAY

INFORMATION
BARS БАРС **1** B3
Police Милиция **2** A3
Rescue Post
    Спасательная Служба **3** A3
Tourist Service Турист Сервис .... (see 9)

SLEEPING
Hotel Crystal
    Гостиница Кристалл **4** A3
Hotel Gornye Vershiny
    Гостиница Горные
    Вершины **5** A3
Hotel Snezhinka
    Гостиница Снежинка **6** A3
Hotel Solnechnaya Dolina
    Гостиница
    Солнечная Долина **7** A3

EATING
Café Crystal Кафе Кристалл .... (see 4)

TRANSPORT
Bus Station
    Автобусная Остановка **8** B3
Cable Car, Lower Station Нижняя
    Станция Канатной
    Дороги **9** A3
Chairlift #1 Канатно-Кресельная
    Дорога **10** B3

While the rescue post could provide some information, it's more usual for climbers to come in organised groups or to hire a guide from one of the local travel agencies.

Tours
The travel agencies and hotels organise tours. Included are walks (R150 to R375, four to nine hours) to various waterfalls and lakes, and jeep excursions (R200 to R400, three to seven hours) to more distant lakes, waterfalls and medieval castle ruins.

Sleeping & Eating
Hotel Snezhinka (Snowflake; ☎ 54321; dombay@ok .ru; d/lyux R1000/3500, 4-person cottage R12,000; ☒ ☒) Just behind Hotel Solnechnaya Dolina, this

is one of the nicest of Dombay's hotels. Rooms are doubles only and there is a romantic three-storey wood-panelled cottage with open fire. Bar, restaurant, sauna and billiards complete the picture.

Hotel Solnechnaya Dolina (Sunny Valley; ☎ 58269; solndol@mail.ru; s/d/tr/q incl breakfast & dinner from R1000/2000/3000/3600; ☒) Built in 1936 as the first hotel in Dombay, this picturesque and friendly place is made entirely of wood and without nails in the manner of north Russian buildings. A hint of pine resin pervades the air. Rooms are all well kitted out and *lyux* come with sitting rooms. Ski equipment can be hired here.

Hotel Crystal (☎ 58555; r low/high season from R800/1000, cottages R500/700; ☒ ☒) The Crystal is a friendly new hotel with standard rooms sharing bathrooms and good luxury wood-panelled rooms with balconies and mountain views. Cottages are simple rooms with shared bathrooms.

Hotel Gornye Vershiny (Mountain Peaks; ☎ /fax 58230; d summer/winter R400/450, full board plus R200, deluxe from R1300, lyux R2400; 🔊) Despite being a relic of the Soviet love affair with concrete monstrosities, this hotel is popular with groups as it's cheap. Rooms are somewhat basic and timeworn, but it's the facilities that score – money exchange and ATM, sauna, bowling alley, disco in winter, free guided walks, skiing and snowboarding instruction with English- and German-speaking guides.

During peak seasons Dombay is blessed with a multitude of cafés and food stalls around the village, cable car stations and chairlift stops.

Café Crystal (meals R110-200; 🕙 9am-midnight) The smell of good cooking will lead you through the porch into a cosy room with refectory tables, where groups of Russians come to eat, tell tall stories, sink vodka and sing; expect to be invited in.

Shopping
The local babushka knitting-circle has stalls all around the village and chairlift stations selling their output of shawls (R150 to R2000), socks (R30 to R100) and felt Georgian-style hats (R50 to R400).

Getting There & Away
Public transport is very limited; a daily *marshrutka* departs Dombay's bus station for Cherkessk (R150, three hours, 8.30am) and returns at 1.30pm. Alternatives are an expensive taxi (up to R2500) or a day excursion from Kislovodsk or Pyatigorsk.

These excursions take you over the 2313m Gumbashi Pass, with gobsmacking views of Mt Elbrus lording it above the whole mountain chain. The coach stops for photographs. Arrange with the tour leader or driver to return another day but remember that the tours aren't daily. Take your passport for crossing borders between the republics.

TEBERDA ТЕБЕРДА
☎ 87872 / 🕙 Moscow
Teberda, 20km north of Dombay, is home to the **Teberdinsky Nature Reserve Headquarters** (☎ 51261; admission R15; 🕙 8.30am-5.30pm). The re-

serve has a nature museum and a small zoo that are covered by the entrance fee. There's decent **accommodation** (☎ 51433; per person with shared bathroom R200-250) in pleasant wood-lined rooms that come with a sitting room. Walks to the **Dzhamagatskie Narzany mineral springs** – west up Dzhamagat Valley and around seven hours for the round trip – start here, as do those to **Mukhinsky Pass** (east). You'll need a border permit for most of the walks and also a permit (R5) from the Nature Reserve headquarters. The reserve can provide guides for groups (five minimum) for R300 a day.

NALCHIK НАЛЬЧИК
☎ 86622 / pop 283,000 / 🕙 Moscow
Nalchik, pleasant capital of the Kabardino-Balkaria Republic, strides the rise of the steppes to the foothills of the Caucasus. It was founded as a fort in 1822 to protect Russian advances into the Caucasus. Apart from a worthwhile museum and a side trips to Chegem Canyon and some medieval villages, visitors come to Nalchik to reach Mt Elbrus.

Orientation
Two parallel streets, pr Lenina and pr Shogentsukova, run southwest through the centre from the train station on Osetinskaya ul. Kiosks on pr Lenina sell the excellent Kartinform Nalchik map that includes regional and detailed Elbrus maps.

Information
BORDER PERMITS
Border police (Pogranzastava; ☎ 916 510; Kabardinskaya ul 192; 🕙 9am-6pm Mon-Fri) See the boxed text, p487, for further details on permits.

INTERNET ACCESS
Internet café (☎ 426 345; pr Lenina 41; per hr R40, after 1MB per MB R2.80; 🕙 10am-8pm).

MONEY
Sberbank (☎ 426 836; ul Khuranova 9; 🕙 9.15am-1pm & 2-3.30pm) Cashes travellers checks, changes currency.

PHOTOGRAPHY
Smart (☎ 423 010; pr Lenina 20; 🕙 9am-8pm) Burn to CD/print digital per photo R3/10.

POST & TELEPHONE
Main post & telephone office (☎ 425 989; pr Shogentsukova 14; 🕙 8am-9pm) Has Internet access on 1st fl, per hr R35.

RUSSIAN CAUCASUS

TRAVEL AGENCIES

Air Communications Agency (Agentstvo Vozdushnykh Soobsheny; ☎ 423 326; ul Lenina 43; ⏰ 8am-6pm) Air ticketing.

KMV (KMB; ☎ 440 470; pr Lenina 32; ⏰ 9am-7pm) Air ticketing; in the foyer of Hotel Rossiya.

Sights

The interesting **Kabardino-Balkar National Museum** (Natsionalny muzey; ☎ 776 880; ul Gorkogo 62; admission R10, camera/video R30/100; ⏰ 10am-5.30pm Tue-Sat) has a good 3-D topographical map of the mountains. Displays cover natural history, prehistory, origins of the Kabardian and Balkarian peoples, the Russian conquest and the industrial development of the state.

A large, fine park with a permanent **fairground** (pr Shogentsukova; ⏰ 9am-dusk) stretches over 2km south of town. A **chairlift** (one way R40; ⏰ 11am-7pm Mon, 9am-7pm Tue-Sun) crosses a lake to wooded hills and the Restaurant Sosruko.

If you're passing, the **Art Gallery** (Izobrazitelnykh iskusstv; ☎ 423 778; pr Lenina 35; admission R10; ⏰ 10am-6pm Sat-Thu) is worth the entrance fee for its rotating exhibitions of local art.

Sleeping & Eating

Grand Caucasus Hotel (☎ 477 266; grand_kavkas@ mail.ru; ul Tarchokova 2; s/d incl breakfast from R1500/2000; Ⓟ) In a wooded suburb southwest of town, this is the stateliest hotel in Nalchik. A carpeted grand staircase sweeps you upstairs to a mixture of fine rooms. Third-floor front rooms have big balconies for viewing the park.

Hotel Rossiya (☎ 775 378; pr Lenina 32; r R600-2100) The central Rossiya has improved since being renovated but guests still don't get any water between 11pm and 5am. Front rooms have little balconies from where guests can

---

LOCAL HERO

Like many other peoples in prehistory, Kabardians enjoyed their fires for warmth, cooking and defence. One day an evil giant called Inizh Nezakve came and stole their fire. The Kabardians suffered for many years until a hero, born out of a large stone, rose up. He was named Sosruko and grew up to meet his destiny – a fight with Nezakve. Victorious, of course, he returned with fire for his people.

---

address the early-morning assembly of stray dogs or lounging taxi drivers.

Restaurant Sosruko (☎ 720 070; off Profsoyuznaya ul; meals R100-345; ⏰ 10am-late) This architecturally unusual restaurant, perched upon a hill, comprises the head of Sosruko (see boxed text, left), an outstretched arm and hand holding a flame. The restaurant is in the head, from where diners can gaze over the Caucasus range and see an ever-changing canvas of moody weather. An outdoor terrace leads to the top chairlift station. Order the Sosruko special, a concoction of mince, mushrooms and herbs in a pastry pear.

Children's World (pr Lenina; meals R60-220; ⏰ 9am-9pm) Never mind the figure of a bearded, hook-handed pirate that greets you by the outline of a pirate ship, as this is not strictly a children's hang-out. Located by Hotel Rossiya, this department store does nice things with ice cream and fruit and is also a full-blown bar. Delectable cakes, snacks, salads and hamburgers are also on offer.

Café Darida (ul Pushkina 66a; meals R25-85; ⏰ 8am-6.30pm) This *stolovaya*-café with cheap eats is near the Rossiya and is good for breakfast.

Supermarket Bosfor Elbrus (☎ 420 265; pr Lenina 43; ⏰ 9am-9pm) Stock up for visits to Elbrus.

Shopping

Cherkess House (☎ 426 171; pr Lenina 49; ⏰ 9am-7pm) This shop sells all manner of Cherkessian items such as Cossack coats complete with breast pockets for gun cartridges (R7000), hats (R500 to R4000) and drinking vessels.

Getting There & Away

There are daily flights to Moscow Vnukovo (R4030). A taxi to the airport is R70.

Buses from the **bus station** (☎ 915 923; ul Gagarina 124) serve Pyatigorsk (R70, 2½ hours, 11 buses daily), Kislovodsk (R75, 2½ hours, 1.10am, 10.40am and 5.05pm) and Mineralnye Vody (R75, 2½ hours, five daily).

From the **train station** (☎ 774 110; ul Osetinskaya) an *elektrichka* runs to Mineralnye Vody (R42, 3¾ hours, 7.16am). Train 41 to Moscow (R2100, 38 hours, 3.25pm) passes through Rostov (R900, 13 hours) and a section splits off to Sochi (R950, 16½ hours).

AROUND NALCHIK

Turn southwest at Chegem-2, 17km northwest of Nalchik, to reach the **Chegem Canyon**. The spectacular part of the canyon is 44km

---

BORDER PERMITS – AN ENCOUNTER WITH BUREAUCRACY

Free permits are issued by the Border Police (Pogranzastava) in Nalchik (p485). Life could be easier, like being on an organised tour where all this is done for you, but solo you'll need three copies of an application form completed in Russian. Detail your routes, dates, who's going – full names, dates of birth, citizenship and passport details. All of this is best done with an interpreter; it takes two days and don't be surprised if a small payment is suggested to ease matters along.

---

up the valley, just past the 30m **Chegem Waterfall**. The canyon is 250m high but only 20m wide, through which both river and road squeeze. The waterfall is spectacular after the snow melts in mid-June.

Verkhny Chegem, another 20km on, has several archaeological sites, including **Lygyt village** with stone mausoleums dating back to the 10th and 11th centuries. Within the village is an 18th-century three-storey defensive tower.

ELBRUS AREA ПРИЕЛЬБРУСЬЕ

☎ 86638 / elevation (Terskol) 2085m /
☾ Moscow

Mt Elbrus rises imperiously on a northern spur of the Caucasus ridge at the end of the Baksan Valley. Surrounding it and flanking the valley are mountains that are lesser in height but equally awe-inspiring.

The tourist facilities that are littered along the valley floor make this potential Switzerland less attractive. Terskol is a disgrace, with its decrepit buildings, half-built or demolished constructions and a scrap yard of rusting steel work. But visitors come for the majestic mountains where there's energetic skiing, exciting hikes and climbing.

The area – known in Russian as Prielbruse – pulls in a more adventurous crowd than Dombay, but day-trippers can use chairlifts or cable cars to reach the slopes of Mt Elbrus, or they can view its peaks from across the valley. Given the visa registration and border permit complexities, most foreign tourists come on a prearranged tour group.

Orientation

The road ends at Azau where the cable car starts up Mt Elbrus which can't be seen from the ground. In busy times stalls sell the knitting output of the local babushkas – mohair mittens, socks and sweaters – and smoky barbecues churn out shashlyks. A few cafés open all year and there's one hotel.

About 3km downhill is Terskol village with a few hotels, basic shops and a post office. Another 1.5km downhill is Cheget Polyana at the base of Cheget mountain. With new private hotels, cafés and market stalls, this little village is a more attractive proposition than Terskol.

The Kartinform Nalchik map includes a good Elbrus map; other maps are available from stalls in Cheget Polyana.

Information

There are no police stations in Cheget, Terskol or Azau. The **Turbaza Terskol Hotel** (☎ 71140; Terskol) does have a MasterCard and Visa ATM.

Doctor on call (☎ 71103) There is no doctor's surgery, the doctor comes to you.

Police (☎ 71102)

Post and telephone office (☎ 71222; Terskol; ☾ post 9am-4pm Tue-Fri, 9am-3pm Sat) The telephone section is open 24 hours and Internet is available until 8pm (per hr R60). Most hotels have international payphones.

Rescue post (Spasatelnaya Sluzhba; ☎ 71489; Terskol; ☾ 24hr) Handles mountain rescue.

Sights & Activities
MT ELBRUS

Mt Elbrus, enigmatically unusual with two peaks – the western at 5642m and eastern at 5621m – bulges nearly 1000m above anything else in the vicinity. It's Europe's highest mountain, lying on the Caucasus ridge that is the geographical divide between Europe and Asia. This volcanic cone has upper slopes reputedly coated in ice up to 200m thick; numerous glaciers grind down its flanks and several rivers start here. The name 'Elbrus', meaning Two Heads, comes from Persian while in Balkar it's 'Mingi-Tau' (meaning 'thousands', ie very big mountain).

The first, unconfirmed climb of Mt Elbrus was in 1829 by a Russian expedition with Killar, a lone Circassian hunter hired as a guide, apparently reaching the peak on his own. The lower peak was officially climbed on 31 July 1868 and the western

RUSSIAN CAUCASUS

peak on 28 July 1874, both by British exped-itions. For propaganda purposes, in Soviet times, there were mass ascents involving hundreds of climbers; a telephone cable was even taken to the top so Comrade Stalin could share the news. Ascent and descent have been done in many ways: by light air-craft, hang gliders, paragliders, a motor-cycle with skis, and even in a Land Rover hauled to the top for advertising purposes. Apparently it's still there, somewhere.

A permit (US$20) is required for ascent above 3700m; it's valid for the whole of the state.

Cable Cars & Chairlift

Azau **cable cars** (per stage return R140; first stage 9am-3.30pm) rise from 2350m to Mir Bar at 3500m, from where you can first see the twin peaks. Mir Bar also has a good café. A **chairlift** (R140, day pass R500; 9am-3pm) contin-ues to 3700m. Both cable cars and chairlift run year-round except for maintenance during October or November.

Skiing

There's skiing and snowboarding to suit all levels and ages. Gear can be hired at many hotels and ski shops at Azau and Cheget Polyana from about R300 a day; ask around for English-speaking instructors who'll charge from R400 an hour.

The Azau slopes are a favourite from De-cember to May, while all-year skiing is pos-sible on the lower slopes above the chairlift which provide gentle skiing. Winter skiing from the upper cable car station has long, steep and challenging runs. From here there are also opportunities for off-piste (free ride) skiing. The ski tow just up from the lower cable car station is good for beginners.

Hiking

Hiking groups can take the cable cars and chairlift up to the Barrels, then walk for about 1½ hours – fairly easy but slow be-cause of the altitude and crevasses – up to Priyut 11 (Priyut odinnadtsat). Take advice at the Barrels as there are crevasses, some open and others concealed. Generally keep 20m to 30m to the left-hand side of marker poles. The walk back down to the chairlift takes about an hour.

Climbers and sightseers can get a ride on a snow cat (group of 10 €200) from the Bar-rels or Mir Bar up to the start of Pastukhov Rocks, 4500m, from where an ascent takes five to eight hours.

Climbing

Mt Elbrus is not technically difficult but is harder than, say, Mt Kilimanjaro with which it is often compared. Climbing exper-ience on ice is advisable, as is a good degree of fitness; most of the work is walking on snow and ice with crampons. Climbers will spend some time at height gaining altitude acclimatisation. Those heading for the top, having acclimatised at Priyut 11, usually do the final assault in a day – about eight to 10 hours up and three to four hours down.

There is a high accident rate from non-guided climbing on Mt Elbrus and guides are strongly recommended.

MT CHEGET

This mountain on the south side of the Baksan Valley is a spur of Mt Donguz-Orunbashi (3769m). Cheget is famous for its difficult piste with moguls while the north side has off-piste opportunities. Either of the lower **chairlifts** (per stage R140; lower 9am-4pm, upper 9am-3.30pm) take you from Cheget Polyana at 2100m to 2700m; another takes you up to 3040m. Riding the chairlift up, the raw majesty of the sur-rounding mountains is quickly revealed. To the west are the smooth milky-white twin peaks of Mt Elbrus, to the east the jagged peaks and near-vertical sides of Mt Donguzorun-Chegetkarabashi (4454m). From the top, an hour's walk takes you to a small peak. Descending, you'll view the length of the deep Baksan Valley as it fades, between craggy sides, into the distance.

Between the lower and upper lifts are several cafés. An easy 7km path round the

---

SEASONS

Peak season is January to mid-May for piste skiing with a mid-April to May season for ski-climbing. This imported Alpine activity has skiers climbing Mt Elbrus on modi-fied skies and then skiing back downhill. The summer climbing and hiking season is June to mid-September. Low season is October and November when chairlifts and cable cars may be under repair.

side of Mt Cheget leads to Donguzorunkyol Lake. Going further will require a permit.

OTHER WALKS

Any walks towards the Georgian border require a border permit. Tour groups will have this arranged for them. The hiking routes to the north and northwest are far better as no permits are required. Keep off glaciers unless you have a guide.

Nonpermit Walks

An easy, two- to three-hour walk leads up the Terskol Valley from behind the white obelisk in Terskol village to a dramatic view of Mt Elbrus behind the 'hanging' **Terskol Glacier**, dripping over a cliff edge.

Day-walk valleys with glaciers at the top include both branches of the Irik River, northwest of Elbrus village. Also there's a five-hour walk up to **Syltrankyol Lake** west of Baksan.

Permit Walks

Take the paved road up Adylsu Valley, south of Elbrus village, to just before the bridge. Then strike southeast with the river on your left and it's about a two-hour walk up a good, gently rising path to the impressive hanging **Shkhelda Glacier**.

Alternatively, from the bridge you can continue up (by car if you wish) to the end of the paved road and walk to **Zelyonaya Gostinitsa** (Green Hotel), a former shelter near

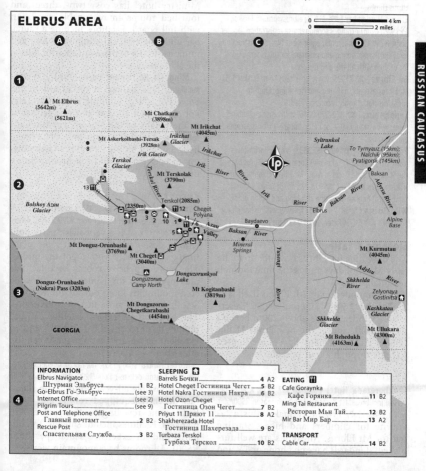

ELBRUS AREA

0 — 4 km
0 — 2 miles

Mt Elbrus (5642m)
(5621m)
Mt Chatkara (3898m)
Mt Irikchat (4045m)
Mt Askerbolbashi-Tersak (3928m)
Irikchat Glacier
Irik Glacier
Terskol Glacier
Mt Terskolak (3790m)
Terskol River
Irikchat
Irik River
Irik River
Syltrankol Lake
To Tyrnyauz (15km); Nalchik (95km); Pyatigorsk (145km)
Baksan
Bolshoy Azau Glacier
(2350m)
Terskol (2085m)
Cheget Polyana
Irik
River
Baksan River
River
Baksan River
Elbrus
Adyrsu River
Alpine Base
Mt Donguz-Orunbashi (3769m)
Mt Cheget (3040m)
Azau Valley
Baydaevo
Mineral Springs
Yasengi
Mt Kurmutau (4045m)
Donguz-Orunbashi (Nakra) Pass (3203m)
Donguzorun Camp North
Donguzorunkyol Lake
Mt Kogitanbashi (3819m)
River
Adylsu River
Shkhelda River
Zelyonaya Gostinitsa
Kashkatau Glacier
Mt Donguzorun-Chegetkarabashi (4454m)
GEORGIA
Shkhelda Glacier
Mt Bzhedukh (4163m)
Mt Ulukara (4300m)

INFORMATION	SLEEPING	EATING
Elbrus Navigator	Barrels Бочки 4 A2	Cafe Goraynka
Штурман Эльбруса.........1 B1	Hotel Cheget Гостиница Чегет......5 B2	Кафе Горянка..............11 B2
Go-Elbrus Го-Эльбрус ......(see 3)	Hotel Nakra Гостиница Накра......6 B2	Ming Tai Restaurant
Internet Office...............(see 2)	Hotel Ozon-Cheget	Ресторан Мын Тай........12 B2
Pilgrim Tours..................(see 9)	Гостиница Озон Чегет......7 B2	Mir Bar Мир Бар 13 A2
Post and Telephone Office	Priyut 11 Приют 11.........8 A2	
Главный почтамт 2 B2	Shakherezada Hotel	TRANSPORT
Rescue Post	Гостиница Шахерезада......9 B2	Cable Car....................14 B2
Спасательная Служба.......3 B2	Turbaza Terskol	
	Турбаза Терскол 10 B2	

little Bashkarinskoe Lake at the head of Adylsu Valley; it's a day-walk destination.

Another day walk is along **River Yusengi Valley**, south of Baydaevo. For more adventure and a spot of camping (or paying US$20 to stay at the Alpine base) there are longer walks south from Baksan up the **River Adyrsu**.

Tours

Rather than being just folk in offices selling tickets, the agencies below are either active tour arrangers and leaders or providers of specialist services for climbers, skiers and hikers.

Adventure Alternative (☎ 44-2890-70 1476; www .adventurealternative.com) UK company: organises Mt Elbrus climbs.

Elbrus Navigator (☎ 71424; elbrus@nm.ru; Terskol; ◷ 9am-9pm) Arranges foreigner visa registration, border permits, Mt Elbrus ascents, equipment hire, ski instruction, local excursions/hiking and program for the elderly. Good for dealing with all the permits.

Go-Elbrus (☎ 71335; www.go-elbrus.com; Terskol 5-5) Mt Elbrus ascents, trekking and heliskiing; English-speaking staff. Highly recommended.

Lenalptours (☎ 812-279 0716; www.russia-climbing .com; ul Vosstaniya 9-4, St Petersburg) Mt Elbrus ascents and ski tours.

Pilgrim Tours (☎ 495-967 3333; www.pilgrim-tours .com; Ostozhenka 41, Moscow) Located at Mt Elbrus base at the Shakherezada Hotel in Azau. Mt Elbrus climbing tours.

Viktor Yanchenko (☎ 928 225 4623; Yanki-viktor@ rambler.ru) English-speaking climbing and skiing guide.

Wild Russia (☎ 812-273 6514; www.wildrussia.spb.ru; Fontanka nab 59, St Petersburg) Mt Elbrus ascents.

Sleeping & Eating

The busy time for Elbrus is winter up to the early May holidays and is the time for high seasonal prices.

Accommodation on Mt Elbrus itself is in the **Barrels** (☎ 903 491 8590; per person R360), a series of cylindrical huts about 200m beyond the chairlift, and at the new **Priyut 11** hut (Diesel Hut) at 4065m. Spaces are limited so book through a tour operator.

AZAU
Shakherezada Hotel (☎ 928 937 2815; Azau; r per person incl breakfast & dinner low/high season R500/600, lyux r R800/1200) Proximity makes this a favourite for climbers and hikers starting out for Mt Elbrus. All rooms are well furnished; standards have no phone or TV and

lyux have sitting rooms. The hotel plans to have Internet soon. There's a downstairs bar, bark-clad and stonewalled with tables you're encouraged to graffiti.

Mir Bar (meals R170-220; ◷ 9am-4pm) A bar at the cable car station for the snow-wet and cold with a large bum-warming open central fire. Once in here forget the weather, you're only two cable cars from a hot shower. Favourites here are a hefty plate of scrambled eggs, speckled with assorted vegetables and *khichin* (bread stuffed with meat or cheese) served with sour cream.

TERSKOL
Turbaza Terskol (☎ 71140; r per person low/high season R430/600, lyux R580/750; ☒) The Defence Ministry hotel has cosy two-, three- and four-bed rooms in reasonable condition with full board. Facilities include a sauna, bar and cafeteria, ski equipment hire and minibus shuttle to the Azau chairlift during the ski season.

Ming Tai Restaurant (meals R190-370; ◷ 2pm-midnight) This Balkarian restaurant in the bowels of a large building is the only Terskol place open all year and can get hectic at the height of the season. Try the Cutlet Ming Tau that arrives on a plate like a hedgehog but hiding within is a tasty stuffing of egg, parsley and mushrooms in an unusual sauce.

CHEGET
Hotel Ozon-Cheget (☎ 71453; Cheget Polyana; s/d with full board low/high season from R2790/3720, deluxe R3410/4340). Ozon is a very swish place built with a designer's flourish. It's *the* place to stay in Elbrus if you've got the means. The more expensive rooms have Jacuzzis plus open fires for winter cosiness while cold mountains loom outside the window. Standard rooms are a little less luxurious. The hotel offers fridges, satellite TV and phones in all rooms, a bar, billiards and an excellent restaurant that nonguests can use after 9pm.

Hotel Nakra (☎ 71357; fax 71220; Cheget Polyana; low/high season deluxe r R600/1200, lyux r R1000/1800; ☒) A possible all-year option. The Nakra has decently equipped rooms and good beds, some revelling in fluffy sheepskin blankets. Facilities include satellite TV, billiards and an expensive sauna (per hour R800). All rooms have mountain views.

RUSSIAN CAUCASUS

Hotel Cheget (☎ 71400; fax 71203; s/d incl breakfast & dinner per person from R155-400) This is a huge, eight-storey ex-Soviet concrete block that's been used by tour groups for years. Consequently it's somewhat timeworn but clean and tidy. Seven- and 14-day stay visitors get chairlift passes, transfer to/from Mineralnye Vody airport and daily transfers to Azau. There's a useful cheap canteen for nonresidents and a cinema, ski equipment rental, shops and sauna.

Café Goryanka (meals R70-220; 7am-midnight) A locals' café, on the corner of Terskol and Cheget Polyana roads, plain but warmed by the friendly reception from the babushka owner. Leave your introduction to borsch until you get here: it'll set the standard, and servings are big enough to stand in for a meal.

Shopping

Cheget Polyana is ringed with stalls selling kitschy souvenirs and useful things like woolly socks, sweaters, gloves and hats. Food stalls hawk shashlyk, *khichin, schorpa* (a Balkar soup) and soft drinks.

Getting There & Away

Public transport is very limited. A daily *marshrutka* links Terskol and Nalchik (R200, three hours, 8am) returning at noon. Alternatively, take a taxi (R250 to R300) to Tyrnyauz and then a frequent *marshrutka* to Nalchik. Arrange with tour operators running out of Kislovodsk and Pyatigorsk to use their excursions as a means of getting to and from Elbrus.

Getting Around

A taxi costs about R100 from Terskol to Azau or Cheget. In season plenty of *marshrutky* operate between Cheget and Azau. Otherwise walk or hitch a ride.

NORTH OSSETIA

Lonely Planet advises against travel in North Ossetia. The state, on the fracture zone between the Russian Federation's loyal republics (of which it's one) and Chechnya, has become embroiled in the latter's tragedy. Four years of bombing incidents in the capital Vladikavkaz reached a crescendo in Beslan in September 2004. Hostage-takers, assumed to be Chechen militants, violently seized a school and held more than 1000 children, teachers and parents hostage in a gym wired with explosives. Claim and counterclaim came from both sides as to who precipitated the massacre – militants or Russian special forces – but regardless more than 300 people died.

Most of the republic's population is Ossetian, thought to be descended from Sarmatians, an Indo-European people who arrived in the 4th century AD. They assimilated with local tribes to form the Alan state that lasted until the 13th century when the Tatars destroyed it. Some escaped deep into the mountains and by the 18th century their descendants, the Ossetians, were found mainly in the valleys west of Vladikavkaz. Ossetia was incorporated into Russia in 1774.

The other inhabitants are the Ingush. Stalin had most Ingush deported to Siberia in 1944 and incorporated western Ingushetia into North Ossetia. The Ingush were rehabilitated during Khrushchev's rule but returned home to find most of their property occupied by Ossetians.

Under Communist rule both Ossetians and Ingush coexisted peaceably, but this was an illusion. In June 1992 an autonomous Ingushetia was set up, leading to bloody clashes between Ossetians and Ingush in October 1992, with hundreds dying.

Russian forces were sent in but according to local accounts they sided with the Ossetians. Together they forced the entire Ingush population (50,000 plus) into Ingushetia to live in extremely poor conditions. Most of their houses were destroyed or confiscated and it's only in the last few years that the Ingush have been allowed to return.

Allegations that Ingush fighters were involved in the Beslan school massacre have led to renewed tensions between both communities.

While the capital Vladikavkaz has several museums, the real attractions are the arcane relics of old Ossetian settlements out in the valleys to the southwest, and the impressive mountain scenery. Dargavs, with its village of the dead, has 13th- and 14th-century family burial chambers whose occupants are still visible. Tsmity, in another valley, contains ruins of a medieval settlement.

CHECHNYA, DAGESTAN & INGUSHETIA Leonid Ragozin

WHY DOES LONELY PLANET NOT GO THERE?

Only official delegations and journalists, who come on heavily guarded trips organised by the Kremlin, are allowed to visit Chechnya. Travelling to the war-torn republic independently would be like walking on the moon without a spacesuit. Neighbouring Dagestan and Ingushetia might seem more peaceful, but grim facts prove that they are almost as dangerous for foreign visitors.

WHAT EXACTLY IS THE DANGER?

At the time of research, reports about casualties in the continuing war between Russian federal forces and the separatist Chechen guerrillas were appearing almost daily. Apart from the obvious risk of being killed in a shootout or a bomb attack, travellers in Chechnya, Dagestan and Ingushetia are exposed to the far greater risk of kidnapping. Many victims of kidnappings in this region have been brutally killed after months of torture.

The Chechen war has spilled over the borders a few times into Dagestan and Ingushetia. Although these regions are not considered war zones, they have proven to be way too dangerous for foreigners after several kidnappings of aid workers.

WHAT IS THE CHECHEN WAR ABOUT?

The roots of the Chechen conflict stretch back to Russia's annexation of the area in the 19th century (see boxed text, p124). The current conflict, which broke out more than a decade ago, is far more complex than being just about a small nation's struggle for independence from a larger one. If you look at local opinion polls, you'll be left wondering why this war is still going on. Ordinary Chechens don't appear to be very much in favour of independence, nor do Russians seem particularly keen to keep Chechnya in their realm. Above all, both people want peace.

It is the story of lost chances. Chechnya enjoyed defacto independence twice in 1990s, but both times moderate leaders failed to rein in gangs of kidnappers and radical Islamists, like Shamil Basayev, who has striven to outdo Osama bin Laden as a murderous terrorist. Brutal treatment of civilians and indiscriminate bombings cost the Russian troops their chance to be seen as a force liberating the republic from gangsters. The international community lost its chance to mediate the conflict through ignorance and the inability to see anything but a black-and-white picture.

Experts point out that the war is fuelled by the money made on arms trade across the frontline, illegal oil extraction and kidnappings. They say it is the dirty economy of the war that needs to be routed, before any lasting peace settlement can be achieved.

IS THERE ANY CHANCE FOR PEACE SOON?

The last possibility of peace talks vanished with the killing of the separatists' nominal leader Aslan Maskhadov. Western governments agree that no deals can be made with Basayev, who leads the resistance, and after Iraq they have found it increasingly difficult to criticise Russia for whatever actions it takes in Chechnya.

The Kremlin understands the need to delegate more power in the republic to the Chechens themselves, including former rebels like Akhmad Kadyrov, who became Chechen president in 2003 but died in a bomb attack a year later. Experts blame the authorities for staking the chance for peace on dealings with just one clan (known as the Kadyrovtsy) instead of creating a broad coalition of people who want to end the war.

Planned local elections will show whether Moscow is keen to resolve this conflict by more democratic means, or if it will stick to the divide-and-rule policy. Even more depends on whether Moscow can help restore Chechnya's shattered economy and provide jobs to thousands of people who live in utter poverty.

WHAT IS THE CURRENT SITUATION?

Russian forces nominally control all of Chechnya and there is certainly more stability than a few years ago, but the separatists' resistance is still very strong, which is reflected by nearly daily killings of policemen and troops. Putin has assigned most of the military operations to units comprised of ethnic Chechens, many of them former rebels, led by Ramzan Kadyrov. Still in his 20s (at the time of writing), the son of the deceased leader seems to have even more power in the republic than Chechen president Alu Alkhanov.

Human rights activists blame Kadyrov for kidnapping civilians, particularly relatives of prominent guerrilla leaders. The authorities have admitted that disappearances of people are the main destabilising factor in the republic. In true Caucasus style, Kadyrov Jr has declared a blood feud on kidnappers, which many in Chechnya found quite ironic. Yet, there are signs of life slowly getting better. Residents of the Chechen capital Grozny say the clatter of builders' hammers is now heard more often than gunshot. The art museum and the puppet theatre have reopened, while in nearby Gudermes, Ramzan Kadyrov has built a modern sports centre, modestly calling it Ramzan.

WHO ARE THE CHECHENS, THE INGUSH & THE DAGESTANI?

The Chechen and Ingush peoples are almost indistinguishable from each other, both culturally and linguistically. Under Soviet rule, they lived together in the Checheno-Ingush republic, but after Dzhokhar Dudayev proclaimed independence in 1991 (see p65), the Ingush preferred to stay within Russia and separate from the Chechens. Dagestan, which means 'mountain country' in Turkish, is an ethnographic wonder, populated by no fewer than 81 ethnic groups of different origins speaking 30 languages, mostly endemic.

The Chechen, Dagestani, Ingush and other groups in northwest Caucasus are known in Russia by the common name *gortsy* (highlanders). By reputation they are very proud, independent-minded and unruly. They live by strict codes of honour and revenge, and clan blood feuds are well entrenched in their patriarchal culture. Most of them are Sunni Muslims.

In the 19th century, the Dagestani-born religious leader Imam Shamil united most of the *gortsy* in a failed war against Russia. This kinship was broken during Soviet times, when Stalin exiled all Chechens and Ingush to Central Asia for alleged collaboration with the Germans during WWII. Returning after Khrushchev's amnesty, many of them found the Dagestani occupying their land and houses. This created the bitterness between the groups that has increased since the Chechen incursion into Dagestan in 1999.

ONCE IT'S SAFE TO GO, WHAT IS THERE TO SEE?

Dagestan has the most tourist sights of the three regions and is more likely to become a travel destination, although in the rather distant future. The 5000-year-old town of Derbent, on the Unesco World Heritage list, is graced by a magnificent ancient fortress and boasts an interesting multicultural population, comprising mountain Jews and Lezgins. In more peaceful times hordes of Russian tourists also used to visit beautiful mountain villages such as Gunib, which is famous for its silverware. Others preferred to bake on the sandy Caspian beaches.

In Soviet times, Checheno-Ingushetia was popular with hikers who came to see medieval clan towers standing amidst the graceful mountain landscape and to walk over mountain passes in Itum-Kale district into Georgia. Now, even after peace is restored, it will take years to clear the Chechen and Ingush mountains of mines and unexploded bombs.

WHERE CAN I LEARN MORE?

Russian journalist Anna Politkovskaya's book *A Dirty War* and *Chienne de Guerre* by another fearless female war reporter, Anne Niva, are both available in English and are worth reading.

You can also find useful information on the following websites:

Free Chechnya (www.chechnyafree.ru/index .php?lng=eng) This pro-Moscow site has tons of information on Chechen life, as well as downloadable Chechen tunes for mobile phones!

Human Rights Watch (www.hrw.org/campaigns /russia/chechnya/) Remains a vocal defender of Chechen civilians against all sides in the conflict.

War and Peace Reporting (www.iwpr.net/caucasus _index1.html) London-based institute with a network of stringers in the North Caucasus who provide an unbiased and detailed look on recent developments in the region.

Siberia
Сибирь

From the Ural Mountains to the great Lena River, the sheer size of Siberia is hard to comprehend. Fearfully cold in winter, swelteringly hot in summer and with a history of banishment and cruelty – for Westerners Siberia's image doesn't readily suggest a tourist destination. But Russians disagree. Southern Siberia's beautiful peak-tickled underbelly offers world-class rafting, hiking and mountaineering. Amid endless forests are ramshackle wooden-cottage villages, and certain Siberian cities hide evocative historic cores behind their harsh Soviet exteriors. Of these, Tomsk and Tobolsk are the most memorable. Irkutsk and Ulan-Ude also have a certain charm and offer launching points to visit Siberia's greatest attraction, Lake Baikal. Visiting all four cities, plus Omsk and Krasnoyarsk, makes sense by breaking a continental crossing into painless overnight hops using the Trans-Siberian Railway. Away from the railway tracks in Tuva, Altai, Buryatiya and Khakassia, local Buddhist and shamanistic beliefs remain closer to those of Mongolia or Tibet. Here local cultures retain their own sports, passions and languages while their fascinating ancient histories are faintly visible in mysterious *kurgany* (burial mounds), standing stones, petroglyphs and *kameny baba* (moustachioed stone idols).

Siberia has friendly inhabitants, rapidly improving restaurants and many new or renovated hotels. Prices are rising but remain much lower than in European Russia. The region remains one of the least touristed areas in all of Asia; you'll really need rudimentary Russian to travel independently as neither museums nor most hotels or restaurants usually have a word of English. However, several cities do have English-speaking tour agencies who can help you out. This is especially helpful for preparing trekking adventures (facilities are minimal *in situ*) and for arranging peak summer-season bookings around Altai and Lake Baikal.

HIGHLIGHTS

- Explore the kremlin and photogenically dishevelled old town of **Tobolsk** (p501), Siberia's former capital

- Observe the Buryat Buddhist revival at **Ivolginsk** (p594), **Aginskoe** (p601) or the glorious **Tsugol datsan** (p601)

- Discover throat-singing and sumo-style *khuresh* wrestling in the wild **Tuva Republic** (p546)

- Beat the rush to **Olkhon Island** (p578), an ecofriendly getaway for meditational hikes, dog-sled rides and shaman encounters

- Cross the world's deepest lake…in a taxi! **Lake Baikal** (p563) looks magical when frozen in March

- Trek in the spectacular **Ergaki** (p545), **Sayan** (p581) or **Altai** (p520) Mountains

★ Tobolsk

Ergaki Mountains ★ Lake Baikal ★ ★ Tsugol Datsan
Sayan Mountains ★ ★
Altai Mountains ★ Tuva Republic ★ Ivolginsk ★ ★ Aginskoe

SIBERIA

History

Siberia's early Altaic people were conceivably progenitors of the Inuit-Arctic cultures and of the Mongol-Turkic groups which expanded in westbound waves with Attila, Chinggis (Genghis) Khaan and Timur (Tamerlane). The name Siberia comes from Sibir, a Turkic khanate and successor-state to the Golden Horde which ruled the region following Timur's 1395 invasion (see p37). From 1563, Sibir started raiding what were then Russia's easternmost flanks. A Volga brigand called Yermak Timofeevich was sent to counter-attack. Though he had only 840 Cossack fighters, the prospect of battle seemed better than the tsar's death sentence which hung over him. With the unfair advantage of firearms, the tiny Cossack force managed to conquer Tyumen in 1580, turning Yermak into a Russian hero. Two years later Yermak occupied Sibir's capital Isker, near today's Tobolsk. Russia's extraordinary eastward expansion had begun.

Initially, small Cossack units would set up an *ostrog* (fortress) at key river junctions. Local tribes would then be compelled to supply Muscovite fur traders, and villages slowly developed. Full-blown colonisation only started during the chaotic Time of Troubles (1598–1613, p39) as Russian peasants fled east in great numbers. Local Altaic peoples were decimated by imported diseases like smallpox. Meanwhile settler numbers were swollen by exiled prisoners. Old Believers then followed after the religious rift of 1653. Other banished troublemakers included the influential Decembrists who'd failed to pull off an 1825 coup (p45).

Siberia's fur-based economy rapidly diversified, and discoveries of gold, copper and ferric metals further encouraged colonisation. Despite quarrels over the status of Altai that weren't resolved until 1864, trade with China brought considerable wealth following the treaties of Nerchinsk in 1689 and Kyakhta in 1728. Lucrative tea caravans continued trudging the seemingly endless Siberian post road until put out of business by the Trans-Siberian Railway after 1901 (see p742). The railway instantly changed the fortunes of cities according to whether or not they were on the line. By 1914 it had carried another five million new Russian settlers east.

Russia's revolutions had reverberations in Siberia. In 1919 Omsk was the centre of Admiral Kolchak's anti-Bolshevik White Russia, and from 1920 to 1922 eastern Siberia was nominally independent as the pro-Lenin Far Eastern Republic centred on Chita. As the USSR stabilised and Stalin's infamous Gulags developed, Siberia reverted to its old role as a land of banishment. Nonetheless unforced colonisation continued apace, especially after WWII when much heavy industry was shifted east for strategic security. Patriotic workers and volunteer labourers as well as prisoners undertook grandiose engineering projects, building dams, railways and whole new cities whose glum concrete realities often belied the dream.

Since the USSR's collapse in 1991, certain settlements built with Soviet disregard for economic logic have withered into gloomy virtual ghost towns. In contrast, discoveries of vast oil and gas deposits in the frozen north have proven Russia's greatest economic asset. Today petroleum as well as timber and minerals provide the wealth that is visibly transforming the region's most prosperous cities, notably Tyumen and Krasnoyarsk.

Climate

Siberia. Impossibly cold, right? Well not necessarily. In some years February can dip to –50°C, which is too cold to do anything. However, March is arguably the best time to visit Siberia, with temperatures oscillating between –5°C and –25°C. On windless, sunny days the latter can even feel pleasant; the snow is crisp underfoot and you'll feel comfy if you're properly wrapped up in good ski wear and gloves. March is great for

---

TICK WARNING

The encephalitis threat (see p750) is often underestimated in Siberia. The ticks *(kleshchi)* that spread this nasty disease are alarmingly plentiful from May to July. The threat is worst in the taiga, but extends to well-trodden footpaths such as those along the Circumbaikal Railway, to the Akokan Gulag near Severobaikalsk and in the Stolby Park (Krasnoyarsk). Recently ticks have even been found in city parks and at the Ethnographic Museum (near Novosibirsk's Akademgorodok). Don't panic but do cover up and be vigilant.

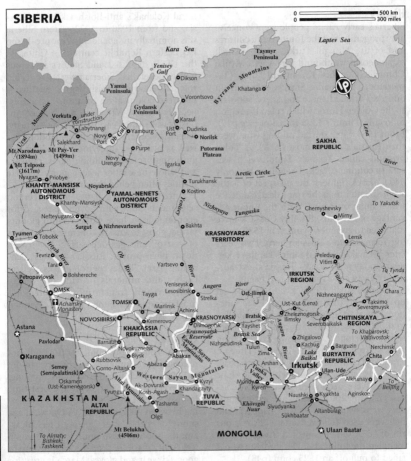

driving across frozen rivers and even Lake Baikal. There's not really any spring. One day it's suddenly 10°C and the compacted blackened snow on the city pavements melts into slush. All those ski clothes soon feel far too warm and by midsummer temperatures can top a sweaty 35°C. Air is obviously cooler and fresh in the Altai or Sayan Mountains though rain there is always possible. In the brief autumn, colours can be beautiful but the seasonal transition is similarly abrupt, albeit with some false starts.

Getting There & Away
TO/FROM RUSSIA
Several Siberian cities have air connections to Germany (from €480 return, p724), the Caucasus, Central Asia and the Far East. Flying from Ürümqi (western China) to Novosibirsk handily saves getting a Kazakhstan transit visa.

Trains run between Novosibirsk and Almaty (Kazakhstan) daily, between Irkutsk and Ulaan Baatar (Mongolia) nine times weekly and between Chita and Manzhouli (China) three times weekly. For all routes a nearby road border allows hop-across independent travel. Since 2004 an exciting new option is the rough road between Kosh-Agach and Olgii (Mongolia) via Tashanta.

WITHIN RUSSIA
If you book three weeks in advance, super-discount air tickets from Moscow to Irkutsk

or Bratsk can cost under R4000 – that's cheaper than the train. Travel agencies and even sometimes the airlines themselves sell them. Other well-connected airports include Krasnoyarsk, hub for **KrasAir** (www .krasair.ru); Novosibirsk with **Siberia Airlines** (www.s7.ru); and Abakan, a secondary hub for **Vladivostok Airlines** (www.vladavia.ru).

First-time visitors often erroneously imagine that there's only one 'trans-Siberian' train running Moscow–Vladivostok. In fact there are dozens operating along sections of the route. In summer several extra cross-Ural services connect from various Siberian cities to Adler (near Sochi) and Kislovodsk (a Caucasus spa). Beware that certain routes cut through a corner of Kazakhstan, with potentially catastrophic consequences for your visas.

Getting Around

Distances are great but travel is remarkably painless if you break journeys into overnight train hops. An ideal routing is Yekaterinburg–Tobolsk–Omsk–Tomsk–Krasnoyarsk–Irkutsk–Ulan-Ude. For the Altai Mountains and Tuva, use Tomsk–Biysk or Krasnoyarsk–Abakan trains respectively then hop on buses or shared taxis. Handy Kyzyl–Irkutsk flights (Saturday) let you continue east from Tuva without backtracking via Abakan.

TYUMEN & OMSK REGIONS
ТЮМЕНСКАЯ И ОМСКАЯ ОБЛАСТИ

The highlight of these regions is the historic and delightfully ramshackle old town of Tobolsk, but en route you could happily spend a day strolling and dining in the vibrant cities of Tyumen or Omsk.

TYUMEN ТЮМЕНЬ

☎ 3452 / pop 507,000 / ⌚ Moscow +2hr

Founded in 1586, Tyumen was the first Russian fort in Siberia. These days the city exudes a sense of growing prosperity as the booming capital of a vast, oil-rich *oblast* (region) stretching all the way to the Arctic Circle. The city has a businesslike drive and youthful bustle, best experienced by strolling through City Park on summer weekend evenings amid the musical fountains. Pleasant and liveable, Tyumen has tree-lined streets and a fair few older buildings amid all the new construction, but if you have limited time you'd be better off seeing Tobolsk instead.

Orientation

From the fine Trinity Monastery to well beyond the bus station the main thoroughfare is ul Respubliki. The train station lies around a kilometre south of ul Respubliki at the end of ul Pervomayskaya.

MAPS

City maps and hard-to-decipher bus-route plans are sold at **Knizhny Magazin** (Poliklinika Bldg, Privokzalnaya ul 28a; ⌚ 8.30am-6pm Mon-Sat, 9am-4pm Sun) near the train station and more expensively at **Knizhnaya Stolitsa** (ul Respubliki 58; ⌚ 10am-7pm).

Information

There are dozens of exchange bureaux and ATMs in the city centre, including at hotels Vostok and Tyumen.

Internet Salon (cnr uls Respubliki & Krasina; Internet per hr R28.80; ⌚ 11am-8pm) Through the phone office on ul Krasina. Prepay at room 3.

Main post office (ul Respubliki 56; ⌚ 8am-8pm Mon-Sat, 9am-6pm Sun)

Sberbank (ul Melnikayte 82; ⌚ 9am-2pm & 3-5pm Tue-Sat) Good dollar and euro rates and 24 hour ATM.

Telephone office (ul Respubliki 51; Internet per min R0.48; ⌚ 24hr)

Trikita (ul Melnikayte 100; Internet per hr R30; ⌚ 24hr) Slow but handy for Hotel Vostok. By day enter through the Megafon cellar-shop, by night good luck!

Tyumen.ru (www.tyumen.ru, in Russian) Has air and railway timetables plus updated cinema listings.

Web Khauz (ul Respubliki 61; Internet per hr R28; ⌚ 11am-8pm) Entry from ul Profsoyuznaya, up two flights of stairs then along a balcony.

Sights

TRINITY MONASTERY

Riverside **Trinity Monastery** (ul Kommunisticheskaya 10) is undoubtedly Tyumen's most appealing architectural complex. Its kremlin-style crenellated outer wall is pierced by a single gate-tower. Behind, black and gold domes top the striking 1727 **Peter & Paul Church**. Its

SIBERIA

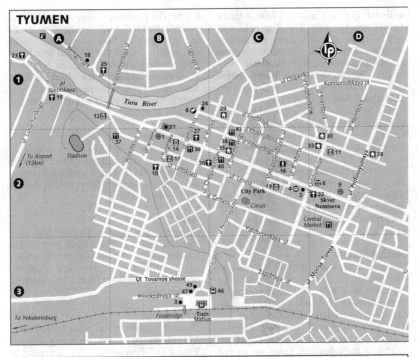

TYUMEN

soaring interior is emphasised by a giant, seven-level candelabra and decorated with murals. Buses 14 and 30 from the city centre stop between here and the attractive 1791 **Krestovozdvizhenskaya Church** (ul Lunacharskogo 1). Backlit at sunset, the monastery domes

glow majestically when viewed from near the **Ukrainian consulate** (ul Semakova 4). It's even more photogenic seen across the ferric-brown river from tree-lined ul Bergovaya with its sprinkling of curiously twisted **old wooden houses** (notably numbers 73 and 53).

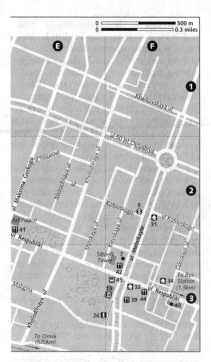

OTHER CHURCHES

With its voluptuously curved baroque towers, the 1786 **Znamensky Cathedral** (ul Semakova 13) is the most memorable of a dozen 'old' churches which are slowly coming back to life. **Saviour's Church** (Spasskaya tserkov; ul Lenina) is structurally similar but lacks the quiet backstreet location while the potentially attractive **Archangel Mikhail Church** (ul Turgeneva) is hemmed in by new construction. Restoration of the **Simeon Bogopriimtsa Church** (ul Respubliki) is bringing new character to the central Skver Nemetsova gardens while the 1789 **Voznesensko-Georgievskaya Church** (Bergovaya ul 77) is rising phoenix-like from the tatty riverside factory of which it once formed a part.

MUSEUMS

The **Fine Arts Museum** (Muzey izobrazitelnykh iskusstv; ☎ 469 115; ul Ordzhonikidze 47; admission R40; ⏱ 10am-5pm Tue-Sun) has an impressive and eclectic collection, ranging from ornate window frames saved from the city's old wooden houses to tiny, intricately carved bone figures. Look for the original Kandinsky canvas.

Near Hotel Vostok and currently undergoing a major renovation, the **Geological Museum** (Muzey Geologi; Nefti i Gaza; ☎ 751 138; ul Respubliki 142) is one of the best of its type with three floors of minerals and petroleum-related exhibits. The fourth floor has ethnographic displays. Immediately south is a unique modern **war memorial** in the shape of a gigantic metal candle.

ARCHITECTURAL ATTRACTIONS

A sprinkling of century-old buildings add a certain charm to the northwesterly stretches of uls Lenin and Respubliki. Most eye-catching is the blue **Selskhoz Academy** (ul Respubliki 7), a brick mansion that was originally a school museum. Most famously Lenin hid here during WWII. Yes, he was already dead! But his embalmed body had been evacuated from Moscow for safe-keeping.

A large **Lenin statue** commands Tsentralnaya pl, flanked by the sturdy buildings of the Tyumen Oblast **Parliament**. A tall **WWII monolith** makes a popular site for wedding photos, beside which the **former town hall** (☎ 461 159; ul Respubliki 2; admission US$2; ⏱ 10am-1pm & 2-5pm Wed-Sun) houses a rather humdrum museum. More fun are the wooden **Marsharov House Museum** (☎ 461 310; ul Lenina 24; admission US$2; ⏱ 9.30am-12.30pm & 1.30-4.30pm Wed-Sun), with original furnishings, and the sweet little **House Museum of 19th & 20th-Century History** (Istoriya Adnovo Doma; ☎ 464 963; ul Respubliki 18; ⏱ 9.30am-4.30pm Wed-Sun) in Tyumen's finest carved cottage. Though brutally interspersed with brand-new structures, there are other delightful **wooden homes** on cross streets such as ul Turgenyeva and notably at ul Semakova 1, perched on a river overlook.

Sleeping

BUDGET

Hotel GUBD (☎ 247 434; ul Sovetskaya 124; s/tw without bathroom R250/400, s/tw with bathroom R500/500) Tyumen's best-value budget choice is small and central, if unaccustomed to foreigners. Bathrooms are newly upgraded.

Hotel Vostok (☎ 205 350; fax 206 124; ul Respubliki 159; s/tw R733/1030) In a lively area just east of the city centre, this vast Soviet monster has repainted but tired rooms with so-so private bathrooms. There are cheaper options at R580/R740 without the crackly TV but receptionists seem reluctant to admit their existence. A few singles at R1158 are pretty comprehensively renovated and sensibly priced. Breakfast included.

MIDRANGE

Hotel Neftyanik (☎ 461 687; fax 460 021; www.neftyanik .ru; ul Chelyuskintsev 12; s/tw/d R1200/1400/2040) Now thoroughly renovated, this concrete slab block has the best position for visiting the nicer old-town areas. Double rooms have sitting areas with flouncy sofas. Some single rooms cost only R1100 but are much less stylish.

Hotel Prometey (☎ 250 021; fax 251 423; 5th fl, Sovetskaya ul 61; s/tw/d R1250/1700/1700) Fully renovated bedrooms have pleasant new furniture though the bathrooms don't quite reach the same standard. Beds in the single rooms are a good size but in twins they're barely wide enough for stick-insects.

Hotel Tura (☎ /fax 282 209; ul Melnikayte 103a; s/tw/d R1370/1950/2160) This relatively small, well-kept hotel near the Vostok has pleasant, subdued décor and new shower-booth bathrooms. One breakfast is included per room.

TOP END

Hotel Tyumen (☎ 494 040; www.hoteltyumen.ru/en/; ul Ordzhonikidze 46; s/d R3500/4400, ste R6000-7700) Nicknamed 'Quality Hotel', typical international business standards come complete with muzak, pinging elevators, a giftshop and great restaurants.

Prezident Hotel (☎ /fax 494 747; ul Respubliki 33; s/d/ste R3200/4000/5500) Reached by a glass elevator through the atrium of the self-proclaimed 'World Trade Centre', the rather overpriced rooms are fully equipped but blandly styleless. Night-time security guards are less than welcoming.

Eating & Drinking

Eateries are dotted along uls Lenina and Respubliki with terrace cafés appearing in summer outside the **Art Palace** (ul Respubliki) cinema-concert complex.

Korolevskaya Trapeza (☎ 451 248; ul Lenina 4; R60 cover after 8pm; biznes lunch R200, meals R250-650; ☻ noon-midnight Mon-Sat) High-vaulted ceilings with Crusader murals and throne chairs give this atmospheric place the feel of a medieval castle. The subtly delicious *svinina po-burgundski* (Burgundy pork) uses prunes to great effect. Enter via a courtyard behind Osminog casino and the Italika pizzeria.

Vienna Café (Hotel Tyumen; meals R400-700; ☻ 6am-3am) With a wide-ranging English-language menu and long opening hours, this smart café-restaurant offers good cakes and tongue-tickling snack meals like Thai rice-noodles (R150) or aubergine in oyster sauce (R160).

Kofeynya (☎ 466 083; ul Semakova 19; espresso R40; ☻ 8am-11pm) Tyumen's top coffee house has an astonishing range of special grinds, delicious cakes and *mate* teas served in curious, wooden bulbs shaped like opium pipes, just as they are in South America.

Pinta Taverna (☎ 250 220; ul Dzerzhinskogo 38; meals R200-400, beers R60-100; ☻ 11am-2am) Waitresses in peasant costumes and a stunted model cow star in this cosy farmyard-styled cellar beneath Vulkan slot-machine casino.

Restaurant Mozart (☎ 455 363; ul Respubliki 34; meals R500-1200, cover R200 after 7pm) Tyumen's top restaurant tries a little too hard to look elegant but its menu (in English) offers extraordinary creations like pistachio-stuffed prawns.

If you're out near Hotel Vostok and in need of a feed, try one of these three options. The low-key *bierkeller* pub **Pivnoy Klub** (☎ 283 669; ul Melnikayte 103; meals R65-140, beers from R40; ☻ 10am-11pm) has heavy wooden seats, displays Gambrinus glasses and serves perfectly cooked chicken ragout using wonderfully crunchy fresh vegetables. Next door is the ever-popular Friday fast-food joint. **Telega** (☎ 782 232; ul Melnikayte 100; meals R350-900; ☻ 11am-2am) is a cute, Ukrainian cellar-restaurant with a carefully contrived village feel and unfiltered *weissbier* (white beer, R100) on tap. The semi-stylish café **Zakusochnaya Teatralnaya** (☎ 246 833; ul Respubliki 36/1; meals R80-250, beers from R30; ☻ 10am-10pm) has reasonably priced if less-than-memorable food with amusingly grouchy staff.

Getting There & Away

AIR

There are daily flights to Moscow (R5000 to R6900), three flights weekly to St Petersburg and various international connections, including flights to Baku (R9100, Wednesday), Kyiv (R7470, Tuesday) and Tashkent (R6730, Wednesday). Tickets are sold by **UtAir Aerokassa** (☎ 453 131; ul Pervomayskaya 58a; ☻ 8am-8pm) opposite the train station and by **Transagenststvo** (ul Respubliki 156; ☻ 8am-8pm) which also sells train tickets.

SIBERIA

BUS

From the **bus station** (ul Permyakova), 3km east of the centre, seven daily buses to Tobolsk (R260, five hours) travel via Pokrovskoe (R89, 1¾ hours).

TRAIN

Useful overnight rail connections include Omsk (R700, eight hours) and Kazan (R1100, 22 hours, departs 4pm). Three daily trains (4½ hours) serve Tobolsk and a *plats-kart* (3rd-class) ticket is R180. While the ugly train station undergoes its long-term reconstruction, rail tickets are sold across the square at ul Pervomayskaya 62.

Getting Around

Tyumen's **Roshchino Airport** (☎ 496 450; http://ros chino.tyumen4u.com/, in Russian) is 30km west of the centre. Take *marshrutka* 35 (R18 plus R8 per bag, 40 minutes) from outside Transagenst-stvo which leaves within 20 minutes of the first passenger getting aboard (last 8.40pm).

From the train station bus 25 serves Hotel Vostok and passes near the bus station – hop off at the Neptun/Stroitel stop then walk a block east, crossing the big clover-leaf junction of uls Permyakova and Respubliki. Metered taxis between bus and train stations cost R70, though freelancers ask R150.

Bus 13 from the train station loops around to the Hotel Neftyanik; switch to frequent buses 30 or 14 in front of the Prezident Hotel for Trinity Monastery. These follow ul Respubliki westbound but return along ul Lenina.

TOBOLSK ТОБОЛЬСК

☎ 34511 / pop 98,000 / ☽ Moscow +2hr

Tobolsk was once Siberia's capital and re-mains its most memorable city. Highlights are its handsome kremlin and a charmingly decrepit old town. Tobolsk is off the trans-Siberian mainline but direct overnight trains to both Yekaterinburg and Omsk make stopping here a perfectly viable op-tion when crossing Russia.

An early visitor to the city was Yermak Timofeevich, whose band of Cossack mer-cenaries sacked the nearby Tatar stronghold of Sibir in 1582. Tobolsk's original fort was built five years later. Although locals were predominantly Muslim Tatars, Tobolsk be-came the seat of Siberia's first bishopric in 1620 as Christianity strove to stamp out

incest, wife-renting and spouse-stealing by sexually frustrated Cossacks.

Tobolsk also became the region's politico-military hub but its strategic importance started to wane in the 1760s, when it was by-passed by the new Great Siberian Trakt (post road). However, until the early 20th century, it remained significant as a centre for both learning and exile. Involuntary guests in-cluded Fyodor Dostoevsky en route to exile in Omsk, and deposed Tsar Nicholas II who spent several doomed months here in 1917.

Hospitable Muslim Tatars still form 30% of the city's population, many living in the quaint, if mosquito-blighted, old town. A handy local greeting is *istimissis* (hello); thank you is *rakhmat*.

Orientation

Buses from the inconvenient train station (some 10km north) give visitors a dismal first impression. Concrete drabness reaches a glum centre around the Hotel Slavyan-skaya, but don't be put off. Tobolsk's glories begin 3km further south around the splen-did kremlin. Immediately beyond and below the kremlin, the old town sinks photogenic-ally into the Irtysh's boggy flood plain.

Information

Gazprombank (ul Oktyabrskaya; ☽ 9am-1pm & 2-4pm Mon-Thu, 9am-3pm Fri) Changes money.

Post office (Komsomolsky pr, M/R 42; ☽ 8am-6pm) Has an attached telephone office.

Servis Tsentr (Internet per hr R28.80; ☽ 8am-10pm) Behind the telephone office.

Sights

KREMLIN

Within the tower-studded 18th-century walls of the **kremlin** (☽ grounds 8am-8pm) are the intriguing but disused **Trading Arches** (Gostiny Dvor) and the glorious 1686 **St Sofia Cathedral**, whose central dome has re-cently been gilded. Less eye-catching from the outside, but with splendid arched ceil-ing murals, is the 1746 **Intercession Cath-edral** (Pokrovsky sobor). Between the two is a 1799 **bell tower**, built for the Uglich bell which had famously signalled a revolt against Tsar Boris Godunov. The revolt failed; in a mad fury Godunov ordered the bell publicly flogged, de-tongued and ban-ished to Tobolsk for its treacherous tolling. A tatty copy of the bell is displayed in the

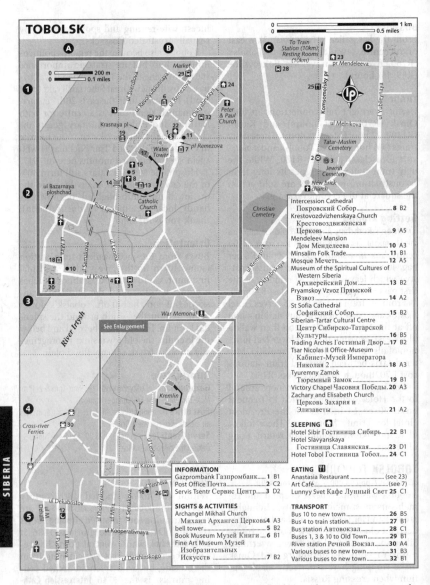

TOBOLSK

Intercession Cathedral
Покровский Собор............8 B2
Krestovozdvizhenskaya Church
Крестовоздвиженская
Церковь...................9 A5
Mendeleev Mansion
Дом Менделеева............10 A3
Minsalim Folk Trade............11 B1
Mosque Мечеть...................12 A5
Museum of the Spiritual Cultures of
Western Siberia
Архиерейский Дом............13 B2
Pryamskoy Vzvoz Прямской
Взвоз...................14 A2
St Sofia Cathedral
Софийский Собор............15 A3
Siberian-Tartar Cultural Centre
Центр Сибирско-Татарской
Культуры...................16 B5
Trading Arches Гостиный Двор....17 B2
Tsar Nicolas II Office-Museum
Кабинет-Музей Императора
Николая 2...................18 A3
Tyuremny Zamok
Тюремный Замок............19 B1
Victory Chapel Часовня Победы.20 A3
Zachary and Elisabeth Church
Церковь Захария и
Элизаветы...................21 A2

SLEEPING
Hotel Sibir Гостиница Сибирь.....22 B1
Hotel Slavyanskaya
Гостиница Славянская............23 D1
Hotel Tobol Гостиница Тобол......24 C1

EATING
Anastasia Restaurant ....(see 23)
Art Café ....(see 7)
Lunnyy Svet Кафе Лунный Свет 25 C1

TRANSPORT
Bus 10 to new town 26 B5
Bus 4 to train station...................27 B1
Bus station Автовокзал...............28 C1
Buses 1, 3 & 10 to Old Town.......29 B1
River station Речной Вокзал.......30 A4
Various buses to new town...........31 B3
Various buses to new town...........32 B1

INFORMATION
Gazprombank Газпромбанк......1 B1
Post Office Почта...................2 C2
Servis Tsentr Сервис Центр.......3 D2

SIGHTS & ACTIVITIES
Archangel Mikhail Church
Михаил Архангел Церковь4 A3
bell tower...................5 B2
Book Museum Музей Книги 6 B1
Fine Art Museum Музей
Изобразительных
Искусств 7 B2

Museum of the Spiritual Cultures of Western Siberia (☎ 23715; admission R20; ⏰ 10am-4pm Wed-Sun), an otherwise entertaining museum within the elegant Arkhiereysky mansion. The upper storey has a stylishly re-created 19th-century drawing room as well as plenty of stuffed animals. The middle floor has a birch-bark *chum* (tepee-shaped tent made of birch bark) amid some interesting ethnographic items. The museum shop sells detailed but hard-to-read city maps.

The eerie 1855 **Tyuremny Zamok** (Krasnaya pl 5; admission R20; ⏰ 10am-4pm Wed-Sun) was once a holding prison. Tsarist exiles were temporarily incarcerated here awaiting a final destination for their banishment.

OUTSIDE THE KREMLIN

Built in 1887 for Tobolsk's 300th anniversary, the delightful **Fine Art Museum** (ul Oktyabrskaya; admission R35, video cameras R100; ☼ 10am-5pm Wed-Sun) was recently renovated and soon after was visited by President Putin. Its celebrated collection of WWI-era Russian avant-garde canvases is arguably less interesting than the fine display of bone carvings. Some of these are by Minsalim Timergazeev, an inspiringly spiritual Tatar eccentric with wild-flowing grey hair. His studio is attached to the nearby art shop **Minsalim Folk Trade** (☎ 22650; dimini@zmail.ru; ul Oktyabrskaya 2; admission free; ☼ 9am-5pm). Here Minsalim will happily demonstrate how to turn antler fragments into little shaman-shapes using Heath Robinson-esque elastic-band technology. His son speaks English.

OLD TOWN

Wooden stairs lead beneath the kremlin's **Pryamskoy Vzvoz** (gatehouse) to the wonderfully dilapidated old town full of weather-beaten churches and angled wooden homes sinking between muddy lanes.

Near the little 1918 **Victory Chapel**, where uls Mira and Kirova meet at a small square, is the grand **Mendeleev mansion** (ul Mira 9) which once housed the family of the famous scientist. The less-eye-catching **Tobolsk Rayon Administration Building** (ul Mira 10) was the exile-home of the last tsar before his fateful journey to execution in Yekaterinburg. Upstairs, beyond a security check, one small room has been restored close to its 1917 appearance as the **Tsar Nicholas II Office-Museum** (Kabinet-muzey Imperatora Nikolaya II; ☎ 22776; admission R15).

Two blocks east, the attractive **Archangel Mikhail Church** (ul Lenina 24) has a colourfully restored interior. The character of Tatiana Larina in Pushkin's epic *Eugene Onegin* is said to have been modelled on Natalya Fonvizina, a Decembrist wife who prayed here when not cultivating pineapples in her hothouse. More photogenic is the somewhat derelict 1759 **Zachary & Elisabeth Church** (ul Bazarnaya Ploshchad) with soaring black-tipped spires. Beyond the main red-brick **mosque** (☎ 22748; ul Pushkina 27), weave through the muddy lanes of attractive Tatar cottages to reach the equally splendid baroque shell of the **Krestovozdvizhenskaya Church**.

The **Siberian-Tatar Cultural Centre** (☎ 22713; ul Yershova 30) has occasional exhibitions and Tatar

musical shows. Upstairs there's a minor **museum** (admission R10; ☼ 9am-noon & 1-5pm Mon-Fri).

Sleeping & Eating

Hotel Sibir (☎ 22390; pl Remezova 1; s R490-650, tw/ste R1300/1330) Across from the kremlin, this good-value hotel has flashes of style, most notably in some of its full-facility suites. Suite 214 has particularly delightful olde-worlde décor with sepia photos and a hint of canopy over the queen-sized bed. Unremarkable standard single rooms have share-pair bathrooms for R490, private ones for R650. Rates include breakfast in the inviting restaurant.

Hotel Slavyanskaya (☎ 99101; www.hotel.tob.ru, in Russian; 9th Mikro-Rayon, pr Mendeleev; s/tw/d from R2000/3500/4300; ℗) Astonishingly well appointed for rural Siberia, the big, modern Slavyanskaya has fully Western-standard comforts. Its only disadvantage is the uninspiring new-town location. Wider beds are available for 10% extra. A few 'imperfect' rooms are significantly discounted. There's tennis, a great downstairs pub and a less appealing small nightclub. The unexpectedly good value **Anastasia Restaurant** (☎ 40138; meals R200-450; ☼ 7am-11pm) serves delicious 'epicure roulette' (apricots and walnuts stuffed into a breast of chicken – though chicken is cunningly misspelt as 'bacon' on the English menu!).

Resting rooms (komnaty otdykha; ☎ 95222; train station; dm R178) Clean and friendly, the location is utterly impractical for visiting the city but ideal if you're arriving blurry-eyed off the Omsk train or awaiting the 5.23am service to Tyumen. Showers cost R35 extra.

Hotel Tobol (☎ 46614; ul Oktyabrskaya 20; s/d/tw R420/780/960) This somewhat dingy concrete slab has bathrooms in each of its old-style Soviet rooms. A few of the sad doubles have been cosmetically repapered. Music blares loud and late from the bar.

Art Café (☎ 24347; Fine Art Museum basement; meals R350, coffee R40) Roast potato dinners or vegetarian curries in Tobolsk? Yes! The town's nicest café now has an Anglo-Iranian owner who can cook up a range of typical British, Russian or international meals to order. Ask about the revolutionary fat-free cakes or Jacob's improbable but true hair-pulling antics.

Lunnyy Svet (Komsomolsky pr 2; meals R100-200, cover R25 from 7pm Thu-Sat) This midrange café has a pleasant summer beer terrace and a

SIBERIA

'night-effect' interior but the music can get appallingly loud in the evenings.

Getting There & Away

Tobolsk is a stop on the railway line to Nizhnevartovsk, Purpe and Novy Urengoy. There are useful overnight connections to/from Yekaterinburg (R850, 12 hours) and Omsk (R890, 12 hours), though the latter arrives at 5am northbound. For Tyumen, trains (R167 *platskart*, 4¾ hours) are supplemented by seven daily buses (R260, five hours) via Pokrovskoe (3¼ hours), Rasputin's home village. Eight buses per day to various destinations pass Abalak.

Big ferries run from June to September out of the **river station** (☎ 96617) about 10 times per year to Salekhard on the Arctic Circle (1st/3rd class R2411/740, four to five days) via Khanty Mansysk and Beryozovo; tickets can be in very short supply. From any of those towns you could fly back to Tyumen, and from Salekhard you can cross the river to Labytnangi from where trains run to Moscow and Vorkuta. See Lonely Planet's *Greenland & the Arctic* guide.

Southbound, the ferries run to Omsk (1st/3rd class R1674/612, 79 hours) via Tara (51 hours).

Getting Around

Bus 4 and *marshrutka* 20 link the train station, new town and kremlin. Buses 1, 3 and 10 travel past the kremlin and loop around the old town. Bus 1 passes the mosque.

AROUND TOBOLSK

Abalak Абалак

From Tobolsk, a quiet road skirts the border of the ancient Tatar kingdom of Isker, continuing 25km to Abalak. Here the region's holiest **monastery** was built on the site of a miraculous materialising icon that was last spotted in Australia long after the Soviets had turned the church into a tractor barn. Today, the monastery is working again, with a copy of the icon over the door. There are charming views over the bend in the Irtysh River, with 249 steps leading down to the riverbank. From Tobolsk, buses bound for Yuzhno Begishebskie, Baygara or Zagbazdina stop at the Abalak bus stop (40 minutes), from which it's an obvious 1.5km walk to the monastery.

OMSK OMCK

☎ 3812 / pop 1.145 million / ⌚ Moscow +3hr

Spending a day in Omsk, 568km southeast of Tyumen, is the best way of breaking a Tobolsk–Tomsk or Tyumen–Novosibirsk train ride into two overnighters. Vast and sprawling, Omsk's industrial suburbs look off-putting but the gently attractive central core has some fine century-old architecture and is dotted with parks, museums, great restaurants and quirky public sculptures.

Starting life as a 1716 Cossack outpost, Omsk grew rapidly and by 1824 had replaced Tobolsk as the seat of Siberia's governor general. Exiled Dostoevsky nearly died from a flogging while jailed here from 1849 to 1853. During the civil war Omsk was briefly the seat of Admiral Kolchak's government until overrun by the Red Army in 1919.

Orientation

The wide Irtysh River divides the city. On the western bank are the airport and bus station. The historic centre, 4km north of the train station, is on the eastern bank at the confluence of the Irtysh with the much smaller Om River. A bookstall upstairs within the train station sells excellent city maps.

Information

Bank Moskovy (pr Marksa 10; ⌚ 10am-1pm & 1.45-4pm Mon-Fri, 10am-3pm Sat) Good euro rates and 24-hour ATM.

Hai Lama! (☎ 287 866; ul Mayakovskogo 15; Internet per MB R3, per hr R25; ⌚ 24hr) Outside is a comical, cross-legged birdman sculpture in a tree.

K2 Adventures (☎ /fax 693 075; www.adventuretravel .ru; office 505, ul Neftezavodskaya 14) Uniquely experienced for extreme rafting and mountaineering expeditions on the toughest rivers and peaks of Siberia and Central Asia. Igor speaks English and can meet you in town, saving you a 6km trip (*marshrutka* 335 to bus stop Magistralnaya).

Navigator Internet Kafe (ul Lenina 14/1; per MB R3, per hr R25-35; beers R30-60; ⌚ 9am-10pm) Night shift R90 to R120 plus R2 per MB.

Omni Travel (☎ 500 070; Hotel Mayak; ⌚ 10am-5pm Mon-Fri) English-speaking travel agency offering simple city tours.

Omskpromstroybank (ul Lermontova 20; ⌚ 10am-2pm & 3-6pm Tue-Fri, 9am-2pm Sat) Good US dollar rates.

Post office (ul Gertsena 1; ⌚ 8am-7pm Mon-Sat, 10am-5pm Sun)

Telephone office (ul Gagarina 34; ⌚ 24hr) For calls prepay a deposit, dial the number (with 8-10 for international), then when connected press '3'.

KOLCHAK'S GOLD TRAIN

The reverberations of Russia's 1917 revolution are full of scarcely believable tales. Few top the incredible journey of the tsar's national gold reserve. With Communist forces closing in, royalists somehow managed to use barges and special trains to scurry east with over 1300 tons of gold, plus silver, platinum and millions of roubles in banknotes. When the retreat reached Omsk, the hoard fell into the hands of Admiral Kolchak. A former national hero for his Arctic explorations, Kolchak was then a minister in Omsk's anti-Lenin coalition. The captured cash allowed him to launch a coup ousting socialist-moderates. Even more money poured in as 'aid' from vehemently anti-Bolshevik Western powers. Thus, while much of Russia starved, 1918–19 in Omsk was a year of surreal extravagance. It couldn't last. Despite some initial successes, Kolchak's brutality as a general as well as his venality meant the movement soon backfired. The Whites collapsed and retreated to Irkutsk where, after a series of intrigues, Kolchak was summarily executed. His body was dumped in the Angara River at the point where his statue now stands (see p567). To pay Japanese agents for military supplies (which failed to arrive), some of the remaining gold was reportedly shipped east to Chita and never seen again. The counter-revolution disappeared with it.

Sights & Activities

Several witty **statues**, including a brass workman emerging from a manhole, add to the elegant, century-old façades of upper ul Lenina. Grandiose flourishes make the **Drama Theatre** (☎ 244 065; www.omskdrama.ru, in Russian; ul Lenina; ✆ cash desk 10am-7pm) Omsk's most ornate historical building. Decrepit but potentially fabulous, the 1905 **Hotel Oktyabrya Building** (Partizanskaya ul 2) faces the pointy little **Serafimo-Alexievskaya Chapel** which looks like it fell off a kremlin. Across Yubileyny Bridge, the **OGIK Museum** (Omsky Gosudarstvenny Istoriko-Kraevadchesky muzey; ☎ 314 747; ul Lenina 23a; admission R25; ✆ 10am-6.30pm Tue-Sun) has a strong historical and ethnographic collection. The next-door **Art Museum** (Omsky muzey iskusstv; ☎ 313 677; admission R100; ✆ 10am-6pm Tue-Sun) displays a lot of fussy decorative arts but the rectilinear 1862 building is a historical curiosity in itself. It was built as the Siberian governor's mansion and hosted passing tsars: note the original Kalmykian throne with its ebony elephant armrests and 7kg of beaten silver. In 1918–19 the building housed Admiral Kolchak's counter-revolutionary government and was thus the very heart of White Russia.

In the gardens behind the art museum are a **war memorial** and a **Lenin statue**, Vlad apparently preening himself in an invisible mirror. Beside the red-brick **former town duma** (pl Lenina) is the **Liberov Centre** (☎ 301 645; Dumskaya ul 3; admission R6; ✆ 10am-5pm Tue-Sun), with a piano room/gallery and a dozen works by renowned artist Alexei Liberov.

The city has several fine churches, including the 1870 **Krestovozdvizhensky Cath**edral (Tarskaya ul 33) and the 1840 neoclassical **St Nicholas Cathedral** (Svyato-Nikolsky sobor; ul Lenina 27a). In a 90-year-old timber house, the **Old Believers' Chapel** (ul Shchetinkina 10) is almost hidden by recent redevelopment.

The limited attractions of the **Literature Museum** (☎ 242 965; ul Dostoevskogo 1; admission R40; ✆ 10am-6pm Tue-Sun) include some Dostoevsky doodles from the unhappy time the writer spent here. One block west a century-old brick building houses the newly renovated **Military Museum** (ul Taubye 7; admission R70; ✆ 10am-5pm Tue-Sun), its garden bristling with artillery.

Chunky but isolated and hardly thrilling, the **Tobolsk** and **Tarskaya Gates** are all that remain of Omsk's second (1791–94) city walls. Across pl Dzerzhinskogo from the latter, the curious **Pozharnaya Kalancha** (ul Internatsionalnaya) is an unusually photogenic, seven-storey firemen's lookout tower. Brick with whitewashed column capitals, it was finished in 1916 and is something of a city icon.

Sleeping
BUDGET

Hotel Omskgrazhdanstroy (☎ 251 247; Gospitalnaya ul 19; dm/s/tw R210/350/660) Remarkably good value, this little-known hotel is the wrong side of the busy ul Frunze intersection, but still walking distance from the centre via ul Gusarova. Rooms are not sexy but are clean, large and all have private bathrooms – even the dormitories.

Hotel Omsk (☎ 310 721; fax 315 222; ul Irtyshskaya Naberezhnaya 30; dm R350, s R650-1200, tw R1200-1600) Halfway between the train station and centre,

SIBERIA

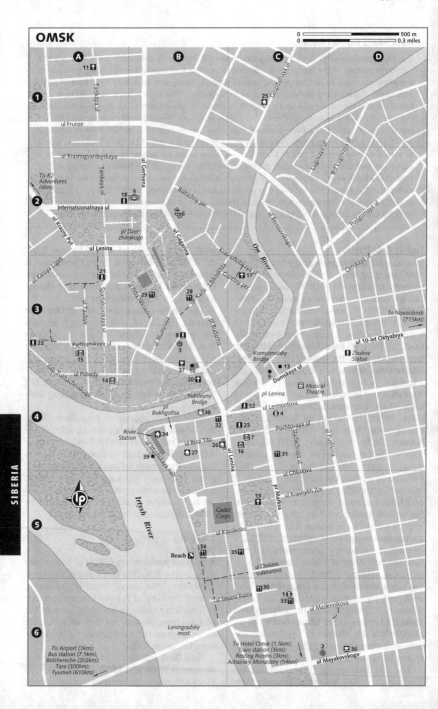

OMSK

0 — 500 m
0 — 0.3 miles

Tarskaya ul

ul Frunze

ul Krasnogvardeyskaya

To K2 Adventures (6km)

Internatsionalnaya ul

ul Krasny Put

pl Dzerzhinskogo

ul Lenina

ul Karoya Ligeti

ul Pavla Nekrasova

ul Spartakovskaya

ul Taubye

ul Gertsena

ul Gagarina

Bolnichny per

Om River

Gospitalnaya ul

Lugovaya ul

Bert ugovskaya ul

Podgornaya ul

ul Berezovskogo

Omskaya ul

To Novosibirsk (715km)

ul 10-let Oktyabrya

Zhukov Statue

Krasnoflotskaya ul

ul Karla Liebknekhta

Gazetny per

ul Muzeynaya

pl Buturina

ul Partizanskaya ul

nab Tukhachevskogo

ul Pobedy

Komsomolsky Bridge

Dumskaya ul

pl Lenina

Musical Theatre

ul Lermontova

Pochtovaya ul

ul Stachechnaya ul

ul Pushkina

Yubileyny Bridge

pl Bukhgoltsa

River Station

ul Irtyshskaya nab

ul Broz Tito

ul Lenina

ul Chkalova

pr Marksa

ul Krasnykh Zor

Irtysh River

Cadet Corps

ul Korolenko

Beach

ul Chokana Valikhanova

ul Stepana Razina

ul Maslennikova

Leningradsky most

To Airport (3km);
Bus station (7.5km);
Bolshereche (202km);
Tara (300km);
Tyumen (610km)

To Hotel Omsk (1.5km);
Train station (3km);
Resting Rooms (3km);
Achairsky Monastery (54km)

ul Mayakovskogo

SIBERIA

this big, drab concrete block is somewhat redeemed by its river views. Rooms are mostly unreconstructed Soviet affairs but a dozen have been fairly thoroughly rebuilt and certain others are half-heartedly redecorated. Very rarely full. Take any bus along ul Karla Marksa to the circus then walk five minutes through Pobedy Park to the riverside.

Resting rooms (komnaty otdykha; ☎ 442 347; train station; dm/tw R250/700) Rebuilt, clean and relatively inviting, they're in a separate building – exit the main station, turn left and find the door before the baggage *kassa*. TV costs R30 per hour extra.

Hotel Sibir (☎ 312 571; 2nd fl, ul Lenina 22; s R500-1300, tw R1300-2400) Despite a great central position in a historical building and some rudimentary improvements, the Sibir remains rather dingy and overpriced. Best deals are the cheapest singles which are very simple with a sink but no bathroom. Cheaper doubles have a basic toilet too. 'Better' rooms have new but clashing floral décor and musty old furniture.

MIDRANGE

Hotel Mayak (☎ /fax 315 431; www.hotel-mayak.ru; ul Lermontova 2; s/tw R1920/2640) Within the rounded end of the vaguely ship-shaped Art Deco river station, the Mayak has small but stylish rooms with artistic lines and good bathrooms. Half-price for 12-hour stays.

Hotel Turist (☎ 316 419; fax 316 414; www.tourist-omsk.ru; ul Broz Tito 2; economy s/tw R1330/1640, standard s/tw R1680/1940, 1st-class s/d/tw R2100/2120/2350) A fairly appealing address with fine views from upper floors. Good 'first-class' rooms are totally rebuilt but the overpriced 'econ-

omy rooms' were remodelled back in the early 1990s and now look very worn.

Eating & Drinking

Chashka (☎ 252 379; www.hollcup.ru; 3rd fl, Pyat Zvyozd shopping mall; ul Karla Libknekhta; meals R150-450; ⏰ 11am-midnight) Delft-style tiles, wooden half-wall panelling and a fireplace give a nominally Dutch décor while the menu (available in English) ranges from Creole pork to Thai beef via a delicious *baklazhany pa-rimski* (cheese-topped aubergine with olives and cream sauce, R127).

Senkyevich (☎ 510 981; ul Sezdovskaya 1) Overlooking the river this stylishly contemporary glass-and-steel building incorporates a small sushi bar (R40 to R140 per piece), an airy business-casual Russian café (meals R260 to R600) and an upscale European restaurant (pastas R150 to R300, meals R400 to R1200) specialising in oysters and duck.

Dom Aktyora (☎ 313 254; ul Lenina 45; meals R230-600) A sedately atmospheric rendezvous for actors whose signed photos grace the walls. Thursday nights there's live jazz without cover charge.

Chudesnitsa (☎ 234 979; ul Nekrasova 8; meals R200-450; ⏰ 10am-midnight) An unpretentious outdoor terrace marked simply 'Kafe' that's ideal for well-made Georgian cuisine on a sunny summer's evening.

Fresh pastries and croissants are sold at **Proviant** (ul Marksa 10; ⏰ 9am-9pm) and from a **bakers' window** (⏰ 10am-8pm) in the side of the traditional, upmarket Russian restaurant **Lygovskaya Sloboda** (☎ 311 540; ul Lenina 20; meals R350-1000; ⏰ noon-1am). **Il Plato** (☎ 310 315; pr Marksa 5; salad-bar lunches R150-215, dinners to R600;

SIBERIA

☺ 9am-midnight Mon-Sat, noon-midnight Sun) does
R90 set breakfasts with bottomless coffee.

Drinking

Ferma (☎ 247 827; Partizanskaya ul 2; beers R45-60,
snacks R80-200) Beneath a splendid old-Omsk
building, communist iconography is delightfully mocked in this amusing cellar
bar-café where Sly Stallone, Elvis, Michael
Jackson and Marilyn Monroe lurk surreptitiously in the Soviet realist paintings.

Coffee Base (☎ 307 578; ul Mayakovskogo 17; coffees
R29-100; ☺ 10am-11pm) Pleasant coffee house
with sensibly priced espressos. If your palate differentiates 80% from 100% Arabica
beans, consider the more expensive 'Elite'
blends. Food includes decent mini-bliny,
pricey cakes and steaks.

Getting There & Away

Flight destinations include Moscow (R5500,
several daily), St Petersburg (R5510, twice
weekly) and Irkutsk (R6050, three times
weekly) plus international connections to
Germany (from US$440, up to twice weekly)
and Tashkent (US$190, Wednesday). Nu-
merous air-ticket agencies at the river station sell rail tickets (R150 commission).

Useful overnight trains from Omsk serve
Tobolsk (No 395, R890, 13¾ hours, 4pm),
Tomsk (No 38 or 272, R850, 14 hours),
Novosibirsk (No 88, R420 platskart, 9½
hours), Yekaterinburg (No 67, 13 hours)
via Tyumen (7½ hours) and Zlatoust (No
59, 17 hours) via Chelyabinsk and Miass.

For Tara the **bus station** (pr Komarova 2) is
across the Irtysh just beyond the Khristo-

Rozhdestbensky Cathedral with its eye-
catching gilded domes.

On a green barge behind the **river station**
(pl Bukhgoltsa) is the **Rechflot** (☎ 398 563; ☺ 9am-
7pm) ticket office. Also here is the jetty for
hydrofoils to Tevriz via Tara and for ferries
cruising the Irtysh River to Salekhard (six
days, 1st/3rd class R3000/1098) via Tobolsk
(R1674/612, two days) roughly three times
monthly. Various **pleasure cruises** depart from
a separate jetty near Yubileyny Bridge, notably for Achairsky Monastery (R160 return,
four times daily mid-May to early October).

Getting Around

From the train station, trolleybus No 4 and
marshrutka 335 run along pr Marksa to pl
Lenina, past the main post office and on
for miles up Krasny Put. Bus 60 crosses the
Irtysh to the **airport** (☎ 517 570; Inzhenernaya ul 1)
while trolleybus 7 or the faster marshrutka
366 head for the bus station. Allow over half
an hour in rush-hour traffic jams.

AROUND OMSK
Achairsky Monastery

This impressive riverside convent is 55km
south of Omsk on the Pavlodar highway. The
original 1905 buildings were destroyed in the
1930s and the site became a Gulag where,
according to local guides, some 200,000
people died or were executed. Since 1992,
impressive gilt-topped brick reconstructions
include a five-storey belfry and a glittering
nine-domed central church. Boat tours from
Omsk (4½ hours return) stay long enough
for you to stroll across the site to a holy
spring that flows out beneath a cute wooden
chapel in the woods. Alternatively, Achair-
bound marshrutky leave roughly hourly
(R30) from the 'Lobkova' stop, just two minutes' walk south of Omsk train station.

TARA ТАРА
☎ 38171 / pop 26,000 / ☺ Moscow +3hr

Founded in 1594 as a defensive outpost for
Tobolsk, Tara recovered from a devastating
fire in 1669 to become a major trade centre. It was later eclipsed by Omsk, 300km
to its south, becoming a dozy backwater
and place of exile for several Decembrists.
Soviet planners ringed an obligatory Lenin
statue with a few small concrete eyesores
on pl Lenina and destroyed five of the city's
six great 18th- and 19th-century churches.

SIBERIA

However, a gentle charm remains, making Tara a possible hop-off if you're taking the river route between Omsk and Tobolsk.

Within a block of each other are a small **museum** (pl Lenina; 🕑 9am-3pm Sun-Fri), the 1761 **Saviour's Church** (Spasskaya tserkov; ul Kuybysheva), a partly reconstructed **ostrog** (timber fortress) and the **Hotel Irtysh** (☎ 21538; pl Lenina 15; dm/d R140/636). The most attractive **wooden cottages** are in the lower town, down a short, steep bank beside a silver toadstool-shaped memorial, a block northeast of the square. With its little **mosque** this lower town straggles 3km along the river valley to the river station for Salekhard ferries (three monthly) and Omsk hydrofoils (alternate days, R170).

Buses (R166, six hours) and minibuses (R170, four hours) to Omsk each leave at least four times daily. The **bus station** (ul Izbisheva) is hidden away, two blocks north of the little market on ul Lenina (the main road from Omsk). Three blocks south of that market is the *ostrog* where you'd turn left walking to pl Lenina.

AROUND TARA
Bolshereche Большеречье
☎ 38169 / pop 11,000 / 🕑 Moscow +3hr
About 100km before Tara, Omsk–Tara buses stop briefly in Bolshereche. Its pleasant outskirts have some old cottages and a renovated church. The central area is mostly unattractive but boasts a locally famous little **zoo** and a trio of small **traders' houses** (Sovetskaya ul) with beautifully carved wooden façades. One of these retains its original interior. The ultrabasic **Hotel Rus** (☎ 21851; ul 50i let VLKSM 7; dm/s/tw R100/290/200) is opposite the market.

NOVOSIBIRSK & TOMSK REGIONS
НОВОСИБИРСКАЯ И ТОМСКАЯ ОБЛАСТИ

Novosibirsk, 530km east of Omsk, is Siberia's biggest city. It's a lively and useful transport hub but you'll thank yourself for choosing Tomsk instead to break your long trans-Siberian journey.

NOVOSIBIRSK НОВОСИБИРСК
☎ 383 / pop 1.5 million / 🕑 Moscow +3hr
If you want nightlife, restaurants with Las Vegas-style glitz or a choice of countless Irish pubs, Novosibirsk might be your Siberian dream come true. For anything else, consider skipping the place or departing the same evening on an overnight train. Novosibirsk hotels, already overpriced, have a weird rule preventing most from accepting foreigners unless prebooked through a tour agency.

Despite its size, Novosibirsk has relatively little to see. It grew up in the 1890s around the Ob River bridge built for the trans-Siberian. Named Novo-Nikolaevsk until 1925 for the last tsar, it grew rapidly into Siberia's biggest metropolis, a key industrial and transport centre exploiting coalfields to the east and mineral deposits in the Urals.

Orientation
Despite its daunting scale, the 'capital of Siberia' has a manageably simple centre focused on pl Lenina. The city's main axis, Krasny pr, runs through this square linking most points of interest. Across the river around Metro Studencheskaya, ul Karla Marksa has numerous dining alternatives at marginally more reasonable prices. Bookshop **Dom Knigi** (Krasny pr 51; 🕑 10am-8pm Mon-Sat, to 7pm Sun) has a good range of maps.

Information
INTERNET ACCESS
Computer Klub Arena (☎ 220 3939; ul 1905 Goda 41; Internet per MB R3, per hr R15; 🕑 8am-9pm) Fun, with submarine-décor, downstairs through an inner courtyard of a school. Night shift R110 from 10pm, booking required.
Internet Tsentr (☎ 291 8841; ul Trudovaya 1; per 30 min R30; 🕑 9am-10pm) Beneath an apartment block; take the first alley off Vokzalnaya magistral when walking from pl Lenina. Night shift R110.

MONEY
TransKreditBank (ul Lenina 86; 🕑 9.30am-1pm & 2-5pm Mon-Fri) Handy for train station; 24-hour ATM.
Vneshtorgbank (Krasny pr 35; 🕑 9am-5pm Mon-Sat) Decent euro rates.

POST
Main post office (ul Lenina 5; 🕑 8am-9pm Mon-Fri, to 7pm Sat & Sun)

TELEPHONE
Telephone office (ul Sovetskaya 33; 🕑 24hr)

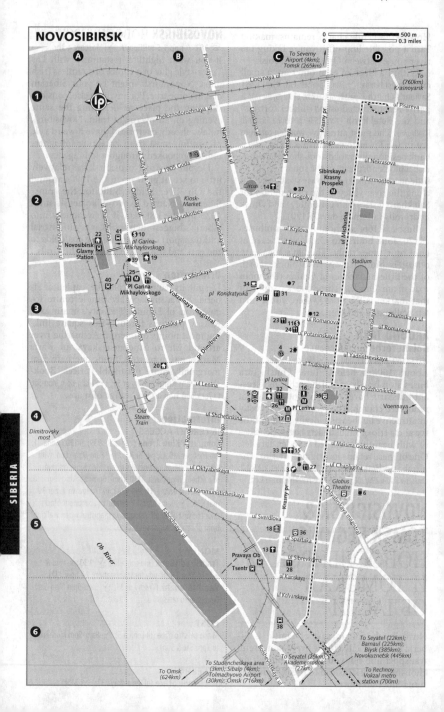

TRAVEL AGENCIES

Novosibirsk's many travel agencies virtually all offer packaged or tailor-made trips to Altai.

Acris (☎ 218 0001; www.acris.ru; 2nd fl, Krasny pr 35; 🕐 10am-6pm Mon-Sat) Offers upmarket Yenisey River cruises from Krasnoyarsk to Dudinka and, given plenty of warning, can sort out the awkward permits. Yuri speaks English.

Altair (☎ 212 5115; www.altairtour.ru; office 15, ul Sovetskaya 65) Helpful, with a wide range of tours and English spoken.

Sibalp (☎ 346 3191; http://sibalp.unpo.ru/; office 515, pr Karla Marksa 2; 🕐 10am-5pm Mon-Fri, longer in summer) Focusing on Altai exploration trips for small-groups and independent foreign travellers, this is a helpful, personal travel service that can also arrange English-speaking homestays and city tours in Novosibirsk. Multilingual staff will meet clients at their hotel.

Sibir Altai (http://sibalt.ru, in Russian; office 607a, ul Frunze 5; 🕐 10am-6pm Mon-Fri, 11am-3pm Sat) Packages Altai trips for local tourists, sold through numerous regional travel agencies. Minimal English. Runs direct weekend buses to Turbaza Katun.

STA-Novosibirsk (☎ 223 9534; www.sibtravel.com /eng/; ul Oktyabrskaya 45a; 🕐 7am-1pm & 2-6pm) English- and German-speaking staff can book you into 'closed' hotels at very short notice for just R100 over normal costs. They offer a variety of Altai trips with set departure dates, prices varying according to take-up. The easily missed office is in a courtyard between the Mexico Kafe and German consulate.

Zhemchuzhina Altaya (☎ 219 2198; www.ozera.sib .ru, in Russian; office 306, Dom Bita, Krasny pr 50) Specialist for Lake Teletskoe.

Sights

Novosibirsk's pl Lenina is dominated by the huge, silver-domed **Opera & Ballet Theatre** (p513). Bigger than Moscow's Bolshoi, its grand interior alone makes performances one of the city's highlights. In front, wearing a flapping coat, the dashing **Lenin statue** is flanked by waving partisans vainly trying to direct the chaotic traffic.

In an elegant mansion, the **Local Studies Museum** (Kraevedchesky muzey; ☎ 218 1773; Krasny pr 23; admission R150; 🕐 10am-5.30pm Tue-Sun) has Altai shaman coats, cutaway pioneer houses and some splendid religious artefacts. The **State Art Museum** (Khudozhestvenny muzey; ☎ 223 3516; http://gallery.nsc.ru/; Krasny pr 5; adult/student R150/80; 🕐 10am-5.20pm Tue-Fri, 11am-5.20pm Sat & Sun) has an extensive collection including icons, Siberian art, Braque-esque works by Nikolai Gritsyuk and numerous distinctive mountainscapes by celebrated spiritual Russian painter Nikolai Rerikh.

CHURCHES

The pretty little **Chapel of St Nicholas** (Chasovnya Svyatitelya Nikolaya; pr Krasny) was said to mark the geographical centre of Russia when built in 1915. Demolished in the 1930s, it was rebuilt in 1993 for Novosibirsk's centenary. The gold-domed 1914 **Cathedral of the Ascension** (Voznesensky sobor; ul Sovetskaya 91) has a wonderful, colourful interior with a soaring central space that's unexpected from its fairly squat exterior appearance. The 1898 **Alexander Nevsky Cathedral** (sobor Alexandra Nevskogo; Krasny pr 1a) is a red-brick Byzantine-style

SIBERIA

building with gilded domes and colourful new murals.

Sleeping

Novosibirsk hotels are poor value by Siberian standards. Most, including the riverside Ob and the nicely renovated but inconvenient Vostok, will only accept foreigners when booked through a tour agency (incurring booking fees and commission).

Hotel Sibir (☎ 223 1215; centre@gk-sibir.sibnet.ru; ul Lenina 21; s/d from R2100/2600; 🏦 🖳) The Sibir considers itself Novosibirsk's international hotel with some English-speaking staff and useful air-ticket and tour bureaux. Only the Hotel Sibir is sure to offer visa registrations, and it will only do so for guests. Excellent king-bedded 'studios' (d R5400) have inviting modern décor and party-sized bathrooms. However, standard rooms lack style or air-conditioning, their parquet floors are worn and some of the furniture is ageing. 'First category' rooms (s/tw R2600/3900) are fully renovated but hardly justify the hefty prices. Rates include breakfast.

Hotel Tsentralnaya (☎ 223 3638; fax 227 660; Lenina 3; s/tw without bathroom R700/1000, s/tw with bathroom R1500/2200) Perfectly central, the no-frills basic rooms with shared, survivable bathrooms are Novosibirsk's best budget option. That's if you're allowed to stay: this seems to depend on having a preregistered visa, on the mood of the receptionist and the wind direction. Sometimes agency bookings are demanded. Lifts are dodgy.

Station Hotel (☎ 229 2376; 2nd fl, Novosibirsk Glavny train station; dm/tw/tr without bathroom R500/1200/1500, s/tw with bathroom R2800/3500). Only for those with onward rail tickets. Half-price for 12-hour stays. It's frequently full.

Hotel Novosibirsk (☎ 220 1120; fax 216 517; Vokzalnaya magistral 1; s/tw from R1100/1700) Opposite Novosibirsk Glavny train station, this glum 23-storey Soviet-era tower has mediocre, overpriced Soviet-era rooms. The cheapest share a toilet and washbasin between pairs of rooms and lack showers altogether. You'll pay over R1800 for a private bathroom. Room rates include a lacklustre breakfast.

Homestays (s R700-1000, tw R1100-1500) can be organised through **Uyut Kvartirnoe Byuro** (☎ 202 009; www.risp.ru/~hotel, in Russian; Novosibirsk Glavny train station) and half-price is charged for stay of 12 hours. For similar rates, tour

agency Sibalp can arrange English-speaking hosts. For marginally less you could take a chance with one of the women loitering outside the train station after 9pm with 'Квартира' (apartment) signs pinned to their jackets.

NOT SLEEPING

No hotel? Budget travellers might consider getting 'locked in' to an Internet Club night shift and typing the night away. Alternatively, for just R280 *platskart* each way you could take an overnight sleeper train to Biysk.

Eating
RESTAURANTS

Choice is almost endless near pl Lenina.

Tbilisi (☎ 222 8181; ul Sovetskaya 65; meals R320-800; 🕑 11am-11pm) Despite growing competition, this atmospheric tavern-cavern still offers the most authentic Georgian cuisine in town. Filling, oozingly cheese-filled *khachapuri po-imeretinsk* (Georgian bread stuffed with salty cheese) cost R100.

Mexico Kafe (☎ 210 3420; Oktyabrskaya magistral 49; meals R350-800; 🕑 noon-1am) Dangling chillies, Aztec icons and a big charcoal grill add atmosphere while Los Gringos serenade. Great Mexican food.

Ieroglif (☎ 222 5712; Krasny pr 35; meals R250-700; 🕑 noon-1am) This hypnotic temple of a restaurant has Chinese, Japanese and Korean offerings.

Aladdin (☎ 222 5233; ul Romanova 28; meals R250-600) Arab-style place with Las Vegas–style entryway and a slightly embarrassed doorman costumed as a harem eunuch. The menu mixes Middle Eastern, Uzbek and Thai. Smoke water pipes from R400.

Prices are relatively reasonable in the very central, Disney-esque 'Siberian village' **Zhili Bili** (ul Lenina 1; meals R130-450; 🕑 11am-11pm), with English menus, a salad bar and great stuffed bliny. It's upstairs above fast-food eatery **Grill-Master** (ul Lenina 1; burgers R39-54) through a central wooden door. Within the same building but entered from the rear (park side) is the super-popular **Lanch Kafe** (☎ 270 581; meals R200-350), above which is a great Italian restaurant and a chilled-out, cushion-floored DJ-bar serving sushi.

QUICK EATS

Vilka-Lozhka (ul Frunze 2; meals R70-130; 🕑 10am-10pm) Simple yet stylishly modern cafeteria decorated with primary-coloured cutlery to remarkably dramatic effect.

Stolovaya Parus (ul Sibrekoma 2; meals R35-50, tea R3; ☺ 9am-4.30pm Mon-Fri) Fill up for a pittance in this easy-to-miss, old-style Soviet chow-room.

SELF-CATERING

Kaskad (ul Vokzalnaya 2; ☺ 7.30am-10pm) Multiroomed grocery with a takeaway, pay-by-weight salad bar and a basic sit-down *pelmenaya*.

Supermarket Khoroshy (Vokzalnaya magistral 4; ☺ 24hr) Groceries any time.

Drinking

Plentiful Irish pubs and Wild West bars are easy to find. Just stroll down ul Lenina, Krasny pr or Vokzalnaya magistral for a block or two from pl Lenina. Almost all serve decent if pricey food as well as drinks.

People's Bar & Grill (☎ 275 5000; Krasny pr; beers from R48, espresso R39; ☺ noon-2am) Performer barmen, hip clientele and a modern vibe (despite items of Anglo-American retrofashion) make this a great people-watching venue. Descend the stairway opposite St Nicholas chapel.

Retro-Kafe Dezhavu (☎ 213 2720; www.v-gosti.ru, in Russian; ul Dimitrova 15; coffees R40-110; ☺ 9am-1am) This very pink piano-café has love niches for romantic couples and menus are presented as old newspapers. Serves breakfasts till 11am.

Entertainment

Dozens of nightclubs, bowling alleys, concert halls and theatres are fully listed in Russian on www.novosibout.ru.

Opera & Ballet Theatre (☎ 227 1537; www.opera -novosibirsk.ru; Krasny pr 36; admission R35-200; ☺ Oct-Jun) For classical culture don't miss an evening at this gigantic theatre.

Philharmonia (☎ 222 1511; www.philharmonia-nsk; ul Spartaka 11) Concerts here range from classical symphonies to Dixieland jazz. Ticket prices vary widely but are usually between R100 and R150.

Rock City (☎ 227 0108; www.rockcity.ru, in Russian; 3rd fl, Krasny pr 37; typical admission R200) With designer metallic factory-style décor, this is Novosibirsk's top spot for everything from Latin dancing to heavy rock concerts. It's above the Old Irish pub.

Getting There & Away

AIR

There are two airports in Novosibirsk. **Severny** (☎ 228 3788), 6km north of the centre, handles shorter hops including three weekly services to Kyzyl (R4800). However, most major airlines use the much bigger **Tolmachyovo** (☎ 216 9230; http://tolmachevoeng.faktura .ru), 30km west of Novosibirsk off the Omsk road. The website gives approximate timetables. Regular international destinations include Ürümqi (R5250, two hours, Tuesday), Beijing, Bangkok, Dubai and Seoul plus several cities in Central Asia (eg Baku R7200). Most weekends there are flights to Hanover (R12,040 return) and/or Frankfurt (R14,600 return). **Siberia Airlines** (toll-free ☎ 8-800 200 0007; www .s7.ru), the biggest regional carrier, is launching online sales and plans links with several international carriers. A comprehensive domestic network includes regular flights to Moscow (R6300, R8600 return), St Petersburg (R7080 booked six days ahead) and Irkutsk (R5490 to R6100, 2¾ hours). The central **Aviakassa** (ul Gogolya 3; ☺ 8.30am-8pm) is one of dozens of places to buy air tickets.

BUS

From the **bus station** (Krasny pr 4) around 20 daily buses serve both Barnaul (R190, 4¾ hours, last at 7.40pm) and Tomsk (R170, five hours). For roughly double the price, shared taxis shave an hour or more off those times.

TRAIN

The city's huge main train station, **Novosibirsk Glavny** (ul Shamshurina 43), has numerous daily long-distance trains.

For Moscow (48 to 55 hours via Omsk, Tyumen and Yekaterinburg), comfortable train 25 (even days) is easy to book. However, the cheaper 339 (1.30am, odd days) takes one night longer, saving on hotel accommodation as well as the fare. Of a dozen possible trains to Omsk, the handiest overnighter is train 87 (R420 *platskart*, nine hours, daily). For Krasnoyarsk (R541 *platskart*, 12 to 14 hours), train 84 (13¾ hours overnight, even days) is well timed and rarely full.

For Altai, the handy 601 runs overnight to Biysk (R280 *platskart*, 10¾ hours, daily)

SIBERIA

via Barnaul (5½ hours). For Khakassia and Tuva you could go to Abakan direct (train 68, 23 hours, daily) or in two overnight hops via Novokuznetsk for which the best option is train 605 (R690, 9½ hours). Trains to Almaty, Kazakhstan (R1500, 32 to 37 hours), run daily at 5pm.

If queues are horrendous at the station's main ticket desks (not normally the case), you can buy them relatively swiftly from the upstairs **service centre** (commission R100; ⊙ 4.30am-2am) – no English spoken.

Getting Around

From the train station, take trolleybus 2 to Severny airport, *marshrutka* 1122 to Tolmachyovo airport or *marshrutka* 1212 for the bus station via pl Lenina. The metro (R8) has a major north–south line running beneath Krasny pr and across the river to Studencheskaya and pl Karla Marksa. For the main train station you'll need metro stop pl Garina-Mikhaylovskogo, which is on a second three-stop line that intersects with the major line at Sibirskaya/Krasny pr. Generally *marshrutky* are handier within the centre.

AROUND NOVOSIBIRSK
Akademgorodok & Seyatel
Академгородок и Сеятель
Akademgorodok suburbs were elite Soviet academic townships full of research institutes. Attached to most Siberian cities, they attracted scientists by offering special perks and relatively spacious apartments in peaceful surroundings. Nearly 30km south of central Novosibirsk, Siberia's biggest Akademgorodok nestles in taiga close to the beaches of the Ob Sea. The idea is interesting, but the reality is frustrating for tourists. Although most institutes have 'museums', most are only for invited academics. A potentially brilliant **open-air**

museum 4km along the Akademgorodok–Klyuchi road contains a superb Yakutian wooden church and partly restored *ostrog* (military stockade) but you can only glimpse them through the high, locked gates. Package tourists get channelled to the **Geological Museum** (☎ 332 837; ul Koptyuga; R150) to endure the tired recitations of Soviet-style slow-motion guides; it's open only by arrangement.

For something vastly more inspiring, jump off *marshrutka* 1015 at Seyatel *elektrichka* station, 2km before Akademgorodok beside an interesting **Railway Locomotive Museum** (☎ 337 9622; admission R50; ⊙ 11am-5pm Sat-Thu). Directly east (but hard to find behind an overgrown playground) is the small but spiritually uplifting **Sun Museum** (Muzey Solntsa; ☎ 339 9126; mobile ☎ 913-943 9835; sun-museum@yandex.ru; 2nd fl, ul Ivanova 11a; adult/child R30/20); call ahead for opening hours. Using carved copies of petroglyphs, religious symbols and popular art, this wonderful place examines sun symbolism across an incredibly diverse range of cultures. For meditative-minded visitors, a highlight is listening to artist-sculptor curator Valery Lipenkov playing the extraordinary *bila* (flat bells) or chanting Tibetan sun mantras. Valery speaks very basic English.

To learn Russian you could enrol in 160-hour, eight-week summer courses at **Novosibirsk State University** (☎ 339 7378; www.nsu .ru) from US$645 including accommodation. Book well ahead.

Marshrutka 1015 (R28, 30 minutes) from Novosibirsk Glavny train station passes the Railway Museum then loops anticlockwise around Akademgorodok. Returning to central Novosibirsk from Seyatel is easier by hourly *elektrichka* trains (R18) or bus 622 (R8, 40 minutes). Bus 7 links Akademgorodok with Seyatel station (east of the rail tracks).

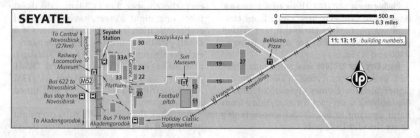

FOR BETTER OR WORSE

Many visitors to Russia unwittingly offend locals by unconsciously assuming that life is better now than in the 'bad old commy days'. The reverse is often true. Perhaps 80% of older Russians (especially non-English speaking) are nostalgic for Brezhnev. Ah, the good old days. Jobs were easy and assured. Arts flourished within ideological limits. Travel was cheap within the vast Soviet world. Life was reassuringly predictable. Predictability and conformism were stultifying for the Western-championed intellectual elite that we hailed as dissidents. But it was just dandy for average Joe Publicski.

Even the relative 'winners' in today's new Russia aren't always happy. Smart and multilingual, Sasha is a young professional working for a Western multinational in a booming Siberian city. Financially he's doing very well. Yet over burritos and a second Stella Artois he confesses that he'd happily bring back the KGB. 'Sure there were certain things you couldn't say, but there was no crime whatever, no poverty, no begging, no homelessness. If you could have a world like that, wouldn't you want it?'

Across the square a maudlin half-forgotten Lenin statue with broken fingers seems to nod.

TOMSK TOMCK

☎ 3822 / pop 473,000 / ⏱ Moscow +3hr

Just 260km from Novosibirsk, but light years ahead in terms of history, ambience and tourist appeal, Tomsk is one of the most enjoyable cities in Siberia. It combines endless examples of fine wooden mansions, some grand century-old commercial buildings and a dynamic, modern outlook. Tomsk's relatively intact architecture was in part preserved by a ghastly commercial miscalculation. The city fathers refused to have the Trans-Siberian Railway pass through, fearing noise, dirt and disruption. Instead they found economic isolation, and the once important trading centre dwindled. However, it survived as a university city and now has half a dozen major academic establishments – hence the youthful, intellectual atmosphere during term time. In summer the city is relatively quiet.

Orientation & Maps

The bus station and Tomsk 1 (main) train station sit together about 2km southeast of the centre. The main axis is fascinating pr Lenina, an architectural and entertainment smorgasbord dotted with banks, shops and cafés. Accurate bus maps are sold at the news kiosks in the bus and train stations. Excellent city maps are available from **Dom Knigi Bookshop** (pr Komsomolsky 49; ⏱ 10am-7pm Mon-Fri, 11am-6pm Sat & Sun) or online in Russian at http://karta.tomsk .ru/. **KnigoMir** (pr Kirova 62 & basement, pr Lenina 5; ⏱ 10am-8pm) stocks the Delovoy Tomsk atlas-directory (R120).

Information

Biznes Tsentr (Hotel Tomsk; Internet per hr 100; ⏱ 24hr) Very pricey but handy when awaiting a train.

Graft Tur (☎ 526 399; http://tour.graft.ru/; ul Gagarina 35; ⏱ 10am-7pm Mon-Fri, 11am-5pm Sat) Helpful travel agency with English-speaking staff.

Internet Salon Plazma (☎ 529 446; ul Kuznetsova 15; Internet per hr R16-28; ⏱ 9am-10pm, night shift R60-110) Faster connection costs R3 per MB extra.

Main post office (pr Lenina 95; Internet per hr R20; ⏱ 9am-7.30pm Mon-Fri, 8am-5pm Sat, 9am-5pm Sun) Cheapest Internet in town.

M@KDEL Internet (☎ 507 808; ul Yakovleva 2; Internet per MB R3, per hr R24; ⏱ 8am-10pm) Near a brick water tower; use bus 11 from the train station or bus 8 from pr Lenina.

Netcafé (☎ 281 441; pr Lenina 32; Internet per MB R2.5, per hr R32; ⏱ 9am-11pm) Night shift costs R130 plus traffic (11pm to 8am). Annoyingly, you must prepay then top up. Half-hour minimum.

Sberbank (pl Lenina 12; ⏱ 9am-7pm Mon-Fri, to 5pm Sat) Changes travellers cheques for 2% commission. Decent euro cash rates with R10 commission.

SibakademBank (☎ 527 489; ul Belinskogo 15a; ⏱ 9am-7pm Mon-Fri, to 5pm Sat) Great rates for US dollars.

Tomskturist (☎ 528 179; pr Lenina 59; ⏱ 9am-7pm Mon-Fri, 11am-4pm Sat) Can arrange individual walking tours of the city, with English-, French- and German-speaking guides. Based in a lovely wooden house opposite the university.

Sights
WOODEN ARCHITECTURE

Tomsk's greatest attraction is its 'wooden-lace' architecture – the carved windows and tracery on old log and timber houses. The

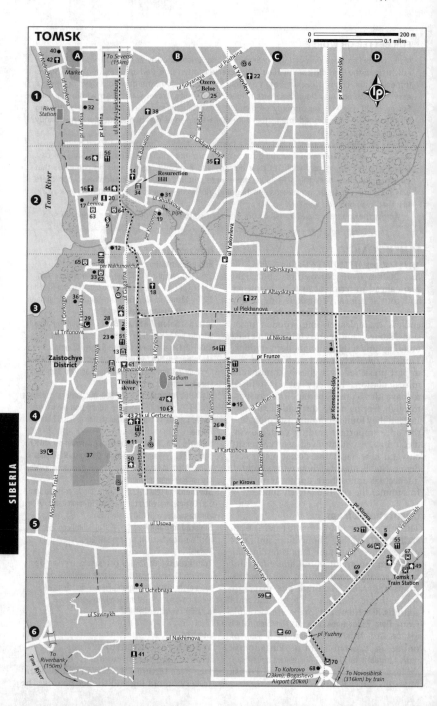

most notable concentration is along **ul Tatarskaya**, accessed via steps beside the lovely old house at **pr Lenina 56**.

Grand, more showy wooden mansions stand along ul Krasnoarmeyskaya, including the spired, bright turquoise **Russian-German House** (1906; ul Krasnoarmeyskaya 71), the **Dragon House** (ul Krasnoarmeyskaya 68) and the fan-gabled **Peacock House** (ul Krasnoarmeyskaya 67a). All are classic landmarks.

Several lesser examples line **per Kononova**, including number 2 where communist mastermind Kirov lodged in 1905. Close by (but hazardous to reach from per Kononova across a slippery pipe) is the splendid, recently restored **Shishkov House** (ul Shishkova 10). The cottage at ul Voykova 14 is all the more photogenic for the **Znameniye bozhyey materi Church** that rises directly behind it. There's even a wooden-lace school, **Shkola 43** (pr Karla Marksa 31).

RESURRECTION HILL
When founded in 1604, Tomsk's original fortress sat atop **Resurrection Hill**. For the city's 400th anniversary, an impressive replica of its 'Golden Gate' was rebuilt in wood complete with domed central tower. Beside it, the well-presented but sparse

Tomsk History Museum (admission R15; 11am-5pm Tue-Sun) has resprouted its wooden **lookout** tower (R10): try to spot the seven historic churches from the top.

Olde-worlde charm continues up cobbled ul Bakunina (named for a 19th-century anarchist) past the Italianate 1833 **Catholic Church** (ul Bakunina 4) and on towards the **Voznesenskaya Church** (ul Oktyabrsky Vzvoz). This Gothic edifice with five gold-tipped black spires has great potential as a Dracula movie set. A truly massive bell hangs from its new lurid-pink belfry.

About 200m beyond is the **Ozero Beloye pond**, whose surrounding park is popular for beer terraces and rides in horse carts or sleighs according to the season. The cute, **Old Believers' Wooden Church** (Staroobryadcheskaya tserkov; ul Yakovleva) is worth a look if you've got any energy left, though its surroundings are relatively uninteresting.

PLOSHCHAD LENINA
Central pl Lenina isn't really a square so much as a jumbled collection of beautifully restored historic buildings interspersed with banal Soviet concrete lumps. The frustrated **Lenin statue**, now relegated to a traffic circle, points at the ugly concrete of

SIBERIA

Tomsk Drama Theatre apparently demanding 'build more like that one'. Fortunately, nobody's listening. The theatre is flanked instead by the splendid 1784 **Epiphany Cathedral**, the former **trading arches** and the elegant 1802 **Magistrat Hotel**. Topped with a golden angel, in a second circle beside Lenin, is the recently rebuilt **Iverskaya Chapel** (10am-6pm) whose celebrated icon is dubbed 'Tomsk's Spiritual Gateway'. The **1000 Melochey Shop** (pr Lenina; 10am-7pm Mon-Sat, to 6pm Sun) has a wonderful 1906 façade featuring griffins and Art Nouveau ironwork flourishes.

PROSPEKT LENINA

Cafés and great architecture continue either way along pr Lenina, most appealingly around per Nakhanovicha where you'll find the thought-provoking **Tomsk Art Gallery** (☎ 514 106; per Nakhanovicha 5; admission R50; 10am-5.30pm Tue-Sun). Amid the dry 19th-century portraiture, wonder how happy SP Obolensky would have felt having been depicted wild-haired with red, hayfeverish (or alcohol-blurred?) eyes. And why does St Christopher have a horse's head on one of the icons?

Built for gold-mining entrepreneur Ivan Atashev in 1842, the **Atashev Palace** (pr Lenina 75) was once used as a church, hence the incongruous steeple tower and wonderful organ hall where concerts are held. Two rooms host the very modest **Regional Museum** (☎ 514 398; http://museum.trecom.tomsk.ru/, in Russian; 10am-6pm Wed-Sun) with a few Atashev furnishings. Outside, a missile launcher points inexplicably at the building's north roof.

The gloomy 1898 brick building across the road is a haunted former school. Closed following the murder of a pupil, it later became the prison for the cruel NKVD (proto-KGB). The building's eerie dungeon is now a memorable **Oppression Museum** (☎ 516 133; rear entrance, pr Lenina 44; admission R18; 2-6pm Mon-Fri). Tours are recommended but are only in Russian. Lighten the mood by peeping into the 1908 **pharmacy** (apteka; pr Lenina 54; 8am-8pm) with its gloriously well-preserved Art Nouveau interior.

The classically colonnaded main buildings of the **university** lie in resplendently leafy grounds, giving Tomsk the soubriquet 'Oxford of Siberia'. Tucked away in unmarked rooms, the university hosts several quietly intriguing museums covering archaeology, geology, zoology and ethnography. Pr Lenina finally ends at the powerful mother-and-son **WWII Memorial** (Lagerny Gardens), behind which are taiga views across the meandering Tom River.

RELIGIOUS BUILDINGS

Tomsk has many more fine churches, including the scoop-domed 1844 **Trinity Church** (Troitskaya tserkov; ul Oktyabrskaya), the very active **Kazansky Icon Church** (ul Krylova 12b) of a former monastery, the pretty new **Nevsky Church** (ul Gertsena) and the Byzantine-style brick **Peter & Paul Cathedral** (Petropavlosky sobor; ul Altayskaya 47) from 1911.

The Zaistochye district was historically the 'Tatar' Muslim quarter. Its unusual, white-washed 19th-century **White Mosque** (Belaya Mechet; Moskovsky Trakt 43) is now fully renovated. The 1904 **Red Mosque** (ul Tatarskaya 4) was sacrilegiously used as a vodka factory in the Soviet era; it's now just a brick shell.

Sleeping
BUDGET

TGU Hotel (☎ 528 386; 5th fl, pr Lenina 49; dm R250, s R500-600, tw R700) Uniquely good-value, clean rooms have kettle, fridge and fully equipped new bathrooms (except in the dorms which share facilities between two triples). In term-time reservations are essential (R100 booking fee) but dropping in might work in midsummer. Enter from the rear; no lift.

Resting rooms (komnaty otdykha; Tomsk 1 train station; dm/tw R200/700) Perfectly clean, new rooms with sparkling shared toilets and shower. No rail-ticket requirement. Curfew 1am to 5am.

Hotel Sputnik (☎ 526 660; www.sputnik.tomskturist .ru; ul Belinskogo 15; s/d/tw/tr R550/750/900/960) A bland tower with lift and smartened-up Soviet rooms sharing refitted bathrooms.

Hotel Severnaya (☎ 512 324; pr Lenina 86; dm/tw/ d R300/900/1300) Don't be fooled by the smart new façade. Most rooms remain ageing Soviet affairs sharing communal squat toilets, though some wallpaper is new and there's a sink in each room. A few doubles (R1300) and twins (R1700) are nicely renovated with full facilities.

MIDRANGE & TOP END

Hotel Magistrat (☎ 511 111; fax 511 200; www.magis trathotel.com; pl Lenina 15; d/tw/ste R2800/3850/4500) Behind the palatial 1802 façade, the luxurious rooms are brand new in a comfortable international style though sadly without historical idiosyncrasies. English is spoken and the restaurant's lavish. Air-conditioning only in suites.

BonApart (☎ 534 650; bon_apart@mail.ru; ul Gertsena 1a; s/tw/d/ste R1550/1850/1850/2400; ✖) In its price range this brand-new, fully fitted private hotel is by far the best. English is spoken, floors have key-card security and the stairs are polished light marble. However, there's no lift and only the suites have air-con.

Hotel Siberia (pr Lenina 91; s/tw/d/ste R1700/1900/2100/2800) This splendidly central old building is now two hotels in one, two reception desks facing-off across the foyer. Choose the **Sibir Forum** (☎ 530 280; www.sibir-forum.tomsk.ru) which operates the appealingly bright, fully renovated 2nd floor and the almost-equivalent 4th floor (rooms discounted R200 for all the stairs). Although prices are the same for the **Hotel Sibir** (☎ /fax 527 225; www.hotelsibir.tomsk.ru) its dingy 3rd-floor corridor is unreconstructed.

Hotel Tomsk (☎ 524 115; www.tomskhotel.best-service .biz; pr Kirova 65; s/tw R1800/1900) Acceptable but rather overpriced, its smartly upgraded Soviet rooms are now reasonably comfortable though baths are very small. A few R1500 rooms have tattier floors and older bathrooms. R200 discount at weekends.

Eating

There are more choices on and around pr Lenina than you can eat through in a week.

Vechny Zov (☎ 528 167; ul Sovetskaya 47; meals R250-800; ☾ noon-4am) Tomsk's top dining option is a Siberian ranch outside and within it has an antique-filled home feel. A menu in English offers 'Louis Armstrong pork', 'Roman Abramovich cutlet' and a wide variety of imaginative Siberian alternatives. Most nights, talented jazz-violinist Viktor Korolev serenades after 7pm (cover charge).

FoodMaster (pr Lenina 83; meals R100-450; ☾ 11am-1am) Despite the ill-fittingly banal name, this is a wonderful *belle époque* café with painstakingly restored plasterwork tracery on the high ceilings. The menu (in English) ranges from Chinese to Mexican to pseudo-Italian; try a strawberry tagliatelle!

People's Bar & Grill (☎ 443 315; ul Krasnoarmeyskaya 31; beers from R60, meals R250-600; ☾ noon-2am) The hip place to drink cocktails or be seen dining on 'Indiana Jones' or 'Some Like It Hot', whatever that might actually mean. Upstairs **Pizza Rio** (☾ 24hr) offers generous slices for R41.

Allegro (☎ 281 586; pr Lenina 32; meals R45-90; ☾ 9am-midnight) Unusually comfortable and pleasantly appointed for such a cheap, basement café. Karaoke threatens after 7pm (R20 per song).

Sibirskoe Bistro (pr Lenina 123 & pr Kirova 66; meals R80-170; ☾ 24hr) Cafeteria chain with lunchtime discounts.

SELF-CATERING

Holiday Supermarket (ul Krasnoarmeyskaya 44; ☾ 24hr) Wide selection, sensible prices

Gastronom (pr Kirova 59; ☾ 24hr) Handy grocery for the train station.

Drinking

Sibirsky Pub (☎ 530 047; www.siberian-pub.ru/, in Russian; ul Novosobornaya 2; mains R100-200, Guinness per pint R140; ☾ noon-3am) Siberia's first British pub was founded over a century ago by a certain Mr Crawley, an Anglo-Egyptian albino who'd got stuck in Tomsk after touring with a circus freak show. Today's pub is no relation. Nonetheless it uses British photo icons from Big Ben to beefeaters and has a menu in English with a filling lunch deal (R144) before 3pm. Bands play live at weekends (cover charge).

Bulanzhe (☎ 516 735; 2nd fl, pr Lenina 80; espresso R40; ☾ 8am-midnight) Tomsk's answer to Starbucks serves great coffee, stuffed bliny (from R30) and superb *chernichniyy pai* (blackcurrant gateau, R33 per 100g). Branches at ul Krasnoarmeyskaya 107 and ul Nakhimova 40.

Prado (☎ 512 685; pr Lenina 78; meals R200-600; ☾ 24hr) Amusing coffee-house restaurant within the Aelita Theatre conceived as an Italian piazza.

Entertainment

Tomsk has a vibrant arts scene. **Tomsk-Life** (http://life.tomsk.ru/, in Russian) has extensive listings.

Aelita Theatre (☎ 516 131; www.aelita.tsk.ru; pr Lenina 78) Mixed offerings from rock concerts to Indian dance.

Philharmonia (☎ 515 965; pl Lenina 1) Classical music and great big-band jazz.

Tomsk Drama Theatre (☎ 512 223; pl Lenina 4)

Youth Theatre (TYuZ; ☎ 513 933; per Nakhanovicha 4)

Getting There & Away

Transport options are comprehensively listed in Russian on http://transport.sibr.ru/.

SIBERIA

Tomsk's **Bogashevo Airport** (☎ 270 084), 22km southeast, has flights to Moscow (R8500) most days on Siberian Airlines, plus some local regional services on **Tomskavia** (☎ 412 466; www.Tomskavia.ru, in Russian; ul Yelizarovkh). The choice is much wider from Novosibirsk's Tolmachyovo Airport (p513), to which there are five direct buses a day (R180, five hours) from Tomsk bus station. Shared taxis (R500, 3½ hours) are much faster than buses (R260, 5½ hours, 20 daily) for Novosibirsk. For Kolorovo (R9, 35 minutes) take one of seven daily services towards Yarskoe, and from pl Yuzhny there are roughly hourly *marshrutky*.

From Tomsk I (main) train station there are daily services to Moscow's Yaroslavsky station (56½ hours). Train 37 leaves about 10am and is handy for Tyumen (22½ hours). For Omsk, the summer-only train 437 (R850, 15 hours, even days) is more convenient. *Platskartny* carriages run to Barnaul (R442, 14¾ hours) on even days and to Irkutsk (34 hours) via Krasnoyarsk (R420, 14½ hours) daily in summer, even days only in winter.

Getting Around

For the airport take the rare bus 119 from pl Lenina. Other city *marshrutky* are very frequent. Handy route 7 runs from near the train station, along pr Frunze, up pr Lenina, then east again on ul Pushkina. *Marshrutka* 11 shows you the wooden houses along ul Krasnoarmeyskaya, 29 does the same for ul Tatarskaya via pl Yuzhny, while bus 4 goes west from the train station and then runs north the length of pr Lenina.

AROUND TOMSK
Kolorovo Колорово
☎ 3822 / pop 280

Picturesquely set on the bank of the meandering Tom River, Kolorovo was once a flourishing way-station for caravans on the tea route from Mongolia. Founded in 1620 it was originally known as Spasskoe. Today the only sign of former glory is the baroque 1799 **church** (new interior). Nonetheless, Kolorovo's utter tranquillity is very refreshing, there are plenty of typical cottages and it's pleasant to stroll south through the river-view meadows along the deserted Yarskoe road. Buses and *marshrutky* to Tomsk (35 minutes) stop opposite the church beside the village shop.

ALTAI АЛТАЙ

Greater Altai (Altay) straddles corners of Kazakhstan, Mongolia and China, as well as southern Siberia. Within the Russian Federation it's divided administratively between the almost flat Altai Territory and the mountainous Altai Republic. Here steppe, mountains, semideserts and over 7000 lakes culminate in the Unesco-cited 'Golden Mountains' including Mt Belukha (4506m), Siberia's highest peak. Celebrated by artists Rerikh and Choros Gurkin, it's called Shambala or Belovodye by Russian New Age groups who revere the region as a major pole of spiritual energy. From do-nothing relaxation to extreme-adventure sports, the region is one of Siberia's tourism magnets.

Altai Culture

Asiatic ethnic-Altai people constitute around 30% of the Altai Republic's 200,000-strong population, and a vastly lower proportion in the heavily Russianised Altai Territory. Despite strong animist undercurrents, most Altai are nominally Christian and villages aren't visually distinct though some rural Altai homes still incorporate a traditional *ail* (tepee-shaped wooden tent). In the Altai language, hello is *yakhshler,* thank you (very

---

RAFTING

Fun-splash rafting is possible at short notice at **Turbaza Katun** (p530) or around **Aya Bridge** (p528).

Increasingly popular five-day raft-and-camp trips start at Kür-Kechü, descending the potentially dangerous Ilgumen Rapids (p532). While not for beginners, they're not Altai's toughest challenge either. Prices (ex Barnaul) start from a bargain US$150 per person but that's likely to mean poor food, no wet suits and mediocre safety standards. You get what you pay for: **Travel Trophy** (☎ 495-502 3145; info@traveltrophy.ru; Moscow) charges US$490-575 for the same tour but readers have praised its vastly higher standards, good guide-to-guest ratio and 'gourmet' cooking. For tailor-made specialist rafting challenges talk to Altour in Barnaul (p522) or English-speaking K2 Adventures in Omsk (p504).

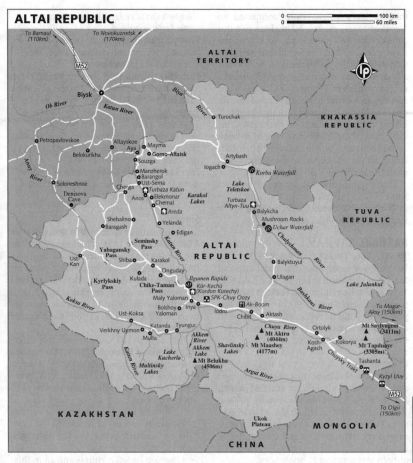

Map: ALTAI REPUBLIC

Scale: 0 — 100 km / 0 — 60 miles

To Barnaul (110km), To Novokuznetsk (170km)

ALTAI TERRITORY

M52

Biysk, Ob River, Katun River, Biya River

Petropavlovskoe, Altayskoe, Aya, Mayma, Turochak

KHAKASSIA REPUBLIC

Belokurikha, Gorno-Altaisk, Souzga, Artybash, Iogach, Korbu Waterfall

Anuy River, Manzherok, Barangol, Ust-Sema, Lake Teletskoe

Soloneshnoe, Cherga, Turbaza Katun, Karakol Lakes, Turbaza Altyn-Tuu, Balykcha

Denisova Cave, Anos, Elekmonar, Chemal, Areda, Mushroom Rocks, Uchar Waterfall

TUVA REPUBLIC

Shebalino, Yelanda, Baragash, Edigan, ALTAI REPUBLIC, Chulyshman River

Seminsky Pass, Yabagansky Pass, Karakol, Balyktuyul, Bashkaus River

Ust-Kan, Shiba, Onguday, Ulagan, Lake Julunkul

Kyrlykskiy Pass, Kulada, Chike-Taman Pass, Ilgumen Rapids, Kür-Kechü (Kordon Kurechy)

Koksa River, Maly Yaloman, SPK-Chuy Oozy, Ak-Boom, To Mugur-Aksy (150km)

Ust-Koksa, Bolshoy Yaloman, Inya, Iodro, Chibit, Aktash, Ortolyk, Mt Saylyugem (3411m)

Verkhny Uymon, Katanda, Tyungur, Chuya River, Mt Aktru (4044m), Kosh-Agach, Kokorya, Mt Tapduayr (3305m)

Multa, Akkem River, Shavlinsky Lakes, Mt Maashey (4177m), Chuysky Trakt, Tashanta

Katun River, Lake Kucherla, Akkem Lake, Mt Belukha (4506m), Argut River, Kyzyl Uuy, M52

Multinsky Lakes

KAZAKHSTAN

Ukok Plateau, To Olgii (150km)

MONGOLIA

CHINA

SIBERIA

much) is *(dyan) biyan/biyan bolzyn* and beautiful is *charash*. Altai tea is served milky: add a bran-rich flour called *talkan* and it becomes a sort of porridge.

Alcohol has a disastrous effect on Altai people. Gentle smiles can turn to unpredictable violence within a bottle. This makes pure-Altai villages like Ulagan and Balyktuyul somewhat dangerous, especially at night.

Some of the Altai Republic's 5% ethnic Kazakhs are still nomadic herders living in traditional felt yurts, notably around Kosh-Agach. Most Kazakhs are Muslims who are keen on kumiss (fermented mare's milk) but don't generally drink vodka, making Kazakh settlements noticeably less hazardous than Altai ones. In the local Kazakh dialect, *salamat sizbe* means hello, *rakhmat* means thank you and *sarlyk* is a handy term for yak meat.

Planning

Remnant old areas of Biysk and Barnaul are worth a passing look, visit Gorno-Altaisk for compulsory visa registration then head for the lakes and mountains. Lake Teletskoe is touted as a 'second Baikal' and is arguably even more picturesque. For glimpses of local culture, rugged valleys, varying scenery and plenty of ancient stones it's quite feasible to potter independently down the memorable Chuysky Trakt by bus or chartered Lada. However, to get closer to the snow-crested mountaintops you'll have to hike. Generally

that requires preparation: compared to
Nepal or New Zealand, hiking here requires
considerable self-sufficiency. Not even the
most popular trails have villages, signs or
teahouses. Sadly, guides and packhorses usually aren't easy to arrange quickly *in situ*,
except perhaps in Tyungur or Chemal. Tour
agencies in Novosibirsk, Barnaul and beyond
can help by prearranging various adventure,
hiking, rafting or relaxation packages. Consider using them in July and August to book
accommodation as demand very often out-
strips supply in summer, especially if you
want the luxury of a sit-down toilet.

Don't ignore the danger posed by ticks
from May to July. For maps try Dom Knigi
in Novosibirsk (p509), which sporadically
stocks 1:200,000 Altai sheets.

BARNAUL БАРНАУЛ

☎ 3852 / pop 575,000 / ☒ Moscow +3hr
Barnaul is a prosperous industrial city and
has been so almost since its foundation in
1730 as Ust-Barnaulskaya. Though far from
the mountains, it hosts the nearest major airport to the Altai Republic and offers enough
cafés and museums to keep you amused between transport connections.

Orientation
Pr Lenina runs 8km northwest from the river
station through pls Sovetov and Oktyabrya.
It's paralleled by Sotsialistichesky pr and
Krasnoarmeysky pr, which almost converge
at pl Pobedy, behind whose large war memorial are both the bus and train stations.
Maps of bus and tram routes (R15) are sold
at both stations and at bookshops.

Information
Altour/Class 5 (☎ 231 698; www.altour.ru; apt 138,
ul Chkalova 89) Specialist for extreme white-water rafting
expeditions. Not for beginners. Office entered through
VIP-Tur at the rear of a big apartment block.
Ekstrim (Komsomolsky pr 75; ☒ 9am-7pm) Sells
climbing, fishing, camping and mountain-bike gear.
Internet Kafe Pl@zma (Apt 27, pr Lenina 58;
Internet per MB R4, per hr R20; ☒ 8am-11pm) Fast web
connection, at the rear of the building through cellar bar.
Knizhny Mir (Sotsialistichesky pr 119a; ☒ 10am-8pm)
Bookshop selling the Barnaul listings pamphlet
Orientir (R60).
Koks-Travel (☎ 669 000; info@kokstravel.ru; 3rd fl,
ul Tolstogo 16a; ☒ 8.30am-12.30pm & 1.30-7pm
Mon-Fri, 10am-5pm Sat) Major Altai tour agency, owners

of Artybash's Turbaza Zolotoe Ozero (holiday camp).
Written English understood.
Penaty Bookshop (pr Lenina 85; ☒ 10am-7pm
Mon-Sat, to 5pm Sun) Stocks many useful maps, atlases,
postcards and Altai picture books.
Post office (pr Lenina 54; ☒ 8am-7pm Mon-Sat, to 6pm
Sun) The attached telephone office stays open until 10pm.
Sputnik-Altai (☎ 367 750; http://sputnik.altai.ru, in
Russian; 2nd fl, Sotsialistichesky pr 87; ☒ 9am-1pm &
2-6pm Mon-Fri, Mon-Sat in summer) This professional,
well-connected tour agency can slot you into Russian Altai
tours, register visas for tour clients (R800) and arrange
tailor-made excursions. English is spoken.
Zern Bank Exchange Booth (pr Lenina 61; ☒ 10am-
1pm & 2-5.45pm Mon-Fri, 9am-4.45pm Sat) Entry via ul
Molodyozhnaya phone shop.

Sights
The impressively eclectic **Altai Arts, Literature
& Culture Museum** (☎ 244 771; ul Tolstogo 2; admission
R20; ☒ 10am-6pm Tue-Sat) occupies a restored,
furnished 1850s mansion in which piano recitals are held on Saturday afternoons. There
are some fine icons, Rerikh sketches, and
even the inevitable WWII room is imaginatively handled through cartoons and theatre
posters.

Founded in 1823, the reasonably interesting **Regional Museum** (☎ 234 551; ul Polzunova
46; admission/photos/videos R20/50/100; ☒ 10am-4pm
Wed-Sun) is Siberia's oldest museum. Top exhibits include safes full of now useless 1910
stocks and bonds, a packing case fashioned
out of former icons, and models of various
18th-century industrial processes.

In an old brick house, the **War History Museum** (☎ 380 041; Komsomolsky pr 73b; admission R20;
☒ 9.30am-5pm Tue-Sat) is simple and all in Russian but the moving understatement of its
Afghanistan memorial rooms is particularly
affecting.

The **Altai Fine Art Museum** (☎ 612 573; pr Lenina
88; admission R20; ☒ 10am-6pm Tue-Sun) is the best of
several galleries in this very cultured city.

Classical **pl Demidov** was once exaggeratedly dubbed a 'slice of St Petersburg'. Now
the slice is itself sliced in half by the tram
tracks of Krasnoarmeysky pr and is hardly
memorable, apart from the 1825 **obelisk**
which is still faintly bullet-pocked from a
1918 skirmish.

Rapacious redevelopment has destroyed
much of Barnaul's older architecture. Nonetheless, century-old remnants are dotted
between the shopping malls of pr Lenina's

BARNAUL

0 ————————————— 1 km
0 ————————————— 0.5 miles

INFORMATION
Altour/Class 5 Алтур............................ **1** B5
Ekstrim Экстрим................................... **2** C3
Internet Kafe Pl@zma.......................... **3** B4
Knizhny Mir Книжный Мир.................. **4** A4
Koks-Travel Кокс-Трэвел...................... **5** D5
Main Post office Почтамт.................... **6** B4
Penaty Bookshop
  Книжный Магазин Пенаты **7** B3
Sputnik-Altai Спутник-Алтай............... **8** B4
Zern Bank Exchange Booth
  Зерн Банк **9** B3

SIGHTS & ACTIVITIES
Altai Arts, Literature & Culture Museum
  Музей Истории, Литературы,
  Искусства и Культуры Алтая **10** D5
Altai Fine Art Musum
  Алтайский Художественный
  Музей.. **11** B3
Barnaul sign БАРНАУЛ........................ **12** D6
Imperator Император......................... **13** C6
Nikolsky Church
  Никольский Храм........................... **14** C4

Pl Demidov, Obelisk
  Площадь Демидов,
  Обелиск.. **15** C6
Pokrovsky Cathedral
  Покровский Собор......................... **16** B6
Regional Museum
  Алтайский Государственный
  Краевой Краеведческий
  Музей.. **17** C6
War-History Museum............................ **18** C3

SLEEPING
Hotel Altai Гостиница Алтай **19** C5
Hotel Barnaul Гостиница
  Барнаул.. **20** A4
Hotel Kolos
  Гостиница Колос **21** B4
Hotel Obsky most
  Гостиница Обский мост................ **22** D6
Hotel Rus Гостиница Русь................... **23** C4
Hotel Siberia
  Гостиница Сибирь **24** B3
Hotel Tsentralnaya
  Гостиница Центральная................ **25** B4

Resting rooms
  Комнаты Отдыха............................ **26** A3

EATING
Bliny Bar Блинный бар........................ **27** D5
Bliny Bar Блинный бар .... (see **35**)
'Coffee Please' Kofeynya **28** B4
Dezhavyu Дежавю................................ **29** C3
Granmulino **30** B4
Khoroshee Nastroenie
  Хорошее Настроение.................... **31** C4
Mexico Мексико **32** C4
Polzunov Restaurant
  Ресторан Ползунов **33** A4
Rok'n'Roll Рок-н-Рол............................ **34** C5
Supermarket.................................. (see **35**)
Voskhod bakery .... (see **35**)

SHOPPING
City Tsentr Shopping Mall
  City Центр.. **35** B5

TRANSPORT
Aerokassa
  Центральная Аэрокасса **36** B3
Bus station Автовокзал..................... **37** A3
KrasAir.. **38** B3
River station
  Речной Вокзал.......................... (see **12**)
Trolleybus 5 to Centre **39** A3

SIBERIA

tree-shaded southern end. A few splendid wooden-lace houses include the famous **Imperator** (Rusky Chay; Krasnoarmeysky pr 131; ⊗ 6pm-6am), now a nightclub, plus ul Korolenko 96 and ul Polzunova 31 and 48. The bulbous-domed, brick **Pokrovskoe** (ul Nikitina 135-7) is the most appealing of the city's many churches with a fine, gilded interior. For wide river views, climb up to the gigantic Hollywood-style **sign** spelling БАРНАУЛ (Barnaul).

Sleeping

BUDGET

Hotel Altai (☎ 239 247; pr Lenina 24; s/tw/tr without bathroom R350/500/600, s/tw/d with bathroom R700/1100/1500) In an early 1940s building this good budget choice has certain elements of faded grandeur. Off corridors green with potted plants, even the simplest rooms and shared facilities are well maintained. Nearby is a 24-hour ATM and a statue of Lenin posing as a bullfighter.

Hotel Rus (☎ 354 382; 2nd fl, ul Chkalova 57a; s/tw/tr from R400/600/690) Very neat, pleasant new rooms have sink and fridge though beds are slightly saggy. Rooms from R700 have bathrooms. Central yet very quiet, it's above the Traktir Nikolsky restaurant. Cannot register foreigners so two-day stays are a maximum.

Hotel Kolos (☎ 228 605; ul Molodyozhnaya 25; dm/tw/tr without bathroom R160/420/540, s/tw/tr with bathroom R510/860/1230) Perfectly acceptable old Soviet rooms though the shared toilets are highly communal with neither seats nor doors.

The train station has decent **resting rooms** (komnaty otdykha; dm per 12hr in d/q R157/136), with clean, shared hot showers.

MIDRANGE

Hotel Siberia (☎ 624 200; www.siberia-hotel.ru; pr Sotsialisticheskky 116; s R2200-2500; tw R2745, d R2530-3250) Barnaul's new business hotel is built almost to international standards though the excellent rooms lack air-conditioning.

Hotel Tsentralnaya (☎ 368 443; www.hotelcentral .ru, in Russian; pr Lenina 57; s/tw R700/800, ste up to R2500) Well renovated, perfectly central and virtually all rooms have good bathrooms.

Hotel Obsky Most (☎ 234 004; ul Bavarina 17a; dm R300-400, tw/tr R1000/1200; ℗) Perhaps the world's only hotel with its own museum of road-building machinery, this surprisingly well-appointed new minihotel is oddly placed in a cloverleaf road junction, though the windows are fairly well soundproofed.

All rooms except the cheaper dormitory have modern, private bathrooms.

Hotel Barnaul (☎ 626 222; info@barnaulhotel.com; pl Pobedy 3; s R750-1200, tw R900-1500) This vast 12-storey block has been thoroughly renovated and some suites are magnificent, but look before paying as quality is uneven. Press ХОД to operate the lift (elevator).

Eating & Drinking

Dozens of appealing options include several summer terraces along pr Lenina.

Polzunov Restaurant (☎ 625 958; pr Krasnoarmeysky 112; meals R280-650) Old copperware and wooden beams add appeal to this delightful upper-market restaurant. The imaginative menu (in English) includes tasty *pork premyera* with pineapple, walnut and mushroom sauce. Attached is a bakery-grocery and the excellent **MasterFood Cafeteria** (meals R70-180; ⊗ 11am-9pm).

'Coffee Please' Kofeynya (☎ 358 983; Sotsialisticheskky pr 78; coffees R45-80; ⊗ 24hr) Maestro macchiatos (R49) and al-dente pasta meals (R70-90) served in a stylish, bean-themed coffee house.

Granmulino (☎ 363 600; Peschanaya ul 83; ⊗ 24hr) Low-key modern café-restaurant with a vast, pictorial menu ranging from sushi (R40-90 per piece) to pizzas (R120-200) and cakes (R50-140). Service very variable.

Rok'n'Roll (☎ 237 606; ul Anatoliya 68; beers from R35; ⊗ 10am-11pm) Designer-graffiti music bar-café whose menu reads like a Beatles lyric sheet.

Mexico (Traktoriya Mekhiko; ☎ 368 688; pr Lenina 44a; meals R150-500, cover R50-100 from 8pm on music nights; ⊗ noon-1am) Plastic flashing palm trees and canned merengue but the Mexican food is underspiced. Beside is a much cheaper beer-and-snack terrace.

Dezhavyu (Komsomolsky pr 75; beers R50-150, meals R160-450; ⊗ 10am-9pm) Relaxed local pub-café serving Staropramen (R55) and Kwak (R120) beers in trademark *ampolo* funnel-glasses.

Bliny Bar (pr Lenina 2b; pancakes R15-80, tea R6) Superb stuffed bliny made to order in a fast-food–style diner. There's another branch on the 3rd floor of the **City Tsentr** (Krasnoarmeysky pr 47a; ⊗ 10am-9pm) shopping mall which has a useful 1st-floor supermarket and whose Voskhod Bakery stand has great cheese strudels (R7.90).

Khoroshee Nastroenie (ul Chkalova 62a; ⊗ 24hr) Grocery with takeaway salad bar.

Getting There & Away

There are flights to Moscow (R7300, twice daily), Krasnoyarsk (R1730 to R3100, four weekly), St Petersburg (R7030, Friday) and Vladivostok (R8190) via either Irkutsk (R5925, Thursday) or Abakan (R1620, Tuesday). For more choice fly from Novosibirsk. Near the main **Aerokassa** (☎ 368 181; ul Sovetskaya 4; ⏰ 8am-7pm Mon-Fri, 8.30am-5pm Sat & Sun), English-speaking **KrasAir** (☎ 242 251; ul Sovetskaya 10; ⏰ 8am-7pm) provides free airport taxis for air-ticket customers.

Trains leave daily to Novokuznetsk (from R210 *platskart*, 7½ hours), Almaty (Kazakhstan, approximately R1250, 31 hours) and most usefully overnight to Tomsk (R442, 15 hours) on odd days at 3.23pm. On even days a train to St Petersburg runs via Moscow. Buses are better for Novosibirsk (R160, five hours, 20 daily), Biysk (R138, three hours, hourly) or Gorno-Altaisk (R200, five hours, seven daily).

Getting Around

From the Aerokassa, rare bus 112 runs to Barnaul's airport in the northwestern suburbs. From the river station frequent buses 1 and 10 go straight up pr Lenina, trolleybus 5 connects to the train station and the handy bus 43 swings past pl Demidov, turns north up Krasnoarmeysky pr, then passes pl Pobedy (near the bus and train stations) before rejoining pr Lenina at pl Oktyabrya.

BIYSK БИЙСК

☎ 3854 / pop 236,000 / ⏰ Moscow +3hr

Friendly Biysk, 160km southeast of Barnaul, is not worth a special detour but its modest attractions may warrant a brief stop en route to or from the Altai Mountains, for which it's the nearest railhead.

In 1709, a group of 70 Russian soldiers with five cannons built a fort at the junction of the Biya and Katun Rivers. This didn't impress the Dzhungarian Mongols, who sent 3000 men to burn it down. Biysk was re-established 20km to the east in 1718, and after the peace of 1756 was rapidly developed as a prosperous trade entrepôt protected by a big, Vauban-style star-shaped fortress (now completely disappeared).

Information

Bars Travel (☎ 328 050; www.tbars.narod.ru; Hotel Tsentralnaya) Runs various Altai tours for Russian groups with weekend rafting trips (R2800 including food, transport and two nights' accommodation) departing most Fridays.
Dobry (ul Lenina 246; ⏰ 10am-6pm Mon-Fri, to 5pm Sat, to 3pm Sun) There's a bookshop for maps (R40) and postcards within this multishop.
Newsstand (☎ 335 500; Krasnoarmeyskaya ul 43; ⏰ 24hr) Also for maps and postcards, beside the air-ticket bureau Aviaflot.
Post office (ul Merlina 17; Internet per MB R3.5, per min R0.35; ⏰ 8.30am-noon & 1-6pm Mon-Fri, 9am-2pm Sat) One block south of the bus station.
Sberbank (ul Lenina 244 & Krasnoarmeyskaya ul 73; ⏰ 9am-1pm & 2-7pm Mon-Sat) Changes money.

Sights

From the market near the bus station take northbound bus 23 to see the tumbledown patches of once-impressive old town which hide intriguingly behind a vast, unprepossessing curtain of Soviet-era concrete. Get off at the once-mighty, now decrepit **Firsova ex-Department Store** (ul Tolstogo 144) with its crown-shaped corner domes. Walk a block east then north to find the excellent **museum** (☎ 337 698; ul Lenina 134; R10; ⏰ 10am-4.30pm Wed-Sat), housed in a grand if dilapidated 1912 merchant's house with its original Art Nouveau fittings. Further east, wobbly wooden homes and a few maudlin mansions hint at long-past wealth, but it's better to walk down towards the riverbank and backtrack along Sovetskaya ul where there are several 1890s brick edifices, the silver-domed **Assumption Church** (Sovetskaya ul 13) and the grand, renovated 1916 **theatre** (Sovetskaya ul 25).

Sleeping

Hotel Tsentralnaya (☎ 338 307; Krasnoarmeyskaya ul; s/tw from R400/600) Three storeys have been pretty well renovated and even the older floors are pleasant for a Soviet-era hotel. All rooms have private bathroom with hot shower.

Hotel Polieks (☎ 236 440; pl 9i Yanvara 3; s/d/tw/tr from R390/550/700/990) Very friendly with great-value en-suite rooms but inconveniently far from the old town. Take westbound bus 23 to Kapelka Kafe (ul Vasilyeva 46) and walk back past Fortuna grocery.

Eating & Drinking

Kavkazskaya Kukhnya (☎ 245 883; ul Lenina 314; meals R90-200, beers R14, cover R20 from 7pm; ⏰ 11am-midnight) Understandably Biysk's most popular dinner spot, with reasonable prices, huge

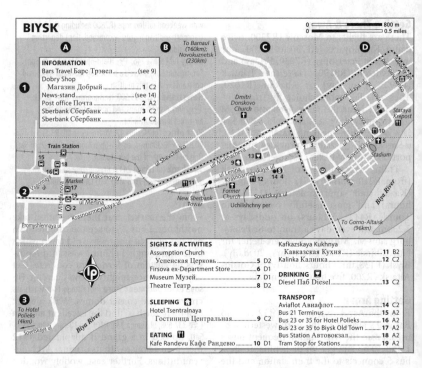

BIYSK

0 ——————— 800 m
0 ——————— 0.5 miles

INFORMATION
Bars Travel Барс Трэвел.................(see 9)
Dobry Shop
  Магазин Добрый...................**1** C2
News-stand.................................(see 14)
Post office Почта..........................**2** A2
Sberbank Сбербанк.......................**3** C2
Sberbank Сбербанк.......................**4** C2

To Barnaul
(160km);
Novokuznetsk
(230km)

Dmitri
Donskovo
Church

Staraya
Krepost

Train Station

ul Shevchenko

ul Mukhacheva

Stadium

ul Maksimovoy

Market

ul Lenina
Krasnoarmeyskaya ul

New Sberbank
Tower

Former
Church

Sovetskaya ul

Uchilishchny per

Krasnoarmeyskaya ul

ul Merlina

Biya River

Promyshlennaya ul

To Gorno-Altaisk
(96km)

SIGHTS & ACTIVITIES
Assumption Church
  Успенская Церковь...................**5** D2
Firsova ex-Department Store.........**6** D1
Museum Музей.............................**7** D1
Theatre Театр...............................**8** D2

SLEEPING
Hotel Tsentralnaya
  Гостиница Центральная............**9** C2

EATING
Kafe Randevu Кафе Рандевю.........**10** D1

Kafkazskaya Kukhnya
  Кавказская Кухня.....................**11** B2
Kalinka Калинка...........................**12** C2

DRINKING
Diesel Паб Diesel..........................**13** C2

TRANSPORT
Aviaflot Авиафлот........................**14** C2
Bus 21 Terminus............................**15** A2
Bus 23 or 35 for Hotel Polieks........**16** A2
Bus 23 or 35 to Biysk Old Town......**17** A2
Bus Station Автовокзал................**18** A2
Tram Stop for Stations...................**19** A2

To Hotel
Polieks
(4km)

Sovetskaya ul

Biya River

---

portions and the best shashlyk in a thousand
kilometres. Slightly raucous and down-to-
earth, but it's easy to miss almost beneath
the tram bridge.

Kafe Randevu (☎ 327 416; Sovetskaya ul 4; meals
R180-450, espresso R30, cover R30 from 7pm; ☒ 11am-
2am) Behind a beautifully renovated old-
town façade, this midrange café has the
most convivial atmosphere of three options
on Sovetskaya ul.

Kalinka (Krasnoarmeyskaya ul 81; meals R140-280,
espresso R30; ☒ 10am-10.30pm) Appealing wood-
interior café within a shop, diagonally opposite the Hotel Tsentralnaya. Good-value
meals but pricey beer.

Diesel (☎ 332 316; ul Lenina 252; lunch R150 till 5pm,
beers R40-100; ☒ 11am-2am) Biysk's own Irish
pub, within the Altai Cinema complex.

Getting There & Away
The bus and train stations face each other
across a large square at the north end of ul
Mitrofanova, 2km west of the Hotel Tsentralnaya and 4km from the historic centre. Useful overnight trains to Novosibirsk
(R280 *platskart*, 11 hours) leave at 8.15pm.

Buses leave frequently until 7.30pm for
Gorno-Altaisk (R65, two hours) and Barnaul (R138, three hours). Shared taxis are
faster. Handy, if slow, daily buses rattle
across to Novokuznetsk (R200, six to seven
hours, four daily).

GORNO-ALTAISK ГОРНО-АЛТАЙСК
☎ 38541 / pop 48,000 / ☒ Moscow +3hr
Gorno-Altaisk, the capital of the Altai Republic, is a narrow ribbon of Soviet concrete
blandness scarring an otherwise attractive
valley. From Mayma on the M52, Gorno-
Altaisk's main street, Kommunistichesky
pr, winds on for 7km before reaching central pl Lenina.

Before heading elsewhere in the Altai Republic you should register your visa at the
MVD Office (☎ 62012; top fl, Kommunistichesky pr 95;
☒ 9am-1pm Mon-Wed & Fri). It's beside the Gorny
Shopping Centre, 500m east of the market,
bus stop Zhilmassiv. Enter via the central
door-stairs. Importantly you'll need a *khod-
ataystsvo* – a letter from whoever sponsored
your visa, listing where in Altai you'll be
visiting. Get this before departing as having

your sponsors fax it to Gorno-Altaisk can cause days of delays and annoyance. With the letter, registration takes only 15 minutes assuming you can figure out the Russian forms. If you list Aktash or Kosh-Agach as destinations the necessary border-zone permits are automatically issued.

Information

The **post office** (Kommunistichesky pr 61; 9am-6pm Mon-Fri) near the bus station has an **Internet centre** (per hr R40; 9am-9pm Mon-Fri, noon-6pm Sat & Sun). **Bank Zenit** (side entrance, ul Churos-Gurkina 28; 9am-1pm & 2-4pm) has good US dollar rates.

Sights

A moustachioed *kameny baba* (standing stone idol, p531) welcomes visitors to the interesting **museum** (27875; ul Churos-Gurkina 46; admission R30; 10am-4.30pm Wed-Sun). There's a reconstruction of a 2000-year-old Pazyryk grave pit and some intriguing archaeological finds from the Turkic and Dzhungarian periods. Much of the top floor is a gallery featuring local landscapes by celebrated Altai artist Grigory Churos-Gurkin (1870–1937). A small but attractive wooden **church** (pr Kommunistichesky 130) is nearing completion towards the market area.

Sleeping & Eating

There's further choice in Mayma, Aya and Souzga.

Hotel Gorno Altaiavtodor (62256; 4th fl, Kommunistichesky pr 182; dm R200-350, tw/d 1600/2500)

Clean, well-kept, three-bed dorms share decent new facilities. Pricier rooms have private bathrooms. Disconcertingly, you have to ring at the rear entry-phone buzzer and give your reservation details before being let in. Book ahead.

Dormoststroy (62149; 3rd fl, per Granitny 1; tw R1000) Five cramped but comfy new twin rooms with kettle and fridge share a sparkling-clean new toilet and hot shower. You can pay per bed (R500).

Hotel Gorny Altai (95086; ul Palkina 5; dm R201, s R350-390, tw/tr R560/603) This crumbling Soviet slab usually has a room available when all else is full. Perfectly central, it has new beds but shared seatless toilets and no showers whatever. Lenin points accusingly to its door.

Kafe Natalya (24393; ul Churos-Gurkina 32; meals R110-170; 10am-11pm) Cosy, with quiet good taste, this remains by far Gorno-Altaisk's nicest. Delicious daily specials are displayed in the heated cabinet making point-and-pick an easy option. The *kuritsa pa-tekhasski* (stuffed chicken breast, R75) is superb. Omelettes (from R25) make a good breakfast. Cover charge R25 on musical nights.

Pelmennaya (22314; 2nd fl, Kommunistichesky pr 178; meals R35-70; 8am-7pm Mon-Fri, to 4pm Sat & Sun) This Soviet-era cafeteria has apparently negatively phototropic pot plants and serves cheap if uninspiring breakfasts.

Getting There & Away

There's no railway but a **booth** (9am-1pm & 2-5pm) within the bus station sells train tickets.

SIBERIA

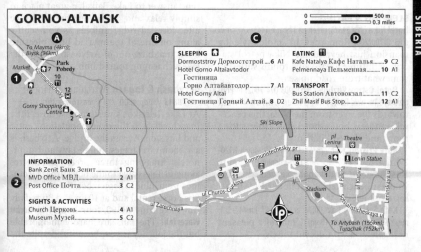

GORNO-ALTAISK

0 — 500 m
0 — 0.3 miles

To Mayma (4km); Biysk (96km)

Market
Park Pobedy
Gorny Shopping Centre
Ski Slope
pl Lenina
Theatre
Lenin Statue
Kommunistecheskiy pr
ul Churos-Gurkina
ul Zarechnaya
Stadium
ul Palkina
ul Kirova
Leninskaya ul
Sotsialisticheskaya ul
To Artybash (155km); Turochak (152km)

Buses run to Barnaul (R200, five hours, seven daily) and Biysk (R65, two hours, eight daily), and serve most Altai Republic villages at least daily including Tyungur (R403, 2.20pm) and Onguday (3.30pm). Timetabled minibuses for Ulagan and Kosh-Agach (both 7.10am, via Aktash) don't run on Tuesday or Saturday. If passenger numbers are low, only one of these buses runs so you might not get beyond Aktash (R265, seven hours).

Private alternatives leave until mid-morning according to demand. Much faster shared taxis usually cost 70% more than buses but can be hard to differentiate from private taxis.

Getting Around

From central Gorno-Altaisk virtually all east-bound city buses take Kommunistichesky pr past the bus station, MVD office and market. Buses numbered over 100 continue to Mayma, with the useful bus 102 (R9) ideal for all of Mayma's restaurants and hotels.

AROUND GORNO-ALTAISK
☎ 38844

Mayma Майма

Hugging the M52 (ul Lenina), Mayma is effectively Gorno-Altaisk's western lobe. There's nothing to see but the settlement does have a large market and Internet-connected post office right where the road turns off to Gorno-Altaisk. Around 2km further south (on bus 102) there are some pleasant eateries and minihotels.

SLEEPING & EATING

Hotel Nika (☎ 21673; ul Lenina 129 at km443/520; s/tw/d R350/700/700) Brand new in an old-style log mansion just beyond the Nika petrol station with three great-value rooms suffering somewhat from road noise.

Hotel Ostrov Yuzhny (☎ 8-903 074 7062; ul Pribrezhnaya 10; tw/d R800/1000) Three minutes' walk towards the river from the Nika, this peaceful, modern house-hotel has a big sitting room and shared kitchen.

Kafe Pristen (☎ 22875; ul Lenina 62; meals R120-250, cover R30 from 7pm; ◷ 11am-midnight) Quality Russian food and kebabs served at heavy wooden bench tables overlooked by hunting trophies.

Kafe Solechny (☎ 23004; ul Lenina 87, km442/521; meals R50-90; ◷ 8am-10pm) Unusually pleasant new cafeteria with decent toilets.

Aya & Souzga Ая и Соузга

The rock-punctuated Katun riverside has many idyllic spots south of Mayma though hotels, *turbazy* (holiday camps) and home-stays dotted every kilometre or two tend to mar the views. Accommodation is most concentrated around **Aya most**, a suspension bridge leading to the famous but laughably pitiful 'warm' Lake Aya. Beside the bridge many agencies offer **rafting trips** (per hr R200-250) and horse rides at short notice; handy if you haven't reserved anything more adventurous.

Souzga village starts 500m beyond the Aya Bridge with the comfortable little **Gostiny Dvor** (☎ 27630; ul Naberezhnaya 64; s/d R1500/1800), whose rooms have good, modern toilets and showers. Prices drop 20% from September to April.

Very basic hut-camps abound here. The cheapest huts are simply two beds and a window. Easy to find and nicely positioned 4km north of Aya most is **Bely Kamen** (☎ 8-903 919 2297; tw R400-600; ◷ Jun-Aug).

Souzga *marshrutky* run very rarely from opposite Mayma market. Chemal and Chuysky Trakt buses also pass by. If you have no accommodation booked consider chartering a taxi from Mayma market to check out various options, saving you very long sweaty walks.

LAKE TELETSKOE
ОЗЕРО ТЕЛЕЦКОЕ

Deep, delightful Lake Teletskoe is Altai's serene answer to Lake Baikal, a great place to simply relax and catch your breath. Ridge after forested ridge unfolds as you scuttle along on one of the myriad little pleasure boats that buzz out of Artybash village, the lake's charming tourist hub.

Artybash & Iogach Артыбаш и Иогач
☎ 38843 / pop 4500 / ◷ Moscow +3hr
At Lake Teletskoe's westernmost nose, little Iogach village is the main population centre and bus stop. Across the bridge, Artybash is a ribbon of cottages, homestays and mini-hotels straggling three pretty kilometres along ul Teletskaya to the big Turbaza Zolotoe Ozera. June to September, the *turbaza* offers horse rental and at 10am and 3pm daily runs lake trips (R250, four hours) to **Korbu Waterfall**. The falls are hardly memorable but the journey is very beautiful despite the

blaring commentary. Most accommodation places can arrange motorboat *(lodki)* rentals. Rafting trips run twice daily from Pensionat Edem. Out of season when the lake is frozen, the village is idyllically peaceful.

SLEEPING & EATING

Iogach is convenient for transport but the walking and views are generally better from Artybash. Many of the cheaper places open peak season only. However, all places listed here (except Turbaza Zolotoe Ozera) operate year-round with reservations highly advisable in July and August.

Iogach

Hotel Tayozhnaya (☎ 27445; ul Naberezhnaya; dm R200-450, tw/d R900/920) Just two minutes east of the bus stand, this handy, friendly place has some very pleasant views of the lake. Cheap rooms share outdoor long-drops (lit and clean) while double rooms share a single indoor loo. Using the *banya* costs extra.

Artybash

Every second house in Artybash seems to have rooms or huts to rent. Prices start from R250 without any facilities but many demand minimum groups of three or more guests in summer. Look for signs marked 'Сдаю Дом' and 'Сдаётся Дом' (house for rent). Beyond Turbaza Zolotoe Ozera, there are more 'mini-resorts', a wide, grassy free-camping area which gets very noisy on weekends plus some cheap but very basic hut-camps. Hotel distances given are from the Iogach-Artybash bridge.

Stary Zamok (☎ 26460; km1.4; off season/summer/ Jul d with bathroom R1600/1800/2000) This sweetly kitsch little 'castle' has the village's best-value upper-range accommodation. There are shared terraces, lake-view sitting rooms and a dining area. Rooms with shared bathrooms cost roughly half.

Pensionat Edem (☎ 26434; km2.5; d/tw from R1000/1400) A variety of comfy rooms and organised activities make the Edem a popular choice though it's in trees slightly set back from the road and lacks any lake views.

Kemping Laguna (☎ 26489; km3; beds/tw R450/ 900 off season, tw R2000-2400 Jun-Aug) Right at the gates of the *turbaza*, the Laguna's fully furnished en-suite rooms are great value out of season. However, in summer they're 99% booked out.

Turbaza Zolotoe Ozera (☎ 26440; km3.2; beds R120-250 Jun & Sep, R170-300 Jul-Aug) Despite the perfect position for views and lake excursions, this big, institutional place has mainly old, shed-like units offering cheap, unappealing accommodation. However, major building works are under way to erect much more attractive hotel-style options.

GETTING THERE & AWAY

From Gorno-Altaisk the 11.05am bus (R137, 5½ hours) detours via Turochak, where you spend over an hour for lunch. In summer a faster direct service should run most afternoons. Returning to Gorno-Altaisk, a few direct shared taxis leave between 6.30am and 7.30am (R200, 2¼ hours). Biysk to Artybash is only 168km but timetables mean that public transport will leave you stranded overnight in Turochak, where the very basic **Hotel Lyzhny Baza** (☎ 22730; ul Nagornaya 1; beds R100) is an awkward 2km walk from the bus stop.

Around the Lake

Around Lake Teletskoe, half a dozen small, simple *turbazy* lie in complete, idyllic isolation accessible only by boat. Novosibirsk's Zhemchuzhina Altaya (p511) organises bookings and access by weekly boat (R800 return, Thursday) from Iogach.

Probably the best choice is **Altyn-Tuu** as it's the closest to the mouth of the dramatic Chulyshman Valley. A 4WD track from here gets you relatively close to the phallic erosional quirks known as **Mushroom Rocks** (Kamennye Griby) and you can hike onwards to see the powerful 160m **Uchar Waterfall**. When the mud road is passable (easiest in autumn) it's possible to reach Altyn-Tuu and Balykcha from the Chuysky Trakt via Balyktuyul (p533). Hike-and-raft adventure tours sold by **STA-Novosibirsk** (www .sibtravel.com) approach this way.

ALONG THE KATUN RIVER TO CHEMAL

Between Mayma and Chemal the rock-dotted Katun River weaves prettily through forests and between tall grey cliffs. Villages all along the route have a range of accommodation from basic summer huts to swanky new hotel-style complexes, many operating from May to September only. Most people simply come to unwind but between all those vodka-drinking sessions

SIBERIA

with holidaying Siberians you can usually arrange easy rafting day trips. Tour agencies in Barnaul, Novosibirsk or beyond have extensive catalogues, but in July and August many have minimum three-day stays and most are heavily prebooked.

Many local homes rent rooms from around R250 per bed without facilities and from R500 with shared indoor bathroom. Nicknamed *Zelyoni Doma,* some are bookable through the Russian-only website www .zel-dom.narod.ru. Otherwise, just look for door signs saying 'Сдаётся Дом'.

Manzherok to Ust-Sema
☎ 38844 / ☽ Moscow +3hr

In the woods towards sprawling **Manzherok** village, there are modestly priced riverside *turbazy* at km461.8, 462.2, 465.2 and 468.3. At km469, **Turkomplex Manzherok** (☎ 24399; dm/d R250/1100) sits behind a mock-Cossack stockade in a riverbank pine grove. Relatively good-value doubles have private shower and toilet.

Manzherok's best homestays are at the village's prettier southern edge around km474.

At km478.7, **Arzhaan Suu** is a 'holy' coldwater spring at the roadside, shrouded by summer souvenir sellers. Just across the new suspension bridge is **Talda Park** with caves and a café in a bizarre wooden galleon.

Further south, development is ever less intrusive. The scenery is prettiest around **Ust-Muni** (where there are some homestays) and **Barangol,** where **Tsarskaya Okhota** (☎ 26410; ram@alt.ru) has an eye-catching, castle-style entrance. Its café is a great place to stop and has arguably the most beautiful Katunside position for miles around. A long suspension bridge allows footpath access to a waterfall (3km). However, its accommodation is rather overpriced.

Ust-Sema to Chemal
☎ 38841 / ☽ Moscow +3hr

A dead end road from Ust-Sema follows the Katun River towards Chemal through thick cedar forests which steadily open out into patchworks of slopes and fields that make for good walking. Several rural accommodation options lie within a few km of the **Turbaza Katun** (dm from R130/190 Jun-Sep/Jul-Aug) which is cheap, if rather institutional, and has an attractive riverside position with regular rafting and other outdoor activities. Bookings

are through Sibir Altai (p511) in Novosibirsk; they can book your stay but if you only want to do some sports it's better just to turn up. Somewhat nicer **Berel** (dm from R300) has cramped huts but also R450 beds in nicer buildings with shared sit-down toilets.

On the 'wrong side' of the Katun, attractive **Anos** village has a tiny Churos-Gurkin museum and a comfortable **guesthouse** (s/tw €20/30) run by Novosibirsk-based Sibalp (p511). Easiest access from the Chemal road is by pedestrian suspension bridge.

Chemal Чемал
☎ 38841 / pop 9000 / ☽ Moscow +3hr

At the attractive junction of the Chemal and Katun Rivers, ever-expanding Chemal is heavily touristed in summer but remains a good base for regional explorations and makes a very pleasant day trip from Gorno-Altaisk, 95km further north.

Chemal **bus station** (☎ 22517; ul Pchyolkina 62) is opposite a cute brick **church** (ul Pchyolkina 69a) with a metal-spired wooden tower. Walk two blocks south past the central shops and a small park, then turn right to find the **Altaysky Tsentr** (☎ 22327; ul Beshpekskaya 6; individual/group R100/300). This comprises three Altai-style wooden *ail*-huts with pointed metal roofs. One is an Altai library, another celebrates Churos-Gurkin's ethnographic work, but most interesting is the traditional 'home' *ail* (tent-like dwelling) where septuagenarian curator Alexander Bardin demonstrates Altai crafts, shows how traditional fire-stones work, explains sheepskin nappies and brews *talkan* Altai tea. It's well worth the entry fee if your Russian (or Altai/Kazakh/Turkish) is good enough; opening hours vary.

Ul Beshpekskaya becomes Sovetskaya ul and, after 700m, dead-ends at a pedestrian suspension footbridge. This dizzyingly wobbly construction leads across a small canyon to a craggy island in the Katun River on which is perched the tiny wooden **Ioanno Bogoslavski Chapel** (☽ 9am-7pm), rebuilt in 2001 to the original 1849 design. Beside it, the rock miraculously shaped like a Madonna-and-child sculpture is supposedly natural.

A narrow but well-trodden footpath winds high along the Katun riverbank into the **Varota Sartikpayev Canyon,** an important place within Altai mythology. Despite power lines and summer crowds, views remain very pretty. After walking for about

15 minutes you emerge behind a small 1935 **dam** (GES in Russian, an acronym for hydroelectric scheme) backed by souvenir stalls. Here you can make 15m **bungee jumps** (pryzhki ve vodu; per jump R90; 10am-1pm & 2-7pm May-Sep) into the frothing outpour waters or 'fly' across on the **kanatnaya daroga** (per ride R150), an amusing elastic-pulley contraption. For much more peaceful Katun views walk, drive or cycle at least 3km further south.

Elekmonar, 5km north of Chemal, is the starting point for multiday hikes or horse rides to the seven attractive **Karakol Lakes** amid picturesque bald mountaintops. The lakes are approximately 30km beyond Elekmonar – start up ul Sadovaya. A sturdy 4WD could get you most of the way.

SLEEPING & EATING

Pensionat Radna (22257; altayradna@inbox.ru; ul Zelyonaya 8; s R500, tw R700-1000) At the northern end of Chemal, three good-humoured lady-doctors have gone 'back-to-nature' milking their cow, growing vegies and baking bread. They rent comfy rooms, some of which share a hot-water bath and sit-down indoor toilet (but go outside for number twos, please!) With bicycle hire (R80 per hour), massage, hiking trips and the best vegetarian food in Altai, you might not want to leave.

Marin Ostrov (22403; ul Yozhanskaya 58; tw Oct-Apr/May-Sep R1800/2400;   ) Large, fully Western-standard rooms have river-facing balconies, while four cheaper rooms (R1200/1600) share two bathrooms. There's a pub and a delightful terrace café. Idyllically quiet, it's 2.5km south of central Chemal towards Areda (a trio of upper-market hotels hidden in a narrow forest gully).

In Elekmonar, very basic homestays are available for under R400 at over a dozen homes, including Sovetskaya ul 53, 107 and 157, and Tsentralnaya ul 32 and 61.

GETTING THERE & AWAY

Buses run thrice daily from Gorno-Altaisk (R91, two hours). In summer additional services run from Barnaul (seven hours) via Biysk (4½ hours) and overnight from Novosibirsk.

CHUYSKY TRAKT ЧУЙСКИЙ ТРАКТ

South of Ust-Sema, the dramatic M52 road to Olgii in Mongolia is known as the Chuysky Trakt. It offers 400km of forested

---

DOMES, STONES AND MOUSTACHES

Kurgany are ancient domed burial mounds. Some are over 2500 years old, while others, like those at Shiba (6km west of Tuetka), date 'only' from the 6th century AD, though to the casual observer they're somewhat more impressive. Nonetheless, even these are still just barely discernable piles of stones. Much more interesting are **kameny baba** figures, literally 'stone granddads'. The best were carved in human form with Terry Thomas moustaches, shown holding a cup that symbolically housed the soul of the dead. Just a few kameny baba have avoided being carted off to museums. Accessible if very eroded (mostly now faceless) examples appear beside the Chuysky Trakt. Much finer is the brilliant Chinggis Khaan stone near Ak-Dovurak (p552). There are also many groups of animal-shaped **petroglyphs** (rock drawings) of debatable origin. These may be fascinating but most are so faint that you might miss the scratches even when you're staring right at them.

---

mountains, canyons and glimpsed vistas, emerging eventually into peak-rimmed steppe dotted with Kazakh yurts. The views are arguably better driving northbound as the woodlands are less dense on the south-facing slopes, leaving visible the photogenic rocky cliffs. Transport is incredibly limited but shared taxis run all the way to Kosh-Agach for around R500 per seat (R1500 to R2000 per car) and drivers are generally happy enough to make brief stops en route for photos of landscapes, stone idols and petroglyphs.

Onguday Area Онгудай

 38845 / pop 5100 / Moscow +3hr

High but relatively unspectacular, the Seminsky Pass is topped with a winter sports training centre and some snack kiosks from which the road descends to **Onguday**. Translating literally as '10 gods' (for the 10 surrounding peaks) the large village isn't especially appealing but its very basic, central **hotel** (21196; ul Erzumasheva 8; dm/tw R300/600) makes a possible base for archaeologists visiting *kurgany* at Karakol, Tuetka and Shiba. There's a small museum in the school and the Torko Chachak handicraft shop sells Altai felts and fur hats. Onguday's Eloyn Festival is a big Altai cultural celebration held some years in early July.

To Onguday's northwest, a dead-end side road to Kulada village passes through **Bichiktu-Boom** (with some traditional tepee-shaped Altai *aily*) and an attractive valley which offers hiking and free-camping possibilities. **Kulada** itself is built around a rocky knob and is a holy place in Burkhanism, a curious but almost extinct Altai religion founded in 1904 by shepherd Chet Chelpan, fusing Orthodox Christianity, Buddhism and folk traditions.

Southeast of Onguday the Chuysky Trakt crosses the beautiful, serpentine **Chike-Taman Pass**. It descends close to the **Ilgumen Rapids**, which offer challenging rafting (grades 4 to 5); five-day adventures to Manzherok start by camping at the beautifully positioned **Kür-Kechü** (Kordon Kurechy; tent sites R50), perched just above the river, 800m east of km681. There are a few summer huts here too. See p520 for more on rafting in Altai.

In a cliff-ringed curl of river, **Maly Yaloman** has a microclimate allowing local villagers to grow cherries, apples and naughty weeds. Up 12km of rough side track **Bolshoy Yaloman** has several *kameny baba*. A faceless but much more accessible trio stand right beside the Chuysky Trakt just beyond the southern end of **Inya** village (km706.4).

At km712.6, overshadowed by an unsightly pylon, picnic tables and prayer flags tempt you to stop for wonderful views of the meeting Ilgumen and Katun Rivers far below. Just beyond, beside the slip road for the Chuy-Oozy truck stop (km714.2), very lightly scored road-side petroglyphs depict little antelope figures. There's another petroglyph group at Kalbak Tash crag, a five-minute walk north of km721. The road then snakes scenically through the Chuya Canyon to Aktash (km790).

Aktash Area

AKTASH АКТАШ

☎ 38846 / pop 3400 / ⏱ Moscow +3hr

This nondescript little garrison-village commands a dramatic area of craggy valleys. If bus timetables leave you stuck here, stroll 3km towards Balyktuyul through the striking rocky canyon named **Red Gate** (Krasnyye Vorota). Aktash could make a base for mountain adventures in the lovely

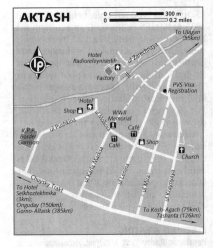

AKTASH

Northern Chuysky Range with its challenging mountaineering on **Mt Aktru** (4044m) and **Mt Maashey** (4177m) or for trekking to the **Shavlinsky Lakes** for idyllic mountain views. However, for all of these you will need outside help as in Aktash itself there are no tourist facilities and no waiting guides. Chartering a suitable 4WD to reach Mt Aktru base camp isn't easy but the trip is lovely if you succeed.

PVS Visa registration (☎ 23381; ul Mira 1a) is required if you missed registering in Gorno-Altaisk. The unmarked **Hotel Radioreleyniserkh** (☎ 23311; ul Zarechnaya 17; d R60) has four excellent rooms for a token fee. It's designed for invited business guests but tourists might be allowed to stay one night by prior arrangement. Finding the keyholder in the bowels of the factory at ul Zarechnaya 15 can be quite an adventure.

Hotel Selkhoztekhnika (Chuysky Trakt km767; dm/s/tw R200/250/500), isolated 3km north of town, is much more basic. A 2003 earthquake left its walls bowed and floors strangely twisted.

The central, two-room unnamed **'hotel'** (gostinitsa; ☎ 23831; ul Pushkina 1; dm R250) is scary – rooms are hidden within a Kafka nightmare of collapsing offices and unidentifiable detritus. Avoid except in case of emergency.

Neither Aktash nor Onguday have professional taxis but shopkeepers can suggest potential drivers. Aktash to Kosh-Agach by car can cost anywhere from R700 to R1200.

ULAGAN & BALYKTUYUL УЛАГАН И
БАЛЫКТЫЮЛ

☎ 38846 / pop 2500 & 1300 / ☻ Moscow +3

From Aktash, a mostly asphalted road
via the disreputable town of **Ulagan** (Ust-
Ulagan, 56km from Aktash) winds through
a lovely high valley to **Balyktuyul** with its cute
wooden Altai church. However, both places
are notorious for dangerous drunkards and
locals suggest reporting your arrival to the
village offices for 'protection'. The excavation sites of the classic **Pazyryk kurgan** (5th
century BC tumuli) are about 5km beyond
Balyktuyul off the very rough jeep track
that continues all the way to Balykcha on
Lake Teletskoe's southern tip. Ulagan has
a small Pazyryk museum and a tiny hotel,
often unmanned.

Kosh-Agach Area Кош Агач

☎ 38842 / pop 4500 / ☻ Moscow +3hr

Clouds allowing, the best views on the
whole Chuysky Trakt are between Aktash
and Kosh-Agach. Wide if distant panoramas of perennially snow-topped peaks
rise formidably behind valleys known
somewhat misleadingly as the Kuray and
Chuy Steppe (km821 to km840 and km870
onwards). These are interspersed by more
great canyons and a colourful mountain-
side that looks like marbled chocolate pudding (km856). The Kuray Steppe hosted
Russia's 2005 paragliding championships
(www.triadaclub.com/kurai).

Kosh-Agach itself has a strange, end-of-
the-world feeling about it, with its shanty-
town homes petering out into magical flat
steppe just beyond the Hotel Tsentralnaya.
When the dusty air clears, the nearby
mountains appear from nowhere like ap-
paritions. A useful landmark is the little
wooden **Khazret Osman Mosque** (ul Sovetskaya
62), which marks the intersection of the
Chuysky Trakt with ul Sovetskaya. It's on
ul Sovetskaya that you'll find the bus stand
and three hotels. Parallel, one block west,
is ul Kooperativnaya with a **post office** and
police station (☎ 22433; ul Kooperativnaya 34) for
visa registration.

Sberbank (ul Pogranichnaya 1a; ☻ 9am-noon & 2-
4.30pm Mon-Fri) changes money if no-one is
in the market will.

Sergei Erlenbaeva, at the Hot Bread
Hotel knows the location of some photogenic local **yurts** where you can sample fresh

kumiss with Kazakh nomad herders. The
nearest are just 5km away on steppe that
rises imperceptibly towards the distant twin
peaks of Mt Saylyugem (3411m) and Mt
Tapduayr (3305m).

Very adventurous travellers with a few
weeks to spare have bought **horses** in Kosh-
Agach and ridden all the way to Tyungur,
Lake Teletskoe or even to Tuva.

SLEEPING

All hotels are small and ultrabasic with outside horror-hole toilets.

Hot Bread Hotel (☎ 22682; ul Sovetskaya 50-52; dm
R150). The nickname 'hot bread' comes from
the bakery sign reading 'Горячий Хлеб'. This
very friendly crash pad has doorless three-
bed dorms upstairs off the baker's family
living room. No English is spoken but the
charming owner understands tourist interests and has travelled the world.

Hotel Tsentralnaya (☎ 22162; ul Pogranichnaya;
s/tw R150/260) Small, very simple governmental
place exaggeratedly criticised by locals. Others include **Hotel Shankhai** (ul Sovetskaya 63; dm
R125) and **Hotel Bazar** (ul Sovetskaya 61; dm R150).

KOSH-AGACH

0	200 m
0	0.1 miles

SIGHTS & ACTIVITIES
Khazret Osman Mosque 1 B3
Mongolian Market Монгольский рынок 2 A3

SLEEPING 🏠
Hot Bread Hotel Гостиница Горячий хлеб...... 3 B3
Hotel Bazar Гостиница Базар........................ 4 B3
Hotel Shankhai Гостиница Шанхай................. 5 B3
Hotel Tsentralnaya Гостиница Центральная 6 A3

EATING 🍴
Stolovaya Столовая 7 B3
Vostochnaya Kukhnya Восточная кухня........8 A3

TRANSPORT
4WD to Mongolia 4WD в Монголию..............(see 2)
Taxis & Minibuses to Gorno-Altaisk
   Такси и маршрутки в Горно-Алтайск 9 A3

CROSSING TO MONGOLIA AT TASHANTA-KYZYL-UUY

In desolately lonely grassland and hills 51km beyond Kosh-Agach, **Tashanta** is a tiny settlement with a wooden-towered stockade. After years of rumours, the **Mongolian border** (☺ 9am-noon & 2-6.30pm) here finally opened to foreigners in 2004. Actor Ewan McGregor and his *Long Way Round* TV crew were among the first across. There's 28km of no-man's-land between Tashanta and **Kyzyl Uuy** (Red Door) which you may not cross on foot. Neither settlements have regular transport so your best bet is to arrange 4WD transport all the way between Kosh-Agach and Olgii markets. Taking your own vehicle into Mongolia requires special paperwork. See www.xor.org.uk/silkroute /siberia2004/for tales and photos.

EATING
Despite posted '24-hour' opening times, most shops and cafés actually close by 6pm. **Vostochnaya Kukhnya** (ul Kooperativnaya 37a) is reckoned best for Central Asian food. The **Stolovaya** (ul Sovetskaya 62a) has simple Russian fare.

GETTING THERE & AWAY
From the **bus stand** (ul Sovetskaya 28), the 7am minibus to Gorno-Altaisk (R370, nine hours) can't be relied upon. Shared taxis (R500 per seat) also leave around 7am; they offer much better views and by arrangement will collect you from your hotel for no extra charge. For transport to the Mongolian town of Olgii (seats R250) it's best to find a 4WD 'UAZ' vehicle at the **Mongolian market** (Mongolski Rynok; ul Kooperativnaya 44). Weekdays around midday are the best times to try.

TOWARDS MT BELUKHA
Tiny Tyungur village sits in an appealing valley. Although lacking viewpoints itself, it's the normal staging point for treks towards **Mt Belukha** (4506m), Siberia's highest peak. Surrounding valleys and lakes are among Russia's most spectacular but access requires strenuous guided hiking.

The road to Tyungur branches off the northern Chuysky Trakt at Cherga and crosses a delightfully isolated, mostly for-ested area via Baragash. After the high grasslands of **Ust-Kan**, there's a brief glimpse of the distant white-tops from the Kyrlyksky Pass as the road descends into the Koksa Valley. Though less dramatic than the Chuysky Trakt, the landscape is attractive with bucolic meadows framed by hills and bluffs.

Ust-Koksa & Tyungur
Усть-Кокса и Тюнгур
☎ 38848 / ☺ Moscow +3hr
The valley meets the Katun River at **Ust-Koksa**, which has the delightful wooden **Pokrovskoe Church** (ul Nagornaya 31). Across the Katun River, around 10km beyond Multa, there's a maral deer farm with a small summer *turbaza* en route to the beautiful **Multinsky Lakes**. These offer yet more great hikes if you can find a guide. In the 1930s the many old believers of the Koksa and Uymon Valleys offered fierce armed resistance to collectivisation, leading to the almost total destruction of their villages by the peeved Soviet state. Nonetheless, **Verkhny Uymon** village has an Old Believers' Museum (Muzey Staroobryadchestva) as well as a small Nikolai Rerikh House Museum.

Tyungur is a tiny village but its well-organised Turbaza Vysotnik (opposite) is a fantastic place to go to organise trekking, rafting or ascents of the mighty Mt Belukha. Decent tents, climbing equipment and even sleeping bags can be rented here. Maps, guides and horses are also available and there's the possibility of meeting other travellers to form a trekking group with. It's worth emailing ahead with your requests. If you speak some Russian ask about joining an existing Russian group (much cheaper, from around US$20 per person per day). Bring trekking supplies as Tyungur has minimal groceries. If you want to spy Mt Belukha without a full-blown expedition, take a long day hike from Tyungur partway up **Mt Bayda**.

HIKING ROUTES
Before setting off on any of Tyungur's five- to 12-day trekking adventures, be aware that you're heading for real wilderness. Discuss your plans carefully with staff at one of the *turbazy* in Tyungur, or join one of the many organised groups by booking

well ahead with one of the many trekking companies, notably those in Barnaul, Novosibirsk, Omsk or beyond.

Hiking alone or without a guide is highly discouraged. Renting packhorses for your baggage will make the treks more pleasant and horsemen often double as guides, though none speak any English.

To reach the lovely **Akkem Lake** from Tyungur you could cross the 1513m Kuzuyak Pass. Alternatively, start by rafting 20km down the Katun River to the mouth of the Akkem River past some *kameny baba*. From there, hiking the forested Akkem River valley (two days) is somewhat dull so consider a four- to five-day high loop to the east, with many marvellous mountain views en route. Camping is popular around Akkem Lake's hydro-meteorological station where there's also a rescue post (but don't play hurt as an 'easy way out' – helicopter evacuation costs from US$6000 minimum).

Stupendous panoramas of Mt Belukha are the reward for crossing the boulder-strewn Kara-Tyurek Pass (3060m), which loops from Lake Akkem to peaceful **Lake Kucherla**; it takes one day if you don't get lost but is tricky for horses. Returning down the Kucherla River valley to Tyungur takes at least two days but add more time for exploring and mishaps.

From the confluence of the Akkem and Katun Rivers it's also possible to hike along the **Katun River** to Inya (three days) on the Chuysky Trakt.

CLIMBING BELUKHA

Ascents of Belukha (grade 3A–5A) are only for experienced mountaineers but don't require special permits. A two-week package (from around US$450 per person) available from Turbaza Vysotnik includes guides, food and acclimatisation climbs for individuals or small groups. Specialist mountaineering groups such as K2 Adventures in Omsk (p504) have successfully guided mountaineers up the toughest 'Bottle' ascent.

SLEEPING & EATING

Ust-Kan has a basic hotel at its bus station, and there's a small hut-camp beside the main Tyungur road 4km east of town near an archaeological cave site.

In Ust-Koksa, the grocery shop **Lada** (Sovetskaya ul 71; beds R200), with multicoloured roof, has decent rooms upstairs, let down by a meet-the-neighbours shared squat toilet. Another unmarked three-room **guesthouse** (Sovetskaya ul 58; beds from R100) has a kitchen and real bathroom, but to get the key you must visit the **Komkhoz office** (☎ 22393; ul Nagornaya 23) during business hours.

There are two options in Tyungur across the suspension bridge from the village. Keep left for the simple but very well organised **Turbaza Vysotnik** (☎ 22024; hut dm/tw/tr/q R150/300/400/500, tent dm R90). Sheets or sleeping bags cost R40 extra. There's a helpful English-speaking manager and a great café which is the nearest you'll find to an international traveller hang-out in Altai. Almost anything you'll need for mountaineering or treks into the wilderness is available for rental here, including tents and guides, but it's worth reserving in advance through Lenalptours (p490) in St Petersburg. Its **Akkem Camp** (dm R60) has pre-erected four-man tents en route to Lake Akkem.

A five-minute walk to the southwest of the Tyungur Bridge is the slightly more comfortable but less traveller-orientated **Turbaza Uch-Sumer** (☎ 29424, 38841-38822; fax 22872; www.uch-sumer.ru; yurt space/dm R150/600). Dorm prices in the hotel section include a shared indoor toilet. There are also some private huts. The owners offer many tour options, notably hunting around Lake Kucherla and elsewhere in the mountains where they maintain cabins.

GETTING THERE & AWAY

From Gorno-Altaisk a strangely timed 2pm bus runs daily to Tyungur (R403, nine hours) arriving just before midnight. It returns at 8am via Ust-Koksa and Ust-Kan. *Marshrutky* run from Gorno-Altaisk to Ust-Koksa (R450) when full, usually two or three times each morning, departing from a corner of the bus station parking area. Departures are possible as late as 10am southbound but northbound all will have usually left by 8am.

Taxis plying the Ust-Koksa–Verkhny Uymon route charge R500 return with waiting time; buses only run twice a week. The Turbaza Vysotnik in Tyungur (above) arranges transfers to Biysk.

SIBERIA

SOUTHERN KEMEROVO REGION

The Kemerovo region is often considered synonymous with the mines of the Kuzbass district. However, south of the industrial mayhem, the Gornaya Shoriya Mountains are locally considered a 'little Switzerland'. While this may be overstating things, there's a popular skiing area at **Sheregesh** (www .sheregesh.ru), 25km from the railhead at **Tashtagol**. A very adventurous trek takes mountaineers over a tough trail to Turochak in Altai.

Visiting Novokuznetsk is a vastly less daring proposition. The Kemerovo region's biggest city, it makes a handy stop between Abakan and Biysk when overlanding between Altai and Tuva.

NOVOKUZNETSK НОВОКУЗНЕЦК
☎ 3843 / pop 563,000 / ☾ Moscow +4hr

Founded on the right bank of the Tom River in 1618, the frequently enlarged Kuznetsk Fortress became one of the most important guardians of imperial Russia's southeastern frontier. The chunky remnants remain Novokuznetsk's modest main attraction. The city's left bank, named Stalinsk until 1961, developed from 1932 as a gigantic steel town and is now the city centre. A day is ample to survey Novokuznetsk's intriguingly pompous early-Stalinist boulevards fanning out to towering smokestacks.

Sights

An easy stroll due north from the cohabiting bus and train stations takes you up pr Metallurgov, which is a good example of Novokuznetsk's memorable 'Brave New 1930s' feel.

To your right in Gagarin Park is the grandly colonnaded main **theatre** (☎ 743 505; pr Metallurgov 28). On the left at the corner of Pionersky pr, the 80-year-old **Regional Museum** (Kraevedchesky muzey; ☎ 741 995; admission R25; ☾ 10am-6pm Tue-Sat) concentrates mostly on mining and steel industries.

If you want to visit the sparse remnants of old Kuznetsk, take frequent *marshrutka* 5 from the stations. You'll pass the vibrant **art museum** (☎ 476 848; ul Kirova 62; admission R15; ☾ 10am-6pm Wed-Sun) and a **Biznes Tsentr** (ul

Kirova 102) in an eye-catching wooden-spired old building before crossing the wide Tom River. Get off at Sovetsky pl and follow the road that leads steeply up beside the beautiful 1792 **Transfiguration Cathedral** (Preobrazhenskoi sobor; ☾ 8am-2pm & 4-7pm). On the hilltop, the restored stone ramparts of the **Kuznetsk Fortress** (krepost; ☎ 360 092; ul Geologicheskaya; admission R35, photography/video R25/50; ☾ 10am-5pm) are massive and topped with canons but represent only 20% of their 1810 extent. There's a great little gift shop upstairs within the copper-domed Barnaul Gate and an exhibition hall in the renovated barrack house.

Return to Sovetsky pl and walk five minutes south down ul Dostoevskogo. One of several wooden homes set in riverside gardens is the artistically presented **Dostoevsky Museum** (☎ 376 586; ul Dostoevskogo 40; admission R25; ☾ 9am-5pm Mon-Fri, 10am-3pm Sat) in the log cabin where the writer stayed for three weeks in 1856–57. Request the key from ul Dostoevskogo 29.

Sleeping

For a fuller Russian-language listing of hotels and cafés consult www.i2n.ru.

Hotel Aba (☎ 424 460; www.aba-hotel.ru; ul Kuybysheva 8; d from R1500; ✳) Rooms in this polite, modern hotel are bright and fairly stylish with clean, new shower booths and toilets. Much bigger R2600 suites have air-conditioning but the same somewhat undersized double beds. It's 1.5km northwest of the stations; three huge blocks up pr Kurako then left.

Hotel Novokuznetsk (☎ 464 647; ul Kirova 53; s R780-1470, tw from R860) This presentable Soviet giant has clean rooms but standards vary widely; few are as smart as the renovated reception area implies. It's on the large traffic circle, 1.5km northeast up pr Bardina from the stations by *marshrutka* 5.

Hotel Metallurg (☎ 746 185; pr Metallurgov 19; s/tw/tr/q R380/500/510/680) Clean, lower-grade Soviet rooms have private sinks but the shared toilets lack seats and the sex-segregated showers are whiffy. A few good-value R850 rooms are much nicer with private facilities and small double beds. It's in a college building beside the main post office with Gorky and Lenin statues loitering outside like a couple of plinthed tramps.

Eating

There are many cheap cafés near the stations. Several places on ul Kirova near the Biznes Tsentr have much more style.

Shafran (☎ 352 609; ul Kirova 103; meals R150-280; ⏰ 11am-11pm) Semimodernist café in a shopping centre with supermarket and ATM. American-style filter coffee R30.

Traktir Zhily-Bili (☎ 392 055; ul Kirova 97; meals R1180-350, salad bar R195) Hansel-and-Gretel ambience beneath a great artificial oak tree for various traditional Russian-Siberian meals. Opposite is a 24-hour Internet club.

Getting There & Around

Handy overnight trains run to Abakan (train 696, R266 *platskart*, 10 hours) and Novosibirsk (train 605, R312 *platskart*, eight hours). The ski-train to Tashtagol (train 679, seven hours) leaves at 6.20am in season.

Slow, bumpy buses run across lonely, undulating agricultural landscapes to Biysk (R200, six to seven hours) departing at 9.30am, 11.25am, 1.27pm and 1.45pm. Infuriatingly, ticket sales normally start only one hour before departure.

Taxis (☎ 390 111) charge around R200 per hour for city tours.

KHAKASSIA REPUBLIC & SOUTHERN KRASNOYARSK TERRITORY
ХАКАССИЯ И ЮЖНЫЙ КРАСНОЯРСКИЙ КРАЙ

The Ireland-sized Khakassia Republic rises from lake-dotted taiga through a vast agricultural plain to meet richly forested mountains on the Tuvan border. Geographically, it is inextricably linked with Southern Krasnoyarsk Territory. For both areas, transport connections focus on on the city of Abakan.

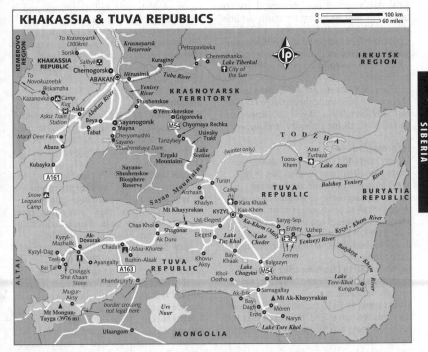

KHAKASSIA & TUVA REPUBLICS

Like culturally similar Altai, Khakassia was a cradle of Siberian civilisation. Standing stones and *kurgan* (burial mounds) pock the landscape; many are more than 3000 years old, though the most visually impressive date from the Turkic period (6th to 12th centuries). The Khyagas (Yenisey Kyrgyz) Empire, from which the name Khakassia is derived, ruled much of Central Asia and central Siberia from around AD 840 until its golden age ended abruptly with the arrival of Chinggis Khaan and company.

Most Khyagas later migrated to what is now Kyrgyzstan. Those who remained were picked on by neighbours until joining the Russian Empire in 1701. Compared to neighbouring Tuva, Russian colonisation in relatively fertile Khakassia was comprehensive. Outnumbered eight-to-one, the shamanist-Khakass people have been largely Christianised and integrated into Russian society, although the area around Askiz remains something of a Khakass cultural stronghold.

ABAKAN АБАКАН
☎ 39022 / pop 163,000 / ⏱ Moscow +4hr
Khakassia's capital is a pleasant, leafy but terminally dull 20th-century transport hub. It started life as a Russian fort in 1707, but until the 1930s remained insignificant compared to suave neighbouring Minusinsk, which was the region's centre of European civilisation.

The main streets are pr Lenina and ul Shchetinkina. The latter becomes pr Druzhby Narodov after 2km as it veers northwest and barrels towards the cathedral and airport.

Information
Abakan Tours (☎ 23284; parkhotel@inbox.ru, attention: Sergei Mechtanov; Hotel Park-Otel; ⏱ 9am-noon & 1-5pm Mon-Fri) Flexible, imaginative and helpful English- and German-speaking tour agency with competitively priced, personalised excursions throughout Khakassia and Tuva for any group size.
A unique six-berth boat experience down the Sayano-Shushenskoe reservoir to Chaa Khol in Tuva runs once a year in autumn.
Elektrorosvyazrkh telephone office (Sovetskaya ul 45; Internet per hr R36; ⏱ 8am-11pm) Modern with an air-conditioned Internet salon.
Khakas Intur (☎ 593 00; rear entrance, ul Krylova 84) Tour agent and owners of Camp Kug near Kazanovka. Enter from behind grocery store through a car lot and unmarked door then venture upstairs.

Main post office (ul Shchetinkina 20; Internet per 5 min R6; ⏱ 8am-9pm)
RosSelkhozBank (ul Vyatkina; ⏱ 9am-4pm Mon-Fri) Good US dollar rates.
TsUM Khakassia (ul Pushkina 127; ⏱ 9am-7pm) Department store which has stalls that sell city and Khakassian maps (R40-50).

Sights & Activities
A superb forest of ancient totem stones welcomes you to the otherwise disappointing **Khakassia Museum** (☎ 22606; ul Pushkina 86; admission R80; ⏱ 10am-5pm Tue-Sun). For similar but better exhibits visit the **Martyanov Museum** (p541) in Minusinsk.

Shimmering golden onion domes make the new **Spasko-Preobrazhenskoy Cathedral** (pr Druzhby Narodov) rather impressive despite the off-white concrete walls and its odd position amid the high-rise apartments of Mikro-Rayon 4. Get there from ul Shchetinkina by bus 11, return by bus 10.

A new **Railway Museum** (Muzey Zheleznoy Dorogi; ☎ 94484; station concourse; admission R30; ⏱ 11am-7pm Wed-Mon) might inspire train buffs with engineers' uniforms through the ages, 22 types of historical rail couplings and a model of Abakan station in 1925.

Other passing curiosities include a latter-day **totem stone** (ul Lenina), an old spired **fire station** (ul Vyatkina), a cross-legged **Lenin statue** (Pervomayskaya pl) and a couple of new **chapels** under construction.

Sleeping
Hotel Persona (☎ 40088; Sovetskaya ul; d R2500-4000) Offer six sparsely stylish rooms whose luxuries and prices are commensurate. Downstairs Abakan's best pub gives access to Orlenok Park.
Hotel Anzas (☎ /fax 25773; anzas@dimetra.ru; ul Vokzalnaya 7a; d R1550-2500) The cheaper rooms are of typical could-be-anywhere international standard while huge *lyux*-suites have more space than style. Sauna costs from R350 per hour. Booking fee only 10%.
Hotel Park-Otel (☎ 27452; fax 23760; parkhotel@inbox.ru; ul Pushkina 54a; ste R1100-1600) The six plush if slightly ageing suites all come with marble bathtub. Central yet quiet, it's hidden behind the 'Kristall' shop and a building site. Some English is spoken.
Hotel Abakan (☎ 23025; pr Lenina 59; s/tw without bathroom 255/360, s with bathroom R585-890, tw with bathroom R900-1080) Behind a misleadingly

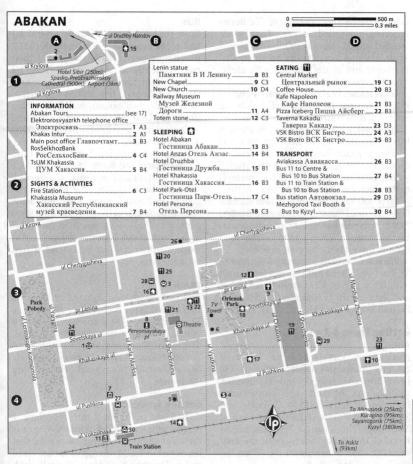

ABAKAN

INFORMATION	
Abakan Tours.............................(see 17)	
Elektrorosvyazrkh telephone office	
Электросвязь...................................**1** A3	
Khakas Intur......................................**2** A1	
Main post office Главпочтамт.........**3** A1	
RosSelkhozBank	
РосСельхосБанк.............................**4** C4	
TsUM Khakassia	
ЦУМ Хакассия...............................**5** B3	

SIGHTS & ACTIVITIES	
Fire Station.....................................**6** C3	
Khakassia Museum	
Хакасский Республиканский	
музей краеведения.....................**7** B4	

Lenin statue	
Памятник В И Ленину.................**8** B3	
New Chapel.....................................**9** C3	
New Church..................................**10** D4	
Railway Museum	
Музей Железной	
Дороги......................................**11** A4	
Totem stone..................................**12** C3	

SLEEPING	
Hotel Abakan	
Гостиница Абакан.....................**13** B3	
Hotel Anzas Отель Анзас...........**14** B4	
Hotel Druzhba	
Гостиница Дружба....................**15** B1	
Hotel Khakassia	
Гостиница Хакассия..................**16** B3	
Hotel Park-Otel	
Гостиница Парк-Отель..............**17** C4	
Hotel Persona	
Отель Персона..........................**18** C3	

EATING	
Central Market	
Центральный рынок.................**19** C3	
Coffee House...............................**20** B3	
Kafe Napoleon	
Кафе Наполеон..........................**21** B3	
Pizza Iceberg Пицца Айсберг.....**22** B3	
Taverna Kakadu	
Таверна Какаду.........................**23** D3	
VSK Bistro ВСК Бистро...............**24** A3	
VSK Bistro ВСК Бистро...............**25** B3	

TRANSPORT	
Aviakassa Авиакасса...................**26** B3	
Bus 11 to Centre &	
Bus 10 to Bus Station.................**27** B4	
Bus 11 to Train Station &	
Bus 10 to Bus Station.................**28** B3	
Bus station Автовокзал..............**29** D3	
Mezhgorod Taxi Booth &	
Bus to Kyzyl..............................**30** B4	

grand façade, this place has simple but perfectly acceptable rooms. Communal showers are clean and modern.

Hotel Khakassia (☎ 23703; pr Lenina 88; s R650-1100, tw R1000-1500) The new reception area sparkles misleadingly; rooms have bathrooms and are passably spruced-up but remain fundamentally Soviet. Higher prices mean bigger not better. Rates include weird breakfasts of gherkin salad and prune yogurt. Half-price for check-ins after 11pm.

Hotel Sibir (☎ 59533; http://siberia.abakannet.ru; pr Druzhby Narodov 9; s R670, tw R1040-1280, d R1340) Rooms, like the staff, range from pleasant and modern to barely reconstructed Soviet. The fully refurbished R1340 doubles are

reasonable value with kettle and minibar. The position is somewhat inconvenient: take bus 11 one stop beyond the Hotel Druzhba then walk through the courtyard play area of pr Druzhba Narodov 13.

Hotel Druzhba (☎ 50244; pr Druzhby Narodov 2; hotel_druzhba@mail.ru; s/tw R430/720) This late-1980s tower is a slightly sleazy last resort.

Eating

Many cheap cafés ring the **central market** (rynok; ul Shevchenko) across from the bus station, with more on ul Pushkina close to the train station.

Kafe Napoleon (☎ 24981; ul Shchetinkina 18; mains R80-130; ✷) The city centre's swankiest restaurant has cork walls, gold-and-magenta colour scheme and a portrait of Old Boney ignoring a startled turkey. Tasty *akula* (stuffed squid) comes with olive-ring 'eyes' while 'Marshal Ney potatoes' are smothered in cheese and gently brushed with garlic. Evening cover charge R70.

Coffee House (☎ 27355; ul Shchetinkina 26; espresso R45; ☯ 9am-11pm; 🔀) Stone and dark-wood interiors. Real coffee.

Pizza Iceberg (☎ 23122; ul Vyatkina 25; pizza slices R35; ☯ 8am-11pm Mon-Fri, 10am-11pm Sat & Sun) Abakan's youth hang-out with pleasant, modern décor. A R40 *kurnik* (pastry stuffed with mushrooms, rice and chicken paste) is better than the microwaved pizza.

Taverna Kakadu (☎ 50336; ul Pushkina 36a; meals R190-450, cover R20 from 8pm; ☯ 11am-4pm & 5pm-2am) Small, dimly lit bar-restaurant with pirate-themed interior. There's good Russian food but the place overheats even in winter.

VSK Bistro (Sovetskaya ul 40; meals R40-100, coffee R9; ☯ 9am-11pm) Cheap but tidy cafeteria chain with bliny (R7 to R29), fresh bread, cakes and light meals. Is that Marilyn Monroe? Second branch at ul Shchetinkina 22.

Getting There & Away

AIR

Abakan's airport is 2km northwest of the city. **Vladivostok Airlines** (www.vladavia.ru) links Moscow (R8350) and Vladivostok (R7920) via Abakan with connections including Barnaul (R1710, Tuesday and Sunday) and Tomsk (R1530, Monday and Thursday). There's also a Thursday hop to Kyzyl (R1690). Buy tickets from the **Aviakassa** (☎ 38363; ul Chertygasheva 104; ☯ 8am-7pm Mon-Fri, to 6pm Sat & Sun).

BUS

From the **bus station** (ul Shevchenko) several day and night buses serve Krasnoyarsk (R215, 6½ to nine hours) via Divnogorsk. Others run frequently to Sayanogorsk (R55, 1¼ hours), eight times daily to Shushenskoe (R50, 1¾ hours), five daily to Yermakovskoe (R77, two hours), hourly to Abaza (R100 to R130, 3½ hours) via Askiz and to Kuragino (R56, 2½ hours) at 1.40pm, 3.20pm and 5.30pm.

Road transport for Tuva leaves from the **Mezhgorod Taxi Booth** (☎ 37888) outside the train station. For Kyzyl, snail-paced, wheezing buses (R280, nine to 11 hours) depart at 7.30am, noon and 7pm daily. Shared taxis ask between R600 and R800 per seat and will collect you from your hotel if you book ahead. No extra charge. To Ak-Dovurak there are no buses and shared taxis are rare.

TRAIN

To Krasnoyarsk, overnight train 124 (R696, 10½ hours) is the best of three alternatives. Train 695 to Novokuznetsk (R504, 10 hours) is handy if you're heading to Altai. The daily *Khakassia* to Moscow's Yaroslavsky vokzal (R3800, 73 hours) runs via Novosibirsk (24 hours) and Yekaterinburg (46 hours).

Getting Around

Bus 15 and trolleybus 3 run from the airport to central ul Shchetinkina. Passing near the train station frequently is bus 11 that heads east to TsUM then up ul Shchetinkina and pr Druzhba Narodov to the cathedral,

---

IN THE MARTYANOV MUSEUM   *Mark Elliott*

'What are you doing here?' gasped Marina. Guard-guide to the 'Minusinsk Life' room, she blankly refused to illuminate the room's darkened exhibits. 'Have you seen the Polish diaspora room? No? Of course not – you're going the wrong way!' Unable to defeat her Russian tirade I dutifully retreated. Elsewhere I examined long-nosed Tashtyk death masks, peeped in a Khakass *ail* and passed cursorily through that requisite Polish room. Finally I dared to return…the 'correct' way. Marina had shed any signs of her previous prickliness. Proudly she now unveiled case after unexotic case of consumer products manufactured in Minusinsk's factories. 'Those biscuits…OUR biscuits, they're…MMMmmm. And our jams. So much fruit – look there. You see. We even TIN the fruits too! Oh we have everything here! You can't imagine.' She extolled the remarkable virtues of Minusinsk yogurt. She swooned over dried milk powder. Then she stunned me with the revelation that the town had not one but TWO mineral water producers. Half bursting with suppressed laughter, half genuinely moved by her heartfelt enthusiasm, I wanted to hug her. What love, what dogmatic energy, what a perfect Siberian experience.

looping back via Mikro-Rayon 4 Market. Bus 10 also passes the train station but adds a loop via ul Marshala Zhukova (beyond the bus station) and pr Lenina before heading up ul Shchetinkina and pr Druzhby Narodov to Mikro-Rayon 4 Market, returning via the cathedral.

AROUND ABAKAN
Minusinsk Минусинск
☎ 39132 / pop 75,000 / ☉ Moscow +4hr

Minusinsk's scattering of partly derelict 18th- and 19th-century buildings offers more architectural interest than Abakan, and its riverside houses can look picturesque when very selectively photographed. The old section is 25km east of Abakan across the protoka Minusinskaya waterway from new-town Minusinsk's domineering concrete blandness. Jump off buses 120 or 10 beside the elegant 1803 **Saviour's Cathedral** (Spasskoe sobor; ul Komsomolskaya 10) and cross the square to find the excellent **Martyanov Museum** (☎ 20752; ul Martyanova 6; admission R50; ☉ 10am-6pm Wed-Sun). Over a century old, highlights include splendid archaeological and cultural exhibits, and the preserved little library in which Lenin occasionally studied while genteelly exiled at Shushenskoe. The museum's gift shop sells town maps.

One block along ul Lenina then two blocks northeast up ul Kravchenko is overgrown pl Lenina, dotted with crumbling mansions including the gutted **Vilner Palace** (ul Oktyabrskaya 65) with maudlin echoes of former grandeur. A block southwest, the complex of wooden buildings where Lenin was a regular guest (1897–1900) is now a **museum** (ul Oktyabrskaya 73; admission R25; ☉ 10am-1pm & 2-5pm Tue-Sun).

The award-winning 1882 **Drama Theatre** (ul Podinskaya 75) is a block northwest of the cathedral, hidden behind an old factory.

SLEEPING & EATING
Hotel Amyl (☎ 51026; ul Lenina 74; dm/s/tw R200/310/560, d with bathroom R740) This old house-hotel, half a block southeast of the Martyanov Museum, has faint hints of style. Most rooms are very basic but the R740 lux doubles are quite inviting.

Hotel Severnoe Siyane (☎ 25906; ul Oborony 32; dm/s/tw R280/350/560) Clean, basic rooms sharing good clean showers (R15 extra) hidden

within an unlikely apartment block five blocks northeast of the theatre.

Kafe Sibir (☎ 21668; ul Lenina 97; meals R35-60, beer R16, tea R3) Unlovely but the only old-town choice. Enter from ul Kravchenko.

GETTING THERE & AROUND
The easy way from Abakan bus station is by big bus 120 (R12, 40 minutes) direct to old-town Minusinsk. But *marshrutky* are faster and much more frequent to new Minusinsk (R15, 25 minutes), where you jump off at the last stop and switch to Minusinsk city bus 10 for the old town. Returning buses are rare after 6.30pm.

Salbyk Салбык
This Stonehenge-sized remnant of a 'royal' *kurgan* is Siberia's most impressive ring of **standing stones**. Excavated in 1956, it's in open fields, 5.6km down unsurfaced tracks south of km38 on the Chernogorsk–Sorsk road. About 2km before Salbyk notice the large, grassy dome of the unexcavated **'Princess' kurgan** which it once resembled. Taxis from Abakan want at least R500 return. Bring buckets of mosquito repellent.

Kuragino & the Vissarion Villages
Курагино
☎ 39136 / ☉ Moscow +4hr

The pleasant market town of **Kuragino** has an eccentric new church but little else to see unless you're interested in Vissarion (see the boxed text, p542). If so, start by contacting the religion's **Info Tsentr** (☎ 23594; www.vissarion.ru; ☉ 8.30am-noon & 1-7pm), a R30 taxi ride from central Kuragino – ask for Motorskoe Obshchizhitye. **Petropavlovka** village, 83km east of Kuragino, is the most accessible Vissarion village with a particularly attractive wooden church. Considerably further east is the utterly isolated **City of the Sun** where Vissarion and his apostles are building their 'new Jerusalem' above beautiful Lake Tiberkul. Entry is by invitation only, and pilgrim jeeps from Cheremshanka to the trailhead (whence you trek the last four hours on foot) generally only run on Sunday so expect to stay a while.

A block from Kuragino bus station, the basic **Hotel Tuba** (ul Partizanskaya 108; s/tw R420/650) has private indoor toilets in a few river-facing rooms. Vissarion villagers in Petropavlovka are often happy to welcome

SIBERIA

VISSARION – MESSIAH OF SIBERIA

Perceiving modern society to be on a destructive collision course with nature, the 30,000-strong Church of the Last Testament follows an ecologically based philosophy for clean living. It was formulated by Vissarion, the 'teacher', who many of his euphoric followers believe to be a second Jesus. He realised his divinity in 1991 and even dresses like a Hollywood Christ. But he was born Sergei Torop and is a former traffic cop from Krasnodar.

Settled in remote, beautiful but harsh Siberian countryside villages, Vissarionites are mostly vegans growing their own food and espousing an eventual goal of independence from the global energy and financial systems. Nonetheless, the community has its own computers, TV- and recording-studios, and doctors from Western, herbal and oriental traditions. Tobacco and alcohol are considered vices, and a woman's place is seen very traditionally as homemaker and loyal supporter for her husband. Horse carts are preferred over polluting tractors, and low-technology agriculture is encouraged both as a meditation and for its ecological sustainability.

The Church calendar's year 1 was 1961 (year of Torop/Vissarion's birth) and 14 January (his birthday) is the Vissarion Christmas. However, the best time to visit Petropavlovka is during the 18 August summer festival.

Devotees continue heading to Siberia to be close to this mysterious messiah, and almost all seem radiantly happy…unlike the families they left behind.

and accommodate guests, feed you great vegetarian food and discuss plenty of interesting philosophy (in Russian, naturally).

Competition is fierce for seats on the two buses each morning from Kuragino to Abakan via Minusinsk (R50, 2¾ hours). Share taxis are an hour faster. Bone-shattering buses from Kuragino to Cherem-shanka via Petropavlovka (R38, 2½ hours) depart at 4pm, returning 6am next day.

Abakan-bound overnight train 768 from Krasnoyarsk arrives at Kuragino's inconveniently located train station at 8.43am.

Shushenskoe Шушенское

☎ 39139 / pop 20,000 / ⊗ Moscow +4hr

As every good Soviet knows, Shushenskoe played host to Lenin for three years of (relatively comfortable) exile. But fewer of them know that in 1898 the young atheist was married in Shushenskoe's **Peter & Paul Church** (ul Novaya; ⊗ 10am-3pm), much to his later embarrassment.

For Lenin's 1970 birth centennial a two-block area of the village centre was reconstructed to look as it had in 1870. These well-kept 'old' Siberian houses now form the **Lenin Memorial Museum** (ul Novaya 1; admission R35, photography/video R20/50; ⊗ 9am-5pm). Many are convincingly furnished, and in summer costumed craftsmen sit around carving spoons. It's gently interesting, but as all trips are guided (in Russian unless you pay R200 extra for a translator) the visit

is somewhat slow and you're locked into spending over an hour seeing everything. At the entrance, a gift shop sells good town maps and a guide to Lenin-related sites in Siberia.

Behind the fenced museum area, but with no direct access from it, a pink **Lenin head** perches on a disproportionately tall plinth. Along ul Pushkina towards the hotel from there is a **sculpture garden** dotted with troll-like figures, and beyond the cinema is a striking mother-and-dove **memorial statue**.

The **post office** (ul Polukoltsevaya 5; ⊗ 9am-1pm & 2-6pm Mon-Fri, 10am-2pm Sat) offers Internet and telephone connection.

Half-hearted restoration continues at **Hotel Turist** (☎ 32841; fax 32941; ul Pushkina 1; upper floors s/tw/tr R290/580/870, 2nd fl s/tw R575/1150), but many rooms remain worn and rather musty. Prices aren't unreasonable given the private bathrooms, though the basic showers tend to flood the toilet floor. Better 2nd-floor rooms are haphazardly redecorated and somewhat more comfy but retain a Soviet soul. There's also ultrasimple summer-only accommodation in old huts at **Turbaza Iskra** (☎ 32151; dm R150), across the river by a footbridge from the Lenin head.

With dark-wooden hunters' décor and great prices, **Medved** (☎ 31 261; ul Pervomayskaya 50; meals R75-160, wine R15-54 per glass; ⊗ 11.30am-3pm & 9pm-4am) is Shushenskoe's most ap-

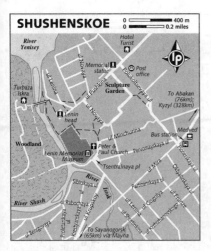

SHUSHENSKOE

0 ———— 400 m
0 ———— 0.2 miles

out. **Sayanogorsk Online** (http://city.sayan.ru/info /map, in Russian) has a basic city map.

Hotel Meridian (☎ 62460; ul Lenina, M/R Sovetsky 40; apt s/d R820/1600) offers large, well-equipped apartments; great value with breakfast included. Behind is a bright cafeteria-style *kofeynya* (espresso R33) and an excellent **restaurant** (☎ 62466; meals R110-250, cover R50-120 evenings; ⏰ noon-2am) which, despite its somewhat Soviet ambience, serves imaginative meals including vegetarian options. For great budget accommodation in a lovely rural valley take a R140 taxi ride to Zharki or Babik.

Zharki Resort (☎ 42378; fax 73811; s Mon-Thu/ Fri-Sun from R250/450) is a former sanatorium 3.5km east of the Maynskaya Dam (18km from Sayanogorsk). The main building *(glavny korpus)* has freshly renovated rooms with showers and toilets shared between pairs of rooms. Rooms in other buildings have private facilities from R600 for a single, R900 for a twin. With chunky beams and wagon-wheel décor the excellent **café-restaurant** (breakfasts R35-80, meals R140-350; ⏰ 8.30am-1am) offers a range of garlic-enriched dishes at very fair prices. Try the trout or the *otbivnaya po-ministersky* (cheesy-pork). In winter, five daily shuttles (R20, 8km) run to the lower Gladenkaya cable car.

Babik Motel (☎ 42701; dm R150) is 2.6km east of Zharki by road but only a 20-minute walk if you head across the boggy fields. Its gloriously lonely riverside position will soon be somewhat diminished as a big ski hotel nears completion nearby. Nonetheless, the motel offers a lovely, budget getaway, with the bonus of strolls in its impressive mountain-sided valley. Accommodation is in simple six-bedded units with shower. However, the toilets are outside unless you pay the R60 supplement for the honour of an in-room chemical portable loo.

Sayanogorsk's bus station, 1km south of the Hotel Meridian, has services to Abakan (R55, 1½ to 2¼ hours, twice hourly), Shushenskoe (R50.50, two hours) at 7.20am, 11.10am and 5.40pm, and Askiz (R72, 2½ hours) at 7.10am and 3.30pm. The latter, via Beya, passes through some archetypal Siberian villages and follows a lovely foothill ridge with wide views over the plains below.

pealing café. It's just 100m from the bus station.

Buses serve Abakan (R50, 1¾ hours, eight daily), Krasnoyarsk (R300, 10½ hours) morning and evening, Kyzyl (R239, eight hours) at 9am and Sayanogorsk (R50, two hours) departing 5.30am, 9.20am and 3.45pm. Ice-cream-stand attendants in the bus station operate a small makeshift baggage room (R2 per hour).

Sayanogorsk Саяногорск

☎ 39042 / pop 57,000 / ⏰ Moscow +4hr

The vast Khakassian grasslands slam into the forested Sayan Mountains at Sayanogorsk. The city is just a huddle of concrete towers but within 30km lie the modern ski resort of **Gladenkaya** (www.sky -gladenkaya.ru, in Russian; ⏰ Nov-Apr), pleasant valley getaways at Zharki and Babik, and the very impressive Sayano-Shushenskaya Dam (p544).

Sberbank (ul Lenina; ⏰ 9am-1pm & 2-5.30pm Mon-Fri) cashes travellers cheques for US$5 commission. **Sayan Tour Service** (M/R Sovetsky 41), behind the Hotel Meridian, and **Gladenkaya Agency** (☎ 26642; fax 73811; gladenkaya@sayan.rusal .ru; M/R Sovetsky 38) can book accommodation at Zharki, Babik or Gladenkaya. They also arrange ski packages and offer tours of the **marble factory** and **Sayano-Shushenskaya Dam** given two working-days' notice to prepare the necessary permits.

Central Sayanogorsk addresses confusingly bear no relationship to the road lay-

SIBERIA

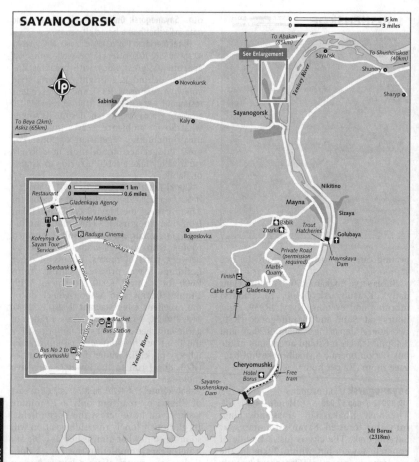

Around Sayanogorsk

SAYANO-SHUSHENSKAYA DAM

САЯНО-ШУШЕНСКАЯ ГЕС

Beside a trout hatchery near the Zharki-Babik turning (15km south of Sayanogorsk) there are pleasant views of the steep-sided river valley from the unremarkable **Mayn-skaya Dam**.

The vastly more impressive **Sayano-Shushenskaya Dam**, Russia's biggest and the world's fourth in terms of energy production, is 15km further south. Privatised in 1993, it cunningly survived a recent rena-tionalisation battle with the Khakassian government by nominally 'relocating' it-self in Krasnoyarsk territory. No physical move was needed as the dam straddles the provincial border. To join by-appointment Russian-language tours of the dam's **turbine rooms** (☎ 71800; admission R300) you'll need cop-ies of your passport, visa and registration plus an invitation letter arranged by a local hotel or Sayanogorsk agency.

Taxis from Sayanogorsk charge R200 re-turn to the dam. Alternatively, Sayanogorsk city bus 2 (R4, 30 minutes, every 40 min-utes) runs as far as 'Tsentralny' in **Cheryo-mushki**, from where the free dam (GES) workers' tram (10 minutes, hourly on the half-hour) continues 4km to the dam. Al-ternatively, observe the dam distantly from the Cheryomushki bridge. Valley views are more photogenic from the main Mayna–Cheryomushki road at around km29, where you'll catch several glimpses of beautiful **Mt Borus** (2318m).

Above the main road in Cheryomushki, **Hotel Borus** (☎ 31919; hotel-borus@yandex.ru; s/tw/ste/apt R1500/2500/3500/10,000) is fairly stylish but rooms are slightly small and not as luxurious as the extensive advertising suggests. Some English is spoken.

The enormous reservoir that the dam created is surrounded by largely untouched wilderness, now constituting the **Sayano-Shushensky Biosphere Reserve**. Sightings of its estimated 30 snow leopards are exceedingly rare, though ibex are easier to spot. Abakan Tours (p538) in Abakan can help you organise a visit and operates a three-day boat ride right down the lake to Chaa Khol in Tuva.

USINSKY TRAKT
УСИНСКИЙ ТРАКТ

First built in 1910, the Usinsky Trakt is the main road between Minusinsk and Kyzyl in Tuva. It skirts the modest, historical township of **Yermakovskoe** and passes the little fruit-growing villages of **Grigorevka** and **Chyornaya Recha** before climbing into pretty birch-wood foothills. After a tea stop in **Tanzybey** (km560) the route climbs more steeply. A truly magnificent view of the crazy, rough-cut Ergaki Mountains knocks you breathless just before km598. Powerful views continue to km601 and resume between km609 and km612. A **roadside cross** (km603–4) marks the spot where hero-of-Chechnya and former Krasnoyarsk governor Alexander Lebed died in 2002 when his helicopter snagged the power lines. Walk 1.5km up the steep track towards the radar station above for fabulous views from the ridge.

As the trakt descends, the scenery morphs through wooded river valleys into Tuva's panoramic roller-coaster grasslands. **Turan**, an attractive village of old wooden homes, has a cute little **museum** (ul Druzhby 44). The big-sky side road barrelling west off the trakt towards Arzhaan passes through Tuva's **Valley of the Kings**. Four pancake-shaped burial mounds here look like mere lumps in the grassland but in 2002 archaeologists found some magnificent artefacts from the 7th century BC within. The dig is featured in Kyzyl's Aldan Maadyr National Museum (p549).

Ergaki Mountains Хребет Ергаки

Rising in magnificent horned peaks above forests and glistening lakes, roadless Ergaki is one of the most beautiful regions in all of Siberia. If you want more than the glimpses from the Usinsky Trakt, consider making a two-day trek to the classic viewpoint above **Lake Svetloe**. Start from Turbaza Yermak where there's guarded parking, a left-luggage service and tent and sleeping-bag rental. A popular forest path follows the stream, dodging fallen trees and swampy patches, flower-filled meadows and fields of eccentric rocks. Wonderful. A guide is sometimes available to show you the way (R350) – recommended, as getting lost is easy. Bring all food supplies. For many mountaineering ideas and some beautiful photos see Russian websites http://ergaki.krasu.ru/gallery.jsp and www.nkz.tourism.ru/climb/ergak/.

Sleeping

Turbaza Yermak (☎ 39138-21762; Tushanchik Most, km622/445) rents one bare room (R500) with a heating stove and a wooden bench-bed big enough for five. The small, new **Tarmazakovski Most Turbaza** (☎ 3912-231 796; km614.5) is used predominantly as a climbing base. There's a further **Baza Otdykha Ergaki** (☎ 39022-56923; www.ergaki.com, in Russian; km605) near Lake Oyskoe, with several multibedded huts from R600 to R1400. All the above are utterly isolated without associated village or shop. Bring food and emergency camping gear. If you're stuck in Yermakovskoe, the friendly **Hotel Oya** (☎ 39138-21274; ul Lenina 7; dm/tw R150/400), on the central square, is perfectly survivable.

Getting There & Away

Buses run from Abakan and Shushenskoe to Yermakovskoe, and from Kyzyl to Arzhaan via Turan, but for the central, spectacular mountain passes the only public transport is on Abakan–Kyzyl buses and shared taxis. The latter are well worth the extra cash and will usually stop for photos if politely requested.

SOUTHWEST KHAKASSIA
Askiz Аскиз

☎ 39045 / pop 24,000 / ⌚ Moscow +4hr

Culturally Askiz is the most Khakass town of Khakassia. However, there's little to

SIBERIA

see and it's really only interesting during Tun Payran (Pasture-Opening Festival). The event features wrestling, horse racing, archery and much merriment. It's held in June but dates are infamously changeable.

About 30km west, appealing **Camp Kug** (Akhtas Yurt Camp; beds US$35) offers comfy *ail* accommodation in a lovely rural setting, close to a series of shamanic sites and sacred bluffs. At the far western end of very quaint Kazanovka village, turn right immediately after crossing the river bridge. Just after you've turned you should see a sign 'Музей' which will confirm you're on the right track. Follow the bumpy track for 4km, bearing right at the only fork. The *aily* have washbasins and chemical toilets plus there are shared hot showers. Khakass cultural shows are performed when tour groups stay. Book ahead through Sayan Ring Travel (p553) in Krasnoyarsk. The camp is deserted when no guests have booked but should you be passing without a reservation you could try calling **Viktoria Kulimeyevna** (☎ 94531; Kazanovka village) who keeps the keys.

Towards Western Tuva

Between Askiz and the iron-ore mining town of **Abaza** are hundreds of ancient **standing stones**, notably at km109/307, where remarkable concentrations stand right beside the A161. If you're not squeamish, visit the roadside **Maral Deer Farm** (admission R35; km163/253) in May when you can watch the cutting of the animals' antlers, valued for their aphrodisiac properties.

Abaza's passable, shared-facility **Hotel Kedr** (☎ 39047-29870; ul Parkovaya 2a) has a pleasant restaurant. Alternatively, hidden within the trees off the Ak-Dovurak road are two decent summer places for those with their own transport; prices for both include full board and *banya*. **Kubayka Camp** (☎ 39022-54855; dm/tw US$35/80) has 10 riverside log houses at a pretty spot 1km off the main road from Kubayka hamlet. Toilets are outside. Abaza tour agency **Rodnik** (☎ 39047-23281; www.rodnikltd.ru, in Russian; ul Filatova 8-1) runs the ecofriendly **Snow Leopard Camp** (Turbaza Snezhny Bars; tw R2120-2700, tr R2880-3710) in thick, tick-free woodland 1.6km west of km296/120. A few R900 single-bed lofts are also available. English-speaking guides can organise hikes and horse treks taking

you to associated hunting lodges and tent camps in the lake-dotted mountains above. In Abaza call ☎ 23893 for a taxi.

TUVA ТУВА

Independent before WWII, fascinating Tuva (Тыва in Tuvan) is culturally similar to neighbouring Mongolia but has an international cult following all of its own. Philatelists remember Tannu Tuva's (opposite) curiously shaped 1930s postage stamps. World-music aficionados are mesmerised by self-harmonising Tuvan throat-singers. And millions of armchair travellers read Ralph Leighton's *Tuva or Bust!*, a non-travel book telling how irrepressible Nobel Prize–winning physicist Richard Feynman failed to reach Soviet-era Kyzyl despite years of trying. Now that visitors are finally allowed in, Leighton's **Friends of Tuva** (www.fotuva.org) organisation keeps up the inspirational work with an unsurpassed collection of Tuvan resources on its website. With forests, mountains, lakes and vast undulating waves of beautiful, barely populated steppe, Tuva's a place you'll long remember.

History

Controlled from the 6th century by a succession of Turkic empires, in the 1750s Tuva became an outpost of China, against whose rule the much-celebrated Aldan Maadyr (60 Martyrs) rebelled in 1885. Tibetan Buddhism took root during the 19th century, coexisting with older shamanist nature-based beliefs; by the late 1920s one man in 15 in Tuva was a lama.

With the Chinese distracted by a revolution in 1911, Russia stirred up a separatist movement and took Tuva 'under protection' in 1914. The effects of Russia's October Revolution took two years to reach Tuva, climaxing in 1921 when the region was a last bolt hole of the retreating White Russians. They were swiftly ejected into Mongolia by 'Red Partisans', to whom you'll see monuments in Kyzyl and Bay Dagh. Tuva's prize was renewed, if nominal, independence as the Tuvan Agrarian Republic (Tyva Arat Respublik, TAR), better known to philatelists as Tannu Tuva. However, to communist Russia's chagrin, Prime Minister Donduk's government dared to declare Buddhism the state religion and favoured reunification with Mongolia. Russia's riposte was to install a dependable communist, Solchak Toka, as prime minister, and, later, to force Tuvans to write their language in the fundamentally inappropriate Cyrillic alphabet, creating a cultural divide with Mongolia. Having 'voluntarily' helped Russia during WWII, Tuva's 'reward' was incorporation into the USSR. Russian immigration increased, Buddhism and shamanism were repressed and the seminomadic Tuvans were collectivised; many Tuvans slaughtered their animals in preference to handing them over.

Today, some people have reverted to traditional pastoralism but, unlike in neighbouring Mongolia, yurt camps are often hidden away in the remoter valleys, largely because gangs of ruthless rustlers have scared herders off the most accessible grasslands. Buddhist-shamanist beliefs survived the oppressions rather better. Even avowed atheists still revere local *arzhaan* (sacred springs), offer food to fire spirits and tie prayer ribbons to cairns and holy trees using the colours of the national flag: blue for sky, yellow for Buddhism and white for purity and happiness.

Tuvan Culture

Of the republic's 310,000 people, about two-thirds are ethnic Tuvans; Buddhist-shamanist by religion, Mongolian by cultural heritage, and Turkic by language. Confusingly in Tuvan *ekii* is 'hello' while *eki* is 'good'. Tuvan Cyrillic has a range of exotic extra vowels and most place names have different Russian and Tuvan variants.

Colourful *khuresh* is a form of Tuvan wrestling similar to Japanese sumo but without the ring, the formality or the huge bellies. Multiple heats run simultaneously, each judged by a pair of referees, flamboyantly dressed in national costume. They'll occasionally slap the posteriors of fighters who seem not to be making sufficient effort. Tuvans also love Mongolian-style long-distance horse races but are most widely famed for their *khöömei* throat-singers. *Khöömei* is both a general term and the name of a specific style in which low and whistling tones, all from a single throat, somehow harmonise with one another. The troll-like *kargyraa* style sounds like singing through a prolonged burp. *Sygyt* is reminiscent of a wine glass being rung by a wet finger: quaintly odd if you hear a recording but truly astonishing when you hear it coming out of a human mouth. Accompanying instruments often include a jew's-harp, a bowed two-stringed *igil* or a three-stringed *doshpular* (Tuvan banjo).

Ironically, it is often easier to get CDs of Tuvan music in the West than in Tuva itself. The most interesting groups are all-star Chirgilchin, inventive Alash and Kaigal-ool's Huun Huur Tu (literally, 'Sun Propeller'). Better-known Kongar-ol Ondar has collaborated with Frank Zappa and worked on the soundtrack for the Oscar-nominated film *Genghis Blues*. You can listen to and download various *khöömei* gems from slow-loading www.tarbagan.com.

Festivals

Tuva's most dramatic festival is **Naadym**, usually held in mid-August. Vastly less touristy than the Mongolian equivalent, Naadym is your best chance to hear *khöömei* concerts, watch horse races and to see if Russia's sumo champion Mongush 'elephant' Ayas (www.sumo.boom.ru/eng/sumotori_m.html) wins the *khuresh* wrestling as usual. Similar elements accompany the **International Khöömei Symposium** (held roughly every three years) and the brilliant but as yet one-off **Dembildey festival**. More significant for local families is **Shagaa**, Tuvan New Year (February), with *sangalyr* purification ceremonies, gift giving and temple rituals.

Tuvan Food

Almost every rural household keeps a vat of *khoitpak* (fermenting sour milk), which tastes like ginger beer with a sediment of finely chopped brie. *Khoitpak* is drunk as is or distilled into alcoholic *araka*. Roast *dalgan* (a cereal, similar to Altai's bran-rich *talkan*) can be added to your salted milky tea, or eaten with *oreme* (sour cream). Local cheeses include stringy *byshtag* and rock-hard Kazakh-style *kurut* balls.

Tuvans are said to have learnt from Chinggis Khaan a special way to kill their sheep without wasting any of the animal's blood. Collected with miscellaneous offal in a handy intestine, this blood makes up the local delicacy, *han* sausage. You may be less than disappointed to find that restaurants rarely serve it – not that there are many restaurants anyway! Beyond Kyzyl, truck stops, *pelmeni* steamers and the temperamental village *stolovaya* are your best hopes for a hot meal unless you're staying with families. Kyzyl residents take their own supplies when travelling to the provinces.

Dangers & Annoyances

Meeting locals is the key to experiencing Tuva but be aware that many friendly Tuvans react badly to alcohol, becoming disproportionately aggressive, even amongst friends. A proliferation of knives and other weapons doesn't help. Chadan in Western Tuva is particularly notorious and even in tiny, apparently peaceful villages, steer well clear of drunks, travel with trusted, sober Tuvans and avoid drinking vodka with local 'friends'. Be streetwise and consider going to bed early!

KYZYL КЫЗЫЛ

☎ 39422 / pop 95,000 / ⏰ Moscow +4hr

The most memorable attractions in Kyzyl are ephemeral – meeting shamans, hearing throat-singing or watching a wrestling competition. Tuva's capital may grandly claim

to be the 'centre of Asia', but architecturally it's mostly disappointing Soviet-era concrete. Fortunately, the central area's streets are pleasantly tree lined. From the riverside are quietly picturesque views across to a tiny Buddhist shrine on the unpopulated north bank. Behind that the steppe is backed by a horizon of arid, low mountains.

The town was founded in 1914 as Belotsarsk (White Tsarville). Whether to be pedantic or humorously ironic, the Soviet regime changed the name to Kyzyl, a Tuvan word which simply means 'red'.

Orientation

The spread-out street grid is centred around the theatre with ul Kochetova as the main commercial thoroughfare. Maps are very hard to find but are sometimes stocked in **Delovye Melochi Bookshop** (basement, Krasnoarmeyskaya ul 100; ⏰ 9am-6pm Mon-Fri, 10am-3pm Sat), which also sells decent Russian-language guides to Tuva (R100). Alternatively, buy maps mail-order from the USA through **Tuva Trader** (www.scs-intl.com/trader/) for US$8 plus postage.

Information

Tuvan visa registration is required and sometimes checked elsewhere in the republic. Kyzyl hotels will do this, or visit **PVS** (Pasportno-Vizovaya Sluzhba; ul Lenina 64; ⏰ 9am-1pm & 2-6pm Tue-Fri), west entrance, window No 2.

Alash Travel (☎ 34826; www.alash-travel.narod.ru, in Russian; ul Kochetova 60/12) Offers full-scale rafting and climbing expeditions, and can arrange horse-back trips between Tuva and Altai. English spoken by some guides but not in the office.

Aldar Tamdyn (☎ 54176; tamdyn@rambler.ru) Instrument-maker and member of group Chirgilchin. He speaks OK English and can help you contact local musicians when he's not on tour.

Aylana Irguit (☎ 13796 home, 34790 work; www .tyvantranslator.com; boraldai@hotmail.com) Charming translator (US$15–40 per hour) with perfect English and many local contacts.

EcoTuva (☎ 10527, 14579; www.ecotuva.ru; ul Kochetova 100/17) Offers horse-back trips with throat-singing and yurt-erections organised by experienced English-speaking agent Rada. Will be moving eventually to Apt 32a, top floor, ul Lenina 43, central rear door.

Post office (ul Kochetova 53; Internet per hr R60; ⏰ 8am-8pm Mon-Fri, to noon Sat) Internet room and telephone office attached. For parcels use entry at ul Druzhby 156a.

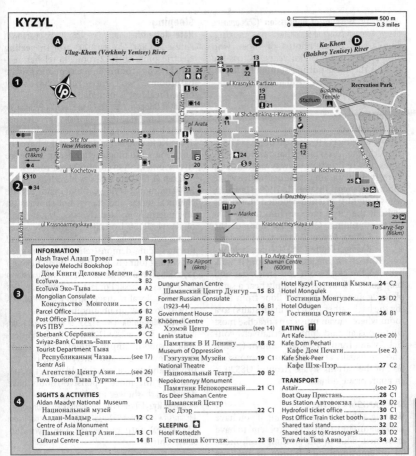

KYZYL

0   500 m
0   0.3 miles

Ulug-Khem (Verkhniy Yenisey) River

Ka-Khem (Bolshoy Yenisey) River

Recreation Park

Buddhist Temple

Stadium

Site for New Museum

Camp Ai (18km)

Market

To Airport (6km)

To Adyg-Eeren Shaman Centre (600m)

To Sarys-Sep (86km)

INFORMATION
Alash Travel Алаш Трэвел	**1** B2
Delovye Melochi Bookshop	
Дом Книги Деловые Мелочи	**2** B2
EcoTuva	**3** B2
EcoTuva Эко-Тыва	**4** A2
Mongolian Consulate	
Консульство Монголии	**5** C1
Parcel Office	**6** B2
Post Office Почтамт	**7** B2
PVS ПВУ	**8** A2
Sberbank Сбербанк	**9** C2
Sviyaz-Bank Свиязь-Банк	**10** A2
Tourist Department Тыва	
Республиканын Чазаа	(see 17)
Tsentr Asii	
Агентство Центр Азии	(see 26)
Tuva Tourism Тыва Туризм	**11** C1

SIGHTS & ACTIVITIES
Aldan Maadyr National Museum	
Национальный музей	
Алдан-Маадыр	**12** C2
Centre of Asia Monument	
Памятник Центр Азии	**13** C1
Cultural Centre	**14** B1

Dungur Shaman Centre	
Шаманский Центр Дунгур	**15** B3
Former Russian Consulate	
(1923-44)	**16** B1
Government House	**17** B2
Khöömei Centre	
Хээмэй Центр	(see 14)
Lenin statue	
Памятник В И Ленину	**18** B2
Museum of Oppression	
Гэгэзунэн Музейи	**19** B2
National Theatre	
Национальный Театр	**20** B2
Nepokorennyy Monument	
Памятник Непокоренный	**21** C1
Tos Deer Shaman Centre	
Шаманский Центр	
Тос Дээр	**22** C1

SLEEPING
Hotel Kottedzh	
Гостиница Коттэдж	**23** B1

Hotel Kyzyl Гостиница Кызыл	**24** C2
Hotel Mongulek	
Гостиница Монгулек	**25** D2
Hotel Odugen	
Гостиница Одугенж	**26** B1

EATING
Art Kafe	(see 20)
Kafe Dom Pechati	
Кафе Дом Печати	(see 2)
Kafe Shek-Peer	
Кафе Шэк-Пээр	**27** C2

TRANSPORT
Astair	(see 25)
Boat Quay Пристань	**28** C1
Bus Station Автовокзал	**29** D2
Hydrofoil ticket office	**30** C1
Post Office Train ticket booth	**31** B2
Shared taxi stand	**32** D2
Shared taxis to Krasnoyarsk	**33** D2
Tyva Avia Тыва Авиа	**34** A2

SIBERIA

Sberbank (ul Kochetova 34a; 8.30am-7pm Mon-Fri, 8.30-noon & 1-6pm Sat) Exchange counter and ATM inside.
Sviyaz-Bank (ul Kochetova 53; 9am-noon & 1-4pm Mon-Fri) Changes US dollars and euros.
Tourist Department (36436; Government House, ul Chuldum 18) Seems to have lost its former energy.
Tsentr Asii (/fax 32326; asiatur@tuva.ru; Hotel Odugen) Helpful, friendly agency that can arrange air tickets and vehicle transfers.

Sights
If you take a map of Europe, cut out Asia and balance the continent on a pin, the pinprick will be Kyzyl. Well, only if you've used the utterly obscure Gall's stereographic projection. However, that doesn't stop the town perpetuating the 'Centre of Asia' idea first posited

by a mysterious 19th-century English eccentric and still marked with a concrete globe-and-obelisk **centre-of-Asia monument** on the riverbank, at the end of Komsomolskaya ul.

Beyond the stuffed animals of the ramshackle **Aldan Maadyr National Museum** (30096; ul Lenina 7; admission US$2; 11am-5pm Tue-Sun) are some banknotes, stamps and photos from the 1930s independence period, a Todzha reindeer-herders' tepee (through dark glass in the WWII room) and some fine *kameny baba* (p531). Many more 6th- to 12th-century stone figures are outside in the back yard (via a padded door between the fish exhibits). A big, new museum building (ul Kochetova) has been built but technical problems currently prevent the collection from moving.

A tiny **Museum of Oppression** (Gööguzuneng muzeyi; Komsomolskaya ul 5; donation) has moving, dog-eared, copied photos of those who disappeared in the Stalin years. Across the grass is the chest-puffing statue of a **Nepok-orennyy** ('undefeated') Aldan Maadyr martyr in his pointy slippers.

Activities

TUVAN MUSIC

Throat-singing is Tuva's great draw, yet finding performances is rather haphazard. Sometimes they're listed on www.tyvantranslator .com. If not, try asking at the distinctive white concrete **National Theatre** (☎ 11566; ul Lenina 33), whose slightly oriental wooden flourishes make it the city's most architecturally distinctive building. On the 1st floor of the sizable **Cultural Centre** (ul Shchetinkina-i-Kravchenko 46), the **Khöömei Centre** (☎ 33424) can help arrange throat-singing lessons – to find it, walk between the cloakroom and snack bar and keep going. However, to simply hear a sample try going up to the 3rd floor from here (by the back rather than the main stairs) to a room where Tuvan musicians practise most afternoons around 2pm. Alternatively, contact Aylana Irguit or Aldar Tamdyn (p548), who can usually arrange a short demonstration of the various styles. Around US$20 is an appropriate donation.

SHAMANISM CENTRES

Visiting a shaman is fascinating if you have a translator and a tangible 'problem' to have examined. This might be a medical, mental or emotional purification or perhaps seeking 'luck' with your travels. Typical ceremony costs are in the R2000 to R3000 range. Less authentic 'shaman shows' are organised for tourist groups.

Riverfront totem poles and reception yurts make **Tos Deer Shaman Centre** (☎ 32 023; ul Krasnykh Partizan 18a; ☼ 8am-8pm) the most photogenic centre. If someone has stumped up the cash, there might be sunset ceremonies here but shamans are touchy about (unpaid) photography.

Adyg-Eeren Shaman Centre ('Bear's Spirit' Shaman Centre; ☎ 14483; ul Shevchenko 225-7; ☼ 8am-8pm) looks like a used-car lot but in one very ordinary room there is a stuffed bear and all the shamanic accoutrements. A third option is **Dungur Shaman Centre** ('Drum' Shaman Centre; ☎ 31909; Rabochaya ul 245; ☼ 8am-8pm).

Sleeping

Hotel Kottedzh (Gostiny Dvor; ☎ 30503; ul Krasnykh Partizan 38; s R700-1200, tw R1200-2000) In peeling electric pink, this 12-room hotel has reasonably cosy rooms and acceptable private bathrooms. Two cheaper rooms have toilet only. Breakfast is included.

Hotel Odugen (☎ 32518; ul Krasnykh Partizan 36; s R700-900, tw R1100-1800, ste R1800) The cheaper rooms here are slightly less comfortable than at the Kottedzh, but top-floor suites have sitting rooms and much better décor. There are river views from even-numbered rooms.

Camp Ai (Biy-Khem Yurta; s/tw R1265/1820; ☼ May-Sep) Traditional-style yurt tents with private chemical toilets and shared hot showers on a wonderfully isolated riverside 18km north of Kyzyl (R150 by taxi). Nearby are some minor petroglyphs. Shaman 'ceremonies' and throat-singing demonstrations are arranged for visiting tour groups. Book ahead through **Sayan Ring Travel** (☎ /fax 3912-522 481; www.gotosiberia .ru) in Krasnoyarsk. For last-minute vacancies try calling local manager **Artur** (☎ 38900). It's unwise to show up unannounced.

Hotel Mongulek (☎ 31253; ul Kochetova 1; dm R400-450, s R530, d R900-1100, tr R1200) Considerable cosmetic improvements have made the rooms bright and fairly fresh, but the private toilets are mostly old Soviet issue, and only the most expensive rooms have dowdy bath-shower units.

Hotel Kyzyl (☎ 11107; ul Tuvinskikh Dobrovoltsev 13; dm/s/tw with toilet R220/350/600, s/tw with bathroom & TV R450/800) Tatty but bearable and wonderfully central.

Eating

Most hotels have basic eateries while the **market** (ul Druzhby) has a range of fresh produce and is ringed by several cheap cafés and shashlyk grills.

Kafe Shek-Peer (☎ 13319; ul Druzhby 151; meals R90-140; ☼ 10am-10pm) Presentable café with a short menu of tasty dishes that include rice or potato garnish in the price. Wine available by vodka-sized glass.

Arlekina Kafe (☎ 10207; ul Kochetova 99; espressos R31, meals R100-230; ☼ 10am-11pm) Bright colours, aquariums and big-screen DVD make this family-friendly place an upbeat choice. The menu is extensive and the R100 lunch is filling if unexotic.

Art Kafe (☎ 14836; Theatre Bldg; meals R120-350) Neither arty nor a café, central Kyzyl's only real restaurant has affordable lunch menus, but R50 evening cover charges.

Kafe Dom Pechati (ul Krasnoarmeyskaya 100; meals R40-100; ☺ 11am-6pm) Unremarkable basement canteen reckoned by most locals to offer the best-value lunch in town.

Getting There & Away

Tyva Avia (☎ 12064; ul Bukhtueva 3; ☺ 9am-1pm & 2-5pm Mon-Sat) flies to Krasnoyarsk (R3210, four weekly), Novosibirsk (R3750, three weekly), Ust-Kut via Irkutsk (R3950, Saturday) and Abakan (R1150, Thursday). To Todzha (four weekly, weather permitting) it's R2050 by plane or R2800 by helicopter. **Astair** (Hotel Mongulek; ☺ 9am-6pm) plans to restart direct flights to Moscow.

For the lovely drive to Abakan, shared taxis (R600 to R800 per seat, 5½ hours) are well worth the difference over the grindingly slow, overbooked buses (R280, 10 hours), which depart from the bus station daily at 6.50am, 8pm and 9pm. Cars congregate behind Hotel Mongulek but if you book ahead through **Mezhgorod** (☎ 14343) they'll collect you from anywhere in town once almost full. Shared taxis/*marshrutky* are best for Chadan (R200/120), Ak-Dovurak (R350/230) and Saryg-Sep (R100/60) but these cannot usually be prebooked.

There's no railway but train tickets ex-Abakan are sold from the post office (special entrance on ul Chuldum).

Summer hydrofoils shoot along the Yenisey rapids up to Toora-Khem in Todzha (R870, 10 hours upstream, seven hours back) on alternate days. Prebook at the **hydrofoil ticket office** (☎ 11897; ul Tuvinskikh Dobrovoltsev; ☺ 9am-4pm) beside the quay. You'll need your passport. Window seats 19, 25 or 31 are best for views with least spray.

Getting Around

The airport is 7km southwest of the centre by bus 1A (R8). Almost all *marshrutka* routes use ul Kochetova. *Marshrutky* 1, 2, 6 and 10 pass the bus station.

AROUND KYZYL

The giant **Kadarchy herder statue** surveys the city from a bare hill, five-minutes' drive from Kyzyl's southernmost edge. Beyond, prayer rags photogenically deck a small roadside **spring** which is the closest such *arzhaan* to the capital. To get a taste for the steppe, con-

sider the relatively easy excursions to **Cheder** salt lake. Slightly more awkward to reach, **Lake Tuz Khol** is crowded with comically mud-blackened health-vacationers; its waters are so salty that you float Dead Sea–style. It's 20km off the main road down sandy, unsurfaced access tracks; taxis charge R650 return plus R100 per hour waiting time.

Following the Ka-Khem (Maly Yenisey) River southeast of Kyzyl, the steppe gives way to agricultural greenery around low-rise **Saryg-Sep,** beyond which an appallingly muddy road continues through woodland to the pretty Old Believers' village of **Erzhey.** Despite the extraordinary inaccessibility, there are several bungalow-hotels and hunting lodges en route and beyond. A good deal is at Bilbey (33km from Saryg-Sep) where the surprisingly pleasant **Turbaza Vasilyevka** (☎ 39432-22253; tw from R250) lies beside a curious cable-ferry in a flower-filled field.

FROM KYZYL TO ERZIN

The paved M54 offers a wonderfully varied scenic feast with archetypal Central Asian grassland, then parkland-style rolling woodlands after Balgazyn, thickening to pine forest beyond the two tiny cafés at **Shurmak.** Spot shamanic cairns and prayer-rag ticker tape on passes and herders' yurts in picturesque meadows. The landscape gets starkly drier descending past Samagaltay and **Bay Dagh,** a former camel-breeding centre where memorials commemorate the last scuffles of the civil war in 1921. Between km1023 and km1024, radar posts look down on the junction of a smooth, scenic but unpaved road to Mören, 18km away, passing near holy mountain **Ak-Khayyrakan.** EcoTuva (p548) can show you its revered spring (whose seasonal flow is aided each summer by multiple shamanic ceremonies) and arrange unforgettable yurt-stays with nomadic cattle herders in the glorious valleys beyond.

The asphalt main road ends at **Erzin,** which has a clean, basic, mural-brightened **hotel** (ul Komsomolskaya 31) near the bus stand and a photogenic competitor for the world's smallest **Buddhist temple** (ul Komsomolskaya 22) competition.

Sandy tracks continue 20km south past Dali-esque rocky outcrops to Lake Tore-Khol, a popular local picnic spot. Although at the edge of the desert zone, herded horses trotting through the shallows give the area a slight feel of the Camargue in France. Across the water is Mongolia but the border is closed to foreigners.

TODZHA (TODZHU)
ТОДЖА (ТОДЖУ)

'If you haven't seen Todzhu you haven't seen Tuva' sighs a popular local saying. Most Tuvans haven't. Mainly lake-dappled forest, this roadless northeastern lobe of the republic has a distinctly different culture, traditionally based on reindeer herding. Above unnavigable rapids on the Biy-Khem (Bolshoy Yenisey) River, salmon-like *taimen* grow to 15kg (even 30kg by some reports), safe from any fisherman unable to fork out nearly US$10,000 for helicopter rental.

Without time and extensive planning casual visitors are limited to the area around Toora-Khem village, accessible from Kyzyl by air or splashing up the beautiful Biy-Khem (Bolshoy Yenisey) River by somewhat claustrophobic hydrofoil. Register immediately with the police upon arrival.

Some 40-minutes' drive down a jeep track from Toora-Khem, the area's main attraction is serene, forest-edged Lake Azas, famed for its water lilies. Beautifully positioned at the lakeside is the basic, astonishingly isolated **Azas Turbaza** (beds R100; ☺ mid-Jun–mid-Sep). Well before leaving Kyzyl ask an agency to warn the manager of your arrival date so he can buy food and pick you up from the boat dock or airfield. At Azas you can row on the lake, walk to smaller **Noghaan Khol** and imagine that the bears in the woods are only aural mirages.

WESTERN TUVA ЗАПАДНАЯ ТУВА

The route looping round to Abakan from Tuva via Askiz is scenically varied, often beautiful and mesmerisingly vast in scale, though the Chinggis Khaan stone near Ak-Dovurak is the only real 'sight'. Independent travellers should be aware of Western Tuva's fearsome reputation for wild lawlessness and unprovoked knife attacks. Even other Tuvans are nervous about travelling without a truly local companion. Sayan Ring tours (opposite) come this way.

At km107, the grassland route from Kyzyl passes dramatic **Mt Khayyrakan**, a spiky ridge blessed by the Dalai Lama in 1992. **Chadan** town (Chadaana) is attractively dotted with wooden cottages and there's an appealing little **museum** (ul Lenina 33; ☺ 9am-4pm Mon-Fri), but the **guesthouse** (aalchylar bazhyngy; ul Pobedy 1) closed in 2003. Stay off those mean streets at night.

Chadan is most famous as Tuva's former spiritual centre. However, the once-great **Ustuu Khuree temple** was utterly devastated in the Soviet era. Only sad, chunky stumps of mud wall now remain, lost in peaceful woodlands some 6km south of Chadan and accessed via tracks off the road to Bazhin-Alaak. Stalled repairs are due to restart in the coming years, and to fund the reconstruction a large annual **music festival** (www .ustuhure.ru) is held on the grounds in late June/early July, embracing everything from *khöömei* to grunge rock. Participants camp in tents and yurts.

From **Khandagayty**, where the Mongolian border remains closed to foreigners, a glorious but notoriously tough truck track runs to Kosh-Agach in Altai via Mugur-Aksy, passing high, bald, glacier-topped **Mt Mongun-Tayga** (3976m). Bring food, a reliable guide, ample extra fuel and spare parts if you plan a truck or jeep convoy. With many deep fords, this route is impassable after rain. It's much more pleasant on horseback; Alash Travel in Kyzyl can help you organise horses. In ideal conditions it's possible to make the trip by mountain bike in around a week but getting lost is dangerously easy. For a mountaineering report see www.mountain.ru/eng/adventure /2004/na_grani/.

Ak-Dovurak Ак-Довурак

☎ 39441 / pop 13,300 / ☺ Moscow +4hr

The world's largest open-pit asbestos mine dominates Ak-Dovurak, Tuva's unlovable second city. Around 10km away, the only 'sight' is the **Chinggis Khaan Stone**, a remarkably well preserved moustachioed stone idol (*kameny baba* in Russian or *kizhigozher* in Tuvan). To find it, cross the Shui River to marginally nicer **Kyzyl-Mazhalik** then drive 8km towards Ayangalty. About 500m after passing the turn-off to tiny Bizhiktigh Haya village, the stone stands all alone in a field, 400m west of the road. Ak-Dovurak taxis want R200 return. Another scenic excursion heads 38km west to Teeli – where there's a very basic hotel, **Chonar Dash** (☎ 24222, 21192; ul Lenina 25, Komsomolskaya ul 121) – and continues to the soapstone-carving village of Kyzyl-Dag. Personal security is a worry.

Ak-Dovurak's **Hotel MPP ZhKKh** (☎ 1255; ul Tsentralnaya 6; tw R320) has Western-style toilets. It's upstairs in the rear of the building whose giant Soviet-era mural faces the east side of bright **Kafe Mirazh** (ul Tsentralnaya 2; ☒ 9am-5pm & 6-11pm). However, Ak-Dovurak's lawless reputation makes it preferable to prearrange a homestay with a trusted local family who can meet you on arrival. Contacts in Kyzyl can help.

GETTING THERE & AWAY

From Kyzyl, sporadic shared taxis (R350) and *marshrutky* (R230) plus three daily buses (R126, departures 9am, 1pm and 4pm) serve Ak-Dovurak (five to seven hours) via Chadan. Two buses a day run from Ak-Dovurak to Teeli, continuing to Kyzyl-Dag on Wednesday and Sunday. For the A161 via Abaza it's sometimes possible to find shared taxis leaving at dawn between Ak-Dovurak bus station and Abakan train station (R700 per seat, six hours), but it's hit and miss. You might have to pay for the whole car. Ak-Dovurak city buses link the centre of town via the bus station (1.5km) to Kyzyl-Mazhalik.

KRASNOYARSK REGION
КРАСНОЯРСКИЙ КРАЙ

Vast and beautiful, the Greenland-shaped Krasnoyarsk Region stretches all the way from the Arctic islands of Servernaya Zemlya to a mountainous tip at Mt Borus near Sayanogorsk. Formerly divided into three autonomous regions, it was reunited following a 2005 referendum. This is likely to further aid the growth of its lucrative petroleum industries which make Krasnoyarsk city such a buzzing, forward-looking metropolis.

KRASNOYARSK КРАСНОЯРСК

☎ 3912 / pop 871,000 / ☒ Moscow +4hr

Vibrant, youthful and backed by attractive spikes of jagged forested foothills, Krasnoyarsk has a much more appealing setting than most typically flat Siberian cities. While

its architecture isn't a particular strength, amid the predominantly unaesthetic concrete of post-WWII industrialisation are a few outstandingly well-embellished timber mansions and a sprinkling of Art Nouveau curves. Pleasant river trips and the nearby Stolby Nature Reserve as well as the region's best concert halls, theatres and museums make Krasnoyarsk a most agreeable place to break a trans-Siberian journey between Tomsk (612km west) and Lake Baikal.

Orientation

Near the Yenisey River's north bank, the centre is a pedestrianised, ferroconcrete square where ul Uritskogo is gashed by thundering ul Veynbauma. The zoo and Stolby Reserve are over 10km west along the Yenisey's south bank. Extremely useful Krasnoyarsk transport maps (R38) are sold within the bus, train and river stations, at bookshops such as **Russkoe Slovo** (ul Lenina 28; ☒ 10am-2pm & 3-7pm Mon-Fri, 10am-3pm Sat) and within the Regional Museum. The museum gift shop also stocks unusually helpful maps of other nearby towns.

Information

Inpexbank (pr Mira 5; ☒ 10am-8pm Mon-Sat, 10am-1pm & 2-5pm Sun) Long hours and good rates for euros.

Internet Klub (ul Lenina 153; per hr R35; ☒ 9am-10pm) Beneath Mister Dzhin.

Internet Termen (☎ 653 290; ul Parizhskoy Kommuny 33; per hr R40; ☒ 9am-10pm Mon-Fri, 11am-10pm Sat & Sun) Has a photocopier.

KBPE (Krasnoyarskoe Byuro Putishestvy i Ekskursy; ☎ 271 626; alftur@hotelkrs.ru; 1st fl, Hotel Krasnoyarsk; ☒ 10am-6pm Mon-Fri, to 3pm Sat) Commercial tour agency.

Paradoks (☎ 239 795; pr Mira 96; Internet per hr R25 for up to 3MB; ☒ 24hr) The best, central Internet access. Enter from an inner courtyard; follow the signs to the Alazani Georgian restaurant, which is opposite Paradoks.

Post office (ul Lenina 62; ☒ 8am-7pm Mon-Sat)

ROSBank (pr Mira 7; ☒ 9am-7pm Mon-Fri, 10am-5pm Sat) Good rates for US dollars; changes travellers cheques.

Sayan Ring Travel (☎ /fax 522 481; www.gotosiberia .ru; office 545, Metropol Bldg, pr Mira 10; ☒ 10am-7pm Mon-Fri) Specialist agency for Tuva-Khakassia tours.

Sberbank (ul Abalakovykh 2; ☒ 9.30am-7pm Mon-Sat) Exchange fairly handy for the train station.

SibTourGuide (☎ 512 654; www.sibtourguide.com) Youthful university teacher Anatoliy Brewhanov offers thoughtfully personalised English-speaking tour services aimed at independent travellers. Useful website, congenial homestays and imaginative trips.

SIBERIA

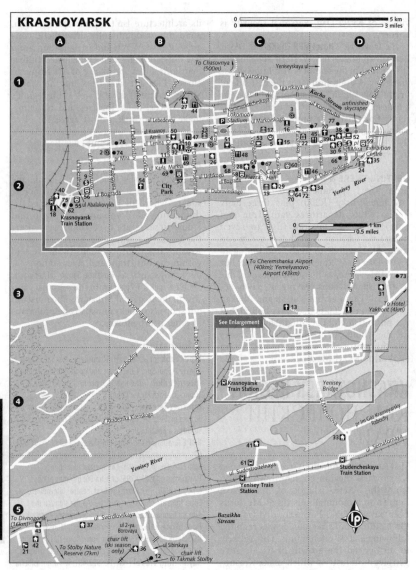

KRASNOYARSK

Telephone office (pr Mira 102 & ul Lenina 49; ☺ 7am-2pm & 3pm-midnight)

Sights
MUSEUMS

The **Regional Museum** (Kraevedchesky muzey; ☎ 226 511; ul Dubrovinskogo 84; admission R30; ☺ 11am-7pm Tue-Sun) is one of Siberia's best. Its wonder-

fully incongruous 1912 building combines Art Nouveau and Egyptian temple–style features. Arranged around a Cossack explorer's ship are models, icons, historical room interiors and nature rooms where you can listen to local birdsong and animal cries. The basement hosts a splendid ethnographic section comparing the historical fashion sense of shamans from various tribal groups. The gift shop sells old coins, medals, postcards and excellent maps.

The **Surikov Museum-Estate** (Muzey-usadba V I Surikova; ☎ 231 507; ul Lenina 98; admission R30; ⏰ 11am-6pm Tue-Sat) preserves the house, sheds and vegetable patch of 19th-century painter Vasily Surikov (1848–1916). The heavy-gated garden forms a refreshing oasis of rural Siberia right in the city centre. More of Surikov's work is on show at the cute **Surikov Art Museum** (☎ 272 558; ul Parizhskoy Kommuny 20; ⏰ 11am-6pm Tue-Sun).

The **Literature Museum** (Literaturny muzey; ☎ 276 202; ul Lenina 66; admission R20; ⏰ 10am-4pm Tue-Sat) is within a glorious 1911 wooden mansion.

A fascinating little **museum** (☎ 277 487; pl Pobedy; admission free; ⏰ 10am-5pm Tue-Sun) at the **Victory Memorial** relates Krasnoyarsk's role in WWII, when much Soviet industry was strategically shifted east away from potential bomber raids.

HISTORIC BUILDINGS

Dotted about Krasnoyarsk are some very fine wooden houses, notably ul Lenina 88 and 67 and ul Karla Marksa 118. There are also many Art Nouveau façades such as pr Mira 76, ul Lenina 62 and ul Parizhskoy Kommuny 13. Attractive old churches abound including the fancy 1795 **Intercession Cathedral** (Pokrovskoe sobor; ul Surikova) and the top-heavy but elegant 1804–22 **Resurrection Church** (Blagoveshchensky tserkov; ul 9 Yanvarya), which was decapitated in the 1930s but retowered in 1998–99. Its icon-filled interior billows with incense. For great city views climb Karaulnaya Hill to the pointy little **Chasovnya** (Chapel) which features on the Russian 10-rouble banknote. At midday there's a deafening one-gun salute here.

LENIN MEMORABILIA

In April 1897 the goateed wonder stayed in Krasnoyarsk at ul Markovskogo 27, now preserved and surveyed by a pensive, replinthed **statue**. A big, much prouder, **Lenin statue** stands opposite the popular city park. Permanently docked below an ugly brown-concrete exhibition centre is the boat **SV Nikolay** which transported Vladimir to exile in Shushenskoe. Other communist curiosities include a splendid **mosaic** (ul Vyborsky 9) on the outer wall of the station

SIBERIA

square post office and a bust of proto-KGB founder **Felix Dzerzhinsky** (ul Dzerzhinskogo).

STOLBY NATURE RESERVE & ROEV RUCHEY ZOO

Arguably Krasnoyarsk's greatest attractions are the spiky volcanic rock pillars called **stolby**. These litter the woods in the 17,000-hectare Stolby Nature Reserve (Zapovednik Stolby) south of the Yenisey River. To reach the main concentration of pillars, start by walking 7km down a track near Turbaza Yenisey. Alternatively, there is much easier access via a long **chair lift** from beside Kafe Bobrovyylog (ul Sibirskaya). This usually runs year-round on request, but was closed throughout 2005 during a massive ski-slope redevelopment. From the top of the chair lift, walk for two minutes to a great viewpoint or around 40 minutes to reach the impressive **Takmak Stolby**. Infected ticks are dangerous between May and July. Tours are available, personalised in English with SibTourGuide (priced according to itinerary) or all in Russian through KBPE (R500/700/1000/1500 per person for groups of many/three/two/one, six hours).

The relatively humane **Roev Ruchey Zoo** (☎ 698 101; adult/child R50/free; 🕙 10am-6pm, to 9pm Wed-Sun Apr-Oct) is home to Siberian species rare and not so rare, along with happily humping camels. Access is on bus 50 or 50A.

Sleeping

There are plenty of accommodation options in Krasnoyarsk, including many budget choices.

Though way out of the centre, there are several small, peaceful hotels in the Stolby area, relatively handy for skiing and trips to the Stolby Nature Reserve. Use bus 50.

For a great insight into local life take an English-speaking homestay organised by SibTourGuide. Most such homestays are in the high-rise Vyetluzhanka area, which is 20-minute's drive west of the centre but well served by bus 91 and close to attractive forest and ski areas. Vyetluzhanka's petal-towered St Nicholas Church is a striking landmark. Prices include a free station pick-up.

BUDGET
City Centre

Hotel Gostiny Dvor (☎ 232 857; pr Mira 81; dm R300-550, s R700-850, tw R600-1100) Superb central position, lovely façade and, despite the ropey recep-

tion area, rooms are fully renovated sharing brand-new toilets and showers between two or three rooms. Kettles in some rooms.

Krasnoyarskstroystrategiya (☎ 276 612; pr Mira 12; s R280-530, tw R650-910) Good value if utterly unpronounceable. Rooms are very pleasant by ex-Soviet standards with share-pair bathrooms. Enter from ul Karatanova.

Hotel-ship Mayak (☎ 276 355; ul Dubrovinskogo; s/tw berths R350/500, lyux berths R650) This antique river steamer is moored handily close to the river station and rents well priced but cramped cabins that can be noisy and are not always secure – windows are rarely lockable. Toilets are shared. Preferable to the musty **Hotel-ship Viktoriya** (☎ 525 152; s/tw berths R500/850).

Other cheap possibilities:

Hotel Kolos (☎ 235 667; ul Kerchinskogo 65; dm/s/tw R300/560/820) Simple, acceptable rooms but with dubious, market-trader clientele.

Hotel Ogni Yeniseyya (☎ 275 262; ul Dubrovinskogo 80; s R590-820, tw R1380-1500) Has miserable rooms off bile-green corridors, but there are private bathrooms and visa registration is possible.

Hotel Sever (☎ 662 266; Hotel-sever@mail.ru; ul Lenina 121; s/tw R500/600) Once grand, now cheap but friendly with some peeling wallpaper and paint.

Resting rooms (komnaty otdykha; ☎ 586 086; train station; dm per 12hr from R180) Excellent brand-new dorm rooms.

South of the Yenisey

Hotel Turist (☎ 361 470; http://tlcom.krs.ru/tourist/index .html, in Russian; ul Matrasova 2; dm/s/tw R500/1100/1600) On a busy roundabout directly across the long Yenisey Bridge from the city centre, this 16-storey Soviet monolith has variable rooms with toilet and shower. Some are pleasantly renovated. At night the dubious disco sets the whole tower vibrating.

Stolby Area

Turbaza Yenisey (☎ 698 110; ul Sverdlovskaya 140/7; d/tw from R400; 🅿 ⊠) Despite the name this is a two-storey hotel not a camp. Good-value renovated rooms are simple but neat and share sparkling-clean showers. Some R1700 doubles have private facilities. There's a glimpse of river view from the small communal terrace but no café.

Khutorok (☎ 698 325; ul Sverdlovskaya 245; d R800) Above this popular Ukrainian restaurant are eight newish if already scuffed rooms with shower and toilet. Sauna R500 per hour.

MIDRANGE
City Centre
All rates include breakfast.

Hotel Oktyabrskaya (☎ 273 780; www.tlcom.krs
.ru/october; pr Mira 15; s/d/tw R2300/2600/2900) Comfortable and professionally run with rooms
approximating chintzy Western standards,
albeit without air-conditioning. Satellite
TV includes CNN and some English is
spoken. The trendy lobby area has a very
stylish juice bar.

Hotel Krasnoyarsk (☎ 273 754; www.hotelkrs.ru;
ul Uritskogo 94; s/tw/ste from R1440/1900/2660; 🔣)
This sprawling eight-storey concrete slab
dominates Krasnoyarsk's central square.
It retains the Soviet-vintage *dezhurnaya*
(floor-lady) system but is well kept with
bright corridors, totally rebuilt full-service
rooms and English-speaking receptionists.
Only the suites have air-conditioning.

Metelitsa Guest House (☎ 625 298; pr Mira 14a;
s R1895-2295, d R2295-2895; 🅿) Small, central
and reasonably comfy but aimed at Russian *biznesmen*.

South of the Yenisey
Siberian Safari Club (☎ 613 335; http://tlcom.krs
.ru/safari/; ul Sudostroitelnaya 117a; s/d R2500/3000)
This intimate 20-room hotel occupies a
pleasantly quiet spot on the riverbank and,
although walls are thin, it's arguably Krasnoyarsk's best option. Attentive staff speak
English, there's a classy terrace restaurant
(meals R300 to R800) and booking is advisable (booking fee is 25% of the cost of
the first night's accommodation). Three
smaller single rooms cost only R1300. Bus
36 stops a 10-minute walk away.

Stolby Area
Iris (☎ 617 762; ul 2nd Borovaya 67; d/ste R1700/2200;
🅿) At the base of a kilometre-long winter-
only ski lift, the position would be wonderfully peaceful in summer if fellow guests
didn't overwork their bedsprings. The comfortable rooms come in various styles, some
in bright primary colours with satin bedspreads and lurid nudes. In winter, ski hire
(R50 per hour) is available at the atmospheric but surprisingly expensive Kashtak
restaurant next door.

Northwestern Suburbs
Hotel Polyot (☎ 651 778; fax 201 047; ul Aerovokzalnaya 16; s R1000, tw R1100-1600) The freshly renovated Polyot is two-minutes' walk from the
bus station; airport buses depart from here,
so it's worth considering for the night before a flight. Presentable rooms have toilets
and short bathtubs; some are much smarter
than others.

Hotel Yakhont (☎ 566 767; www.yahont.ru; ul Telmana 44a; s/d/ste R2100/3000/3300) Popular with
tour groups; rooms are modern and well
furnished, but prices seem excessive given
the very inconvenient suburban location
near the far end of trolleybus route 7. Singles with share-pair bathrooms cost R1500.
There's juvenile amusement in mispronouncing the hotel's name and in observing
the free minibar's postmodernist selection:
Sprite, water and a tea bag.

TOP END
Stolby Area
Snezhnaya Dolina (☎ 693 033; d R3000-5450; 🅿)
Excellent full-facility cottages form slightly
cramped rows within a peaceful walled
orchard. Each has kitchen, covered terrace
and no reservation fee. There's also a shared
tennis court.

Eating
There are plenty of eateries along pr Mira,
summer cafés on the promenade near the
river station and cheap stalls selling *samsas*
(Central Asian pastries), *shawarma* (grilled
meat and salad wrapped in flat bread)
and *khachapuri* (Georgian cheese bread)
in the extensive **central market** (🕙 8am-6pm).
On summer evenings, lively beer bars and
shashlyk grills give the concrete, fountain-
filled square outside Hotel Krasnoyarsk a
convivial piazza feel.

RESTAURANTS
Telega (☎ 595 987; pr Mira 91; biznes lunch R120;
🕙 noon-2am) Enter Telega beneath a dangling cart, and you'll find an extensive hot
and cold buffet, ideal for avoiding linguistic
problems. All-you-can-eat deals for R250.

Sultan Suleyman (☎ 270 070; ul Perensona 20;
meals R180-350; 🕙 10am-11pm Mon-Sat, noon-11pm
Sun) Behind the lovely 1913 Dom Ofitserov
building, midpriced Turko-Russian food is
served in a semi-oriental basement. In front
is a handy fast-food joint.

Luch (☎ 662 064; www.kinoluch.ru; ul Karla Marksa
149) The Luch entertainment complex contains several eateries, including fast food,

fine Russian cuisine and notably the airy glassed-in **Terrasa Kafe** (top fl; meals R100-350, coffees R50-80; ☺ noon-6am). Enjoy fine views across pl Lenina, menus ranging from Japanese to Uzbek and a remarkably filling R100 lunch deal, available daily.

Mama Roma (☎ 661 072; www.mamaroma.ru; pr Mira 50a; pizzas R192-480, pastas R144-256; ☺ 11am-1am) Herb-filled air wafts temptingly from the best Italian eatery in town. Pizzas are freshly baked, menus bilingual.

QUICK EATS

Stolovaya OK (ul Uritskogo 33; meals R20-50; ☺ 11am-6pm Mon-Sat term-time) Super-cheap student canteen with perfectly acceptable R17 *plov* (Uzbek rice dish with diced meat and carrot).

Subito (ul Lenina 110; pizza slices R38; ☺ 10am-10pm) Relatively well-laden microwave pizza and various alternatives.

Drinking

Krem (☎ 581 538; pr Mira 10; ice creams R65-100, coffees R50-80; ☺ 10am-1am) Krasnoyarsk's top coffee house has black-and-white photography and dark, modern wooden furniture, spotlit by metallic pod-lamps.

Tsentr (☎ 273 737; pr Mira 80; meals R190-350, coffees R54-101) Inviting patisserie-café ambience, though the cakes (R30 per 100g) aren't Krasnoyarsk's best.

Kinopark Pikra (☎ 277 531; ul Perensona 29a; beers R25) An atmospheric, great-value basement pub within a cinema-beat complex that's easily spotted by the plane crashing through its front wall. The bar is easy to miss though: follow signs to the toilets.

Bar Chemodan (☎ 230 259; ul Oboron 2b; biznes lunch R200, beers R159-169) is a wonderfully atmospheric if fiercely expensive 1920s-themed pub-restaurant stocking dozens of whiskies. There's also a smoky **bar** (R50; ☺ 6pm-midnight) attached to the Literature Museum.

Entertainment

Krasnoyarsk has a variety of concert halls and theatres.

Opera-Ballet Theatre (☎ 278 697; ul Perensona 2; tickets from R60) The architecturally nondescript theatre has up to five early-evening shows per week October to June.

The **Philharmonia** (☎ 274 930; pl Mira 2b) has three concert halls showcasing folk, pop and classical music. Organ concerts are held in the twin-spired **Catholic Church** (☎ 210 566; ul Dekabristov 20).

Luch (☎ 661 595; www.kinoluch.ru; ul Karla Marksa 149) A futuristically angular entertainment complex with cinemas, video games, pool tables and a Moai-guarded nightclub. Plenty of fun for children.

Che Guevara (☎ 595 857; ul Bograda; admission after 7pm R300-500, cocktails R100-190; ☺ noon-1am Sun-Wed, to 5am Thu-Sat) Has dancing or live music in a fun saloon-club with 1950s pin-ups and a commie-Cuba theme.

Rock-Jazz Kafe (☎ 523 305; ul Perensona 20; admission R80, beers R30) Entered through a small bar beside the Dublin Irish Pub, this dark venue showcases live bands around an upturned motorcycle from 6pm on weekends.

Havana Club (☎ 216 416; ul Abalakovykh; admission R30-180) A big nightclub with three dance floors and celebrity DJs on Saturday. Themed nights include Russian nostalgia (Monday), student night (Wednesday) and Latin dance (Thursday).

Getting There & Away

AIR

From Krasnoyarsk's Yemelyanovo Airport, you can fly to Germany plus almost anywhere in Russia. Handy **KrasAir** (www.krasair .ru, in Russian) connections include Moscow (R8700, three daily), Barnaul (R3100, four weekly) and Kyzyl (R3210, four weekly). **SIAT** (SibAviaTrans; www.siat.ru, in Russian) flies to Igarka and Turukhansk. Just a handful of flights use Cheremshanka Airport, 3km south of Yemelyanovo: double check that yours isn't one of them.

BOAT

Every few days in summer passenger boats from Krasnoyarsk's spired **river station** (☎ 274 446; ☺ 8am-7pm) ply the Yenisey to Dudinka (1989km, 4½ to five days) but foreigners may not proceed beyond Igarka (p560).

Summer hydrofoils to Divnogorsk depart at 11am, 1pm, 3pm and 5pm daily plus 7pm at weekends, returning an hour later. Buy tickets (R70) on board.

BUS

The main **bus station** (☎ 230 512; ul Aerovokzalnaya 22) is reached by trolleybus 2 from the train station or bus 53 from ul Karla Marksa. Destinations include Yeniseysk (R243, seven hours, nine daily), Abakan (R294, 8¾ hours, five daily), Shushenskoe (10½ hours at 10am and 9.30pm) and Sayanogorsk (R354, 10½ hours, six daily).

From the lower west side of the river station, *marshrutka* 106 to Divnogorsk (R25, one hour) runs 30 times per day from 7.10am to 9.10pm, albeit with timetable gaps. Buy tickets from a window halfway down the steps. Several Yeniseysk *marshrutky* (R250, 5½ hours) use this bus stand too.

TRAIN
Useful overnight hops include Tomsk (R420 *platskart,* 14 hours) and Lesosibirsk (R320 *platskart,* 11 hours) for Yeniseysk. Six or more trains daily take around 19 hours to Irkutsk (R520 *platskart*). Train 055 is the best sleeper choice for Novosibirsk (R541 *platskart,* 12½ hours), Yekaterinburg (33 hours) and Moscow (60 hours). Train 092 along the BAM takes 30 hours to Severobaikalsk, continuing alternate days to Tynda. Three overnight trains run to Abakan; train 124 (*kupe* R630, 11 hours) is much the fastest, while train 658 is better for Kuragino. All services use the main Krasnoyarsk station.

There are railway **booking offices** (☉ 9am-6pm) in the river and bus stations.

Getting Around
Bus 135 (R26, 1¼ hours) runs 14 times daily from the bus station to Yemelyanovo Airport, 46km northwest of the city. It passes Cheremshanka Airport en route. The 3am, 5.50am, 8.30pm and 10pm buses cost R70.

Within the city centre, almost all public transport runs eastbound along ul Karla Marksa or pr Mira, returning westbound on ul Lenina. Eastbound buses marked 'Matrasovo' will veer south, stopping at both ends of the long Yenisey Bridge; this is handy for hotels Krasnoyarsk and Turist respectively.

Frequent, if slow, trolleybus 7 trundles from the train station via ul Karla Marksa, up ul Surikova passing Hotel Yakhont after more than half an hour. Bus 21 from ul Karla Marksa is faster. Trolleybus 2 links bus and train stations via pr Mira. Useful bus 50 starts beyond the zoo, passes the Turbaza Yenisey and comes through the centre of town, winding on to the bus station. Bus 50A repeats the first half of the

route then turns left along ul Lenina and passes the train station.

AROUND KRASNOYARSK
Divnogorsk Дивногорск
☎ 39144 / pop 29,000 / ☉ Moscow +4hr

From Krasnoyarsk a popular day trip by bus and/or summer hydrofoil follows the Yenisey River 27km to Divnogorsk town through a wide, wooded canyon. Some 5km beyond Divnogorsk's jetty is a vast 90m-high dam. Turbine-room visits are not permitted but if you're lucky you might see ships being lifted by a technologically impressive inclined plane to the huge Krasnoyarsk Sea reservoir behind. A few kilometres beyond you can observe ice fishing from December to March or rent boats and yachts from **Aly Parus** (☎ 3912-403 187; per hr R700-1000; ☉ summer).

The Krasnoyarsk–Divnogorsk road has a panoramic overlook point at km23 and passes quaint **Ovsyanka** village. From the main road walk 100m (crossing the train tracks) to Ovsyanka's cute though new wooden **St Inokent Chapel** (ul Shchetinkina) then 50m right to find the **House Museum** (ul Shchetinkina 26; admission R30; ☉ 10am-6pm Tue-Sun) of famous local writer Victor Astafiev, who died in 2001. Directly opposite in Astafiev's grandma's cottage-compound is the more interesting **Last Bow Museum** (ul Shchetinkina 35; admission R30; ☉ 10am-6pm Tue-Sun), giving a taste of rural Siberian life.

SLEEPING
Under five-minutes' walk south of Divnogorsk's jetty (bus 1 from Divnogorsk bus stand), the riverside **Hotel Biryuza** (☎ 23761; 2nd fl, ul Lenina 55; s/tw with toilet R280/400, s/tw/tr with bathroom R500/600/1000) is much nicer than it looks. Rooms with river views cost R200 extra.

Beside Aly Parus yacht club on the Krasnoyarsk Sea, **SKIF** (☎ 3912-581 682) has basic but acceptable **summer cabins** (beds R280-400).

GETTING THERE & AWAY
Both hydrofoils (R70, 45 minutes, five daily) and *marshrutky* (R25, 30 daily) depart from behind Krasnoyarsk's river station. Taxis meet boats on arrival in Divnogorsk and want around R200 return to shuttle you to a dam-overlook point. **SibTourGuide** (p553) offers various tailored excursions in

English (US$50 to US$65 per car) or will include the Divnogorsk loop as part of its '10-Rouble Tour'.

Buses going from Krasnoyarsk to Abakan pick up in Divnogorsk and drive right in front of the dam.

NORTH ALONG THE YENISEY

From the end of May to early October, elegant Yenisey passenger ships with wood panelling and shiny brass fittings depart Krasnoyarsk for Dudinka (4½ days) via Yeniseysk (17 hours) and the depressing ex-Gulag town of Igarka (R1800 to R4278, 74 to 79 hours), which is somewhat redeemed by its award-winning **permafrost museum** (Vechnoy Merzloty muzey; ☎ 24110; fax 23011; www .museum.ru/M1405; ul Bolshoy Teatr 15a; admission R200; 9am-12.45pm & 2-5pm Sun-Fri). There are three to four sailings per week, most departing at 7am. Returning upstream, journeys take 50% longer. Trips are more meditational than scenic, days merging as the northern sun barely sinks below the Arctic horizon. Beware that independent travellers may not go beyond Igarka: Dudinka and nearby Norilsk are 'closed' to foreigners. It might be possible to get Dudinka permits by joining a luxury 12-day return cruise with **Acris** (www.acris.ru; US$810-2000) but triple check well in advance and allow a couple of months' processing time. For more details of this route see Lonely Planet's *Greenland & the Arctic* guide. Visiting Yeniseysk is vastly easier.

Yeniseysk Енисейск

☎ 39115 / pop 16,000 / Moscow +4hr

Using Lesosibirsk overnight trains, historic Yeniseysk makes a pleasant two-night, one-day excursion from Krasnoyarsk, 340km away. Founded in 1619, this was once Russia's great fur-trading capital, with world-famous 18th-century August trade fairs and 10 grand churches gracing its skyline. Eclipsed by Krasnoyarsk despite a burst of gold-rush prosperity in the 1860s, the town is now a delightfully peaceful backwater with a good **Regional Museum** (ul Lenina 106; 9am-5pm Mon-Sat), the faded commercial grandeur of ul Lenina and many old houses; over 70 are considered architectural monuments. Most appealing of the surviving churches are the walled 1731 **Spaso-Pereobrazhensky Monastery** (ul Raboche-Krestyanskaya 105) and the **Assumption Church** (Uspenskaya tserkov; ul Raboche-Krestyanskaya 116) with its unusual metal floor and splendid antique icons.

Should you wish to linger, **Hotel Yenisey** (☎ 23149; ul Khuzinskogo 2; dm/s/tw R105/490/660), near the quay, has burping old toilets and washbasins in the best rooms. The cheap **Hotel Avtovokzal** (☎ 22030; ul Babkina 13; dm R190) is a handful of ultrabasic beds above the bus station.

Between Yeniseysk and Krasnoyarsk there are buses (R243, seven hours, two daily), *marshrutky* (R260, 5½ hours, nine daily), hydrofoils (R468, 10 hours, weekly) and Yenisey River passenger ships (R685 to R1487, 17 hours downstream, several monthly).

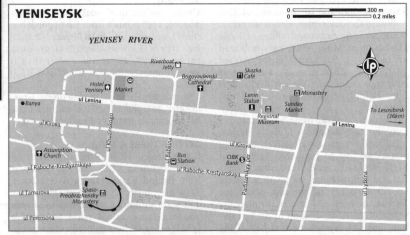

YENISEYSK

0 _____ 300 m
0 _____ 0.2 miles

YENISEY RIVER

Riverboat Jetty

Bogoyavlenski Cathedral

Skazka Café

Hotel Yenisey

Market

Banya

ul Lenina

Lenin Statue

Monastery

Sunday Market

Regional Museum

To Lesosibirsk (36km)

ul Kirova

ul Khuzinskogo

ul Babkina

ul Lenina

Assumption Church

Bus Station

ul Kirova

OBK Bank

ul Raboche-Krestyanskaya

ul Raboche-Krestyanskaya

Partizanskaya per

ul Vitkina

ul Tamarova

Spaso-Preobrazhensky Monastery

ul Perensona

SIBERIA

Lesosibirsk Лесосибирск

☎ 39145 / pop 77,000 / ☾ Moscow +4hr

This uninteresting timber town is only really useful as the railhead for Yeniseysk, 36km further north. But do stop to admire its breathtaking new **Krestovozdvizhensky Church**, south of ul Gorkogo 81, with gleaming clusters of golden domes. To Yeniseysk there are buses (R30, 45 minutes) from the bus station at least hourly, plus one direct service from the train station departing 15 minutes after the arrival of the overnight train from Krasnoyarsk (R320 *platskart*, 11 hours). Bus 13 links the bus and train stations very infrequently.

WESTERN BAM
ЗАПАДНЫЙ БАМ

The 3100km-long Baikal-Amur Mainline (Baikalo-Amurskaya Magistral, BAM) is an astonishing victory of belief over adversity. This 'other' trans-Siberian line runs from Tayshet (417km east of Krasnoyarsk) around the top of Lake Baikal to Sovetskaya Gavan on the Pacific coast. Begun in the 1930s to access the timber and minerals of the Lena Basin, work stopped during WWII. Indeed the tracks were stripped altogether and re-used to lay a relief line to the besieged city of Stalingrad (now Volgograd). Work effectively started all over again in 1974 when the existing Trans-Siberian Railway was felt to be vulnerable to attack by potentially hostile China. Much of the route was cut through virgin taiga and pesky mountain ranges. To encourage patriotic volunteer labourers the BAM was labelled 'Hero Project of the Century'. Even so, building on permafrost pushed the cost of the project to US$25 billion, some 50 times more than the original Trans-Siberian Railway.

New 'BAM towns' grew with the railway, often populated by builders who decided to stay on. However, the line's opening (1991) coincided with the collapse of the centrally planned USSR and the region's bright Soviet future has not really materialised. While Bratsk and Severobaikalsk have thrived, many other smaller, lonely settlements have become ghost towns.

The BAM route crosses virtually virgin territory that is more impressively moun-tainous than anything along the trans-Siberian mainline. For most travellers the most popular BAM stop is Severobaikalsk, as a hub for visiting north Baikal. For details on eastern BAM towns Tynda, Komsomolsk-na-Amure, Vanino and Sovetskaya Gavan, see the Russian Far East chapter.

The official start of the BAM is Tayshet, but through services from Krasnoyarsk and Moscow and elsewhere mean there's little reason to stop there. Bratsk is famous for its giant dam. Ust-Kut–Lena has irregular hydrofoil services along the Lena River to Lensk for Yakutsk. Between the two is the claustrophobic 1960s iron-ore processing town of Zheleznogorsk-Ilimsky (train station Korshunikha Angarskaya), whose sole, modest attraction is the **Yangel Museum** (☾ 9am-4pm Mon-Fri), celebrating a local astro-scientist friend of Yuri Gagarin.

There are particularly fine mountain views between Kunerma and minispa Goudzhekit, with the line performing a full 180-degree switchback before tunnelling through to Daban.

The line between Severobaikalsk and Nizhneangarsk offers flashes of dazzling Lake Baikal views. It then continues to Tynda via Dzelinda, another tiny spa, and the 15km-long Severomuysk Tunnel.

BRATSK БРАТСК

☎ 3953 / pop 258,000 / ☾ Moscow +5hr

A stop in Bratsk neatly breaks a Krasnoyarsk to Severobaikalsk trip into two overnight rides, but a day here is plenty. Its *raison d'être* is a gigantic 1955 **dam** (GES), which caused the drowning of the original historic town. New Bratsk is a confusing necklace of disconnected concrete 'subcities' with a high-rise Tsentralny area that is spirit-crushingly dull. It does, however, have two English-speaking tour agencies: **Taiga Tours** (☎ 413 951; taigat@bratsk.net.ru; 2nd fl, Hotel Taiga) and **Lovely Tour** (Lavli Tur; ☎ 433 290; baikal@lovelytour.ru; ul Sovetskaya 3, Tsentralny; ☾ 10am-8pm Mon-Fri, to 5pm Sat). Given two days' notice, either agency can organise permits and guides to visit the dam's turbine rooms.

The dam itself is 30km further north in Energetik and the BAM trains go right across it.

Between the two, the impressive **Angara Village** (☎ 412 834; locals/foreigners R12/90; ☾ 10am-5pm Tue-Sun, longer hr in summer) is an

SIBERIA

open-air ethnographic museum featuring a rare wooden watchtower and buildings rescued from drowned old Bratsk. A series of shaman sites and Evenki (also known as Tungusi) *chum* (tepee-shaped conical dwellings) lie in the woods behind. The attractive lakeside site is a lonely 3km walk from Sibirsky Traktir, an isolated highway café off the main *marshrutka* routes 10 or 50. Taking a taxi makes more sense.

Sleeping

PANDUN/ENERGETIC

Hotel Turist (☎ 378 743; ul Naymushina 28, Energetik; s R350-900, tw R700-1800, ste R2500-3000) Good-value cheaper twins (half-price for single occupancy) are clean if typically Soviet with just-functional bathrooms. 'First-class' rooms look better but new wallpaper and carpet don't justify paying almost triple prices. You can walk to the dam in 15 minutes.

Hotel Lyuks (☎ 363 146; ul Naberezhnaya 62, Padun; s/d/ste R1000/1200/1400) In a quiet, low-rise neighbourhood in woods beside the Bratsk Sea, this six-room wooden mansion was once an exclusive Communist Party retreat. Opt for the large of unstylish suites with their superb lake views and extensive, somewhat ageing bathrooms. Khrushchev, Brezhnev, Yeltsin and even Jacques Chirac have all stayed here. Cheaper rooms are forgettable and wantonly overpriced. It's a R80 taxi ride from Padunskie Porogie station.

TSENTRALNY

Hotel Taiga (☎ 414 000; ul Mira 35; s/d/tw R1800/1800/2100) Behind a smart new façade, wobbly Soviet-era corridors host very green bedrooms – good singles but cramped, overly intimate doubles. Some staff speak English, guest visas are registered and rates include breakfast.

Hotel Bratsk (☎ 438 436; ul Deputatskaya 32; s/tw from R350/700; P) Upstairs a wide variety of clean but essentially Soviet rooms all have private bathrooms and peeling paint, so unless you want a malfunctioning old TV, take the cheapest available.

Eating

Kalipso (☎ 376 781; ul Naymushina 54; meals R150-400; noon-7pm & 8pm-3am) The nicest pub-café in Energetik is at bus stop GES. It has a nautical interior, porthole windows and a beer-garden terrace that almost overlooks the lake.

Getting There & Away

The three main train stations are an hour's ride apart. Padunskie Porogie is closest to Energetik and Padun. Gidrostritel is several kilometres east of the dam. For Tsentralny, get off at Anzyobi and transfer by bus or *elektrichka*.

Eastbound there are afternoon and night trains to Severobaikalsk (R760, 15 hours) via Lena–Ust-Kut (R650, eight hours). On odd days a useful 3pm train runs overnight to Krasnoyarsk (16 hours). For Irkutsk there's daily train 87 (R970, 18 hours), buses (R500, 11 hours) from the Tsentralny **bus station** (ul Yuzhnaya) and, in summer, hydrofoils (13 hours, three per week) down the Angara River from a river station in southeast Tsentralny.

Getting Around

Marshrutky 10 and 50 shuttle regularly between Hotel Turist in Energetik and Tsentralny bus station (45 minutes).

Bus 8 starts at the GES stop beside the Kalipso café and wiggles around Energetik's Mikro-Rayon 7 estate to a no-man's-land bus stop nearly opposite Padunskie Porogie train station. For taxis call ☎ 368 482 or 377 707.

UST-KUT & LENA
УСТЬ-КУТ И ЛЕНА

☎ 39565 / pop 70,000 / Moscow +5hr

Quietly attractive old Ust-Kut, centred 8km west of Lena station, is worth a stroll if you're stuck here a while, but the only real reason to stop is for hydrofoils up the Lena River towards Yakutsk, 2000km downstream. This requires changing boats in Lensk, for which departures leave several times weekly in summer. The Osetrovo river station is handily across the central square from Lena train station past the **Lena Hotel** (☎ 51507; ul Kirova 88; s R550-900; d R1100), which has neat rooms with shower and toilet.

Lena station (not the tiny Ust-Kut halt) is a major stop on the BAM railway with useful overnight trains to Severobaikalsk (7½ hours) via Goudzhekit (seven hours) leaving nightly around midnight. At least two westbound trains a day stop here, including one bound for Moscow.

LAKE BAIKAL
ОЗЕРО БАЙКАЛ

Crystal-clear Lake Baikal is a vast body of the bluest water, surrounded by rocky or tree-covered foreshores behind which mountains float like phantoms at indeterminable distances. Baikal's meteorological mood swings are transfixing spectacles, whole weather systems dancing for your delectation over Siberia's 'climatic kitchen'.

Shaped like a banana, Baikal is 636km from north to south and up to 1637m deep, making it the world's deepest lake. Incredibly, it contains nearly one-fifth of the planet's unfrozen fresh water, more than North America's five Great Lakes combined, and despite some environmental worries (p106) it's drinkably pure.

In the past, foreign tourists have typically visited Baikal from Listvyanka via Irkutsk, but options are rapidly expanding and it's now equally feasible to approach via Ulan-Ude (for eastern Baikal) or Severobaikalsk (on the BAM railway). Choosing well is important as there's no round-lake road nor even a trekking path, at least not until the **Great Baikal Trail** (www.baikal.eastsib.ru/gbt/index_en.html) is completed. Hydrofoil-ferry connections are limited to local services plus the Irkutsk–Olkhon–Severobaikalsk–Nizhneangarsk run. Round-Baikal cruises can be fiercely expensive: Irkutsk agencies quote between US$600 and US$850 per day for liveaboards (where you sleep on board during the trip) holding between eight and 12 people, though you can pay vastly less

by starting in Nizhneangarsk. March is arguably one of the best times to visit the region: the scenery is pristine white and there's no need to charter expensive excursion boats as (in places) you can hop in a taxi and drive across the world's deepest lake – a thrilling proposition. Other adventurous if potentially foolhardy crossing methods include **kayaking** (www.chargelife.com), **motor-biking** (www.iceride.com) and **skating** (www.transbaikal.nl).

Note that this section also includes the beautiful inland Tunka and Barguzin Valleys as they're accessed via Baikal towns.

IRKUTSK ИРКУТСК
☎ 3952 / pop 591,000 / ⏰ Moscow+5hr

Historic if vaguely seedy Irkutsk, 1090km southeast of Krasnoyarsk, is the nearest big city to glorious Lake Baikal, though it's still 70km inland. With some fancifully rebuilt churches and areas of grand 19th-century architecture it's well worth at least a brief stop. If your Russian is poor, Irkutsk has plenty of Anglophone agencies eager to help, and now has some real (if small) hostels too.

Founded in 1651 as a Cossack garrison to control the indigenous Buryats, Irkutsk was the springboard for 18th-century expeditions to the far north and east including Alaska, then known as 'Irkutsk's American district'.

As eastern Siberia's trading and administrative centre, Irkutsk dispatched Siberian furs and ivory to Mongolia, Tibet and China in exchange for silk and tea. Three-quarters of the city burnt down in the disastrous fire of 1879. However, the 1880s Lena Basin gold rush quickly saw its grand brick mansions and public buildings restored. Known

SIBERIA

FISHY FUN

No trip to Baikal is complete without tasting **omul**, a distant relative of salmon that's delicious raw and better still freshly smoked. Over 50 other varieties of Baikal fish include perch, black grayling, ugly frilly nosed bullheads and tasty sig (whitefish). While the lake isn't Russia's greatest place for anglers, from February to April it offers the unusual spectacle of **ice fishing**. There are two forms: individuals with immense patience dangle hooked lines through Eskimo-style ice holes; elsewhere, especially in shallow waters, whole teams of villagers string extraordinarily long thin nets beneath the ice and pull out omul by the hundred, carting them home on horse-drawn troikas.

You can get beneath the ice yourself with Irkutsk's very professional scuba-diving outfits **Aqua-Eco** (Akva-Eko; Map p568; ☎ 3952-334 290; www.aquaeco.eu.org; ul K Libknekhta 12) and **SVAL** (Map p568; ☎ 3952-211 748; http://svaldiving.com; ul Dekabrskikh Sobyty 55). But the lake's greatest divers are the almost-unique **nerpa** (freshwater seals). Their moist, black eyes are so lovably emotional that few observers fail to be smitten.

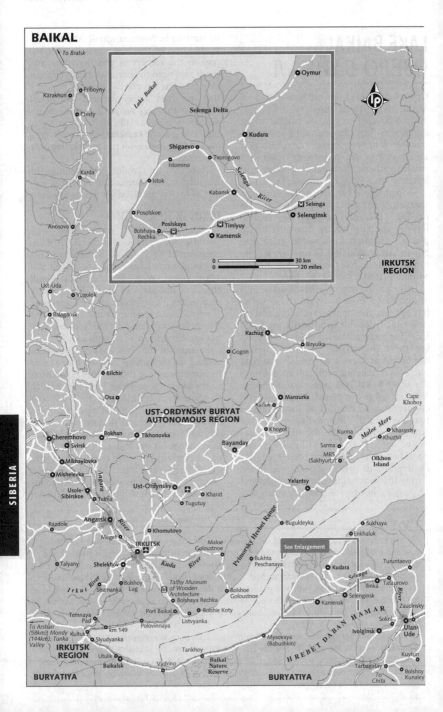

BAIKAL

To Bratsk

Karakhun Priboyny

Chisty

Lake Baikal

Selenga Delta

Oymur

Kudara

Shigaevo Tvorogovo

Istomino

Istok

Kabansk Selenga River Selenga

Selenginsk

Posolskoe

Poslskaya Timlyuy

Bolshaya Rechka Kamensk

Karda

Anosovo

0   30 km
0   20 miles

IRKUTSK
REGION

Ust-Uda Yugolok

Balagansk

Kachug Biryulka

Gogon

Bilchir

Osa Manzurka

Karluk Cape Khoboy

UST-ORDYNSKY BURYAT
AUTONOMOUS REGION Khogot Kurma Kharantsy

Cheremhovo Bokhan Tikhonovka Bayanday Sarma Khuzhir

Svirsk MRS Olkhon
(Sakhyurta) Island

Mikhaylovka

Mishelevka Yelantsy

Usole- Ust-Ordynsky
Sibirskoe Telma Kharat

Tugutuy

Razdole Buguldeyka Sukhaya

Angarsk Khomutovo Enkhaluk

Meget Maloe
Goloustnoe See Enlargement

IRKUTSK Kudara

Kuda River Bukhta
Peschanaya Selenga Tataurovo

Talyany Shelekhov Ilinka

Bolshoy Taltsy Museum Selenginsk Zaudinsky
Shamanka Lug of Wooden
Irkut River Architecture Bolshoe Kamensk Sokol
Bolshaya Rechka Goloustnoe Ivolginsk Ulan-
Temnaya Port Baikal Bolshie Koty Ude
Pad km 149 Listvyanka Kuytun
To Arshan Polovinnaya Mysovaya
(58km); Mondy Kultuk (Babushkin) Tarbagatay Bolshoy
(144km); Tunka Slyudyanka H R E B E T D A B A N H A M A R Kunaley
Valley Utulik Tankhoy To
IRKUTSK Baikalsk Baikal Chita
REGION Vydrino Nature
Reserve

BURYATIYA BURYATIYA

SIBERIA

as the 'Paris of Siberia', Irkutsk did not welcome news of the October Revolution. The city's well-to-do merchants only succumbed to the Red tide in 1920, with the capture and execution of White army commander Admiral Kolchak, whose statue has recently been reerected. Soviet-era planning saw Irkutsk develop as the sprawling industrial and scientific centre that it remains today.

Orientation

Grand ul Karla Marksa is the historic commercial centre. Paralleling the Angara River, main axis ul Lenina runs from the administrative centre (pl Kirova) to the Raising of the Cross Church, where it becomes ul Sedova. Nearly 6km further south this road's continuation reaches the Angara Dam (GES). Beyond are the SibExpo area, several hotels and the 'Raketa' hydrofoil station.

The attractive train station is across the Angara River, and is bypassed by ul 2-Zheleznodorozhnaya. This becomes ul Lermontova, the main west-bank axis, leading to the unexotic Akademgorodok and Yubileyny suburbs en route to the Angara Dam (9km).

Many hotels, souvenir stalls and bookshops sell various city maps. Shop around as prices vary drastically.

Information

INTERNET ACCESS

Epitsentr (ul Sukhe-Batora 18; per hr R45-60; 🕑 24hr) Best Internet connection in town.
Kofeynya Karta (ul Marata 38; per hr R45; 🕑 9am-11pm) An inviting cellar Internet coffee shop serving real espressos (R33).
Web-Ugol (ul Lenina 13; per hr R45; 🕑 10am-10pm) Downstairs and easy to miss.

INTERNET RESOURCES

Baikal.ru (www.baikal.ru) Partly translated with old-postcard portraits of various Irkutsk streets.
ICC (www.irkutsk.com) History, maps and tourist information.
IrkutskOut (www.irkutskout.ru, in Russian) A wealth of practical details including café and restaurant listings, some with menus and photos.

MONEY

ATMs abound.
Bank Soyuz Booth (Hotel Baikal) Changes money 22 hours a day including Chinese yuan.

Guta Bank (foyer booth, ul Dzerzhinskogo; ☺ 11am-3pm & 4-6.45pm Mon-Fri) Good US dollar rates.

Valyutnaya Kassa No 1 (Guta Bank, ul Dzerzhinskogo; ☺ 9am-2pm & 3-5pm Mon-Fri) Travellers cheques swiftly cashed.

PHOTOGRAPHY
Yustas Photo-Salon (ul Sukhe-Batora; ☺ 10am-6pm) Passport photos for those Mongolian visas.

POST
Post office (ul Stepana Razina 23; ☺ 8am-8pm Mon-Fri, 9am-8pm Sat & Sun) Bigger branches at per Bogdanov 8 and ul Karla Marksa 28.

TELEPHONE
Main telephone office (ul Proletarskaya 12) Also has 24-hour ATMs.

TOURIST INFORMATION
Visitor Information Office (☎ 406 706; http://baikal info.ru; ul Karla Marksa 26b; ☺ 9am-8pm Mon-Fri, to 4pm Sat & Sun) Useful and very unusual for Russia, but this information office is also commercial and not always very imaginative beyond the tours it sells. The website is extensive if clunky.

TRAVEL AGENCIES
Local tour operators are useful not only for organising excursions (of which there are many) but also for booking hotels and train tickets. Note that most have only one or two overstretched English speakers, so you may need some patience.

BaikalComplex (☎ 389 205; www.baikalcomplex.irk .ru) Busy, well-organised operation, offering homestays and trips tailored for Western travellers. Call to arrange a meeting.

Baikal Discovery (☎ 243 715; www.baikal-discovery .com/en; Cheremchovski per 1a)

Baikaler (☎ 336 240; www.baikaler.com) Imaginative Jack Sheremetoff speaks good English and is well tuned to budget-traveller needs. Imaginative, personalised tours and a great central house-hostel.

BaikalExplorer (☎ 172 440; www.baikalex.com)

Baikalhostel (☎ 527 798; www.baikalhostels.com; ul Lermontova 136-1) Tours, a hostel and lots of useful information.

Baikal Safari (☎ 287 527; www.baikal-safari.ru; ul Chkalova 35/3) Offers homestays in Bolshoe Goloustnoe and Maloe More trips; competitive but mostly for local tourists. Minimal English is spoken.

Green Express (☎ 563 400; www.greenexpress.ru; 7th fl, ul Baikalskaya 291; ☺ 9am-6pm Mon-Fri) Big, professional outfit with a hotel in Listvyanka, yurts on

Olkhon Island and many mountain-biking, horse-riding and other tour options.

Sputnik (☎ 341 733; www.baikalsp.com; ul Chkalova 33; ☺ 9am-1pm & 2-6pm Mon-Fri) Publishes a comprehensive guidebook, *Mini-Encyclopaedia Bokrug*, which it plans to translate into English.

Sights
MUSEUMS
Irkutsk's pleasant if fairly standard **Regional Museum** (Kraevedchesky muzey; ☎ 333 449; ul Karla Marksa 2; foreigner admission R100; ☺ 10am-6pm Tue-Sun) is within a fancy 1870s brick building that formerly housed the Siberian Geographical Society, a club of Victorian-style gentlemen-explorers. The small gift shop is good for birch-bark boxes (from R80) and jewellery made from purple chaorite, a unique Siberian mineral. Across the road, a newly recast **statue of Tsar Alexander III** stands bushy-bearded on the riverfront promenade, copying a 1904 original.

A short walk behind the pretty pink **Preobrazheniya Gospodnya Church** (ul Timiryazeva) then through big heavy gates is the **Volkonsky House Museum** (☎ 207 532; per Volkonskogo 10; admission R50; ☺ 10am-6pm Tue-Sun). It's the preserved home of Decembrist Count Sergei Volkonsky, whose wife Maria Volkonskaya cuts the main figure in Christine Sutherland's book *The Princess of Siberia*. The mansion is set in a courtyard with stables, barn and servant quarters (beware of the dog). Downstairs is an (over-) renovated piano room; upstairs is a photo exhibition including portraits of Maria and other 1820s women who romantically followed their husbands and lovers into exile (see the boxed text, opposite). Labels are only in Russian but a R70 English-language pamphlet tells the stories. On Monday, when the museum is closed, the smaller **Trubetskoy House Museum** (☎ 275 773; ul Dzerzhinskogo 64; admission R40; ☺ 10am-6pm Thu-Mon) offers a similar Decembrist experience.

The grand old **Art Gallery** (ul Lenina 5; foreigner admission R50; ☺ 10am-6pm Wed-Mon) has a valuable though poorly lit collection ranging from Mongolian *thangka* (Buddhist religious paintings) to Russian-Impressionist canvases. Behind a photogenic 1909 façade its **sub-gallery** (ul Karla Marksa 23; admission R60; ☺ 10am-6pm Tue-Sun) is strong on Siberian landscapes and petroglyph rubbings and has some superb 17th-century icons.

A collection of Soviet tanks and missile launchers guard the **Dom Ofitserov** (ul Karla Marksa 47) which has a sporadically open museum and occasional concerts of patriotic songs.

Small, far from central, but well presented, the **City History Museum** (ul Chaikovskogo 5; admission R30; ✪ 10am-6pm Thu-Tue) shows various eras through shop window–style displays. Take the rare bus 11 about 2km west of town.

ARCHITECTURE & CHURCHES

Don't miss strolling along ul Karla Marksa, whose grand brick façades exude 19th-century architectural charm. Some fine **wooden houses** are sparsely dotted around town, notably on ul Dekabrskikh Sobyty, east of ul Timiryazeva.

The magnificent Annunciation Cathedral that once dominated pl Kirova was demolished during one of Stalin's bad moods. It was replaced by a hulking concrete **regional administrative building**, the ex-Communist Party headquarters. Tragic. Behind this ugly centrepiece, however, two notable churches survive. The whitewashed 18th-century **Saviour's Church** (Spasskaya tserkov; admission R100; ✪ 10am-6pm Tue-Sun) has remnants of murals on its façade and contains an ethnographic museum which is most exciting for allowing access to the bell tower – great views if you're allowed to the very top. Much more eye-catching is the fairy-tale ensemble of the **Bogoyavlensky Cathedral** (ul Nizhnaya Naberezhnaya; ✪ 8.30am-5pm), whose on-going restoration continues to add a colourful dazzle to the otherwise rather grimy riverfront.

Set in a leafy garden behind a noisy traffic circle, the 1762 **Znamensky Monastery** is 1.5km northeast of the Bogoyavlensky Cathedral. Echoing with mellifluous plainsong, the interior has splendidly muralled vaulting, a towering iconostasis and a gold sarcophagus holding the miraculous relics of Siberian missionary St Inokent. Celebrity graves outside include that of Grigory Shelekhov, the man who claimed Alaska for Russia. White-Russian commander Admiral Kolchak was executed by Bolsheviks near the spot where his **statue** was controversially erected in November 2004 at the entrance to the monastery grounds, on a plinth that's exaggeratedly high enough to reduce vandalism.

The 1758 baroque **Raising of the Cross Church** (Krestovozdvizhenskaya tserkov; ul Sedova 1; donation) has a fine interior of gilt-edged icons and several examples of unusually intricate brickwork in a rounded style that's unique to Irkutsk and the Selenga Delta village of Posolskoe.

Nearing completion, the gigantic **Kazansky Church** is a Disneyesque confection of salmon-pink walls and fluoro turquoise domes topped with gold baubled crosses. Get off tram 4 two stops northeast of the bus station.

NERPA SEALS

Nessie and Tito, two much-loved nerpa (freshwater seals), live at **Akvarium Nerpy** (☎ 435 047; ul 2-Zheleznodorozhnaya 66; admission R70; ✪ 11am-6.30pm Wed-Sun) and perform 'shows' every half-hour with no minimum attendance. Unlike some small 'zoos' elsewhere, the experience is positive and relatively humane. Feats include 'singing' (nasal flatulence?), break-dancing, ball-tossing and even basic mathematics.

THE DECEMBRIST WOMEN

Having patently failed to topple Tsarist autocracy in December 1825, many prominent 'Decembrist' gentlemen-revolutionaries were exiled to Siberia. They're popularly credited with bringing civilisation to the rough-edged local pioneer-convict population. Yet the real heroines were their womenfolk who cobbled together the vast carriage fares to get themselves to Siberia: in prerailway 1827, the trip from St Petersburg to Irkutsk cost the equivalent of US$200. And that was just the start. Pauline Annenkova, the French mistress of one aristocratic prisoner, spent so long awaiting permission to see her lover in Chita that she had time to set up a fashionable dressmakers' shop in Irkutsk. By constantly surveying the prisoners' conditions, the women eventually shamed guards into reducing the brutality of the jail regimes while their food parcels meant that Decembrists had more hope of surviving the minimal rations of their imprisonment. The Decembrist women came to form a core of civil society and introduced 'European standards of behaviour'. As conditions eventually eased, this formed the basis for a liberal Siberian aristocracy, especially in Chita and Irkutsk where some Decembrists stayed on even after finishing their formal banishment.

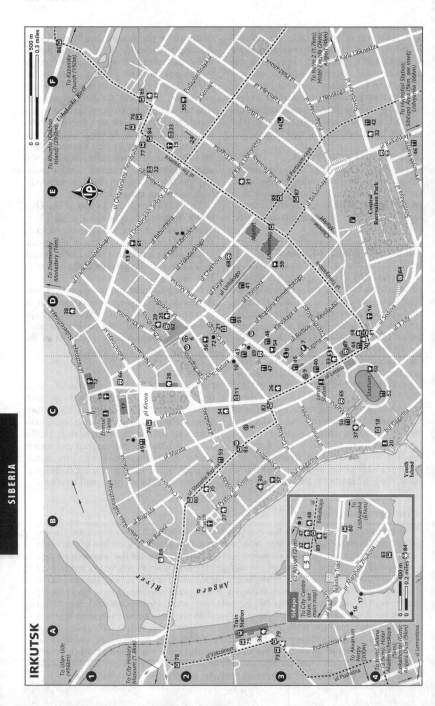

INFORMATION
Baikal Safari 1 C1
Bank Soyuz Booth Банк Союз .... (see 30)
Epitsentr Епицентр 2 D3
Guta Bank Гута Банк 3 D4
Jewish Cultural Centre 4 E2
Kofeynaya Karta Кофейная Карта 5 C3
Main Telephone Office
   Междугородный телефонный
   пункт 6 D2
Mongolian Consulate
   Консульство Монголии 7 D3
Sputnik .... (see 49)
Visitor Information Office 8 D3
Web-Ugol Web-Угол 9 C3
Yustas Photo-Salon
   Юстас Фото-Салон 10 C3

SIGHTS & ACTIVITIES
Art Gallery
   Художественный Музей 11 C1
Bogoyavlensky Cathedral
   Богоявленский Собор 12 C1
Dom Ofitserov Дом Офицеров 13 D1
Islamic Cultural Centre 14 F3
Preobrazheniya Gospodnya Church
   Преображения
   Господня Церковь 15 E2
Raising of the Cross Church
   Крестовоздвиженская
   церковь 16 D4
Regional Administrative Building 17 C1
Regional Museum
   Краеведческий Музей 18 C4
Saviour's Church
   Спасская Церковь 19 C1
Statue of Tsar Alexander III
   Памятник Александр III 20 C4
sub-gallery
   Художественный Музей 21 D2
Trubetskoy House Museum
   Дом Трубецкого 22 E2
Volkonsky House Museum
   Дом Волконского 23 F2
Wooden Houses 24 E2

SLEEPING 🛏
Arena Obshchezhitiye
   Арена Общежитие 25 D2
Baikaler Hostel 26 C3
Hotel Agat Гостиница Агат 27 B2
Hotel Angara Гостиница Ангара 28 C2
Hotel Arena Гостиница Арена 29 D2
Hotel Baikal Гостиница Байкал 30 B3
Hotel Delta Отель Дельта 31 E3
Hotel Gloria Отель Глория 32 F4
Hotel Gornyak Гостиница Горняк 33 C4
Hotel Rus Гостиница Русь 34 C2
Irkutsk Downtown Hostel 35 B2
Resting Rooms Комнаты Отдыха 36 A3
Retro 1 Ретро 1 .... 37 C4
Santerra Bar-Hotel
   Бар-Гостиница Сантерра 38 D1
Uzory Узоры 39 F2

EATING 🍴
Arbatski Dvorik
   Арбатский Дворик .... (see 41)
Domino Домино 40 C3
Fiesta Фиеста 41 D3
Figaro Pizza Фигаро Пицца 42 F4
Kafe 16 Кафе 16 .... 43 D3
Kafe Temp 44 D4
Kino Kafe 45 C3
Korchma 46 E4
Kyoto 47 C3
Lancelot *8 D3
Pervach 49 C2
Russkaya Chaynaya
   Русская Чайная 50 C4
Snezhinka Снежинка 51 D2
U Dzhuzeppe У Джузеппе 52 C4
Wiener Café Венское Кафе 53 C2

DRINKING 🍷
Bierhaus 54 D3
Cheshskaya Pivovarnaya
   Чешская Пивоварная 55 F2
Liverpool Паб Ливерпуль 56 D2
Monet 57 B3
Na Zamorskoy 58 D4

Ryumochnaya Рюмочная 59 D3
Shch17 Щ17 .... 60 C4
U Shveyka У Швейка 61 E1

ENTERTAINMENT 🎭
Circus Цирк 62 D2
Kukol Theatre Театр Кукол 63 E4
Musical Theatre
   Музыкальный Театр 64 D4
Okhlopkov Drama Theatre
   Драматический Театр
   Имени Охлопкова 65 C4
Organ Hall Органный Зал 66 C1
Philharmonic Hall Филармония 67 D4
Poznaya Disko-bar
   Позная Диско-Бар 68 D3
Stratosphera Night Club
   Ночной Клуб Стратосфера 69 D3

SHOPPING 🛍
Fanat Фанат 70 D4

TRANSPORT
Bus station Автовокзал 71 F1
Central Air Agency
   Центральная Аэрокасса 72 D2
Marshrutka 12 .... 73 A3
Marshrutka 16 to Raketa 74 C2
Marshrutky 16 & 20 .... 75 A3
MIAT .... (see 7)
Minibuses to Listvyanka 76 F1
Private buses to Bratsk 77 E2
Tram 1 & 2 .... 78 A2
Tram 1 & 2 .... 79 A3
Tram 1 & 2 .... 80 B2
Tram 1 & 2 .... 81 D4
Tram 1 & 2 from train station 82 C3
Tram 1 & 2 to train station 83 C3
Tram 4 .... 84 E2
Tram 4 .... 85 F2
Tram 4 stop for Kazansky Church 86 F1
Tram 4 terminus 87 E3
Tram 5 to SibExpo area 88 E3
VSRP Hydrofoils to Bratsk
   Речной Вокзал 89 B2

DAM & SIBEXPO AREA

Some 6km southeast of the centre, the 1956 **Angara Dam** is 2km long. Its construction raised Lake Baikal by up to 6m, causing various human and environmental problems, but the dam itself is hardly an attraction. Moored nearby, the **Angara steamship** is an ice-breaker ferry originally imported in kit form from England to carry Trans-Siberian Railway passengers across Lake Baikal (the trains went on her bigger sister ship *Baikal*, which sank years ago). Officially closed to visitors, the ship is currently used as drinks storage for a nearby summer café, but the impressive engines still work, as you might see, should the café owner decide to befriend you.

Sleeping

Although options are expanding, Irkutsk accommodation still gets very full in summer. Bookings are generally a very good idea.

Travel agencies arrange homestays in Irkutsk and villages around Lake Baikal. Prices typically start at R500 per bed, though R800 (sometimes with full board) is more common. Check the location: the cheapest places can be 10km or more from the city centre.

BUDGET
Hostels

Irkutsk has three tiny new private hostels. All have good, shared toilets, shower and kitchen. They are ideal for finding English-speaking assistance, arranging tours or meeting fellow travellers, and unlike hotels they don't charge booking fees.

Baikaler Hostel (☎ 336 240; apt 11, ul Lenina 9; www .baikaler.com; dm R500; 🖳) Beds are limited at this wonderful, super-central homestay-hostel. No drop-ins without prior reservation.

Irkutsk Downtown Hostel (☎ 334 597; www.down townhostel.irkutsk.ru; apt 12, ul Stepana Razina 12; dm/d R400/1080) Cosy, 10-bed apartment-hostel above the Yantar grocery. Enter using the rear door spray-painted with the word 'Hostel'; phone ahead for the door entry code. Though central this area is slightly dubious at night. Take tram 1 from the train station.

Baikalhostel (☎ 525 742, 527 798; www.baikal hostels.com; apt 1, ul Lermontova 136; dm €8-10) This German-owned hostel receives rave reviews from several travellers, despite the inconvenient and insalubrious location, several kilometres south of the train station; take *marshrutka* 12 to stop Mikrochirurgia Glaza. Excellent website.

Hotels

Hotel Profsoyuznaya (Obshchezhitiye Gostinichogo Tipa Profsoyuznaya; ☎ 357 963; fax 357 855 for bookings; ul Baikalskaya 263; dm/tr R295/826, tw R590-708) Simple but well-kept Soviet-era rooms, albeit far from the centre in the distant SibExpo area. Tram 5 stops outside.

Hotel Gornyak (☎ 243 754; ul Lenina 24; s R900-1200, tw R1800) Friendly, central and small, this hotel has reasonably presentable rooms with private shower and toilet, though some are affected by road noise. Per-hour rates available. The entrance is on ul Dzerzhinskogo.

Hotel Akademicheskaya (☎ 427 872; ul Lermontova 271a; s R1070-1210, d R1390) Were it nearer the centre, the renovated standard rooms with new toilet and curtained shower here would be fairly decent value. However, it's way out in Akademgorodok: take *marshrutka* 3 to Gosuniversitet stop then walk across a grassy area from ul Lermontova 265 (map at www.irkutsk.org/fed/pic/akad.jpg). There are cheaper R820 doubles (5th floor, no lift) with toilet and washbasin, but these are rather miserable unreconstructed affairs.

Uzory (☎ 209 239; ul Oktyabrskoy Revolyutsi 17; s/tw/tr R550/800/1200) Clean, unpretentious rooms with leopard-skin–patterned blankets. The communal toilets and shower are being rebuilt. Apocryphal backpacker folklore claims that impecunious travellers can get discounts for sleeping on the billiard table.

Arena Obshchezhitiye (☎ 334 663; ul Sverdlova 39; s/tw/tr/q R300/600/900/1200) Staff are grumpy and rooms are ragged but no worse than you'd expect for the price. Entered through a warren of prison-like brown-metal doors, this place is very central and often full.

Hotel Agat (☎ 242 320; ul Pyatoy Armii 12; tw R1000) Uninspired but with clean communal toilets and showers. Plenty of peeling paint.

Hotel Selena (☎ 397 859; ul Igoshina 1; dm/s/tw R680/750/1040) Overlooking the new Angara bridge site on the west bank, this crumbling eyesore is depressing and awkward to reach but might have rooms available when

everything else is full. It's a 15-minute walk from the southern terminus of tram 1, passing the Technical University, around which there are many eateries.

There are also **resting rooms** (komnaty otdykha; R18 per hr plus R40 for sheets) at the train station.

MIDRANGE & TOP END
Central

Hotel Zvezda (☎ 540 000; www.zvezdahotel.ru; ul Yadrintseva 1ж; s/d 2900/3300, ste R5500-9000; ⓟ ✖ ▣) Within a new, Swiss chalet–style building, rooms here are modern and comfortable, service is pleasant and English is spoken. The peaceful location is 300m south of Retro 2. Its atmospheric restaurant specialises in game and exotic meats.

Hotel Gloria (☎ 540 326; www.gloriahotel.ru; Sovetskaya ul 58; s R3200, tw/d R3600, ste R5000-5500; ✖) This new pastel-beige tower has nine international-class rooms and two bigger suites which have bath as well as shower. English is spoken and the minibars overflow with alcoholic choice.

Santerra Bar-Hotel (☎ 201 518; ul Nizhnaya Naberezhnaya 126; s/d R3000/3100) This tiny all-suite minihotel has very stylish, fully equipped accommodation, bamboo screens shading generously sized king beds. Oddly, guests must access their rooms through the director's private office. No English. Rooms are half-price for 12-hour stays.

Hotel Delta (☎ 217 876; www.grandbaikal.ru; ul Karla Libknekhta 58; s/d R2000/3000) The functional new motel-standard rooms here have little panache, but are good value for their relatively central position; vastly preferable to the old Soviet hotels.

Irkutsk has two exclusive house-hotels in restored historic buildings with plush if sometimes over-fussy décor. Both open only by appointment. **Retro 1** (☎ 333 251; http://rus.baikal.ru/english/hotels/retro1/; ul Karla Marksa 1; ste R2640-4580) is perfectly central and was reconstructed for a presidential visit. **Retro 2** (☎ 271 534; http://rus.baikal.ru/english/hotels/retro2/; ul Yadrintseva 1; ste R2660-3620) is in a small park off Sovetskaya ul, three stops from the airport on *marshrutka* 20.

Location is the only advantage of Irkutsk's old Soviet-era hotels which mostly offer budget quality rooms at midrange prices. Despite their overpriced mediocrity, most are still full in summer. **Hotel Angara** (☎ 255 105; www.angarahotel.ru; ul Sukhe-Batora 7) is central but outrageously overpriced; beware of considerable quality variation between and within different floors. The standard rooms on the 3rd floor (single/double R1400/2100) are the Angara's worst, with worn carpets and dizzying wallpaper, but the 3rd floor's upgraded rooms (single/double R2000/2500) are the Angara's best. Despite crooked lamps and scratchy towels, these are generally more presentable than the pokey little renovated rooms on the 5th to 7th floors (single/twin R2240/3680); rooms on the 6th floor have fridge and safe. Rooms on the 2nd and 4th floors (single/double R1600/2360) are repainted but retain scuffed Soviet-era furniture and teeny tiny toilets.

Other Soviet-era dinosaurs:

Hotel Arena (☎ 344 642; ul Zhelyabova 8a; s/tw R1206/1872) The small rooms renovated some years ago are now getting increasingly scruffy with dirty carpets and battered furniture. Reasonable bathrooms are shared between room-pairs.

Hotel Baikal (Hotel Intourist, Hotel Irkutsk; ☎ 250 167; fax 250 314; www.baikal-hotel.ru; bul Gagarina 44; s/tw R1500/2370, d R2370-3200) Rooms are upgraded but only the most expensive doubles come close to Western standards in this riverside slab-hotel. Some have good views.

Hotel Rus (☎ 242 715; http://rus.baikal.ru; ul Sverdlova 19; s R1457-1603, d R1845, ste R2710-2981) Cosy by Soviet standards but redecoration of the rooms is skin deep. Breakfast is included and the contrastingly appealing Siberian cottage–style restaurant is recommended.

SibExpo Area
The SibExpo-Solnichny area is some 6km south of the centre by tram 5. Rates include breakfast.

Sun Hotel (☎ 255 910; www.xemi.com/sunhotel; ul Baikalskaya 295b; s €100-115, d €120-135; P 🍴 🖳) Impressive bathrooms and minibar complement stylish dark-wood furnishings in the Sun's modern rooms. Reception staff speak English but the lobby lacks facilities.

Solnyshonok (3rd fl, ul Baikalskaya 259; s/d €50/65) Sister hotel to the Sun Hotel, this has cheaper motel-standard rooms. The rooms have more style than pricier equivalents at the Baikal Business Centre, but their bathrooms are slightly musty and lack shower curtains. The Solnyshonok's three flights of stairs (no lift) are off-putting in midsummer heat.

Baikal Business Centre (☎ 259 120; www.bbc.ru; s/tw R3400/4200; P 🍴) This functional business hotel is a white and blue-glass tower approximating international standards.

Bathrooms have showers but no bathtub, and there is BBC World TV.

Eating
RESTAURANTS
Pervach (☎ 202 288; ul Chkalova 33; meals R240-350) Pervach offers imaginative Baikal-based menus in a vaulted stone-and-brick cellar, heated by real fires in winter. Some English is spoken.

Arbatski Dvorik (☎ 200 633; ul Uritskogo; meals R450-800; 🕙 11am-midnight) An upmarket restaurant with English menu and a remarkable interior of imitation houses, doorways and lanterns. Incongruously, access is by walking through Fiesta fast food.

Korchma (☎ 209 102; ul Krasnykh Madiyar 52; meals R230-580; 🕙 noon-last client) Home-cooked traditional Russian food in a one-room cottage restaurant. It's set amid other more-genuine Siberian log homes which have so far survived rapid development pressures. Meals are presented on two-tone ceramics while an accordionist accompanies a talented, costumed folk singer (R40 cover). There's a 10% service charge.

Snezhinka (☎ 344 862; opposite ul Karla Marksa 25; meals R220-330; 🕙 11am-midnight) Warm, cosy *belle époque* café-restaurant with attentive service and consistently good food. The swirling ironwork furniture is suitably padded.

Lancelot (☎ 202 328; ul Kievskaya 2; meals R350-800; 🕙 noon-midnight Sun-Thu, noon-2am Fri & Sat) Flaming torches lead down through a portcullis into an amusing neomedieval castle interior. There's a menu in English with Arthurian-named dishes and European prices.

U Dzhuzeppe (☎ 258 348; stadium arches; meals R70-170; 🕙 11am-11pm) Cloyingly cute puppy photos undermine the otherwise understated elegance of high ceilings and wrought-iron fittings. Fruity eggplant (R90) and stuffed squid (R110) are much better than the microwaved pizza slices (R35). Menu in English.

The most authentic pizzeria in town is **Figaro Pizza** (☎ 270 607; ul Sovetskaya 58; pizzas R100-270, beers from R50; 🕙 10am-midnight), while at **Kyoto** (Kioto; ☎ 550 505; ul Karla Marksa 15a; meals R400-1000; 🕙 10am-2am) there's Japanese ambience and non-Japanese rice.

CAFÉS
Kafe 16 (☎ 242 682; ul Sukhe-Batora 16; meals R270-500, coffees R40-80; 🕙 10am-11pm) Enticing brown and beige tones purring with jazz beckon you

---

BEST OF BAIKAL – WHAT'S BEST WHERE?

Accommodation (choice) Listvyanka, Maloe More
Accommodation (charm) Port Baikal, Olkhon Island
Beaches (photogenic) Eastern Baikal
Beaches (swimming) Maloe More
Buddhist datsans Tunka Valley
Cruises (best value) Nizhneangarsk
Cycling Olkhon Island
Day trip Irkutsk–Bolshie Koty
Dog-sledding (winter) Listvyanka
Dog-sledding (summer) Olkhon Island
Easiest lake access Slyudyanka
English-speaking help Irkutsk, Severobaikalsk, Olkhon
Gulag near Nizhneangarsk
Hiking (easy) Port Baikal, Arshan
Hiking (expedition) Goudzhiket
Hot springs Khakusy

Ice driving Severobaikalsk
Ice fishing (through a hole) off Slyudyanka or Severobaikalsk
Ice fishing (with a net) Katun village (Chivyrkuysky Gulf)
Lakeside church Posolskoe
Meeting foreign travellers Khuzhir (Olkhon), Irkutsk hostels
Nerpa seals (captive) Irkutsk
Nerpa seals (wild) Ushkanny Islands (Svyatoy Nos)
Quaint villages Baikalskoe, Uro (Barguzin Valley)
Scenic train rides Baikalsk to Slyudyanka, Circumbaikal Railway
Scenery Ust Barguzin, Barguzin Valley, Tunka Valley
Scuba diving Irkutsk agencies
Shamanism Olkhon Island
Skiing and snowboarding Baikalsk

---

through a unique Art Deco clamshell archway. Try the hard-hitting espressos (R40), and tastily garlic-edged fried cheese starters.

Wiener Café (Venskoe Kafe; ☎ 202 116; ul Stepana Razina 19; meals R180-300, coffees R40-70; ☻ 10am-11pm) Alluring coffee house with marble-top tables, Parisian-bar chairs and sepia photos. Reasonably priced pastries are available to takeaway.

Na Zamorskoy (☎ 290 891; ul Timiryazeva; meals R200-400, coffees R35-200; ☻ 9am-11.30pm) Fresh roses, rattan furniture, raffia-threaded blinds and lots of potted plants make this a comforting breakfast oasis. Enjoy delicious ham-and-cheese stuffed bliny (R65) and an excellent latte (R45). Nice church views.

Russkaya Chaynaya (☎ 201 678; ul Karla Marksa 3; meals R200-350, coffees R40-100; ☻ 10am-11pm) Boasts a splendid *fin de siècle* interior and summer beer garden.

Kino Kafe (ul Karla Marksa 22; snacks R10-40, tea R3, beers R20; ☻ 11am-10pm) Ultrabasic, super-cheap snack tables and a handy toilet, all within the foyer of the architecturally delightful Khudozhestveny Cinema.

QUICK EATS

Fiesta fast food (ul Uritskogo; snacks R45-120; ☻ noon-11pm) is the most atmospheric and congenial of Irkutsk's numerous fast-food outlets, though **Domino** (ul Lenina 13a; meals R70-140; ☻ 24hr) is popular for its all-night service.

Most appealing of the city's cheap cafeterias is the neat little **Blinnaya** (ul Sukhe-Batora;

meals R40-90; ☻ 10am-6pm Mon-Fri, 10am-4pm Sat). However, for a slice of pure Soviet ambience try **Kafe Temp** (ul Lenina 25; meals R40-70; ☻ 10am-8pm), a sit-down cafeteria with archetypal 1970s décor. Amusingly surly staff bark bad-temperedly from behind gently vibrating displays of typical pre-served *stolovaya* stodge.

Drinking

Liverpool (☎ 202 512; ul Sverdlova 28; imported beers R50-100; ☻ noon-last client) Superbly idiosyncratic Beatles theme-pub with a room for live acoustic music and a second bar decorated with typewriters and antiquated reel-to-reel tape recorders. Newcastle Brown Ale in Irkutsk – whatever next? Food is imaginatively named but so-so.

U Shveyka (☎ 242 687; ul Karla Marksa 34; beers R50-55, meals R170-400; ☻) This olde-worlde cavern with staring elk head and yin-yang condiments has a good summer beer terrace. Much better value than Bierhaus.

Bierhaus (☎ 550 555; ul Karla Marksa; beers R120-180; ☻ noon-2am) Upmarket Bavarian-style *bierstube* (beer-hall with heavy wooden furniture) serving Hoegaarden and Guinness as well as German beers and sausages.

Cheshskaya Pivovarnaya (☎ 538 482; ul Krasnoarmeyskaya 29; beers R47-53, meals R180-300) Irkutsk's unpretentious microbrewery-pub creates its own Czech-style Pils.

Monet (☎ 201 771; bul Gagarina 42; coffees R75-150, meals R250-650; ☻ 9am-11pm) Overpriced and pretentiously dubbed a 'coffee fashion club', the Monet's most intriguing feature is its cushioned oriental parlour downstairs for smoking water pipes (R450 to R850).

Shch17 (☎ 203 109; stadium arches; beers R34-40; ☽ 24hr) The extraordinary interior here is designed like a submarine.

Ryumochnaya (ul Litvinova 16; vodkas R14, beers R28-40; ☽ 24hr) Get slammed with rough-edged locals at tables that are too chunky to be thrown at anyone…hopefully.

Entertainment
On summer evenings romantic couples and jolly groups of locals stroll the Angara promenade and the grassy areas behind the fine **Okhlopkov Drama Theatre** (☎ 333 361; ul Karla Marksa 14).

Circus (☎ 336 139; ul Zhelyabova; tickets R100-250) Puts on eye-boggling Cirque du Soleil–style performances. Avoid the cheapest front seats where you'll get poor views and a regular splashing.

Other options:

Kukol Theatre (☎ 270 666; Sovetskaya ul) Puppet shows.

Musical Theatre (☎ 342 131; ul Sedova; tickets R60-300; box office ☽ 11am-6.30pm Tue-Sun) Pantomimes, ballets and costumed musical-comedy shows in a big concrete auditorium.

Organ Hall (pl Kirova) Organ concerts are held in the Polish Catholic church.

Philharmonic Hall (☎ 245 076; ul Dzerzhinskogo 2) Historic building staging regular children's shows and musical programmes from pop to classical.

Poznaya Disko-bar (ul Chekhova 17; admission R50; beers R45; ☽ 9pm-late) Tobacco-fugged dive popular with student drinkers on modest budgets.

Stratosphera Night Club (www.strata-club.ru; ul Karla Marksa 15; cover from R100; ☽ 6pm-6am Fri-Sun) Irkutsk's late-night hotspot, with bowling alley, two-storey disco and three-storey drink prices.

Shopping
Fanat (ul Timiryazeva; ☽ 10am-7pm Mon-Fri, to 6pm Sat) Sells Western-brand camping, fishing and skiing equipment, hiking boots and mountain bikes.

Getting There & Away
For regularly updated boat, bus and local train schedules consult kbzd.irk.ru/Eng /shedule.htm.

AIR
Irkutsk's antiquated little 'international' airport is handily placed near the city centre. Foreign destinations include Baku (US$250), Tashkent (US$280) and Dushanbe (US$290), as well as the Chinese cities Shenyang (US$170, Tuesday and Saturday) and Tianjin (US$330, Thursday and Sunday). **MIAT** (☎ 203 458; www.miat.com; Mongolian consulate, ul Lapina) flies thrice weekly to Ulaan Baatar (US$210). Prices are discounted to as little as US$64 in winter.

There are dozens of domestic destinations. For Moscow Domodedovo there are direct flights with Siberian (R7980 to R10,150, daily) and TransAero (R6650, twice weekly). Bargain deals abound for early bookings possibly via Omsk (Friday and Sunday) or Krasnoyarsk (three weekly). Tickets are sold by a convenient **Central Air Agency** (☎ 201 517; ul Gorkogo 29; ☽ 8am-7pm).

Some other options:

Destination	Cost	Frequency
Barnaul	R6100	Fri
Bratsk	R2870	daily
Chita	R2700	5 weekly
Khabarovsk	R5450-6200	6 weekly
Kyzyl	R3940	Sat
Magadan	R8500	Fri
Nizhneangarsk	R2160	2 weekly
Novosibirsk	R6500	7 weekly
St Petersburg	R7500-9000	3 weekly
Yekaterinburg	R7680	8 weekly
Yuzhno Sakhalinsk	R7600	Mon & Thu

BOAT
In July and August hydrofoils buzz up Lake Baikal to Severobaikalsk and Nizhneangarsk (R1400, 11½ hours) stopping off in Port Baikal and Olkhon Island (R1100). Departures from Irkutsk are timetabled at 8.50am on Tuesday and Friday returning next day but changes and cancellations are frequent. An extra Irkutsk–Olkhon–Irkutsk service might run on certain summer Thursdays. There's an airline-style baggage limit.

Between once and four times daily, June to September, hydrofoils also serve Listvyanka (R130, 1¼ hours) and Bolshie Koty (R180, 1¾ hours).

All of the above depart from the Raketa hydrofoil station beyond the Angara Dam in Solnechny Mikro-Rayon, two-minutes' walk from bus 16 stop 'Raketa'.

From a different jetty beside floating Kafe Iveriya, **VSRP** (☎ 287 467) hydrofoils run

SIBERIA

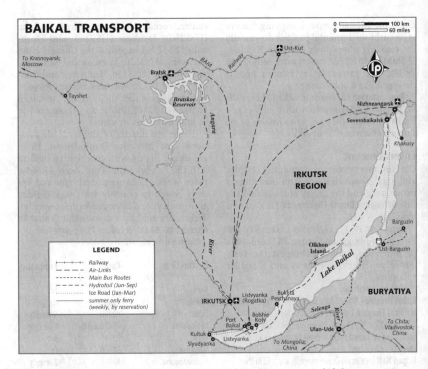

BAIKAL TRANSPORT

LEGEND

+—+—+	Railway
– – –	Air-Links
--------	Main Bus Routes
– – –	Hydrofoil (Jun-Sep)
....	Ice Road (Jan-Mar)
————	summer only ferry (weekly, by reservation)

to Bratsk (R460, 12½ hours) on Tuesday, Saturday and certain Thursdays, June to late September.

BUS

From the **bus station** (☎ 209 115; ☉ 6am-7pm) book tickets ahead for Arshan (R220, 8am) and Khuzhir on Olkhon Island (R370, 9am, frequency varies seasonally). Listvyanka buses (R30, 1¼ hours, five daily) are supplemented by regular *marshrutky* (R60, 50 minutes) leaving when full. For Bratsk, comfortable private express buses have special ticket booths opposite the bus station.

The Visitor Information Office organises seasonal minibuses to Maloe More and Olkhon Island, departing from the yard outside its office.

TRAIN

The elegant old train station has numbered sections. Northernmost section No 1 has advance domestic ticketing; No 2 sells same-day tickets. Upstairs in area No 3 is the **Servis Tsentr** (☎ 636 501; ☉ 8am-7pm) for international tickets and the resting rooms,

while downstairs is left-luggage. An unnumbered fourth area beyond sells *elektrichka* tickets (eg to Slyudyanka, R38.20) and is the access route to all platforms.

The best, if most expensive, train to/from Moscow is the No 9/10 *Baikal* (R4150, 77 hours) but *platskart* berths on slower trains such as No 240/250 (87 hours) cost only R1820 via Krasnoyarsk (R505, 19 hours).

There are several alternate-day trains for Vladivostok including No 2 (R3840, 72 hours) and No 230 (R3400, 75 hours) via Khabarovsk (58 to 60 hours). Trains for Beijing (R3800, 73 hours) via Chita pass through Irkutsk on Tuesday at 9am. Those via Mongolia depart Saturday at 6am. Alternatively, for Ulaan Baatar (R1600) fast train No 6 (Friday and Saturday) is a full 10 hours quicker than the daily No 364 (35 hours). If you're heading east, consider stopping first in Ulan-Ude (eight hours), enjoying views of Lake Baikal en route. Train tickets are sold at the Central Air Agency (commission R80), upstairs in the airport (commission R70) and in Hotel Baikal (commission R100 domestic, R300 international).

Getting Around

Within the central area, walking is usually the best idea as one-way systems make bus routes confusing. Expect some routes to change significantly if and when the big new Angara bridge is completed.

Frequent *marshrutka* 20 runs from the airport, up ul Dekabrskikh Sobyty, ul Karla Marksa and ul Lenina before passing the Hotel Angara and crossing to the train station. Trolleybus 4 (R5) takes a similar route but via ul Sovetskaya and Hotel Gloria.

From the train station trams 1 and 2 run to uls Lenina and Timiryazeva, while bus 7 crosses to pl Kirova, then loops round the centre and out past the Znamensky Monastery. Bus 16 continues down ul Lenina, past the Raising of the Cross Church and (eventually) the Angara Dam. It then passes within 500m of the SibExpo hotels before looping back beside the Raketa hydrofoil station to the *Angara* steamship. Slow tram 5 from the Sun Hotel trundles to the central market, and from here tram 4 goes past the bus station and Kazansky Church.

For the west bank, both bus/*marshrutka* 3 from the central market and *marshrutky* 12 and 72 (to Solnichny) from the train station cover the whole length of ul Lermontova.

AROUND IRKUTSK
Taltsy Museum of Wooden Architecture

Музей Деревянного Зодчества Тальцы
About 47km east of Irkutsk, 23km before Listvyanka, **Taltsy** (locals/foreigners R20/80 plus photography permit; ☼ 10am-6pm summer, to 4pm winter) is an impressive outdoor collection of old Siberian buildings set in a delightful riverside forest. Amid the renovated farmsteads are two chapels, a church, a watermill, some Tungusi graves and the eye-catching 17th-century Iliminsk Ostrog watchtower. Listvyanka–Irkutsk buses stop on request at Taltsy's apparently deserted entrance access road. Don't worry; the ticket booth is only a minute's walk through the forest.

LISTVYANKA ЛИСТВЯНКА

☎ 3952 / pop 2500 / ☼ Moscow +5hr
The nearest Lake Baikal village to Irkutsk, Listvyanka offers winter dog-sledding and summer boat and horse rides, and is ideal for watching the Siberian nouveau riche at play. Outside busy weekends, the village is still reasonably quiet with inspiring views

towards the distant snow-capped Kamar Daban Mountains. Basic maps are available on www.irkutsk.org/fed/maps/listmap .jpg and from a **tourist information booth** at the port's bus stand, which also has accommodation listings.

Sights & Activities

Having glimpsed Lake Baikal and eaten fresh-smoked omul fish at the port, many visitors are left wondering why they came. Fishing-boat rides (charters from R800 per hour) or gentle strolls are a common time-filler with old log cottages to photograph up uls Gudina and Chapaeva, though ongoing gentrification is starting to impinge on their architectural integrity. About 2km west in **Krestovka**, the pretty if unremarkable **Svyato-Nikolskaya Church** was named for an apparition of St Nicholas who supposedly saved its sponsor from a Baikal shipwreck.

Another 2km towards Irkutsk at **Rogatka**, tour groups are herded into the **Limnological Institute** (☎ 250 551; ul Akademicheskaya 1; locals/foreigners R180/80; ☼ 9am-5pm Oct-May, to 7pm Jun-Sep), where gruesomely discoloured fish samples and seal embryos in formaldehyde are now supplemented with tanks containing a sad, living nerpa seal and various Baikal fish that you'd otherwise encounter on restaurant menus.

From December to March, the **Baikal Dog Sledding Centre** (☎ 112 829, 112 799; ole-tbaik sledog@mail.ru; ul Gornaya 17, Krestovka) offers thrilling dog-sledding on forest tracks. The shortest run, 3km with three dogs, costs R600, but whole multiday cross-Baikal expeditions are possible with bigger dog-teams. The owners' sons speak English.

On warmer winter weekends snowmobiles and even horses can be informally hired on the ice near the Proshli Vek restaurant, while hovercraft rides are available from the main port area. On the beachfront, locals photograph one another in front of weirdly shaped frozen waves.

Sleeping

There is a vast choice of accommodation. However, with minimal public transport, no taxi service and no left-luggage office, finding a room in summer without reservations can take some tiresome trekking around. Leave heavy bags in Irkutsk. Anything under R500 is likely to be very basic with outside squat toilet, dorm-style beds or both. Virtually every Irkutsk tour agent has its own guesthouse or homestay in Listvyanka; value varies.

In the port area, handy but predominantly unexotic homestays abound on lakefront ul Gorkogo and along the two ribbons of attractive wooden cottages rising steeply up inland valleys nearby, ul Chapaeva (eg Nos 6, 44 and 64) and ul Gudina (Nos 77 and 13a). Slightly less convenient than the port area for public transport, Krestovka is nonetheless more of a 'real' village and offers an ever-expanding choice of accommodation.

BUDGET

Galina Vasilievna's homestay (☎ 112 798; ul Kulikova 44, Krestovka; dm/tr R300/900) Galina offers cheap, saggy dorm beds in a delightfully genuine old home with a large traditional stove-heater but minimal facilities. Ask for keys at the Dariya grocery shop in front. An indoor toilet functions in summer.

Spitting distance from the lake in the port area, **Priboy** (☎ 112 839; upper fl, ul Gorkogo 101; dm/tw R250/1200) has cheap if unappealing dorms and some basic rooms with shared toilet, shower and dubious taste in wallpaper. Add R300 for lake views. Request keys from the **Askat shop** (☉ 8am-8pm) or the **restaurant** (☉ noon-11pm) downstairs.

MIDRANGE
Port Area

Ersi (☎ 112 546; www.ersi.baikal.ru; ul Chapaeva 65; tw R1000-1289) In the garden behind the house is a Mongolian *ger* (yurt) which tourists pay R25 to visit – but you can sleep inside for R480. There's a good indoor toilet and shower. Helpful Nikolai speaks English and can arrange boat and bicycle excursions. However, when he's away his lovable granny gets quickly flummoxed by foreigners.

Devyaty Val (☎ 112 814; ul Chapaeva 24; d R1200-1400) The better rooms are relatively good value with big beds, TV and private shower and toilet in a long timber extension. Out of season, single occupancy costs half.

Baikal Dream (☎ 112 758; ul Chapaeva 69; d R1300-1800) Baikal Dream offers big bright comfortable rooms with flush toilets, but décor is minimal; a chip-chinned Lenin in one room is the only adornment. The urban-

style brick architecture cruelly disregards its rural surroundings.

Briz (☎ 250 468; www.baikal-briz.ru/; ul Gudina 71; standard s/tw R1500/1700 summer, s/tw R1200/1400 winter) A good price–quality balance with in-room toilets and distant Baikal views from the nicer rooms, plus more basic hut beds are available for R750 in summer only. Out of season a few basic singles cost only R400 but call ahead to have them prewarmed.

Krestovka Area

Derevenka (☎ 250 459; www.village2002.narod.ru; ul Gornaya 1; s/d R1300/1400, s/d midsummer R1400/1700, banya R200) On a ridge behind the Baikal-front road, lovely little wooden huts with stove-heaters, private toilets and hot water (but shared showers) offer Listvyanka's most appealing semibudget choice. Very friendly owners can organise snowmobile, sled and boat rentals.

Baikalskie Terema (☎ 112 599; info@greenexpress .ru; ul Gornaya 16; s/d R2500/2700) For Western comforts this fully equipped pine-furnished hotel remains Listvyanka's snazziest option so far. There are half-price room rates for 12-hour stays – handy if you arrive on the last bus from Irkutsk and are continuing next day by hydrofoil to Bolshie Koty. There's a sports-activities centre but compare prices.

U Ozera (☎ 250 444; Irkutsk Hwy km3; d winter/summer R1800/2500) New, reasonably comfortable if cramped motel overlooking the lake between Krestovka and Rogatka.

Eating

Near the port numerous vendors pedal delicious smoked omul fish, and café **Shury Mury** (☎ 250 452; meals R150-350, sandwiches R25-60; ☉ 10am-11pm) has a lakeside summer terrace. The most atmospheric eatery is the **Proshli Vek** (☎ 112 554; ul Lazlo 1; meals R200-470) 2.5km west of the port between U Ozera and Krestovka. The hotel Baikalskie Terema also has an excellent restaurant.

Several cheaper homestays allow their guests use of communal cooking facilities, but note that grocery shops are rather rare and poorly stocked. The best are in Krestovka, either the Dariya (in front of Galina Vasilevna's homestay) or another on the coast road at the ul Kulikova junction. There's a sporadically open bakery stand beside the port and a small grocery 800m east of the port, some way beyond the turning for ul Gudina.

Getting There & Away

Five daily buses (R30, 1¼ hours) and roughly hourly *marshrutky* run from Listvyanka port to Irkutsk passing the Limnological Institute and Taltsy museum. Taxis from Irkutsk want at least R1000.

Mid-May to late September, hydrofoils stop at Listvyanka port between Irkutsk (R180) and Bolshie Koty (R80) at least daily, more frequently at weekends.

Year-round a tiny, battered car-ferry lumbers across the never-frozen Angara River–mouth to Port Baikal from Rogatka. It supposedly departs at 8.15am, 4.15pm and 6.15pm but times are by no means guaranteed.

Various short trips by yacht, fishing boat or even hovercraft are available at the main port depending on the season. For longer cruises inquire well ahead through Irkutsk agencies.

AROUND LISTVYANKA

Hydrofoils (in summer), ferries (all year-round) or taxis (across the winter ice) lead on to more isolated roadless villages. Port Baikal and Bolshie Koty are the most accessible and are easy to visit as a day trip. In winter, Jack Sheremetoff at Baikaler (p566) runs a one-day excursion from Irkutsk to Listvyanka, Bolshie Koty and across the ice to a tunnel on the Circumbaikal Railway for R1200 per person.

Port Baikal Порт Байкал
☎ 3952

Seen from Listvyanka across the unbridged mouth of the Angara River, Port Baikal looks like a rusty semi-industrial eyesore. But the view is misleading. A kilometre southwest of Stanitsa (the port area), Baranchiki is a ramshackle 'real' village with lots of unkempt but authentic Siberian cottages and a handy selection of accommodation options. The village rises steeply, making excellent Baikal viewpoints easily accessible. Awkward ferry connections mean that Port Baikal remains largely uncommercialised, lacking Listvyanka's 'attractions' but also its crowds. Thus it's popular with meditative painters and walkers, but its main draw is the Circumbaikal train ride from Slyudyanka.

From 1900 to 1904 the Trans-Siberian Railway tracks led to Port Baikal from Irkutsk. They continued on Lake Baikal's far eastern shore at Mysovaya (Babushkin), and the rail-less gap was plugged by ice-breaking steamships, including the *Angara*, now restored and on view in Irkutsk (p569). Later, the tracks were extended south and around the lake. This Circumbaikal line (see below) required so many impressive tunnels and bridges that it earned the nickname 'The Tsar's Jewelled Buckle'. With the damming of the Angara River in the 1950s, the original Irkutsk to Port Baikal railway section was submerged and replaced with an Irkutsk–Kultuk shortcut (today's trans-Sib). That left poor little Port Baikal to wither away at the dead end of a rarely used branch line.

SLEEPING & EATING

B&B Baikal (☎ 250 463; www.baikal.tk, in Russian; ul Baikalskaya 12, Baranchiki; bed R500, bed with half-board R800) Set 400m back from the lakeside in a house with a conspicuous, wood-framed new picture window. Various newly decorated but unpretentious rooms share two Western-style toilets and a shower.

Anastasia Shishlonova's homestay (ul Naburezhnaya 12-1, Baranchiki; bed R150, bed with half-board R300) This delightful, ever-smiling family offer rooms in their wonderfully positioned Baikal-facing home and a cute but minuscule hut-room in the yard. There's fresh milk from the cow who greets you on the walk to the challenging pit toilet. No running water.

AUTHOR'S CHOICE

Yakhont (☎ 250 496, 622 977; www.yahont.irk.ru, in Russian; ul Naberezhnaya 3, Baranchiki; dm/tw R800/2400) could be the Siberian boutique hotel you've been dreaming of. It's a traditionally designed log house decorated with eclectic good taste by well-travelled, English-speaking owners. There's even a little hookah-smoking salon. Guests congregate in the stylish communal kitchen/dining room, above which rooms have perfect Western bathrooms. For those on tighter budgets a cute but waterless cliff-front cottage offers an appealing dormitory option. Advance bookings are essential.

SIBERIA

Lyudmila Masalitina's homestay (ul Vokzalnaya 7/2, Stanitsa; dm/q R150/600) In the unattractive Stanitsa area, this homestay is great value and very handy for the Listvyanka ferry. The toilet is a scary outhouse.

As yet Port Baikal has no café but there are three grocery kiosks at Baranchiki and two in Stanitsa. All accommodation options listed here have either kitchen or meals included (or both).

GETTING THERE & AWAY

The ferry to Rogatka near Listvyanka (20 minutes) runs year-round, supposedly three times daily at 7.10am, 3.50pm and 5.15pm, but times can change at whim. There are direct hydrofoils to Irkutsk (50 minutes) in summer. All trains come via the very slow Circumbaikal route. For guests, the Yakhont offers speedboat charters (R2000 per hour) and R300 pick-ups to/from Listvyanka.

Circumbaikal Railway

Кругобайкальская Железная Дорога
Excruciatingly slow or a great social event? Opinions are mixed but taking one of the four weekly Slyudyanka to Port Baikal trains along this scenic, lake-hugging branch line remains a very popular tourist activity. You'll need to juggle sunglasses, fan and torch as the carriages are unventilated and unlit. The most picturesque sections of the route are the valley, pebble beach and headland at Polovinnaya (around halfway), and the bridge area at km149 where there's also a small **Rerikh museum** (one hour from Slyudyanka). Views are best if you can persuade the driver to let you ride on the front of the locomotive – possible on certain tour packages. Note that most trains *from* Port Baikal travel by night and so are useless for sightseeing.

The old stone tunnels, *stolby*-cliff cuttings and bridges are an attraction even for nontrain-buffs who might drive alongside sections of the route on winter ice roads from Kultuk. Hiking sections of the peaceful track is also popular. Walking from Port Baikal leads to some pleasant if litter-marred beaches. Or get off an Irkutsk–Slyudyanka *elektrichka* at Temnaya Pad and hike down the stream valley for about an hour. You should emerge at km149 on the Circumbaikal track, from where you can continue by train to Port Baikal if you time things well.

SLEEPING

There are roughly a dozen isolated *turbazy* of varying quality along the route. Perhaps the most usefully positioned is the rambling, very basic **Baza Alpinistov** (☎ 902-178 3502; Ludmilla Arteminka; dm R100) at km149. Bring your own food.

GETTING THERE & AWAY

From a side platform at Slyudyanka I station, short, wooden-seated Matanya trains (R32, six hours) currently depart at 1pm, two to four times weekly – check timetables carefully. To get a seat you'll need to join the scrum to board around half an hour before departure. Get off at Baranchiki, the penultimate halt, for Port Baikal's best accommodation. In summer an additional tourist train direct from Irkutsk departs at around 7am on Saturday. Wonderfully detailed website http://kbzd.irk.ru/Eng/ has regularly updated timetables plus photographs of virtually every inch of the route.

Several Irkutsk agencies run organised Circumbaikal tours. BaikalComplex (p566) includes a charter ferry to get you to Listvyanka, avoiding a forced overnight stay in Port Baikal.

Bolshie Koty Большие Коты

Founded by 19th-century gold miners, roadless Bolshie Koty makes an easy day trip by boat or ice-drive from Listvyanka or a picturesque if somewhat hair-raising hike. The little **museum** opposite the jetty has a few pickled crustaceans and stuffed rodents. Otherwise, the village is simply a pleasant place to stroll, snooze and watch fish dry. A few basic homestays include ul Baikalskaya 55 (lovely lakeside position) and neater, inland ul Zarechnaya 11b. Great fresh-smoked omul are sold at the port when boats arrive.

Hydrofoils originating in Irkutsk (R180) depart Listvyanka (R80, 25 minutes) at least daily in summer, staying nearly two hours before returning. That's plenty for most visitors.

OLKHON ISLAND ОСТРОВ ОЛЬХОН

pop 1500 / ⊙ Moscow +5hr
Halfway up Lake Baikal's western shore and reached by a short ferry journey from Sakhyurta (aka MRS), the serenely beautiful Olkhon Island is a wonderful place from

which to view the lake and relax during a tour of Siberia. Considered one of five global poles of shamanic energy by the Buryat people, the 72km-long island's main settlement is Khuzhir, which has seen something of a tourist boom over the last few years mainly thanks to the inspiring efforts of Nikita's Guest House, which also runs the **tourist information office** (9am-9pm) outside its premises. For a good map of the island go to www .baikalex.com/info/map_olkhon.html.

Although peak season is July and August, also consider visiting during the quiet winter months, when you can drive across the ice to the island until early April. Olkhon was reconnected to the electricity grid in 2005 and mobile phones now work in Khuzhir.

Sights & Activities

There are unparalleled views of Baikal from sheer cliffs that rise at the island's northern end, culminating in dramatic **Cape Khoboy**. Day-long jeep trips here including lunch (R350) can be arranged through Nikita's and Khuzhir's other guesthouses.

Khuzhir's small **museum** (ul Pervomayskaya 24; admission free; 10am-6pm), next to the village school, is worth a look. Consider dropping by Nikita's even if you aren't staying there to admire the inventive kid's playground and general atmosphere of the place. A short walk north of Nikita's, the unmistakable **Shaman Rocks** are neither huge nor spectacular, but they make a perfect meditational focus for the ever-changing cloudscapes across the picturesque Maloe More (Little Sea). East of the rocks is a long strip of sandy beach.

The island's southern end is rolling grassland – great for off-road mountain biking or gentle hiking, and if Baikal proves too cold for a dip you can cool off in the small **Shara-Nur Lake**.

Sleeping & Eating

The large complex of upmarket-looking wooden cabins under construction on the north edge of town at the time of research will be the latest in an ever-growing range of places to stay in Khuzhir. Irkutsk agencies (p566) offer a choice of basic cottage homestays in Khuzhir at around R600 with full board. If you just show up there's a fair chance of finding a similar place from around R450. Toilets are always outside the rooms and the *banya* will typically cost

extra. The village is small enough that it won't take you long to find the following recommended places.

Nikita's Guest House (http://olkhon.info/; ul Kirpichnaya 8, Khuzhir; full board per person R530) Run by a former Russian table-tennis champ and his wife, Siberia's premier travellers hang-out is a wonderful place to stay and ecofriendly to boot. If it's full (as it often is in high season) the owners will find you a place to stay elsewhere in the village. The basic rooms on site are attractively decorated. Scrub up in an authentic *banya* and pig out on delicious home-cooked meals. There's a tourist information centre out front and a packed schedule of excursions and activities.

Solnechnaya (3952-389 103; www.web-olkhon .com; ul Solnechnaya 14; full board R510-570) Not quite as happening a scene as Nikita's but still a pleasant place to stay offering a good range of activities. Accommodation is in two-storey cabins, cooler 1st-floor rooms being the more expensive.

Ventsak (ul Baikalskaya 42; full board per person R480) The most appealing of Khuzhir's smaller guesthouses has a handful of cabins in a quiet spot just off the village's main street. The shower and *banya* block is in good condition and there's a comfortable communal lounge area.

Several kilometres north of Khuzhir near the tiny hamlet of Kharansty, Green Express (p566) runs **Yurt Camp Harmony** (www.green express.ru; full board per person in 4-bed yurt R800) with some 20 large circular felt tents shaded by trees in a lakeside camp site. It's used for the company's tours but independent travellers can stay if there's room. Curious dog-cart rides are available in summer.

Getting There & Away

From June to August there are at least two and usually three daily buses between Khuzhir and Irkutsk (R370, seven hours), with an additional minibus leaving from Nikita's daily at 8.30am (R300). Frequency drops off drastically outside peak summer season. With a little warning, agencies or hostels can usually find you a ride in a private car to Irkutsk (5½ hours), R700 per seat, R2500 for the whole car. Prices include the short ferry ride to MRS – mid-January to March an ice road replaces that ferry. When ice is partly formed or partly melted, the island is completely cut off for a few weeks.

In summer a hydrofoil service operates three times weekly from Irkutsk to Olkhon (R1100, seven hours), dropping passengers near the ferry terminal, from where it's possible to hitch a lift into Khuzhir.

Maloe More Малое Море

The relatively warm, shallow waters of the Maloe More (Little Sea) offer a primary do-nothing holiday attraction for Siberians. Main attractions are swimming, hiking to waterfalls and drinking. Dozens of camps, huts and resorts are scattered amid attractive multiple bays backed by alternating woodland and rolling grassland scenery. Since each widely spaced 'resort' is frequently pre-booked and hard to access without private transport, you'd be wise to first visit Irkutsk agencies and leaf through their considerable catalogues. Booking something not too far from MRS makes it easier to continue later to Olkhon Island. Arguably the most appealing bay is **Bukhta Kurkutskaya** where the Baza Otdykha Naratey has showers and bio-toilets. Several new resorts offer weekly transfers from Irkutsk for guests (around R400), including **Baikal-Dar** (☎ 3952-266 336; www.dar.irk .ru; d/tr incl full board R1600/2400). The further north, Olkhon-facing **Khadarta Bay** between Sarma and Kurma is becoming ever more popular.

From June to late August *marshrutky* run to Kurma (R380, 5½ hours) at 9am via Sarma (R320) from the courtyard of Irkutsk's Visitor Information Office. They return at 2pm the same afternoon. Public buses from Irkutsk serve MRS.

SOUTH BAIKAL

From trans-Siberian train windows there are attractive lake-glimpses along much of Baikal's south coast. Lacking any architectural charm, neither Slyudyanka nor smelly Baikalsk tempt many Westerners off the train, yet these drab, functional places have superb mountain-backed lakeside settings and accommodation that's cheaper than Irkutsk's. Slyudyanka is also the best place to start Circumbaikal train rides or excursions to the lovely Tunka Valley.

Slyudyanka Слюдянка

☎ 39544 / pop 18,800 / ⏱ Moscow +5hr
Slyudyanka 1, the famous all-stone **train station**, is a mere five-minutes' walk from Lake Baikal's shore. En route you pass a photogenic timber **church** in multicoloured, Scooby Doo style. Across the tracks, former locomotive workshops host an interesting though all-in-Russian **museum** (Kraevedchesky muzey; ☎ 2351; ul Zheleznodorozhnaya 22; admission R30; ⏱ 11am-5pm Sun-Thu) with archaeological finds, old railway-switching boxes and an identification guide to 47 locomotive types.

The simple, friendly **hotel** (☎ 23071; ul Frunze 4, M/R Perival; dm/s/tw R300/400/800), with shared showers and seatless toilets, charges half-price for 12-hour stays. To get there from the train station cross the long footbridge and walk two blocks further to a little **bus station** (ul Lenina); from here the hotel is 4km west by very frequent *marshrutka* 1 (last at 11pm). A taxi costs R40. Lugubriously UV-lit **Kafe Germez** (☎ 51089; ul Lenina 54; meals R50-70) is halfway along.

Trains from Irkutsk take around 3¼ hours *(elektrichka)* or 2½ hours (express). Slyudyanka 1 is the usual starting point for the **Circumbaikal Railway** trip (p578). Two cheap but very scenic *elektrichky* run daily to Baikalsk (R18) and *marshrutky* from outside the station depart to both Kyren and Arshan at an ungodly 4.45am (or earlier depending on when train 125 arrives from Ulan-Ude). An additional bus to Arshan (R75, two hours) leaves at 2pm from the bus station. From here bus 103 also runs six times daily to Baikalsk.

Baikalsk Байкальск

☎ 39542 / pop 15,500 / ⏱ Moscow +5hr
Lakeside Baikalsk is the site of a huge, controversial Baikal-polluting pulp mill (p106) which gives the town a faint but unpleasantly pervasive perfume of decomposing cellulose. However, the mountains that rise abruptly behind town offer the region's best **snowboarding** (www.worldsnowboardguide.com/resorts /Russia/Baikalsk/) and skiing at the very active **Gora Sobolinaya Resort** (http://baikalsk.irk.ru, in Russian). The complex has a handy **left-luggage office** (per day R80) as well as modern **ski-lifts** (per hr/half-day/day R150/200/300; ⏱ 10am-5pm) which cost double at weekends. Equipment rentals range from R200 to R1000 for ski-boot-pole sets or R500 to R750 for snowboards.

SLEEPING

All hotels charge a 50% first-day booking premium and ask big weekend and seasonal surcharges.

Hotel Uyut (☎ 37312; www.baikaltur.ru; Stroitelnaya 13; d low/mid-season R800/1000, d high season R1200-1600) Comfortable new rooms are individually designed though the tiger-skin, floral and wave motifs may not appeal to every taste. You can also watch BBC World TV from vivid lemon-yellow settees in the airy communal hallway/billiard room. The hotel is 5km from the ski slopes and 400m from a pretty Baikal beach where the gregarious Armenian owner can arrange water-skiing, boat trips and ice-pulls on the frozen lake (you ski while being towed behind a 4WD).

Hotel Sobolinaya (☎ 32455; dm R240, s R540-600, d R800-100, tr R1050-1200) Just 600m from the ski-pulls, Hotel Sobolinaya is somewhat dreary but all rooms have a good new toilet and shower (some shared between pairs). The R2580 *lyux* suite hosted President Putin when he slapped on his skis in 2002.

Taxi driver and part-time chainsaw sculptor **Yuri Sklyarov** (☎ 8-9025 681 807; www.sklyarowtur.boom.ru, in Russian) speaks a few words of English and can arrange homestays from R300.

GETTING THERE & AWAY

Baikalsk's main station on the trans-Siberian mainline is bizarrely inconvenient, 9km east of the centre – that's 12km from the ski slopes. Handier Baikalsk Passagersky station is only used by the twice-daily *elektrichka* services to Slyudyanka.

Selenga Delta Villages

Posolskoe was the site where Imperial Russia's first trans-Baikal diplomatic mission to the Mongolian khan got ambushed and robbed in 1651; by the 1680s its monastery was spearheading the evangelism of Buryatiya. Closed in the 1920s but recently renovated, the monastery's **Spaso-Preobrazhensky Church** dominates what is now a quiet little wooden-cottage fishing village. The church stands on a slight rise overlooking a long, pebbly beach where inhabitants quietly fill horse-drawn barrels with Baikal water.

Tvorogovo also has a notable old church, beside the Posolskoe–Kabansk road. Quietly attractive **Kabansk** has a museum and a big Soviet 'flame' monument.

Shared taxis (R10) run between Kabansk and Timlyuy station on the Trans-Siberian Railway. Posolskoe buses are rare from Kabansk and run twice daily from Ulan-Ude train station (3½ hours, last return at 6pm).

TUNKA VALLEY
ТУНКИНСКАЯ ДОЛИНА
☽ Moscow +5hr

When the clouds clear, sawtooth Sayan peaks rise spectacularly above the cute Buddhist villages of the wide, rural Tunka Valley, which starts about 30km west of Kultuk and continues all the way to the Mongolian border near Mondy. Smoke rising gently from cottage chimneys adds to the wisps of romantic morning mist. Beyond justifiably popular Arshan, there's minimal tourist infrastructure and the grandly panoramic mountains are generally set too far back for easy access. Nonetheless, hiking maps are sold in Irkutsk and **Tunkinskiye Goltsy** (http://tunki.baikal.ru, in Russian) has great photos and useful mountaineer's schematics.

Arshan Аршан
☎ 30156 / pop 900–3800, seasonal

This popular hot-springs village is nestled right at the foot of soaring forested mountains. Relaxing short walks take you to a series of rapids and waterfalls but there are plenty of longer, more challenging treks and climbs with detailed information (in Russian) on http://tunki.baikal.ru/.

From the big, six-storey Sayan Sanatorium, Arshan's patchily attractive main street (ul Traktovaya) fires itself 2km straight towards the mountains. Beyond the post office, **Internet Zal** (ul Traktovaya 32, per hr R50; ☽ 11am-1pm & 2-6pm Mon-Fri, 12.30-6pm Sat & Sun) and **bus-ticket kiosk** (ul Traktovaya 3), it swerves west past the **Altan Mundarga Information Booth** (☎ 97502; ul Traktovaya 6) and the sprawling Kurort Arshan resort. Keep walking 20 minutes through the forest to find the dinky little **Badkhirkharma Datsan** (Buddhist temple), set in an idyllic mountain-backed glade, or walk up the stream to access the mountain footpaths.

SLEEPING & EATING

Many log cottages offer basic homestays from R100 per bed. Look for 'Дом Жильё' signs.

Priyut Alpinista (☎ 97697; www.iwf.ru; ul Bratev Domshevikh 8; tw R800-1000, tr R1300) This characterful new climbers' centre has the atmosphere of a Western youth hostel, but rooms have private toilets and better ones have hot showers. Rent bicycles (R65 per hour), buy climbing maps (R25) and watch videos of Arshan's attractions in the comfortable sitting room before adding comments to the

SIBERIA

'magic tree'. It's a modest wooden building three-minutes' walk along ul Pavlova from the bus stand. The owners offer pre-erected tent places, including supplies, high in the mountains (R350 per person including food) so that hikers and mountaineers don't need to carry a rucksack.

Hotel Zamok Gornogo Korolya (☎ 97384; ul Gagarina 18; d R1700-2100) This modern pseudo-castle has crenellations, green-tipped towers and four comfortable rooms with questionable 'artistic' taste in nude derrières.

Kurort Arshan (☎ 97745; ul Traktovaya 1; dm/s R150/215; ☯ reception 8am-8pm summer, 9am-1pm & 4-7pm winter) Basic institutional sanatorium with various sized buildings spread through the forest, used mostly by those seeking a cure at its hot springs.

Pensionat Sagaan Dali (☎ 97468; www.sagaan.ru; ul Deputatskaya 14; s/d/ste R390/780/1170; ℗) Inexpensive but with all the charm of a 1970s council block, rooms here are cosmetically upgraded but still have rather sad old toilets. Suites are bigger but not better. The access footpath from ul Traktovaya skirts the Sayan Sanatorium, passing a spluttering sulphurous spring-water faucet marked by prayer flags.

Easily missed within the grounds of the Sayan Sanatorium, the small **Sayan Kafe** (meals R200-400; ☯ noon-11pm) is Arshan's nicest eatery. Much cheaper snacks are available from a rustic unmarked **teahouse** (ul Traktovaya 1; beers R30) beside Visit grocery shop and from a bright if unrepentantly Soviet **stolovaya** (ul Traktovaya 13; meals R35-50; ☯ 9am-7pm) near the post office.

GETTING THERE & AWAY
Buses or *marshrutky* (slightly more expensive) run to Kyren (R35, 1¼ hours, 10.30am, noon and 2pm), Slyudyanka (R75, 7.30am and 2pm), Ulan-Ude (R332, 11 hours, 7.30am Tuesday to Sunday) and Irkutsk (R220, 2pm).

Kyren Кырен
☎ 30147 / pop 5500
The valley's unkempt, low-rise little 'capital' is home to the **Tunka National Park HQ** (☎ 91793; ul Lenina 69). Its small, onion-topped **church** (ul Kooperativenaya) adds foreground to the photogenic alpine backdrop. Walk south between the cottages of muddy ul Kooperativenaya to find open fields for carefree strolls across bird-serenaded grasslands. A few hours is probably enough in Kyren, and a 150%

supplement dissuades foreign guests from using the very basic **Hotel Druzhba** (☎ 91580; upstairs, ul Lenina 109; dm/s/tw R312/557/991), with shared toilet and no showers whatsoever.

From outside the **Poznaya Chayna** (ul Lenina 112; meals R30-50; ☯ 10am-5pm Mon-Fri), about 1km east of the hotel, buses or *marshrutky* depart for Slyudyanka (R70, three hours, 6am and 6pm), Arshan (R35, 1¼ hours, 10am and 2pm), Nilova Pustyn (11.40am) and Irkutsk (3.30pm).

Beyond Kyren
The Tunka Valley road leads to **Mondy** near the peak of Munko-Saridak, the highest mountain in eastern Siberia. Proposals to open the nearby Mongolian border to foreigners were rejected again in 2005, but one day it might be feasible to join Russian vodka-and-fishing tourists who already visit Mongolia's appealing Khövsgöl Lake. Check with Irkutsk tour agents, notably Baikal Discovery (p566). En route the road passes near **Nilova Pustyn**, a minor spa where locals voluntarily subject themselves to radioactive radon baths. It's tucked into an attractive pine valley, from where a tough 70km trek crosses a 2700m pass to reach the wild, forested **Shumak** region, famous for its medicinal rhododendrons.

EASTERN BAIKAL
☯ Moscow +5hr
Sparsely scattered beach villages of old-fashioned log cottages dot the pretty east Baikal coast. They are well described in a usefully practical Prebaikalsky booklet, available for free download from www.tahoebaikal.org. Further north is the dramatic Barguzin Valley, from which Chinggis Khaan's mother, Oilun-Ehe, is said to have originated. Access is across a forested pass from Ulan-Ude via tiny **Baturino** village with its elegantly renovated Sretenskaya Church.

After around 2½ hours' drive, the road first meets Lake Baikal at pretty little **Gremyachinsk**. Buses stop at a roadside café from which Gremyachinsk's sandy but litter-strewn beach is a 15-minute walk up Komsomolskaya ul past several shadoof-style lever-wells. *Marshrutky* back to Ulan-Ude are often full so consider prebooking your return. If you're stuck overnight there's a basic one-room **homestay** (Komsomolskaya ul 41) and a fortress-themed tourist complex is under construction at the north end of the beach. Approximately 5km from Gremyachinsk (no taxis), many more tourist camps and rest huts are strung around **Kotokel Lake**, whose thermal springs keep it warm year-round.

The main road offers surprisingly few Baikal views until fishing port **Turka**, which has a small, rather overpriced house-hotel (US$35 to US$60) and a museum. Bigger **Goryachinsk**, around 3km inland, is centred on a typically institutional hot-springs **kurort** (sanatorium complex; ☎ 55135; beds from R220) with cheap cottage homestays in the surrounding village. *Marshrutky* run to Ulan-Ude (R140, 3½ hours) at 8am and 4pm. Picturesque Baikal beaches stretch northwest of quaint little **Maksimikha** fishing hamlet with several huts and *turbazy* including **Svetlaya Polyana** (tw R1200-1800; ☺ Apr-Oct). Book ahead through agencies in Ulan-Ude or Ust-Barguzin.

Ust-Barguzin Усть-Баргузин
☎ 30131 / pop 10,200
Low-rise Ust-Barguzin has streets of traditional log homes with blue-and-white carved window frames. These are most attractive towards the northern end of the main street, ul Lenina, where it reaches the Barguzin River ferry. From here, views are magical towards the high-ridged peaks of the Svyatoy Nos Peninsula. Nearby **Shik Poznaya** (☎ 91913; ul Lenina 2b; ☺ 10am-10pm; meals R35-60) is a wholesome if modest eatery. There's no formal accommodation but experienced tour agent **Alexander Loginov** (☎ 91591; aloginov@bk.ru, alex157@mail.ru; ul Komsomolskaya 19) speaks passable English, arranges various standards of homestay (R100 to R700) and organises boat trips. He lives one block west of ul Lenina, about 600m south of the river ferry.

Buses to Barguzin leave at 8.15am and 5pm (R42, 1¼ hours) from either the north ferry quay (summer) or the distant town office on ul Chernoshevskogo (other seasons). When the river is part-thawed, buses divert via a long, rough forest track. Several daily buses and *marshrutky* to Ulan-Ude (R192, six hours) depart around 8am. In February or March driving across Lake Baikal to Severobaikalsk takes around five hours.

Svyatoy Nos (Holy Nose) Peninsula
Полуостров Святой Нос
Rising 1800m almost vertically out of shimmering waters, dramatic Svyatoy Nos is one of Lake Baikal's most impressive features. It's within the mostly impenetrable **Barguzin National Reserve** (Barguzinsky zapovednik) and joined to Ust-Barguzin by a muddy 20km sand-bar that's possible but painful to drive along (toll). **Nerpa seals** are particularly abundant off the peninsula's west coast around the **Ushkanny Islands**, accessible by charter boat from Ust-Barguzin. You'll pay around R3000 (speedboat) or R7000 (sailing boat). Add R1000 per person and R500 per boat park fees if caught by rangers.

The warm and fish-filled waters of the **Chivyrkuysky Gulf** appeal to rich-but-hardy Russian tourists who pay absurd sums to stay in minimalist boat-hotels off **Kurbulik** village or in **Snake Bay** (up to US$200 without bathrooms). Access is by boat from uninhabited Monakhovo where the already bad Ust-Barguzin track degenerates into a mudslide. Gulf access is much easier in February and March when the ice-road to Severobaikalsk passes right beside **Katun** village, a great place to observe villagers ice fishing in teams.

Barguzin & the Barguzin Valley
Баргузин
☎ 30131 / pop 7000
The road north from Ust-Barguzin emerges from thick forests at Barguzin, a low-rise town of wooden cottages that dates back to 1648. Walking from the bus station you can see its handful of dilapidated historic buildings in about 20 minutes by heading along ul Krasnoarmeyskaya then around pl Lenina towards the cursorily renovated old **church**. Opposite the quaint little post office, the wooden-colonnaded **former Uezdnogo Bank** (ul Krasnoarmeyskaya 54) was once the grand home of Decembrist Mikhail Kyukhelbeker.

Barguzin's real interest is as a base for visiting the timeless Barguzin Valley as it opens out into wide horse-grazed meadows, gloriously edged by a vast Toblerone of mountain peaks. These are most accessibly viewed across the meandering river plain from **Uro** village. Similarly inspiring panoramas continue for miles towards the shamanist-Evenki village of **Suvo**, passing near **Bukhe Shulun** (Byk), a rocky outcrop considered to have magical powers. You'll pass through widely scattered, old-fashioned villages where horse carts and sleighs outnumber cars. Way up on the valley's mountainous west side, **Kurumkan** has a small but photogenic peak-backed *datsan*.

Barguzin's friendly but basic **hotel** (☎ 41229; ul Lenina 25; s R225-335, tw R450) suffers power cuts for unpaid arrears. Better rooms have private toilets but there are no showers and the fridges are pretty useless when the electricity is off. Irina Maganova offers a **homestay** (☎ 41133; ul Stroiteley 30) in a rather dishevelled house with a dog called Tyson and many disturbing Marilyn Manson posters. There's a decent bathroom but it's 4km south of the centre and prices vary at whim (R500-750 with meals per person).

Two blocks south of the hotel, simple **Kafe Brigantina** (ul Dzerzhinskogo; 🕙 8am-8pm Mon-Thu, to 11pm Fri-Sun) is the only eatery.

Buy tickets ahead for Ulan-Ude buses (R227.50, seven hours), departing 8am and 10.30am. *Marshrutky* (R350) run when full until around 10am. Buses also run to Ust-Barguzin (1¼ hours) at 7am and 4pm, to Uro (R12, 35 minutes) at 7am, 1pm and 5.40pm and to Kurumkan (R85, 2½ hours) at 9am and 4pm. Taxi driver Sergei Kuznetsov parks at the bus station and offers climbing and fishing trips.

SEVEROBAIKALSK
СЕВЕРОБАЙКАЛЬСК
☎ 30139 / pop 35,000 / 🕙 Moscow +5hr

With friendly, English-speaking help at hand, Severobaikalsk makes a convenient base from which to explore the beautiful yet little-visited North Baikal area. It's a refreshingly uncommercial sort of place and although the centre is a depressingly typical regiment of prefabricated 1970s apartment blocks, just a short walk across the train tracks are some peaceful Baikal viewpoints.

Information
INTERNET ACCESS
Internet Klub Mega (Leningradsky pr 6; per MB R5, per hr R20; 🕙 9am-9pm) Popular with gamers.
Internet Klub Rikom (basement, per Proletarsky 2; per MB R10, per hr R30; 🕙 10am-1am) Fast but pricey connection. Entered from the forest side.
Library (Leningradsky pr 5; 🕙 11am-7pm Mon-Thu, 10am-2pm Fri, 10am-6pm Sat) Internet available. Enter through the video stall.

INTERNET RESOURCES
North Baikal Tourist Portal (www.sbaikal.ru) Comprehensive regional overview.

MONEY
Sberbank (per Proletarsky; 🕙 8.30am-5.30pm Mon-Thu, to 1pm Fri) Changes travellers cheques in 20 minutes for 3% commission.
POST & COMMUNICATIONS
Post office (Leningradsky pr 6; 🕙 10am-2pm & 3-7pm Mon-Fri, 10am-2pm & 3-5pm Sat) Internet room (per hr R30) entered via separate rear entrance.
Telephone office (per Proletarsky 1; 🕙 24hr)

TRAVEL AGENCIES & HELPERS
The following agencies and individuals can help you arrange accommodation and Baikal boat trips, but check very carefully what is and is not included in any deal you arrange. See also Nizhneangarsk (p588).
Baikal Service (☎ /fax 23912) This tour agency is a professional outfit with its own boat, hotel, permit arrangements and tour programme, but staff don't speak English.
Khozyain (☎ /fax 24512; irina@myBaikal.ru; apt 43, Leningradsky pr 5; 🕙 8am-6pm Mon-Fri) Coordinates accommodation at Goudzhekit and sells Khakusy excursions (mostly two-week stays).
Maryasov family (☎ 26491; kolonok2004@yandex .ru; ul Mostovstroitely 12/1) Alyona speaks English and her father Yevgeny organises adventure tours through Tyozhik (☎ 20323). Their homestay is 3km out of town in Zarechny.
Rashit Yakhin/BAM Tour (☎ /fax 21560; www .gobaikal.com, ul Oktyabrya 16/2) This experienced full-time travel-fixer, guide and ex-BAM worker suffered an immobilising stroke in the mid-1990s rendering his spoken English somewhat hard to follow. Nonetheless he is quick to reply to emails and is always keen to please. He rents a brilliant, central apartment (US$15, negotiable).
Vladimir Yatskovich (☎ 20111; Y_V_N@hotmail.com; apt 112, ul Polygrafistov 5) This proverb-spouting John Cleese lookalike is a local schoolteacher with great English and the contacts to help with a range of activities. Family homestay (US$15) includes meals.

Sights & Activities
For **lake views** that hint at Baikal's enormous size, head for the summer shashlyk stand at the eastern end of town (*marshrutka* 3 or 103). A steep path leads down from here onto a scenic pebble beach. In winter you can walk across the ice to the Neptuna area where unsophisticated but curiously photogenic dachas incorporate boat sheds into their lower storeys. A short winter taxi ride onto the 'desert' of lake ice is memorable – watch offshore fishermen freezing their hands baiting omul through little holes in

SEVEROBAIKALSK

the ice. In warmer months Severobaikalsk makes a great base for relatively high-endurance hiking and for very pleasant boat rides on Lake Baikal. Yacht club **Bely Parus** (☎ 23950; Severobaikalsk port) rents windsurfers (ails parusniye), water-skis (vodnye lyzhi) and wet suits but the water's very chilly.

The friendly little **museum** (☎ 27644; ul Mira 2; admission R20; ☼ 10am-12.30pm & 1.30-5pm Tue-Sun) has limited exhibits on BAM railway history and some Buryat artefacts. There's also an associated art gallery. While not historic, the blue-and-white plank-clad **church** (ul Truda 21; ☼ services 6pm Tue, 6pm Sat, 8.30am Sun) has a lovably dishevelled, wobbly appearance.

Sleeping

Homestays are organised by many helpers listed above and by staff at Podlemore when rooms there are full. Alternatively, consider sleeping in Nizhneangarsk.

Baikal Resort (Dom u Baikala; ☎ 23950; Baikal-kruiz@ Rambler.ru; ul Neptuna 3; tw R700) Unusually comfortable for this price range, this 'resort' is really just a house in a quiet area, walking distance from the lake. Rooms have a new shower and toilet. Summer-only huts are much more cramped and have no shower. Owner Alex Rudkovsky speaks English.

Podlemore (☎ 23179; pr 60 let SSSR 21a; s/tw/tr R452/904/975) The obvious if unmarked red-and-yellow tower beside the train station is a sanatorium that rents decent-value 7th-floor rooms with attached hot showers. Views of Baikal are across the railway marshalling yard – light sleepers might tire of the ever-disgruntled train dispatcher and her distorting loudspeaker.

Zolotaya Rybka (☎ 22231; ul Sibirskaya 14; tw R1100-1700) Thoroughly renovated 'cottages', each containing three rooms which share a modern shower, kitchen, tasteful sitting area and two toilets. The pleasant setting between pine trees offers glimpses of Baikal and the Neptuna area below. Search for the receptionist in unrenovated cottage No 1.

Baikal Service Bungalows (☎ /fax 23912; dm €15, d/tr incl breakfast €50/90) Hidden in a peaceful pine grove at the otherwise unpromising northeast end of town, Baikal Service (p584) has comfortable chalets with well-appointed doubles and less appealing upstairs triples with sitting room. Cheaper options include summer yurts, camping pitches and dorm beds in the 'student' house sharing a fridge and good hot shower.

Resting rooms (komnaty otdykha; train station; dm per hr R16-30) Clean, cheap dorm beds are charged by the hour with a six-hour minimum. Hot shared showers.

Hotel Cherenbas (☎ 23654; dm R150-250) Springy beds are packed together in a tidy but very basic former youth centre. There is a kitchen for self-catering.

Eating & Drinking

Most cafés and restaurants double as drinking dens and the music can be deafening. To avoid ear damage and cover charges (common after 7pm) eat at one of the cheap but unlovely *poznye* (cafés serving Central Asian food) beside the market such as **Goryache Pozi** (pr Leningradsky 6; pozi R12; 9am-8pm;).

Restaurant Rus (☎ 23914; pr 60 let SSSR 28; mains R40-90, garnish R30, cover R50; 8pm-1am Mon-Sat) Lively tavern restaurant with wood-and-stone alcoves in which to sup full-bodied home-brewed beer (R25).

Gril Bar (pr Leningradsky 6; meals R60-80, cover R30-50; 8pm-2am Mon-Sat) Small cellar bar-restaurant where you can avoid the cover charge by sitting at bar stools. Perhaps.

Sportsbar OverTaim (meals R80-120, beers R40; 8pm-1am) No sports but no cover charge either, this slightly more upmarket new pub-restaurant is popular with the youth crowd.

Kafe Ayana (☎ 21224; pr Leningradsky 6; meals R60-100, beers R30, cover after 7pm R60; 10am-11pm) Puls-ing coloured lights and the arrangement of tables around a central dance floor set the tone, though food prices are reasonable.

Kafe Tyya (☎ 22292; pr Leningradsky 6; meals R60-100, beers R21; 10am-11pm) Furnished with a more modern interior than the Ayana, Kafe Tyya is a fundamentally similar concept.

Kafe Nostalgie (2nd fl, per Proletarsky 7; mains R270-300; noon-3pm & 7pm-1am) Ostensibly a plush, upmarket Chinese restaurant but the strobe light might put you off your Manchurian *goyuju*. UN weapons inspectors should examine the murderously bone-barbed fish dumplings.

For cheap groceries try **VIST supermarket** (pr Leningradsky 5; 8.30am-9pm).

Getting There & Away

An **aerokassa** (☎ 22746; Tsentralny pl; 9am-noon & 1-4pm Wed-Fri & Sun-Mon) in Dom Kultury Zhelezne Dorognikov sells tickets for flights from Nizhneangarsk, 30km northeast.

BOAT

From late June to late August a hydrofoil service should run the length of Lake Baikal between Nizhneangarsk, Severobaikalsk and Irkutsk (R1400, 12 hours) via Olkhon Island. Unfortunately, the precise timetable is only announced days before the service begins, making advance planning difficult.

Boat trips are fun and reveal the lake's vastness. Baikal's mountain backdrop looks most spectacular from about 3km offshore, so going all the way across doesn't add a lot scenically and you'll need permits to land on the almost uninhabited east coast (p588). It's possible to negotiate cheap charters with fishermen at Severobaikalsk, Nizhneangarsk or Baikalskoe, but think carefully before taking a boat that's small, slow or seems unreliable if you're going far: storms can come from nowhere and getting help in the middle of icy-cold Baikal is virtually impossible. To rent better, long-distance boats typically costs from R1000 to R1800 per hour. For a reliable charter, contact the charming Viktor Kuznetsov in Nizhneangarsk (p588).

BUS

From outside Severobaikalsk's train station *marshrutky* run to Baikalskoe (six per week) and Goudzhekit (four daily). The half-hourly *marshrutky* 103 to Nizhneangarsk airport

(R29, 25 minutes) passes Severobaikalsk's hydrofoil port and yacht club (2km), then follows the attractive Baikal shore.

In February and March locals regularly drive across Lake Baikal to Ust-Barguzin, en route to Ulan-Ude. For a paid hitchhike to Ust-Barguzin, around R800 per person is appropriate. Ideally, ask local contacts to find you a ride, offering to pay 'petrol money'. Otherwise, try going out to a lonely but well-known hitching spot on the ice near the Profilaktoriya (Lager) children's camp. It's on an attractive curve of Baikal shore: take a *marshrutka* 2km south of the museum towards Zarechny, then turn left and walk another 2km via either fork. Best chances are between 6am and 9am on Friday and Saturday but it's hit and miss, and waiting can get lonely and very cold.

TRAIN

Heading towards Moscow, locals consider train 91 (even-numbered days) somewhat better than train 75 (odd days). Train 91 attaches a Tomsk-bound carriage (42½ hours). On odd days train 71 loops round to Irkutsk (33 hours) while on even days train 347 runs to Krasnoyarsk (33 hours). All go via Lena (seven hours), Bratsk (14 to 16 hours) and Tayshet (24 hours). They also stop in Goudzhekit (R130, 35 minutes), though the trip is vastly cheaper by *elektrichka* (R20, one hour, twice daily).

Eastbound trains 76 (28½ hours, odd days) and 98 (26 hours, Tuesday and Saturday) go all the way to Tynda (train 76, 28½ hours). There are also daily trains to Novaya Chara (14½ hours) and very slow *elektrichki* to Uoyan via Kichera (departs 6.15am).

Getting Around

Marshrutka 3 connects the low-rise Zarechny suburb to Tsentralnaya pl via the museum, then continues to the train station and loops right around to the far side of the tracks, passing the Baikal Resort one way. *Marshrutka* 1 passes the access road for Baikal Service en route to the train station, Tsentralnaya pl and the museum.

AROUND SEVEROBAIKALSK

Baikalskoe Байкальское

This timeless little fishing village 45km south of Severobaikalsk has an old bridge and a jawdroppingly picturesque lakeside location. From the fishing port, walk past the cute **wooden church** and 20 minutes up the cliff-side path towards the radio mast for particularly superb **views**. Continue to the bay beyond for possible camping spots. With a knowledgeable guide you might even find Baikalskoe's shamanic **petroglyphs**, as pictured in the Severobaikalsk museum.

Marshrutky leave Severobaikalsk at 8am and 5pm on Tuesday, Friday and Sunday, returning an hour or so later. A taxi for the ¾-hour drive costs from R250 each way plus waiting time; you can stop at an appealing viewpoint en route.

You'll need to charter a boat to reach **Cape Kotelnikovsky**, from which a difficult trek on overgrown, ill-defined trails leads to lovely **Gitara Lake**, several waterfalls around **Tazik Lake** and eventually to the glaciers which descend from **Mt Chersky**, the region's highest peak. A guide is essential.

Goudzhekit Гоуджекит

Goudzhekit's lonely BAM station is beautifully situated between bald, high peaks that stay dusted with snow until early June. Five-minutes' walk to the right, the only habitation is a low-rise spa and **hotel** (dm R200-350, d R800-1000) where the best bungalows have private toilets and showers. Tour agency Khozyain in Severobaikalsk handles bookings. With suitable guides, a 12-day trekking expedition can take you through the lovely, though mosquito-plagued, mountains behind Goudzhekit into the impressive, very isolated **Tyya Valley**.

Nizhneangarsk Нижнеангарск

Severobaikalsk might be much bigger but Nizhneangarsk, 30km northeast, is much older and remains the administrative centre of northern Baikal. A small **museum** in the high school traces the history of the settlement back to the 17th century. Most buildings are wooden and the town forms a quietly attractive low-rise ribbon of long parallel streets stretching 5km along the lakeside from the port to the airport. Opposite a red triangular monument on the coast road, the centre is marked by the **tourist office** (room 1, ul Pobedy 55; ☼ 10am-5pm Mon-Fri). Staff book rooms and ferry tickets for Khakusy, and issue permits for Khakusy, Frolikha and Ayaya Bay. In the same building are a small commercial **art** salon (✆ 10am-5pm Tue-Sat) and a seasonal *poznaya*. For boat rentals or expeditions track down hunter, fisherman and connoisseur of nature **Viktor Kuznetsov** (☎ 47005; fax 47030; frolicha@mail.ru, baikal.nordtour@mail.ru; ul Pobedy 9/7). Though he understands minimal English or German, Viktor's enthusiasm, humanity and energy are utterly infectious. His bigger boats (R1000 per hour, US$200 per day) have a decent turn of speed and basic berths for five people, offering shelter from unpredictable weather. He also has an *aerosami* (propeller-powered sledge), several horses and reindeer to act as pack animals when trekking.

The very appealing **Gostiny Dom Portal** (☎ 47280; ul Rabochaya 10; tw/ste R720/960) is a new wooden house-hotel. Well-appointed standard rooms have attached bathrooms. The two suites have big double beds and great views across the mudflats towards Baikal. It's 2.8km east of the tourist office: a wonderfully peaceful location but there's no restaurant nor any nearby café.

Curiously, the town's **hospital** (☎ 47719) maintains two no-frills, saggy-bed hostels ideal for penny-pinching escapists. Open year-round are eight beds in the east wing of the green-and-white **Polyclinic** (ul Lenina 123; dm R220), accessed from the rear. In summer more beds are available in a block further east in a red-brown timber **clinic** (ul Lenina 133; beds R176). There's a communal kitchen and toilet but no showers.

GETTING THERE & AWAY

Scenic low-altitude flights cross Lake Baikal to Ulan-Ude (R1810, four to six per week) and Irkutsk (R2250, two per week) when weather conditions allow.

Marshrutka 103 from Severobaikalsk runs every 30 minutes along ul Pobedy to the tourist office. It continues along the coast road (ul Rabochaya) to the airport then returns via uls Kozlova and Lenina. The last service is at 8pm, or 6pm on weekends.

Akokan Gulag

The northernmost part of Baikal has a shallower, marshy persona most photogenically viewed from tiny **Dushkachan** hamlet. Some 15km beyond, 3km north of the turning to Kholodnaya village, a track to your left is the start of a forest hike to remnants of the small mica-mining **Akokan Gulag** (1931–33). Assuming you have a reliable guide, it's about an hour's walk to reach some 'officers' huts'. Above is the main prison-camp ruins with a collapsed watchtower and a kitchen area, where three Marie Celeste–like cauldrons seem to await use. About 15-minutes' climb beyond, a small railway has tiny bucket wagons and a magical pile of mica remnants leading to the collapsed mine entrance.

Nikolai Sorokin, a hearty taxi driver who can usually be found at Severobaikalsk train station, speaks no English but manages to guide foreigners to the site, show them animal tracks and point out various Gulag secrets. Reckon around R800 including transport. Don't forget to bring good tick-protection.

Khakusy & Northeast Baikal

The virtually impenetrable **Frolikha Reserve** (Frolikhinsky zapovednik) is the northern extension of the Barguzin National Park (Russia's oldest). Despite being on Baikal's east coast, access is generally from Nizhneangarsk where you can also get the necessary permits. These are required to land your boat on lovely, shaman-haunted **Ayaya Bay** or to trudge seven mud-soaked kilometres to visit biologically unique **Lake Frolikha**.

Khakusy, an idyllically isolated hot-spring **turbaza** (dm/tw/tr R400/1100/1450; ✆ mid-Jun–early Sep) also requires permits in summer but these are waived in February and March when it takes about an hour to drive across the ice from Severobaikalsk (around R1200 return taxi). Bathing (per person R40) is fun in the snow and frozen steam creates curious ice-patterns on the otherwise unremarkable wooden spa buildings. Most local summer guests stay two weeks (from R7586 per person full board including ferry ride from Nizhneangarsk). This ferry is generally fully prebooked, but if there's space it offers the cheapest way for individual travellers to cross the unfrozen lake (R800 return, R914 if booked through Khozyain in Severobaikalsk).

Even less accessible, the mostly deserted village at **Davsha** (population five) has been partly restored as a scientific hamlet and there's now a little museum.

In spring and autumn, when the ice is half-melted or half-formed, all these places are totally cut off.

SOUTHERN BURYATIYA & CHITA REGION
ЮЖНАЯ БУРЯТИЯ И ЧИТИНСКАЯ ОБЛАСТЬ

Scenically magnificent, Buryatiya crouches on the Mongolian border like a cartographic crab squeezing Lake Baikal with its right pincer. Much of the Baikal region covered above also falls within the republic, including Severobaikalsk and the Tunka Valley. Though its English version is limited, Buryatiya now has a tourism website at www.baikaltravel.ru.

The vast, sparsely populated Chita region stretches as far east as the wild Chara Mountains on the BAM railway, but in its more accessible southern reaches it's most interesting for the vibrant capital (Chita), the Buddhist culture of its autonomous Agin-Buryat enclave and as an access route to China.

Buryat Culture

Indigenous ethnic Buryats are a Mongol people who now comprise around 30% of Buryatiya's population, as well as 65% of the Agin-Buryat Autonomous District southeast of Chita. Culturally there are two main Buryat groups. During the 19th century, forest-dwelling western Buryats retained their shamanic animist beliefs, while eastern Buryats from the southern steppelands mostly converted to Tibetan-style Buddhism, maintaining a thick layer of local superstition. Although virtually every Buryat *datsan* (Buddhist temple) was systematically wrecked during the Communists' antireligious mania in the 1930s, today Buryat Buddhism is rebounding. Many (mostly small) *datsans* have been rebuilt and seminaries for training Buddhist monks now operate at Ivolginsk and Aginskoe. The Buryat language is Turkic, though very different from Tuvan and Altai. Dialects vary considerably between regions but almost everyone speaks decent Russian. Hello is *sainbena/sambaina*, thank you (very much) is *(yikhe) bai yer la*. Buryat

oral history is traditionally recited to the twangs of a *khuchir* (two-stringed lute).

ULAN-UDE УЛАН-УДЕ
☎ 3012 / pop 380,000 / ⏰ Moscow +5hr

The appealing capital of Buryatiya, 'UU' is 456km east of Irkutsk by rail and makes a sensible staging post for visiting Mongolia or eastern Lake Baikal. Founded as Verkhneudinsk in 1775, the city prospered as a major stop on the tea-caravan route from China via Troitskosavsk (now Kyakhta). Ulan means 'Red' in Buryat, yet Ulan-Ude is pleasantly green, cradled attractively in rolling hills. Despite the inevitable concrete suburban sprawl, it remains one of the most likable cities in eastern Siberia.

Orientation

The city's heart is pl Sovetov and its backbone ul Lenina, but most traffic bypasses the latter on uls Borsoeva and Baltakhinova. The commercial centre is increasingly focused around 'Elevator', a clothing market and new shopping mall across the railway tracks on pr 50-let Oktyabrya.

Information

There are exchange bureaus in the Geser and Buryatiya hotels. Witty, widely travelled schoolteacher **Petr Ishkin** (☎ 410 334; mobile 8-914 843 3287; petr_first@mail.ru, petr_great@hotmail.com, petroishkin@yahoo.com) speaks great English and enjoys voluntarily helping foreign visitors find their feet during his free time.

BOOKSHOP
Knigi Bookshop (ul Kuybysheva 28; ⏰ 10am-1pm & 2-7pm Mon-Fri, 10am-5pm Sat) Sells excellent *Karta-Skhema* city maps (R30) and Turistskaya Buryatiya advertorial tourist pamphlets (R70).

MONEY
MDM Bank (Sovetskaya ul 32a; ⏰ 9am-1pm & 2-4pm Mon-Fri) Decent rates for US dollars.

PHOTOGRAPHY
PhotoPlus (ul Kommunisticheskaya 16; ⏰ 9am-7pm Mon-Sat, 10am-5pm Sun) Three-minute passport photos for that Mongolian visa, R70.

POST
Post office (ul Lenina 61; ⏰ 8am-7pm Mon-Fri, 9am-6pm Sat & Sun) The rather slow Internet room (per hour R35) stays open longer.

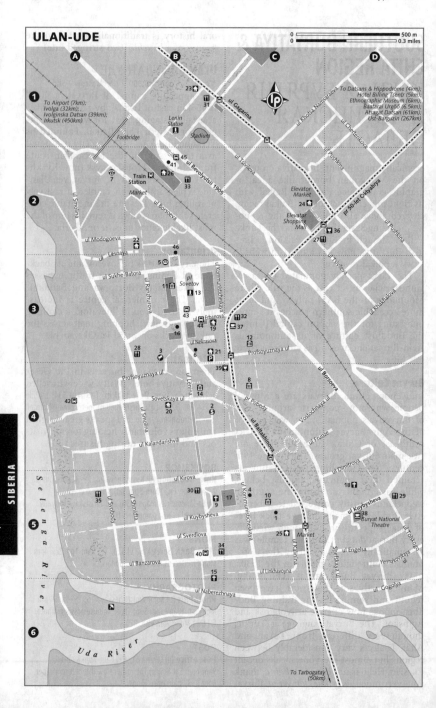

ULAN-UDE

0 _____ 500 m
0 _____ 0.3 miles

To Airport (7km);
Ivolga (32km);
Ivolginska Datsan (39km);
Irkutsk (450km)

To Datsans & Hippodrome (4km);
Hotel Billing Tsentr (5km);
Ethnographic Museum (6km);
Baatarai Urgöö (6.5km);
Atsagat Datsan (61km);
Ust-Barguzin (267km)

ul Gagarina

ul Khotka Namsaraeva
ul Chertenkova
ul Pushkina

Footbridge

Lenin
Statue
Stadium

ul Tsivileva

ul Revolyutsii 1905

Train
Station
Market

ul Borsoeva

ul Smolina

ul Modogoeva

ul Lesnaya

ul Sukhe-Batora

ul Ranzhurova

Elevator
Market

Elevator
Shopping
Mall

pr 50-let Oktyabrya

ul Pushkina

ul Tsivileva

ul Khakhalova

pl
Sovetov

ul Kommunisticheskaya

ul Erbanova

ul Nekrasova

Profsoyuznaya ul

ul Borsoeva

Profsoyuznaya ul

ul Lenina

Sovetskaya ul

ul Smolina

ul Kalandarishvili

pr Pobedy

ul Baltakhinova

Vostochnaya ul

ul Frunze

ul Dimitrova

SIBERIA

S e l e n g a   R i v e r

ul Svoboby

ul Shmidta

ul Kirova

ul Kommunisticheskaya

ul Kuybysheva

ul Sverdlova

ul Banzarova

ul Kuybysheva

ul Kalinina

Market

ul Linkhovoyna

ul Kuybysheva

Buryat National
Theatre

ul Engelsa

Sherskaya ul

ul Tolstogo

Yermotovskaya ul

ul Gogolya

ul Naberezhnaya

U d a   R i v e r

To Tarbogatay
(50km)

INFORMATION		
Buryat-Intour		(see 19)
Firn Travel		(see 4)
Knigi Bookshop Книги	**1**	C5
MDM Bank MDM Банк	**2**	B4
Mongolian Consulate		
Консульство Монголии	**3**	B3
MorinTur		(see 24)
Naran Tur		(see 21)
PhotoPlus ФотоПлюс	**4**	C5
Post Office Почтамт	**5**	B3
Siberia Tours	**6**	B3
Telephone Office		
Телефон и Интернет	**7**	A2

SIGHTS & ACTIVITIES		
Buryatiya Literary Museum		
Литературный Музей Бурятии	**8**	C4
Chapel Часовня	**9**	B5
Fine Arts Museum		
Художественный Музей	**10**	C5
Geological Museum		
Геологический Музей Бурятии	**11**	B3
Historical Museum		
Исторический Музей	**12**	C3
Lenin Head Голова Ленина	**13**	B3
Nature Museum		
Музей природы Бурятии	**14**	B4

Odigitria Cathedral	**15**	B5
Opera House		
Театр Оперы и Балета		
Бурятии	**16**	B3
Trading Arcades Гостиный Двор	**17**	C5
Trinity Church	**18**	D5

SLEEPING 🏠		
Hotel Baikal Гостиница Байкал	**19**	B3
Hotel Barguzin		
Гостиница Баргузин	**20**	B4
Hotel Buryatiya		
Гостиница Бурятия	**21**	B3
Hotel Geser Гостиница Гэсэр	**22**	B2
Hotel Odon Гостиница Одон	**23**	B1
Hotel Sagaan Morin		
Отель Сагаан Морин	**24**	C2
Hotel Zolotoy Kolos		
Гостиница Золотой Колос	**25**	C3
Resting Rooms Комнаты Отдыха	**26**	B2

EATING 🍴		
Blues Café Блюз Кафе	**27**	C3
Drakon Дракон	**28**	B3
Ekonomi Supermarket		
Супермаркет Экономи	**29**	D5
Geser Restaurant		(see 22)
King's Burger Кинг'c Бургер	**30**	B5
Samovar Самовар	**31**	B1

Sputnik Supermarket		
Супермаркет Спутник	**32**	C3
Stolitsa Столица	**33**	B2
Zakusochnaya Real		
Закусочная Реаль	**34**	B5
Zolotoy Drakon Золотой Дракон	**35**	A5

DRINKING 🍷		
Kakadu Какаду	**36**	D2
Kofeynya Marco Polo		
Кофейня Marco Polo	**37**	C3
Kofeynya Shokolad		
Кофейня Шоколад	**38**	D5
Mir Igry Мир Игры	**39**	C4

TRANSPORT		
Air Ticket Booth		(see 21)
Banzarova bus station		
Автостанция Банзарова	**40**	B5
Buses & marshrutky to Chita,		
Irkutsk and Arshan	**41**	B2
Main Bus Station		
Центральный автовокзал	**42**	A4
Marshrutka 55 to airport	**43**	B3
Marshrutka 8 to Ethnographic		
Museum	**44**	B3
Marshrutky to pl Sovetov	**45**	B2
Siberia Airlines	**46**	B2

TELEPHONE

Telephone office (ul Borsoeva; ⏱ 9am-9pm) Internet access here is R30 per hour.

TRAVEL AGENCIES

Ulan-Ude has many agencies happy to sell you Buryatiya and Baikal tours. The following companies are among those more orientated to Westerners and have at least some English-speaking staff.

Buryat-Intour (☎ 219 207; tgomboeva@yahoo.com; room 209, Hotel Baikal) Very well organised with its own bus service to Ulaan Baatar. Also sells air tickets.

Firn Travel (☎ 216 250; http://firntravel.ru/; Kommunisticheskaya ul 16) Ecological projects and tours.

MorinTur (☎ 443 647; info@morintour.com, tgomboeva@yahoo.com; Hotel Sagaan Morin) Focuses on east Baikal, offering various ice and fishing adventures, a horse-sledge trip, seal-watching, rafting in the Barguzin Valley and climbing on Svyatoy Nos (Holy Nose) Peninsula.

Naran Tur (☎ 215 097; baikalnarantour@mail.ru; room 105, Hotel Buryatiya) Director Sesegma (aka Svetlana) is infectiously passionate about Buryatiya, offers horse-riding adventures and has dozens of fascinating one-off ideas.

Siberia Tours (☎ 222 277; ul Nekrasova; ⏱ 9am-7pm Mon-Fri, 10am-6pm Sat) New, English-speaking travel and tour agency.

Sights

CITY CENTRE

A certain 19th-century opulence is still visible in the attractive commercial buildings on and around ul Lenina. Viewed from near the splendid **Opera House**, this street is given a photogenic focus by the gold-tipped spires of the 1785 **Odigitria Cathedral** (ul Lenina 2), which was rescued from near collapse in the late 1990s. It commands an appealing area of the old town, with carved wooden cottages extending as far as ul Kirova. At the other end of ul Lenina the main square, pl Sovetov, is awesomely dominated by the world's largest **Lenin head** which looks less domineering than comically cross-eyed. Located beside a recently rebuilt 1830 **chapel** (ul Lenina), the renovated 1838 **trading arcades** are now filled with modern shops. Ul Lenina's pedestrianised section, extending two blocks north, is a popular early-evening hang-out.

Backed by a park with a Ferris wheel and Gaudi-esque fountain, the active **Trinity Church** (ul Dimitrova 5a) sprouts a series of green bulb-domes.

The **Historical Museum** (☎ 215 961; Profsoyuznaya ul 29; admission per fl R80; ⏱ 10am-5.30pm Tue-Sun) charges per single-room floor. The best is *Buddiyskoe Iskustvo* (3rd floor), displaying *thangka*, Buddhas and icons salvaged from Buryatiya's monasteries before their Soviet destruction. Note-sheets in English fail to explain the fascinating, gaudy papier-mâché models of Khvashan's eight unruly sons urinating at one another. Note the Gungarba shrine table (every Buryat home once had one), the Atsagat medical charts (Tibetan medicine was apparently standard here until the 1940s) and the walnut necklace on grey, clown-faced Sagan Obugen (walnuts were exotic in Buryatiya). The less-interesting 2nd floor traces Buryat history in maps,

SIBERIA

documents and artefacts. Spy it for free from the balcony above.

In an attractive 1847 wooden house, the **Buryatiya Literary Museum** (Literaturny muzey; ☎ 213 722; admission R50; ⏱ 9am-5pm Tue-Sat) contains old photos and manuscripts. A rare 108-volume Atsagat Ganzhur (Buddhist chant book) is inscribed in multicoloured Tibetan script on special black lacquer made from blood, sugar and pounded sheep's vertebrae.

The **Nature Museum** (Muzey Pripody Buryati; ☎ 214 833; ul Lenina 46; admission R30; ⏱ 10am-6pm Wed-Sun) has big stuffed animals and a scale model of Lake Baikal showing you just how deep it is.

The **Geological Museum** (Geologchesky muzey; ul Lenina 59; admission free; ⏱ 1-4pm Mon-Fri) is modest but well presented, while the **Fine Arts Museum** (Khudozhestvenny muzey; ☎ 212 909; ul Kuybysheva 29; admission per exhibition R30-70; ⏱ 10am-6pm Wed-Sun) has small, regularly changing exhibitions.

OUTSKIRTS

In a forest clearing 6km from central Ulan-Ude is the worthwhile **Ethnographic Museum** (Etnografichesky muzey; ☎ 443 210; adult/student/child R60/35/25, photography/video R60/120; ⏱ 9am-5pm Tue-Sun), an outdoor collection of local architecture plus some reconstructed burial mounds and the odd stone totem. Although lacking the pretty lakeside setting of equivalents in Bratsk and Irkutsk, it features occasional craft demonstrations, has a splendid wooden church and sports a whole strip of Old Believers' homesteads. *Marshrutka* 8 from pl Sovetov passes within 1km and upon request will detour to drop you at the door for no extra charge.

En route you'll notice Ulan-Ude's attractive new pair of **datsans** (Barguzinsky Trakt) backed by stupas and trees that flutter with prayer flags; there are services from 9am to 11am most mornings. The nearby **hippodrome** is the venue for major Buryat festivals, including the Buryatiya Folk Festival, which features horse riding, wrestling and other folky delights.

Sleeping

In summer, when the city's central hot water system goes off, showers can run very cold.

BUDGET

Hotel Baikal (☎ 213 718; ul Erbanova 12; s R650-700, tw R900-1000, tr R1200) The Baikal has unreconstructed Soviet rooms, but with water heaters in most attached bathrooms and a perfect position overlooking pl Sovetov.

Hotel Zolotoy Kolos (top floors; ul Sverdlova 43; dm R140, s R187-252, tw R304-804) Repainted, simple but modestly priced, the best singles here have private toilets but showers cost R25 extra. This is a reasonable budget option, though the area is slightly dubious late at night and there's an 11pm curfew.

Hotel Barguzin (☎ 215 746; Sovetskaya ul 28; s/tw/tr R600/820/990) Well positioned for the old town, the lacklustre Barguzin has faded corridors and a stuffed bear lurking in the foyer. Just two twins have their own water heaters.

Hotel Odon (☎ 342 983; ul Gagarina 43; s R330-540, tw R650-890) Uninspiring and usually full of Chinese merchants but only five-minutes' walk from the train station, the Odon has a popular though pricey Chinese restaurant.

Resting rooms (komnaty otdykha; Ulan-Ude train station; dm R500) These decent resting rooms charge R270 for half-days, or R150 for three hours. Showers cost R60.

MIDRANGE

Hotel Sagaan Morin (White Horse; ☎ 444 019; fax 443 647; www.morintour.com/tours/acc_uu/index.php, in Russian; ul Gagarina 25; s/tw/tr R800/1700/1925) This perfectly appointed new three-star tower is so obviously the best hotel in town that you might need to book (by fax) months ahead for summer. The entrance is somewhat hidden by the melee of Elevator market.

Hotel Buryatiya (☎ 211835; ul Kommunisticheskaya 47a; s R725-860, tw R910-1100) A big Soviet tower with decent rooms but no hot water in summer. English-speaking receptionists are friendly but watch out for the room-cleaners' trick of 'tidying away' items of your luggage into the back corners of wardrobes and drawers.

Hotel Geser (☎ /fax 216 151; ul Ranzhurova 11; s/tw/ste R1850/2800/6000) For a Soviet place this former Party hang-out has relatively spacious rooms, some of which have been passably modernised. However, others retain clunky old toilets and one would expect vastly better facilities for these prices. Rates include breakfast and drop 20% October to April. One or two staff members speak English.

Hotel Billing Tsentr (☎ 267 770; km9, Barguzinsky Trakt) This new complex, near the Ethnographic Museum, is nearing completion. Fully equipped, totally rebuilt wooden houses are dotted about a partly wooded field, which should make this a pleasantly relaxing retreat. Prices aren't yet decided but are estimated at around R1500 to R2000 a night.

Eating

In summer many open-air cafés appear near the river and around the opera house serving mostly beers and shashlyk. A few fast-food vans sell burgers and snacks near the trading arches.

RESTAURANTS

Samovar (☎ 464 188; ul Gagarina 41; meals R130-250; ⏰ 11am-11pm) Friendly, costumed staff add to the old-Russia atmosphere of this cute basement restaurant with wooden ceiling beams, spinning wheels and garlands of medicinal herbs.

Stolitsa (☎ 552 836; ul Revolyutsy 1905 31; meals R160-320; ⏰ 11am-11pm) This elegant upstairs restaurant has red, black and gold décor, modernist Buddhist-influenced art and old photos of Ulan-Ude. There's a menu in English and a vastly cheaper *zakusochnaya* (café; meals from R40 to R70) around the side. Handy for the train station.

Geser Restaurant (☎ 211 178; Hotel Geser, ul Ranzhurova 11; meals R120-280; ⏰ noon-4pm & 6-11pm) Smart restaurant with a menu in English and a variety of sensibly priced Siberian specialities, including omul fillet in cream sauce (R101) and five vegetarian options.

Zolotoy Drakon (☎ 212 109; ul Kirova 8; meals R150-350; ⏰ 11am-midnight) Redecorated in contemporary scarlet-and-white chinoiserie, Ulan-Ude's best predominantly Chinese restaurant usefully offers choices of portion sizes plus several European options. One room has an open fire in winter.

Drakon (☎ 215 283; ul Smolina 38; mains R25-50; ⏰ 11am-1am) Enjoy enormous servings of great Chinese food in this dungeon-effect chamber. Vegetarians might try the delicious *chi-san-tsi* (braised aubergines).

Baatarai Urgöö (Yurta; ☎ 447 492; Barguzin Rd; pozi for 4 people R59.30; ⏰ noon-11pm) Two carved Mongol warriors guard this unusual collection of restaurant yurts. The central dining hall is how you'd imagine Chinggis Khaan's spaceship, powered by a central dragon-stove. The menu includes many Buryat specialities: liver and onions, battered omul, *shangi* (scone-bread) and *khuushuur* (meat turnovers) washed down with astringent *arsa* (a warm, sour milk concoction).

Blues Café (Kafe Blyuz; ☎ 443 333; pr 50-let Oktyabrya 6; beers R30; ⏰ 10am-11pm) It's not Beale St, but there's a short menu of good-value meals and a cup of Nescafé costs only R6.

QUICK EATS & SELF-CATERING

Zakusochnaya Real (ul Banzarova 11; meals R21-30, pozi R12, beers R20; ⏰ 10am-11pm) A friendly, unadorned, ultracheap snack-café facing the cathedral. Next door is a gorgeous wooden-lace house.

King's Burger (ul Lenina 21; burgers R30-38, pizzas R90-110; ⏰ 8am-10pm) is a tasteful fast-food emporium, or you can get pizzas delivered from **Pepino** (☎ 272 366; ⏰ 24hr).

Sputnik Supermarket (ul Kommunisticheskaya 48; ⏰ 24hr) is a handy central grocery, but **Ekonomi Supermarket** (ul Tolstoy 3; ⏰ 9am-9pm) is the cheapest around.

Drinking

Mir Igry (ul Kommunisticheskaya 52; meals R90-220, beers R37-60; ⏰ 10am-11pm) This casino complex has three great bar-restaurants, each with its own atmosphere. It's popular with young professionals and a great place to strike up conversations over a shot of vodka or 10. Food menus are appealing but the more-intriguing Buryat options have limited availability.

Kakadu (☎ 440 553; pr 50-let Oktyabrya 10; snacks R18-30, beers R23; ⏰ 10am-11pm) Smoky, upbeat basement pub with a very nominal Mexican theme. Entry is from a side alley opposite the Dauriya bar (a real dive).

Kofeynya Shokolad (☎ 223 659; ul Kuybysheva 38; coffees R30-55, ice creams from R30; ⏰ 8.30am-11pm) Remarkably suave for the surroundings, this minicafé makes the best macchiato in town. It's built into the front terrace of the Buryat National Theatre building and uniquely enjoys simultaneous views of Ulan-Ude's two finest churches.

Kofeynya Marco Polo (ul Kommunisticheskaya 46; coffees R45-60; ⏰ 10am-10pm) Cosy, fairly characterful Western-style coffee house with great cakes and cocktails.

Getting There & Away

AIR

Siberia Airlines (☎ 220 125; ul Sukhe-Batora 63; ⏰ 9am-7pm Mon-Fri, to 5pm Sat & Sun) flies to Novosibirsk and Vladivostok, and offers deep discounts for early-purchase tickets to Moscow (daily, R9980 full price, R3500 two-week advanced purchase). Buryatavia has very scenic flights to Nizhneangarsk near Severobaikalsk (R1860, four to six per week) purchasable through Buryat Intour (p591).

BUS
At 8am on Tuesday, Thursday and Sunday, Buryat Intour runs buses from outside the Hotel Baikal to the Bayangol Hotel in Ulaan Baatar (R750, 12 hours) via Kyakhta.

Use the **main bus station** (Sovetskaya ul) for Barguzin (R228, 8.10am), Kurumkan (R295, 8am) and Ust-Barguzin (R192, six to seven hours, 7am) supplemented by similarly timed *marshrutky* from the yard opposite. *Marshrutky* to Goryachinsk (R140, 3½ hours) leave at noon and 4pm and to Kyakhta (R150, 4½ hours) via Novoselenginsk in the morning when full. There's also a 7.45am bus to Arshan (R332, 11 hours).

Marshrutky to Arshan (R350), Irkutsk and Chita run overnight from the courtyard of the train station, usually departing around 9pm. Sporadic daytime *marshrutky* serve Kabansk and Posolskoe from the same place.

From the Banzarova bus station bus 104 departs for Ivolginsk Datsan at 7am, noon and 4.20pm. Alternatively, use frequent bus 130 to Ivolga then switch to a taxi.

TRAIN
Beijing-bound trains pass through Ulan-Ude on Tuesday (via Chita) and Saturday (via Mongolia). Fast trains to Ulaan Baatar pass through on Sunday and Monday at 1.30am and waste vastly less time at the border than train 364 (R1350, 24 hours), which departs 6am daily. Buy international tickets from the **servis tsentr** (☎ 282 696; ⏱ 8am-1pm & 2-6.45pm) upstairs at the train station. For Chita, train 340 (R295 *platskart*, 10¾ hours) is the handiest overnight option. Towards Irkutsk day trains (from R280 *platskart*, from seven to 10½ hours) are popular for Baikal views.

Getting Around
Ulan-Ude has a vast, frequent but confusing public transport web. From pl Sovetov *marshrutka* 55 (R10, 20 minutes) runs a few times hourly to the airport while *marshrutka* 8 passes the *datsans*, hippodrome, Ethnographic Museum and Baatarai Urgöö restaurant – last return around 9pm. Tram 7

(R6) between ul Baltakhinova and the Hotel Odon is a relatively direct way to approach the train station, avoiding the sometimes convoluted *marshrutka* routes.

AROUND ULAN-UDE
The most popular attractions are the local *datsans* (Buddhist temples) although even interesting Ivolginsk, Buryatiya's biggest, is somewhat 'tinny' and far less visually impressive than the Tibetan-style equivalents at Tsugol and Aginskoe in Chita region.

First founded in 1741, **Tamchinski Datsan** (160km south of Ulan-Ude by rail) was Buryatiya's first Buddhist monastery. The original was destroyed in the 1930s, and the modern reconstruction is fairly small and surrounded by the disappointing little town of Gusinoe Ozero (30km south of Gusinoozersk). It's briefly visible from the west-facing windows of Naushki–Ulan-Ude trains.

Atsagat Datsan was once the centre of Buryat Buddhist scholarship and has an important scriptorium. Fine examples of Atsagat manuscripts are displayed in Ulan-Ude's literary museum (p592). Like Tamchinski, the *datsan* was completely destroyed in the 1930s, but has crawled back to life and has a tiny **Ayvan Darzhiev museum** commemorating the Atsagat monk who became a key counsellor to the 13th Dalai Lama. Photogenically gaudy, the little monastery sits on a lonely grassy knoll set back from km54 of the old Chita road – there's no convenient public transport. Tours from Ulan-Ude cost around US$70 for up to three people.

The hilly steppe around Ulan-Ude is pimpled with forgotten **Hun 'castles'**, so ancient that they are effectively invisible undulations in the flower-filled grass. Naran Tur (p591) can show you one such area but butterflies, flowers and the guide's enthusiasm are the biggest attractions of the trip. There are several relatively accessible **Old Believers' villages**, notably Tarbagatay (50km south) with its new church, but visits are only really interesting when costumed shows are put on (ie for larger tourist groups).

Ivolginsk (Ivolga) Datsan
Иволгинский Дацан
This multibuilding **datsan complex** (admission free, guided tour R60) was founded in 1946 and is the centre of Siberian Buddhism. Flanked by a few log cottages and a small canteen, it

---

DATSAN ETIQUETTE

Datsans, the temples of Siberian Buddhism, are easy-going places that visitors are generally welcome to explore. However, whether spinning prayer wheels or just walking around, you should politely maintain a clockwise direction, keeping your right side respectfully towards the shrines. Enter any temple via the left door and don't use the central stairs unless you're a self-realised lama. Bowing prayer-style with clasped-palms or prostrating yourself using wheelie-board contraptions is optional. If joining in the prayers and prostrations, do so three or seven times – 108 times is even better but that's just showing off. There's no entry fee but donation boxes abound. Once inside you could light *zula* (butter candles, R10) or fill in wish slips to post in the *Amgalanay* box for wellbeing or the *Yurööl* box to remember the dead. Don't forget to attach the cash register receipt – the more you pay, the better the chances of a wish come true, right?

---

sits in a wide green valley edged by mountain foothills. Viewed distantly across grassy fields, low morning sunlight glints enthrallingly from the gilded roof-wings of the 1972 main temple building. Closer up, however, the exterior is less impressive, with slapdash paintwork, tacky tiger guardian statues and brick-patterning painted onto the whitewashed walls. Some of the lovably basic prayer wheels are crafted from old tin cans. The main temple's interior (no photography please) is colourful and very atmospheric despite discordantly chuntering cash registers. Nearby notice the glassed-in **bodhi tree**, convolutedly descended from the Bodh Gaya original beneath which the Buddha achieved enlightenment.

Nearing completion within the *datsan* complex is the beautiful, Korean-style wooden **Etigel Khambin Temple** honouring the 12th Khambo Lama, whose body was recently exhumed. To general astonishment, seven decades after his death his flesh had still not decomposed. Some 'experts' have even attested that the corpse's hair is still growing, albeit extraordinarily slowly. The new temple plans to display the revered cadaver in a refrigerated display box that looks more suited to housing soft drinks.

The *datsan*'s unheated **hostel** (dm R250) is for pilgrims but Buddhist-minded tourists just might be accommodated upon polite request.

The first direct bus from Ulan-Ude arrives well before the 9am *khural* (prayer service), giving ample time to wander among the prayer flags of the mosquito-infested surrounding swamp. Returning buses leave at 1.30pm, 5.30pm and 8.30pm. Alternatively, share a taxi to uninteresting Ivolga (Ivolginsk town, R12 per seat, R35

per car). From here, *marshrutka* 130 shuttles to Ulan-Ude several times hourly (R20). Several Ulan-Ude tour agencies offer small group excursions combining visits to Ivolginsk, a local stupa and a hill-top *oova* (sacred whitewashed boulders) site with lovely views and shamanistic overtones. The typical cost is US$30 to US$40 per person.

TOWARDS MONGOLIA

Although there are faster weekend expresses, the daily Ulaan Baatar–bound train from Irkutsk is excruciatingly slow, taking a mind-numbing 11 hours to clear the borders. It's just one or two *kupe* carriages appended to train 364, which has no restaurant car and doesn't make food stops between Naushki (on the border) and Ulan-Ude (six to eight hours). Southbound you can save money by travelling *platskart* to Naushki, buying the Naushki–Sükhbaatar ticket separately then purchasing a Sükhbaatar to Ulaan Baatar ticket on arrival in Mongolia (paid in Mongolian tögrög).

Much faster is the through bus to Ulaan Baatar organised three times weekly by Buryat Intour in Ulan-Ude (opposite). More interesting than either is to make *marshrutka* hops to the Mongolian border via Novoselenginsk and the once-opulent tea-route city of Kyakhta.

Novoselenginsk Новоселенгинск

☎ 30145 / pop 9500 / ⊙ Moscow +5hr

Stockades and wooden houses on broad dust-blown roads give this small, 19th-century town a memorable Wild West feel. Learn something of Novoselenginsk's interesting history at the **Decembrist Museum** (Muzey Dekabristov; ☎ 96716; ul Lenina 53; admission R10; ⊙ 9am-5pm Wed-Sun), which is housed in an unmissable

SIBERIA

200-year-old colonnaded house in the town's centre. Lower floors are stocked with 19th-century furnishings, while upstairs are maps and photos relating to the Decembrist exiles and their wives (p567), as well as a long-armed naive-style crucifixion scene rescued from the town's 18th-century church.

If you walk a couple of kilometres east of the museum through the town towards the Selenginsk River you'll see on the grassy far bank the isolated ruins of the whitewashed **Spassky Church**; this is all that remains of Staroselenginsk, the original settlement which was abandoned around 1800 due to frequent floods. Some low hills here provide photogenic viewpoints across the landscape. You'll also find an unremarkable **obelisk** commemorating Glaswegian missionaries Robert Yuille and Martha Cowie who worked here back in 1829.

GETTING THERE & AWAY
Marshrutky from Ulan-Ude (R100, 1½ hours, six or seven daily) all pause here on their way to Kyakhta. Novoselenginsk has no hotel, and just a simple *pozi* canteen where the bus stops, but there's little reason to linger beyond the couple of hours it takes to see the town. Beware: we have received one horrific though fortunately atypical report of foreign visitors being brutally mugged at 4am while they were camping near Novoselenginsk.

Kyakhta Кяхта
☎ 30142 / pop 18,400 / ◷ Moscow +5hr
Kyakhta lacks the cinemascope landscapes of Novoselenginsk but retains three once-grand churches, a great museum and a surprisingly good hotel. Formerly called Troitskosavsk, Kyakhta was a town of tea-trade millionaires whose grandiose cathedral was reputed to have had solid silver doors embedded with diamonds. By the mid-19th century, as many as 5000 cases of tea a day were arriving via Mongolia on a stream of horse- or camel-caravans, which returned loaded with furs. Compressed tea 'bricks' were used as money, a practice continued by Buryat nomads as recently as the 1930s.

This gloriously profitable tea trade was brought to an abrupt end with the completion of the Trans-Siberian Railway. Almost overnight, all commerce was redirected via Vladivostok or Harbin and Kyakhta withered

into a remote border garrison town, bristling with weapons instead of gilded spires.

Modern Kyakhta is effectively two towns. The main one is centred around ul Lenina, where you'll find the bus terminus next to the 1853 trading arcade *(ryady gostinye)*. Kyakhta's smaller Sloboda district, 4km south of the commercial centre (R50 by taxi), is where you'll find the border post.

SIGHTS
The impressive shell of the 1817 **Trinity Cathedral** (Troitsky sobor) lies at the heart of the overgrown central park. Northeast along ul Lenina, the delightfully eccentric **museum** (ul Lenina 49; admission R40; ◷ 10am-6pm Tue-Sat) retains its original 1922 hardwood exhibition cases full of pickled foetuses and pinned butterflies. Enjoy imaginative displays of treasures salvaged from Soviet-plundered churches and *datsans*.

Running parallel to ul Lenina, ul Krupskaya has several attractive wooden buildings, including No 37 where the first meeting of the Mongolian Revolutionary Party was held in 1921. The street ends at Kyakhta's only working church, the **Uspenskaya Church**, with a subdued iconostasis and frescoed dome.

In Sloboda, a dwarfish Lenin glares condescendingly at the extraordinarily grand but sadly ruined **Voskresenskaya Church** (1838) and its splendid Italianate cupola. Behind Lenin is the big but rather mutilated 1842 **Historic Customs Warehouse** (Zdanie Gostinogo Dvora) with appended Communist-era spire. Directly behind is the frontier station for crossing into Mongolia.

SLEEPING & EATING
Hotel Druzhba (☎ 91 321; ul Krupskaya 8; dm from R280, ste R560) Beside the Uspenskaya Church, 10-minutes' walk south of Kyakhta's main centre, this place has good-value suites with hot water, sitting room and king-size bed. Its restaurant-bar is one of the better places to eat in town, too.

Hotel Turist (☎ 92431; cnr uls Lenina 21 & Sovetskaya; beds R135) With shared cold showers, this small, basic place is in a chocolate-box wooden house near the market.

Eating options are very limited. **Kafe Viola** (upstairs, ul Lenina 40; meals from R50; ◷ 10am-3am), near the market, is a reasonably pleasant place with booth seating and a decent menu.

For a snack try **Buryatskaya Kukhnya** (ul Menina; pozi each R9; ✆ 10am-1am), a small Buryat-style decorated room tucked between the trading arches and Sberbank.

GETTING THERE & AWAY

Ulan-Ude–Kyakhta *marshrutky* (R150, 3½ hours) take a pleasantly scenic route with a meal break in Novoselenginsk.

The **Mongolian border** (✆ 9am-noon & 2-6pm) is open to bicycles and vehicles, and some officials speak English. You can't walk across, so pedestrians need to negotiate passage with private drivers. Start asking as close as possible to the front of the chaotic queue: processing takes about an hour with only a handful of vehicles allowed through at any one time. The going rate is R150 per passenger across no-man's-land, but it's well worth negotiating a ride all the way to Sükhbaatar train station (around R100 extra) rather than becoming prey to rip-off taxi drivers in Altanbulag, the dreary Mongolian border village. From Sükhbaatar to Ulaan Baatar, nightly trains (*obshchiy/ kupe* 3300/8400 tögrög, nine hours) depart around 9.20pm – they're rarely full.

Naushki Наушки

The only reason to come here is to catch the border-hop train to Sükhbaatar (R230 *kupe*, one hour). This is often a single carriage, but when officially 'full', a suitably tipped *provodnik* might still be prepared to get you aboard. Naushki to Ulan-Ude (R210 *platskart*) is an attractive but excruciatingly slow ride, taking six to eight hours to travel 255km. Two or three buses shuttle the 35km between Kyakhta and Naushki (R35, one hour) to connect with Ulaan Baatar–Irkutsk trains.

CHITA ЧИТА

☎ 3022 / pop 370,000 / ✆ Moscow +6hr

The golden domes of Chita's new cathedral entice train travellers to hop off and explore this historic, patchily attractive city. If its architectural gems were less widely dispersed the city might be considered one of Siberia's more appealing. Sadly, each attractive area is a little too diffuse to make the overall impact particularly memorable. Nonetheless, the friendly, go-ahead atmosphere and lack of (non-Chinese) tourists makes Chita a pleasant place to spend a day or two.

Founded in 1653, Chita developed as a rough-and-tumble silver-mining centre till force-fed a dose of urban culture after 1827 by the arrival of more than 80 exiled Decembrist gentlemen-rebels – or more precisely by their wives and lovers who followed, setting up homes on what became known as ul Damskaya (Women's St). That's now the southern end of ul Stolyanova, where sadly only a handful of wooden cottages remain amid soulless concrete apartment towers.

As gateway to the new East Chinese Railway, Chita boomed in the early 20th century, despite flirting with socialism. Following the excitement of 1905, socialists set up a 'Chita Republic' which was brutally crushed within a year. After the 'real' revolutions of 1917, history gets even more exciting and complex. Bolsheviks took over, then lost control to Japanese forces who possibly intercepted part of the famous gold train (p505) before retreating east. By 1920 Chita was the capital of the huge, short-lived Far Eastern Republic, a nominally independent, pro-Lenin buffer state whose parliament is now garishly over-renovated at ul Anokhina 63. The republic was absorbed into Soviet Russia in December 1922 once the Japanese had withdrawn from Russia's east coast. Closed and secretive for much of the Soviet era, today Chita is prosperous, rejuvenated and once again flooded with Chinese traders.

Orientation

Three blocks north of the main Chita 2 train station, uls Butina and Leningradskaya form the sides of the wide pedestrianised expanse of pl Lenina. Perpendicular to this, attractively tree-lined ul Lenina parallels the train tracks from either side of the square. Parallel uls Amurskaya and Babushkina are major thoroughfares.

Information

Bookshop (Dom Knigi shopping centre; ul Amurskaya 58; ✆ 10am-2pm & 3-7pm Mon-Sat) Stocks various local and regional maps.

Dauria Ecology-Centre (☎ 232 619; http://dauria .chita.ru/english/index.html; ul Chkalova 120) Protecting and promoting the gorgeous, little-known landscapes of the Transbaikal region. It hosts some great web photos, but is not tourist orientated.

Flamingo Travel (☎ 359 353; www.flamingo.chita.ru, in Russian; office 7, ul Lenina 120; ✆ 9am-6pm) Small tour agency, with some English-speaking staff.

CHITA

0 _____ 500 m
0 _____ 0.3 miles

INFORMATION
Bookshop Книжный Магазин **1** B4
Dauria Ecology-Centre
  Эко-Центр Даурия.......................... **2** C3
Flamingo Travel Фламинго Трэвел **3** A3
Foreign Languages Faculty **4** B3
KiberPocht КиберПочт **5** B3
Lanta Ланта **6** B3

Magellan Internet
  Интернет Магеллан **7** B3
Main Post Office Почтамт **8** B3
Promstroibank Промстройбанк **9** B5
Telephone Office
  Междугородный телефон **10** B3

SIGHTS & ACTIVITIES
Archangel Michael Log Church
  Михайло-Архангельская
  Церковь **11** D5
Art Museum
  Картинная галерея....................... **12** C3
Former Far Eastern Republic
  Parliament Building **13** C4
Former Synagogue **14** D5
Kuznetzov Regional Museum
  Краеведческий Музей
  им А К Кузнецова........................ **15** C3
Lenin Statue
  Памятник В И Ленину.................. **16** B3
Military Museum Музей
  Истории Войск ЗабВО.................. **17** B4
Mosque Мечеть.................................... **18** D5

Officers' Club Дом Офицеров **19** B4
Tanks and Artillery..........................**20** B4
Wooden House, ul Anokhina 53........**21** C4
Wooden House, ul Babushkina 82....**22** B2
Wooden House, ul Chkalova 125......**23** B3
Wooden House, ul Lenina 104..........**24** B3

SLEEPING 🛏
Hotel AChO
  Гостиница Управления
  делами Администрации
  Читинской Области....................**25** B4
Hotel Chitaavtotrans
  Гостиница Читаавтотранс...........**26** B3
Hotel Dauria Гостиница Даурия......**27** B4
Hotel Ingoda Гостиница Ингода..**28** B4
Hotel Taiga Гостиница Тайга **29** C4
Hotel Zabaikale
  Гостиница Забайкалье..............**30** B3

EATING 🍴
Evrika Эврика.................................**31** C4
Gril Master Гриль Мастер...............**32** B3
Kafe Kollazh Кафе Коллаж **33** A2

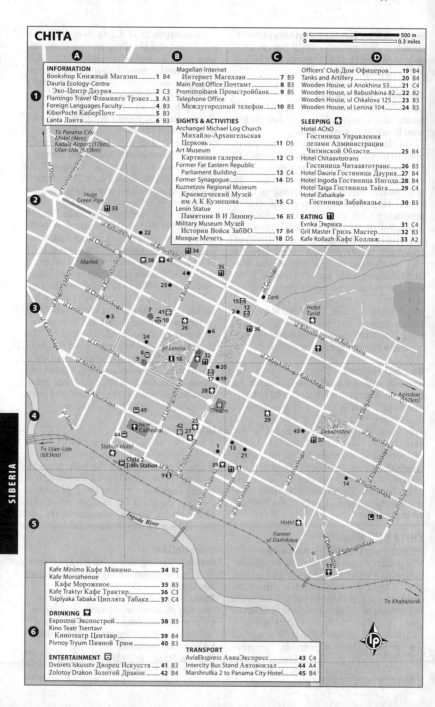

Kafe Minimo Кафе Минимо **34** B2
Kafe Morozhenoe
  Кафе Мороженое **35** B3
Kafe Traktyr Кафе Трактир................ **36** C3
Tsiplyaka Tabaka Циплята Табака.... **37** C4

DRINKING 🍷
Expostroi Экспострой **38** B3
Kino Teatr Tsentavr
  Кинотеатр Центавр........................ **39** B4
Pivnoy Tryum Пивной Трюм **40** B3

ENTERTAINMENT 🎭
Dvorets Iskusstv Дворец Искусств **41** B3
Zolotoy Drakon Золотой Дракон **42** B4

TRANSPORT
AviaEkspress АвиаЭкспресс **43** C4
Intercity Bus Stand Автовокзал **44** A4
Marshrutka 2 to Panama City Hotel..... **45** B4

SIBERIA

Foreign Languages Faculty (ul Butina 65) Helpful students here are keen to practise their English with those rare tourists.

KiberPocht (ul Butina 35; per MB R4, per hr R25; ☺ 8am-9pm) Internet access and stamps.

Magellan Internet (ul Chaikovskogo 24; per hr R50; ☺ 9am-7pm Mon-Fri, to 5pm Sat)

Main post office (ul Butina 37; ☺ 8am-7pm Mon-Fri, to 6pm Sat & Sun) Quaintly spired wooden building on pl Lenina.

Promstroibank (ul Petrovskaya 41) Changes US dollars, euros and Chinese yuan.

Telephone office (ul Chaikovskogo 22; ☺ 8am-11pm) Has an ATM.

Sights

Chita has a wealth of grand, century-old mansions liberally mixed with modern and Stalinist edifices of lesser quality. To enjoy the greatest concentration, walk along uls Anokhina, Amurskaya and Lenina for three blocks southeast of pl Lenina. That central square is also fairly imposing, dominated by a constipated-looking pink granite **Lenin statue**, surrounded in midwinter by ice sculptures. Chita also has a fair sprinkling of delightful old **wooden houses**, notably at ul Lenina 104, ul Chkalova 125, ul Babushkina 82 and ul Anokhina 53. Although the former historic centre is now mostly trampled by concrete towers, some timber cottages also remain on ul Dekabristov, southeast of the city centre. Hemmed in behind apartment blocks is the lovely 1771 **Archangel Michael log church** (ul Selenginskaya). It houses a small but interesting **Decembrist's Museum** (Muzey Dekabristov; ☎ 356 223; admission R20; ☺ 10am-6pm Tue-Sun), with a cooing nest of lovable babushkas as potential guides. The church's position close to an impressive 1907 **former synagogue** (ul Ingodinskaya 19) and eye-catching 1909 brick **mosque** (ul Anokhina 3a) has led certain Chita residents to declare rather absurdly that the area is some sort of 'Siberian Jerusalem'.

The excellent **Kuznetzov Regional Museum** (Kraevedchesky muzey; ☎ 226 709; ul Babushkina 113; admission R50; ☺ 10am-6pm Tue-Sun) is housed in an early-20th-century mansion. Beyond the gratuitous stuffed elk, you'll find some pretty interesting local exhibits, including a very thorough examination of the heritage and architectural renaissance of the city and region.

The **Art Museum** (Oblastnoy khudozhestvenny muzey; ul Chkalova 118; admission R15; ☺ 10am-6pm Tue-Sun) shows frequently changing exhibitions by school children and local artists, not always especially talented.

The previously interesting **Military Museum** (Muzey istori voysk ZaBVO; ul Lenina 86) was under reconstruction at the time of research. Its collection of tanks and artillery can still be seen by walking up the passage between the museum and the impressive Officers' Club building next door.

Sleeping

BUDGET

Chita's big military presence means many transients and lots of accommodation, but cheap dorms can be uncomfortably male dominated and off-putting for individual women travellers.

Hotel Dauria (☎ 262 350; Profsoyuznaya ul 12; dm R350, s R600-800, tw/tr R1200/1200) Big, unsophisticated old rooms are repainted and airy. Beds in a dormitory triple (with attached toilet and bathrooms) are Chita's best backpacker option. It's above the Kharbin Chinese Restaurant.

Hotel Taiga (☎ 262 332; 4th fl, ul Lenina 75; dm R190; ✗) Sheets in this survivable crash pad are clean and guests are usually segregated by gender. There's a shared kitchen and shower. The front door is locked at midnight.

Hotel Chitaavtotrans (☎ 355 011; ul Kostyushko-Grigovicha 7; s/tw R550/1000) Cosmetically improved rooms retain wobbly old shower floors. Quiet yet central.

Hotel Ingoda (☎ 356 356; Profsoyuznaya ul 25; s/tr R550/1500, tw R600-1100) Peeling paint bubbles off the walls of these unreconstructed Soviet rooms. Pay only R300 per person for rooms where the toilets don't work.

MIDRANGE

Hotel AChO (Gostinitsa Upravleniya delami Administratsi Chitinskoi Oblastu; ☎ 351 966; ul Profsoyuznaya 19; tw R1400-2700) Painted taupe and white, this fine brick mansion was built in 1906 for a printing magnate and used as a WWI hospital and tobacco factory before becoming a hotel. Rooms are now fully renovated with polished wooden floors, a fridge and showers with doors! Admire the wrought ironwork of the grand doorway and banisters.

Hotel Zabaikale (☎ 359 819; Hotel-zabaikal@yandex .ru, zabaikalie@yandex.ru; ul Leningradskaya 36; s/tw R1450/2000; 🖳) Unbeatably located overlooking the main square, a thorough Western makeover has given the Zabaikale's rooms minibars and Russian MTV. Showers are piping hot if poorly mounted. Rates include ham-and-egg breakfast in the kitschily grand new 2nd-floor restaurant.

Panama City Motel (☎ 443 747; http://panama.chita .ru/, in Russian; M/Я Severny 64; d R1950-2950; P X) Fully equipped Western-style motel rooms off a poorly lit corridor cost from R2350. Older octagonal cottages at R1950 are somewhat better value. There's a bar, restaurant and bowling alley (lanes per hour R360 to R600) but otherwise the motel's stuck in a suburban no-man's-land, some 5km north of the centre – take *marshrutka* 2 eastbound from ul Amurskaya (opposite the cathedral) or from uls Butina or Babushkina.

Eating

RESTAURANTS

Kafe Kollazh (☎ 978 138; ul Bogomyagkova 27; meals R110-300; ✹ 11.30am-11pm) Mood-lit and cosy with spinning wheels, old samovars and dried flowers. The food is tasty and beautifully presented.

Kafe Traktyr (☎ 352 229; ul Chkalova 93; meals R170-400; ✹ noon-2am) Russian home-style cooking is served at heavy wooden tables in this rebuilt wooden-lace cottage, with a quietly upmarket Siberian-retro atmosphere.

Kafe Minimo (☎ 323 338; ul Babushkina 62a; meals R80-240; ✹ noon-2am, last food 11pm) Genuine, if somewhat underspiced, Georgian food is easy to select from helpful picture menus. Dine in the beamed upstairs restaurant-hall (music show and R30 cover after 7pm) or in the small, pleasant bar area. *Khachapuri* (R50) takes 25 minutes to cook.

Tsiplyaka Tabaka (☎ 239 739; ul Ostrovskogo 20; meals R180-250; ✹ noon-5pm & 6pm-1am) Floral murals and fake stone carvings contrast intriguingly with Austin Powers–style lighting. Roast chicken priced by weight is the only main course (reckon R130 for a half bird). Add salads, julienne vegetables and reasonably priced wine.

Kafe Morozhenoe (☎ 266 867; ul Babushkina 50; meals R30-70; X) In primary blue and yellow this striking ice-cream parlour serves cheap meals, wine by the glass (from R20) and trendy terracotta pots of Chinese green tea.

QUICK EATS

Evrika (ul Amurskaya 67; ✹ 8.30am-8pm) From behind a historic façade, this plain but well-

kept *stolovaya* doles out very cheap *chebureki* (meat turnovers) and *pozi*.

Gril Master (ul Pushkina 5; burgers R42-56; ✹ 11am-11pm) Chita's fast-food joint is better for stuffed chicken roulade (R50) than for its microwaved burgers.

Drinking

Several dive bars fill basements on ul Amurskaya, two blocks north of the train station. Super-cheap beers (R15) mean you'll meet many swaying, overfriendly local drunks.

Expostroi (ul Chkalova 144; espresso R40; ✹ 10am-2pm & 3-7pm Mon-Sat) This tiny but excellent coffee bar is plonked incongruously within a hardware store.

Pivnoy Tryum (☎ 352 680; ul Babushkina 127; meals R100-190, beers from R30) Guarded by a hook-handed pirate, this nautically themed pub-restaurant is entered down a stairway from ul Zhuraleva.

Kino Teatr Tsentavr (ul Amurskaya 69; beers from R25; ✹ 10am-midnight) The inexpensive bar of this cinema complex is a popular youth hang-out.

Entertainment

Zolotoy Drakon (☎ 371 288; ul Amurskaya 78; admission R200-250; ✹ 9pm-6am) This discordant glass and yellow-concrete monstrosity is Chita's top disco and bowling alley.

Dvorets Iskusstv (ul Butina; concerts R20-70) Cultural centre with mixed offerings of theatre and music including local rock bands. Events often start around 5pm.

Getting There & Away

Kadala airport (☎ 338 404) is 18km west of central Chita on *marshrutka* 12 or 14. Limited flights connect to Moscow (R7000), Krasnoyarsk (R5900) and Yekaterinburg. **AviaEkspress** (☎ 371 288; www.aviaexpress.ru, in Russian; ul Lenina 55; ✹ 9am-7am Mon-Sat) sells tickets from anywhere to anywhere else with sharp discounts for purchasing three weeks ahead.

The main train station is Chita 2. For China the *Vostok* (train 020) runs to Beijing (R2950, 56½ hours) very early Wednesday morning while trains to Manzhouli (R1100, 25 hours) depart on Thursday and Saturday evening. Alternatively, take the nightly service to the border town of Zabaikalsk (R660 to R940, 14 hours) then bus hop into China.

Other destinations include Blagoveshchensk (train 250, R1470, 34½ hours, odd days), Tynda (train 078, R1250, 27 hours) and several Ulan-Ude services (R700, eight to 12 hours), some overnight. For R72 commission, the helpful **service centre** (Chita 2 train station; ☺ 8am-noon & 1-7.30pm) issues tickets while you relax on comfy settees.

From near Chita 2 train station buses and *marshrutky* run to Olovyannaya (R220, 8.30am) and Aginskoe (R120, three hours, hourly), shared taxis (R180 to R200) taking up any slack. Buy bus tickets in advance from the kiosks opposite. For Alkhanay use services to Duldurga, Uzon or Aksha.

AROUND CHITA
Aginskoe & Mogoytuy
Агинское и Могойтуй

For an intriguing trip from Chita, take a shared taxi (R180, two hours) to the dusty Buryat town of **Aginskoe** (☎ 30289, population 15,000), capital of the Agin-Buryat Autonomous District. Scenery en route transforms from patchily forested hills via river valleys into rolling grassy steppe. In Aginskoe, visit the beautiful old Buddhist **datsans** (5.5km west of the centre), see the shaman's *gabala* cup (made from a human skull) in the **Tsybikova Museum** (☎ 34462; ul Komsomolskaya 11; admission R30; ☺ 9am-1pm & 2-6pm Mon-Fri) and take a taxi to have lunch at one of the three great restaurants at **Hotel Sapsam** (☎ /fax 34590; www.megalink.ru/sapsan/, in Russian; tw/d R1200/1500, meals R200-500). Around 2km north of the centre, the **Hotel Dali** (☎ 34196; 3rd fl, ul Komsomolskaya 79; dm/d R400/600) offers cheaper, simpler rooms with bathrooms, though it's easy enough to get a *marshrutka* back to Chita until mid-afternoon.

Continuing the same day to brilliant Tsugol Datsan is feasible but more awkward. First take the hourly *marshrutka* (R30) across the endlessly undulating grasslands to **Mogoytuy** (population 7400), where there's a dismal, unmarked **hotel** (☎ 30255-21656; ul Zvaskaya 6; dm R88.60) but no reason to linger. From Mogoytuy, trains to Olovyannaya are poorly timed but trains ask only R800 to Tsugol including waiting time and a drop-off in Olovyannaya.

Tsugol, Olovyannaya & Zabaikalsk
Цугол, Оловянная и Забайкальск

Set just 2km from the 'holy' Onon River, Tsugol village is not particularly pretty but the perfectly proportioned **Tsugol Datsan** is surely the most memorable Buddhist temple in Russia. Built in 1820, it is just four years younger than Aginskoe Datsan and even more photogenic, with gilded Mongolian script-panels, wooden upper façades and tip-tilted roofs on each of its three storeys. The interior is less colourful than Ivolginsk, but clinging to the front is a unique, colourfully painted wrought-iron staircase. Make sure your taxi waits unless you're happy to walk the 13km to **Olovyannaya**, home to the nearest train station. The nightly train to Chita (R210 *platskart,* five hours) reaches this depressing railway town at 2.30am, so consider hopping on the 5pm *elektrichka* south to **Borzya**. As that's much further south, returning to Chita from Borzya gives you two hours' extra sleep en route. Alternatively, from Borzya you could attempt to find transport into the **Dauria Biosphere Reserve** (Daursky Zapavednik; www.nature.chita.ru), whose vast, periodically emptying **Torey Lakes** attract rare crane species and where you'll find the magical but very hard-to-reach **Adon-Chelon Oboo** (Buddhist-shamanist pilgrim stones).

Before leaving from Chita, consider prebooking the return train ticket from Borzya or Olovyannaya as train occupancy is high, with Chinese traders on board. Alternatively, if you're heading for China there are *elektrichky* (3½ hours from Borzya) to the bustling border town of **Zabaikalsk**, then minibuses ferry you across no-man's-land.

Alkhanay & Duldurga
Алханай и Дулдурга
☎ 30256 / pop 7000

Alkhanay, a Buryat-run national park 130km south of Chita, is reckoned by local Buddhists to be the religion's fifth most important holy 'mountain'. In fact you'll see forested hills, not mountains, through which a devotional six- to seven-hour return trek takes pilgrims to a small stupa and a window rock (a curtain of rock with a hole in it), considered the Gate of Shambala, an entry to spiritual paradise. The beautiful flowers, pious pilgrims and bird-watching opportunities are as interesting as the scenery. Alkhanay's entrance is 20km (R200 by taxi) from **Duldurga** village, where there's a helpful **Alkhanay National Park Office** (☎ 21458; alkhanai@yandex.ru; ul Gagarina 47) and two simple hotels. There's more accommodation in *turbazy* around the park entrance including a **yurt camp** (beds R500).

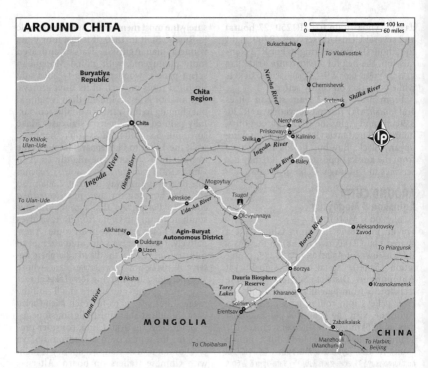

July to September, Chita-based agency **Lanta** (Map p598; ☎ 3022-262 368; ul Leningradskaya 56; ☺ 9am-6pm Mon-Sat) runs R1000 weekend tours, departing Friday and including two-nights' accommodation; no English is spoken. *Marshrutky* from Chita to Duldurga (R150, three hours) run several times daily and a single daily bus links Duldurga to Aginskoe (90km) on a terribly bumpy road.

NERCHINSK НЕРЧИНСК

☎ 30242 / pop 15,300 / ☺ Moscow +6hr

Once one of eastern Siberia's foremost towns, forgotten Nerchinsk is quietly intriguing. While hardly worth a special 300km trip from Chita, a day here handily breaks up a long Chita–Blagoveshchensk journey.

Founded in 1654 by Petr Beketov's Cossacks, Nerchinsk was the venue where China signed the immensely important 1689 border treaty recognising Russia's claims to the trans-Baikal region. The town profited from resultant Sino-Russian trade and boomed from the 1860s with the region's development of rich silver mines. Mikhail Butin, the local silver baron, also created steel and

wine industries and built himself an impressive crenellated palace, furnished with what were then claimed to be the world's largest mirrors. He'd bought the mirrors at Paris's 1878 World's Fair and miraculously managed to ship them unscathed all the way to Nerchinsk via the China Sea and up the Amur River.

Sights

Butin's mirrors form the centrepiece of the recently restored **Butin Palace Museum** (☎ 44515; lit@rambler.ru; Sovetskaya ul 83; admission R50; ☺ 9am-1pm & 2-6pm Tue-Sat), along with a delightful pair of hobbit-style chairs crafted from polished tangles of birch roots. Three-quarters of the palace, including the grand, triple-arched gateway (demolished in 1970), have yet to be rebuilt.

A block from the museum, the active 1825 **Voskresensky Cathedral** (ul Pogodaeva 85) looks like an opera house from the outside; its interior is plain and whitewashed.

Head across the sports pitch, passing a little silver Lenin, to the imposing though somewhat dilapidated 1840 **Trading Arches** (*gostiny dvor*). Nearby is a fine colonnaded pharmacy and the very grand façade of the pink former **Kolobovnikov Store** (ul Shilova 3), now a barn-like Togorvy Tsentr filled with some desultory stalls and kiosks. Trains stop just behind at an unmarked platform facing Kolobovnikov's former wooden-lace home, now the **children's music school** (ul Yaroslavskaya 24).

About 1km south of the museum, just before the post office and bank, a little pink column-fronted building was once the **Dauriya Hotel** (Sovetskaya ul 32). As locals will proudly tell you, Chekhov stayed here in June 1890. Diagonally across the same junction, the Uglavoy shop doubles as a minuscule bus station with a minibus to Chita at 6am and a few daily runs to Priiskovaya.

In **Kalinino village**, 25km away, the terribly neglected shell of the **Uspensky Monastery church** sits in a picturesque small village that was in fact the original 17th-century site of Nerchinsk (it moved twice). Kalinino is some 10km from Priiskovaya but taxis are easier to arrange from Nerchinsk (R200 including drop-off at Priiskovaya station).

Sleeping & Eating

Hotel PU (☎ 41745; ul Dostovalova 3; dm R150) This unmarked small white building has a green fence and turquoise metal gate, and is half a block west of the museum. Camp beds share a kitchen and sitting room but there's no shower and toilets are outdoor longdrops.

Kafe Russkaya Dusha (☎ 47523; Gostiny Dvor; meals R30-50; ◷ 11am-4pm & 5pm-late) Simple meals are served here, beneath plastic grapes and disco balls that hardly suit the crumbling grandeur of the old trading arches.

Getting There & Away

Nerchinsk is up a 10km dead-end railway spur from Priiskovaya on the trans-Siberian mainline. A single Nerchinsk-bound *platskartny* carriage from Chita (R209, 10 hours) is attached to the Erofey Pavlovich–bound train 392 departing Chita at 10pm daily. For much more choice, taxi-hop back to Priiskovaya, where connections include the 1.20pm train to Blagoveshchensk, the 8.55pm to Khabarovsk or the 6.11pm back towards Irkutsk: all run on odd days only. Taxis *from* Priiskovaya evaporate when there's no train due, so don't hang around too long if arriving there.

Russian Far East
Дальний Восток

Commonly mistaken for 'Siberia', the Russian Far East is actually further from Moscow, more remote and colder. It's also pretty big. Larger than Europe, it is comprised of taiga forest, snow-splattered or forested mountains, and northward rivers. Few foreigners make it here. Even trans-Siberian goers usually cut south from Baikal to Mongolia, missing the Far East entirely. There's a lot of thrillingly untouched turf though, with great (often costly) options for hiking, rafting, cross-country skiing, dog sledding and fishing. Best are encounters – on streets, in train carriages – with locals who may be surprised you made it here at all.

The southern strips of towns run along the eastern stretches of the pan-Russian trans-Siberian and BAM railways. The former sees more life, as it reaches the region's cosmopolitan leaders Khabarovsk and Vladivostok, both with tsarist-era buildings and sushi. The BAM is a gritty Soviet effort to connect Russia with some purpose-built '70s wasteland towns and more appealing, tsar-styled communist creations like Komsomolsk-na-Amure. Across the Tatar Strait is oil-booming Sakhalin Island and the Kuril Islands, still claimed by Japan.

Up north, beyond train tracks or reasonable roads, surprising Yakutsk is the heart of Russia's largest political division: Sakha Republic, home to many Yakut people (and a lot of horse meat on menus). The rugged 'Kolyma Highway' leads a couple of thousand kilometres over mountains and marsh to Magadan, a Gulag-built town overlooking the Sea of Okhotsk. Dangling towards Alaska, the Kamchatka Peninsula is simply one of the world's most beautiful places. Dotted with smoking volcanoes, fields of hardened lava and bear tracks, much of Kamchatka requires some money and a tour to reach.

HIGHLIGHTS

- Explore one of Russia's great natural highlights, **Kamchatka** (p642), a rugged paradise of volcanoes, geysers and bear hangouts
- Travel to the isolated home of the Yakut, **Yakutsk** (p627), a city on stilts above the permafrost, with a thrilling Yakut festival
- Experience bustling **Khabarovsk** (p607), an Amur River city on the Trans-Siberian Railway, with its European-style centre and the region's best museum
- Ride the funicular railway in **Vladivostok** (p614) to get a great view of the city's snaking bays and Russia's Pacific Fleet
- Visit Russia's 'Gateway to Hell', **Magadan** (p632), a Sea of Okhotsk town set amidst mountains with great whale-watching opportunities

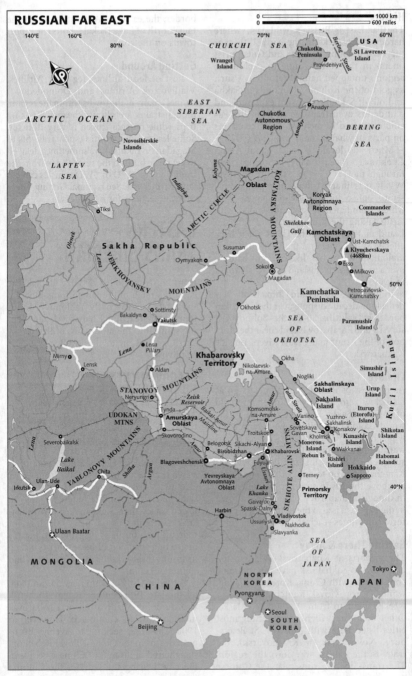

RUSSIAN FAR EAST

0 _____ 1000 km
0 _____ 600 miles

140°E   160°E   180°   70°N   60°N   80°N

CHUKCHI   SEA

Chukotka Peninsula
Wrangel Island
St Lawrence Island
USA
Providabiya

EAST SIBERIAN SEA

Chukotka Autonomous Region

ARCTIC   OCEAN

Anadyr

BERING   SEA

Novosibirskie Islands

LAPTEV SEA

Koryak Avtonomnaya Region

Commander Islands

Tiksi

Shelekhov Gulf

Kamchatskaya Oblast

Ust-Kamchatsk

Magadan
Oblast

▲ Klyuchevskaya (4688m)

S a k h a   R e p u b l i c

Susuman

Esso
Milkovo

Oymyakon

Sokol
Magadan

50°N

Kamchatka Peninsula

Petropavlovsk-Kamchatsky

Bakaldyn
Sottinsty
Yakutsk

Okhotsk

SEA OF OKHOTSK

Paramushir Island

Mirny
Lensk

Lena Pillars
Aldan

Khabarovsky Territory

Okha

Nikolaevsk-na-Amure

Nogliki

Simushir Island

Urup Island

Sakhalinskaya Oblast

STANOVOY MOUNTAINS
Neryungri
Zeisk Reservoir
Tynda

Komsomolsk-na-Amure

Vanino

Sakhalin Island

Iturup (Etorofu) Island

Amurskaya Oblast

Soveatskaya Gavan

Yuzhno-Sakhalinsk

Korsakov

Shikotan Island

UDOKAN MTNS

Skovorodino

Troitskoe

Kholmsk
Moneron Island

Kunashir Island
Wakkanai

Severobaikalsk

Belogotsk
Sikachi-Alyan

Birobidzhan

Khabarovsk
Fuyuan

Rebun Is

Hokkaido

Rishiri Island

Habomai Islands

Lake Baikal

Blagoveshchensk

Terney

Sapporo

Ulan-Ude
Chita

Yevreyskaya Avtonomnaya Oblast

Lake Khanka

Irkutsk

YABLONOVY MOUNTAINS

Harbin

Gaivaron
Spassk-Dalny

Primorsky Territory

40°N

Ulaan Baatar

Ussuriysk
Vladivostok
Nakhodka
Slavyanka

SEA OF JAPAN

M O N G O L I A

Tokyo

C H I N A

NORTH KOREA

Pyongyang

J A P A N

Beijing

Seoul
SOUTH KOREA

ARCTIC CIRCLE

KOLYMSKY MOUNTAINS

VERKHOYANSKY

MOUNTAINS

Lena
Lena

Onenek

Indigirka

Kolyma

Anadyr

Kuril Islands

SIKHOTE ALIN MTNS

Amur

Ussuri

Argun

Shilka

Zeya

Baikal-Amur Mainline

RUSSIAN FAR EAST

History

The Far East is Russia's 'wild east,' where hardened Cossacks in the early 17th century – and young Soviets (and Gulag prisoners) in the 20th – came to exploit the region's untapped natural resources – such as gold of the Kolyma, diamonds of Sakha and oil off Sakhalin. Russian explorers and plunderers even leapfrogged from the Pacific coast and Kamchatka to stake claims on parts of what is today the USA (p42).

Much ado locally is made about Anton Chekhov's (occasionally whoring) trip through the Far East to Sakhalin in 1890. WWII gets much tribute in regional museums, but so does the Russo-Japanese War, which humiliated Russia and ended with Japan taking the southern half of Sakhalin Island in 1905 (p47); the USSR got it back after WWII. China and the USSR had their diplomatic burps too, like outright battling over a worthless river island near Khabarovsk in 1969.

In June 2005 Russia and China finally settled a four-decade dispute over their 4300km border by splitting 50–50 the Bolshoy Ussurysky and Tarabarov Islands near the junction of the Amur and Ussuri Rivers, outside Khabarovsk.

Climate

As in most of Russia, thermometers go as far below zero as above. Winters are cold of course – Sakha Republic is home to the world's coldest inhabited town (Oymyakon, which hits –50°C in January). The sea brings warmer temperatures in winter, cooler in summer – Vladivostok and Petropavlovsk-Kamchatsky drop to only –10°C, and rarely go above the 20s in summer (fog often fills in though). Khabarovsk, the sunniest town in the Far East, is also the hottest – temperatures sometimes reach the mid-30s in July.

Getting There & Away

The airports at Khabarovsk, Vladivostok and Yuzhno-Sakhalinsk have international connections with China, Korea and Japan, while Petropavlovsk-Kamchatsky has a weekly flight to/from Anchorage, Alaska. Other than direct flights (connecting most cities listed here with Moscow, St Petersburg, Novosibirsk or Krasnoyarsk), the train is the easiest way into the region. The trans-Siberian runs near the Chinese border; the eastern BAM cuts through the taiga north of Lake Baikal – both reach port towns on the coast.

Getting Around

A host of local airlines (eg Sibir Airlines, Vladivostok Airlines and Domodedovo) connect many of the towns within the region, though trains are always cheaper. Booking trips while outside Russia is very difficult. Some less frequent routes (such as flights to Magadan or Yakutsk) are sometimes delayed to get more butts in the seats. Aside from the train, vans or 4WD or 6WD vehicles can get your further out. See regional Getting There & Away sections for more details.

EASTERN TRANS-SIBERIAN

Running from south of Lake Baikal, the eastern stretch of the famed trans-Siberian mostly flattens east of the Yablonovy Mountains before reaching Khabarovsk and turning south into the mountains of Primorsky Territory and on to the lovely naval port Vladivostok.

BLAGOVESHCHENSK
БЛАГОВЕЩЕНСК

☎ 4162 / pop 210,000 / ☯ Moscow +6hr

About 110km south of the trans-Siberian tracks, where Chinese and Russians rub shoulders, is Blagoveshchensk, a city set on the wide Amur River across from the Chinese town of Heihe. Since opening as a free trade zone in 1994, folks from either side swish-swash across the border (Russians for cheaper goods, Chinese for jobs – at lower wages than Russians). Blagoveshchensk (meaning 'good news') is less for tourism than business or gambling, but it's interesting watching Chinese tourists posing in front of tsar-era European buildings and statues of Lenin.

Settled as Ust-Zaysk military post in 1644, by the late 19th century Blagoveshchensk was outdoing Vladivostok or Khabarovsk in Sino-Russian commerce. However in 1900 Cossacks, seeking to avenge European deaths in the Chinese Boxer Rebellion, slaughtered thousands of Chinese people in the city. During the years of the Cultural

Revolution, citizens of Blagoveshchensk dealt with 24-hour propaganda blasted from loudspeakers across the river.

Orientation & Information

The train station is 4km north of the river. The main cross-town artery is north–south ul 50 Let Oktyabrya, which meets pl Lenina (and east–west ul Lenina) a block from the river. Another key hub of action is a few blocks north at the corner of ul 50 Let Oktyabrya and ul Amurskaya.

Amur Tourist (☎ 53005; tour@amur.ru; ul Kuzhnechnaya 1; ☼ 8am-noon & 1-5pm) Caters to Russians and Chinese, but may help you with regional advice.

Internet Access (☎ 391 276; ul Lenina 142; per hr R36; ☼ 9am-1pm & 2-8.30pm) Second floor of century-old red building, about 1km west of pl Lenina.

Sights

Central **ploshchad Lenina** – with Lenin's bronze self, fountains and promenade leading along the river in both directions – is a sort of beer-drinking focal point in good weather.

About 500m west on tree-lined ul Lenina, the large and well laid-out **Amur Regional Museum** (Amursky Oblastnoi Kraevedchesky muzey; ☎ 422 414; ul Lenina 165; admission R80; ☼ 10am-6pm Tue-Sun) is in a smartly kept red building dating from the turn of the 20th century.

Just south, around the WWII-themed **ploshchad Pobody** (a block south of ul Lenina), you can see several prerevolutionary buildings in their faded glory. Look for the **Anton Chekhov bust** on the red building on the square's south side – he stayed here in 1890 on his way to Sakhalin.

Many 100-year-old wooden buildings – some rather dilapidated – offer a break from the modern block housing seen in much of the Far East.

Sleeping & Eating

Most restaurants – found along ul Lenina – surrender to the temptation of the karaoke mic or slot machines: *pa-ching*.

Druzhba Hotel (☎ 376 140, 534 789; www.hotel druzhba.ru, in Russian; ul Kuznechnaya 1; s/d R650/800-1000) About 600m east of pl Lenina, this riverside Soviet survivor is the town's best, with friendly service and clean basic rooms – many of which get full-frontal views of China.

Zeya Hotel (☎ 539 996; hotel_zeya@amur.ru; ul Lenina 122; r per person from R744) Grey high-rise with clean rooms, just west of pl Pobody.

Russkaya Izba (☎ 446 661; ul Lenina 48; meals around R250-350; ☼ 11am-11pm) Tiny (four tables) and dachalike (with samovars and engraved wood details – and no gambling!), the homy Izba cooks up good Russian meals. It's about 800m east of the Druzhba.

Getting There & Away

Blagoveshchensk is 110km off the trans-Siberian, on a branch line from Belogorsk (where taxi vans also meet oncoming trains for the two-hour ride; R150).

From the Blagoveshchensk train station, daily trains 185/186 lead to/from Vladivostok, passing through Khabarovsk (R1090, 16 hours). On odd-numbered days, trains 249/250 connect Blagoveshchensk with Moscow, stopping in Irkutsk (R2500, 53 hours); and trains 81/82 go to/from Tynda (R1260, 20 hours).

The wild **Passazhirskoe Port Amurasso** (☎ 440 703, 555 754; ul Chaykovskogo 1), about 500m east of the Druzhba, sends teams of bag-toting Chinese and Russians on four daily boats to Heihe, China (R600, 15 minutes); five boats make the return trip. You'll need a Chinese visa and a multientry Russian one if you plan on coming back. The nearest consulate is in **Khabarovsk** (Map p608; ☎ 4212-302 519; fax 328 390; Lenin Stadium 1); visa applications are taken from 10.30am to 1pm Monday, Wednesday and Friday. A visa can be arranged in a day for about R4200 or in a week for R2400. We hear it's quite hectic on the Chinese side. Be sure to fill out a yellow form for entry, or a blue one for exit. If you're coming back to Russia, you may have to insist on a migration card.

KHABAROVSK ХАБАРОВСК

☎ 4212 / pop 620,000 / ☼ Moscow + 7hr

After dozens of hours of taiga and the isolated Soviet towns of eastern Siberia, Khabarovsk can put a jolt in the most rail weary. A booming river town 25km from China, Khabarovsk gives off an air of a coastal, almost Mediterranean, resort with tree-lined streets, squares with fountains, 19th-century brick buildings, popular parks overlooking the wide Amur, and real Japanese sushi, imported here to serve the frequent Japanese business travellers.

Such business has brought in hope and money to locals – and prices show it. One Khabarovsk resident told us it's brought a

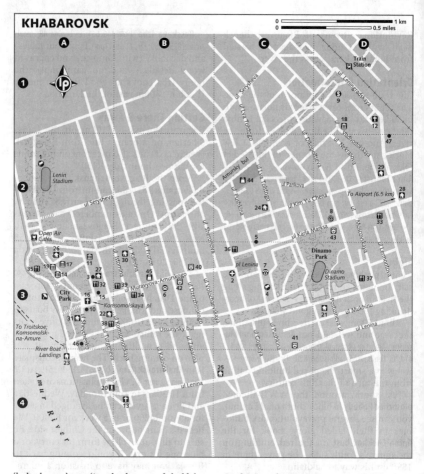

'baby boom' too: 'just look around, half the women are pregnant!'

If you stop for just a day, try to take in the Regional History Museum, the best in the Far East.

History

Khabarovsk was founded in 1858 as a military post by eastern Siberia's governor general, Count Nikolai Muravyov (later Muravyov-Amursky), during his campaign to take the Amur back from the Manchus. It was named after the man who got the Russians into trouble with the Manchus in the first place, 17th-century Russian explorer Yerofey Khabarov.

The trans-Siberian rail line arrived from Vladivostok in 1897. During the Russian

Civil War, the town was occupied by Japanese troops for most of 1920. The final Bolshevik victory in the Far East was at Volochaevka, 45km to the west.

In 1969 Soviet and Chinese soldiers fought a bloody hand-to-hand battle over little Damansky Island in the Ussuri River. Since 1984, tensions have eased. Damansky and several other islands were handed back to the Chinese in 1991.

The Japanese are also back – this time for business and pleasure. They make up 80% of all foreign visitors here.

Eighty per cent of Khabarovskians are native Russian-speakers. The only indigenous people here in any number are the Nanai, whose capital is Troitskoe, three hours north on the Amur.

INFORMATION	Far Eastern Art Museum	**EATING** 🍴
Chinese Consulate	Дальневосточный	Chocolate Шоколад **32** A3
Китайское Консульство **1** A2	Художественный Музей **14** A3	Citi HK Supermarket................**33** D2
City Hospital No 2	Far Eastern State Research Library	Dalny Vostok Cafe
Городская больница номер 2 ..**2** C3	Библиотека Дальне-Восточное	Дальний Восток Кафе........**34** B3
Dalgeo Tours Далгео Тур..............**3** A3	Иследования **15** A3	Kafe Utyos Кафе Утёс.............**35** A3
Exchange Bureau ....(see 26)	Khram Uspeniya Bozhey Materi	Maly Hotel Restaurant ....(see 30)
Internet Mir Интернет Мир ....(see 6)	Храм Успения Божей Матери ..**16** A3	Metro Метро **36** C3
Intour-Khabarovsk	Military Museum Военный Музей...**17** A3	Overtime...................................**37** D3
Интур-Хабаровск ....(see 26)	Museum of History of the Far Eastern	Russky Restaurant
Japanese Consulate	Railway Музей Истории	Русский Ресторан **38** A3
Японское Консульство **4** C3	Дальневосточной Железной	Tsentralnaya Gastronom
Khabarovsk-Tourist	дороги **18** D1	Центральный Гастроном......**39** B3
Хабаровск-Турист...................(see 28)	Regional History Museum	Unikhab....................................(see 26)
Knizhny Mir Книжный Мир **5** C2	Краеведческий Музей **19** A3	
Main Post Office Главпочтамт **6** B3	Tower.....................................(see 35)	**ENTERTAINMENT** 🎭
Main Telephone Office	Tsentralny Gastronom	Drama Theatre Театр Драмы.....**40** B3
Центральный Переговорный	Центральный Гастроном......(see 39)	Rio **41** C3
Пункт.......................................**7** C3	WWII Memorial Памятник	SovKino СовКино......................**42** B3
P@RTY......................................**8** D2	Второй Мировой Войны.......**20** A4	Theatre of Musical Comedy
Sberbank Сбербанк.....................**9** D1		Театр Музыкальной Комедии .**43** D2
	SLEEPING 🛏	
SIGHTS & ACTIVITIES	Ali Hotel Гостиница Али **21** D3	**SHOPPING** 🛍
Amur Steamship Company	Ekspress Vostok Експресс Восток...**22** A3	Market Рынок **44** C2
Параходная Компания Амур **10** A3	Gostinitsa Гостиница..................**23** A4	Tainy Remesla Тайны Ремесла...**45** B3
Archeology Museum	Hotel Amethyst	
Музей Археологии...................**11** A3	Гостиница Аметист **24** C2	**TRANSPORT**
Church of Christ's Birth	Hotel Amur Гостиница Амур **25** C4	Boat Ticket Office.....................**46** A3
Христорождественская	Hotel Intourist	Train Ticket Office
Церковь **12** D1	Гостиница Интурист **26** A3	Железнодорожные кассы **47** D2
Church of the Transfiguration	Hotel Sapporo Гостиница Саппоро **27** A3	Transport Service Transit............(see 33)
Преображенская церковь **13** B4	Hotel Turist Гостиница Турист ...**28** D2	
Duma Дума ....(see 45)	Hotel Zarya Гостиница Заря **29** D2	
	Maly Hotel Гостиница Малая **30** B3	
	Parus Парус **31** A3	

Orientation

Khabarovsk's train station is about 3.5km northeast of the Amur waterfront at the head of broad Amursky bul; the airport is 9km east of the centre. Running more or less perpendicular to the river is the busiest street, ul Muravyova-Amurskogo, which becomes ul Karla Marksa east of pl Lenina.

MAPS

Knizhny Mir (☎ 328 250; ul Karla Marksa 37; ⌚ 9am-8pm) stocks a good range of city and regional maps for the entire Russian Far East (city maps are about R50).

Information

INTERNET ACCESS

Internet Mir (☎ 304 613; ul Muravyova-Amurskogo 28; per hr R40; ⌚ 8am-9pm Mon-Fri, 9am-7pm Sat & Sun) Web access, next to post office.

P@RTY (☎ 308 350; ul Karla Marksa 52; per hr R30; ⌚ 10am-8pm) Rather unfestive actually.

MEDICAL SERVICES

City Hospital No 2 (☎ 306 585, 304 620; ul Muravyova-Amurskogo 54)

MONEY

Exchange offices and ATMs can be found across the city.

Exchange bureau (Hotel Intourist; Amursky bul 2; ⌚ 8.45am-11pm) Changes travellers cheques.

Sberbank (Amursky bul 66; ⌚ 8am-8pm Mon & Wed-Fri, 9am-8pm Tue, 9am-7pm Sat & Sun) With 24-hour ATM, across from the train station.

POST

Main post office (ul Muravyova-Amurskogo 28; ⌚ 8am-9pm Mon-Fri, 9am-7pm Sat & Sun) You can make calls from here or the centre just below.

TELEPHONE

Main telephone office (ul Pushkina 52; ⌚ 8.30am-10pm)

TRAVEL AGENCIES

Any of the following can help book rail or plane tickets. Popular city tours incorporate beer-included peeks at the Baltika brewery (US$40 per person) or Russian cuisine classes with dinner (about US$60 per person).

Dalgeo Tours (☎ 318 829; www.dalgeotours.com; ul Turgeneva 78; ⌚ 10am-7pm Mon-Fri) Very helpful English-speaking staff offer a range of local tours.

Intour-Khabarovsk (☎ 312 186; fax 327 634; www.intour-khabarovsk.com; Hotel Intourist, Amursky bul 2; ⌚ 10am-6pm Mon-Fri) Friendly staff have plenty of experience with foreigners (mostly prebooked group tours).

Khabarovsk-Tourist (☎ 439 423; ul Sinelnikova 9, Hotel Turist; ⌚ 9am-6pm Mon-Fri) Arranges Chinese visas in a week for R2400, or in a day for R4500.

Sights & Activities
ULITSA MURAVYOVA-AMURSKOGO

Khabarovsk is the nicest city in the region to see by foot. A stroll along ul Muravyova-Amurskogo provides a chance to admire the graceful architecture that survived the civil war. The pretty fountains at pl Lenina are a magnet for locals relaxing in the evening, where Lenin still looks down from the front of a handsome 1903 red-brick building. During January, the square hosts an ice sculpture fest.

The striking old parliament building, or **duma** (ul Muravyova-Amurskogo 17), became the House of Pioneers (Dom Pionerov) in Soviet times. It now houses a souvenir shop called Tainy Remesla.

A statue of Mercury tops **Tsentralny Gastronom** (ul Muravyova-Amurskogo 9), a glamorous 1895 mint-green Style Moderne building with a decent café of the same name. The **Far Eastern State Research Library** (ul Muravyova-Amurskogo 1), with its intricate red-and-black brick façade, was built from 1900 to 1902.

At Komsomolskaya pl is the newly reconstructed Orthodox church **Khram Uspenya Bozhey Materi**, a replica of one destroyed during communist times. On the south side of the square is the headquarters of the **Amur Steamship Company**.

WATERFRONT & RIVER TRIPS

Steps from Komsomolskaya pl lead to the waterfront and a strip of beach that's very popular with sunbathers on hot days. Heading south, there's a string of summertime food stalls and the landing stages for suburban river boats. Further on, as you climb the steps back up to ul Lenina, you'll encounter Khabarovsk's bombastic **WWII memorial** and the new multidomed **Church of the Transfiguration**.

A pleasant **city park** stretches 1.5km downriver (northwards). On the promontory is a cliff-top **tower** in which a troupe of WWI Austro-Hungarian POW musicians was shot dead for refusing to play the Russian Imperial anthem. It now contains a café, Kafe Utyos. Opposite the tower is a statue of Count Nikolai Muravyov-Amursky.

For a short local ride along the Amur, various hydrofoils and boats set off from May to October on hour-long beer-soaked trips for R70; 90-minute evening cruises cost R130. There are no set schedules – just watch for one and jump on. Call **Amurrechturist** (☎ 398 269) for more information.

MUSEUMS

Four of Khabarovsk's museums are bunched together in impressive century-old buildings. One of the Far East's best attractions, the **Regional History Museum** (Kraevedchesky muzey; ☎ 312 054; ul Shevchenko 11; admission R140, photo permits R100; ⊗ 10am-6pm Tue-Sun) earns it rubles with six well laid-out (and well-lit) halls in an evocative 1894 red-brick building. Highlights are many, particularly a far better than average look into native cultures, including eerie larger-than-life-size spear-toting wooden figurines. Stuffed animals feature – *sacré bleu!* – and there are some English captions. Another highlight is the full-on panorama of the snowy 1922 civil war battle at Volochaevka. Judging by the lone White soldier aiming his musket at you, you are a Red (game: first one to find him *wins*). The museum also has a Soviet-fest room complete with medals, photos, stamps and banners (skimps on Gulag coverage though).

The nearby **Military Museum** (Voyenny muzey; ☎ 326 350; ul Shevchenko 20; admission R84; ⊗ 10am-5pm Tue-Sun) is a not uninteresting four-room frenzy of battle-axes, guns, knives, and busts and photos of moustached heroes of past conflicts. In the back courtyard are a line of army trucks, cannons, tanks and a luxury officers-only rail carriage dating from 1926.

The highlights of the small **Archaeology Museum** (Muzey Arkheologii; ☎ 324 177; ul Turgeneva 86; admission R120; ⊗ 10am-5.30pm Tue-Sun) are the reproductions and diagrams of the wide-eyed figures found at the ancient Sikachi-Alyan petroglyphs (p614). Lots of pot parts and spearheads – some dating, reportedly, from 30,000 years ago. We particularly like the mural of hunters sending spears into a thick-lashed, very submissive seal.

The **Far Eastern Art Museum** (Dalnevostochny Khudozhestvenny muzey; ☎ 328 338; ul Shevchenko 7; admission US$4; ⊗ 10am-5pm Tue-Sun) has religious icons, Japanese porcelain and 19th-century Russian paintings.

Closed at research time (but apparently reopening) is the small **Museum of History of the Far Eastern Railway** (☎ 383 035; ul Vladivostokskaya 40; admission free; ⊗ 8.30am-5.30pm Mon-Fri), which has plenty of photos and models.

OTHER ATTRACTIONS

Dinamo Park, behind the Theatre of Musical Comedy, brims with sun and shade seekers in good weather; the ponds on the south side are popular swim-and-splash spots, and there are some small rides and a mechanical bull, of course.

Among the few churches that survived the Soviet years is the cute, red, blue, and white **Church of Christ's Birth** (Khristorozhdestvenskaya tserkov; ul Leningradskaya 65). with a kaleidoscopic interior of coloured glass and icons. Two-hour services are held most days at 7am and 5pm.

Sleeping

Dalgeo Tourist arranges homestays (from US$35 including breakfast) with advance notice.

BUDGET

All rooms come with private bathroom, TV and refrigerator. The first two are not far from the train station.

Hotel Zarya (☎ 310 101; fax 310 103; hotel_zarya@mail.ru; ul Kim Yu Chena 81/16; s/d incl breakfast from R850/1600; ✖ 🖳) Modern makeover of a rather drab building gives Zarya a nearly 'boutique hotel' feel. Rooms are small – some have air-con. Staff is great, and the Internet's available 24 hours.

Hotel Turist (☎ 439 674; fax 439 421; postmaster@khabturist.kht.ru; ul Karla Marksa 67; s/d from R1100/1320) Facing a busy street, the eight-storey Turist looks every bit of its 40 years, but its rooms are well kept up – the cheapies are frequently full.

Hotel Amur (☎ 221 223; fax 217 141; ul Lenina 29; s/d incl breakfast from R1500/1600; ✖) Grand old building with 75 rooms (some with air-con) on the busy residential ul Lenina.

Ekspress Vostok (☎ 384 797; ul Komsomolskaya 67; s/d R1300/1800; ✖) New hotel geared to Russians – all 29 rooms are clean, with a writing desk and rather cheap vinyl floors.

At last pass, it was possible to bunk on a late-night disco cruise ship from June to September; it's simply called **'gostinitsa'** (hotel; ☎ 398 980; s/d R400/800).

MIDRANGE & TOP END

Hotel Intourist (☎ 312 313; fax 326 507; www.intour.khv.ru; Amursky bul 2; s/d from R2352/2604; 🖳) This big bolshevik is another monster of the past, but it's quite good. The halls – with darkwood

doors and small, but clean rooms – look over the nearby Amur, and most of the package tourists who come seem to like it. Prices fall in winter. Ask for 7th or higher floors on the north side for best views. There's a tourist agency and three restaurants.

Hotel Amethyst (☎ 420 766; fax 324 699; amethyst@hotel.kht.ru; ul Lva Tolstogo 5a; s/d from R2600/3100; ✖) A boutique-style hotel with just 16 spacious, nicely decorated rooms. The staff are great and there's a sauna. Breakfast is R200.

Maly Hotel (☎ 305 802; fax 305 939; ul Kalinina 83a; s/d US$110/180; ✖) Behind a bank, in a small, quiet brick courtyard, the Maly has just 11 rooms – the doubles a lot bigger than the singles.

Ali Hotel (☎ 217 888; fax 304 403; ul Mukhinu 17; s/d incl breakfast US$120/162; ✖ 🖳 ♨) Ali's 20 rooms are Khabarovsk's roomiest, with sparkling bathrooms – though the hotel's a bit stranded (between apartments and garages). Fitness centre with pool and sauna.

Hotel Sapporo (☎ 306 745; fax 306 075; sapporo1@gin.ru; ul Komsomolskaya 79; s/d R2983/3297; ✖ 🖳) Just off the main crawl, the Sapporo's 20 rooms are geared to the many visitors from Japan; small, clean (not particularly remarkable) rooms in a simple red-brick building. There's a good sauna on the premises.

Parus (☎ /fax 649 510; guest@parus.vic.ru; ul Shevchenko 5; s/d incl breakfast R3100/4400; ✖ 🖳) Part of a century-old red-and-brick building near the water, the Parus seems more 'business centre' than hotel, though its spacious rooms are comfortable (all but four rooms are in a newer annex). Its bar opens at 7pm.

Eating

Eating is easy in Khabarovsk: new spots open frequently on and off ul Muravyova-Amurskogo. Also you'll see – weather permitting – tons of street vendors selling pizza and the ever-present hot dog (R13).

RESTAURANTS

Russky Restaurant (☎ 306 587; Ussuriysky bul 9; meals R800-1200; ⏱ noon-1am) Cosy and slightly kitsch, Russky has four dacha-style cellar rooms decorated with balalaikas and stuffed owls – one with live traditional music at 8pm, which fills first. The food is very good. Sizzling sturgeon is a favourite, as is the breaded pork chop covered in dill.

Chocolate (☎ 420 097; ul Turgeneva 74; meals R400-700; ⏱ 24hr) Stylish eatery where the cool folk go (and the air-con is cranking in summer) for international snacking (fajitas, burgers) and some superb desserts (the namesake brownie is R180).

Kafe Utyos (☎ 777 050; ul Shevchenko 15; meals R800-1500) In the tower in the park overlooking the river, Utyos is one of Khab's swankier restaurants – mostly Russian and Japanese food.

Metro (ul Muravyova-Amurskogo 35; meals R400-700, lunches R100-150; ☺ 11am-5pm & 6pm-2am Mon-Fri, 11am-2am Sat & Sun) Below a university building on pl Lenina, the Metro occupies (it's whispered) the spot where medical students once poked at cadavers. Now it's a flashy subterranean drink 'n' eat spot – best for the cheap lunch.

Maly Hotel Restaurant (☎ 305 802; meals R600-1000; ☺ 9am-11pm) The hotel's small restaurant is known for the best Japanese in town (all imported) and rather slow service. Worth calling ahead.

Unikhab (☎ 312 315; Amursky bul 2, 11th fl; meals R600-1000 ☺ noon-3pm & 6-11pm) The best of Hotel Intourist's three restaurants, the top-floor Japanese restaurant offers imported-from-Japan sushi with views.

Overtime (☎ 318 547; ul Dikopoltseva 12, Platinum Arena; meals R600-1000) If you're here in hockey season, Overtime's primary red, white and blue décor overlooks the rink; photos of local hockey greats adorn walls all year. The 'goalkeeper' is a spiced Sicilian fish (R350).

CAFÉS & SELF-CATERING

Tsentralny Gastronom (ul Muravyova-Amurskogo 9; meals R150-300; ☺ 10am-10pm) In a 19th-century building, upstairs from a good 24-hour supermarket, this cute modern-retro self-service café has a good selection of meals, beer-on-tap and a refrigerator full of desserts.

Dalny Vostok Cafe (ul Muravyova-Amurskogo 18; meals R150-300; ☺ 9am-midnight) Plump blue booths overlook the street action at this two-line cheapie fast-food pick-and-point stop (go past the doors in the front bar).

Citi HK Supermarket (ul Karl Marksa 76; ☺ 9am-11pm) Best grocery in town with lines to prove it.

Drinking

Most drinking occurs at open-air cafés; good ones are along the river, north of the Hotel Intourist.

Rio (☎ 238 420; ul Lenina 49; cover R300; ☺ 9pm-4am Fri-Sun) The city's largest club on two levels –

photos show what to expect: topless women engaging in mud conflict.

Entertainment

Those who cannot speak Russian cannot be entertained. Pushkin said that, right? These options require Russian (or enjoyment of confusion).

Drama Theatre (Teatr Dramy; ☎ 310 809; ul Dzerzhinskogo 44) Bet you a kopeck Chekhov's on.

Theatre of Musical Comedy (Teatr Muzykalnoy Komedii; ☎ 211 403; ul Karla Marksa 64; tickets R80-800) Talking, joking, and the occasional heavy metal concert. Dio started its 2005 tour here.

SovKino (☎ 324 065; ul Muravyova-Amurskogo 32) Often shows dubbed Hollywood flicks.

Shopping

Tainy Remesla (☎ 327 385; ul Muravyova-Amurskogo 17; ☺ 11am-6pm or 7pm) Best souvenir shop in town, in the old House of Pioneers building. Plenty of traditional items, though you may have to use your credit card to take many with you.

The main **market** (cnr bul Amursky & ul Tolstogo; ☺ 8am-7pm) covers everything from plug adaptors and fishing gear to underwear and fresh produce.

Getting There & Away
AIR

The **airport** (☎ 393 758) offers the following domestic services:

Destination	Duration	Frequency	Fare
Irkutsk	3hr	daily	R5800
Magadan	2½hr	4 weekly	R2630-3100
Moscow	8½hr	daily	R11,500
Nikolaevsk-na-Amure	1½hr	daily	R4100
Petropavlovsk-Kamchatsky	2½hr	6 weekly	R5975
Vladivostok	1¾hr	daily	R2500
Yakutsk	3hr	6 weekly	R6200
Yuzhno-Sakhalinsk	1½hr	2 daily	R4200

There are international flights to Harbin (US$170) and Guau (US$320) in China, Seoul (from US$300) in Korea, and Niigata (US$340) and (July to September) Aomori (US$340) in Japan. All international flights are subject to a R800 departure tax, usually included in ticket price.

The foreign airlines all have offices at the airport's international terminal (to the left of the new one). **Intour-Khabarovsk** (☎ 312 154; Hotel Intourist; ⏱ 9am-8pm) books tickets, as does **Transport Service Transit** (☎ 291 692; ul Karl Marksa 76; ⏱ 10am-2pm & 3-8pm), in the HK Citi Mall.

BOAT & BUS

From Khabarovsk's river station boats sail down the Amur to Fuyuan in northern China (p614). Between May and October, hydrofoils run north on the Amur between Khabarovsk and Komsomolsk-na-Amure (R446, six hours) and Nikolaevsk-na-Amure (R2332, 17 hours). You'll save money taking the night bus from here to Komsomolsk-na-Amure then, catching a boat up. At research time, boats left here at 7am. The pink river station *(rechnoy vokzal)* houses the **boat ticket office** (☎ 398 654; ⏱ 8am-10pm).

TRAIN

Heading west, apart from the No 1 *Rossiya,* which departs for Moscow (R8500, five days 10 hours) and Irkutsk (R5000, 60 hours) on even-numbered dates, there's also the daily No 43 service to Moscow (R5700, five days 17 hours) and Irkutsk (60 hours, R3350) and the No 7 to Novosibirsk (R4550, 91 hours). Heading east, Vladivostok is best reached on the daily train 6 *Okean* service (R1500, 13 hours). See right for details on getting to Birobidzhan.

Other daily services (all leaving in the evening) include train 226 to Tynda (R1351, 30 hours), and on to Neryungri; the No 67 and No 953 to Komsomolsk (R860, eight hours), the latter continuing to Sovetskaya Gavan and Port Vanino for the ferry across to Sakhalin; and the No 385 to Blagoveshchensk (R1090, 16 hours).

Buy tickets at the station or the quieter (and nearby) **train ticket office** (zheleznodorozhne-avia kassy; ul Leningradskaya 56V; ⏱ 9.30am-7.20pm), where you'll pay a R60 booking fee.

Getting Around

Trolleybus 1 (R9) runs regularly from the airport to ul Muravyova-Amurskogo, taking around 30 minutes to cover the 5km; *marshrutky* (fixed-route minivans) also do the journey (R10). A taxi to/from the Hotel Intourist should cost no more than R250.

The easiest way to get into the city centre from the train station at the eastern end of Amursky bul is by way of tram 1, 2, 4 or 6 (R10), which cross ul Muravyova-

Amurskogo along ul Sheronova. Bus 35 connects the airport and the train station.

Travel agents can get you a car with driver for US$15 per hour.

AROUND KHABAROVSK

Contact a Khabarovsk travel agent for a full list of (sometimes rather touristy) regional tours, including dacha tours and the more intriguing Khekhtsir, a nature park near China with hiking trails and wildlife (about US$50 per person).

Birobidzhan Биробиджан

☎ 42162 / pop 90,000 / ⏱ Moscow + 7hr

A couple hours shy of Khabarovsk on the trans-Siberian line (if you're heading east), Birobidzhan is actually a more attractive town, with shady streets and a quiet pace. It's interesting mostly for its history, as the big Hebrew letters spelling out the station's name indicate.

Birobidzhan (named for the swampy meeting place of the Bira and Bidzhan Rivers) is capital of the 36,000-sq-km Jewish Autonomous Region (Yevreyskaya Avtonomnaya Oblast). It was opened to settlement in 1927, when the Soviet authorities conceived the idea of a homeland for Jews. Some 43,000 Jews, mainly from Belarus and Ukraine but also from the US, Argentina and even Palestine, made the trek. In the 1930s growing anti-Semitism – fuelled by Stalin's paranoia that Jewish doctors were plotting to kill him – led to the ban of Yiddish and synagogues.

Since 1991 diplomatic ties between Russia and Israel have led to an outward flood of Jews. Of the estimated 22,000 who lived here then, only 4800 remain – about 2.4% of the region's population. Today Hebrew and Yiddish are once again taught in schools, and Khabarovsk's nearby boom has prompted some Jews to return from overseas.

For most visitors, an easy DIY day trip from Khabarovsk is more than enough time.

ORIENTATION & INFORMATION

All is quite walkable. Parallel to the tracks to the south are the main streets ul Lenina, then ul Sholom-Aleykhema. An **Internet centre** (cnr uls Gorkogo & Lenina; per hr R40; ⏱ 8am-10pm) faces pl Pobedy.

SIGHTS

Across from the train station, pl Pobedy is devoted to WWII. Halfway along the square, west on ul Lenina, are the two main sights in town. **Freid** (☎ 27708; ul Sholom-Aleykhema 14A), reached from ul Lenina (look for the giant menorah on your left), is Birobidzhan's Jewish culture centre. Ask to see if you can chat with the lively director about local history, pick up the Jewish newspaper or buy a souvenir yarmulke (skull cap). Next door is a new synagogue you can visit.

About 100m further west, the **Regional Museum** (Kraevedchesky muzey; ☎ 68321; ul Lenina 25; admission R100; ☉ 10am-1pm & 2-6pm Tue-Fri) has a smattering of exhibits on local Jewish history (including an ad for a cheesy 1980s band), plus boars and bears and a mini-diorama of the Volochaevka civil war battle (akin to Khabarovsk's bigger and better one, but here blood pours from the 3-D dead guy's head).

SLEEPING & EATING

Hotel Vostok (☎ 65330; ul Sholom-Aleykhema 1; s/d R850/1146) Birobidzhan's only hotel has nice rooms, and is next to a lively market. The hotel's restaurant serves meals, including filling R100 lunch specials.

GETTING THERE & AWAY

Most trans-Siberian trains stop in Birobidzhan. The easiest way here is by the morning *elektrichka* (suburban train) from Khabarovsk (R90 to R120, 2¾ hours). It leaves Khabarovsk at 8am, and returns around 6pm. You can also catch buses from the Khabarovsk train station.

Fuyuan (China) Фуюань

From mid-May to mid-October, daily hydrofoils leave Khabarovsk for the small Chinese town of Fuyuan (one way R1400, return R2000, 1½ hours) at 8am and 10am, returning in the evening (with tons of shopping bags). If you're planning to return to Russia, you'll need a Chinese visa and a double/multiple entry Russian visa. There's a Chinese consulate in Khabarovsk (see p607 for details). From Fuyuan you can take a bus to Jiamusi and then on to Harbin.

Sikachi-Alyan Сикачи-Алян

The main attraction at Sikachi-Alyan, 40km north of Khabarovsk, is the enigmatic stone carvings of strange graphic figures, dating from the 11th century BC. They can be found on the basalt boulders at the water's edge. Bring mosquito repellent in summer. There's a couple of competing museums here: the Ecological Tourist Complex was made by Russians, the local museum by local Nanai. It's not possible to just show up to the latter without prior arrangements.

An eight-hour tour – with guide, lunch and transport, usually looking at how Nanai locals make crafts out of fish skin – costs about US$130.

VLADIVOSTOK ВЛАДИВОСТОК

☎ 4232 / pop 650,000 / ☉ Moscow + 7hr

It has the rep, everyone around the Far East seems to look up to it, and Vladivostok is indeed pretty good to look at for a couple days. Some streets are a bit drab, but the setting is remarkable: a series of peaks and peninsulas curl around Golden Horn Bay (bukhta Zolotoy Rog; named after Istanbul's similar-looking harbour), which is home to huge icebreakers and the Russian Pacific Fleet.

Quite the port-town bustler before communism (back when the Swiss family Brynner brought a bald Yul into the world here in 1920), Vladivostok's cosmopolitan urges have slowly returned after the long Soviet snooze. Vladivostok was firmly off limits to all foreigners (and most Russians) during the life of the USSR. Today you can (fairly freely) hop on ferries to far-off beaches on former navy-only islands, tour century-old forts or a Soviet sub, and weave past battalions of Chinese, Japanese and Korean summer tourists.

On the downside, summer is wet and foggy, and power outages plague winter. One transplant from Moscow exaggerated, 'I've been here four years and still haven't seen the sun.' September and October, locals swear, are best.

History

Founded in 1860, Vladivostok (meaning 'Lord of the East') became a naval base in 1872. Tsarevitch Nicholas II turned up in 1891 to inaugurate the new trans-Siberian rail line. By the early 20th century, Vladivostok teemed with merchants, speculators and sailors of every nation in a manner more akin to Shanghai or Hong Kong than to Moscow. Koreans and Chinese, many of

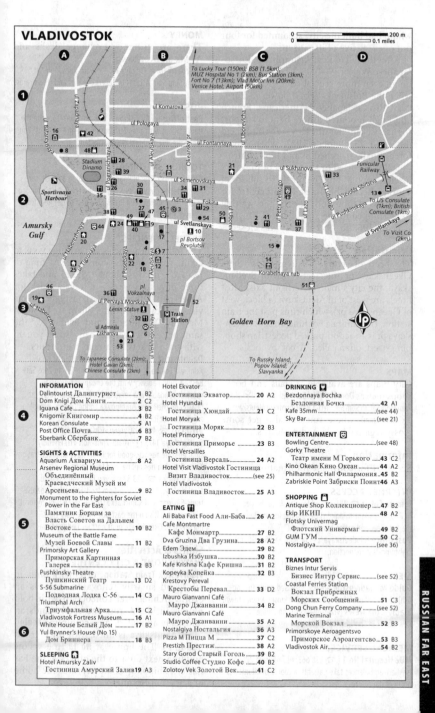

VLADIVOSTOK

INFORMATION
Dalintourist Далинтурист............1 B2
Dom Knigi Дом Книги...............2 C2
Iguana Cafe..................................3 B2
Knigomir Книгомир...................4 B2
Korean Consulate.........................5 A1
Post Office Почта........................6 B3
Sberbank Сбербанк.....................7 B2

SIGHTS & ACTIVITIES
Aquarium Аквариум 8 A2
Arsenev Regional Museum
    Объединённый
    Краеведческий Музей им
    Арсеньева........................9 B2
Monument to the Fighters for Soviet
    Power in the Far East
    Памятник Борцам за
    Власть Советов на Дальнем
    Востоке..........................10 B2
Museum of the Battle Fame
    Музей Боевой Славы 11 B2
Primorsky Art Gallery
    Приморская Картинная
    Галерея..........................12 B3
Pushkinsky Theatre
    Пушкинский Театр 13 D2
S-56 Submarine
    Подводная Лодка С-56 ...14 C3
Triumphal Arch
    Триумфальная Арка........15 C2
Vladivostok Fortress Museum...16 A1
White House Белый Дом 17 B2
Yul Brynner's House (No 15)
    Дом Бриннера 18 B3

SLEEPING
Hotel Amursky Zaliv
    Гостиница Амурский Залив19 A3

Hotel Ekvator
    Гостиница Экватор........20 A2
Hotel Hyundai
    Гостиница Хюндай........21 C2
Hotel Moryak
    Гостиница Моряк........22 B3
Hotel Primorye
    Гостиница Приморье 23 B3
Hotel Versailles
    Гостиница Версаль........24 B2
Hotel Visit Vladivostok Гостиница
    Визит Владивосток.........(see 25)
Hotel Vladivostok
    Гостиница Владивосток.......25 A3

EATING
Ali Baba Fast Food Али-Баба 26 A2
Cafe Montmartre
    Кафе Монмартр............27 B2
Dva Gruzina Два Грузина........28 A2
Edem Эдем..................................29 B2
Izbushka Избушка.....................30 B2
Kafe Krishna Кафе Кришна....31 B2
Kopeyka Копейка.......................32 B3
Krestovy Pereval
    Крестобы Перевал....33 D2
Mauro Gianvanni Café
    Мауро Джанванни........34 B2
Mauro Gianvanni Café
    Мауро Джанванни........35 A2
Nostalgiya Ностальгия..............36 A3
Pizza M Пицца М......................37 C2
Prestizh Престиж.......................38 A2
Stary Gorod Старый Гоголь ...39 B2
Studio Coffee Студио Кофе 40 B2
Zolotoy Vek Золотой Век........41 C2

DRINKING
Bezdonnaya Bochka
    Бездонная Бочка............42 A1
Kafe 35mm..............................(see 44)
Sky Bar...................................(see 21)

ENTERTAINMENT
Bowling Centre........................(see 48)
Gorky Theatre
    Театр имени М Горького ...43 C2
Kino Okean Кино Океан 44 A2
Philharmonic Hall Филармония.45 B2
Zabriskie Point Забриски Поинт46 A3

SHOPPING
Antique Shop Коллекционер 47 B2
Ekip ИКИП..............................48 A2
Flotsky Univermag
    Флотский Универмаг....49 B2
GUM ГУМ..............................50 C2
Nostalgiya..............................(see 36)

TRANSPORT
Biznes Intur Servis
    Бизнес Интур Сервис..........(see 52)
Coastal Ferries Station
    Вокзал Прибрежных
    Морских Сообщений....51 C3
Dong Chun Ferry Company ....(see 52)
Marine Terminal
    Морской Вокзал 52 B3
Primorskoye Aeroagentsvo
    Приморское Аэроагентство...53 B3
Vladivostok Air........................54 B2

whom had built the city, accounted for four out of every five of its citizens.

After the fall of Port Arthur in the Russo-Japanese War of 1904–05, Vladivostok took on an even more crucial strategic role, and when the Bolsheviks seized power in European Russia, Japanese, Americans, French and English poured ashore here to support the tsarist counterattack. Vladivostok held out until 25 October 1922, when Soviet forces finally marched in and took control.

Stalin deported or shot most of the city's foreign population. The northern suburb of Vtoraya Rechka became a transit centre for hundreds of thousands of prisoners waiting to be shipped to the gold fields of Kolyma.

From 1958 to 1992 the city was closed.

Orientation

The heart of central Vladivostok is where Okeanskaya pr intersects with ul Svetlanskaya, the city's main waterfront axis. Most hotels are west of ul Aleutskaya (a block west of Okeanskaya pr), which runs past the train station. Ul Admirala Fokhina, west of Okeanskaya pr is an action-packed pedestrian shopping street, often called 'Arbat' by locals.

MAPS

City maps are available at stalls and bookshops such as **Dom Knigi** (ul Svetlanskaya 43; 🕑 10am-7pm Mon-Sat, to 5pm Sun) and **Knigomir** (ul Aleutskaya 23; 🕑 10am-8pm), where you can also get some glossy regional books and postcards.

Information

See p704 for consulate information.

INTERNET ACCESS

Iguana Cafe (☎ 481 367; ul Svetlanskaya 23; per hr R60; 🕑 10am-midnight) Behind the indoor flower market. Beer and coffee handy.

Post office (ul Aleutskaya; per hr R50; 🕑 8am-8pm) Lightning-fast connection.

MEDIA

Guide to Vladivostok Annual ad-based guide (in English) of limited usefulness; available at kiosks around town.

Vladivostok News (vn.vladnews.ru) An online newspaper in English.

MEDICAL SERVICES

MUZ Hospital No 1 (☎ 258 663; ul Sadovaya 22) This is where ambulances take patients, a couple of kilometres north of the centre.

MONEY

There are currency exchange desks and ATMs all over town.

Sberbank (ul Aleutskaya 12; 🕑 9am-7pm Mon-Sat, 10am-5pm Sun) Accepts travellers cheques and credit cards.

POST

Post office (ul Aleutskaya; 🕑 8am-8pm) Opposite the train station, with a modern business centre upstairs. You can make international calls downstairs.

TOURIST INFORMATION

PVU (☎ 432 576; ul Pogranichnaya 6) In a pinch, can help extend your visa by a day – for a fee if it isn't for good reason – so you can exit Russia. It's best to get help from a travel agent.

TRAVEL AGENCIES

The following agencies can arrange visas to China from the new consulate. At time of research, it costs about US$125 and takes three days to a week – always a week for Americans. Otherwise the consulate accepts visa applications from 9.30am to 12.30pm Monday, Wednesday and Friday for the same price. The agencies can also set you up with train tickets, homestays and tours.

Dalintourist (☎ 222 949; www.dalintourist.ru; ul Admirala Fokina 8; 🕑 10am-5pm Mon-Fri, to 2pm Sat) Best all-round agency with the cheapest homestays, most-dependable visa service, good side trips to Vityaz beach and their new Arkhipovka Lodge (rooms including all meals cost R530).

Vizit Co (☎ 499 799; www.visitfareast.com; ul Svetlanskaya 147; 🕑 10am-7pm Mon-Fri) Friendly smaller-scale agency, good for homestays and registration, Trans-Siberian tips online, and local tours.

Lucky Tour (☎ 223 333; www.luckytour.com; ul Moskovskaya 1; 🕑 10am-6pm Mon-Fri) Helps organise trans-Siberian and Kamchatka trips – and has many local trips on offer. It's on the east side of the park (just northeast of Okeanskaya pr at northern edge of map).

Sights & Activities

WATERFRONT & CITY CENTRE

Vladivostok Train Station, originally built in 1912 and smartly renovated since, is an exotic architectural concoction with bold murals inside. Across the road stands an unusually animated, finger-pointing **Lenin**.

Ul Aleutskaya is lined with once-grand buildings. The house at **No 15** (the yellow building next door to the offices of the Far Eastern Shipping Company) was the home of actor Yul Brynner.

Pl Bortsov Revolutsy has the impressive **Monument to the Fighters for Soviet Power in the Far East** as its centrepiece. The square, a focal point for performers and protesters of all kinds, hosts a market every Friday. The monolithic slab at the square's western end is the **White House** (Bely dom), home to the regional administration.

Heading east from the square, and just below the reconstruction of a **triumphal arch** (are they ever failure arches?) built originally for Tsar Nicholas II in 1902, you'll see the green-and-grey **S-56 submarine** (Memornalnoi Gvargeiskoi Podvodnoi Lodke S-56; ☎ 216 757; Korabelnaya nab; adult/child R50/25; ✆ 10am-8pm). Lots of original gear inside (plus photos), but best is just clambering around inside a WWII sub that sunk 10 enemy ships (if you don't mind elbow-wrestling tour groups).

The bulk of local strolls, beer-drinking and ice cream–eating is back west along the **Sportivnaya Harbour**, where you'll find plenty of food stalls, an amusement park and a statue of a topless woman in the Amursky Gulf (Amursky zaliv) facing a rather trashy small beach. Just north is an **Aquarium** (Okeanarium; ul Batareynaya 4; admission R80; ✆ 10am-8pm Tue-Sun, 11am-8pm Mon).

ARSENEV REGIONAL MUSEUM

Most intriguing in its unexpectedness, the **Arsenev Regional Museum** (Kraevedchesky muzey Arseneva; ☎ 413 977; ul Svetlanskaya 20; adult/child R70/35; ✆ 10am-7pm Tue-Sun) is named for a late-19th-century ethnographer. It features two floors of thematic rooms – some revel in mixing it up (water fountain and fake plants amid modern photographs, 'CCCP' sign atop a green-and-red candy cane, the warring embrace of a bear and Siberian tiger that looks a little like ballroom dancing). Surprisingly not dozing or barking orders, the old lady guards here are pretty chipper, and are often fond of pointing out photos of Yul Brynner and other 'Western' celebrities who've visited Vladivostok.

FUNICULAR

Vladivostok's favourite attraction may just be the smoothest running operation in the Far East: the freshly renovated **funicular railway** (funikulyor; ticket R5; ✆ 7am-8pm), which every few minutes makes a fun 60-second ride up a 100m hill. At the top, go under ul Sukhanova via the slummy underpass to a great (but

also slummy) lookout beside the buildings of DVGTU (Far Eastern State Technical University) – best view in town, no doubt.

You'll find the base of the funicular beside the elegantly restored **Pushkinsky Theatre** (ul Pushkinskaya).

FORTS

Attention fort fans: Vladivostok teems with sprawling, rather unique subterranean forts built a century ago to repel potential Japanese attacks. Neophytes are best sticking with the accessible **Vladivostok Fortress Museum** (Muzey Vladivostokskaya Krepost; ☎ 400 896; ul Batereynaya 4A; admission R70; ✆ 10am-6pm), which blasts a giant gun at noon daily (drawing huge crowds of Asian tourists) and stages a knight fight, of all things, on Sunday. Inside the renovated fort you can see guns, bombs and fort models. The fort is just north of the aquarium, but is best accessed from ul Zapadnaya.

Sixteen protective forts encircle Vladivostok. The best (but pricey) is the hill-top **Fort No 7**, 14km north of the centre. It has 1.5km of tunnels, pretty much untouched since the last 400 soldiers stationed here left. (The sole inhabitants now include two pet cats to keep rats out.) Views are good too. Visiting on your own is very difficult, as the fort doesn't keep regular hours and it's hard to find. Organise a trip through an agency instead (about US$30 or US$40 per person including guide, transport and admission).

ISLANDS & BOAT TOURS

To catch ferries to the nearby Russky and Popov Islands, part of the archipelago that stretches southwards from Vladivostok towards North Korea, go to the **coastal ferries station** (☎ 220 823), 100m east from the S-56 submarine. Locals will be going with you – bags of cucumbers and *kolbasa* (sausage) in tow – to offshore dachas.

There's still the question of whether foreigners are technically allowed to visit the once-closed Russky Island – at research time, we heard everything between 'no way' and 'no problem'. When we went, no-one said 'no' anything, but there's a chance you won't be able to leave the boat. There's no restriction to visiting the smaller Popov Island, where there is a better beach and guesthouses for an overnighter. Camping's possible on both.

At least three daily boats head to a couple of points on Russky (R40 return, 30 minutes) – around 7am, noon and 6.30pm – staying for 10 minutes, then returning to Vladivostok, making for an easy DIY shoestring bay cruise past the Russian Pacific Fleet and giant icebreakers. If you're planning to tour the island, boats stopping at 'podnozhye' (past an island canal) are best. Only one daily boat heads to Popov (R60 return, 1½ hours) – leaving at 1pm, and returning at 3pm.

A 90-minute bay cruise with a travel agent runs a little high: anywhere from US$100 to US$225 depending on the size of the group.

OTHER SIGHTS

At the **Museum of the Battle Fame** (Muzey Boevoy Slavy; ☎ 217 904; ul Semenovskaya 17-19; admission R20; ✆ 9am-1pm & 2-6pm Tue-Sat, closed last Fri of month), in a fine old pillared building, a guy in a navy outfit will probably help you put shoe covers on for the carpeted floors of the three-floor exhibit. The museum is geared chiefly to border patrol history (despite its more marketable 'war-oriented' name), with imaginative 'boat' and 'plane' doors to such-themed rooms. Up top you can spy on hipsters outside through high-definition binoculars.

The **Primorsky Art Gallery** (Primorskaya kartinnaya galereya; ☎ 411 195; ul Aleutskaya 12; admission R100; ✆ 10am-1pm & 2-6.30pm Tue-Sat, 11am-5pm Sun) was temporarily closed for renovation at the time of research. Its collection – a surprising range of 17th-century Dutch works and excellent works by Russian artists Repin and Vasily Vereshchagin – should be back before you arrive.

Sleeping

Vladivostok is poorly served by budget accommodation; if funds are tight it's best to arrange a homestay for around US$20 to US$30, including breakfast, with one of the travel agencies listed earlier. Visa registration can be tricky – some agents can arrange it for a fee of US$25 or so. Also note that the cheaper hotels get very busy during the summer months with package-tour groups from China and Korea – try to book well ahead. To make matters worse, you'll have to pay extra for breakfast at most hotels.

Note: in winter, Vladivostok routinely experiences energy shortages, which means hot water can be a rarity, and even cold water disappears on occasion. Check what the situation is and keep your bathtub full.

MIDRANGE

Hotel Primorye (☎ 411 422; admin@hbotel.primorye .ru; ul Posetskaya 20; s/d from R1000/1200) A favourite central hotel on a rather quiet street, this renovated five-storey hotel has half of its quite nice rooms facing the harbour. (Smaller) cheapies go first, so call ahead. Fourth-floor café offers a R180 breakfast.

Hotel Moryak (☎ /fax 499 499; ul Posetskaya 38; s/d from R1000/1100) Cheapest rooms fill with tour groups first, but it's still a good back-up to Primorye with (very) small but bright rooms – many with a peek at the bay or Vladivostok hills. At the crest of a hilly street. No lift.

Hotel Vladivostok (☎ 412 808; www.vladhotel .vl.ru; ul Naberezhnaya 10; economy s/d R725/1450, standard s/d R1830/2330; ☐) One-time flagship of the Soviet era has the best economy single deal in the city, while the standard's slight extra comfort hardly justifies the price hike. Half the rooms have great views over the Amursky Gulf. Also see Hotel Visit Vladivostok.

Hotel Ekvator (☎ 412 060; www.hotelequator.in Russian; ul Naberezhnaya 20; s/d from 1300/1800) Rather seedy (fading dark-wood panelling, exposed wiring), but facing the water, the Ekvator is often nevertheless full with groups in summer. Rooms are OK.

Hotel Amursky Zaliv (☎ 225 520; fax 221 430; ul Naberezhnaya 9; s/d from R550/1100) An enigmatic rambling place dug into the cliff-side right on the water (the top floor is at street level), this hotel is packed with Chinese and Russian tour groups from May to September. Several price ranges – all were full when we last dropped by.

Hotel Gavan (☎ 495 363; www.gavan.ru; ul Krygina 3; economy s/d R2000/2400, standard s/d incl breakfast R3600/4000; ☐ ☐) About 2km south of the city centre, the Gavan's harbour views are blocked by old-school Soviet-style apartments, but rooms are nice enough. Economy rooms are nearly identical to standard ones, but don't get free use of the 25m indoor pool (anyone can swim if they pay R130 entry, plus R25 to use the hilarious slide). Several buses get here from the centre, including Nos 57 to 62.

TOP END

Hotel Hyundai (☎ 407 205; www.hotelhyundai.ru; ul Semenovskaya 29; s/d incl breakfast R6000/6500; ☐) Probably the city's nicest hotel – with comfortable rooms offering excellent views on either side, plus an air ticket agency, casino, sauna, Korean restaurant and top-floor bar on hand.

Hotel Versailles (☎ 264 201; www.versailles.vl.ru; ul Svetlanskaya 10; s/d R4000/5000) Quite a regal place in the centre, with a bring-out-the-tsar dining room and 40 nice rooms that get frequently filled with upmarket tour groups. The buffet breakfast is R280. Save your French skills, it's called 'Versal' here.

Hotel Visit Vladivostok (☎ 413 453; www.vizit .vl.ru; ul Naberezhnaya 10; s/d incl breakfast R2650/2950) Occupying the 4th floor of the Hotel Vladivostok, these refurbished rooms come with maybe a few more comforts than in the main hotel. Has a nice small bar handy.

Vlad Motor Inn (☎ 331 351; www.vlad-inn.ru; ul Vosmaya 11, Sanatornaya; r from US$139) For a respite from Russia, this Canadian-Russian joint venture, 20km north of the centre in the leafy coastal suburb of Sanatornaya, is quiet, very comfortable and very Western. Rates include free airport transfers and the restaurant is superb. Sanatornaya is six stops from the city on the local train or a 30-minute bus ride.

Venice Hotel (☎ 307 600; fax 307 602; ul Portovaya 39; s/d US$76/94) Near the airport. A fine place if you arrive late or leave early.

Eating
RUSSIAN
Izbushka (☎ 510 269; ul Admirala Fokhina 9; meals R250-500; ☽ 11am-11pm) Trad Russian eatery attracting local couples, most opting for the 'forest' room rather than the front 'dacha'. The food's particularly good (start with the bread-covered bowl of *shchi*, soup of cabbage, potato and beef, R95). Mugs of Russian beer here, not the usual costly imports.

Kopeyka (ul Aleutskaya; meals R100-200; ☽ 8am-midnight) Fast-food, pick-and-point cafeteria with Soviet-era posters and McDonald's-style seating in the modern pyramid across from the train station. The mezzanine café has good espressos for R20.

Nostalgiya (☎ 410 513; ul Pervaya Morskaya 6/25; meals R600-1000; ☽ 8am-11pm) This long-established upscale restaurant and café serves fine, good-value Russian cuisine, such as chopped chicken fillet stuffed with vegetables (R200). Those diners just off seven days of noodles from train samovars may faint at the tsarist elegance in the small restaurant – for the less-tender few, it's a little too plush.

Stary Gorod (☎ 205 294; ul Semenovskaya 1/10; meals from R600) Good Russian meals in a village-style interior that's mod-retro, with stars shining above and waterfalls and fish tanks.

GEORGIAN
Dva Gruzina (Two Georgians; ☎ 268 580; ul Pogranich-naya; meals R250-500; ☽ 10am-1am) Wagon-wheel benches and murals of Zapata-moustached men greet mostly local diners. The food's very good – the lone daily soup is especially flavourful – but there's little but pork and beef (and no English menu). Beer is a merciful R50.

Krestovy Pereval (☎ 265 640; ul Lutskogo 12; meals R700-1000; ☽ 11am-late) Great two-storey restaurant designed like a rock-garden treehouse. Plenty of fish dishes to add to faves like bowl-of-rabbit-and-potatoes (R350) or mutton stew (R360).

ITALIAN
Mauro Gianvanni (☎ 220 782; ul Admirala Fokina 16; meals R400-800) Slick mirror-windowed Italian restaurant near the water, run by a big Italian guy. The thin-crusted pizza (around R200) is easily the best east of the Urals. The café location (Okeansky pr 9) is slightly cheaper, with pastas and lots of cocktail action (but no pizza).

Pizza M (☎ 268 511; ul Svetlanskaya 51A; meals R350-700) Classier than its name might suggest, the M (near Gorky Theatre) is rather rustic inside, despite the videos on the TV above the painted fireplace. The pizza is pretty good, and there's several pasta and meat or fish dishes (around R350 to R500).

JAPANESE
Edem (☎ 261 990; ul Admirala Fokina 22; meals R1200-1800; ☽ 11am-midnight Sun-Thu, 11am-2am Fri & Sat) Vladivostok's first and still best sushi bar is in an attractive cellarlike space with nooks to sit in. Sushi and sashimi combos start at R1200. 'Sushi time' is 11am to 5pm, and 6pm to 11pm only.

CAFÉS
Studio Coffee (☎ 552 222; ul Svetlanskaya 18; meals R300-500; ☽ 24hr) Vladivostok's cool kids (and parents) come here to this indoor-outdoor café to enjoy a good range of drinks, excellent hamburgers (R190) and appealing salads (R100 to R250). A big set lunch is R300 (served from noon to 4pm).

Kafe Krishna (Okeansky pr 10/12; meals R100-200; ☸ 11am-7pm Mon-Sat) At press time this excellent cheap-lunch turf – with Indian, blissful all-veggie lunches and lots of local Hare Krishnas supping – was getting muscled out of its prime location. Hopefully it's still here, or at a new location, as its freshly baked items draw streams of nose-following passers-by in.

Cafe Montmartre (☎ 412 789; ul Svetlanskaya 9/6; meals R300-600; ☸ 9am-3am) Down a small alley, the Montmarte offers good desserts, set lunches for R180, and a R120 'English breakfast' (cream-of-wheat, not eggs and ham).

QUICK EATS & SELF-CATERING

For fresh fruit and vegetables, there are daily stalls along ul Posetskaya, behind the post office.

Ali Baba Fast Food (☎ 264 887; ul Pogranichnaya 6/3; ☸ 10am-midnight) Cheap Middle Eastern–style pita-bread sandwiches, soup and a Coke cost R70. Ice cream and salads too. Caravan-style décor and hangings block the fast-food view from view. Bear loops may be on the TVs, Pink Floyd on the stereo. Nearby you can get a *shawarma* (shish kebab) at a stand by Sportivnaya Harbour for about R50.

Other recommendations:

Prestizh (ul Svetlanskaya 1/2; ☸ 24hr) Supermarket with good bakery.

Zolotoy Vek (ul Svetlanskaya 29; ☸ 8am-10pm) Another grocery.

Drinking

Cafés can be good for a quiet drink, but best are the outdoor beer gardens by Sportivnaya Harbour – for views and cheaper brews.

Bezdonnaya Bochka (Bottomless Barrell; ☎ 221 383; ul Fontannaya 2; ☸ noon-4am Sun-Thu, to 6am Fri & Sat) This cavernlike bar is Vlad's best beer bingeing ground and is a pretty popular place, particularly on weekends, when you should book a table if you want a seat.

Kafe 35mm (ul Naberezhnaya 3; ☸ 11am-2am) Spacious, laid-back bar upstairs at Kino Okean. Local students enjoy it.

Sky Bar (Hotel Hyundai, ul Semenovskaya 29, 12th fl; ☸ 6pm-2am) Excellent bay views, but just a beer hits you for R180 a pop.

Entertainment

Bowling Centre (☎ 400 728; ul Batereynaya 8; per game R50-100; ☸ 10am-2am) Very Soviet eight-laner

upstairs in sports complex (note the old athletic mosaics).

Stadium Dinamo (ul Pogranichnaya) The popular local football team, Luch-Energiya, plays games here April to November. Many seats have bay views too.

BSB (☎ 456 250; Krasnogo Znameni pr 67; admission R100-300; ☸ 9pm-4am) This is the city's best club-disco, drawing rather young students. On weekends rock bands hit the stage at midnight.

Zabriskie Point (☎ 215 715; ul Naberezhnaya 9A; cover Mon-Thu R300, Fri-Sun R500; ☸ 8pm-4am) Attached to the rear of the Hotel Amursky Zaliv, Zabriskie is Vladivostok's main rock and jazz club. Live music at 11pm every night but Monday, DVD concerts fill in the gaps. Staff told us 'we are the same as Hard Rock Café', except there's a sushi bar instead of bad burgers and we couldn't find Jimi Hendrix's guitar on the collection of rock posters on the wall. Pricey, but not without character.

Other options:

Kino Okean (☎ 406 406; ul Naberezhnaya 3) Multiplex cinema shows dubbed movies only.

Philharmonic Hall (Filarmoniya; ☎ 260 821; ul Svetlanskaya 15) For classical music performances.

Gorky Theatre (Teatr Gorkogo; ☎ 260 520; ul Svetlanskaya 49) The city's main venue for drama.

Shopping

Plenty of souvenir stands sell *matryoshka* dolls, lacquered boxes and postcards. Here's the cream of the crop.

Flotsky Univermag (ul Svetlanskaya 11; ☸ 10am-7pm Mon-Fri, to 6pm Sat & Sun) Great army and navy supply store with those cute blue-and-white striped navy undershirts (R95) and flap-back shirts (R400), plus army ties, badges and hats.

Antique shop (ul Svetlanskaya 20; ☸ 9.30am-6pm) Small but interesting collection of yesteryear titbits: medals, arts, flags, cameras, coins (some obviously picked up abroad by vacationing Russians).

Nostalgiya (ul Pervaya Morskaya 6/25; ☸ 10am-8pm) Nice range of traditional handicrafts, plus Vladivostok-themed artwork and Putin refrigerator magnets.

GUM (ul Svetlanskaya 35; ☸ 10am-8pm Mon-Sat, 10am-7pm Sun) If you collect GUMs (Soviet-style department stores), this is the Far East's most Art Deco elegant. Some traditional souvenirs on the ground floor.

Ekip (☎ 400 914; ul Batereynaya 8; ⏰ 10am-7pm)
Sporting gear including sleeping bags,
tents, windsurfing boards and bikes.

Getting There & Away
AIR
Direct flights go to Moscow (R16,700, nine
hours, twice daily); flights via Novosibirsk
are cheaper (R12,300). Other domestic
service includes Khabarovsk (R2500, 1¼
hours, daily), Irkutsk (R6000, four hours,
six weekly), Magadan (R5000, three hours,
two weekly), Petropavlovsk-Kamchatsky
(from R7000, four hours, three weekly),
Yakutsk (R8500, two weekly) and Yuzhno-
Sakhalinsk (R4900 to R6500, 1¾ hours,
daily).

Vladivostok Air offers fligths to Harbin (R5900, two weekly) and to \Tianjin
(R7300, one weekly), China. There are less
frequent flights to Dailin.

For Japan, Vladivostok Air flies to Niigata
(R10,500, two weekly), Toyama (R12,700,
two weekly) and once weekly in August to
Tokyo (R6900) and twice weekly in summer to Osaka (R15,000).

Both Vladivostok and Korean Air fly direct six times weekly to Seoul (R11,000) or
Pusan (R11,000).

Primorskoye Aeroagentsvo (☎ 407 707; www
.airagency.ru; ul Posetskaya 17; ⏰ 8am-7pm) is a reliable chain for tickets with offices around
much of the Russian Far East. **Vladivostok
Air** (☎ 205 133; ul Svetlanskaya 22; ⏰ 9am-7pm) is in
a convenient location for the main carrier
serving Vladivostok.

BOAT
The **Biznes Intur Servis** (☎ 497 391; www.bisintour
.com; 3rd fl, Morskoy Vokzal, Okeansky pr 1; ⏰ 10am-
6pm Mon-Fri) sells tickets for the fairly regular ferries (it claims to offer them every
Monday and Saturday, but check first) between Vladivostok and the Japanese port of
Fushiki from late February to early January. The often rough trip takes 42 hours
and the ship is rarely full. Four categories
of berths range from US$228 to US$888
one way (meals included) – minus student
discounts.

Dong Chun Ferry Company (☎ 494 060; www
.dongchunferry.co.kr, not in English; 2nd fl, Morskoy Vokzal,
Okeansky pr 1; ⏰ 10am-5.30pm Mon-Fri, 7am-9am Sat)
sells tickets for weekly ferry service to Sokcho, Korea (US$168 to US$312 one way, 24

hours), generally leaving at 10.30am Saturday. In Sokcho, you can catch a bus to
Seoul (W15,000, three hours) every couple
of hours. 'It's not such a great boat,' an
agent warned us. 'It's Chinese.'

BUS
The **bus station** (☎ 323 378; ul Russkaya), 3km
north of the centre, sends many buses
around the Primorsky Territory. You can
catch a bus every 30 or 40 minutes to Nakhodka (R180, four hours) or three times
daily to Khabarovsk (R665, 15 hours). Some
southbound destinations may be off-limits
to foreigners without a permit.

TRAIN
At the time of writing, the No 1 service,
the *Rossiya,* leaves the **train station** (☎ 491
005) for Moscow (R9100, 6½ days) on even-
numbered days, passing through Irkutsk
(R6300, 73 hours). A cheaper service, also
on even-numbered days, is the No 239 – it's
R6300 for a Moscow *kupe* ticket. On odd-
numbered days No 7 *Sibir* to Novosibirsk
(R5150, four days) is a cheaper option for
Irkutsk (R4200).

Other trains include the daily No 5
Okean overnight to Khabarovsk (R1500, 13
hours), the daily No 351 via Khabarovsk
and Komsomolsk-na-Amure (on the BAM)
to Vanino (R1700, 41 hours), where you can
get a ferry service to Sakhalin Island. The
No 53 service to Kharkiv, Ukraine – going
on odd-numbered days – has a (possibly
deserved) less-than-stellar reputation for
comfort and cleanliness.

Leaving (local time) at 2am on Tuesday
and Friday, the No 185 connects Vladivostok with Harbin, China (R1500, about
30 hours) in the Heilongjiang province of
northern China, from where there are daily
connections to Beijing. There are many delays and border checks. The train crosses
the border at the Chinese town of Suifenhe
and also stops at Mudanjiang.

Tickets for long-distance trains are sold
in the office beside the main platform. If
there are long queues here you can buy
tickets at the **Service Centre** (☎ 210 404; ⏰ 8am-
6.45pm), at the southern end of the building,
for a whopping commission of R104, plus
R48 if you need information first. Travel
agents (p616) will also get tickets for you
for similar fees.

Getting Around

TO/FROM THE AIRPORT

Painfully, no direct bus or train links the airport with the centre (50km south). From the centre, take a local train three stops to Vtoraya Rechka (near the bus station, *avtovokzal*), or one of the several buses (including bus 23) that goes from the stand at the corner of ul Aleutskaya and ul Semenovskaya (R7, 30 to 40 minutes).

From the bus station, 150m east of the railway, 'bus' (actually *marshrutka*) 101 goes to the airport (R50, one hour) about every hour from 6.30am to 6pm; call the **bus station** (☎ 322 751) for information. Coming from the airport it's the reverse procedure. The whole trip takes about two hours.

A taxi is far easier. A taxi to the airport is about R500 (45 minutes), while the airport taxi gang will try to charge triple (or more) going the other way. Look for minivan taxis heading to the centre.

LOCAL TRANSPORT

Trolleybuses and trams cost R7 a ride; pay when exiting. From in front of the train station, trams 4 and 5 run north then swing east onto ul Svetlanskaya, to the head of the bay; tram 7 stays on ul Aleutskaya, running north past the market. The many buses are quicker.

For local ferry information, see p617.

AROUND PRIMORSKY TERRITORY

It's hard to explore or raft any of mountainous Primorsky Territory without the help of a travel agent. Prices vary wildly – check a few. Trips to Gaivoron to see the tigers, for example, start around US$50 or US$60 per person (with a group of four or more) and go up to about US$125 or US$150.

Some of these places can be seen on day trips from Vladivostok.

Slavyanka Славянка

Locals enjoy making a day trip by ferry to the port of Slavyanka, 50km south towards the (off-limits) North Korean border. The small town is nice enough, but best are nearby beaches, such as **Vityaz**, reached by a hour-long drive south by 4WD. Dalintourist (p616) in Vladivostok can help make transport and accommodation arrangements.

From the **coastal ferries station** (☎ 220 823) three daily boats leave for Slavyanka. At research time, a lone hydrofoil left Vladivostok at noon (R300 return, one hour), and a bigger boat left at 8.50am and 6.30pm (R300, 2½ hours).

Buses also go to Slavyanka from Vladivostok, but sometimes foreigners are not permitted to go by land.

Gaivoron & Lake Khanka
Гаиворон и Озеро Ханка

Museums around the Russian Far East look for any excuse to fit in a stuffed Amur tiger or two, but only here are you guaranteed to see the real thing in a natural setting – up close. About 235km north of Vladivostok, near the 4000-sq-metre Lake Khanka spanning the Chinese border, **Gaivoron** is the location of the Russian Academy of Sciences biological research reserve, home to two rare Amur tigers. **Dr Victor Yudin** (☎ 42352-74249) keeps the duo safely behind an electrified high wire fence in a 2-hectare compound, beside which Yudin has several bears and other orphaned animals passed on to him by locals.

The nearby **Lake Khanka** is home to around 350 different species of bird every summer. The lake's shallow waters – only around 4m at the deepest – famously bloom with giant lotus flowers.

It's possible to organise an 11- or 12-hour day trip from Vladivostok to see the tigers (starting at US$200 to US$250 for four people), but it's worth tacking on a couple of hours to see the lake (for about US$30 or US$50 extra, at least). Some agencies charge more.

Partizanskaya River
Партизанская Река

Vladivostok tour agencies also offer day rafting trips in summer to the Partizanskaya River, a couple of hours' drive north. This is a generally gentle run; more experienced rafters should look into the longer trips along the Kema River further north. Trips cost about US$400 for up to four people.

Nakhodka Находка

The eastern terminus of the Trans-Siberian Railway, Nakhodka was little more than a landing after WWII but is now a major fishing port. Its sheltered bay was discovered by a storm-tossed Russian ship in the 1850s (its name means 'discovery').

During the Soviet-era, Nakhodka was the only Pacific port open to foreign ships. The main reason for heading out this way is to inspect the dramatic coastal rock formations near the city; there are several guesthouses in town.

A couple of daily trains leave Vladivostok for Nakhodka (R90, 3½ hours), and more frequent buses (R180, four hours).

Sikhote-Alin Nature Reserve
Сихоте-Алинский Заповедник
Home to the Russian-American Siberian Tiger project, this 3440-sq-km forested reserve, headquartered in the coastal town of Terney, stretches from the Sikhote-Alin Mountains past clear salmon streams and a savannalike oasis to the Pacific coast and rocky beaches. Chances of seeing a tiger are slim, but it's beautiful.

It's an 11- or 12-hour ride one way. Most visitors go on five-day trips. You'll need permission to visit. Contact a Vladivostok agency; they can also sort out transport and accommodation. Dalintourist's five-night 'Tigerland' trip hits several points of the reserve; it costs about R10,000 per person if a group of four goes. You can also travel on your own to their lodge in the south of the reserve for far cheaper access to the area.

EASTERN BAM

Mocked by Moscow brass (and much of Russia), the one-track BAM makes its greatest construction achievements on this 80-hour stretch east of Lake Baikal, where it passes more taiga, and through a 15.7km tunnel cut through solid rock. Most of the towns aren't much to look at – 1970s housing blocks put up 'so leaders wouldn't look like idiots for spending so much on the railroad,' one local cynic suggested – and with a greater stench of vodka in many passers-by. But many locals will be delighted at your interest (and maybe get you drunk). The best stop-off point is Komsomolsk-na-Amure, a European-styled town built in the 1930s.

TYNDA ТЫНДА
☎ 41656 / pop 39,000 / ◷ Moscow + 6hr
If BAM gets you giddy, Tynda's your town. Flanked by low-lying, pine-covered hills, Tynda is BAM HQ and a hub for trains

between Severobaikalsk and Komsomolsk-na-Amure. The 'Little BAM' connects with Blagoveshchensk to the south; the AYaM (Amuro-Yakutskaya Magistral) heads north, getting as far as Aldan – plans to reach Yakutsk remain on hold. Tynda shows off its Soviet roots: it was a shack village before BAM centralised its efforts here in 1974.

Orientation & Information
The train station – the city's most striking landmark – is across the Tynda River. A pedestrian bridge leads 1km north to the central ul Krasnaya Presnaya. At research time, the only ATM (good for Cirrus and Eurocards) was at the train station. You can get online at the station's **Service Centre** (per hr R65; ◷ 8am-7pm), but better connections are at the **Post Office** (ul Krasnaya Presnaya 53; per hr R40; ◷ 8am-noon & 1-7pm Mon-Fri, 8am-2pm Sat & Sun), at the street's east end.

Travel agent **Nadezhda Nizova** (☎ 29655; td_nadejda@amur.ru; ul Festivalnaya 1; ◷ 9am-1pm & 2-6pm Mon-Sat) may be able to help with area tours. Contact feisty adventurer **Alexey Podprugin** (☎ 29126; bamland@mail.ru) for kayaking, hiking and cross-country skiing trips.

Sights & Activities
The **BAM Museum** (☎ 41690; ul Sportivnaya 22; admission R60; ◷ 10am-1pm & 2-6pm Mon-Fri, 10am-7pm Sat), a couple of blocks southwest of the red-brick Orthodox cathedral (Sobor Svyatoy Troitsy), covers native Evenki culture, local art, WWII and regional wildlife, but is known for its four rooms of BAM relics and photos (no English). Two rooms cover the railway's early years – and the Gulag prisoners who built it. Look for sci-fi author Ivan Efremov's photo, who secretly wrote while in the Gulag.

Zarya is a native Evenki village nearby. Bus 105 from the train station goes eight times daily (30 minutes).

Clean and well-patronised, Tynda's public **banya** (bathhouse; ☎ 40030; ul Amurskaya; admission R60, lyux from R300; ◷ for women 2pm-8.30pm Thu & 10am-8.30pm Sat, ◷ for men 2-8.30pm Fri & 10am-8.30pm Sun) is the real McCoy when it comes to the hellishly hot steam room and chilly dunks in a pool. Freshly cut birch branches are available. The 'lyux' banya is open 9am to 9pm Tuesday to Sunday. It's in a red-brick building 50m south of a dramatic sledgehammer-wielding **statue** at the eastern end of ul Krasnaya Presnaya.

AUTHOR'S CHOICE

Decorated when the nation still mourned Brezhnev, and hidden away atop an enigmatic yester-year Soviet shopping centre, the **Hotel Nadezhda** (☎ 27021; 4th fl, ul Festivalnaya 1; r per person with shared bathroom R290-450) somehow feels homy and certainly offers that only-when-in-the-Russian-Far-East glory. It's clean and central, there's a kitchen, and staff don't complain even if a drunk guest vomits in the hallways (self-less research methods back this up). The 15 rooms sometimes fill with construction workers. You pay per bed; two or three beds per room. It's in the Torgovy Dom Nadezhda, behind Hotel Yunost.

Sleeping

Komnaty Otdykha (☎ 73297; train station; beds per 6/12/24hr R150/240/420, lyux beds R198/335/610, showers R55) Surprisingly comfy and clean 'rest' rooms.

Vagon Gostinitsa (per 6/12/24hr R101/161/261) A parked *kupe* (compartment) carriage on platform No 1.

Hotel Yunost (☎ 23534; ul Krasnaya Presnaya 49; r from R500) This crumbling hotel has over-priced rooms with cold-water only.

Eating

Tynda is low-key meal-wise.

Midina (ul Krasnaya Presnaya 49; dishes R120-170; 11am-2am Mon-Sat) Behind the Yunost, this funky restaurant is rather splashy. It's located above a casino that serves big, shareable portions of Chinese (and some Russian) dishes. Karaoke at 8pm.

50/50 (ul Krasnaya Presnaya 43; dishes from R30) About 150m west of Midina, this is a half beer bar, half snack bar with surprisingly tasty Russian meals served on its outside porch.

Getting There & Around

Trains 75/76 link Tynda with Moscow on even-numbered days, and Nos 77/78 on odd-numbered dates with Novosibirsk via the western BAM. These stop in Severobaikalsk (R1335, 26 hours). Trains 963/964 connect Tynda with Komsomolsk (R1351, 37 hours, daily), Nos 81/82 with Blagoveshchensk (R1260, 16 hours, daily), and Nos 325/326 with Khabarovsk (R1351, 30 hours, daily). Many of these trains go

on to Neryungri (R411, five hours), as does Tynda–Neryungri link Nos 958/957.

You can buy regional air tickets at **Vesta Service Centre** (ul Krasnaya Presnaya 39; 9am-noon & 1-6pm).

Bus 5 outside the train station goes every 20 or 30 minutes along ul Krasnaya Presnaya (R10). A taxi ride is R60.

NERYUNGRI НЕРЮНГРИ

☎ 8247 / population 70,000 / Moscow +6hr

Set on a flat-top hill about 220km north of Tynda, modern Neryungri loses most views due to its 30-year-old housing blocks. It's worth a visit only for the land link with Yakutsk, 800km north. The banks have no ATMs.

One of the world's largest open-cut **coal mines** *(razrez)* is just outside town – where adventurers can fairly freely wander the facilities and see *mammoth* trucks that transport chunks of coal. Take bus 3 (R7, 25 minutes).

Book ahead for one of **Hotel Arigus'** (☎ 30173; arigus@rambler.ru; pr Druzhby Narodov 27; s/d R850/1100) four clean rooms. **Hotel PLINZ** (☎ 44234; ul Yuzhno-Yakutskaya 18/5; bed per person R180-400) is a scrappy back up. The cosy, central **Pizzeria** (ul Karla Marksa 23; meals R200-300; noon-2am) focuses more on its Russian dishes.

See Tynda (left) for train links here. Taxi vans leave from the train station, 3km east of the centre, a couple of times daily to Yakutsk (R1800, 20 to 24 hours), usually following morning train arrivals from Tynda.

KOMSOMOLSK-NA-AMURE
КОМСОМОЛЬСК-НА-АМУРЕ

☎ 4217 / pop 305,000 / Moscow + 7hr

By far the eastern BAM's best place to stop, Komsomolsk-na-Amure (the 'City of Youth'; a whopping 1500km east of Tynda) sports a carefully planned tree-lined, bricked pavement centre with long prospekts, European-style buildings and rattling trams. Built in a hey-ho fervour in 1932, Komsomolsk was a Soviet-dream transformation of a swamp into a planned city for the Young Communist League *(komsomol)* to help populate the east – and strengthen area defences, with steelworks, an aircraft factory and ship-building yards on the Amur River. Activity has slowed since the glory days.

It's a convenient hub between Tynda, Khabarovsk (290km to the south), Vanino's ferry service to Sakhalin Island, and Nikolaevsk-na-Amure up the river.

Information

Far Eastern Mutual Bank (pr Mira 26; ⊙ 9am-7pm Mon-Fri, to 6pm Sat & Sun) ATM open 24-hours.

Gladiator (pl Lenina, Dom Kulturi Stroiltini, 2nd fl; per hr from R25; ⊙ 10am-10pm) In a pillared building behind Lenin's statue, this Internet café has a King Arthur theme inside.

Nata Tour (☎/fax 530 332; www.amurnet.ru/natatour /index.html; pr Pervostroiteley 31, Hotel Voskhod room 104; ⊙ 10am-2pm & 3-6pm Mon-Fri) Experienced travel service books rafting, birding, fishing, skiing, Gulag, windsurfing and other trips in the region. Ask for overnight stays in the Nanai village of Nizhny Khlabny upriver (about US$20).

Post office (pr Mira 27; ⊙ 8am-7pm Mon-Fri, to 6pm Sat, to 3pm Sun)

Telephone office (pr Mira 31; ⊙ 8am-11pm)

Sights

Just northwest of the river station, Komsomolsk's landmark sight is the **WWII memorial**, which features stoic faces chipped from stone, with pillars marking the years of WWII nearby.

Worth it even if you can't read Russian, the **Regional Museum** (☎ 592 640; pr Mira 8; admission R25; ⊙ 10am-1pm & 2-6pm Tue-Fri, 11am-6pm Sat & Sun) features several rooms filled with old, but well cared for, exhibits (we like the BAM construction hats best) showing how Komsomolsk came to be.

The **Fine Art Museum** (☎ 590 822; pr Mira 16; admission R100; ⊙ 10am-5.45pm Tue-Sun) has a couple of floors of changing exhibits.

It's a long shot, but you could ask Nata Tour about (rare) visits of the Yury Gagarin Aircraft Factory east of the centre. Look around for **Soviet mosaics** beside housing blocks on back streets. There's a simple **Japanese POW memorial**, off pr Mira. If things seem quiet on a sunny day, probably half of town's at the **beach**, just east of the river station.

Sleeping

Three good ones. All come with TV and private bathroom.

Hotel Voskhod (☎ 535 131; pr Pervostroiteley 31; s/d from R560/800) This eight-storey grey hotel has boxy rooms – some renovated, all quite clean. The top-floor café serves good food and there's bowling and a disco next door.

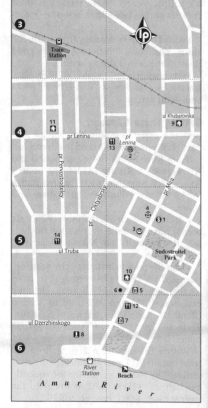

KOMSOMOLSK-NA-AMURE

INFORMATION
Far Eastern Mutual Bank 1 B5
Gladiator Гладиатор 2 B4
Nata Tour Ната Тур .... (see 11)
Post Office Почта 3 B5
Telephone Office 4 B5

SIGHTS & ACTIVITIES
Fine Art Museum Художественный музей .. 5 B5
Japanese POW Memorial 6 B5
Regional Museum Краеведческий музей .. 7 B6
WWII Memorial
Памятник Второй Мировой Войне .. 8 A6

SLEEPING
Dacha Khrushcheva Дача Хрущёва .. 9 B4
Hotel Amur Гостиница Амур .. 10 B5
Hotel Voskhod Гостиница Восход .. 11 A4

EATING
Cafe Rodnik Кафе Родник .. 12 B6
Pelmennay Пельменная .. 13 B4
Rodnik Родник .. 14 A5
Voshkod Cafe Восход Кафе .. (see 11)

Dacha Krushcheva (☎ 540 659; ul Khabarovska 47; r R1500 & R2500) Built for Nikita Khrushchev – Gorbachev and Brezhnev have slept here – the 'dacha' (a concrete villa with small shady yard) is a step back in time. Nikita's room is a massive suite with private balcony; his gun-toting goons probably took the cheaper rooms downstairs. It's behind a green plank fence.

Hotel Amur (☎ 590 984; ruma@kmscom.ru; pr Mira 15; r R925 & R1425) Fifteen renovated rooms in a bright, lovely 1932 building.

Eating

Komsomolsk isn't Russian for 'spirited dining scene.'

Rodnik (☎ 531 396; pr Pervostroiteley 15; meals R500-1000; ⌚ noon-3pm) Slightly formal two-floor restaurant-bar with private banquet rooms and nightly music – plus their own beer Flora on tap (R50 for a frosted mug; it's a little sweet). More relaxed is their cheaper option **Cafe Rodnik** (pr Mira 12; ⌚ 8am-11pm).

Voshkod Cafe (pr Pervostroiteley 31; meals R150-300) Hotel Voshkod's 8th-floor café has good Russian meals in a simple setting.

Pelmennay (pr Lenina 21; meals R150-250; ⌚ 10am-8pm Mon-Fri, 11am-7pm Sat) Old-school, pick-and-point eating.

Getting There & Around

Between early June and the end of August, it's possible to travel by hydrofoil to/from Khabarovsk (R466, six hours) and Nikolaevsk-na-Amure (R1350, 12 hours). At research time, boats left the **river station** (☎ 592 935) for Nikolaevsk at 7.30am and 11am.

Buses bound for Khabarovsk (R300, six hours) leave from the river station (including after the boat from Nikolaevsk arrives) and pl Lenina.

From the pink **train station** (pr Pervostroiteley), trains 67/68 run daily overnight to/from Khabarovsk (R860, 9½ hours). Heading east, trains 954 and 352 head to Vanino (R660, 18 hours), for ferries to Sakhalin. Train 964 heads west to Tynda (R1351, 37 hours).

Within the city tram 2 runs from the train station (R7), past all hotels to the river station. Bus 102 leads from the infrequently used airport (25km west of town) to the river station; a taxi there costs R250.

NIKOLAEVSK-NA-AMURE
НИКОЛАЕВСК-НА-АМУРЕ

☎ 42135 / pop 35,000 / ⌚ Moscow + 7hr

Historic and humbled, the grim port town of Nikolaevsk feels like a lost corner of earth compared to Komsomolsk, 12 hours south via the northward-drifting Amur River. It's a bit rough at the edges, with some leering locals and crumbling concrete apartment blocks mixed with more evocative wooden homes.

Named after the tsar, this shipbuilding port was founded in 1850 as a fortress near the mouth of the river and the Tatar Strait. Many convicts bound for the tsarist-era penal colony on Sakhalin Island (20km away) came through here, as did Gulag-era convicts in the 20th century. The one-time cosmopolitan flavour was wiped out by Bolsheviks, who killed any Japanese person they could find.

You may be able to get online at the library next to Hotel Sever (about R80 per hour). At the overpriced **Regional Museum** (☎ 23412; ul Gorkogo 27A; admission R140; ⌚ 10am-1pm & 2-6pm Wed-Fri, 10am-5pm Sat & Sun), look for the sad bust of Stalin tucked away behind a cannon, exhibits on the 2300 locals sent to the Gulags in 1937–38 alone, and 15th-century Chinese-style pottery excavated nearby.

Sleeping & Eating

Hotel Sever (☎ 22174; ul Sibirskaya 117; s/d from R620/661) Chekhov couldn't find a hotel here in 1890; you get this paint-peeling hotel. Higher-priced rooms aren't worth the splurge; all have hot-water showers. From the river station, it's a 20-minute walk – go past the smokestacks, turn left on ul Sovetskaya, right on ul Volodarskogo (across from a park), past ul Gorkogo a couple of blocks to the parking-lotlike pl Lenina. A taxi is about R60.

Hotel Sever restaurant (ul Sibirskaya 17; meals R250-350; ⌚ 12.30-4.30pm & 7pm-2am) This place is, according to one waitress and our experience, 'not bad'.

Maestro (ul Kantera 2; meals R150-200; ⌚ 9am-4pm & 5pm-2am) This is better, just off ul Sovetskaya in the blue loghouse centre.

Getting There & Away

From late May through August or so, the daily hydrofoil leaves the **river station** (☎ 23297; ⌚ 9am-4pm) headed for Komsomolsk (R1350,

12 hours) at 5am (a nice ride actually), and for Khabarovsk (R2330, 17 to 18 hours) at midnight. Year-round there are daily flights to Khabarovsk (R4000, 1½ hours).

VANINO ВАНИНО

☎ 42137 / ☯ Moscow +7hr

The reason for heading some 500km east of Komsomolsk is to take the (supposedly daily in summer) ferry from Vanino to Kholmsk, on Sakhalin (around R780, 16 hours). Weather (and indecision) plagues the sailing schedule at times. If you have to wait, the **Hotel Vanino** (☎ 7473; ul Chekhova 1; s/d incl breakfast R680/900) is located above the train station (where boat tickets often attract hordes). Try calling ahead to prebook a seat from the **ferry station** (☎ 57708).

Daily trains en route to/from Sovetskaya Gavan (the next, and last, stop east) connect Vanino with Komsomolsk (R660, 18 hours). Trains 351/352 connect Vanino with Vladivostok (R1700, 41 hours) via Khabarovsk and Komsomolsk.

OUTER FAR EAST

Looming like a tip of a giant inverted iceberg north of the BAM line, the sprawl of remote Sakha Republic (the country's largest), Khabarovsky Territory and (further up) Magadan Region take time and effort to reach (or an air ticket). Life is noticeably different here. The buildings of Yakutsk – a friendly place where Russians are the minority – stand on stilts. Built by Gulag labour, Magadan embraces its natural setting of mountains, salmon streams and rocky beaches facing the Sea of Okhotsk.

YAKUTSK ЯКУТСК

☎ 4112 / pop 240,000 / ☯ Moscow + 6hr

For somewhere that's over 1000km from anywhere much, Yakutsk comes as a pleasant, and sometimes surreal, surprise. Over half of its inhabitants are Yakut – and a good portion of the remainder are Chinese immigrants – so it feels (despite the Lenin statue) less Russian than many places across the Far East. Most of its buildings stand on stilts above a cruel permafrost that never thaws. It's most isolated when the weather's misbehaving – as winter frozen-river highways thaw, and earth turns into an unnavigable slop.

People are particularly friendly in Yakutsk. Visitors often find themselves quickly connected with the local scene.

History

One of the oldest cities in the Far East, Yakutsk was founded in 1632 as a Cossack fort, and later served as a base for expeditions to the Pacific coast. The most unrepentant dissidents (including Decembrists and Bolsheviks) were exiled here. It was a 'jail without doors,' as the swamps, mountains, ice and bug-infested forests did a pretty good job of keeping people from going anywhere. In the late 19th century, Yakutsk became a kind of 'wild east' version of Dodge City – a boozy, bawdy rest-and-recreation centre for the region's increasing number of gold-miners.

Today, money is more noticeably being spent on striking modern architecture around the city, the legacy of former republic president Mikhail Nikolayev. A good example is the angular Sakha Theatre on pl Ordzhonikidze.

Orientation & Information

The main street is pr Lenina, most of it between pl Druzhby to the west and pl Ordzhonikidze to the east. The Lena River and river boat station is east of Ordzhonikidze, the bus station on ul Oktyabrskaya just 500m north of Lenina.

There are many places to change money along pr Lenina. Call ☎ 03 in case of a health emergency.

Globus (☎ 423 072; pr Lenina 18; ☯ 10am-8pm Mon-Fri, to 7pm Sat & Sun) Excellent selection of maps of the city (R70), Sakha Republic and globby jobs of Russia.
Post & telegraph office (pl Ordzhonikidze; ☯ 8am-8pm Mon-Fri, 9am-7pm Sat & Sun)
Siberia Tour (☎ 422 652; siberia_tour@sakha.ru; Dom Torgovy, ul Yaroslavskogo, 4th fl; ☯ 10am-7pm Mon-Sat) Offers regional tours.
Telephone & Internet Centre (pr Lenina 10; ☯ 11am-2pm & 3pm-9.30pm) Best Internet connections (R55 per hour).
Tour Service Centre (☎ 350 897; www.yakutiatravel .com; ul Poyarkova 12; ☯ 9am-6pm Mon-Fri) Experienced, helpful English-speaking staff arrange all kinds of tours of Yakutsk and Sakha. Also have a network of homestays around the republic that could make for a fascinating trip.

Sights

A visit to the **Permafrost Institute** (Institut Merzlotovedeniya; ☎ 334 423; ul Merzlotnaya; admission

R300; ⊙ by appointment), about 2km west of the centre, may sound as exciting as a lump of frozen soil, but is actually quite fascinating. Two-thirds of Russia (and all of Yakutsk) sits atop permafrost and this institute explores how life can coexist with ground that thaws and freezes, killing trees and collapsing buildings. A tour includes a short film in English and a trip 12m below the institute, where temperatures stay a constant of 5°C (wrap up warmly). It looks like an icicle basement, but is really an underground lab in the frozen earth. You'll see 10,000-year-old deposits of vegetation and a model of a baby mammoth discovered on the Kolyma River in 1977 (the original is at St Petersburg's Museum of Zoology, p264).

A good place to delve deeper into Yakut culture, the **Regional Museum** (☎ 425 174; pr Lenina 5/2; ⊙ 10am-4pm Tue-Sun) packs nine rooms devoted to wildlife (including a 2900-year-old human skeleton), Yakut culture, first Russian settlers, regional minerals, revolution, WWII (with plenty of Yakut soldiers with medals) and Soviet life – watch for the B&W photo of Brezhnev speaking, for the priceless expression of exasperation from the committee members behind him. The museum is off pr Lenin, in a big courtyard, with a whale skeleton outside and statue of Bolshevik Yemelyan Yaroslavsky, who once lived in the wooden home nearby.

The one-time fascinating **Museum of Music & Folklore** was looking for new premises

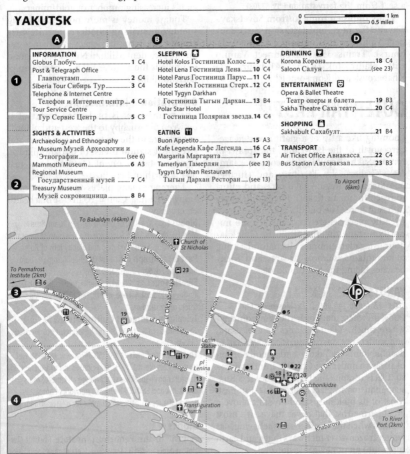

YAKUTSK

0 — 1 km
0 — 0.5 miles

INFORMATION
Globus Глобус...................................**1** C4
Post & Telegraph Office
   Главпочтамп..............................**2** C4
Siberia Tour Сибирь Тур...............**3** C4
Telephone & Internet Centre
   Телефон и Интернет центр...**4** C4
Tour Service Centre
   Тур Сервис Центр.....................**5** C3

SIGHTS & ACTIVITIES
Archaeology and Ethnography
   Museum Музей Археологии и
   Этнографии.........................(see 6)
Mammoth Museum.........................**6** A3
Regional Museum
   Государственный музей.......**7** C4
Treasury Museum
   Музей сокровищница..............**8** B4

SLEEPING 🛏
Hotel Kolos Гостиница Колос.....**9** C4
Hotel Lena Гостиница Лена......**10** C4
Hotel Parus Гостиница Парус...**11** C4
Hotel Sterkh Гостиница Стерх..**12** C4
Hotel Tygyn Darkhan
   Гостиница Тыгын Дархан....**13** B4
Polar Star Hotel
   Гостиница Полярная звезда.**14** C4

EATING 🍴
Buon Appetito.................................**15** A3
Kafe Legenda Кафе Легенда....**16** C4
Margarita Маргарита..................**17** B4
Tamerlyan Тамерлян...................(see 12)
Tygyn Darkhan Restaurant
   Тыгын Дархан Ресторан.....(see 13)

DRINKING 🍷
Korona Корона..............................**18** C4
Saloon Салун................................(see 23)

ENTERTAINMENT 🎭
Opera & Ballet Theatre
   Театр оперы и балета........**19** B3
Sakha Theatre Саха театр.........**20** C4

SHOPPING 🛍
Sakhabult Сахабулт....................**21** B4

TRANSPORT
Air Ticket Office Авиакасса.......**22** C4
Bus Station Автовакзал............**23** B3

To Airport
(6km)

To Bakaldyn (46km)

Church of
St Nicholas

To Permafrost
Institute (2km)

Lenin
Statue

pl
Druzhby

pl
Lenina

Pr Lenina

pl Ordzhonikidze

Transfiguration
Church

To River
Port (2km)

RUSSIAN FAR EAST

YSYAKH

One of Russia's better kept secrets, the major Yakut festival of Ysyakh is celebrated all over the Sakha Republic each year following the summer solstice (21 and 22 June). The biggest occurs in a field near the village of Zhetai, about 20km north of Yakutsk centre, on the Saturday and Sunday after the summer solstice. Best is at noon on Saturday, at the short opening ceremony, when there are hundreds of costumed performers (including Chinggis (Genghis) Khaan–like soldiers reenacting battles) and people handing out free skewers of horse meat and offering sips of horse milk.

Stands are filled by Yakut from across Sakha, often set up around modern *irasa* (teepees); the rare foreigner is likely to be drawn in for more horse meat (as we were by the local communist party offering looks at their embroidered Stalins and – no joke – hugs).

It's surprisingly sober during the day. Less so later, as dancing and revelry continues all night – dawn is the goal, for young and old. It's well worth planning your Yakutsk detour around this event.

Packed buses head to/from the festival regularly from pr Lenina in Yakutsk (R20, 45 minutes).

---

at research time. Apparently the English-speaking curator – who gave lively, singing tours of traditional instruments and cultures – will reopen it sometime in 2006.

The Sakha Republic was once mammoth country, and the permafrost helped protect some of the world's best preserved mammoth skeletons. If time is ample, see some mammoths at the two-pack museums, the **Mammoth Museum** and **Archaeology & Ethnography Museum** (☎ 361 647; ul Kulakovskogo 48, UGU Bldg; admission R100; ○ 10am-1pm & 2-5pm Tue-Fri, 11am-1pm & 2-4pm Sat), with skeleton sketches comparing the hair and trunk of mammoths with those of elephants. Take bus 17 or walk – taxi drivers don't know it.

Ask at a travel agent to see if you can visit the (often VIP only) repository of Sakha's amazing minerals and jewels at the **Treasury Museum**, behind the Hotel Tygyn Darkhan.

Sleeping
BUDGET
Tour Service Centre offers homestays for R750 including breakfast.

Hotel Kolos (☎ 366 124; ul Kurashova 28/1; s R800-900, d R1200-1400) Behind the official-looking blue-and-white complex, the Kolos offers 28 basic rooms – all with private bath; cheaper ones come without TV.

MIDRANGE
Hotel Lena (☎ 424 892; fax 424 214; pr Lenina 8; s/d incl breakfast from R1350/1880) Pricey for its old but comfortable rooms with TV; single guests

can sometimes get half a double for R940. Private bathrooms have dolphin shower curtains. There's usually an open slot in its 96 rooms.

Hotel Sterkh (☎ 342 701; fax 342 701; pr Lenina 8; s/d incl breakfast 1600/2200; ✷) Fifty rooms are simple but offer little details – raised ceiling, fake-brick hallways – and they face the square rather than the busy street. Some rooms have air-con.

Hotel Parus (☎ 423 727; fax 425 309; pr Lenina 7; s/d incl breakfast R2400/2500; ✷) Across the street, the Parus aims for elegance it can't quite achieve in its small, boxy rooms. Nice though – all have air-con, and there's a sauna on the premises. Dinner here is R150. Sparkling tiled bathrooms are art, but the single price is a rip off.

TOP END
Polar Star Hotel (☎ 341 215; www.alrosahotels.ru /eng/polar; pr Lenina 24; s/d incl breakfast from R3000/4000; ✷ 💻 🅿) Yakutsk's top choice for business and cash-happy travellers, the modern Polar Star has new, carpeted rooms (nothing to stop the world for, but comfy), plus a bar, restaurant, café and bowling alley. Book ahead in summer. Nonguests can cannonball in the pool for R200.

Hotel Tygyn Darkhan (☎ 435 109; fax 435 354; ul Ammosova 9; s/d incl breakfast from R2540/4550; ✷ 💻 ☎) Steps from pl Lenina, the TD's deluxe rooms (only) have air-con. All are carpeted and clean. Singles are tight, but have a nice armoire and writing desk. There's an indoor pool-sauna combo.

Eating

Tygyn Darkhan Restaurant (Hotel Tygyn Darkhan; ul Ammosova 9; meals R500-600; ☺ 8am-10am, noon-3pm & 6-11pm) If you have just one meal in Yakutsk, come here. The place is simple enough, but has a menu filled with Yakut specialities. Locals love the *indigirka* (frozen raw fish and onions – it's like eating frozen fish in a ball of snow); far easier for the uninitiated is the fine tender fillet of *khalakhty* (colt meat) and a glass of kumis (sour horse milk).

Buon Appetito (☎ 321 733; ul Ikrupskaya 37; meals R500-600; ☺ noon-2am) Hipster-stop for whisky or wood-oven pizzas (R250), with outdoor-indoor seating near the pedestrian bridge on a Lena River canal.

Tamerlyan (☎ 342 802; pl Ordzhonikidze; meals R200-300; ☺ 10am-midnight Mon-Thu, to 1am Fri-Sun) Mongolian BBQ meals (pick your own meats for the chef to grill) in a somewhat snazzy, self-service setting – Yakut raiders and battleaxes add to the décor. A mug of local beer is R40.

Kafe Legenda (☎ 420 506; pr Lenina 11; meals R150-350; ☺ 9am-11pm Mon-Sat, 11am-11pm Sun) Good for a quick, cheap snack-type meal. A burger or Central Asian rice 'n' pork bowl of *plov* is R55.

Margarita (☎ 435 514; pr Lenina 23; meals R500-600) Smoking locals come for the faux Tuscan décor (and imported beer) as much as the dozen OK pizzas (R180 to R250) or Japanese hand rolls (R120).

Drinking

Saloon (ul Oktyabrskaya 24; ☺ 9am-7pm & 9pm-4am) At the bus station, this rather humorous drinkin' spot is a not uncosy 'Wild West' bar with cowboy paintings on the dark-wood walls.

Korona (☎ 424 343; pr Lenina 10; admission R500; ☺ 9am-3am or 4am Tue-Sun) A favourite new, nose-raised disco behind the telephone centre.

Entertainment

Opera & Ballet Theatre (☎ 435 635; pr Lenina 46) Grand theatre with more accessible programmes than the Sakha.

Sakha Theatre (☎ 341 331; pl Ordzhonikidze) This strikingly modern venue has performances in Yakutian (with headphones for Russian).

Shopping

Sakhabult (☎ 435 537; sakhabult@sakha-ru; pr Lenina 25; ☺ 10am-2pm & 3-7pm Tue-Sat) Long-running shop where locals go for coats, boots and hats made of rabbit, muskrat, reindeer and other pelts. It's pricey but quality: big *norka* (mink) hats costs R2000 to R5000. A (real) reindeer Christmas ornament is R250.

Getting There & Away

See p634 for information on the Kolyma Hwy between Yakutsk and Magadan.

AIR

Reminding you that you are in fact in Asia, the often frantic airport, 6km northeast of centre, sends daily flights to Moscow (R15,000, six hours); four weekly connections to Khabarovsk (R6200, two hours); three weekly to Novosibirsk (R7500, four hours); two to Irkutsk (R7000, three hours), Blagoveshchensk (R8500, two hours) and Vladivostok (R8500, three hours). The weekly flight to Magadan was suspended at last pass.

The main **air ticket office** (☎ 425 782; ul Ordzhonikidze 8; ☺ 8am-7pm Mon-Fri, to 4pm Sat & Sun) also sells boat tickets.

BOAT

June through September it's possible to boat between Yakutsk and Lensk (R4000, 32 hours to Lensk, 26 hours back to Yakutsk) by hydrofoil, timed to jump on another boat to Ust-Kut on the BAM line. (It's possible the previously available direct service to Ust-Kut may resume in the future.) The boat for Lensk left at 5am Tuesday at research time. The Yakutsk **river port** (rechnoy port; ☎ 219 013), 2km northeast of the centre, has information. Cruises north to Tiksi, on the Laptev Sea, go twice a summer (R6415 each way).

At research time, service to Sottintsy (R313, 2½ hours) was suspended. It normally runs twice-daily Friday to Sunday, with return times allowing a day trip.

BUS & TAXI

Hardened souls can venture to Neryungri on a very rough 1200km highway (see p624). The Yakutsk **bus station** (avtovokzal; ☎ 355 987; ul Oktyabrskaya 24) sends buses there on Tuesday and Friday morning only (R1200, 20 to 24 hours). Slightly more regular, more expensive (and less comfortable) taxi vans to Neryungri are advertised on STS and TNT TV channels, or call ☎ 366 847.

Getting Around

A handy city bus line is No 8 (R8) which goes past pr Lenina's hotels on its way between the river port and bus station. Bus 4 goes to the airport. Taxis charge R100 and up for most rides.

AROUND SAKHA REPUBLIC

Many of the sites outside Yakutsk in the massive Sakha Republic (also called Sakha-Yakutia) are strung along the 4265km Lena River, a wide northward-running river that inspired a certain Vladimir to change his name to Lenin.

Lena Pillars Ленские Столбы

Sakha Republic's top attraction are the 80km long Lena Pillars (Lenskie Stolby), a 35-million-year-old stretch of Kimberly limestone on the edge of the Lena River, about 220km south of Yakutsk. Jagged spires and picturesquely crumbling fronts (almost bricklike) look like ancient ruins if you squint. The only real way to see them is by cruise (or you could drive on the river in winter). A two-night cruise in a particularly comfy 70-cabin Austrian-made ship costs about US$400/700 (single/double). Trips leave Yakutsk Tuesday and Friday (around 7pm) from June to September; weekends can be tighter. Meal deals are R1200 extra.

You'll have plenty of time (five to eight hours) at the pillars to climb up for sweeping views. The trip is quite laid back. Most Russians go to see the pillars a bit, sing some karaoke in the bar, and maybe fish from shore. It's best to book places ahead via a Yakutsk tour agency. You could ask about paying the cheaper Russian rate.

Bakaldyn Бакалдын

In the taiga, 46km northwest of Yakutsk, is Bakaldyn, a family-run Evenki ethnographical complex and base for reindeer-pulled sledge rides. Day trips here are around US$50, and seven-day sledge tours in winter can be arranged too. See p627 for tour agency details. The complex sometimes moves south in the summer months; check with a travel agent beforehand.

Even without the snow it's still a great place to learn more about the Evenki culture and shamanism in an appropriate setting. You can trek through the forest to find grazing reindeer, learn how to lasso one, and try on the lightweight but warm reindeer coats and hats.

Sottintsy Соттинцы

At this village on the Lena River, 60km north of Yakutsk, is the **Druzhba Historical Park** with a collection of original wooden buildings, Yakutian and Russian. There are hydrofoils that take you part of the way, but they don't run to a regular schedule any more and the park itself, a state-run enterprise, has erratic opening times. If you want to visit here, contact one of the Yakutsk tour agencies. It's about US$85 per person (including ferry, guide and meals) for a group of four.

IT'S AS COLD AS SIBERIA HERE

When thermometers dip as far below zero as they go above, and as many as two out of three days of your life is spent slipping on snow, you make some adjustments. In many towns around the Far East, hot-water pipes are elevated above the damaging permafrost below. Giant fur coats aren't fashion but (an expensive) necessity.

Since *perestroika*, many Siberian and Far Eastern towns have seen a rise in heated garages, as locals now enjoy owning cars and need a place to keep them warm. Cars must run constantly when outdoors – that means leaving it running when stopping off for a new supply of *kolbasa*. 'If your engine goes off, that's it – you have to wait till spring,' one local warned.

One problem, seen in some towns, is cracked or blackened teeth, which happens – over time – when drinking hot tea or coffee in temperatures 30 or 40 degrees below zero.

But one Yakutsk local shrugged off the winters, 'Twenty or 30 below is no problem, but I don't know how they live in Oymyakon at 50 below.'

Life certainly doesn't stop in winter. Travel options actually improve – riverways freeze offering new 'roads' to reach otherwise isolated areas. Contact travel agents about potentially exciting cross-country skiing, dogsledding and ice fishing trips or about just going to places where 'you can't hammer a nail into a frozen banana'.

Oymyakon Оймякон

The reason for visiting this remote village, a breeding station for reindeer, horses and silver foxes 650km north of Yakutsk, is that it holds the record as the coldest inhabited spot on earth (it's known locally as the 'pole of cold'). Temperatures have been recorded as low as −71°C (in the nearby valleys they go down to −82°C). At such times, according to Yakut lore, if you shout to a friend and they can't hear you, it's because all the words have frozen in the air. But when spring comes, all the words thaw and if you go back at the right time you can hear everything that was said months ago. Certainly if you blow bubbles they freeze and fall like table tennis balls.

The best time to visit is in March, when the temperatures are a relatively balmy −25°C. Again, the Yakutsk tour agencies can help you get here.

Tiksi Тикси

Where the Lena drops into the Arctic Ocean, Tiksi (a strategic air force town in Soviet times, and still a controlled zone requiring a permit to visit) is best reached on a 14-day cruise from Yakutsk (twice in July). The cruise takes in Sottintsy, the Lena Pillars and several other stops. Some visitors come for taimen fishing. See p630 for travel information.

MAGADAN МАГАДАН

☎ 41322 / pop 120,000 / ⏰ Moscow +8hr

Tucked between hills facing the Sea of Okhotsk, and a world away from anything but the bear droppings and gold nuggets of the wide Kolyma Region, Magadan is a quiet city with an almost cute, rather European centre in pastels. Not exactly what you expect from the so-called 'gateway to hell,' as it was called by its builders: the estimated two million Stalin-era Gulag prisoners who passed through here.

These days, most of the friendly folk you'll meet came in the 1960s after Stalin's death in a rebuild, positive-energy frenzy. That said, probably no other town in Russia wears the stigma of the Gulags more – and probably no other place (including Moscow) has done as good a job of paying tribute to the victims.

The rare visitor – other than business people selling construction equipment to gold mines up north in the mountainous Kolyma Region – can camp at a Gulag, fish or raft on the Arman River, cross-country

---

'GATEWAY TO HELL'

Though you're pretty near a Gulag site anywhere in Russia, Magadan and the surrounding Kolyma Region is most often linked to the terror of the Gulag. Following the discovery of gold here in 1932, prisoners poured in. The setting was 'perfect' for Gulag overseers – ice-locked and 9000km from Moscow, with mountains and ice providing barriers in winter, sludge and mosquitoes in summer: escape was impossible.

As in most of Russia, prisoners lacked proper clothing or housing for the freezing temperatures, food to keep up with 14-hour workdays, or even tools with which to build roads or dig mines. The trip here, aboard packed trains and boats, consumed many. One ship tried to beat winter, but was stuck in ice on the way from Vladivostok. It reached the Kolyma coast nine months later, all 3000 prisoners aboard frozen to death. It's estimated two million came here between the arrest-fest of Stalin's 'Great Terror' (1937–38) and his death in 1953.

Gulag prisoners all over knew about Kolyma and dreaded a move to what they called 'the Planet' (for its remoteness) or 'gateway to hell' (for its conditions). Winter jobs clearing trees for new roads often left only a few survivors and thousands of frozen bodies – thus, the Kolyma Hwy linking Magadan with Yakutsk is called the 'road of bones'.

Many visitors to Russia remark on how little is said or seen on the subject of Gulags in Russia. In Alexander Solzhenitsyn's famous *The Gulag Archipelago: 1918–1956,* he constantly calls for a film to show the horrors, but nearly four decades on nothing akin to *Schindler's List* has retold the tragedy. Actually Magadan – built largely by Gulag prisoners (as well as Japanese POWs) – has confronted its past more than Moscow or other places. Its Mask of Sorrow may be the most moving symbol for Gulag victims in the country. For more information, the best book to read more is Anne Applebaum's *Gulag: A History.*

MAGADAN

ski, see birds, or hike. The trip to Yakutsk on the Kolyma Hwy is a classic rugged overland journey.

Orientation

Surrounded by hills and mountains, Magadan's compact city centre stems from ul Lenina, reaching Gorodskoy Park at pr Marksa.

Information

The very helpful English-speaking staff at **DVS-Tour** (☎ 23296; www.dvs-tour.ru; pr Lenina 3; ⌚ 9am-1pm, 2-6pm Mon-Fri) can arrange bay cruises (from US$100 for one day) for birdwatching, hunting, fishing or relaxing trips in bear country at their two remote wilderness lodges (about US$100 to US$120 per day including meals, transport and guide), or arrange Gulag trips including 6WD transport (about US$1000).

The **post office** (ul Proletarskaya 10; per hr R38; ⌚ 8am-9pm) has Internet access.

There are many ATMs and currency-exchange services on and around pr Lenina.

Sights

On a small hill overlooking the town, the striking **Mask of Sorrow** (Maska Skorbi) was built in 1991 in memory of those who perished in Kolyma's camps. Names of old camps are along the small hillside down from the monument – a grey stone face, with minifigures, an inner cell and a weeping woman behind. Views take in two bays. The monument is about 500m south of the bus station (visible the whole way).

The **Regional Museum** (☎ 51148; pr Karla Marksa 55; admission R50; ⌚ 11am-7pm Wed-Sun) is worth seeing for the upstairs Gulag exhibit that features relics and the top of a watchtower.

The two bays near town – Gertner and Nagaeva – have **beaches**. Probably the best beach – called Novaya Vesolaya – is at Gertner Bay, reached by bus 3.

Sleeping

Hotel VM-Tsentralnaya (☎ 21200; hotelvm@dtcom .ru; Lenina pr 13; s/d incl breakfast from R1000/1600) Magadan's best hotel, central and clean. Higher-priced rooms are probably not worth the extra. All rooms come with TV and hot water in a private bathroom. There's a bar on the 2nd floor.

Other options:

Hotel Magadan (☎ 99557; ul Proletarskaya 8, 5th fl; s/d from R700/800) Smaller rooms, older bathrooms.

Okean Hotel (☎ 31085; ul Portovaya 36/10; s/d R850/1200) A heartbroken, old Soviet grey monster facing the sea.

Eating

Toragi (☎ 24795; ul Pushkina 1; meals R200-400; ☺ noon-10pm) This appealing eight-table restaurant serves a mix of Korean and Central Asian meals. The *kuksu* (beef-and-cabbage soup with noodles) is great.

Sloboda (☎ 22962; pr Karla Marksa 36/20; meals R300-500; ☺ noon-2am) Small Russian restaurant proud of its 'hangover cure' soup and Cossack-styled chicken breast (R90).

Supermarket (pr Karla Marksa 48; ☺ 10am-10pm Mon-Sat, to 9pm Sun) Big grocery store.

Getting There & Away
AIR

The airport is 61km northeast in the town of Sokol. Direct services connect Magadan with Khabarovsk (R5000, 2½ hours, three weekly), Krasnoyarsk (R9900, two weekly), Moscow (about R15,000 to R18,000, four weekly), Petropavlovsk (R3000, 1½hours, one weekly), and Vladivostok (R4500, three hours, two weekly). The less-popular flight to Yakutsk was suspended at research time.

Admiral-Tur (☎ 23496; ul Portovaya 1; ☺ 9am-9pm Mon-Fri, 10am-4pm Sat & Sun) can help with domestic and international tickets.

BUS & TRUCK

The Magadan **bus station** (☎ 22897; cnr pr Lenina & ul Proletarskaya) has daily bus services around the region; the furthest route goes to Susuman (R1010, 10 hours), on the way to Yakutsk. Bus 111 goes to the airport from here (R55, 70 minutes) every 45 minutes or so from 6.30am to 8.30pm.

One of the great 'extreme' trips is a rough multiday trip between Magadan and Yakutsk (2200km west) on the Kolyma Hwy, the so-called 'road of bones,' in reference to the many Gulag prisoners who perished building it. It's most reliably travelled along the frozen Indigerka River in winter (after December, about two days); spring and summer conditions (6WD only) can turn the road to impassable slop

(slushy May is an outright no-go) – other times it'll take at least four days. Hitching isn't recommended as we've heard many unlicensed gold prospectors create a somewhat criminal atmosphere, though technically it's possible to hitch from Susuman or Magadan. Hiring a vehicle from Magadan will cost about US$2000 (in winter) to US$4000 (in summer).

CHUKOTKA ЧУКОТКА

Brushing its (icy) nose with Alaska's, the Chukotka peninsula is Russia's (and Asia's) most northeastern tip – and seriously 'out there'. Backed by eroded mountains of permafrost (some as high as 1800m), Chukotka is almost solely inhabited by indigenous peoples, including the Chukchi, Evenki, Yupik and Chuvantsi. Coming on a tour simplifies permit headaches and can get you to traditional villages and offshore to witness whales and walruses. Famously, Roman Abramovich (the Chelsea Football Club owner and governor of Chukotka) has poured a lot of money into the region in recent years.

The main two access points are Anadyr and Providenya, where a number of US-based tours come by charter flight via Nome, Alaska (June to August). Check www.chukotka.org for more information. There are weekly flights from Moscow, monthly from Khabarovsk.

Circumpolar Expeditions (☎ 907-2720 9299; www.arctictravel.net/tourprov.htm; Anchorage, Alaska), has four-/12-day trips for US$1300/3500. Moscow-based **Tours to Russia** (☎ 495-921 8027; www.tourstorussia.com) offer 18-day rafting trips from US$900.

SAKHALIN ISLAND
ОСТРОВ САХАЛИН

Fought for, lost, won, debated over, called 'hell' by a literary great, sought after by oil-eyed businessfolk – Sakhalin is the 948km-long heart of the Sakhalinskaya Oblast (Sakhalin Region) which includes 59 islands, including Moneron Island and the disputed Kuril Islands. By map, the area looks pretty darn Japanese but since WWII, the region has been all Russian.

Most visitors – and there are many – are here on business, with rigs off Sakhalin's

SAKHALIN ISLAND

0 ——————— 200 km
0 ——————— 120 miles

Cape Schmidt

Sakhalin Bay

Nekrasovka • Okha

• Nikolaevsk-na-Amure

Tatar Strait

SEA OF OKHOTSK

• Nogliki

• Tymovskoe

Alexandrovsk-Sakhalinsky •

• Pervomaysk

Lesogorskoe •   • Poronaisk   Cape Terpeniya
Shakhtersk •   *Terpeniya*   • Tyuleny
Uglegorsk •   *Bay*   *Island*

• Makarov

Krasnogorsk •

To Vanino

• Tikhy   To Kuril Islands →

• Dolinsk
Kholmsk •   Yuzhno-Sakhalinsk   *Lake Tunaycha*
Aniva •   • Korsakov
Nevelsk •   *Aniva*
Moneron   *Bay*
Island •
Le Perouse Strait   • To Wakkanai

---

northern shores pulling millions of dollars of crude oil. Travellers will find getting far very difficult (and costly) – but if they do, there's great natural beauty (three-quarters of Sakhalin is wild terrain of forests and mountains, islands of seals, bears wandering around 1500m mountain tops, clear rivers to fish, slopes to ski). March to June can be wet and grey, mid-September and October brings on foliage.

Beyond that, Sakhalin is a bit of an enigma. It's seven time zones from Moscow, but some locals like to claim about 95% of all revenue goes to the capital. Even gas plucked from its reserves goes to Komsomolsk and Khabarovsk by pipeline, and is then sold back to the island at inflated prices. Russian transplants from Moscow and St Petersburg complain that life is harder and more costly than back home.

It has the makings of a liberalised port on the Asian front. A glimpse of a 1930s photo shows members of the *komsomol* of different races side by side, and today lunching Russians walk the pavements with Korean Russians (who constitute 10% of the popula-

tion, most descendants of force labourers – aka 'slaves' – brought by the Japanese during WWII). Yet the booming island has a flair for ultraconservative, pro-Russian politics. A 2004 survey showed the island had a 60% support rating for Stalin!

History

The first Japanese settlers came across from Hokkaido in the early 1800s, attracted by marine life so rich that one explorer wrote 'the water looked as though it was boiling'. The island already had occupants in the form of the Nivkhi, Oroki and Ainu peoples but, just as this didn't give pause to the Japanese, the Russians were equally heedless when they claimed Sakhalin in 1853. Japan agreed to recognise Russian sovereignty in exchange for the rights to the Kuril Islands.

In 1882 the tsar made the remote island into one huge penal colony. Anton Chekhov visited in 1890, resulting in his *A Journey to Sakhalin,* in which he wrote: 'I have seen Ceylon which is paradise and Sakhalin which is hell.' (Though he said Sakhalin's experiences influenced all his writing thereafter.)

Japan restaked its claim, seizing the island during the Russo-Japanese War and getting to keep the southern half, which they called Karafuto, under the terms of the Treaty of Portsmouth, 1905. In the final days of WWII, though, the Soviet Union staged a successful invasion of the island. Sakhalin became a highly militarised eastern outpost of the Soviet empire, loaded with aircraft, missiles and guns. Just how sensitive Sakhalin had become was illustrated in 1983, when the off-course Korean Airlines flight 007 was shot down by the Russians. All 267 on board were killed.

YUZHNO-SAKHALINSK
ЮЖНО-САХАЛИНСК

☎ 4242 / pop 240,000 / ☽ Moscow +7hr

Sprawling between mountains, landlocked Yuzhno-Sakhalinsk is the booming capital of Sakhalin. At times on its main strips (ul Lenina or Kommunistichesky pr – still keeping Marx happy with newly made street signs) you have to struggle to see Russia. There's not a lot to do – that is if you're not in town bound for oil rigs or construction projects – but it's a good (and the only)

YUZHNO-SAKHALINSK

0 ━━━━━ 500 m
0 ━━━━━ 0.3 miles

INFORMATION
American Express .... (see 4)
Bookstore .... (see 4)
Evrika Эврика 1 C3
International SOS Clinic .... (see 4)
Intourist Sakhalin
  Интурист Сахалин 2 B5
Post Office Почта 3 A5
Sakhalin Centre Сахалин центр . 4 C4
Servisny Tsentr Сервисный Центр 5 A4
Telephone Office
  Переговорный пункт .... (see 5)

SIGHTS & ACTIVITIES
AP Chekov Book Museum
  Книги А П Чехова-музей 6 B4
Art Museum
  Художественный музей 7 A4
Officers' Club Дом Офицеров 8 D4
Regional Museum
  Краеведческий музей 9 C4

SLEEPING 🏠
Eurasia Евразия 10 A5
Gagarin Hotel
  Гагарин Гостиница 11 D3
Hotel Sakhalin-Sapporo
  Гостиница Сахалин-Сапоро 12 A5
Moneron Монерон 13 A5
Natalya Наталя 14 B5
Oriental Ориенталь 15 C3
Rubin Hotel Рубин Гостиница .. 16 B6
Rybak Рыбак 17 A5
Tourist Hotel
  Турист Гостиница 18 C3

EATING 🍴
Chyornaya Koshka
  Чёрная Кошка 19 B6
Kafe Kolobok Кафе Колобок 20 A4
Nihon Mitai Нихон Митай......... 21 D6
Pacific Café .... (see 4)
Rendezvous Рандеву 22 D4

Slavyanka Славянка 23 B3
Taj Mahal ....(see 14)
Torgovy Kompleks Pervy
  Торговый Комплекс Первый 24 A6

DRINKING 🍷
Kona Bar .... (see 4)
Mishka Pub .... (see 16)

ENTERTAINMENT 🎭
777 .... 25 B6
Chekhov Theatre
  Драматический театр
  им Чехова 26 C5
Holiday Palace Холидей Палас .. 27 B4

TRANSPORT
Primorskoye Aeroagentsvo
  Приморское Аэроагентство 28 B5
Sakhalin Fantastic 29 A3
SAT CAT .... (see 24)

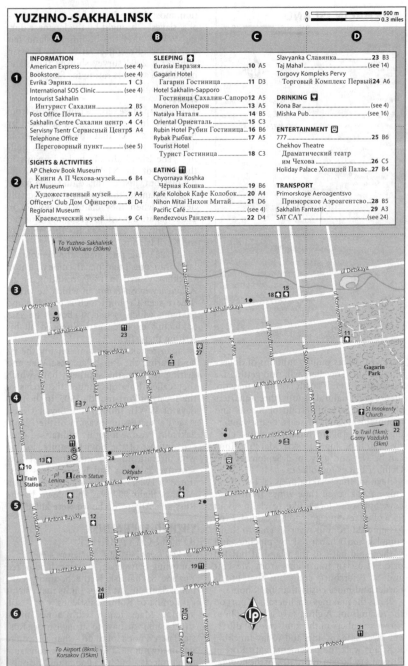

starting point to the rest of the relatively unexplored island or the Kuril Islands, and it offers some flashy restaurants and bars.

History

Vladimirovka (Yuzhno's first of three names) was basically a hamlet of convicts when the Japanese renamed it Toiohara and developed it into a thriving township. After WWII, the USSR Russified the new centre (main Russian communities were further north), renaming it Yuzhno-Sakhalinsk (Southern Sakhalin).

In 1990 the city achieved international fame as the site of the 'Sakhalin experiment,' when new governor, Muscovite Valentin Fyodorov, vowed to create capitalism on the island. He privatised retail trade and transformed the communist HQ into a business centre, but most people soon found themselves poorer. Fyodorov hightailed it back to Moscow in 1993.

The demise of the Soviet Union and the influx of thousands of expat oil-industry people and their entourages have achieved what Fyodorov couldn't. New businesses are opening up all the time and there are several shiny new joint-venture buildings in the town.

Orientation

The town's main axis, running roughly north–south, is ul Lenina with pl Lenina and the train station at its midpoint. Kommunistichesky pr runs east from the square.

MAPS

Cyrillic maps of the city and region are available at bookshops (K85 each).

Information

BOOKSHOPS

Bookstore (Sakhalin Centre, Kommunistichesky pr 32; 10am-5pm Mon-Fri, 11am-3pm Sat) A few English-language books available.

Evrika (ul Sakhalinskaya 8; 10am-7pm Mon-Fri, to 6pm Sat, to 5pm Sun) Sells maps and coffee-table style volumes on the island (from R240 to R2000).

INTERNET ACCESS

Pacific Cafe (Kommunistichesky pr 32; per hr R100; 8am-8pm) Wi-fi access.

Servisny Tsentr (Service Centre; ☎ 721 672; ul Lenina 220; per hr R60; 10am-8pm)

MEDIA

Sakhalin Times (www.sakhalintimes.ru) Weekly English-language newspaper distributed at the major hotels and Sakhalin Centre.

Sovietski Sakhalin Local Russian-language paper still carries the USSR name.

MEDICAL SERVICES

International SOS Clinic (☎ 727 550, 499 911; Sakhalin Centre basement, Kommunistichesky pr 32) English-language doctors attend to emergency needs around the clock.

MONEY

Currency can be exchanged at several banks and ATMs are abundant.

American Express (☎ 499 693; Sakhalin Centre, room 405) Russia's third Amex office (after Moscow and St Petersburg).

Sakhalin Centre (Kommunistichesky pr 32; 10am-4pm Mon-Fri) Money is exchanged at Bank Moscow in the basement. The ATM in the lobby gives rubles or dollars from 6am to 11pm.

POST

Post office (pl Lenina; 8am-7.30pm Mon-Fri, 9am-4pm Sat & Sun)

TELEPHONE

Telephone office (ul Lenina; 7.30am-10pm) Between the post office and Internet centre.

TRAVEL AGENCIES

Really the only way to get around the island is on a guided tour. These agencies can tailor trips.

Intourist Sakhalin (☎ 424 386; intourist-sakhalin@isle.ru; ul Dzerzhinskogo 36, office 207; 9am-1pm & 2-5pm Mon-Fri) Long-running agency offering group tours. Were a little less helpful at last pass, but should be able to help you get to the Kurils.

Sakhalin Outdoor Club (trio@sakhalin.su) Sasha Dashersky is one of the city's most knowledgeable guides, and offers many entertaining trips, such as day and overnight fishing trips to Tambuka River, 80km south (from US$200 per person). A five-day trip to the Chamgu Pass includes hiking up a 1510m mountain with the option of summer skiing (US$800 to US$1200 per person).

Sights & Activities

Home to the Karafuto administration before the USSR seized the island from the Japanese in 1945, the pagoda-roofed **Regional Museum** (☎ 727 555; Kommunistichesky pr 29; admission R70, photo/video permit R50/70; 11am-5pm

Tue, to 6pm Wed-Sun) is the city's best museum. On the 1st floor are photos of the island's (and the Kurils') natural features and Chekhov-era prisons, plus 19th century seal-hide tunics worn by the Ainu (some of the island's indigenous population). The wildlife room – a taxidermy-rama – features a seal exhibit complete with a model of a bird dung–splattered cliff. Upstairs highlights the Soviet days – best is the photo of the 1931 *komsomol* group with a mix of races sitting side by side. A small Korean exhibit has recently been added. It's all in Cyrillic (except for details in English on how to purchase art in the gallery).

Next door, at the old **Officers' Club** (Dom Ofitserov), a jet fighter overlooks nine armoured vehicles and cannons: a free climbing zone for the area's tots.

Scrappy but loved, the 220-acre **Gagarin Park**, at the city's east side, is Yuzhno's greenest hang-out spot, with loads of rides, shaded walkways and free concerts in summer, at 2pm Sunday.

Nearby, from the east end of Kommunistichesky pr, is a **trail** you can climb for a view of town (and the smokestacks), which is near the **Gorny Vozdukh** ski area in winter. Head south at ul Gorkogo, then follow the trail to the east.

The **Art Museum** (☎ 722 925; ul Lenina 137; admission R30; ☺ 10am-6pm Tue-Sun) is in another Japanese-era building. Its permanent collection (on the 2nd floor) features Japanese and Korean textiles, plus 100-year-old Russian art. The best (usually) is part of the temporary exhibit downstairs.

Devoted to Chekhov's 1890 visit to Sakhalin, the **AP Chekhov Book Museum** (☎ 423 349; ul Kurilskaya 42; admission R15; ☺ 11am-6pm Tue-Sat) was closed for renovation at last pass. It's supposedly going to expand from its small collection of photos and artwork.

Sleeping

The island's oil boom has tapped out the hotel infrastructure, meaning booking ahead is almost essential (particularly in summer). If you choose to, savvy hotels charge a 10% to 20% fee. Sadly homestays are not commonly arranged; ask a travel agent, who may be able to hook you up for R1500 to R2000 per night.

The airport **info booth** (☎ 788 390) can help find a room on arrival.

BUDGET

In a rare perverse sense of justice, the cheapies have the best location.

Moneron (☎ 714 323; fax 723 454; Kommunistichesky pr 86; s/d R800/1000) This sky-blue building facing pl Lenina and the train station is the best cheapie. The location's great, the rooms small, the staff friendly, the (shared) toilets clean, the (shared) shower (note lack of plural) situation a bit enigmatic (it costs R25; ask at room 343). Rooms have TV, sink and refrigerator.

Rybak (☎ 723 768; fax 722 712; ul Karla Marksa 51; s/d R1050/1400, lyux R2200-2650) Across the square, this place has less enigmatic shared bathrooms, and slightly more updated rooms. Luxury rooms have private bathrooms (with panda bear toilet covers). Rooms have TV and refrigerator.

MIDRANGE

Most hotels in this range are priced to bring sarcastic laughter. Laugh, then submit. At all you'll get TV, phone and private bathroom with hot water.

Gagarin Hotel (☎ 498 400; gagarinhotel@yahoo.com; ul Komsomolskaya 133; s/d R3500/4000) Popular with business travellers, the Gagarin is a notch up from other slightly cheaper options. Quite mod toilets, fancy doors. The tiny basement bar is guarded by a dinosaur robot.

Tourist Hotel (☎ 467 811; ul Sakhalinskaya 2; incl breakfast r R3000, lyux s/d R5000/5200) This new hotel, in a less appealing area of town (though near Gagarin Park), is a well-done conversion of an old building with stylish rooms, but there's no lift for its four floors.

Oriental (☎ 721 972; orientalsakhalin@mail.ru; ul Sakhalinskaya 2A; s/d R2400/3400) Looking a bit haggardly next to the Tourist, the Oriental's rooms are clean, the Korean-Russian staff is friendly, and there's free billiards.

Natalya (☎ 36683; fax 462 701; ul Antona Buyukly 38; s/d incl breakfast from R3500/4700) Fine modern rooms on a side street.

Eurasia (☎ 713 560; eurtur@sakhmail.sakhalin.ru; ul Vokzalnaya 54; s/d R2300/2400) Connected to the train station, and a glory of grey outside, the friendly Eurasia has clunky but reasonably well-kept rooms (some with hilariously retro carpets).

TOP END

Rubin Hotel (☎ 422 212; www.rubinhotel.ru, in Russian; ul Chekhova 85; s/d from R5500/6200) New three-storey hotel on the backstreets justifies the extra R1500 on its price tag with a kitchen in all rooms. Mishka Pub in the basement is a popular pub-style expat hangout.

Hotel Sakhalin-Sapporo (☎ 721 560; fax 723 889; ul Lenina 181; s/d incl breakfast R4372/4922) Surely poorly paid prison architects could've outdone the exterior (a white brick boxy cube), but the Sapporo is swankier inside – with all rooms upgraded for Japanese tourist standards – and its restaurant is tip-top.

Eating

RUSSIAN

Kafe Kolobok (ul Lenina 218; meals R80-150; ☿ 8am-7pm) This quick self-service eatery – a modern take on the Russian *stolovaya* (cafeteria) – serves excellent food (omelettes, goulash, salads, pork cutlets, bliny and happy breakfast bowls of *kasha*) for dirt cheap.

Slavyanka (☎ 429 667; ul Sakhalinskaya 45; meals R500-750; ☿ noon-4pm & 5pm-10pm) *Matryoshka* dolls and wooden spoons encircle (mostly Russian) diners at this homy, eight-table restaurant that fills for all meals. The stage sees a balalaika trio from 6pm or 7pm nightly. Food's good and there's an English menu.

Chyornaya Koshka (☎ 420 263; ul Chekhova 43A; dishes R750-1300; ☿ noon-11pm) Tucked behind a pavilion of drab housing blocks, the new 'Black Cat' is a very popular eatery for wine-sipping locals dining on big portions of beef, pork, fish and – ! – Mexican *quesadillas* (cheese pastries) or Spanish paella. Reserve on weekends.

WESTERN & ASIAN

Take expat repellent if you're looking for independence.

Pacific Cafe (Kommunisticheskya pr 32; meals R250; ☿ 8am-8pm) In the Sakhalin Centre, this all-Western standard self-serve café is a de facto business meeting point. A full American breakfast is R160, while pizza slices (from R60) get rolling later on. The machine-made espresso is R50 – OK, but probably not what you're looking for.

Nihon Mitai (☎ 551 901; pr Pobedy 28B; meals R500-750; ☿ noon-10pm) The smoke-filled, slick sushi bar sends sushi around in twos (from R30 to R180). Soba noodles are R200. Fish is fresh; we just hope grumpy management will follow suit.

Rendezvous (☎ 429 434; Kommunistechsky pr 15A; meals R300-400; ☿ noon-2am) This small, window-less, modern parlour-style place serves tasty, authentic Korean food. Squid fans should try *odinopokum* (squid with chilli paste and rice). Photo menu, with some English.

Taj Mahal (☎ 499 488; ul Antona Buyukly 38; meals R350-500; ☿ 11.30-2.30pm & 5.30-10.30pm Mon-Thu, 11.30am-2.30pm & 5.30pm-midnight Fri & Sat, 11.30am-10pm Sun) Happy place with colourful murals and very good Indian curries – plenty of veggie items.

SELF-CATERING

Torgovy Kompleks Pervy (cnr uls Lenina & Popovicha; ☿ 24hr) Well-stocked supermarket.

Drinking

Kona Bar (Sakhalin Centre, Kommunistichesky pr 32; ☿ 11am-midnight) Dancing girls at 9pm could give an idea of who visits: oil-talking busin* men*. It's not really that seedy, with cut-off ties hanging over the entry and enough bamboo to house the homeless of Hokkaido. You can bring in pizza from Pacific Cafe. A half-litre mug of beer is R75.

Mishka Pub (☎ 422 811; ul Chekhova 85; ☿ noon-midnight Sun-Thu, to 1am Fri & Sat) Here in the small basement bar of Rubin Hotel, rugby-watching expats chew on cheeseburgers (R185) and down beer (R35 to R125).

Entertainment

Holiday Palace (☎ 728 489; ul Dzerzhinskogo 21; admission R150-200; ☿ 9pm-4am or 5am) Upstairs in the monolith that is the Holiday Palace Entertainment Complex, the Holiday is a popular disco. There's also a casino.

777 (☎ 429 462; ul Chekhova 71) Another popular disco.

Chekhov Theatre (☎ 505 235; ul Kommunistichesky; tickets R250-400) Across from the Sakhalin Centre, the Chekhov irregularly holds popular music comedy shows.

Getting There & Away

AIR

The airport is 8km south of the centre. There are daily flights to/from Khabarovsk (R4300, 1½ hours), Moscow (R8000 to R12,000, nine hours) and Vladivostok (R5700, two hours), and to Kunashir on the Kuril Islands four times weekly (R6600 return) and once weekly to Komsomolsk (R4750, 1½ hours). There are also less-regular flights to Blagoveshchensk, Irkutsk, Krasnoyarsk, Novosibirsk and St Petersburg.

In addition to domestic flights, **SAT** (☎ 422 782; Kommunisichesky pr 49; ☻ 10am-7pm) flies three times weekly to/from Hakodate (US$360, two hours) and twice weekly to Sapporo (US$360, 1½ hours), both on the Japanese island of Hokkaido; and five times weekly to Seoul (US$390, three hours). There's an international departure tax of around R600, payable on check-in.

You can buy domestic or international tickets at **Primorskoye Aeroagentstvo** (☎ 437 474; Kommunisichesky pr 74; ☻ 8am-7pm).

BOAT & BUS

Boat services leave from various ports around southern Sakhalin. Buses (about R60) leave for the port towns regularly from outside the Yuzhno-Sakhalinsk train station.

From April to December, ferries run to Wakkanai on Hokkaido (from US$182 one way, five hours) from Korsakov. Book tickets at **Sakhalin Fantastic** (☎ /fax 420 917; www .sakhalin-fantastic.ru; ul Lenina 154, room 502; ☻ 9am-1pm & 2-5pm Mon-Fri). Bus 115 runs every half hour to Korsakov. Microbuses stop at the port; bigger ones stop inland, where you'll need to grab a local bus to the water.

Leave-when-full ferries head regularly to Vanino (and the BAM rail line) on the mainland from Kholmsk. For ferry information from Yuzhno-Sakhalinsk, call ☎ 8233-66098 or 8233-66516 a day ahead to snag a space and find departure times (R760 to R1021, 14 hours). It's *not* easy arranging this by phone. To reach Kholmsk, take bus 518. The bus continues on to Nevelsk, where (expensive) charter boats sail to Moneron Island. Boats need to be prebooked through an agent in Yuzhno-Sakhalinsk.

Bus 111 leaves regularly for Aniva, a kilometre from the water. A bay-direct summer bus leaves from 777 (ul Chekhova).

TRAIN

From the often-quiet train station, facing pl Lenina, the fastest train is 1, which heads north at 6.55pm daily, stopping at Ty-movskoe (R992, 12½ hours) and the end of the line Nogliki (R1193, 14½ hours). Train 2 comes back, leaving Nogliki daily at 3pm and leaving Tymovskoe at 7.40pm.

Getting Around

Although Yuzhno is compact enough to walk around, *marshrutky* run regular routes

about the city, most leaving from the train station. Bus 63 leaves for the airport from in front of Kino Oktyabr, bus 68 from outside the telephone centre (R9, 30 minutes). A taxi from the train station to the airport will cost around R200.

AROUND SAKHALIN ISLAND

Locals like to say Japan held the island's southern half from 1905 to 1945 because it's the pretty part. Further north, trees are shorter, temperatures cooler – 'it's just tundra up there,' said a proud southerner. Most who go are oil folks (workers and managers). All over the island, wide pockets of nature – off the main rail or road links – endure relatively unexplored (particularly great for fishing and trekking), though sadly little of the glory is easily available to the independent traveller on public transport. Hiring a car from a travel agent is costly (try US$17 per hour – no discounts for extended use).

See p627 for some travel agents that can tailor trips here. You could try to pay a friendly local gas money to check some daytrip sights out.

Note: places such as Aleksandrovsk-Sakhalinsky and Tambovka River require a *propusk* (special border permit); a travel agent can help arrange one.

Southern Sakhalin

Fishers should contact the **Sakhalin Outdoor Club** (trio@sakhalin.su) for day or overnight camping trips to their private Tambovka River to fish cherry salmon, East Siberian char and the catch-and-release taimen (from US$200).

LAKE TUNAYCHA ОЗЕРО ТУНАЙЧА

One of the nicest places to go to from Yuzhno-Sakhalinsk is the Lake Tunaycha region in the extreme southeast, where there's a string of lakes, some only separated from the sea by narrow causeways a few metres wide. For its shallowness, locals call it the 'warm lake,' and some wind-surfers have sought gusts here. Many birds come here during the migrating seasons and the coastline is favoured by seals. Amber gets washed up on the beaches, and it's a favourite place for locals to go crab hunting and camping.

Tunaycha is 45km southwest of Yuzhno.

YUZHNO-SAKHALINSK MUD VOLCANO

ЮЖНО-САХАЛИНСКИЙ ГРЯЗЕВОЙ ВУЛКАН

Sakhalin doesn't actually have any volcanoes, but this 6-hectare field of volcanic mud appeared in the midst of the forest, some 30km north of Yuzhno-Sakhalinsk near the village of Klyuchi, in 1959. Another big eruption of mud occurred in 2002, following an earthquake in the region, and the ground here still bubbles with small fumaroles.

It can only be reached by privately arranged transport via a hill track (about 90 minutes), though it's possible you could hike here with a guide.

KORSAKOV КОРСАКОВ

About 40km south of Yuzhno-Sakhalinsk is the grimy port of Korsakov, centre of the island's hugely profitable fishing industry, and the place to come for the ferry to Wakkanai on Hokkaido and to Kunsahir of the Kuril Islands. Bus 115 comes here from Yuzhno's train station regularly (R60, 90 minutes). The lone hotel is **Alfa** (☎ 8235-41010; ul Krasnoflotskaya 3).

ANIVA АНИВА

This simple, mostly wooden town, about 50km southwest of Yuzhno-Sakhalinsk, is just inland from the wide Aniva Bay – and actually can be reached via bus 111 from the Yuzhno train station. As beaches go, it's Sakhalin's best – but not great: a stretch of slightly trashy brown sand facing (often) grey water. Locals set up tents much of the year (peaking in August) for a little fishing, maybe a swim, and a lot of drinking.

KHOLMSK ХОЛМСК

Southern Sakhalin's other major port, Kholmsk, 40km west, is where ferries connect the island with Vanino on the mainland. If you're awaiting a ride (likely), sleep at **Hotel Kholmsk** (☎ 42433-52854; fax 51824; ul Sovetskaya 60; r R700-1200).

MONERON ISLAND ОСТРОВ МОНЕРОН

In the Tatar Strait, 50km southwest of Sakhalin, is the largely uninhabited Moneron Island, surrounded by a marine park popular with divers and snorkellers. Unfortunately an increase in poaching has wreaked havoc on the underwater world, but it's still possible to go. Many birds – such as black-tailed gulls and long-billed guillemot –

flock here. You must charter a boat that leaves from Nevelsk (south of Kholmsk, also reached by bus 518 from Yuzhno). Inquire with travel agents (p637).

Central & Northern Sakhalin

Daily trains connect Yuzhno with Tikhy, Poronaysk, Tymovskoe and Nogliki, nearly 15 hours north. To get anywhere but some grisly towns on the line usually requires prearranged (and costly) transport. See opposite for information on trains heading north.

TIKHY ТИХИИ

Heading two hours north from Yuzhno-Sakhalinsk (about 135km) brings you to Tikhy, where the Zhdanko Mountains drop into the ocean in volcanic-rock formations and hardened lava flows. Ask an agent about camping tours along the dramatic coastline here. A good two- or three-day hike leads over a pass to north.

ALEKSANDROVSK-SAKHALINSKY
АЛЕКСАНДРОВСК-САХАЛИНСКИЙ

About two-thirds up the island, the train stops at Tymovsk (the station for Tymovskoe town). Here, a bus *usually* waits before departing for Aleksandrovsk-Sakhalinsky on the west coast (two hours). Chekhov spent most of his time here during his 1890 visit (the house is now a small museum). Little is left of the penal camps he wrote about, but the rugged coastline is attractive. There's a simple hote. In a pinch, you can stay at the **Agrolitsey** (☎ 8247-21636; ul Sovetskaya 4) in Tymovskoe.The daily train 2 returns to Yuzhno (R992, 12 hours) at 7.40pm.

NOGLIKI НОГЛИКИ

The train terminates at this drab town, which hardly seems to have benefited from the billions of dollars being sunk on oil-drilling platforms anchored just offshore. The town centre is 5km from the station; *marshrutky* run there regularly. In town, the comfortable **Hotel Nogliki** (☎ 42444-96805; fax 96865; ul Sovetskaya 6; s/d US$82/97) often fills its rooms with oil-industry guests.

The daily train 2 heads back to Yuzhno-Sakhalinsk (R1193, 14½ hours) at 3pm.

OKHA & NEKRASOVKA ОХА И НЕКРАСОВКА

An irregular 6WD bus service meets oncoming trains in Nogliki for a service to

Okha, a 250km dirt-road ride north. We heard it's best to prearrange transport with a Yuzhno travel agent. Okha, another ugly oil-town base, is 28km from the village of Nekrasovka, home to over a thousand Nivkhi (over half of the island's remaining population). The village holds traditional holiday festivals in early January and mid-to-late June; at any other time it's depressing to visit.

KURIL ISLANDS
КУРИЛЬСКИЕ ОСТРОВА

The stunningly beautiful, rugged 56-island chain of the Kuril Islands arc like stepping stones between the southern tip of Kamchatka and the Japanese island of Hokkaido. The islands, which form part of the Pacific 'Ring of Fire', are actually the tips of a volcanic mountain range. Among the peaks protruding from the sea are 49 active volcanoes, many of which erupt frequently and violently. Of these, Mt Tyatya is considered to be the most picturesque. The islands are indeed stunningly beautiful, with circular azure-blue lagoons, steaming rivers and hot springs, boiling lakes such as Lake Kupashi, the moon-like landscape of Mendelyev volcano, and some spectacular cliff formations, notably the Stolbchaty Cape.

Plan way ahead on a trip as fog delays, permits and lack of infrastructure make a solo trip all but impossible. A one-week visit (not including delays) should cost from US$800 to US$1500. A permit takes at least three days to arrange in Yuzhno-Sakhalinsk and costs about US$50. Contact Intourist (p637) in Yuzhno-Sakhalinsk for information.

As a geographic link between Russia and Japan, the Kurils have only been a wedge politically. A treaty of 1855 divided possession of the chain between Russia and Japan; the latter received the islands of Habomai, Shikotan, Kunashir and Etorofu. A second treaty, in 1875, gave Tokyo sovereignty over the whole lot in exchange for recognising the Russians' right to Sakhalin. But then, in the last days of WWII, the Soviets reneged on the deal and invaded the Kurils. For three years the new Russian settlers and the existing Japanese residents lived side-by-side, but in 1948 Stalin ordered all the Japanese to leave. The Kurils have been a diplomatic minefield between the two nations ever since and, technically, Japan and Russia have never concluded a peace treaty after WWII because of them.

The main centre is Yuzhno-Kurilsk on Kunashir, the southernmost and most accessible of the islands; here you'll find the **Storitel Hotel** (☎ 8255-21689) where tour groups get put up. Other centres are Severo-Kurilsk on Paramushir Island and Kurilsk on Iturup Island.

Getting There & Away

This can be tricky. Thick fog wreathes the islands all too regularly. And the airport works on vision only (no radar). To be safe, count on a delay of up to five days or a week getting to or off the islands – this goes for boats too. Five weekly flights connect Yuzhno-Sakhalinsk with Yuzhno-Kurilsk on Kunashir (R6000, 1¾ hours). A travel agent may be able to help you go by a ferry from Korsakov (about US$200 return, 24 hours).

KAMCHATKA
КАМЧАТКА

Dangling across from Alaska between the Sea of Okhotsk and the Bering Sea, the 1000km-long Kamchatka Peninsula (also known as Kamchatskaya oblast) is without doubt one of Russia's – and possibly the world's – most beautiful regions. A 'mini-Alaska,' Kamchatka is more often called, accurately, the 'land of fire and ice'. It boasts more than 200 volcanoes that bubble, spurt and spew in a manner that suggests that Creation hasn't quite finished yet. Hikes up them take you through lush (mosquito-filled) forest, over clear streams filled with salmon, and past herds of reindeer to fields of hardened lava so unworldly that the Soviet space program tested 'moonwalker' vehicles here.

Still awakening from its closed-off days under the USSR, Kamchatka is simply an adventure traveller's dream – well, adventure travellers with money and time. The best attractions are well away from the hub Petropavlovsk-Kamchatsky. Many places require a 6WD, a helicopter or a couple of

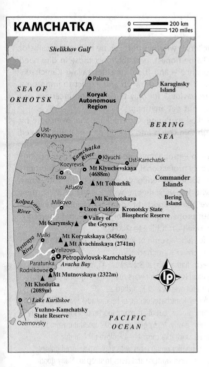

KAMCHATKA

0 — 200 km
0 — 120 miles

Shelikhov Gulf

SEA OF
OKHOTSK

Palana

Koryak
Autonomous
Region

Karaginsky
Island

BERING
SEA

Ust-
Khayryuzovo

Kamchatka River

Klyuchi
Ust-Kamchatsk

Kozyrevsk
Mt Klyuchevskaya
(4688m)

Esso

Mt Tolbachik

Atlasov

Mt Kronotskaya

Commander
Islands

Bering
Island

Kolpakova
River

Milkovo

Uzon Caldera
Kronotsky State
Biospheric Reserve

Mt Karymsky
Valley of
the Geysers

Bystraya River

Malki

Mt Koryakskaya (3456m)
Mt Avachinskaya (2741m)

Yelizovo

Paratunka
Petropavlovsk-Kamchatsky

Rodnikovoe
Avacha Bay

Mt Mutnovskaya (2322m)

Mt Khodutka
(2089m)

Lake Kurilskoe

Yuzhno-Kamchatsky
State Reserve

Ozernovsky

PACIFIC
OCEAN

days' hike. The help of a local travel agency and guide is crucial.

August is the peak travel season, though winter trips are equally enticing. Be prepared for varying conditions – and potential delays. We've sunk in groin-deep snow on volcano tops in July; fog is common in Petropavlovsk, often grounding helicopter rides and even boat trips.

History

The man credited with the discovery of Kamchatka, in 1696, was the half-Cossack, half-Yakut adventurer Vladimir Atlasov who, like most explorers of the time, was out to find new lands to plunder. He established two forts on the Kamchatka River that became bases for the Russian traders who followed.

The native Koryaks, Chukchi and Itelmeni warred with their new self-appointed overlords, but fared badly and their numbers were greatly diminished. Today, the remnants of the Chukchi nation inhabit the isolated northeast of Kamchatka, while the Koryaks live on the west coast of the peninsula with their territorial capital at Palana. There's also a community of Even, related to the Evenki of the Sakha Republic, based around Esso, where they migrated to some 150 years ago. Some of these peoples still maintain a traditional existence as reindeer-herders and hunters of various sea creatures, the animals being a source of food and raw materials for clothing. While much of their culture and language have been lost, the tradition of storytelling through mime, dance and song has survived; see p651.

Kamchatka was long regarded as the least hospitable place in the Russian Empire – half a year's journey away and with nothing to offer beyond a dwindling supply of furs. When Alaska was sold off in 1867, Kamchatka might also have been up for grabs if the Americans had shown enough interest.

During the Cold War, Kamchatka took on new strategic importance and foreign interest was definitely no longer welcome. It became a base for military airfields and early-warning radar systems, while the coastline sheltered parts of the Soviet Pacific Fleet. Isolated regions of Kamchatka also served as target areas for missile testings. No foreigners, nor even nonresident Russians, were allowed anywhere near the peninsula.

In August 2005 Kamchatka made newspapers worldwide when a training submarine which had become entangled in fishing line had to be rescued by a US and British team, just a few hours before the sub's air supply was up.

Getting Around

Locals are fond of repeating that on Kamchatka 'there are no roads, only directions.' You will have a hard time getting 'out there,' where the bulk of Kamchatka's glory is (volcano bases, rivers, geysers), without an arranged 6WD truck or helicopter (or several-day hike). Daily buses do go between Petropavlovsk and Paratunka, as well as north via Milkovo to Esso.

Used by vulcanologists and travellers alike, Mi-2 (capacity: six or eight people) and Mi-8 (capacity: 20 people) helicopters charge by time travelled in the air (usually about R40,000 per hour, plus a set pilot fee). An hour or so in the air (return) costs around

---

GOING ALONE OR ON A TOUR?

The biggest question for Kamchatka-bound travellers is whether trips can be arranged locally for cheaper (or at all) and what agent to go with. To be honest, probably only those in dire need of saving money should not book a tour in advance – and if so, consider saving Kamchatka for when you have the money or things change. If you just show up and expect to jump on a tour, you'll be lucky to sit around expensive Petropavlovsk for only three or four uncertain and unexciting days before finding a spot. You might not get anything.

And you do need a guide. Many locals have died exploring Kamchatka alone, overcome by sulphurous fumes on volcanoes, crashing through thin crusts into boiling pits, or being mauled by a bear. This ain't Disneyworld.

Considering there are over 120 travel agencies in Petropavlovsk and nearby Yelizovo, options certainly abound. Some are well seasoned and highly professional, monitoring climate conditions and running smooth, infinitely rewarding trips. Some are renegade entrepreneurs with some hiking boots and a pal who knows someone who knows someone with a 4WD or 6WD; their goal is 'get the money, then figure it out.' We've heard reports of some experienced travellers being flat-out scared on frightening hikes without proper equipment or instruction. Reportedly, a couple of Czech tourists on a cheap trip were killed on a hike in 2004.

Don't be scared though. Here are a few good agencies (some of which have deals with foreign agencies). Also see p729 for overseas agents that cover Kamchatka.

Explore Kamchatka (☎ 41531-26601; www.explorekamchatka.com; ul Bolshokova 41, Yelizovo) Run by an American living here, Explore hosts several interesting tours and is looking for ways to avoid costly (and polluting) helicopter rides. Their free annual visitors guide provides a useful overview of Kamchatka.

Kamchatintour (Map p646; ☎ 41522-7134, 73776; inform@kamchatintour.ru; ul Leningradskaya 124B) Another long-running, reliable agency. Often works with Japanese tour groups, but offers many shorter tours from mid-July to August that individuals can piece together for a full trip fairly easily. Many guides are 20-something youngsters.

Lost World (Map p646; ☎ /fax 4152-198 328; www.travelkamchatka.com; 4/1-4 Frolova ul) A highly professional operation with lots of experience. It specialises in smaller group tours with very experienced guides (some are vulcanologists who have lived in the mountains over harsh winters) and tents to sleep in. Many good itineraries, including winter dog-sled tours out of Esso to meet the reindeer-herders, and major treks through central and southern Kamchatka. Sometimes can help independent travellers hook up with groups.

If you do go on your own, the following contacts may help you join other tours or flights:

Hotel Petropavlovsk Travel Agency (Map p646; ☎ 41522-91400; travel@petropavlovsk-hotel.ru; ul Marksa 31, Petropavlovsk; ✆ 10am-6pm Mon-Sat) Mostly sets up independent travellers on weekend bay cruises or rafting trips on weekends only.

Kamchatka Regional Parks Dept (Map p646; ☎ 41522-90723; www.park.kamchatka.ru; ul Karl Marksa 29/1, room 305) Independent travellers can sometimes hop on scientist rides to take day trips to various volcanoes – for US$200 or so return. Also offers full tours.

Vision of Kamchatka (Map p646; ☎ 41522-57785; www.kamchatka.org.ru; ul Pobedy 29-58, Petropavlovsk)

Those insistent on going without a travel agent can easily visit Paratunka's hot springs, or arrange their own rafting or horseback adventures from Esso. Volcano climbs will be tougher, though Avachinskaya is near Petropavlovsk.

US$200 per person in a group of eight or ten. Rides can be exciting (and loud) with windows you can open and room to roam about. Some travellers have complained that some trips adhere to strictly predetermined times at stops, but we had no problems.

The tour agencies listed in boxed text, above, can help arrange both helicopters and suitable road transport.

PETROPAVLOVSK-KAMCHATSKY
ПЕТРОПАВЛОВСК-КАМЧАТСКИЙ
☎ 41522 for 5-digit Nos, 4152 for 6-digit Nos
pop 255,000 / ✆ Moscow + 9hr

Some see Petropavlovsk as a necessary evil, a hub to Russia's most beautiful scenery, others focus on the setting, one of the world's most beautiful – facing Avacha Bay and looking out at two giant volcanoes (when the fog behaves) and a long line of snow-capped mountains. Though it's one of Russia's oldest towns in the Far East, Petropavlovsk's 25km-long bay is filled with mostly grim Soviet block housing, but there are enough attractions to warrant a day (maybe two), and people are quite nice.

History

Petropavlovsk was founded in 1741 by Vitus Bering, the Danish-born Russian captain who discovered the straits that bear his name. The slowly developing town was named for Bering's two ships, the *Svyatoy Pyotr* (St Peter) and *Svyatoy Pavel* (St Paul); 'Kamchatsky' was added to distinguish it from all the other Petropavlovsks. It became the tsars' major Pacific sea port and was used as the base for explorations that turned up the Aleutian Islands and Alaska.

There were some unlikely visitors in 1779, when Captain Clerke, sailing under the British flag, entered the Petropavlovsk harbour in command of Captain James Cook's former ships (Cook had lost them, and his life, two years before in Hawaii). Clerke intended to travel the Arctic, but shortly after setting out was stricken with consumption and died. In August 1854 more British (with the French in tow) sailed into Avacha Bay with more permanent goals in mind. This seaborne Crimean War invasion was successfully and unexpectedly repulsed by the small Petropavlovsk garrison.

During the Soviet era the town became a sizable Pacific Fleet submarine base, but its present prosperity is owed completely to the fishing industry. Rusting Petropavlovsk trawlers bring in a million tonnes of fish a year, of which nearly half is sold to Japan.

Orientation

Petropavlovsk is strung along one main axis, the road that runs in from the airport 30km west. It enters the city limits as pr Pobedy and, for the hell of it, changes its name 11 times as it snakes around the rippling contours of the bayside hills. Although nominally pl Lenina is the 'historic centre' (quotes intended), there is no one focal point of Petro action.

Information

Make sure to get registered on your first night. Some travellers have been fined about US$150 when leaving Kamchatka for not doing so.

BOOKSHOPS

A couple of good places to pick up maps and postcards:

Detskaya Kniga (pr 50 let Oktyabrya 7; ☉ 11am-7pm Mon-Fri, to 5pm Sat)

Rossiyskaya Kniga (pr 50 let Oktyabrya; ☉ 11am-7pm Mon-Fri, to 5pm Sat)

INTERNET ACCESS

Tet-A-Tet (☎ 267 540; ul Lukashevskogo 4; per hr R60; ☉ 24hr) Several computers, and Twix bars, coffee and vodka for sale.

MEDICAL SERVICES

Hospital (☎ 128 610; ul Leningradskaya 114)

MONEY

Planeta shopping centre (ul Lukashevskogo 5) 24-hour ATM offering dollars and rubles.

Sberbank (ul Lukashevskogo 2; ☉ 9am-7.30pm Mon-Fri, 9am-5pm Sat, 10am-3.30pm Sun) Currency exchange window.

POST & TELEPHONE

Main post office (ul Leninskaya 56; ☉ 8am-7pm Mon-Fri, 10am-4pm) A telephone centre is across the street.

Main telephone & telegraph office (ul Vladivostokskaya 5)

Post office (ul Tushkanova 9; ☉ 9am-7pm Mon-Fri, 10am-4pm Sat & Sun)

Sights & Activities

Most package tours include a well worthwhile boat tour of Avacha Bay, surely one of the most beautiful harbours in the world with fascinating rock formations all around it. Best are full-day tours that reach Starichkov Island, a haven for bird life. Contact travel agencies (opposite) to see if you can hop on a group tour – it's about US$55 per person, including lunch; US$600 for the whole boat.

An excellent way to begin a volcano-centric trip is taking in an expert's lecture at the one-room exhibit in the **Institute of Volcanology** (☎ 59546; bul Piypa 9; admission per group R500; ☉ 10am-6pm Mon-Fri). You'll need to prearrange an interpreter (about R500 to R1000 per group) with a travel agency.

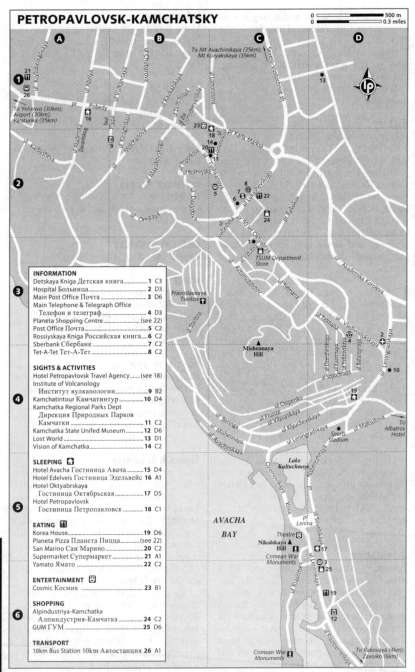

PETROPAVLOVSK-KAMCHATSKY

INFORMATION

Detskaya Kniga Детская книга.............................1 C3
Hospital Больница...2 D3
Main Post Office Почта.....................................3 D6
Main Telephone & Telegraph Office
    Телефон и телеграф....................................4 D3
Planeta Shopping Centre...........................(see 22)
Post Office Почта..5 C2
Rossiyskaya Kniga Российская книга............6 C2
Sberbank Сбербанк...7 C2
Tet-A-Tet Тет-А-Тет..8 C2

SIGHTS & ACTIVITIES

Hotel Petropavlovsk Travel Agency........(see 18)
Institute of Volcanology
    Институт вулканологии................................9 B2
Kamchatintour Камчатинтур.........................10 D4
Kamchatka Regional Parks Dept
    Дирекция Природных Парков
    Камчатки..11 C2
Kamchatka State Unifed Museum..................12 D6
Lost World..13 D1
Vision of Kamchatka......................................14 C2

SLEEPING

Hotel Avacha Гостиница Авача.....................15 D4
Hotel Edelveis Гостиница Эдельвейс...........16 A1
Hotel Oktyabrskaya
    Гостиница Октябрьская..............................17 D5
Hotel Petropavlovsk
    Гостиница Петропавловск..........................18 C1

EATING

Korea House..19 D6
Planeta Pizza Планета Пицца.................(see 22)
San Marino Сан Марино................................20 C2
Supermarket Супермаркет............................21 A1
Yamato Ямато...22 C2

ENTERTAINMENT

Cosmic Космик 23 B1

SHOPPING

Alpindustriya-Kamchatka
    Алпиндустрия-Камчатка............................24 C2
GUM ГУМ...25 D6

TRANSPORT

10km Bus Station 10km Автостанция............26 A1

The **Kamchatka State Unified Museum** (☎ 125 411; ul Leninskaya 20; admission R150; ⏰ 10am-5pm Wed-Sun) is housed in an attractive half-timbered building overlooking the bay. The museum features an imaginative mix of relics and murals that outline Kamchatka's history, for example dioramas of nomadic herders, old cannon balls and flags, photos of the 1975 Tolbachik eruption, maps showing Alaskan expansion). Note that the sign that reads 'free on first Sunday of the month' (in English) does *not* apply to foreigners.

The most walkable part of Petropavlovsk is around the 'historic centre', particularly up from pl Lenina at bayside **Nikolskaya Hill**, where there's a small chapel and several **monuments** to those who fell in the failed Crimean War invasion in 1854. Some buses (including 1 and 22) continue south of town along the hillside road to Rakovaya village, with even better bay views. Just south is Zavoiko (reached by taxi or by foot), where there's a **black-sand beach**, one of the area's nicest, and a good spot from which to spot puffins and other sea birds.

Sleeping

Conditions at Petro's hotels are all about the same – pretty good and overpriced. All have friendly staff, and Soviet-era rooms with TV, refrigerator, private bathroom with hot water, and free breakfast.

Travel agencies such as Lost World (see p644) arrange good-value homestays with *all* meals for US$30 per person. Check for flat rentals in local (Russian) papers for about R700 or R800 per night.

Hotel Petropavlovsk (☎ 50374; www.petropavlovsk-hotel.ru; pr Karla Marksa 31a; r per person R1600; 🖳) This cubey block of a building is where most tour groups go to stay, and it definitely has the best overall rooms; some of the 21 face the volcanoes. Travel agency on hand.

Hotel Edelveis (☎ 53324; hotel@idelveis.ru; pr Pobedy 27; s/d R2220/2960) Street-cred from outside (wrecked cars in dreary 'hood), rather grandmotherly inside, with comfy rooms and great staff.

Hotel Avacha (☎ /fax 11008; www.avacha-hotel .ru; ul Leningradskaya 61; s/d R2400/3300) The most central location of the four hotels, with inland views. Rooms are a bit small, but

bathrooms are quite nice. There's a sauna, air ticket agency and (formal) casino.

Hotel Oktyabrskaya (☎ 112 684; hotelok2@mail .kamchatka.ru; ul Sovetskaya 51; s/d US$85/108) Best location, with easy access for bay strolls amidst the 'historic centre.' Staff sometimes, enigmatically, won't allow visitors to stay here – even when empty.

Albatros Hotel (☎ 76806; express-k@mail.kam chatka.ru; ul Kutuzova 18; r from R1700) Further from the centre.

Eating

All the hotels have cafés. In summer, beer and shashlyk stands set up along the small beach, near pl Lenina.

Yamato (☎ 267 700; Planeta shopping centre; ul Lukashevskogo 5; meals R250-350; ⏰ noon-midnight Sun-Thu, to 3am Fri & Sat) Past the shopping centre's video games, Yamato serves surprisingly tasty sushi amidst soothing Japanese-style screens – to the tune of dance music. Set lunches (R100 to R150) are a steal.

Planeta Pizza (☎ 230 368; Planeta shopping centre; meals R250-350; ⏰ 9am-midnight) Next to Yamato, Planeta's tables get filled with locals following good pizzas (from R120) with milkshakes.

San Marino (☎ 93355; ul Karl Marksa 29/1; meals R700-1000; ⏰ noon-1am) Colourful, stylish restaurant on the backside of a grim office building has a full nautical theme in décor (only half the menu is fish). It's quite good and draws locals who park their new Japanese import SUVs outside.

Korea House (☎ 121 193; ul Leninskaya 26; meals R700-1000; ⏰ 11am-4pm & 5pm-1am) Classy Korean food in bay-view historic building.

Supermarket (⏰ 9am-9pm) Behind the 10km bus station you'll find Petropavlovsk's best supermarket.

Entertainment

Cosmic (☎ 94990; ⏰ bowling 1pm-6am Mon-Fri, noon-6am Sat & Sun, ⏰ disco 10pm-6am) Next to the Hotel Petropavlovsk, 1st-floor lanes cost R360 to R780 per hour (cheapest in afternoon) – also air hockey and booze in the house; basement disco charges R50 to R150 cover.

Shopping

Alpindustriya-Kamchatka (☎ 230 246; malkov@mail .iks.ru; pr 50 let Oktyabrya 22; ⏰ 11am-7.30pm Mon-Fri, to 6pm Sat, to 5pm Sun) This valuable camping-gear shop has about all you'll need for overnight volcano treks. You can also rent stuff –

backpacks are R30 per day, sleeping bags R40, tents R150.

GUM (ul Leninskaya 54; ◯ 9am-7pm Mon-Fri, 10am-6pm Sat) Clothes and souvenirs.

Getting There & Away

There are flights to/from Irkutsk (R12,721, four hours, weekly), Khabarovsk (R6000, 2½ hours, daily), Moscow (R12,000, nine hours, daily), St Petersburg (R12,400, 10 hours, four weekly) and Vladivostok (R8400, three hours, six weekly). Also, a weekly flight on Magadan Air comes from Anchorage, Alaska (US$1400 return, four hours) stopping en route to Magadan (R3000, 1½ hours).

From the 10km bus station you can catch daily buses to Paratunka, Yelizovo, Milkovo, Esso and a few other destinations. See those sections for details.

Getting Around

Buses (R10) run from the 10km bus station (*avtostantsiya desyaty kilometr*), on pr Pobedy at the northern end of town, to the Regional Museum. *Marshrutky* (R15) provide most of the rest of the town's transportation.

All buses and *marshrutky* for the airport (R20, 45 minutes) depart from the 10km station; take anything marked 'Aeroport' or 'Yelizovo', which is the name of the settlement close by the airport. To get into town from the airport, catch any bus at the Petropavlovsk stop across from the airport

---

> **AUTHOR'S CHOICE**
>
> Well worth making time for is a meal at Paratunka's surprisingly genuine **Exotic Picnic with a Farmer** (choom@pochta.ru; about US$25-35 per person), set up by tour agencies; one-time Muscovite Sasha offers very lively sing-song meals with vodka toasts and smoked fish plus loads of veggie dishes pulled from wild plants near his lakeside home (near Golubaya Laguna). Meals are in an all-wooden building or teepee (bring repellent). At last pass, a young college student (also 'Sasha') added her honey-dewed, heart-melting voice to Big Sasha's gruffer backups. Lots to take in: sailor songs, great food and quality entertainment in rustic Russian setting.

---

entrance. A taxi costs R300 or R400. A taxi around town is R60 to R150.

AROUND PETROPAVLOVSK-KAMCHATSKY

Yelizovo Елизово

The 'airport town' – a junction town some 30 kilometres west of Petropavlovsk – is actually a nicer town with shaded promenades, proximity to the helipad, and the three-room **B&B** (☎ 41531-26601; www .explorekamchatka.com; 41 Bolshakova ul; r per person incl breakfast US$40), run by an American woman who operates Explore Kamchatka. All 'Yelizovo' buses from Petropavlovsk stop at the airport to/from Yelizovo.

Paratunka Паратунка

Sprawled-out Paratunka (25km south of Yelizovo) is a leafy network of spa resorts set up around natural or pool-like hot springs. Most tours fit in a day here. Many are geared more to Russian locals or tourists, but it's a possible back-up base. One of a couple of dozen, **Golubaya Laguna** (Blue Lagoon; ☎ 4152-124 718; www.bluelagoon.ru; r with/without private bathroom from R2700/1530) is surrounded by woods, with a couple popular pools (slides, Jacuzzi) and near more natural hot-spring pools. If you have private transport and a local guide, the natural springs on the slopes of **Goryachaya**, 15km further south, are better.

Several *marshrutky* (R20) plus bus 111 connect Paratunka with Yelizovo and Petropavlovsk.

Mt Avachinskaya & Mt Koryakskaya
Горы Авачинская и Корякская

The nearest volcanoes to Petropavlovsk are these two giants looming 20km north of town (about 35km by road). The smaller one on the east, Mt Avachinskaya (2741m) is generally included on tours and is one of Kamchatka's 'easier' volcanoes to summit (about six to eight hours up). Avachinskaya last erupted in 1991, but you can see it smoking daily.

More forbidding Mt Koryakskaya (3456m) takes experienced climbers about 12 hours to climb up.

Unfortunately there's no public transportation here – getting there on your own can be shockingly expensive (about US$160 for a return van with 'guide' and

ACTIVITIES

Rafting

From Petropavlovsk, the **Bystraya River** is the easiest to get to and easiest trip to arrange; the most-travelled section is the 120km southwest-flowing stretch between the village of Malki, 80km west of Yelizovo, and the Ust-Bolsheretsk bridge just before the Bystraya empties into the Sea of Okhotsk. The name means 'fast', but there are only a few rapids; the journey takes a leisurely two days. A two-night trip (with guides, transport, meals, tents) arranged locally costs about US$250 per person.

Guesthouses in Esso can arrange trips to lovely, more rapid stretches of the Bystraya from about R2000 per person per day.

Horseback Riding

Near Petropavlovsk, you can ride on day and overnight trips, starting at R500 per hour. One agency, **Kamchatka Tour** (☎ 166 128; ul 3a Kosmichevsky proezd 201, Petropavlovsk-Kamchatsky; www.kamchatka-tour .com, in Russian; ☷ 10am-6pm Mon-Sat), sets off on one-day/two-day trips from its ranch about 20km from the centre for R1000/3500 per person (most commonly on Saturday and Sunday).

Guesthouses in more-remote Esso arrange trips – with some more appealing overnighter options to surrounding lakes – from about R600 to R800 per person.

Skiing

Agents like Lost World (p644) arrange heli-skiing and snowboarding trips, with daily rides up volcanoes. But it'll cost you. A 10-day tour (not including lunch and dinner) costs about €3650 per person.

Fishing

Kamchatka is home to a quarter of the world's salmon. Proceeds from fishing trips with nonprofit **Wild Salmon Rivers** (☎ 425-742-1938; www.steelhead.org; 16300 Mill Creek Blvd Ste 115B, Mill Creek, Washington, USA) help study and protect local fish populations. Weeklong trips run about US$5000.

You can get more information online from the US-based **Wild Salmon Center** (www.wild salmoncenter.org), which works to protect salmon on both sides of the Pacific.

interpreter). Try hitching. The volcanoes are great, but the base camp is rather bustling – in comparison to the remoteness of other volcanoes – with Petro views, and a complex of cabins that see much traffic in summer from locals and tour groups.

It's possible to hike 40km from here to **Nalychevo National Park** in two days.

SOUTHERN KAMCHATKA

Mt Mutnovskaya Гора Мутновская

Kamchatka vulcanologists love all their 'kids' – the many steaming, cratered, lonely, tall, squat volcanoes – but more than a couple of crusty vets told us Mutnovskaya (2322m) is probably the best – for studying, climbing or looking at. Hiking up takes three or four hours depending on where you start, though it can be snowy even in mid-July. It's considered one of the easier climbs, though when weather turns against

you, it can quickly become gruelling. The effort is worth it; its bubbling, steaming caldera feels like another planet, and for the really fearless it's possible to go to the very crumbly edge of the beast. No wonder engineers are working on tapping the volcano's thermal power to generate electricity for Kamchatka.

Many tours climb the oval-shaped caldera of nearby **Gorely** (1829m). Base camps here are tent only and far more remote than Avachinskaya.

It's possible to go snowboarding from June to August in **Rodnikovoe**, about 15km north of Mt Mutnovskaya in the Vilyucha River valley.

Lake Kurilskoe Озеро Курильское

Reached by helicopter towards the southern tip of the peninsula, Lake Kurilskoe (part of the mountainous Yuzhno-Kamchatsky

State Reserve) is Kamchatka's most famed spot to view wildlife, chiefly in August when brown bears come in droves to feast on over a million salmon en route to spawn in nearby streams. Soaring above are many Steller's sea eagles. It's beautiful too, dotted with an island and rimmed by volcanoes.

Don't wander alone. In 2000 a Japanese photographer was eaten by a bear here.

Some bigger trips take in the lake. Some agents, such as Explore Kamchatka (p644), offer a six-day trip here including guide, meals, basic cabin accommodation and transport for about US$1600.

NORTHERN KAMCHATKA

Milkovo and Esso are easily reached by public transport – much of the rest of the north requires a helicopter, 4WD or 6WD.

Valley of the Geysers & Uzon Caldera
Долина Гейзеров

About 200km north of Petropavlovsk and most commonly accessed by helicopter is the spectacular Valley of the Geysers (Dolina Geyzerov). Discovered in 1941, the 6km-long valley cut through by the Geysernaya River is part of the protected Kronotsky State Biospheric Reserve. Here, around 200 geothermal pressure valves sporadically blast steam, mud and water heavenwards. The setting is exquisite and walking tours along a boardwalk take you past some of the more colourful and active geysers. The valley is closed for a 40-day period between May and June because of migrating birds.

There's a bit of heist in price. **Krechet** (☎ 41531-24347; www.krechet.com; ul Izluchina 4, Yelizovo) runs the helicopter market and, in 2004, doubled prices from about US$250 per person to US$500 for a day-trip tour (about four or five hours travel time). Many visitors feel it's simply too much for what you get.

If you splurge, be sure to go for a trip that adds a stop at Uzon Caldera (about US$50 more), the remains of an ancient volcano, now a 10km crater with steamy lakes.

Milkovo Милково
☎ 41533 / pop 13,000 / ⏱ Moscow + 9hr

Some 300km north of Petropavlovsk, close to the Kamchatka River, is the down-at-

heel fishing and agricultural town of Milkovo, where you'll find a surprisingly interesting **museum** (admission R140; ⏱ 11am-1pm & 2-6pm Wed-Sun), with a collection of native artefacts, shamans' hats, and pictures depicting the traditional lives of the area's Itelmeni people. The cross-shaped, Siberian-style building was designed by local artist Mikhail Ugrin, who made many of the wall paintings around town. Also in town is a replica of a Cossack *ostrog* (fort).

The **Hantai Travel Company** (☎ 22937; www.iks.ru/~balanev/index2.htm; ul Pobedi 6/37) offers a few trips to places not often visited by other groups.

The **Hotel Dolina** (☎ 22892; s/d R800/1400), on the main square (two blocks from the bus stop), is an OK hotel on the top floor of a Soviet-style building.

There's a café beside the bus stop; there are four buses daily from Petropavlovsk (R240, four hours). At research time, buses left Petropavlovsk at noon, 5pm and 6pm. Call ☎ 52202 in Petropavlovsk for more information.

Esso Эссо
☎ 41542 / pop 3000 / ⏱ Moscow +9hr

Easily reached by public bus, the snug-in-valley village of Esso is a quiet, lovely place with the scent of pine and friendly locals who live in picturesque wooden cottages (many of which let rooms cheaply). Locals like to call it the 'Switzerland of Kamchatka'; locals also go rather un-Swiss in heating their greenhouses for year-round tomatoes – tapping into the abundant hot springs. It's easy to arrange rafting or horseback trips here for less than in Petropavlovsk.

Evenki people migrated here 150 years ago from what is now the Sakha Republic, becoming the distinct Even people in the process. Here they met the local Itelmeni and Koryak people as well as Russians. Although Esso remains a mixed community, the nearby village of Anavgay is 100% Even.

There's no ATM in town. The library has a very iffy Internet connection.

SIGHTS & ACTIVITIES
You can find out much about the history of the area's peoples in the local **museum**

DANCERS OF ESSO

One of the best reasons to make the long trip to Esso is the chance to see the folk dance group Nulgur (meaning 'strangers' or 'travellers'). Established in 1985, the group plays a couple of hundred shows around Kamchatka and Russia annually – check with a Petropavlovsk agent to arrange a 60-minute show. The 18-member troupe performs traditional dances and songs from native people around Kamchatka – the director casually explains some of the moves between numbers.

It's touristy, but no tourist trap. The troupe constantly searches out traditions, costumes and songs to stage – and so is instrumental in keeping some alive.

Some throat chants replicate the sounds of reindeer, while Even shoulder-movements replicate riding a reindeer. One highlight is the young master Mikhail, who joined the group in 1999 at just three years old.

The hour-long shows are held in the ugly cultural building in town. You may be able to join another group for about US$25.

(☎ 21319; admission with/without guide R80/50; ⊙ 10am-6pm), a small but nicely designed wooden building set beside the burbling river that flows through Esso. Here also is a picturesque wooden bridge and a **souvenir shop** (admission R5) selling local handicrafts. The museum guides really care about what they do – one bragged about putting an 'old Englishman' to sleep after a four-and-a-half hour tour! Warning: a visit usually includes a dance lesson. Trying to sit it out is futile.

Other than checking out the outdoor **hot springs pool** and hopefully seeing the dance group Nulgur (above), the main reason for coming here is to fly in a helicopter and track down one of the three Even-managed **reindeer herds**. A flight into a small nomadic camp, where you should be able to watch the Even round up (and sometimes slaughter) at least one of their 1500-strong herd of snorting reindeer is certainly an unforgettable experience. The high alpine scenery, carpeted with wild flowers (and alive with mosquitoes) in summer is probably worth the flight alone. Costs are based on how long it takes to reach the camp (at R40,000 per hour), plus a US$300 excursion fee. Make sure the 'fee' actually gets to the nomads (for example, you can prepay the fee by taking a predetermined value of groceries on board with you). You stay three hours maximum. You may be able to arrange this via a guesthouse in town (do so a day or two in advance). Call ☎ 41542-21345 for information.

Flights out to **Kozyrevsk**, the base camp from which to launch an ascent of the re-

gion's giant volcano **Klyuchevskaya** (4688m), must be arranged through an agency.

SLEEPING & EATING

Many Kamchatka residents treat Esso as a holiday base, and there are several small, simple hotels and private rooms to let. All arrange meals.

Alyona Tur (☎ 21271; altour@mail.kamchatka.ru; s/d R450/900; ⊠) A small complex with shared bathrooms (and often partying Koreans). There's a small hot-springs pool in the back.

Hotel Altai (☎ 41542-21218; ul Mostovaya 12A; r per person with/without bathroom R500/300; ⊠) Less toury, but this hotel has small rooms in a ginger breadlike house. They can help you get in a raft or on a horse.

GETTING THERE & AWAY

A daily bus runs here from the 10km station in Petropavlovsk (R520); at research time it left at 9am, taking nine to 12 hours depending on the condition of the largely unsealed road.

For the return trip, buy tickets ahead of time in Esso at the plank-wood **ticket office** (☎ 21399; ul Mostovaya 9), which doubles as the station.

Tolbachik Толбачик

Passing dense forest and a river ferry, about six hours to the east of Esso by 6WD, Tolbachik features the site of interconnected volcanoes and a wild mix of terrain. The main volcano to climb is Plosky Tolbachik, a flat-top, often snow-splattered volcano that erupted in 1941, creating a 3km crater. You can reach the crater by taking a six-hour hike up the volcano. To the south are three black volcano craters created from flat ground in 1975. Chunks of volcanic rock line the road, atop are sulphuric craters, and just past this is a dead forest with the bare tops of birch sticking up from a sea of hardened lava. The area is so moonlike, the Soviet space programme tested its 'moonwalker' vehicle here before sending it out into space.

Groups sometimes include Tolbachik on tours.

Belarus

Belarus
Беларусь

BELARUS

Belarus
Беларусь

Those who are aware of Belarus at all have probably heard nothing but negative reports: The last dictatorship in Europe! An 'outpost of tyranny'! A Soviet Union time capsule! Radiation and political oppression! Rusty tractors and tacky 1970s fashion!

True, the current governmentis backward and repressive in almost all ways, yet tourists will be undisturbed by its machinations. True, fashion police are the only kind of law enforcers *not* found on the streets of Belarus, but who's forcing you to go clothes shopping there? While Belarus' reputation as a living museum of the USSR should be tempered by the visible bursts of capitalism in Minsk, visitors can indeed get a better taste of what life resembled in the 'good old days' here than in Russia. The rule of law is more strongly felt here, and the clean city streets are lined with more Soviet iconography and statues than you can shake a sickle at. The capital, Minsk, is a shining testament to neoclassical Stalinist architecture but straining to become Westernised; its residents are urbane and savvy even as their government does its best to block all Western influence. It's communism with a cappuccino.

Friendly Belarus is a country with few traditional attractions to offer tourists. The best way to enjoy Belarus is to sample city life but spend as much time as possible in the countryside or in small towns, getting to know the locals. Some parts of the country retain a haunting beauty, especially when fields of birch groves are interspersed with wooden villages that seem frozen in 19th-century isolation. Urbanisation is a relatively new phenomenon for the country and the heart of the nation still resides in the least populated areas.

That said, Minsk offers thoroughly modern city entertainment but without the consumerist glut of Western Europe. Here fun is stripped down to the essentials: letting go, partying in kicking clubs, and getting to know interesting, attractive people – all in the KGB's shadow. This is Belarus – have fun!

HIGHLIGHTS

- Exploring the last truly Soviet capital, quirky and vibrant **Minsk** (p669)

- Discovering local art in Marc Chagall's cosy home city of **Vitsebsk** (p691)

- Plunge back into the 19th century (and sample some moonshine!) in the reconstructed village of **Dudutki** (p680)

- Chase after 1000-year-old healing stone crosses, ancient legends and rare wildlife in and around **Turau** (p693)

- Let your jaw drop in front of the monumental **Brest Fortress** (p684) war memorial

★ Vitsebsk

Minsk
★
★ Dudutki

★ Brest   ★ Turau

HISTORY
Arrival of the Slavs

Evidence of human presence in Belarus goes back to the early Stone Age. Eastern Slavs from the Krivichi, Dregovichi and Radimichi tribes arrived here in the 6th to 8th centuries AD. The principalities of Polatsk (first mentioned in 862), Turau (980), Pinsk and Minsk were formed, all falling under the suzerainty of Prince Vladimir's Kyivan Rus by the late 10th century. The economy was based on slash-and-burn agriculture, honey farming and river trade, particularly on the Dnjapro (Dnepr in Russian).

Lithuanian & Polish Control

When Kyivan Rus was smashed by the Mongol Tatars in 1240, many Belarusian towns, left relatively unscathed by the invasions, became Tatar vassals. In the 14th century, the territory of modern-day Belarus became part of the Grand Duchy of Lithuania. It was to be 400 years before Belarus came under Russian control, a period in which Belarusians became linguistically and culturally differentiated from the Russians to their east and the Ukrainians to their south.

After Lithuania became Roman Catholic following the uniting of its crown with Poland's in 1386, the Belarusian peasantry remained Orthodox but were reduced to serf status.

Lithuania nonetheless permitted its subjects a fair degree of autonomy, even using Belarusian as its state language during the early 15th century – an important fact for patriotic Belarusians today as proof of their historical legitimacy. All official correspondence, literature, doctrines and statutes at the time were written in Belarusian.

In 1596 the Polish authorities arranged the Union of Brest, which set up the Uniate Church (also known as Ukrainian Catholic or Greek Catholic), bringing much of the Orthodox Church in Belarus under the authority of the Vatican. The Uniate Church insisted on the pope's supremacy and Catholic doctrine, but permitted Orthodox forms of ritual.

Over the next two centuries of Polish rule, Poles and Jews controlled trade and most Belarusians remained peasants. Only after the three Partitions of Poland (1772, 1793 and 1795–96) was Belarus absorbed into Russia.

WHY WHITE?

Belarus means 'White Russia'. What makes Belarusians 'whiter' than run-of-the-mill Russians? One version has it that the name refers to the people's fair complexions. Others point to the whiteness of traditional folk costumes. The most likely explanation, however, is that the term *bely* ('white', but also 'pure, clean') was applied to the peoples living on the only major territory of Kyivan Rus to be left relatively unscathed by the Mongol ravages.

Tsarist Rule

Under Russian rule a policy of Russification was pursued, and in 1839 the Uniate Church was abolished, with most Belarusians returning to Orthodoxy. The Russian rulers and the Orthodox Church regarded Belarus as 'western Russia' and tried to obliterate any sense of a Belarusian nationality. Publishing in the Belarusian language was banned.

The economy slowly developed in the 19th century with the emergence of small industries such as timber-milling, glass-making and boat-building. However industrial progress lagged behind that of Russia, and poverty in the countryside remained at such a high level that 1.5 million people – largely the wealthy or educated – emigrated in the 50 years before 1917, mostly to Siberia or the USA.

During the 19th century, Belarus was part of the Pale of Settlement, the area where Jews in the Russian Empire were required to settle. The percentage of Jews in many Belarusian cities and towns before WWII was between 35% and 75%. The vast majority of Belarusians remained on the land, poor and illiterate. Due to their cultural stagnation, their absence from positions of influence and their historical domination by Poles and Russians, any sense among Belarusian speakers that they were a distinct nationality was very slow to emerge. Nonetheless, Belarusian intellectuals were part of a wave of nationalism across Europe and it was in the 19th century that the concept of Belarusians as a distinct people first emerged.

World Wars & Soviet Rule

In March 1918, under German occupation, an independent Belarusian Democratic

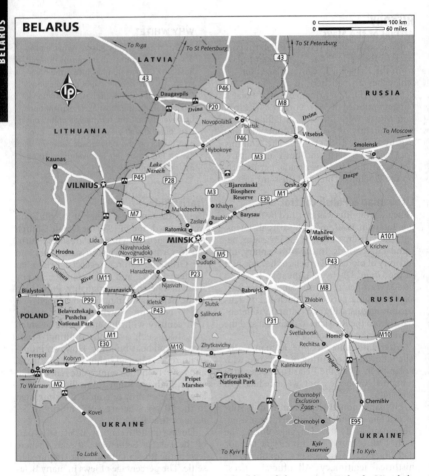

BELARUS

0 ——— 100 km
0 ——— 60 miles

Republic was declared, but in January 1919 the Soviets declared the Belarusian Soviet Socialist Republic (BSSR) in Smolensk and soon after the Red Army moved in and occupied most of present-day Belarus. The Polish-Soviet war of 1919–20 saw Polish forces occupy Minsk for over a year. The 1921 Treaty of Rīga allotted roughly the western half of modern Belarus to Poland. Rough-handed Polonisation followed, in turn provoking armed resistance by Belarusians.

The Bolshevik-controlled area, the redeclared BSSR, became a founding member of the USSR in 1922. This small area, centred on Minsk, was enlarged a few years later with the transfer from the USSR's Russian Republic of the eastern Polatsk, Vitsebsk, Orsha, Mahileu and Homel areas, all with large Belarusian populations.

The Soviet regime of the 1920s encouraged Belarusian literature and culture and supported the formation of many nationalist-tinged organisations, but in the 1930s under Stalin, nationalism and the Belarusian language were discouraged and their proponents ruthlessly persecuted. The 1930s saw industrialisation, agricultural collectivisation, and purges in which hundreds of thousands were executed – many in the Kurapaty forest outside Minsk. These purges effectively obliterated the nationalist elite and put a decisive stop to cultural development among Belarusians. While these atrocities were unveiled in the late 1980s and the government in the early 1990s made an attempt to honestly confront them, President Alexander Lukashenka has undertaken a thorough cover-up of the issue.

When Nazi Germany began WWII by invading Poland in September 1939, the Red Army took the chance to seize a swath of Poland, now western Belarus. Belarus again found itself on the front line when the Nazis turned around and invaded the USSR in 1941. The resulting occupation was savage and partisan resistance widespread until the Red Army drove the Germans out in 1944. There were big battles around Vitsebsk, Barysau and Minsk, where barely a stone was left standing. At least 25% of Belarus' population (some three million people) died between 1939 and 1945. Many of them died in one of the more than 200 concentration camps; the third-largest Nazi concentration camp was set up at Maly Trostenets, where more than 200,000 Jews and others were executed.

Belarus remained in Soviet hands at the end of the war. In 1945 it became one of the founding members of the United Nations and afterwards had its own seat on the Security Council. Belarus was turned into the industrial powerhouse of western USSR, with major factories (most notably the Minsk Tractor Plant) set up there. As a consequence, it became one of the USSR's most prosperous republics, with relatively high standards of living in the cosmopolitan centres.

Protest & Independence

The 1986 Chornobyl nuclear disaster left Belarus more affected than any other country (propaganda theorists and scientists alike say that Moscow had clouds seeded to keep radionuclides from falling over Russia proper), with one quarter of the country contaminated. This was one of the few issues that crystallised political opposition among a traditionally placid population of staunch communist supporters.

In 1988 the Belarusian Popular Front was formed to address the issues raised by the Chornobyl disaster, the discoveries at Kurapaty and the declining use of the Belarusian language. The leader of the Popular Front from its inception has been archaeologist Zjanon Paznjak, now residing in the USA after seeking political asylum.

In response to the growth of nationalist feeling, on 27 July 1990 the republic issued a declaration of sovereignty within the USSR. That same year, Belarusian was declared the republic's official language (the Russian language joined it in 1995). The leadership instituted its own financial system and state currency, and set about trying to establish an open, free market system.

After the failed anti-Gorbachev coup in August 1991, the Supreme Soviet (parliament) issued a declaration of full national independence on 25 August. The country's name was changed to the Republic of Belarus. With no history whatsoever as a politically or economically independent entity, Belarus was one of the oddest products of the disintegration of the USSR.

Postindependence

Stanislau Shushkevich, a physicist supported by the Popular Front who had campaigned to expose official negligence over Chornobyl, was chosen as head of state of a new government which nonetheless remained dominated by the communist old guard. In December 1991 Belarus became a founding member of the Commonwealth of Independent States (CIS), with Minsk its headquarters.

With the communists regaining popularity during economically difficult times, Shushkevich came into increasing conflict with them. He was dismissed in January 1994 over trumped-up corruption charges.

In July 1994, in Belarus' first direct presidential election, Alexander Lukashenka, formerly director of a collective chicken farm (a common derogatory nickname for him is *kolkhoznik*, from kolkhoz: collective farm), won with a majority. Lukashenka campaigned on promises to reverse inflation, stop privatisation and move closer to Russia.

Lukashenka was the first to call himself autocratic and authoritarian; most of his 10-plus years in power has been about gaining ever-tighter control over all aspects of Belarusian society and shielding it from foreign influence. His first major move came in 1996, with what the West still regards as an illegitimate referendum which stripped the authority of the parliament, increased the length of his term and made the entire government subservient to the president. He's been busy accruing more power ever since.

Lukashenka won a majority in the 2001 elections, despite international criticism and opposition accusations of illegality. The next elections are scheduled for 2006, and seeing as he has the right to run for president for life (another referendum in 2004 handily gave him the right to remain in office without any term restrictions), he's widely expected to win. The fact that in the year preceding the referendum he raised pensions three times, raised the average wage for the first time in years, and tripled the price paid for wheat to state farms goes some way to explaining his sustained popularity among rural folk.

Politically, the country has become an isolated island in the centre of Europe. Belarus is the only European country without Council of Europe membership – it even lost its status as special guest due to its blatant disregard for human rights. Lukashenka's isolationist policies have shown little regard for what the 'outside world' thinks, save for Russia, with whom the president has been trying with, varying degrees of success, to forge closer ties (see p660).

Belarus has 'enjoyed' a higher international profile since the US administration seemed to suddenly notice the country's existence. In 2004 George W Bush signed the Belarus Democracy Act, threatening sanctions against the country for continuing its undemocratic ways, and in 2005 Secretary of State Condoleezza Rice named Belarus as one of the world's six 'outposts of tyranny.' This belated interest is probably due to intelligence about Belarus' arms sales to Iraq.

Arms sales are a major contributing factor of the Belarusian economy; for the last decade Belarus has been one of the world's top-ten arms exporters. Some of its regular clients have been Kosovo, Palestine and Libya. In 2004 Veranika Cherkasava, a journalist preparing an exposé of her government's dealings with Iraq, was brutally slain in her Minsk apartment (see www.isn.ch/news/sw/details_print.cfm?id=10853 for astonishing details).

The list of acts which show the lengths the government will go to to protect itself is long and sadly astonishing (see boxed text, below). In the public sector, even cracking a joke about Lukashenka can get you fired.

Lukashenka has vowed to preserve his freedom, 'at whatever cost'. Worryingly, he passed into law in late 2004 amendments that essentially make his word law of the land. His commands to military and interior ministry troops are to be followed

---

'OUTPOST OF TYRANNY' TOP FIVE

Selecting only five bizarre examples of Lukashenka-inspired repression over the years is a tall order. Some have been shocking, others merely absurd. Here are some of the more striking ones:

- September 1995. An air balloon manned by two Americans taking part in an international race accidentally drifted into Belarusian airspace and was shot down by a military helicopter. Both ballooners were killed. Lukashenka praised his country's efficient air force.

- June 1998. It's hard to close down a foreign embassy, but getting them to up and leave in a huff can be fun. Ambassadors from the EU and USA were locked out of their residence complex at Drozby, a quiet suburb of Minsk. Lukashenka said that the building was in need of repairs. This followed other neighbourly gestures such as welding shut the gate to the US ambassador's residence. The EU and US ambassadors packed up and left.

- July 2004. A Russian TV office in Minsk was closed after authorities accused it of broadcasting a report exaggerating the size of an antigovernment demonstration.

- December 2004. Opposition politician Mikhail Marinich was jailed for five years for allegedly stealing office equipment from the US embassy – even though the US had no complaint against him!

- January 2005. Radio stations were from then on forced to play 75% Belarusian music to spare locals' ears from poisonous 'foreign' music (including Russian!). Radio stations scramble for music to play as many top Belarusian groups are already blacklisted after having performed at an opposition rally in 2004. Listeners groan to the beat.

in all cases at all times, even when they contravene international law, as during martial law or states of emergency. The use of weapons and military equipment is now possible under any circumstance, at the president's discretion, and soldiers are unable to refuse to, say, shoot unarmed civilians if so ordered. A Ukrainian-styled 'revolution' looks highly unlikely in the years to come.

THE CULTURE
The National Psyche

One of the first things foreigners notice in Belarus is the cleanliness of cities and towns. Even in Soviet times, Belarusians had a reputation of being exceptionally neat and tidy. Even tipsy teens assiduously use rubbish bins for their beer bottles. People are also loath to walk on park grass or cross streets where they're supposed to use an underpass. This undercurrent of respect for (or fear of) the law is felt in many aspects of society (as in the Soviet era, people are never quite sure who's working for whom), and this sometimes bleeds into a reluctance to do anything deemed out of the ordinary. It has also fostered a slight wariness of strangers, which may likely dissipate after a few beers.

Though the vast majority of Belarusian city dwellers deride Lukashenka and his oppressive policies, you might sense that the Belarusian people nonetheless are a tad on the passive side and like a firm leader; throughout history the Belarusian people have been the underclass in their own country, with little distinct culture or history of their own. Less demonstrative and approachable than Russians, they are just as friendly, if not more so, once their reserve is melted away in the joy of companionship.

In further comparison to their Russian cousins, Belarusians tend to be harder workers and more polite. However in the service industries you are likely to encounter blunt, even rude service. When you do – and you will – consider another fact: in a survey measuring happiness levels in 50 countries, Belarus was third in the world for declaring themselves not very or not at all happy – 54% saw themselves this way (Belarus was topped only by party-poopers Bulgaria and Moldova). In comparison, only 13% of their Polish neighbours saw themselves as unhappy.

Nonetheless, the Slavic gene for having fun often overrides daily concerns and you'll find Belarusians generous, genuinely helpful and giving of their time.

A certain level of anomie – social alienation – exists among Belarusians due to an uncertain cultural affiliation. Throughout the Soviet era, official policies tried to erase the notion that Belarusians were distinct from Russians. A brief burst of nationalism and revival of the Belarusian language in the early 1990s has been followed by continued erosion of a separate Belarusian identity on an official level. While this identity is kept alive by expatriates and passionate nationalistic groups inside Belarus (and also quietly by many others), the present government does what it can to diminish the sense of Belarusians as a separate people.

The language issue is a bizarre one for foreigners: no-one in cities speaks Belarusian in public; street signs are in Belarusian but all maps are printed in Russian. What to expect in a country where the president himself is famed for his embarrassing command of Belarusian?

Lifestyle

With the majority of the population earning around US$150 a month, there isn't much disposable income for leisure and extravagance. However, Belarusians are creative, innovative folk who know how to make their roubles stretch. Cafés, bars and pool halls are often full; people love to treat themselves by going out, but do so frugally. Even those without extra cash to frequent cafés gather in parks or in homes and expertly built a good time with few raw materials. Fancier restaurants and nightclubs are filled with people with lots of disposable income to spend lavishly and conspicuously.

Curiously, Belarusians seem not to be overly talented in selecting marriage partners. The country is always at or near the top of the list of highest divorce rates: one worldwide survey saw Belarus in first place, with 68% of marriages ending in divorce. Children tend to live with their mothers after a divorce, so the number of single-parent families headed by a mother is relatively high.

Gender role stereotyping remain rigidly traditional, from a Western perspective.

People are encouraged to act as their gender traditionally dictates, and you'll see a lot of public posturing on both sides of the gender divide, resulting in anything from amusing encounters to more serious problems (see p662).

Population

The population of Belarus is 9.89 million and declining slowly. Ethnic Belarusians make up 81.2% of the population, 11.4% are Russian, 4% Polish and 2.4% Ukrainian. This results in a rather homogenous population, with many shared physical attributes such as fair hair and piercing, round blue eyes. The only sizable (10,000–15,000), non-Slavic minority in the country is the Romany, who live primarily in towns and cities in the south and southeast. Their presence is not well tolerated and there is virtually no mixing between the groups.

There was once a huge Polish and Jewish population as well as a substantial German minority – all of whom were either killed or fled during WWII, or were sent off to Siberia in its aftermath. Belarus lost one million citizens during WWI and some three million during WWII. There are approximately three million Belarusians living outside Belarus.

The country's population density is low at 48.2 people per sq km. As with other countries in the region, the death rate exceeds the birth rate: in Belarus it is about 40% higher. The average life expectancy for males is an unimpressive 62.3 years; for females it's 74.6.

Government & Politics

In theory, Belarus is a democracy with an executive president, chosen in direct popular elections. The president chooses a prime minister, who is responsible for many of the day-to-day affairs of government. The country's parliament is the National Assembly, consisting of two chambers. In practice, however, the country is run by the sitting president, Alexander Lukashenka.

Aside from the fact that most of Lukashenka's opponents have either been intimidated into silence, sacked or have conveniently disappeared, opposition groups have done themselves no great favours by bickering among themselves, failing to elect a populist leader and allowing corruption to seep into its midst by accepting generous handouts from various Western (mainly US) organisations. The general public, regularly treated to derisive reports about opposition groups on state-run TV, view these groups as unstable and uncomfortably anti-Russian. Moreover, participation in an unofficial protest (defined as a meeting of more than two persons) can lead to imprisonment or a heavy fine.

Lukashenka has cracked down on the media (in the past, open-forum websites have been blocked for 'technical reasons' during elections and referendums, and gay-themed sites have also been blocked), halted or reversed economic reforms, stifled political opposition, and isolated Belarus from the West and its 'corruptive' influence. Instead, he has been forging ties with such stalwarts of world democracy as Libya, Syria and Zambia. Russian president Vladimir Putin has several times publicly humiliated Lukashenka, partly for his unrealistic demands on Russia with regards to proposed reunification.

The country is divided into six administrative regions centred on the cities of Minsk, Brest, Hrodna, Vitsebsk, Homel and Mahileu.

Economy

Belarus has one of the most restricted economies on the planet. Despite attempts at reform in the early 1990s, the country has devolved continually under Lukashenka's spectacularly unsuccessful attempts at 'market socialism'. The economy is largely state controlled and closed. The government has placed controls on prices and wages and greatly expanded the right of the state to intervene in enterprises. Starting any private enterprise involves months of paperwork, permission seeking and bribery – only to pay 18 kinds of taxes once it's opened. It makes more economic sense for people to find unofficial second or third jobs on the side to survive.

Inflation was such that for the 1990–2001 period, the country had the planet's fourth highest inflation rate overall (318%). During the same period, it's GDP growth rate was a mighty –0.6%. The inflation rate was 'down' to 28% in 2004.

On the plus side, the country has one of the lowest foreign debts on earth (under

US$1billion), official unemployment is a low 2.1% (though underemployment is another matter), industrial output was up 13% in 2004, and the economy grew by 6.1% in 2003 with 8–10% growth forecasted for 2005. In part, this is explained by the state continually pumping money into key industries; there are hundreds of millions of dollars worth of products sitting in warehouses, but at least the workers are employed and production figures look rosy!

In early 2005 the average monthly wage was US$170; workers in state institutions, the police and military make salaries of US$400 to US$500.

Industry contributes over 40% of GDP. Some of Belarus' major export items (aside from arms) include potassium fertilisers, chemicals, wood fibreboards, refrigerators, tractors and trucks. Belarus' biggest export partners are Russia (some 54%), Latvia, Ukraine, Lithuania and Germany. Russia provides 68% of all Belarusian imports.

The country is almost totally dependent on Russia for oil and gas supplies, and in part on Lithuania for electricity. It is rich in peat, which is used as fuel for power stations, and in chemical manufacturing. It also has substantial deposits of potassium salts, used in fertiliser.

Belarus' economy is almost completely state run. In 2005 Lukashenka announced that any private enterprise found not to be performing up to standard can be forcibly taken over by the state without explanation or compensation.

Media

Lukashenka's administration has been battling the free press for years, forcing many independent papers out of business by refusing to grant operating licences, imposing exorbitant fines for supposed violations, and driving them out of their operating premises; however, several independent papers still exist. They regularly publish scathing critiques of the president, and articles are sometimes so venomous that many moderate readers find them off-putting.

State-run newspapers such as *Sovetskaya Belorussia* dominate the market, often featuring an impressive photo of Lukashenka on the cover, framed by headlines bellowing how the country is following the right path. Popular among the independ-

ent press is *Belorusskaya Delovaya Gazetta,* which features many articles about the sorry political path the country is actually on, and *Vecherny Minsk* (Evening Minsk), an apolitical paper with listings of cultural events.

With its fine tradition of harassing and arresting both domestic and foreign journalists, in 2003 Belarus was voted one of the world's ten worst places to be a journalist by the Committee to Protect Journalists. This honour didn't make the state TV news.

Newspaper kiosk vendors will inform you which papers are *gosudarstveniy* (government) or *nyezavisimiy* (independent). For English-language news of what's really going on in Belarus, check out the weekly *Belarus Today* (www.belarustoday.info). *The International Minsk Times* is a weekly which often sees Lukashenka in a favourable light.

The most popular station is FM 104.6 Radio BA, the first private radio station in the country. Also well liked is Radius FM (103.7 in Minsk). FM 106.2 is Belarus State Radio. Since a 2005 law forced all stations to play at least 75% made-in-Belarus music, there is little difference between stations anymore. And now you can satisfy all your desires to hear Belarusian radio stations live from your computer! Check out www.tvradioworld.com/region3/blr/Radio_TV_On_Internet.asp.

Most TV channels are from Russia. There is a national Belarusian TV channel, where you can see exciting reports following Lukashenka's every move (especially when he takes part in a ski or skating marathon: watch him win!), and there are a few local stations across the country as well, with a mix of Belarusian- and Russian-language programming. Belarus TV launched a satellite station in 2005, to broadcast its version of Belarusian news to other countries.

Religion

Belarus, like Ukraine, has always been a crossing point between Latin and Eastern Orthodox Christianity, with Polish Catholics to the west and Orthodox Russians to the east. Some 80% of the populace is Eastern Orthodox. In 1990 the Belarusian Orthodox Church was officially established.

As a legacy of centuries of Polish rule, 20% of the population (about two million

JEWISH BELARUS

Around the corner from Hotel Jubileynaja in Minsk, on the corner of vuls Zaslavskaja and Melnikajte is the haunting **Jewish Ghetto Monument** (Map p670), which marks the site of a pit where on 2 March 1942 – in one day – 5000 Jews were shot and buried. It depicts bronze figures, people of all ages, descending a staircase to face certain death.

There were just under one million Jews in Belarus before WWII, making up from one-third to three-quarters of the population of Minsk, Brest, Hrodna, Vitsebsk, Mir and other towns. Over 80% were exterminated in the 164 ghettos set up throughout the country – one of the largest in Europe was in Minsk (over 100,000 people lived there). Today there are some 25,000 Jews in Belarus divided into 10 orthodox and six progressive Jewish communities.

The Lukashenka administration has garnered the ire of local and international Jewish organisations for its refusal to return most historical synagogues to the Jewish community and for not cracking down on the desecration of Jewish monuments. In 2003 in Hrodna, construction of a sports stadium on the site of a 17th-century Jewish cemetery resulted in human remains being dug up and carelessly treated, mixed with dirt and used for road repaving. An official statement from a member of parliament stated that it's acceptable to bulldoze historic synagogues or mosques if they stand in the way of city planning.

Belarus' Jewish community dates from the 14th century, when Brest and Hrodna grew as cultural centres and when Jews were encouraged to settle in these areas by the liberal Lithuanian rulers. After control switched to Russia in the late 18th century, Belarus was part of the Pale of Settlement where Jews were forced to live. However, a series of brutal pogroms in 1881 and uncontained anti-Semitism and cultural persecution thereafter caused many to flee west.

Current attitudes towards Jews remain two-sided. While the average person professes tolerance, the official Orthodox calendar of 2003 printed as one of its holy remembrance days 20 May 1690, the day a young boy named Belostoksy was allegedly murdered by Jews near Hrodna in a religious ritual that required fresh, young blood. Such apocryphal tales of Jews as baby killers led to widespread pogroms that killed thousands of Jews across Eastern Europe. The church's prayer for that day refers to Jews as 'real beasts'.

For more information, contact the **Israeli Cultural Centre in Minsk** (☎ 017-230 1874; vul Uralskaja 3; Ⓜ Ploshcha Peramohi).

people) are Roman Catholic, of whom 15% are ethnic Poles. Their presence can be especially felt in Hrodna, where they hold services in Polish.

In the early 1990s the Uniate Church – an Orthodox sect that looks to Rome, not Moscow – was reestablished and now has a following of over 100,000, many of them Ukrainians living in Belarus. There's also a small Protestant minority, the remnant of a once large German population. There are also small numbers of Tatars practising Islam, and Jews (see boxed text, above).

In 2002 the president signed into force a new law on religion despite international criticism. The Belarus Orthodox Church was given wide privileges while other groups' activities have been severely limited. Following in the footsteps of such beacons of democracy as Turkmenistan, Belarusian authorities use the law to harass almost every religious group in the coun-

try. Police have threatened to close Baptist churches and people have been arrested and fined for holding illegal gatherings – even prayer meetings inside private apartments!

Women in Belarus

Local and international women's groups have identified domestic violence and workplace discrimination as social problems in Belarus: some 30% of women have experienced violence at home and 12% sexual harassment at work. There are other social problems which place Belarusian women behind their Western European counterparts: very few women occupy public positions of power (only 10% of female government employees hold managerial positions); women's salaries are on average 80% of men's; and women tend not to be land or business-owners (women own only 5% of all small and medium-sized enterprises). All this, combined with the high number of single mothers, ensure that women are more prone to poverty than men.

There are signs of improvement, however. Since 1999 the government has made several legal amendments as well as set up a committee with the goal of ameliorating the social and economic situation for women.

Sport

The state spends a lot of money on sports and on building new sports stadiums. As in the USSR, showing sports prowess is a way of suggesting political might.

Dinamo Minsk is Belarus' top soccer club and plays frequently in its home stadium in central Minsk, but there's no denying that ice hockey is the number one spectator sport in the country, especially since Lukashenka has gone all-out to help popularise it. Nearly every Minsk resident will tell you that Lukashenka practises three times a week and that his team always wins (security agents reportedly tell players from other teams to pass the puck the president's way whenever they can!).

After Belarus placed fourth in the ice hockey tournament at the 2002 Winter Olympics, the sport was given an extra boost. Cross-country skiing is another popular winter sport.

In Olympic events, Belarus has in the past been a major power in the biathlon, gymnastics, shooting and rowing. Vitaly Shcherbo, considered one of the world's finest gymnasts, is a six-time Olympic gold medallist and has won 14 world championship medals. In 2004 Belarus took home gold medals in judo and track and field and excelled in boxing and weightlifting. Two of the strongest men in the world, Alexander Kurlovich and Leonid Taranenko, are also Belarusian.

Sadly, even the world of sports has been affected by politics. In 2004 the sports minister Yury Sivakov was denied a visa to attend the Olympic Games in Greece as his name was linked to the disappearance of opposition figures.

Arts

Without control of its own destiny, Belarusian cultural identity was, outside the rural framework, subdued and often suppressed, with only brief periods of revival in the 16th, 19th and 20th centuries.

LITERATURE & DRAMA

The hero of early Belarusian literary achievement was Francyska Skaryny (after whom many main streets in Belarus are named). Born in Polatsk but educated in Poland and Italy, the scientist, doctor, writer and humanist became the first person to write a Slavic translation of the Bible: into Belarusian. This, as well as other editions by Skaryny between 1517 and 1525, was one of the first books to be printed in all of Eastern Europe. In the late 16th century, the philosopher and humanist Simon Budny printed a number of works in Belarusian, including controversial editions such as *Justification of a Sinner Before God*. The 17th-century Belarusian poet Symeon of Polatsk was the first writer to introduce the baroque style of literature to Russia.

The 19th century saw the beginning of modern Belarusian literature, with works by writers and poets such as Maxim Haradsky, Maxim Bohdanovish, Janka Kupala and, most notably, Jakub Kolas. Many of these writers were active in the influential nationalist newspaper *Nasha Niva* (Our Cornfield), which had to be published in Lithuania from 1906 to 1916, as nationalist literature in Belarus was banned by the tsar at the time. Haradsky's novel *Two Souls* (1919) and Kupala's play *The Locals* (1922) are poignant expressions of the repressed state of Belarus before and after WWI. Kolas is considered to be the pioneer of classical Belarusian literature, and both he and Kupala are revered for having promoted the literary and poetic use of Belarusian. You can read full versions of translated Belarusian prose and poetry from the 20th century at Belarusian Bookcase: www.knihi.com/index-en.html.

A period of cultural revival in the 1920s saw the rise of many talented poets and writers, including Jazep Pushcha and satirist playwright Kandrat Krapiva. Another minirevival occurred in the 1960s, with works by Vladimir Karatkevich and Vasyl Bykov, who wrote several books depicting the efforts of partisans. The modern literature scene in Belarus is not exactly bustling, partly due to government censorship of all printed material. Though local authors face censorship and have trouble getting published, a 700-page book glorifying Stalin was given a major release in bookshops in

2005. *To Stalin Bow, Europe* is no doubt an extension of Lukashenka's own fantasies.

MUSIC

Belarusian folk music and shows are energetic and colourful. Modern folk music originated from ritualistic ceremonies – either based on peasant seasonal feasts or, more commonly, on the traditions of church music (hymns and psalms), which became highly developed in Belarus from the 16th century. The band Pesnyary have been extremely popular since the 1960s for having put a modern twist on traditional Belarusian folk music. Other modern bands that utilise folk songs as a base include Troitsa and Stary Olsa; both sing in Belarusian.

Classical music in the modern sense only developed in Belarus within the last 100 years, with composers such as Kulikovich Shchehlov and Yevheny Hlebov, the latter composing the operas *Your Spring* (1963) and *Alpine Ballad* (1967). Though you can't get more American than Irving Berlin, composer of *God Bless America, White Christmas* and *There's No Business Like Show Business*, he was born in Mahileu, Belarus, in 1888.

Guitar-oriented rock is king among local bands. Popular modern groups from Belarus include: the hard rock NRM; the equally hard but more melodic Palats; Krama, an excellent and versatile group which sings in Russian, Belarusian and English (check out their *Vodka on Ice*); the rock-blues champions Plan (their *Blues* is recommended); and the well-known Lyapis Trubetskoi, whose catchy light rock-pop has found many fans.

ENVIRONMENT
The Land

Landlocked and flat as a board (the highest point is just 345m), Belarus may not sound very appealing, but belying its dull description on paper, it boasts many pastoral landscapes of calm beauty, criss-crossed with rivers (the longest being the Dnjapro, which traverses through 700km of Belarus) and lakes (the largest being Narach at 79.6 sq km). There are some 10,000 lakes dotting the country. Europe's largest marsh area is here too.

At 207,600 sq km, Belarus is slightly smaller than the UK. It borders Russia in the north and east, Latvia and Lithuania

in the northwest, Poland in the west and Ukraine in the south.

Wildlife

Marshlands make a perfect breeding ground for many animal species and as such, the most interesting wildlife can be seen in the southern swamp regions, along the Dvina River's northern marshes near Polatsk and in the thick forests of the Belavezhskaja Pushcha National Park. As many as 74 species of animals including elk, deer, boars, lynx, wolves, foxes, squirrels, martens and hares can be spotted traipsing among the abundant silver birch groves, and mixed deciduous and coniferous forests which make up 45% of the overall territory.

The Pripet River is Europe's largest migratory circuit of waterfowl; some 250 bird species live, nest or pass through the region. White (and more rarely black) storks are visible in the villages in southern Belarus, and other commonly spotted birds include owls, hawks, grouse, woodcocks, cuckoos and partridges.

National Parks

The Belavezhskaja Pushcha National Park (p686), on the western border with Poland, is Europe's largest surviving primeval mixed forest. Once used as private hunting grounds for Polish and Russian royalty, the forest has always been renowned for its European bison, Europe's largest mammal.

The Pripyatsky National Park (p693) encompasses haunting marshland in the country's south. Excursions – from exotic sauna sessions to bird-watching – will convince anyone that swamps are more interesting than they sound on paper!

In all there are 903 areas in Belarus under protection – 100 more than in all of China – but they only cover 4.2% of the total land.

Environmental Issues

The 1986 disaster at Chornobyl has been the defining event for the Belarusian environment, if not for the republic as a whole. While there are some heavily polluted areas in the country's southeast, some completely off limits, visitors will be unaffected by the disaster's aftereffects (see p694).

Since the USSR's break-up and the resulting closure of many factories, pollution levels have dropped steadily throughout the

1990s, though air in the larger cities, especially in the eastern sectors of the republic (for instance, around Polatsk) is polluted by emissions from ageing factories and outdated cars. The flipside is that most of the countryside is unspoiled, and old farmsteads have slowly been reclaimed by new forests.

Other problems of concern to European environmentalists are commercial logging in the Belavezhskaja Pushcha National Park and a low level of transparency in government decision making. While Belarus signed many environmental agreements and treaties with its neighbours in the early 1990s, one of the only progressive steps of the Lukashenka administration was the 2000 ratification of the UN Framework Convention of Climate Change.

FOOD & DRINK

In a word: potatoes. It's a stereotype – and slight exaggeration – that Belarusians eat potatoes with every meal, but it's not far from the mark either! The bumbling little veggie has found its way into the hearts and minds, folk songs, proverbs and plates of Belarusians for centuries. Yet dull as it may sound, this tips you off to an important element in Belarusian cuisine: tradition. A traditional country meal will be simple – and simply satisfying. A good rule to follow when ordering food in Belarus: keep it simple. Ordering fancy-sounding dishes will likely result in disappointment.

Otherwise, the kind of fare on offer in cafés and bistros throughout the country is very much like what you'd find in western Russia (can you say: *pelmeni* and *plov*?); the smaller the town, the more limited the choice. See p107 for more food-related insights, information and Russian phrases.

Staples & Specialities

The Belarusians love their mushrooms; mushroom-gathering is a traditional expedition in Belarus. It's hard to avoid the fungus, as they pop up in one way or another everywhere. *Hribnoy sup* is a mushroom and barley soup, and *kotleta pokrestyansky* is a pork cutlet smothered with a mushroom sauce.

Draniki are potato pancakes – perhaps *the* Belarusian dish. When fresh, plump, lightly crispy and served with sour cream, they can be delicious. Unfortunately, in most restaurants they are often deep fried and greasy. *Kolduni* are delectable, thick potato dumplings stuffed with meat, while *kletsky* are dumplings stuffed with either mushrooms, cheese or – you guessed it – potatoes.

Golubtsy are cabbage rolls stuffed with meat and rice. *Matchanka* is pork sausages and pork steak served with sour cream atop a pancake.

There's more information about Belarusian cuisine than you could have ever imagined possible – including myriad pork and potato recipes – at http://txt.knihi.com/kuchnia/cuisine.html.

Drinks

Try Belarusian *kvas*, a popular elixir ideally made of malt, flour, sugar, mint and fruit (though you might only find the regular, fermented bread variant).

Among the hard stuff, vodka and beer predominate, of course. Among the best of local vodkas are Crystal Luks and Belaya Rus. Belovezhskaja is a bitter herbal alcoholic drink considered the best of its kind; it's, shall we say, an acquired taste. There are also some local *balzams* (herbal infusions); among the best is Chyorni Rytsar. These are great on cold days.

TRAVEL YOUR TASTEBUDS

Salo is usually what makes foreigners' noses wrinkle most in the food markets of Belarus. It's basically a huge lump of pig's fat, salted, spiced or smoked, which you then slice up and serve, ideally before the main meal, and usually with vodka. It's a Ukrainian national delight but is also found everywhere in Belarus. If you can get over the sight of these white, fibrous chunks – and imbibe enough vodka – they do have a charm of their own.

KNOW YOUR BEER

The most popular brands of Belarusian beer are Lidskoe, Krynitsa and Alevaria, in that order. Beer from local microbreweries is favoured. Half-litre bottles cost around BR1400. Russian brands like Baltika are often more in style than domestic brands.

BELARUS TOP 5

Here are our favourite places to wine and dine in Belarus! Head there now, thank us later!

- Dudutki open-air museum, Dudutki (p680)

- Khutorok, Minsk (p675)

- Taj, Minsk (p675)

- Jules Verne, Brest (p685)

- Vitebsky Traktir, Vitsebsk (p692)

Vegetarians & Vegans

Meat is ever-present on menus throughout Belarus. Most people don't consider it a meal if meat isn't part of it. That said, because of the love affair with the potato, there are always vegetarian side dishes available. Borsch is usually made with beetroots and potatoes only, though sometimes it has chunks of meat. Some *golubtsy* are stuffed with rice only. The increasing number of ethnic restaurants in the big cities has also given rise to a greater variety of vegetarian meals. Thus, while it's a bit of a challenge to maintain your vegetarianism in Belarus (not to mention veganism – medals should be awarded for those who manage that!), it's much easier to do so than even a few years ago.

MINSK МИНСК

☎ 017 / pop 1.7 million

Minsk is a mind-blowing experience. Ostensibly, it's a European capital, but officially, the city hearkens back to Soviet times: the KGB building is impossible to miss, and people speak about spies, wire taps and stool pigeons in their midst. Police and the military are everywhere. News is that Lukashenka is ready to send in tanks to squash protests. Yet never mind, a slick new nightclub is rolling out drum 'n' bass tonight. Before that, drop in to the new sushi bar.

Communist chic. Cappuccino communism. Minsk is a living oxymoron. When it all gets too bizarre to figure out – and it will – just abandon yourself and have a blast.

There's a palpable pride about Minsk, the pride of a survivor. It has come back from the dead several times in its almost millennium of existence (the city's official birthday is 3 March 1067), each time triumphantly. Currently, it's the defiant capital of one of the few countries to actively snub US and European attempts at 'intervention', and the city which best approximates what life was like in the Soviet heyday of the 1970s: insular, cocooned, fun.

After Minsk was reduced to rubble during WWII, Moscow architects were given a blank slate to transform ruins into a model Soviet city. An excess of monumental classicism was to give the impression of a workers' utopia. The wide boulevards, expansive squares and grandiose proportions of the buildings in the centre do initially impress, but eventually they take on an oppressive weight. Aside from a minuscule reconstructed Old Town, the city has few cosy corners as antidotes to the concrete, colonnaded grandeur. Evenings, when buildings are beautifully illuminated, offer a softer view of the city.

Minsk, as a clean, safe city and with few tourist attractions, is best enjoyed as the locals do – hanging out in the parks and cafés, meeting people and trying to forget about what goes on behind the Presidential Palace's doors.

HISTORY

First mentioned in 1067 and capital since 1101 (first of the Minsk principality, later of the Belarusian province of the Russian Empire and more recently of an independent Belarus) Minsk has been pushed to the brink of extinction several times. It has been frequently destroyed by fire, sacked by Crimean Tatars in 1505, trampled to ruin by the French in 1812, and damaged by the Germans in 1918 and the Poles in 1919–20. Its greatest suffering came in WWII, when half the city's population died, including most of its 50,000 Jews. Virtually every building here has been erected since 1944, when Minsk's recapture by the Soviet army left barely a stone standing.

Over the past 50 years Minsk has watched its population triple with the pouring in of industry. Before independence, it was the industrial and economic powerhouse of the western USSR. It is currently the headquarters of the Commonwealth of Independent States (CIS).

ORIENTATION
Minsk stretches about 15km from north to south and east to west, the Brest–Moscow highway crossing it from southwest to northeast. The highway is the six-laned monster pr Francyska Skaryny, the city's main artery. The most interesting section is between the stubbornly austere pl Nezalezhnastsi and pl Peramohi. To cross the busier streets, there are often underground passageways, called *perekhodi*.

For information on getting into town from the airport, see p679.

Maps
Kvadrograph publishes a great map and 'panoramic' drawing showing every building in Minsk (BR1500). Trivium publishes a very detailed 1:27,000 scale Minsk map (with a 1:10,000 centre map), listing every city street (BR1600). These are easily found in kiosks and bookshops.

INFORMATION
Bookshops
Dom Knihi Znanie (☎ 226 1090; vul Karla Marksa 36; ⊙ 10am-7pm Mon-Fri, to 6pm Sat; Ⓜ Kupalawskaja/Kastrychnitskaja) Maps, postcards and souvenir books plus a used section with Soviet-era gems.
Tsentralnaja Kniharnya Mahazin (☎ 227 4918; pr Francyska Skaryny 19; ⊙ 10am-8pm Mon-Fri, to 6pm Sat; Ⓜ Kupalawskaja/Kastrychnitskaja) The city's largest bookshop. Lots of dictionaries, souvenir books about Belarus and posters of Lukashenka.

Cultural Centres
Goethe Institute (☎ 236 3433; vul Frunze 5; library ⊙ 9.30am-2pm Wed, 2.30-7pm Thu & Fri, 9.30am-3pm Sat; Ⓜ Ploshcha Peramohi) Well-stocked reading and lending library; also hosts events.

Emergency
Ambulance ☎ 03
Fire ☎ 01
Pharmacy Infoline ☎ 069
Police ☎ 02 – knowledge of English not to be taken for granted.

Internet Access
Ploshadka (☎ 226 4243; vul Njamiha 8; per hr BR1900; ⊙ 9am-11pm; Ⓜ Njamiha) Friendly, can-do staff. Has printing and burning facilities.
Soyuz Online (☎ 226 0279; vul Krasnaarmejskaja 3; per hr BR2100; ⊙ 24hr; Ⓜ Kupalawskaja/Kastrychnitskaja) The largest in the city. Has printing facilities and a smoke-infested café-bar. Look for the building with the tank out front and climb to the 2nd floor.
Train Station (per hr BR2000; ⊙ 24 hr; Ⓜ Ploshcha Nezalezhnastsi) On the 4th floor of the train station.

Internet Resources
Andreas Haack (http:ahaack.net) This home page has many quirky anecdotes about one person's multiple travels to Minsk and Belarus. Funny, invaluable information from that rare someone who repeatedly travelled to Belarus just because he wanted to! Find out why it's fun to do so…
In Your Pocket (www.inyourpocket.com/belarus/minsk /en) A funny and well-written, if occasionally dated and

---

THE NAME GAME

As we were heading to press, President Lukashenka unexpectedly decided to change the names of Minsk's two largest streets. As if the street name situation in the country weren't complicated enough! Minsk's longest street, praspekt Francyska Skaryny, named after Belarus' main national hero and symbolising Belarusian language and culture, has been renamed praspekt Nezalezhnastsi (Independence boulevard) and praspekt Masherava renamed praspekt Peramozhtsau (boulevard of the Victors). How original!

This name change set off street protests and a petition to cancel the change. While chances are good that the changes will be pushed through, local usage is likely to stubbornly stick to the original names, and the millions of references to them in books, brochures, websites, documents and on business cards will take years to be completely replaced. Therefore, we print all addresses here with the original street names. Here are the main changes.

Previously	Now
praspekt Francyska Skaryny	praspekt Nezalezhnastsi (prospekt Nenavisimosti in Russian)
praspekt Masherava	praspekt Peramozhtsau (prospekt Pobeditelei in Russian)
vulitsas Varvasheni, Ierusalimskaja and Drozda	praspekt Masherava

MINSK IN...

Two Days

Start with a walk down **praspekt Francyska Skaryny** (opposite), pop into **London** (p676) for a killer coffee, tea or cocktail before visiting the **Museum of the Great Patriotic War** (p670). Unwind with a stroll along the river or in one of the parks, and a walk through **Traetskae Prodmestse** (p672) where you can have another cocktail at **Banana** (p676) before dinner at **Khutorok** (p675). Take your pick of clubs or bars for the evening.

The next day, head out to **Dudutki** (p680), and in the evening continue exploring Minsk, in the cafés and bars but also in the parks and side streets of the **Upper Town** (p672).

Four Days

Same as above, only add in a visit to some local **art galleries** (p673) and definitely more nightlife, like a visit to wild and friendly **Babylon** (p677) and a visit to **West World Club** (p677), just for the spectacle of it all. You'll also have time to visit **Mir** (p681) and **Njasvizh** (p681), or, on a hot summer's day, **Minskae Mora** (p673).

inaccurate, description of all the places you'll want and need to see in Minsk.

Minsk in the Fifties (www.data.minsk.by/minsk /fifties) Some brilliant Technicolour postcards of Minsk in its carefree heyday, when its population was a third of today's and everyone wore a smile – imagine!

Laundry

As in Russia, there are no laundrettes. Hotels usually provide a laundry service, or you can make a deal with the cleaning ladies.

Left Luggage

There are lockers at the central bus station and downstairs at the train station.

Medical Services

Medical service is, predictably, well behind Western Europe.

EcoMedservices (☎ 200 4581; vul Tolstoho 4; 🕑 24hr; Ⓜ Ploshcha Nezalezhnastsi) No reliable, Western-run clinics operate, but this place comes the closest. Drop-ins are possible, but you'll need to reserve a time with a doctor. Consultations cost between BR10,000 and BR30,000. Also contact your embassy to see who they recommend.

Minsk Emergency Hospital (☎ 227 7621; vul Leitenanta Kizhevatava 58; 🕑 24hr)

Money

There are exchange bureaus in every hotel, in most big shops, lining major streets and inside bus and train stations. The most popular foreign currencies are euros and US dollars. Typically, exchange bureaus in main hotels offer the most varied services,

including cashing travellers cheques. ATMs are omnipresent (inside bus, train and metro stations, major stores and all hotels); the ones at Hotel Minsk (p675) and Zhuravinka (p675) dispense US dollars and euros. There's a 24-hour exchange bureau inside **Hotel Jubileynaja** (☎ 226 9024; pr Masherava 19).

Post

Central post office (glavpashtamt; pr Francyska Skaryny 10; 🕑 8am-8pm Mon-Fri, 10am-5pm Sat & Sun; Ⓜ Ploshcha Nezalezhnastsi) Worth visiting if only for the impressive neobaroque, domed interior. You can also send faxes and receive them on ☎ 375-17-226 0530, upon presentation of your passport.

DHL (☎ 228 1108) Has offices in major hotels, including the Hotel Jubileynaja and the Hotel Complex Oktjabrsky.

Express Mail Service (EMS; ☎ 227 8512) On the post office's 2nd floor.

UPS (☎ 227 2233) Has offices in major hotels, including the Hotel Jubileynaja and the Hotel Complex Oktjabrsky.

Telephone & Fax

Telegraph offices (tsentralny telegraf; 🕑 7am-11pm) Inside the central post office, this is one of the numerous places where you can make national and international calls.

Beltelekom (☎ 236 7124; vul Enhelsa 14; 🕑 24hr; Ⓜ Kupalawskaja/Kastrychnitskaja) Another convenient calling centre.

Toilets

Outside Minsk, public toilets – when you can find them – are better left unfound, though in the capital they're pretty decent. Your best bets are at large hotels and restaurants. Always keep some spare tissues with you, as toilet paper can either be sparse or as rough as steel wool.

Tourist Information

There are no Western-styled tourist information offices anywhere in Belarus, so travel agencies are your best source of information.

Travel Agencies

Belintourist (☎ 203 1143; www.belintourist.by; pr Masherava 19A; ⏰ 8am-8pm; Ⓜ Njamiha) The agency mainly deals with groups, but individuals can be accommodated with some convincing and wrangling. A city tour runs at around US$50 per group; trips to Khatyn cost around US$65. They organise a wealth of country tours, can help with visa support and can get discounts at the huge concrete hotels they usually do business with.

Sakub (☎ 209 4250; www.sakub.com, in Russian; pr Masherava 17; Ⓜ Njamiha) Sakub are flexible when it comes to individual requests, and offer creative, thematic tours throughout Belarus. They also offer visa support.

U Zheni (☎ 211 2605; www.uzheni.com/en/; vul Kamsamolskaja 8/18; Ⓜ Njamiha) Offers Jewish-themed tours (plus others) of the country, ranging from a few hours to several days. Its staff are extremely resourceful and helpful, and can also get discounts at some Minsk hotels.

DANGERS & ANNOYANCES

Run-ins with the authorities can be unpleasant, so don't do things to antagonise them! Do not overtly photograph the Presidential Administrative Building, don't carry the white-red-white national Belarusian flag in use before Lukashenka came to power, and avoid participating in opposition rallies and protests, unless you're willing to chance being arrested or questioned – or just photographed for the KGB archives!

Minsk has relatively little street crime, unless you count jaywalking, for which the police will quite eagerly fine you!

SIGHTS
Praspekt Francyska Skaryny

Minsk's main thoroughfare impresses in its sheer girth. Hectic and huge, it tripled in width when it was rebuilt after WWII and extends over 11km from the train station to the outer city. The busiest section – with the best architectural examples of Soviet monumentalism – is sandwiched between pl Nezalezhnastsi and pl Peramohi, with the block between vul Lenina and vul En-

helsa doubling as a popular evening youth hangout.

The stubbornly austere and expansive **ploshcha Nezalezhnastsi** (Independence Square; ploshchad Nezavisimosti in Russian) is dominated by the **Belarusian Government Building** (behind the Lenin statue) on its northern side, and the equally proletarian **Belarusian State University** on its southern side. A massive, underground shopping centre was built in 2005 in front of the one element that breaks the theme of Soviet classicism dominating the square: the 1910 red-brick Catholic **Church of St Simon & Elena** (Red Church; vul Savetskaja 15; ⏰ 8.30am-7.30pm).

The church's tall, gabled bell tower and attractive detailing are reminiscent of many brick churches in the former Teutonic north of Poland. Used as a cinema studio in the Soviet era, it became a key opposition meeting place in the last years of the USSR. The interior is dark, lavish, mysterious, and downstairs is a small exhibition hall and Polish library.

Northwest of the square are many of Minsk's main shops and cafés. An entire block is occupied by a yellow neoclassical building with an ominous, temple-like Corinthian portal – the **KGB building** (pr Francyska Skaryny 17; Ⓜ Ploshcha Nezalezhnastsi). On the opposite side of the street is a long, narrow park with a **bust** of terror-monger Felix Dzerzhinsky, the founder of the KGB's predecessor, the Cheka. The downing of his statue in Moscow was one of the defining moments of the breakup of the USSR in 1991; this is one of the world's last remaining statues to the person responsible for much bloodshed.

Between vul Enhelsa and vul Janki Kupaly is the city's busiest square, still referred to

---

LONG LIVE MINSK SLOGANS!

Want to know what those large letters looming over your head mean?

■ Above the Museum of the Great Patriotic War: ПОДВИГУ НАРОДА ЖИТЬ В ВЕКАХ (The Feats of the People Will Live Forever)

■ Across two buildings on pl Peramohi: ПОДВИГ НАРОДА БЕССМЕРТЕН (The Feats of The People are Eternal)

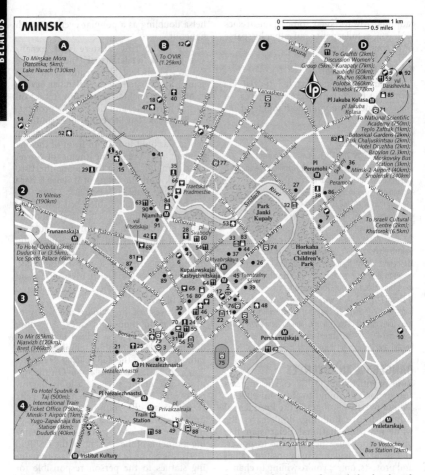

by its Russian name **Oktyabrskaya ploshchad**. Here you'll find the impressively severe **Palats Respubliki** (Palace of the Republic; 216 2098; www.palace.by; Oktyabrskaya pl 1; Kupalawskaja/ Kastrychnitskaja). The city's premier concert hall, it resembles a massive mausoleum on the outside, and is decorated in 1960s-style gaudy splendour inside.

Also on this square is the classical-style, multicolumned **Trade Unions' Culture Palace**. Next to this is the highly recommended **Museum of the Great Patriotic War** (277 5611; pr Francyska Skaryny 25A; admission BR5000; 10am-5pm Tue-Sun; Kupalawskaja/Kastrychnitskaja). The 28 well-designed rooms display the horrors of WWII and go a long way towards explaining Belarus' apparent obsession with

the war, which transformed the land and the people of the country. Particularly harrowing are the photos of partisans being executed in recognisable central Minsk locations. The museum also graphically depicts the Nazi atrocities against Jews during the war, giving special attention to the Maly Trostenets concentration camp where more than 200,000 Jews from Minsk and surrounding cities were murdered. All the texts are in Russian and Belarusian but it's still worth a visit.

Across the street is **Tsentralny Skver** (Central Square), a small park on the site of a 19th-century marketplace. People gather around the small statue of a boy and a swan, play guitar and drink beer until the last metro.

The dark grey building on the far side of the square is **Dom Ofitserov** (Officer's Building) – you can't miss the tank outside it, a memorial to the Soviet soldiers who liberated Minsk from the Nazis. Behind Tsentralny Skver, well lit and peering through the trees, is the **Presidential Administrative Building**, where Lukashenka makes most of his wise decisions. It's also his residence and as such is well guarded. It's best seen from afar.

As pr Francyska Skaryny crosses the Svislach River, it passes two of the city's main parks; **Park Janki Kupaly** on the southwestern bank opposite the **circus** (p677) and the larger **Horkaha Central Children's Park**, where there's a section with rides, attractions and fast-food kiosks. Just across the bridge, in a green wooden house by the banks of the river, is the **Museum of the First Congress of the Russian Social Democratic Workers' Party** (☎ 236 6847; pr Francyska Skaryny 31; admission free; ⏰ 10am-6pm Thu-Tue; Ⓜ Ploshcha Peramohi), where the Russian Social-Democratic Workers Party – Russia's original Marxist party – held its illegal founding congress in 1898. Today, you can wander around the small museum inside, just as Fidel Castro did in 1972.

Diagonally opposite is the **apartment building** (Kamunistychnaja vul 4; Ⓜ Ploshcha Peramohi) where Lee Harvey Oswald – the alleged assassin of US president John F Kennedy – lived for a few years in his early 20s. Few locals know or are interested in this fact, though the building – and Oswald's stay in the city – remains a curiosity for most tourists. He was lucky enough to have lived on one of the city's prettiest streets, excellent for riverside strolling.

Just 100m northeast of here, **ploshcha Peramohi** (Victory Square; ploshchad Pobedy in Russian) is hard to miss. A giant **victory obelisk** rises up from the centre of the busy intersection, the eternal flame at its feet. Parades on 9 May (Victory Day) and

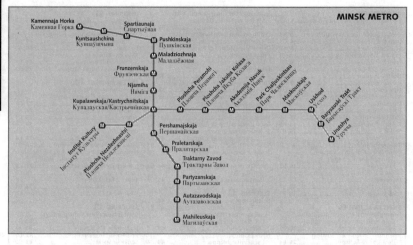

7 November (Anniversary of the October Revolution) often end up here. The eternal flame is accessible from the underground passageway.

Further north is **ploshcha Jakuba Kolasa**, another expansive square, this one softened by pleasant parkland and a sitting area near the elephantine monument to the Belarusian writer.

Pr Francyska Skaryny continues northeast, becoming a bit of a student ghetto around metro Akademija Navuk; various faculties of the state university are located nearby, as well as the impressive, multicolumned **National Scientific Academy** (Akademija Navuk; pr Francyska Skaryny 66). Beyond the hohum, 96-hectare **Botanical Gardens** (284 1484; pl Kalinina; admission BR1000; 10am-6pm early May–late Oct; Park Chaljustkintsau) and the adjacent, sprawling **Chaljuskintsau Park** (another major summer hangout and site of outdoor concerts and festivities) the praspekt's shops, cafés and commercial buildings give way to residential buildings.

Upper Town & Old Town (Traetskae Prodmestse)

The congested overpass that now carries vul Lenina over vul Njamiha near the Njamiha metro station was the site of Minsk's main marketplace in the 12th century. In May 1999 the metro entrance was the site of a brutal stampede in which 53 people died. The tragedy occurred when hundreds of young people ran into the pedestrian tunnel to escape a sudden thunderstorm at a beer festival. There is now a touching memorial at the metro entrance, with a bronze rose for each of the people who died.

Ploshcha Svabody, to the southeast of the overpass, bordered by vul Lenina, became the new city centre in the 16th century. The surrounding area is known as Upper Town (Verkhny Garad). The baroque, twintowered Orthodox **Holy Spirit Cathedral**, off the northern end of the small square, stands defiantly on a small hill overlooking its rather bleak surroundings. It was once part of a Polish Bernardine convent (founded in 1628) along with the former **Bernardine Church** next door, which now houses city archives. The former monastery buildings further to the right (east) have been restored and now house a music academy affiliated with the classical-looking conservatory building at the far southwestern end of pl Svabody.

A new **Town Hall** was quickly constructed in 2003 on the square using old photographs and drawings to replicate the long-destroyed original. A general reconstruction plan for the Upper Town has been drawn up which will see many buildings in the area repaired, restored or rebuilt.

There are several side streets in the triangle formed by vuls Lenina, Torhovaja and Internatsjanalnaja, on which some houses remain from the pre-WWII period. They are in poor condition, but their old-world charm offers a welcome respite in a city whose past is little felt.

Across the vul Lenina overpass sits the attractively restored 17th-century **SS Peter & Paul Church** (vul Rakovskaja 4; M Njamiha), the city's oldest church (built in 1613, restored in 1871), awkwardly dwarfed by the morose concrete structures surrounding it. It's worth dropping in to see the unusual icons.

A minuscule area on the eastern bank of the Svislach River, bordered by vul Maxima Bahdanovicha, has been rebuilt in 17th- and 18th-century style to recreate the look and feel of what much of Minsk once looked like. This Old Town is known as **Traetskae Prodmestse** (Trinity Suburb). It is the city's most photographed area, and there are a few cafés, bars, restaurants and craft-gift shops to tempt you for a lazy hour. By the river banks is the **Ostrov Slyoz** (Island of Tears), in memory of Belarusians who lost their lives to war. There sits a fantastic monument in the shape of a chapel, ornamented with mourning female figures; nearby a guarding angel weeps for having failed to protect his charges.

The nicest small church in the city is about 600m north of here near Hotel Belarus. The attractive little **St Mary Magdeline Church** (Tsarkva Svyati Mary Magdaleny; vul Kisjaleva 42; M Njamiha) was built in 1847 in the ancient Orthodox style, with a pointed octagonal bell tower over the entrance and a single sweeping dome over the cruciform plan.

Other Museums & Art Galleries

There is so much history and culture at the **Belarus National Museum of History & Culture** (☎ 227 3665; vul Karla Marxa 12; admission BR7000; ☺ 11am-7pm Thu-Tue; M Kupalawskaja/Kastrychnitskaja), most visitors leave with their head spinning (Belarusian-only explanation panels don't help). It takes you on a journey into the turbulent history of the nation, and features a replica of the printing press used by national hero Francyska Skaryny.

More interesting is the **Belarusian State Art Museum** (☎ 227 7163; vul Lenina 20; admission BR5000; ☺ 11am-7pm Wed-Mon; M Kupalawskaja/Kastrychnitskaja). Here you'll find the country's largest collection of Belarusian art, in two rooms devoted to works depicting the depopulated agrarian bliss of the 1920s and 1930s. There are also impressive works by Arkhip Kuindji, Nikolai Ghe, Ilya Repin, Isaak Levitan and Konstantin Makovsky.

A cool place to hang out in is **Palats Mastatsva** (Art Palace; ☎ 213 3549; vul Kazlova 3; admission free; ☺ 10am-7pm Tue-Sun; M Ploshcha Peramohi). There are several exhibition halls showing modern art, used book and antique stalls and a general buzz of free-spirited activity. The **Mastatsky Salon** (Art Gallery; ☎ 227 8363; pr Francyska Skaryny 12; ☺ 10am-8pm Mon-Sat; M Ploshcha Nezalezhnastsi) also features rotating exhibits of local artists and overpriced souvenirs.

ACTIVITIES

Wintertime, join the crowds of skaters strutting their stuff in front of the Palats Respubliki on the gigantic **skating rink** (adult/child skate rental BR5000/3000; ☺ 8am-10pm; M Kupalawskaja/Kastrychnitskaja). Year-round, you can drop in on expat Friday nights at the bowling alley inside the Zhuravinka (p675) hotel. See also p678 for more sporting options.

There's swimming and beach fun at **Minskae Mora** (Minsk Sea), an artificial reservoir 5km north of the city (buses leave regularly from the central bus station). There's a free public beach (plus a nudist beach!), and pedal-boat and catamaran rental. By car, head north along the P28 and watch for the signs after the village of Ratomka.

MINSK FOR CHILDREN

Let's hope the kids aren't too fussy when it comes to entertainment options. Definitely head to the circus (p677). The **State Puppet Theatre** (☎ 227 0532; vul Enhelsa 20; M Kupalawskaja/Kastrychnitskaja) is one of the other few places

---

FREETHINKING MINSK

When the novelty of wondering if your hotel room is bugged wears off, try spending time at these relative oases of freethinking. Cosy, liberal and as 'alternative' as you'll get, these are the places in which you might feel like you're in another country!

Enjoy the city's best coffee and tea selection at both **Stary Mensk** (p676) and **London** (p676) before relaxing with a waterpipe at **Banana** (p676) or taking in a kick-ass live show in the inimitable **Graffiti** (p677). Hanging out at **Podzemka** (p678) will do the trick when all those government department stores start weighing heavy upon you!

you can bring your children, and the National Academic Opera & Ballet Theatre (p677) often has performances geared towards kids on weekend afternoons. Otherwise, your best bet is the Horkaha Central Children's Park (p671) where there's a children's amusement section and occasional planned activities, as well as the sprawling Chaljuskintsau Park (p672).

FESTIVALS & EVENTS

Minsk's biggest party is on **City Day**, September 11. Celebrations (with parades, concerts and many organised events) often stretch over several days. The **Belarusian Musical Autumn** in the last 10 days of November is a festival of folk and classical music and dance held in various locales.

SLEEPING

With few exceptions, hotels in Minsk follow a predictable mould – unremarkable and overpriced. Budget travellers face a meagre choice, but those willing to dent their credit cards can enjoy full splendour.

Budget

Bus Station Dorms (dm BR23,000) Moskovsky Bus Station (☎ 219 3651; M Maskouskaja); Vostochny Bus Station (☎ 247 6374; M Partyzanskaja) For a small *gostinitsa* (hotel) with super-friendly staff that is kept spotlessly clean and is surprisingly quiet, head to either of these two bus stations. Rooms have a sink and mirror but share toilet and showers in the corridor. There are lockers to keep your valuable Minsk purchases safe. These are the city's cheapest beds – but note that they do not register your visa (p720).

Hotel Sputnik (☎ 229 3619; vul Brilevskaja 2; s US$28-42, d US$50-63; P ; M Institut Kultury) This place has been well known for years for its very cheap accommodation and its off-the-scale rude service. Well, it's not that cheap anymore, but at least other things haven't changed! The rooms are spacious and unmemorable. However, there's a great Indian restaurant in the same building (Taj, see opposite) and bus 100 quickly whisks you up to pr Francyska Skaryny.

Hotel Ekspress (☎ 225 6463; pl Privakzalnaja 4; dm/s/d/ste BR33,000/94,000/168,000/200,000; P ; M Ploshcha Nezalezhnastsi) Attached to the eastern end of the train station, this is OK as a budget affair only if you take the dorm doubles (no

showers at all though), but the singles and doubles are way overpriced for what you get. All rooms have toilets.

Midrange

Hotel Belarus (☎ 209 7537; belarus@hotel.minsk.by; vul Starazhouskaja 15; s US$46-80, d US$60-90, ste US$170-410; P ✕ ♨ ; M Njamiha) There are several renovated floors with such amenities as new carpets, but aside from having great views (ask for a room facing the centre), there is nothing noteworthy about this otherwise stodgy 23-storey giant. There are three restaurants, including a top-floor one with panoramic views.

Hotel Druzhba (☎ 266 2481; vul Tolbukhina 3; s/d/ste US$40/50/70; M Park Chaljustkintsau) Near the leafy Chaljuskintsau Park, Druzhba has spartan rooms and a slightly seedy atmosphere, but at least it's a quick 10-minute trip to the centre.

Hotel Orbita (☎ 252 3208; pr Pushkina 39; s US$45-60, d US$50-90; P ; M Pushkinskaja) Rising above a concrete suburb, Orbita boasts friendly, attentive service (something you'll end up appreciating) and dull but decent rooms. Hop on the metro heading north from the Kupalawskaja/Kastrychnitskaja station; this tall hotel can be seen as soon as you exit the Pushkinskaja station.

Hotel Planeta (☎ 226 7855; pr Masherava 31; s/d US$92/110, ste US$140-160; P ✕ ; M Njamiha) Planeta has a pretty, marbled lobby and the rooms are decent sized but dull. Each room has slightly different furniture and bed sizes –

ask to see a few before you choose, but go for one with a park view. It prides itself on its business facilities, offered via a Swedish business centre on the ground floor.

Hotel Complex Oktjabrsky (☎ 222 3289; vul Enhelsa 13; s/d/ste from BR158,000/210,000/280,000; P ⚒ ; M Kupalawskaja/Kastrychnitskaja) For years considered the tops in Minsk, this hotel has a rather humorous, starchy formality to it, perhaps due to its location right behind the Presidential Administrative Building. Rooms are conservatively tasteful.

Top End

Hotel Minsk (☎ 209 9074; www.hotelminsk.by; pr Francyska Skaryny 11; s US$130-170, d US$170-190, d US$210-840; P ⚒ 🖥 ✕ ; M Ploshcha Nezalezhnastsi) Where the diplomats and rock stars stay. Its four-star rooms are formal and on the wee side for the price (single beds in the single rooms are Lilliputian!), but all are fully furnished. Access to the gym, Jacuzzi, saunas, and business centre, as well as a buffet breakfast and secure parking, are included in the price. It's wheelchair accessible and has two rooms for handicapped guests.

Zhuravinka (☎ 206 6900; vul Janki Kupaly 25; s US$170-190, d US$210-230, ste US$800; P ⚒ 🖥 ; M Kupalawskaja/Kastrychnitskaja) All 12 rooms overlook the river in this super-modern, gleaming complex sporting a bowling alley, pool, fitness centre and restaurant where you can hobnob with the Belarus elite.

EATING

Quality has improved along with choice over recent years, though don't hope for too much authenticity in the city's 'ethnic' restaurants. 'Peasant food' has become quite a back-to-roots fad in Belarus' big cities. Expect a high level of stiffness and formality in many places: you'd be forgiven for thinking that you're disturbing the staff by entering. You can also find decent food in the places listed under Drinking (p676).

Restaurants

BELARUSIAN

Staroe Ruslo (☎ 217 8470; vul Uljanauskaja; mains BR2000-18,000; ⏰ noon-11pm; M Pershamajskaja) Don't be fooled by the lacklustre exterior, inside is some of the best food in town. There are several soups to choose from, and lots of cheesy or mushroomy dishes.

Pivnoi '0.5' (☎ 226 0643; vul Herzena 1; mains BR8000-16,000; ⏰ 10am-2am; M Kupalawskaja/Kastrychnitskaja) Beer is accented here, and as such the meals are hearty, heavy and manly. Their Belarusian specialities include *machanka* (pork, sausage, egg and pancake all combined into one). The interior is lavish and modern but in a traditional beer-hall style.

Traktir Na Parkavoi (☎ 223 6991; pr Masherava 11; mains BR7000-15,000; M Njamiha) A good bet for Belarusian favourites, this pleasant early 20th-century country kitchen is tucked behind a row of cement blocks.

Café Traktir Na Marxa (☎ 226 0361; vul Karla Marxa 21; mains BR3000-7000; M Kupalawskaja/Kastrychnitskaja) Another excellent choice serving decent Belarusian food such as *draniki*. The relaxed atmosphere in this cellar café-cum-bar is more authentic than the food, but then again, you can't beat the prices. It's also a good place to hang out and have a few beers.

INTERNATIONAL

Taj (☎ 229 3592; vul Brilevskaja 2; mains BR12,000; ⏰ noon-midnight; M Institut Kultury) Where Buddha statues meet wooden Russian *matryoshka* dolls! The North Indian food here is sublime and provides a welcome explosion of spices. The dhal and samosas are fantastic, and vegetarians will find heaven here (veggie dishes around BR6000). The menu has English explanations and photos.

Teplo Zaftrak (☎ 205 5483; pr Francyska Skaryny 78; mains BR8000; ⏰ 8am-11pm; M Akademija Navuk) This bistro-style restaurant sets itself apart from the competition with friendly service, a menu boasting 37 different kinds of pizza (and other Italian fare), a full – yes, full –

AUTHOR'S CHOICE

Of all the folk-style traditional restaurants in town, this one takes the prize. Set southeast of the centre, **Khutorok** (☎ 299 6194; pr Partizansky 174; mains BR7000-14,000; M Mahileuskaja) has several thematically decorated rooms to choose from, a leafy summer terrace and a menu filled with meat-heavy country cooking (their shashlyk is among the city's best). It's either an 800m walk east of metro Mahileuskaja or a BR5000 to BR6000 cab ride from the centre.

breakfast menu (a rarity in these parts) and client-friendly specials like free coffee with breakfast.

Planeta Sushi (☎ 210 5645; pr Francyska Skaryny 18; mains from BR10,000; 🕑 noon-1am; Ⓜ Kupalawskaja/Kastrychnitskaja) A great alternative to meat and potatoes is this little slice of paradise. Options range from very affordable sushi to decadent, intricate meals, and the interior is perfect for both a quick lunch or a relaxed meal.

Grunwald (☎ 210 4255; vul Karla Marxa 19; mains BR12,000-26,000; 🕑 10am-11.30pm; Ⓜ Kupalawskaja/Kastrychnitskaja) A great place for a splurge. The décor is lightly medieval, the atmosphere relaxed, and the superb food a mix of European and Belarusian (delicious soups and *draniki*, filling enough for a meal). There's a dazzling array of inventive fish and meat dishes.

Also recommended:

Byblos (☎ 289 1218; vul Internasianalnaja 21; mains BR4000-7000; Ⓜ Kupalawskaja/Kastrychnitskaja) Pseudo-Lebanese food and icy service (waitresses as icy as Hitchcock heroines!) but good for a quick kebab.

Kasbar (☎ 220 8155; vul Vakzalnaja 23; mains BR7000-20,000; 🕑 10am-2am; Ⓜ Ploshcha Nezalezhnastsi) Not quite the Kasbah, but the Persian food on offer is decent, if not terribly spicy and served in teeny portions. Smoke a waterpipe for additional flavours. There are several vegetarian options. Their nightly exotic dance shows are an eyeful.

Quick Eats

Lido (☎ 224 2729; pr Francyska Skaryny 49; mains BR5000-11,000; 🕑 10am-11pm; Ⓜ Ploshcha Jakuba Kolasa) This Latvian restaurant injects vitality into the local restaurant scene. It's sprawling (but always jam-packed) self-serve food emporium is done up like a country village, waterfalls and all. The food's on the heavy and greasy side, but you can point to or grab what you like, and the choice is staggering.

Express Krynitsa (☎ 226 1708; pr Francyska Skaryny 18; mains BR3000-10,000; 🕑 11am-11pm; Ⓜ Kupalawskaja/Kastrychnitskaja) The Soviet *stolovaya* (cafeteria) tradition meets modernity here in this huge place where all the food, happily swimming in grease, is visible (a pointer's delight). People-watch out the large windows.

Self-Catering

Kamarowski Rynok (vul Very Haruzaj 6; 🕑 8am-7pm Tue-Sun; Ⓜ Ploshcha Jakuba Kolasa) Northwest of pl Jakuba Kolasa is this immense minicity of market mayhem. Inside you'll find nuts,

spices, breads, honey, dried fish, meat carcasses, CDs – the lot.

There are dozens of grocery shops throughout the city; one of the best stocked is **Tsentralny Universam** (☎ 227 8876; pr Francyska Skaryny 23; 🕑 9am-11pm; Ⓜ Kupalawskaja/Kastrychnitskaja).

DRINKING

Stary Mensk (☎ 289 1400; pr Francyska Skaryny 14; 🕑 10am-11pm; Ⓜ Ploshcha Nezalezhnastsi) Spy on the KGB building across the street! Similar menu and atmosphere as at London (below), with a bit more space and more books. Highly recommended.

Banana (☎ 289 5079; vul Staravilenskaja 7; 🕑 10am-2am; Ⓜ Njamiha) The Turkish-style so-called VIP lounge on the 1st floor is the city's best place to relax with a cocktail and smoke a flavoured waterpipe *(sheesha)*. The pillowed couches and dimly-lit interiors make it one of the city's cosiest corners.

Rakovsky Brovar (☎ 206 6404; vul Vitsebskaja 10; Ⓜ Njamiha) This is the best place for a Belarusian pint. Because of its four brewed-on-site beers, both light and dark, this is the city's most popular place for suds-lovers. Its food is largely unsurprising, however.

Air Grip (☎ 201 3793; vul Kamsamolskaja 19; 🕑 10am-1am; Ⓜ Kupalawskaja/Kastrychnitskaja) By day it's a hangout for wealthy foreigners enjoying the excellent Italian espresso and *gelato* (the specialities here), by evening it's one of the city's premier meeting points for a younger, rowdier crowd. This place has the right attitude: to try to reduce the billows of smoke from their customers, they sometimes offer free coffee for those who actually don't smoke!

Karchma Stavravilenskaja (☎ 289 3754; vul Staravilenskaja 2; 🕑 11am-midnight; Ⓜ Njamiha) In

---

AUTHOR'S CHOICE

Charming, eccentric and crammed with trinkets, the miniscule café **London** (☎ 289 1529; pr Francyska Skaryny 17; 🕑 10am-11pm; Ⓜ Kupalawskaja/Kastrychnitskaja) is an oasis of laid-back cool, just one step off of the city's main drag but another world entirely. The city's best tea and coffee selection is right here too, plus a bevy of creative cocktails to be enjoyed in the upstairs 'lounge' and a small but very tasty food menu. It's where Minsk's intellectuals, artists, DJs and generally cool folk meet.

the Old Town along the riverfront, this café has a breezy summer terrace and a low-key interior. Its food is good, if overpriced, but it's the beer and coffee that most head here for.

ENTERTAINMENT
Nightclubs

Discos are widespread, but as prices are prohibitive for ordinary Belarusians (cover prices range from BR5000 to BR20,000), most of them boast a predictable crowd – leather jackets, short skirts, wads of cash. You're almost guaranteed an 'erotic show' around midnight too, and many hotel clubs are filled with sex workers. Check out www .mixtura.org for the latest club happenings and pics from past events – it's all in Russian, but makes Minsk look like Europe's party central.

Babylon (☎ 8-029 677 0445; vul Tolbukhina 4; ☺ 10pm-6am Tue-Sun; Ⓜ Park Chaljustkintsau) The city's main gay (now gay-friendly) club, and probably the least pretentious and most fun-spirited club in town. Here people of all persuasions gather just to have a down-to-earth good time. It's on the 3rd floor of a commercial building – just walk in the open door and follow the music.

Bronx (☎ 288 1061; vul Varvasheni 17; ☺ noon-5am; Ⓜ Ploshcha Peramohi) Though it's definitely a place for Minsk's moneyed crowd (count the Mercedes out front and sip on their US$12 bowls of soup in the restaurant downstairs!), the two-floor club isn't awash in pretentiousness; it attracts some of the city's best DJs, plays some of its most progressive music, has the city's nicest pool hall, and is tastefully decked out in 1930s American-gangster chic.

Blindazh (☎ 219 0010; vul Timiryazeva 9; ☺ 11pm-6am Wed-Sun; Ⓜ Fruzenskaja) Boasting the city's best sound system, this club is strong on techno and house and has a stylish, neon-bathed interior. Attracts a young crowd with energy to burn. Take a taxi there (2km).

West World Club (☎ 239 1798; vul Starazhouskaja 15; ☺ 8pm-6am; Ⓜ Njamiha) Because of its circular shape, locals dub this place *shaiba* (hockey puck). Visiting it once is part of the quintessential Minsk experience. Here, the city's dubiously nouveau riche and prostitutes aplenty mingle with innocent (or not-so-innocent) foreigners. The doormen alone must be seen to be believed.

Theatre, Opera, Ballet & Circus

If you like the performing arts, you're in for a treat. Some of the best ballet in Eastern Europe takes place in Minsk. During Soviet times the Belarusian Ballet was considered second only to Moscow's Bolshoi Ballet. Ballet costs from BR2000 to BR12,000 and performances are at 7pm on Tuesday, Wednesday, Friday and Sunday. Opera only costs between BR2500 and BR6000 and performances are held at 7pm on Thursday, Saturday and Sunday.

National Academic Opera & Ballet Theatre (☎ 234 0652; pl Parizhskoy Kamuni 1; Ⓜ Njamiha) Ballets and operas are regularly performed at this bulky theatre (it's more attractive inside, fear not), whose main season runs from September to April.

Belarusian State Philharmonia (☎ 284 4427; pr Francyska Skaryny 50; Ⓜ Ploshcha Jakuba Kolasa) Also has an excellent reputation – it features folk ensembles as well as a symphony orchestra, and performs everything from classical to jazz.

To buy advance tickets or to find out what's playing in Minsk, head to the **theatre ticket office** (teatralnaja kasa; ☎ 288 2263; pr Francyska Skaryny 13; Ⓜ Ploshcha Nezalezhnastsi); tickets for pretty much every performance in all theatres, with some exceptions, can be bought here. There are other ticket sales points scattered along pr Francyska Skaryny and in the underground passageways. Same-day tickets are usually available only from the theatres.

Another popular theatre is the **Janka Kupala National Academic Theatre** (☎ 227 1717; vul Enhelsa 7; Ⓜ Kupalawskaja/Kastrychnitskaja), which stages plays mainly in Belarusian. Those needing their trapeze fix should check out the **circus** (☎ 227 7430; pr Francyska Skaryny 32; Ⓜ Kupalawskaja/Kastrychnitskaja).

BELARUS

Sport

Dinamo Minsk, Belarus' top soccer club (often appearing in European competitions), plays at the 55,000-capacity **Dinamo Stadium** (☎ 227 2611; vul Kirava 8; Ⓜ Pershamajskaja). The **Ice Sports Palace** (☎ 252 5022; vul Prititskoho 27; Ⓜ Pushinskaja) and sometimes the **Sports Palace** (☎ 223 4483; pr Masherava 4; Ⓜ Njamiha) host stellar ice-hockey matches.

About 20km northeast of Minsk is the large **Raubichi Sports Complex** (☎ 598 4447; Raubichi village; ⏱ year-round). It's at its busiest during winter, with cross-country skiing and ski trampolines for practising aerial skiing; local and world championships are held here, too. During summer, there's swimming, tennis courts and small-boat rentals.

SHOPPING

Folk art is the main source of souvenirs, which include carved wooden trinkets, ceramics and woven textiles. Unique to Belarus are wooden boxes intricately ornamented with geometric patterns composed of multicoloured pieces of straw. These are easily found in city department stores and in some museum kiosks. Most days, a small outdoor **souvenir market** (⏱ 9am-6pm) operates in the small space between the Trade Unions' House of Culture and the Museum of the Great Patriotic War, just off pr Francyska Skaryny. Breeze past the cheesy paintings and you'll find crafts in the back. **Suvenirnaja Lavka** (☎ 234 5451; vul Maxima Bahdanovicha 9; ⏱ 10am-7pm Mon-Fri, to 6pm Sat; Ⓜ Njamiha) is another good bet for souvenirs, vodka included.

Even if you're not in the mood for shopping, pop into **Podzemka** (☎ 288 2036; pr Francyska Skaryny 43; Ⓜ Ploshcha Peramohi). Here you'll find local art and sculptures which could make creative souvenir gifts, as well as locally-designed clothes and blessedly cheap CDs and DVDs (not that we're suggesting you buy anything pirated, mind you!). Another place for local art is the relatively expensive **Mastatsky Salon** (☎ 227 8363; pr Francyska Skaryny 12; Ⓜ Ploshcha Nezalezhnastsi).

It can be fun to wander through one of the big department stores to see what's for sale. Try **GUM** (☎ 226 1048; pr Francyska Skaryny 21; Ⓜ Kupalawskaja/Kastrychnitskaja), **TsUM** (☎ 284 8164; pr Francyska Skaryny 54; Ⓜ Ploshcha Jakuba Kolasa), and the **Na Nemige shopping centre** (☎ 220 9747; vul Njamiha 8; Ⓜ Njamiha). Here you can also get good-quality, inexpensive lingerie made by the Belarusian company Milavitsa (www .milavitsa.com.by).

GETTING THERE & AWAY
Air

Most international flights use **Minsk-2 airport** (☎ 279 1032), some 40km east of the city off the Moscow highway. A few shorter flights to neighbouring countries use **Minsk-1 airport** (☎ 222 5418), at the end of vul Chkalava, about 3km south of pl Nezalezhnastsi. Flights to Moscow and St Petersburg use both. For more information on international flights to/from Minsk and the contact details of airlines serving Belarus, see p745.

Belarus' national airline, **Belavia** (☎ 210 4100; www.belavia.by; vul Njamiha 14; Ⓜ Njamiha), has an office near Na Nemige shopping centre. For international flight information call ☎ 225 0231.

Bus

Minsk has several bus stations.

Central (tsentralny avtovokzal; ☎ 004, 227 3725; Babrujskaja vul 12; Ⓜ Ploshcha Nezalezhnastsi) Most buses for international destinations leave from here, just east of the train station. No matter what station you leave from, you can buy advance tickets from here.

Moskovsky (☎ 219 3622; vul Filimonova 61; Ⓜ Maskouskaja) About 600m northeast of metro Maskouskaja.

Vostochny bus (☎ 248 0882; vul Vaneeva 34; Ⓜ Partyzanskaja) About 3km southeast of the centre; bus 8 and trolleybus 20 travel between the central station and Vostochny.

Yugo-Zapadnaja (☎ 226 3188; vul Zheleznodorozhnaja 41) To get here, take bus 1, 32 or 41 from vul Druzhnaja at the central bus station. Get off at Yugo-Zapadnaja Stantsija.

See the boxed text, opposite, for the major domestic and international bus services from Minsk's four bus stations.

Car & Motorcycle

Brestskoe sh, the road from Minsk to Brest (E30/M1), is one of the best in the country – an excellent two-laner all the way. Minsk to Smolensk has a few narrow, slow stretches, and patches of forest alleviate its tedium.

Car-rental agencies in Minsk include **Avis** (☎ 234 7990), upstairs at Hotel Belarus and at Minsk-2 airport, and **Europcar** (☎ 226 9062; pr Masherava 11; Ⓜ Njamiha). Rates start at around

DOMESTIC & INTERNATIONAL BUS SERVICES FROM MINSK

Destination	Frequency	Duration	Cost	Station
Brest	5 daily	5½hr	BR22,000	Central
Dudutki	3 daily	1½hr	BR7000	Yugo-Zapadnaja
Homel	4-6 daily	7hr	BR23,000	Vostochny
Hrodna	20 daily	4-6hr	BR25,000	Central
Kaunas	2 daily	6hr	BR30,000	Central
Lake Narach	10 daily	2½hr	BR8000	Central
Mahileu	8 daily	4hr	BR18,000	Vostochny
Minskae Mora	dozens daily	45min	BR5000	Central
Moscow	2 weekly	14½hr	BR34,000	Central
Paris	2 weekly	41hr	BR432,000	Central
Pinsk	2-3 daily	7hr	BR23,000	Vostochny
Polatsk	2-3 daily	5hr	BR20,000	Moskovsky
Prague	9 weekly	23hr	BR142,000	Central
Riga	daily	10hr	BR45,000	Central
St Petersburg	weekly	19hr	BR50,000	Central
Turau	3 daily	4-6½hr	BR13,000	Vostochny
Vilnius	3 daily	4hr	BR18,000	Central
Vitsebsk	7 daily	4-5½hr	BR23,000	Moskovsky
Warsaw	2 daily	11hr	BR49,000	Vostochny

US$55 per day, and cars can often be hired with drivers for an extra fee.

Train

The train station is an impressive, super-modern construction with full services on all its four floors, including left luggage in the basement.

Times in red on station timetables are for weekends and holidays only; those in black are daily. Major domestic and international destinations from Minsk's main train station (prices are for *kupeyny*, 2nd-class, travel):

Destination	Frequency	Duration	Cost
Brest	8 daily	4½hrs	BR24,000
Homel	3 daily	4½hr	BR25,000
Hrodna	5 daily	6½hr	BR13,000-17,000
Kaliningrad	2 daily	13hr	BR77,000-130,000
Kyiv	daily	12hr	BR45,000
Moscow	20 daily	11hr	BR66,000-104,000
Polatsk	2 daily	6-8hr	BR18,000
Prague	daily	24hr	BR240,000
Riga	3-4 weekly	7½hr	BR98,000
Smolensk	15 daily	4hr	BR31,000
St Petersburg	daily	16hr	BR113,000
Vilnius	daily	4½hr	BR32,000
Vitsebsk	2-3 daily	4½-6hr	BR12,000-18,000
Warsaw	3 daily	9-11hr	BR94,000-120,000

RESERVATIONS

Ticket counters (pl Privakzalnaja; ☎ 005, 596 5410; Ⓜ Ploshcha Nezalezhnastsi) are on either side of the main entrance hall of Minsk's train station. However, for non-CIS international destinations such as Prague and Warsaw, counter 13 sells tickets only on the day of departure (open from 8pm to 8am daily). Ask at counters 14 and 15 for train information. Tickets for the slow electric trains to suburban destinations are sold in the smaller building just west of (to the right if facing) the train station.

To save a trip to the station, and to book international tickets in advance, book through any of the city's travel agencies (p669), or at the **international ticket office** (☎ 225 3067; vul Voronyanskoho 6; ◷ 8am-6pm Mon-Fri, 10am-4pm Sat; Ⓜ Institut Kultury). To purchase tickets for domestic and CIS destinations, you can also use the convenient **ticket office** (☎ 225 6124; pr Francyska Skaryny 18; ◷ 9am-8pm Mon-Fri, to 7pm Sat & Sun; Ⓜ Kupalawskaja/Kastrychnitskaja), much quieter than the train station.

GETTING AROUND
To/From the Airports

The taxi drivers who lurk around Minsk-2 airport (outside terminals five and six) are vultures who all want about US$40 for the

40-minute ride into the city (it should cost around US$25, what you'd pay to get to the airport from the city). You can try to bargain them down, or else wait for one of the hourly buses that cost BR3000 (80 minutes) and take you to the central bus station. Better are the regular *marshrutky* that make the trip in under an hour and cost only BR5000. Both the buses and *marshrutky* head to/from the central bus station. Bus 100 runs regularly between Minsk-1 airport and pr Francyska Skaryny.

Public Transport

Public transport operates from about 5.30am to 1am daily and serves all parts of the city. You will find trolleybuses 1, 2 and 18 plying pr Francyska Skaryny between pl Nezalezhnastsi and pl Peramohi. The frequent bus 100 is among the most convenient, running northeast along pr Francyska Skaryny to Akamedija Navuk. There are also many *marshrutky* zipping around the city, with their routes displayed in Russian on signs in their windows.

Minsk has two metro lines. Note that some stations still have their Russian names on signs – namely Ploshcha Nezalezhnastsi, in places alternatively marked as Ploshchad Lenina; Ploshcha Peramohi, marked as Ploshchad Pobedy; and Kastrychnitskaja, which is almost always referred to as Oktyabrskaya. The metro closes around 12.30am.

TICKETS & PASSES

Individual tickets (or *zhetony*, plastic tokens for the metro) for all modes of transport cost BR360. Except for on the metro, they can be bought inside the vehicle from the person on board wearing a bright vest. Get the ticket and validate it by punching it through one of the red punching machines on the poles. Ten-day and monthly passes are also available for one or all modes of transport. A ten-day/monthly pass on all modes of transport costs just BR8840/25,200. These can be conveniently bought at metro stations.

AROUND MINSK

DUDUTKI ДУДУТКІ

Near the sleepy, dusty village of Dudutki, 40km south of Minsk (15km east after a cut-off from the P23 highway), is an open-air museum (☎ 213-7 2525; unguided admission BR9000; ☼ 10am-8pm Tue-Sun May-Oct), where 19th-century Belarusian country life comes to life. Guided tours are offered for BR33,000 per person; an English-speaking guide costs US$25 per group. If you only make one day trip from Minsk let this be the one.

Traditional crafts, such as carpentry, pottery, handicraft-making and baking are on display in old-style wood-and-hay houses. You can wander around the grounds, taking in the fresh air, spying on a working farm as it was a century ago. Nearby is a working windmill which you can climb. You can also go horse riding or just rest on bales of hay.

Best of all though is the meal you can order, prepared on site using traditional recipes and techniques. Homemade cheeses, bread, *draniki, kolduni*, and pork sausages all go down so well, especially with a shot of local *samagon* (moonshine) – make sure you're not the one driving home! A scrumptious meal will cost only BR25,000 to BR35,000.

Getting There & Away

Public transport to Dudutki is iffy. About three daily buses go to Ptich from Minsk's Yugo-Zapadnaja bus station, letting you off at the village of Dudutki, a 2km walk from the museum complex. Hailing a cab from central Minsk and convincing the driver to wait for you for a few hours there will cost about BR75,000. While all travel agencies organise trips there, **Dudutki Tur** (☎ 017-251 0076; dudutki@telecom.by; vul Dunina Martsinkevicha 6) in Minsk is your best bet. Their prices are practically the same as at the museum, plus they can organise transport (US$50 there and back for up to seven persons), sauna (US$40 per hour), snowshoeing (US$13 per hour) and other activities.

KHATYN ХАТЫНЬ

The hamlet of Khatyn, 60km north of Minsk, was burned to the ground with all its inhabitants in a 1943 Nazi reprisal. The site is now a sobering memorial centred around a sculpture modelled on the only survivor, Yuzif Kaminsky. Also here: the Graveyard of Villages, commemorating 185 other Belarusian villages annihilated by the

Germans; the Trees of Life (actually concrete posts) commemorating a further 433 villages that were destroyed but rebuilt; and a Memory Wall listing the Nazi concentration camps in Belarus and some of their victims.

Khatyn is about 5km east of the Minsk–Vitsebsk road (M3). The turn-off is about 15km north of Lohoysk, opposite the village of Kazyry. There's no reliable public transport out there, but a taxi will cost around BR70,000 for the return journey from Minsk. Pricey trips organised by **Belintourist** (p669) cost US$70 for two people, US$90 for three to nine people.

MIR MIP
☎ 01596 / pop 2500

About 97km southwest of Minsk and 8km north off the Minsk–Brest road is the small town of Mir where the 16th-century **Mir Castle** sits overlooking a pond.

Once owned by the powerful Radziwill princes, the castle is now under Unesco protection. Built predominantly out of stone and red brick, it's a walled complex with five towers surrounding a courtyard. The exterior detailing was intended to be aesthetic as well as defensive. Though most of the decidedly ho-hum complex is under reconstruction, one tower is open as an **archaeological museum** (☎ 23610; admission BR5000, guided tour in Russian BR20,000; ✆ 10am-5pm Wed-Sun).

From the central bus station in Minsk, some 12 buses a day head to the town of Navahrudak (Novogrudok in Russian) and stop in Mir (BR7000, 2½ hours) shortly after they turn off the main highway. For an alternative way of getting to Mir, see right.

NJASVIZH НЯСВІЖ
☎ 01770 / pop 15,000

Njasvizh, 118km southwest of Minsk, is one of the oldest sites in the country, dating from the 13th century. It reached its zenith in the mid-16th century while run by the mighty Radziwill magnates, who had the town rebuilt with the most advanced system of fortification known at the time.

Over the centuries, war, fire and neglect diminished the town's status and today, it's a random mix of painted wooden cottages and bland housing, but with enough fine pieces of 16th-century architecture and a great park to happily occupy you for a few hours.

There's a small but interesting **Local History Museum** (☎ 55874; Leninskaja vul 96; admission BR5000; ✆ 8am-5pm), a healthy 2km walk from the bus station, with everything from farm tools to maps and photos depicting life over the centuries in Njasvizh.

From the bus station, walk southeast (to your right) down Savetskaja vul for five blocks to the 16th-century **town hall**, one of the oldest of its kind in the country. Two blocks south is the impressive **Farny Polish Roman Catholic Church**. Large and sombre, it was built between 1584 and 1593 in early baroque style and features a splendidly proportioned façade.

Adjacent to the Farny Church is the red-brick arcaded **Castle Gate Tower**. Built in the 16th century, it was part of a wall and gateway controlling the passage between the palace fortress and the town. There's an **excursion bureau** (☎ 54145; admission BR5000, Russian-language guided tours BR40,000; ✆ 8am-5pm) in the gate tower, where you pay to enter the palace fortress grounds; the staff can help organise guided tours.

Further on is a causeway leading to the **Radziwill Palace Fortress** (1583), designed by the Italian architect Bernardoni, who was also responsible for the Farny Church. In Soviet times the fortress was turned into a sanatorium, and there are vague plans to turn it into a full-fledged museum. Only a few halls have been preserved.

Unesco protection and money would be better going to this fine architectural ensemble, rather than Mir; the splendid, lush parkland and nearby lake make for fitting surroundings. Across another causeway, you can reach a lazy picnic area by the sleepy banks of Lake Dzinkava, where you'll find pedal and rowboat rental.

Getting There & Away
From Minsk's Vostochny bus station, there are four to six daily buses to Njasvizh (BR10,000, 2½ hours).

There are two buses daily running between Njasvizh and Mir, making it possible, though tricky, to visit both from Minsk in one day.

ELSEWHERE IN BELARUS
ПА БЕЛАРУСІ

As if Minsk doesn't provide enough of an exotic adventure, wait until you leave its classicist confines. It's outside the big city where things get really interesting. Belarus' capital is already off the beaten track, but the other dots on the country's map are even more devoid of foreigners, even more of a throw-back to the Soviet Union but without the potentially creepy oppressiveness that the KGB and police on every corner lend the capital.

The rest of Belarus is The Land Capitalism Forgot (despite the occasional pseudo-flourish here and there). Take a rest from advertising and hard-sell consumerist living; here there are still shops called 'Bread' and 'Shoes'.

The countryside is peaceful and pastoral, with stretches of meandering roads and meekly hilly landscapes interspersed with rivers, lakes and patches of forest. Not quite the sunny, agrarian bliss of Soviet children's books once you start counting the rusting and closed collective farms and noticing how difficult life is for the locals, but it's serene enough to clear your head.

Belarus' other main cities are in some ways more interesting than Minsk and offer an even greater sense of discovery. This is the magical terrain which begat Marc Chagall, where stone crosses rise from the

---

TOP FIVE REASONS TO GET OUT OF MINSK

- Letting your jaw drop at the Brest Fortress

- Discovering Marc Chagall's roots in Vitsebsk

- Going hunting for thousand year-old magic crosses in Turau

- Trying to find one Western advertisement in Hrodna (go on, we dare you!)

- Counting bisons in the Belavezhskaja National Park

---

ground and where resurrected bison roam free. Brest and Vitsebsk are especially out-of-the-ordinary cities, each boasting major trump cards: the mother of all war memorials in the former and a creative art scene and killer folk festival in the latter. In Hrodna and Polatsk many historic vestiges like castle ruins, narrow winding streets and fantastic churches remain. The tiny town of Turau and the nearby Pripyatsky National Park will dot the 'i's and cross the 't's of your Belarus experience by offering a slice of village life, mysterious reflections of a majestic past and stunning swamp – yes, swamp – landscape where you can 'get away from it all' more than you'd have thought possible.

BREST БРЕСТ
☎ 0162 / pop 300,000

Brest, snug up on the border with Poland, has a more Western feel than elsewhere in the country, excluding Minsk. In addition, it has very much its own vibe going on. Locals boast that within Belarus, Brest is a world apart.

Located on one of the busiest road and rail border points in Eastern Europe, some sections have the bustle associated with a border town, but mostly the pace is laid-back and comfortable. This, along with the relentless friendliness of the locals, some great places to eat and lovely, tree-lined streets of wooden houses, gives the city a breezy charm unique in Belarus. As a bonus, here is one of the wonders of the Soviet era – Brest Fortress.

First mentioned in 1019 and originally known as Bereste, Brest was sacked by the Tatars in 1241 and tossed between Slavic, Lithuanian and Polish control for decades until it finally settled under the control of the Grand Duchy of Lithuania. The Uniate Church was set up here in 1596 at the Union of Brest, forming a branch of Orthodox Christians who were faithful to Rome as a way of drawing together the largely Slavic populace and their Polish rulers. The peace was short lived, as Russians invaded in 1654 and a series of wars levelled Brest.

The Treaty of Brest-Litovsk (as the city was named until WWI) was negotiated here in March 1918, buying time for the new Soviet government by surrendering Poland, the Baltic territories and most of Ukraine and Belarus to German control.

As a result, Brest was well inside Poland from 1919 to 1939, and became the front line when Germany attacked the USSR on 22 June 1941. Two hugely outnumbered regiments in Brest's fortress held out for almost a month – a heroic defence for which Brest was named one of the former Soviet Union's 11 'Hero Cities' of WWII.

Brest puts on its party best every July 28, its City Day. Belaya Vezha, an international theatre festival is held every October to November.

Orientation

Central Brest fans out southeast from the train station to the Mukhavets River. Vul

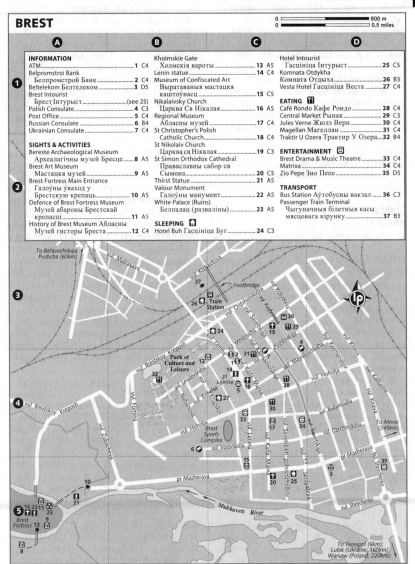

BREST

0   800 m
0   0.5 miles

INFORMATION
ATM...1 C4
Belpromstroi Bank
  Белпромстрой Банк....................2 C4
Beltelekom Белтелеком.................3 D5
Brest Intourist
  Брест Інтурыст.........................(see 25)
Polish Consulate...............................4 C3
Post Office..5 C4
Russian Consulate............................6 B4
Ukrainian Consulate.........................7 C4

SIGHTS & ACTIVITIES
Bereste Archaeological Museum
  Археалагічны музей Бресце.......8 A5
Brest Art Museum
  Мастацкя музей.............................9 A5
Brest Fortress Main Entrance
  Галоўны ўваход у
  Брэстскую крепаць...................10 A5
Defence of Brest Fortress Museum
  Музей абароны Брэстскай
  крепасці.......................................11 A5
History of Brest Museum Абласны
  Музей гысторы Бреста.............12 C4

Kholmskie Gate
  Холмскія вароты.......................13 A5
Lenin statue......................................14 C4
Museum of Confiscated Art
  Выратаваныя мастацкя
  каштоўнасц.................................15 C5
Nikalaivsky Church
  Царква Св Нікалая....................16 A5
Regional Museum
  Абласны музей...........................17 C4
St Christopher's Polish
  Catholic Church............................18 C4
St Nikolaiv Church
  Царква св Нікалая....................19 A5
St Simon Orthodox Cathedral
  Праваславны сабор св
  Сымона.......................................20 C5
Thirst Statue.....................................21 A5
Valour Monument
  Галоўны манумент....................22 A5
White Palace (Ruins)
  Белпалац (развалiны)..............23 A5

SLEEPING
Hotel Buh Гасцініца Буг................24 C3

Hotel Intourist
  Гасцініца Інтурыст...................25 C5
Komnata Otdykha
  Комната Отдыха........................26 B3
Vesta Hotel Гасцініца Веста.........27 C4

EATING
Café Rondo Кафе Рондо.................28 C4
Central Market Рынак.....................29 C3
Jules Verne Жюлз Верн..................30 C4
Magellan Магеллан.........................31 C4
Traktir U Ozera Трактир У Озера...32 B4

ENTERTAINMENT
Brest Drama & Music Theatre.........33 C4
Matrixa..34 C4
Zio Pepe Зио Пепе..........................35 D5

TRANSPORT
Bus Station Аўтобусны вакзал.......36 C3
Passenger Train Terminal
  Чыгуначныя білетныя касы
  мясцовага кірунку....................37 B3

Savetskaja is the main drag and has several pedestrian sections. Brest Fortress lies at the confluence of the Buh and Mukhavets Rivers, about 2km southwest of the centre down pr Masherava.

Information

Belpromstroi Bank (pl Lenina; ☺ 8.30am-7.30pm Mon-Fri, to 6.30pm Sat, to 5.30pm Sun) Has a currency exchange, Western Union and nearby ATM.

Beltelekom (☎ 221 315; pr Masherava 21; ☺ 7am-10.30pm) Long-distance calls can be made from here, plus there's Internet access for BR1800 per hour (pay first at Booth 2).

Brest Intourist (☎ 200 510; pr Masherava 15; ☺ 9am-6pm Mon-Fri) Inside Hotel Intourist, this office is superfriendly and highly recommended. They offer 90-minute tours of Brest Fortress with a translator for US$25 for up to four people. They're also your best bet to get to Belavezhskaja Pushcha National Park (p686) and to get discounts for Hotel Intourist.

www.brestregion.com English-language news about the city, plus photos and discussion boards to help you get excited about your visit.

Sights

BREST FORTRESS

If you are going to see only one Soviet WWII memorial in your life, make it **Brest Fortress** (Brestskaja krepost; ☎ 204 109; pr Masherava; admission free; ☺ 9.30am-6pm Tue-Sun). The scale of the fortress is so massive and the heroism of its defenders so vast, even the giant stone face and glistening obelisk are dwarfed in comparison.

Between 1838 and 1842 the entire town of Brest was moved east to make way for this massive fort. During the interwar period it was used mainly for housing soldiers and had lost most of its military importance. Nevertheless, two regiments bunking here at the time of the sudden German invasion in 1941 defended the aged fort for an astounding month. The whole structure withstood incredible attacks, including at least 500 cannon fires and 600 bombs. What is left of the fortress is too overwhelming to be poignant, but too emotional to be gauche.

At the **main entrance**, a looped recording of soldier songs, gunfire and a radio broadcast informing of the German attack echo from a large, star-shaped opening in a huge concrete mass on top of the old brick outer wall. Just inside to the left is the harrowing **Thirst statue**. Across a small bridge and to

your right are the ruins of the **White Palace**, where the 1918 Treaty of Brest-Litovsk was signed. Further to the right is the **Defence of Brest Fortress Museum** (☎ 200 365; admission BR2100; ☺ 9.30am-6pm Tue-Sun). Its extensive and dramatic exhibits demonstrate aptly the plight of the defenders.

The centrepiece of the fortress ensemble is the huge **Valour monument**, a stone soldier's head projecting from a massive rock. Adjacent is a sky-scraping obelisk, with an eternal flame and stones bearing the names of those who died. There are often men and women in period military uniforms marching to sombre orchestral music.

Behind the Valour rock is the attractive Byzantine **Nikalaivsky Church**, the oldest in the city, which dates from when the town centre occupied the fortress site. Once part of a large monastery before being turned into a soldier's garrison club, it was gutted during the 1941 siege but has since been restored and now holds regular services.

Heading south, to your left, there's the **Brest Art Museum** (☎ 200 826; admission BR2100; ☺ 10am-6pm Wed-Sun), which showcases local arts and crafts. To the right is the unmistakable **Kholmskie Gate**; its bricks are decorated with crenulated turrets and its outer face is riddled with hundreds of bullet and shrapnel holes. Beyond the gate is the small **Bereste Archaeological Museum** (☎ 205 554; admission BR2100; ☺ 9.30am-6pm Tue-Sun) which exhibits several log cabins found on land nearby.

To get to the fortress, walk to the end of pr Masherava (about 2km from the centre); or wait for the hourly bus 17 which starts at the bus station and goes along pr Masherava.

OTHER SIGHTS

The city's most interesting museum is the **Museum of Confiscated Art** (☎ 204 195; vul Lenina 39; admission BR2100; ☺ 10am-5pm Tue-Sun), a display of valuable international art pieces (paintings, sculptures, ceramics) seized by Brest border guards as they were being smuggled out of the country. It is no doubt the most eclectic art collection in Belarus. It often has great temporary exhibits.

In the **History of Brest Museum** (☎ 231 765; vul Levatevskaha 3; admission BR2100; ☺ 10am-5pm Wed-Sun) there's a small exhibit on the city in its different guises throughout history. Check the painting of Brest-Litovsk in medieval times to see what a vibrant European city it was then. The quiet neighbourhood around the museum, lined with quaint wooden houses, is worth strolling through. Just behind the museum is the sprawling **Park of Culture and Leisure** (Park Kultury i Otdykha), with a few children's rides, scupltures and a great restaurant (right). The **Regional Museum** (☎ 239 116; vul Karla Marxa 60; admission BR2100; ⊙ 10am-5pm Tue-Sat), has an odd exhibit on the history of science, and a small display on the Chornobyl disaster.

With its gold cupolas and yellow-and-blue façades shining gaily in the sunshine, the finely detailed 200-year-old Orthodox **St Nikolaiv Church** (cnr vuls Savetskaja & Mitskevicha) is one of several lovely churches in Brest. On pl Lenina, a **statue** of Lenin faces east towards Moscow, but it appears to be pointing accusatorily across the street to the 1856 **St Christopher's Polish Catholic Church** (pl Lenina). Just a block west of Hotel Intourist is the peach-and-green **St Simon Orthodox Cathedral** (cnr pr Masherava & vul Karla Marxa), built in 1865 in the Russian Byzantine style (the gold on the cupolas was added in 1997).

Sleeping

Hotel Vesta (☎ 237 169; vul Krupskoi 16; s/d €33/50, ste €64-137; ❄) A bit pricier than the rest, but head over heels better too. Pleasant, quaint and as comfy as your granny's home (all rooms have TV and fridge), the hotel is surrounded by peaceful, green streets.

Komnata Otdykha (resting rooms; ☎ 273 967; dm BR11,000) For true and proud penny-pinchers, this is a sort-of hostel on the 2nd floor of the train station's main building. It's among Belarus' cheapest places to stay, so don't expect showers – you're lucky to get a toilet! It's kept tidy, however. The colourful characters who stay here make this inappropriate for lone female travellers.

Hotel Intourist (☎ 202 082; www.brest-intourist .com; pr Masherava 15; s/d BR78,000/106,000; P) Set in a typical 1970s Soviet building, with all the expected rigid formalities. Staff are helpful and rooms are spacious and bright.

Hotel Buh (☎ 236 417; vul Lenina 2; s/d from BR78,000/106,000) This stately building with neoclassical entryway and pagan-themed murals has seen better days (we hope). On the dreary side, but the rooms are spacious and have a certain old-world charm. If your room faces the main street, it'll be noisy.

Eating

For self-catering, head to the well-stocked **Central Market** (cnr vuls Pushkinskaja & Kuybisheva; ⊙ 8am-6pm).

Jules Verne (☎ 236 717; vul Hoholja 29; mains BR8000-20,000) Despite the maritime décor and seafood slant at this fabulous restaurant, the menu is a dizzying and odd combination of Indian and Chinese – but it works. Best is that everything from nan bread to dim sum is mouthwatering and sumptuous. A highly attentive staff (who appear from nowhere to refill your water glass) adds to the dining pleasure. Vegetarians will find plenty to purr about.

Traktir U Ozera (☎ 235 763; Park Kultury i Otdykha; mains BR6000-20,000; ⊙ noon-11pm) This wins hands-down for best location, perched as it is by a pond in the city's prettiest park. The terrace sits under willow trees. Inside the spacious, country-style dining hall, you can feast on simple shashlyks as well as tasty, more elaborate fish and grilled meat meals.

Café Rondo (☎ 264 134; vul Savetskaja 45; mains BR3000-6000; ⊙ 11am-11pm) An exotic trip back to the USSR is assured in this café, where there's a shot glass set at every place, waiting to be filled with cheap vodka. A great place for an inexpensive, quick fill-up on standards like *pelmeni* (Russian-style ravioli), bliny and borsch.

Magellan (☎ 236 292; vul Kamsomolskaja 36; mains BR2000-6000; ⊙ 10am-11pm) Where Soviet cafeteria meets modern fast-food bistro. A slick and comfortable place where you can point to what you want before ordering. Nothing fancier here than meat *kotlety* (cutlets) and salads but all perfectly tasty. Come evening, it's a barlike hangout for young people before they hit the clubs.

Entertainment

Good bars in Brest are few and far between; most locals chill at the many all-purpose places listed here and under Eating – restaurants or clubs which also double as bars (or casinos, or cinemas...).

Matrixa (☎ 238 245; vul Savetskaja 73; billiards ⊙ 9am-1am, club ⊙ 9pm-5am) In a gleaming, hypermodern building is this entertainment complex, with a huge pool hall and hyperhip nightclub, expertly decorated to recall every second person's favourite film, *The Matrix*.

Zio Pepe (☎ 205 053; bul Shevchenko 4; ⊙ noon-6am) One of the country's many all-purpose hangouts, this is a nightclub (after 9pm), bowling alley, bar, casino and eatery all rolled into one. If the chrome-and-black lights don't give you indigestion, the thin-crust pizzas are very good, as are the other Italian dishes.

Brest Drama & Music Theatre (☎ 266 440; vul Lenina 21) Puts on government-approved pieces and classics.

Getting There & Away

BUS

The **bus station** (☎ 004, 238 142; vul Mitskevicha) is in the centre of town, next to the city's main market. There are about six *marshrutky* and buses a day to Hrodna (BR25,000, four to six hours). There are also four buses daily to Warsaw (BR52,000, five hours) and services several times a week to various cities in Germany.

TRAIN

Brest's impressive, classical **train station** (☎ 005, 273 277) is a busy place. There are at least three daily trains to Warsaw (BR70,000, four to five hours). Seven daily trains head to Moscow (BR80,000, 12 to 15 hours), and one a day to St Petersburg (BR90,000, 19 hours). There are two daily trains to Berlin (BR197,000, 12 hours) and one to Prague (BR240,000, 16 hours).

Domestic trains include a daily train to Hrodna (BR19,000, 8½ hours), two a day to Vitsebsk (BR27,000, ten to 20 hours), and two a day to Homel (BR27,000, 12 hours).

Moscow, St Petersburg, Sverdlovsk and Vitsebsk-bound trains also stop in Minsk, as well as four other daily trains (BR19,000 to BR40,000, four to 10 hours). The slowest train does the trip overnight, saving you a night in a hotel. Generally, the trains with final destinations other than Minsk are the most expensive.

For all trains leaving Brest for Europe, you have to go through customs at the station, so get there early. Tickets for trips outside Belarus are purchased from the *mezhdunarodny kassi* (international ticket windows) in the main hall of the ticketing building.

Tickets for domestic electric trains (to Minsk, Hrodna, Homel or Vitsebsk) are sold in the *passazhirskiy pavilon* (passenger train terminal) behind the train station, away from the city.

AROUND BREST

Belavezhskaja Pushcha National Park

A Unesco World Heritage Site some 60km north of Brest, **Belavezhskaja Pushcha National Park** (☎ 01631-56370, 56396) is the oldest wildlife refuge in Europe and the pride of Belarus. The reserve went from obscurity to the front page in late 1991 as the presidents of Belarus, Russia and Ukraine signed the death certificate of the USSR – a document creating the Commonwealth of Independent States (CIS) – at the Viskuli dacha, now the occasional residence of Lukashenka. The park is coadministered by Poland, where half of the park's territory lies.

Some 1300 sq km of primeval forest survive here. Today it's all that remains of a canopy that eight centuries ago covered northern Europe. Some oak trees here are more than 600 years old, some pines at least 300 years old.

At least 55 mammal species, including deer, lynx, boars, wild horses, wolves, elks, ermines, badgers, martens, otters, mink and beavers call this park home, but the area is most celebrated for its 300 or so European bison, the continent's largest land mammal. These free-range *zoobr* – slightly smaller than their American cousins – were driven to near extinction (the last one living in the wild was shot by a hunter in 1919) and then bred back from 52 animals that had survived in zoos. Now a total of about 2000 exist, most of them in and around western Belarus, Lithuania, Poland and Ukraine.

There's a nature museum and *volerei* (enclosures), where you can view bison, deer, boars and other animals (including the rare hybrid tarpan horse, a crossbreed of a species that was also shot into near extinction).

GETTING THERE & AWAY

The national park rarely sees individual tourists, partly as the area is a border zone and visitors not in a prearranged group need special permission to be there. However, you can take a *marshrutka* (1½ hours, BR5500) there – they leave regularly throughout the day from Brest's bus station; the destination is Kamjanjuky. You are unlikely to be asked to show special permission, however to avoid problems it's best to book an excursion through Brest Intourist (p684). It's about US$50 for a small group, generally under five persons, and they can custom-make tours according to budget. They're a fun bunch to go with, and also include visits at historical spots along the way to the park, can fix a summer picnic in a lovely area, and arrange overnight accommodation in the park itself for roughly US$30 per double room.

HRODNA ГРОДНА

☎ 0152 / pop 310,000

Hrodna (Grodno in Russian) in many parts has the look and feel of an overgrown village; it's hard to believe that this is one of the country's largest cities. As in a big village, there's not much to do here other than hang out, watch life go by, peer across the Nioman River and check out some fine churches. Hrodna survived the war better than elsewhere in Belarus and has some picturesque corners, yet oddly enough these are more impressive in photographs than in person.

A novelty for foreigners is how un-Western the city looks and feels, sitting in Europe yet as if capitalism passed it by. Devoid of Western advertisements and shops or any sense of a customer-geared industry, Hrodna really does feel 'far away'.

Hrodna has been tossed back and forth between major powers for its entire existence. Settled since ancient times and first mentioned in 1128, it was an important town under the Princedom of Polatsk and was a crucial outpost on the fringes of Kyivan Rus until it was absorbed by Lithuania in the late 14th century. Russia took over in the 1770s. After being overrun in WWI, the city found itself back under Polish control until 1939.

During WWII, Hrodna's large Jewish contingent was wiped out. Today, Hrodna has a substantial Polish Catholic population, whose presence gives it a welcome whiff of multiculturalism.

Orientation

The city centre is about 1km southwest of the train station and occupies an elevated portion of land overlooking a shallow bend in the Nioman River to the south. The mostly pedestrianised vul Savetskaja is a favourite strolling venue. At its northern end is the city's main department store, and its southern end spills into the wide, hectic pl Savetskaja, which in turn extends towards the river.

Information

Belpromstroi Bank (vul Telegrafnaja 8; ☺ 9am-6.30pm Mon-Fri, 9am-4pm Sat) Currency exchange and ATM.

Beltelekom (☎ 730 061; vul Telegrafnaja 24; per hr BR1900; ☺ 8am-10pm Mon-Sat, 9am-5pm Sun) Fast computers and phones for long-distance calls in a modern setting.

Main post office (☎ 441 792; vul Karla Marxa 29; ☺ 9am-5pm Mon-Fri, to 2pm Sat)

Ranitsa Book Store (☎ 721 705; vul Mastovaja 33) Sells city maps.

Sights

The sight in Hrodna is the **Catholic Farny Cathedral** (☎ 442 677; pl Savetskaja 4; ☺ 7.30am-8.30pm), one of Belarus' most impressive churches. Inside is a row of splendidly ornate altars leading to a huge main altarpiece constructed of multiple columns interspersed with sculpted saints. The sense of space and history inside is almost dizzying. It was built up from the late 17th century and throughout the 18th century, as foreign masters (especially Kristof Peykher from Königsberg) designed altars and drew frescoes. Another church once stood on the opposite side of the square. It was damaged in WWII and later razed by the Soviet regime; fragmented **foundation ruins** now mark the spot.

The 16th-century Catholic **Bernadine Church & Seminary** (Parizhskoy Kamuni 1) was built predominantly in the Renaissance style, and the bell tower was redone with a defiant baroque flair 250 years later, and again after WWII. It stands atop a hill opposite the bizarre, spiderlike **Drama Theatre** (☎ 453 428; vul Mastovaja 35), looking much like a spacecraft about to lift off.

Near the train station is the attractive 1904–05 **Pokrovsky Cathedral** (vul Azhyeshka 23), a candy-striped house with blue-and-gold domes. Nearby is the **Museum of Garadnitsa History** (☎ 721 669; vul Azhyeshka 37; admission BR2100; ☺ 10am-6pm Tue-Sat). This tiny city history museum has almost nothing in it, but it's pleasant to walk around the 18th-century wooden home it's housed in, and they sell curious handcrafted items and souvenirs.

About 400m west of the bus station is the **Pobrigitski Monastery** (vul Karla Marxa 27), built in 1651, which has some lovely ornaments on its façade, as well as some 18th-century wooden buildings inside the complex.

Along vul Vjalikaja Traetskaja is a dilapidated 19th-century **synagogue**, the largest still
standing in Belarus. Just to the north of the
synagogue, take a left turn down a shaded
lane and across a wooden bridge through the
park, which will take you to an **obelisk** marking Hrodna's 850th anniversary. From there
head south (left) and you'll find on a hillside
by the riverbank the very attractive **Church of
SS Boris & Hlib** (☎ 723 145), a small, unassuming church, unusual looking as half of it is
made of stone, half of wood. The stone sections date from the 12th century, making it
the second-oldest surviving structure in the
country after St Sophia Cathedral in Polatsk.
It's a candidate for Unesco World Heritage
List. There are weekend services.

CASTLES

There are two castles facing each other
in the city centre. In reality, these are
less impressive than they sound, but still
worth poking around. The Novi Zamak
(New Castle) is to the southeast and the
Stari Zamak (Old Castle) to the northwest.
Each houses a branch of the Historical and
Architectural Museum. Between the castles
is a wooden carving of Vytautas the Great,
the Lithuanian leader responsible for **Stari
Zamak** (☎ 446 056; admission BR3500; ⌚ 10am-6pm
Tue-Sun), which was built in the 14th century
on a site the Kyivan Rus settlers had established a few centuries earlier. The only
original remains are the sections of wall to
the left as you enter, from which there are

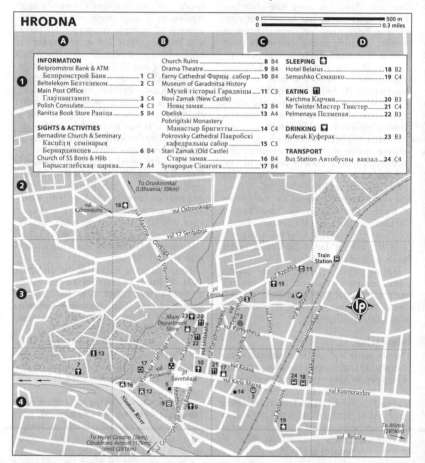

nice views across the river. The rest was cheaply refurnished in a pseudomodern style (including linoleum floors). The extensive exhibits in the museum focus on the wars that ravaged Hrodna.

On the opposite side of the bluff overlooking the river is the **Novi Zamak** (Governor's Palace; ☎ 447 269; admission BR3000; ❂ 10am-6pm Tue-Sun), built in 1737 as the royal palace for the Polish king August III. Originally built in opulent rococo-style, it was gutted by fire when the Soviets retook Hrodna from the Germans in 1944 and rebuilt in a yawn-inspiring classical style (notice the Soviet emblem above the columns).

Sleeping

Semashko (☎ 750 299; vul Antonova 10; s/d BR100,000/ 120,000; **P**) A burst of modernity on the Hrodna scene (save for the old-world security goons who size you up suspiciously as you enter). Rooms are comfortable and secure, if on the official side. You won't find a nicer place in town.

Hotel Belarus (☎ 441 674; vul Kalinovskoho 1; s/d BR70,000/106,000) Dank, dark and slightly creepy – all what you'd want and expect from a hotel stuck in the Soviet 1960s. The staff are friendly, though. Single males can expect regular late-night calls from sex workers offering their company, and the walls are thin enough to hear which of your neighbours took advantage of the offers. Bus 15 from the train station goes to the hotel.

Hotel Grodno (☎ 224 233; vul Popovicha 5; s/d BR75,000/115,000) In a typical 1970s high-rise; rooms are clean and functional, if a bit austere. From pl Savetskaja, take trolleybus 1 or bus 3, the latter originating from the train station.

Eating & Drinking

Karchma (☎ 723 411; vul Savetskaja 31; mains BR6000-12,000; ❂ 8am-midnight) By far your best bet in the city, this folk-styled tavern-restaurant has a wide selection of tasty dishes, including lots of salads and vegetarian options.

Mr Twister (☎ 470 989; vul Karla Marxa 10; mains BR6000-12,000) This smoky bar-café serves decent fare while a soothing mix of techno and heavy metal blares from the speakers. At least they try – mashed potatoes come in the shape of a bunny!

Pelmenaya (vul Savetskaja 23; mains BR2000; ❂ 10am-10pm) As long as you're in a city that's already

a blast from the past, continue the theme in this Soviet-style bistro with some of the cheapest fill-ups in town, including *pelmeni*, meat patties of uncertain origin and other greasy snacks.

Kuferak (vul Azezhka 6; ❂ 10am-11pm) A tiny basement bar for friendly, 20-something locals, this is a fun place for cheap drinks, down-to-earth service and a chance to meet energetic locals.

Getting There & Away

AIR

Gomel Avia (☎ 0232-531 415 in Gomel) operates a weekly flight to/from Kaliningrad (US$88 one-way), landing at the little-used **Obukhovo** airport (☎ 445 382), 15km from Hrodna.

BUS

From the main **bus station** (☎ 723 724), there are some 20 daily buses and *marshrutky* to Minsk (BR25,000, four to 5½ hours) and between three and six buses or *marshrutky* per day to Brest (BR25,000, four to 5½ hours).

To Lithuania, there are twice-daily buses to Kaunas (BR8200, four hours) and one daily bus to Vilnius (BR28,000, five hours). Express buses run by **Intaks** (☎ 720 230) go six times daily to Bialystok (BR14,000, 3½ hours), twice daily to Warsaw (BR16,000, six hours) and twice weekly to Rīga (BR45,000, 13 hours). The Intaks ticket counter is outside the main bus station building, facing the platforms; it also sells tickets for express *marshrutky* to Brest.

TRAIN

From the **train station** (☎ 448 556) there are at least five trains a day to Minsk (BR17,000, 6½ hours), plus one overnight train to Brest (BR19,000, 12 hours) and a daily train to Vitsebsk (BR18,000, 11 hours).

About three trains a day head across the border to Warsaw (BR55,000, seven hours), stopping in Bialystok along the way. Three trains a week go to St Petersburg (BR89,000, 22 hours) and one a day goes to Moscow (BR74,000, 17 hours). Buy your tickets in advance from cashiers seven to 14.

POLATSK ПОЛАЦК

☎ 0214 / pop 85,000

Polatsk, 261km north of Minsk, is a sleepy riverfront town with a rich history. It was the birthplace of the Belarusian nation as well

BELARUS

as that of the country's national hero, Francyska Skaryny, who published the first Bible in a Slavonic language in 1517–19. Today, however, its lovely monastery and cathedral are the only sights of interest to tourists.

The Princedom of Polatsk, first mentioned in 862, was one of the earliest Slavic settlements. It was absorbed by the Kingdom of Lithuania in 1307 and later by Poland, which introduced Catholicism. Polatsk prospered as a river port, but was continually flung back and forth between the feuding Muscovy tsars and the Polish crown, being reduced to rubble more than once. Ivan the Terrible had his day here in 1563 when he had the entire city council drowned or impaled for daring to show too much independence. The new city of Novopolatsk, a grey concrete industrial centre, has grown up right next to Polatsk, making the immediate surroundings rather unattractive.

Orientation

The centre lies 1km south of the train and bus stations (along vul Hoholja). The main axis is the east–west pr Karla Marxa, which has pl Francyska Skaryny at its eastern end and pl Lenina at its western end. The oldest and most interesting area is along vul Lenina, parallel to and one street south of pr Karla Marxa.

Information

Belarusbank (pr Karla Marksa 7; ☉ 9am-6pm Mon-Fri, to 2pm Sat) Currency exchange and 24-hour ATM.
Travel Bureau (☎ 491 745; vul Pushkina 21/31; ☉ 9am-6pm Mon-Fri) Organises local excursions, translation services and accommodation.

Sights
ST SOPHIA CATHEDRAL
Atop a small hill past the western end of vul Lenina is the finely moulded façade of the St Sophia Cathedral, its twin baroque bell towers rising high over the Dvina River. It's the oldest surviving monument of architecture in Belarus and one of two original 11th-century Kyivan Rus cathedrals (the other is in Novgorod) modelled and named after the St Sophia Cathedral in Kyiv. Its original appearance, however, has long gone. Damaged by fire in the 15th century, it was turned into an armoury which was subsequently destroyed by retreating Russians in 1710. About 40 years later the

Poles reconstructed it – inside and out – as a baroque Catholic cathedral.

The interior is a **museum** (☎ 445 340; vul Zamkovaja 1; admission BR3000; ☉ 10am-5pm Tue-Sun), and parts of the 11th-century foundations can be seen in the vaulted basement. Out front is a large stone on which a cross was carved in the 12th century by Prince Boris, who etched Christian symbols on every formerly pagan rock or stone he could find.

ST EFRASINNIA MONASTERY
This **monastery** (☎ 445 679; vul Efrosini Polotskoi 59; admission free; ☉ noon-4pm) was founded in 1125 by St Efrasinnia (1110–73), Belarus' first saint and the first woman to be canonised by the Orthodox Church. She was the founder of the city's first library and had a strong independent streak, shunning numerous offers of marriage to establish her own convent here and to commission the Holy Saviour Church. Still standing, it's one of the finest examples of early 12th-century religious architecture in Belarus, and the small, dark interior is mesmerisingly beautiful, with haunting frescoes. The saint's embalmed remains are in a glass-covered coffin inside.

The small **Church of the Transfiguration** (Spaso-Preobrazhenski Sabor), on the right as you enter the grounds, was originally built in the 17th century, although the current façade dates from 1833.

In the centre of the ensemble stands the large **Kresto-Vozdvizhenskom Cathedral** (1897). The impressive interiors, where most services are held, contain, in finely gilded cases, the sanctified remains of 239 saints, as well as miracle-performing icons. The monastery restarted religious services in 1990 and today, there are 90 female monks living here.

To get to the monastery, you can either walk due north from pl Lenina on vul Frunza for a brisk half-hour, watching for the complex on your right, or take the infrequent buses 4 or 17 three stops from the northern end of pl Lenina. The monastery is used to accepting visitors into its grounds outside official opening hours, but not all of its buildings may be open.

Sleeping & Eating
Hotel Dzvina (☎ 442 235; pr Karla Marxa 13; s/d BR48,000/60,000) This is the only hotel in town, with average but adequate rooms. Its res-

taurant serves a mediocre meal, which will do nicely in a pinch.

If you're really stuck for cash, there's a converted **train wagon** (☎ 446 237; BR7000) at the train station, with no showers. **Bratchina** (☎ 490 769; vul Lenina 22; mains BR3000-7000; ✆ 10am-11pm) is a decent little café serving standard fare at low prices.

Getting There & Away
The modern-looking building next to (east of) the older train station sells long-distance train tickets, while tickets for the five daily electric trains connecting Polatsk and Vitsebsk (BR8000, two hours) are sold inside the train station itself. Most long-distance routes are served by through-trains.

Two trains a day run to Minsk (BR18,000, six to eight hours), and one train daily goes to Moscow (BR62,000, 13 hours) via Smolensk (BR40,000, five hours).

The bus station is 100m east of the train station, with two or three daily buses to Minsk (BR20,000, five hours) and Vitsebsk (BR8000, two hours), and one daily to Homel (BR32,000, 12 hours). Left-luggage lockers are available.

Getting Around
Getting around this town is an easy stroll, even with a moderate backpack; the half-hour walk out to the monastery will be as far as you'll need to go.

VITSEBSK ВИЦЕБСК
☎ 0212 / pop 350,000
Vitsebsk (Vitebsk in Russian), 277km north of the capital, is in some ways the most intriguing and dynamic Belarusian city outside Minsk, mainly due to its artistic heritage. Marc Chagall was born here, studying under an unheralded master, Yudel Pyen, who opened the country's first art school here in 1897; the artists Vasili Kandinsky, Ilya Repin and Kasimir Malevich also spent some time in what was then a dynamic city.

Aside from this, the city boasts what even Minsk cannot – a sense of the past. Several small areas of pre-WWII houses lend a delicate elegance to the relatively hilly city sitting at the confluence of three rivers, the dramatic Dvina, and the smaller Vitba and Luchesa.

Its past, however, is as painful as that of other Belarusian cities. Its history goes back to the 6th-century Varangian explorers from

Scandinavia who settled here. Part of the Princedom of Polatsk, Vitsebsk was also pulled into the sphere of Kyivan Rus, then fell under the Lithuanian and Polish umbrella before being finally pinched by Moscow.

It was burned to ashes by Ivan the Terrible in the mid-16th century, and was savagely razed in WWII, when only 118 people out of a prewar population of 170,000 survived. Each year on 26 June, the city celebrates the day in 1944 when the Red Army liberated it from the Nazis. Though less developed than Minsk, Vitsebsk has a down-to-earth quality that visitors will appreciate.

Orientation
The remnants of the old town lie along a picturesque, steep ridge about 2km northeast of the train station and across the Dvina River. Heading due east from the station is the main thoroughfare, vul Kirava, which becomes vul Zamkovaja after it crosses the river, and vul Frunze after it crosses vul Lenina, the main north–south axis.

Information
There's a 24-hour ATM inside a kiosk on the northeast corner of vuls Lenina and Zamkovaja.
Internet Club (☎ 372 966; per hr BR1900; ✆ 24hr) Handily located on the 2nd floor of the train station.
Sputnik (☎ 240 556; vul Smolenskaja 9) Friendly travel agency which can organise city and regional tours.

Sights
Immerse yourself in what distinguishes Vitsebsk from other Belarusian cities: art. Nowhere else in the country will you get such a concentrated dose of quality art! Absolute musts are the Chagall-related museums (see boxed text, p692). The grand halls of the **Art Museum** (☎ 362 231; vul Lenina 32; admission BR3000; ✆ 11am-6pm Wed-Sun) are decked out with mainly local art, both old and new. There are numerous 18th- to 20th-century works, including those by Repin and Vladimir Egorovic Makovsky. A highlight is the collection of very moving realist scenes of early 20th-century Vitsebsk street life by Yudel Pyen. Of the 793 paintings he donated to the city before he died, only 200 have survived, most of them held here.

A few houses away, past the **town hall** distinguishable by its clock tower, is the **Regional Museum** (☎ 364 712; vul Lenina 36; admission

BELARUS

BR3000; ☿ 11am-6pm Wed-Sun), where you are guaranteed something interesting and thought provoking. There are up to five temporary exhibitions (usually paintings and photography) plus a permanent one full of 11th- to 14th-century artefacts from the city and region.

From here, taking a walk up vul Suvorava and exploring the surrounding side streets is a pleasant way to experience what's left of old Vitsebsk, with some fine 18th and 19th-century buildings and a laid-back old-world ambience.

The **Museum of the Belarusian Army** (☎ 223 972; vul Voinov Internatsionalistov 20; admission BR3000; ☿ by appointment), set up by veterans of the Afghan War, has some touching exhibits on the history of war on Belarusian soil from the 6th century, as well as of Belarusians participating in foreign wars. The museum is difficult to find on your own; take a BR8000 taxi from the centre.

While Vitsebsk does not have many churches of note, there is a pair of very different **Orthodox churches** on the eastern bank of the Dvina, near the main bridge on vul Zamkovaja. These are reconstructions built in 1998 of 10th- (wooden) and 13th-century (white stone) styles. Both hold regular services; the atmospheric wooden church is especially worth visiting.

Festivals & Events
Belarus' best-loved cultural event is held here; the immensely popular **Slavyansky Bazar** (Slavic Bazaar) in mid-July brings together dozens of singers and performers from Slavic countries for a weeklong series of concerts. The annual event attracts tens of thousands of visitors, creating a huge citywide party.

Sleeping
Hotel Dvina (☎ 377 173; vul Ilinskoho 2; s/d BR32,000/45,000) This enormous student residence on the western banks of the Dvina is a great deal. The *Shining*-like endless corridors are creepy, but all rooms have toilet and showers (leaky though they may be).

Hotel Eridan (☎ 362 456; vul Savetskaja 21/17; s/d/ste BR141,000/159,000/267,000) In the quiet old town, this is intimate and upscale. Extremely comfortable and modern, the hotel also boasts an excellent (and expensive) restaurant.

Vetrazh (☎ 217 204; pr Cherniahovsky 25/1; s/d BR72,000/90,000) With 300 beds and the classic concrete look of a huge bomb shelter, the Vetrazh is a standard post-Soviet hotel just south of the city centre (tram 4 from the bus and train stations goes there).

Eating & Drinking
Vitebsky Traktir (☎ 362 957; vul Suvorava 4; mains BR6000-9000) Hands-down the best place in

---

MARC CHAGALL

One of the most important names in 20th-century art, visionary Marc Chagall (1887–1985), often grouped in with the surrealists, was born in Vitsebsk on 7 July 1887. He spent from 1897 to 1910 in what is now the **Marc Chagall House Museum** (☎ 363 468; vul Pokrovskaja 11; admission BR3000; ☿ 11am-7pm Tue-Sun), now charmingly kitted out with early-20th-century Jewish knick-knacks and photos. To get there, turn left when exiting the bus or train station, walk one block, then turn right onto vul 1-ja Krasina. After a block you'll see a fanciful **monument** to the artist; turn left here onto vul Pokrovskaja.

Chagall left Vitsebsk to go on to greater fame in St Petersburg and Moscow, finally settling in Paris from 1923, where he lived until his death, churning out fantastically poetic and often humorous murals and artwork. Many of his pieces reflect the Jewish country life of his childhood, largely influenced by his beloved Vitsebsk.

Nestled in a pretty park, the **Chagall Museum** (☎ 360 387; www.chagall.vitebsk.by; vul Punta 2; admission BR3000; ☿ 11am-7pm Tue-Sun) has two floors filled with 300 original, colourful lithographs (all donations), as well as reproductions of some of his famous paintings, including the infamous murals he did for the Moscow Jewish Theatre, considered so mesmerising that they were banned from the stage for distracting the audience.

There would be more originals at the museum had Soviet authorities accepted Chagall's offer to donate some to the city of his birth; they didn't think much of his art and declined. To get to the museum from Vitsebsk's Regional Museum, head north along vul Suvorava to vul Uritsoho, make a left and walk to the end; the museum will be on your right.

town – once you try it you'll not want to bother looking any further. It boasts charming, cavelike rooms, friendly service and a diverse menu, chock-full of inventive, tasty dishes such as gazpacho.

XXI Vek (☎ 364 913; vul Lenina 40; mains BR4000-9000; ⏱ 11am-3am) With a reputation for being alternative, this restaurant has a slightly underground look and feel, and decent, if unexciting, food. After 11pm on weekends, the place turns into a fun disco with that retro, secretive Eastern European feel that foreigners love. It's also the city's only gay-friendly establishment.

Kafe Teatralnaja (☎ 369 966; vul Zamkovaja 2; mains BR6000-12,000; ⏱ noon-6am) This cavernous, pseudomodern restaurant-disco (after 11pm) has artistic pretensions and attracts a well-to-do over-30 crowd. Its menu is as large as the place itself, and the service slightly starchy.

Getting There & Away

Vitsebsk is on one of the major railway lines heading south from St Petersburg into Ukraine. There are two or three daily trains to Minsk (BR12,000 to BR18,000, 4½ to six hours) and one to St Petersburg (BR95,000, 13 hours). On even-numbered days of the month trains run to Kyiv (BR56,000, 16 hours). There's also a daily train to both Moscow (BR40,000, 11 hours) and Brest (BR25,000, 16 hours), and on odd-numbered days to Hrodna (BR20,000, 12 hours). Domestic electric trains connect Polatsk and Vitsebsk (two hours, BR8000) five times daily, but most southbound or westbound trains also stop at Polatsk.

There are at least seven daily buses and *marshrutky* to Minsk (BR23,000, four to 5½ hours). Buses head two or three times daily to Polatsk (BR8000, two hours).

Getting Around

While Vitsebsk is larger than most other regional centres, the city is pleasant to explore on foot. Buses ply the 1.5km main drag from the bus and train stations into town; get off just after crossing the Dvina and you'll be just 500m from the Art Museum.

TURAU ТУРАЎ

☎ 02353 / pop 2000

At first glance this tiny speck on the map may seem like a dusty village-cum-town; one main road, on which cows and chickens vie for space with tractors and cars. Hard to believe that this was once the seat of the great Principality of Turov, one of the first and main principalities in ancient Kyivan Rus. Here once stood an elaborate fortress, 70 churches, six monasteries and four cathedrals; Turau (Turov in Russian) was a major cultural and educational centre.

Most visitors come here as part of a tour of the nearby Pripyatsky National Park (below) – or to see the town's two magic crosses. In a cemetery near the site of the ancient fortress is a **small cross** that is supposedly rising from the ground at a rate of 1.9cm a year. It's also apparently widening at the same rate, which leads locals to believe that the cross has magical powers. Locals and people from far away now visit the cross to heal themselves or pray.

Another stone cross stands inside the **Vsesvyatskaya church** (vul Leninskaja 95). It reportedly floated upriver from Kyiv and planted itself upright in the Pripet River in Turau 1000 years ago. The cross' unusual appearance inside the wooden church adds an almost pagan touch to the Russian Orthodox surroundings.

The **Regional Museum** (☎ 75375; vul Kirava; admission BR500; ⏱ 8.30am-5.30pm Wed-Sun) is a good source of information on Turau's history. Informal town excursions can be booked from here (as well as from the Pripyatsky National Park, who can also find you a translator; see below), and there is a lovingly designed exhibit on Turau's grand history. This is your best source for the myriad legends about the region – there are enough to fill a book and their mysteriousness will add exponentially to your visit.

The Pripyatsky National Park (below) can arrange accommodation in town, either in a private home or in a guesthouse. See p694 for information on transport to and from Turau.

PRIPYATSKY NATIONAL PARK ПРИПЯТСКИЙ НАЦИОНАЛЬНЫЙ ПАРК

The 82,460 hectares covered by this **national park** (☎ 75644, 75173; vul Leninskaja 127, Turau) offer a unique chance to explore a vast, relatively untouched swath of marshes, swampland and floodplains. As unattractive as 'swamp' might sound, the landscape here is striking, even haunting, and provides a welcome

BELARUS

CHORNOBYL

Most of us don't remember where exactly we were on 26 April 1986. Yet everyone in Belarus, Ukraine and western Russia old enough to remember knows exactly what they were doing when news came that the fourth reactor at the Chornobyl nuclear plant, just a few kilometres south of the Belarusian border, exploded.

Some 70% of Chornobyl's released radioisotopes fell on Belarus (primarily in the Homel and Mahileu districts in the south and east, but caesium-137 fallout was registered in many other regions of the country), contaminating about a quarter of its territory on which 2.2 million people lived. Most continue to live in these regions.

Compounding the lack of proper response by the authorities at the time of the accident and the reports underestimating its dangers, the percentage of Belarus' state budget dealing with lingering aftereffects has been more than halved under Lukashenka's rule, to under 8%. Financial benefits to people living in contaminated areas have been gradually cut, and the government encourages resettlement of effected areas. Scientists and officials who dare speak out about continuing consequences have been intimidated and jailed on trumped-up charges. Fewer children who suffered from the fallout (or whose parents did) are being sent abroad for treatment; Lukashenka has stated that Belarus' children need not be poisoned by Western culture.

The dangers of exposure to radiation for the casual tourist are negligible, even for those who visit areas that experienced fallout (these regions are not covered in this book).

contrast to the stretches of flat, dry fields that cover most of Belarus.

Locals dub the area the 'lungs of Europe' as air currents passing over wetlands are reoxygenated. Flora and fauna particular to wetlands are found here, including more than 800 plant species, some 50 mammal species and more than 200 species of birds. At the **park headquarters & museum** (☎ 75644; vul Leninskaja 127) you can tour a great display of the flora and fauna specific to the area, and make all the arrangements you need. Excursions range from one day to a week, and can include extended fishing, hunting and boating expeditions deep into the marshlands. Cruises on the river are particularly recommended.

Park staff can also put you up at one of their guesthouses in town, arrange accommodation in a private home or, even better, put you up in the middle of the park's nature itself. Several comfy cottages have been kitted out with kitchens and saunas and are set in sublimely peaceful settings. The park organises winter ice-fishing expeditions (followed by vodka and sauna, of course) and many summer activities. Prices vary, but generally a person need only spend about €60 per day, including accommodation, three meals and guided tours.

From the UK, a yearly, eight-day trek throughout the national park can be organised for about £1000 per person via **Nature Trek** (www.naturetrek.co.uk).

Getting There & Away

Transport is tricky. Two buses each day (BR13,000, 6½ hours), plus one early morning *marshrutka,* (BR22,000, four hours) make the long trip to Turau from Minsk's Vostochny bus station. By car, take the P23 south from Minsk until the end, drive east on the M10 for 26km, south on the P88 for 25km, then head west for 6km to Turau. Staff at the park headquarters can also arrange private transport to or from anywhere in Belarus, though it might end up being pricey.

Directory

CONTENTS

RUSSIA

ACCOMMODATION

The choice of accommodation in Russia is constantly improving, with everything from cosy homestays to five-star luxury hotels on offer. You'll occasionally come across hotels (Novosibirsk is infamous) that refuse to let you stay because you're a foreigner, or that will only allow you to stay in the most expensive rooms. Otherwise you can generally stay where you like though beware a few of the cheapest hotels will rarely be able to register your visa.

It's a good idea to book a few nights in advance for Moscow and St Petersburg, but elsewhere it's usually not necessary. Make

PRACTICALITIES

- Russia uses the metric system (see the inside front cover). Menus often list food and drink servings in grams: a teacup is about 200g, a shot-glass 50g. The unit for items sold by the piece, such as eggs, is *shtuka* ('thing' or 'piece') or *sht*.

- Access electricity (220V, 50Hz AC) with a European plug with two round pins. A few places still have the old 127V system. Some trains and hotel bathrooms have 110V and 220V shaver plugs.

- TV channels include Channel 1 (Pervy), Rossiya, NTV, Kultura, Sport, RenTV, STS, MTV-Russia, and Russia Today, an English-language satellite channel. Each region has a number of local channels, while in many hotels you'll have access to CNN and BBC World, plus several more satellite channels in English and other languages.

- Radio is broken into three bands: AM, UKV (66MHz to 77MHz) and FM (100MHz to 107MHz). A Western-made FM radio usually won't go lower than 85MHz. BBC's World Service's short-wave (SW) frequencies in the morning, late evening and night are near 9410kHz, 12,095kHz (the best) and 15,070kHz, though exact settings vary depending on your location; see www .bbc.co.uk/worldservice.

- Russia's main video format, SECAM, is incompatible with the system used in Australia and most of Europe (France and Greece are among the exceptions), and with North America's NTSC.

bookings by email or fax rather than telephone – so you get a written copy of your reservation – and note that many hotels charge a booking surcharge *(bron)* which can be up to 50% of the first night's accommodation rate.

If you're looking for cheaper places to stay, head for the smaller towns or consider a homestay; many travel agencies can arrange these. Inexplicably, twin rooms are occasionally cheaper than singles. Especially in small towns it's often possible to pay half again when only one person is staying (though you may end up sharing with a stranger): ask for *potselenye*.

Camping

Camping in the wild is allowed, except in those areas signposted Не разбивать палатку (No putting up of tents) and/or Не разжигать костры (No camp fires). Check with locals if you're in doubt.

Kempingi (organised camp sites) are rare and usually only open from June to September. Unlike Western camp sites small wooden cabins often take up much of the space, leaving little room for tents. Some *kempingi* are in quite attractive woodland settings, but communal toilets and washrooms are often in poor condition and other facilities few.

Homestays

Taking a room in a private flat, shared with the owners – often referred to as 'bed & breakfast' (B&B) or 'homestay' – enables you to glimpse how Russians really live. Most flats that take in guests are clean and respectable, though rarely large! If you stay in a few you'll be surprised how, despite outward similarities, their owners can make them so different.

Moscow and St Petersburg have organisations specifically geared to accommodating foreign visitors in private flats at around US$20 or US$30 per person, normally with English-speaking hosts, breakfast and other services, such as excursions and extra meals. Many travel agencies and tourism firms in these and other cities can also find you a place for around US$25 per person, but the price may depend on things like how far the flat is from the city centre, whether the hosts speak English, and whether any meals are provided.

It's possible to pay less by staying with one of the people who approach travellers arriving off major trains in Moscow, St Petersburg and other major cities. But be sure you can trust them, establishing how far from the city centre their place is – you'll find many such people are genuine, and just in need of some extra cash. It's better to avoid committing yourself before you actually see the place.

HOMESTAY AGENCIES

The following agencies can arrange homestays mainly in Moscow and St Petersburg (as can some travel agencies; see individual city listings for details). It's worth knowing that your host family usually only gets a small fraction of the price you pay the agent.

Host Families Association (HOFA; ☎ /fax 812-275 1992 in St Petersburg; www.hofa.us)

Interchange (☎ 020-8681 3612 in London; www.interchangeuk.com)

Russian Home Travel (☎ 1-800 861 9335 in the USA; russiahome@aol.com)

Uncle Pasha (www.unclepasha.com)

Way to Russia (www.waytorussia.net/services /accommodation.html)

You can contact many Russian homestay agents from overseas (if you do, check they provide visa support), and can even book through travel agencies in your own country.

Hostels

A hostel movement has yet to emerge across Russia although you will find them in Moscow, St Petersburg and Irkutsk (see the individual city listings for details). For a dorm bed in a hostel you can expect to pay around R600.

Hotels

Russian hotels run the gamut from dirt-cheap flophouses to megabuck five-star palaces. Some hotels have one price for Russians and a higher price for foreigners – this is increasingly rare but there is little you can do about it, even if you arrive with Russian friends. In such cases this book lists the prices hotels charge foreigners.

At most hotels, you can just walk in and get a room on the spot. A few very basic hotels aren't registered for foreign guests or will only take you if you've already registered your visa, though these are fairly rare. In the Soviet era, receptionists had a habit of pretending that their half empty hotels were actually full. These days that classic theatricality is uncommon, though some old-style places do sometimes have a spare room or two salted away for the politely persistent traveller.

PROCEDURES

When you check in practically all hotels will ask to see your passport – most will be able to stamp and register your immigration card (p714) at the same time.

At typical Soviet-style hotels each floor has a *dezhurnaya* (floor lady) who guards the keys for all the rooms in her little kingdom. When the *dezhurnaya*'s dozing or away for lunch you'll be effectively locked out of your room until she deigns to return.

Modern hotels generally have a checkout time (usually noon) as in the west. However, many older Russian hotels charge by *sutki*, ie for a stay of 24 hours. Check which you've paid for before rushing to pack your bags. If you want to store your luggage somewhere safe for a late departure, arrange it with the *dezhurnaya* or front-desk staff.

ROOMS

Most hotels have a range of rooms at widely differing prices. Receptionists tend to automatically offer foreigners the most expensive ones, often feeling quite genuinely that cheaper rooms are 'not suitable'. Fortunately for the budget conscious, there's always a price list displayed (on the wall or in a menu-style booklet on the counter) listing the price for every category. Staff are increasingly obliging about allowing guests to look around before checking in: ask *'Mozhno li posmotret nomer?'* (May I see the room?).

Not all hotels have genuine single rooms and 'single' prices often refer to single occupancy of a double room. Some hotels, mainly in the bottom and lower-middle ranges, have rooms for three or four people where the price per person comes to much less than a single or double. Beds are typically single and where there is a double bed you'll generally pay somewhat more than for a similarly sized twin room.

Hot water supplies are fairly reliable, but since hot water is supplied on a district basis, whole neighbourhoods can be without it for a month or more in summer when the system is shut down for maintenance (the best hotels have their own hot water systems).

A *lyux* room equates to a suite with a sitting room in addition to the bedroom and bathroom. A *polu-lyux* room is somewhat less spacious. Size doesn't always equate to better quality.

Budget

Rooms may have their own toilet, washbasin or shower, or you may have to use facilities shared by the whole corridor. Some places are clean, if musty, and even include a TV or huge, Soviet-era fridge in the rooms; others are decaying, dirty and smelly, and lack decent toilets and washing facilities. Take care with security in some cheap hotels.

A double room with bathroom in a budget hotel in Moscow and St Petersburg will cost anything up to R2500. Elsewhere budget hotels can be as cheap R300 a night with shared facilities, although R600 is a more realistic minimum for many cities.

Midrange

Until recently, Russia had disappointingly few cosy, moderately priced 'minihotels'. This is rapidly changing, however, with a particular boom in St Petersburg, around Lake Baikal and in parts of the Altai region. Elsewhere the midrange niche is filled mostly by Soviet-era hotels. Some are formerly top-rated monsters that are starting to look worn while others are once dismal places which have been given a good facelift. Don't always trust the sparkling new façades, however. Sometimes the rooms have not received the same treatment.

Nonetheless, rooms are usually clean, reasonably comfortable with private bathrooms (standards vary greatly), and there'll be a restaurant along with a bar or *bufet* (snack bar). These are the most common hotels in cities and you'll pay R600 to R1500 for a midrange twin (except in Moscow and St Petersburg, where it's R2500 to R5000).

Top End

Luxury hotels in the major cities are up to the best international standards, with very comfortable rooms boasting satellite TV, minibars, fawning service, fine restaurants, health clubs, and prices to match, from around US$200/400 for singles/doubles. (Prices will usually be quoted in dollars, sometimes euros, and will typically include the 20% VAT, but the 5% local tax will sometimes be on top of that.)

In provincial cities, the 'top end' (where it exists) is composed mainly of the very best Soviet-era tourist hotels, along with the occasional former Communist Party hotel or smaller, newer private ventures.

Expect to pay upwards from R2000, although you may get better prices through a travel agent.

Resting Rooms

Komnaty otdykha (resting rooms) are found at all major train stations and several smaller ones. Generally, they have basic (but often quite clean) shared accommodation with communal sink and toilet. Some have showers but you'll often pay an extra fee to use them. Sometimes there are single and double rooms and, rarely, more luxurious ones with private bathroom. The beds are usually rented by the hour (from R10), half-day (from R120) or 24-hour (from R240) period. Some will ask to see your train ticket before allowing you to stay.

Turbazy, Rest Houses & Sanatoriums

A great way to get a feel for the average Russian's holiday is to book into a *turbaza,* typically a no-frills holiday camp aimed at outdoor types. Cheap, basic accommodation is usually in spartan multiroom wooden bungalows or small huts *(domiky).* Don't expect indoor plumbing. In the Soviet era *turbazy* were often owned by a factory or large company for use by its employees. Many became somewhat decrepit, but these days more and more are privatised and being rebuilt. At some, you can arrange boating, skiing, hiking or mountaineering.

Doma otdykha (rest houses) are similar to *turbazy,* although generally somewhat more luxurious. In peak seasons it's often essential to book through travel agencies in regional cities as demand can be very high.

Sanatoriums *(sanatory),* usually booked through local travel agencies, have professional medical staff on hand to treat your illnesses (real or imagined), design your diet and advise you on correct rest. Generally most are ugly concrete eyesores in otherwise attractive rural or coastal settings. Sanatoriums can be spas, sea resorts (there are several good ones in Sochi), or resorts where you can get some kind of nontraditional treatment (for instance with kumis, fermented mare's milk).

University Accommodation

In Moscow, St Petersburg and other cities with large universities, it's possible to stay in Russian student accommodation, sometimes for as little as R300 a night (the conditions are not unlike the kind you find in hostels and guesthouses). Getting in can sometimes be a bit iffy, dependent upon availability or even the administrator's mood – a student card, and looking like a student, certainly helps.

ACTIVITIES

Russia offers ample opportunities for all the usual outdoor activities such as hiking, skiing and canoeing. There are also some uncommon ones too, such as sweating it out in a *banya* (p71) or zooming up into the stratosphere in a jet plane (p163).

For information about outdoor activities, it's best to inquire locally. There will often be a group of enthusiasts more than happy to share their knowledge and even equipment with a visitor; you might also be able to locate guides for trekking and other activities where detailed local knowledge is essential.

Specialist agencies are listed under the respective activities sections. Give people as much advance warning as possible; even if you can't hammer out all the details, give them an idea of your interests. While there are several professional operations out there, it's best to be flexible, patient, and prepared for things not to go as smoothly as you may hope.

Boating, Canoeing & Rafting

Although the water quality of many rivers discourages even getting near the water, the coasts offer many canoeing and kayaking possibilities. The Solovetsky Islands in northern European Russia are an example of the remote and fascinating places that can be toured by boat during the summer. The Volga River delta, with its fascinating flora and fauna below Astrakhan, is another good place for exploring. In towns and parks with clean lakes, there are usually rowing boats available for rent during the warmer months, with yacht clubs in St Petersburg and Moscow.

Rafting trips can be arranged with agencies in Barnaul, Omsk, Novosibirsk, Kyzyl, Vladivostok, Komsomolsk-na-Amure and Kamchatka. The Altai region offers full-blown expedition-grade rafting but also easy fun splashes possible on a 'turn up' basis.

Agencies offering boating, kayaking and rafting trips include Reinfo in Sochi (p465), Samara Intour in Samara (p417), Nizhny

Novgorod's Team Gorky (p407), and in St Petersburg Solnechny Parus (p269) and Wild Russia (p269).

Cycling

Deteriorated roads and manic drivers are two of the main hazards for cyclists in Russia. Otherwise, rural Russians are quite fascinated with and friendly towards long-distance riders. Just make certain you have a bike designed for the harshest conditions and carry plenty of spare parts. Agencies offering organised bike tours include Ekaterinburg Guide Center (p437) and Urals Expeditions & Tours (p438) in Yekaterinburg, Team Gorky (p407) in Nizhny Novgorod, Monchegorsk's Kola Travel (p379).

Diving

Fancy diving Lake Baikal or within the Arctic Circle? Such specialist trips can be arranged through **Diveworldwide** (☎ 0845-130 6980; www.diveworldwide.com) in the UK. Russian-based dive operators include Aqua-Eco and SVAL (both p563) in Irkutsk, Moscow's **MGU** (Map pp126-7; ☎ 495-105 7799; www .dive.ru/english; Serpukhovsky val 6; Ⓜ Tulskaya) and St Petersburg's Red Shark Dive Club (p269).

Fishing

Serious anglers drool at the opportunity to fish the rivers and lakes of northern Euro-

pean Russia, the Russian Far East and Siberia: Kamchatka is a particular draw, with steelhead fishing in the peninsula reckoned to be the best in the world; see p649.

Start saving up: organised fishing trips in Russia can be heart-stoppingly expensive. While it's possible to go it alone and just head off with rod and tackle, most regions have severe restrictions on fishing so you'd be wise to at least check these out before departure. A curious alternative take is ice fishing for Lake Baikal's unique omul (p563).

See p365 for some specialist agencies with trips to the Kola Peninsula. Other agencies in northern European Russia include Flait in Murmansk (p367), Yug Kola in Apatity (p382), and Umba Discovery (p385) in Umba.

Hiking & Mountaineering

Among the best areas to road-test your hiking boots and climbing skills are the Elbrus area of the Caucasus, the western Ural Mountains, around Lake Baikal, the Altai Mountains and Kamchatka. Before setting off it's especially important to seek out local advice, information and even guides.

Reliable agencies include K2 (Omsk, p504), Kola Travel (Monchegorsk, p379), Lenalp Tours (Elbrus area, p490), Wild Russia (St Petersburg, p269), **Megatest** (☎ 495-126

SAFETY GUIDELINES FOR HIKING

Before embarking on a hike, consider the following:

■ Be sure you're healthy and feel comfortable about hiking for a sustained period. The nearest village in Russia can be vastly further away than it would be in other countries.

■ Get the best information you can about the physical and environmental conditions along your intended route. Russian 'trails' are generally nominal ideas rather than marked footpaths so employing a guide is very wise.

■ Walk only in regions, and on trails, within your realm of experience.

■ Be prepared for severe and sudden changes in the weather and terrain; always take wet-weather gear.

■ Pack essential survival gear including emergency food rations and a leak-proof water bottle.

■ If you can, find a hiking companion. At the very least tell someone where you're going and refer to your compass frequently so you can find your way back.

■ Unless you're planning a camping trip, start early so you can make it home before dark.

■ Allow plenty of time.

■ Consider renting or even buying (then later reselling) a pack horse, especially in southern Siberia where this is fairly inexpensive.

9119 in Moscow; www.megatest.ru), Reinfo (Sochi, p465) and Sibalp (Novosibirsk, p511).

Mineralogical (Rock-Hunting) Tours
This unusual activity in northern European Russia will appeal to the geologically minded. Contact Kola Travel (p379) or Yug Kola (p382) to organise a trip.

Paragliding
The Caucasus is a popular area for this aerial sport. Contact Paraguide in Krasnaya Polyana (p470), and BARS or Tourist Service in Dombay (p482) for more.

Winter Sports
Downhill ski slopes are scattered throughout the country, although cross-country skiing is more common, attracting legions of skiers during the long winters. Given the wealth of open space (even near Moscow), you won't have a problem finding a place to hit the trail. The few sporting goods stores carry decent, inexpensive Russian-made equipment.

For details on resorts across Russia that are particularly good for snowboarding check out www.worldsnowboardguide.com /resorts/russia/.

Russians skate with abandon during the long winter. Outdoor rinks are common and easy to find, and equipment rentals are cheap. There are also many indoor rinks open throughout the year.

Ski resorts include Abzakovo, Asha, Baikalsk, Kirovsk, Krasnaya Polyana and Dombay. Ekaterinburg Guide Center (p437) organises skiing trips around Yekaterinburg.

For snowmobile safaris and activities in the arctic see Kola Travel in Monchegorsk (p379), **Megatest** (☎ 495-126 9119; www.megatest .ru) in St Petersburg, or Yug Kola in Apatity (p382).

BUSINESS HOURS
Usual business hours are listed inside the front cover. Exceptions to this have been noted in individual listings in this book.

Almost all services and businesses post official opening hours on their doors but restaurants will frequently close earlier if there's nobody to serve and museums can be reluctant to let you in anywhere near their closing or lunch hours. Note that exchange operations at banks sometimes have a very different timetable to the posted opening times of the bank itself.

Government offices open from 9am or 10am to 5pm or 6pm weekdays.

In major cities 24-hour kiosks selling food and drink are common. Restaurants typically open from noon to midnight except for a break between afternoon and evening meals.

Museum hours are not uniform, but most commonly they close on Mondays.

CHILDREN
Russians love children and travelling there with them can be fun as long as you come well prepared with a relaxed attitude and a degree of patience. See p171, p272, and p465 for ideas of how to entertain the little ones in Moscow, St Petersburg and Sochi respectively. If you're heading for Siberia, Nikita's on Olkhon Island (p579) has a fantastic kids' playground.

Practicalities
Baby changing rooms are not common and many public toilets you wouldn't want to use yourself, let alone change your baby's nappy in. Instead head back to your hotel, to one of the coffee house chains, or to a fast-food joint where the toilets, while typically small, should be clean. Nappies, powdered milk and baby food are widely available except in very rural areas.

Finding English-language kids' publications will be a challenge, although there's no shortage of toy shops.

Lonely Planet's *Travel with Children* contains useful advice on how to cope with kids on the road and what to bring to make things go more smoothly.

CLIMATE CHARTS
It's no surprise that Russia has long, cold winters. Other seasons do get a look in, though, and summers can be scorchers. See p20 for more information concerning climate and when to go. Sample climate charts follow.

COURSES
Apart from Russian-language courses, there are a handful of other courses that may appeal to those who like to combine travel with learning. In Moscow, Dom Patriarshy Tours (p171) offers a Russian cooking course. In Rostov-Veliky you can learn

about Russian decorative crafts at Khors (p219). And throat singing lessons can be taken at the Khöömei Centre in Kyzyl (p550) by negotiation.

Language

There are plenty of opportunities to study Russian in Russia. The English-language publications in Moscow and St Petersburg regularly carry advertisements for Russian-language schools and tutors. The cost of

formal coursework varies widely, but one-on-one tutoring can be a bargain given the low local wage levels – numerous professors and other highly skilled people are anxious to augment their incomes by teaching you Russian.

Another option for learning Russian is through one of the many international universities operating in Moscow and St Petersburg. These are usually affiliated with a school in either Britain or the USA. Or

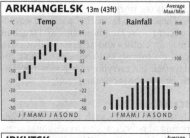

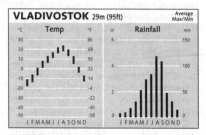

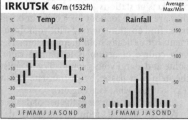

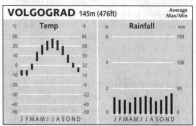

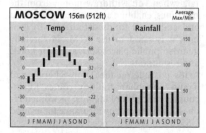

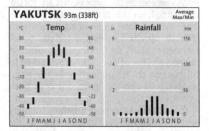

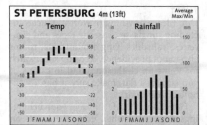

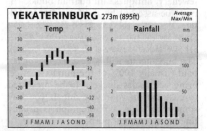

you could take a course through the **Eurolingua Institute** (www.eurolingua.com/russian_in_russia .htm), which offers homestays combined with language courses.

For other specific course recommendations see p170 and p272.

CUSTOMS

Customs controls in Russia are relatively relaxed these days. Searches beyond the perfunctory are quite rare. This said clearing customs, especially when you leave Russia by a land border, can be lengthy. Apart from the usual restrictions, bringing in and out large amounts of cash is limited, although the amount at which you have to go through the red channel changes frequently. At the time of writing visitors are allowed to bring in US$10,000 (or equivalent) in currency and take out US$3000 without making a customs declaration.

On entering Russia you might be given a customs declaration (deklaratsia) on which you should list any currency you are carrying as well as any items of worth. Make sure you list any mobile phones, cameras and laptops to avoid any potential problems on leaving Russia.

It's best if you can get your customs declaration stamped on entry (to do so go through the red lane at the bigger airports) and then simply show the same declaration when you exit Russia. However, sometimes customs points are totally unmanned, so this is not always possible. The system seems to be in total flux, with officials usually very happy for you to fill out declarations on leaving the country if necessary. One of our authors was asked to fill out two copies on leaving Russia to go to Mongolia and was given one copy back as a souvenir!

If you plan to export anything vaguely 'arty' – manuscripts, instruments, coins, jewellery, antiques, antiquarian books – it must be assessed by the **Committee for Culture** (Moscow Map pp132-3; ☎ 495-244 7675; ul Arbat 53; Ⓜ Smolenskaya; St Petersburg Map pp230-1; ☎ 812-311 5196; Malaya Morskaya ul 17; Ⓜ Nevsky Prospekt). The bureaucrats will issue a receipt for tax paid (usually 100% of the purchase price; bring your sales docket), to be presented to customs on your way out. If you buy something large, a photograph is usually fine for assessment purposes.

DANGERS & ANNOYANCES
Crime
STREET CRIME

The streets of big cities such as Moscow and St Petersburg are about as safe (or as dangerous) as those of New York or London: there's petty theft, pickpocketing, purse-snatching and all the other crimes endemic to big cities anywhere. Travellers have reported problems with groups of children who surround foreigners, ostensibly to beg, closing in with dozens of hands probing pockets (or worse).

The key is to be neither paranoid nor insouciant – use common sense and try to fit in: shun clothes and accessories that show you're a tourist; and consider scraping the day pack and carrying your goods in a plastic bag, as the locals do.

SCAMS

Be wary of officials, such as police (or people posing as police), asking to see your papers or tickets at stations – there's a fair chance they are on the lookout for a bribe and will try to find anything wrong with your documents, or basically hold them ransom. The only course of action is to remain calm, polite and stand your ground. Try to enlist the help of a passer-by to translate (or at least witness what is going on).

Another scam involves the use of devices in ATMs that read credit card and PIN details when you withdraw money from the machines, enabling accounts to be accessed and additional funds withdrawn. In general, it is safest to use ATMs in carefully guarded public places such as major hotels and restaurants.

It's possible on the Trans-Siberian and Trans-Mongolian Railway routes to encounter official-looking men or women requesting that you buy insurance for around US$10 – there is no need to do this.

THEFT

Don't leave anything of worth in a car, including sunglasses, cassette tapes and cigarettes. Valuables lying around hotel rooms also tempt providence. At camp sites, watch for items on clotheslines and in cabins. If you stay in a flat, make sure it has a well-bolted steel door.

Generally it's safe to leave your belongings unguarded when using the toilets on

DON'T WORRY ABOUT THE MAFIA

In Russia, 'Mafia' is a broad term encompassing the country's small- and big-time gangsters, as well as the many thousands of corrupt officials, businesspeople, financiers and police. However, they will be the least of your problems while travelling in the country. Despite occasional beat-ups in the Western media, the lawless situation of the early 1990s has largely disappeared – big-time crime's impact on tourists is now pretty much nonexistent.

trains, but you'd be wise to get to know your fellow passengers first.

Dangerous Regions
Check with your government's foreign affairs ministry at home or your embassy in Russia for the latest danger zones. Heading to Chechnya is obviously a dumb idea, as is going to Dagestan another location of civil unrest and general lawlessness; see p492 for more details. Certain very isolated villages suffer from the unpredictable side effects of chronic alcoholism, especially in western Tuva where locals are frequently armed with knives, as well as drunk.

In more remote areas of the country specific natural hazards include bears and, in late May to July, potentially fatal tick-borne encephalitis (particularly in Siberia and Ussuriland in the Russian Far East). And if trekking in Kamchatka, remember many of those volcanoes are volatile.

Transport & Road Safety
See p732 for details on air travel safety and p741 for precautions to take on trains.

Take care when crossing the road in large cities: some crazy drivers completely ignore traffic lights, while others tear off immediately when the lights change (which can be suddenly), leaving you stranded in the middle of the road.

Annoyances
Customer service is certainly improving but the single most annoying thing the majority of travellers encounter in Russia is the combination of bureaucracy and apathy that turns some people in 'service' industries into surly, ill-mannered, ob-

structive goblins. At times you still have to contend with hotel-desk staff struck deaf (or, at best, monosyllabic) by your arrival, as well as shop 'assistants' with strange paralyses that make them unable to turn to face customers. 'What do you want?' is a strange but frequent welcome to provincial museums, as though you'd ended up there by mistake.

Russians also have very specific rules for queuing (holding someone's place in the line while they shop or whatever for several hours is common, as is pushing in at the last minute if you're at the train station, say, and the train is about to go). In most cases, neither politeness nor anger will help. If you have the head for it, sharpen your elbows, learn a few scowling phrases, and plough head first through the throng. Good luck.

Prostitution is common, and unsolicited prostitutes still visit or telephone hotel rooms offering sex; you'll usually be left alone though if you make it clear you're not interested. Be prepared for strip shows, male and female, at many nightclubs and some restaurants.

Racism & Discrimination
Sadly, racism is a problem in Russia; see p75. It's a good idea to be vigilant on the streets around Hitler's birthday (20 April), when bands of right-wing thugs have been known to roam around spoiling for a fight with anyone who doesn't look Russian. Frightening reports of racial violence appear from time to time in the media, and it's a sure thing that if you look like a foreigner you'll be targeted with suspicion by many (the police, in particular). Moscow, St Petersburg and Voronezh have all seen violent attacks on non-Russians.

DISABLED TRAVELLERS
Disabled travellers are not well catered for in Russia. Many footpaths are in poor condition, hazardous even for the mobile. There's a lack of access ramps and lifts for wheelchairs. However, attitudes are enlightened and things are slowly changing. Major museums such as the Hermitage offer good disabled access.

Before setting off get in touch with your national support organisation (preferably with the travel officer, if there is one). The following organisations offer general travel advice:

Australia
Nican (☎ 02-6285 3713; www.nican.com.au; PO Box 407, Curtin, ACT 2605)

UK
Holiday Care Service (☎ 0845-124 9974; www.holidaycare.org.uk; Sunley House, 7th fl, 4 Bedford Park, Croydon, Surrey CR0 2AP)

USA
Accessible Journeys (☎ 800-846 4537; www.disability travel.com) Agency specialising in travel for the disabled.

Mobility International USA (☎ 541-343 1284; www.miusa.org; PO Box 10767, Eugene, Oregon, 974400)

DISCOUNT CARDS
Full-time students and people aged under 26 can sometimes (but not always) get a substantial discount on admissions – always flash your student card or International Student Identity Card (ISIC) before paying. If you're not a student but are under 26, ask a student agency at home for an ISIC Youth Card.

Senior citizens also *might* get a discount, but no promises: carry your pension card or passport anyway.

EMBASSIES & CONSULATES
Russian Embassies & Consulates
Check out www.russianembassy.net for a full list of Russian embassies and consulates overseas. The best advice is to get your Russian visa in your home country – it's practically impossible (ridiculously expensive and time consuming) to get a visa for Russia in China or Mongolia, for example.

Australia (☎ 02-6295 9033; 78 Canberra Ave, Griffith, ACT 2603) Also a consulate in Sydney.

Belarus Minsk Embassy (Map p670; vul Staravilenskaya 48; ☎ 250 3666; fax: 250 3664; M Njamiha); Minsk Consulate (Map p670; ☎ 222 4985; fax 250 3664; vul Gvardeiskaja 5a; M Fruzenskaja); Brest (Map p683; ☎ 0162-25 5670; fax 22 2473; vul Vorovskaha 19)

Canada (☎ 613-235 4341; 285 Charlotte St, Ottawa) Also consulates in Montreal and Toronto.

France (☎ 1-4504 0550; 40-50 Blvd Lannes, 75116 Paris) Also consulate in Marseilles.

Germany (☎ 030-220 2821; Unter den Linden 63-65, 10117 Berlin) Also consulates in Bonn, Hamburg, Leipzig, Munich, Rostock and Strasbourg.

Ireland (☎ 01-492 3525, 492 2048; russiane@indigo.ie; 184-186 Orwell Rd, Rathgar, Dublin 14)

Japan (☎ 03-3583 4224; 2-1-1 Azabudai, Minato-ku, Tokyo 106-0041) Also consulates in Niigata and Sapporo.

Netherlands (☎ 70-345 1300, 345 1301; ambrusnl@euronet.nl; Andries Bickerweg 2, 2517 JP Den Haag)

New Zealand (☎ 04-476 6113; 57 Messines Rd, Karori, Wellington)

UK (☎ 020-7229 3628; fax 7727 8625; www.rusemblon .org; 5 Kensington Palace Gardens, London W8 4QX) Also consulate in Edinburgh.

USA (☎ 202-298 5700; russianembassy@mindspring .com; 2650 Wisconsin Ave, NW, Washington DC 20007) Also consulates in New York, San Francisco and Seattle.

Embassies & Consulates in Russia
If you will be travelling in Russia for a long period of time (say a month or more), and particularly if you're heading to remote locations, it's wise to register with your embassy. This can be done over the telephone or by email. For a full list of embassies in Moscow, check www.themoscowtimes.ru /travel/facts/embassies.html. When calling Kaliningrad, be aware that the telephone area code is ☎ 22 when calling from within the region, and ☎ 4112 when calling from elsewhere.

Australia Moscow Embassy (Map p131; ☎ 495-956 6070, fax 956 6170; www.australianembassy.ru; Podkolokolny per 10A/2; M Kitay-Gorod)

Belarus Moscow Consulate (Map p131; ☎ 495-924 7031; fax 928 6633; Maroseyka ul 17/6, 101000; M Kitay Gorod); Kaliningrad Consulate (Map p346; ☎ 214 412; ul Dm Donskogo 35A); St Petersburg Consulate (Map pp234-5; ☎ 812-273 0078; Office 66, nab Robespiera 8/64; M Chernyshevskaya)

Canada Moscow Embassy (Map pp132-3; ☎ 495-105 6000, fax 105 6025; Starokonnyusheny per 23; M Smolenskaya); St Petersburg Consulate (Map pp236-7; ☎ 812-325 8448; fax 325 8364; Malodetskoselsky pr 32B; M Teknologichesky Institut)

China Moscow Embassy (Map pp126-7; ☎ 495-143 1540; ul Druzhby 6; M); Khabarovsk Consulate (Map p608; ☎ 4212-302 519; fax 328 390; Lenin Stadium 1); St Petersburg Consulate (Map pp236-7; ☎ 812-114 6230; nab kanala Griboedova 134; M Sadovaya/Sennaya Ploshchad); Vladivostok Consulate (Map p615; ☎ 4232-495 037; Hotel Gavan, ul Krygina 3) In Khabarovsk, visa applications are taken from 10.30am to 1pm Monday, Wednesday and Friday. A visa can be arranged in a day for about R4200 or in a week for R2400. In Vladivostok, visa applications are accepted 9am to 12.30pm Monday, Wednesday and Friday. A visa costs about US$125 and takes three to seven days.

Finland Moscow Embassy (Map pp132-3; ☎ 495-246 4220; fax 230 2738; Kropotkinsky per 15/17; M Park Kultury); Murmansk Consulate (Map p366; ☎ 8512-543 275; ul Karla Marksa 25A); Petrozavodsk Consulate (Map p358; ☎ 8142-761 564; Pushkinskaya ul 15); St Petersburg Consulate (Map pp234-5; ☎ 812-273 7321; ul Chaykov-skogo 71; M Chernyshevskaya)

France Moscow Embassy (Map pp132-3; ☎ 495-937 1500, fax 937 1577; www.ambafrance.ru; ul Bolshaya Yakimanka 45; M Oktyabrskaya); St Petersburg Consulate (Map pp230-1; ☎ 812-312 1130; fax 311 7283; nab reki Moyki 15; M Nevsky Prospekt)

Germany Moscow Embassy (Map pp126-7; ☎ 495-937 9500, fax 938 2354; www.germany.org.ru; Mosfilmovskaya ul 56); Kaliningrad Consulate (Map p346; ☎ 326 923; ul Demyana Bednogo 13A); Novosibirsk Consulate (Map p510; ☎ 383-223 1411; www.nowosibirsk.diplo.de, not in English; Krasny pr 28); St Petersburg Consulate (Map pp234-5; ☎ 812-327 2400; fax 327 3117; Furshtatskaya ul F39; M Chernyshevskaya); Yekaterinburg Consulate (Map p438; ☎ 343-359 6399; gk_jeka@yahoo.de; ul Kuybysheva 44)

Ireland Moscow Embassy (Map p131; ☎ 495-937 5911, fax 975 2066; Grokholsky per 5; M Prospekt Mira)

Japan Moscow Embassy (Map pp128–9; ☎ 495-291 8500; fax 200 1240; Kalashny per 12; M Arbatskaya); Khabarovsk Consulate (Map p608; ☎ 4212-326 907; fax 4212-327 212; ul Pushkina 38a); Vladivostok Consulate (Map p615; ☎ 4232-267 513; ul Verkhne-Portovaya 46)

Korea Vladivostok Consulate (Map p615; ☎ 4232-402 222; ul Pologa 19)

Latvia Kaliningrad Consulate (Map p346; ☎ 9022 176 060; Velichavaya ul 2)

Lithuania Kaliningrad Consulate (Map p346; ☎ 959 487; Proletarskaya ul 133)

Mongolia Moscow Embassy (Map pp128-9; ☎ 495-290 6792, 290 3061, 290 6481, 241 1548; Borisoglebsky per 11; M Arbatskaya); Irkutsk Consulate (Map p568; ☎ 3952-342 145; fax 342 143, irconsul@angara.ru; ul Lapina 11; ☽ 9.30am-noon, 2.30-5pm Mon, Tue, Thu & Fri); Ulan-Ude Consulate (Map p590; ☎ 3012-211 078; ul Profsoyuznaya 6; ☽ Mon, Wed & Fri); Kyzyl Consulate (Map p549; ☎ 3942-210 445; ul Internatsionalnaya 9; ☽ 10am-noon, 2-4.30pm Mon-Thu, 10am-1pm Fri) In Kyzyl two-day processing for a single-entry, 20-day visa costs US$25; a double-entry, one-month version is US$50; and a transit visa US$15. Prices are doubled for same-day service. In Irkutsk one month/three-day visas cost US$30/20 processed in nine days, $43/28 in three to six days, $55/45 in two days or $105/85 in 24 hours. Visas for longer stays require invitation letters. Apply for visas from 10am to 12.30pm; collect them at 5pm. In Ulan-Ude, one-month tourist visas cost US$30 issued in nine days, $35 in a week, $45 in two days, $55 same day. Transit visas US$20-35.

Netherlands Moscow Embassy (Map pp128-9; ☎ 495-797 2900, fax 797 2904; Kalashny per 6; M Arbatskaya)

New Zealand Moscow Embassy (Map pp128-9; ☎ 495-956 3579; fax 956 3583; Povarskaya ul 7; www.nzembassy .msk.ru; M Arbatskaya)

Norway Murmansk Consulate (Map p366; ☎ 8152-400 620, 453 879; ul Sofyi Perovskoy 5)

Poland Kaliningrad Consulate (Map p346; ☎ 950 419; polcon@kaliningrad.ru; Kashtanovaya Alleya 51)

Sweden Kaliningrad Consulate (Map p346; ☎ 577 806; Borodinskaya ul 23); Murmansk Consulate (Map p366; ☎ 8152-400 620, 453 879; ul Sofyi Perovskoy 5)

UK Moscow Embassy (Map pp128-9; ☎ 495-956 7200, fax 956 7201; www.britemb.msk.ru; Smolenskaya nab 10; M Smolenskaya); St Petersburg Consulate (Map pp234-5; ☎ 812-320 3200; fax 325 3111; pl Proletarskoy Diktatury 5; M Chernyshevskaya); Vladivostok Consulate (Map p615; ☎ 4232-300 070; ul Pushinskaya 32); Yekaterinburg Consulate (Map p438; ☎ 343-379 4931; britcon@sky.ru; ul Gogolya 15)

Ukraine Rostov-On-Don Consulate (☎ 8632-262 5789; ul Seraphimovicha 25; ☽ 9am-noon & 1-4pm Mon-Fri)

USA Moscow Embassy (Map pp128-9; ☎ 495-728 5000, fax 728 5090; http://moscow.usembassy.gov/; Bolshoy Devyatinsky per 8; M Barrikadnaya); St Petersburg Consulate (Map pp234-5; ☎ 812-275 1701; fax 110 7022; ul Furshtatskaya 15; M Chernyshevskaya); Yekaterinburg Consulate (Map p438; ☎ 343-379 4691; www.uscgyekat .ur.ru; ul Gogolya 15)

FESTIVALS & EVENTS

January
Russian Orthodox Christmas (Rozhdestvo; 7 January) Begins with midnight church services.

February to April
Pancake Week (Maslenitsa; late February and/or early March) Folk shows and games celebrate the end of winter, with lots of pancake eating before Lent (pancakes were a pagan symbol of the sun).

Winteriada: International Baikal Nordic Games Festival (www.winteriada.ru/) Winter games festival held near Irkutsk from February to March.

Tibetan Buddhist New Year (Tsagaalgan) A movable feast lasting 16 days, Tsagaalgan celebrates the lunar new year and hence advances by about 10 days annually. It's mainly celebrated at family level in Buryatiya and Tuva, where it's known as Shagaa.

Festival of the North (last week of March) Murmansk and other northern towns hold reindeer races, ski marathons and so on; see p368 for more information.

Easter (Pashka; March/April) The main festival of the Orthodox Church year. Easter Day begins with celebratory midnight services. Afterwards, people eat *kulichy* (dome-shaped cakes) and *paskha* (curd cake), and may exchange painted wooden

Easter eggs. The devout deny themselves meat, milk, alcohol and sex during Lent's 40-day pre-Easter fasting period.

May
Victory Day (9 May) A public holiday celebrating the end of WWII, or what Russians call the Great Patriotic War. Big military parades are held in Moscow and St Petersburg and are well worth attending.
Graduates Day (traditionally 25 May) A day for those finishing school, who parade about their hometowns in traditional student garb.

June
Glinka Festival (1–10 June) In the composer's hometown of Smolensk, an annual festival (p325) is held in Mikhail Glinka's honour.
Stars of the White Nights Festival (June) Involves general merrymaking and staying out late, as well as a dance festival in Russia's cultural capital, St Petersburg.
Tun-Payram (Opening-of-Summer-Pastures Festival) With traditional food, costumes and sports, this festival is celebrated in Askiz (p545), usually on the first or second Sunday of the month, and then in villages.
Ysyakh (around 22 June) Eat traditional food while watching local sports and spectacular costumed reenactments of battles near Yakutsk (p629).

July
Maitreya Buddha Festival Held at Ivolginsk *datsan* (monastery) near Ulan-Ude.
Buryatiya Folk Festival Celebrated at the hippodrome near the ethnographic museum in Ulan-Ude; highlights include horse-riding and wrestling.

August
Naadym The main summer festival in Tuva (p547) with *khuresh* (Tuvan wrestling), long-distance horse racing and throat-singing.

November
National Reconciliation Day (7 November) The old Great October Socialist Revolution Anniversary – still a big day for Communist Party marches. Otherwise, monarchists mourn and others drink while closing down their dachas for winter.

December
Sylvester and New Year (31 December & 1 January) The main winter and gift-giving festival, when gifts are put under the *yolka*, (traditional fir tree). See out the old year with vodka and welcome in the new one with champagne while listening to the Kremlin chimes on TV.
Russian Winter Festival Features tourist-oriented *troika* (horse-drawn sleigh) rides and folklore performances at Irkutsk through into January.

FOOD
Dining options throughout Russia have improved immeasurably over recent years and you should have little problem in most parts of the country finding somewhere or something decent to eat; see p112 for more details.

Restaurant and café listings in this book give an indication of how much you'll pay for a main course or a meal (with starter and drink). In general for a budget meal you'll be looking at R100 or less, with a midrange place costing around R500 and top end places over R1000.

GAY & LESBIAN TRAVELLERS
While girls holding hands and drunken men showing affection towards each other are common sights throughout Russia, open displays of same-sex love are not condoned. In general, however, the idea of homosexuality is well tolerated (particularly by the urban younger generation), although overt gay behaviour is frowned upon.

There are active gay and lesbian scenes in both Moscow and St Petersburg, and newspapers such as the *Moscow Times* and *St Petersburg Times* feature articles and listings on gay and lesbian issues, clubs, bars and events (although you shouldn't expect anything nearly as organised as you might find in other major world centres). Away from these two major cities, the gay scene tends to be much less open – and in fact even in Moscow, the founder of the Gay & Lesbian Archive (a centre for gay literature and writing) prefers to remain anonymous for fear of being sacked from her regular job.

For a good overview, visit www.gay.ru /english, with up-to-date information, good links and a resource putting you in touch with personal guides for Moscow and St Petersburg. St Petersburg's **Krilija** (Wings; ☎ 812-312 3180; www.krilija.sp.ru) is Russia's oldest officially registered gay and lesbian community organisation.

Cracks in the Iron Closet: Travels in Gay & Lesbian Russia, by David Tuller and Frank Browning, is a fascinating account of modern Russia's gay and lesbian scene. A combination of travel memoir and social commentary, it reveals an emerging homosexual culture surprisingly different from its US counterpart.

HOLIDAYS
Public Holidays
New Year's Day 1 January
Russian Orthodox Christmas Day 7 January
International Women's Day 8 March
International Labour Day/Spring Festival 1 & 2 May
Victory Day (1945) 9 May
Russian Independence Day (when the Russian republic of the USSR proclaimed its sovereignty in June 1991) 12 June
Unity Day 4 November

Many businesses are also closed from 1 to 5 January. Other widely celebrated holidays are Defenders of the Motherland Day (23 February) and Easter Monday.

School Holidays
Russia's academic year runs from September to June with major school breaks around the end of December through to the beginning of January, and typically also in April and May for the Easter, International Labour Day and Victory Day holidays.

INSURANCE
It's wise to take out travel insurance to cover theft, loss and medical problems. There are many policies available, so check the small print for things like ambulance cover or an emergency flight home. Note: some policies specifically exclude 'dangerous activities', which can include scuba diving, motorcycling and trekking.

You may prefer for the insurance policy to provide for payment to doctors or hospitals directly, rather than having you paying on the spot and claiming it back later (if you do have to claim the money back later, make sure you keep all documentation). Some policies ask you to call back (reverse charge) to a centre in your home country, where an immediate assessment of your problem is made.

INTERNET ACCESS
Internet cafés are common across Russia – all but the smallest towns have connections. The best place to start is the main post office or telephone office, as they often have the cheapest rates (typically around R28.80 an hour.

Wireless Internet (wi-fi) is becoming more common, particularly in Moscow and St Petersburg, where several bars and regular cafés have it as well as many top-end hotels. Go to the Russian-language website www.intel.com/products/services/emea/rus/mobiletechnology/unwire/hotspots.htm for a listing of wi-fi hotspots in the major cities.

There are several connection options if you have your own computer:
- Regular dial-up – some hotels will sell you an 'Internet card'; it's just like a phonecard and sometimes the same can be used for both. Use the number listed on the card to connect via a land line to slow-speed Internet. These cards can also be bought in the same places telephone cards are bought.
- Via high-speed link – many business and top-end hotels have high-speed links and many provide the connection cords you'll need for your computer.
- Via wi-fi.

For both high-speed and wi-fi check with the hotel to see whether this is free or whether you pay an hourly or daily rate – at some hotels, particularly top-end ones, the rates charged can be ridiculous.

To access your home account, you'll need your incoming (POP or IMAP) mail server name, your account name, and your password; your ISP or network supervisor will be able to give you these. It also pays to become familiar with the process for accessing mail from a net-connected machine before you leave home.

See p22 for a list of useful Russian web resources.

LAUNDRY
While self-service laundries are almost unheard of in in Russia, you can get laundry done in most hotels: ask the floor attendant. It usually takes at least a day and costs around R200 a load, but if you plan on doing it yourself, bring along a universal sink plug.

LEGAL MATTERS
In general it's best to avoid contact with the myriad types of police. Some are known to bolster their puny incomes by robbing foreigners – either outright or through sham 'fines'. If you do need police assistance (ie you've been the victim of a robbery or an assault) it's best to go to a station with a

---

COMING OF AGE

- Russians can vote once they're 18.
- The legal age for driving is 18.
- The legal drinking age is 18.
- Both heterosexual and homosexual sex is legal at 16.

Russian for both language and moral support. You will have to be persistent and patient, too.

Arrest

If you are arrested, the Russian authorities are obliged to inform your embassy or consulate immediately and allow you to communicate with it without delay. Although you can insist on seeing an embassy or consular official straight away, you can't count on the rules being followed, so be polite and respectful towards officials and hopefully things will go far more smoothly for you. In Russian, the phrase 'I'd like to call my embassy' is *'Pozhaluysta, ya khotel by pozvonit v posolstvo moyey strany'*. Note there is zero tolerance for alcohol consumption by drivers.

MAPS

Moscow and St Petersburg maps are available from many outlets in the respective cities, and outside the country. Russian country maps are also readily available. For other city maps, as well as detailed regional maps useful for hiking and other activities,

---

RUSSIAN STREET NAMES

We use the Russian names of all streets and squares in this book to help you when deciphering Cyrillic signs and asking locals the way. To save space the following abbreviations are used:

bul – bulvar бульвар – boulevard
nab – naberezhnaya набережная – embankment
per – pereulok переулок – side street
pl – ploshchad площадь – square
pr – prospekt проспект – avenue
ul – ulitsa улица – street
sh – shosse шоссе – road

---

the choices are limited – check this book's listings for each individual destination.

Good overseas sources for maps:

Australia
Mapland (☎ 03-9670 4383; www.mapland.com.au; 372 Little Bourke St, Melbourne)
Travel Bookshop (☎ 02-9261 8200; www.travelbooks .com.au; Shop 3, 175 Liverpool St, Sydney)

France
Librairie Ulysse (☎ 01-43 25 17 35; www.ulysse.fr in French; 26 rue Saint Louis en L'Isle, 75004, Paris)

UK
Stanfords Map Centre (☎ 020-7836 1321; www .stanfords.co.uk; 12-14 Long Acre, London)

USA
Map Link (☎ 1-800 962 1394; www.maplink.com; Unit 5, 30 S La Patera Lane, Santa Barbara, CA)

MONEY

We've listed most prices in this book in roubles (abbreviated to R), with the main exceptions being some (but not all) hotel prices, which are often quoted in US dollars and tied to that currency. A few hotels and tour agencies quote in euros (€).

Consult the inside front cover for a table of exchange rates and refer to p20 for information on costs.

For rules on taking money in or out of the country, see p702.

ATMs

ATMs, linked to international networks such as AmEx, Cirrus, MasterCard and Visa, are common right across Russia – look for signs that say *bankomat* (БАНКОМАТ). Using a credit card or the debit card you use in ATMs at home, you can obtain cash as you need it – usually in roubles, but sometimes in dollars, too.

If you are going to rely on ATMs, make certain you have a few days' supply of cash at hand in case you can't find a machine to accept your card. Memorise PINs for all cards you intend to carry and check p704 for information on ATM scams.

Black Market

Don't risk changing money on the street – there are plenty of exchange bureaus and banks where you'll get a decent rate. Should some shadowy character offer to exchange money for you, remember that they can't give you a substantially better rate than banks and still make a profit.

Credit Cards

Across Russia credit cards are becoming more accepted, but don't rely on them outside of the major cities. Most sizable cities have banks or exchange bureaus that will give you a cash advance on your credit card, but be prepared for paperwork in Russian.

Currency

The Russian currency is the rouble (*ru*-bl), written as 'рубль' and abbreviated as 'ру' or 'р'. There are 100 kopecks in a rouble and these come in coin denominations of one (rarely seen), five, 10 and 50. Also issued in coins, roubles come in amounts of one, two and five, with banknotes in values of 10, 50, 100, 500 and 1000 roubles. Finding change can sometimes be a problem – while it's wise to hang on to a stash of smaller notes and coins, be insistent at shops, restaurants and so on if the staff are doubtful about giving change for larger notes.

It's illegal to make purchases in any currency other than roubles. When you run into prices in dollars (or the pseudonym 'units', often written as 'ye' – the abbreviation for *uslovnye yedenitsy*, conventional units) or euros in expensive restaurants and hotels you will still be presented with a final bill in roubles.

Exchanging Money

You'll usually get the best exchange rates for US dollars, though euros are increasingly widely accepted and in rare cases get even better rates, for instance in bigger cities where there's a specialist bank. British pounds are sometimes accepted in big cities, but the exchange rates are not so good; other currencies incur abysmal rates and are often virtually unchangeable.

Any currency you bring should be pristine: banks and exchange bureaus do not accept old, tatty bills with rips or tears. For US dollars make certain they are the new design, with the large offset portrait, and are looking and smelling newly minted.

Carrying around wads of cash isn't the security problem you might imagine. Divide your money into three or four stashes

hidden out of view about your person, and take solace in the fact that nowadays there are a lot of Russians with plenty more money on them than you.

Every town of any size will have at least one bank or exchange office – be prepared to fill out a lengthy form and show your passport. Your receipt is for your own records as customs officials no longer require documentation of your currency transactions. As anywhere, rates can vary from one establishment to the next so it's always worth shopping around.

International Transfers

Larger cities will have at least one bank that can handle Western Union money wires. Ask at any bank for this information – they will be happy to steer you to a bank in town that can handle wire transfers.

Taxes

Value Added Tax (VAT, or NDS in Russian) is 20% and is usually included in the listed price for purchases – ask to make sure. In Moscow and St Petersburg there's also a 5% sales tax, usually only encountered in top hotels.

Tipping & Bargaining

Tipping is common in the better restaurants, about 10%; elsewhere, 5% to 10% is fine. It's accepted practice to tip your guide, if you have one, at around US$5 to US$10 a day; a small gift (skin cream, imported chocolates, CDs) is appropriate if service is especially good.

Prices in stores are usually firm; for goods at markets and souvenir stalls, make a counter bid somewhat lower than the merchant's price. Russia is not really the place for protracted haggling.

Travellers Cheques

It can be difficult to exchange travellers cheques outside the largest cities and the process can be lengthy, involving trips to numerous different cashiers in the bank, each responsible for a different part of the transaction. Expect to pay 1% to 2% commission. Unless you spend all your time in Moscow and St Petersburg, it is not a good idea to carry your fortune in travellers cheques – you might not be able to use them.

Not all travellers cheques are treated as equal by those Russian establishments that are willing to handle them. In descending order of acceptance the favourites are American Express (AmEx), Thomas Cook and Visa; you'll have little or no luck with other brands. The most likely bank to cash travellers cheques is Sberbank, with branches in all the major cities.

PHOTOGRAPHY

Film & Equipment

Any town or city will have several photographic shops where you can download digital snaps to CD, and buy memory cards and major brands of print film. Slide film is not widely sold so bring plenty of rolls with you. The same rare specialist shops that sell slide film will also have a smattering of camera gear by leading brands such as Nikon and Canon.

Photographing People

As anywhere, use good judgement and discretion when taking photos of people. It's always better to ask first and if the person doesn't want to be photographed, respect their privacy; a lifetime living with the KGB may make older people uneasy about being photographed, although a genuine offer to send on a copy can loosen your subject up. Remember that many people will be touchy if you photograph 'embarrassments' such as drunks, run-down housing and other signs of social decay.

In Russian, 'May I take a photograph of you?' is *'Mozhno vas sfotografirovat?'*.

Restrictions

You should be particularly careful about photographing stations, official-looking buildings and any type of military-security structure – if in doubt, don't snap! Travellers, including an author of this book, have been arrested for such innocent behaviour.

Some museums and galleries forbid flash pictures, some ban all photos and most will charge you extra to snap away. Some caretakers in historical buildings and churches charge mercilessly for the privilege of using a still or video camera.

Technical Tips

Avoid running films through airport X-ray machines. No matter what the attendant says, these machines are not film-safe: effects are cumulative and too much will fog your pictures. Lead 'film-safe' pouches help, but the best solution is to have your film and camera inspected by hand. You can minimise officials' annoyance by having all film in clear plastic bags.

Camera batteries get sluggish in the cold, so carry your camera inside your coat and keep spare batteries warm in your pocket. Film gets brittle at very low temperatures and a motor drive's fast advance or rewind can break it and leave static marks. Frame-filling expanses of snow come out a bit grey unless you deliberately *overexpose* about one-half to one stop. Deep cold can play tricks with exposure, so 'bracket' your best pictures with additional shots about one stop underexposed and overexposed each.

Avoid magenta-tinted pictures by protecting your film from fierce summer heat. Leave it at the hotel, or line a stuff-sack with a piece cut from an aluminised Mylar 'survival blanket' – your film will stay cool inside all day.

For more professional tips on taking decent photos, read Lonely Planet's *Travel Photography,* by Richard I'Anson.

POST

Pochta (ПОЧТАМТ) refers to any post office, *glavpochtamt* to a main post office, and *mezhdunarodny glavpochtamt* to an international one. The main offices are open from 8am to 8pm or 9pm Monday to Friday, with shorter hours on Saturday and Sunday; in big cities one office will possibly stay open 24 hours a day.

Sending Mail

Outward post is slow but fairly reliable; if you want to be certain, use registered post (*zakaznaya pochta*). Airmail letters take two to three weeks from Moscow and St Petersburg to the UK, longer from other cities, and three to four weeks to the USA or Australasia. To send a postcard or letter anywhere in the world costs R10 or R14, respectively.

You can address outgoing international mail just as you would in any country, in your own language, though it might help to *precede* the address with the country name in Cyrillic.

Some Cyrillic country names:

America (USA)	Америка (США)
Australia	Австралия
Canada	Канада
France	Франция
Germany	Германия
Great Britain	Великобритания
Ireland	Ирландия
New Zealand	Новая Зеландия

In major cities you can usually find the services of at least one of the international express carriers, such as FedEx or DHL.

Incoming mail is so unreliable that many companies, hotels and individuals use private services with addresses in Germany or Finland (a private carrier completes the mail's journey to its Russian destination). Other than this, your *reliable* options for receiving mail in Russia are nil: there's no poste restante and embassies and consulates won't hold mail for transient visitors.

If sending mail to Russia or trying to receive it, note that addresses should be in reverse order: Russia (Россия), postal code (if known), city, street address, then name.

SHOPPING

Russia offers plenty of attractive souvenirs, if you know where to look – the shopping sections in each chapter will help. Most regions have some local craft specialities (see p95) and, of course, vodka is available everywhere: see p110 for some recommendations of what to buy.

Traditional Souvenirs

Few visitors leave Russia without buying a *matryoshka* (a set of wooden dolls nesting within dolls). In recent years they have become something of a true folk art, with all manner of intricate painted designs. Hunt around because sometimes *matryoshki* can be seedy little things, poorly painted dolls depicting Soviet and Russian leaders, the Keystone Cops – you name it. Small, mass-produced sets go for just a couple of dollars, but the best examples of the craft could set you back US$100. For this price you can also take along a family photograph to Moscow's Izmaylovsky Park (p185) market. Come back the following week to collect your very own personalised *matryoshka* set.

Quality is similarly varied with the enamelled wooden boxes known as *palekh* (after the town east of Moscow where they originated), each with an intricate scene painted on its lid – but they're usually even more expensive. Several hundred dollars are asked for the best. Cheaper but cheerful are the gold, red and black wooden bowls, mugs and spoons from Khokhloma, a bit further east, which are widely available.

Another attractive Russian craft is the blue-and-white ornamental china called *gzhel* (after its home town, east of Moscow).

The trademark Russian textile is the 'babushka scarf' – officially the Pavlovsky Posad kerchief (*pavlovoposadsky platok*), again named after its home town east of Moscow. These fine woollen scarves with floral designs go for R500 or more in shops, but you may find cheaper ones in markets. Other Russian textiles include wool shawls so fine they look almost like lace, and flax products (tablecloths, clothes, dolls) in Smolensk.

Other regional specialities including: amber (*yantar*) from the Baltic coast (though beware of fake stuff in St Petersburg and Moscow markets and shops) – a good necklace or ring might be US$50 to US$200; big hairy Cherkessian hats and domed felt Georgian hats in the Caucasus; intricately beautiful *beresta* bark boxes from across Siberia; and bone carvings, a speciality of Tobolsk.

Other Items

Russia is one of the world's largest markets for bootleg recorded music, videos and computer software – you'll find all manner of pirated versions on sale in kiosks, underground passageways, markets and all kinds of stores. Just remember, you get what you pay for with such black market products. Be especially wary of cheap software; it's rumoured that 75% of all computer program CD-ROMs sold in Russia have a defect or virus on them.

More souvenir ideas: paintings from street artists and art markets (there's some talent amid the kitsch); art and children's books from bookshops; posters, both old Socialist exhortation and modern social commentary, from bookshops or specialist poster (*plakat*) shops; and little Lenin busts at street stands and in tourist markets.

DIRECTORY

TELEPHONE & FAX

Fax
Faxes can be sent from most post offices and the better hotels.

Telephone
Russian city codes are listed in this book under the relevant section heading. The country code for Russia is ☎ 7.

Local calls from homes and most hotels are free. To make a long-distance call from most phones first dial ☎ 8, wait for a second dial tone, then dial the city code and phone number. To make an international call dial ☎ 8, wait for a second dial tone, then dial ☎ 10, then the country code etc. See boxed text, below, for details of future changes to this system, though. Some phones are for local calls only and won't give you that second dial tone.

From mobile phones, just dial + then the country code to place an international call.

MOBILE PHONES
A mobile phone revolution has occurred across Russia in the past few years. There are several large networks, including Beeline, Megafon, MTS and Skylink, most of which operate on the pay-as-you-go system. However, beware that depending on the SIM card you opt for, you might only be able to call from local parts of the network. Reception is increasingly spreading to more rural areas and is already available right along the Trans-Siberian Railway. MTS probably has the widest network at the time of writing.

To call a mobile phone from a landline, the line must be enabled to make paid (ie

---

CHANGING TELEPHONE NUMBERS

Russian authorities have an annoying habit of frequently changing telephone numbers, particularly in cities. We've listed the correct phone number as at the time of research, but it's likely that some will change during the lifetime of this book. All city codes that used to start with zero (chiefly in and around Moscow and Kaliningrad) have now substituted a 4 for the initial 0. The reason for this is that in 2007/2008 intercity and international connection codes will be changed to 0 and 00 respectively (from the current 8 and 8 + 10).

---

nonlocal) calls. SIM and phone call-credit top-up cards, available at any mobile phone shop and costing as little as US$15, can be slotted into your regular mobile phone handset during your stay. Call prices are very low within local networks, but charges for roaming larger regions can mount up; cost-conscious locals switch SIM cards when crossing regional boundaries.

PAY PHONES
Taksofon (pay phones, ТАКСОФОН) are located throughout most cities, usually in working order. Most take prepaid phonecards. There are several types of cardphones, and not all cards are interchangeable. Cardphones can be used for either local and domestic calls, or for international long-distance calls.

PHONECARDS & CALL CENTRES
Local phonecards (*telefonnaya karta*), in a variety of units, are available from shops and kiosks everywhere and metro stations in Moscow and St Petersburg, and can be used to make local, national and international calls.

Sometimes better value for international calls is a call centre, where you give the clerk the number you want to call, pay a deposit and then go to the booth you are assigned to make the call. Afterwards you either pay the difference or collect your change. Such call centres are common in Russian cities and towns – ask for *mezhdunarodny telefon*.

TIME
From Kaliningrad in the west to Kamchatka in the far east, the time in Russia varies in a 10-hour range around the standard time calculated from Moscow. From the early hours of the last Sunday in September to the early hours of the last Sunday in March, Moscow is GMT/UTC plus three hours. From the last Sunday in March to the last Sunday in September, 'summer time' is in force: GMT/UTC plus four hours.

The following international relationships will be wrong by an hour for short periods, as other cities change to 'summer time' on different dates. See p768 for a map showing the world's time zones. When it's noon in Moscow and St Petersburg, the time in other cities around Russia and the world is:

TRAIN TIME

It's important to remember that Russian train timetables (except for suburban services) are generally written according to Moscow time everywhere. Station clocks in most places are also set to Moscow time. In this guide we list how far ahead cities and towns are of Moscow time, eg ☽ Moscow +5hr, meaning five hours ahead of Moscow.

- Tbilisi and Samara   1pm
- Tyumen   2pm
- Novosibirsk   3pm
- Irkutsk   4pm
- Ulan-Ude and Beijing   5pm
- Chita   6pm
- Vladivostok and Sydney   7pm
- Magadan   8pm
- Kamchatka and Auckland   9pm
- San Francisco   1am
- New York   4am
- London   9am
- Paris and Berlin   10am
- Kaliningrad, Helsinki and Minsk   11am

TOILETS

Pay toilets are identified by the words платный туалет (*platny tualet*). In any toilet Ж (*zhensky*) stands for women's, while M (*muzhskoy*) stands for men's.

In cities, you'll find clusters of temporary plastic toilets in popular public places, although other public toilets are rare and often dingy and uninviting. A much better option are the loos in major hotels or in modern food outlets such as McDonald's.

In all public toilets, the babushka you pay your R5 to R10 to can also provide miserly rations of toilet paper; it's always a good idea to carry your own.

TOURIST INFORMATION

Tourist offices as you may be used to elsewhere are extremely rare in Russia; the best we've found is in Novgorod (p329). Moscow doesn't have one at all, and the one for St Petersburg is barely worth bothering with. And, that's about it folks, for tourist offices in the world's largest country!

Instead you're mainly dependent for information on the moods of hotel receptionists and administrators, service bureaus and

travel firms. The latter two exist primarily to sell accommodation, excursions and transport – if you don't look like you want to book something, staff may or may not answer questions.

Russia has no overseas tourist offices and most of its consulates and embassies have little practical information. Travel agencies specialising in Russian travel can be useful (see p729).

VISAS

Everyone needs a visa to visit Russia and it's likely to be your biggest single headache in organising a trip there, so allow yourself at least a month before you travel to secure one. There are several types of visa, but for most travellers a tourist visa (single or double entry and valid for a maximum of just 30 days from the date of entry), will be sufficient. If you plan to stay longer than a month, it's best to apply for a business visa. The good news is that these days getting a visa is, usually (but not always), a straightforward process. The process has three stages – invitation, application and registration.

Invitation

To obtain a visa, you first need an invitation. Hotels and hostels will usually issue anyone staying with them an invitation (or 'visa support') free or for a small fee (typically around US$30). If you are not staying in a hotel or hostel, you will need to buy an invitation – costs typically range from US$10 to US$30. This can be done through most travel agents and online through websites such as www.waytorussia.com, www.expresstorussia.com and www.russiadirect.co.uk – all can also help arrange invitation letters for business visas (p714). Also some hotels and hostels issue invites for the equivalent cost of one night's accommodation with them.

Note that if you are flying directly from abroad into any of the following cities, special invitation rules may apply (see www.waytorussia.net/russianvisa/types.html for more details): Barnaul, Kaliningrad, Kazan, Khabarovsk, Irkutsk, Murmansk, Nizhny Novgorod, Omsk, Petropavlovsk-Kamchatsky, Petrozavodsk, Pyatigorsk, Rostov-on-Don, Samara, Ufa, Vladivostok and Yuzhno-Sakhalinsk.

DIRECTORY

Application

Invitation in hand you can then apply for a visa at any Russian embassy. Costs vary – anything from US$20 to US$200 – depending on the type of visa applied for and how quickly you need it. Rather frustratingly, Russian embassies are practically laws unto themselves, each with different fees and slightly different application rules – avoid potential hassles by checking well in advance what these rules might be. It's also best to apply for your visa in your home country rather than on the road: trans-Mongolian travellers should note that attempting to get visas for Russia in both Beijing and Ulaan Baatar can be a frustrating, costly and ultimately fruitless exercise.

Registration

On arrival in Russia, you will need to fill out an immigration card – a long white form issued at passport control throughout the country. You surrender one half of the form immediately to the passport control, while the other you keep for the duration of your stay and give up only on exiting Russia. Take good care of this as you'll need it for registration and could face problems while travelling in Russia, and certainly will on leaving, if you cannot produce it.

You must register your visa within three working days of arrival. Registration essentially means getting a stamp on the immigration card from your hotel or hostel. Note that the very cheapest places sometimes can't oblige. Novosibirsk is notorious for forcing visitors into overpriced hotels to get that registration stamp, so it makes a bad arrival point.

If staying in nonhotel accommodation, you'll need to pay a travel agency (about US$30) to register your visa for you (most agencies will do this through a hotel). Every time you move city or town and stay for more than three days it's necessary to get another stamp on the immigration card. There's no need to be overly paranoid about this but the more stamps you have on the card the safer you'll be. Also keep all transport tickets (especially if you spend nights sleeping on trains) to prove to any overzealous police officers exactly when you arrived in a new place.

Registrations are regularly checked in Moscow by fine-hungry cops who lurk around train stations and other places hoping to catch tourists too hurried or disorganised to be able to explain long gaps in their registration. Also note that application and registration rules for trips to the Altai (p526) are slightly different.

VISA AGENCIES

If you're really pressed for time, or especially badly affected by impersonal bureaucracies, there are agencies that specialise in getting visas. In the USA, try **Zierer Visa Services** (☎ 1-866 788 1100; www.zvs.com) which has offices in Chicago, Houston, New York, San Francisco and Washington DC, as well as London in the UK.

In the UK, **Thames Consular Services** (☎ 020-7494 4957; www.visapassport.com; 3rd fl, 35 Piccadilly, London) charges from £50 (plus VAT) on top of the Russian visa fees.

Types of Visa

Apart from the tourist visa, other types of visas could be useful to travellers.

BUSINESS VISA

A business (or commercial) visa supported by a Russian company is far more flexible and desirable for the independent traveller than a tourist visa. These can be issued for three months, six months or two years, and are available as single-entry, double-entry or multiple-entry visas.

To obtain a business visa you must have a letter of invitation from a registered Russian company guaranteeing to provide accommodation during the entire length of your stay, and a covering letter from your company (or you) stating the purpose of your trip. **Way to Russia** (www.waytorussia.net), **Express to Russia** (www.expresstorussia.com) and **Russia Direct** (www.russiadirect.co.uk) can arrange this for you.

TRANSIT VISA

This is for 'passing through', which is loosely interpreted. For transit by air it's usually good for 48 hours. For a nonstop Trans-Siberian Railway journey it's valid for 10 days, giving westbound passengers a few days in Moscow; those heading east, however, are not allowed to linger in Moscow.

Visa Extensions & Changes

The Interior Ministry's passport and visa agency is called the PVU (Passportno-Vizovoye Upravleniy), although you'll still often hear the old acronym OVIR used. It's to this agency that you must apply if you wish to extend or change your visa.

Extensions are time consuming, if not downright difficult; tourist visas can't be extended at all. Try to avoid the need for an extension by asking for a longer visa than you might need. Note that many trains out of St Petersburg and Moscow to Eastern Europe cross the border after midnight, so make sure your visa is valid up to and including this day. Don't give border guards any excuses for making trouble.

WOMEN TRAVELLERS

Russian women are very independent and in general you won't attract attention by travelling alone as a female. Sexual harassment on the streets is rare, but be prepared for it elsewhere. Any young or youngish woman alone in (or near) flashy bars full of foreigners risks being mistaken for a prostitute. A woman alone should also certainly avoid ad-hoc taxis at night – have one called for you from a reputable company.

Sexual stereotyping remains strong. If you're with a man, finer restaurants may hand you a 'ladies' menu' without prices. Russian men will also typically rush to open doors for you, help you put on your coat, and, on a date, act like a 'traditional' gentleman. In return they may be expecting you to act like a 'traditional' lady.

Russian women dress up and wear lots of make-up on nights out. If you wear casual gear, you might feel uncomfortable at a restaurant, a theatre or the ballet; in rural areas, revealing clothing will probably attract unwanted attention.

WORK

Given the vast number of unemployed and well-educated Russians, the chances of foreigners finding work in the country are slim. The most likely positions available are as English teachers (look in the *Moscow* and *St Petersburg Times* for ads); your odds for other positions will be slightly increased if you speak fluent Russian.

Starting a business is a hassle given the amount of bureaucracy involved, although the government says it would actually like to increase the level of foreign investment in the country. In the event that you do find work in Russia or are sent there by your company, it would be wise to use a professional relocation firm to navigate the country's thicket of rules and regulations surrounding employment of foreigners.

BELARUS

ACCOMMODATION

Foreigners are on the top of a three-tier pricing system; Belarusians pay least, citizens of CIS states are in the middle. The logic of this system is debatable, but it means that there are few real bargains to be had.

Accommodation has been listed in a general budget order, and within that, by preference. Generally, budget places are those which offer a bed or room for under US$30 a night; midrange goes up to US$100, and top-end over US$100.

Apartments

Where you can find a reliable agency, renting your own city apartment is a good idea, if you don't mind not having the security of a doorman and front desk staff staring you down as you walk in. They are usually conveniently-located, fully equipped and clean. There are not many reliable agencies in Belarus; one is listed in the Minsk section (see p674). Otherwise, ask at travel agencies for their recommendations.

PRACTICALITIES

- The electrical system standard is 220V, 50Hz AC.
- The video system is SECAM though PAL is also read and used.
- Belarus is in the GMT+2 time zone.
- Belarus boasts three state-run (completely) TV channels, though several Russian ones are available to most viewers.
- There are five main radio stations.
- There are some 1200 registered periodicals in the country, many of which open and close (or are closed) quite quickly!

Camping

Farmers and villagers are generally generous about allowing campers to pitch a tent on their lot for a night. Outside national parks you may camp in forests and the like, provided you don't make too much of a ruckus. Camping in or near a city is asking for trouble from the police.

Homestays

Not developed into a cohesive system as yet in Belarus, homestays are possible, though usually through personal connections. If you are invited to spend the night at someone's house, it is customary to buy them a small gift or, preferably, tactfully leave them some money. Remember the need to register your visa (p720) however, which you cannot easily do if staying with someone. Agencies dealing with homestays in the Minsk area include:

Gateway Travel (☎ 02-9745 3333; 48 The Boulevarde, Strathfield, NSW 2135, Australia)

Host Families Association (HOFA; ☎ 812-275 1992; http://webcenter.ru/~hofa; 5-25 Tavricheskaya ulitsa, St Petersburg, Russia)

Hotels

While budget and midrange accommodation standards in Belarus tend to be lower than in the West, they are still generally acceptable and often better (cleaner!) than in Russia or Ukraine. The few top-end places are for the most part equitable to what you would expect from a top-end place in the West.

ACTIVITIES

While the visitor to Belarus will not exactly be overtaxed with things to do (no difficult decisions to make like 'Should I go mountain climbing or snorkelling today?'), locals love the outdoors and there should be no problem finding activities. Being a flat land, Belarus is good for cycling; however the often poor road conditions and lack of rental, repair and purchase outlets are drawbacks. Cycling from Minsk to Njasvizh would take you through some small villages and picturesque countryside, and the region around Lake Narach, 130km north of Minsk, is worth exploring on two wheels. There are lots of outdoor sporting and forest hiking options around Lake Narach. It's a popular outdoor recreational area, with a large **tourist complex** (☎ 297-47 443; vul Turistkaja)

where boat rentals and many summer-oriented activities can be organised. For other sporting tips, see p673 and p678.

BUSINESS HOURS

Offices are generally open 9am to 6pm during the working week, with banks closing at 5pm. Shops are open from about 9am or 10am to about 9pm Monday to Saturday, closing on Sunday around 6pm if they're open at all that day. Restaurants and bars usually open around 10am and close anywhere from 10pm to midnight.

CHILDREN

Though a challenging destination for children (there's not much for them to do!), you should have no problem finding items like nappies (diapers) and baby formula in the larger supermarkets in Minsk and Brest. If travelling elsewhere and if you need specialised items, bring your own. You might consider apartment rental for ease of cooking at home. For helpful hints on what to do with the kids in Minsk, see p673.

CLIMATE CHART

Belarus is in a transitional climate zone between continental and maritime, giving it warm, moist summers and cold winters – they can be frigid, but less so than Moscow's. The rainiest months are June and August, but these are also the most pleasant times to visit. See also p20.

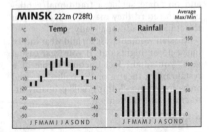

CUSTOMS

Upon arrival in Belarus, you may be given a *deklaratsia* (customs declaration form) to fill out. You are allowed to bring in the equivalent of US$3000 and take out US$10,000 (where you'll make such money in Belarus is a mystery, but good luck!) without filling in a form, but border guards are known to make up their own rules at times. You're allowed to carry one video camera per person and are limited to one litre of alcohol going in or out of the country.

If you're given a form to fill out, keep it until your departure as you may be asked to show it. Generally, border inspections and proceedings are less rigorous on buses than on trains.

For more detailed information, see the Belarusian US embassy website at www .belarusembassy.org, or contact the **State Customs Office** (☎ 17-234 4355; vul Khoruzhoy 29, Minsk).

DANGERS & ANNOYANCES

The level of crime in Belarus, thanks to the omnipresence of police on city centre streets and the relative lack of tourists, is quite low, far below that of Western countries. As a foreigner you have a slightly higher chance of being targeted – don't flash your money around or put yourself in a vulnerable situation. For further information and general advice, see p702.

DISABLED TRAVELLERS

Wheelchair-bound travellers will find that many locations in Minsk are accessible: metro entrances and underground walkways, hotels and some museums. Still, Belarusian society is not used to serving disabled tourists and is much less equipped than in the West. Hotel, restaurant and museum staff will usually be happy – if caught unawares – to help.

The **Association of Disabled in Wheelchairs** (☎ 17-213 8743; vad@open.by) in Minsk can provide general advice. An organisation called **VOVHY** (☎ 17-223 1473; ysovip@tut.by; Amuratorskaja vul 4, Minsk) has developed special programmes for the blind and sight-impaired.

DISCOUNT CARDS

See www.isic.org for the handful of Belarus locations which offer discounts to ISIC card-holders. Discounts are often available to seniors on public transport and in some museums and concert halls.

EMBASSIES & CONSULATES
Belarusian Embassies & Consulates

Belarus' diplomatic representation abroad includes the following:

Canada Embassy (☎ 613-233-9994; Suite 600, 130 Albert St, Ottawa, Ontario K1P 5G4)

France Embassy (☎ 01 44 14 6979; fax 01 44 14 6970; 38 Blvd Suchet, 75016 Paris)

Germany Embassy (☎ 030-5 36 35 929; fax 5 36 35 923; Consular department ☎ 030-5 36 35 934; fax 5 36 35 924; Am Treptower Park 32, 12435 Berlin); Embassy representative (☎ 0228-201 1310; fax 201 1319; Consular department ☎ 0228-201 1330; fax 201 1339; Fritz-Schäffer-Strasse 20, 53113 Bonn)

Latvia Embassy (☎ 732 3411; fax 732 2891; Jezus baznicas iela 12, Riga 1050) Consulate (☎ 54-37 573; fax 52 945; 18-Noyabrya 44, Daugavpils)

Lithuania Embassy (☎ 5-226 2200; fax 279 1363; Mindaugo gatvė 13, Vilnius) Consulate (☎ 5-223 2255; fax 223 3322; Muitinės gatvė 41, Vilnius)

Poland Embassy (☎ 022-617 2391; fax 617 8441; ulica Atenska 67, 03-978 Warsaw) Consulate (☎ 0583-41 0026; fax 41 4026; ulica Yackova Dolina 50, 80-251 Gdansk) Consulate (☎ 085-44 5501; fax 44 6661; ulica Warshiskeho 4, 15-461 Bialystok)

Russia Moscow Embassy (Map p131; ☎ 495-924 7031, fax 928 6633; Maroseyka ul 17/6, 101000; Ⓜ Chistye Prudy); Moscow Consulate (☎ 495-928 7813; fax 928 6403; Armyansky per 6, 101000 Moscow); Kaliningrad Embassy (Map p346; ☎ 214 412; ul Dm Donskogo 35A); St Petersburg Consulate (Map pp234-5; ☎ 812-273 0078; ul Robespierra 8/46-66 St Petersburg; Ⓜ Chernyshevskaya)

UK Embassy (☎ 020-7937 3288; fax 7361 0005; 6 Kensington Court, London W8 5DL)

Ukraine Embassy (☎ 044-290 0201; fax 290 3413; vul Sichnevogo povstannya 6, 252010 Kyiv)

USA Embassy (☎ 202-986 1604; fax 986 1805; 1619 New Hampshire Ave NW, Washington, DC 20009) Consulate (☎ 212-682 5392; fax 682 5491; 708 Third Ave, New York, NY 10017)

Embassies & Consulates in Belarus

Unless otherwise indicated, the following addresses are in Minsk, telephone area code ☎ 017.

France (Map p670; ☎ 210 2868; fax 210 2548; pl Svabody 11; Ⓜ Kupalawskaja/Kastrychnitskaja)

Germany (Map p670; ☎ 284 8714; fax 284 8552; vul Zakharava 26; Ⓜ Ploshcha Peramohi)

Latvia (Map p670; ☎ /fax 284 7475; vul Darashevicha 6a; Ⓜ Ploshcha Jakuba Kolasa)

Lithuania (Map p670; ☎ 285 2448; fax 285 3337; vul Zakharava 68; Ⓜ Ploshcha Peramohi)

Poland (Map p670; ☎ 283 2310; fax 236 4992; vul Krapotkina 91a; Ⓜ Njamiha); Brest (Map p670; ☎ 0162-22 2071; fax 0162-20 3829; vul Kubysheva 34); Hrodna (Map p688; ☎ 0152-96 7469; fax 0152-75 1587; vul Budzyonaha 48a)

Russia Embassy (Map p670; vul Staravilenskaya 48; ☎ 250 3666; fax: 250 3664; Ⓜ Njamiha); Consulate (☎ 222 4985; fax 250 3664; vul Gvardeiskaja 5a;

Ⓜ Fruzenskaja); Brest (Map p683; ☎ 0162-25 5670; fax 22 2473; vul Vorovskaha 19)
UK (Map p670; ☎ 210 5920; fax 229 2306; vul Karla Marxa 37; Ⓜ Kupalawskaja/Kastrychnitskaja)
Ukraine (Map p670; ☎ /fax 283 1958; vul Staravilen-skaja 51; Ⓜ Njamiha); Brest (Map p683; ☎ 0162-23 7526; vul Pushkinskaja 16-1)
USA (Map p670; ☎ 210 1283; fax 234 7853; vul Staravilenskaja 46; Ⓜ Njamiha)

FESTIVALS & EVENTS

The night of 6–7 July is a celebration with pagan roots called **Kupalye**. Similar to St John's Day, celebrated in the Baltic States and Scandinavia on 24 June, young girls gather flowers and throw them into a river as a method of fortune-telling, and everyone else sits by lakeside or riverside fires drinking beer.

In mid-July in Vitsebsk is the **Slavyansky Bazar**, a major musical event that gathers Slavic singers and performers from many countries (see p692). The Belarusian Musical Autumn is an international folk dance and folk and classical-music festival, which takes place in different Minsk locales during the last ten days of November.

Another festival worth checking out is **Bely Zamak** (White Castle; alterego@tut.by), usually held at the end of March in Maladzechna, 80km from Minsk. It's a medieval-themed festival, where costumed folk engage in tournaments and contest, but it's more than just Dungeons and Dragons; there are concerts, costume balls, food kiosks and general merry-making.

GAY & LESBIAN TRAVELLERS

Homosexuality is less tolerated in Belarus than in Russia. Officially, the government retains a confrontational and intolerant attitudes towards gays and lesbians. There are gay clubs, but no official ones. Gay websites have been blocked on Belarusian servers, attempts to stage Gay Pride parades have been stymied, and even the rainbow flag was confiscated by police during a 1999 exhibit of an AIDS quilt. Most gays keep their orientation largely a secret. Belarusians are generally tolerant of homosexual behaviour itself – it's the gay identity most have problems with.

However, there is a lively and popular gay bar in Minsk, Babylon (see p677), and the **Belarus Lambda League** (☎ 017-221 9205;

www.bll.apagay.com in Russian/Belarusian; Minsk), can also provide assistance and advice.

HOLIDAYS

The main public holidays, which may or may not be recognised due to presidential whims, are:
New Year's Day 1 January
Orthodox Christmas Day 7 January
International Women's Day 8 March
Constitution Day 15 March
Catholic Easter March/April
Orthodox Easter March/April
Radunitsa 9th day after Orthodox Easter
International Labour Day 1 May
Victory Day (1945) 9 May
Day of the Coat of Arms & the State Flag of the Republic of Belarus 2nd Sunday in May
Independence Day 3 July
Dzyady (Memory Day) 2 November
Anniversary of the October Revolution 7 November
Catholic Christmas Day 25 December

Note that Independence Day is the date Minsk was liberated from the Nazis, not the date of independence from the USSR, which is uncelebrated.

INSURANCE

Visitors are required to possess medical insurance from an approved company covering their entire stay. It's unlikely you'll ever be asked for it. Insurance is sold at entry points and is relatively cheap; see www.belarusconsul.org for costs and details. Note that medical coverage is not required for holders of transit visas (see p720).

INTERNET ACCESS

While accessible wi-fi is still a long way away in Belarus, and while only top-end hotels may have Internet access in rooms, there is a proliferation of fast-speed Internet cafés throughout the country, where an hour's access costs under BR2000. Just don't bother trying to access some anti-government sites which might have been blocked!

LANGUAGE

Belarusian is closely related to both Russian and Ukrainian. Today Russian dominates in nearly all aspects of social life and has been an official language since 1995. There is little state support for Belarusian and many citizens are quite apathetic, if slightly embarrassed, about the subject. While much of the signage is in Belarusian (street signs, inside train and bus stations), usage is indiscriminate. There is a small but strong and growing group of student nationalists who are working to support the use of Belarusian; thanks to them, Belarusian is now considered to be a language of the intellectual elite.

LEGAL MATTERS

Possession of any amount of illegal narcotic could possibly result in prosecution and jail terms; Belarus has one of the world's highest incarceration rates, so it doesn't pay to risk anything. A large number of traffic violations are still handled by surreptitious bribes, though it is not recommended to offer bribes to police who may wish to fine you for some indiscretion.

MAPS

Good maps are available in book stores and newspaper kiosks in all main cities in Belarus. Small, user-friendly maps of Minsk, Hrodna, Brest and Vitsebsk are published by Interpresservis and cost about BR1800 each. They double as handy bus, trolleybus and metro maps as well, and are easy to find in bookshops and kiosks in those cities. Trivium publishes an excellent 1:750,000 scale map of Belarus and a very detailed 1:20,000 scale Minsk map (with a 1:10,000 city centre map). These cost about BR2300 each.

MONEY

All prices are listed in Belarusian roubles (abbreviated to BR) in this book. These are

---

COMING OF AGE

In Belarus, you need to be the following ages to do the following fun things:

- Get married: 18
- Work: 14
- Be criminally responsible: 16 (grave offences: 14)
- Have sex (heterosexual or homosexual): 16
- Vote: 18
- Purchase cigarettes: 18
- Purchase alcohol: 21

---

better known as *zaichiki* or 'rabbits', named after the one rouble note issued in 1992 that featured a leaping rabbit. The extinct rabbits have since been replaced and devalued many times, and the currency has been the subject of many jokes.

There is thankfully no coinage in Belarus; notes range from 1 to 50,000 roubles which means you'll always be left with a fistful of bills after every purchase.

Plans are in place for a monetary union between Belarus and Russia to be in effect by 2007 or 2008 (whereby Belarus will adopt the Russian rouble as its official currency).

See the inside front cover for exchange rates, as well as (p20).

Exchanging Money

The most easily convertible currencies in Belarus, aside from the mighty euro and US dollar, are the Russian rouble, Lithuanian lita, Polish zloty and to a lesser extent the Ukrainian hryvna. These – and other currencies – are freely exchanged in any of the dozens of exchange booths along pr Francyska Skaryny.

POST

The word for post office is *pashtamt*. Addresses are written as in Russia, basically in the opposite direction to the West, with the country first and the name last.

Sending a 20g letter surface mail within Belarus costs BR160, to Russia BR350 and to any other country BR560. Air mail costs BR900. The best way to mail important, time-sensitive items is with Express Mail Service (EMS), offered at most main post offices, or better (but more expensive) one of the multinational services such as UPS or DHL in Minsk (see p668).

SHOPPING

Aside from a Lukashenka poster for all your friends and some wrapped candy with cool designs and lettering (available at all supermarkets), folk art is the way to go here. See p678 for other suggestions of things to stuff your bags with before departure!

TELEPHONE & FAX

Payphones are found throughout the country. They accept prepaid chip cards (from BR1520 to BR12,060) sold at newspaper kiosks, post offices and Beltelekom

DIRECTORY

locations. These last are state-run and often open 24 hours. You can access the Internet, place international and domestic calls, and send and receive faxes at these offices. Calls to the UK cost BR1660 per minute; to other European destinations BR645 or cheaper; to the US BR1370; to Australia BR1400.

To dial within Belarus, dial ☎ 8, wait for the tone, then city code (including the first zero) and the number. To dial abroad, dial ☎ 8, 10, country code, city code and the number. To phone Belarus from abroad, dial ☎ 375 followed by the city code (without the first zero) and number. For operator inquiries in English (9am to 5pm), call ☎ 017- 221 8448.

Getting a prepaid SIM card for your mobile phone in Belarus is extremely expensive and not worth the hassle.

See p668 for some handy emergency numbers.

TOURIST INFORMATION

There are no tourist information offices in the formal sense in Belarus, but there are some hotel service bureaux and excursion offices that may be helpful. Otherwise, travel agencies are your best bet – see p669 for more details. Outside Belarus, information on the country is rare; however, there is a good deal of information available on the Internet (see p22).

VISAS

Belarusian visa regulations change frequently, so check the Belarusian US embassy website at www.belarusembassy.org for more information.

All Western visitors need a visa, and arranging one before you arrive is essential. Visas are not issued at border points except at Minsk-2 international airport – however, you will still need to show hotel reservations or your personal or business invitation. It's not a recommended course of action. Even if you are passing through Belarus by train or bus en route to another country, you need a transit visa (right) – without one, you will be removed from the vehicle and sent back to where you came from.

To get a visa, you will need a photograph, an invitation from a private person or a business, or a confirmation of reservation from a hotel, and your passport. There are three main types of visas: tourist, issued if you have a tourist voucher or hotel reservation; visitor, if your invitation comes from an individual; and business, if your invitation is from a business. Tourist and visitor visas are issued for 30 days, while business visas are valid for 90 days and can be multientry.

Citizens of 13 countries, including UK and Canada, do not require an invitation to receive a tourist visa; they merely need to complete an application and submit a photograph at a Belarusian embassy or consulate (see www.belarusembassy.org for more details).

Note that there is effectively no border between Belarus and Russia, so if you're arriving from Russia (on a train with a final destination in Belarus) you may not encounter any border guards and in theory it's possible to enter and leave (back to Russia) without a visa. However, you are risking trouble this way and remember, you cannot stay at any hotel without a valid visa.

Registration

Once you enter the country you must be officially registered. Most hotels do this automatically, and sometimes for a small fee. They'll give you small pieces of papers with stamps on them, which you keep to show to customs agents upon departure if asked. In theory, you'll be fined if you don't provide proof of registration for every day of your stay; in practice, it is rarely asked for (typically asked for more frequently on trains than on buses). If you've received a personal invitation, you'll need to seek out the nearest PVU (*passportno-vizovoye upravleniye*), or passport and visa department or try to convince hotel staff somewhere to register your visa for the cost of one night's stay. The **PVU main office** (Map p670; ☎ 017-231 9174; vul Francyska Skaryny 8; Ⓜ Nezalezhnastsi) is in Minsk.

Transit Visas

All persons passing through Belarusian territory are required to possess a transit visa, which can be obtained at any Belarusian consulate upon presentation of travel tickets clearly showing the final destination as being outside of Belarus. The possession of a valid Russian visa is not enough to serve as a transit visa. Be sure to check your train or bus routing, as you could be removed and not allowed to travel onwards. Transit visas are not available at the border.

Applying for a Visa

By far the simplest – although the most expensive – way to get a visa is to apply through a travel agency. Alternately, you can take a faxed confirmation from your hotel to the nearest Belarusian embassy and apply for one yourself.

Tallinn, Rīga and Vilnius have numerous travel agencies specialising in Belarusian visas. In Vilnius, the most convenient point to jump off, try **Viliota** (☎ 370 5-265 2238; www .viliota.it in Lithuanian; Basanaviciaus gatvė 15), where you can get a visa hassle-free with a photo of yourself and US$50 to US$100.

Many Belarusian travel agencies (see p669) can send you an invitation. The Host Families Association (HOFA) (see p716 for details) can do the same.

Getting an invitation from an individual can be a long, complex process. Your friend in Belarus needs a *zapreshenne* (official invitation) form from their local PVU office and should then send it to you. With this, you apply at the nearest Belarusian embassy.

Visa costs vary depending on the embassy you apply at and your citizenship. Typically, single-entry visas cost about US$50 for five working–days service and US$90 for next-day service; double-entry visas usually cost double that. Business visas are more expensive than tourist visas. Transit visas typically cost from US$20 to US$35.

Visa Extensions

Nontransit visas cannot be extended beyond the 30-day limit for tourists, or the 90-day limit for holders of business visas; you will need to apply for a new visa. Try at the **Belintourist** (Map p670; ☎ 017-226 98 85; pr Masherava 19A; Ⓜ Njamiha) office or the **Ministry of Foreign Affairs** (Map p670; ☎ 017-222 2674; vul Lenina 19; Ⓜ Kupalawskaja/Kastrychnitskaja), both in Minsk.

WOMEN TRAVELLERS

Women travelling on their own is a rare sight in these parts, and may be looked upon as an oddity ('Oh, those foreigners!'), but those wishing to do so should encounter no particular problems or harassment. The restaurants listed in this book would all serve as appropriate hang-outs for single women, but in bars and pubs, women alone may be mistaken for prostitutes and may be approached as such. On the streets, you need not dress conservatively however, young women here often express their femininity through fashion styles that would be considered provocative or sexy in the West. As this is the norm, they are not pestered in public places for it. Travellers should be aware that traditional sex roles are quite firmly in place here, with both sexes straining to act in ways seen to be in accordance with their genders.

The **Discussion Women's Club** (Map p670; vul Karbysheva 11-48 ☎ 017-263 7736; beluwi@minsk.sovam .com), in Minsk, is a nongovernmental organisation (NGO) that regularly hosts forums and meetings about women's issues in Belarus.

Transport

CONTENTS

THINGS CHANGE...

The information in this chapter is particularly vulnerable to change. Check directly with the airline or a travel agent to make sure you understand how a fare (and ticket you may buy) works and be aware of the security requirements for international travel. Shop carefully. The details given in this chapter should be regarded as pointers and are not a substitute for your own careful, up-to-date research.

RUSSIA

GETTING THERE & AWAY
Entering the Country

Bordering 13 countries and with flights and even boats to many more around the world, there's no shortage of options for getting to and from Russia.

Unless you have a transit visa (p714), you can enter the country on a one-way ticket (even if your visa is only good for one day, it's unlikely anyone will ask to see your outgoing ticket), so you have a great deal of flexibility once inside Russia to determine the best way of getting out again.

For information on travel between Russia and Belarus, see p746.

Air
AIRPORTS & AIRLINES

Moscow's **Sheremetyevo-2** (airport code SVO; ☎ 495-956 4666; www.sheremetyevo-airport.ru) and the much more congenial **Domodedovo** (airport code DME; ☎ 495-933 6666; www.domodedovo

.ru) airports host the bulk of Russia's international flights. There are also many daily international services to St Petersburg's **Pulkovo-2** (airport code LED; ☎ 812-704 3444; eng .pulkovo.ru) airport.

It's worth noting that you don't necessarily have to fly into either Moscow or St Petersburg – plenty of other cities have direct international connections, including Arkhangelsk (airport code ARH), Irkutsk (airport code IKT), Kazan (airport code KZN), Khabarovsk (airport code HNV), Krasnodar (airport code KRR), Krasnoyarsk (airport code KJA), Kavkazskie Mineralnye Vody (airport code MRV), Murmansk (airport code MMK), Nizhny Novgorod (airport code GOJ), Novosibirsk (airport code OVB), Perm (airport code PEE), Vladivostok (airport code VVO), Yekaterinburg (airport code SVX) and Yuzhno-Sakhalinsk (airport code UUS).

Airlines flying into Russia include the following. Phone numbers are given for the Moscow office, where applicable.

Aeroflot Russian International Airlines (airline code SU; ☎ 495-753 5555; www.aeroflot.com /eng; hub Sheremetyevo Airport, Moscow)

Air China (airline code CA; ☎ 495-292 3387, 292 5440; www.china-airlines.com/en/index.htm; hub Beijing Capital Airport, Beijing)

Air France (airline code AF; ☎ 495-937 3839; www.air france.com; hub Charles de Gaulle Airport, Paris)

Alitalia (airline code AZ; ☎ 495-258 3601; www.alitalia .it; hub Malpensa Airport, Milan)

Austrian Airlines (airline code OS; ☎ 495-995 0995; www.aua.com; hub Vienna International Airport, Vienna)

Bashkir Airlines (BAL; airline code V9; ☎ 3472-733 656 in Ufa; www.bal.ufanet.ru, in Russian; hub Ufa)

British Airways (airline code BA; ☎ 495-363 2525; www.britishairways.com; hub London Heathrow, London)

ČSA (Czech Airlines; airline code OK; ☎ 495-973 1847, 978 1745; www.csa.cz/en/; hub Prague)

Delta Air Lines (airline code DL; ☎ 495-937 9090; www.delta.com; hub Hartsfield Atlanta International Airport, Atlanta)

El Al Israel Airlines (airline code LY; ☎ 495-232 1017; www.elal.co.il; hub Ben Gurion Airport, Tel Aviv)

Finnair (airline code AY; ☎ 495-933 0056; www.finnair .com; hub Helsinki-Vantaa Airport, Helsinki)

Japan Airlines (airline code JL; ☎ 495-921 6448, 921 6648; www.jal.co.jp/en; hub Narita Airport, Tokyo)

KLM (airline code KL; ☎ 495-258 3600; www.klm.com; hub Amsterdam Schiphol Airport, Amsterdam)

Korean Air (airline code KE; ☎ 495-725 2727; www .koreanair.com; hub Incheon International Airport, Seoul)

Krasair (airline code 7B; ☎ 3912-555 999 in Krasnoyarsk; www.krasair.ru in Russian; hub Krasnoyarsk)

LOT Polish Airlines (airline code LO; ☎ 495-229 5771; www.lot.com; hub Fredrick Chopin Airport, Warsaw)

Lufthansa (airline code LH; ☎ 495-737 6400; www .lufthansa.com; hub Frankfurt International Airport, Frankfurt)

Magadan Airlines (airline code H5; ☎ 41322-97610 in Magadan; http://mavial.magtrk.ru in Russian; hub Magadan)

MIAT Mongolian Airlines (airline code OM; ☎ 495-241 0754 in Moscow, ☎ 976-11-379935 in Ulaan Baatar; www.miat.com; hub Ulaan Baatar)

Pulkovo (airline code FV; ☎ 495-925 4747; http://eng .pulkovo.ru; hub Pulkovo International Airport, St Petersburg)

SAS (airline code SK; ☎ 495-925 4747; www.scandinavian.net; hub Copenhagen Airport, Copenhagen)

Siberia Airlines (airline code S7; ☎ 495-777 9999 in Moscow, ☎ 383-359 9090 in Novosibirsk; www.s7.ru; hub Novosibirsk)

Swissair (airline code LX; ☎ 495-937 7799; www.swissair.com; hub Zurich Airport, Zurich)

Transaero Airlines (airline code UN; ☎ 495-241 4800, 241 7676; www.transaero.com/noframes/eng/home.htm; hub Sheremetyevo-2 Airport, Moscow)

Turkish Airlines (airline code TK; ☎ 495-292 1667; www.turkishairlines.com; hub Istanbul Ataturk International Airport, Istanbul)

Ural Airlines (airline code U6; ☎ 343-264 3600 in Yekaterinburg; www.uralairlines.ru; hub Yekaterinburg)

Vladivostok Air (airline code XF; ☎ 4232-426 296 in Vladivostok; www.vladavia.ru; hub Vladivostok)

TICKETS

Good deals on tickets can be found online and with discount agencies. Use the fares quoted in this book as a guide only. They are approximate and based on the rates advertised by agencies and online at the time of research. Quoted air fares do not necessarily constitute a recommendation for the carrier.

There are many websites specifically aimed at selling flights; sometimes these fares are cheap, but often they're no cheaper than those sold at a standard travel agency, and occasionally they're way too expensive. However, it's certainly a convenient way of researching flights from the comfort of your own home or office. Many large travel agencies also have websites, but not all of them allow you to look up fares and schedules. See p729 for a list of agencies who specialise in tours to Russia: some of these will offer discount fares, too.

TRANSPORT

RUSSIA THROUGH THE BACK DOOR

There are plenty of options to reach Moscow or St Petersburg using budget flights out of European cities. Germany is particularly well served with **Germania Express** (airline code ST; ☎ 49-01805-737 100 in Germany; www.gexx.de; hubs Berlin, Düsseldorf & Munich) connecting Berlin, Düsseldorf and Munich with Moscow's Domodedovo, and **German Wings** (airline code 4U; ☎ 49-01805-955 855 in Germany; www27.germanwings.com; hubs Hamburg, Cologne/Bonn, Stuttgart & Dresden) flying Berlin, Bonn and Cologne to Moscow's Vnukovo airport. SAS's budget airline **Snowflake** (www.flysnowflake.com; ☎ 46-8-797 4000 in Stockholm; hubs Stockholm & Copenhagen) has services from Copenhagen and Stockholm to both Moscow's Sheremetyevo-2 and St Petersburg. From the Baltic States, you can fly Tallinn to Sheremetyevo on **Estonian Air** (airline code OV; ☎ 372-640 1160 in Tallinn; www.estonian-air.ee; hub Tallinn) and Rīga to Moscow and St Petersburg with **Air Baltic** (airline code BT; ☎ 371-720 7473 in Rīga; www.airbaltic.com; hub Rīga).

Finland is also a popular back-door way into Russia with both Helsinki and Tampere being connected by various budget airlines to other parts of Europe. From either city you can take a bus or trains to St Petersburg. Also check out www.waytorussia.net/Transport/International /Budget.html for some ideas of how to get cheaply to Moscow or St Petersburg from London or Germany via the Baltic States. One more option is to get yourself through Poland to Kaliningrad and then take an internal Russian flight from there.

There are also (particularly during the summer season) charter flights to and from Russia, mainly to resort towns in Turkey, Greece, Egypt and other countries. These flights, which never show up on regular schedules, may be cheap, but sometimes the planes being used leave a lot to be desired in terms of comfort and, more worryingly, safety. Buyer beware!

Websites worth checking:

www.cheapflights.co.uk Really does post some of the cheapest flights (out of the UK only), but get in early to get the bargains.

www.dialaflight.com Offers worldwide flights out of Europe and the UK.

www.expedia.com A good site for checking worldwide flight prices.

www.lastminute.com This site deals mainly in European flights, but does have worldwide flights, mostly package returns. There's also a link to an Australian version.

www.statravel.com STA Travel's US website. There are also UK and Australian sites (www.statravel.co.uk and www.statravel.com.au).

www.travel.com.au A good site for Australians to find cheap flights. A New Zealand version also exists (www.travel.co.nz).

To bid for last-minute tickets online try **Skyauction** (www.skyauction.com). **Priceline** (www.priceline.com) aims to match the ticket price to your budget. Another cheap option is an air courier ticket but it does carry restrictions: for more information check out organisations such as **Courier Association** (www.aircourier.org) or the **International Association of Air Travel Couriers** (IAATC; www.courier.org).

AUSTRALIA

Flights from Australia to Europe generally go via Southeast Asian capitals, involving stopovers at Kuala Lumpur, Bangkok or Singapore. If a long stopover between connections is unavoidable, transit accommodation is sometimes included in the price of the ticket. If the fare means you have to pay for transit accommodation yourself, it may be worth your while upgrading to a more expensive ticket.

Two well-known agencies for cheap fares, with offices throughout Australia, are **Flight Centre** (☎ 133 133; www.flightcentre.com.au) and **STA Travel** (☎ 1300 733 035; www.statravel.com.au).

The cheapest flight you're going to get would be something like Sydney to Seoul and then Seoul to Moscow: a Korean Air deal starts at return A$1400. Seoul is also the most convenient transfer point for flights on to Vladivostok or Khabarovsk.

CANADA

Canadian discount agencies, also known as consolidators, advertise their flight specials in major newspapers such as the *Toronto Star* and the *Vancouver Sun*. The national

student travel agency is **Travel CUTS** (☎ 800-667 2887; www.travelcuts.com).

In general, fares from Canada to Russia cost 10% more than from the USA. From Vancouver to Moscow return flights start from C$1145 (with two changes of plane); from Montreal C$1400 (with one change of plane).

CHINA

There are multiple options for getting to and from China. Moscow, naturally, has the best connections with daily flights offered by Air China and Aeroflot to Beijing (return Y8700). There are five flights a week between Shanghai and Moscow (return Y8700). Transaero flies occasionally from Moscow to Hong Kong. There are also flights from Beijing to Novosibirsk (US$505), Guangzhou to Khabarovsk (US$320), Harbin to Khabarovsk (US$170) and Vladivostok (R5900), Shenyang to Irkutsk (from US$170), and Ürümqi to Novosibirsk (US$184). Tainjin and Dalian also have infrequent connections with Vladivostok.

CONTINENTAL EUROPE

Generally there is not much variation in air fare prices from the main European cities. All the major airlines usually offer some sort of deal, as do travel agencies, so shop around.

Return fares to Moscow from major Western European cities start at around €250.

France

French travel agencies with branches around the country specialising in youth and student fares include **OTU Voyages** (www.otu.fr in French) and **Nouvelles Frontières** (☎ 0825 000 747; www.nouvelles-frontieres.fr in French). Also try **Anyway** (☎ 0892 893 892; www.anyway.fr in French) and **Lastminute** (☎ 0892 705 000; www.fr.lastminute.com in French).

Germany

Germany is an excellent jumping-off point for Russia, with not only plenty of connections to a range of Russian cities with Lufthansa but also connections through budget airlines such as Germania Express and German Wings (see the boxed text, p723). The following airlines also fly direct between Germany and the Caucasus: **Kuban Air** (www.alk.ru/eng/alk), **Don Aeroflot** (www.aeroflot-don.ru in Russian) and **KMV Avia** (www.kmvavia.ru/engl). Krasair and Siberia Airlines have direct connections to Krasnoyarsk and Novosibirsk respectively.

Recommended agencies in Germany include **Just Travel** (☎ 089-747 3330; www.justtravel .de), **STA Travel** (☎ 01805-456 422; www.statravel.de) and **Travel Overland** (☎ 01805-276370; www.travel -overland.de in German). **J&S ONG** (☎ 02361-904 7981; jsohg@gmx.de; Hernerstrasse 26, 45657 Recklinghausen) is useful for booking tickets on the regional Russian airlines.

Italy
CTS Viaggi (☎ 06 462 0431; www.cts.it in Italian) specialises in student and youth travel fares.

Netherlands
A recommended agency is **Airfair** (☎ 020-620 5121; www.airfair.nl in Dutch).

Spain
Try **Barcelo Viajes** (☎ 902 116 226; www.barcelo viajes.com in Spanish).

JAPAN
Reliable discount agencies in Japan include **No 1 Travel** (☎ 03-3200 8871; www.no1-travel.com) and **Across Travellers Bureau** (☎ 03-3373 9040; www.across-travel.com), as well as **STA Travel** (☎ 03-5485 8380; www.statravel.co.jp) with branches in both Tokyo and Osaka.

One-way/return flights from Tokyo to Moscow are around ¥130,000/221,000, although at certain times of the year 60-day excursion fares on Aeroflot can go as low as ¥60,000 return.

Other useful connections are from Vladivostok to Niigata (one way/return from ¥41,000/48,000), Osaka (¥46,000/42,000) and Toyama (¥47,000/58,000). In August there are also weekly direct flights between Tokyo and Vladivostok (R6900). From Japan's northern island of Hokkaido there are flights from Hakodate and Sapporo to Yuzhno-Sakhalinsk (p639). From Khabarovsk there are weekly flights to Niigata and from July to September, a service to Aomori (both one way/return ¥42,000/60,000).

MONGOLIA & CENTRAL ASIA
Ulaan Baatar is connected with Moscow (one way/return from US$330/580) and Irkutsk (US$210), though the latter can be discounted to under $70 in winter.

There are dozens of connections to Central Asia. From Moscow there are many direct flights. Also from Novosibirsk you can reach Almaty (US$160) in Kazakhstan; Andizhan (US$125) and Tashkent (US$135) in Uzbekistan; Dushanbe (US$145) and Khujand/Khodzhent (US$140) in Tajikistan; and Bishkek (US$170) in Kyrgyzstan. Tyumen, Omsk and Krasnoyarsk have a slightly smaller range of similar destinations.

NEW ZEALAND
The *New Zealand Herald* has a travel section in which travel agencies advertise fares. **Flight Centre** (☎ 0800 243 544; www.flightcentre.co.nz) and **STA Travel** (☎ 0508 782 872; www.statravel.co.nz) have branches in Auckland and elsewhere in the country; check the websites for complete listings.

Air fares from New Zealand to Russia are similar to those from Australia.

SINGAPORE
In Singapore, **STA Travel** (☎ 737 7188; www.sta travel.com.sg) offers competitive discount fares for Asian destinations and beyond. Singapore, like Bangkok, has hundreds of travel agents, so you can compare prices on flights.

SOUTH KOREA
Seoul in South Korea is a possible international travel hub for Siberia and the Russian Far East, with weekly flights to Khabarovsk (from US$300) and Novosibirsk (one way/return US$490/670) and at least twice-weekly services to Vladivostok (R11,000) and Yuzhno-Sakhalinsk (US$390). There are also flights connecting Pusan to/ from Vladivostok and Yuzhno-Sakhalinsk.

THAILAND
Although most Asian countries are now offering fairly competitive deals, Bangkok is still one of the best places to shop around for discount tickets. Khao San Rd in Bangkok is the budget travellers' headquarters. Bangkok has a number of excellent travel agencies but there are also some suspect ones; ask the advice of other travellers before handing over your cash. **STA Travel** (☎ 02-236 0262; www.statravel.co.th; Rm 1406, 14th fl, Wall St Tower, 33/70 Surawong Rd) is a reliable place to start. Aeroflot has direct flights to Moscow from Bangkok. Siberia Airlines flies to Novosibirsk (US$303), and several other Russian airlines offer seasonal charters.

TURKEY, THE CAUCASUS & THE MIDDLE EAST
Summer charter flights to Turkey, especially Antalya, are available from several major airports. Moscow has regular flights to all the major cities in the Caucasus and Middle East. Competition is so intense on the Baku to Moscow route that you can pay as little as US$120.

There are also weekly flights from the Russian Caucasus towns of Rostov-on-Don and Kavkazskie Mineralnye Vody to Turkey. Elsewhere in Russia there are weekly flights to Baku, Azerbaijan, from Tyumen (US$320), Krasnoyarsk (US$205), Irkutsk (US$250) and Novosibirsk (US$250); from the latter there are also twice-weekly flights to Yerevan, Armenia (US$220), as well as weekly services to Tel Aviv, Israel (US$425).

Emirates and Qatar Airways provide very useful connections in the Gulf and some of the best value-for-money options for all over Asia. They fly to Moscow's Domodedovo airport.

UK & IRELAND
Newspapers and magazines such as *Time Out* and *TNT Magazine* in London regularly advertise low fares to Moscow. Start your research with the major student or backpacker-oriented travel agencies such as STA and Trailfinders. Through these reliable agents you can get an idea of what's available and how much you're going to pay – however, a bit of ringing around to the smaller agencies afterwards will often turn up cheaper fares.

Reputable agencies in London:
ebookers (☎ 0870-010 7000; www.ebookers.co.uk)
Flight Centre (☎ 0870-499 0040; www.flightcentre.co.uk)
STA Travel (☎ 0870-160 0599; www.statravel.co.uk)
Trailfinders (☎ 0207-938 3939; www.trailfinders.co.uk)
Travelbag (☎ 0870-814 6794; www.travelbag.co.uk)

Shop around and you may get a low-season one-way/return fare to Moscow for £150/200. Flights to St Petersburg are a bit more expensive at around £200/250. Aeroflot generally offers the cheapest deals.

USA
Discount travel agencies in the USA are known as consolidators (although you won't see a sign on the door saying Consolidator), and they can be found in the *Yellow Pages* or the travel sections of major daily newspapers such as the *New York Times*, the *Los Angeles Times* and the *San Francisco Examiner*. You'll generally come across good deals at agencies in San Francisco, Los Angeles, New York and other big cities.

STA Travel (☎ 1-800 781 4040; www.statravel.com) has a wide network of offices. A specialist agency is **Interactive Russia** (☎ 1-866-680 1373; http://travel.in-russia.com).

Economy-class air fares from New York to Moscow can go as low as US$700 return. From Los Angeles you're looking at return fares to Moscow of around US$880. Also see p648 for details of Magadan Airlines' flights connecting Anchorage with Magadan and Kamchatka in the Russian Far East.

Land
There are numerous land routes to Russia from both Europe and Asia. Many people approach the country on trains and buses from Central and Baltic European countries or on either the trans-Manchurian or trans-Mongolian train routes from China and Mongolia. Russian Railways has a series of discounts with neighbouring countries' rail systems on international tickets: see www.eng.rzd.ru/static/index.html?he_id=249 for details.

BORDER CROSSINGS
Russia shares borders with Azerbaijan, Belarus, China, Estonia, Finland, Georgia, Kazakhstan, Latvia, Lithuania, Mongolia, North Korea, Norway, Poland and Ukraine: all except Azerbaijan, Georgia and North Korea are open to non-Russian travellers. Before planning a journey into or out of Russia from any of these countries, check out the visa situation for your nationality.

On trains, border crossings are a straightforward but drawn-out affair, with a steady stream of customs and ticket personnel scrutinising your passport and visa. If you're arriving by car or motorcycle, you'll need to show your vehicle registration and insurance papers, and your driving licence, passport and visa. These formalities are usually minimal for Western European citizens.

On the Russian side, chances are your vehicle will be subjected to a cursory inspection by border guards (your life will be made much easier if you open all doors and the boot yourself, and shine a torch for the guards at night). You pass through customs separately from your car, walking through a metal detector and possibly having hand luggage X-rayed.

Train fares for trips to/from Russia listed under individual countries in this section are for a *kupe* (compartment) in a four-berth compartment. Certain routes also offer cheaper *platskartny* (3rd-class open carriage) fares.

BELARUS
See p746 for information on getting there and away by train and road.

CHINA
Car & Motorcycle
The road from Manzhouli to Zabaikalsk in the Chitinskaya Region is open to traffic and it's also possible to cross from Heihe to Blagoveshchensk (p607) using a ferry across the Amur River.

Train
The classic way into Russia from China is along the trans-Mongolian and trans-Manchurian rail route; see p742 for details.

Also see Vladivostok (p621) and Khabarovsk (p614) for other options on travelling overland to China.

ESTONIA
The nearest border crossing from Tallinn is at Narva. There's a daily train between Moscow and Tallinn (R1560, 15 hours) and seven express buses daily from St Petersburg (R550 to R650, 7½ hours).

FINLAND
Bus
There are many daily buses between Helsinki and St Petersburg. For more details see p291. Also see p354 for routes into and out of Finland from Northern European Russia.

Car & Motorcycle
Highways cross at the Finnish border posts of Nuijamaa and Vaalimaa (Brusnichnoe and Torfyanovka, respectively, on the Russian side). Fill up with petrol on the Finnish side (preferably before you get to the border petrol station, which is more expensive than others and closes early). Note – there's a speed trap just outside the St Petersburg

city line, where the limit is 60km/h. Be sure to watch for all road signs; a few roads involve tricky curves and signposting is not all it should be. It's best to make this drive for the first time during daylight hours.

Train
There are two daily trains between St Petersburg and Helsinki: see p293 for details. There's also the daily 31/34 'Leo Tolstoy' service between Moscow and Helsinki (R3220, 13½ hours).

KAZAKHSTAN
Car & Motorcycle
Roads into Kazakhstan head east from Astrakhan, and south from Samara, Chelyabinsk, Orenburg and Omsk.

Train
There are trains every two days between Moscow and Almaty (R4100, 78 hours) and daily from Astrakhan to Atyrau/Guryev, in addition to a variety of services from Siberia. Beware that some domestic Russian trains cut through Kazakhstan en route, including Chelyabinsk–Omsk, Chelyabinsk–Magnitogorsk and those Yekaterinburg–Omsk services routed via Kurgan. Visa checks are not always made leaving Russia, but coming back in you may find yourself in serious trouble if you don't have a Kazakhstan visa and a double/multiple entry Russian visa, too.

LATVIA
Bus
There are two daily buses from Rīga to St Petersburg (R500, 11 hours); see p291. There are also daily buses between Rīga and Kaliningrad (R360, 10 hours) and two to three buses daily to Moscow (R720, 14 to 16 hours).

Car & Motorcycle
The M9 Rīga–Moscow road crosses the border east of Rezekne (Latvia). The A212 road from Rīga leads to Pskov, crossing a corner of Estonia en route.

Train
From Latvia, handy overnight trains run daily between Rīga and Moscow (R1404 *platskartny*, 15 hours) and St Petersburg (R1812, 13 hours).

TRANSPORT

TRANSPORT

LITHUANIA
Bus
There are at least four buses daily from Kaliningrad to Smiltyne in Lithuania; see p348 for details.

Car & Motorcycle
The A229 to Kaliningrad crosses the border at Kybartai. Most roads to the rest of Russia cross Belarus.

Train
A service leaves Vilnius for Kaliningrad (R1000, seven hours) five times a week, for Moscow (R1588, 15 hours) three times a week and for St Petersburg (R1387 to R1499, 15 hours and 15 minutes) every other day. The St Petersburg trains cross Latvia, and the Moscow ones cross Belarus (see p720 for transit visa information).

MONGOLIA
Bus
There are direct buses three times a week between Ulaan Baatar and Ulan-Ude (p594).

Car & Motorcycle
It's possible to drive between Mongolia and Russia at the Tsagaanuur–Tashanta, Altanbulag–Kyakhta and Erdeentsav–Borzya borders. The process of getting through these borders can be very slow, and it's a good idea to have written permission from a Mongolian embassy if you wish to bring a vehicle through.

Train
Apart from the trans-Mongolian train connecting Moscow and Beijing (p742), there's a direct train twice a week from Ulaan Baatar to Moscow (R3800, four days and five hours) as well as a daily service to and from Irkutsk (R1600, 25 to 35 hours).

NORWAY
For details of bus connections between Norway and Russia, see p355.

POLAND
Bus
There are two daily buses between both Gdansk and Oltshyn and Kaliningrad as well as daily buses to/from Warsaw. For further details on buses to/from towns in Poland, see p348.

Car & Motorcycle
The main border crossing between Poland and Kaliningrad is near Bagrationovsk on the A195 highway. Be warned; queues can be very long.

Train
There are daily services linking Warsaw with Moscow (R2200, 20 hours) and St Petersburg (R2240, 29 hours). The Moscow trains enter Belarus near Brest. The St Petersburg trains leave Poland at Kuznica, which is near Hrodna (Grodno in Russian) in Belarus. Changing the wheels to/from Russia's wider gauge adds three hours to the journey.

UK & EUROPE
Train
Travelling overland by train from the UK or Western Europe takes a minimum of two days and nights. It is, however, a great way of easing yourself into the rhythm of a long Russian journey, such as one on the Trans-Siberian Railway.

There are no direct trains from the UK to Russia. The most straightforward route you can take is on the **Eurostar** (www.eurostar .com) to Brussels, and then a two-night direct train to Moscow via Warsaw and Minsk (Belarus). The total cost can be as low as £217 one way. See www.seat61.com/Russia .htm for details of this and other train services to Moscow.

Crossing the Poland–Belarus border at Brest takes several hours while the wheels are changed for the Russian track. All foreigners visiting Belarus need a visa, including those transiting by train – sort this out before arriving in Belarus. For more details on visas, see p720.

To avoid this hassle consider taking the train to St Petersburg from Vilnius in Lithuania, which runs several times a week via Latvia. There are daily connections between Vilnius and Warsaw.

From Moscow and St Petersburg there are also regular international services to European cities including Berlin, Budapest, Prague, Vienna and Warsaw; see p188 for Moscow, and p293 for St Petersburg details.

For European rail timetables check www .railfaneurope.net, which provides a central link to all of Europe's national railways.

UKRAINE
Bus
There is a handful of weekly buses travelling from Kharkiv across the border into Russia on the E95 (M2) road. The official frontier crossing is 40km north of Kharkiv, and is near the Russian border town of Zhuravlevka.

Car & Motorcycle
The main autoroute between Kyiv and Moscow starts as the E93 (M20) north of Kyiv, but becomes the M3 when it branches off to the east some 50km south of Chernihiv.

Driving from Ukraine to the Caucasus, the border frontier point is on the E40 (M19) road crossing just before the Russian town of Novoshakhtinsk at the Ukrainian border village of Dovzhansky, about 150km east of Donetsk.

Train
Most major Ukrainian cities have daily services to Moscow, with two border crossings: one used by trains heading to Kyiv, the other by trains passing through Kharkiv.

Trains from Kyiv to Moscow (US$23, 15 hours, nine services daily) go via Bryansk (Russia) and Konotop (Ukraine), crossing at the Ukrainian border town of Seredyna-Buda. The best trains to take (numbers are southbound/northbound) between Moscow and Kyiv are the 1/2 and 3/4. The best train between Moscow and Lviv is 73/74 (28 hours, daily via Kyiv). Between Moscow and Odessa (28 hours, daily via Kyiv) there's the 23/24, the *Odesa*. There are also daily trains to/from St Petersburg to Lviv (31 hours via Vilnius) and Kyiv (26 hours).

Trains between Kharkiv and Moscow (13 hours, about 14 daily via Kursk) cross the border just 40km north of Kharkiv. The best train is the night train, the *Kharkiv*, 19/20. Between Moscow and Simferopol (26 hours, daily via Kharkiv), the best train is 67/68, the *Simferopol*. Trains between Moscow and Donetsk (22 hours, three daily), Dnipropetrovsk (20 hours, twice daily), Zaporizhzhya (19 hours, twice daily) and Sevastopol (29½ hours, daily) all go through Kharkiv.

Many trains travelling between Moscow and the Caucasus go through Kharkiv, including a daily service to Rostov-on-Don (12 hours). There are also daily international trains passing through Ukraine to/ from Moscow's Kyivsky vokzal (station). These include the 15/16 Kyiv–Lviv–Chop–Budapest–Belgrade train, with a carriage to Zagreb three times a week.

Sea
There is a handful of opportunities to reach Russia by sea:
- from Helsinki (Finland), Tallinn (Estonia) and Kaliningrad (p349) to St Petersburg (p290)
- from Istanbul or Trabzon (Turkey) to Sochi (p468) and Novorossiysk (p461)
- from Fushiki on Japan's main island of Honshu to Vladivostok (p621) and from Wakkanai on the northern Japanese island of Hokkaido to Korsakov on Sakhalin (p641)

Tours
If you have time, and a certain degree of determination, organising your own trip to Russia is easily done. But for many travellers, opting for the assistance of an agency in drawing up an itinerary, booking train tickets and accommodation, not to mention helping with the visa paperwork, is preferable.

Also, you may want to arrange an outdoor activity, such as hiking or rafting, for which the services of an expert agency is almost always required. Or you may choose to go the whole hog and have everything taken care of on a fully organised tour.

The following agencies and tour companies provide a range of travel services; unless otherwise mentioned they can all help arrange visas and transport tickets within Russia. Numerous, more locally based agencies can provide tours once you're in Russia; see the destination chapters for details. Many work in conjunction with overseas agencies, so if you go to them directly you'll usually pay less.

Australia
Eastern Europe/Russian Travel Centre (☎ 02-9262 1144; www.eetbtravel.com)
Passport Travel (☎ 03-9867 3888; www.travelcentre .com.au)
Russian Gateway Tours (☎ 02-9745 3333; www .russian-gateway.com.au)
Sundowners (☎ 03-9672 5300; www.sundowners travel.com) Specialises in trans-Siberian packages and tours.

TRANSPORT

Travel Directors (☎ 08-9242 4200; www.traveldirect
ors.com.au) Upmarket trans-Siberian tour operator.

Canada

Trek Escapes (☎ 1800-267 3347; www.theadventure
centre.com) Canada's top adventure tour agency offers Sundowners' and Imaginative Traveller trans-Siberian packages.
Also has branches in Calgary, Edmonton and Vancouver.

China

Beijing Tourism Group (BTG; tour@163bj.com; ☎ 8610-
6515 8562; Beijing Tourist Building, 28 Jianguomen Wai
Dajie, Beijing) Can arrange train tickets on trans-Siberian,
trans-Manchurian and trans-Mongolian trains.
Monkey Business (☎ 8610-6591 6519; www
.monkeyshrine.com) Offers tours on the trans-Siberian,
trans-Manchurian and trans-Mongolian trains.
Moonsky Star Ltd (☎ 852-2723 1376) Monkey
Business's Hong Kong partner.

Germany

Lernidee Reisen (☎ 030-786 0000; www.lernidee
-reisen.de in German)

Japan

MO Tourist CIS Russian Centre (☎ 03-5296 5783;
wwkw.motcis.com in Japanese) Can help arrange ferries
and flights to Russia.

UK

GW Travel Ltd (☎ 0161-928 9410; www.gwtravel
.co.uk) Offers luxury trans-Siberian tours on private
Pullman-style carriages with restaurants, showers and
lectures.
Imaginative Traveller (☎ 0800-316 2717; www
.imaginative-traveller.com) Trans-Siberian tours.
Intourist Travel (☎ 020-7538 8600; www.intourist
.co.uk)
Page & Moy Holidays (☎ 08700-106 230; www.page
-moy.co.uk) Specialises in river cruises.
Regent Holidays (☎ 0117-921 1711; www.regent
-holidays.co.uk)
Russia Experience (☎ 020-8566 8846; www.trans
-siberian.co.uk) Also runs the Beetroot Bus (www.beetroot
.org), a backpacker-style tour between St Petersburg and
Moscow, as well as adventurous programmes in the Altai
and Tuva.
Russian Gateway (☎ 08704-46 1690; www.russian
gateway.co.uk) Web-based agency.
Steppes East (☎ 01285-880 980; www.steppeseast
.co.uk) Specialises in catering to offbeat requirements.
Travel for the Arts (☎ 020-8799 8350; www
.travelforthearts.co.uk) Specialises in luxury culture-based
tours to Russia for people with a specific interest in opera
and ballet.
Voyages Jules Verne (☎ 020-7616 1000; www.vjv
.co.uk) Offers a variety of upmarket tours in Russia.

INDEPENDENT VS GROUP TOUR

Independent travel in Russia can be a lot of fun, although you shouldn't expect it to be necessarily cheap or easy to organise. The important factor to note is that your enjoyment will be
directly in proportion to your ability to speak and read Russian. Away from the major cities, your
odds of meeting anyone who speaks English are slim. With limited language skills, everything
you attempt will likely be more costly and difficult. However, it's far from impossible; if you really
want to meet locals and have a flexible itinerary, independent travel is the way to go.

To help things along, it's a good idea to consider using a specialist travel agency to arrange
your visa and to make some of your transport and accommodation bookings. Most will be happy
to work on any itinerary. It's also possible to arrange guides and transfers – the prices can sometimes be better than those you'd be able to negotiate yourself (with or without language skills).
Using a tour agency to buy train tickets only, though, can work out much more expensive than
if you were to do it yourself in Russia: check prices carefully and only consider doing this if you
absolutely must travel on certain dates and want a specific class of ticket.

Once in Russia, excursions and trips can be booked through agencies in all large cities; elsewhere, it's usually not too difficult to find locals ready to escort you on nature expeditions, treks
and the like. Many interesting places are far off the beaten path and the best way to reach them
is often through a local guide or travel agent. We have noted some examples in the various
destination listings.

On group tours everything is taken care of; all you need to do is pay and turn up. Tours
can cater to special interests and range from backpacker basics to full-on tsarist luxury. Bear in
mind that you'll seldom be alone, which can be a curse as well as a blessing (depending on the
company). This will also reduce your chances of interacting with locals, with opportunities to
head off the beaten track or alter the itinerary limited, if not impossible.

TRAVELLING THE SCIENTIFIC WAY

Four floors up in a Soviet apartment block in the north of Moscow is the **Academy of Free Travels** (☎ 495-457 8949; www.avp.travel.ru; apt 547, Leningradskoe sh 112-2), home of Russian hitchhiker extraordinaire Anton Krotov. Plastered in maps outlining his travels and full of photographs and small souvenirs, with a bed in one corner, a heavily laden desk in another and stockpiles of the many books he has written and published, Krotov's world is a fascinating one.

Krotov's travels have taken him from one end of Russia to the other on less than an old Soviet 10-kopeck coin, not to mention to India, the Middle East, Central Asia and Africa on little more. His travelling philosophy: 'The world is good and belongs to everyone. There are many cars, many empty seats, many empty houses, food for all to eat, many possibilities! We try to use it!'

Krotov's 'scientific' method of travelling assumes that most people are kind and happy to give bed and board to a traveller – you only need to find the key to their heart. How to do that is the subject of his books, containing frequently hilarious accounts of his travels in which you'll discover that the Russian approach to hitchhiking includes scrounging lifts not only in cars, but also cargo trains, ships, military planes – basically, anything that moves.

Don't be fooled into thinking Krotov is a throwback hippie. It actually takes some organisation, and not a little guts, to undertake the type of expeditions Krotov and his followers do: to the geographical centre of Russia, for example, 1200km north of Krasnoyarsk and only accessible in winter because there are no permanent roads, just tracks in the snow; or through some of the most war-torn, poverty-ridden and disease-stricken parts of Africa and Central Asia. So impressed was Krotov by the hospitality of the people in Islamic countries through which he travelled that he became a Muslim himself.

Krotov disdains travelling in the comfortable parts of the world (because he realises that in Europe and the USA people will not be so willing to put him up every step of the way), but he's certainly not above practising what he preaches. Any traveller who calls in advance and sincerely wants to tap into his and his followers' principles of 'free' travel is welcome to turn up at his flat, buy one of his books (all in Russian), have a cup of tea, even crash for the night. Assuming that he's not on the road, of course.

Wallace Arnold Tours (☎ 0113-263 4234; www .wallacearnold.co.uk) Runs bus tours to Russia aimed at older travellers.

USA
Cruise Marketing International (☎ 800-578 7742; www.cruiserussia.com) Books tours on cruises along Russian waterways such as the Volga River.
Far East Development (☎ 206-282 0824; www .traveleastrussia.com) Ecoadventure tour company specialising in Far East Russia.
Mir Corporation (☎ 206-624 7289; www.mircorp.com) Options include private train tours along the trans-Siberian route in Pullman-style carriages.
Ouzel Expeditions (☎ 907-783 2216; www.ouzel.com) Specialises in Kamchatka fishing trips.
Red Star Travel (☎ 206-522 5995; www.travel2 russia.com)
Russiatours (☎ 800-633 1008; www.russiatours.com) Specialises in luxury tours to Moscow and St Petersburg.
Sokol Tours (☎ /fax 1-724 935 5373; www.sokoltours .com) Tour options include train trips, Tuva and Kamchatka.
Viking Rivers Cruises (☎ 818-227 1234; www.viking rivercruises.com) Upmarket Russian cruise operator.

White Nights (☎ /fax 916-979 9381; www.wnights .com; 610 La Sierra Dr, Sacramento CA 95864) Also has offices in Germany, the Netherlands, Russia and Switzerland.

GETTING AROUND
Getting around Russia is a breeze thanks to a splendid train network and a packed schedule of flights between all major and many minor towns and cities. In the summer months many of the rivers and lakes are navigable and have cruises and ferry operations. For hops between towns there are buses, most often *marshrutky* (fixed-route minibuses).

Don't underestimate the distances involved: Russia is huge. From Yekaterinburg at the western limits of Siberia to Vladivostok on the Pacific coast is about the same distance as from Berlin to New York, while even a relatively short overland hop, such as the one from Irkutsk to its near neighbour Khabarovsk, is still roughly equivalent to the distance from London to Cairo. And you were wondering about taking a bus?

TRANSPORT

TRANSPORT

Air

Flying in Russia is like the country itself – a unique experience. Many flights (except those between major cities) are delayed, often for hours and with no explanation.

Almost every small town has an airport but don't expect much; most of these places have fewer facilities than the average bus shelter. If nothing else, it will at least have flights to the nearest big town or city, and from there you'll be able to make nation-wide connections. Recent years have seen the emergence of small, regional airlines, but most use old Aeroflot machines with a fresh coat of paint (see below).

It's no problem buying a ticket at *avia-kassa* (ticket offices) found in most large towns and cities. Note that some city ticket offices still have a huge Aeroflot sign over the door, even if none of the airlines serving that town actually use the Aeroflot name. Generally speaking, you'll do better booking internal flights once you arrive in Russia, where more flights and flight information

are available, and where prices may be lower. Fares are generally 30% cheaper (60% on major Moscow routings) for advance book-ings or evening departures. Finding out fares before you arrive can be tricky; try the air-line websites we list, or contact **Primorskoye Aeroagentsvo** (☎ 4232-407 707; www.airagency.ru), a Vladivostok-based agency with branches in Moscow and St Petersburg, as well as across the Russian Far East, who will quote fares and have English-speaking agents.

Whenever you book airline tickets in Russia you'll need to show your passport and visa. Tickets can also be purchased at the airport right up to the departure of the flight and sometimes even if the city centre office says that the plane is full. Return fares are usually double the one-way fares.

Make sure you reconfirm your flight at least 24 hours before takeoff: Russian air-lines have a nasty habit of cancelling un-confirmed tickets. Airlines may also bump you if you don't check in at least 90 minutes before departure.

AIRLINE SAFETY IN RUSSIA

Since the break up of Aeroflot, the former Soviet state airline, Russia has witnessed the boom and bust of hundreds of smaller airlines ('baby-flots'). Following a crash in Irkutsk in August 2001, in which 145 people died, President Vladimir Putin ordered a purge of Russian airlines – as a result, almost half of the total number of airlines lost their licences.

Obtaining reliable statistics is difficult, but people familiar with the Russian aviation scene say that the safety of domestic airlines varies widely. For information on flight accidents in Russia check www.airsafe.com/events/airlines/fsu.htm. Tales of Russian airline-safety lapses are common, though often apocryphal. The vast majority of crashes involve small airlines in Siberia (connecting district centres with remote villages or mines) or military planes.

Of more concern is the checking procedure that's meant to prevent terrorist bombings and hijacks. Two crashes in 2004 involved explosive devices where the bombers were allowed on the planes after they bribed officials. In the wake of these and other terrorist incidents around the world, security checks at Russian airports have increased – however, they are not yet at the same level as those in the US or Europe.

Generally, **Aeroflot Russian Airlines** (www.aeroflot.com) is considered to have the highest stand-ards. This airline took over the old international routes of the Soviet-era Aeroflot and today offers Western-style services on mostly Western-made aircraft such as Boeing 757s and 737s. The airline also offers domestic services on many routes; check out the website for further information. **Transaero** (www.transaero.com/noframes/eng/home.htm) and **Krasair** (www.krasair.ru in Russian) are other Russian airlines with a consistent safety record.

If you're worried about airline safety, the good news is that for many destinations in Rus-sia, getting there by train or bus is practical, and often preferable (if you have the time). Also, on routes between major cities it's possible that you may have a choice of airlines (although given the dearth of hard information and continually changing circumstances, it's impossible to recommend one operator over another). But in some cases – where you're short of time or where your intended destination doesn't have reliable rail or road connections – you will have no choice but to take a flight.

To minimise the danger of loss or theft, try not to check in any baggage: many planes have special stowage areas for large carry-on pieces. Also note that you put your carry-on luggage under your own seat, not under the one in front of you. However, Russian airlines can be very strict about charging for bags that are overweight, which generally means anything over 20kg. One way of getting around this is to bulk out your coat and clothes' pockets with heavier items and repack once you're through the check-in procedure.

Have your passport and ticket handy throughout the various security and ticket checks that can occur right up until you find a seat. Some flights have assigned seats, others do not. On the latter, seating is a free-for-all.

Beware: most internal flights in Moscow use either Domodedovo or Vnukovo airports; if you're connecting to Moscow's Sheremetyevo-2 international airport, allow a few hours to cross town.

Boat

The great rivers that wind across Russia are the country's oldest highways. A millennium ago the early Russians based their power on control of the waterborne trade between the Baltic and Black Seas. River transport remains important and in summer it's possible to travel long distances across Russia on passenger boats. You can do this either by taking a cruise, which you can book through agencies in the West or in Russia, or by using scheduled river passenger services. The season runs from late May through to mid-October, but is shorter on some routes.

To find out what's running, go down to the *rechnoy vokzal* (river station), where you can check timetables and fares. Note that Raketa, Kometa and Meteor are all types of hydrofoil; windows are sealed and spray splattered and the experience can be somewhat claustrophobic.

Teplokhod is a large passenger boat, *kater* a smaller river or sea boat and *parom* a ferry. *Vverkh* means upstream and *vniz* downstream, while *tuda* means one way and *tuda i obratno* return.

There are also ferry services along the coasts and across to islands that combine a pleasant sea journey with public transport.

MOSCOW TO ST PETERSBURG

There are numerous boats plying the routes between Moscow and St Petersburg, many stopping at some of the Golden Ring cities on the way. Most of the trips are aimed at foreign tourists. See p729 for the names of some overseas travel companies that can book such trips.

You can also sail on a boat aimed at Russian holiday-makers. The price is much less than for the foreigner cruises but the food and accommodation are also less lavish, though adequate. **Cruise Company Orthodox** (Map pp126-7; ☎ 495-943 8560; www.cruise .ru; ul Alabyana 5, Moscow; Ⓜ Sokol) and **Solnechny Parus** (Map pp234-5; ☎ 812-279 43 10; www.solpar .ru; ul Vosstania 55, St Petersburg; Ⓜ Chernyshevskaya) sell tickets for cruises from Moscow to St Petersburg as well as for cruises further south along the Volga.

THE VOLGA

See p406 for details of cruises along the Volga from Moscow and other points along the river.

NORTHERN EUROPEAN RUSSIA

Northern European Russia (including St Petersburg) is well served by various waterborne transport options. Apart from hydrofoil services along the Neva River and the Gulf of Finland from St Petersburg to Petrodvorets, there are also very popular cruises from St Petersburg to Valaam in Lake Ladoga (p363), some continuing on to Lake Onega, Petrozavodsk and Kizhi (p362). Also from Kem (Karelia) and Arkhangelsk you can take boats to the Solovetsky Islands (p395).

BLACK SEA

Between June and September, frequent hydrofoils connect the Black Sea port of Novorossiysk and the resort of Sochi.

SIBERIA & THE RUSSIAN FAR EAST

Siberia and the Russian Far East have a short navigation season (mid-June to September), with long-distance river transport limited to the Ob and Irtysh Rivers (Omsk–Tara–Tobolsk–Salekhard), the Lena (Ust-Kut–Lensk–Yakutsk) and the Yenisey (Krasnoyarsk–Igarka–Dudinka). You can also make one-day hops by hydrofoil along several sections of these rivers, along the

TRANSPORT

Amur River (Khabarovsk–Komsomolsk–Nikolaevsk) and across Lake Baikal (Irkutsk–Olkhon–Severobaikalsk–Nizhneangarsk). Other Baikal services are limited to short hops around Irkutsk/Listvyanka and from Sakhyurta to Olkhon unless you charter a boat (about US$200 per day), most conveniently done in Listvyanka, Nizhneangarsk, Severobaikalsk or Ust-Barguzin. Irkutsk agencies can help.

Ferries from Vanino cross the Tatar Strait to Sakhalin, but it can be murder trying to buy a ticket in the summer months; although sailings are supposed to take place daily, in reality there is no set schedule. There are also irregular sailings from Korsakov, on Sakhalin, across to Yuzhno-Kurilsk in the Kuril Island chain.

Out of Vladivostok there is a range of ferries to nearby islands and to beach resorts further south along the coast. For the truly adventurous, with a month or so to spare, it's possible to hitch a lift on one of the supply ships that sail out of Nakhodka and Vladivostok up to the Arctic Circle towns of Anadyr and Providyeniya.

Beware that boat schedules can change radically from year to year (especially on Lake Baikal) and are only published infuriatingly near to the first sailing of each season. When buying tickets for a hydrofoil, try to avoid *ryad* (rows) one to three – spray will obscure your view, and, although enclosed, you'll often get damp.

Bus & Marshrutky

Long-distance buses complement rather than compete with the rail network. They generally serve areas with no railway or routes on which trains are slow, infrequent or overloaded.

Most cities have a main intercity bus station (автовокзал, *avtovokzal*). Like long-distance bus stations everywhere, they are often scoundrel magnets and are rarely pleasant places to visit after dark. Tickets are sold at the station or on the bus. Fares are normally listed on the timetable and posted on a wall. As often as not you'll get a ticket with a seat assignment, scribbled almost illegibly on a till receipt. Prices are comparable to 2nd-class train fares; journey times depend on road conditions. A sometimes hefty fee is charged for larger bags.

Marshrutky (a Russian diminutive form of *marshrutnoye taksi*, meaning a fixed-route taxi) are minibuses that are quicker than the rusty old buses and rarely cost much more. Where roads are good and villages frequent, *marshrutky* can be twice as fast as buses, and are well worth the double fare.

Car & Motorcycle

Bearing in mind the frequently dire quality of the roads, lack of adequate signposting, keen-eyed highway police and the occasional difficulty of obtaining petrol (not to mention spare parts), driving in Russia will not be everybody's cup of tea. But if you've

---

DRIVING & CYCLING ACROSS RUSSIA

In 2004 the final missing link in a trans-Russian highway was filled when a section of road opened between Chita and Khabarovsk. It's now possible to drive or cycle the 10,000 plus kilometres from St Petersburg to Vladivostok, although only about one-quarter of the eastern section of the highway is paved. The rest is gravel-topped, with plans to have the entire highway paved by 2008.

A few intrepid souls have been known to rise to the challenge of driving, even cycling, across the country. Most famously, *Corriere della Sera* journalist Luigi Barzini documented the road trip he made from Beijing to Paris in 1907, led by Prince Scipione Borghese. The journey took them two months, during which time they frequently resorted to driving along the railway rather than the mud tracks that constituted Siberian roads.

More recently, Ewan McGregor and Charley Boorman wrote about their Russian adventures in *Long Way Round* (www.longwayround.com/lwr.htm); their round-the-world route took them from Volgograd all the way to Yakutsk and Magadan via Kazakhstan and Mongolia. The celebrity bikers had a camera crew and support team following them. For tales of how to cross part of Russia the hard way check out www.roundtheworldbybike.com, the website of Alastair Humphreys, who cycled from Magadan to Vanino in the depths of winter!

a sense of humour, patience and a decent vehicle, it's an adventurous way to go.

Motorbikes will undergo vigorous scrutiny by border officials and highway police, especially if you're riding anything vaguely flashy. Motorcyclists should also note that while foreign automobile companies now have an established presence in Moscow, St Petersburg and other major cities, motorcycles in the former Soviet Union are almost exclusively Russian- or East German–made: a Ural-brand carb will not fit your Hog.

BRING YOUR OWN VEHICLE

Apart from your licence, you'll also need your vehicle's registration papers and proof of insurance. Be sure your insurance covers you in Russia. A customs declaration promising that you will take your vehicle with you when you leave is also required. A departure road tax of about US$10 is collected at the border.

DRIVING LICENCE

To legally drive your own or a rented car or motorcycle in Russia you'll need to be over 18 years of age and have a full driving licence. In addition, you'll need an International Driving Permit with a Russian translation of your licence, or a certified Russian translation of your full licence (you can certify translations at a Russian embassy or consulate).

FUEL & SPARE PARTS

Western-style gas stations are common. Petrol will come in four main grades: 76, 93, 95 and 98 octane. And prices are cheap by European standards: R15.50 for a litre of 80 octane, R17.60 a litre for 92 octane and R18.60 for 95 octane. Unleaded gas is available in major cities; BP gas stations usually always sell it. *Dizel* (diesel) is also available (around R13 a litre). In the countryside, petrol stations are usually not more than 100km apart, but you shouldn't rely on this.

RENTAL & HIRE CARS

You can rent self-drive cars in Moscow (p187) and St Petersburg (p291). Elsewhere, renting a car that comes with a driver is the norm. This can be a blessing, given the nature of Russian roads.

Private cars sometimes operate as cabs over long distances and can be a great deal if there's a group of you to share the cost. Since they take the most direct route between cities, the savings in time can be considerable over slow trains and meandering buses. Typically you will find drivers offering this service outside bus terminals. Someone in your party must speak Russian to negotiate a price with the driver that typically works out to about R10 to R12 per kilometre.

Select your driver carefully, look over their car and try to assess their sobriety before setting off. Note that you'll always have to pay return mileage if renting 'one way', and that many local drivers want to get home the same night, even if that's at 3am.

ROAD CONDITIONS

Russian main roads are a mixed bag – sometimes smooth, straight dual carriageways, sometimes rough, narrow, winding and choked with the diesel fumes of the slow, heavy vehicles that make up a high proportion of Russian traffic. Driving much more than 300km in a day is pretty tiring.

Russian drivers use indicators far less than they should, and like to overtake everything on the road – on the inside. Russian drivers rarely switch on anything more than sidelights – and often not even those – until it's pitch black at night. Some say this is to avoid dazzling others, as, for some reason, dipping headlights is not common practice.

If you use a hired driver or taxi, the driver will probably be offended if you wear your seat belt (except when passing through a GAI (State Automobile Inspectorate) police post when everyone in a taxi suddenly pulls the belt half-heartedly for show). Even if you say, 'It's not your driving, it's those other crazies I'm worried about,' drivers will often request you leave it off. Of course, you have the final word, but it's not unheard of for passengers to get a new driver who won't mind if the seat belt is fastened.

ROAD RULES

Russians drive on the right and traffic coming from the right generally (but not always) has the right of way. Speed limits are generally 60km/h in towns but usually there are no signs to say so – you have to intuit from a town's name plate that the limit applies on an otherwise fast, straight road. Limits are between 80km/h and 110km/h on highways. There may be a 90km/h zone,

TRANSPORT

enforced by speed traps, as you leave a city. Children under 12 may not travel in the front seat, and seat belt use is mandatory (though few motorists seem to realise this!). Motorcycle riders (and passengers) must wear crash helmets.

Technically, the maximum legal blood-alcohol content is 0.04%, but in practice it is illegal to drive after consuming *any* alcohol at all. This is a rule that is strictly enforced. Police will first use a breathalyser test to check blood-alcohol levels – in Moscow and other big cities the equipment is fairly reliable, but old Soviet test kits are not. You have the legal right to insist on a blood test (which involves the police taking you to a hospital).

Traffic lights that flicker green are about to change to yellow, then red. Beware, you will be pulled over if the police see you going through a yellow light, so drive cautiously.

The GAI

The State Automobile Inspectorate, GAI (short for Gosudarstvennaya Avtomobilnaya Inspektsia), skulks about on the roadsides, waiting for speeding, headlightless or other miscreant vehicles. Officers of the GAI are authorised to stop you, issue on-the-spot fines and, worst of all, shoot at your car if you refuse to pull over.

The GAI also hosts the occasional speed trap – the Moscow–Brest, Moscow–Oryol and Vyborg–St Petersburg roads have reputations for this. In Moscow and St Petersburg, the GAI is everywhere, stopping cars and collecting 'fines' on the spot.

There are permanent GAI checkpoints at the boundary of many Russian regions, cities and towns. Random spot checks are rarer than in previous years but still occur. For serious infractions, the GAI can confiscate your licence, which you'll have to retrieve from the main station. If your car is taken to the GAI's parking lot, you should try to get it back as soon as possible, since you'll be charged a huge amount for each day that it's kept there.

Get the shield number of the 'arresting' officer. By law, GAI officers are not allowed to take any money at all – fines should be paid via Sberbank. However, in reality Russian drivers normally pay the GAI officer approximately half the official fine, thus saving money and the time eaten up by Russian bureaucracy, both at the police station and the bank.

Hitching

Hitching is never entirely safe in any country in the world, and Lonely Planet doesn't recommend it. Travellers who hitch should understand that they are taking a small but potentially serious risk.

That said, hitching in Russia is a very common method of getting around (see p731). In cities, hitching rides is called hailing a taxi, no matter what type of vehicle stops (see opposite). In the countryside, especially in remote areas not well served by public transport, hitching is a major mode of transport.

Rides are hailed by standing at the side of the road and flagging passing vehicles with a low, up-and-down wave (not an extended thumb). You are expected to pitch in for petrol; paying what would be the normal bus fare for a long-haul ride is considered appropriate.

While hitching is widely accepted – and therefore safer than in some other countries – you should still use common sense to keep safe. Avoid hitching at night. Women should exercise extreme caution. You should avoid hitching alone and let someone know where you are planning to go.

Local Transport

Most cities have good public transport systems combining bus, trolleybus and tram; the biggest cities also have metro systems. Public transport is very cheap and easy to use, but you'll need to be able to decipher some Cyrillic. Taxis are plentiful and usually cheap by Western standards.

BOAT

In St Petersburg, Moscow and several other cities located on rivers, coasts, lakes or reservoirs, public ferries and water excursions give a different perspective on the place. For details, see Getting Around in the relevant chapters or sections.

BUS, MARSHRUTKY, TROLLEYBUS & TRAM

Even in cities with metros you'll often need to use above-ground forms of public transport. Services are frequent in city centres but more erratic as you move out towards the edges. They can get jam-packed in the late afternoon or on poorly served routes.

A stop is usually marked by a roadside A sign for buses, T for trolleybuses, and ТРАМВАЙ or a T hanging over the road for trams. The normal fare (R7 to R20) is usually paid to the conductor; if there is no conductor, pass the money to the driver. You may be charged extra if you have a large bag.

Within most cities, *marshrutky* double up official bus routes but are more frequent. In certain towns they're prepared to stop between official bus stops, which can save quite a walk.

METRO

Moscow, St Petersburg, Nizhny Novgorod and Yekaterinburg have excellent metro systems. The only confusing element is that a metro station can have several names – one for each line that crosses at that station. See the Getting Around sections of the relevant city chapters for details on riding these systems.

TAXI

There are two main types of taxi in Russia. The official ones are either taxis you order by phone (see city listings for numbers), or the rarer four-door sedans with a chequerboard strip down the side and a green light in the front window that cruise the streets of Moscow. There are also 'private' taxis (any other vehicle on the road).

Official taxis have a meter that they sometimes use, though you can always negotiate an off-the-meter price. There's a flag fall, and the number on the meter must be multiplied by the multiplier listed on a sign that *should* be on the dashboard or somewhere visible. Extra charges are incurred for radio calls and some night-time calls. Taxis outside of luxury hotels often demand usurious rates, although, on the whole, official taxis are around 25% more expensive than private taxis.

To hail a private taxi, stand at the side of the road, extend your arm and wait until something stops. When someone stops for you, state your destination and be prepared to negotiate the fare – it's best to fix this before getting in. If the driver's game, they'll ask you to get in (*sadites*), but always act on the cautious side and consider your safety before doing this.

Check with locals to determine the average taxi fare in that city at the time of your visit; taxi prices around the country vary widely. Practise saying your destination and the amount you want to pay so that it comes out properly. The better your Russian, the lower the fare (generally). If possible, let a Russian friend negotiate for you: they'll do better than you will.

Risks & Precautions

Avoid taxis lurking outside foreign-run establishments, luxury hotels, railway stations and airports. They charge far too much and get uppity when you try to talk them down. Know your route: be familiar with how to get there and how long it should take. Never get into a taxi that has more than one person already in it, especially after dark.

Keep your fare money in a separate pocket to avoid flashing large wads of cash. If you're staying at a private residence, have the taxi stop at the corner nearest your destination, not the exact address. Trust your instincts – if a driver looks creepy, take the next car.

Tours

Once in Russia, you'll find many travel agencies specialising in city tours and excursions. Sometimes these are the best way to visit out-of-the-way sights. See the travel agencies listed in the relevant city sections.

Train

Russia has the world's second-largest rail network. Tickets can be cheap and are seldom difficult to buy: for a small extra charge, typically R100, there are service bureaus at most major stations that allow you to skip the queues, if there are any, at the general service windows. Trains are relatively comfortable, making them an excellent way to get around, see the countryside and meet Russians from all walks of life. A good 1st- or 2nd-class berth on a Russian sleeper train could prove more civilised than one in Western Europe, as they're larger and often more comfortable.

Trains are rarely speedy but have a remarkable record for punctuality, with most departing each station to the minute allotted on the timetable. However, there are underlying reasons for this punctuality: managers have a large portion of their pay determined by the timeliness of their trains. This not only inspires promptness, but it results in the creation of fairly generous schedules. You'll notice this when you find your train stationary for hours in the middle of nowhere only suddenly to start up and roll into the next station right on time.

All trains have numbers. The lower the number, the higher the standard and the price; the best trains are under 100. Odd-numbered trains head towards Moscow; even ones head east away from the capital.

READING A TRAIN TIMETABLE

Russian train timetables vary from place to place but generally list a destination; train number; category of train; frequency of service; and time of departure and arrival, in Moscow time unless otherwise noted (see the following information on arrival and departure times).

Trains in smaller city stations generally begin somewhere else, so you'll see a starting point and a destination on the timetable. For example, when catching a train from Yekaterinburg to Irkutsk, the timetable may list Moscow as the point or origin and Irkutsk as the destination. The following are a few key points to look out for.

Number – Номер (*nomer*). The higher the number of a train, the slower it is; anything over 900 is likely to be a mail train.

Category – Скорый Пассажирский Почтово-багажный Пригородный (*Skory, Passazhirsky, Pochtovo-bagazhny, Prigorodny* – and various abbreviations thereof). These are train categories and refer, respectively, to fast, passenger, post-cargo and suburban trains. There may also be the name of the train, usually in Russian quotation marks, eg 'Россия' ('Rossiya').

Frequency – Ежедневно (*yezhednevno*, daily); чётные (*chyotnye*, even-numbered dates); нечётные (*nechyotnye*, odd-numbered dates); отменён (*otmenyon*, cancelled). All of these, as well, can appear in various abbreviations, notably еж, ч, не, and отмен. Days of the week are listed usually as numbers (where 1 is Monday and 7 Sunday) or as abbreviations of the name of the day (Пон, Вт, Ср, Чт, Пт, С and Вск are, respectively, Monday to Sunday). Remember that time-zone differences can affect these days. So in Chita (Moscow + 6hr) a train timetabled at 23.20 on Tuesday actually leaves 5.20am on Wednesday. In months with an odd number of days, two odd days follow one another (eg 31 May, 1 June). This throws out trains working on an alternate-day cycle so if travelling near month's end pay special attention to the hard-to-decipher footnotes on a timetable. For example, '27/V – 3/VI Ч' means that from 27 May to 3 June the train runs on even dates. On some trains, frequency depends on the time of year, in which case details are usually given in similar abbreviated small print: eg '27/VI – 31/VIII Ч; 1/IX – 25/VI 2, 5' means that from 27 June to 31 August the train runs on even dates, while from 1 September to 25 June it runs on Tuesday and Friday.

Arrival & Departure Times – Corresponding trains running in opposite directions on the same route may appear on the same line of the timetable. In this case you may find route entries like время отправления с конечного пункта (*vremya otpravlenia s konechnogo punkta*), or the time the return train leaves its station of origin. Most train times are given in a 24-hour time format, and almost always in Moscow time (Московское время, *Moskovskoye vremya*). But suburban trains are usually marked in local time (местное время, *mestnoe vremya*). From here on it gets tricky (as though the rest wasn't), so don't confuse the following:

время отправления (*vremya otpravleniya*) Time of departure.

время отправления с начального пункта (*vremya otpravleniya s nachalnogo punkta*) Time of departure from the train's starting point.

время прибытия (*vremya pribytiya*) Time of arrival at the station you're in.

время прибытия на конечный пункт (*vremya pribytiya v konechny punkt*) Time of arrival at the destination.

время в пути (*vremya v puti*) Duration of the journey.

Distance – You may sometimes see the расстояние (*rastoyaniye*) – distance in kilometres from the point of departure – on the timetable as well. These are rarely accurate and usually refer to the kilometre distance used to calculate the fare. Note that if you want to calculate where you are while on a journey, keep a close look out for the small black-and-white kilometre posts generally on the southern side of the track. These mark the distance to and from Moscow. In between each kilometre marker are smaller posts counting down roughly every 100m. The distances on train timetables don't always correspond to these marker posts (usually because the timetable distances are the ones used to calculate fares).

LONG DISTANCE

The regular long-distance service is a *skory poezd* (fast train). It rarely gets up enough speed to really merit the 'fast' label. The best *skory* trains often have names, eg the *Rossiya* (the Moscow to Vladivostok service) and the *Baikal* (the Moscow to Irkutsk service). These 'name trains', or *firmeny poezda*, generally have cleaner cars, polite(r) attendants and more-convenient arrival and departure hours; they sometimes also have fewer stops, more first-class accommodation, and functioning restaurants.

A *passazhirsky poezd* (passenger train) is an intercity stopping train, found mostly on routes of 1000km or less. Journeys on these can take rather longer, as the trains clank from one small town to the next. However, they are inexpensive, and often well timed to allow an overnight sleep between neighbouring cities. Avoid trains numbered over 900. These are primarily baggage or postal services and are appallingly slow, often sitting in stations for several hours.

SHORT DISTANCE

A *prigorodny poezd* (suburban train), commonly nicknamed an *elektrichka*, is a local service linking a city with its suburbs or nearby towns, or groups of adjacent towns – they are often useful for day trips, but can be fearfully crowded. There's no need to book ahead for these – just buy your ticket and go. In bigger stations there may be separate timetables, in addition to *prigorodny zal* (the usual name for ticket halls) and platforms for these trains.

TIMETABLES

Timetables are posted in stations and are revised twice a year. It's vital to note that the whole Russian rail network mostly runs on Moscow time, so timetables and station clocks from St Petersburg to Vladivostok will be written in and set to Moscow time. The only general exception is suburban rail services, which are listed in local time.

Most stations have an information window; expect the attendant to speak only Russian and to give a bare minimum of information. Sometimes you may have to pay a small fee (around R10) for information. See the boxed text, opposite for ways to crack the timetable code on your own.

CLASSES

> In Europe and America people travel in a train fully aware that it belongs either to a state or company and that their ticket grants them only temporary occupation and certain restricted rights. In Russia people just take them over.
>
> Laurens van der Post,
> Journey into Russia

Russians have the knack of making themselves very much at home on trains. This often means that they'll be travelling with plenty of luggage. It also means inevitable juggling of the available space in all classes of compartment.

In all but local trains there's a luggage bin underneath each of the lower berths that will hold a medium-sized backpack or small suitcase. There's also enough space beside the bin to squeeze in another medium-sized canvas bag. Above the doorway (in 1st and 2nd class) or over the upper bunks (in 3rd class) there's room to accommodate a couple more rucksacks.

In all classes of carriage with sleeping accommodation you'll be asked if you want *pastil*. If you accept (recommended) you'll be given two sheets, a washcloth, a pillowcase and a blanket; you'll usually have to pay extra (R40 to R60) for this to the *provodnitsa* (the female carriage attendant; see boxed text, p740). In 1st class the bed is often made up already and with some types of fare the cost of bedding is already included.

1st Class/SV

Most often called SV (which is short for *spalny vagon*, or sleeping wagon), 1st-class compartments are also called *myagky* (soft class) or *lyux*. They are the same size as 2nd class but have only two berths, so there's more room and more privacy for double the cost. Some 1st-class compartments also have TVs on which it's possible to watch videos or DVDs supplied by the *provodnitsa* for a small fee (there's nothing to stop you from bringing your own). You could also unplug the TV and plug in your computer or other electrical equipment. These carriages also have the edge in that there are only half as many people queuing to use the toilet every morning. So far, on only a couple of services (Moscow to St Petersburg and Moscow to Kazan)

TRANSPORT

TRANSPORT

SHE WHO MUST BE OBEYED

On any long-distance Russian train journey you'll soon learn who's in charge: the *provodnitsa*. Though sometimes male *(provodniks)*, these carriage attendants are usually women, with some of the most distinctive hairdos you'll come across this side of a drag-queen convention.

Apart from checking your ticket before boarding the train, doling out linen, and shaking you awake in the middle of the night when your train arrives, the *provodnitsa's* job is to keep her carriage spick-and-span (some are more diligent at this than others) and to make sure the samovar is always fired up with hot water. They will have cups, plates and cutlery to borrow, if you need them, and can provide drinks and snacks for a small price; some have even been known to cook up meals and offer them around.

On long journeys the *provodnitsa* works in a team of two; one will be working while the other is resting. Butter them up the right way and your journey will be all the more pleasant.

---

will you find luxury SV compartments each with their own shower and toilet.

2nd Class/Kupe

The compartments in a *kupeyny* (2nd-class, also called 'compartmentalised' carriage) – commonly shortened to *kupe* – are the standard accommodation on all long-distance trains. These carriages are divided into nine enclosed compartments, each with four reasonably comfortable berths, a fold-down table and just enough room between the bunks to turn around.

In every carriage there's also one half-sized compartment with just two berths. This is usually occupied by the *provodnitsa*, or reserved for railway employees, but there's a slim chance that you may end up in it, particularly if you do a deal directly with a *provodnitsa* for a train ticket.

3rd Class/Platskartny

A reserved-place *platskartny* carriage, sometimes also called *zhyostky* ('hard class') and usually abbreviated to *platskart*, is essentially a dorm carriage sleeping 54. The bunks are uncompartmentalised and are arranged in blocks of four down one side of the corridor and in twos on the other, with the lower bunk on the latter side converting to a table and chairs during the day.

Platskart is ideal for one-night journeys. However, on multiday journeys the scene often resembles a refugee camp, with clothing strung between bunks, a great swapping of bread, fish and jars of tea, and babies sitting on potties while their snot-nosed siblings tear up and down the corridor. That said, many travellers (women in particular) find this a better option than being cooped

up with three (possibly drunken) Russian men. It's also a great way to meet ordinary Russians. *Platskart* tickets cost half to two-thirds the price of a 2nd-class berth.

If you do travel *platskart*, it's worth requesting specific numbered seats when booking your ticket. The ones to avoid are 1 to 4, 33 to 38, 53 and 54, found at each end of the carriage, close to the samovar and toilets, where people are constantly coming and going. Also note that 39 to 52 are the doubles with the bunk that converts to a table – you may want to avoid these ones too, especially if you're tall.

4th Class/Obshchiy

Obshchiy (general) is unreserved. On long-distance trains the *obshchiy* carriage looks the same as a *platskartny* one but, when full, eight people are squeezed into each unenclosed compartment, so there's no room to lie down. Suburban trains normally have only *obshchiy* class, which, in this case, means bench-type seating. On a few daytime-only intercity trains there are higher grade *obshchiy* carriages with more-comfortable, reserved chairs.

COSTS

In this book we typically quote 2nd-class *(kupe)* fares. Expect 1st-class (SV) fares to be double this, and 3rd-class *(platskartny)* to be about 40% less. Children under five travel free if they share a berth with an adult; otherwise, children under 10 pay half-fare for their own berth.

Complicating matters is Russian Railways' policy of varying fares by to season. At peak travel times, for example early July to early August and around key holidays such as Easter and New Year, fares can be between 12% and 16% higher than the regular fare. The inverse happens at slack times of the year such as early January to March when there are discounts on fares. On *skory* and *firmeny* trains it's also possible to have two grades of *kupe* fare: with or without meals.

Fares quoted in this book were collected between March and July so please take them as a general guide only.

DANGERS & ANNOYANCES

Make certain on all sleeper trains that your baggage is safely stowed, preferably in the

---

HOW TO READ YOUR TICKET

When buying a ticket in Russia, you'll always be asked for your passport so that its number and your name can be printed on your ticket. The ticket and passport will be matched up by the *provodnitsa* (female carriage attendant) before you're allowed on the train – so make sure the ticket-seller gets these details correct.

Most tickets are printed by computer and come with a duplicate. Shortly after you've boarded the train the *provodnitsa* will come around and collect the tickets: sometimes they will take both copies and give you one back just before your final destination; sometimes they will leave you with the copy. It's a good idea to hang on to this ticket, especially if you're hopping on and off trains, since it provides evidence of how long you've been in a particular place if you're stopped by police.

Sometimes tickets are also sold with separate chits for insurance in the event of a fatal accident (this is a small payment, usually less than R30); for linen; and for some or all meals. The following is a guide for deciphering the rest of what your Russian train ticket is about.

1. Train number
2. Train type
3. Departure date – day and month
4. Departure time – always Moscow time for long-distance trains
5. Carriage number and class: Л = two-bed SV, М = four-bed SV, К = *kupe*, П = *platskartny*, О = *obshchiy*
6. Supplement for class of ticket above *platskartny*
7. Cost for *platskartny* ticket
8. Number of people travelling on ticket
9. Type of passenger: полный (*polny*, adult); детский (*detsky*, child); студенческий (*studenchesky*, student)
10. From/to
11. Bed number
12. Passport number and name
13. Total cost of ticket
14. Tax and service fee
15. Arrival date
16. Arrival time – always Moscow time for long-distance trains

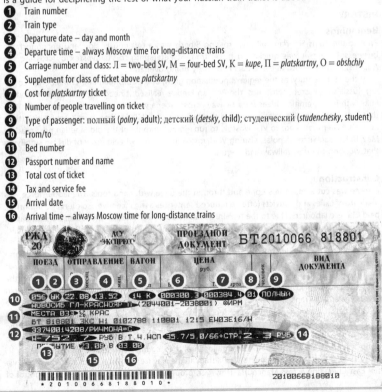

TRANSPORT

TRANSPORT

THE TRANS-SIBERIAN RAILWAY

Extending 9289km from Moscow to Vladivostok on the Pacific, the Trans-Siberian Railway and connecting routes are one of the most famous and potentially enjoyable of the world's great train journeys. Rolling out of Europe and into Asia, through eight time zones and over vast swaths of taiga, steppe and desert, the Trans-Siberian – the world's longest single-service railway – makes all other train rides seem like once around the block with Thomas the Tank Engine.

Don't look for the Trans-Siberian Railway on a timetable, though. The term is used generically for three main lines and the numerous trains that run on them. The trains most people use are the daily *Rossiya* 1/2 service linking Moscow and Vladivostok (or the *Baikal* 9/10 service from Moscow to Irkutsk for part of the way); the weekly 3/4 trans-Mongolian service via Ulaan Baatar to Beijing; and the weekly 19/20 trans-Manchurian service, also from Moscow to Beijing but via Harbin in China.

For the first four days' travel out of Moscow's Yaroslavsky vokzal, the trans-Siberian, trans-Manchurian and trans-Mongolian routes all follow the same line, passing through Nizhny Novgorod on the way to Yekaterinburg in the Ural Mountains and then into Siberia. Many travellers choose to break their journey at Irkutsk to visit Lake Baikal (we recommend you do) but, otherwise, the three main services continue on round the southern tip of the lake to Ulan-Ude, another possible jumping off point for Baikal. From here trans-Siberian trains continue to Vladivostok, while the trans-Mongolian ones head south for the Mongolian border, Ulaan Baatar and Beijing. The trans-Manchurian service continues past Ulan-Ude to Chita, then turns southeast for Zabaikalsk on the Chinese border.

HISTORY

Beginnings

Prior to the Trans-Siberian Railway, crossing Siberia was a torturously slow and uncomfortable business. In fact, it was quicker to travel from St Petersburg to Vladivostok by crossing the Atlantic, North America and the Pacific than by going overland.

In the 19th century, as the region's population grew, and both Japan and China began coveting Russia's far-eastern territories, the Russian Empire realised it needed better communication links with its extremities. Ideas for a railway across Siberia were floated, but it wasn't until 1886 that Tsar Alexander III finally authorised the building of a 7500km line from Chelyabinsk (then Russia's eastern railhead) to Vladivostok, to run along the route of the old Siberian post road. In May 1891, Tsarevitch Nicholas, visiting Vladivostok, emptied a wheelbarrow of dirt, so signifying that work on the new railway had begun.

Construction

A route was cut across the steppe and through the taiga with hand tools. The labour force was made up of exiles and convicts (offered reduced sentences as an incentive), soldiers and imported, paid Chinese labourers. Due to the terrain, climate, floods and landslides, disease, war and bandit attacks, not to mention shoddy materials and bad planning, the railway took 26 years to build. But it remains the most brilliant engineering feat of its time.

The railway was divided into six sections, with construction taking place simultaneously along the route. The Ussuri line (Vladivostok to Khabarovsk) was built between 1891 and 1897, followed by the western Siberian line (Chelyabinsk to Novosibirsk), built between 1892 and 1896, and the mid-Siberian line (Novosibirsk via Irkutsk to Port Baikal), built between 1893 and 1898. Within seven years, the Trans-Siberian Railway stretched 5200km from Moscow to the western shore of Lake Baikal. Baikal was initially crossed by two icebreakers built at Newcastle-upon-Tyne in England and sent in pieces to be assembled in Irkutsk. The huge, four-funnelled *Baikal* was the larger of the two, and her decks were laid with three lines of track that could accommodate an entire express train and its load. The smaller ship, the *Angara*, was used for passengers.

By 1904, it was finally possible to take a train all the way from St Petersburg to Vladivostok, via the East China line across Manchuria. However, propelled by fears that they may lose control of

Manchuria to the Japanese, the Russians embarked upon the alternative Amur line, from Sretensk to Khabarovsk. Finished in 1916, with the bridge over the Amur River at Khabarovsk, it was the final link in the world's longest railway.

Early Services

Following Russia's orgy of self-publicity at the Paris Universal Exposition of 1900, the earliest trans-Siberian travellers were lured on to the rails even before the line was fully completed. To attract overseas clientele, the *State Express* (as it was then known) was presented at the exposition as a palace on wheels. It included sleeping carriages, a gymnasium car, a restaurant car with a large tiled bathroom, a reading lounge and piano, and even a fully functioning church car crowned with a belfry – in a mock-up landscape of stuffed seals, papier-mâché icebergs and mannequins of native hunters. The same year saw the publication of the official *Guide to the Great Siberian Railway*.

The primary reason for the construction of the railway had been to further the economic and social development of Siberia, and the bulk of passengers were emigrants escaping overpopulation in European Russia. Their travelling conditions were a far cry from the sumptuousness on offer to the international set – 'stables on wheels' was one eyewitness description. But a few weeks of hardship on the rails was far preferable to crossing Siberia on foot, and in 1908 alone 750,000 peasants rode east.

Postrevolution

Civil war interrupted the development of the railway. When the Reds finally prevailed, upgrading the Trans-Siberian Railway was a major priority in their plans for economic rebirth by linking the iron-ore reserves of the Ural region with the Kuznetsk coalfields and the great industrial plants being developed throughout western Siberia.

In the 1920s, the railway was extended southwest from Novosibirsk to Almaty in Kazakhstan (the present-day Turkestan–Siberian Railway, known as the Turk–Sib). In 1940, a branch line was built between Ulan-Ude and Naushki, on the border with Mongolia. By 1949 it had connected with Ulaan Baatar, the Mongolian capital. The line from Ulaan Baatar to Beijing was begun four years later and completed by 1956.

Although work on the alternative Trans-Siberian Railway, the Baikal–Amur Mainline (BAM), began in the 1930s, this 'Hero Project of the Century' wasn't officially opened until 1991 – for details, see p561.

Despite the ascendancy of the aeroplane and the demise of the Soviet system, the importance of the Trans-Siberian Railway has not diminished; it's the glue that holds Russia together. Rail is still the only viable option for heavy freight, a fact underlined by tentative plans made for a trans-Korean line, which raises the possibility of travelling all the way by train from Seoul to the far west of Europe.

BOOKING TICKETS

There's no such thing as a stopover ticket. If you are travelling from Moscow to Beijing, and plan on spending a night or two in Irkutsk and Ulaan Baatar, you'll need three separate tickets: Moscow–Irkutsk, Irkutsk–Ulaan Baatar and Ulaan Baatar–Beijing. The tickets will all be for a specific berth on a specific train on a specified day.

Tickets can be booked a month in advance and you'd be wise to do this over the busy summer months when securing berths at short notice on certain trains can be difficult. Many travel agencies can make advance bookings, but for anyone with flexible travel plans, independent rail travel within Russia is easy enough, and tickets along the Moscow–Vladivostok route in particular are rarely hard to get.

For full details of the journey, read Lonely Planet's *Trans-Siberian Railway* guide. For general information on buying tickets and travelling on trains in Russia, see p737. Also see www.transsib .ru/eng, the best website on the Trans-Siberian Railway.

TRANSPORT

TRANSPORT

steel bins beneath the lower bunks. In 1st- and 2nd-class compartments you can lock the door but remember that it can be unlocked with a rather simple key; on the left side of the door, about three-quarters of the way up, there's a small steel switch that flips up, blocking the door from opening more than a few centimetres. Flip this switch up and make sure to stuff a piece of cork in the cavity so it can't be flipped back down by a bent coat hanger. At station halts it's also a good idea to ask the *provodnitsa* to lock your compartment while you go down to stretch your legs on the platform. Ironically, in cheaper *platskartny* carriages your unguarded possessions are often safer as there are more people around to watch.

Generally, Russians love speaking with foreigners; on long train rides, they love drinking with them as well. Avoiding this is not always as easy as it would seem. Choose your drinking partners very carefully on trains, and only drink from new bottles and only when you can watch the seal being broken.

LEFT LUGGAGE

Many train stations have a left-luggage room (камера хранения, *kamera khranenia*) or left-luggage lockers (автоматические камеры хранения, *avtomaticheskiye kamery khranenia*). These are generally secure, but make sure you note down the room's opening and closing hours and, if in doubt, establish how long you can leave your stuff for. Typical costs are R40 to R80 per bag per day (according to size) or R72 per locker.

Here is how to work the left-luggage lockers (they're generally the same everywhere). Be suspicious of people who offer to help you work them, above all when it comes to selecting your combination.

1. Buy two *zhetony* (tokens) from the attendant.
2. Put your stuff in an empty locker.
3. Decide on a combination of one Russian letter and three numbers and write it down.
4. Set the combination on the inside of the locker door.
5. Put one token in the slot.
6. Close the locker.

To open the locker, set your combination on the outside of your locker door. Note that even though it seems as if the knobs on the outside of the door should correspond directly with those on the inside, the letter is always the left-most knob, followed by three numbers, on both the inside and the outside. After you've set your combination, put a token in the slot, wait a second or two for the electrical humming sound and then pull open the locker.

ON THE JOURNEY

There is nothing quite like the smell of a Russian train: coal smoke, coffee, garlic, sausage, sweat, vodka and dozens of other elements combine to form an aroma that's so distinctive it will be permanently etched in your sensual memory.

Smoking is forbidden in the compartments, but permitted in the spaces at the ends of the cars, past the toilets.

Sleeping compartments are mixed sex; when women indicate that they want to change clothing or get out of bed, men go out and loiter in the corridor. Be aware that toilets can be locked long before and after station stops (there's a timetable on the door) and that except on a very few trains there are no shower facilities – improvise with a sponge, flannel, or a short length of garden hose that you can attach to the tap for a dowsing.

Food & Drink

It's a safe bet you won't go hungry. On long trips Russian travellers bring great bundles of food that they spread out and, as dictated by railway etiquette, offer to each other; you should do the same. Always remember to bring along bottled water for the trip, although every sleeping carriage has a samovar filled with boiling water that's safe to drink and is ideal for hot drinks or instant noodles.

The quality of food in dining cars varies widely. Rather than for eating they become the place to hang out, drink beer and play cards, particularly on the long trans-Siberian trip. Note also on the trans-Mongolian and trans-Manchurian trains that the dining cars are changed at each border, so en route to Beijing you get Russian, Chinese and possibly Mongolian versions. Occasionally, between the Russian border and Ulaan Baatar there is no dining car.

A meal in a restaurant car will rarely cost more than R300. If you don't fancy what's on offer – which is highly likely – there's often a table of pot noodles, chocolate, alcohol, juice and the like being peddled by the staff. They sometimes make the rounds of the carriages, too, with a trolley of snacks and drinks. Prices are cheap but still more than you'd pay at the kiosks or to the babushkas at the station halts.

Shopping for supplies at the stations is part of the fun of any long-distance Russian train trip. The choice of items is often excellent, with fresh milk, ice cream, grilled chicken, boiled potatoes, home cooking such as *pelmeni* (Russian-style ravioli dumplings) or pirozhki (savoury pies), buckets of forest berries and smoked fish all on offer. Prices are low and it's a good idea to have plenty of small change on hand.

RESERVATIONS
At any station you'll be confronted by several ticket windows. Some are special windows reserved exclusively for use by the elderly or infirm, heroes of the Great Patriotic War or members of the armed forces. All will have different operating hours and generally unhelpful staff.

The sensible option, especially if there are horrendous queues, is to avail yourself of the *servis tsentr* (service centre) now found at most major stations. At these air-conditioned centres – a godsend in summer – you'll generally encounter helpful, sometimes English-speaking staff who, for a small fee (typically around R100), can book your ticket. In big cities and towns it's also usually possible to buy tickets at special offices and some travel agencies away from the station – individual chapters provide details.

From whomever you end up buying your ticket, it's a good idea to have the following written down, in Cyrillic, to hand over to the sales assistant:
- destination;
- train number;
- date and time of departure;
- class of ticket required;
- number of tickets; and
- your name (though they'll check on your visa anyway).

When writing dates, use ordinary (Arabic) numerals for the day of the month and Roman numerals for the month. See boxed text, p738 for more information.

Even if the ticket-sellers tell you a particular service is sold out, it still may be possible to get on the train by speaking with the chief *provodnitsa*. Tell her your destination, offer the face ticket price first, and move slowly upwards from there. You can usually come to some sort of agreement.

Tickets for suburban trains – which are very cheap – are often sold at separate windows or from an *avtomat* (automatic ticket machine). A table beside the machine tells you which price zone your destination is in.

BELARUS

GETTING THERE & AWAY
Travel for foreigners into Belarus is unrestricted at all international border points (see p746), provided you have a valid visa. All international flights arrive and depart from Minsk.

Air
International flights entering and departing Belarus do so at the **Minsk-2 airport** (☎ 017-279 1032), about 40km east of Minsk. Some domestic flights, as well as flights to Kyiv, Kaliningrad and Moscow, depart from the smaller **Minsk-1 airport** (☎ 017-222 5418), only about 3km from the city centre. Departure taxes are included in the ticket price.

Belavia (Map p670; ☎ 017-210 4100; www.belavia .by; vul Njamiha 14, Minsk; Ⓜ Njamiha), Belarus' national airline, which also has offices in Berlin, London and Moscow, has direct connections to a number of destinations, including London (US$370 return), Berlin (US$315 return), Kyiv (US$200 return), Paris (US$400 return), Frankfurt, Rome, Stockholm and Tel Aviv (all once to three times a week). Belavia also flies up to three times daily to Moscow (US$160 return), twice daily to Vienna and daily to Warsaw, and has weekly flights to a number of other cities in Russia.

A number of other airlines service Minsk. Airline offices in the capital:

Austrian Airlines (Map p670; airline code OS; ☎ 017-289 1970; www.austrianair.com; hub Vienna International Airport, Vienna)

El Al Airlines (Map p670; airline code LY; ☎ 017-211 2605; www.elal.co.il; hub Ben Gurion Airport, Tel Aviv)

LOT Airlines (Map p670; airline code LO; ☎ 017-226 6628; www.lot.com; hub Fredrick Chopin Airport, Warsaw)

Lufthansa Airlines (Map p670; airline code LH; ☎ 017-284 7130; www.lufthansa.com; Frankfurt International Airport, Frankfurt)

Transaero (Map p670; airline code UN; ☎ 289 1510; www.transaero.ru; Sheremetyevo-2 Airport, Moscow)

Land

BORDER CROSSINGS

Long queues at border crossings are common. The most frequently used bus crossings are those on the quick four-hour trip between Vilnius (Lithuania) and Minsk, and the seven-hour trip between Minsk and Bialystok (Poland). Buses stop at the border for customs and passport controls.

If you're driving your own vehicle, there are 10 main road routes into Belarus that have border stations through which foreigners can pass (see p656). International driving permits are recognised in Belarus. Roads in Belarus are predictably bad, but main highways are decent. On intercity road trips, fill up when exiting the city; fuel stations may be scant before you hit the next big town.

BUS

International buses are less comfortable and endlessly bumpier than trains; their pluses include less-complicated border crossing procedures and sometimes faster service.

For detailed information about international destinations and prices to and from Minsk, Brest and Hrodna, see p678, p686 and p689 respectively.

TRAIN

Prices (in Belarusian roubles) are listed as *kupeyny/platskartny*. *Kupeyny* will get you a place in a four-person car. *Platskartny* compartments, while cheaper, have open bunk accommodations and are not great for those who value even a modicum of privacy. In 1st class, you share with one other person.

For detailed information about international destinations and prices to and from Minsk, Brest and Hrodna, see p679, p686 and p689 respectively.

Tours

Very few travel agencies abroad specialise in trips to Belarus. See p729 for agencies that specialise in Russian travel but which may include Belarus in their itineraries.

There are a number of agencies inside Belarus, such as Belintourist and Sakub, which happily organise personalised individual or group tours, starting from your country of origin (see p669). The Pripyatsky National Park deals with a UK-based travel agency (p694).

GETTING AROUND

Travel within Belarus, although not always easy, is unrestricted. The exceptions are the military installations and some border areas where signs may be posted that forbid entry without special permission. The country is linked by a system of train lines and bus routes, and the cities themselves are navigable by trolleybus, tram, city bus and, in Minsk, a metro. Local transport can often be crowded, grungy and slow, but in general it is efficient.

Air

There are several regional airports in Belarus, but the only domestic flight left operating regularly in the country is Minsk to Homel (an astoundingly low BR24,000, one way), run by **Gomel Avia** (☎ 017-222 5429; Minsk-1 airport).

Bus

Buses and the zippy little *marshrutky* are often the better option than trains for travellers on most routes, due to more-convenient and more-frequent departure times, and faster journey times. It's possible to get to most destinations inside Belarus for just a few dollars. See the Getting There & Away and Getting Around sections for each city for more details.

Car & Motorcycle

With spare parts rare, road conditions rugged and getting lost always a tantalising possibility, driving or riding in Belarus can be problematic. However, it is always an adventure and is the best way to really see the country.

The E30 (M1) highway dissects Belarus and is the major route between Warsaw and Moscow; it's in relatively good shape. For information on road conditions, rules and regulations, fuel, repairs and motorbikes, see p734.

Road police are not usually very forgiving (though they can usually be made so with the surreptitious offer of a few dollars), so be sure to obey all legal limits and make sure you have all the necessary documents handy. Take care whenever you see a ГАИ sign (ДАЙ in Belarusian); that's the traffic police's acronym and means there'll be a control booth soon – reduce your speed.

Cars drive in the right-hand lane, children 12 and under must sit in a back seat, and your blood-alcohol level should be no higher than zero.

HIRE
Cars can be rented in Belarus with or without a driver, but it may be cheaper to bargain with a taxi driver if you just want to go to one way and back for a day trip. For details of car-rental agencies, see p678.

Hitching
Hitching is never entirely safe in any country in the world, and Lonely Planet does not recommend it. Nevertheless, in Belarus it is a very common method to get around the country, especially for students, who

wait for rides near the major exits of cities and towns.

Local Transport
Local transport in all large cities, especially Minsk, is efficient. See p679 for more details about modes and prices of city transport.

An A sign indicates a bus stop, T indicates a tram stop, Tp a trolleybus stop, and M a metro station.

Tours
Once you're in the country and you wish to have a tour or excursion arranged, contact Belintourist or the other travel agencies listed in the Minsk chapter (p669).

Train
Train stations are called *zhelznadarazhniy* or *vokzal* (station). Local electric trains *(elektrichka)* are the cheapest of all trains, but also the slowest – be sure to check the timetable carefully for departure and arrival times. Several trains may make your journey, each with a different duration.

Health

CONTENTS

HEALTH

TRAVEL HEALTH WEBSITES

It's usually a good idea to consult your government's travel health website before departure, if one is available:
Australia www.smartraveller.gov.au
Canada www.hc-sc.gc.ca/english/index.html
UK www.doh.gov.uk
US www.cdc.gov/travel/

BEFORE YOU GO

Prevention is the key to staying healthy. A little planning, particularly for preexisting illnesses, will save trouble later. See your dentist before a long trip, carry a spare pair of contact lenses and glasses, and take your optical prescription with you. Bring medications in original, labelled containers. A letter from your physician describing your medical conditions and medications, including generic names, is also a good idea. If carrying syringes or needles, have a physician's letter documenting their medical necessity.

INSURANCE

Good emergency medical treatment is not cheap in Russia and Belarus, so seriously consider taking out a policy that covers you for the worst possible scenario, such as an accident requiring an emergency flight home. Find out in advance if your insurance plan will make payments directly to providers (the preferable option) or reimburse you later for overseas health expenditures.

RECOMMENDED VACCINATIONS

No vaccinations are required for travel to Russia, but the World Health Organization (WHO) recommends that all travellers should be covered for diphtheria, tetanus, measles, mumps, rubella and polio, regardless of their destination. Since most vaccines don't produce immunity until at least two weeks after they're given, visit a physician at least six weeks before departure.

INTERNET RESOURCES

The WHO's publication *International Travel and Health* is revised annually and is available online at www.who.int/ith/.

IN TRANSIT

DEEP VEIN THROMBOSIS (DVT)

Blood clots may form in the legs during plane flights, chiefly because of prolonged immobility. The longer the flight, the greater the risk. The chief symptom of DVT is swelling or pain of the foot, ankle or calf, usually but not always on just one side. If a blood clot travels to the lungs it may cause chest pain and breathing difficulties. Travellers with any of these symptoms should immediately seek medical attention.

To prevent DVT on long flights you should walk about the cabin, contract the leg muscles while sitting, drink plenty of fluids and avoid alcohol. If you have previously had DVT speak with your doctor about preventive medications (usually given in the form of an injection just prior to travel).

JET LAG & MOTION SICKNESS

To avoid jet lag (common when crossing more than five time zones) try drinking plenty of nonalcoholic fluids and eating light meals. Upon arrival, get exposure to natural sunlight and readjust your schedule (for meals, sleep and so on) as soon as possible.

Antihistamines such as prochlorperazine (Phenergan), dimenhydrinate (Dramamine), and meclizine (Antivert, Bonine) are usually the first choice for treating motion sickness. The main side effect of these medications is drowsiness. A herbal alternative is ginger.

IN RUSSIA & BELARUS

AVAILABILITY & COST OF HEALTH CARE

Medical care is readily available across Russia and Belarus but the quality can vary enormously. The biggest cities and towns have the widest choice of places, with Moscow, St Petersburg and to some extent Minsk well served by sparkling international-style clinics that charge handsomely for their admittedly generally excellent and professional service: expect to pay around US$50 for an initial consultation.

Some foreigners, Brits for instance, are theoretically entitled to free treatment in state-run noncommercial clinics, according to bilateral agreements from Soviet times. In practice this means that in Moscow they might be treated for free in cases of major injury. In remote areas doctors won't usually charge travellers, although it's recommend to give them a present – such as a bottle of Armenian cognac, chocolate or just money.

In some cases, medical supplies required in hospital may need to be bought from a pharmacy and nursing care may be limited. Note that there can be an increased risk of hepatitis B and HIV transmission via poorly sterilised equipment.

INFECTIOUS DISEASES
Rabies

Spread through bites or licks on broken skin from an infected animal, rabies is always fatal unless treated promptly. Animal handlers should be vaccinated, as should those travelling to remote areas where a reliable source of postbite vaccine is not available within 24 hours.

Tickborne Encephalitis

Spread by tick bites, tickborne encephalitis is a serious infection of the brain and vaccination is advised for those in risk areas

who are unable to avoid tick bites (such as campers, forestry workers and walkers). Two doses of vaccine will give a year's protection, three doses up to three years'. For more information see the website www .masta.org/tickalert/.

Typhoid & Hepatitis A

Both of these diseases are spread through contaminated food (particularly shellfish) and water. Typhoid can cause septicaemia (blood poisoning); hepatitis A causes liver inflammation and jaundice. Neither is usually fatal but recovery can be prolonged.

TRAVELLER'S DIARRHOEA

To prevent diarrhoea, avoid tap water unless it has been boiled, filtered or chemically disinfected (with iodine tablets) and steer clear of ice. Only eat fresh fruits or vegetables if cooked or peeled; be wary of dairy products that might contain unpasteurised milk. Eat food which is hot through and avoid buffet-style meals. If a restaurant is full of locals the food is probably safe.

If you develop diarrhoea, be sure to drink plenty of fluids, preferably an oral rehydration solution (eg Dioralyte). A few loose stools don't require treatment, but if you start having more than four or five stools a day, you should start taking an antibiotic (usually a quinolone drug) and an antidiarrhoeal agent (such as Loperamide). If diarrhoea is bloody, persists for more than 72 hours or is accompanied by fever, shaking, chills or severe abdominal pain you should seek medical attention.

ENVIRONMENTAL HAZARDS
Altitude Sickness

Lack of oxygen at high altitudes (over 2500m) affects most people to some extent. As far as Russia is concerned only those climbing mountains in the Caucasus, the Altai or Kamchatka need be concerned.

Symptoms of Acute Mountain Sickness (AMS), such as headache, lethargy, dizziness, difficulty sleeping and loss of appetite, usually develop in the first 24 hours at altitude but may be delayed up to three weeks. There is no hard-and-fast rule as to what is too high: AMS has been fatal at 3000m, although 3500m to 4500m is the usual range.

Treat mild symptoms by resting at the same altitude until recovery, usually a day or two. Paracetamol or aspirin can be taken for headaches. If symptoms persist or become worse, however, *immediate descent is necessary*; even 500m can help. Drug treatments should never be used to avoid descent or to enable further ascent.

Diamox (acetazolamide) reduces the headache of AMS and helps the body acclimatise to the lack of oxygen. It is only available on prescription and those who are allergic to the sulfonamide antibiotics may also be allergic to Diamox.

In the UK, fact sheets are available from the **British Mountaineering Council** (177-179 Burton Rd, Manchester, M20 2BB). Also check out the **Travel Health Zone website** (www.travelhealthzone.com/away/altitude/).

Heat Exhaustion & Heat Stroke

Best avoided by drinking water on a constant basis, heat exhaustion occurs following excessive fluid loss with inadequate replacement of fluids and salt. Symptoms include headache, dizziness and tiredness. Dehydration is already happening by the time you feel thirsty. To treat heat exhaustion, replace lost fluids by drinking water and/or fruit juice, and cool the body with cold water and fans. Treat salt loss with salty fluids such as soup or Bovril, or add a little more table salt to foods than usual.

Heat stroke is much more serious, resulting in irrational and hyperactive behaviour and eventually loss of consciousness and death. Rapid cooling by spraying the body with water and fanning is ideal. Emergency fluid and electrolyte replacement by intravenous drip is recommended.

Hypothermia & Frostbite

Proper preparation will reduce the risks of getting hypothermia. Even on a hot day in the mountains the weather can change rapidly; carry waterproof garments and warm layers, and inform others of your route.

Acute hypothermia follows a sudden drop of temperature over a short time. Chronic hypothermia is caused by a gradual loss of temperature over hours.

Hypothermia starts with shivering, loss of judgment and clumsiness. Unless rewarming occurs, the sufferer deteriorates into apathy, confusion and coma. Prevent further heat loss by seeking shelter, warm dry clothing, hot sweet drinks and shared bodily warmth.

Frostbite is caused by freezing and subsequent damage to bodily extremities. As it develops the skin blisters and then becomes black. Adequate clothing, staying dry, keeping well hydrated and ensuring adequate calorie intake best prevent frostbite. Treatment involves rapid rewarming. Avoid refreezing and rubbing the affected areas.

Insect Bites & Stings

TICKS

Always check all over your body if you have been walking through a potentially tick-infested area as ticks can cause skin infections and other more serious diseases. If you find a tick attached, press down around its head with tweezers, grab the head and gently pull upwards. Avoid pulling the rear of the body as this may squeeze the tick's gut contents through the attached mouth parts into the skin, increasing the risk of infection. Smearing chemicals on the tick will not make it let go and is not recommended.

From May to July, tickborne encephalitis is a risk anywhere in rural Russia and Belarus.

MOSQUITOES

A problem in summer all across Russia and Belarus, mosquitoes here may not carry malaria but can cause irritation and infected bites. Use a DEET-based insect repellent.

From May to September in rural areas bordering Mongolia, China and North Korea, take extra care as mosquito bites can cause Japanese encephalitis. If visiting rural areas you should consider immunisation.

LYME DISEASE

This is a tick-transmitted infection that may be acquired throughout the region. It usually begins with a spreading rash at the site of the tick bite, accompanied by fever, headache, extreme fatigue, aching joints and muscles and mild neck stiffness. If untreated, these symptoms usually resolve over several weeks, but over subsequent months disorders of the nervous system, heart and joints may develop. There is no vaccination against the disease. Treatment should be sought as soon as possible for best results.

LEECHES

You'll often find leeches in damp forest conditions; they attach themselves to your skin to suck your blood. Trekkers often get them on their legs or in their boots. Salt or a lighted cigarette end will make them fall off. Do not pull them off, as the bite is then more likely to become infected. Clean and apply pressure if the point of attachment is bleeding. An insect repellent may keep them away.

Snake Bites
Avoid getting bitten – do not walk barefoot or stick your hand into holes or cracks. Keep an eye out for snakes in forest areas, particularly in western European Russia and the Russian Far East. Half of those bitten by venomous snakes are not actually injected with poison (envenomed). If bitten by a snake, do not panic. Immobilise the bitten limb with a splint (eg a stick) and apply a bandage over the site firmly, similar to a bandage over a sprain. Do not apply a tourniquet, or cut or suck the bite. Get the victim to medical help as soon as possible so that antivenin can be given if necessary.

Water
In at least 50% of places tap water isn't safe to drink so it is best to stick to bottled water, boil water for 10 minutes, or use water purification tablets or a filter. Do not drink water from rivers or lakes as it may contain bacteria or viruses that can cause diarrhoea or vomiting.

TRAVELLING WITH CHILDREN
All travellers with children should know how to treat minor ailments and when to seek medical treatment. Make sure the children are up to date with routine vaccinations, and discuss possible travel vaccines well before departure as some vaccines are not suitable for babies aged under a year.

If your child has vomiting or diarrhoea, lost fluid and salts must be replaced. It may be helpful to take rehydration powders for reconstituting with boiled water.

Children should be encouraged to avoid and mistrust any dogs or other mammals because of the risk of rabies and other diseases. Any bite, scratch or lick from a warm-blooded, furry animal should immediately be thoroughly cleaned. If there is any possibility that the animal is infected with rabies, immediate medical assistance should be sought.

WOMEN'S HEALTH
Tampons and sanitary towels are readily available across Russia and Belarus.

Travelling during pregnancy is usually possible but always consult your doctor before planning your trip. The most risky times for travel are during the first 12 weeks of pregnancy and after 30 weeks.

SEXUAL HEALTH
Condoms are available across Russia and Belarus from all pharmacies and certainly should be used: see 'HIV & AIDS' below. Emergency contraception (ie the morning after pill, available from doctors by prescription) is most effective if taken within 24 hours after unprotected sex. The **International Planned Parent Federation** (www.ippf.org) can advise about the availability of contraception in different countries. When buying condoms, look for a European CE mark, which means they have been rigorously tested, and then keep them in a cool, dry place or they may crack and perish.

HIV & AIDS
Infection with HIV may lead to AIDS, a fatal disease. Russia is experiencing one of the fastest rises of reported HIV and AIDS cases in the world. By the end of 2002, Russia had nearly 250,000 official cases of HIV/AIDS, but most experts believe the true figure is at least 1 million and rising rapidly.

Rates of infection are over four times lower in neighbouring Belarus, which had reported 6581 cases as of mid-2005. The country's highest infection rates by far are in the Homel region – almost five times higher than Minsk's. Over the last few years, there has been a dramatic increase in the number of infections through (mainly heterosexual) sexual transmission; it's now 55% of all new cases, versus 27% in 2001.

Any exposure to blood, blood products or body fluids may put the individual at risk. HIV/AIDS is often transmitted through sexual contact or dirty needles – vaccinations, acupuncture, tattooing and body piercing can be potentially as dangerous as intravenous drug use. It can also spread through infected blood transfusions; Russia's record of blood screening is not perfect. If you need an injection, ask to see the syringe unwrapped in front of you, or take a needle and syringe pack with you.

HEALTH

Language

CONTENTS

Just about everyone in Russia speaks Russian, though there are also dozens of other languages spoken by ethnic minorities. Russian and most of the other languages are written in variants of the Cyrillic alphabet. It's relatively easy to find English speakers in St Petersburg and Moscow, but not so easy in small cities and towns.

Russian grammar may be daunting, but your travels will be far more interesting if you at least take the time to learn the Cyrillic alphabet (see p753), so that you can read maps and street signs. For a more in-depth handling of Russian, grab a copy of Lonely Planet's *Russian Phrasebook*.

TRANSLITERATION

There's no ideal system for going from Cyrillic to Roman letters; the more faithful a system is to pronunciation, the more complicated it becomes. The transliteration system used in this language guide differs from that used in the rest of this book (which follows the US Library of Congress System I – good for deciphering printed words and rendering proper names); it's intended to assist you in pronouncing Russian letters and sounds, with an emphasis on practicality. Most letters are transliter-ated in accordance with the sounds given in the alphabet table. In this system Cyrillic **e** (pronounced 'ye') is written as Roman 'e' except at the start of words where it's written as 'ye' (eg Yeltsin). The combination **кс** becomes 'x'.

Italicised syllables in the transliterations indicate where the stress falls in a word.

PRONUNCIATION

The 'voiced' consonants (ie when the vocal cords vibrate) **б**, **в**, **г**, **д**, **ж**, and **з** are not voiced at the end of words (eg хлеб, 'bread', is pronounced *khlyep*) or before voiceless consonants. The **г** in the common adjective endings -**его** and -**ого** is pronounced 'v'; Mayakovskogo, for example, is pronounced 'Maya-*kov*-skovo'.

Two letters have no sound but are used to modify the pronunciation other letters. A consonant followed by the 'soft sign' **ь** is spoken with the tongue flat against the palate, as if followed by a faint 'y'. The 'hard sign' **ъ** is rarely seen; it occurs after consonants and indicates a slight pause before the next vowel.

ACCOMMODATION

Where's a ...?
gdye ...   Где ...?
   boarding house
   pan·si·a·*nat*   пансионат
   camping ground
   kem·ping   кемпинг
   hotel
   ga·*sti*·ni·tsa   гостиница
   youth hostel
   ap·shche·*zhi*·ti·e   общежитие

How much is a room?
   skol'·ka *sto*·it *no*·mer
   Сколько стоит номер?
Do you have a cheaper room?
   u vas yest' de·*shyev*·le *no*·mer
   У вас есть дешевле номер?
What's the address?
   ka·*koy a*·dres
   Какой адрес?
Could you write it down, please?
   za·pi·*shi*·te pa·*zhal*·sta
   Запишите, пожалуйста.

THE RUSSIAN CYRILLIC ALPHABET

Cyrillic	Roman	Pronunciation
А, а	a	as the 'a' in 'father' (in stressed syllable); as the 'a' in 'ago' (in unstressed syllable)
Б, б	b	as the 'b' in 'but'
В, в	v	as the 'v' in 'van'
Г, г	g	as the 'g' in 'god'
Д, д	d	as the 'd' in 'dog'
Е, е	ye/e	as the 'ye' in 'yet' (in stressed syllable and at the beginning of a word); as the 'e' in 'ten' (in unstressed syllable)
Ё, ё *	yo	as the 'yo' in 'yore'
Ж, ж	zh	as the 's' in 'measure'
З, з	z	as the 'z' in 'zoo'
И, и	i	as the 'ee' in 'meet'
Й, й	y	as the 'y' in 'boy' (not transliterated after ы or и)
К, к	k	as the 'k' in 'kind'
Л, л	l	as the 'l' in 'lamp'
М, м	m	as the 'm' in 'mad'
Н, н	n	as the 'n' in 'not'
О, о	o/a	as the 'o' in 'more' (in stressed syllable); as the 'a' in 'hard' (in unstressed syllable)
П, п	p	as the 'p' in 'pig'
Р, р	r	as the 'r' in 'rub' (rolled)
С, с	s	as the 's' in 'sing'
Т, т	t	as the 't' in 'ten'
У, у	u	as the 'oo' in 'fool'
Ф, ф	f	as the 'f' in 'fan'
Х, х	kh	as the 'ch' in 'Bach'
Ц, ц	ts	as the 'ts' in 'bits'
Ч, ч	ch	as the 'ch' in 'chin'
Ш, ш	sh	as the 'sh' in 'shop'
Щ, щ	shch	as 'sh-ch' in 'fresh chips'
Ъ, ъ	-	'hard sign' (see opposite)
Ы, ы	i	as the 'i' in 'ill'
Ь, ь	'	'soft sign'; (see opposite)
Э, э	e	as the 'e' in 'end'
Ю, ю	yu	as the 'u' in 'use'
Я, я	ya/ye	as the 'ya' in 'yard' (in stressed syllable); as the 'ye' in 'yearn' (in unstressed syllable)

* Ё, ё are often printed without dots

How much is it per/for ...?
skol'·ka sto·it za ...   Сколько стоит за ...?
night
noch'   ночь
two people
dva·ikh   двоих
week
ned·yel·yu   неделю

Do you have a ... room?
u vas yest' ...   У вас есть ...?
single
ad·na·myest·ni no·mer   одноместный номер
double
no·mer z dvu·spal'·ney   номер с двуспальней
kra·va·t'yu   кроватью
twin
dvukh·myes·ni no·mer   двухместный номер

hotel
gas·ti·ni·tsa   гостиница
room
no·mer   номер
key
klyuch   ключ
blanket
a·de·ya·la   одеяло
toilet paper
tu·a·lyet·na·ya bu·ma·ga   туалетная бумага

The ... isn't working.
... ne ra·bo·ta·et   ... не работает.
electricity
e·lek·tri·chest·va   электричество
heating
a·ta·plye·ni·e   отопление
hot water
ga·rya·cha·ya va·da   горячая вода
light
svyet   свет
tap/faucet
kran   кран

Can I see it?
mozh·na pas·mat·ryet'   Можно посмотреть?
Where is the toilet?
gdye zdyes' tu·al·yet   Где здесь туалет?
I'm leaving now.
ya sey·chas u·ez·zha·yu   Я сейчас уезжаю.
We're leaving now.
mi sey·chas u·ez·zha·em   Мы сейчас уезжаем.

CONVERSATION & ESSENTIALS

Two words you're sure to use are the universal 'hello', здравствуйте (zdrast·vuy·te), and пожалуйста (pa·zhal·sta), the word for 'please' (commonly included in all polite requests), 'you're welcome', 'pardon me', 'after you' and more.

Hello.
zdrast·vuy·te   Здравствуйте.
Hi.
pri·vyet   Привет.

Good morning.
do·bra·e *u*·tra — Доброе утро.

Good afternoon.
do·bri dyen' — Добрый день.

Good evening.
dob·ri vye·cher — Добрый вечер.

Goodbye.
da svi·*da*·ni·ya — До свидания.

Bye.
pa·*ka* — Пока.

Yes.
da — Да.

No.
nyet — Нет.

Please.
pa·*zhal*·sta — Пожалуйста.

Thank you (very much).
(bal'·*sho*·e) spa·*si*·ba — (Большое) спасибо.

You're welcome.
pa·*zhal*·sta — Пожалуйста.

Excuse me.
pras·*ti*·te — Простите.

Sorry.
iz·vi·*ni*·te — Извините.

No problem/Never mind.
ni·che·*vo* — Ничего.

Can you help me?
pa·ma·*gi*·te pa·*zhal*·sta — Помогите, пожалуйста.

May I take a photo?
mozh·na sfa·ta·gra·*fi*·ra·vat' — Можно сфотографировать?

I like ...
mnye *nra*·vits·ya ... — Мне нравится ...

I don't like ...
mnye nye *nra*·vits·ya ... — Мне не нравится ...

Just a minute!
mi·*nut*·ku — Минутку!

When introducing yourself use your first name, or first and last name. Russians often address each other by first name plus patronymic, a middle name based on their father's first name – eg Natalya Borisovna (Natalya, daughter of Boris), Pavel Nikolayevich (Pavel, son of Nikolay).

What's your name?
kak vas za·*vut* — Как вас зовут?

My name is ...
me·*nya* za·vut ... — Меня зовут ...

Pleased to meet you.
o·chen' pri·*yat*·na — Очень приятно.

How are you?
kak de·*la* — Как дела?

Where are you from?
at·*ku*·da vi — Откуда вы?

I'm from ...
ya iz ... — Я из ...

DIRECTIONS

House numbers are not always in step on opposite sides of the street. Russian addresses are written back-to-front, with Russia at the top of the address and the adressee at the bottom.

Where is ...?
gdye ... — Где ...?

How do we get to ...?
kak da·*brat'*·sya k ... — Как добраться к ...?

Turn (at the) ...
pa·ver·*ni*·te ... — Поверните ...

corner
za·*u*·gal — за угол

left
na·*lye*·va — налево

right
na·*pra*·va — направо

traffic lights
na sve·ta·*fo*·re — на светофоре

straight ahead	*prya*·ma	прямо
here	tut	тут
there	tam	там
near	da·le·*ko*	далеко
far	*blis*·ka	близко
behind ...	za ...	за ...
in front of ...	*pye*·ret ...	перед ...
next to ...	*rya*·dam s ...	рядом с ...
opposite ...	na·*pro*·tif ...	напротив ...

SIGNS

Вход	Entrance
Выход	Exit
Мест Нет	No Vacancy
Справки	Information
Запрещено	Prohibited
Открыт	Open
Закрыт	Closed
Касса	Cashier/Ticket Office
Больница	Hospital
Милиция	Police
Туалет	Toilet
Мужской (М)	Men
Женский (Ж)	Women

EMERGENCIES

Help!
  pa·ma·*gi*·te   Помогите!
Thief!
  vor   Вор!
Fire!
  pa·*zhar*   Пожар!
I'm lost.
  ya za·blu·*dil*·sya/za·blu·*di*·las' (m/f)
  Я заблудился/заблудилась.
Leave me alone!
  pri·*va*·li·vay
  Приваливай!
There's been an accident.
  pra·i·za·*shol* ne·*shas*·ni *slu*·chay
  Произошёл несчастный случай.
Call ...!
vi·za·vi·te ...   Вызовите ...!
  a doctor
  vra·*cha*   врача
  the police
  mi·*li*·tsi·yu   милицию

north	*sye*·ver	север
south	yuk	юг
east	vas·*tok*	восток
west	*za*·pad	запад
avenue	pras·*pyekt*	проспект (просп.)
beach	plyazh	пляж
bridge	most	мост
boulevard	bul'·*var*	бульвар
castle	*za*·mak	замок
cathedral	sa·*bor*	собор
church	*tsyer*·kof'	церковь
highway	sha·*sye*	шоссе
island	*ost*·raf	остров
lake	*o*·ze·ra	озеро
lane	pe·re·u·lak	переулок (пер.)
market	*ri*·nak	рынок
museum	mu·*zyey*	музей
palace	dvar·*yets*	дворец
ruins	raz·*va*·li·ni	развалины
sea	*mo*·re	море
square/plaza	*plo*·shchat'	площадь (пл.)
street	*u*·li·tsa	улица (ул.)
theatre	te·*atr*	театр
tower	*bash*·nya	башня

HEALTH

I'm ill.
  ya *bo*·len/bal'·*na* (m/f)   Я болен/больна.

I need a doctor.
  mnye *nu*·zhen vrach   Мне нужен врач.
It hurts here.
  zdyes' ba·*lit*   Здесь болит.

Where's the nearest ...?
  gdye bli·*zhay*·sha·ya ...?   Где ближайшая ...
  chemist (night)
  ap·*tye*·ka (nach·*na*·ya)   аптека (ночная)
  dentist
  zub·*noy* vrach   зубной врач
  doctor
  vrach   врач
  hospital
  bal'·ni·tsa   больница

I need a doctor (who speaks English).
  mnye *nu*·zhen vrach (an·*gla*·ga·va·*ryash*·chi)
  Мне нужен врач (англоговорящий).

I have (a) ...
  u me·*nya* ...   У меня ...
  diarrhoea
  pa·*nos*   понос
  fever
  tem·pe·ra·*tu*·ra   температура
  headache
  ga·la·*vna*·ya bol'   головная боль
  pain
  bol'   боль
  stomachache
  ba·lit zhe·*lu*·dak   болит желудок

I'm allergic to ...
  u men·*ya* a·ler·*gi*·ya na ... У меня алергия на...
  antibiotics
  an·ti·bi·*o*·ti·ki   антибиотики
  aspirin
  a·spi·*rin*   аспирин
  penicillin
  pe·ni·*tsi*·lin   пеницилин
  bees
  pche·*li*·ni u·kus   пчелиный укус
  nuts
  ar·*ye*·khi   орехи
  peanuts
  a·*ra*·khi·si   арахисы

antiseptic
  an·ti·*syep*·tik   антисептик
condom
  pre·zer·va·*tif*   презерватив
contraceptives
  pra·*ti*·va za·*cha*·tach·ni·e противо-зачаточные
  sryets·tva   средства

BELARUSIAN

Russian is by far the most dominant language in Belarus. No matter how noble it may be of you to try a little Belarusian, be aware you're more likely than not to be greeted with consternation and confusion – it's far less problematic to use Russian.

Belarusian belongs to the Eastern Slavonic branch of Indo-European, closely related to both Russian and Ukrainian, though its written form shares with Ukrainian only its ancestor in the now extinct language called Ruthenian. It began to differ from Old Russian (also called Church Slavonic) in the Middle Ages. It's normally written with the Cyrillic alphabet, but there does exist a written form using accented Latin characters. This latter is dubbed Lacinka, and it is different than transliterated Belarusian. While Russian and present-day Belarusian are very close, there are significant differences in pronunciation and spelling, and some case endings and many words are completely different; a Russian-speaker would at best understand 60% of spoken Belarusian heard for the first time.

Belarusian, like Ukrainian (but not Russian), has the letter **i**, pronounced *ee*. It also has the unique letter **ў**, pronounced like 'w' in the word 'west'. Transliteration is also different, with **й** transcribed as *j*, **ю** as *ju*, **я** as *ja* and **ё** as *io*. **Г** is pronounced and transcribed *h*. The Russian letter **o** is often written as **a** in Belarusian – making, for example, Komsomolskaya into Kamsamolskaja, which looks closer to its pronunciation in any case. The Russian Gogolya becomes Hoholja in Belarusian.

You'll see an apostrophe used in written Belarusian to separate a consonant from the syllable that follows it.

Hello.	*do·bree dzhen*	Добры дженн.
Goodbye.	*da pa·ba·chen·nya*	Да пабачэньня.
Yes.	*tak*	Так.
No.	*nye*	Не.
Please.	*ka·lee las·ka*	Калі ласка.
Thank you.	*dzya·koo·uee*	Дзякуй.
good	*dob·ree*	добры
bad	*dren·nee*	дрэнны

Saturday	*su·bo·ta*	субота
Sunday	*nyad·ze·lya*	нядзеля
Belarus	*be·la·roos*	Беларусь
Entrance	*u·va·khod*	Уваход
Exit	*vy·khad*	Выхад
Information	*da·ved·ka*	Даведка
Left Luggage Room		
	ka·mera za·khau·vannya ba·ha·zha	
	Камера Захоўвання Багажа	

Belarusian on Signs & Timetables

Monday	*pan·ya·dzel·ak*	панядзелак
Tuesday	*aut·o·rak*	аўторак
Wednesday	*se·ra·da*	серада
Thursday	*chats·ver*	чацвер
Friday	*pyat·ni·tsa*	пятніца

on even days	*pa tsot·nykh*	па цотных
on odd days	*pa nya·tsot·nykh*	па няцотных
daily	*shtod·zyo·nna*	штодзюнна
departure	*ad·prau·len·nje*	адпраўленне
arrival	*pry·by·tssje*	прыбыцце

nausea
tash·na·*ta*   тошнота
sunblock cream
soln·tse·zash·*chit*·ni kryem   солнцезащитный крем
tampon
tam·*pon*   тампон

LANGUAGE DIFFICULTIES

Do you speak English?
vi ga·va·*ri*·te pa an·*gli*·ski
Вы говорите по-английски?

Does anyone (here) speak English?
kto·ni·bud' ga·va·rit pa·an·*gli*·ski
Кто-нибудь говорит по-английски?

I don't speak Russian.
ya nye ga·va·*ryu* pa rus·ki
Я не говорю по-русски.

I understand.
ya pa·ni·*ma*·yu
Я понимаю.

I don't understand.
ya nye pa·ni·*ma*·yu
Я не понимаю.

What does 'пуп' mean?
shto a·baz·na·*cha*·et *slo*·va pup
Что обозначает слово 'пуп'?

How do you say ... in Russian?
kak *bu*·det ... pa·*ru*·ski
Как будет ... по-русски?

Could you write it down, please?
za·pi·*shi*·te pa·*zhal*·sta
Запишите, пожалуйста?

Can you show me (on the map)?
pa·ka·*zhi*·te mnye pa·*zhal*·sta (na *kar*·te)
Покажите мне, пожалуйста (на карте).

NUMBERS

How much/many?

skol'-ka | | Сколько?

1	a-din	один
2	dva	два
3	tri	три
4	che-ti-re	четыре
5	pyat'	пять
6	shyest'	шесть
7	syem'	семь
8	vo-sem'	восемь
9	dye-vyat'	девять
10	dye-syat'	десять
11	a-di-na-tsat'	одиннадцать
12	dve-na-tsat'	двенадцать
13	tri-na-tsat'	тринадцать
14	che-tir-na-tsat'	четырнадцать
15	pyat-na-tsat'	пятнадцать
16	shest-na-tsat'	шестнадцать
17	sem-na-tsat'	семнадцать
18	va-sem-na-tsat'	восемнадцать
19	de-vyat-na-tsat'	девятнадцать
20	dva-tsat'	двадцать
21	dva-tsat' a-din	двадцать один
22	dva-tsat' dva	двадцать два
30	tri-tsat'	тридцать
40	so-rak	сорок
50	pyat'-des-yat	пятьдесят
60	shihs-des-yat	шестдесят
70	syem'-des-yat	семьдесят
80	vo-sem'-des-yat	восемьдесят
90	de-vya-no-sta	девяносто
100	sto	сто
1000	ti-sya-cha	тысяча
1,000,000	(a-din) mi-li-on	(один) миллион

PAPERWORK

name
ri-nak | рынок
nationality
na-tsi-a-nal'-nast' | национальность
date of birth
da-ta razh-dye-ni-ya | дата рождения
place of birth
mye-sta razh-dye-ni-ya | место рождения
passport
pas-part | паспорт
visa
vi-za | виза

QUESTION WORDS

Who? kto | кто
What? shto | что
When? kag-da | когда
Where? gdye | где
Which? ka-koy | какой
Why? pa-che-mu | почему
How? kak | как

SHOPPING & SERVICES

I need ...
mnye nuzh-na ... | Мне нужно ...
Do you have ...?
u vas yest' ... | У вас есть ...?
How much is it?
skol'-ka sto-it | Сколько стоит?
Can I look at it?
pa-ka-zhi-te pa-zhal-sta | Покажите, пожалуйста.
I'm just looking.
ya pros-ta smat-ryu | Я просто смотрю.
Do you have any others?
u vas yest' dru-gi-e | У вас есть другие?
That's too expensive.
e-ta o-chen' do-ra-ga | Это очень дорого.
I'll take it.
vaz'-mu | Возьму.

Do you accept ...?
vi pri-ni-ma-e-te a-pla-tu ... | Вы принимаете оплату ...?
  credit cards
  kre-dit-nay kar-tach-kay | кредитной карточкой
  travellers cheques
  da-rozh-nim chye-kam | дорожным чеком

good
kha-ra-sho | хорошо
bad
plo-kha | плохо
more/bigger
bol'-she | больше
less/smaller
myen'-she | меньше

bookshop
knizh-ni ma-ga-zin | книжный магазин
department store
u-ni-ver-sal'-ni ma-ga-zin | универсальный магазин
market
ri-nak | рынок
newsstand
ga-zet-ni ki-osk | газетный киоск
pharmacy
ap-tye-ka | аптека

bank
bank | банк
currency exchange
ab-myen va-lyu-ti | обмен валюты

money
dyen'-gi — деньги
small change
raz-myen — размен
travellers cheques
da-rozh-ni-e chye-ki — дорожные чеки

post office
poch-ta — почта
postcard
at-krit-ka — открытка
stamp
mar-ka — марка
telephone
te-le-fon — телефон
fax
fax/te-le-fax — факс/телефакс
telephone office
te-le-fo-ni punkt — телефонный пункт

TIME & DATES
What time is it?
ka-to-ri chas — Который час?
It's (ten) o'clock.
(dye-syat') chi-sof — (Десять) часов.
At what time?
f ka-to-ram chi-su — В котором часу?
At (ten).
v (dye-syat') chi-sof — В (десять) часов.

hour
chas — час
minute
mi-nu-ta — минута
am/in the morning
u-tra — утра
pm/in the afternoon
dnya — дня
in the evening
vye-che-ra — вечера
local time
myes-na-e vrye-mya — местное время
Moscow time
mas-kov-ska-e vrye-mya — московское время

When? — kag-da — когда
today — se-vod-nya — сегодня
tomorrow — zaft-ra — завтра
yesterday — vche-ra — вчера

Dates are given day-month-year, with the month usually in Roman numerals. Days of the week are often represented by numbers in timetables (Monday is 1).

Monday — pa-ne-dyel'-nik — понедельник
Tuesday — ftor-nik — вторник
Wednesday — sre-da — среда
Thursday — chet-vyerk — четверг
Friday — pyat-ni-tsa — пятница
Saturday — su-bo-ta — суббота
Sunday — vas-kre-syen'-e — воскресенье

January — yan-var' — январь
February — fev-ral' — февраль
March — mart — март
April — ap-ryel' — апрель
May — may — май
June — i-yun' — июнь
July — i-yul' — июль
August — av-gust — август
September — sen-tyabr' — сентябрь
October — ok-tyabr' — октябрь
November — na-yabr' — ноябрь
December — de-kabr' — декабрь

TRANSPORT
Public Transport
When does it leave?
kag-da at-prav-lya-et-sya — Когда отправляется?
How long does it take to get to (Volgograd)?
skol'-ka vrye-me-ni nuzh-na ye-khat' da (vol-ga-gra-da)? — Сколько времени нужно ехать до (Волгограда)?
How long will it be delayed?
na skol'-ka on a-paz-di-va-et — На сколько он опаздывает?

A ... ticket (to Novgorod).
bil-yet ... (na nov-ga-rat) — Билет ... (на Новгород).
1st-class
f pyer-vam kla-se — в первом классе
2nd-class
va fta-rom kla-se — во втором классе
one-way
v a-din kan-yets — в один конец
return
v o-ba kan-tsa — в оба конца

bus — af-to-bus — автобус
taxi — tak-si — такси
train — poy-ezt — поезд
tram — tram-vay — трамвай
trolleybus — tra-lyey-bus — троллейбус

cancelled
at-me-ni-li — отменили
delayed
a-paz-di-va-et — опаздывает

ROAD SIGNS

Берегись (Трамвая)!	Watch For (Trams)!
Внимание	Caution
Уступи Дорогу	Give Way
Опасно	Danger
Стоянка Запрещена	No Parking
Объезд	Detour
Впереди Ведутся Работы	Roadworks In Progress
Въезд	Entry
Проезд Запрещен	No Entry
Стоп	Stop
Одностороннее Движение	One Way
Выезд	Exit

first
pyer·vi · первый
last
pas·lyed·ni · последний
map
kar·ta · карта
metro token, tokens
zhe·ton, zhe·to·ni · жетон, жетоны
platform
plat·for·ma · платформа
railway station
zhe·lez·na·da·rozh·ni · железнодорожный (ж. д.)
vag·zal · вокзал
stop (bus, tram etc)
a·sta·nof·ka · остановка
ticket, tickets
bi·lyet, bi·lye·ti · билет, билеты
ticket office
bi·lyet·na·ya ka·sa · билетная касса
timetable
ras·pi·sa·ni·e · расписание
transport map
skhye·ma trans·par·ta · схема транспорта

Private Transport
I'd like to hire a ...
ya bi kha·tyel/kha·tye·la vzyat' ... na pra·kat (m/f)
Я бы хотел/хотела взять ... на прокат.
  car
  ma·shi·nu · машину
  4WD
  ma·shi·nu s pol·nim · машину с полным
  pri·vo·dam · приводом
  bicycle
  ve·la·si·pyet · велосипед
  motorbike
  ma·ta·tsikl · мотоцикл

Is this the road to (Kursk)?
e·ta da·ro·ga ved·yot f (kursk)
Эта дорога ведёт в (Курск)?
Where's a petrol station?
gdye za·praf·ka
Где заправка?
Please fill it up.
za·pol·ni·te bak pa·zhal·sta
Заполните бак, пожалуйста.
I'd like (15) litres.
(pyat·na·tsat') li·traf pa·zhal·sta
(Пятнадцать) литров, пожалуйста.

diesel
di·zel'·na·e to·pli·va
дизельное топливо
regular
ben·zin no·mer tri de·vya·no·sta
бензин номер 93
unleaded
a·chish·che·ni ben·zin
очищенный бензин

(How long) Can I park here?
(skol'·ka) zdyes' mozh·na sta·yat'
(Сколько) Здесь можно стоять?
Do I have to pay?
nuzh·na pla·tit'
Нужно платить?
I need a mechanic.
mnye nu·zhen af·ta·me·kha·nik
Мне нужен автомеханик.
The car/motorcycle has broken down (at Kursk).
ma·shi·na sla·ma·las'/ma·ta·tsikl sla·mal·sya v (kur·ske)
Машина сломалась/Мотоцикл сломался в (Курске).
The car/motorbike won't start.
ma·shi·na/ma·ta·tsikl nye za·vo·dits·ya
Машина/Мотоцикл не заводится.
I have a flat tyre.
u men·ya lop·nu·la shi·na
У меня лопнула шина.
I've run out of petrol.
u men·ya kon·chil·sya ben·zin
У меня кончился бензин.
I've had an accident.
ya pa·ter·pyel/pa·ter·pye·la a·va·ri·yu (m/f)
Я потерпел/потерпела аварию.

TRAVEL WITH CHILDREN
Do you mind if I breast-feed here?
mozh·na zdyes' pa·kar·mit' reb·yon·ka grud'·yu
Можно здесь покормить ребёнка грудью?
Are children allowed?
dyet·yam fkhot raz·re·shon
Детям вход разрешён?

I need a/an ...
ya kha-*chu* ...   Я хочу ...

baby seat
dyet-ska-e sid-*yen'*-e
детское сиденье

disposable nappies/diapers
ad-na-*ra*-zav-ni-e pel-*yon*-ki
одноразовые пелёнки

(English-speaking) babysitter
nyan-yu ga-var-*yash*-chu-yu (pa-an-*gli*-ski)
няню, говорящую (по-английски)

highchair
dyet-ski *stul'*-chik
детский стульчик

potty
gar-*shok*
горшок

stroller
dyet-sku-yu kal-*yas*-ku
детскую коляску

Is there a/an ...?
yest' ...   Есть ...?

baby change room
kom-na-ta a-ba-*ru*-da-va-na-ya dlya u-*kho*-da za
mlad-*yen*-tsa-mi
комната, оборудованная для ухода за
младенцами

child-minding service
sluzh-ba pa pris-*mo*-tru za det'-*mi*
служба по присмотру за детьми

children's menu
dyet-ska-e men-*yu*
детское меню

Also available from Lonely Planet:
Russian Phrasebook

Glossary

You may encounter some of the following terms and abbreviations during your travels in Russia and Belarus. See also the Language chapter (p752).

aeroport – airport
aerovokzal – airline terminal
ail – hexagonal or tepee-shaped yurt
apteka – pharmacy
arzhaan – Tuvan sacred spring
ataman – Cossack leader
aviakassa – air-ticket office
avtobus – bus
avtomat – automatic ticket machine
avtostantsiya – bus stop
avtovokzal – bus terminal

babushka – literally, 'grandmother', but used generally in Russian society for all old women
BAM (Baikalo-Amurskaya Magistral) – Baikal-Amur Mainline, a trans-Siberian rail route
bankomat – automated teller machine (ATM)
banya – bathhouse
bashnya – tower
baza otdykha – literally, 'relaxation base'; often used to describe lodges and sanatoriums
benzin – petrol
biblioteka – library
bilet – ticket
biznesmen, biznesmenka – literally, 'businessman', 'businesswoman'; often used to mean a small-time operator on the fringe of the law
bolnitsa – hospital
boyar – high-ranking noble
bufet – snack bar selling cheap cold meats, boiled eggs, salads, bread, pastries etc
bulochnaya – bakery
bulvar – boulevard
buterbrod – open sandwich
byliny – epic songs

chum – tepee-shaped tent made of birch bark
CIS – Commonwealth of Independent States; Sodruzhestvo Nezavisimykh Gosudarstv (SNG); an alliance (proclaimed in 1991) of independent states comprising the former USSR republics (less the three Baltic States)

dacha – country cottage, summer house
datsan – Buddhist monastery
deklaratsia – customs declaration

detsky – child's, children's
Detsky Mir – Children's World, name for many toy shops
devushki – young women
dezhurnaya – woman looking after a particular floor of a hotel
dolina – valley
dom – house
dorogoy – expensive
duma – parliament
dvorets – palace
dvorets kultury – literally, 'culture palace'; a meeting, social, entertainment, education centre, usually for a group such as railway workers, children etc

elektrichka – suburban train
etazh – floor (storey)

finift – luminous enamelled metal miniatures
firmeny poezda – trains with names (eg *Rossiya*); these are generally nicer trains

GAI (Gosudarstvennaya Avtomobilnaya Inspektsia) – State Automobile Inspectorate (traffic police)
gallereya – gallery
gastronom – speciality food shop
gavan – harbour
gazeta – newspaper
glasnost – literally, 'openness'; the free-expression aspect of the Gorbachev reforms
glavpochtamt – main post office
gora – mountain
gorod – city, town
gostinitsa – hotel
gostiny dvor – trading arcade
granitsa – border
gril-bar – grill bar, often limited to roast chicken
Gulag (Glavnoe Upravlenie Lagerey) – Main Administration for Camps; the Soviet network of concentration camps
GUM (Gosudarstvenny Univermag) – State Department Store

i – and
ikra – caviar
imeni – 'named after' (often used in names of theatres and libraries, eg Moscow's Konsertny zal imeni Chaykovskogo is the Tchaikovsky Concert Hall)
inostranets – foreigner
Intourist – old Soviet State Committee for Tourism, now privatised, split up and in competition with hundreds of other travel agencies

GLOSSARY

istochnik – mineral spring
izba – traditional, single-storey wooden cottage
izveshchenie – notice of permission (for visas)

kafe – café
kameny baba – standing stone idol
kamera khranenia – left-luggage office
kanal – canal
karta – map
kassa – ticket office, cashier's desk
kater – small ferry
Kazak – Cossack
kemping – camp site; often has small cabins as well as tent sites
KGB (Komitet Gosudarstvennoy Bezopasnosti) – Committee of State Security
khleb – bread
khokhloma – red, black and gold lacquered pine bowls
khöömei – Tuvan throat-singing
khram – church
khuresh – Tuvan-style of wrestling
kino – cinema
kipyatok – boiled water
kladbishche – cemetery
kleshchi – ticks
klyuch – key
kniga – book
kokoshniki – colourful gables and tiles laid in patterns
kolkhoz – collective farm
kolonna – column, pillar
koltsevaya doroga – ring road
kombinat – complex of factories
komnaty otdykha – resting rooms found at all major train stations and several smaller ones
Komsomol – Communist Youth League
kopek – kopeck; the smallest, worthless unit of Russian currency
korpus – building (ie one of several in a complex)
kray – territory
krazha – theft
kreml – kremlin, a town's fortified stronghold
kruglosutochno – around the clock
krugovoy – round trip
kulak – Stalinist name for a wealthier peasant
kupeyny, kupe – 2nd-class compartment on a train
kurgan – burial mound
kvartira – flat, apartment
kvitantsia – receipt

lavra – senior monastery
lednik – glacier
les – forest
lyux – a kind of hotel suite, with a sitting room in addition to bedroom and bathroom; a *polu-lyux* suite is the less spacious version

Mafia – anyone who has anything to do with crime, from genuine gangsters to victims of their protection rackets
magazin – shop
manezh – riding school
marka – postage stamp or brand, trademark
marshrut – route
marshrutka, marshrutnoe taxi – minibus that runs along a fixed route
mashina – car
matryoshka – set of painted wooden dolls within dolls
mavzoley – mausoleum
medovukha – honey ale
mestnoe vremya – local time
mesto – place, seat
mezhdugorodny – intercity
mezhdunarodny – international
militsia – police
mineralnaya voda – mineral water
monastyr – monastery
more – sea
morskoy vokzal – sea terminal
Moskovskoe vremya – Moscow time
most – bridge
muzey – museum; also some palaces, art galleries and nonworking churches
muzhskoy – men's (toilet)

naberezhnaya – embankment
nomenklatura – literally, 'list of nominees'; the old government and Communist Party elite
novy – new

obed – lunch
oblast – region
obmen valyuty – currency exchange
obmenny punkt – exchange point (bureau, counter)
obshchiy – 4th class place on a train
obyavlenie – handwritten bulletin
okrug – district
ostanovka – bus stop
ostrog – fortress
ostrov – island
OVIR (Otdel Viz I Registratsii) – Department of Visas and Registration; now known under the acronym PVU, although outside Moscow OVIR is still likely to be in use
ozero – lake

palekh – enamelled wood boxes
pamyatnik – monument, statue
Paskha – Easter
passazhirsky poezd – intercity stopping train
perekhod – underground walkway
pereryv – break (when shops, ticket offices, restaurants etc close for an hour or two during the day; this always happens just as you arrive)

perestroika – literally, 'restructuring'; Mikhail Gorbachev's efforts to revive the Soviet economy
pereulok – lane
peshchera – cave
pivo – beer
plan goroda – city map
platskartny, platskart – 3rd-class place on a train
ploshcha (Belarusian), ploshchad (Russian) – square
plotinka – little dam
plyazh – beach
pochta, pochtamt – post office
poezd – train
poliklinika – medical centre
polu-lyux – less spacious version of a *lyux*, a kind of hotel suite with a sitting room in addition to the bedroom and bathroom
poluostrov – peninsula
polyana – glade, clearing
posilka – parcel
posolstvo – embassy
praspekt (Belarusian), prospekt (Russian) – avenue
prichal – landing, pier
priglashenie – invitation
prigorodny poezd – suburban train
prigorodny zal – ticket hall
prodazha – sale
produkty – food store
proezd – passage
prokat – rental
propusk – permit, pass
prospekt (Russian), praspekt (Belarusian) – avenue
provodnik (m), provodnitsa (f) – carriage attendant on a train
PVU (Passportno-Vizovoye Upravleniye) – passport and visa department, formerly OVIR (an acronym which is still likely to be in use outside Moscow)

rabochy den – working day (Monday to Friday)
rayon – district
rechnoy vokzal – river station
reka – river
remont, na remont – closed for repairs (a sign you see all too often)
restoran – restaurant
Rozhdestvo – Christmas
rubl – rouble
ruchnoy – handmade
rynky – food markets
rynok – market

sad – garden
samolyot – aeroplane
sanitarny den – literally, 'sanitary day'; the monthly day when shops, museums, restaurants, hotel dining rooms etc shut down for cleaning

schyot – bill
schyotchik – taxi meter
selo – village
sever – north
shlagbaum – checkpoint, barrier
shosse – highway
shtuka – piece (many produce items are sold by the piece)
skhema transporta – transport map
skory poezd – literally, 'fast train'; a long-distance train
sneg – snow
sobor – cathedral
Sodruzhestvo Nezavisimykh Gosudarstv (SNG) – Commonwealth of Independent States (CIS)
soviet – council
spalny vagon – 1st class place on a train
spravka – certificate
spusk – descent, slope
Sputnik – former youth-travel arm of Komsomol; now just one of the bigger tourism agencies
stanitsa – Cossack village
stary – old
stolovaya – canteen, cafeteria
sutok – period of 24 hours
suvenir – souvenir

taiga – northern pine, fir, spruce and larch forest
taksofon – pay telephone
talon – bus ticket, coupon
tapochki – slippers
teatr – theatre
teatralnaya kassa – theatre ticket office
telegramma – telegram
thangka – Buddhist religious paintings
traktir – tavern
tramvay – tram
troyka – vehicle drawn by three horses
tserkov – church
tsirk – circus
TsUM (Tsentralny Univermag) – name of department store
tualet – toilet
tuda i obratno – literally, 'there and back'; return ticket
turbaza – tourist camp

ulitsa (Russian), vulitsa (Belarusian) – street
univermag, universalny magazin – department store
ushchelie – gorge, canyon
uzhin – supper

val – rampart
valyuta – foreign currency
vanna – bath
vareniki – dumplings with a variety of possible fillings
velosiped – bicycle
venik – birch branch

vezdekhod – all-terrain vehicle
vkhod – way in, entrance
voda – water
vodapad – waterfall
vodny vokzal – ferry terminal
vokzal – station
vorovstvo – theft
vostok – east
vrach – doctor
vulitsa (Belarusian), ulitsa (Russian) – street
vykhod – way out, exit
vykhodnoy den – day off (Saturday, Sunday and holidays)

yantar – amber
yezhednevno – every day

yug – south
yurt – nomad's portable, round tent-house made of felt or skins stretched over a collapsible frame of wood slats

zakaz – reservation
zakaznoe – registration (of mail)
zakuski – appetisers
zal – hall, room
zaliv – gulf, bay
zamok – castle, fortress
zapad – west
zapovednik – (nature) reserve
zavtrak – breakfast
zheleznodorozhny vokzal – train station
zhenskiy – women's (toilet)
zheton – token (for metro etc)

Behind the Scenes

THIS BOOK

This fourth edition of *Russia & Belarus* was coordinated by Simon Richmond with Mark Elliott, Patrick Horton, Steve Kokker, John Noble, Robert Reid, Regis St Louis and Mara Vorhees.

THANKS from the Author

Simon Richmond I was fortunate to have a great commissioning editor in Fiona Buchan, a talented production crew led by Imogen Bannister, and an unbelievably ace team of co-authors who all pulled out the stops to make this the fine book that it is. In St Petersburg a huge *spasibo* goes to Peter Kozyrev who always gives me new insights into the city. Chris Hamilton did sterling service checking on elusive facts and was good company. Thanks to Katya and her mum Natalia for an illuminating Dostoevsky walk and to Anton and Anna for creating the perfect bar so convenient to my apartment (for which I must thank Yegor and his helpful colleagues at Wild Russia for arranging). Aileen Exeter and Steve Caron both shared their wisdom as did Matt Brown at the *St Petersburg Times*. And cheers to Yulia at the tourist office for persevering with me through the whole police report business. In Moscow, Leonid did a splendid job of keeping me abreast of the latest news and correcting my mistakes. In Siberia, thanks to Jack for helping me get to Olkhon and to Nikita and Natasha for creating such a wonderful place to stay there. I very much enjoyed the company and feedback I received from the many travellers I met along the way

including Alexandra Stark, Ruby and Ron, Monica and Magda, Rebecca, and Eric and Katrina.

Mark Elliott Thanks to the hundreds of people who helped with tips, directions, e-mails, and suggestions as well as for continual guidance, kindness and hospitality right across Siberia. Particular thanks to Igor in Omsk, the ever-inspiring Minsalim in Tobolsk, Petr in Severobaikalsk, Jack in Irkutsk, Rada, Vera, Aylana and Aldar in Tuva, Alatoliy and family in Krasnoyarsk, Valentina in Aktash and the team at LP. As ever my work is dedicated to my beloved wife and parents whose love and support allow me to live with happily opening eyes.

Patrick Horton Big thanks go to many people who have helped me put all this together. To Lubov Slavkina, translator and fixer extraordinaire, who cajoled even the most reluctant to divulge essential information on trains, planes, buses and hotels. Thanks to Liza Pahl of Go-Elbrus for the complete low down on the Elbrus scene and also to the gods of travel who this time permitted me to ascend part of that beautiful mountain. *Spasiba* to Vitali of Nalchik who transported me to Elbrus and on the way surprised me with a car lift ascending the side of a hill. Let me buy a coffee for the very young, 20-something, manager of Krasnodar train station who spent a fruitful half hour explaining the Russian railway system, information thatwas augmented by her colleagues across the region. A large shot of vodka for Fiona Buchan at Lonely Planet for another chance to understand Russia

THE LONELY PLANET STORY

The story begins with a classic travel adventure: Tony and Maureen Wheeler's 1972 journey across Europe and Asia to Australia. There was no useful information about the overland trail then, so Tony and Maureen published the first Lonely Planet guidebook to meet a growing need.

From a kitchen table, Lonely Planet has grown to become the largest independent travel publisher in the world, with offices in Melbourne (Australia), Oakland (USA) and London (UK). Today Lonely Planet guidebooks cover the globe. There is an ever-growing list of books and information in a variety of media. Some things haven't changed. The main aim is still to make it possible for adventurous travellers to get out there – to explore and better understand the world.

At Lonely Planet we believe travellers can make a positive contribution to the countries they visit – if they respect their host communities and spend their money wisely. Every year 5% of company profit is donated to charities around the world.

and a big glass of Georgian red to Simon Richmond who has knitted it all together. Last but not least thanks to my partner and family for their support, interest and restorative cups of tea.

Steve Kokker In Minsk, warm and full-hearted *dziakuy* to the inimitable Inna Bukshtynovich who was not only a personal delight to hang out with but of invaluable help; to clever Miroslaw and his sad, bright eyes – may providence be kind to him; to DJ Laurel for the music; and to Alexander and Konstantin. In Brest, big thanks to talented Slava Titov (and Julia) for such an unforgettable meeting; to the wonderful persons at Belintourist; and to Andrei. In Turau, much gratitude to Anna Ivanovna, Irina Yevgenina, Irina Klaus, the staff at the National Park and Museum, everyone at the church for a great meal, and Igor on the bus. To Misha Shpynev, thanks for being a *velikalepny sputnik* and good friend. At LP, my full respect to Fiona Buchan, the tireless Simon Richmond, Imogen Franks and Wendy Taylor, previously Queen of Belarus.

John Noble A host of people in northern European Russia gave me a lot of their time and help and I thank all of you for your kindness and generosity – especially Andrey and Vita on Solovki, Ulrich Kreuzenbeck, Svetlana and Frank de Wit, Irina Volkova, Sergey Burenin, Andrey Primak, Sergey of Solovki Travel, Eivind Tvedt, Elena Zhirina, Sigfred Palmar Giskegaerde, Marina Barandina and Vadim Lesonen. Above all, thanks to Susan for keeping my alive while I wrote it all up.

Robert Reid Thanks to Fiona Buchan of Lonely Planet for offering this superb opportunity, and to Simon Richmond for flapping wings of coordinating-authorship with greater intensity than I've seen before. Thanks to Imogen Bannister and all the LP production crew for cleaning up the text and maps.

Many many many people offered great advice and kindness on the road: Leonid Ragozin of Moscow, Nick Yakubovsky of Yakutsk (for hockey statistics), the former Coloradan Jeff Valkar of Yuzhno-Sakhalinsk, the Swiss Force Five in Kamchatka (for letting me join the tour), the St Petersburg con man for the free ride in Yuzhno, the customs police for the free ride in Vladivostok, the Hungarian film crew for the offer to camp at a Gulag, the Nikolaevsk hotel staff for showing me around, the Kenny G lookalike for the pencil drawing outside Khabarovsk, and many others.

Also travel agencies helped out with info, including Igor and Olga of Magadan, Dima of Yakutsk, Anastasia in Khabarovsk, Julia of Vladivostok, everyone at Vizit in Vladivostok, Andrei of Petropavlovsk, and Sasha Dashevsky of Yuzhno-Sakhalinsk. Thanks to Mai for putting up with such a long road trip.

Regis St Louis Many thanks to Fiona Buchan for sending me to Russia and for her astute guidance throughout. I'd also like to thank Simon Richmond for his excellent work coordinating this tome and for his comradeship in St Petersburg. Along the way, I met some extraordinary people who shared their love of this great country, and it really made my trip. In particular, I'd like to thank Misha, Albert and other staff at Baltma Tours in Kaliningrad; Svetlana, for the edifying tour of Smolensk; Tatiana for explaining Novgorod's rich history; Olga for showing me the splendour of Kaliningrad. I'd also like to thank the staff at the Novgorod tourist office for providing such great resources to the city, and for being the friendliest agency in the country (at least by my reckoning) – though the Smolensk tourist office also deserves special thanks. I'm also grateful to Steve Kokker for tips on Kaliningrad. Lastly, I'd like to thank my family for their support and Cassandra for putting up with my long absences and my sometimes stress-filled temperament.

Mara Vorhees Of all the places to stay in Moscow, none is so comfortable, convenient and completely welcoming as Tommo and Julia's flat, where accommodation comes with guaranteed good company, not to mention a friendly, fat cat. Thanks to Jimmy and Belen (et al), who showed me first-hand what to do with kids in Moscow. Kathleen Pullman and Dmitry and Anna Lebedeva were all fonts of information about the capital.

I appreciated meeting Viktor Aleksandrovich and Igor Nikolaevich at Perm-36; Konstantin Bryliakov and Oleg Demiyanenko in Yekaterinburg; Dasha in Ufa; and Paul van Oostveen in the Golden Ring. Returning to Yekaterinburg is always a highlight, especially when I can hang out with Tim O'Brien and Nadia Altukhova and take advantage of their wealth of knowledge about my favourite Russian city. Somehow 'Nasha Pasha' Yesin still manages to help me out every time I go to Russia, even though he lives in Prague.

Back at LP, I am grateful Fiona Buchan, Simon Richmond, Mark Elliott and the rest of my co-authors. Thanks to Yakov Klots and Donald Tyson for their contributions. And thank you Jerz: you are my creative inspiration, even when you're thousands of miles away.

CREDITS

This guidebook was commissioned in Lonely Planet's London office, and produced by:

Commissioning Editor Fiona Buchan, Imogen Hall, Alan Murphy
Coordinating Editor Imogen Bannister
Coordinating Cartographer Valentina Kremenchutskaya
Coordinating Layout Designer Katie Thuy Bui
Managing Cartographer Mark Griffiths
Assisting Editors & Proofers Janet Austin, Emma Gilmour, Craig Kilburn and Joanne Newell
Assisting Cartographers David Connolly, James Ellis, Tony Frankhauser, Jack Gavran, Kusnandar, Jacqueline Nguyen and Anthony Phelan
Colour Designer Wibowo Rusli
Cover Designer Jim Hsu
Project Manager Ray Thomson
Language Content Coordinator Quentin Frayne

Thanks to Sally Darmody, Bruce Evans, Mark Germanchis, Adriana Mammarella, Malisa Plesa, Nicholas Stebbing, Dmitri Verbuk, Celia Wood.

THANKS from Lonely Planet

Many thanks to the hundreds of travellers who used the last edition and wrote to us with helpful hints, useful advice and interesting anecdotes.

A MiRee Abrahamsen, Bob Audretsch, **B** Tom Barnes, Andy Barrett, Nick Berry, Robert Braun, Allen Breen, Oliver Buckley, John Burke, **C** Julia Chong, Jemetha Clark, Yvonne Clark, Eleanor Crook, **D** Vivien Debenham, Janet Denye, Andy Diamond, Stephan Dorrenberg, Tom Drummond, Eddie Dry, Euan Duncan, **E** Michael Eckett, Nick Evreinow, **F** Tommaso Ferigo, Fernando Ferreira Lima, **G** Karin Gallagher, Andy Ganner, Sam Golledge, **H** EP Hamilton, Nigel Harper, Joshua Hartshorne, Lisa & Rune Henriksen, Henri Hovine, Jane Huglin, Nam Seok Hwang, **I** Ruth Imershein, Giovanni Introno, Olga Ivanova, **J** Antonio Navas Jaquete, Martin Jennings, Joel Johansson, **K** John Kilmartin, Jon Kjernlie, **L** Kam Lam, Rebecca Lange, Philip Livingstone, Thomas Lohr, **M** Eamonn McCallion, Jay & Carolyn MacInnes, Jan Macutek, Arthur Markham, Michael & Beatrix Mathew, Loic Meuley, Cynthia Milton, **N** Susan Neill, Ellen Nemhauser, Paige & Gabriel Newby, Sara Normington, **P** Maarten Peeters, Simon Penner, Lea Ann Pestotnik, James Phillips, Clemencia Pineda, Pam Poole, **Q** Bernadette Quin, **R** Karen & John Reilly, Jason Rico, Chris Riede, Gregory Rose, Bruce Rumage, Shimon Rumelt, Victor Ruskin, **S** Bob Schnelle, Tobi Schwarzmueller, Craig & Mel Scutchings, Laura Sheahen, Adam Skordinski, Juuk Slager, Barney Smith, Chris Smith, **T** Stephen Tannas, Justin Templemore-Finlayson, Ben Tettlebaum, Fred Thornett, Robert & Mauri Thornton, Allan Tighe, Daystan Tiller, Donald Tyson, **V** Leander van Delden, Theijs van Wlij, Howard Vickers, **W** Adrian Wagner, Frans Weiser, **Z** Evan Zoldan

ACKNOWLEDGMENTS

Many thanks to the following for the use of their content: Globe on back cover; map data contained in colour highlights map – Mountain High Maps® © 1993 Digital Wisdom, Inc.

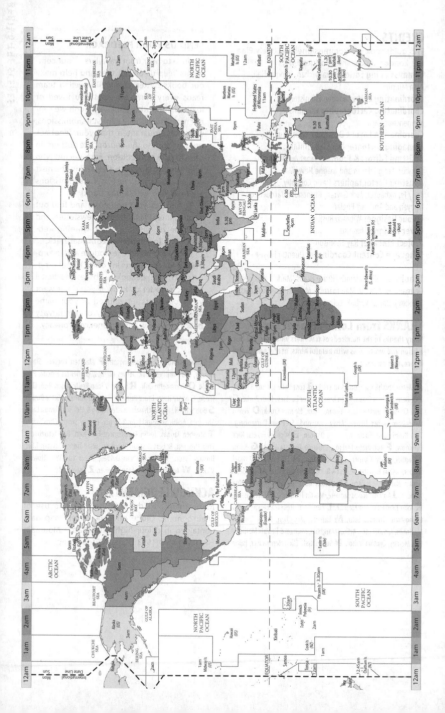

Index

INDEX

INDEX

INDEX

INDEX

000 Map pages
000 Location of colour photographs

INDEX

INDEX

INDEX

INDEX

INDEX

INDEX

MAP LEGEND

ROUTES

Tollway	One-Way Street
Freeway	Street Mall/Steps
Primary Road	Tunnel
Secondary Road	Walking Tour
Tertiary Road	Walking Tour Detour
Lane	Walking Trail
Under Construction	Walking Path
Track	Pedestrian Overpass
Unsealed Road	

TRANSPORT

Ferry	Rail
Metro	Rail (Underground)
Cable Car, Funicular	Tram

HYDROGRAPHY

River, Creek	Canal
Intermittent River	Water
Swamp	Lake (Dry)
Reef	Lake (Salt)
Glacier	

BOUNDARIES

International	Regional, Suburb
State, Provincial	Ancient Wall
Disputed	Cliff
Marine Park	

AREA FEATURES

Airport	Land
Building	Mall
Campus	Market
Cemetery, Christian	Park
Cemetery, Other	Sports
Forest	Urban

POPULATION

CAPITAL (NATIONAL)	CAPITAL (STATE)
Large City	Medium City
Small City	Town, Village

SYMBOLS

Sights/Activities
- Beach
- Buddhist
- Castle, Fortress
- Christian
- Islamic
- Jewish
- Monument
- Museum, Gallery
- Point of Interest
- Pool
- Ruin
- Skiing
- Winery, Vineyard
- Zoo, Bird Sanctuary

Eating
- Eating

Drinking
- Drinking
- Café

Entertainment
- Entertainment

Shopping
- Shopping

Sleeping
- Sleeping
- Camping

Transport
- Airport, Airfield
- Border Crossing
- Bus Station
- General Transport
- Taxi Rank

Information
- Bank, ATM
- Embassy/Consulate
- Hospital, Medical
- Information
- Internet Facilities
- Police Station
- Post Office, GPO
- Telephone
- Toilets

Geographic
- Lighthouse
- Lookout
- Mountain, Volcano
- National Park
- Pass, Canyon
- River Flow
- Waterfall

LONELY PLANET OFFICES

Australia
Head Office
Locked Bag 1, Footscray, Victoria 3011
☎ 03 8379 8000, fax 03 8379 8111
talk2us@lonelyplanet.com.au

USA
150 Linden St, Oakland, CA 94607
☎ 510 893 8555, toll free 800 275 8555
fax 510 893 8572
info@lonelyplanet.com

UK
72-82 Rosebery Ave,
Clerkenwell, London EC1R 4RW
☎ 020 7841 9000, fax 020 7841 9001
go@lonelyplanet.co.uk

Published by Lonely Planet Publications Pty Ltd
ABN 36 005 607 983

© Lonely Planet Publications Pty Ltd 2006

© photographers as indicated 2006

Cover photographs: Laughing Priest, Olivier Martel/APL/Corbis (front); The Museum of Anthropology and Ethnography, reflected in the beautiful blue waters of Bolshaya Neva – St Petersburg, Georgi S Shablovsky/Lonely Planet Images (back). Many of the images in this guide are available for licensing from Lonely Planet Images: www.lonelyplanetimages.com.

Printed through Colorcraft Ltd, Hong Kong.
Printed in China